Panic Disorder with Agoraphobia

Agoraphobia Without History of Panic Disorder

Specific Phobia

Social Phobia

Obsessive-Compulsive Disorder

Posttraumatic Stress Disorder

Acute Stress Disorder

Generalized Anxiety Disorder

SOMATOFORM DISORDERS

Somatization Disorder

Undifferentiated Somatoform Disorder

Conversion Disorder

Pain Disorder

Hypochondriasis

Body Dysmorphic Disorder

FACTITIOUS DISORDERS

DISSOCIATIVE DISORDERS

Dissociative Amnesia

Dissociative Fugue

Dissociative Identity Disorder

Depersonalization Disorder

SEXUAL AND GENDER IDENTITY DISORDERS

Sexual Dysfunctions

Sexual Desire Disorders

Hypoactive Sexual Desire Disorder

Sexual Aversion Disorder

Sexual Arousal Disorders

Female Sexual Arousal Disorder

Male Erectile Disorder

Orgasmic Disorders

Female Orgasmic Disorder

Male Orgasmic Disorder

Premature Ejaculation

Sexual Pain Disorders

Dyspareunia (Not Due to a General Medical Condition)

Vaginismus (Not Due to a General Medical Condition)

Paraphilias

Exhibitionism

Fetishism

Frotteurism

Pedophilia

Sexual Masochism

Sexual Sadism

Transvestic Fetishism

Voyeurism

Gender Identity Disorders

Gender Identity Disorder in Children

Gender Identity Disorder in Adolescents or Adults

EATING DISORDERS

Anorexia Nervosa

Bulimia Nervosa

SLEEP DISORDERS

Primary Sleep Disorders: Dyssomnias

Primary Insomnia

Primary Hypersomnia

Narcolepsy

Breathing-Related Sleep Disorder

Circadian Rhythm Sleep Disorder

Primary Sleep Disorders: Parasomnias

Nightmare Disorder

Sleep Terror Disorder

Sleepwalking Disorder

IMPULSE-CONTROL DISORDERS NOT ELSEWHERE CLASSIFIED

Intermittent Explosive Disorder

Kleptomania

Pyromania

Pathological Gambling

Trichotillomania

ADJUSTMENT DISORDERS

Adjustment Disorder

With Depressed Mood

With Anxiety

With Mixed Anxiety and Depressed Mood

With Disturbance of Conduct

With Mixed Disturbance of Emotions and Conduct

PERSONALITY DISORDERS

Note: These are coded on Axis II.

Paranoid Personality Disorder

Schizoid Personality Disorder

Schizotypal Personality Disorder

Antisocial Personality Disorder

Borderline Personality Disorder

Histrionic Personality Disorder

Narcissistic Personality Disorder

Avoidant Personality Disorder

Dependent Personality Disorder

Obsessive-Compulsive Personality Disorder

MULTIAXIAL SYSTEM

Axis 1

Clinical Disorders
Other Conditions That May Be a Focus of Clinical Attention

Axis II

Personality Disorders
Mental Retardation

Axis III

General Medical Condition

Axis IV

Psychosocial and Environmental Problems

Axis V

Global Assessment of Functioning

Understanding Abnormal Behavior

EIHTH EDITION

David Sue

Western Washington University

Derald Wing Sue

Teachers College, Columbia University

Stanley Sue

University of California — Davis

Houghton Mifflin Company   Boston   New York

To our parents, Tom and Lucy Sue, who never suspected they would produce three psychologists, and to our wives and families who provided the emotional support that enabled us to complete this edition.

Publisher & Editor-in-Chief: Charles Hartford
Sponsor: Jane Potter
Development Editor: Laura Hildebrand
Senior Project Editor: Aileen Mason
Editorial Assistant: Susan Miscio
Composition Buyer: Chuck Dutton
Art & Design Manager: Gary Crespo
Art & Design Coordinator: Jill Haber
Manufacturing Manager: Karen Banks
Marketing Manager: Laura McGinn
Marketing Assistant: Erin Lane

Cover Image: Jenn Roycroft, © Images.com

Chapter Opener Credits
Chapter 1: ©Janusz Kapusta/SIS Illustration/Veer; *Chapter 2:* ©Janusz Kapusta/SIS Illustration/Veer; *Chapter 3:* ©Janusz Kapusta/SIS Illustration/Veer; *Chapter 4:* ©Joyce Hesselberth/SIS Illustration/Veer; *Chapter 5:* ©Janusz Kapusta/SIS Illustration/Veer; *Chapter 6:* ©Janusz Kapusta/SIS Illustration/Veer; *Chapter 7:* ©Joyce Hesselberth/SIS Illustration/Veer; *Chapter 8:* ©Sandra Dionisi/Images.com; *Chapter 9:* Spots Illustration/Veer; *Chapter 10:* ©Jose Ortega/Images.com; *Chapter 11:* Spots Illustration/Veer; *Chapter 12:* ©Cheri/Images.com; *Chapter 13:* ©John Nelson/Images.com; *Chapter 14:* ©Janusz Kapusta/SIS Illustration/Veer; *Chapter 15:* ©Ryoichi Yosumoto/Images.com; *Chapter 16:* Digital Visions/Veer; *Chapter 17:* ©Joyce Hesselberth/SIS Illustration/Veer: *Chapter 18:* ©Janusz Kapustra/SIS Illustration/Veer.

Credits continue on page C-1 at the end of the text.

Printed in China

Library of Congress Control Number: 2005924907

ISBN-13: 978-0-618-52828-8

ISBN-10: 0-618-52828-8

3 4 5 6 7 8 9-SDP-10 09 08 07 06

Brief Contents

Contents

16 Eating Disorders and Sleep Disorders 526

17 Therapeutic Interventions 558

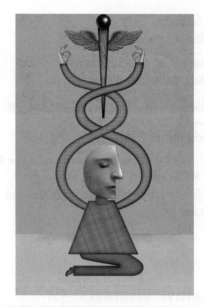

18 Legal and Ethical Issues in Abnormal Psychology 594

Features

Preface

Abnormal behaviors both fascinate and are of concern to scientists and the general public. Why people exhibit abnormal behaviors, how they express their disturbances, and how such behaviors can be prevented and treated are questions that continue to intrigue us. We now know that all human beings are touched in one way or another by mental disturbance in their lives, either directly through their own struggles to deal with mental disorders or indirectly through affected friends or relatives.

Over the years, major research discoveries in genetics, neurobiology, and psychology have made unprecedented contributions to our understanding of abnormal behaviors. This is clearly evident in the Human Genome Project, where scientists have mapped the location of all genes in the human nucleus. The hope among mental health professionals is that the "map of life" will allow for increased understanding of mental disorders and their subsequent treatments. In addition to this tremendous biological breakthrough, we also know that psychological forms of intervention are effective in treating abnormal behaviors. The move to identify empirically supported treatments has taken the profession by storm. Finally, research has revealed the great cultural variations in abnormal behaviors and what other cultures consider effective treatments. In the Eighth Edition of our book, we examine all of these areas.

In writing and revising this book, we have sought to engage students in the exciting process of understanding abnormal behavior and the ways that mental health professionals study and attempt to treat it. In pursuing this goal, we have been guided by three major objectives:

■ To provide students with scholarship of the highest quality,

■ To offer an evenhanded treatment of abnormal psychology as both a scientific and a clinical endeavor, giving students the opportunity to explore topics thoroughly and responsibly, and

■ To make our book inviting and stimulating to a wide range of students.

In each edition, we have strived to achieve these objectives, working with comments from many students and instructors and our own work in teaching, research, and practice. The Eighth Edition, we believe, builds on the achievements of previous editions and surpasses them.

Our Approach

We take an eclectic, multicultural approach to the field, drawing on important contributions from various disciplines and theoretical stances. The text covers the major categories of disorders listed in the *Diagnostic and Statistical Manual of Mental Disorders* (DSM-IV-TR), but it is not a mechanistic reiteration of DSM. We believe that different combinations of life experiences and constitutional factors influence behavioral disorders, and we project this view throughout the text.

One vital aspect of life experience comprises cultural norms, values, and expectations. Because we are convinced that cross-cultural comparisons of abnormal behavior and treatment methods can greatly enhance our understanding of disorders, we pay special attention to cultural and gender phenomena. Indeed, *Understanding Abnormal Behavior* was the first textbook on abnormal psychology to integrate and emphasize the role of multicultural factors, and although many texts have since followed our lead, the Eighth Edition continues to provide the most extensive coverage and integration of multicultural models, explanations, and concepts available. Not only do we discuss how changing demographics have increased the importance of multicultural psychology, but we also introduce multicultural models of psychopathology in the opening chapters. As with other models of psychopathology (such as psychoanalytic, cognitive, behavioral, and biological), we address multicultural issues throughout the text whenever research findings and theoretical formulations allow. For example, cultural factors as they affect assessment, classification, and treatment of various mental disorders are presented to students. Such an approach adds richness to our understanding of mental disorders. To aid students in integrating new research and work in abnormal behavior, we present in Chapter 2 a tripartite approach to viewing disorders through the lens of individual, group, and universal dimensions.

As psychologists (and professors), we know that learning is enhanced whenever material is presented in a lively and engaging manner. We achieve these qualities in part by providing case vignettes and clients' descriptions of their experiences to complement and illustrate research-based explanations. In addition, we highlight and explore controversial topics in depth, including the following questions:

■ Has managed care made it more difficult to seek psychological help? (Chapter 1)

■ Are there disorders (culture-bound syndromes) unique to a particular culture? (Chapter 3)

■ Is the fear of spiders due to disgust or perceived danger? (Chapter 5)

■ Was Sybil a genuine case of dissociative identity disorder? (Chapter 6)

■ Do ethnic minorities receive inferior medical treatment? (Chapter 7)

■ Do women have higher rates of anxiety and depressive disorders? (Chapters 5 and 11)

■ What are the effects of club drugs? (Chapter 9)

■ Can people be addicted to sex? (Chapter 10)

■ What are the causes of sexual aggression in society? (Chapter 10)

■ Should we assist in suicide and allow the "right to die"? (Chapter 12)

■ Do individuals with schizophrenia in developing countries have a better prognosis than those in developed countries? (Chapter 13)

■ Can social psychological factors be a cause of schizophrenia? (Chapter 13)

■ Should Web sites advocating anorexia nervosa be shut down? (Chapter 16)

■ Is psychotherapy effective and useful? (Chapter 17)

■ Should culture-specific approaches in therapy be used in treating racial/ethnic minority populations? (Chapter 17)

■ How well can psychologists predict dangerousness? (Chapter 18)

■ Should therapists maintain confidentiality with AIDS clients? (Chapter 18)

We clarify complex material by providing students with case descriptions, real-life situations, and research findings. Examples of this approach can be seen in our discussions of the phenomenon of recovered memories and our careful examination of the various factors that affect clients with mood disorders. Our goal is to encourage students to think critically rather than merely assimilate a collection of facts and theories. As a result, we hope that students will develop an appreciation of the study of abnormal behavior.

Special Features

Contributing to the strength of the Eighth Edition are features that were popularized in earlier editions and, in some cases, have been revised and enhanced. These features are aimed at aiding students in organizing and integrating the material in each chapter.

■ *Disorder, prevalence, onset, and course charts* have been found to be among the most popular and helpful features for students and teachers alike. They help readers to conceptualize and define disorders; each chapter has a chart that provides information about the DSM-IV-TR diagnostic category and about the prevalence rate, onset, and course of various disorders. This should facilitate even greater understanding of the disorders and their relationship to each other.

■ *Critical Thinking boxes* provide factual evidence and thought-provoking questions that raise key issues in research, examine widely held assumptions about abnormal behavior, or challenge the student's own understanding of the text material. This feature prompts students to think about issues as a psychologist would, weighing the evidence and applying theoretical perspectives and personal experiences to arrive at an evaluation. The feature can spark lively class discussion and debate.

■ *New interactive Critical Thinking boxes* are designated by a mouse icon that indicates there is a corresponding web activity on the student Web site. These hands-on, Internet-based activities further promote critical thinking skills.

■ *Updated Mental Health and Society boxes* deal with controversial issues with wide implications for our society. These boxes stimulate critical thinking, evoke alternative views, provoke discussion, and draw students into issues that help them better explore the wider meaning of abnormal behavior in our society.

■ *Chapter outlines and opening Focus Questions,* appearing in the first two pages of every chapter, provide a framework and stimulate active learning—with questions in mind, students begin thinking about the concepts they are about to explore within the chapter.

■ *Integrated chapter Summaries keyed to the Focus Questions* provide students with a concise recap of the chapter's most important concepts and with tentative answers to the chapter opener's Focus Questions. This heuristic device to learning helps students to form an integrated understanding of the content contained in each chapter.

- *Updated Myth and Reality discussions* help dispel students' preconceived notions regarding mental health issues. This feature challenges the many myths and false beliefs that have surrounded the field of abnormal behavior and also helps students realize that beliefs, some of which may appear to be "common sense," must be checked against scientific facts and knowledge.

- *New and updated case studies and examples* make issues of mental health and mental disorders "come to life" for students and instructors. Many of the cases are taken from actual clinical files, and are clearly designated within the text's design.

- *Key terms* are highlighted in the text, appear at the end of each chapter, and are defined in the glossary at the back of the book.

New and Updated Coverage of the Eighth Edition

Our foremost objective in preparing this edition was to update thoroughly and present the latest trends in research and clinical thinking. This has led throughout the text to expanded coverage of dozens of topics, including the following:

- The growing ethnic and cultural diversity in the United States and its implications for mental health research, theory, and practice.

- Expanded and balanced coverage of the biological perspective and the latest research strategies and findings on genetic factors in mental disorders.

- Integrated coverage of the growing prevalence of psychoactive drug use in U.S. society.

- Coverage of violence and its mental health meaning for our society.

- New developments concerning the implications of managed health care on mental health services and the use of evidence-based treatments.

- Research findings concerning the rates of each mental disorder and the prevalence of disorders according to gender, ethnicity, and age.

- Updated suicide coverage.

- Coverage of date rape and recommendations for young people on the avoidance of at-risk situations.

- Expanded coverage on sleep disorders.

- Expanded coverage on eating disorders.

- Identification of psychotherapies and treatments that are likely to increase or decrease in use in the future.

- Developmental and clinically significant decline in memory associated with aging.

- Recent findings and analyses of elimination disorders.

- Ethical and legal issues raised by recent cases involving insanity pleas, courtroom testimony by psychologists, and assisted suicide.

- Comprehensive coverage of culture-specific therapeutic guidelines and strategies for treating African American, Asian American, Latino American, and Native American clients.

The design of the book has been refined to present the content in the clearest, most accessible way. As in the previous edition, the Eighth Edition contains an abundance of tables, illustrations, figures, and photographs that graphically show research data, illustrate comparisons and contrasts, and enhance the understanding of concepts or controversies in the field.

In addition to updating the book's coverage, its look, and its special features, we have maintained a streamlined organization of the book, as described next.

Organization of the Text

To make covering the book's contents over the course of a quarter or semester more manageable, the text is eighteen chapters long, in keeping with feedback from users of the book. Long-time users of our text will immediately notice that we continue to offer features that have been helpful, and that we continue to have a chapter on eating disorders (Chapter 16) and to provide coverage of mental retardation in the chapter on cognitive disorders (Chapter 14). In addition, all of the chapters have been thoroughly revised and updated with an eye toward balancing research findings with clinical implications.

Chapters 1 through 4 provide a context for viewing abnormal behavior and treatment by introducing students to definitions of abnormal behavior and historical perspectives (Chapter 1), the key theoretical perspectives used to explain deviant behavior (Chapter 2), methods of assessment and classification (Chapter 3), and the research process involved in the study of abnormal behavior (Chapter 4). Especially noteworthy is our updated coverage on the biological bases of abnormal behavior and a discussion of the scientific method.

The bulk of the text, Chapters 5 through 16, presents the major disorders covered in DSM-IV-TR. In each chapter, symptoms of the disorder are presented first, followed by diagnosis, theoretical perspectives, etiology, and treatment. Our disorders charts include not only the definitions of disorders but also their prevalence, onset, and course, so, at a glance, students are able to gain an important overview of the disorders. Highlights of the coverage in this part of the book include an entire chapter devoted to suicide (Chapter 12), which was deemed important because of its increasing visibility in the mental health professions and our society. In addition, major contemporary issues involving the right to die, assisted suicide, and our aging population have thrust it into the public limelight as well. This chapter presents information on the reasons for suicide and also on its moral, legal, and ethical implications. Chapter 16 still provides thorough coverage of eating disorders, but in response to reviewer feedback, we have greatly expanded our discussion of sleep disorders and have renamed the chapter to reflect its dual coverage of these two subjects. The bulk of the chapter is devoted to eating disorders, as it is a problem that continues to be prevalent in our society, especially among younger people. Research now links eating disorders to situational factors, biological proclivity, and other interlocking mental disorders. The fact that the majority of those who suffer from eating disorders are women is also a powerful statement of how the images society portrays to them may result in unhealthy behaviors.

Chapters 17 and 18 conclude the book with a look at therapy and the legal and ethical issues in psychopathology. Discussions of treatment approaches are included in each of the chapters on disorders, allowing students some closure in covering particular disorders. Chapter 17 then looks at treatment more broadly. Unique to the therapy chapter are sections that deal with suggesting guidelines in the treatment of various racial/ethnic minority groups. Chapter 18 covers the issues and controversies surrounding topics such as the insanity defense, patients' rights, confidentiality, and mental health practices in general.

The text is manageable for a one-semester class. While research findings and knowledge in the field of psychopathology have grown considerably, we have tried to provide the most important and significant developments in the field without sacrificing the scholarly and comprehensive nature of the book.

Ancillaries

This text is supported by a rich set of supplementary materials designed to enhance the teaching and learning experience. Several new components make use of new instructional technologies.

For Instructors

- *New! Abnormal Psych in Film® DVD/VHS:* This DVD/VHS is a hybrid product that contains clips from popular films such as *The Deer Hunter,* and *Apollo Thirteen* that illustrate key concepts in abnormal psychology, as well as thought-provoking footage from documentaries and client interviews. Each clip is accompanied by overviews and discussion questions to help bring the study of abnormal psychology alive for students. This DVD works in tandem with the *Abnormal Psychology,* Eighth Edition *Student CD-ROM* as a unique learning system. On the *Student CD-ROM* are select, corresponding video clips with overviews, multiple-choice and essay questions, designed to stimulate critical thinking about the diagnosis and treatment of various disorders. *Punctuate your lecture with engaging videos from the DVD; then have your students use the Student CD-ROM to further study the concepts presented in those videos.*

- *HM ClassPrep CD-ROM with HM Testing:* This CD-ROM provides one convenient location for testing and presentation materials. It contains PowerPoint slides, the *Instructor's Resource Manual,* and the Computerized Test Bank. Our HM Testing program offers delivery of test questions in an easy-to-use interface, compatible with both Mac and Windows platforms.

- *Instructor's Resource Manual:* The *Instructor's Resource Manual* includes an extended chapter outline, learning objectives, discussion topics, classroom exercises, handouts, and a list of supplementary readings and multimedia resources. For instructors switching from the Seventh to the Eighth Edition of the text, the manual also includes a detailed transition guide. The *Instructor's Resource Manual* is available on the instructor Web site and the HM ClassPrep CD-ROM with HM Testing.

- *Test Bank:* The *Test Bank* features 100 multiple-choice and three essay questions (with sample answers) per chapter. Each question is labeled with the corresponding text page reference as well as the type of question being asked for easier test creation. The *Test Bank* is available on our HM ClassPrep CD-ROM with HM Testing.

- *New! PowerPoint Slides:* A completely revamped set of PowerPoint slides is available with the Eighth Edition. Each chapter's show contains dozens of slides that include tables and illustrations that help highlight the major topics in abnormal psychology. The PowerPoint slides are available on the instructor Web site and the HM ClassPrep CD-ROM with HM Testing.

- *Instructor Web Site:* For maximum flexibility, much of the material from the HM ClassPrep CD-ROM is also available on our Web site, which may be accessed at **http://psychology.college.hmco.com/instructors.** Easy to navigate, this site offers a range of instructional strategies and tools.

■ *Course Cartridges for WebCT and Blackboard:* Course cartridges for WebCT and Blackboard are available for the Eighth Edition, allowing instructors to use text-specific material to create an online course on their own campus course management system.

For Students

■ *Study Guide:* The *Study Guide* provides a complete review of the chapter with chapter outlines, learning objectives, fill-in-the-blank review of key terms, and multiple-choice questions. Answers to test questions include an explanation for both the correct answer and incorrect answers.

■ *Student CD-ROM:* The CD that accompanies every copy of the student text is designed to reinforce concepts presented in the textbook as well as provide engaging, interactive activities that sharpen critical thinking skills. The CD includes select video clips accompanied by overviews, multiple-choice and essay questions, Flashcards, Focus Question Activities, Myth vs. Reality Exercises, and Case Study Exercises, all of which provide extra review of concepts and terms studied in the abnormal psychology course.

■ *Student Web Site:* The Student Web Site contains additional study aids, including Ace Self-tests, interactive Critical Thinking exercises and multimedia tutorials—all designed to help students improve their grades while learning more about abnormal psychology. All Web resources may be accessed by logging onto the Web site at **http://psychology.college.hmco.com/students.**

■ *Case Studies in Abnormal Psychology:* Case Studies in Abnormal Psychology, by Clark Clipson, California School of Professional Psychology, and Jocelyn Steer, San Diego Family Institute, contains 16 studies and can be shrink-wrapped with the text at a discounted package price. Each case represents a major psychological disorder. After a detailed history of each case, critical-thinking questions prompt students to formulate hypotheses and interpretations based on the client's symptoms, family and medical background, and relevant information. The case proceeds with sections on assessment, case conceptualization, diagnosis, and treatment outlook, and is concluded by a final set of discussion questions.

■ *Abnormal Psychology in Context: Voices and Perspectives:* This supplementary text, written by David Sattler, College of Charleston, Virginia Shabatay, Palomar College, and Geoffrey Kramer, Grand Valley State University, features 40 cases and can be shrink-wrapped with the text at a discounted package price. This unique collection contains first-person accounts and narratives written by individuals who live with a psychological disorder and by therapists, relatives, and others who have direct experience with someone suffering from a disorder. These vivid and engaging narratives are accompanied by critical-thinking questions and a psychological concept guide that indicates which key terms and concepts are covered in each reading.

Acknowledgments

We continue to appreciate the critical feedback received from reviewers and colleagues. The following individuals helped us prepare the Eighth Edition by sharing with us valuable insights, opinions, and recommendations.

Lorry Cology, Owens Community College

Greg A. R. Febbraro, Drake University

Jerry L. Fryrear, University of Houston, Clear Lake

Michele Galietta, John Jay College of Criminal Justice

George-Harold Jennings, Drew University

Robert Hoff, Mercyhurst College

Kim L. Krinsky, Georgia Perimeter College

Sherry Davis Molock, George Washington University

Michael D. Spiegler, Providence College

Ma. Teresa G. Tuason, University of North Florida

Theresa A. Wadkins, University of Nebraska, Kearney

Fred Whitford, Montana State University

We also wish to thank Richeal Barnes and Sarah Jaffe, Western Washington University, and to acknowledge the continuing support and high-quality of work done by Houghton Mifflin personnel including Laura Hildebrand, Development Editor; Liz Hogan, Editorial Assistant; Jane Potter, Sponsoring Editor; Aileen Mason, Senior Project Editor; Susan Miscio, Editorial Assistant; Laura McGinn, Marketing Manager; and Erin Lane, Marketing Assistant. We also thank text designer and art editor Jean Hammond, photo editor Martha Shethar, copyeditor Elaine Lauble Kehoe, proofreader Angela Hoover Morrison, and indexer Lizbeth Miller.

D. S.
D. W. S.
S. S.

About the Authors

David Sue is Professor of Psychology at Western Washington University, where he is an associate of the Center for Cross-Cultural Research and has served as the Director of both the Psychology Counseling Clinic and the Mental Health Counseling Program. He and his wife are currently writing a book *Counseling and Psychotherapy in a Diverse Society*. He received his Ph.D. in Clinical Psychology from Washington State University. His research interests revolve around issues in cross-cultural counseling. He, his wife, and their three children enjoy tennis, hiking, and snowshoeing.

Derald Wing Sue is Professor of Psychology and Education in the Department of Counseling and Clinical Psychology at Teachers College, Columbia University. He has written extensively in the field of counseling psychology and multicultural counseling/therapy and is author of a best-selling book, *Counseling the Culturally Diverse: Theory and Practice*. Dr. Sue has served as president of the Society of Counseling Psychology and the Society for the Psychological Study of Ethnic Minority Issues. He received his doctorate from the University of Oregon and is married and the father of two children. Friends describe him as addicted to exercise and the Internet.

Stanley Sue is University Distinguished Professor of Psychology and Asian American Studies at the University of California, Davis. He received his B.S. from the University of Oregon and Ph.D. from UCLA. He was Assistant and Associate Professor of Psychology at the University of Washington (1971–1981) and Professor of Psychology at UCLA (1981–1996). His research interests lie in the areas of clinical-community psychology and ethnicity and mental health. His hobbies include working on computers, which has resulted in an addiction to the Internet, and jogging with his wife.

Understanding Abnormal Behavior

CHAPTER 1
Abnormal Behavior

FOCUS QUESTIONS

■ What is abnormal psychology?

■ What criteria are used to determine normal or abnormal behaviors?

■ How common are mental disorders?

■ How have the explanations of abnormal behavior changed over time?

■ Are mental disorders due primarily to biological or to psychological factors?

■ What are some contemporary trends in abnormal psychology?

It was a very tense hour we spent together. The silences were long, awkward, and uncomfortable. Art, a college junior, had come for his third therapy session and continued to have difficulty disclosing much about his personal life and the problems that brought him to the university counseling center. Several times he seemed on the verge of telling me a dark secret, but each time he hesitated and went on to another topic. I knew, however, from his records that Art had been diagnosed in the past as suffering from multiple disorders such as paranoid schizophrenia, manic-depression (bipolar disorder), and antisocial personality disorder. In our sessions together, he showed many signs of paranoia, as he obviously was guarded in what he disclosed to me and seemed mistrustful of my motives and those of his parents, as well.

In our first session together, he asked me many questions regarding my background, training, and qualifications, and specifically my racial background. He wanted to know whether I was Chinese or Japanese. When I informed him that I was Chinese, he seemed relieved. He stated that he did not trust the Japanese since they bombed Pearl Harbor (even though the event occurred some thirty years ago). Art was adamant in not wanting our therapy sessions audiotaped, and he requested that I not take notes. It was like pulling teeth in each session to get Art to talk about himself and the reasons he sought counseling.

Although the first session seemed to be a feeling-out process for Art, our second one was different. He was quite animated and talkative, and he rambled in his speech. I wondered whether he was on LSD or some other drug. He alluded to multiple conspiracies from the government and especially the campus police. He frequently lost his train of thought, glanced away, blinked rapidly, and occasionally seemed to appear disoriented. I was certain that Art was hallucinating and probably hearing voices or seeing things. For example, he would turn his head quickly to the right, stare into space, and occasionally nod his head. When I asked whether he was hearing voices or seeing things, he would either not respond or shrug his shoulders. He refused my suggestion to visit the psychiatric clinic.

It was during the third session with Art that I really felt quite uncomfortable and scared. Yes, I will use the word "scared" because that was precisely the impact Art had on me. Not only was he physically imposing (tall, husky, and muscled), but I knew that Art was quite capable of antisocial behavior and that he had been involved in many student demonstrations and had participated in several campus "sit-ins" and public "riots" that resulted in property destruction. He had informed me that he belonged to a group of community activists intent on "bringing down a corrupt government."

Don't ask me how I knew, but I was certain that he had chosen today to inform me about some potential plans to destroy property as part of a wider social protest. When he stated, "I know I can trust you because you're Chinese and not one of them," I panicked. Rather than dealing with the situation in a therapuetic manner, I quickly informed Art that there were limits to confidentiality. If he disclosed anything that bordered on criminal behavior, I didn't want to hear it. Further, I told him, I would be compelled to report it to the proper authorities.

The disclosure greatly angered Art. He rose from his seat quickly, looked at me in a menacing fashion, and left my office. For one brief moment during that encounter, I was concerned that he would become violent.

Art never returned for any of his other appointments after that incident.

Although I take full responsibility for the poor way I handled the situation, no amount of reading and course work could have prepared me for such an experience. Since that day, I have often used the case of Art to illustrate how complex the study of abnormal psychology becomes in real life. We can ask many questions generated from this incident.

1. What was wrong with Art? Was he truly mentally disturbed, suffering from paranoid schizophrenia, or was he a common criminal? How much do mental disorders contribute to antisocial behavior?

2. What role do race and culture play in the treatment of mental disorders and their manifestations? How did my culture and race—and his—affect the therapeutic process? Why was it important for him to know whether I was Chinese or Japanese? Why did an event that occurred some thirty years ago make such an impact upon this nineteen-year-old student?

3. What disorder did he suffer from? How does one determine normality and abnormality? Art was said to suffer from schizophrenia. Are hallucinations, delusions, suspiciousness, and tangential thinking symptoms of this disorder? How does a therapist tell whether a client is delusional or hallucinating?

4. Did Art pose a physical threat to me? Are people who suffer from mental disorders more likely to harm others or more likely to engage in criminal behavior? My professors had always reassured us that fears of violence and injury from mentally disturbed individuals were unfounded. Yet I could not shake the feeling that I was in some form of danger.

5. What type of therapy would best help Art? It seemed that individual therapy did not have much impact on him. What other forms of treatment are available to the clinician? Should he be on medication to control his hallucinations and delusions? Would he be better off hospitalized rather than wandering around on campus? Are some mental disorders more difficult to cure than others?

6. As a therapist, what are the limits of confidentiality? If I hear about wrongdoing or possible future criminal acts from clients, am I obligated to report it? Should all clients be told immediately about the limits of confidentiality before therapy begins? If clients are told that whatever they say may not be confidential, doesn't it make honest communication from clients more difficult?

In a sense, the purpose of this book, *Understanding Abnormal Behavior,* is to help you answer such questions. To do so, however, requires us first to examine some basic aspects of the study of abnormal behavior, including some of its history and emerging

changes in the field. Periodically, we will return to the case of Art, for it illustrates many complex issues in the field.

The Concerns of Abnormal Psychology

Abnormal psychology is the scientific study whose objectives are to describe, explain, predict, and control behaviors that are considered strange or unusual. Its subject matter ranges from the bizarre and spectacular to the more commonplace—from the violent homicides and "perverted" sexual acts that are widely reported by the news media to such unsensational (but more prevalent) behaviors as stuttering, depression, ulcers, and anxiety about examinations.

Describing Abnormal Behavior

The description of a particular case of abnormal behavior must be based on systematic observations by an attentive professional. These observations, usually paired with the results of psychological tests and with the person's psychological history, become the raw material for a **psychodiagnosis,** an attempt to describe, assess, and systematically draw inferences about an individual's psychological disorder. For example, Art had a long psychiatric history and had been diagnosed as suffering from paranoid schizophrenia. Observations during his sessions revealed the possibility of hallucinations, delusions, and tangential thought processes. These symptoms are certainly consistent with a diagnosis of schizophrenia (American Psychiatric Association, 2000).

Diagnosis is obviously an important early step in the treatment process. But a diagnosis that is not developed with great care can end up as nothing more than a label that tends to hinder rather than aid treatment. Such labels present two major problems. First, like the term *schizophrenic* (a term once used to refer to a particular psychotic disorder) applied to Art, labels can cover a wide range of behaviors and can mean different things to different psychologists. A label may therefore be too general—it may describe something other than a client's specific behaviors. Second, a label describes only a current condition rather than a past or changing circumstance. A person's psychological problems (especially those of a young person) are likely to change over time. A previous diagnosis can quickly become obsolete, a label that no longer describes that person. To guard against these problems, sensitive therapists ensure that labels, either old or new, are not substitutes for careful investigation of a client's condition.

Explaining Abnormal Behavior

To explain abnormal behavior, the psychologist must identify its causes and determine how they led to the described behavior. This information, in turn, bears heavily on how a program of treatment is chosen.

As you will see in later chapters, explanations of abnormal behavior do vary, depending on the psychologist's theoretical orientation. For example, Art's therapist might stress his client's *intrapsychic conflicts* and the need to resolve and control extreme feelings of rage and hostility toward authority figures. Especially pronounced was his deep resentment of early childhood experiences of abandonment by parents. (Art's mother and father were primarily absent parents, more interested in their own careers than in their son.) Other psychologists might concentrate on his *social isolation,* being cared for by a strict Japanese caretaker who spoke no English but who would force him to stay in his room when he misbehaved. Unable to communicate with her, he became suspicious and paranoid about her motives and actions. Although it would be difficult to prove, Art's obvious aversion toward the Japanese (bombing of Pearl Harbor) might be related to his experiences with the race of the caretaker. Explanations offered by still other psychologists might be more *biological* in nature, emphasizing genetics or a biochemical imbalance. And still others might see and treat Art's behavior as resulting from a *combination* of these causes.

Predicting Abnormal Behavior

If a therapist can correctly identify the source of a client's difficulty, he or she should be able to predict the kinds of problems the client will face during therapy and the symptoms the client will display. But therapists have difficulty predicting the future course of many disorders. Even an experienced professional finds it hard to foretell how a particular client will behave.

For example, consider Art's behavior. Was he a danger to people and to the therapist? Does his past proclivity to destroy property and participate in demonstrations indicate an affirmative response? Research shows that mental health professionals do a poor job of predicting dangerousness; they tend to greatly overpredict violence (Buchanan, 1997). Further, as we shall see in the chapter on legal and ethical issues, mental health professionals do not operate in a therapeutic bubble apart from the greater good of society. Mental health laws have codes of conduct that place limits on confidentiality and outline specific actions that must be taken should a client pose a danger to self or others.

Controlling Abnormal Behavior

Abnormal behavior may be controlled through **therapy,** which is a program of systematic intervention whose purpose is to modify a client's behavioral, affective (emotional), and/or cognitive state. For example, many therapists believe that allowing Art an opportunity to get in touch with and to vent his anger would reduce his chances of doing harm to others. Some mental health professionals might also recommend family therapy, social skills training, or medication. Some might even recommend hospitalization. Those who see schizophrenia as caused by a chemical imbalance might rely on a primarily biological means of intervention and prescribe antipsychotic drugs. As we shall shortly see, the treatment for abnormal behavior generally follows from its explanation. Just as there are many ways to explain abnormal behaviors, there are many proposed ways of conducting therapy and an equal number of professional helpers offering their services. Along with the demand for mental health treatment, the numbers and types of qualified helping professionals have grown. In the past, mental health services were controlled primarily by psychiatrists, psychologists, and psychiatric social workers. The list of acceptable (licensed) providers in different fields has expanded rapidly. In 1968 there were 12,000 clinical psychologists in the United States; today there are more than 40,000. As Figure 1.1 illustrates, nearly 300,000 professional therapists now practice in the United States (primarily in clinical psychology, counseling psychology, school psychology, psychiatry, psychoanalysis, social work, and marriage and family counseling). Someone once observed that there are more professional therapists than librarians, firefighters, or mail carriers, and there are twice as many therapists as dentists and pharmacists.

The qualifications, training, and functions of the people who work as mental health professionals are briefly described in Table 1.1. Today, students desiring to enter practice can choose from a variety of professional careers.

Defining Abnormal Behavior

Implicit in our discussion so far is the one overriding concern of abnormal psychology: abnormal behavior itself. But what exactly is abnormal behavior, and how do psychologists recognize it? To answer this question, we examine four types of definitions of abnormal behavior: conceptual, practical, integrated, and the combined definitions given in *Mental Health: A Report of the Surgeon General* (Department of Health and Human Services [DHHS], 1999) and in the *Diagnostic and Statistical Manual of Mental Disorders*

(The same) Behavior can be looked at in many ways

FIGURE 1.1 Number of Professional Therapists in the United States   From 1945 to 1968 the number of clinical psychologists in the United States more than tripled; from that time until today, it quadrupled again. Clinical psychologists represent only a small portion of mental health professionals, whose numbers now approach nearly three hundred thousand. Professional therapists include psychiatrists, social workers, counseling psychologists, marriage and family counselors, and others.

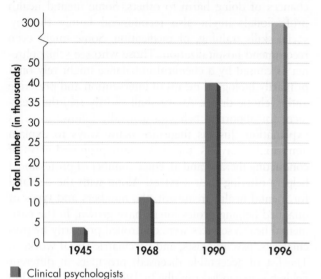

Clinical psychologists

All mental health professionals

Source: Data from Zilbergeld (1983); N. A. Cummings (1995).

(DSM-IV-TR; American Psychiatric Association, 2000). Figure 1.2 summarizes the criteria for each of these definitions.

Conceptual Definitions

Conceptual definitions present a broad framework based on theoretical principles or standards for evaluating normal and abnormal functioning. They define abnormal behavior as, essentially, deviations from what is considered normal or most prevalent in a sociocultural context. The underlying criteria for judging normality and abnormality may be a statistical average, a concept of ideal mental health, or a concept of cultural universality or specificity. In one form or another, the three conceptual definitions form the basis for diagnosing a mental disorder in nearly all criteria used by mental health professionals.

Statistical Deviation   Statistical criteria equate normality with those behaviors that occur most frequently in the population. Abnormality is therefore defined in terms of those behaviors that occur least frequently. For example, data on IQ scores may be accumulated and an average calculated. Then IQ scores near that average are considered normal, and relatively large deviations from the norm (in either direction) are considered abnormal. In spite of the

Intervening Through Therapy
Group therapy is a widely used form of treatment for many problems, especially those involving interpersonal relationships. In this group session, participants are learning to develop new and adaptive social skills in coping with social problems rather than relying on alcohol or drugs to escape the stresses of life.

word *statistical*, however, these criteria need not be quantitative in nature: people who talk to themselves incessantly, undress in public, or laugh uncontrollably for no apparent reason are considered abnormal according to statistical criteria simply because most people do not behave that way. Art's behaviors (hallucinations and tangential thinking) can certainly be considered a violation of a statistical norm.

Definitions based on statistical deviation may seem adequate in some specific instances, but they present many problems. One problem is that they fail to take into account differences in place, community standards, and cultural values. For example, some lifestyles that are acceptable in San Francisco and New York may be judged abnormal by community standards in other parts of the nation. Likewise, if deviations from the majority are considered abnormal, then many ethnic

---

TABLE 1.1 The Mental Health Professions

Clinical psychology Clinical psychology is the professional field concerned with the study, assessment, treatment, and prevention of abnormal behavior in disturbed individuals. Clinical psychologists must hold a Ph.D. degree from a university or a Psy.D. (doctor of psychology) degree, a more practitioner-oriented degree granted by several institutions. Their training includes course work in psychopathology, personality, diagnosis, psychological testing, psychotherapy, and human physiology. Apart from these and other course requirements, there are two additional requirements for the Ph.D. degree. In addition, they are required to complete a doctoral dissertation and usually a one-year internship. Clinical psychologists work in a variety of settings, but most commonly they provide therapy to clients in hospitals and clinics and in private practice. Some choose to work in academic settings in which they can concentrate on teaching and research. Other clinical psychologists are hired by government or private organizations to do research.

Counseling psychology To a great extent, a description of clinical psychology applies to counseling psychology as well. The academic and internship requirements are similar, but the emphasis differs. Whereas clinical psychologists are trained to work specifically with a disturbed client population, counseling psychologists are usually more immediately concerned with the study of life problems in relatively normal people. Furthermore, counseling psychologists are more likely to be found in educational settings than in hospitals and clinics.

School psychology School psychology is the field of study concerned with the processes of cognitive and emotional development of students in educational settings. Thus it focuses on the processes of learning, remembering, and thinking and on human development as it applies to the educational process. School psychologists may hold either a master's or a doctoral degree. They are often employed by school districts to help with assessment and testing and with the treatment of learning difficulties.

Psychiatry Psychiatrists hold an M.D. degree. Their education includes the four years of medical school required for that degree, along with an additional three or four years of training in psychiatry. Of all the specialists involved in mental health care, only psychiatrists can prescribe drugs in the treatment of mental disorders.

Psychoanalysis Psychoanalysis has been associated with medicine and psychiatry because its founder, Sigmund Freud, and his major disciples were physicians. But Freud was quite adamant in stating that one need not be medically trained to be a good psychoanalyst. Nevertheless, most psychoanalysts hold either the M.D. or the Ph.D. degree. In addition, psychoanalysts receive intensive training in the theory and practice of psychoanalysis at an institute devoted to the field. This training includes the individual's own analysis by an experienced analyst.

Psychiatric social work Those entering psychiatric social work are trained in a school of social work, usually in a two-year graduate program leading to a master's degree. Included in this program is a one-year internship in a social-service agency, sometimes a mental health center. Some social workers go on to earn the D.S.W. (doctor of social work) degree. Traditionally, psychiatric social workers work in family counseling services or community agencies, where they specialize in intake (assessment and screening of clients), take psychiatric histories, and deal with other agencies.

Marriage and family counseling A specialty in marriage and family counseling has recently emerged with its own professional organizations, journals, and state licensing requirements. Marriage and family counselors have varied professional backgrounds, but their training usually includes a master's degree in counseling and many hours of supervised clinical experience.

Mental health counselors As of this writing, mental health counselors are recognized and licensed for clinical/counseling practice in 48 states. They work in a variety of settings, receive intensive training in personal, emotional, vocational and human development, and have their own professional association. Mental health counselors must meet many hours of supervised clinical experience and possess a master's degree in counseling.

FIGURE 1.2 Abnormal Behavior Defined   There are numerous definitions of abnormal behavior that have been used by mental health professionals. Some of the most current and widely used ones are briefly described here.

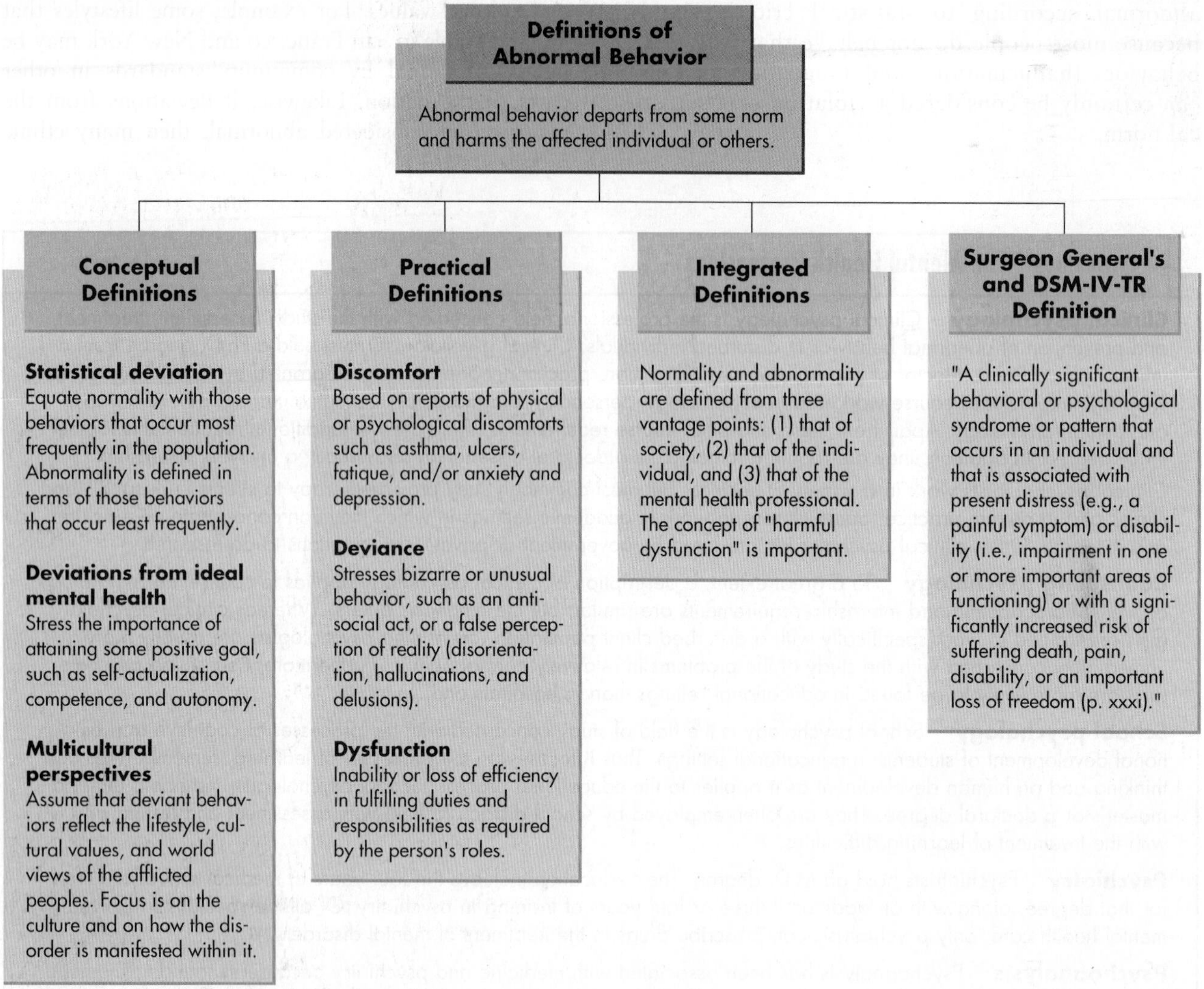

Definitions of Abnormal Behavior

Abnormal behavior departs from some norm and harms the affected individual or others.

Conceptual Definitions

Statistical deviation
Equate normality with those behaviors that occur most frequently in the population. Abnormality is defined in terms of those behaviors that occur least frequently.

Deviations from ideal mental health
Stress the importance of attaining some positive goal, such as self-actualization, competence, and autonomy.

Multicultural perspectives
Assume that deviant behaviors reflect the lifestyle, cultural values, and world views of the afflicted peoples. Focus is on the culture and on how the disorder is manifested within it.

Practical Definitions

Discomfort
Based on reports of physical or psychological discomforts such as asthma, ulcers, fatigue, and/or anxiety and depression.

Deviance
Stresses bizarre or unusual behavior, such as an antisocial act, or a false perception of reality (disorientation, hallucinations, and delusions).

Dysfunction
Inability or loss of efficiency in fulfilling duties and responsibilities as required by the person's roles.

Integrated Definitions

Normality and abnormality are defined from three vantage points: (1) that of society, (2) that of the individual, and (3) that of the mental health professional. The concept of "harmful dysfunction" is important.

Surgeon General's and DSM-IV-TR Definition

"A clinically significant behavioral or psychological syndrome or pattern that occurs in an individual and that is associated with present distress (e.g., a painful symptom) or disability (i.e., impairment in one or more important areas of functioning) or with a significantly increased risk of suffering death, pain, disability, or an important loss of freedom (p. xxxi)."

and racial minorities that show strong subcultural differences from the majority must be classified as abnormal. When we use a statistical definition, the dominant or most powerful group generally determines what constitutes normality and abnormality.

In addition, the statistical criteria do not provide any basis for distinguishing between desirable and undesirable deviations from the norm. An IQ score of 100 is considered normal or average. But what constitutes an abnormal deviation from this average? More important, is abnormality defined in only one direction or in both? An IQ score of 55 is considered abnormal by most people, but should people with IQ scores of 145 or higher also be considered abnormal? How

does one evaluate such personality traits as assertiveness and dependence in terms of statistical criteria?

Two other central problems also arise. First, people who strike out in new directions—artistically, politically, or intellectually—may be seen as candidates for psychotherapy simply because they do not conform to normative behavior. Second, statistical criteria may "define" quite widely distributed but undesirable characteristics, such as anxiety, as normal.

In spite of these weaknesses, statistical criteria remain among the most widely used determinants of normality and abnormality. Not only do they underlie the layperson's evaluation of behaviors, but they are also the most frequently used criteria in psychology.

Determining What's Abnormal By most people's standards, the full-body tattoo of this man would probably be considered unusual at best and bizarre at worst. Yet despite the way his body appears, this person may be very functional in his work and personal life. This leads to an important question: What constitutes abnormal behavior and how do we recognize it?

Many psychological tests and much diagnosis and classification of behavior disorders are based in part on statistical criteria.

Deviation from Ideal Mental Health

The concept of ideal mental health was proposed as a criterion of normality by humanistic psychologists Carl Rogers and Abraham Maslow. Deviations from the ideal are taken to indicate varying degrees of abnormality.

This type of definition stresses the importance of attaining some positive goal. For Maslow and his followers, the goal was *self-actualization* or *creativity*. Psychoanalytically oriented psychologists have used the concept of *consciousness* (awareness of motivations and behaviors) and *balance of psychic forces* as criteria for normality. Others have proposed aspects of maturity, such as *competence*, *autonomy*, and *resistance to stress*. But using any of these constructs as the sole criterion for defining normality leads to a number of problems.

First, which particular goal or ideal should be used? The answer depends largely on the particular theoretical frame of reference or values embraced by those proposing the criterion. Second, most of these goals are vague; they lack clarity and precision. If resistance to stress is the goal, are the only healthy persons those who can always adapt? Study of the experiences of prisoners of war indicates that many of them eventually break down under repeated stress. Should we label them as unhealthy? A third problem is that ideal criteria exclude too many people: most persons would be considered mentally unhealthy by these definitions.

Multicultural Perspectives

All behaviors, whether normal or abnormal, originate from a cultural context. Psychologists are increasingly recognizing that this is an inescapable conclusion and that culture plays a major role in our understanding of human behavior. But what is culture? There are many definitions of "culture." For our purposes, culture is "shared learned behavior which is transmitted from one generation to another for purposes of individual and societal growth, adjustment, and adaptation: culture is represented externally as artifacts, roles, and institutions, and it is represented internally as values, beliefs, attitudes, epistemology, consciousness and biological functioning" (Marsella, 1988, pp. 8–9). Three important points should be emphasized:

1. Culture is not synonymous with *race* or *ethnic group*. Jewish, Polish, Irish, and Italian Americans represent diverse ethnic groups whose individual members may share a common racial classification. Yet their cultural contexts may differ substantially from one another. Likewise, an Irish American and an Italian American, despite their different ethnic heritages, may share the same cultural context. And even within the same ethnic group, small groups of individuals may develop and transmit shared behavior patterns that in essence constitute a form of culture.

2. Every society or group that shares and transmits behaviors to its members possesses a culture. European Americans, African Americans, Latino/Hispanic Americans, Asian Americans/Pacific

Islanders, Native Americans, and other social groups within the United States have a culture. For example, a strong argument can be made that hearing impaired or deaf people possess a culture (Olkin, 1999). "Signing" represents a language.

3. Culture is a powerful determinant of worldviews (Sue & Sue, 2003). It affects how we define normal and abnormal behaviors and how we treat disorders encountered by members of that culture. Even racial or ethnic groups that possess many similarities may have quite different cultural constellations.

These three points give rise to a major problem: one group's definition of mental illness may not be shared by another. This contradicts the traditional view of abnormal psychology, which is based on **cultural universality**—the assumption that a fixed set of mental disorders exists whose obvious manifestations cut across cultures (Kim & Berry, 1993). This psychiatric tradition dates back to Emil Kraepelin (discussed later in this chapter), who believed that depression, sociopathic behavior, and especially schizophrenia were universal disorders that appeared in all cultures and societies. Early research supported the belief that these disorders occurred worldwide, had similar processes, and were more similar than dissimilar (Howard, 1992). From this flowed the belief that a disorder such as depression is similar in origin, process, and manifestation in all societies, such as Asia, Africa, and Latin America. As a result, no modifications in diagnosis and treatment need be made; western concepts of normality and abnormality can be considered universal and equally applicable across cultures.

In contrast to the traditional view of cultural universality has been **cultural relativism,** the belief that lifestyles, cultural values, and worldviews affect the expression and determination of deviant behavior. This concept arose from the anthropological tradition and emphasized the importance of culture and diversity in the manifestation of abnormal symptoms. For example, a body of research supports the conclusion that acting-out behaviors associated with mental disorders are much higher in the United States than in Asia and that even Asian Americans in the United States are less likely to express symptoms via acting out (Asian American Federation of New York, 2003; Chun, Eastman, Wang, & Sue, 1998; Hong & Domokos-Cheng Ham, 2001). Researchers have proposed that Asian cultural values (restraint of feelings, emphasis on self-control, and need for subtlety in approaching problems) all contribute to this restraint. Proponents of cultural relativism also point out that cultures vary in what they consider to be normal or abnormal behavior. In some societies and cultural groups, hallucinating (having false sensory impres-

Cultural Relativism Cultural differences often lead to misunderstandings and misinterpretations. In a society that values technological conveniences and clothing that comes from the runways of modern fashion, the lifestyles and cultural values of others may be perceived as strange. The Amish, for example, continue to rely on traditional modes of transportation (horse and buggy). And women in both the Amish and Islamic cultures wear simple, concealing clothing; in their circumstances, dressing in any other way would be considered deviant.

sions) is considered normal in specific situations. Yet in the United States, hallucinating is generally perceived to be a manifestation of a disorder.

Which view is correct? Should the criteria used to determine normality and abnormality be based on cultural universality or cultural relativism? Few mental health professionals today embrace the extreme of either position, although most gravitate toward one or the other. Proponents of cultural universality focus on the disorder and minimize cultural factors, and proponents of cultural relativism focus on the culture and on how the disorder is manifested within it. Both views have validity. It is naive to believe that no disorders cut across different cultures and share universal characteristics. For example, even though hallucinating may be viewed as normal in some cultures, proponents of cultural universality argue that it still represents a breakdown in biological-cognitive processes. Likewise, it is equally naive to believe that the relative frequencies and manner of symptom formation for various disorders do not reflect dominant cultural values and the lifestyles of a society (American Psychiatric Association, 2000). A third point to consider is that some common disorders, such as depression, are manifested similarly in different cultures.

A more fruitful approach to studying multicultural criteria of abnormality is to explore two questions:

- What is universal in human behavior that is also relevant to understanding psychopathology?

- What is the relationship between cultural norms, values, and attitudes and the incidence and manifestation of behavior disorders?

These are important questions that we hope you will ask as we continue our journey into the field of abnormal psychology. In the chapter on models of abnormal behavior, we try to address these questions directly by presenting a tripartite model to view how culture is an intimate aspect of our identity and functioning.

Practical Definitions

Practical definitions of abnormal behavior are based on pragmatic or clinical criteria concerning the effect of the behavior on the person exhibiting it or on others. These definitions are subject to many of the same criticisms discussed earlier. Nonetheless, they are often the basis on which people who are labeled abnormal or unhealthy come to the attention of psychologists or other mental health specialists. Moreover, clinicians often must act primarily on the basis of pragmatic manifestations. The practical criteria for abnormality include subjective *discomfort, deviance* (bizarreness), and *dysfunction* (inefficiency in behavioral, affective, and/or cognitive domains).

Discomfort   Most people who seek the help of therapists are suffering physical or psychological discomfort. Many physical reactions stem from a strong psychological component; among them are disorders such as asthma, hypertension, and ulcers, as well as physical symptoms such as fatigue, nausea, pain, and heart palpitations. Discomfort can also be manifested in extreme or prolonged emotional reactions, of which anxiety and depression are the most prevalent and common. Of course, it is normal for a person to feel depressed after suffering a loss or a disappointment. But if the reaction is so intense, exaggerated, and prolonged that it interferes with the person's capacity to function adequately, it is likely to be considered abnormal.

Societal Norms and Deviance   Societal norms often affect our definitions of normality and abnormality. When social norms begin to change, standards used to judge behaviors or roles also shift. Here we see two examples of role reversal that are becoming more acceptable over time: a woman working as a stonemason cutting limestone blocks and a husband who staggers his work schedule with his wife's so that they can share in caring for their children.

Deviance   As a practical criterion for abnormality, deviance is closely related to statistical criteria. Bizarre or unusual behavior is an abnormal deviation from an accepted standard of behavior (such as an antisocial act) or a false perception of reality (such as a hallucination). This criterion is extremely subjective; it depends on the individual being diagnosed, on the diagnostician, and, as we have seen, on the particular culture.

Certain sexual behaviors, delinquency, and homicide are examples of acts that our society considers abnormal. But social norms are far from static, and behavioral standards cannot be considered absolute. Changes in our attitudes toward human sexuality provide a prime example. During the Victorian era, women wore six to eight undergarments to make sure that every part of the body from the neck down was covered. Exposing an ankle was roughly equivalent to wearing a topless bathing suit today. Taboos against publicly recognizing sexuality dictated that words be chosen carefully to avoid any sexual connotation. Victorians said "limb" instead of "leg" because the word *leg* was considered too erotic. (Even pianos and tables were said to have limbs.) People who did not adhere to these strict codes of conduct were considered immoral or even perverted. One can only wonder what people of the Victorian era would have thought had they encountered anything as sexually graphic as the newspaper and media accounts of the President Clinton and Monica Lewinsky affair.

Although these accounts drew comments from many critics, many American magazines and films now openly exhibit the naked human body, and topless and bottomless nightclub entertainment is hardly newsworthy. Various sex acts are explicitly portrayed in NC-17-rated movies. Women are freer to question traditional sex roles and to act more assertively in initiating sex. Such changes in behavior make it difficult to subscribe to absolute standards of normality.

Nevertheless, some behaviors can usually be judged abnormal in most situations. Among these are severe disorientation, hallucinations, and delusions. *Disorientation* is confusion with regard to identity, place, or time. People who are disoriented may not know who they are, where they are, or what historical era they are living in. *Hallucinations* are false impressions—either pleasant or unpleasant—that involve the senses. People who have hallucinations may hear, feel, or see things that are not really there, such as voices accusing them of vile deeds, insects crawling on their bodies, or monstrous apparitions. *Delusions* are false beliefs steadfastly held by the individual despite contradictory objective evidence. A *delusion of grandeur* is a belief that one is an exalted personage, such as Jesus Christ or Joan of Arc; a *delusion of persecution* is a belief that one is controlled by others or is the victim of a conspiracy.

Dysfunction   Dysfunctions in a person's biological, mental, and emotional states are often manifested in role performance. One way to assess dysfunction is to compare an individual's performance with the requirements of a role. In everyday life, people are expected to fulfill various roles—as students or teachers; as workers and caretakers; as parents, lovers, and marital partners. Emotional problems sometimes interfere with the performance of these roles, and the resulting role dysfunction may be used as an indicator of abnormality.

Another related way to assess dysfunction is to compare the individual's performance with his or her potential. An individual with an IQ score of 150 who is failing in school can be labeled inefficient. (The label *under-achiever* is often hung on students who possess high

intelligence but obtain poor grades in school.) Similarly, a productive worker who suddenly becomes unproductive may be experiencing emotional stress. The major weakness of this approach is that it is difficult to accurately assess potential. How do we know whether a person is performing at his or her peak? To answer such questions, psychologists, educators, and the business sector have relied heavily on testing. Tests of specific abilities and intelligence are attempts to assess potential and to predict performance in schools or jobs.

Integrated Definitions

Different definitions of abnormality carry different implications, and there is no easy consensus on a best definition. All the criteria we have discussed have shortcomings. Many of these deficiencies and their sociopolitical implications have been well articulated by Thomas Szasz (1987). In a radical departure from conventional beliefs, he has asserted that mental illness is a myth, a fictional creation by society used to control and change people. According to Szasz, people may suffer from "problems in living," not from "mental illness." His argument stems from three beliefs: that abnormal behavior is so labeled because it is different, not necessarily because it is a reflection of "illness"; that unusual belief systems are not necessarily wrong; and that abnormal behavior is frequently a reflection of something wrong with society rather than with the individual. Individuals are labeled "mentally ill" because their behaviors violate the social order and their beliefs challenge the prevailing wisdom of the times. Szasz finds the concept of mental illness to be dangerous and a form of social control used by those in power. Hitler branded Jews as abnormal. Political dissidents in many countries, including both China and the former Soviet Union, have often been cast as mentally ill. And the history of slavery indicates that African Americans who tried to escape their white masters were often labeled as suffering from *drapetomania*, defined as a sickness making the person desire freedom.

Few mental health professionals would take the extreme position advocated by Szasz, but his arguments highlight an important area of concern. Those who diagnose behavior as abnormal must be sensitive not only to such variables as psychological orientation but also to individual value systems, societal norms and values, and potential sociopolitical ramifications.

Perhaps, then, definitions of abnormality should not be viewed from a single perspective or in accordance with a single criterion but rather should be an integrated statement incorporating multiple perspectives. Two early researchers (Strupp & Hadley, 1977) proposed a three-part method for defining normality and abnormality; their method continues to represent one of the more useful conceptualizations of abnormality. They identified three vantage points from which to judge a person's mental health: (1) that of society, (2) that of the individual, and (3) that of the mental health professional. Each "judge" operates from a different perspective, perhaps using different criteria. At times, three people taking these viewpoints would agree that a person is either mentally disturbed or mentally healthy. At other times, they might disagree. Nonetheless, using an integrated set of criteria alleviates the problems inherent in imposing a single criterion to define behavior.

We·must carefully consider two important points as we assess the value of the multiple-perspectives concept. First, a person who feels subjectively contented—mentally sound—may be perceived as unhealthy from a societal perspective. For example, people who commit antisocial acts such as rape, murder, or robbery may not feel remorseful but may be quite contented with their acts. Similarly, an artist living a very unconventional lifestyle may be judged maladapted from society's perspective; from that individual's perspective and the perspective of many health professionals, however, he or she is intact and sound. Second, a judgment must be recognized as stemming from one of the three vantage points. Otherwise, even greater confusion could result.

Another proposal for an integrated definition comes from Wakefield (1992), who has advocated defining the concept of mental disorder from the perspective of biological facts and social values. He argues that a mental disorder is a "harmful dysfunction," wherein the term *harmful* is based on social norms, and *dysfunction* is a scientific term referring to the "failure of a mental mechanism to perform a natural function for which it was designed by evolution." This definition considers the following points to be essential:

1. Understanding dysfunction requires identifying the natural functions of an organ or organ system; the function of the heart, for example, is to pump blood.

2. We must distinguish between functions and effects; the sound of a beating heart is an effect and not a function—thus a quiet heart is not a dysfunction.

3. We must ultimately look for our definition of disorder in the biological sciences.

4. Dysfunction must involve the harm requirement—seen from a social and cultural perspective—if it is to be considered a disorder.

This fourth point is an important one. Wakefield (1992) argues that dysfunctions must cause significant harm to the person according to current environmental and cultural standards. Thus albinism, reversal of heart position, or fused toes would not be considered a disor-

der even though each involves a breakdown of natural functions. Likewise, hallucinations may be a manifestation of a mental disorder because they represent a *dysfunction* of a normal biological process. Yet a cultural group that values "visions" would not consider them harmful but would view them as a positive development. And certainly a man whose aging mechanism suffers a dysfunction that slows the aging process would not be considered disordered but lucky! A truly adequate understanding of mental illness and health can be reached through comprehensive evaluation from all points of view. It may not be enough to rely solely on the judgments of mental health professionals, who are not immune to biases and shortcomings.

The Surgeon General's and DSM-IV-TR Definitions

Thus we may define **abnormal behavior** as behavior that departs from some norm and that harms the affected individual or others. This definition encompasses—or at least allows room for—the various criteria and perspectives on behavior. It also accurately implies that no precise, universally acknowledged line delineates normal behavior from abnormal behavior. And by a *mental disorder* or *mental disturbance* we mean some recognizable pattern of abnormal behavior.

This definition is also consistent with the ones used in both the Surgeon General's report on mental health (DHHS, 1999) and the DSM-IV-TR (American Psychiatric Association, 2000): "a clinically significant behavioral or psychological syndrome or pattern that occurs in an individual and that is associated with present distress (e.g., a painful symptom) or disability (i.e., impairment in one or more important areas of functioning) or with a significantly increased risk of suffering death, pain, disability, or an important loss of freedom" (American Psychiatric Association, 2000, p. xxxi).

The Frequency and Burden of Mental Disorders

A student once asked one of the authors, "How crazy is this nation?" This question, put in somewhat more scientific terms, has occupied psychologists for some time. Psychiatric epidemiology provides insights into factors that contribute to the occurrence of specific mental disorders. Prior to our discussion, however, some terms need to be clarified. The **prevalence** of a disorder indicates the percentage of people in a population who suffer from a disorder at a given point in time; **lifetime prevalence** refers to the total proportion of people in the population who have ever had a disorder in their lives. **Incidence** refers to the onset or occurrence of a given disorder over some period of time. From this information, we can find out how frequently or infrequently various disturbances occur in the population. We can also consider how the prevalence of disorders varies by ethnicity, gender, and age and whether current mental health practices are sufficient and effective.

Current Research into the Epidemiology of Mental Disorders

An early but highly regarded and frequently cited study, the Midtown Manhattan Study, was performed in 1950 (Srole, Langer, Michael, Opler, & Rennie, 1962). Fifteen hundred New Yorkers were interviewed and rated on their psychological health. The results were startling: approximately 25 percent of those interviewed showed severe impairment, about 55 percent were mildly impaired, and only 20 percent (one in five) were rated unimpaired.

Some social commentators contend that our mental health has deteriorated since the Midtown Manhattan Study was conducted. They point to such "evidence" as the mushrooming of cults; a revival of belief in the supernatural; the increased incidence of mass murder (Oklahoma City bombing of the Federal Building) and serial murder; children killing fellow classmates in Littleton, Colorado, and Santee, California; the increase in incidents of hate crimes; mass suicides such as those of the Jonestown and Heaven's Gate cult followers; and attempts at political assassination.

More recently, the destruction of the World Trade Center in New York City, the attack on the Pentagon near Washington, D.C., and the downing of an airliner in Pennsylvania by terrorists have left a nation stunned and shocked. This has been followed by a threat of bioterrorism with reports of anthrax contamination and several deaths. Many believe that the September 11, 2001, tragedy has severely traumatized Americans and that an increase in the incidence of mental disorders is likely to follow.

To ascertain whether the population's mental health was deteriorating, researchers carried out a similar study in the 1970s (Srole & Fischer, 1980). Although the investigators found no support for this contention, neither did they find any evidence that the mental health of Americans had improved in the intervening decades.

Perhaps the most thorough and comprehensive study of the incidence of mental disorders in the U.S. adult population (eighteen years and older) was conducted by the National Institute of Mental Health (NIMH, 1985; see also Eaton et al., 1984; Freedman, 1984; Myers et al., 1984; Regier et al., 1988; Regier et al., 1993; Robins et al., 1984; Robins, Locke, & Regier, 1991). The NIMH epidemiological study included data collected in

Long-term Effects of Trauma   On September 11, 2001, terrorist attacks destroyed the World Trade Center in lower Manhattan, killing thousands and traumatizing a nation. What are the mental health consequences of extreme disasters? How are these effects measured?

three major cities: New Haven, Baltimore, and St. Louis. The study had several features that distinguished it from others. It included a large sample of approximately 20,000 persons, and it used the categories in the *Diagnostic and Statistical Manual* of the American Psychiatric Association in the construction of the research instruments.

As in the previous studies cited, participants reported a high rate of disorders. Approximately 29 to 38 percent (percentage range accounts for variations in the three cities) of the sample reported that they experienced at least one mental disorder! Schizophrenia, often one of the most severe mental disturbances, affects 1 percent of the population, or approximately 2.5 million Americans. Figure 1.3 presents one-year and lifetime-prevalence rates of various mental disorders as percentages of the total U.S. population.

Researchers also found that although men and women were equally likely to suffer from mental disorders, they differ in the kinds of disorders they experience. For example, alcohol abuse or dependence occurs in 24 percent of men but in only 4 percent of women; drug abuse is more likely to occur in men; and depression and anxiety are more likely to occur in women. Age was also an important factor. Alcoholism and depression are most prominent in the twenty-five- to forty-four-year-old age group; drug dependence in the eighteen- to twenty-four-year-old age group; and cognitive impairment in people age sixty-five and older. Phobias, however, were equally represented at all ages. Studies on even the young (children and adolescents) suggest that nearly 17 percent suffer from a serious disorder (Kessler et al., 1994; Regier et al., 1993). Figure 1.4 summarizes the rates of psychiatric disorders in various demographic categories. Some of the findings are not surprising—for example, common sense might cause us to guess that financially dependent or less educated Americans would have higher rates of disorders. The relationship of disorders to other characteristics is more obscure, and sometimes downright baffling: how would you explain the fact that the lowest percentages are found for people sixty-five or older or that rural dwellers have a lower rate than their urban counterparts? Such findings require critical analyses.

The cost and burden of mental disorders to our nation are indeed a major source of concern. The recognition of this problem was the impetus for *Mental Health: A Report of the Surgeon General* (DHHS, 1999) and *Achieving the Promise: Transforming Mental Health Care in America* (President's New Freedom Commission on Mental Health, 2003), two comprehensive reports on the state of mental health in our nation. Their conclusions were very troubling: (1) at least 30 percent of the nation's adults suffer from a diagnosable mental disorder; (2) 20 percent of children show signs of a diagnosable disorder in the course of a year; (3) by the year 2020, neuropsychiatric disorders for children will increase by 50 percent and become one of the five most common forms of disability; (4) we continue to lack adequate knowledge and information regarding the causes, treatment, and prevention of mental disorders;

FIGURE 1.3 Rates of Various Mental Disorders This figure shows the one-year and lifetime-prevalence rates of mental disorders as percentages of the population. It is clear that the most common mental disorders in the United States are phobias, followed by alcohol-related problems, anxiety, and depressive episodes.

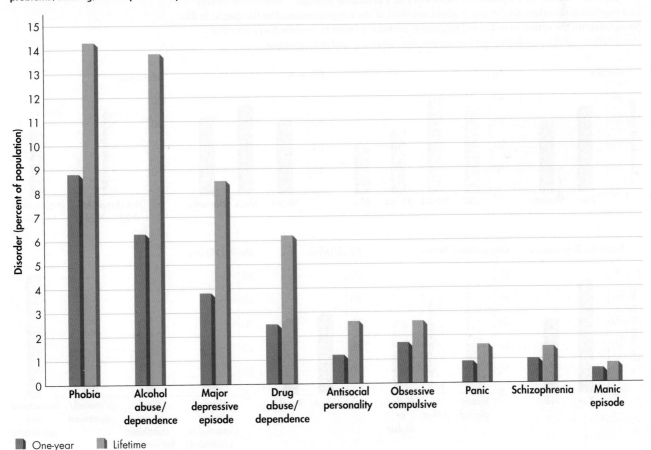

Source: Data from Robins & Regier (1991).

(5) the major obstacle to mental health progress is "stigma"; (6) collectively, mental disorders account for more than 15 percent of the overall burden of disease from all causes; and (7) mental illness and mental health must become part of a public health policy.

To indicate the profound impact mental disorders have on our health and productivity, the measure of disease burden, Disability Adjusted Life Years (DALYs), compares a disease (mental illness) across many different disease conditions (DHHS, 1999). DALYs record lost years of healthy life regardless of whether the years were lost to premature death or some form of disability. Mental illness ranks higher than cancer and all other malignant diseases! More frightening, however, is the point strongly made in the Surgeon General's report that many people suffer from "mental health problems" that do not meet the criteria for a mental disorder. These problems, the report observes, may be equally debilitating unless adequately treated.

These epidemiological findings are troubling, to say the least. Clearly, mental disturbances are widespread,

and many persons are currently suffering from them. What is more troubling is that two-thirds of all people suffering from a diagnosable mental disorder are not receiving or seeking mental health services (President's New Freedom Commission on Mental Health, 2003). Yet spending on mental health services has declined over 54 percent, from $154 per person in 1988 to $69 per person in 1998, and the period from 1988 to 1997 saw mental health care benefits slashed 670 percent more than general health care benefits (Reed, Levant, Stout, Murphy, & Phelps, 2001)!

Stereotypes About the Mentally Disturbed

Americans tend to be suspicious of people with mental disorders. Are most of them really maniacs who at any moment may be seized by uncontrollable urges to murder, rape, or maim? Such portrayals seem to emerge from the news media and the entertainment industry, but they are rarely accurate. Like other minority groups in the United States, people with mental disturbances are the subject of rampant stereotyping and

FIGURE 1.4 Rates of Psychiatric Disorders in Particular Groups   Research indicates that psychiatric disorders are present in about one-third of the U.S. population. The bar graphs in this figure illustrate the extent to which any psychiatric disorder is found in combination with other characteristics of the population, such as gender, age, ethnicity, and marital status.

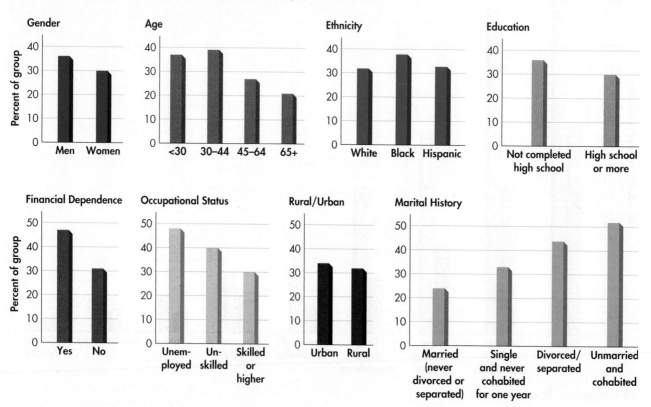

Source: Data from Robins & Regier (1991).

popular misconceptions. It is worthwhile at this point to dispel the most common of these misconceptions or myths.

Myth vs Reality

Myth: "Mentally disturbed people can always be recognized by their consistently deviant abnormal behavior."

Reality: Mentally disturbed people are not always distinguishable from others on the basis of consistently unusual behavior. Even in an outpatient clinic or a psychiatric ward, distinguishing patients from staff on the basis of behavior alone is often difficult. There are two main reasons for this difficulty. First, as already noted, no sharp dividing line usually exists between "normal" and "abnormal" behaviors. Rather, the spectrum of behaviors is continuous, ranging from abnormal to normal. Depending on the situational context and the perspective of the person judging the behavior, many behaviors could be considered either normal or deviant. Second, even when people are suffering from some form of emotional disturbance, that experience may not always be detectable in their behavior.

Myth: "The mentally disturbed have inherited their disorders. If one member of a family has an emotional breakdown, other members will probably suffer a similar fate."

Reality: The belief that insanity runs in certain families has caused misery and undue anxiety for many people. Although the data are far from conclusive, heredity does not seem to play a major role in most mental disorders, except for some cases of schizophrenia and depression, certain types of mental retardation, and the bipolar disorders. Evidence suggests that, even though heredity may predispose an individual to certain disorders, environmental factors are extremely important. When many family members suffer from mental disorders, a stress-producing environment is usually acting on the family predisposition. If the environment is benign, however, or if predisposed individuals modify a stressful environment, psychopathology may never occur.

Myth: "The mentally disturbed person can never be cured and will never be able to function normally or hold a job in the community."

Reality: This erroneous belief has caused great distress to many people who have at some time been labeled mentally ill. Former mental patients have endured social discrimination and have been denied employment because of the public perception that "once insane, always insane." Unfortunately, this myth may keep former mental patients or those currently experiencing emotional problems from seeking help. Although most people don't hesitate to consult a doctor, dentist, or lawyer for help, many who need mental health services are fearful and anxious about the social stigma attached to being labeled "mentally ill." Nearly three-fourths of clients who are hospitalized with severe disorders will improve and go on to lead productive lives. Many recovered mental patients make excellent employees, and employers frequently report that they outperform other workers in attendance and

Incidence of Abnormal Behavior By all appearances, this photo seems to depict a well-functioning group of college graduates from many facets of life. Yet studies reveal that approximately one in three persons suffers from at least one mental disorder.

punctuality. Some famous examples of persons who have recovered from mental disorders are President Abraham Lincoln; philosopher William James; *60 Minutes* news anchor Mike Wallace; writer Art Buchwald; a former vice president's wife, Tipper Gore; and talk show host Rosie O'Donnell.

Myth: "People become mentally disturbed because they are weak-willed. To avoid emotional disorders or cure oneself of them, one need only exercise will power."

Reality: These statements show that the speaker does not understand the nature of mental disorders. Needing help to resolve difficulties does not indicate a lack of will power. In fact, recognizing one's own need for help may be a sign of strength rather than a sign of weakness. Many problems stem from situations that are not under the individual's immediate control, such as the death of a loved one or the loss of a job. Other problems stem from lifelong patterns of faulty learning; it is naive to expect that a simple exercise of will can override years of experience.

Myth: "Mental illness is always a deficit, and the person suffering from it can never contribute anything of worth until cured."

Reality: Many persons who suffered from mental illness were never "cured," but they nevertheless made great contributions to humanity. Ernest Hemingway, who was one of the great writers of our time and who won the Nobel Prize for literature in 1954, suffered from lifelong depressions, alcoholism, and frequent hospitalizations. In 1961 he put a shotgun in his mouth and killed himself. The famous Dutch painter Vincent van Gogh produced great works of art despite the fact that he was severely disturbed. Not only did he lead an unhappy and tortured life, he frequently heard voices, he cut off a piece of his left ear as a gift to a prostitute, and he finally committed suicide. Others, such as Pablo Picasso and Edgar Allan Poe, contributed major works to humanity while seriously disturbed. The point of these examples is not to illustrate that madness and genius go hand in hand but that many who are less severely disturbed can continue to lead productive and worthwhile lives. Because people suffer from psychological problems does not mean that their ideas and contributions are less worthy of consideration.

Myth: "The mentally disturbed person is unstable and potentially dangerous."

Reality: This misconception has been perpetuated by the mass media. Many murderers featured on television are labeled "psychopathic," and the news media concentrate on the occasional mental patient who kills. But the thousands of mental patients who do not commit crimes, do not harm others, and do not get into trouble with the law are not news. According to the Surgeon General's report (DHHS, 1999), there is a small elevation of risk of violence, especially among individuals with dual diagnosis (suffering from a mental disorder and substance abuse), but the risk is minimal (Swanson, 1994; Eronen, Angermeyer, & Schulze, 1998). Unfortunately, the myth persists.

Historical Perspectives on Abnormal Behavior

In this section and the next, we briefly review the historical development of western thought concerning abnormal behavior. We must be aware, however, that our journey is necessarily culture-bound and that other civilizations (nonwestern) have histories of their own.

The task of reconstructing what our ancestors believed about abnormal behavior is further complicated for two reasons. First, we lack specific facts about the historical past and must piece them together. Until other information is uncovered, these gaps in our knowledge could lead us to mistaken conclusions. For example, disagreements now exist over the psychiatric interpretation of witchcraft.

Second, historical interpretation depends on the perspective of the researcher. For example, an anthropological approach to the study of history may differ from a psychological one. Within each discipline, one's biases and point of view may affect how an interpretation is made. Even given these limitations, many current attitudes toward abnormal behavior, as well as modern ideas about its causes and treatment, appear to have been influenced by early beliefs. In fact, some psychologists contend that modern societies have, in essence, adopted more sophisticated versions of earlier concepts. For example, the use of electroconvulsive therapy to treat depression is in some ways similar to ancient practices of exorcism in which the body was physically assaulted. The Greek physician Hippocrates, 2,500 years ago, believed that many abnormal behaviors were caused by imbalances and disorders in the brain and the body, a belief shared by many contemporary psychologists.

Most ideas about abnormal behavior are firmly rooted in the system of beliefs that operate in a given society at a given time. Perhaps for that reason, change—especially in the form of new ideas—does not come quickly or easily. People who dare to voice ideas that differ from the prevalent beliefs of their time have often been made outcasts or even, in some periods, executed. Yet in spite of the difficulties, we have evolved a humanistic and scientific explanation of abnormal behavior. It remains to be seen whether such an explanation will still be thought valid in decades to come. (Much of this history section is based on discussions of deviant behavior by Alexander & Selesnick, 1966; Hunter & Macalpine, 1963; Neugebauer, 1979; Spanos, 1978; and Zilboorg & Henry, 1941).

Prehistoric and Ancient Beliefs

Prehistoric societies some half a million years ago did not distinguish sharply between mental and physical disorders. Abnormal behaviors, from simple headaches to convulsive attacks, were attributed to evil spirits that inhabited or controlled the afflicted person's body. According to historians, these ancient peoples attributed many forms of illness to demonic possession, sorcery, or the behest of an offended ancestral spirit. Within this system of belief, called *demonology*, the victim was usually held at least partly responsible for the misfortune.

It has been suggested that Stone Age cave dwellers may have treated behavior disorders with a surgical method called **trephining,** in which part of the skull was chipped away to provide an opening through which the evil spirit could escape. People may have believed that when the evil spirit left, the person would return to his or her normal state. Surprisingly, some trephined skulls have been found to have healed over, indicating that some patients survived this extremely crude operation. As pointed out earlier, however, disputes often arise from the interpretation of historical data: a different explanation of trephining is that it was used to remove bone splinters and blood clots resulting from blows to the head in fights between men (Maher & Maher, 1985). This explanation is consistent with findings that most trephined skulls were those of men and that many had fractures (suggesting a vigorous blow).

Another treatment method used by the early Greeks, Chinese, Hebrews, and Egyptians was exorcism. In an **exorcism,** elaborate prayers, noises, emetics (drugs that induce vomiting), and extreme measures such as flogging and starvation were used to cast evil spirits out of an afflicted person's body.

Naturalistic Explanations (Greco-Roman Thought)

With the flowering of Greek civilization and its continuation into the era of Roman rule (500 B.C.–A.D. 500), naturalistic explanations gradually became distinct from supernatural ones. Early thinkers, such as Hippocrates (460–370 B.C.), a physician who is often called the father of medicine, actively questioned prevailing superstitious beliefs and proposed much more rational and scientific explanations for mental disorders.

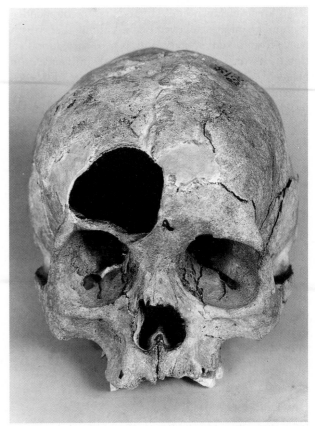

An Early Surgical Treatment There are two theories about trephining. The most widely accepted postulates that trephining was a form of surgery that enabled an evil spirit to leave the body. The other theory rejects this idea, proposing instead that the holes were actually the result of wounds.

The beliefs of many thinkers of this era were based on incorrect assumptions. They all relied heavily on observations and explanations, however, that form the foundation of the scientific method. Also, they denied the intervention of demons in the development of abnormality and instead stressed organic causes. Because of these factors, the treatment they prescribed for mental disorders tended to be more humane than previous treatments.

Hippocrates believed that, because the brain was the central organ of intellectual activity, deviant behavior was caused by **brain pathology**—that is, a dysfunction or disease of the brain. He also considered heredity and environment important factors in psychopathology. He classified mental illnesses into three categories—mania, melancholia, and phrenitis (brain fever)—and for each category gave detailed clinical descriptions of such disorders as paranoia, alcoholic delirium, and epilepsy. Many of his descriptions of symptoms are still used today, eloquent testimony to his keen powers of observation.

To treat melancholia, Hippocrates recommended tranquility, moderate exercise, a careful diet, abstinence from sexual activity, and, if necessary, bloodletting. His belief in environmental influences on behavior sometimes led him to separate disturbed patients from their families. He seems to have gained insight into a theory popular among psychologists today: that the family constellation often fosters deviant behavior in its own members.

Other thinkers who contributed to the organic explanation of behavior were the philosopher Plato and the Greek physician Galen, who practiced in Rome. Plato (429–347 B.C.) carried on the thinking of Hippocrates; he insisted that the mentally disturbed were the responsibility of the family and should not be punished for their behavior. Galen (A.D. 129–199) made major contributions through his scientific examination of the nervous system and his explanation of the role of the brain and central nervous system in mental functioning. His greatest contribution may have been his codification of all European medical knowledge from Hippocrates' time to his own.

Reversion to Supernatural Explanations (the Middle Ages)

With the collapse of the Roman Empire and the rise of Christianity, rational and scientific thought gave way to a reemphasis on the supernatural. Religious dogma included the beliefs that nature was a reflection of divine will and beyond human reason and that earthly life was a prelude to the "true" life (after death). Scientific inquiry—attempts to understand, classify, explain, and control nature—was less important than accepting nature as a manifestation of God's will.

The Dark Ages (Fifth Through Tenth Centuries)

Early Christianity did little to promote science and in many ways actively discouraged it. The church demanded uncompromising adherence to its tenets. Christian fervor brought with it the concepts of heresy and punishment; certain truths were deemed sacred, and those who challenged them were denounced as heretics. Scientific thought that was in conflict with church doctrine was not tolerated. Because of this atmosphere, rationalism and scholarly scientific works went underground for many years, preserved mainly by Arab scholars and European monks. Natural and supernatural explanations of illness were fused.

People came to believe that many illnesses were the result of supernatural forces, although they had natural causes. In many cases, the mentally ill were treated gently and with compassion in monasteries and at shrines, where they were prayed over and allowed to rest. In other cases, treatment could be quite brutal, especially if illnesses were believed to be due to God's wrath. Because illness was then perceived to be punishment for sin, the sick person was assumed to be guilty of wrongdoing, and relief could come only through atonement or repentance.

During this period, treatment of the mentally ill sometimes consisted of torturous exorcistic procedures seen as appropriate to combat Satan and eject him from the possessed person's body. Prayers, curses, obscene epithets, and the sprinkling of holy water—as well as such drastic and painful "therapy" as flogging, starving, and immersion in hot water—were used to drive out the devil. The humane treatments that Hippocrates had advocated centuries earlier were challenged severely. A time of trouble for everyone, the Dark Ages were especially bleak for the mentally ill.

Mass Madness (Thirteenth Century)

Belief in the power of the supernatural became so prevalent and intense that it frequently affected whole populations. Beginning in Italy early in the thirteenth century, large numbers of people were affected by various forms of **mass madness,** or group hysteria, in which a great many people exhibit similar symptoms that have no apparent physical cause. One of the better known manifestations of this disorder was *tarantism,* a dance mania characterized by wild raving, jumping, dancing, and convulsions. The hysteria was most prevalent during the height of the summer and was attributed to the sting of a tarantula. A victim would leap up and run out into the street or marketplace, jumping and raving, to be joined by others who believed that they had also been bitten. The mania soon spread throughout the rest of Europe, where it became known as Saint Vitus' Dance.

Another form of mass madness was *lycanthropy,* a mental disorder in which victims imagine themselves to be wolves and imitate wolves' actions. (Motion pictures about werewolves—people who assume the physical characteristics of wolves during the full moon—are modern reflections of this delusion.)

How can these phenomena be explained? Stress and fear are often associated with outbreaks of mass hysteria. During the thirteenth century, for example, there was enormous social unrest. The bubonic plague had decimated one-third the population of Europe. War, famine, and pestilence were rampant, and the social order of the times was crumbling.

A more recent example of mass hysteria apparently occurred in the small town of Berry, Alabama, where elementary school children became ill. A fifth-grader came to school with a rash and began scratching vigorously and uncontrollably. Classmates began to scratch at an imaginary itch. The incident resulted in

Casting Out the Cause of Abnormality During the Middle Ages, people suffering from a mental disorder were often perceived as being victims of a demonic possession. The most prevalent form of treatment was exorcism, usually conducted by religious leaders who used prayers, incantations, and sometimes torturous physical techniques to cast the evil spirit from the bodies of the afflicted.

more than 150 schoolchildren afflicted with a frenzy of scratching, fainting, vomiting, numbness, crying, and screaming. Medical authorities concluded after months of study that the culprit could not be an infectious disease or food poisoning. Rather, the symptom pattern, onset, and manifestation suggested mass hysteria (Kramer, 1973).

Witchcraft (Fifteenth Through Seventeenth Centuries) During the fifteenth and sixteenth centuries, the authority of the church was increasingly challenged by social and religious reformers. Reformers such as Martin Luther attacked the corruption and abuses of the clergy, precipitating the Protestant Reformation of the sixteenth century. Church officials viewed such protests as insurrections that threatened their power. According to the church, Satan himself fostered these attacks. By doing battle with Satan and with people supposedly influenced or possessed by Satan, the church actively endorsed an already popular belief in demonic possession and witches.

To counter the threat, Pope Innocent VIII issued a papal bull (decree) in 1484 calling on the clergy to identify and exterminate witches. This resulted in the 1486 publication of the extremely influential *Malleus Maleficarum* (The Witch's Hammer). The mere existence of this document acted to confirm the existence of witches, and it also outlined means of detecting them. For example, red spots on the skin (birthmarks) were supposedly made by the claw of the devil in seal-

ing a blood pact and thus were damning evidence of a contract with Satan. Such birth defects as clubfoot and cleft palate also aroused suspicion.

The church initially recognized two forms of demonic possession: unwilling and willing. God let the devil seize an unwilling victim as punishment for a sinful life. A willing person, who made a blood pact with the devil in exchange for supernatural powers, was able to assume animal form and cause disasters such as floods, pestilence, storms, crop failures, and sexual impotence. Although unwilling victims of possession at first received more sympathetic treatment than that given those who willingly conspired with the devil, this distinction soon evaporated.

People whose actions were interpreted as peculiar were often suspected of witchcraft. It was acceptable to use torture to obtain confessions from suspected witches, and many victims confessed because they preferred death to prolonged agony. Thousands of innocent men, women, and even children were beheaded, burned alive, or mutilated.

Witch hunts occurred in both colonial America and in Europe. The witchcraft trials of 1692 in Salem, Massachusetts, were infamous. Authorities there acted on statements taken from children who may have been influenced by the sensational stories told by an old West Indian servant. Several hundred people were accused, many were imprisoned and tortured, and twenty were killed. It has been estimated that some 20,000 people (mainly women) were killed as witches in Scotland alone and that more than 100,000 throughout Europe were executed as witches from the middle of the fifteenth to the end of the seventeenth century.

It would seem reasonable to assume that the mentally ill would be especially prone to being perceived as witches. Indeed, most psychiatric historians argue that mental disorders were at the roots of witchcraft persecutions (Alexander & Selesnick, 1966; Deutsch, 1949; Zilboorg & Henry, 1941). Support for the belief that many accused witches were mentally ill was based on the following evidence: (1) some witches claimed that they could do impossible acts (such as fly and cause floods) and thus must have been deluded (schizophrenic); (2) they participated in sabbats (nocturnal orgies) and must have been psychopaths or nymphomaniacs; (3) they evidenced localized sensitivity to pain in various parts of their bodies and must have been hysterics; and (4) they evidenced symptoms associated with high suggestibility, delusions, or hallucinations. Spanos (1978), however, in a comprehensive critical analysis, concluded that very little support could be found to indicate that accused witches were mentally ill.

Indeed, the lines of evidence just mentioned either have no basis in fact or were misinterpreted. Sabbats, for example, seem to have existed only in the imaginations of the witch hunters. Claims of supernatural powers were obtained from the accused only after prolonged and painful torture, and trickery was often used to diminish body sensitivity. It appears that, although some accused witches may have been mentally ill, most were normal (Schoeneman, 1984).

The Rise of Humanism (the Renaissance)

A resurgence of rational and scientific inquiry during the Renaissance (fourteenth through sixteenth centuries) led to great advances in science and **humanism,** a philosophical movement that emphasizes human welfare and the worth and uniqueness of the individual. Until this time, most asylums were at best custodial centers in which the mentally disturbed were chained, caged, starved, whipped, and even exhibited to the public for a small fee, much like animals in a zoo. But the new way of thinking held that if people were "mentally ill" and not possessed, then they should be treated as though they were sick. A number of new methods for treating the mentally ill reflected this humanistic spirit.

In 1563 Johann Weyer (1515–1588), a German physician, published a revolutionary book that challenged the foundation of ideas about witchcraft. Weyer asserted that many people who were tortured, imprisoned, and burned as witches were mentally disturbed, not possessed by demons. The emotional agonies he was made to endure for committing this heresy

are well documented. His book was severely criticized and banned by both church and state, but it proved to be a forerunner of the humanitarian perspective on mental illness. Others eventually followed his lead.

The Reform Movement (Eighteenth and Nineteenth Centuries)

In France, Philippe Pinel (1745–1826), a physician, was put in charge of La Bicêtre, a hospital for insane men in Paris. Pinel instituted what came to be known as the **moral treatment movement**—a shift to more humane treatment of the mentally disturbed. He ordered that inmates' chains be removed, replaced dungeons with sunny rooms, encouraged exercise outdoors on hospital grounds, and treated patients with kindness and reason. Surprising many disbelievers, the freed patients did not become violent; instead, this humane treatment seemed to foster recovery and improve behavior. Pinel later instituted similar, equally successful, reforms at La Salpêtrière, a large mental hospital for women in Paris.

In England William Tuke (1732–1822), a prominent Quaker tea merchant, established a retreat at York for the "moral treatment" of mental patients. At this pleasant country estate, the patients worked, prayed, rested, and talked out their problems—all in an atmosphere of kindness quite unlike that of the lunatic asylums of the time.

In the United States, three individuals—Benjamin Rush, Dorothea Dix, and Clifford Beers—made important contributions to the moral treatment movement. Benjamin Rush (1745–1813), widely acclaimed as the father of U.S. psychiatry, attempted to train physicians to treat mental patients and to introduce more humane treatment policies into mental hospitals. He insisted that patients be accorded respect and dignity and that they be gainfully employed while hospitalized, an idea that anticipated the modern concept of work therapy. Yet Rush was not unaffected by the established practices and beliefs of his times: his theories were influenced by astrology, and his remedies included bloodletting and purgatives.

Dorothea Dix (1802–1887), a New England schoolteacher, was the preeminent American social reformer of the nineteenth century. While teaching Sunday school to female prisoners, she became familiar with the deplorable conditions in which jailed mental patients were forced to live. (Prisons and poorhouses were commonly used to incarcerate these patients.) For the next forty years, Dix worked tirelessly for the mentally ill. She campaigned for reform legislation and funds to establish suitable mental hospitals and asylums. She raised millions of dollars, established more than thirty modern mental hospitals, and greatly improved conditions in countless others. But the struggle for reform was far from over. Although the large hospitals that replaced jails and poorhouses had better physical facilities, the humanistic, personal concern of the moral treatment movement was lacking.

That movement was given further impetus in 1908 with the publication of *A Mind That Found Itself,* a book by Clifford Beers (1876–1943) about his own mental collapse. His book describes the terrible treatment he and other patients experienced in three mental institutions, where they were beaten, choked, spat on, and restrained with straitjackets. His vivid account aroused great public sympathy and attracted the interest and support of the psychiatric establishment, including such eminent figures as psychologist-philosopher William James. Beers founded the National Committee for Mental Hygiene (forerunner of the National Mental Health Association), an organization dedicated to educating the public about mental illness and about the need to treat the mentally ill rather than punish them for their unusual behaviors.

It would be naive to believe that these reforms have totally eliminated inhumane treatment of the mentally disturbed. Books such as Mary Jane Ward's *The Snake Pit* (1946) and films such as Frederick Wiseman's *Titicut Follies* (1967) continue to document harsh treatment of mental patients. Even the severest critic of the mental health system, however, would have to admit that conditions and treatment for the mentally ill have improved in this century.

Causes: Early Viewpoints

Paralleling the rise of humanism in the treatment of mental illness was an inquiry into its causes. Two schools of thought emerged. The *organic,* or *biological, viewpoint* holds that mental disorders are the result of physiological damage or disease; the *psychological viewpoint* stresses an emotional basis for mental illness. It is important to note that most people were not extreme adherents of one or the other. Rather, they tended to combine elements of both, predating the biopsychosocial model widely used today.

The Biological Viewpoint

Hippocrates' suggestion of an organic explanation for abnormal behavior was ignored during the Middle Ages but revived after the Renaissance. Not until the nineteenth century, however, did the organic, or **biological, view**—the belief that mental disorders have a physical or physiological basis—become important.

Dorothea Dix (1802–1887) During a time when women were discouraged from political participation, Dorothea Dix, a New England schoolteacher, worked tirelessly as a social reformer to improve the deplorable conditions in which the mentally ill were forced to live.

The ideas of Wilhelm Griesinger (1817–1868), a German psychiatrist who believed that all mental disorders had physiological causes, received considerable attention. Emil Kraepelin (1856–1926), a follower of Griesinger, observed that certain symptoms tend to occur regularly in clusters, called **syndromes.** Kraepelin believed that each cluster of symptoms represented a mental disorder with its own unique—and clearly specifiable—cause, course, and outcome. He attributed all disorders to one of four organic causes: metabolic disturbance, endocrine difficulty, brain disease, or heredity. In his *Textbook of Psychiatry* (1883/1923), Kraepelin outlined a system for classifying mental illnesses on the basis of their organic causes. That system was the original basis for the diagnostic categories in the *Diagnostic and Statistical Manual of Mental Disorders* (DSM), the classification system of the American Psychiatric Association.

The acceptance of an organic or biological cause for mental disorders was accelerated by medical breakthroughs in the study of the nervous system. The effects of brain disorders, such as cerebral arteriosclerosis, on mental retardation and on senile and other psychoses led many scientists to suspect or advocate organic factors as the sole cause of all mental illness. And, as we will see in the chapter on models of abnormal behavior, the drug revolution of the 1950s made medication available for almost every disorder. The issues of the therapeutic effectiveness of these drugs and of how they work, however, are still hotly debated today.

The biological viewpoint gained even greater strength with the discovery of the organic basis of *general paresis,* a progressively degenerative and irreversible physical and mental disorder (*paresis* is syphilis of the brain). Several breakthroughs had led scientists to

Emil Kraepelin (1856–1926) In an 1883 publication, psychiatrist Emil Kraepelin proposed that mental disorders could be directly linked to organic brain disorders and further proposed a diagnostic classification system for all disorders.

suspect that the deterioration of mental and physical abilities exhibited by certain mental patients might actually be caused by an organic disease. The work of Louis Pasteur (1822–1895) established the germ theory of disease (invasion of the body by parasites). Then in 1897 Richard von Krafft-Ebing (1840–1902), a German neurologist, inoculated paretic patients with pus from syphilitic sores; when the patients failed to develop the secondary symptoms of syphilis, Krafft-Ebing concluded that the patients had been previously infected by that disease. Finally, in 1905 a German zoologist, Fritz Schaudinn (1871–1906), isolated the microorganism that causes syphilis and thus paresis. These discoveries convinced many scientists that every mental disorder might eventually be linked to an organic cause.

The Psychological Viewpoint

Some scientists noted, however, that certain types of emotional disorders were not associated with any organic disease in the patient. Such observations led to another view that stressed psychological factors rather than biological factors as the cause of many disorders. For example, the inability to attain personal goals and resolve interpersonal conflicts could lead to intense feelings of frustration, depression, failure, and anger and to consequent disturbed behavior.

Mesmerism and Hypnotism   The unique and exotic techniques of Friedrich Anton Mesmer (1734–1815), an Austrian physician who practiced in Paris, presented an early challenge to the organic point of view. It is important to note, however, that Mesmer was really an anomaly and not part of mainstream scientific thinking. Mesmer developed a highly controver-

sial treatment that came to be called *mesmerism* and that was the forerunner of the modern practice of hypnotism.

Mesmer performed his most miraculous cures in the treatment of *hysteria*—the appearance of symptoms such as blindness, deafness, loss of bodily feeling, and paralysis that seem to have no organic basis. According to Mesmer, hysteria was a manifestation of the body's need to redistribute the magnetic fluid that determined a person's mental and physical health. His techniques for curing this illness involved inducing a sleeplike state, during which his patients became highly susceptible to suggestion. During this state, their symptoms often disappeared. Mesmer's dramatic and theatrical techniques earned him censure, as well as fame. A committee of prominent thinkers, including U.S. ambassador to France Benjamin Franklin, investigated Mesmer and declared him a fraud. He was finally forced to leave Paris.

Although Mesmer's basic assumptions were discredited, the power of suggestion proved to be a strong therapeutic technique in the treatment of hysteria. The cures he effected stimulated scientific interest in, and much bitter debate about, the **psychological view**—the belief that mental disorders are caused by psychological and emotional factors rather than organic or biological factors.

An English physician, James Braid (1795–1860), renamed mesmerism *neurohypnotism* (later shortened to *hypnotism*) because he believed that the technique induced sleep by producing paralysis of the eyelid muscles. (The Greek word *hypnos* means "sleep.") Braid's trance-inducing technique of having a subject gaze steadily at an object has now become almost a standard procedure in hypnosis.

The Nancy School   About ten years after Mesmer died, a number of researchers began to experiment actively with hypnosis. Among them was Jean-Martin Charcot (1825–1893), a neurosurgeon at La Salpêtrière Hospital in Paris and the leading neurologist of his time. His initial experiments with hypnosis led him to abandon it in favor of more traditional methods of treating hysteria, which he claimed was caused by organic damage to the nervous system. Other experimenters had more positive results using hypnosis, however, which persuaded Charcot to try it again. His subsequent use of the technique in the study of hysteria did much to legitimize the application of hypnosis in medicine.

The experimenters most instrumental in Charcot's conversion were two physicians practicing in the city of Nancy, in eastern France. First working separately, Ambroise-Auguste Liébeault (1823–1904) and Hippolyte-Marie Bernheim (1840–1919) later came together to work as a team. As a result of their

Anton Mesmer (1734–1815) Mesmer's techniques for treating hysteria by inducing a sleeplike state in which his patients were highly susceptible to suggestion was a forerunner of the modern practice of hypnotism. Though highly controversial and ultimately discredited, Mesmer's efforts stimulated inquiry into psychological and emotional factors, rather than organic factors, as causes of mental disorders.

experiments, they hypothesized that hysteria was a form of self-hypnosis. The results they obtained in treating patients attracted other scientists, who collectively became known as the "Nancy School." In treating hysterical patients under hypnosis, they were often able to remove symptoms of paralysis, deafness, blindness, and anesthesia. They were also able to produce these symptoms in normal persons through hypnosis. Their work demonstrated impressively that suggestion could cause certain forms of mental illness; that is, symptoms of mental and physical disorders could have a psychological rather than an organic explanation. This conclusion represented a major breakthrough in the conceptualization of mental disorders.

Breuer and Freud   The idea that psychological processes could produce mental and physical disturbances began to gain credence among several physicians who were using hypnosis. Among them was the Viennese doctor Josef Breuer (1842–1925). He discovered accidentally that, after one of his female patients spoke quite freely about her past traumatic experiences while in a trance, many of her symptoms abated or disappeared. He achieved even greater success when the patient recalled previously forgotten memories and relived their emotional aspects. This latter technique became known as the **cathartic method,** a therapeutic use of verbal expression to release pent-up emotional conflicts. It foreshadowed psychoanalysis, whose founder, Sigmund Freud (1856–1939), was influenced by Charcot and was a colleague of Breuer. Freud's theories have had a great and lasting influence in the field of abnormal psychology.

Behaviorism   Whereas psychoanalysis offered an intrapsychic explanation of abnormal behavior, another viewpoint that emerged during the latter part of this period was more firmly rooted in laboratory science: *behaviorism.* The behavioristic perspective stressed the importance of directly observable behaviors and the conditions or stimuli that evoked, reinforced, and extinguished them. As we will see in the chapter on models of abnormal behavior, behaviorism not only offered an alternative explanation of the development of both normal and abnormal behavior but also demonstrated a high degree of success in treating maladaptive behaviors.

Contemporary Trends in Abnormal Psychology

Earlier, we made the statement that our current explanations of abnormal behavior have been heavily influenced by the beliefs of the past. Much has changed, however, in our understanding and treatment of psychopathological disorders. Twentieth-century views of abnormality continue to evolve in the twenty-first century as they incorporate the effects of several major events and trends in the field: (1) the drug revolution in psychiatry, (2) potential prescription privileges for psychologists, (3) managed health care, (4) increased appreciation for research in abnormal psychology, and (5) the influence of multicultural psychology.

The Drug Revolution

Many mental health professionals consider the introduction of psychiatric drugs in the 1950s as one of the great medical advances in the twentieth century (Nemeroff, 1998; Norfleet, 2002; Lickey & Gordon, 1991). Although some might find such a statement excessive, it is difficult to overemphasize the impact that drug therapy has had. It started in 1949 when an Australian psychiatrist, John F. J. Cade, reported on his successful experiments with lithium in radically calming manic patients who had been hospitalized for years. Several years later, French psychiatrists Jean Delay and Pierre Deniker discovered that the drug chlorpromazine (brand name, Thorazine) was extremely effective in treating agitated schizophrenics. Within a matter of years, drugs were developed to treat disorders such as depression, schizophrenia, phobias, obsessive-compulsive disorders, and anxiety. Large classes of drugs were developed for depression (antidepressant drugs), anxiety (antianxiety drugs), and grossly impaired thinking (antipsychotic drugs).

These drugs were considered revolutionary because they rapidly and dramatically decreased or eliminated troublesome symptoms experienced by patients. As a result, other forms of therapy became available to the mentally ill, who were now more able to focus their attention on their therapy. Their stays in mental hospitals were shortened and were more cost effective than prolonged hospitalizations. In addition, they were allowed to return home while receiving treatment.

The new drug therapies were credited with the depopulation of mental hospitals, often referred to as *deinstitutionalization* (see discussion in the chapter on legal and ethical issues). This decline can be attributed not to a decrease in new admissions but rather to shorter stays and earlier releases (Lickey & Gordon, 1991; Manderscheid & Sonnenschein, 1992; NIMH, 1995). To handle the large number of patients returning to the community, outpatient treatment became the primary mode of service for the severely disturbed. In addition to changing the way therapy was dispensed, the introduction of psychiatric drugs revived strong belief in the biological bases of mental disorders (Fox & Sammons, 1998).

Prescription Privileges for Psychologists

As can be seen in Table 1.1, one of the major distinguishing features between psychiatrists and psychologists has been the right to prescribe medication. Should psychologists have a legal right to prescribe medication? Within the mental health field, the opposing answers to this question have been extremely divisive (Albee, 2002; Caccavale, 2002; Hayes & Chang, 2002). Psychologists have increasingly exerted pressure on state legislatures to allow them to prescribe medication in treating the mentally disturbed. They have argued that such a move would be cost effective and benefit the American public by containing escalating health care costs (Wedding, 1995).

Even though surveys suggest that most nonmedical mental health organizations favor prescription privileges for psychologists, and even though current statutes have never stipulated that only physicians can prescribe medication, the American Medical Association has adamantly opposed any such move. Although a good part of this stance may be due to psychiatry's fears of economic losses and the blurring of boundaries between professions, other reasons are cited as well. The medical establishment has argued that granting such privileges could endanger the public because psychologists lack medical training and the expertise to recognize medical risks and potential drug-interaction effects (Tatman, Peters, Greene, & Bongar, 1997).

Even many psychologists have expressed grave reservations, which tend to take three forms (Gutierrez & Silk, 1998; Klusman, 1998; Norfleet, 2002):

1. Pharmacology interventions may supplant psychological ones, causing a loss of professional identity for psychologists.

2. Rather than compete with medicine, psychologists should use their unique skills to deal with broader societal needs.

3. Prescription privileges would increase the length of education and burden training programs.

Still, proponents of prescription privileges present compelling reasons for approval, as follows (Foxhall, 2001; Gutierrez & Silk, 1998):

- Studies show that psychologists would be more cautious than psychiatrists in prescribing medication and therefore safer.

- Prescribing medications is a logical extension of the psychologist's role. It would lead to better patient care and better communication with physicians.

- Psychologists are equally if not better trained than their psychiatric counterparts to understand mind, body, and environmental causes of mental disorders.

- Restrictions on prescription privileges prevent psychologists from functioning as fully autonomous health-service providers.

- Those wishing to prescribe medications would have to undergo a rigorous psychopharmacology curriculum.

In 1995, the American Psychological Association (APA) voted to pursue prescription privileges for appropriately trained professional psychologists by initiating actions along several fronts. First, it developed model state legislation aimed at prescription privilege laws. Second, it developed both a model curriculum for predoctoral training in psychopharmacology and an examination to determine competence (Dunivin & Orabona, 1999; Sammons & Olmedo, 1997). As of this writing, organized psychology has achieved a number of successes. The U.S. territory of Guam passed a prescription privilege statute for psychologists several years ago; and history was made in 2002 when New Mexico became the first state to pass such legislation. As a result, a dozen programs now exist to train psychologists to provide psychotropic medications to their patients. Legislation granting psychologists the right to prescribe has been proposed in California, Florida, Hawaii, Louisiana, Missouri, and Tennessee (Gutierrez

& Silk, 1998). Many believe it is just a matter of time before psychologists will be granted such privileges widely at the state level (Ax & Resnick, 2001). There is little doubt that if prescription privileges are granted, it will change the public's perception of psychologists and may affect their professional identity as well.

Managed Health Care

Health care costs in the United States have exploded from $27.1 billion in 1960 to $1.1 trillion in 1998 and are estimated to exceed $2 trillion by 2007 (Reed et al., 2001). The U.S. public spends increasing amounts each year in either direct or indirect expenses for mental health care. Some twenty years ago we spent $40 billion, of which nearly 40 percent went for direct care, including therapy and hospitalization (Levine & Willner, 1976). From 1974 to 1985 the number of psychologists in health care increased by more than 100 percent (Dorken, Stapp, & VandenBos, 1986; Enright, Welch, Newman, & Perry, 1990). One recent report (NIMH, 1995) indicates that when the costs of mental health problems are calculated to include decreased productivity in the workplace, educational problems, an aging society, drug and alcohol abuse, and health and violence in the United States, more than $150 billion is spent each year! One can surmise that the rise of the managed care industry was partially a reaction to these spiraling costs.

Managed health care refers to the industrialization of health care, whereby large organizations in the private sector control the delivery of services. In the past, psychotherapy was carried out primarily by individuals in solo offices or in small-group practices. Some clients paid for services out of their own pockets. Others had health plans that covered treatment, generally with minimal restrictions on the number of sessions the client could attend, and usually with reimbursable treatment for a broad array of "psychological problems." The fees, number of sessions, and types of treatment were determined by the mental health practitioner. When mental health costs rapidly escalated in the 1980s, attempts were made to contain costs via managed health care or some form of health reform (Cummings, 1995; J. Hall, 1995; Sammons, 2004). This industrialization of health care has brought about major changes in the mental health professions:

- Business interests are exerting increasing control over psychotherapy by determining reimbursable diagnoses, limiting the number of sessions psychologists may offer clients, and imposing other such restrictions.

- Current business practices are depressing the income of practitioners. Some organizations prefer hiring therapists with master's degrees rather than those with doctoral degrees, or they reimburse at rates below those set by the therapist.

- Psychologists are being asked to justify the use of their therapies on the basis of whether they are empirically based—established treatments with research support. This last point is especially important. For example, if research reveals that cognitive-behavioral forms of treatment are more successful than psychodynamic approaches for a certain form of phobia, then therapy using the latter approach might be denied by the insurance carrier.

These trends have alarmed many psychologists, who fear that decisions will be made not so much for health reasons but for business ones, that the need for doctoral-level practitioners will decrease, and that the livelihood of clinicians will be threatened. Although no one can say with certainty whether these fears will be realized, recent studies suggest that managed care policies are not based on scientific foundations and that patients are being deprived of adequately skilled treatment on a massive scale (see the Mental Health and Society feature "Managed Care: Will Someone Please Help Me?"; Holloway, 2004; Scribner, 2001; Seligman & Levant, 1998). As a result, lawsuits against major health-care plans over accountability, patient access, and both patient and provider rights threaten to change the managed care landscape (Holloway, 2004). A class-action lawsuit in Florida against eight of the nation's largest managed care providers accuses them of conspiring to reduce and delay payments to physicians. In November 2003, the U.S. Supreme Court agreed to reenter the debate over patients' legal rights when their plans refuse to pay for recommended treatments (Holloway, 2004). It is expected that a decision in the summer of 2005 may alter how managed care will operate.

Appreciation for Research

Breakthroughs in neuroanatomy, identification of the role that neurotransmitters play in mental disorders, and increasing interest in exploring empirically validated forms of psychotherapy have produced another contemporary trend: a heightened appreciation for the role of research in the study of abnormal behavior. The success of psychopharmacology spawned renewed interest and research into brain-behavior relationships (DHHS, 1999). Indeed, more and more researchers are now exploring the biological bases (chemical and structural) of abnormal behavior. Within recent years,

MENTAL HEALTH AND SOCIETY

Managed Care: Will Someone Please Help Me?

In 1973, David Rosenhan published a highly controversial study titled "On Being Sane in Insane Places (see the Mental Health and Society feature: "Normal or Abnormal: The Consequences of Labeling," in the chapter on assessment and classification). In essence, eight normal individuals without any history of psychiatric illness were admitted and kept in a mental hospital for an average of nineteen days even though they behaved normally during their stay on the hospital ward. Rosenhan and others believe that the study illustrates how easily mental health professionals read pathology into behavior and the ease of obtaining unnecessary treatment for a nonexistent disorder.

In light of the managed health care movement and constant complaints from health care providers and patients about the difficulty in obtaining adequate treatment, Christopher Scribner (Scribner, 2001) asked the question: "Would today's health care environment affect the ease of obtaining treatment even when such intervention is warranted?"

Scribner uses a satirical commentary to answer the question by using fictionalized accounts of seven patients (composites of experiences people have had in encountering the managed care system). The following is a thumbnail sketch of the seven patients' experiences as they tried to obtain treatment:

1. Male patient 1 was refused treatment "because we don't have anyone on our panel who specializes in your sort of problem." He was, however, told that new providers were always being added to the panel of therapists

and to check back in a few weeks. When the patient protested and reiterated his need for therapy, the intake worker simply handed him a well-worn binder containing a 1987 listing of self-help groups.

2. Female patient 2 experienced communication problems with the psychiatrist. While she tried in vain to relate and describe her mental disorder, the doctor constantly interrupted her in his broken English, saying, "The chemical brain imbalance is your problem; you need medicine like a diabetes person need medicine." Although she tried to explain to the doctor that the medication had not worked for her in the past, he persisted in suggesting the medication. Frustrated and upset, the patient screamed, "You're not listening!" At that point, the psychiatrist summoned the security guard, stating that the patient had no intention of complying with treatment; the patient was escorted off the grounds.

3. Female patient 3 was told that she was not eligible for service until she accessed her employer's "employee assistance program" first. The irony of this rule was that the patient was unemployed.

4. Female patient 4 encountered a young interviewer who seemed more interested in straightening the frames surrounding her new master's degree and her certificate naming her "Intake Clinician/Customer-Service Representative of the Month." The patient was told that the acute psych beds were full and

that giving her a diagnosis of chemical dependency (even though incorrect) might lead to treatment. Appalled at the suggestion, the patient requested to speak to a supervisor. A well-dressed male psychologist came in. After listening to the patient, he indicated that "people with schizophrenia need to accept their illness and just learn to live with it."

5. Patients 5 and 6 were turned away because they did not receive proper authorization for services. Both had difficulty dealing with their gatekeeper physicians. In one case the patient was told that the next available appointment with her physician was in five weeks, and in the other case the physician did not send the proper forms because "We ran out of those forms."

6. Male patient 7 was severely symptomatic, displayed loose cognitive associations in his speech, hadn't bathed for days, and heard terrifying voices and other grossly unusual behaviors. The intake worker, however, informed the patient that his disorder did not appear severe enough to warrant admission. He was admitted only when he stated, "But I fear that I'm at significant risk to do harm to myself or others."

In all seven hypothetical cases the patients were crying for help: "Will someone please help me?" The possibility that these things could happen is disturbing.

biological factors have been associated with many psychological disorders, such as depression, suicide, schizophrenia, learning disabilities, alcoholism, and Alzheimer's disease (Dick & Rose, 2002; Hollon, Thase, & Markowitz, 2002).

On another front, many researchers are focusing on aspects of mental illness that are primarily psychological rather than biological. As we shall see in the chapter on models of abnormal behavior, the behavioral school of thought and the recent interest and work in cognitive psychology have been instrumental not only in expressing this point of view but also in advocating the use of scientific research in understanding human behavior (Hollon, DeRubeis, & Seligman, 1992; Lipman & Kendall, 1992). Currently, researchers are seeking insights into the most effective means of understanding and treating specific disorders through studies comparing the effectiveness of drug treatment with that of cognitive treatment and through the development of empirically based treatments (D. M. Chambless, 1993; Nathan, 1998).

The move toward empirically based or supported treatments is one of the most visible aspects of the profession's use of research to determine the most effective forms of therapy for various disorders (Norcross, 2004; Wampold, Lichtenberg, & Waehler, 2002). The early work by the Division of Clinical Psychology Task Force (Task Force on Promotion and Dissemination of Psychological Procedures, 1995) listed treatments for various disorders as to their effectiveness and can be found at www.apa.org/divisions/div12/rev_est/index.html.

Although the move to evidence-based practice is accepted by the profession as important, it is not without controversy. Some claim the call for empirically based treatments to be biased against certain theoretical orientations (humanistic-existential, psychodynamic, etc.). For example, studies reveal that 60 percent to 80 percent of those identified as most effective are cognitive-behavioral treatments (Norcross, 2004). Others assert that evidence-based practice is too restrictive and does not recognize clinical intuition and the dynamic basis of therapy. Further, the majority of disorders identified are those that can be easily measured and have a discrete but narrow symptom cluster, such as phobias. What about disorders that are more global and less susceptible to precise description, such as alienation in life, feelings of meaninglessness, and so on (Messer, 2001)? Lastly, some fear that managed care companies will use this information to place more restrictions on types of treatments they are willing to reimburse.

Diversity and Multicultural Psychology

We are fast becoming a multicultural, multiracial, and multilingual society (see Figure 1.5). The recently released 2000 U.S. Census reveals that within several decades, racial and ethnic minorities will become a numerical majority (Atkinson, Morten, & Sue, 1998). These changes have been referred to as "the diversification of the United States" or, literally, the "changing complexion of society." Much of this change is fueled by two major trends in the United States: the increased immigration of visible racial and ethnic minorities and the differential birth rates among the various racial and ethnic groups in our society. In 1990, 76 percent of the population was composed of white Americans; in the year 2000, their numbers had declined to 69 percent of the population. The "diversity index," which measures the probability of selecting two randomly chosen individuals from different parts of the country who differ from each other in race or ethnicity, stands at 49. In other words, there is nearly a 50 percent chance these two individuals would be of a different race or ethnicity. Nowhere is the explosive growth of minorities more noticeable than in our public schools, where students of color now make up 45 percent of those attending. To give readers some idea of the impact on certain regions of the United States, one only has to look at these figures:

- Over 50 percent of the state of California is composed of minority groups.

- 30 percent of New York City residents were born in other countries.

FIGURE 1.5 Census 2000 Racial/Ethnic Composition of the United States The rapid demographic transformation of the United States is illustrated in the fact that minorities now constitute an increasing proportion of the population. Several major trends are evident. First, within several short decades, people of color will constitute a numerical majority. Second, the population of Hispanic Americans nearly equals that of African Americans and will soon surpass them. Because the 2000 Census now allows citizens to claim more than one racial category, the accuracy of counts have been made more difficult. There is little doubt, however, that mental health providers will increasingly be coming into contact with client groups who differ from them in race, ethnicity, and culture.

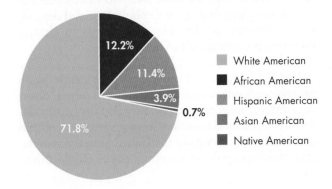

12.2%
11.4%
3.9%
0.7%
71.8%

- White American
- African American
- Hispanic American
- Asian American
- Native American

- 70 percent of the District of Columbia is African American.

- 37 percent of San Francisco is Asian American/Pacific Islander.

- 67 percent of Detroit is African American.

- 67 percent of Miami is Latino/Hispanic American.

Diversity has had a major impact on the mental health profession, creating a new field of study called **multicultural psychology**. As we saw earlier in this chapter, the multicultural approach stresses the importance of culture, race, ethnicity, gender, age, socioeconomic class, and other similar factors in its effort to understand and treat abnormal behavior. There is now recognition that mental health professionals need to (1) increase their cultural sensitivity, (2) acquire knowledge of the worldviews and lifestyles of a culturally diverse population, and (3) develop culturally relevant therapy approaches in working with different groups (American Psychological Association, 2003; D. W. Sue et al., 1998). Although issues of race, culture, ethnicity, and gender have traditionally been ignored or distorted in the mental health literature, these forces are now increasingly recognized as powerful influences on many aspects of normal and abnormal human development (Sue & Sue, 2003). Four primary dimensions related to cultural diversity—social conditioning, cultural values and influence, sociopolitical influences, and bias in diagnosis—seem to explain how cultural forces exert their influence.

Social Conditioning   How we are raised, what values are instilled in us, and how we are expected to behave in fulfilling our roles seem to have a major effect on the type of disorder we are most likely to exhibit. Traditionally, in our culture men have been raised to fulfill the masculine role, to be independent, assertive, courageous, active, unsentimental, and objective. Women, in contrast, have been raised to be dependent, helpful, fragile, self-abnegating, conforming, empathetic, and emotional. Some mental health professionals believe that, as a result, women are more likely to internalize their conflicts (resulting in anxiety and depression), whereas men are more likely to externalize and act out (resulting in drug or alcohol abuse and dependence). Although gender roles have begun to change, their effects continue to be widely felt.

Cultural Values and Influences   Mental health professionals now recognize that types of mental disorders differ from country to country and that major differences in cultural traditions among various racial and ethnic minority groups in the United States may influence their susceptibility to certain emotional disorders.

In 1994, the *Diagnostic and Statistical Manual of Mental Disorders* (American Psychiatric Association) acknowledged the existence of "culture-bound" syndromes in other societies (see Table 3.3 in the chapter on assessment and classification of abnormal behavior). Among Hispanic/Latino Americans and Asian Americans, experiencing physical complaints is a common and culturally accepted means of expressing psychological and emotional stress (Hong & Domokos-Cheng Ham, 2001; Santiago-Rivera, Arredondo, & Gallardo-Cooper, 2002). People with these cultural backgrounds believe that physical problems cause emotional disturbances and that the emotional disturbances will disappear as soon as appropriate treatment for the physical illness is instituted. In addition, mental illness among Asians is seen as a source of shame and disgrace, although physical illness is acceptable. Asian values also emphasize restraint of strong feelings. Thus when stress is encountered, the mental health professional is likely to hear complaints involving headaches, fatigue, restlessness, and disturbances of sleep and appetite.

Sociopolitical Influences   In response to a history of prejudice, discrimination, and racism, many minorities have adopted various behaviors (in particular, behaviors toward whites) that have proved important for survival in a racist society (Ridley, 1995; Sue & Sue, 2003). Mental health professionals may define these behaviors as abnormal and deviant, yet from the minority group perspective, such behaviors may function as healthy survival mechanisms. Early personality studies of African Americans concluded that, as a group, they tend to appear more "suspicious," "mistrustful," and "paranoid" than their white counterparts. But are African Americans inherently pathological, as studies suggest, or are they making healthy responses? Members of minority groups who have been victims of discrimination and oppression in a society not yet free of racism have good reason to be suspicious and distrustful of white society. The "paranoid orientation" may reflect not only survival skills but also *accurate reality testing*. We are pointing out that certain behaviors and characteristics need to be evaluated not only by an absolute standard but also by the sociopolitical context in which they arise.

Bias in Diagnosis   Epidemiological studies reporting the distribution and types of mental disorders that occur in the population may be prone to bias on the part of the clinician and researcher. The mental health professional is not immune to inheriting the prejudicial attitudes, biases, and stereotypes of the larger society. Even the most enlightened and well-intentioned mental health

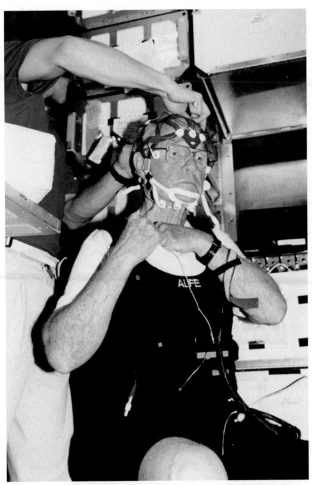

Age Bias In making diagnoses and conducting research, clinicians and researchers must be careful to avoid age bias, as well as race, gender, and social class biases. In 1998, John Glenn, shown here in the Space Lab training module, returned to space, in part, to participate in studies about how age (Glenn was seventy-seven at the time of the flight) is affected by weightlessness. It may be that some of the findings may help clinicians better diagnose and treat older individuals.

professional may be the victim of race, gender, and social class bias. One source of bias is the tendency to over-pathologize—to exaggerate the severity of disorders—among clients from particular socioeconomic, racial, or ethnic groups whose cultural values or lifestyles differ markedly from the clinician's own. The overpathologizing of disorders has been found to occur in evaluation of African Americans, Hispanic Americans, and women (Lopez & Hernandez, 1987; Sue & Sue, 2003).

It is clear that one of the most powerful emerging trends in the mental health field is in increased interest, appreciation, and respect for multicultural psychology. Understanding abnormal behavior requires a realistic appraisal of the cultural context in which behavior

occurs and an understanding of how culture influences the manifestations of abnormality. This recognition led the American Psychological Association to adopt "Guidelines on Multicultural Education, Training, Research, Practice, and Organizational Change for Psychologists" (APA, 2003). It states explicitly that the guidelines "reflect the continuing evolution of the study of psychology, changes in society at large, and emerging data about the different needs of particular individuals and groups historically marginalized or disenfranchised within and by psychology based on their ethnic/racial heritage and social group identity or membership" (p. 277).

Some Closing Thoughts

As you can see, the study of abnormal psychology is not only complex but also heavily influenced by the tenor of the times. As we begin our journey into attempts to explain the causes of certain disorders, we encourage you not to become rigidly locked into one system or model. It is our contention that no one model is equally applicable to all situations, problems, and populations. All have something of worth to add. And, in reality, few contemporary psychologists or psychiatrists take the extreme of adhering just to one position. Indeed, most psychologists believe that mental illness probably springs from a combination of not only biological and psychological factors but societal and environmental influences as well. The realization that biological, psychological, and sociocultural factors must all be considered in explaining and treating mental disorders has been termed the **biopsychosocial approach.** It would be a serious oversight to neglect the powerful impact on mental health of family upbringing and influence, the stresses of modern society (unemployment, poverty, loss of a loved one, adapting to technological change, and so on), experiences of oppression (prejudice, discrimination, stereotyping), effects of natural disasters (earthquakes, floods, hurricanes), human-made conflicts such as wars, and our current battle against terrorism.

Finally, we close this chapter with a word of caution. To be human is to encounter difficulties and problems in life. A course in abnormal psychology dwells on human problems—many of them familiar. As a result, we may be prone to the "medical student syndrome": reading about a disorder may lead us to suspect that we have the disorder or that a friend or relative has it when indeed that is not the case. (See the Mental Health and Society feature "I Have It, Too!" for more on this syndrome.) This reaction to the study of abnormal behavior is a common one, and one we must all guard against.

MENTAL HEALTH AND SOCIETY

"I Have It, Too": The Medical Student Syndrome

Medical students probably caught it first. As they read about physical disorders and listened to lecturers describing illnesses, some students began to imagine that they themselves had one disorder or another. "Diarrhea? Fatigue? Trouble sleeping? That's me!" In this way, a cluster of symptoms—no matter how mild or how briefly experienced—can lead some people to suspect that they are very sick.

Students who take a course that examines psychopathology may be equally prone to believe that they have a mental disorder that is described in their text. It is possible, of course, that some students do suffer from a disorder and would benefit from counseling or therapy. Most, however, are merely experiencing an exaggerated sense of their susceptibility to disorders. In one study, it was found that one of every five individuals responded "yes" to the ques-

tion, "Have you ever felt that you were going to have a nervous breakdown?" Of course, most of those people never suffered an actual breakdown.

Two influences in particular may make us susceptible to these imagined disorders. One is the universality of the human experience. All of us have experienced misfortunes in life. We can all remember and relate to feelings of anxiety, unhappiness, guilt, lack of self-confidence, and even thoughts of suicide. In most cases, however, these feelings are normal reactions to stressful situations, not symptoms of disease. Depression following the loss of a loved one or anxiety before giving a speech to a large audience may be perfectly normal and appropriate. Another influence is our tendency to compare our own functioning with our perceptions of how other people are functioning. The outward behav-

iors of fellow students may lead us to conclude that they experience few difficulties in life, are self-assured and confident, and are invulnerable to mental disturbance. If we were privy to their inner thoughts and feelings, however, we might be surprised to find that they share our apprehension and insecurities.

If you see yourself anywhere in the pages of this book, we hope you will take the time to discuss your feelings with a friend or with one of your professors. You may be responding to pressures that you have not encountered before—a heavy course load, for example—and to which you have not yet adjusted. Other people can help point out these pressures to you. If your discussion supports your suspicion that you have a problem, however, then by all means consider getting help from your campus counseling and/or health clinic.

SUMMARY

What Is Abnormal Psychology?

■ Abnormal psychology is the field that attempts to describe, explain, predict, and control behaviors that are considered strange or unusual.

What Criteria Are Used to Determine Normal or Abnormal Behaviors?

■ Four types of definitions are used to describe such behaviors, and they differ in the criteria they apply.
  • Conceptual definitions include statistical deviation, deviations from ideal mental health, and multicultural perspectives.
  • Practical definitions use discomfort, deviance, and dysfunction to assess abnormality.

  • Integrated definitions use an approach in which behavior is judged from a number of different perspectives.
  • The *Diagnostic and Statistical Manual of Mental Disorders* (DSM-IV-TR) definition is used by most mental health practitioners.
■ In light of these multiple perspectives, abnormality is probably best defined from the combined vantage points of society, the individual, and the mental health professional.

How Common Are Mental Disorders?

■ Mental health problems are widespread in the United States, and the human and economic costs are enormous. Among the many problems encountered by those who are suffering or have suffered from a mental disturbance are the many myths and stereotypes that have plagued them.

How Have the Explanations of Abnormal Behavior Changed Over Time?

- Ancient peoples believed in demonology and attributed abnormal behaviors to evil spirits that inhabited the victim's body. Treatments consisted of trephining, exorcism, and bodily assaults.
- Rational and scientific explanations of abnormality emerged during the Greco-Roman era. Especially influential was the thinking of Hippocrates, who believed that abnormal behavior was due to organic, or biological, causes, such as a dysfunction or disease of the brain. Treatment became more humane.
- With the collapse of the Roman Empire and the increased influence of the church and its emphasis on divine will and the hereafter, rationalist thought was suppressed and belief in the supernatural again flourished. During the Middle Ages, famine, pestilence, and dynastic wars caused enormous social upheaval. Forms of mass hysteria affected groups of people. In the fifteenth century, some of the men, women, and children killed in church-endorsed witch hunts were people we would today call mentally ill.
- The Renaissance brought a return to rational and scientific inquiry along with a heightened interest in humanitarian methods of treating the mentally ill. The eighteenth and nineteenth centuries were a period characterized by reform movements.

Are Mental Disorders Due Primarily to Biological or to Psychological Factors?

- In the nineteenth and twentieth centuries, major medical breakthroughs fostered a belief in the biological roots of mental illness. An especially important discovery of this period was the microorganism that causes general paresis. Scientists believed that they would eventually find organic causes for all mental disorders.
- Mesmerism, and later hypnosis, supported another view, however. The uncovering of a relationship between hypnosis and hysteria corroborated the belief that psychological processes could produce emotional disturbances.

What Are Some Contemporary Trends in Abnormal Psychology?

- Five contemporary developments have had a major influence in the mental health professions: (1) the drug revolution in psychiatry, which not only allowed many of the more severely disturbed to be treated outside of a hospital setting but also lent credence to the biological viewpoint; (2) the push by psychologists for prescription privileges; (3) the development of managed health care; (4) an increased appreciation for the role of research; and (5) increasing diversity in the United States, leading to reliance on multicultural psychology.

KEY TERMS

abnormal behavior (p. 13)
abnormal psychology (p. 4)
biological view (p. 23)
biopsychosocial approach (p. 31)
brain pathology (p. 19)

cathartic method (p. 25)
cultural relativism (p. 10)
cultural universality (p. 10)
exorcism (p. 19)
humanism (p. 22)
incidence (p. 13)

lifetime prevalence (p. 13)
managed health care (p. 27)
mass madness (p. 20)
moral treatment movement (p. 22)
multicultural psychology (p. 30)

prevalence (p. 13)
psychodiagnosis (p. 4)
psychological view (p. 24)
syndrome (p. 23)
therapy (p. 5)
trephining (p. 19)

MULTIMEDIA PREVIEW

For additional study aids, we invite you to explore our media resources accompanying *Understanding Abnormal Behavior*, Eighth Edition. The Student CD-ROM includes videos, quizzing, and critical thinking activities that help to reinforce key concepts in a fun and engaging manner. The Student Web Site provides additional interactive activities, chapter outlines, and research links that further support and complement the text. All Web resources may be accessed by logging onto the Web site at **http://psychology.college.hmco.com/students**.

CHAPTER 2
Models of Abnormal Behavior

In the chapter on abnormal behavior, we described how the rise of humanism influenced society's attitude toward mental disorders. As rational thought replaced superstition in the eighteenth and nineteenth centuries, the mentally disturbed were increasingly regarded as unfortunate human beings who deserved respectful and humane treatment, not as monsters inhabited by the devil.

This humanistic view gave rise, in the late nineteenth and early twentieth centuries, to two different schools of thought about the causes of mental disorders. According to one group of thinkers, mental disorders are caused primarily by biological problems, and the disturbed individual is displaying symptoms of physical disease or damage. The second group of theorists believed that abnormal behavior is essentially psychosocial, rooted not in cells and tissues but in the invisible complexities of the human mind or in environmental forces.

In this chapter, we continue to trace the evolution of these two schools of thought and bring them up to date. We begin with the biological perspective and then examine several major psychosocial perspectives. A chart outlining these various approaches appears in Figure 2.1. The theories we examine in this chapter are by no means the only possible explanations of abnormal behavior. Estimates (Corey, 2005; Corsini & Wedding, 1995; Day,

2004) place the number of such theories between 240 and 400 in the United States alone. Many are variants of the more basic theories discussed here; others have never gained widespread acceptance.

Let's begin by clarifying two terms you will encounter frequently. The first is **psychopathology,** which clinical psychologists use as a synonym for abnormal behavior. The second is **model,** a term that requires a more elaborate explanation.

Models in the Study of Psychopathology

Scientists who need to discuss a phenomenon that is difficult to describe or explain often use an analogy, which enables them to liken the phenomenon to something more concrete. A *model* is such an analogy, and scientists most often use it to describe a phenomenon or process that they cannot directly observe. In using an analogy, the scientist borrows terms, concepts, or principles from one field and applies them to another, as when a physician describes the eye as a camera.

Psychologists have used models extensively to help conceptualize the causes of abnormal behavior, to ask probing questions, to determine relevant information and data, and to interpret data. For example, when psychologists refer to their "patients" or speak of

FIGURE 2.1 The Major Models of Psychopathology   Attempts to explain abnormal
behavior have resulted in more than a hundred explanations. The major models of psychopathology,
however, are displayed here.

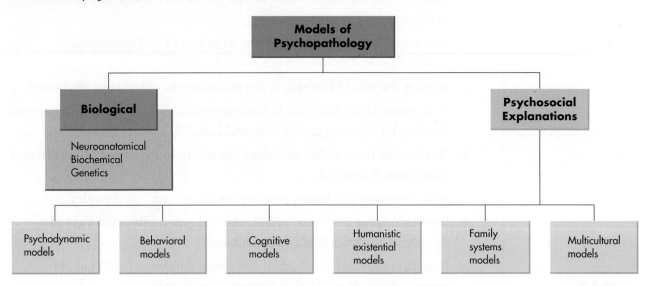

deviant behavior as "mental illness," they are borrowing the terminology of medicine and applying a *medical model* of abnormal behavior. They may also describe certain external symptoms as being visible signs of deep underlying conflict. Again, the medical analogy is clear: just as fevers, rashes, perspiration, or infections may be symptoms of a bacterial or viral invasion of the body, bizarre behavior may be a symptom of a mind "invaded" by unresolved conflicts. Psychologists use a variety of such models, each embodying a particular theoretical approach. Hence we tend to use the terms *model, theory, viewpoint,* and *perspective* somewhat interchangeably. Most theorists realize that the models they construct will be limited and will not correspond in every respect to the phenomena they are studying (Sommers-Flanagan & Sommers-Flanagan, 2004). Because of the complexity of human behavior and our relatively shallow understanding of it, psychologists do not expect to develop the definitive model. Rather, they use the models to visualize psychopathology as if it truly worked in the manner described by the models.

To aid us in our analyses, we present the case of Steve V. We begin our discussion of each model with a thumbnail sketch of Steve's situation as it might be seen by a clinician conceptualizing Steve's problems and recommending treatment within the parameters of the model being discussed.

Steve V., a twenty-one-year-old college student, had been suffering from a crippling and severe bout of depression. Eighteen months earlier, Steve's friend,

Linda, had broken off her relationship with him. However, Steve's long psychiatric history had begun well before he first sought help from the therapist at the university's psychological services center. Steve had been in and out of psychotherapy since kindergarten and had been hospitalized twice for depression when he was in high school. His case records, nearly two inches thick, contained a number of diagnoses, including labels such as *schizoid personality disorder, schizophrenia (paranoid type),* and *bipolar mood disorder.* Although his present therapist did not find these labels particularly helpful, Steve's clinical history did provide some clues to the causes of his problems.

Steve V. was born in a suburb of San Francisco, California, the only child of an extremely wealthy couple. His father, who is of Scottish descent, was a prominent businessman who worked long hours and traveled frequently. On those rare occasions when he was at home, Mr. V. was often preoccupied with business matters and held himself quite aloof from his son. The few interactions they had were characterized by his constant ridicule and criticism of Steve. Mr. V. was greatly disappointed that his son seemed so timid, weak, and withdrawn. Steve was extremely bright and did well in school, but Mr. V. felt that he lacked the "toughness" needed to survive and prosper in today's world. Once, when Steve was about ten years old, he came home from school with a bloody nose and bruised face, crying and complaining of being picked on by his schoolmates. His father showed no sympathy but instead berated Steve for losing the fight. In his father's presence, Steve usually felt worthless, humiliated, and fearful of doing or saying the wrong thing.

Mrs. V. was very active in civic and social affairs, and she, too, spent relatively little time with her son. Although she treated Steve more warmly and lovingly than his father did, she seldom came to Steve's defense when Mr. V. bullied him. She generally allowed her husband to make family decisions. In reality, Mrs. V. was quite lonely. She felt abandoned by Mr. V. and harbored a deep resentment toward him, which she was frightened to express.

When Steve was a child, his mother at times had been quite affectionate. She had often allowed Steve to sleep with her in her bed when her husband was away on business trips. She usually dressed minimally on these occasions and was very demonstrative—holding, stroking, and kissing Steve. This behavior had continued until Steve was twelve, when his mother abruptly refused to let Steve into her bed. The sudden withdrawal of this privilege had confused and angered Steve, who was not certain what he had done wrong. He knew, though, that his mother had been quite upset when she awoke one night to find him masturbating next to her.

Most of the time, Steve's parents seemed to live separately from each other and from their son. Steve was raised, in effect, by a full-time maid. He rarely had playmates of his own age. His birthdays were celebrated with a cake and candles, but the only celebrants were Steve and his mother. By age ten, Steve had learned to keep himself occupied by playing "mind games," letting his imagination carry him off on flights of fantasy. He frequently imagined himself as a powerful figure—Superman or Batman. His fantasies were often extremely violent, and his foes were vanquished only after much blood had been spilled.

As Steve grew older, his fantasies and heroes became increasingly menacing and evil. When he was fifteen, he obtained a pornographic videotape that he viewed repeatedly on a video player in his room. Often, Steve would masturbate as he watched scenes of women being sexually violated. The more violent the acts against women, the more aroused he became. He was addicted to the *Nightmare on Elm Street* films, in which the villain, Freddie Kreuger, disemboweled or slashed his victims to death with his razor-sharp glove. Steve now recalls that he spent much of his spare time between the ages of fifteen and seventeen watching X-rated videotapes or violent movies, his favorite being *The Texas Chainsaw Massacre*, in which a madman saws and hacks women to pieces. Steve always identified with the character perpetrating the outrage; at times, he imagined his parents as the victims.

At about age sixteen, Steve became convinced that external forces were controlling his mind and behavior and were drawing him into his fantasies. He was often filled with guilt and anxiety after one of his mind games.

Although he was strongly attracted to his fantasy world, he also felt that something was wrong with it and with him. After seeing the movie *The Exorcist*, he became convinced that he was possessed by the devil.

Biological Models

Steve V. is a biological being, and his mental disorders are caused by some form of biological malfunctioning. Environmental influences are important but probably secondary to the manifestation of psychopathology. I believe that the causes of Steve's problems reside in a possible genetic predisposition to mental disorders, an imbalance of brain chemistry, or, perhaps, in structural abnormalities in his neurological makeup. The fact that he suffers from paranoid schizophrenia and a bipolar affective disorder (disorders that have an increased probability of being present in blood relatives) seems to support such an explanation. The most effective way to treat this disorder is through drug therapy or some variation of somatic intervention.

Myth vs Reality

Myth: We should attempt to clearly identify those disorders that have a biological base and those that do not. Disorders that are shown to originate from biological causes warrant exclusive biological interventions. Disorders that are caused psychologically should be treated through psychological means.

Reality: Although it is important to identify biological and psychological correlates of psychopathology, this dichotomous and simplistic thinking is unfortunate and has served to hinder integrated approaches to explaining and treating mental disorders. We now realize, for example, that gene activity and changes in biology are influenced by the psychological environment and vice versa. The relationship between the biological and psychological makeup of people is complex and interrelated (Miller & Keller, 2000). DSM-IV-TR, for example, states explicitly that the mind-body dualism is a false one. There is much that is biological/physical in "mental disorders" and much that is mental in "physical disorders."

Modern biological explanations of normal and abnormal behavior continue to share certain assumptions: (1) the things that make people who they are—their physical features, susceptibility to diseases, temperaments, and ways of dealing with stress—are embedded in the genetic material of their cells; (2) human thoughts, emotions, and behaviors are associated with nerve cell activities of the brain and spinal cord; (3) a change in thoughts, emotions, or behaviors will be associated with a change in activity or structure (or both) of the brain; (4) mental disorders are highly correlated with some form of brain or other organ dysfunction; and (5) mental disorders can be treated by drugs or somatic intervention (Cottone, 1992; Department of Health and Human Services, 1999; Kolb, Gibb, & Robinson, 2003; Strohman, 2001).

Biological models have been heavily influenced by the neurosciences, a group of subfields that focus on brain structure, function, and disorder. Understanding biological explanations of human behavior requires knowledge about the structure and function of the central nervous system (composed of the brain and spinal cord). Especially important is knowledge about how the brain is organized, how it works, and, particularly, the chemical reactions that enhance or diminish normal brain actions.

The Human Brain

The brain is composed of billions of **neurons,** or nerve cells, that transmit messages throughout the body. The brain is responsible for three very important and highly complicated functions. It receives information from the outside world, it uses the information to decide on a course of action, and it implements decisions by commanding muscles to move and glands to secrete. Weighing approximately three pounds, this relatively small organ continues to amaze and mystify biological researchers.

The brain is separated into two hemispheres. A disturbance in either one (such as by a tumor or by electrical stimulation with electrodes) may produce specific sensory or motor effects. Each hemisphere controls the opposite side of the body. For example, paralysis on the left side of the body indicates a dysfunction in the right hemisphere. In addition, the right hemisphere is associated with visual-spatial abilities and emotional behavior. The left hemisphere controls the language functions for nearly all right-handed people and for most left-handed ones.

Viewed in cross section, the brain has three parts: forebrain, midbrain, and hindbrain. Although each part is vital for functioning and survival, the forebrain is probably the most relevant to a discussion of abnormality.

The Forebrain   The *forebrain* probably controls all the higher mental functions associated with human consciousness, learning, speech, thought, and memory. Within the forebrain are the thalamus, hypothalamus, reticular activating system, limbic system, and cerebrum (see Figure 2.2). The specific functions of these structures are still being debated, but we can discuss their more general functions with some confidence.

FIGURE 2.2 The Internal Structure of the Brain   A cross-sectional view of the brain reveals the forebrain, midbrain, and hindbrain. Some of the important brain structures are identified within each of the divisions.

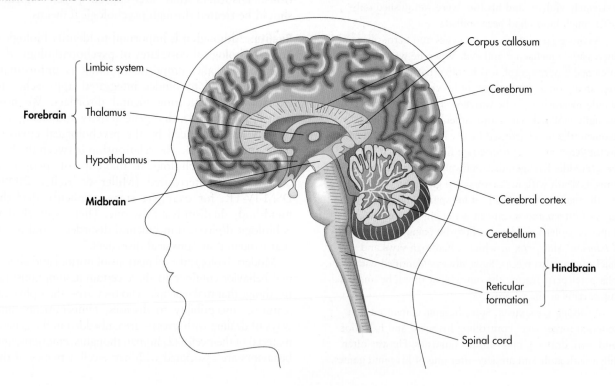

The *thalamus* appears to serve as a "relay station," transmitting nerve impulses from one part of the brain to another. The *hypothalamus* ("under the thalamus") regulates bodily drives, such as hunger, thirst, and sex, and body conditions, such as temperature and hormone balance. The *limbic system* is involved in experiencing and expressing emotions and motivation—pleasure, fear, aggressiveness, sexual arousal, and pain. The largest structure in the brain is the *cerebrum,* with its most visible part, the *cerebral cortex,* covering the midbrain and thalamus.

The Midbrain and Hindbrain The midbrain and hindbrain also have distinct functions:

- The *midbrain* is involved in vision and hearing and—along with the hindbrain—in the control of sleep, alertness, and pain. Mental health professionals are especially interested in the midbrain's role in manufacturing chemicals—serotonin, norepinephrine, and dopamine—that have been implicated in certain mental disorders.

- The *hindbrain* also manufactures serotonin. The hindbrain appears to control functions such as heart rate, sleep, and respiration. The *reticular formation,* a network of nerve fibers that controls bodily states such as sleep, alertness, and attention, starts in the hindbrain and threads its way into the midbrain.

Because the brain controls all aspects of human functioning, it is not difficult to conclude that damage or interruption of normal brain function and activity could lead to observable mental disorders. There are, of course, many biological causes for psychological disorders. Damage to the nervous system is one: As Fritz Schaudinn demonstrated (see the chapter on abnormal behavior), general paresis results from brain damage caused by parasitic microorganisms. Tumors, strokes, excessive intake of alcohol or drugs, and external trauma (such as a blow to the head) have also been linked to cognitive, emotional, and behavioral disorders. Two specific biological sources—body chemistry and heredity—have given rise to important biological theories of psychopathology.

Biochemical Theories

The basic premise of the biochemical theories is that chemical imbalances underlie mental disorders. This premise relies on the fact that most physiological and mental processes, from sleeping and digestion to reading and thinking, involve chemical actions within the body. Support for the biochemical theories has been found in research into anxiety disorders, mood disorders (both depression and bipolar disorder), Alzheimer's disease, autism, dyslexia, and schizophrenia (G. Carey & DiLalla, 1994; Lickey & Gordon, 1991; Plomin, Owen, & McGuffin, 1994). Some researchers have even claimed that our gene pool affects such characteristics as alienation, leadership, career choice, risk aversion, religious conviction, and pessimism (Colt & Hollister, 1998). To see how biochemical imbalances in the brain can result in abnormal behavior, we need to understand how messages in the brain are transmitted from nerve cell to nerve cell.

Nerve cells (neurons) vary in function throughout the brain and may appear different, but they all share certain characteristics. Each neuron possesses a cell membrane that separates it from the outside environment and regulates the chemical contents within it. On one end of the cell body are **dendrites,** numerous short rootlike structures whose function is to receive signals from other neurons. At the other end is an **axon,** a much longer extension that sends signals to other neurons, some a considerable distance away. Under an electron microscope dendrites can be distinguished by their many short branches (see Figure 2.3).

FIGURE 2.3 Major Parts of a Neuron The major parts of a neuron include dendrites, the cell body, the axon, and the axon terminals.

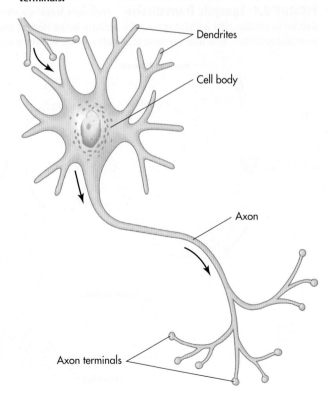

Dendrites

Cell body

Axon

Axon terminals

Messages travel through the brain by electrical impulses via neurons: an incoming message is received by a neuron's dendrites and is sent down the axon to bulblike swellings called *axon terminals,* usually located near dendrites of another neuron. Note that neurons do not touch one another. A minute gap (the **synapse**) exists between the axon of the sending neuron and the dendrites of the receiving neuron (see Figure 2.4). The electrical impulse crosses the synapse when the axon releases chemical substances called **neurotransmitters.** When the neurotransmitters reach the dendrites of the receiving neuron, they attach themselves to receptors and, if their "shapes" correspond, bind with them (see Figure 2.5). The binding of transmitters to receptors in the neuron triggers either a synaptic excitation (encouragement to produce other nerve impulses) or synaptic inhibition (a state preventing production of nerve impulses).

The human body has many different chemical transmitters, and their effect on neurons varies (see Table 2.1). An imbalance of certain neurotransmitters in the brain is believed to be implicated in mental disorders. As discussed in the chapter on abnormal behavior, the search for chemical causes and cures for mental problems accelerated tremendously in the early 1950s with the discovery of psychoactive drugs. Since that time, three convincing lines of evidence have contributed to the search for biochemical causes and cures:

1. Studies showed that antipsychotic drugs have beneficial effects on schizophrenics, that lithium is useful in controlling affective disorders, and that tricyclic and monoamine oxidase inhibitors alleviate symptoms of severely depressed patients.

2. Biochemical studies (Department of Health and Human Services, 1999; Lickey & Gordon, 1991) indicated that these drugs seem to work by blocking or facilitating neurotransmitter activity at receptor sites. Most current psychiatric drugs seem to affect one of five different transmitters: norepinephrine, dopamine, serotonin, acetylcholine, and gamma aminobutyric acid (GABA).

3. Certain chemical imbalances appear to be disorder specific. Insufficient dopamine, for example, is a possible cause of Parkinson's disease. Ironically, an excess of dopamine has been implicated in the development of schizophrenia (J. R. Cooper, Bloom, & Roth, 1986; Lickey & Gordon, 1991; Snyder, 1986). Two hypotheses have been proposed: that people with schizophrenia may have too many postsynaptic dopamine receptors (a structural explanation) or that their receptors may be supersensitive to dopamine. The effect of drug therapy on receptor sites has been shown with other disorders. Drugs used to treat depression alter norepinephrine and serotonin

FIGURE 2.4 Synaptic Transmission   Messages travel via electrical impulses from one neuron to another. The impulse crosses the synapse in the form of chemicals called neurotransmitters. Note that the axon terminals and the receiving dendrites do not touch.

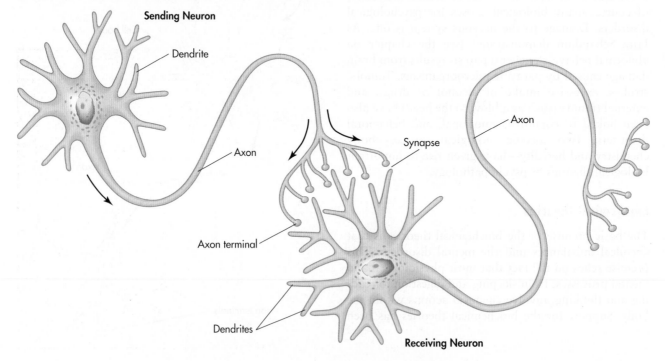

FIGURE 2.5 Neurotransmitter Binding

Neurotransmitters are released into the synapse and travel to the receiving dendrite. Each transmitter has a specific shape that corresponds to a receptor site. Like a jigsaw puzzle, binding occurs if the transmitter fits into the receptor site.

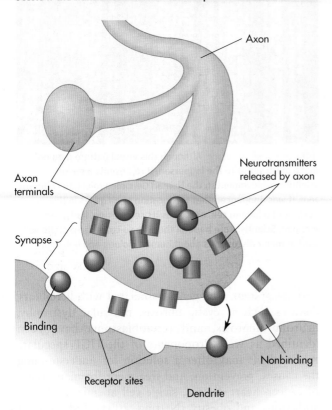

sensitivity and receptivity at the receptor sites. Drugs used in the treatment of anxiety affect receptor reactivity to GABA.

Research into biochemical mechanisms holds great promise for our understanding and treatment of mental disorders. It appears unlikely, however, that biochemistry alone can provide completely satisfactory explanations of the biological bases of abnormal behavior. Researchers should instead expect to find hundreds—or perhaps even thousands—of pieces in the biological puzzle.

Genetic Explanations

Research strongly indicates that genetic makeup plays an important role in the development of certain abnormal conditions. For instance, "nervousness" can be inherited in animals; this finding was demonstrated some thirty-seven years ago through the breeding of generations of dogs that were either fearful or friendly (Murphree & Dykman, 1965). There is evidence that autonomic nervous system (ANS) reactivity may be inherited in human beings as well; that is, a person may be born with an ANS that makes an unusually strong response to stimuli (Andreasen, 1984; Baker & Clark, 1990). Other studies (G. Carey & DiLalla, 1994; Cloninger, Reich, Sigvardsson, Von Knorring, & Bohman, 1986; Gatz, 1990; Plomin, Owen, & McGuffin, 1994) implicate heredity as a causal factor in alcoholism, schizophrenia, and depression. To show that a particular disorder is inherited, however, researchers must demonstrate that it could not be caused by environmental factors alone, that closer genetic relationships produce greater similarity of

TABLE 2.1 Major Neurotransmitters and Their Effects

Neurotransmitter	Source and Function
Acetylcholine (ACH)	One of the most widespread neurotransmitters. Occurs in systems that control the muscles and in circuits related to attention and memory. Reduction in levels associated with Alzheimer's disease.
Dopamine	Concentrated in small areas of the brain, one of which is involved in the control of the muscles. In excess, dopamine can cause hallucinations. Associated with schizophrenia.
Endorphins	Found in the brain and spinal cord. Suppresses pain.
Gamma amino-butyric acid (GABA)	Widely distributed in the brain. Works against other neurotransmitters, particularly dopamine.
Norepinephrine	Occurs widely in the central nervous system. Regulates moods and may increase arousal and alertness. Often associated with mood disorders and eating disorders.
Serotonin	Occurs in the brain. Works more or less in opposition to norepinephrine, suppressing activity and causing sleep. Linked with anxiety disorders, mood disorders, and eating disorders.

the disorder in human beings, and that people with these problems have similar biological and behavioral patterns (S. Siegel, 1990).

Biological inheritance is transmitted by genes. A person's genetic makeup is called his or her **genotype.** Interaction between the genotype and the environment results in the person's **phenotype,** or observable physical and behavioral characteristics. At times, however, it is difficult to determine whether genotype or environment is exerting a stronger influence. For example, characteristics such as eye color are determined solely by our genotype—by the coding in our genes. But other physical characteristics, such as height, are determined partly by the genetic code and partly by environmental factors. Adults who were undernourished as children will be shorter than the height they were genetically capable of reaching, but even the most effective nutrition would not have caused them to grow taller than their "programmed" height limit.

As is detailed more fully in the chapter on schizophrenia, twin studies and correlational associations between genetics and certain mental disorders lend strong support to the behavioral genetics model.

The Human Genome Project Perhaps the greatest breakthrough in our attempt to understand the impact of genes on human life comes from the astounding accomplishments of the Human Genome Project (HGP). In June 2000, the International Human Genome Sequencing Consortium (composed of several academic and government labs) and its rival in the private sector (Celera Genomics) announced that they had mapped the location of all genes in the nucleus of a human cell; in February 2001, they also completed its sequencing (the order of the DNA chemical subunits in each cell). Oftentimes referred to as the "map of life" or the "total body manual," the HGP was successful in creating a basic blueprint of the entire genetic material found in each cell of the body. The human **genome** is composed of all the genetic material in the chromosomes of a particular organism and is the most complex instruction manual ever conceived on how the body works. Many scientists believe that the successful mapping and sequencing of the human genome will reveal life secrets: how our physical characteristics are determined, how we age, our susceptibility to diseases, personality traits, and the proclivity to develop mental disorders, for example. The challenge is our inability to fully read the manual or to understand what it means!

However, we have begun to accumulate scientific data that suggest the potential importance of the HGP. In 1993, for example, scientists discovered the gene that determines the occurrence of Huntington's disease, which causes an irreversible degeneration of the

Genome Sequencing Although this visual pattern may not make much sense to the layperson, it represents a major scientific achievement in the Human Genome Project. In February 2001, it was announced that the location of all genes in the nucleus of a human cell, as well as its sequencing, had been mapped. Scientists are hopeful that the so-called map of life will lead to major discoveries about human biology and behavior.

nervous system. The genes associated with hereditary diseases such as cystic fibrosis, muscular dystrophy, neurofibromatosis, and retinoblastoma have been identified as well. Proponents of the HGP speculate that findings may offer a solution for understanding the causes, prevention, and treatment for many types of cancer, heart disease, sickle cell anemia, and even addictions and obesity (Netting, 2001). Indeed, data coming out of the HGP could benefit those with sleep disorders or night-shift workers with the identification of eight "clock genes" that play a role in the body's timekeeping mechanism. Already, a new field called *pharmacogenomics,* the science of understanding the correlation between a patient's genetic makeup and his or her response to drug treatment, has drug manufacturers poised to develop more effective pharmacological treatments. Biologists, anthropologists, and evolutionary psychologists are also looking at the HGP as potentially providing answers to questions in comparative and evolutionary biology; much of the human genome contains families of genes conserved from ancient snippets of DNA (Rios, 2001).

Lest we get carried away with unrealistic optimism for solving the secrets of life and finding the genes that cause all human diseases, the HGP seems to raise many difficult questions as well. Whereas scientists had expected to find 100,000 genes in the human genome, less than 25,000 were found—only two to three times more than that of a fruit fly or nematode worm (Wade, 2004). Of those, only 300 unique genes distinguished us from the mouse. In other words, human and mouse genomes are about 85 percent identical! Although these findings may be a blow to our dignity, the more important question is how such relatively few genes can account for our "humanness." Some scientists believe the promise of the HGP is based on two false premises: genetic determinism and the simple model of "one gene for one disease" (Strohman, 2001). Muscular dystrophy, for example, was found to be traceable to a single gene. Such a relationship is often cited as evidence of the power of heredity. A one-to-one correspondence such as this one is, however, a rarity in behavioral genetics. Such diseases account for only 2 percent of the disease load, whereas disorders associated with the genes for cancers, heart disease, and bipolar disorders together make up 70 percent of the disease load (Strohman, 2001). The majority of human diseases are multifactorial, caused by many genes interacting in a cellular environment of hormones, electrical signals, and nutrient supplies, as well as in our physical and social environment (Miller & Keller, 2000). If the majority of diseases are indeed multifactorial, then any single gene or group of genes has small effects, not large ones. Strohman (2001) concludes, "The wider environment and complex cellular processes—not just genes—play important roles in shaping our lives" (p. 27).

Criticisms of Biological Models

The biological model of abnormal behavior, which drifted out of favor when psychoanalysis was at the peak of its influence in the 1940s, has regained its popularity, especially with the completion of the mapping and sequencing of the human genome. Indeed, rarely does a week go by without news reports linking genetics to intelligence, homosexuality, obesity, alcohol abuse, learning disabilities, temperament, personality, or susceptibility to stress. Structural differences in the brain have been linked to schizophrenia, and new "miracle" drugs are being discovered for various disorders. But the biological model has some major shortcomings if viewed as the sole explanation for mental disorders.

First, one of its basic tenets is that abnormal behavior results from an underlying physical condition, such as damage to the brain or malfunction of neural processes. The model implies that treatment should be aimed at controlling the underlying disease by changing the individual's biochemistry or removing toxic substances. This approach does not adequately account for abnormal behavior for which no biological *etiology*, or cause, can be found. Some mental disorders, such as bipolar and unipolar psychotic mood states and schizophrenia, may have primary biological causes, but strong evidence exists that phobias, eating disorders, and other disorders have a predominantly social cause. Many disorders are probably a mix of predisposition and environment.

Second, the biological model implicitly assumes a correspondence between organic dysfunction and mental dysfunction, with only a minimal impact from environmental, social, or cultural influences. But rarely are the equations of human behavior so uncomplicated. More often there are a multitude of causes behind any human behavior, and environmental factors seem to play as important a role as any other. Increasingly, mental health research has focused on the diathesis-stress theory, originally proposed by Meehl (1962) and developed further by Rosenthal (1970). The **diathesis-stress theory** holds that it is not a particular abnormality that is inherited but rather a *predisposition* to *develop illness* (diathesis). Certain environmental forces, called *stressors*, may activate the predisposition, resulting in a disorder. Alternatively, in a benign and supportive environment, the abnormality may never materialize.

A third shortcoming, related to the preceding one, is revealed by our accumulating knowledge that biochemical changes often occur because of environmental forces. We know, for example, that stress-produced fear and anger cause the secretion of adrenaline and noradrenaline. Similarly, schizophrenia, rather than resulting from the presence of such chemicals as dopamine, could *cause* the secretion of excess amounts of the chemicals in persons with the disorder.

A fourth shortcoming is the inherent danger in using a genetic-determinist paradigm that oversimplifies our lives as the sole result of genes. Genetic determinism is an incomplete scientific model because, by itself, a genome is passive, and it must utilize a second informational system in order to assemble a meaningful story. As we mentioned earlier, the "map of life" has no meaning until it is assembled in such a manner as to give it one. How this occurs represents a major challenge to scientists.

A final shortcoming is that wholesale adoption of the biological model could foster patients' helplessness by eliminating their responsibility in the treatment process. Patients might be seen—both by their therapists and by themselves—as passive participants, to be treated only with appropriate drugs and medical interventions. For patients who are already suffering from feelings of helplessness or loss of control, such an approach could be devastating.

Psychodynamic Models

At the core of Steve's problems are his early childhood experiences, his inability to confront his own intense feelings of hostility toward his father (fears of castration), his unresolved Oedipal longing toward his mother. As a psychodynamically oriented therapist, I believe that, at crucial psychosexual stages, Steve did not receive the love and care a child needs to develop into a healthy adult. He was neglected, understimulated, and left on his own. As a result, he felt unloved and rejected. Therapy should be aimed at uncovering Steve's unconscious conflicts, letting him relive his early childhood traumas, and helping him to attain insight into his motivations and fears.

Psychodynamic models of abnormal behavior have two main distinguishing features. First, they view disorders in adults as the result of childhood traumas or anxieties. Second, psychodynamic models hold that many of these childhood-based anxieties operate unconsciously; because they are too threatening for the adult to face, they are repressed through mental defense mechanisms. As a result, people exhibit symptoms they are unable to understand. To eliminate the symptoms, the therapist must make the patient aware of these unconscious anxieties or conflicts.

The early development of psychodynamic theory is generally credited to Sigmund Freud (1938, 1949), a Viennese neurologist who gave up his practice to enter psychiatry. During his clinical work, Freud became convinced that powerful mental processes could remain hidden from consciousness and could cause abnormal behaviors. He believed that the therapist's role was to help the patient achieve insight into these unconscious processes. Although he originally relied on hypnosis for this purpose, Freud soon dropped it in favor of other techniques. He felt that cures were more likely to be permanent if patients became aware of their problems without the aid of hypnosis. This view eventually led Freud to his formulation of **psychoanalysis**, the therapy technique based on the view that unconscious conflicts must be aired and understood by the patient if abnormal behavior is to be eliminated.

Myth vs Reality

Myth: Psychoanalysis is history. Although it makes interesting reading and has some useful concepts, contemporary mental health professionals no longer find it useful as an explanation of abnormal behavior, nor do they use it in their practices.

Reality: Although traditional psychoanalytic conceptualizations may have waned over the years, little doubt exists that its interpretation of the importance of early childhood experiences in explaining abnormal

Sigmund Freud (1856–1939) Freud began his career as a neurologist. He became increasingly intrigued with the relationship between illness and mental processes and ultimately developed psychoanalysis, a therapy in which unconscious conflicts are aired so that the patient can become aware of and understand his or her problems.

behavior, the role of the unconscious, and the use of insight continue to exert a pervasive influence on mental health practice. First, the practice of psychoanalytic approaches has evolved into what is now called object relations, brief analytic, or interpersonal approaches (James & Gilliland, 2003). In fact, the terms *psychoanalytic* and *psychoanalysis* are used to refer to traditional Freudian theory, whereas the term *psychodynamic* is used to refer to all psychoanalytic explanations, including their modern counterparts. These approaches emphasize the importance of understanding relationships formed from early childhood. Second, one study revealed that 18 percent of clinical psychologists, 12 percent of counseling psychologists, 35 percent of psychiatrists, 33 percent of social workers, and 11 percent of counselors describe their orientation as "psychoanalytic/psychodynamic" (Prochaska & Norcross, 1999).

Personality Structure

Freud believed that personality is composed of three major components—the *id,* the *ego,* and the *super-ego*—and that all behavior is a product of their inter-action. The *id* is the original component of the personality; it is present at birth, and from it the ego and superego eventually develop. The id operates from the **pleasure principle**—the impulsive, pleasure-seeking aspect of our being—and it seeks immediate gratifica-tion of instinctual needs, regardless of moral or realis-tic concerns.

In contrast, the *ego* represents the realistic and rational part of the mind. It comes into existence because the human personality must be able to cope with the external world if it is to survive. The ego is influenced by the **reality principle**—an awareness of the demands of the environment and of the need to adjust behavior to meet these demands. The ego's deci-sions are dictated by realistic considerations rather than by moral judgments.

Moral judgments and moralistic considerations are the domain of the *superego;* they often represent soci-ety's ideals or values as interpreted by our parents. The superego is composed of the *conscience,* which instills guilt feelings about engaging in immoral or unethical behavior, and the *ego ideal,* which rewards altruistic or moral behavior with feelings of pride.

The energy system from which the personality oper-ates occurs through the interplay of *instincts.* Instincts give rise to our thoughts and actions and fuel their expression. Freud emphasized *sex* and *aggression* as the dominant human instincts because he recognized that the society in which he lived placed strong prohi-bitions on these drives and that, as a result, people were taught to inhibit them. A profound need to express one's instincts is often frightening and can lead a person to deny their existence. Indeed, Freud felt that even though most impulses are hidden from one's con-sciousness, they nonetheless determine human actions.

Psychosexual Stages

According to psychodynamic theory, human personal-ity develops through a sequence of five **psychosexual stages,** each of which brings a unique challenge. If unfavorable circumstances prevail, the personality may be drastically affected. Because Freud stressed the

Psychosexual Stages During the oral stage, the first stage of psychosexual development, the infant not only receives nourishment but also derives pleasure from sucking and being close to its mother. Later, during the anal stage, toilet training can be a time of intense emotional conflict between parent and child, or it can be a time of cooperation.

importance of early childhood experiences, he saw the human personality as largely determined in the first five years of life—during the *oral* (first year of life), *anal* (around the second year of life), and *phallic* (beginning around the third or fourth years of life) stages. The last two psychosexual stages are the *latency* (approximately six to twelve years of age), and *genital* (beginning in puberty) stages.

The importance of each psychosexual stage for later development lies in whether fixation occurs during that stage. (*Fixation* is the arresting of emotional development at a particular psychosexual stage.) If the infant is traumatized (harmed) in some way during the oral stage, for example, some of the infant's instinctual energy becomes trapped at that stage. Consequently, the personality of that person as an adult will retain strong features of the oral stage. Passivity, helplessness, obesity, chronic smoking, and alcoholism may all be characteristics of an oral personality. According to the psychodynamic model, each stage is characterized by distinct traits and, should fixation occur, by distinct conflicts.

Freud believed that a person who could transcend the various stages without fixation would develop into a normal, healthy individual. Heterosexual interests, stability, vocational planning, marriage, and other social activities would become a person's prime concern during the genital stage.

Anxiety and Psychopathology

Anxiety is at the root of Freud's theory of psychopathology, and he identified three types (shown diagrammatically in Figure 2.6) that arise from conflicts among the id, ego, and superego. *Realistic anxiety* occurs when there is potential danger from the external environment. For example, you smell smoke in a building and experience realistic anxiety as your ego warns you to take action to protect yourself from physical harm. *Moralistic anxiety* results when someone does not live up to his or her own moral standards

or engages in unethical conduct. In this case, the ego warns of possible retaliation from the superego. *Neurotic anxiety* often results when id impulses seem to be getting out of hand, bursting through ego controls. In all these cases, anxiety is a signal that something bad is about to happen and that appropriate steps should be taken to reduce it.

Although Freud studied and treated all three types of anxiety, he concentrated mainly on neurotic anxiety. We shall do the same, although much of our discussion applies to the other two types of anxiety as well. (Recent editions of the *Diagnostic and Statistical Manual of Mental Disorders*, including DSM-IV-TR, have replaced the traditional subcategories of neurotic behavior with other, more refined concepts. We use the term *neurotic* here because of its importance to Freud's theory.)

Defense Mechanisms

Neurotic behavior develops from the threat of overwhelming anxiety, which may lead to full-scale panic. To forestall this panic, the ego often resorts to defense mechanisms, such as those listed in Table 2.2. **Defense mechanisms** share three characteristics: they protect the individual from anxiety, they operate unconsciously, and they distort reality.

All individuals use some strategies to reduce anxiety. The defense mechanisms in Table 2.2 are considered maladaptive, however, when they are overused—that is, when they become the predominant means of coping with stress and when they interfere with one's ability to handle life's everyday demands. The difference is one of degree, not of kind.

Psychodynamic Therapy

Traditional psychodynamic therapy attempts to rid people of maladaptive behaviors by inducing ego weakness. According to Freud, ego weakness occurs during the natural state of sleep and under conditions

FIGURE 2.6 Three Types of Anxiety Freud believed that people suffer from three types of anxiety, arising from conflicts involving the id, ego, and superego. Each type of anxiety is, in essence, a signal of impending danger.

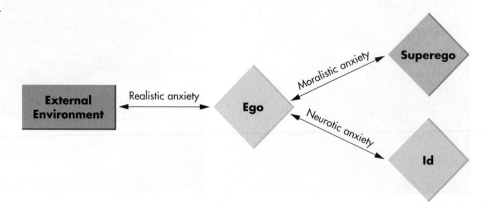

TABLE 2.2 Defense Mechanisms

Repression The blocking of forbidden or dangerous desires and thoughts to keep them from entering one's consciousness; according to Freud, the most basic defense mechanism. *Example:* A soldier who witnesses the horrible death of his friend in combat may force the event out of consciousness because it symbolizes his own mortality.

Reaction formation Repression of dangerous impulses, followed by converting them to their direct opposite. *Example:* A woman who gives birth to an unwanted child may become an extremely overprotective mother who is afraid to let the child out of her sight and who showers the child with superficial attention.

Projection Ridding oneself of threatening desires or thoughts by attributing them to others. *Example:* A worker may mask unpleasant feelings of inadequacy by blaming his poor performance on the incompetence of fellow workers or on a conspiracy in which enemies are disrupting his life.

Rationalization Explaining one's behavior by giving well-thought-out and socially acceptable reasons that do not happen to be the real ones. *Example:* A student may explain flunking a test as follows: "I'm not interested in the course and don't really need it to graduate. Besides, I find the teacher extremely dull."

Displacement Directing an emotion, such as hostility or anxiety, toward a substitute target. *Example:* A meek clerk who is constantly belittled by her boss, builds up tremendous resentment and snaps at her family members instead of at her boss, who might fire her.

Undoing A symbolic attempt, often ritualistic or repetitive, to right a wrong or negate some disapproved thought, impulse, or act. *Example:* In Shakespeare's play, Lady Macbeth goads her husband into slaying the king and then tries to cleanse herself of sin by constantly going through the motions of washing her hands.

Regression A retreat to an earlier developmental level—according to Freud, the person's most fixated stage—that demands less mature responses and aspirations. *Example:* A dignified college president drinks too much and sings old school songs at a reunion with college classmates.

of excessive fatigue. Therapists—called *psychoanalysts,* or just *analysts*—attempt to induce this state through such techniques as hypnosis and *projective tests,* in which ambiguous stimuli such as inkblots, word associations, or pictures provoke revealing verbal responses. These techniques give the analyst some access to unconscious material, which is used to help patients achieve insight into their inner motivations and desires. The basic premise of the psychodynamic approach is that a cure can be effected only through this process. (Psychodynamic methods are discussed further in the chapter on therapeutic interventions.)

Post-Freudian Perspectives

Freud's psychoanalytic approach attracted many followers. Some of Freud's disciples, however, came to disagree with his insistence that the sex instinct is the major determinant of behavior. Many of his most gifted adherents broke away from him and formulated coherent psychological models of their own. Despite their new ideas, they remained strongly influenced by Freud's constructs. For example, nearly all of them continued to believe in the power of the unconscious, in the use of "talking" methods of psychotherapy that rely heavily on the patient's introspection, in the three-part structure of personality, and in the one-to-one analyst-patient approach to therapy.

The major differences between the various post-Freudian theories and psychoanalysis lie in the emphasis that the former placed on five areas: freedom of choice and future goals, ego autonomy, social forces, object relations (past interpersonal relations), and treatment of seriously disturbed people (see Table 2.3).

Criticisms of Psychodynamic Models

Psychodynamic theory has had a tremendous impact on the field of psychology. Psychoanalysis and its variations are very widely employed. Nonetheless, three major criticisms, discussed here, are often leveled at psychodynamic theory and treatment (Joseph, 1991).

First, the empirical procedures by which Freud validated his hypotheses have grave shortcomings. His observations about human behavior were often made under uncontrolled conditions. For example, he relied heavily on case studies and on his own self-analysis as a basis for formulating theory. His patients, from whom he drew conclusions about universal aspects of personality dynamics and behavior, tended to represent a narrow spectrum of one society. Although case studies can be a rich source of clinical data, Freud's lack of verbatim notes means that his recollections were subject to distortions and omissions. Furthermore, he seldom submitted the material related by his patients to any form of external corroboration—statements from relatives or friends, test data, documents, or medical records. Using such private and uncontrolled methods of inquiry as a basis for theory is fraught with hazards.

Second, is a theory of human behavior adequate if it does not apply to more than one-half the population of

---

TABLE 2.3 Contributions of Post-Freudians and Psychoanalytic Therapists

Traditional psychoanalytic theory has changed over the years due to the work of post-Freudians and others. Although most of the individuals listed here accept many of the basic tenets of the theory, they have stressed different aspects of the human condition. Some differences are listed below.

1. Freedom of choice and future goals People are not just mechanistic beings. They have a high degree of free choice and are motivated toward future goals.

> *Alfred Adler (1870–1937)* Stressed that people are not passive victims of biology, instincts, or unconscious forces. Stressed freedom of choice and goals directed by means of social drives.

> *Carl Jung (1875–1965)* Believed in the collective unconscious as the foundation of creative functioning. Believed that humans were goal directed and future oriented.

2. Ego autonomy The ego is an autonomous entity and can operate independently from the id. It is creative, forward moving, and capable of continual growth.

> *Anna Freud (1895–1982)* Emphasized the role, operation, and importance of the ego. Believed ego is an autonomous component of the personality and not at the mercy of the id.

> *Erik Erikson (1902–1994)* Perhaps the most influential of the ego theorists. Formulated stages of ego development from infancy to late adulthood—one of the first true developmental theorists. Considers personality to be flexible and capable of growth and change throughout the adult years.

3. Social forces Interpersonal relationships are of primary importance in our psychological development. Especially influential are our primary social relationships.

> *Karen Horney (1885–1952)* Often considered one of the first feminist psychologists who rejected Freud's notion of penis envy. Stressed that behavior disorders are due to disturbed interpersonal childhood relationships.

> *Harry Stack Sullivan (1892–1949)* Major contribution was his interpersonal theory of psychological disorders. Believed that the individual's psychological functions could be understood only in the context of his or her social relationships.

4. Object relations The technical term *object relations* is roughly equivalent to "past interpersonal relations." it refers to how people develop patterns of living from their early relations with significant others.

> *Heinz Kohut (1913–1981)* Felt it was especially important to study the mother-child relationship. Known for his work on the narcissistic personality.

> *Otto Kernberg (1928–)* Known especially for his studies of the borderline personality. Especially interested in understanding how clients seem to have difficulty in forming stable relationships because of pathological objects in the past.

5. Treatment of the seriously disturbed Freud believed that psychoanalysis could not be used with very seriously disturbed individuals because they were "analytically unfit." By this he meant that they did not have sufficient contact with reality to benefit from insight.

> *Hyman Sponitz* Demonstrated that modern psychoanalysis could be used with severely disturbed clients. Associated with new treatment techniques that do not require clients to be intellectually capable of understanding interpretations. Techniques provide feedback that helps client resolve conflicts by experiencing them rather than understanding them.

---

the world? Freud's theory of female sexuality and personality has drawn heavy criticisms from feminists for many years. Phallic-stage dynamics, penis envy, unfavorable comparisons of the clitoris to the penis, the woman's need for a male child as a penis substitute, and the belief that penetration is necessary for a woman's sexual satisfaction all rest on assumptions that are biologically questionable and that fail to consider social forces that shape women's behavior. Such theories, at face value, seem to depreciate female sexuality and legitimize male sexuality (McBride, 1990; Schaef, 1981).

"Since man is the measure of all things—man, literally, rather than human beings—we have all tended to measure ourselves by men" (J. Miller, 1976, p. 69).

A third criticism of psychoanalysis is that it cannot be applied to a wide range of disturbed people. Among them are individuals who have speech disturbances or are inarticulate (talking is important in therapy); people who have urgent, immediate problems (classical psychoanalysis requires much time); and people who are very young or old. Research studies have shown that psychoanalytic therapy is best suited to well-educated people of the middle and upper socioeconomic classes who exhibit anxiety disorders rather than psychotic behavior (Corey, 2005). It is more limited in therapeutic value with people of lower socioeconomic levels and with people who are less verbal, less intelligent, and more severely disturbed (Sloane, Staples, Cristol, Yorkston, & Whipple, 1975). More disturbing are findings that indicate that psychodynamic therapies are only minimally more effective than placebo treatments or no treatments at all (Nietzel, Bernstein, & Milich, 1994; Prochaska & Norcross, 1994). To be fair, however, it must be acknowledged that newer and more short-term psychodynamic approaches may be helpful to some patients (Crits-Christoph, 1992).

Behavioral Models

The roots of Steve's problems can be traced to his behavioral repertoire. Many of the behaviors he has learned are inappropriate, and his repertoire lacks useful, productive behaviors. He has had little practice in social relationships, lacks good role models, and has difficulty distinguishing between appropriate and inappropriate behavior. Furthermore, his delusion that he is controlled by demonic forces and his continual thinking about Satanism may be unwittingly reinforced by those around him. When Steve discusses or acts out these beliefs, he garners much attention from his parents, peers, and onlookers (perhaps a form of reinforcement). In sum, I recommend behavioral therapy that includes modeling and role playing to enhance Steve's social skills and a program to eliminate or control his delusional thoughts.

The **behavioral models** of psychopathology are concerned with the role of learning in abnormal behavior.

The differences among them lie mainly in their explanations of how learning occurs. Although some models appear to disagree, they generally tend to complement one another (Corey, 2005; Kottler, 2002). The three learning models discussed here—classical conditioning, operant conditioning, and observational learning—are usually applied to different types of behavior.

The Classical Conditioning Model

Early in the twentieth century, Ivan Pavlov (1849–1936), a Russian physiologist, discovered a process known as **classical conditioning,** in which responses to new stimuli are learned through association. This process involves the involuntary responses (such as reflexes, emotional reactions, and sexual arousal), which are controlled by the autonomic nervous system.

Pavlov's discovery was accidental. He was measuring dogs' salivation as part of a study of their digestive processes when he noticed that the dogs began to salivate at the sight of an assistant carrying their food. This response puzzled Pavlov and led to his formulation of classical conditioning. He reasoned that food is an **unconditioned stimulus (UCS)**, which, in the mouth, automatically elicits salivation; this salivation is an unlearned or **unconditioned response (UCR)** to the food. Pavlov then presented a previously *neutral* stimulus (one, such as the sound of a bell, that does not initially elicit salivation) to the dogs just before presenting the food. He found that, after a number of repetitions, the sound of the bell alone elicited salivation. This learning process is based on association: the neutral stimulus (the bell) acquires some of the properties of the unconditioned stimulus (the food) when they are repeatedly paired. When the bell alone can provoke the salivation, it becomes a **conditioned**

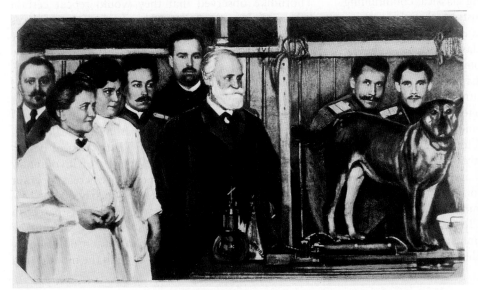

Ivan Pavlov (1849–1936) A Russian physiologist, Pavlov discovered the associative learning process we know as classical conditioning while he was studying salivation in dogs. Pavlov won the Nobel Prize in physiology and medicine in 1904 for his work on the principal digestive glands.

FIGURE 2.7 A Basic Classical Conditioning Process   Dogs normally salivate when food is provided (left drawing). With his laboratory dogs, Ivan Pavlov paired the ringing of a bell with the presentation of food (middle drawing). Eventually, the dogs would salivate to the ringing of the bell alone, when no food was near (right drawing).

  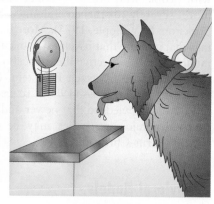

Stimulus:	UCS (food)	UCS & CS (food & bell)	CS (bell alone)
Response:	UCR (salivation)	UCR (salivation)	CR (conditioned salivation)

stimulus (CS). The salivation elicited by the bell is a **conditioned response (CR)**—a learned response to a previously neutral stimulus. Each time the conditioned stimulus is paired with the unconditioned stimulus, the conditioned response is said to be *reinforced,* or strengthened. Pavlov's conditioning process is illustrated in Figure 2.7.

Classical Conditioning in Psychopathology

Pavlov never fully explored the implications of classical conditioning for human behavior; John B. Watson is credited with recognizing the importance of associative learning in the explanation of abnormal behavior. In a classic and oft-cited experiment, Watson (J. B. Watson & Rayner, 1920), using classical conditioning principles, was able to demonstrate that the acquisition of a *phobia* (an exaggerated, seemingly illogical fear of a particular object or class of objects) could be explained by classical conditioning.

As we shall see in later chapters, classical conditioning has provided explanations not only for the acquisition of phobias but also for certain unusual sexual attractions and other extreme emotional reactions. It has also served as a basis for effective treatment techniques (Day, 2004). Yet the "passive nature" of associative learning limited its usefulness as an explanatory and treatment tool. Most human behavior, both normal and abnormal, tends to be much more active and voluntary. To explain how these behaviors are acquired or eliminated necessitates an understanding of operant conditioning.

The Operant Conditioning Model

An **operant behavior** is a voluntary and controllable behavior, such as walking or thinking, that "operates" on an individual's environment. In an extremely warm room, for example, you would have difficulty consciously controlling your sweating—"willing" your body not to perspire. You could, however, simply walk out of the uncomfortably warm room—an operant behavior. Most human behavior is operant in nature.

Edward Thorndike (1874–1949) first formulated the concept of **operant conditioning**, which he called *instrumental conditioning.* This theory of learning holds that behaviors are controlled by the consequences that follow them. In working with cats, Thorndike observed that they would repeat certain behaviors that were followed by positive consequences and would reduce behaviors that were followed by unpleasant consequences. This principle became known as the **law of effect.** Some fifty years later, B. F. Skinner (1904–1990) started a revolution in the field by innovatively applying Thorndike's law of effect, which he renamed *reinforcement.*

Operant conditioning differs from classical conditioning primarily in two ways. First, classical conditioning is linked to the development of involuntary behaviors, such as fear responses, whereas operant conditioning is related to voluntary behaviors.

Second, as we discussed earlier, behaviors based on *classical* conditioning are controlled by stimuli, or events *preceding* the response: salivation occurs only when it is preceded by a UCS (food in the mouth) or a

Operant Conditioning in the Classroom In operant conditioning, positive consequences increase the likelihood and frequency of a desired response. This is particularly important in a classroom setting in which a child knows that appropriate behavior will be rewarded and inappropriate behavior will be punished.

CS (the thought of a sizzling, juicy steak covered with mushrooms, for example). In *operant* conditioning, however, behaviors are controlled by reinforcers—consequences that influence the frequency or magnitude of the event they follow. Positive consequences increase the likelihood and frequency of a response. But when the consequences are negative, the behavior is less likely to be repeated. For example, a student is likely to raise his or her hand in class often if the teacher recognizes the student, smiles, and seems genuinely interested in the student's comments.

Operant Conditioning in Psychopathology

Studies have demonstrated a relationship between environmental reinforcers and certain abnormal behaviors. For example, self-injurious behavior, such as head banging, is a dramatic form of psychopathology that is often reported in psychotic, autistic, and mentally retarded children. It has been hypothesized that some forms of head banging may be linked to reinforcing features in the environment (Corey, 2005; Sommers-Flanagan & Sommers-Flanagan, 2004). In one classic study, experimenters used bananas as reinforcement to shape a self-injurious behavior, head hitting, in two monkeys (Schaefer, 1970). The experimenters rewarded the monkeys for successive approximations of the behavior: first, for raising a paw; then for holding the paw over the head; and finally for bringing the paw down on the head. This sequence of behaviors was shaped in about sixteen minutes in both monkeys. Each time the investigators gave the reinforcement, they said, "Poor boy!

Don't do that! You'll hurt yourself." Head hitting later occurred whenever these words were spoken. It seems clear from these findings that self-injurious behaviors can be developed and maintained through reinforcement. Likewise, some forms of alcohol or substance abuse may be due to the initial pleasurable feelings and lowered anxieties people experience (K. B. Carey & Carey, 1995).

Although positive reinforcement can account for some forms of self-injurious or other undesirable behaviors, in some instances other variables seem more important. *Negative reinforcement* (the removal of an aversive stimulus), for example, can also strengthen and maintain unhealthy behaviors. Consider a student who has enrolled in a class in which the instructor requires oral reports. The thought of doing an oral presentation in front of a class produces anxiety feelings, sweating, an upset stomach, and trembling in the student. Having these feelings is aversive. To stop the unpleasant reaction, the student switches to another section in which the instructor does not require oral presentations. The student's behavior is reinforced by escape from aversive feelings, and such avoidant responses to situations involving "stage fright" will increase in frequency.

The principles of operant conditioning, like those of classical conditioning, have proven invaluable in the treatment of psychopathology. In many cases, the therapist must be ingenious in devising successful strategies. In later chapters on specific psychological disorders and in the chapter on therapeutic interventions, we discuss a variety of ways in which

B. F. Skinner (1904–1990) Skinner was a leader in the field of behaviorism. His research and work in operant conditioning started a revolution in applying the principles of learning to the psychology of human behavior. He was also a social philosopher, and many of his ideas fueled debate about the nature of the human condition. These ideas were expressed in his books, *Walden II* and *Beyond Freedom and Dignity*.

operant conditioning has been applied to the treatment of abnormal behaviors.

Myth vs Reality

Myth: Behavioral approaches assume that people are completely the products of their conditioning histories, that they are passive participants in the developmental process, and that they have little free will. These approaches deny the importance of "mental life" in people. They seem more focused on behaviors and seem to believe people are mechanistic and robotic in their actions.

Reality: Whereas early behaviorism, under the influence of John B. Watson (and to some extent B. F. Skinner), saw people as primarily the products of their conditioning histories and felt that speculating about the "inner life" of a person was unscientific, such rigid concepts have given way to a more holistic and integrated interpretation of the learning process. Behaviorally oriented mental health professionals are now very much involved in understanding how the internal mental life of the person affects the acquisition and treatment of certain disorders. They now acknowledge that people are not passive beings and have increasingly moved toward using social modeling and cognitive processes to supplement the principles of both classical and operant learning models.

The Observational Learning Model

The traditional behavioral theories of learning—classical conditioning and operant conditioning—require that the individual actually perform behaviors to learn them. **Observational learning theory** suggests that an individual can acquire new behaviors simply by watching other people perform them (Bandura, 1997; Cormier & Cormier, 1998). The process of learning by observing models (and later imitating them) is called *vicarious conditioning* or **modeling.** Direct and tangible reinforcement (such as giving praise or other rewards) for imitation of the model is not necessary, although reinforcers are necessary to maintain behaviors learned in this manner. Observational learning can involve both respondent and operant behaviors, and its discovery has had such an impact in psychology that it has been proposed as a third form of learning.

Observational Learning in Psychopathology

Models that attribute psychopathology to observational learning assume—as do those that emphasize classical and operant conditioning—that abnormal behaviors are learned in the same manner as normal behaviors. More specifically, the assumption is that exposure to disturbed models is likely to produce disturbed behaviors (James & Gilliland, 2003). For example, when monkeys watched other monkeys respond with fear to an unfamiliar object, they learned to respond in a similar manner (Cook, Hodes, & Lang, 1986). Observational learning can have four possible effects on an observer:

1. New behaviors can be acquired by watching the model.

2. The model may serve to elicit particular behaviors by providing the observer with cues to engage in those behaviors.

Learning by Observing
Observational learning is based on the theory that behavior can be learned by observing it. Although much has been made of the relationship between violence and aggression viewed on television and in movies and violent behavior in real life, observational learning can have positive benefits as well.

3. Behaviors formerly inhibited because of anxiety or other negative reactions may be performed after they have been observed.

4. A behavior may become inhibited if the observer sees that a similar behavior performed by the model resulted in aversive consequences.

Criticisms of the Behavioral Models

Behavioral approaches to psychopathology have had a tremendous impact in the areas of etiology and treatment, and they are a strong force in psychology today. The contributions of behaviorist perspectives include: (1) questioning the adequacy of the biological model of psychological disorders, (2) stressing the importance of external influences on behavior, (3) requiring strict adherence to scientific methods, and (4) encouraging continuing evaluation of the techniques employed by psychologists. These features endow behaviorism with a degree of effectiveness and accountability that is lacking in the insight-oriented perspectives.

Opponents of the behavioral orientation point out that it often neglects or places a low importance on the inner determinants of behavior. They criticize the behaviorists' extension to human beings of results obtained from animal studies. Some also charge that because of its lack of attention to human values in relation to behavior, the behaviorist perspective is mechanistic, viewing people as "empty organisms." And some critics complain that behaviorists are not open-minded and that they tend to dismiss out of hand the advances and data accumulated by other approaches to therapy. Criticism that behavioral approaches ignore the person's inner life are less applicable to proponents of modeling. As you will see in the next section of this chapter, a recent trend among behaviorists is to place increasing importance on cognitive processes and to deemphasize the importance of intrapsychic dynamics. This has led to the development of cognitive models. Many theorists and practitioners, however, find it hard to believe that clients can help themselves by simply changing their thinking.

Cognitive Models

Steve is a "thinking being." The psychological problems he is experiencing derive from two main cognitive sources: his irrational thoughts or belief system about himself and others and his distorted thought processes, which lead him to misinterpret events. Steve's tendency to interpret all events to his disadvantage is obvious. For example, because his father constantly criticized and belittled him, Steve believes he is a "worthless" person and will always be "worthless." A cognitive approach to Steve's therapy would be highly cognitive and behavior-oriented. As a therapist in this tradition, I would recommend a program that would emphasize three points. First, Steve needs to recognize the role that thinking and belief systems play in his problems. Second, he must learn to identify self-statements, belief systems, or assumptions that are irrational and maladaptive and to respond to them by rationally disputing them. Finally, he must learn to replace irrational self-statements with productive ones.

Cognitive models are based on the assumption that conscious thought mediates, or modifies, an individual's emotional state and/or behavior in response to a stimulus. According to these models, people actually create their own problems (and symptoms) by the ways they interpret events and situations. For example, one person who fails to be hired for a job may become severely depressed, blaming himself for the failure. Another might become only mildly irritated, believing that failure to get the job had nothing to do with personal inadequacy. How does it happen that events (not being hired for a job) are identical for both people but the responses are very different? To explain this phenomenon, we have to look at *mediating processes*—the thoughts, perceptions, and self-evaluations that determine our reactions and behaviors.

Cognitive theories argue that modifying thoughts and feelings is essential to changing behavior. How people label a situation and how they interpret events profoundly affect their emotional reactions and behaviors. How a person interprets events is a function of his or her **schema**—a set of underlying assumptions heavily influenced by a person's experiences, values, and perceived capabilities. Cognitive psychologists usually search for the causes of psychopathology in one of two processes: in actual irrational and maladaptive assumptions and thoughts or in distortions of the actual thought process. Although many theorists have contributed greatly to this area, we will concentrate primarily on the contributions of Albert Ellis and Aaron Beck.

Irrational and Maladaptive Assumptions and Thoughts

Almost all cognitive theorists stress heavily that disturbed individuals have both irrational and maladaptive thoughts. Ellis (1962, 1987, 1997) labels these thoughts "irrational" assumptions; Beck (1976, 1991, 1997) calls them dysfunctional "automatic thoughts"; and D. H. Meichenbaum (1977, 1985, 1993) refers to them as counterproductive "self-statements." As a practicing therapist for many years, Beck became interested in the way many of his clients would engage in an almost rigid, inflexible, and automatic interpretation of

events they had experienced. These negative thoughts seemed to "just happen" as if by reflex, even in the face of objective contrary evidence. For example, Beck believes that depression revolves around firmly entrenched "negative views of self, experience and the future" and that the paranoid individual persists in assuming that other people are deliberately abusive, interfering, or critical (Beck & Weishaar, 1989).

In working with his clients, Beck concluded that cognitive content is organized in a hierarchy along three levels. At the first level are our most accessible and least stable cognitions, the voluntary thoughts that we have the greatest ability to control and summon at will. Clients suffering from an anxiety disorder, for example, are readily able to describe their symptoms and to offer superficial causes and solutions for them. Most people do not, however, have such ready access to the second level of cognitions, the automatic thoughts that occur spontaneously. The cognitions at this second level are triggered by circumstances and intercede between an event or stimulus and the individual's emotional and behavioral reactions. A student who must make an oral presentation in class may think that "everyone will see I'm nervous." Such thoughts are given credibility without being challenged and usually derive from the third level of cognitions: underlying assumptions about ourselves and the world around us. For example, the belief that one is a failure and an ineffectual person in all aspects of life moderates interpretation of all events. These assumptions are quite stable and almost always outside of the person's awareness.

One of the most prominent psychologists associated with implicating the role of irrational beliefs and assumptions in maladaptive emotions and behaviors is Albert Ellis. According to Ellis, psychological problems are produced by irrational thought patterns that stem from the individual's belief system. Unpleasant emotional responses that lead to anger, unhappiness, depression, fear, and anxiety result from one's *thoughts* about an event rather than from the *event itself*. These irrational thoughts have been conditioned through early childhood, but we also add to the difficulty by reinstilling these false beliefs in ourselves by autosuggestion and self-repetition. Ellis hypothesized that irrational thinking operates from dogmatic, absolutist "shoulds," "musts," and "oughts." Some examples are such self-statements as "I must be loved by my mother or father," "I ought to be able to succeed in everything," and "If I don't get what I want, it will be awful." Cynically, Ellis has referred to the many "musts" that cause human misery as "musturbatory activities."

Although being accepted and loved by everyone is desirable, it is an unrealistic and irrational idea, and as such it creates dysfunctional feelings and behaviors. Consider a student who becomes depressed after an unsuccessful date. An appropriate emotional response in such an unsuccessful dating situation might be frustration and temporary disappointment. A more severe depression will develop only if the student adds irrational thoughts, such as "Because this person turned me down, I am worthless. ... I will never succeed with anyone of the opposite sex. ... I am a total failure."

Distortions of Thought Processes

The study of cognitions as a cause of psychopathology has led many therapists to concentrate on the process (as opposed to the content) of thinking that characterizes both normal and abnormal individuals. Ellis (1962, 1997) believed that human beings are born with the potential for both rational and irrational thinking. Ellis described the process by which an individual acquires irrational thoughts through interactions with significant others, and he called it the *A-B-C theory of personality*. *A* is an event, a fact, or the individual's behavior or attitude. *C* is the person's emotional or behavioral reaction. The activating event *A* never causes the emotional or behavioral consequence *C*. Instead, *B*, the person's beliefs about *A*, causes *C*.

Think back to the two job hunters. Job hunter 1, whose activating event *A* was being turned down for the position, may think to himself (irrational beliefs *B*), "How awful to be rejected! I must be worthless. I'm no good." Thus he may become depressed and withdraw (emotional and behavioral consequence *C*). Job hunter 2, on the other hand, reacts to the activating event *A* by saying (rational beliefs *B*), "How unfortunate to get rejected. It's frustrating and irritating. I'll have to try harder" (healthy consequence *C*). The two sets of assumptions and expectations are very different. Job hunter 1 blamed himself and was overcome with feelings of worthlessness; job hunter 2 recognized that not every person is right for every job (or vice versa) and left the situation with self-esteem intact. Job hunter 1 interprets the rejection as "awful and catastrophic" and, as a result, reacts with depression and may cease looking for a job. Job hunter 2 does not interpret the rejection personally, reacts with mild irritation and annoyance, and redoubles his efforts to seek employment. Figure 2.8 illustrates the *A-B-C* relationship and suggests a possible path for a cognitive approach to treatment.

Cognitive Approaches to Therapy

Certain commonalities characterize almost all cognitive approaches to psychotherapy. These have been summarized by Beck and Weishaar (1989):

Cognitive therapy consists of highly specific learning experiences designed to teach patients (1) to monitor their negative, automatic thoughts (cognitions); (2) to recognize the connections between cognition, affect, and behavior; (3) to examine the evidence for and against distorted automatic thoughts; (4) to substitute more reality-oriented interpretations for these biased cognitions; and (5) to learn to identify and alter the beliefs that predispose them to distort their experiences. (p. 308)

Criticisms of the Cognitive Models

In many respects, cognitive models share many characteristics of the traditional behavioral models. Cognitive models emphasize learned cognitions that occur within people as they interact with internally generated stimuli and external events. Both types of models stress the altering of behavior and both deemphasize childhood experiences; neither considers insight into a problem necessary to alleviate it. In addition, successful treatment is measured by changes in overt behavior, and therapists rely on experimental methods to validate techniques.

Yet some behaviorists remain quite skeptical of the cognitive schools. Just before his death, B. F. Skinner (1990) warned that cognitions are not observable phenomena and cannot form the foundations of empiricism. In this context, he echoed the historical beliefs of John B. Watson, who stated that the science of psychology was observable behaviors, not "mentalistic concepts." Although Watson's reference was to the intrapsychic dynamics of the mind postulated by Freud, Watson might have viewed cognitions in the same manner.

Cognitive theories have also been attacked by more humanistically oriented psychologists who believe that human behavior is more than thoughts and beliefs (Corey, 2005). They object to the mechanistic manner by which human beings are reduced to the sum of their cognitive parts. Do thoughts and beliefs really cause disturbances, or do the disturbances themselves distort thinking?

Criticisms have also been leveled at the therapeutic approach taken by cognitive therapists. The nature of the approach makes the therapist a teacher, expert, and authority figure. The therapist is quite direct and confrontive in identifying and attacking irrational beliefs and processes. In such interactions, clients can readily be intimidated into acquiescing to the therapist's power and authority. Thus the therapist may misidentify the client's disorder, and the client may be hesitant to challenge the therapist's beliefs.

Cognitive learning approaches, with their emphasis on the powerful influence of internal mediating processes, seem to offer an exciting new direction for behaviorists. It is clear that psychology has undergone a "revolution" in that cognitive and behavioral approaches have been integrated into mainstream psychological thought.

Humanistic and Existential Approaches

Steve is a flesh-and-blood person, alive, organic, and moving, with thoughts, feelings, and emotions. I object to the use of diagnosis because labels serve only to pigeonhole people and act as barriers to the development of a therapeutic relationship. In my attempt to understand the subjective world of Steve's experience, it appears that he is feeling trapped, immobilized, and lonely and that he is externalizing his problems. In this way Steve may be evading responsibility for making his own choices and may be protecting himself by staying in the safe, known environment of his "illness." Steve needs to realize that he is responsible for his own actions, that he cannot find his identity in others, and that his life is not predetermined.

The humanistic and existential approaches evolved as a reaction to the determinism of early models of psychopathology. For example, many psychologists were disturbed that Freudian theory did not focus on the inner world of the client but rather categorized the client according to a set of preconceived diagnoses (R. May, 1967). Psychoanalysts, these critics said, described clients in terms of blocked instinctual forces and psychic complexes that made them victims of some mechanistic and deterministic personality structure. Similarly, critics noted, the cognitive-behavioral schools of thought seemed to describe human beings as "learned responses," "automatic beings," and "deterministic creatures" who were victims of their conditioning histories.

Although the humanistic and existential perspectives represent many schools of thought, they nevertheless share a set of assumptions that distinguishes them from other approaches or viewpoints. The first of these assumptions is that an individual's reality is a product of that person's unique experiences and perceptions of the world. Moreover, that individual's

FIGURE 2.8 Ellis's A-B-C Theory of Personality   The development of emotional and behavioral problems is often linked to a dysfunctional thinking process. The cognitive psychologist is likely to attack these problematic beliefs using a rational intervention process, resulting in a change in beliefs and feelings.

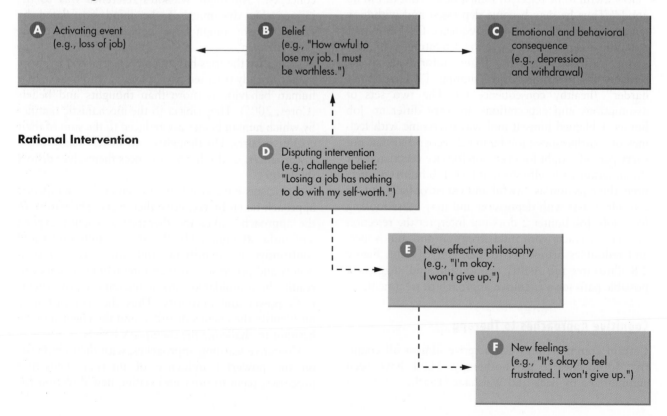

Irrational Cognitive Process

A Activating event
(e.g., loss of job)

B Belief
(e.g., "How awful to lose my job. I must be worthless.")

C Emotional and behavioral consequence
(e.g., depression and withdrawal)

Rational Intervention

D Disputing intervention
(e.g., challenge belief: "Losing a job has nothing to do with my self-worth.")

E New effective philosophy
(e.g., "I'm okay. I won't give up.")

F New feelings
(e.g., "It's okay to feel frustrated. I won't give up.")

subjective universe—how he or she construes events—is more important than the events themselves. Hence, to understand why a person behaves as he or she does, the psychologist must reconstruct the world from that individual's vantage point.

The second point that humanistic and existential theorists stress is that individuals have the ability to make free choices and are responsible for their own decisions. Third, these theorists believe in the "wholeness" or integrity of the person. They view as pointless all attempts to reduce human beings to a set of formulas, to explain them simply by measuring responses to certain stimuli. And a final important point, according to the humanistic and existential perspectives, is that people have the ability to become what they want, to fulfill their capacities, and to lead the lives best suited to themselves.

The Humanistic Perspective

One of the major contributions of the **humanistic perspective** is its positive view of the individual. Carl Rogers (1902–1987) is perhaps the best known of the humanistic psychologists. Rogers's theory of personality (1959) reflects his concern with human welfare and his deep conviction that humanity is basically "good," forward-moving, and trustworthy.

Besides being concerned with treating the mentally ill, psychologists such as Rogers and Abraham Maslow (1908–1970) focused on improving the mental health of the person who is considered normal (Maslow, 1954; Rogers, 1961, 1980, 1987). This focus has led humanistic psychologists and others to explore the characteristics of the healthy personality.

The Actualizing Tendency

Instead of concentrating exclusively on behavior disorders, the humanistic approach is concerned with helping people *actualize* their potential and with bettering the state of humanity. Humanistic psychological theory is based on the idea that people are motivated not only to satisfy their biological needs (for food, warmth, and sex) but also to cultivate, maintain, and enhance the self. The *self* is one's image of oneself, the part one refers to as "I" or "me."

The quintessence of this view is the concept of **self-actualization**—a term popularized by Maslow—which is an inherent tendency to strive toward the realization of one's full potential. The actualizing tendency can be viewed as fulfilling a grand design or a genetic blueprint. This thrust of life that pushes people forward is manifested in such qualities as curiosity, creativity, and joy of discovery. According to Rogers (1961), this inherent force is common to all living organisms. How

one views the self, how others relate to the self, and what values are attached to the self all contribute to one's **self-concept**—the individual's assessment of his or her own value and worth.

Development of Abnormal Behavior

Rogers believed that if people were left unencumbered by societal restrictions and were allowed to grow and develop freely, the result would be fully functioning people. In such a case, the self-concept and the actualizing tendency would be considered congruent.

However, society frequently imposes *conditions of worth* on its members, standards by which people determine whether they have worth. These standards are transmitted via *conditional positive regard*. That is, significant others (such as parents, peers, friends, and spouse) in a person's life accept some but not all of that person's actions, feelings, and attitudes. The person's self-concept becomes defined as having worth only when others approve. But this reliance on others forces the individual to develop a distorted self-concept that is inconsistent with his or her self-actualizing potential, inhibiting that person from being self-actualized. A state of disharmony or *incongruence* is said to exist between the person's inherent potential and his or her self-concept (as determined by significant others). According to Rogers, this state of incongruence forms the basis of abnormal behavior.

Rogers believed that fully functioning people have been *allowed* to *grow* toward their potential. The environmental condition most suitable for this growth is called *unconditional positive regard* (Rogers, 1951). In essence, people who are significant figures in someone's life value and respect that person *as a person*. Giving unconditional positive regard is valuing and loving regardless of behavior. People may disapprove of someone's actions, but they still respect, love, and care for that someone. The assumption that humans need unconditional positive regard has many implications for child rearing and psychotherapy. For parents, it means creating an open and accepting environment for the child. For the therapist, it means fostering conditions that will allow clients to grow and fulfill their potential; this approach has become known as *nondirective* or *person-centered therapy*.

Person-Centered Therapy

Carl Rogers emphasized that therapists' attitudes are more important than specific counseling techniques. The therapist needs to have a strong positive regard for the client's ability to deal constructively with all aspects of life. The more willing the therapist is to rely on the client's strengths and potential, the more likely it is that

Carl Rogers (1902–1987) Rogers believed that people need both positive regard from others and positive self-regard. According to Rogers, when positive regard is given unconditionally, a person can develop freely and become self-actualized.

the client will discover such strengths and potential. The therapist cannot help the client by explaining the client's behavior or by prescribing actions to follow. Therapeutic techniques involve expressing and communicating respect, understanding, and acceptance.

The way a person-centered therapist most commonly communicates understanding of a client's subjective world is through *reflecting feelings*. In "saying back" to the client what he or she understood the client to say, the therapist provides a "mirror" for the client. The client can then actively evaluate thoughts and feelings with less distortion. Even in very strained situations, the person-centered therapist relies on reflection of feelings and on acceptance in working with the client.

Myth vs Reality

Myth: A humanistically oriented clinician does not need training in developing good clinical skills and techniques in working with clients because it is the attitude that is important. If you view clients with unconditional acceptance and have faith in their ability to help themselves, then that is therapeutic enough.

Reality: Although the humanistic schools do believe that people are able to advance and grow on their own and that it is a therapeutic mistake to be concerned with the use of specific strategies and techniques in therapy, the reality is that learning good therapy skills is essential for

several reasons. First, the perception of unconditional positive regard from the therapist may differ across cultural groups. When a client wants advice or feedback from a therapist, the withholding of such input may be perceived by some groups as lacking in respect for them. Second, studies on how humanistic clinicians work in therapy suggests that they are highly trained in using therapeutic techniques in aiding their clients.

The Existential Perspective

The **existential approach** is really not a systematized school of thought but a set of attitudes. It shares with humanistic psychology an emphasis on individual uniqueness, a quest for meaning in life and for freedom and responsibility, a phenomenological approach (understanding the person's subjective world of experience) to understanding the person, and a belief that the individual has positive attributes that will eventually be expressed unless they are distorted by the environment. The existential and humanistic approaches differ in several dimensions.

1. Existentialism is less optimistic than humanism; it focuses on the irrationality, difficulties, and suffering all humans encounter in life. Although humanism allows the clear possibility of self-fulfillment and freedom, existentialism deals with human alienation from the social and spiritual structures that no longer provide meaning in an increasingly technological and impersonal world.

2. Both approaches stress phenomenology—the attempt to understand the person's subjective world of experience—but their perspectives are slightly different. Humanists focus on the individual. Humanistic therapists attempt to reconstruct the subjective world of their clients through empathy. Existentialists believe that the individual must be viewed within the context of the human condition and that moral, philosophical, and ethical considerations are part of that context.

3. They differ in their views on responsibility. Humanism stresses individual responsibility: the individual is ultimately responsible for what he or she becomes in this life. Existentialism stresses not only individual responsibility but also responsibility to others. Self-fulfillment is not enough.

Criticisms of the Humanistic and Existential Approaches

Criticisms of the humanistic and existential approaches point to their "fuzzy," ambiguous, and nebulous nature and to the restricted population in which these approaches can be applied. Although these phenomenological approaches have been extremely creative in describing the human condition, they have been less successful in constructing theory. Moreover, they are not suited to scientific or experimental investigation. The emphasis on subjective understanding rather than prediction and control, on intuition and empathy rather than objective investigation, and on the individual rather than the more general category all tend to hinder empirical study.

Carl Rogers has certainly expressed many of his ideas as researchable propositions, but it is difficult to verify scientifically the humanistic concept of people as rational, inherently good, and moving toward self-fulfillment. The existential perspective can be similarly criticized for its lack of scientific grounding because of its reliance on the unique subjective experiences of individuals to describe the inner world. Such data are difficult to quantify and test. Nevertheless, the existential concepts of freedom, choice, responsibility, being, and nonbeing have had a profound influence on contemporary thought beyond the field of psychology.

Another major criticism leveled at the humanistic and existential approaches is that they do not work well with severely disturbed clients. They seem to be most effective with intelligent, well-educated, and relatively "normal" individuals who may be suffering adjustment difficulties. In fact, Carl Rogers's person-centered counseling originated from his work with college students who were bright, articulate, and psychology-minded—what some psychologists describe as the "worried well." This limitation, along with the occasional vagueness of humanistic and existential thought, has hindered broad application of these ideas to abnormal psychology.

The Family Systems Model

Steve's problem is not an isolated phenomenon. It resides in the family system, which should be the primary unit of treatment. Although Steve is manifesting the disorders, his father and mother are also suffering, and their pathological symptoms are reflected in Steve. Attempts to help Steve must therefore focus on the entire family. It is obvious that the relationships between Steve and his father, between Steve and his mother, and between his father and his mother are unhealthy. Furthermore, the relationship of Mr. and Mrs. V. can be characterized as isolative. Each seems to live a separate life, even when they are together in the same house. Each has unfulfilled needs, and each denies and avoids interactions and conflicts with the other. As long as Steve is the "identified patient" and is seen as "the problem," Mr. and Mrs. V. can continue in their mutual self-deception that all is well between them. I recommend that Steve's entire family be included in a program of therapy.

Almost all of the theories of psychopathology discussed so far in this chapter have focused on the individual. Given the emphasis in the United States on individual achievement and responsibility—on "rugged individualism"—it is not surprising that these approaches have been very popular in the United States.

In contrast, the **family systems model** emphasizes the family's influence on individual behavior. This viewpoint holds that all members of a family are enmeshed in a network of interdependent roles, statuses, values, and norms. The behavior of one member directly affects the entire family system. Correspondingly, people typically behave in ways that reflect family influences.

We can identify three distinct characteristics of the family systems approach (Corey, 2005). First, personality development is ruled largely by the attributes of the family, especially by the way parents behave toward and around their children. Second, abnormal behavior in the individual is usually a reflection or "symptom" of unhealthy family dynamics and, more specifically, of poor communication among family members. Third, the therapist must focus on the family system, not solely on the individual, and must strive to involve the entire family in therapy. As a result, the locus of disorder is seen to reside not within the individual but within the family system.

Family Treatment Approaches

The family system model has spawned a number of approaches to treatment. Three of the major ones are the communications (Satir, 1983), strategic (Haley, 1987), and structural (Minuchin, 1974) approaches.

Among those who have emphasized the importance of clear and direct *communications* for healthy family system development is Virginia Satir (Satir, 1967, 1983; Satir & Bitter, 1991). Her *conjoint family therapeutic approach* stresses the importance of teaching message-sending and message-receiving skills to family members. Like other family therapists, Satir believes that the identified patient is really a reflection of the family system gone awry.

The term *strategic* as applied to family therapy grew out of the ideas of Don Jackson and Jay Haley (Haley, 1963, 1977, 1987). Therapy is conceived as a power struggle between client and therapist. According to this viewpoint, the identified patient is in control, making other family members feel helpless. To shift the balance of power, the therapist must devise strategies (hence the term *strategic*) to effect change.

In the *structural family approach* advocated by Salvatore Minuchin (1974), disorder is seen simply as a result of a system of relationships that need to be basically modified or restructured. Most family problems arise because members are either too involved or too little involved with one another.

All three of these approaches focus on communications, unbalanced power relationships among family members, and the need to restructure the troubled family system.

Criticisms of the Family Systems Model

There is no denying that we are social creatures, and by concentrating on this aspect of human behavior, the family systems approach has added an important social dimension to our understanding of abnormal behavior. In fact, much evidence shows that unhealthy family relationships can contribute to the development of disorders. But the family systems model is subject to a number of criticisms. For one thing, the definition of *family* used by these models may be culture bound. Also, the basic tenets and specific applications of this approach are difficult to study and quantify.

As we have stated frequently, a psychologist who places too much emphasis on any one model may overlook the influence of factors not included in that model. Exclusive emphasis on the family systems model may have particularly unpleasant consequences. Too often,

psychologists have pointed an accusing finger at the parents of children who suffer from certain disorders, despite an abundance of evidence that parental influence may not be a factor in those disorders. The parents are then burdened with unnecessary guilt over a situation they could not have otherwise controlled.

Models of Diversity and Psychopathology

Steve V. is not only a biological, feeling, behaving, thinking, and social being but also a person with a culture. The cultural context in which his problems arise must be considered in understanding Steve's dilemma. He is a European American of Scottish descent, born to an extremely wealthy family in the upper socioeconomic class. He is a male, raised in a cultural context that values individual achievement. All of these characteristics mean that many of his experiences are likely to be very different from those of a person who is a member of a minority group, is economically indigent, or is female. One might argue, for example, that Steve's father values American individualistic competitiveness and achievement in the extreme. He has succeeded by his own efforts, but, unfortunately, his success has come at the emotional cost of his family. To truly understand Steve, we must recognize that the many multicultural variables—race, culture, ethnicity, gender, religion, sexual orientation, and so on—are powerful factors. As such, they influence the types of social-psychological stressors

Family Dynamics and Positive Self-Image Family interaction patterns can exert tremendous influence on a child's personality development, determining the child's sense of self-worth and the acquisition of appropriate social skills. This picture shows a Hispanic family at dinner. Notice the attentiveness of the parents toward their children (communicating a sense of importance to them) and how every family member is present during the meal (emphasizing family cohesion and belonging).

Multicultural Perspectives Multicultural models of human behavior regard race, culture, and ethnicity as central to the understanding of normality and abnormality. As diversification in the United States has increased, multicultural psychology has become increasingly important and has raised our awareness of different assumptions of healthy human development. In China, children are taught to value group harmony over individual competitiveness. In contrast, in the United States, individual efforts are valued and often encouraged, a cultural value that may have influenced this woman to start her own electrical business. Still, racial and ethnic minorities in the United States often possess a more collectivistic source of identity.

Steve is likely to experience, the ways he will manifest disorders, and the types of therapeutic approaches most likely to be effective.

Minority groups have always expressed dissatisfaction with European American standards of mental health, but this dissatisfaction assumed a more specific form during the 1960s with the civil rights movement. At that point, the models of psychopathology, especially those applied to racial and ethnic minorities, came under systematic criticism by minority mental health professionals (Sue & Sue, 2003). The cry for the development of multicultural models of psychology has been fueled by a rapid increase in racial and ethnic minority populations in the United States and by a renewed interest in indigenous psychologies (psychologies developed in other countries). As described in the chapter on abnormal behavior, the United States is undergoing some rapid and radical demographic changes, which can be referred to as the "diversification of the United States." The reality of cultural diversity in the United States has already had tremendous impact on educational, political, economic, and social systems. That same diversity is now having an impact on the mental health professions and on models traditionally used to explain both normal and abnormal behavior (Sue & Sue, 2003; D. W. Sue, Ivey, & Pedersen, 1996).

Multicultural psychology encompasses more than the study of issues related to racial and ethnic minorities; it also focuses on issues concerning sexual orientation, religious preference, socioeconomic status, gender, physical disabilities, and other such factors (Sue, 2001). In the following discussion, however, we use racial and ethnic minority groups to illustrate the major premises of the multicultural models. To avoid misunderstanding and potential stereotyping, we urge you to read carefully the Mental Health and Society feature "Problems in Using Racial and Ethnic Group References" before you continue with this topic.

Multicultural Models of Psychopathology

Early attempts to explain differences between various minority groups and their white counterparts tended to adopt one of two models. The first, the inferiority model, contends that racial and ethnic minorities are inferior in some respect to the majority population. For example, this model attributes low academic achievement and higher unemployment rates among African Americans and Latinos to low intelligence (heredity). The second model—the deprivations or deficit model—explained differences as the result of "cultural deprivation." It implied that minority groups lacked the "right" culture. Both models have been severely criticized as inaccurate, biased, and unsupported in the scientific literature (Samuda, 1998).

During the late 1980s and early 1990s, a new and conceptually different model emerged in the literature. Often referred to as the "multicultural model" (W. Johnson, 1990; J. White & Parham, 1990), the "culturally different model" (Sue & Sue, 2003), the "culturally pluralistic model," or the "culturally diverse model" (Ponterotto & Casas, 1991), the new model emphasizes that to be culturally different does not equal deviancy, pathology, or inferiority. The model recognizes that each culture has strengths and limitations and that

MENTAL HEALTH AND SOCIETY
Problems in Using Racial and Ethnic Group References

African American, American Indian, Asian American, and *Hispanic American* have emerged as commonly used terms to refer to four recognized racial and ethnic minority groups in the United States. These terms, however, are not without controversy, nor are they universally accepted by those who are classified as belonging to the group (Atkinson, Morten, & Sue, 1998). This task has been made even more difficult with changes in the 2000 U.S. Census that allow for sixty-three possible racial categories. Because we will refer to racial and ethnic groups throughout our text, we want to avoid potential confusion by clarifying some problematic issues.

1. *Terms may be accepted in some regions but not in others, and some generations will prefer one over the other.* For example, we use the term *Hispanic* to refer to individuals with ancestry from Mexico, Puerto Rico, Cuba, El Salvador, the Dominican

Republic, and other Latin American countries (Sue & Sue, 1999). Some individuals, however, prefer to be called *Latinos* or *La Raza* (the race). Some younger ethnically conscious Hispanics with roots in Mexico may refer to themselves as *Chicanos,* a statement indicating racial pride and consciousness. Many older Mexican Americans, however, consider *Chicanos* to be an insulting reference associated with the uneducated and exploited farm hands of the Southwest.

Those individuals who trace their ancestry to Africa may prefer the term *black* to *African American.* The latter term links identification to country of origin, whereas *black* is a much more political statement of identity arising from the late 1960s. Likewise, many older individuals of Asian ancestry prefer the term *Oriental,* whereas younger mem-

bers prefer *Asian American,* which for them reflects a self-identification process rather than an identity imposed by the larger society.

2. *Racial/ethnic references can create problems by failing to acknowledge ethnic and cultural differences within a group, thereby submerging many groups under one label.* The term *Asian American,* for example, technically encompasses between twenty-nine and thirty-two distinct identifiable Asian subgroups (Chinese, Japanese, Korean, Filipinos, Vietnamese, Asian Indian, Laotian, Cambodians, etc.)—each with its own culture, language, customs, and traditions. The same can be said of the label "Hispanic American" as well (Mexican American, Puerto Rican American, Cuban American, etc.).

3. *An increasing number of people have mixed ancestry, and many*

differences are inevitable. Behaviors are to be evaluated from the perspective of a group's value system, as well as by other standards used in determining normality and abnormality.

The multicultural model makes an explicit assumption that all theories of human development arise from a particular cultural context (Sue & Sue, 2003; J. White & Parham, 1990). Thus many traditional European American models of psychopathology are culture bound, evaluating and viewing events and processes from a worldview not experienced or shared by other cultural groups. For example, individualism and autonomy are highly valued in the United States and are equated with healthy functioning. Most European American children are raised to become increasingly independent, to be able to make decisions on their own, and to "stand on their own two feet." In contrast, many traditional Asians and Asian Americans place an equally high value on "collectiv-

ity," in which the psychosocial unit of identity is the family, not the individual (D. W. Sue, 1995). Similarly, whereas European Americans fear the loss of "individuality," members of traditional Asian groups fear the loss of "belonging."

Given such different experiences and values, unenlightened mental health professionals may make biased assumptions about human behavior—assumptions that may influence their judgments of normality and abnormality among various racial and ethnic minorities. For example, a mental health professional who does not understand that Asian Americans value a collectivistic identity might see them as overly dependent, immature, and unable to make decisions on their own. Likewise, such a person might perceive "restraint of strong feelings"—a valued characteristic among some Asian groups—as evidence of being "inhibited," "unable to express emotions," or "repressed."

of them prefer not to be identified with one specific racial or ethnic group (Root, 1996). For the first time in history, the number of biracial babies is increasing at a faster rate than the number of monoracial babies (U.S. Bureau of the Census, 1992). People of mixed ancestry may prefer to be known as *biracial, biethnic, bicultural, multiethnic,* or some other term. A whole new vocabulary associated with this phenomenon is increasingly finding its way into the social science literature, including, for example, *Afroasian,* meaning people of African and Asian heritage; *Eurasian,* people of mixed white European and Asian ancestry; and *Mestiza,* people of Indian and Spanish ancestry. Indeed, in recognition of the increasing number of "mixed racial heritage" persons, the year 2000 U.S. Census allows individuals to mark off more than one racial and ethnic descriptor.

With 63 racial categories and the fact that "Hispanics" can be of any race, the dimension Hispanic and non-Hispanic makes for the possibility of 126 different racial/ethnic groups!

4. *Reference to* European American, white, Caucasian American, *and* Anglo *is also filled with controversy.* Anglo is perhaps least appropriate because it technically refers to people of English descent (or more distantly, of Germanic descent). People who trace their ancestry to Italy, France, and the Iberian peninsula may object to being called *Anglo American.* Our experience has been that many *whites* in our society also react quite negatively to that term; they prefer to refer to themselves as *Irish American, Jewish American, Italian American,* and so on. The terms *white* and *European American* are, however, gaining wider usage, the latter in part because of the emerging trend of identifying the region or country of ancestry for Americans.

In this text, we use the four terms *African American, American Indian, Asian American,* and *Hispanic American,* and we do so for the following reasons:

- These terms are labels created and used by government reporting agencies, such as the U.S. Office of Management and Budget and the U.S. Census Bureau.
- Such terms are necessary for purposes of discussing group differences and organizing our discussion around multicultural and diversity variables.
- Reference to any group is necessarily fraught with hazards involving overgeneralization.

We are aware that such groupings are oversimplifications, and we apologize to readers who find any of them offensive.

The multicultural model suggests that European American perspectives of pathology place too much emphasis on locating the problems within the person (intrapsychic). Although these perspectives do not deny that problems may originate outside the individual, they are likely to consider external or system forces equally important for all individuals, regardless of social or ethnic group (Sue & Sue, 2003). In contrast, the multicultural model suggests that problems are often located in the social system rather than within the person. Minority group members, for example, may have to deal with greater and more unique stressors than do their white counterparts. Racism, bias, discrimination, economic hardships, and cultural conflicts are just a few of the sociopolitical realities with which racial and ethnic minorities must contend. As a result, the role of therapist may be better served by ameliorating oppressive or detrimental social conditions than by attempting therapy aimed at changing the individual.

Appropriate individual therapy may, however, be directed at teaching clients self-help skills and strategies focused on influencing their immediate social situation.

Criticisms of the Multicultural Model

In many respects, the multicultural model operates from a relativistic framework; that is, normal and abnormal behavior must be evaluated from a cultural perspective. The reasoning is that behavior considered disordered in one context—seeing a vision of a dead relative, for example—might not be considered disordered in another time or place. As indicated in DSM-IV-TR, some religious practices and beliefs consider it normal to hear or see a deceased relative during bereavement. In addition, certain groups, including some American Indian and Hispanic/Latino groups, may perceive "hallucinations" not just as not disordered but actually as positive events.

TABLE 2.4 A Comparison of the Most Influential Models of Psychopathology

	Biological	Psychodynamic	Behavioral
Motivation for behavior	State of biological integrity and health	Unconscious influences	External influences
Basis for assessment	Medical tests, self-reports, and observable behaviors	Incorrect data, oral self-reports	Observable, objective data, overt behaviors
Theoretical foundation	Animal and human research, case studies, and other research methods	Case studies, correlational methods	Animal research, case studies, experimental methods
Source of abnormal behavior	Biological trauma, heredity, biochemical imbalances	Internal: early childhood experiences	External: learning maladaptive responses or not acquiring appropriate responses
Treatment	Biological interventions (drugs, ECT, surgery, diet)	Dream analysis, free association, transference; locating unconscious conflict from early childhood; resolving the problem and reintegrating the personality	Direct modification of the problem behavior; analysis of the environmental factors controlling the behavior and alteration of the contingencies

Some critics of the multicultural model argue that "a disorder is a disorder," regardless of the cultural context in which it is considered. For example, a person suffering from schizophrenia and actively hallucinating is evidencing a malfunctioning of the senses (seeing, hearing, or feeling things that are not there) and a lack of contact with reality. Regardless of whether *the person* judges the occurrence to be desirable or undesirable, it nevertheless represents a disorder (biological dysfunction), according to this viewpoint.

Another criticism leveled at the multicultural model is its lack of empirical validation concerning many of its concepts and assumptions. The field of multicultural counseling and therapy, for example, has been accused of not being solidly grounded in research (Ponterotto & Casas, 1991). Most of the underlying

concepts of the multicultural model are based on conceptual critiques or formulations that have not been subjected to formal scientific testing. There is generally heavy reliance on case studies, ethnographic analyses, and investigations of a more qualitative type.

Multicultural psychologists respond to such criticisms by noting that they are based on a Western worldview that emphasizes precision and empirical definitions. They point out that there is more than one way to ask and answer questions about the human condition.

Myth vs Reality

Myth: Because people are people, mental disorders are shared by all cultures and groups across all societies.

Cognitive	Humanistic	Existential	Family systems	Multicultural
Interaction of external and cognitive influences	Self-actualization	Capacity for self-awareness; freedom to decide one's fate; search for meaning in a meaningless world	Interaction with significant others	Cultural values and norms (race, culture, ethnicity, socioeconomic status, gender, sexual orientation, religious preference, physical disabilities, and so on)
Self-statements, alterations in overt behaviors	Subjective data, oral self-reports	Subjective data, oral self-reports, experiential encounter	Observation of family dynamics	Study of group norms and behaviors; understanding of societal values and interplay of minority and dominant group relations
Human research, case studies, experimental methods	Case studies, correlational and experimental methods	An approach to understanding the human condition rather than a firm theoretical model	Case studies, social psychological studies, experimental methods	Study of cultural groups; data from anthropology, sociology, and political science
Internal: learned pattern of irrational or negative self-statements	Internal: incongruence between self and experiences	Failure to actualize human potential; avoidance of choice and responsibility	External: faulty family interactions (family pathology and inconsistent communication patterns)	Culture conflicts and oppression
Understanding relationship between self-statements and problem behavior; modification of internal dialogue	Nondirective reflection; no interpretation; providing unconditional positive regard; increasing congruence between self and experience	Provide conditions for maximizing self-awareness and growth, to enable clients to be free and responsible	Family therapy involving strategies aimed at treating the entire family, not just the identified patient	Understanding of minority group experiences; social system intervention

We all belong to the species *Homo sapiens,* so psychopathologies and their treatments are not influenced by racial or cultural factors.

Reality: Race, culture, and ethnicity are powerful mediators in determining the type of disorder an individual is likely to suffer. Although we share many commonalities, it has been found that different racial groups not only have different rates of specific mental disorders but also manifest their psychological problems differently. Asian Americans, for example, are more likely to somaticize (to have stomach cramps, sleeplessness, headaches, et al.) than are their European American counterparts when under stress. DSM-IV-TR also recognizes culture-bound syndromes or disorders that occur more frequently in one culture and less frequently in another.

An Integrative Approach to Models of Psychopathology

Table 2.4 compares the models of psychopathology discussed in this chapter. (You can also review the models by applying them to the hypothetical case of Bill in the Critical Thinking feature "Applying the Models of Psychopathology.") Each model—whether biological, psychodynamic, behavioral, cognitive, existential-humanistic, family systems, or multicultural—represents different views of pathology. Each details a different perspective from which to interpret reality, the nature of people, the origin of disorders, the standards for judging normality and abnormality, and the therapeutic cure. Biological models focus on genetic, neuroanatomical, or biochemical explanations; psychodynamic models stress

Applying the Models of Psychopathology

A useful learning exercise to evaluate your mastery of the various models is to apply them to a case study. We invite you to try your hand at explaining the behavior of Bill, a hypothetical client. Table 2.4 summarizes the various models, and the following hints will help you to begin this exercise:

- Consider what each theory proposes as the basis for the development of a mental disorder.
- Consider the type of data that each perspective considers most important.
- Compare and contrast the models.
- Because there are eight models represented, you might wish to do a comparison only between selected models (psychodynamic, humanistic, and behavioral, for example).

As you attempt to explain Bill's behavior, notice how your adoption of a particular framework influences the type of data you consider important. Is it pos-

sible that all the models hold some semblance of truth? Are their positions necessarily contradictory? Is it possible to integrate them into a unified explanation of Bill? (Again, you might wish to consult Table 2.4.)

Bill was born in Indiana to extremely religious parents who raised him in a rather strict moralistic manner. His father, a Baptist minister, often told Bill and his two sisters to "keep your mind clean, heart pure, and body in control." He forbade Bill's sisters to date at all while they lived at home. Bill's own social life and contacts were extremely limited, and he recalls how anxious he became around girls.

Bill's memories of his father always included feelings of fear and intimidation. No one in the family dared disagree with the father openly, lest they be punished and ridiculed. The father appeared to be hardest on Bill's two sisters, especially when they expressed any inter-

est in boys. The arguments and conflicts between father and daughters were often loud and extreme, disrupting the typical quietness of the home. Although it was never spoken of, Bill was aware that one of his sisters suffered from depression, as did his mother; his sister had twice attempted suicide.

Bill's recollections of his mother were unclear, except that she was always sick with what his father referred to as "the dark cloud," which seemed to visit her periodically. His relationships with his sisters, who were several years older, were uncomfortable. When Bill was a young child, they had teased him mercilessly, and when he reached adolescence, they seemed to take sadistic delight in arousing his raging hormones by flaunting their partially exposed bodies. The result was that Bill became obsessed with having sex with one of his sisters, and he tended to masturbate compulsively. Throughout his adolescence and

unconscious forces, the historical past, and the need for insight; cognitive-behavioral models assert that behaviors and cognitions are learned and that maladaptive ones can be unlearned; existential-humanistic approaches stress the need for growth, attaining one's potential, self-actualization, and autonomy; family systems theories promote wider family dynamics in structure and communications that affect human development; and the multicultural models focus on how cultural context affects the manifestation of mental disorders.

Each model has devout supporters who, in turn, are influenced by the model they support. But even though theory building and the testing of hypotheses are critical to psychology as a science, it seems evident that we can best understand abnormal behavior only by integrating the various approaches. These models of psychopathology are describing the same phenomena but from different vantage points. A folk tale from India, in

which three blind men try to describe an elephant, symbolizes the situation. The blind man who felt the elephant's trunk described the great animal as thin at one end and broad at the top; the man who felt the leg described the elephant as thick, immobile, and firm; and the man who felt the tail described the elephant as thin and constantly twitching. Who was correct?

Like the three men, many models of psychopathology focus on one aspect to the exclusion of most or all others, overlooking the person as a "total package" and resulting in a distorted view. Some models emphasize *feeling* (humanistic-existential), others *thinking* (cognitive), still others *behavior* (behavioral) or *social* aspects (family systems). A truly comprehensive model of human behavior, normal and abnormal, must address the possibility that people are all of these—*feeling, thinking, behaving,* and *social* persons—and probably much more: biological, cultural, spiritual, and political ones as well.

early adulthood he was tortured by feelings of guilt and believed himself to be, as his father put it, "an unclean and damned sinner."

By all external standards, Bill was a quiet, obedient, and well-behaved child. He did well in school, attended Sunday School without fail, never argued or spoke against his parents, and seldom ventured outside of the home. Although Bill did exceptionally well in high school some of his teachers were concerned about his introverted behavior and occasional bouts of depression. When they brought Bill's depression to the attention of his father, however, Mr. M. seemed unconcerned and dismissed it as no reason to worry. Indeed, Mr. M. complimented Bill on his good grades and unobtrusive behavior, rewarding him occasionally with small privileges, such as a larger portion of dessert or the choice of a television program. To some degree of awareness, Bill felt that his worth as a person was dependent only on "getting good grades" and "staying out of trouble."

As a young child, Bill had exhibited excellent artistic potential, and his teachers tried to encourage him in that direction. In elementary school he had won several awards with his drawings, and teachers frequently asked him to paint murals in their classrooms or to draw and design flyers and posters for school events. His artistic interests continued into high school, where his art instructor entered one of Bill's drawings in a state contest. His entry won first prize. Unfortunately, Mr. M. discouraged Bill from his interests and talents and told him that "God calls you in another direction." Attempting to please his father, Bill became less involved in art during his junior and senior years and concentrated more on math and the sciences. He did very well in these subjects, obtaining nearly straight A's at the finish of his high school years.

When Bill entered college, his prime objective was to remain a straight-A student. Although he had originally loved the excitement of learning, achieving, and mastering new knowledge, he now became cautious and obsessed with "safety"; he was fearful of upsetting his father. As his string of perfect grades became longer and longer, safety (not risking a B grade) became more and more important. He began to choose safe and easy topics for essays, to enroll in very easy courses, and to take incompletes or withdrawals when courses appeared tough.

Toward the end of his sophomore year, Bill suffered a mental breakdown characterized by pessimism and hopelessness. He became very depressed and was subsequently hospitalized after he tried to take his own life.

Interestingly, it appears that practicing clinicians have intuitively begun a framework of integration. In practice, most remain open to more than one perspective, recognizing that the different models do not completely contradict one another on every point. Rather, the elements of various models can complement one another to produce a broad and detailed explanation of a person's condition (Corey, 2001). In fact, many therapists seek the best ideas and techniques from all the psychotherapies (Goldfried & Castonguay, 1992).

It is clear from recent writings and research publications that a major evolution, or revolution, is occurring in the field. This movement may lead to an integration of some of the currently contrasting views of psychopathology and treatment, in line with a more eclectic approach (Corey, 2005; Norcross & Newman, 1992; Sommers-Flanagan & Sommers-Flanagan, 2004). Such theoretical integration is a long way off, and there are still a number of strong fundamental dif-

ferences among the major schools of psychotherapy. Whatever form it ultimately takes, integration must be holistic, addressing both the multiple levels of human development and the multiple perspectives inherent in our current models of psychopathology. We believe that adopting a tripartite framework of human identity and applying it to understanding psychopathology may be an important step toward this integration. We examine this type of framework next, as we close our discussion of models of abnormal behavior.

A Tripartite Framework for Understanding Abnormal Psychology

There is an old saying that goes something like this: "All individuals, in many respects, are (1) *like no other individuals*; (2) *like some individuals*; and (3) *like all other individuals*." Although this statement may sound confusing and even contradictory, we believe

FIGURE 2.9   A Tripartite Framework of Personal Identity   Each of us has multiple dimensions of identity. On the individual level, each person is unique, unlike any other. On the group level, we share cultural values and beliefs with our reference groups. At the universal level, we share common features of our species. Cultural models that fail to consider all of these levels will lead to conclusions that may be culture-bound, class-bound, or gender-bound. The tripartite model attempts to represent the complexity of human psychology. Although this schematic representation shows discrete boundaries between the levels, the levels are in fact permeable and ever changing.

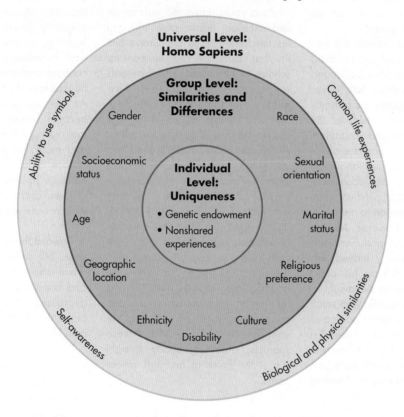

these words to have great wisdom and to be entirely true with respect to human development and identity. To help us understand the multiple models of abnormal psychology better, it might be possible to view them through a tripartite framework (see Figure 2.9).

Individual Level   *"All individuals are, in some respects, like no other individuals."* There is much truth in the saying that no two individuals are identical. We are all unique biologically, and no two of us share exactly the same experiences in our society. Human inheritance almost guarantees differences because no two individuals ever share the same genetic endowment. Even identical twins, who might prove to be the exception, are likely to exhibit differences because of different environmental experiences. For example, identical twins raised in the same family are exposed to both "shared" and "nonshared" environmental influences (Plomin, 1989; Plomin & Daniels, 1987). Their shared influences might encompass

poverty, marital discord, familial values, and so on. Even so, each twin will experience powerful forces in the shape of nonshared environmental influences, such as different experiences in school, with peers, and even qualitatively different treatment by parents, which will contribute to that twin's uniqueness. There is evidence to indicate that psychological characteristics and forms of psychopathology are more affected by experiences specific to a child than by shared experiences (Rutter, 1991). The tradition of psychology that has developed in the United States has always placed great emphasis on the study of individual differences.

Group Level   *"All individuals are, in some respects, like some other individuals."* Each of us is born into a cultural context of existing beliefs, values, rules, and cultural practices (Sue, 2001). Individuals who share the same cultural matrix with us exhibit similar values and belief systems. The process of being socialized is generally the function of the family, through participation in cultural groups. As a result of these circumstances, each person is a cultural entity with a personal culture.

Our reference groups exert a powerful influence over us. Some of these group markers, such as gender, culture, ethnicity, age, and race, are relatively *fixed* and unchangeable. Those that are *nonfixed*—such as educational background, socioeconomic status, marital status, and geographic location—are more fluid and changeable. But all of your group markers—whether you are a man or a woman, black or white, young or old, rich or poor; have a physical disability or an able body; live in Appalachia or San Francisco; are married or single, gay or straight—result in your sharing with certain groups many similar experiences and characteristics. And as a result of these same experiences and characteristics, you may differ significantly from members of groups different from your own. One of the ways these cultural group dimensions exert their powerful force is in affecting and mediating our susceptibility to, and manifestation of, mental disorders.

Universal Level *"All individuals are, in some respects, like all other individuals."* As Shylock, in Shakespeare's *The Merchant of Venice*, points out, "When you prick us, do we not bleed?" We are all members of the human race by virtue of our membership in the species *Homo sapiens*. Indeed, the Human Genome Project findings indicate that the DNA of every person on Earth is 99.9 percent identical (Wade, 2004). Each of us is therefore also like all others, and much of the tradition of psychology has been to develop theories and methods that are applicable to the human condition. Psychology's goals have always been to discover universal facts, principles, and laws in explaining human behavior (Kim & Berry, 1993). Universal to our human identity are biological and physical similarities, common life experiences (among them birth, death, stress, love, and sadness), self-awareness, and our ability to use symbols (such as language).

Thus it is possible to conclude that all people possess individual, group, and universal levels of identity. Current theories of psychopathology typically address only portions of this tripartite framework. Yet a model that neglects any level of our identity ignores an important part of our existence. What is needed is for psychologists to describe the totality of the whole person, both in research and in practice.

SUMMARY

How much of mental disorder can be explained through our biological makeup?

Biological models cite various organic causes of psychopathology:
- Damage to the nervous system.
- Biochemical imbalances. Several types of psychological disturbances have been found to respond to drugs. In addition, a good deal of biochemical research has focused on identifying the role of neurotransmitters in abnormal behavior.
- Hereditary predisposition. The Human Genome Project has provided renewed interest in the role of genes in the cause and potential biological treatment of mental disorders. Researchers have found correlations between genetic inheritance and certain psychopathologies.
- Mental health research increasingly focuses on the diathesis-stress theory—the idea that a predisposition to a disorder, not the disorder itself, may be inherited.

How important are early childhood experiences and unconscious motivations in determining our mental health?

- Psychodynamic models emphasize childhood experiences and the role of the unconscious in determining adult behavior.
- Sigmund Freud, the founder of psychoanalysis, believed that personality has three components: the id, which represents the impulsive, selfish, pleasure-seeking part of the person; the ego, which represents the rational part; and the superego, which represents society's values and ideals. Each component checks and balances the others.
- Instincts, the energy system from which the personality operates, manifest themselves in various ways during the five psychosexual stages: oral, anal, phallic, latency, and genital. Each of these life stages poses unique challenges that, if not adequately resolved, can result in maladaptive adult behaviors.
- According to Freud, abnormal behavior results from neurotic anxiety and the threat that unconscious thoughts will attain consciousness. To repress forbidden thoughts and impulses, the ego

uses defense mechanisms. Psychoanalytic therapy attempts to help the patient achieve insight into his or her unconscious.

■ Post-Freudians accept basic psychodynamic tenets but differ from traditional strict Freudian theorists along five dimensions: freedom of choice and future goals, ego autonomy, the influence of social forces, the importance of object relations, and treatment of seriously disturbed people.

What is the role of learning in the development of behavior disorders?

■ Behavioral models focus on the role of learning in abnormal behavior.

■ The traditional behavioral models of psychopathology hold that abnormal behaviors are acquired through association (classical conditioning) or reinforcement (operant conditioning).

■ Negative emotional responses such as anxiety can be learned through classical conditioning: a formerly neutral stimulus evokes a negative response after it has been presented along with a stimulus that already evokes that response.

■ Negative voluntary behaviors may be learned through operant conditioning if those behaviors are reinforced (rewarded) when they occur.

■ In observational learning, a person learns behaviors, which can be quite complex, by observing them in other people and then imitating, or modeling, those behaviors. Pathological behavior results when the imitated behavior is inappropriate or inappropriately applied.

How powerful are thoughts in causing mental disorders, and can positive thinking be used to combat irrational beliefs?

■ According to the cognitive model, perceptions of events are mediated by thoughts and feelings, and the perception may have a greater influence on behavior than the event itself. Despite this emphasis, the cognitive perspective shares many characteristics with the traditional behavioral models. Cognitive therapeutic approaches are generally aimed at normalizing the client's perception of events.

Don't we all have within ourselves the ability to move toward health and away from disorders?

■ The humanistic perspective actually represents many perspectives and shares many basic assumptions with the existential perspective. Both view an individual's reality as a product of personal perception and experience. Both see people as capable of

making free choices and fulfilling their potential. Both emphasize the whole person and the individual's ability to fulfill his or her capacities.

■ The best-known humanistic formulation is Carl Rogers's person-centered approach, which has as a strong tenet the belief that humanity is basically good. Rogers believed that people are motivated not only to meet their biological needs but also to grow and to enhance the self, to become actualized or fulfilled. If the actualizing tendency is thwarted, behavior disorders may result.

■ Although the existential perspective shares similarities with its humanistic counterpart, it is generally less optimistic, focusing on the irrational, human alienation, and the search for meaning. It stresses that the individual has a responsibility not only to oneself but also to others.

What role does the family play in making us "sick" or "healthy"?

■ The family systems model asserts that family interactions guide an individual's development of personal identity, as well as his or her sense of reality.

■ Abnormal behavior is viewed as the result of distortion or faulty communication or unbalanced structural relationships within the family. Children who receive faulty messages from parents or who are subjected to structurally abnormal family constellations may develop behavioral and emotional problems. Therapeutic techniques generally focus on the family as a whole rather than on one disturbed individual.

Does belonging to a racial/ethnic minority group affect the type of disorder a person is likely to experience?

■ Increases in racial and ethnic minority populations have corresponded with a renewed interest in multicultural models of psychology.

■ Proponents of this approach believe that race, culture, ethnicity, gender, sexual orientation, religious preference, socioeconomic status, physical disabilities, and other variables are powerful influences in determining how specific cultural groups manifest disorders, how mental health professionals perceive disorders, and how disorders will be treated.

■ Cultural differences have been perceived in three ways: (1) the inferiority model, in which differences are attributed to the interplay of undesirable elements in a person's biological makeup; (2) the deprivations or deficit model, in which differences in traits or behaviors are blamed on not having the "right culture"; and (3) the multicultural model, in which differences do not necessarily equate with deviance.

How do we reconcile individual and group differences with human commonalities in explaining abnormal behavior?

■ Models of abnormal pathology may represent different perspectives on the same phenomena. An integrative approach recognizes three levels of human existence: (1) the individual level of uniqueness; (2) the group level, in which group consciousness is developed; and (3) the universal level of commonality.

KEY TERMS

axon (p. 39)

behavioral model (p. 49)

classical conditioning (p. 49)

cognitive models (p. 54)

conditioned response (CR) (p. 50)

conditioned stimulus (CS) (p. 49)

defense mechanism (p. 46)

dendrite (p. 39)

diathesis-stress theory (p. 43)

existential approach (p. 58)

family systems model (p. 59)

genome (p. 42)

genotype (p. 42)

humanistic perspective (p. 57)

law of effect (p. 50)

model (p. 35)

modeling (p. 52)

neuron (p. 38)

neurotransmitter (p. 40)

observational learning theory (p. 52)

operant behavior (p. 50)

operant conditioning (p. 50)

phenotype (p. 42)

pleasure principle (p. 45)

psychoanalysis (p. 44)

psychodynamic model (p. 44)

psychopathology (p. 35)

psychosexual stages (p. 45)

reality principle (p. 45)

schema (p. 54)

self-actualization (p. 57)

self-concept (p. 57)

synapse (p. 40)

unconditioned response (UCR) (p. 49)

unconditioned stimulus (UCS) (p. 49)

MULTIMEDIA PREVIEW

For additional study aids, we invite you to explore our media resources accompanying *Understanding Abnormal Behavior,* Eighth Edition. The Student CD-ROM includes videos, quizzing, and critical thinking activities that help to reinforce key concepts in a fun and engaging manner. The Student Web Site provides additional interactive activities, chapter outlines, and research links that further support and complement the text. All Web resources may be accessed by logging onto the Web site at **http://psychology.college.hmco.com/students.**

CHAPTER 3
Assessment and Classification of Abnormal Behavior

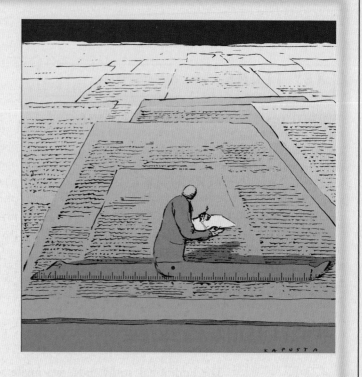

FOCUS QUESTIONS

■ In attempting to make an accurate evaluation or assessment of a person's mental health, what kinds of standards must tests or evaluation procedures meet?

■ What kinds of tools do clinicians employ in evaluating the mental health of people?

■ How are mental health problems categorized or classified?

Finding the nature and rate of mental disorders, the factors that cause or affect mental disorders, and an effective means of treating and preventing disorders are some of the most important tasks in the mental health field. To accomplish these tasks, therapists must collect information on the well-being of individuals and organize information about a person's condition. Among the assessment tools available to clinicians are observations, conversations and interviews, a variety of psychological and neurological tests, and the reports of the patient and his or her relatives and friends. When the data gathered from all sources are combined and analyzed, a therapist can gain a good picture of the patient's behavior and mental state.

As we noted in the chapter titled "Abnormal Behavior," the evaluation of the information leads to a psychodiagnosis, which involves describing and drawing inferences about an individual's psychological state. Psychodiagnosis is often an early step in the treatment process. For many psychotherapists it is the basis on which a program of therapy is first formulated.

To arrive at a psychodiagnosis, the therapist attempts to obtain a clear description of the client's behavioral patterns and to classify or group them based on the symptom picture that emerges. This classification performs several functions. First, it helps clarify the therapist's "picture" of the client's mental state; once the data are organized, they are easier to analyze. Second, if the classification scheme is an effective one, it can lead the therapist to possible treatment programs. Third, the names of the categories within a classification scheme provide concise descriptions of, or referents to, symptoms and disorders; these descriptions facilitate communication among psychologists who try to use the same categories to convey information about clients. Finally, using a classification scheme standardizes psychological assessment procedures. That is, if particular information is required for classi-

fication, therapists will tend to use the assessment techniques that provide that information. Thus classification may affect the entire psychodiagnostic process, as well as the therapy that follows it. Classification is at the heart of science (Barlow, 1991).

Reliability and Validity

To be useful, assessment tools and classification systems must demonstrate reliability and validity. **Reliability** is the degree to which a procedure or test—such as an evaluation tool or classification scheme—will yield the same results repeatedly under the same circumstances. There are many types of reliability (Robinson, Shaver, & Wrightsman, 1991).

Test-retest reliability determines whether a measure yields the same results when given to an individual at two different points in time. For example, if we administer a measure of anxiety to an individual in the morning and then readminister the measure later in the day, the measure is reliable if the results show consistency or stability (that is, the results are the same) from one point in time to another.

In reliability that involves *internal consistency,* a measure is considered reliable if various parts of the measure yield similar results. For example, if responses to different items on a measure of anxiety are not related to one another, the items may be measuring different things, not just anxiety.

Finally, *interrater reliability* determines consistency of responses when different judges or raters administer the measure. For instance, let us imagine that two clinicians are trained to diagnose individuals according to a certain classification scheme. Yet one clinician diagnoses the patient's disorder as schizophrenia and the other diagnoses mental retardation. There is a reliability problem here, either in the raters' judgments or in the classification scheme. The problem may be interrater reliability; one clinician may simply be a poor judge. Or in test-retest reliability, inconsistent results may reflect real changes in the behavior of the individual. Nevertheless, in such circumstances, the reliability of the classification scheme or measurement instrument is open to question.

Validity is the extent to which a test or procedure actually performs the function it was designed to perform. If a measure that is intended to assess depression instead assesses anxiety, the measure demonstrates poor validity for depression. As in the case of reliability, there are several ways to determine validity. The most important are predictive, criterion-related, construct, and content validity.

Predictive validity refers to the ability of a test or measure to predict or foretell how a person will behave, respond, or perform. Colleges and universities often use applicants' high school achievement test scores to predict their future college grades. If the test scores have good predictive validity, they should be able to differentiate students who will perform well from those who will perform poorly in college. However, psychological assessment is generally worse at predicting what people will do than at describing what people are like (Weiner, 2003).

Criterion-related validity determines whether a measure is related to the phenomenon in question. Assume, for example, that we devise a measure that is intended to tell us whether persons recovering from alcoholism are likely to return to drinking. If we find that those who score high on the measure start drinking again and that those who score low do not, then the measure is valid.

Determining *construct validity* is actually a series of tasks with one common theme: all are designed to test whether a measure is related to certain phenomena that are empirically or theoretically thought to be related to that measure. Let us say that a researcher has developed a questionnaire to measure anxiety. To determine construct validity, the researcher should show that the questionnaire is correlated with other measures, such as existing tests of anxiety. Furthermore, we would have increased confidence that the questionnaire is measuring anxiety if it is related to other phenomena that (based on our theory of anxiety) appear in anxious people, such as muscle tension, sweating, tremors, and startle responses. The questionnaire should also be unrelated to characteristics that are not consistently associated with anxiety, such as paranoia.

Finally, *content validity* refers to the degree to which a measure is representative of the phenomenon being measured. For example, we know that depression involves cognitive, emotional, behavioral, and physiological features. If a self-report measure of depression contains items that assess only cognitive features, such as items indicating pessimism, then the measure has poor content validity because it fails to assess three of the four known components of the disorder.

Reliability and validity are also influenced by the conditions in which a test or measure is administered. Standard administration requires that those who administer a test strictly follow common rules or procedures. If an instructor creates a tense and hostile environment for some students who are taking final exams for a course but not for others, for example, the students' test scores may vary simply because the instructor is not treating all students in a similar or standard fashion.

An additional concern is the standardization sample—a group of people who have taken the measure and whose performance can be used as a standard or norm. The performance of another person can therefore be interpreted against this norm. However, the standardization sample must be appropriate to the person being evaluated. Our interpretations may not be valid if we compare the test score of a twenty-year-old African American woman with the scores of forty-year-old white American men in a standardization sample.

Questions of reliability and validity are essential to address in assessment tools and in any diagnostic system. In this chapter, we examine assessment methods and clinicians' use of assessment tools. We also discuss the most widely employed diagnostic classification system, DSM-IV-TR, as well as the issues of reliability and validity.

The Assessment of Abnormal Behavior

Assessment is the process of gathering information and drawing conclusions about the traits, skills, abilities, emotional functioning, and psychological problems of the individual, generally for use in developing a diagnosis. Assessment tools are necessary to the study and practice of mental health. Without them, data could not be collected, and psychologists could not conduct meaningful research, develop theories, or engage in psychotherapy. Data collection necessarily involves the use of tools to systematically record the observations, behaviors, or self-reports of individuals. Four principal means of assessment are available to clinicians: observations, interviews, psychological tests and inventories, and neurological tests. In general, assessment should be conducted using multiple methods and tests in order to get a more accurate view of

---

TABLE 3.1 Assessment Techniques

Observation Controlled observations; naturalistic observations

Interviews Clinical interview; mental status examination

Psychological Tests and Inventories

Projective personality tests Rorschach technique; Thematic Apperception Test; sentence-completion tests; draw-a-person tests

Self-report inventories Minnesota Multiphasic Personality Inventory; Beck Depression Inventory

Intelligence tests Wechsler Adult Intelligence Scale; Stanford-Binet Intelligence Scale; Wechsler Intelligence Scale for Children; Wechsler Preschool and Primary Scale of Intelligence; Kaufman Assessment Battery for Children

Tests for cognitive impairment Bender-Gestalt Visual Motor Test; Halstead-Reitan Neuropsychological Test Battery; Luria-Nebraska Neuro-psychological Battery

Neurological tests Computerized axial tomography; positron emission tomography; electroencephalograph; magnetic resonance imaging

---

clients (Kendall, Holmbeck, & Verduin, 2004). Assessment techniques and some specific tools for conducting them are discussed in the following pages and are summarized in Table 3.1.

Observations

Observations of overt behavior provide the most basic method of assessing abnormal behavior; indeed, behavioral observation is the most basic tool in all of science. Research methods are examined in the chapter titled "The Scientific Method in Abnormal Psychology"; we concentrate here on clinical observations, which can be either controlled or naturalistic. *Controlled* (or *analogue*) *observations* are often made in a laboratory, clinic, or other contrived setting, and clients may be given instructions, stimuli, or tasks that allow the observers to evaluate responses to specific situations (Haynes, 2001). *Naturalistic observations*, which are much more characteristic of the clinician's work, are made in a natural setting—a schoolroom, an office, a hospital ward, or a home—rather than in a laboratory. Although we focus our discussion primarily on observing a client alone, interpersonal interactions, such as those between client and family, also

offer important insights for determining the factors that produce and maintain disturbed behaviors (Guerin & Chabot, 1992; Norton & Hope, 2001). Observations can be highly structured and specific, as when an observer notes the frequency of stuttering and the circumstances under which stuttering occurs in a client. Sometimes, clients are asked to role-play social interactions, and these interactions are evaluated (Norton & Hope, 2001). On other occasions, observations may be less formal and specific, as when a clinician simply looks for any unusual behaviors on the part of a client. In such a situation, the observations and interpretations of the behaviors may be subjective in nature. Leichtman (1995) believes that this subjectivity has certain advantages in fully understanding clients and their circumstances.

Observations of behavior are usually made in conjunction with an interview, although verbal interaction is not necessary. A trained clinical psychologist watches for external signs or cues and expressive behaviors that may have diagnostic significance. The client's general mode of dress (neat, conventional, sloppy, flashy), significant scars or tattoos, and even choice of jewelry may be correlated with personality traits or, perhaps, with disorder. Likewise, other expressive behaviors, such as posture, facial expression, language and verbal patterns, handwriting, and self-expression through graphic art may all reveal certain characteristics of the client's life. Here is an example of some typical observations.

Margaret was a thirty-seven-year-old depressive patient who was seen by one of the authors in a hospital psychiatric ward. She had recently been admitted for treatment. It was obvious from even a casual glance that Margaret had not taken care of herself for weeks. Her face and hands were dirty. Her long hair, which had originally been done up in a bun, had shaken partially loose on one side of her head and now hung down her left shoulder. Her beat-up tennis shoes were only halfway on her stockingless feet. Her unkempt and disheveled appearance and her stooped body posture would lead one to believe she was much older than her actual age.

When first interviewed, Margaret sat as though she did not have the strength to straighten her body. She avoided eye contact with the interviewer and stared at the floor. When asked questions, she usually responded in short phrases: "Yes," "No," "I don't know," "I don't care." There were long pauses between the questions and her answers. Each response seemingly took great effort on her part.

Naturalistic vs. Controlled Observations Naturalistic observations are made in settings that occur naturally in one's environment. Here, on the left, a rater, sitting on a bench, observes children at play in a playground. The playground is a natural setting for the children to play. Controlled observations, on the other hand, are made in a laboratory or in a contrived setting that allows researchers or clinicians to regulate many of the events that occur. In the clinic laboratory on the right, a researcher is observing a two-year-old boy and his mother, who are given a task to perform with the blocks. What are the advantages and disadvantages of the different observational techniques?

Some psychologists rely on trained raters or on parents, teachers, or other third parties to make the observations and gather information for assessment and evaluation. Others prefer their own observations to those of a third party. Regardless of who conducts the observation, two problems may occur (Sundberg, Taplin, & Tyler, 1983). First, observers must check the validity of their own interpretations of the patient's behaviors. This is particularly important when the patient is from a culture different from that of the observer. Second, observers must try to minimize the impact of their observations on the patient's behaviors. This effort is necessary because a person who is aware of being observed or assessed may change the way he or she usually responds, a phenomenon known as **reactivity**.

Interviews

The clinical interview is a time-honored tradition as a means of psychological assessment. It lets the therapist observe the client and collect data about the person's life situation and personality. Verbal and nonverbal behaviors, as well as the content (what the client is saying) and process (how the client is communicating—with anxiety, hesitation, or anger) of communications are important to analyze (Reiser, 1988).

Depending on the particular disciplinary training of the interviewer, the interview's frame of reference and its emphasis may vary considerably. (This variability has been a source of inconsistency and error in the assessment of clients.) Psychiatrists, being trained in medicine, may be much more interested in biological or physical variables. Social workers may be more concerned with life history data and the socioeconomic environment of the client. Clinical psychologists may be most interested in establishing rapport with clients as a form of therapy.

Likewise, variations in therapeutic orientation within the discipline of psychology can affect the interview. Because of their strong belief in the unconscious origin of behavior, psychoanalysts may be more interested in psychodynamic processes than in the surface content of the client's words. They are also more likely to pay particular attention to life history variables and dreams. Behaviorists are more likely to concentrate on current environmental conditions related to the client's behavior. In practice, however, mental health practitioners with different therapeutic orientations can also exhibit a great deal of similarity in psychotherapeutic style.

Standardization and Structure As mentioned in the earlier discussion of reliability and validity, standard administration means that common rules or procedures must be strictly followed. Interviews can vary in the degree to which they are structured, the manner in which they are conducted, and the degree of freedom of response on the part of the client. In some interviews, the client is given considerable freedom about what to say and when to say it. The clinician does little to interfere with conversation or to direct its flow. Psychoanalysts, who use free association, and Rogerians, who carry on nondirective therapy, tend to conduct highly unstructured interviews. Behaviorists tend to use more structured interviews.

The most highly structured interview is the *formal standardized interview,* in which questions are usually arranged as a checklist, complete with scales for rating answers. The interviewer uses the checklist to ask each interviewee the same set of questions, so that errors are minimized. One widely used structured interview is the Composite International Diagnostic Interview. The purpose of an interview is to enable a trained interviewer to arrive at a diagnosis. The interviewer asks questions, makes clinical judgments, and, depending on the interviewee's previous responses, may ask follow-up questions (Kessler et al., 1994). Although structured interviews often do not permit interviewers to probe interviewees' responses in depth, they have the advantage of allowing consistent data to be collected across interviewees and they are less subject to interviewers' biases (Hill & Lambert, 2004).

A less structured but also widely used interview procedure is the *mental status examination.* The intent of this examination is to determine in a general way a client's cognitive, psychological, and behavioral functioning by means of questions, observations, and tasks posed to the client (Othmer & Othmer, 1994). The clinician considers the appropriateness and quality of the client's responses (behaviors, speech, emotions, intellectual functioning) and then attempts to render provisional evaluations of the diagnosis, prognosis, client dynamics, and treatment issues. Another structured interview is the Structured Clinical Interview for DSM-IV-TR (Spitzer, Gibbon, & Williams, 1996). This interview is intended to render a diagnosis. It gives precise procedures for rating clients and for asking questions, including follow-up questions and probes.

Errors In the field of mental health, straightforward questions do not always yield usable or accurate information. Believing personal information to be private, patients may refuse to reveal it, may distort it, or may lie about themselves. Furthermore, many patients may be unable to articulate their inner thoughts and feelings. An interview should therefore be considered a measurement device that is fallible and subject to error (Wiens, 1983).

There are three main sources of interviewing errors (Kleinmutz, 1967). One is the interview process itself and the relationship between the interviewer and interviewee. Information exchange may be blocked if either the client or the clinician fails to respect the other or if one or the other is not feeling well. A second source of error may be intense anxiety or preoccupation on the part of the interviewee; his or her revelations may be inconsistent or inaccurate. Third, the interviewer may be a source of error. A clinician's unique style, degree of experience, and theoretical orientation will definitely affect the interview.

Psychological Tests and Inventories

Psychological tests and inventories are a variety of standardized instruments that have been used to assess personality, maladaptive behavior, development of social skills, intellectual abilities, vocational interests, and cognitive impairment. Tests have also been developed for the purpose of understanding personality dynamics and conflicts. They vary in form (that is, they may be oral or written and may be administered to groups or to individuals), structure, degree of objectivity, and content. To varying degrees (less so in the case of projective personality tests), they share two characteristics that involve standard administration and use of a standardization sample. First, they provide a standard situation in which certain kinds of responses are elicited. The same instructions are given to all persons who take the same test, the same scoring is applied, and similar environmental conditions are maintained to ensure that the responses are due to each test taker's unique attributes rather than to differences in situations. Second, by comparing an individual test taker's responses with norms, established by the standardization sample, the therapist can make inferences about the underlying traits of the person. For instance, the test taker may answer "yes" to questions such as "Is someone trying to control your mind?" more frequently than is the norm. The therapist might infer that this pattern of response is similar to that of individuals diagnosed with paranoia.

In the remainder of this section, we examine two different types of personality tests and measures (projective and self-report inventories) and tests of intelligence and cognitive impairment. It should be noted that two-thirds of the assessments used by clinical psychologists are evaluations of personality-psychopathology and intellectual achievement. The second most popular use of psychological testing is for neuropsychological assessment and adaptive-functional behavior assessment, according to half of the clinical psychologists surveyed for their assessment practices (Camara, Nathan, & Puente, 2000).

Projective Personality Tests   In a **projective personality test,** the test taker is presented with ambiguous stimuli, such as inkblots, pictures, or incomplete sentences, and asked to respond to them in some way. The stimuli are generally novel, and the test is relatively unstructured. Conventional or stereotyped patterns of response usually do not fit the stimuli. The person must "project" his or her attitudes, motives, and other personality characteristics into the situation. The nature of the appraisal is generally well disguised: participants are often unaware of the true nature or purpose of the test and usually do not recognize the

significance of their responses. Based largely on a psychoanalytic perspective, projective tests presumably tap into the individual's unconscious needs and motivations or dynamics of perception and motivation (Meyer et al., 2003).

No matter which form of test is used, the goal of projective testing is to get a multifaceted view of the total functioning person, rather than a view of a single facet or dimension of personality. The use of projective tests is becoming more controversial because many evidence-based assessment psychologists believe that projective tests generally lack evidence for their reliability and validity (Hunsley, Crabb, & Mash, 2004). Nevertheless, we present information on inkblot descriptions and storytelling because they are both popular and typical of projective tests.

Swiss psychiatrist Hermann Rorschach devised the *Rorschach technique* for personality appraisal in 1921. A Rorschach test consists of ten cards that display symmetrical inkblot designs. The cards are presented one at a time to participants, who are asked (1) what they see in the blots and (2) what characteristics of the blots make them see that. Inkblots are considered appropriate stimuli because they are ambiguous, are nonthreatening, and do not elicit learned responses.

What people see in the blots, whether they attend to large areas or to details, whether they respond to

The Rorschach Technique
Devised by Swiss psychiatrist Hermann Rorschach in 1921, the Rorschach technique uses a number of cards, each showing a symmetrical inkblot design similar to the one shown here. The earlier cards in the set are in black and white; the later cards are more colorful. A client's responses to the inkblots are interpreted according to assessment guidelines and can be compared by the therapist with the responses that other clients have made.

color, and whether their perceptions suggest movement are assumed to be symbolic of inner promptings, motivations, and conflicts. Test takers react in a personal and "unlearned" fashion because there are no right or wrong answers. The psychologist then interprets the individual's reactions. Both the basic premise of the Rorschach test and the psychologist's interpretation of the symbolism within the patient's responses are strongly psychoanalytic. For example, seeing eyes or buttocks may imply paranoid tendencies; fierce animals may imply aggressive tendencies; blood may imply strong uncontrolled emotions; food may imply dependency needs; and masks may imply avoidance of personal exposure (Klopfer & Davidson, 1962). The single most important rationale for using the Rorschach and other projective tests is that they presumably provide information about personality dynamics that are outside the conscious awareness of the test takers (Clarkin, Hurt, & Mattis, 1999).

There are actually a variety of approaches to interpreting and scoring Rorschach responses. The most extensive and recent is that of Exner (1983, 1990), whose scoring system is based on reviews of research findings and studies of the Rorschach technique. Exner thinks of the Rorschach technique as a problem-solving task; test takers are presented with ambiguous stimuli that they interpret according to their preferred mode of perceptual-cognitive processing. Exner's system has also yielded indexes of specific disorders such as depression, although the adequacy of the Rorschach technique in assessing specific disorders is a matter of continuing research (Ball, Archer, Gordon, & French, 1991). Because it relies on research findings and normative data, Exner's system has become the standard for scoring the Rorschach test (D. Weiss, 1988).

The Rorschach is employed by a number of psychologists. In one survey (Exner, 1995) of psychologists, 75 percent reported that they used psychological tests in their practice; of those who used such tests, 43 percent used the Rorschach at various times. Use of the Rorschach is not confined solely to the evaluation of psychopathology. P. Lerner (1995) has developed a means to analyze the adaptive capacities of individuals. Rather than solely trying to determine disturbance and mental disorders, he uses projective tools such as the Rorschach to reveal positive features such as adaptation and creativity in individuals.

The *Thematic Apperception Test (TAT)* was first developed by Henry Murray in 1935 (H. Murray & Morgan, 1938). It consists of thirty picture cards, each typically depicting two human figures. Their poses and actions are vague and ambiguous enough to be open to different interpretations. Some cards are designated for specific age levels or for a single gender,

The Thematic Apperception Test In the Thematic Apperception Test, clients tell a story about each of a series of pictures they are shown. These pictures—often depicting one, two, or three people doing something—are less ambiguous than Rorschach inkblots.

and some are appropriate for all groups. Like the Rorschach technique, the TAT relies on projection to tap underlying motives, drives, and personality processes. Most clinicians agree, however, that the TAT is best when it is used to uncover aspects of interpersonal relationships.

Generally, twenty TAT cards are shown to the participant, one at a time, with instructions to tell a story about each picture. Typically, the tester says, "I am going to show you some pictures. Tell me a story about what is going on in each one, what led up to it, and what its outcome will be." The entire story is recorded verbatim. There is usually no limit on time or the length of the stories.

A trained clinician interprets the participant's responses, either subjectively or by using a formal scoring system. Both interpretations usually take into account the style of the story (length, organization, and so on); recurring themes, such as retribution, failure, parental domination, aggression, and sexual concerns; the outcome of the story in relationship to the plot; primary and secondary identification (the choice of hero or secondary person of importance); and the handling of authority figures and sexual relationships. The purpose is to gain insight into the individual's conflicts and worries, as well as clues about his or her core personality structure. Woike and McAdams (2001) found that the TAT is particularly valuable in ascertaining an individual's personality and motivation.

Other types of projective tests include sentence-completion and draw-a-person tests. In the sentence-completion test, the participant is given a list of partial sentences and is asked to complete each of them. Typical partial sentences are "My ambition ... ," "My mother was always ... ," and "I can remember ... ." Clinicians try to interpret the meaning of the individual's responses. In draw-a-person tests, such as the Machover D-A-P (Machover, 1949), the participant is actually asked to draw a person. Then he or she may be asked to draw a person of the opposite sex. Finally, the participant may be instructed to make up a story about the characters that were drawn or to describe the first character's background. Many clinicians analyze these drawings for size, position, detail, and so on, assuming that the drawings provide diagnostic clues. For example, persons suffering from brain impairments may draw disproportionately large heads. The validity of such assumptions is open to question, and well-controlled studies cast doubt on diagnostic interpretations (Anastasi, 1982).

The analysis and interpretation of responses to projective tests are subject to wide variation. Clinicians given the same data frequently disagree with one another about scoring. Much of this disparity is caused by differences in clinicians' orientations, skills, and personal styles. But, as noted earlier, the demonstrably low reliability and validity of these instruments means that they should be used with caution and in conjunction with other assessment measures (D. Weiss, 1988). And even when projective tests exhibit reliability, they may still have low validity. For example, many clinicians agree that certain specific responses to the Rorschach inkblots indicate repressed anger. The fact that many clinicians agree makes the test reliable, but those specific responses could indicate something other than repressed anger. Illusory correlations may exist, and clinicians may erroneously link a patient's response to the existence of a syndrome (Chapman & Chapman, 1967). In a major review of the research evidence, Lilienfeld, Wood, and Garb (2000) concluded that the reliability and validity of the Rorschach are problematic. Although some indicators in the Rorschach can identify a narrow range of disorders in a valid fashion, there are some serious shortcomings in its diagnostic use for disorders. In general,

projective tests may yield important information when they are interpreted by clinicians who are highly skilled and insightful in their use. Because many projective tests are subjectively interpreted by clinicians in accordance with their intuition, however, overall validity of the tests is low. Exner's (1990) work in developing norms and in using empirical research in the Rorschach scoring system has been a major step in reducing subjectivity problems.

Self-Report Inventories   Unlike projective tests, **self-report inventories** require test takers to answer specific written questions or to select specific responses from a list of alternatives—usually self-descriptive statements. Participants are asked to either agree or disagree with the statement or to indicate the extent of their agreement or disagreement. Because a predetermined score is assigned to each possible answer, human judgmental factors in scoring and interpretation are minimized. In addition, participants' responses and scores can be compared readily with a standardization sample.

Perhaps the most widely used self-report personality inventory is the Minnesota Multiphasic Personality Inventory, or MMPI (Hathaway & McKinley, 1943). The MMPI-2, a revision by Butcher and colleagues (see Butcher, 1990; Graham, 1990; Greene, 1991), restandardized the inventory, refined the wording of certain items, eliminated items considered outdated, and attempted to include appropriate representations of ethnic minority groups. The MMPI-2 consists of 567 statements; participants are asked to indicate whether each statement is true or false as it applies to them. There is also a "cannot say" alternative, but clients are strongly discouraged from using this category because too many such responses can invalidate the test.

The test taker's MMPI-2 results are rated on ten clinical scales and a number of validity scales. The ten clinical scales were originally constructed by analyzing the responses of diagnosed psychiatric patients (and the responses of normal participants) to the 567 test items. These analyses allowed researchers to determine what kinds of responses each of the various types of psychiatric patients usually made, in contrast to those of normal individuals. The validity scales, which assess degrees of candor, confusion, falsification, and so forth on the part of the respondent, help the clinician detect potential faking or special circumstances that may affect the outcome of other scales (Bagby et al., 1997). Figure 3.1 shows possible responses to ten sample MMPI-2 items and the kinds of responses that contribute to a high rating on the ten MMPI clinical scales.

FIGURE 3.1 The Ten MMPI-2 Clinical Scales and Sample MMPI-2 Test Items   Shown here are the MMPI-2 clinical scales and a few of the items that appear on them. As an example, answering "no" or "false" (rather than "yes" or "true") to the item "I have a good appetite" would result in a higher scale score for hypochondriasis, depression, and hysteria.

SAMPLE ITEMS

TEN MMPI CLINICAL SCALES WITH SIMPLIFIED DESCRIPTIONS	I like mechanics magazines.	I have a good appetite.	I wake up fresh and rested most mornings.	I think I would like the work of a librarian.	I am easily awakened by noise.	I like to read newspaper articles on crime.	My hands and feet are usually warm enough.	My daily life is full of things that keep me interested.	I am about as able to work as I ever was.	There seems to be a lump in my throat much of the time.
1. **Hypochondriasis (Hs)**—Individuals showing excessive worry about health with reports of obscure pains.	NO	NO					NO		NO	
2. **Depression (D)**—People suffering from chronic depression, feelings of uselessness, and inability to face the future.	NO			YES				NO	NO	
3. **Hysteria (Hy)**—Individuals who react to stress by developing physical symptoms (paralysis, cramps, headaches, etc.).	NO	NO			NO		NO	NO	NO	YES
4. **Psychopathic Deviate (Pd)**—People who show irresponsibility, disregard social conventions, and lack deep emotional responses.								NO		
5. **Masculinity-Femininity (Mf)**—People tending to identify with the opposite sex rather than their own.	NO			YES						
6. **Paranoia (Pa)**—People who are suspicious, sensitive, and feel persecuted.										
7. **Psychasthenia (Pt)**—People troubled with fears (phobias) and compulsive tendencies.			NO						NO	YES
8. **Schizophrenia (Sc)**—People with bizarre and unusual thoughts or behavior.								NO		
9. **Hypomania (Ma)**—People who are physically and mentally overactive and who shift rapidly in ideas and actions.										
10. **Social Introversion (Si)**—People who tend to withdraw from social contacts and responsibilities.										

Source: Adapted from Dahlstrom & Welsh (1965). These items from the original MMPI remain unchanged in the MMPI-2.

A basic assumption of the original version of the MMPI was that a person whose MMPI answers are similar to those of diagnosed patients is likely to behave similarly to those patients. However, single-scale interpretations are fraught with hazards. Although a person with a high rating on Scale 6 may be labeled paranoid, this scale does not detect many persons with paranoia. Interpretation of the MMPI-2 scales can be quite complicated and requires special training. Generally, multiple-scale interpretations (pattern analysis) and characteristics associated with the patterns are examined.

Although the MMPIs of clients are subjected to pattern and statistical analyses, client responses can also be viewed as direct communications of important content: information about the client's symptoms, attitudes, and behaviors (Butcher, 1995). The MMPI-2 should be used by clinicians who have mastered its intricacies, who understand relevant statistical concepts, and who can interpret the client's responses (Butcher, 1995; Graham, 1990; Newmark, 1985). Although labeled as a personality test, the MMPI was constructed to assess mental disorders (Clarkin, Hurt, & Mattis, 1999).

Whereas the MMPI-2 assesses a number of different personality characteristics of a person, some self-report inventories or questionnaires focus on only certain kinds of personality traits or emotional problems, such as depression or anxiety. For example, the Beck Depression Inventory (BDI) is composed of twenty-one items that measure various aspects of depression, such as mood, appetite, functioning at work, suicidal thinking, and sleeping patterns (Beck, Ward, Mendelson, Mock, & Erbaugh, 1961).

Though widely used, personality inventories have limitations. First, the fixed number of alternatives can hinder individuals from presenting an accurate picture of themselves. Being asked to answer "true" or "false" to the statement "I am suspicious of people" does not permit an individual to qualify the item in any way. Second, a person may have a unique response style or response set (a tendency to respond to test items in a certain way regardless of content) that may distort the results. For example, many people have a need to present themselves in a favorable light, and this can cause them to give answers that are socially acceptable but inaccurate. Some individuals may fake having a disorder or try to avoid appearing deviant. Third, interpretations of responses of people from different cultural groups may be inaccurate if norms for these groups have not been developed.

Despite these potential problems, personality inventories are widely used. Some, such as the MMPI-2, have been extensively researched, and in many cases their validity has been established. Sophisticated means have also been found to control for response sets and for faking, and, as noted earlier, attempts have been made to establish the cross-cultural validity of instruments such as the MMPI-2. For example, although individuals can lower their psychopathology scores by trying to hide their symptoms on the MMPI (as in trying to fake being healthy when they are not), the MMPI has scales that can help alert clinicians to possible faking (Bagby et al., 1997). The MMPI-2 has also been translated into a variety of languages and used in a number of countries, including Japan, Korea, Thailand, Vietnam, China, Chile, Argentina, Norway, Russia, Greece, France, Iran, and Israel (see Butcher, 1996). In general, inventories are inexpensive and more easily administered and scored than are projective tests. (In fact, many inventories are scored and interpreted by computer.) These features make the use of self-report inventories desirable, especially in a busy clinic or hospital environment.

Moreover, although progress has been slow, the predictive ability and validity of personality assessment tests have been improved. **Psychometrics**—mental measurement, including its study and techniques—is becoming increasingly sophisticated. Further refinement will be achieved when situational variables that help determine behaviors can be taken into account and when fluctuations in mood and other, more stable personality processes can be measured.

Intelligence Tests   Intelligence testing has two primary diagnostic functions and one secondary function. The first is to obtain an estimate of a person's current level of cognitive functioning, called the *intelligence quotient (IQ)*. An IQ score indicates an individual's level of performance relative to that of other people of the same age. As such, an IQ score is an important aid in predicting school performance and detecting mental retardation. (Through statistical procedures, IQ test results are converted into numbers, with 100 representing the mean, or average, score. An IQ score of about 130 indicates performance exceeding that of 95 percent of all same-age peers.) The second diagnostic function of intelligence testing is assessing intellectual deterioration in psychotic disorders. And, finally, an individually administered intelligence test may yield additional useful data for the clinician. The therapist may find important observations of how the person approached the task (systematic versus disorganized), handled failure (depression, frustration, or anger), and persisted in (or gave up) the task.

The two most widely used intelligence tests are the Wechsler Scales (Wechsler, 1981) and the Stanford-Binet Scales (Terman & Merrill, 1960; Thorndike,

Hagen, & Sattler, 1986). The *Wechsler Adult Intelligence Scale* (the *WAIS* and its revised version *WAIS-III*) is administered to persons age sixteen and older. Two other forms are appropriate for children ages six to sixteen (the *Wechsler Intelligence Scale for Children,* or *WISC-III*) and four to six (the *Wechsler Preschool and Primary Scale of Intelligence,* or *WPPSI-III*). The WAIS-III consists of six verbal and five performance scales, which yield verbal and performance IQ scores. These scores are combined to present a total IQ score. The WAIS consists of four factors: Verbal Comprehension, Perceptual Organization, Working Memory, and Processing Speed (Saklofske, Hildebrand, & Gorsuch, 2000). Table 3.2 shows subtest items similar to those used in the WAIS-III.

The *Stanford-Binet Intelligence Scale* is used for individuals age two and older. Much more compli-

cated in administration and scoring, and not standardized on an adult population, the Stanford-Binet requires considerable skill in its use. The test procedure is designed to establish a basal age (the participant passes all subtests for that age) and a ceiling age (the participant fails all subtests for that age), from which an IQ score is calculated. In general, the WISC is preferred over the Stanford-Binet for school-age children (LaGreca & Stringer, 1985). It is easier to administer and yields scores on different cognitive skills (such as verbal and performance subtests).

Some interesting research has been conducted on possible physiological measures of intelligence. When individuals are exposed to an auditory stimulus, electroencephalograph (EEG) recordings of the brain waves can monitor brain reactions to the stimulus. Brain wave patterns appear to be strongly correlated with IQ scores on the WAIS (Matarazzo, 1992). Moreover, a review of research also showed that measures of intellectual functioning seem to be related to the rate of glucose metabolism in certain brain regions, as revealed by positron emission tomography (Matarazzo, 1992). (We discuss positron emission tomography later in this chapter.) Even if such findings prove to be valid, however, the results are difficult to interpret. We cannot assume that as indicators of intelligence, physiological measures are somehow "superior" to performance on the WAIS.

There are four major critiques of the use of IQ tests. First, some investigators believe that IQ tests have been popularized as a means of measuring innate intelligence, when in truth the tests largely reflect cultural and social factors (Garcia, 1981; R. Williams, 1974). The issue of racial differences in innate intelligence has a long history of debate, but the publication of *The Bell Curve* (Herrnstein & Murray, 1994) refocused attention on this issue. The authors of that book propose that racial differences in IQ scores are determined by heredity and that social and status differences between intellectually different classes are therefore difficult to overcome (see Figure 3.2). Critics (S. Gould, 1994) have charged that the basic premises of Herrnstein and Murray's book are faulty and that the frequent assumption that IQ tests measure innate intelligence is false.

Second, the predictive validity of IQ tests has been criticized. That is, do IQ test scores accurately predict the future behaviors or achievements of different cultural groups? Proponents and critics disagree on this point (Anastasi, 1982).

Third, investigators often disagree over criterion variables (in essence, what is actually being predicted by IQ tests). For example, two investigators may be interested in the ability of IQ tests to predict future

---

TABLE 3.2 Items Similar to Those for the Wechsler Adult Intelligence Scale-III

Information

1. How many pennies make a nickel?

2. What is ice made of?

3. What is salt?

Comprehension

1. Why do some people save rubber bands?

2. Why is copper often used in water pipes?

Arithmetic (all calculated "in the head")

1. Susan had 3 pieces of candy and John gave her 2 more. How many pieces of candy did Susan have altogether?

2. Four women divided 20 pieces of candy equally among themselves. How many pieces of candy did each person receive?

Similarities

In what way are the following alike?

1. horse/zebra

2. rake/lawn mower

3. triangle/rectangle

Vocabulary

This test consists simply of asking, "What is a _____?" or "What does _____ mean?" The words cover a wide range of difficulty.

success. One may try to find a correlation between test scores and grades subsequently received in school. The other investigator may argue that grades are a poor indicator of success—that leadership skills and the ability to work with people are better indicators of success.

Fourth, some researchers have questioned whether our current conceptions of IQ tests and intelligence are adequate. A number of researchers have proposed that intelligence is a multidimensional attribute. E. H.

FIGURE 3.2 A Bell Curve, Showing Standard Deviations The *bell curve* refers to the fact that the distribution of IQ scores in a population resembles the shape of a bell, with most scores hovering over the mean and fewer scores falling in the outlying areas of the distribution. IQ scores are transformed so that the mean equals 100, and deviations from the mean are expressed in terms of standard deviations. One standard deviation from the mean (about 15 IQ points above or below the mean, or IQ scores between 85 and 115) represent about 68 percent of the scores. Two standard deviations (about 30 IQ points above or below the mean, or IQs between 70 and 130) account for over 95 percent of the scores.

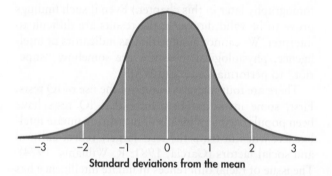

Standard deviations from the mean

Taylor (1990) stated that an important aspect of intelligence, and one that cannot be adequately assessed using IQ tests, is social intelligence or competency. Social skills may be important in such areas as problem solving, adaptation to life, social knowledge, and the ability to use resources effectively.

The controversies over the validity and usefulness of IQ testing may never fully subside. Some continue to claim that IQ tests demonstrate predictive validity for many important attributes, including future success (Barrett & Depinet, 1991). Others maintain that such tests are biased and limited (Helms, 1992). Reliance on IQ scores has resulted in discriminatory actions. In California, for example, African American children were, in the past, disproportionately assigned to classes for the educable mentally retarded on the basis of IQ results. Mercer (1979) has argued that all cultural groups have the same average intellectual potential and that members of a cultural minority may score low on a given IQ test because they are less familiar with the tasks required on such tests, not because of mental retardation. She developed the System of Multicultural Pluralistic Assessment, an assessment procedure that compares a person's performance on the WISC with those of groups of people who have similar social and cultural backgrounds, rather than with others from different backgrounds. This procedure results in fewer children who represent ethnic minorities being assigned to classes for the mentally retarded.

The Kaufman Assessment Battery for Children (K-ABC) An increasingly popular means of evaluating

Intelligence Testing as a Diagnostic Tool Intelligence tests can provide valuable information about intellectual functioning and can help psychologists assess mental retardation and intellectual deterioration. Although many of these tests have been severely criticized as being culturally biased, if used with care, they can be beneficial tools. Here, a child is shown taking the Stanford-Binet test. Can you think of anything in the photograph that would make a child feel comfortable or uncomfortable in the testing structure?

the intelligence and achievement of children ages two and one-half to twelve and one-half years is the *Kaufman Assessment Battery for Children (K-ABC)*. Based on theories of mental processing developed by neuropsychologists and cognitive psychologists, the K-ABC is intended for use with both the general and special populations. For example, the assessment battery has been used with children who have hearing or speech impairments and with those who have learning disabilities. Because of its reliance on visual stimuli, the K-ABC is unsuitable for individuals with visual impairments (Kaufman, Kamphaus, & Kaufman, 1985).

The K-ABC can be used with exceptional children and members of ethnic minority groups. Its applicability to diverse groups has been attributed to measures that (1) are less culturally dependent than those found on traditional tests and (2) focus on the process used to solve problems rather than on the specific content of test items. Children are administered a wide variety of tasks, such as copying a sequence of hand movements performed by the examiner, recalling numbers, assembling triangles to match a model, and demonstrating reading comprehension. Their verbal performance and nonverbal performance are then assessed. For certain language-disordered children or those who do not speak English, nonverbal performance can be used to estimate intellectual functioning.

A Spanish-language version of the K-ABC is available, and norms for African American and Hispanic children have been developed. Interestingly, differences in performance between white and ethnic minority children are much lower on the K-ABC than on traditional IQ tests. The K-ABC tends to have high reliability and validity (Kaufman, Kamphaus, & Kaufman, 1985; Kaufman & Kaufman, 1983), and it may provide a comprehensive, unique, and useful assessment tool for children (Reynolds, Kamphaus, & Rosenthal, 1989). The K-ABC has been one of the most well-studied instruments with reference to cross-cultural applicability, and results have generally been very favorable (Meller & Ohr, 1996). Because many of the K-ABC subscales measure performance using social information, it may be more likely than traditional IQ tests to assess social intelligence (Taylor, 1990). This approach offers promise in the effort to devise more culturally unbiased tests of intelligence. Also available is a short form of the instrument (Kaufman Brief Intelligence Test), which requires about fifteen to thirty minutes to complete (Kamphaus, Petoskey, & Rowe, 2000).

Tests for Cognitive Impairment Clinical psychologists, especially those who work in a hospital setting, are concerned with detecting and assessing **organicity** (an older term referring to damage or deterioration in the central nervous system), or cognitive impairments due to brain damage. Such damage can have profound effects both physically (e.g., motor behavior) and psychologically (memory, attention, thinking, emotions, etc.; Gass, 2002). The use of individual intelligence tests such as the WAIS-III can sometimes identify such impairments. For example, a difference of twenty points between verbal and performance scores on the WAIS-III may indicate the possibility of brain damage. Overall, IQ scores have been found to be signficantly correlated with neuropsychological test performance (Diaz-Asper, Schretlen, & Pearlson, 2004). Certain patterns of scores on the individual subtests, such as those that measure verbal concept formation or abstracting ability (comparison and comprehension), can also reveal brain damage. Because impaired abstract thinking may be characteristic of brain damage, a lower score on this scale (when accompanied by other signs) must be investigated.

One of the routine means of assessing cognitive impairment is the *Bender-Gestalt Visual-Motor Test* (Bender, 1938; Brannigan, Decker, & Madsen, 2004), shown in Figure 3.3. Nine geometric designs, each drawn in black on a piece of white cardboard, are presented one at a time to the test taker, who is asked to copy them on a piece of paper. Certain errors in the copies are characteristic of neurological impairment. Among these are rotation of figures, perseveration (continuation of a pattern to an exceptional degree), fragmentation, oversimplification, inability to copy angles, and reversals. In addition to assessing brain damage and neurological impairment, the Bender-Gestalt is often used for the evaluation of visual-motor maturity and for screening children for developmental delays. Although some have found the reliability and validity of the test to be good (Koppitz, 1975), it may be subject to misinterpretation, and it is affected by gender and culture. The Bender-Gestalt should be used only as one assessment tool among others.

The *Halstead-Reitan Neuropsychological Test Battery*, developed by Reitan from the earlier work of Halstead, has been used successfully to differentiate patients with brain damage from those without brain damage and to provide valuable information about the type and location of the damage (Boll, 1983). The full battery consists of eleven tests, although several are often omitted. Clients are presented with a series of tasks that assess sensorimotor, cognitive, and perceptual functioning, including abstract concept formation, memory and attention, and auditory perception. The full battery takes more than six hours to administer, so it is a relatively expensive and time-consuming assessment tool. Versions of the Halstead-Reitan Battery are available for children age five and older (Nussbaum & Bigler, 1989), and normative data for

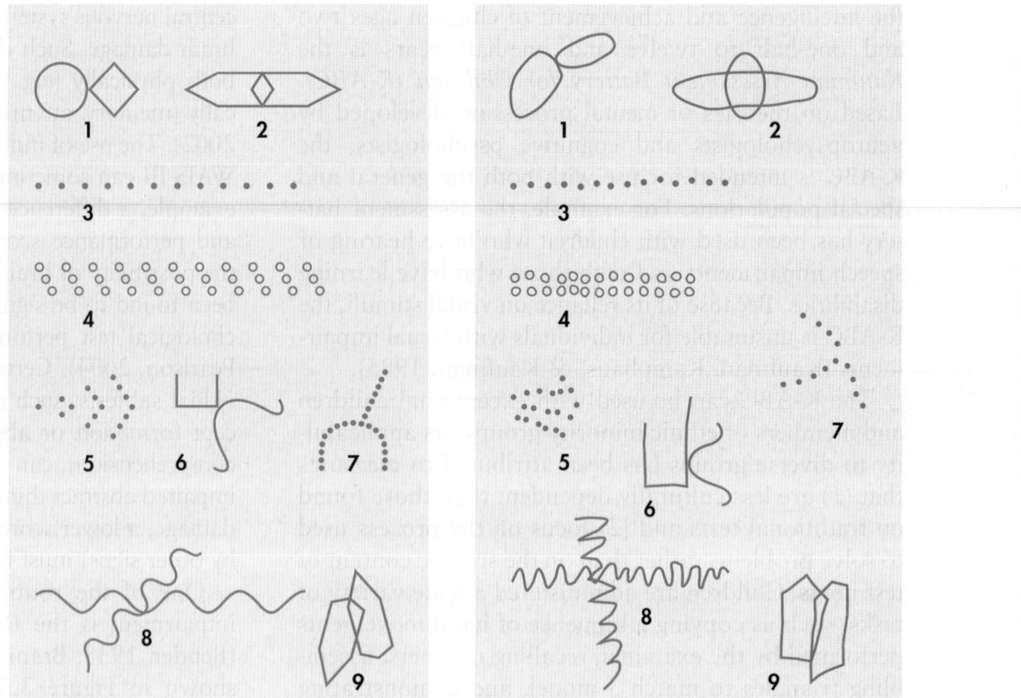

FIGURE 3.3 The Nine Bender Designs The figures presented to participants are shown on the left. The distorted figures drawn by participants are possibly indicative of organicity (brain damage) and are shown on the right.

Source: Bender (1938).

children have been collected. Reliability and validity of the tests are well established (Clarkin, Hurt, & Mattis, 1999).

A less costly test for cognitive impairment is the *Luria-Nebraska Neuropsychological Battery,* which requires about two hours to administer and is more standardized in content, administration, and scoring than is the Halstead-Reitan Battery. Developed by C. J. Golden and colleagues (Golden et al., 1981), this battery includes twelve scales that assess motor functions, rhythm, tactile functions, visual functions, receptive and expressive speech, memory, writing, intellectual processes, and other functions. Validation data indicate that the battery is highly successful in screening for brain damage and quite accurate in pinpointing damaged areas (Anastasi, 1982). A children's version has been developed (Golden, 1989). Although the battery has been shown to differentiate brain-damaged children from normal children, its ability to discriminate between different types of learning disabilities has been questioned (Morgan & Brown, 1988). When clinicians must make detailed analyses of specific diagnostic decisions, using other tests in conjunction with the Luria-Nebraska may be desirable (Golden, 1989).

Neuropsychological tests are widely used (Camara, Nathan, & Puente, 2000) and are effective and valid in evaluating cognitive impairment due to brain damage. In fact, they are far more accurate than evalua-

tions made simply through interviews or informal observations (Kubiszyn et al., 2000).

Neurological Tests

In addition to psychological tests, a variety of neurological medical procedures are available for diagnosing cognitive impairments due to brain damage or abnormal brain functioning. For example, x-ray studies can often detect brain tumors. A more sophisticated procedure, *computerized axial tomography (CAT) scan,* repeatedly scans different areas of the brain with beams of x-rays and, with the assistance of a computer, produces a three-dimensional image of the structure of the brain. That image can provide a detailed view of brain deterioration or abnormality. In addition to the study of brain damage, CAT scans have been used to study brain tissue abnormalities among patients diagnosed with schizophrenia, affective disorders, Alzheimer's disease, and alcoholism (Coffman, 1989).

The *positron emission tomography (PET) scan* enables study of the physiological and biochemical processes of the brain, rather than the anatomical structures seen in the CAT scan. In PET scans, a radioactive substance is injected into the patient's bloodstream. The scanner detects the substance as it is metabolized in the brain, yielding information about brain functioning. PET scans, like CAT scans, have

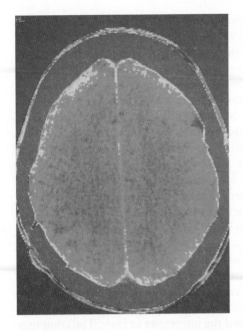

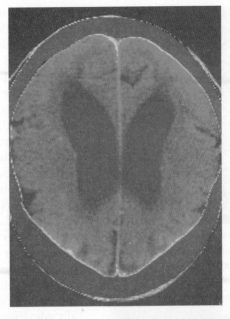

CAT Scans Neurological tests, such as CAT scans, PET scans, and MRIs, have dramatically improved our ability to study the brain and to assess brain damage. Shown here on the left is a normal CAT scan; on the right, a CAT scan showing the enlarged ventricles (butterfly shape in the center) of an individual suffering from senile dementia.

been used to study a variety of mental disorders and brain diseases. Characteristic metabolic patterns have been observed in many of these disorders (Holcomb, Links, Smith, & Wong, 1989).

An older and more widely used means of examining the brain is the *electroencephalograph (EEG)*. Electrodes attached to the skull record electrical activity (brain waves), and abnormalities in the activity can provide information about the presence of tumors or other brain conditions.

A final technique, *magnetic resonance imaging (MRI)*, creates a magnetic field around the patient and uses radio waves to detect abnormalities. MRIs can produce an amazingly clear "picture" of the brain and its tissues. Because of these superior pictures, which are reminiscent of postmortem brain slices, MRIs may eventually supplant CAT scans; some lesions are seen better using the MRI (Andreasen, 1989; Morihisa et al., 1999). In functional magnetic resonance imaging, both the structures and also those changes that occur in specific brain functions can be observed. It provides high resolution, noninvasive views of neural activity detected by a blood-oxygen-level-dependent signal.

These neurological techniques, coupled with psychological tests, are increasing diagnostic accuracy and understanding of brain functioning and disorders. Some researchers predict that in the future such techniques will allow therapists to make more precise diagnoses and to pinpoint precise areas of the brain affected by disorders such as Alzheimer's and Huntington's diseases (Matarazzo, 1992).

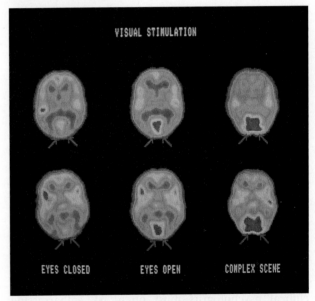

PET Scans This PET scan reveals increased brain activity as a function of visual stimulation. The areas in red show the most intense stimulation, and as you can see, the more complex the information being processed, the more active the brain is.

Myth vs Reality

Myth: Psychological tests are less accurate than are medical tests because one's psychological status is more difficult to assess.

Reality: The widely held belief that medical tests are more reliable and valid than psychological tests

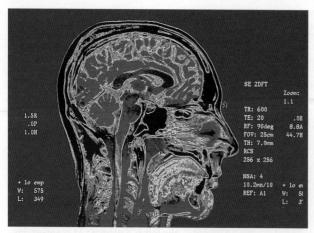

Magnetic Resonance Imaging (MRI) In magnetic resonance imaging, a magnetic field is created around the patient, and radio waves are then used to produce amazingly detailed pictures of the brain.

appears to be false. Meyer and colleagues (2001) conducted an evaluation of the validity of psychological and medical tests. Both kinds of tests were found to vary in reliability and validity. However, many psychological tests were found to be as good as or better than medical tests in detecting conditions. For example, neuropsychological tests were as accurate as the MRI in detecting dementia. Psychological tests are valuable tools.

The Ethics of Assessment

Over the years, a strong antitesting movement has developed in the United States. Issues such as the confidentiality of client records, invasion of privacy, client welfare, cultural bias, and unethical practices have increasingly been raised (Bersoff, 1981; Weiner, 1995). In assessing and treating emotionally disturbed people, clinical psychologists must often ask embarrassing questions or use tests that may be construed as invasions of privacy. In many cases, a clinician may not know beforehand whether the test results will prove beneficial to the client. Yet to exclude testing because it may offend clients or place them in an uncomfortable position could ultimately deprive those clients of the test's long-range benefits.

Some people strongly criticize tests on the grounds that they can have undesirable social consequences. They ask, "Who will use the test results, and for what purpose is the test employed?" Test results may be used to the client's detriment in some instances. Tests may also be inaccurate, causing serious misdiagnosis and its consequences. Note the fears and concerns over

the possible widespread use of tests to detect antibodies to the HIV virus (AIDS) and drug abuse, as well as the use of the polygraph in job settings. Attention has also focused on the increased role of computers in assessment. For decades, computers have been used to score the test results and to provide psychological profiles of clients. More recently, computer programs have become available to administer clinical interviews, IQ tests, personality inventories, and projective tests. They may also interpret responses of clients or other persons, such as applicants for jobs. The computers are programmed, for example, to simulate a structured clinical interview. Individuals who are being assessed sit before a keyboard and answer questions shown on the computer screen.

Computer assessment has some advantages over face-to-face assessment. First, with the rising costs of mental health care, this technique can free up the time of clinicians and other personnel who have traditionally administered the interviews or tests. The computer can easily perform scoring and interpretation. Second, the motivation and attention of clients may be increased because clients often enjoy using a computer. Third, because clinicians often differ in interviewing styles and backgrounds, computer assessment may provide superior standardization of procedures. But although the use of computers in assessment is increasing, the application of computer technology remains largely in the scoring rather than in the administration of tests (Camara, Nathan, & Puente, 2000). Two important questions remain: How reliable and valid are computer assessments, and can they be a substitute for face-to-face assessment between client and clinician? How can standardization occur when respondents may have very different settings under which the online responses are given (e.g., while simultaneously watching television, having others "help" complete the tests, eating while responding, etc.)? Can security and privacy of responses be assured when tests are completed online? Thus, although there are advantages to Internet testing, a number of problems need to be addressed (Naglieri et al., 2004).

Some studies of computer assessment have yielded encouraging results. Some findings indicate that the assessment has good reliability and validity and that patients have favorable views of rated computerized interviews (Strong & Farrell, 2003). One investigation (Farrell, Stiles-Camplair, & McCullough, 1987) evaluated the ability of a computer interview to assess the target complaints of clients. The clients completed a computer interview in which they were told to answer a series of questions by pressing the appropriate keyboard selections that corresponded to their feelings. Depending on their answers, further programmed questions were asked to refine their responses. The researchers also used traditional forms of assessment—clinical interviews and psychological tests—with these clients and compared those results with the computer interview results. The computer interview findings generally agreed with those of the traditional clinical interview and test results. However, most of the clients preferred being interviewed by the clinician.

Although some studies have provided positive results, critics of computer assessment are concerned about the proliferation of computer assessment techniques, the paucity of research studies that have established their validity, and the unwarranted impression that computerized assessments are scientifically precise (Butcher, 1995; Matarazzo, 1986). As computer assessment becomes more popular, there is also a risk that untrained individuals, or even clients themselves, may be unaware of the limits of this form of assessment and may misinterpret the meaning of the findings. Computer assessment research should therefore address issues involving validity, use and abuse of test results, and ethical concerns, such as privacy.

Psychological testing has ethical, legal, and societal implications that go beyond the field of psychology. Psychologists should be aware of these implications and should guard against the misuse of test results. They should also carefully weigh the consequences of permitting such considerations to interfere with devising, improving, and applying tests that will benefit their patients. The mental health professions and the general public are increasingly aware of the need to guard against possible abuses and to continually refine and improve classification systems and assessment procedures. The professions themselves have to engage in evidence-based assessments. That is, the use of tests, measures, and assessment procedures should be based on research evidence concerning their value rather than on tradition or popular beliefs.

A final problem relating to the use of psychological tests or assessment procedures addresses their ability to assess the status of individuals from different cultures. Evidence exists that biases often occur in the assessment of individuals from different cultures and that therapists of different ethnicities evaluate the same client behaviors differently (Okazaki & Sue, 1995). In one study (Li-Repac, 1980), five Chinese American and five European American male therapists rated Chinese American and European American male clients who appeared on a videotaped interview. The therapists evaluated clients of other ethnicities more negatively than they evaluated clients of their own

ethnicities. European American therapists rated Chinese American clients as anxious, awkward, confused, and nervous, whereas Chinese American therapists perceived the same clients as alert, ambitious, adaptable, honest, and friendly. Chinese American therapists deemed their European American clients active, aggressive, rebellious, and outspoken, whereas European American therapists viewed these people as affectionate, adventurous, sincere, and easygoing. In addition, European American therapists rated Chinese American clients as being more depressed, more inhibited, and less socially poised and as having a lower capacity for interpersonal relationships than did Chinese American therapists. Similarly, Chinese American therapists rated European American clients as more severely disturbed than did European American therapists.

These findings suggest that judgments about psychological functioning depend at least in part on whether therapists are of the same ethnic background as their clients. Because tests or procedures may not be normed, standardized, or widely used on individuals from different cultural groups, or because cultural biases may intrude on judgments, clinicians should consider the issues discussed in the Critical Thinking feature "Can We Accurately Assess the Status of Members of Different Cultural Groups?" New assessment strategies are also needed to overcome problems in the evaluation of people from different cultures. One researcher (Dana, 1998) has suggested implementing a number of cultural competency skills in the assessment process: ensuring the use of an appropriate language (by having bilingual clinicians or interpreters); noting culture-specific behaviors on the part of clients; considering culture-bound syndromes (see Table 3.3); determining clients' cultural orientation; and drawing implications for etiology, course, and prognosis of disorders.

The Classification of Abnormal Behavior

The goal of having a **classification system** for abnormal behaviors is to provide distinct categories, indicators, and nomenclature for different patterns of behavior, thought processes, and emotional disturbances. Thus the pattern of behavior classified as *paranoid schizophrenia* should be clearly different from the pattern named *borderline personality*. At the same time, the categories should be constructed in such a way as to accommodate wide variation in these patterns. That is, the clinician should be able to categorize paranoid schizophrenic behavior as such, even when

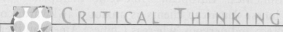

CRITICAL THINKING

Can We Accurately Assess the Status of Members of Different Cultural Groups?

We often have a difficult time evaluating the behaviors of people from other cultures. Cultural groups differ in many aspects, including dietary practices, type of clothing, religious rituals, and social interactions. How do we decide whether an individual from a different culture is behaving in a certain way because of a mental disorder or because of cultural practices? What signs or clues indicate that someone is truly mentally and emotionally disturbed? Can we use assessment measures standardized in the United States with people from other countries?

These questions are only a sampling of the kinds of issues clinicians must consider when trying to assess members of ethnic minority groups or individuals from different cultures. Brislin (1993) has identified several major problems, including the equivalence of concepts and scales.

First, certain concepts may not be equivalent across cultures. For instance, Americans living in the United States and the Baganda living in East Africa have different concepts of intelligent behavior. In the United

States, one indicator of intelligence is quickness in mental reasoning; among the Baganda, slow, deliberate thought is considered a mark of intelligence. Obviously, tests of intelligence devised in the two cultures would differ. Individuals taking the tests could be considered intelligent on one culture's measure but not on the other.

Second, scores on assessment instruments may not really be equivalent in cross-cultural research. For example, many universities use the Scholastic Aptitude Test (SAT), which has a verbal and a quantitative component, as a criterion for admissions. Do the test scores mean the same thing for different groups in terms of assessing academic potential, achievements, and ability to succeed? SAT scores do tend to be moderately successful predictors of subsequent university grades. Sue and Abe (1988), however, found that the SAT score's ability to predict success varies according to ethnicity and the components of the SAT. Whereas the SAT verbal component was a good predictor of university

grades for white American students, the SAT quantitative portion was a good predictor of grades for Asian American students. Thus Asian American and white American students with the same overall SAT scores may receive very different grades in individual courses. In every phase of testing, including test construction, test administration, and test interpretation, cultural factors are important to consider (Dana, 2000).

Third, the manner in which symptoms are expressed may vary from culture to culture, and certain cultural groups may have disturbances that are specific to those groups (Griffith, Gonzalez, & Blue, 1999). For example, culture-bound syndromes shown in Table 3.3 refer to syndromes that are often found in one cultural group but not others.

What are the implications of these findings? Should we abolish measures of performance for members of groups that have not been part of the standardization process? If so, how can we evaluate them? These are only a few of the dilemmas involved in assessment.

---

the patient does not show the "perfect" or "textbook" paranoid schizophrenic pattern.

Problems with Early Diagnostic Classification Systems

As discussed in Chapter 1, Emil Kraepelin, toward the end of the nineteenth century, devised the first effective classification scheme for mental disorders. Kraepelin held the organic view of psychopathology, and his system had a distinctly biogenic slant. Classification was based on the patient's symptoms, as in medicine. It was hoped that disorders (similar groups of symp-

toms) would have a common **etiology** (cause or origin), would require similar treatments, would respond to those treatments similarly, and would progress similarly if left untreated.

Many of these same expectations were held for the first edition of the *Diagnostic and Statistical Manual of Mental Disorders* (DSM-I), published by the American Psychiatric Association in 1952 and based on Kraepelin's system (Clarkin & Levy, 2004). These expectations, however, were not realized in DSM-I. The DSM was revised in 1968 (DSM-II), 1980 (DSM-III), 1987 (DSM-III-R), 1994 (DSM-IV), and 2000 (DSM-IV-TR). Each revision was made to increase the

TABLE 3.3   Culture-Bound Syndromes

Culture-bound syndromes are recurrent, locality-specific patterns of aberrant behavior and troubling experience that may or may not be classified in a particular DSM-IV-TR diagnostic category. Many of these patterns are indigenously considered to be illnesses or afflictions. The particular symptoms, course, and social response are very often influenced by local cultural factors. Among the culture-bound syndromes that DSM-IV-TR recognizes are the following:

Amok   A dissociative episode characterized by a period of brooding followed by an outburst of violent, aggressive, or homicidal behavior directed at people and objects. The episode tends to be precipitated by a perceived slight or insult and seems to be prevalent only among males. The episode is often accompanied by persecutory ideas, amnesia, exhaustion, and a return to a premorbid state following the episode. Some instances of amok may occur during a brief psychotic episode or constitute the onset or an exacerbation of a chronic psychotic process. The original reports that used this term were from Malaysia. A similar behavior pattern is found in Laos, the Philippines, Polynesia, Papua New Guinea, and Puerto Rico, and among the Navajo.

Ataque de nervios   An idiom of distress principally reported among Latinos from the Caribbean but recognized among many Latin American and Latin Mediterranean groups. Commonly reported symptoms include uncontrollable shouting, attacks of crying, trembling, heat in the chest rising into the head, and verbal or physical aggression. Dissociative experiences, seizurelike or fainting episodes, and suicidal gestures are prominent in some attacks but absent in others. A general feature of an ataque de nervios is a sense of being out of control. Ataques de nervios frequently occur as a direct result of a stressful event relating to the family (such as news of the death of a close relative, a separation or divorce from a spouse, conflicts with a spouse or children, or witnessing an accident involving a family member). People may experience amnesia for what occurred during the ataque de nervios, but they otherwise return rapidly to their usual level of functioning. Although descriptions of some ataques de nervios most closely fit with the DSM-IV-TR description of panic attacks, the association of most ataques with a precipitating event and the frequent absence of the hallmark symptoms of acute fear or apprehension distinguish them from panic disorder. Ataques span the range from normal expressions of distress not associated with having a mental disorder to symptom presentations associated with the diagnoses of anxiety, mood, dissociative, or somatoform disorders.

Ghost sickness   A preoccupation with death and the deceased (sometimes associated with witchcraft) frequently observed among members of many American Indian tribes. Various symptoms can be attributed to ghost sickness, including bad dreams, weakness, feelings of danger, loss of appetite, fainting, dizziness, fear, anxiety, hallucinations, loss of consciousness, confusion, feelings of futility, and a sense of suffocation.

Hwa-byung   A Korean folk syndrome literally translated into English as "anger syndrome" and attributed to the suppression of anger. The symptoms include insomnia, fatigue, panic, fear of impending death, dysphoric affect, indigestion, anorexia, dyspnea, palpitations, and generalized aches and pains.

Koro   A term, probably of Malaysian origin, that refers to an episode of sudden and intense anxiety during which the penis (or, in females, the vulva and nipples) will recede into the body and possibly cause death. The syndrome is reported in South and East Asia, where it is known by a variety of local terms. It is occasionally found in the West. Koro at times occurs in localized epidemic form in East Asian areas.

Rootwork   A set of cultural interpretations that ascribe illness to hexing, witchcraft, sorcery, or the evil influence of another person. Symptoms may include generalized anxiety and gastrointestinal complaints (such as nausea, vomiting, and diarrhea), weakness, dizziness, the fear of being poisoned, and sometimes fear of being killed ("voodoo death"). "Roots," "spells," or "hexes" can be "put" or placed on other persons, causing a variety of emotional and psychological problems. The hexed person may even fear death until the root has been eliminated, usually through the work of a root doctor (a healer in this tradition), who can also be called on to bewitch an enemy. Rootwork is found in the southern United States among both African American and European American populations and in Caribbean societies.

Shenjing shuairuo   ("neurasthenia") In China, a condition characterized by physical and mental fatigue, dizziness, headaches, other pains, concentration difficulties, sleep disturbance, and memory loss. Other symptoms include gastrointestinal problems, sexual dysfunction, irritability, excitability, and various signs suggesting disturbance of the autonomic nervous system. In many cases, the symptoms would meet the criteria for a DSM-IV-TR mood or anxiety disorder.

Source: Adapted from American Psychiatric Association (2000).

reliability, validity, and usefulness of the classification scheme. As mentioned previously, reliability and validity are crucial to any diagnostic scheme and, in fact, to any scientific construct.

Reliability Early studies of the DSM that compared the diagnoses of pairs of clinicians found poor agreement (interrater reliability) between the members of each pair (Ash, 1949; Schmidt & Fonda, 1956). The greatest disagreement was found in specific categories. In about 80 percent of the pairs, both clinicians agreed on the general category (organic, psychotic, or personality disturbance) in which a particular disorder belonged. As a rule, reliability was higher for broad distinctions than for fine distinctions (Phares, 1984). A fine distinction, for example, would focus on the precise type of personality disturbance or disorder.

In other reliability studies, the same information was presented to clinicians on two occasions or at different times (test-retest reliability). These studies showed that the clinicians' later diagnoses often did not agree with their earlier ones (Beck, 1962; Wilson & Meyer, 1962). Thus even a single clinician's diagnosis was not very reliable over time.

Much unreliability of early DSM editions can be attributed to the diagnostic categories themselves. Three sources of diagnostic error have been identified. Of the errors, 5 percent were attributable to the patients, who gave different material to different interviewers. Nearly one-third (32.5 percent) of the errors were due to inconsistencies among diagnosticians in interview techniques, in interpreting similar data, and in judging the importance of symptoms. Most significantly, however, 62.5 percent of the errors derived from inadequacies of the diagnostic system (Ward et al., 1962). It was simply not clear which behavior patterns belonged in which categories.

In view of these problems, each subsequent version of DSM was developed to have greater interrater reliability. Results of field trials indicated that good to excellent interrater reliability could be obtained for many, but not all, of the major classes of disorders (J. B. Williams, 1999).

Validity Many critics questioned the validity and usefulness of psychiatric classification (Ferster, 1965; Kanfer & Phillips, 1969; Ullmann & Krasner, 1965). They claimed that DSM did not adequately convey information about underlying causes, processes, treatment, and prognosis. (A **prognosis** is a prediction of the future course of a particular disorder.) The problem arose because early versions of DSM were strongly influenced by the biological model of mental illness, in

which cause is supposed to be a basis of classification. With the exception of the categories involving brain damage, which may parallel diseases, most DSM categories were purely descriptive. In addition, a prerequisite for high validity is high reliability. Because the reliability of early versions of DSM was questionable, the validity of the DSM was also limited. Indeed, it is difficult to talk about the validity of the entire diagnostic system because reliability and validity vary from one category to another. Moreover, empirical tests of the construct validity of DSM have been largely absent.

DSM tried to respond to new research findings. Although Kraepelin's concepts still formed the basis for some of its categories, successive versions of DSM contained substantial revisions. For example, to improve reliability, DSM specified the exact criteria clinicians should use in making a diagnosis. What has helped to increase reliability and validity has been the development of structured interviews (e.g., Structured Clinical Interview for DSM-IV) that gather information pertinent to making a DSM diagnosis (J. B. Williams, 1999). DSM was intended to be atheoretical and descriptive, making it more useful to clinicians of varying orientations. In a survey of use and attitudes among mental health professionals in forty-two countries, DSM was widely used and considered useful, although respondents noted that certain diagnostic categories, such as personality disorders, were very problematic (Maser, Kaelber, & Weise, 1991).

The Current System: DSM-IV-TR

After DSM-III-R, the American Psychiatric Association published DSM-IV (1994), which took into account the accumulating research on psychopathology and diagnosis. In 2000, revisions were made to DSM-IV with respect to updating research findings and other minor changes, and the DSM-IV-TR version was published. Criteria for disorders largely remain the same in DSM-IV and DSM-IV-TR. Thus comments regarding DSM-IV are applicable to DSM-IV-TR and vice versa. The adequacy of DSM-IV-TR has been under investigation. Field trials or studies are being conducted on certain diagnostic categories. One test of whether symptom measures could differentiate between clients with DSM-IV-TR anxiety and mood disorders (Brown, Chorpita, & Barlow, 1998) found evidence that the different disorders could be distinguished from one another. Brown, Di Nardo, Lehman, and Campbell (2001) also found good to excellent reliability for the majority of DSM-IV-TR anxiety and mood disorder categories. Factors decreasing reliability included disagreements over whether symptoms were sufficient in number, severity, or duration to meet DSM-IV-TR criteria. Such studies provide support for the meaningfulness of the disorders as listed by DSM-IV-TR.

DSM-IV-TR recommends that clinicians examine and evaluate the individual's mental state with regard to five factors or dimensions (called axes in the manual). Axes I, II, and III address the individual's present mental and medical condition. Axes IV and V provide additional information about the person's life situation and functioning. Together, the five axes are intended to provide comprehensive and useful information.

Axis I—Clinical Syndromes and Other Conditions That May Be a Focus of Clinical Attention

Any mental disorder listed in the manual (except those included on Axis II) is indicated on Axis I. If an individual has more than one mental disorder, they are all listed. The principal disorder is listed first.

Axis II—Personality Disorders and Mental Retardation

Personality disorders, as well as prominent maladaptive personality features, are listed on Axis II. Personality disorders may be present either alone or in combination with a mental disorder from Axis I. If more than one personality disorder is present, they are all listed. Also included on Axis II is mental retardation.

Axis III—General Medical Conditions

Listed on Axis III are any medical conditions that are potentially relevant to understanding and treating the person.

Axis IV—Psychosocial and Environmental Problems

These problems may affect the diagnosis, treatment, and prognosis of mental disorders. For example, a client may be experiencing the death of a family member, social isolation, homelessness, extreme poverty, and inadequate health services. The clinician lists these problems if they have been present during the year preceding the current evaluation or if they occurred before the previous year and are clearly contributory to the disorder or have become a focus of treatment. The clinician has various categories in which to classify the type of problems.

Axis V—Global Assessment of Functioning

The clinician provides a rating of the psychological, social, and occupational functioning of the person. Normally, the rating is made for the level of functioning at the time of the evaluation. The clinician uses a 100-point scale in which 1 indicates severe impairment in functioning (for example, the individual is in persistent danger of severely hurting self or others or is unable to maintain minimal personal hygiene) and 100 refers to superior functioning with no symptoms.

The disorders (categories) for Axes I and II that are included in DSM-IV-TR are shown on the inside covers of this book. The Mental Health and Society feature "An Example of Classification Using DSM-IV-TR" provides an example of the classifications that result from the five-axis evaluation.

DSM-IV-TR Mental Disorders

The task of making a diagnosis of mental disorder involves classifying individuals on Axes I and II. Most disorders found in clients are listed under either Axis I or Axis II, but some clients may have disorders on both axes or more than one on each axis. The following are the broad categories of mental disorders, most of which are discussed in this book.

Disorders Usually First Diagnosed in Infancy, Childhood, or Adolescence

A variety of problems are included in the category of disorders that begin before maturity. The problems include impairment in cognitive and intellectual functioning, language or motor deficiencies, disruptive behaviors, poor social skills, anxiety, eating disorders, and so on (see the chapters on disorders of childhood and adolescence and eating and sleep disorders). (Mental retardation is discussed in the chapter on cognitive disorders.)

Delirium, Dementia, Amnestic, and Other Cognitive Disorders

The essential feature of the cognitive impairment disorders is a psychological or behavioral abnormality that is associated with a transient or permanent identifiable dysfunction of the brain. Included in this category are cognitive, emotional, and behavioral problems that arise from head injuries, ingestion of toxic or intoxicating substances, brain degeneration or disease, and so on (see the chapter on cognitive disorders).

Mental Disorders Due to a General Medical Condition

Medical conditions can be an important cause of mental disorders. When there is evidence that general medical conditions are causally related to a disorder and explain it, the client is considered to have a mental disorder due to a general medical condition. For example, hypothyroidism can be a direct cause of major depressive disorder. In that case, the diagnosis would be "major depressive disorder due to a general medical condition (hypothyroidism)." Many of the major diagnostic categories (mood disorders or

MENTAL HEALTH AND SOCIETY

An Example of Classification Using DSM-IV-TR

The client

Mark was a fifty-six-year-old machine operator who was referred for treatment by his supervisor. The supervisor noted that Mark's performance at work had deteriorated during the past four months. Mark was frequently absent from work, had difficulty getting along with others, and often had a strong odor of liquor on his breath after his lunch break. The supervisor knew Mark was a heavy drinker and suspected that Mark's performance was affected by alcohol consumption.

In truth, Mark could not stay away from drinking. He consumed alcohol every day; during weekends, he averaged about sixteen ounces of Scotch per day. Although he had been a heavy drinker for thirty years, his consumption had increased after his wife divorced him six months previously. She claimed she could no longer tolerate his drinking,

extreme jealousy, and unwarranted suspicions concerning her marital fidelity.

Coworkers avoided Mark because he was a cold, unemotional person who distrusted others.

During interviews with the therapist, Mark revealed very little about himself. He blamed others for his drinking problems: if his wife had been faithful or if others were not out to get him, he would drink less. Mark appeared to overreact to any perceived criticisms of himself. A medical examination revealed that Mark was developing cirrhosis of the liver as a result of his chronic and heavy drinking.

The evaluation

Mark's heavy use of alcohol, which interfered with his functioning, resulted in an alcohol abuse diagnosis on Axis I. Mark also exhibited a personality disorder, which was diagnosed as paranoid personality

on Axis II because of his suspiciousness, hypervigilance, and other behaviors. Cirrhosis of the liver was noted on Axis III. The clinician noted Mark's divorce and difficulties in his job on Axis IV. Finally, Mark was given a 54 on the Global Assessment of Functioning (GAF) scale, used in Axis V to rate his current level of functioning, mainly because he was exhibiting moderate difficulty at work and in his social relationships. Mark's diagnosis, then, was as follows:

Axis I—Clinical syndrome: alcohol abuse

Axis II—Personality disorder: paranoid personality

Axis III—Physical disorder: cirrhosis

Axis IV—Psychosocial and environmental problems: (1) Problems with primary support group (divorce), (2) occupational problems

Axis V—Current GAF, 54

---

anxiety disorders) have specific categories that include disorders caused by medical conditions.

Substance-Related Disorders Psychoactive substances, such as alcohol, amphetamines, marijuana, cocaine, and nicotine, are those that affect the central nervous system. Whenever use of these substances continues despite social, occupational, psychological, or physical problems, it is considered a mental disorder. Individuals with substance use disorders are often unable to control intake and have a persistent desire to use the substance (see the chapter on substance-related disorders). Some disorders (anxiety or mood) occur because of the ingestion of substances. In these cases, they are considered substance-induced disorders and are listed by DSM-IV-TR not in the section on substance-related disorders but in the section for those disorders that share the same symptoms. (For example,

substance-induced major depressive disorder would be classified under mood disorders.)

Schizophrenia and Other Psychotic Disorders The disorder known as schizophrenia is marked by severe impairment in thinking and perception. Speech may be incoherent, and the person often has delusions (false belief systems), hallucinations (such as hearing imaginary voices), and inappropriate affect. Schizophrenia, as well as other psychotic disorders, seriously disrupts social, occupational, and recreational functioning (see the chapter on schizophrenia).

Mood Disorders A separate class of disorders is composed of disturbances in mood or affect. The mood may be one of serious depression, in which the person shows marked sadness, diminished interest, and loss of energy. Extreme elation or mania is also

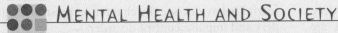

MENTAL HEALTH AND SOCIETY

The Diagnosing and Classification of a Disorder: Depression

Views of mental disorders and criteria by which to diagnose disorders have changed over time. As noted by Dubovsky and Buzan (1999) in the case of depression, the condition was recognized from the very beginning of human existence. It has been described throughout history. In the fourth century B.C., Hippocrates used the terms *melancholia* (black bile) and *mania* (to be mad) to refer to mood disorders and mental illness. At the beginning of the twentieth century, Emil Kraepelin differentiated schizophrenia from "manic-depressive insanity" in that the former resulted in a deteriorating course, whereas the latter occurred in episodes. He believed that manic-depressive insanity was a single illness that included periods of melancholia and mania.

Beginning in 1952, the early editions of DSM considered psychotic depressive reaction as a severe disorder that lacked a precipitant. In cases in which there was a marked depressive reaction to an external event or stressor, it was considered neurotic depressive reaction. In 1968, DSM-II added involutional melancholia and manic-depressive psychosis to the mood disorders. In subsequent editions of DSM mood disorder diagnoses were based on symptom clusters rather than on the presence or absence of a precipitant. They also more clearly distinguished between different mood disorders and their features (see the chapter on mood disorders). In the most recent edition, DSM-IV-TR, mood disorders are divided into Depressive Disorders (including major depressive disorders and dysthymic disorder), Bipolar Disorders (including bipolar I disorders, bipolar II disorder, and cyclothymic disorder), and Other Mood Disorders. Detailed symptom features and specifiers are included in the diagnosis. For example, sometimes depression may occur during certain seasons, which would result in a seasonal pattern specifier for the disorder. Thus, over time, the diagnosing and categorizing of disorders such as depression have become much more detailed and articulated.

included in these disorders. People with mania frequently have grandiosity, decreased need for sleep, flight of ideas, and impairment in functioning. Severity of mood disorders can vary, and sometimes, in bipolar conditions, both depression and mania are exhibited (see the chapter on mood disorders, and the Mental Health and Society feature "The Diagnosing and Classification of a Disorder: Depression").

Anxiety Disorders Anxiety is the predominant symptom in anxiety disorders, and avoidance behaviors are almost always present. For example, people with phobias fear an object or situation and avoid encountering the feared object. People with other anxiety disorders may not know the reasons for their extreme feelings of anxiety or may exhibit obsessions (recurrent thoughts) or compulsions (repetitive behaviors), which, when not performed, cause marked distress (see the chapter on anxiety disorders).

Somatoform Disorders Symptoms of a physical disorder that cannot be fully explained by a known general medical condition are usually classified as somatoform disorders. Individuals with these disorders usually complain of bodily problems or dysfunctions, are preoccupied with beliefs of having a disease or health problem, or experience pain. Yet the symptoms may be inconsistent with anatomical structures, and the discrepancy suggests a psychological basis for the symptoms (see the chapter on dissociative and somatoform disorders).

Factitious Disorders In factitious disorders, there is intentional feigning of physical or psychological symptoms. The individual with this disorder is motivated not by external incentives, such as economic gain or avoiding legal responsibility, but by a psychological need to assume the sick role.

Dissociative Disorders The essential feature of these disorders is a disturbance or alteration in memory, identity, or consciousness. The disturbance may be reflected in people who cannot remember who they are, who assume new identities, who have two or more distinct personalities, or who experience feelings of depersonalization in which the sense of reality is lost (see the chapter on dissociative and somatoform disorders).

Sexual and Gender Identity Disorders Two main groups of disturbances are included in sexual disorders: paraphilias and sexual dysfunctions. Paraphilias are characterized by intense sexual arousal and fantasies involving nonhuman objects, the suffering or humiliation of oneself or one's partner, or children or nonconsenting people. Paraphilias are considered disorders only if the person has acted on the fantasies or is markedly distressed by them. Sexual dysfunctions may involve inhibitions in sexual desires, inhibited orgasms, premature ejaculations among males, or recurrent pain during the process of sexual intercourse. In gender identity disorders, there is a strong cross-gender identification and a desire to be the other sex, coupled with a persistent discomfort with one's own sex (see the chapter on sexual and gender identity disorders).

Eating Disorders Included in this category are such disorders as refusal to maintain body weight above a minimally normal weight and binge eating and purging (that is, eating excessively and then intentionally vomiting; see the chapter on eating and sleep disorders).

Sleep Disorders The primary symptoms in these disorders involve sleeping difficulties: problems in initiating or maintaining sleep, excessive sleepiness, sleep disruptions, repeated awakening from sleep associated with extremely frightening nightmares, sleepwalking, and so on.

Impulse Control Disorders Not Elsewhere Classified A separate class of disorders involves the failure to resist an impulse or temptation to perform some act that is harmful to oneself or to others. Included are disorders involving loss of impulse control over aggression, stealing, gambling, setting fires, and pulling hair. Disorders of impulse control that are listed under other disorders (such as drug use or paraphilias) are not classified in this group of disorders (see the chapter on personality and impulse control disorders).

Adjustment Disorders These disorders are characterized by marked and excessive distress or significant impairment in social, occupational, or academic functioning because of a recent stressor. The symptoms do not meet the criteria for Axis I or II disorders and do not include bereavement.

Personality Disorders Whenever personality traits are inflexible and maladaptive and notably impair functioning or cause subjective distress, a diagnosis of personality disorder is likely. The patterns of these disorders are usually evident by adolescence. They typically involve odd or eccentric behaviors, excessive dramatic and emotional behaviors, or anxious and fearful behaviors (see the chapter on personality disorders and impulse control disorders).

Throughout DSM-IV-TR, there are categories entitled "Not Otherwise Specified." These categories are intended to include disorders that do not fully meet the criteria for a particular disorder. For example, a disorder that is cognitive in nature but that does not meet all of the criteria for delirium, demential, amnestic, or other specified cognitive disorders would be considered a "cognitive disorder, not otherwise specified." Furthermore, after each diagnosed disorder, clinicians can use specifiers that indicate severity and remission status. Severity is rated as mild, moderate, or severe, depending on the symptoms and degree of impairment. Remission refers to a disorder in which the full criteria for making the diagnosis were met at one time but in which the current symptoms or signs of the disorder are only partially apparent (partial remission) or no longer remain (full remission).

It should be noted that many individuals who have one mental disorder also suffer from another. For example, an individual who is diagnosed with depression may also have a second disorder such as substance abuse. **Comorbidity** refers to this co-occurrence of different disorders. One large-scale survey (Kessler et al., 1994) found that the rate of comorbidity is high—79 percent of those with one disorder also had another disorder. One possible explanation is that factors involved in one disorder, such as stress, may actually influence the development of other disorders (Krueger, Caspi, Moffitt, & Silva, 1998).

Figure 3.4 shows the prevalence rate (the percentage of the population with the disorder) of certain disorders, as determined by the largest epidemiologic investigation (the study of the rate and distribution of disorders) ever conducted in the United States (Robins, Locke, & Regier, 1991).

Finally, DSM-IV-TR emphasizes cross-cultural assessment issues far more than previous versions of DSM did. It has an introductory section that places diagnosis within a cultural context. It provides a description of pertinent culture, age, and gender features for each disorder, and it supplies guidelines for addressing the cultural background of the client and the context for evaluating the client. DSM-IV-TR also contains an outline of culture-bound syndromes, disorders unique to a particular cultural group. Table 3.3 describes some of these syndromes. Many culture-bound syndromes involve not only psychological symptoms but also bodily or somatic symptoms (Dana, 1998); this reflects the fact that the mind-body distinction prevalent in western societies is absent in many other societies (Dana, 1998).

These improvements make DSM-IV-TR far more culturally sensitive than were the previous editions. This trend might be taken even further by incorporating into DSM another axis that specifies the extent to which cultural factors influence the client's clinical condition (Draguns, 1996). With this addition, DSM and the assessment process could be a great deal more appropriate for clients from different cultural backgrounds.

Evaluation of the DSM Classification System

Continuing research is needed to monitor the reliability and validity of DSM-IV-TR in relation to different populations and to study the social and research consequences of its use. Because research findings helped shape DSM-IV-TR, reliability and validity are stronger than in the previous versions (Brown et al., 2001). In general, with the greater precision in specifying the criteria for making a diagnosis and with the increased role of research findings in defining disorders, reliability of diagnosis of disorders is higher in DSM-IV-TR than in earlier versions of DSM. However, increased reliability may not mean increased validity. As one critic (Sarbin, 1997) observes, sixteenth-century witch hunters developed explicit and reliable criteria (such as bodily abnormalities) for determining whether a person is a witch. Nevertheless, the diagnosis ("witch") had no validity.

Most objections to DSM have been about the system in general, and many are applicable to DSM-IV-TR. For example, some clinicians and researchers believe

FIGURE 3.4 Lifetime and One-Year Prevalence Rates for Mental Disorders, as Percentage of U.S. Population As this graph shows, anxiety, alcohol abuse, and depressive disorders are among the most common.

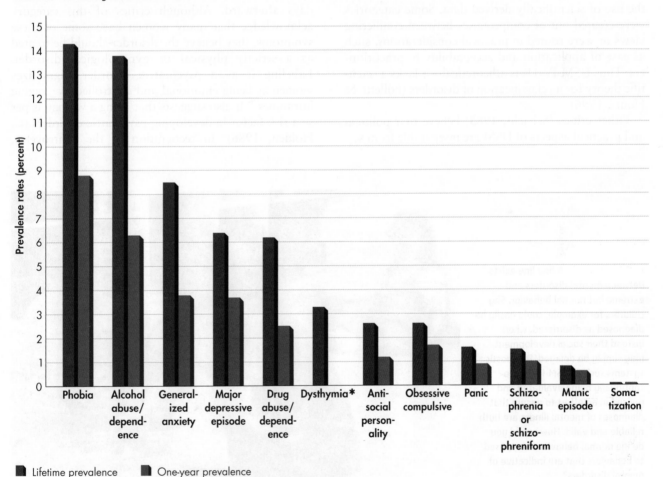

■ Lifetime prevalence ■ One-year prevalence

*One-year prevalence not ascertained.

Source: Data from Robins, Locke, & Regier (1991).

that DSM has a strong medical orientation, even though more than one-half of the disorders listed are not attributable to known or presumed organic causes and should not be considered biological in nature (Nelson-Gray, 1991; Schacht, 1985; Schacht & Nathan, 1977). Some psychologists see DSM's medical emphasis in part as a response to psychiatrists' need to define abnormality more strongly within their profession. A survey of psychotherapists who are psychologists rather than psychiatrists indicated little enthusiasm for DSM (D. Smith & Kraft, 1983). Most of those respondents rejected the notion that mental disorders form a subset of medical disorders. They preferred a social and interpersonal, rather than a medical, approach to mental disorder. However, no such alternative to DSM enjoys widespread use at present.

Other psychologists question the usefulness of the DSM classification scheme for research. One critique (Sarbin, 1997) observes that the procedures leading up to the development of DSM-IV-TR primarily involved committees negotiating the nomenclature rather than the use of scientifically derived data. Some categories were created out of compromises between conflicting views or were rooted in practical considerations, such as ease of application and acceptability to practitioners. Thus DSM-IV-TR is atheoretical—it lacks a scientific theory for its classification of disorders (Follette & Houts, 1996).

Other critics (Schacht, 1985) believe that political and practical aspects of DSM are inseparable from sci-

entific considerations. For example, certain diagnostic categories in DSM have been characterized as being sexist. In other words, specific behaviors sometimes seen among women may be inappropriately interpreted as signs of mental disorders (D. Franklin, 1987; M. Kaplan, 1983; see also the Critical Thinking feature in the chapter on personality and impulse control disorders). One example of this controversy is the continuing discussion of whether to establish premenstrual dysphoric disorder as a DSM diagnostic category. Premenstrual dysphoric disorder, many times associated with women experiencing premenstrual syndrome (PMS), has been a hotly debated category (Tavris, 1991). According to DSM-IV-TR, the symptoms include marked changes in mood, persistent anger, depression, or anxiety, often accompanied by complaints of breast tenderness and bodily aches. There is often an increase in interpersonal conflicts and a marked interference with work or social activities and relationships. These symptoms occur in a cyclical pattern a week before menses and remit a few days afterward. Although critics of this category acknowledge that many women have some of these symptoms, they believe the disorder should be treated as a strictly physical or gynecological disorder. Labeling it as a psychiatric disorder stigmatizes women as being emotional and controlled by "raging hormones." It also suggests that being a woman is per se a risk factor in developing psychiatric disorders (C. Holden, 1986). In recognition of the controversy,

The DSM-IV-TR A fine line exists between mental disorders and extreme but normal behavior. Shy children, for example, could easily be diagnosed as disordered, when instead their social development may simply be delayed. Diagnostic systems such as DSM-IV-TR are continually being evaluated and revised in an effort to ensure that diagnoses of mental illness are both reliable and valid. How would you define normal behavior as opposed to behaviors that are indicative of mental disorders?

DSM-IV-TR considers premenstrual dysphoric disorder to be a proposed condition requiring further study rather than a new disorder category.

Several other lines of criticism also have been made. One is that the study of the symptoms of a disorder is more valuable than research on diagnosed disorders because many patients may be misdiagnosed (Persons, 1986). By placing patients in diagnosed categories, important information regarding the severity of symptoms is lost. Another question is whether a diagnostic system that categorizes disorders is appropriate, or whether a model that views disorders on dimensions (that is, having more or less of certain characteristics) would be preferable (R. Carson, 1991). Others (Hayes, Wilson, Gifford, Follette, & Strosahl, 1996; Krueger et al., 1998) have also suggested that the mental health field develop a system in which disorders are viewed as continuous or dimensional in nature. There is evidence that in some disorders, such as depression, the distinction between major and less severe mood states is a matter of degree rather than kind (Ruscio & Ruscio, 2000). Taxometric analysis has emerged as a means of investigating whether a disorder is better conceptualized as being categorical or continuous. Through the use of statistical procedures in examining data on disorders to discover the data's structure, it is possible to confirm whether a disorder tends to be one or the other (Cole, 2004).

An attempt to clarify the intent of DSM and respond to its critics noted that the classification system was not intended to imply that all mental disorders have an organic basis (Millon, 1983). Rather, the important question is whether the DSM revised editions are a substantial improvement over past systems. Proponents of this position believe they are, and they argue that constructing a diagnostic classification system is an ongoing process, requiring continual revision and improvement. The limitations in the usefulness of DSM may therefore partly reflect holes in our knowledge of psychopathology (Goldman & Foreman, 1988).

DSM-IV-TR, like other classification systems, was constructed by people, and the philosophical and scientific orientation and cultural beliefs of the developers are important considerations. One can imagine that a group of individuals who believe that spiritual forces influence human behavior would devise a system completely different from DSM-IV-TR. Even within DSM-IV-TR, according to some critics, the psychopathology found in nonwestern societies may not be easily classified. This points once again to the need to continually attend to issues of cross-cultural usefulness (Frances et al., 1991).

The debates over the usefulness of the DSM system have been valuable in suggesting new research directions, increasing the role of research in developing the system, and stimulating the examination of conceptual, methodological, philosophical, and clinical assumptions in the classification of mental disorders. Future research, particularly research that examines the construct validity of DSM, is essential to evaluating the usefulness of the system.

Alternatives to DSM classification are available, such as Goldfried and Davison's (1976) behavioral classification scheme in which deviant behaviors are classified according to the variables that are maintaining the behaviors. For example, a child may learn to be physically aggressive while playing football and then bring such behavior into the classroom (inappropriate behavior). The inappropriate behavior is classified as a stimulus control problem. Stimulus control is defective because the behavior does not conform to the appropriate stimulus (the child should be physically nonaggressive in the classroom). The change of stimuli (playing field to classroom) fails to change the child's behavior. Because this classification scheme emphasizes the variables that maintain behavioral patterns, it lets the therapist isolate those variables for treatment purposes (Goldfried & Davison, 1976). The behavioral classification approach also tends to be superior to DSM in reliability and validity (Bellack & Hersen, 1980). However, DSM continues to be the dominant diagnostic system. Others have proposed different classification schemes that can supplement DSM-IV-TR. For example, Berenbaum, Raghavan, Le, Vernon, and Gomez (2003) have constructed a taxonomy of emotional disturbances. The taxonomy divides emotional disturbances (which cut across the spectrum of psychiatric disorders) into emotional valence disturbances, emotional intensity/regulation disturbances, and emotional disconnections. The type of emotional disturbance, sometimes neglected in DSM disorders, can be the target of treatment.

Objections to Classification and Labeling

Classification schemes can be of immense aid in categorizing disorders and in communicating information about them and conducting research on them. They have nevertheless been criticized on the grounds that classification schemes foster belief in an erroneous all-or-nothing quality of psychopathology. As we noted in the chapter on abnormal behavior, behaviors lie on a spectrum from normality to abnormality. To place a diagnostic label on someone categorizes that person as "abnormal" and implies that he or she is qualitatively different from normal. Many psychologists now perceive that, for many disorders, the differences between normal and abnormal are differences of degree, not of kind (Persons, 1986). Many good arguments can be made for using alternatives to a categorical system, such as scores indicating the degree to which symptoms and traits are characteristic of a person (Clarkin & Levy, 2004), particularly for those disorders found through taxometric analysis to be more continuous in nature.

In the chapter on abnormal behavior, we also touched on two problems that can arise when a diagnosis becomes a label. Here are four more:

1. *A label can predispose people to interpret all activities of the affected individual as pathological.* An excellent example of this occurred when a young psychology intern, training in the psychiatric ward of a VA hospital, talked very openly about his feeling of inadequacy. Most people have such feelings, but his openness gave him the reputation of being anxious. On the basis of this prejudgment and label, his supervisor became concerned about the young intern's competence and watched him very closely. One of the supervisor's chief complaints was that the intern's anxiety prevented him from acquiring sufficient information during interviews with patients. Frustrated by his inability to shake this impression from the supervisor's mind, the intern took copious notes on all his patients. When he was next scheduled to present a case to his supervisor, the young intern prepared thoroughly and memorized details of the patient's life. He displayed a remarkable knowledge of the patient's life history to his supervisor that day, but the supervisor's response was not at all what he expected. The supervisor felt that the intern's anxiety had caused him to become so compulsive in obtaining information from patients that he was not listening to their feelings! Thus a label or first impression can predispose the observer to distort even contradictory evidence to fit into the suggested frame of reference.

2. *A label may lead others to treat a person differently.* A study by Rosenthal and Jacobson (1968) showed that responses to a label can cause differential treatment. They tested schoolchildren and then randomly assigned them to either of two groups. Teachers were told that tests of one group indicated that they were potential intellectual "bloomers" (gaining in competence and maturity); the other group was not given this label. After a one-year interval, children from both groups were retested. Children identified as bloomers showed dramatic gains in IQ scores. How did this occur? Many have speculated that the label led teachers to have higher intellectual expectations for the bloomers and thus

The Risks of Labeling A number of problems can occur when a diagnosis is used more as a convenient label. For one thing, if others know about the diagnosis, they may see everything the individual does as due to the disorder.

She's being treated for melodrama.

to treat them differently. Even though there was no significant difference in IQ levels between the two groups to begin with, differences were present by the end of the year. The Rosenthal and Jacobson study has been criticized on the basis of its methodology and statistical analysis. Nevertheless, other studies have yielded similar results (Rappaport & Cleary, 1980).

3. *A label may lead those who are labeled to believe that they do indeed possess such characteristics.* Labels can become self-fulfilling prophecies. In the Rosenthal and Jacobson study just cited, the label not only caused teachers to behave differently but also may have affected the children. When people are constantly told that they are stupid or smart, they may come to believe such labels. It is reasonable to believe that people who ascribe certain stereotypical traits to a racial minority or an ethnic group will behave differently toward the group and will cause cognitive and behavioral changes among members of that group. Rosenhan (1973) showed how people labeled mentally ill can become trapped by this label. (Rosenhan's most renowned research study is discussed in the Mental Health and Society feature "Normal or Abnormal: The Consequences of Labeling.") The effect of labeling may be pronounced among children who are forming their self-identities and self-concepts. Reschly (1992) noted that labeling a child as mentally retarded is not only demeaning but also problematic. Many people believe that mental retardation is a biological anomaly, a permanent disability, and a gross intellectual handicap. Such beliefs and the accompanying reactions can have a profound effect on a child's self-image.

4. *A label may not provide the precise, functional information that is needed.* Today, many forms of managed care organizations (MCOs)—such as health maintenance organizations, preferred provider organizations, and others—are gaining popularity in the provision of health and mental health care (Pallack, 1995). MCOs are less concerned about classifying or labeling clients' mental disorders than about finding a more precise means of measuring client functioning. Given this trend, the assessment of functioning at work, home, school, and elsewhere may be of greater interest than the validity of the clinician's diagnosis of schizophrenia or another disorder.

MENTAL HEALTH AND SOCIETY
Normal or Abnormal: The Consequences of Labeling

Can "normal" people be diagnosed as disturbed? To find out, psychologist D. L. Rosenhan (1973) sent eight experimenters as pseudopatients to different psychiatric hospitals. Their assignment was first to simulate psychiatric symptoms to gain admission into psychiatric wards and, once there, to behave in a normal manner. Rosenhan wanted the pseudopatients to record their experiences as patients without hospital staff members becoming aware of the experiment.

Several interesting and provocative findings emerged. First, no one on the ward staff in the hospitals ever detected that the pseudopatients were normal—despite the fact that many patients suspected the pseudopatients were not abnormal but were merely "checking up on the hospital." In fact, the pseudopatients' length of hospitalization ranged from seven to fifty-two days. Second, nearly all pseudopatients were initially diagnosed as schizophrenic. And many of their normal behaviors on the ward were subsequently interpreted as manifestations of schizophrenia; one example was "excessive note-taking." Third, the staff failed to interact much with patients, who were treated as powerless, irresponsible individuals.

Rosenhan concluded that it is difficult to distinguish normal and disturbed behaviors in persons in mental hospitals, that the labels applied to patients often outlive their usefulness, and that the hospital environment is harsh and frequently maintains maladaptive behaviors. His study has generated a great deal of controversy (Millon, 1975; B. Weiner, 1975). One critic argued that, because patients did report abnormal symptoms at the time of hospital admission, it is understandable that they were hospitalized (Spitzer, 1975). And, although the pseudopatients were not detected by the staff, they were all released within sixty days. All were said to be "in remission."

Of course, over the past thirty years, improvements have been made in our assessment procedures and hospitalization practices. Rosenhan's study served as a stimulus to examine and reform such practices.

SUMMARY

In attempting to make an accurate evaluation or assessment of a person's mental health, what kinds of standards must tests or evaluation procedures meet?

■ Assessment and classification of disorders are essential in the mental health field.

■ In developing assessment tools and useful classification schemes, researchers and clinicians have been concerned with issues regarding:
  • reliability (the degree to which a procedure or test yields the same results repeatedly, under the same circumstances)
  • validity (the extent to which a test or procedure actually performs the function it was designed to perform).

What kinds of tools do clinicians employ in evaluating the mental health of people?

■ Clinicians primarily use four methods of assessment: observations, interviews, psychological tests and inventories, and neurological tests.

■ Observations of external signs and expressive behaviors are often made during an interview and can have diagnostic significance.

■ Interviews, the oldest form of psychological assessment, involve a face-to-face conversation, after which the interviewer differentially weighs and interprets verbal information obtained from the interviewee.

■ Psychological tests and inventories provide a more formalized means of obtaining information.

■ Most testing situations share two characteristics: a standard situation in which certain responses are elicited and the measurement and use of the responses to infer underlying traits.

■ In personality testing, projective techniques, in which the stimuli are ambiguous, or self-report inventories, in which the stimuli are much more structured, may be used.

■ Two of the most widely used projective techniques are the Rorschach inkblot technique and the Thematic Apperception Test (TAT).

■ Unlike projective tests, self-report personality inventories, such as the MMPI-2, supply the test taker with a list of alternatives from which to select an answer. Intelligence tests can be used to obtain an estimate of a person's current level of cognitive functioning and to assess intellectual deterioration.

■ Behavioral observations of how a person takes the test are additional sources of information about personality attributes.

■ The WAIS, Stanford-Binet, and Bender-Gestalt tests can be used to assess brain damage. The Halstead-Reitan and Luria-Nebraska test batteries specifically assess brain dysfunction.

■ Neurological medical procedures, including x-rays, CAT and PET scans, EEG, and MRI, have added highly important and sophisticated means to detect brain damage.

How are mental health problems categorized or classified?

■ The first edition of DSM was based to a large extent on the biological model of mental illness and assumed that people who were classified in a psychodiagnostic category would show similar symptoms that stem from a common cause, that should be treated in a certain manner, that would respond similarly, and that would have similar prognoses. Critics questioned the reliability and validity of earlier versions of DSM.

■ The current DSM-IV-TR contains detailed diagnostic criteria; research findings and expert judgments were used to help construct this latest version. As a result, its reliability appears to be higher than that of the previous manuals. Furthermore, data are collected on five axes so that much more information about the patient is systematically examined.

■ General objections to classification are based primarily on the problems involved in labeling and the loss of information about a person when that person is labeled or categorized.

■ A number of ethical questions have been raised about classifying and assessing people through tests. These include questions about confidentiality, privacy, and cultural bias. Concerned with these issues, psychologists have sought to improve classification and assessment procedures and to define the appropriate conditions for testing and diagnosis. In spite of the problems and criticisms, classification and assessment are necessary to psychological research and practice.

KEY TERMS

assessment (p. 74)

classification system (p. 89)

comorbidity (p. 96)

etiology (p. 90)

organicity (p. 85)

prognosis (p. 92)

projective personality test (p. 78)

psychological test and inventory (p. 77)

psychometrics (p. 82)

reactivity (p. 76)

reliability (p. 73)

self-report inventory (p. 80)

validity (p. 74)

MULTIMEDIA PREVIEW

For additional study aids, we invite you to explore our media resources accompanying *Understanding Abnormal Behavior,* Eighth Edition. The Student CD-ROM includes videos, quizzing, and critical thinking activities that help to reinforce key concepts in a fun and engaging manner. The Student Web Site provides additional interactive activities, chapter outlines, and research links that further support and complement the text. All Web resources may be accessed by logging onto the Web site at **http://psychology.college.hmco.com/students**.

CHAPTER 4
The Scientific Method in Abnormal Psychology

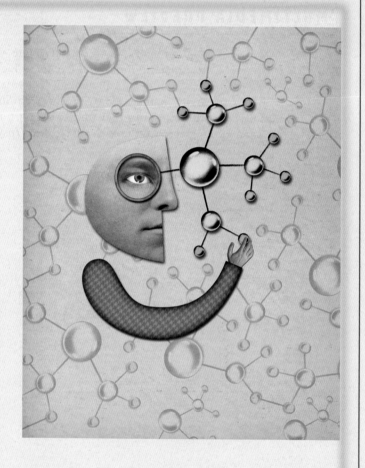

- Should the scientific method be used to evaluate psychotherapy?

- How does the experimental design differ from other ways of investigating phenomena?

- Child sexual abuse is relatively common and is correlated with a number of disorders and symptoms. Why can we not consider it the causal factor of these disorders?

- Can experimental findings obtained from college students with subclinical fears be applied to individuals with phobias?

- If you were using a field study, what would you investigate in the aftermath of a tragedy such as the terrorist attack on the World Trade Center or the devastation produced by the tsunami in Indonesia and other countries?

- How can you determine a cause-and-effect relationship when using only one participant?

- What are some of the advantages and shortcomings of the biological approach in abnormal psychology?

- Obtaining the prevalence rate of mental disorders is important. Why do some surveys show large discrepancies in the rates for disorders?

- Is it ethical to withhold treatment from mentally ill individuals because they are part of the control group?

The process involves "noninvasive touch on the head, chest, arms, legs, and feet, with varying extents of health-related conversation, for approximately 40 minutes—usually while the subject lies comfortably on a treatment bed. (Weze, Leathard, Grange, & Stevens, 2004)

Healing by a "gentle touch" is thought to restore and energize the human energy fields that surround the body. It is an alternative therapy that has been used to reduce anxiety in psychiatric patients and discomfort in oncology patients (Cook, Guerrerio, & Slater, 2004). In one study, the use of the "gentle touch" on seventy-six individuals with musculoskeletal disorders resulted in a significant reduction on self-report measures of stress, pain, anxiety, depression, and disability (Weze, Leathard, & Stevens, 2004). However, concerns have been expressed regarding the findings of this study (Ernst, 2004). Specifically, Ernst

argued that the relief reported by the patients could be due to placebo effects, as studies have found that "pain sufferer's response to sham healing is indistinguishable to 'real' healing of a similar type" (p. 1074). In addition, he argues that controversial processes such as spiritual healing should be examined using clinical trials that meet the standards of "scientific rigor."

According to Ernst, patients' responses on the self-report questionnaires that indicate improvement could also be due to demand characteristics (responding in a manner to please the researcher) or because the people administering the touch were "kind and empathetic." These criticisms lead to intriguing possibilities regarding the interpretation of the findings. First, are there genuine reductions in anxiety and pain that are due to the placebo effect or to some other factor? For some disorders, such as depression, placebos have been found to produce changes in regional metabolic rates in the same parts of the brain that are associated with the effects of antidepressant medications (Mayberg et al., 2002). It is possible, therefore, that the "gentle touch" therapy does produce actual therapeutic changes but as a placebo or because of relief obtained due to physical comfort from "kind and empathetic" individuals. Second, it is possible that no actual improvement in the symptoms occurred but that the patients were responding to demand characteristics and reported feeling better to please the therapist. How could a researcher determine whether these factors are responsible for the patient's responses? Third, if genuine positive changes have occurred with "gentle touch" therapy, is there a way of determining whether they are due to the restoration of the "human energy field" or the other possibilities listed? As you can see, when opinions differ on clinical or research findings, the scientific method can offer important insights.

Scientists are often described as skeptics. Rather than accept the conclusions from a single study, scientists demand that the results be *replicated,* or repeated by other researchers. Replication lessens the chance that the findings were due to experimenter bias, methodological flaws, or sampling errors. The following list gives some examples of findings that were initially reported as "conclusive" by the mass media and describes their current status after further investigation:

■ The majority of sexually abused children exhibit signs or symptoms of trauma that can be reliably detected by experienced mental health experts in the child sexual abuse field. *Status:* There are no signs or symptoms that characterize the majority of abused children; a significant number appear to be asymptomatic (Hagen, 2003).

■ Traumatic memories are fixed and indelible. *Status:* Fifty-nine veterans of Operation Desert Storm were interviewed about highly traumatic combat events twenty-six months after their return from the Gulf War. Nearly 90 percent exhibited inconsistent recall. The greater the symptoms of posttraumatic stress disorder, the greater the inaccuracies were (Southwick, Morgan, Nicolaou, & Charney 1997).

■ A specific gene, the A1 allele of DRD2, plays a key role in alcoholism. *Status:* Subsequent research (Comings et al., 1991; Gelernter et al., 1991) found that the gene is present in fewer than 50 percent of people with alcoholism and that the gene was found in individuals with other disorders and in individuals who did not have drinking problems. The gene is neither sufficient nor necessary for the development of alcoholism.

■ Early trials have shown a computer test based on brain scans for blood flow characteristics to be 100 percent accurate in identifying patients with schizophrenia. *Status:* Needs replication. As one researcher, Robin Murray, points out, "Nobody has ever found a specific brain abnormality that all schizophrenics have that nobody else has" (Press Association, 2001).

■ Hyperactivity in children is due to reactions to specific food groups or food additives. *Status:* Probably not supported (Eigenmann & Haenggeli, 2004). In general, experimental studies using biological challenge or double-blind methods (described later in this chapter) have reported no change in behavior as a result of food or additives.

■ An individual's attitude or personality can influence both the development and course of diseases such as cancer. *Status:* Unresolved. Little evidence exists that attitude or personality influences the development of cancer.

■ Specific negative family communication patterns may be responsible for the development of schizophrenia. *Status:* Little support exists for this view, although a negative family environment might be associated with relapses and increased stress for a number of disorders.

■ Childhood sexual abuse is a major causal factor in the development of eating disorders. *Status:* Still controversial. When methodological problems are controlled for, there is little support for this position (Conners & Morse, 1993; H. Pope & Hudson, 1992; H. Pope, Mangweth, Negrao, Hudson, & Cordas, 1994).

As you can see, the search for "truth" is often a long journey. Answers to the causes of abnormal behavior have come and gone. In this chapter, we discuss the components of the scientific method. Understanding different research designs and their shortcomings is necessary to be able to critically evaluate reported findings in abnormal psychology.

The Scientific Method in Clinical Research

A videotape segment showed a seventy-minute session in which a ten-year-old girl was begging for her life. Candace had been wrapped in a blanket and surrounded with pillows pressing against her by four adults. She was undergoing "rebirthing therapy." Candace was purportedly diagnosed with a reactive attachment disorder, a condition that prevents the formation of loving relationships. The purpose of the therapy was to enable Candace to be "reborn" and to be able to bond with her adoptive mother. The session involved the simulation of birth, in which the blanket represented the womb. On the tape, Candace complains about not being able to breathe. After being unwrapped, Candace wasn't breathing and had no pulse. The cause of death was suffocation (Kohler, 2001). The two therapists, Julie Ponder and Connell Watkins, were convicted of reckless child abuse. The governor of Colorado signed a law outlawing rebirthing therapy. (Associated Press, 2001)

Hundreds of different forms of psychotherapies exist. Should the scientific method be employed to evaluate their effectiveness and safety or as a means to certify "empirically supported treatments" (Waehler, Kalodner, Wampold, & Lichtenberg, 2000)? As Perez (1999, p. 206) argues, "We must decide if we want to foster an environment in which clinicians can practice whatever they want, even in the absence of scientific evidence that what they practice actually works. Conversely, we may choose to protect the rights of clients to receive the most effective treatments available." Before employing a therapy such as rebirthing, should we know whether it has received any validation trials? What do you see as the advantages and disad-

vantages of requiring some type of experimental support for the different therapies?

The **scientific method** is a method of inquiry that provides for the systematic collection of data through controlled observation and for the testing of hypotheses. A **hypothesis** is a conjectural statement that usually describes a relationship between two variables. Different theories may result in different hypotheses for the same phenomenon. A **theory** is a group of principles and hypotheses that together explain some aspect of a particular area of inquiry. For example, hypothesized reasons for eating disorders have included biological or neurochemical causes, fear of sexual maturity, societal demands for thinness in women, and pathological family relationships. Each of these hypotheses reflects a different theory.

Characteristics of Clinical Research

Clinical research can proceed only when the relationship expressed in a hypothesis is clearly and systematically stated and when the variables of concern are measurable and defined. We need to define clearly what we are studying and make sure that the variables are measured with reliable and valid instruments. Clinical research relies on these characteristics of the scientific method—the potential for self-correction, the hypothesizing of relationships, the use of operational

Controlled Observation The systematic collection of data through controlled observations is the hallmark of the scientific method. Although this child's behavior can be precisely measured and recorded in a laboratory setting, how likely is he to behave in a similar manner in school or at home?

MENTAL HEALTH AND SOCIETY

Antidepressant Medication and Suicide in Children: Attack on Scientific Integrity?

Dr. Andrew Mosholder, an FDA medical reviewer, stated that he had been pressured to alter and hide information on a document submitted to congressional investigators concerning the possible link between antidepressant use and suicide in children (Richwine, 2004b).

An internal GlaxoSmithKline (a pharmaceutical company) memo concerning a study of paroxetine (an antidepressant) use in children stated, "It would be unacceptable to include a statement that efficacy had not been demonstrated, as this would undermine the profile of paroxetine" (Anonymous, 2004, p. 1335).

Dr. Gregory D. Curfman, who is the executive editor of the *New England Journal of Medicine,* states, "We know that some clinical trials, especially those with results unfavorable to drug companies, are never published" (Barclay, 2004, p.1).

The scientific method requires that researchers be committed to the search for truth and to remain objective in the study of phenomena. When we allow personal beliefs, values, political position, or conflicts of interest to influence our interpretation of data, our scientific integrity is threatened. The dependence on research for making informed decisions necessitates that scientists hold and maintain high ethical standards. Unfortunately, when financial considerations intersect with science, research can become the tool of the interested party rather than a mechanism to promote the welfare of society. In the case of some antidepressant medications and their effects on children, "The story of research into selective serotonin reuptake inhibitors (SSRIs) is one of confusion, manipulation, and institutional failure. Although published

research evidence was inconsistent at best, use of SSRIs to treat childhood depression has been encouraged by pharmaceutical companies and clinicians worldwide" (Anonymous, 2004, p. 1334). This assessment was published in the medical journal *The Lancet.* Because there is little evidence on the effectiveness of antidepressant medications with children, the UK Committee on Safety of Medicines prohibited the treatment of childhood depression with any SSRI except fluoxetine in 2003.

Questions have been raised about why the Food and Drug Administration (FDA) in this country has been so slow to act. Research evidence on the effectiveness of antidepressants with children and adolescents has been equivocal at best, but continued use of these medications has been recommended by psychiatrists, mental health professionals, and pharmaceutical

---

definitions, the consideration of reliability and validity, and the acknowledgment of base rates.

Potential for Self-Correction   Perhaps the unique and most general characteristic of the scientific method is its *potential for self-correction.* Under ideal conditions, data and conclusions are freely exchanged and experiments are replicable (reproducible), so that all are subject to discussion, testing, verification, and modification. The knowledge developed under these conditions is as free as possible from the scientist's personal beliefs, perceptions, biases, values, attitudes, and emotions. When a researcher does not follow this guideline, ethical concerns can arise (see the Mental Health and Society feature "Antidepressant Medication and Suicide in Children: Attack on Scientific Integrity?").

Hypothesizing Relationships   Another characteristic of the scientific method is that it attempts to identify and explain (hypothesize) the relationship

between variables. Examples of hypotheses are statements such as: "Some seasonal forms of depression may be due to decreases in light," "Autism [a severe disorder beginning in childhood] is a result of poor parenting," and "Eating disorders are a result of specific family interaction patterns."

Operational Definitions   Operational definitions are definitions of the variables that are being studied. For example, an operational definition of depression could be (1) a score representing some pattern of responses to a self-report questionnaire on a depression inventory, (2) a rating assigned by an observer using a depression checklist, or (3) a laboratory identification of specific neurochemical changes. Operational definitions are important because they force an experimenter to clearly define what he or she means by the variable. This allows others to agree or disagree with the way the variable was defined. When operational definitions of a phenomenon differ, comparing research is problematic, and conclusions can be faulty.

companies. Part of the problem is the vested interest that researchers often have in the drug companies themselves. Research funding by pharmaceutical companies rose from $1.5 billion to $22 billion between 1980 and 2001 (Warner & Roberts, 2004). Equally problematic is the substantial percentage of researchers in academic medical centers who have financial interests in or receive funding from for-profit companies. This percentage is increasing (Warner & Roberts, 2004). These ties with pharmaceutical companies can produce a conflict of interest that threatens scientific integrity. Researchers may be less likely to report findings that are considered unfavorable to their source of funding. In some cases, the publication of data is subject to the approval of the funding source. There is suspicion that research findings unfavorable to "interested parties" are not being published.

Whittington and colleagues (2004) performed a meta-analysis of published and unpublished studies on the effectiveness of SSRIs for children. In published studies, although there appeared to be little meaningful reduction of depressive symptoms with SSRIs (with the possible exception of fluoxetine), a favorable risk-benefit profile was found—that is, suicide ideation or attempts were extremely low, and there was a slight benefit with the SSRIs. However, when unpublished studies were factored in, sertraline, citalopram, and venlafaxine were considered to have "unfavorable risk-benefit profiles" in that there was little evidence of efficacy for these SSRIs and a small increased risk of suicidal ideation or suicide attempts. The different findings between published and unpublished research has led to requests that the results of all research trials be posted and the results published in a registry that is available to researchers (Lundberg, 2004). This position is supported by international medical organizations and, in the United States, by the *New England Journal of Medicine* and the *Journal of the American Medical Association* (JAMA).

The U.S. Food and Drug Administration Advisory Panel, which reviewed the evidence concerning antidepressant use in children, suggested the use of a black box warning on the drug label of these medications (Richwine, 2004a). On October 15, 2004, the FDA indicated that all antidepressants must now carry a black box warning, which is the strongest safety alert, linking its use in children and teenagers with increases in suicidal thoughts and behavior. However, questions remain regarding means of minimizing the influence on research by conflicts of interest. With researchers receiving funding from, and even sitting on the board of directors of, pharmaceutical companies, how can the interests of society in general be promoted and scientific integrity be maintained?

Let us consider the recent studies or reports linking child sexual abuse with panic disorder, phobias, depression, alcohol and substance abuse, multiple personality and dissociative disorders, and bulimia and anorexia nervosa (Briere, 1992; Pribor & Dinwiddie, 1992; Terr, 1991). Unfortunately, these studies employ different operational definitions (Haugaard, 2000). Consider the following different definitions of *child sexual abuse:*

■ Any sexual activity, overt or covert, between a child and an adult (or older child), where the younger child's participation is obtained through seduction or coercion. (Ratican, 1992, p. 33)

■ Any self-reported contact—ranging from fondling to sexual intercourse—experienced by a patient on or before age 18 and initiated by someone 5 or more years senior or by a family member at least 2 years senior. (Brown & Anderson, 1991, p. 56)

Other definitions of child sexual abuse include "any unwanted sexual experience before 14," "any attempted or completed rape before 18 years," and "contact between someone under 15 and another person 5 years older" (Briere, 1992, p. 198). The use of so many different definitions of child sexual abuse makes any general conclusions difficult (Mallinckrodt, McCreary, & Robertson, 1995; H. Pope et al., 1994; Rind, Tromovitch, & Bauserman, 1998).

Operational definitions need to be clear and precise. How should "any unwanted sexual experience before 14" be interpreted? What behaviors can this definition include? It is no wonder that the reported rate of sexual abuse in different studies ranges from 6 to 62 percent for females and from 3 to 31 percent for males (Watkins & Bentovim, 1992). In evaluating or comparing research, the operational definition of the phenomenon must be considered.

Reliability and Validity of Measures and Observations The scientific method requires that the measures we use be reliable or consistent.

CRITICAL THINKING

Repressed Memories—Issues and Questions

Patricia Burgus claimed that during treatment, which included hypnosis and hypnotic drugs, therapists had induced recovered memories of her participation in a cannibalistic satanic cult and of her having sexually abused her two sons (Ewing, 1998). Burgus's memories were later discovered to be false and were attributed to suggestions and techniques used by the therapists. She was awarded $10.6 million in damages.

According to one survey (Golding, Sanchez, & Sego, 1996), 13 percent of undergraduates (14 percent of women and 9 percent of men) report having recovered *repressed memories* (memories of traumatic events forced from consciousness). Although college students express some degree of belief in repressed memories, they also believe that these memories can be implanted by therapists. Furthermore, gender differences are evident in the findings: Males are more likely to have doubts about repressed memories than are females.

The controversy over the existence of "repressed memory" is especially pronounced between experimental psychologists and clinicians (clinical psychologists and social workers). In one study, only 34 percent of the experimental psychologists reported that they believed in the validity of the phenomenon, compared with over 60 percent of the clinicians (Dammeyer, Nightingale, & McCoy, 1997). The study also revealed some differences among the clinicians themselves. Those with psychoanalytic, psychodynamic, or eclectic orientations believed more strongly in repressed memories than did those with cognitive orientations. And the clinicians believed that some therapeutic techniques could lead to false memories. The techniques they identified as the most problematic were trance work (behaviors performed under an altered state of consciousness induced by hypnosis or drugs), body memories, hypnotic age regression, coercive group therapy, and trance writings (Knapp & VandeCreek, 1996). Drugs such as sodium amytal ("truth serum"), barbiturates, and other medications have also been used as memory-recovery techniques. Like hypnosis, these drugs increase clients' suggestibility (Stocks, 1998).

The case of Patricia Burgus points out several important issues. First, if she was never a part of a satanic cult, how did she come to believe this? Under what kinds of conditions are clients susceptible to the acceptance of false memories? Second, what did the therapist do to produce these false memories? A number of therapists use techniques such as hypnosis, age regression, body memories, and trance states with their clients. Should these techniques be regulated? Should a therapist be held liable if procedures he or she uses are found to have resulted in false memories? Third, cases of genuine recovered memory have also been reported or have received external verification. How can therapists determine whether a memory is true or inaccurate? Should they be involved in determining the veracity of clients' memories? Fourth, females are more likely to believe in the accuracy of recovered memories than are males. What might account for this gender difference?

Reliability refers to the degree to which a measure or procedure will yield the same results repeatedly (see the chapter on assessment and classification of abnormal behavior). Consider, for example, an individual who has been diagnosed, by means of a questionnaire, as having an antisocial personality. If the questionnaire is reliable, the individual should receive the same diagnosis after taking the questionnaire again. Results must be consistent if we are to have any faith in them. Diagnostic reliability is low for many of the childhood disorders and for some of the personality disorders.

Even if consistent results are obtained, questions can arise over the *validity* of a measure (see the chapter on assessment and classification of abnormal behavior). Does the testing instrument really measure what it was developed to measure? If we claim to have developed a

test that identifies multiple personality disorder, we have to demonstrate that it can accomplish this task. Many of the clinical tests used in studies have not been evaluated to determine their validity. We return to this topic later in this chapter. See the Critical Thinking feature "Repressed Memories—Issues and Questions" for a look at just one construct—repressed memories—whose validity is considered highly controversial.

Base Rates   A **base rate** is the rate of natural occurrence of a phenomenon in the population studied. When the base rate is not known or considered, research findings can be misinterpreted. For example, both unwanted sexual events and eating problems are reported by a high percentage of females (Conners & Morse, 1993; H. Pope & Hudson, 1992). As a result, clinicians may find that the majority of individuals treated for eating problems report a history of sexual abuse. An investigator, not recognizing that these are both high-frequency behaviors (high base rates), may mistakenly conclude that one is the cause of the other.

Base rate data is helpful in interpreting phenomenon such as sexual behaviors in children. Is the presence of "sexualized" behaviors a sign of sexual abuse or a normative type of behavior? Specific sexual behavior in 1,114 children between the ages of two and twelve were rated by primary caregivers (see Table 4.1). A broad range of sexual behaviors was reported in children who had not been sexually abused. As the researchers state, "Simply because a 5-year-old boy touches his genitals occasionally, even after a weekend visit with his noncustodial parent, it does not mean he

has been sexually abused. Rather, it is a behavior that is seen in nearly two-thirds of boys at that age" (Friedrich, Fisher, Broughton, Houston, & Shafran, 1998, p. 8). Base rate data allow the identification of sexual behaviors that are unusual or rare for the gender or age of the child. For example, behaviors such as "tries to have sexual intercourse," "puts mouth on sex parts," "puts objects in vagina/rectum," and "asks others to do sex acts" were reported only infrequently. Base rate data, however, provide only a context in which to evaluate behavior. Whether "normative" or low-percentage sexual behaviors are due to abuse must be determined in each case.

The importance of base rates in clinical research can be seen in the responses of a control group to a psychotic-traits questionnaire. Persons with severe mental disorders

TABLE 4. 1 Reported Sexual Behaviors in Children

Age	Behavior	% Endorsed	
		Boys	**Girls**
Children (2–5 years)	Touches sex parts in public	26.5	15.1
	Masturbates with hand	16.7	15.8
	Touches breasts	42.0	43.7
	Masturbates with toy/object	3.5	6.0
	Touches sex part at home	60.2	43.8
	Shows sex part to adults	15.4	13.8
	Hugs adults not well known	15.4	12.8
	Touches other child's sex parts	4.6	8.8
Children (6–9 years)	Touches sex parts in public	13.8	6.5
	Masturbates with hand	12.8	5.3
	Touches breasts	14.3	15.9
	Masturbates with toy/object	2.7	2.9
	Touches sex part at home	39.8	20.7
	Shows sex part to adults	6.4	5.4
	Hugs adults not well known	3.7	6.6
	Touches other child's sex parts	8.0	1.2
Children (10–12 years)	Touches sex parts in public	1.2	2.2
	Masturbates with hand	3.7	5.3
	Touches breasts	1.2	1.1
	Masturbates with toy/object	1.2	4.3
	Touches sex part at home	8.7	11.6
	Shows sex part to adult	2.5	2.2
	Hugs adults not well known	0.0	4.3
	Touches other child's sex parts	1.2	1.1

Source: Friedrich et al. (1998).

are believed to have "unusual" thoughts or reactions. On a psychotic-traits questionnaire, however, a large percentage of a control group gave positive answers to the questions in Figure 4.1. Although individuals with schizophrenia are twice as likely as normal persons to endorse such statements (M. Jackson & Claridge, 1991), "normal" individuals in control groups also report disturbing thoughts and urges, "paranoid ideation," and "magical thinking." That an individual or client reports having odd or bizarre thoughts of sex or being bothered by the feeling of being watched may therefore not be indicative of a disorder.

Statistical Versus Clinical Significance The scientific method also requires that research findings be evaluated in terms of their *statistical significance*—the likelihood that the relationship could be due to chance alone. Even a statistically significant finding may have little practical significance in a clinical setting, however. For example, various articles based on a study by Phillips, Van Voorhees, and Ruth (1992) have stated that women are more likely to die the week after their birthdays than in any other week of the year. This find-

ing seemed to show that psychological factors have a powerful effect on biological processes. The study involved 2,745,149 persons, and the findings were statistically significant (not due to chance). The number of deaths for the weeks after the birthdays, however, was only 3.03 percent higher than would be expected in any other week. Thus psychological factors associated with deaths and birthdays, although statistically significant, play a relatively small role in deaths among women. When evaluating research, you must determine whether the statistical significance reported is really "clinically" significant. This problem is most likely to occur in studies with large sample sizes.

Experiments

The **experiment** is perhaps the best tool for testing cause-and-effect relationships. In its simplest form, the experiment involves the following:

1. An **experimental hypothesis,** which is the prediction concerning how an independent variable affects a dependent variable in an experiment

2. An **independent variable** (the possible cause), which the experimenter manipulates to determine its effect on a dependent variable

3. A **dependent variable** that is expected to change as a result of changes in the independent variable

As we noted, the experimenter is also concerned about controlling extraneous or *confounding variables* (factors other than the independent variable that may affect the dependent variable). For example, expectancies of both the research participants and the researchers may influence the outcome of a study. Participants in a study may try to "help" the researcher succeed and, in so doing, may nullify the results of the study (T. Anderson & Strupp, 1996). If the experimenter is effective in eliminating confounding variables in a study, the study has high **internal validity.** That is, we can be relatively certain that changes in the dependent variable are due only to the independent variable.

The experimenter is also interested in **external validity.** This refers to whether the findings in a particular study can be generalized to other groups or conditions. Let us clarify these concepts by examining an actual research study.

FIGURE 4.1 Responses to Psychotic-Traits Questionnaire This figure shows the percentage of "normal" individuals endorsing items on a questionnaire used to identify psychotic thinking and beliefs.

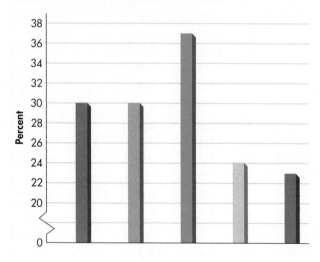

■ Bothered by the feeling that others are watching you

■ Thought that people were talking when it was only a noise

■ Believed that you were communicating with others through telepathy

▨ Felt urge to injure yourself

■ Have odd and bizarre thoughts about sex

Source: Data from M. Jackson & Claridge (1991).

Melinda N. was a nineteen-year-old sophomore who sought help from a university psychology clinic for dental phobia. Her strong fear of dentists began when she was about twelve years old. It was suggested to her that she might have a low pain threshold or had experienced some type of traumatic incident during dental work. Melinda had several cavities that were painful, so she decided to see if the counselor could offer her some help. Because she had an appointment to see the dentist the following week, Melinda wanted something that could work quickly. The therapist had heard that an antianxiety medication, benzodiazepine, and psychological methods (relaxation training and changing thoughts about the procedure) were both successful in treating this disorder. Before deciding which treatment to use, the therapist searched the research literature to determine whether studies had compared the effectiveness of these approaches.

A study by Thom, Sartory, and Johren (2000) seemed to provide some direction. In that study, fifty dental-phobic patients were assigned to either a psychological treatment, a medication (benzodiazepine), or a no-treatment group. Of the patients, forty-one needed a tooth extraction, and the others required endodontic work. The psychological treatment took only one session and involved stress management training (relaxation exercises, visualization of dental work, and the identification and use of coping thoughts). The exercises were to be performed daily for a period of one week. Those in the medication group received a benzodiazepine (midazolam hydromaleate) thirty minutes before the dental procedure. Those in the control condition were told that their surgeon specialized in patients with dental anxiety and would treat them carefully.

The Experimental Group

An *experimental group* is the group that is subjected to the independent variable. In their study, Thom and her colleagues (2000) created two experimental groups: one exposed to stress management training and imaginal exposure to dental scenes for a single session and the other provided with medication before dental work. The psychological treatment included cognitive, relaxation, and breathing training, which the patients were to practice daily for one week.

Because the investigators were interested in how treatment affects level of anxiety and reports of panic attacks, the dependent variables were measured in several ways. Pre- and posttreatment measures were obtained for dental fear, as well as subjective ratings for pain during the procedure. The investigators also tabulated how many of the patients completed dental treatment with further appointments.

The Control Group

If the participants in the two experimental groups in the study by Thom and her colleagues (2000) showed a

reduction of anxiety on the outcome measures from pretesting to posttesting, could the researchers conclude that the treatments were effective forms of therapy? The answer would be no. The patients may have shown less anxiety about dental procedures merely as a result of the passage of time or as a function of completing the assessment measures. The use of a control group enables researchers to eliminate such possibilities.

A *control group* is a group that is similar in every way to the experimental group except for the manipulation of the independent variable. In the study by Thom and her colleagues (2000), the control group also took the pretest measures, received dental work, and took the posttest measures. The participants did not receive any of the experimental treatments. Because of this we can be more certain that any differences found between the control and experimental groups were due to the treatments. The findings revealed that the groups treated with either stress management or benzodiazepine had significantly larger reductions on the Dental Fear Scale and Pain Scale than the control group. However, those treated with benzodiazepine showed a relapse following dental surgery while those in the stress management condition showed further improvement and continued treatment. Of those who completed additional dental procedures, 70 percent had been in the stress management group, 20 percent in the benzodiazepine group, and 10 percent in the control group. Given these findings, the therapist might tell Melinda that both treatments can reduce her dental fear but that stress management might offer a more long-term solution.

Myth vs Reality

Myth: Increasing controls over an experiment always results in greater generalizability of the findings.

Reality: Although a tightly controlled study increases internal validity, problems can occur with external validity—that is, the findings may not be generalizable to other populations since the conditions existing in an experimental setting may not resemble those found in real-life situations. Both internal and external validity have to be considered when designing a study.

The Placebo Group

You should note that the results of the experiment may also be challenged for another reason. For example, what if the participants in the treated experimental groups improved not because of the treatment but because they had faith or an expectancy that they would improve? Some researchers have found that if participants expect to improve from treatment, this expectancy—rather than specific treatment—is responsible for the outcome.

One method by which to induce an expectancy in students without using the specific treatment is to include a placebo control group. The study by Thom and her colleagues (2000) could have included a condition in which participants would be told that they were being provided with a medication for dental anxiety but were actually given an inert drug (a placebo) that could have no chemical impact on their anxiety. A plausible psychological placebo condition (one that the experimenter believes should not reduce dental fear) could also be developed. If the therapy groups improved more than the placebo control group, then one could be more confident that therapy, rather than expectancy, was responsible for the results.

Additional Concerns in Clinical Research

Although researchers hope to control expectations of outcome through the use of a placebo control group, two types of problems can occur. First, the placebo control group may also report significant improvements. In one study of a group of fifty patients with mild depression, all reported that they were "much or very much" improved after taking a placebo (Rabkin et al., 1990). This finding would make it difficult to separate treatment from expectancy effects. Second, participants may "guess" correctly that they are receiving a placebo, thereby reducing any expectancy effects.

Experimenter or participant expectations can also influence diagnosis and the outcome of a study. When parents are aware that food additives are either removed or added to the diets of children, they often report a link between the additives and hyperactive behavior (Kurdyak, 2004). In genetic studies, interviews or diagnoses are often made with the patients' relatives to determine whether they have the same or related disorders. When clinicians are aware that they are interviewing the patient's relatives, they report higher rates of psychopathology than when they are not aware of the family connections (Gottesman & Shields, 1982). To control for experimenter expectations, the researcher may use a *blind design,* in which the clinicians doing the interviewing are not aware of the purpose of the study. Even in this case we may not be totally satisfied that clinician ratings are not influenced in some way. In family history studies, relatives are often contacted by the researcher or the patient (Alexander, Lerer, & Baron, 1992). The knowledge that they are participating in a genetic study could cause the relatives of the patients to behave differently than a person in the control group would during the interview. These behavioral differences may be picked up by the clinician and influence diagnostic decisions.

A method to reduce the impact of both experimenter and participant expectations is the *double-blind design.* In this procedure, neither the individual working directly with the participant nor the participant is aware of the experimental conditions. However, the effectiveness of this design is dependent on the "blindness" of

"MR. HARRIS, YOU'RE A HYPOCHONDRIAC...TAKE THESE TWO PLACEBOS AND CALL ME IN THE MORNING!"

the participants, which may not always be ensured. In a randomized, double-blind study (Margraf et al., 1991), patients with panic disorder were given one of two antidepressants (alprazolam or imipramine) or a placebo. All of the substances were dispensed in identical capsules. Were the patients and physicians "blind" to the conditions? Apparently not. The great majority of patients and physicians were able to assess the physiological responses and accurately rate whether the patient was taking an antidepressant. Further, the physicians were able to distinguish between the two types of active drugs based on the reaction of the patients. These findings indicate the need to modify experimental designs so that the degree of "blindness" is increased. Otherwise, the results may be influenced by both client and experimenter expectations.

As you can see, researchers have a difficult time controlling extraneous or confounding variables. External validity is also very important to determine. In the study by Thom and her colleagues (2000), we would want to know whether behavior therapy and benzodiazepines are also effective in reducing anxiety in other populations and situations. Sometimes importing a therapy from a research setting to a real-life environment is difficult. Martin Seligman (1996) points out that research designs that produce high internal validity (such as those that use a manual to specify steps in therapy, a fixed number of sessions, and random assignment of clients with well-diagnosed and uncomplicated disorders) may have problems with external validity. "Real" therapy often does not

follow treatment manuals and may not be of fixed duration. Patients frequently have multiple problems, and they are not randomly assigned to therapists. Thus, in some cases, designing research with very high internal validity may reduce the generalizability of the findings. (For some additional problems, see the Critical Thinking feature "Research Alliance: A 'Wild Card' in Comparative Research?")

Correlations

A **correlation** is the extent to which variations in one variable are accompanied by increases or decreases in a second variable. The variables in a correlation, unlike those in an experiment, are not manipulated. Instead, a statistical analysis is performed to determine whether increases in one variable are accompanied by increases or decreases in the other. The relationship is expressed as a statistically derived *correlation coefficient*, symbolized by the symbol r, which has a numerical value between -1 and $+1$. In a positive correlation, an increase in one variable is accompanied by an increase in the other. When an increase in one variable is accompanied by a decrease in the other variable, it is a negative correlation. The greater the value of r, positive or negative, the stronger the relationship. See Figure 4.2 for examples of correlations.

Correlations indicate the degree to which two variables are related but not the reason for the relationship. Consider a study reported in the *American*

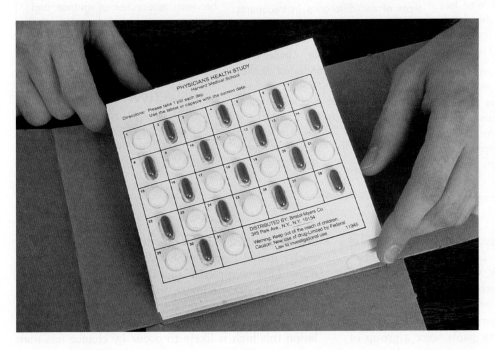

Double-Blind Design When researching the effects of a drug, experimenters will often use a double-blind design to ensure that neither participants nor experimenter are aware of the experimental conditions. Shown here is a prepared card of drugs that could be used in a research study in such a way that neither patient nor doctor actually knows whether the patient is receiving a drug or a placebo. How would you determine if this manipulation was successful?

CRITICAL THINKING

Researcher Allegiance: A "Wild Card" in Comparative Research?

Once upon a time, in the dark ages, psychotherapists practiced however they liked, without any scientific data guiding them. Then a group of courageous warrior ... embarked upon a campaign of careful scientific testing of therapies under controlled conditions. Along the way, the Knights had to overcome many obstacles. Among the most formidable were the wealthy Drug Lords who dwelled in Mercky moats filled with Lilly pads. Equally treacherous were the fire-breathing clinician-dragons, who roared, without any basis in data, that their ways of practicing psychotherapy were better. After many years of tireless efforts, the Knights came upon a set of empirically supported therapies that made people better. They began to develop guidelines so that patients would receive the best possible treatments for their specific problems. And in the end, Science would prevail, and there would be calm (or at least less negative affect) in the land. (Westen, Novotny, & Thompson-Brenner, 2004, p. 631)

The move to develop empirically supported treatments has resulted in research that compares two or more forms of therapy to determine which ones are the most effective for specific disorders. Although this appeared to be a clear-cut task, reviewers became

puzzled as to why the results of comparative studies were so contradictory. In some, psychodynamic therapies would be superior to behavioral therapy in treatment outcome, and in other cases the reverse might be true. To determine what might be producing these discrepant findings, Luborsky and his colleagues (1999) reviewed twenty-nine studies that compared two therapies. Of these, nine involved cognitive versus behavioral therapy, seven involved behavioral versus psychodynamic therapy, four compared psychodynamic with cognitive therapy, and nine examined psychopharmacology versus psychotherapy. Because the reviewers were suspicious that the theoretical position or "alliance" to a specific approach by researchers in the studies might influence the outcome, ratings of the researcher's alliance were obtained through self-ratings, ratings by colleagues, and reprints of research. These three measures combined correlated .85 with the effect sizes of the difference in treatments compared. In other words, researcher allegiance was a very important influence. For example, behavioral researchers who conducted studies comparing behavioral versus dynamic therapies would find that their favored approach would be "more effective." The reverse was also true for psychodynamic researchers.

Luborsky and his colleagues (1999) speculated on how the researcher's allegiance to a treatment might be associated with the outcome in comparative research:

1. A less effective comparison treatment might have been selected when compared with the favored treatment.
2. Research that reflected negatively on the researcher's favored treatment may be shelved and not submitted for publication.
3. The therapist or therapy that is provided for the nonfavored treatment may differ in a way that favors the researcher's allegiance; for example, the therapist may have less training with the treatment.
4. Subtle reinforcements or positive expectations may be conveyed subtly to therapists providing the favored treatment.

If the Luborsky study is correct in finding a very strong relationship between researcher allegiance and treatment outcome, what does this mean in terms of the validity of research that compares several types of treatment? Other than the preceding speculations by Luborsky and his colleagues (1999). What additional explanations can you give for the findings? What are different ways of identifying and minimizing research allegiance effects?

"Dissociation and Childhood Trauma in Psychologically Disturbed Adolescents." The researchers (Sanders & Giolas, 1991) hypothesized that dissociation (disturbance or change in function of identity, memory, or consciousness) during adolescence is positively correlated with childhood stress and abuse. Their participants were a group of

institutionalized adolescents (thirty-five females and twelve males) between the ages of thirteen and seventeen. They completed the Dissociative Experiences Scale and a questionnaire on child abuse and trauma. Statistically significant correlations were obtained between these measures ($r = 0.38$, $p > 0.01$). A correlation this high is likely to occur by chance less than

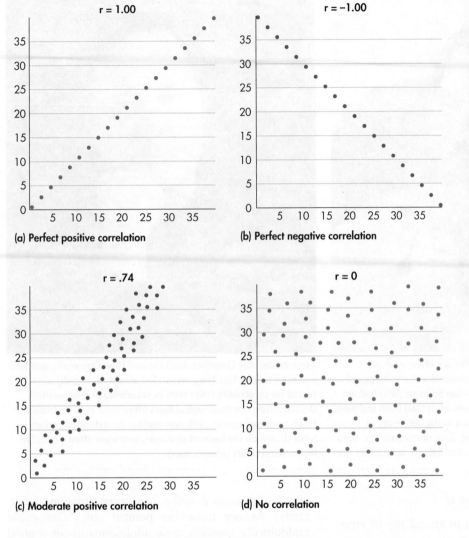

FIGURE 4.2 Possible Correlation Between Two Variables The more closely the data points approximate a straight line, the greater the magnitude of the correlation coefficient r. The slope of the regression line rising from left to right in example (a) indicates a perfect positive correlation between two variables, whereas example (b) reveals a perfect negative correlation. Example (c) shows a lower positive correlation. Example (d) shows no correlation whatsoever.

r = 1.00

(a) Perfect positive correlation

r = −1.00

(b) Perfect negative correlation

r = .74

(c) Moderate positive correlation

r = 0

(d) No correlation

one time out of a hundred. The researchers concluded that "these findings support the view that dissociation represents a reaction to early negative experience."

If we adopt the scientific method, what questions might we raise about this study? We must first remember that correlations do not necessarily imply a cause-and-effect relationship. Many alternative reasons for the relationship may exist. A third variable, such as environmental stress, might make it more likely for parents to physically abuse the child and for the child to develop a range of problem behaviors. Poverty or poor living conditions may cause both the dissociation in the adolescent and the abusive behavior on the part of the parents. Such third-variable possibilities in correlations are numerous. Consider the following actual observations. What third-variable explanations can you suggest for them?

■ The number of storks nesting on rooftops in certain New England communities is positively correlated with the human birthrate.

■ The number of violent crimes committed in a community is positively correlated with the number of churches in the community.

In correlations, it is also often difficult to determine the direction of the causation. If we accept the findings of Sanders and Giolas (1991), we must then determine whether the physical abuse caused dissociation or whether the child's early dissociative behaviors produced more negative parenting.

This study also raises other issues. Do we agree or disagree with the operational definitions used in the study?

How were *child abuse* and *trauma* defined and measured? Because the questionnaire devised by Sanders and Giolas (1991) did not appear to undergo validation procedures, we cannot be certain that the questionnaire actually measured the variables the researchers intended to measure (child abuse and trauma). Consider, for example, these sample questions from their questionnaire:

Correlational Studies Identical twins are often used in correlational studies in an attempt to determine the influence of genetic factors. The twins shown here—Jim Springer (left) and Jim Lewis (right)—were separated four weeks after their birth and lived in different communities. As participants in the University of Minnesota Study of Twins Reared Apart, they discovered that they were incredibly similar: both chain-smoked Salems, both drove the same model blue Chevrolet, both chewed their fingernails, and both had dogs named Toy. They responded almost identically when tested for personality traits such as sociability and self-control. Unfortunately, methodological flaws often exist in twin studies. Many have had contact with one another for extended periods, were chosen on the basis of similarity, and were often evaluated by nonblind raters (Joseph, 2001).

Do you feel safe living at home?

Were your parents unwilling to attend any of your school-related activities?

Were you physically mistreated as a child or a teenager?

When you didn't follow the rules of the house, how often were you severely punished?

Did your parents ridicule you?

Were there traumatic or upsetting sexual experiences when you were a child or teenager that you couldn't speak to adults about?

As a child did you feel unwanted or emotionally neglected?

Did you ever think you wanted to leave your family and live with another family?

Do these questions measure "child abuse and trauma" exclusively, or could they measure something else? Would other groups of adolescents give similar or different answers to these questions? Might institution-alized adolescents describe their home situation inaccurately? As one researcher pointed out, "One could undoubtedly question these adolescents about a good many things and produce interesting correlations and comparisons to others whose mind set is more objective" (Furlong, 1991, p. 1423). We would be more certain about the validity of the child abuse trauma questionnaire if we had some independent verification of the severity of actual abuse suffered by the adolescents. Unfortunately, in the Sanders and Giolas (1991) study, responses on their questionnaire were not even related to abuse ratings obtained by clinicians at the institution.

Even if we accepted the operational definitions in this study, we could not say that child abuse is specifically related to dissociation. We would have to give both questionnaires to control groups and to other psychiatric populations to determine how they would respond.

In summary, a correlation indicates the degree to which two variables are related. It is a very important method of scientific inquiry because there are many variables we cannot control, such as genetic makeup, gender, and socioeconomic status. Manipulating other variables that we might be able to control, such as exposing a child to trauma or abuse, would be unethical. Correlations can tell us how likely it is that two variables can occur together. Even when the variables are highly related, however, we must exercise caution in interpreting causality. The two variables may not be causally related, or both may be influenced by a third variable. Even if they are causally related, the direction of causality may be unclear.

Analogue Studies

As we have noted, ethical, moral, or legal standards may prevent researchers from devising certain studies on mental disorders or on the effect of treatment. In other cases, studying real-life situations is not feasible because researchers would have a difficult time controlling all the variables. In such cases, researchers may resort to an **analogue study**—an investigation that attempts to replicate or simulate, under controlled conditions, a situation that occurs in real life (Noble & McConkey, 1995). The advantage of this type of investigation is that it allows us to study a phenomenon using experimental designs that are not possible with correlational studies. Here are some examples of analogue studies:

1. To study the possible effects of a new form of treatment on patients with anxiety disorders, the researcher may use students who have high test anxiety rather than patients with anxiety disorders.

2. To test the hypothesis that human depression is caused by continual encounters with events that one cannot control, the researcher exposes rats to uncontrollable aversive stimuli and examines the increase of depressivelike behaviors (such as lack of motivation, inability to learn, and general apathy) in these animals.

3. To test the hypothesis that sexual sadism is influenced by watching sexually violent films and television programs, an experimenter exposes "normal" participants to either violent or nonviolent sexual programs. The participants then complete a questionnaire assessing their attitudes and values toward women and their likelihood of engaging in violent behaviors with women.

Obviously, each example is only an approximation of real life. Students with high test anxiety may not be equivalent to individuals with anxiety disorders. Findings based on rats may not be applicable to human beings. And exposure to one violent sexual film and the use of a questionnaire may not be sufficient to

Correlational Findings Depression has been found to be inversely related to activity level. How could you determine the direction of the relationship? Does an increase in depression cause a reduction in physical activity or does inactivity result in greater depression? What other factors might be involved in the correlation between the two variables?

allow a researcher to draw the conclusion that sexual sadism is caused by long-term exposure to such films. However, analogue studies give researchers insight into the processes that might be involved in abnormal behaviors and treatment.

Field Studies

In some cases, analogue studies would be too contrived to be accurate representations of the real-life situation. Investigators may then resort to the **field study,** in which behaviors and events are observed and recorded in their natural environment. The participants in a field study are most often members of a given social unit—a group, an institution, or a community. However, the investigation may also be limited to a single individual; single-participant studies are discussed in the next section.

Field studies sometimes employ data collection techniques, such as questionnaires, interviews, and the

Field Studies The catastrophic damage wrought by the tsunami on December 26, 2004, caused nearly 100,000 fatalities in Meulaboh, Indonesia alone. The majority of victims were women and children. Here survivors survey the ruins. Many individuals involved in or witnessing the disaster suffered severe emotional and physical trauma. Disasters such as this provide a unique if unwelcome opportunity to observe events and reactions of individuals in the natural environment. Can social scientists remain detached and objective when recording a tragedy of such magnitude?

analysis of existing records, but the primary technique is observation. The observers must be highly trained and have enough self-discipline to avoid disrupting or modifying the behavior processes they are observing and recording.

A field study may be used to examine mass behavior after events of major consequence, such as wars, floods, and earthquakes. It may also be applied to the study of personal crises, as in military combat, major surgery, terminal disease, or the loss of loved ones. An example of a field study is the in-person interviews conducted in New York City after the terrorist attacks on the World Trade Center. Nearly 11 percent of the interviewees had lost a close family member or friend. The most frequent symptoms reported were recurring painful memories of the event. Although 18.5 percent displayed posttraumatic stress disorder (PTSD) symptoms, only 11.3 percent had received any psychiatric help or were taking medications for the symptoms (DeLisi et al., 2003).

Although field studies offer a more realistic investigative environment than other types of research, they suffer from certain limitations. First, as with other nonexperimental research, determining the direction of causality is difficult in field studies because the data are correlational. Second, so many variables are at work in real-life situations that it is impossible to control—and sometimes even distinguish—them all. As a result, they may contaminate the findings. Third, observers can never be absolutely sure that their presence did not influence the interactions they observed.

Single-Participant Studies

Most scientists advocate the study of large groups of people to uncover the basic principles governing behavior. This approach, called the *nomothetic orientation*, is concerned with formulating general laws or principles while deemphasizing individual variations or differences. Experiments and correlational studies are nomothetic. Other scientists advocate the in-depth study of one person. This approach, exemplified by the single-participant study, has been called the *idiographic orientation*. There has been much debate over which method is more fruitful in studying psychopathology.

Although the idiographic method has many limitations, especially its lack of generality, it has proved very valuable in applied clinical work. Furthermore, the argument over which method is more fruitful is not productive because both approaches are needed to study abnormal behavior. The nomothetic approach seems appropriate for laboratory scientists, whereas the idiographic approach seems appropriate for their clinical counterparts, the psychotherapists, who daily face the pressures of treating disturbed individuals.

There are two types of single-participant studies: the case study and the single-participant experiment. Both techniques may be used to examine a rare or an unusual phenomenon, to demonstrate a novel diagnostic or treatment procedure, to test an assumption, to generate future hypotheses on which to base controlled research, and to collect comprehensive information for a better understanding of the individual. Only the single-participant experiment, however, can determine cause-and-effect relationships.

The Case Study

Physicians have used the case study extensively in describing and treating medical disease. In psychology, a **case study** is an intensive study of one individual that relies on clinical data, such as observations, psychological tests, and historical and biographical information. A case study thus lacks the control and objectivity of many other methods and cannot be used to demonstrate cause-and-effect relationships. It can serve as the primary source of data in cases in which systematic experimental procedures are not feasible. It is especially valuable for studying rare or unusual phenomena. Hatcher (1989), for example, reported a case in which a fourteen-year-old boy would "scream with terror" when seeing a doll with mobile eyes or with the roots of the hair showing. The origin of such a specific fear can be investigated by examining historical data. Case studies can also be helpful in determining diagnosis, characteristics, course, and outcome of a disorder, as illustrated in the following case study:

Stephen Shore, an individual diagnosed in childhood with atypical development with autistic features (a disorder characterized by impairments in social interaction and restricted interest in activities), now serves on the Board of Directors for the Autism Society of America. According to his mother, Stephen developed normally during his first year of life but stopped talking during his second year. At the time, little was known about autistic-like disorders. When his mother talked to Stephen, he did not respond. Using trial and error, she discovered that making nonsensical statements would attract his attention. She also found that he would not imitate her, but he acknowledged her with a glance when she made peculiar noises. At the age of four, Stephen became fascinated by watch motors and would take watches apart and put them back together again. He later attributed his obsession with watches to the fact that they provided structure. During later schooling, he became absorbed with reading, although his teachers did not appear to understand his ability to do so. One teacher told Stephen's parents about his difficulty with reading. The parents responded by saying that Stephen read newspapers at home.

Based on his own experiences, Stephen believes that he can offer suggestions for working with individuals who have autistic disorders. For example, he suggests that topics such as airplanes, astronomy, bicycles, cats, chemistry, electricity, hardware, locks, music, and watches might be attractive to these children. Interactions can be structured around specific activities, such as bicycling or computers. This allows conversation to revolve around an activity rather than "small talk," which is difficult for people with autistic disorders. He also believes that individuals with autism can benefit by furnishing precise explanations of social interactions since they are often unaware of the "rules" involved. In working with George, an individual with Asperger's disorder (a disorder related to autism), Stephen explained to him, "When people look at their watch, it means they're bored with what you're talking about. ... Now George, I'm looking at my watch. What does this mean?" (Shore, 2003, p. 89). Initially, George did not understand and responded by talking about watches with Roman numerals and other characteristics of watches. With correction and practice, George began to understand this rule in social interaction.

In this case, Stephen relayed his life experience, explaining how he perceived the world and events. His account gives some clues as to the reasons for some of the unusual behaviors shown by individuals with autistic disorders, as well as suggested interventions. Case studies are also useful in helping clinicians formulate hypotheses that can be tested later in research.

Goldman and Gutheil (1991) reported in the *American Journal of Psychiatry* that *bruxism* (clenching and grinding of teeth, especially during sleep) may be associated with sexual abuse. They based this preliminary observation on their work with five patients in whom this relationship was found. From their work with three patients, Coons and Bowman (1993) believe that psychiatric patients who are unable to lose weight from dieting may suffer from dissociation. (Remember that these are hypothesized relationships that have to be verified in more rigorous studies.)

The Single-Participant Experiment

The **single-participant experiment** differs from the case study in that the former is actually an experiment in which some aspect of the person's own behavior is used as a control or baseline for comparison with future behaviors. To determine the effectiveness of a treatment, for example, the experimenter begins by plotting a baseline to show the frequency of a behavior before intervention. Then the treatment is introduced, and the person's behavior is observed. If the behavior changes, the treatment is withdrawn. If after the withdrawal of treatment the person's behavior again resembles that observed during the baseline condition, we can be fairly certain that the treatment was responsible for the behavior changes observed earlier. In the final step, the treatment is reinstated. In a second type of single-participant experiment (multiple baseline), baselines are obtained on two or more behaviors. The same intervention is introduced with each. If the behaviors change only with the intervention, confidence is increased that the intervention caused the changed behavior. The following case illustrates the multiple-baseline procedure:

Juanita, a twenty-four-year-old African American woman, developed assault-related flashbacks and nightmares related to the trauma of being raped by an acquaintance. The clinicians wanted to evaluate the effectiveness of a therapeutic intervention called eye movement desensitization (EMD) over that of supportive counseling. During the baseline period, the frequency of self-reported flashbacks and nightmares were obtained. With supportive counseling, the average number of flashbacks Juanita experienced per week was about four. After EMD, the number of flashbacks dropped dramatically (see Figure 4.3). To make certain that it was EMD that produced the change, the therapy was then used to treat the nightmares, which averaged about two to three per week. After EMD was introduced, the frequency of nightmares was reduced. The treatment was most effective when it involved scenes with the attacker (Lundervold & Belwood, 2000).

In this case, EMD clearly was more effective than supportive counseling. Although there may be questions about the generalizability of the findings obtained from single-participant experiments, the method has many advantages for the clinician or therapist. The individual, rather than the group average, is the focus, and the approach facilitates clinical innovation and accountability (Blampied, 2000; Morgan & Morgan, 2001).

Biological Research Strategies

More and more biological research is being performed on the causes and treatment of mental disorders. Some of these research strategies are applicable to psychological research.

Human Genome Project

In the year 2000, the entire 3.1 billion nucleotide basis of human DNA was identified. The focus of future research will turn away from identifying genes to understanding how they affect behavior. Efforts will be directed to determining how genes work and how they will lead to gene-based diagnoses and treatment programs. For most forms of psychopathology, this approach will be most helpful in early identification rather than in genetic engineering, as multiple genes are involved in complex traits. For example,

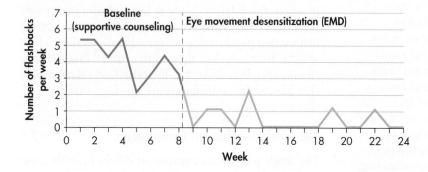

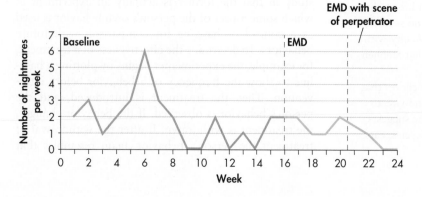

FIGURE 4.3 A Multiple-Baseline Study   A multiple-baseline study is an experimental design in which two or more behaviors are observed prior to intervention. Intervention is then applied to first one behavior and then another. In this case, eye movement desensitization (EMD) was first applied to flashbacks, resulting in a dramatic decrease in frequency. It was then applied to nightmares, but it became more effective when scenes of the perpetrator were included.

Source: From Lundervold & Belwood (2000).

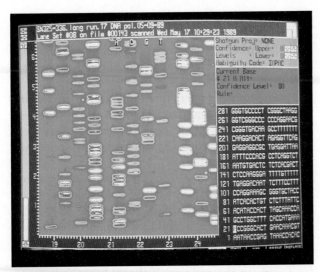

The Human Genome Project This massive undertaking involved deciphering, mapping, and identifying DNA sequencing patterns and variations in approximately 30,000 genes in human DNA. Scientists hope to determine the "message" contained in the DNA patterns that may contribute to human attributes and diseases. The knowledge of the factors involved in human development raises ethical, legal, and social concerns.

phenylketonuria (PKU), a metabolic disorder that can produce mental retardation, is treated not by technological methods but by altering diet to prevent damage (Plomin & Crabbe, 2000).

Genetic Linkage Studies

Genetic linkage studies attempt to determine whether a disorder follows a genetic pattern. If a disorder is genetically linked, individuals closely related to the person with the disorder (who is called the *proband*) should be more likely to display that disorder or a related one. Genetic studies of psychiatric disorders often employ the following procedure (Alexander et al., 1992):

1. The proband and his or her family members are identified.

2. The proband is asked for the psychiatric history of specific family members.

3. These members are contacted and given some type of assessment to determine whether they have the same or a "related" disorder.

4. Assessment of the proband and family members may include psychological tests, brain scans, and neuropsychological examinations.

This research strategy depends on the accurate diagnosis of both the proband and the relatives. One com-

plication is that the criteria for specific disorders have changed with each new edition of the *Diagnostic and Statistical Manual of Mental Disorders* (DSM). Are the findings based on the DSM-IV-TR categories applicable to their earlier counterparts in DSM-II, DSM-III, DSM III-R, or DSM-IV? Kendler, Silberg, and colleagues (1991) have pointed out another possible source of error. In the family history interview method, the proband is asked whether relatives also have the same disorder. Kendler and colleagues used this method in a study of female twin pairs who were discordant for major depression, generalized anxiety disorder, and alcoholism—that is, in each pair, one twin had the disorder, and the other did not. When asked whether her parents also had the disorder, the "sick" twin was more likely than the "well" twin to report that they did. As this study indicates, caution must be used in employing the family history method in genetic linkage studies. An individual's psychiatric status ("sick" or "well") may influence the accuracy of his or her assessment of the mental health of relatives. This bias in reporting may be reduced by using multiple informants or assessing the family members directly.

Biological Markers

Genetic studies may attempt to identify **biological markers** (biological indicators of a disorder that may or may not be causal) for specific disorders. Indicators that have been noted in these studies include differences in variables such as cerebral blood-flow patterns, responses to specific medications, and brain structure. Some researchers believe that for schizophrenia, for example, differences in eye movement pursuit, attention and information-processing deficits, and reduced brain size are biological markers. Although some of these biological markers have been reported in close relatives of the patients, they have also been seen in populations that do not have the disorder. Several researchers concluded that "No definite 'biological marker' for schizophrenia or related spectrum conditions has been identified" (Szymanski, Kane, & Lieberman, 1991, p. 106). They based their view on the criteria needed for a biological marker: (1) it is distributed differently in the patient group than in control populations; (2) it is stable over time; (3) it appears more frequently in relatives of the patients than in the general population; and (4) it is associated with and precedes the development of the disorder in high-risk children. Many psychologists hoped that biological markers could be included in DSM-IV's diagnostic criteria, but this has not been possible. Mass media constantly report that some biological marker has been found that either causes or is diagnostic of mental disorders. Unfortunately, most of these reports have not been supported with subsequent research.

Other Concepts in Biological Research

Iatrogenic refers to the unintended effects of therapy—an intended change in behavior resulting from a medication prescribed or a psychological technique employed by the therapist. The therapist may not recognize the behavior change as a side effect of the medication or technique and may treat it as a separate disorder. For example, therapists have mistakenly diagnosed memory losses—which can be side effects from antidepressant medication—as Alzheimer's disease or other organic conditions.

Psychological interventions or techniques may also produce unexpected results. Researchers and therapists believe that some cases of multiple-personality disorder may be inadvertently produced by hypnotism, the very method used to investigate it (Coons, 1988; Merskey, 1995; Ofshe, 1992). Hypnotism has been used to retrieve memories reported by the different personalities, and clinicians often believe that the information obtained in this manner is accurate. The Council on Scientific Affairs (1985), however, concluded the following in its investigation of hypnosis:

1. Traumatic memories retrieved may reflect an emotional reality rather than an accurate recollection.

2. Hypnosis produces a state in which an individual is more vulnerable to subtle cues and suggestions that often distort recollections.

3. Hypnosis increases both accurate and inaccurate information.

4. Without independent verification, neither the hypnotist nor the subject can distinguish between accurate and inaccurate information.

5. Hypnosis can "increase the subject's confidence in his memories without affecting accuracy and ... increase errors while also falsely increasing confidence" (p. 1921).

6. In general, recollections obtained during nonhypnotic recall are more accurate than those obtained during hypnosis.

These conclusions and a recent research review (Barber, 1997) indicate the need to question the accuracy of material obtained during a hypnotic state.

Penetrance refers to the degree to which a genetic characteristic is manifested by individuals carrying a specific gene or genes associated with it. Complete penetrance occurs when a carrier always manifests the characteristic associated with the gene or genes. In mental disorders, incomplete penetrance is the rule. Even in cases of schizophrenia, only about half of the identical twins of the proband develop this disorder, even though their status as identical twins means that they carry the same genes.

Pathognomonic refers to a biological or psychological symptom or characteristic on which a diagnosis can be made. A great deal of research has been directed to discovering a symptom that is specifically distinctive of a disorder.

Biological challenge tests are often used to determine the effect of a substance on behavior. If we believe that a specific additive or food is responsible for hyperactivity in a child, we might observe the child's behavior after he or she eats food with the additive (the "challenge" phase) and after he or she eats food without the additive. If the additive and disruptive behaviors are linked, the behavior should be present during the challenge phase and absent during the other phase.

We now examine the major techniques of clinical research. They vary in their adherence to the scientific method.

Epidemiological and Other Forms of Research

In the field of abnormal and clinical psychology, investigators may employ experimental, correlational, case-study, or field-observation strategies in their research. The following strategies are important sources of information about disorders and their treatment.

Survey research Collecting data from all or part of a population to assess the relative prevalence, distribution, and interrelationships of naturally occurring phenomena.

Longitudinal research Observing and evaluating people's behaviors over a long period of time so that the course of a disorder or the effects of some factor such as a prevention program can be assessed over time.

Historical research Reconstructing the past by reviewing and evaluating evidence available from historical documents.

Twin studies Focusing on twins as a population of interest because twins are genetically similar. Twin studies are often used to evaluate the influence of heredity and environment.

Treatment outcome studies Evaluating the effectiveness of treatment in alleviating mental disorders. Outcome is concerned with answering the question of whether treatment is effective.

Treatment process studies Analyzing how therapist, client, or situational factors influence one another during the course of treatment. Process research focuses on how or why treatment is effective.

Program evaluation Analyzing the effectiveness of intervention or prevention programs.

The reliance on experimental, correlational, and single-participant methods varies with the research strategy. For instance, survey researchers often collect data and then correlate certain variables, such as social class and adjustment, to discover whether they are related. Researchers may also combine elements of different methods in their research. For example, an investigator conducting treatment outcome studies may use surveys and longitudinal studies.

Surveys are frequently used in **epidemiological research,** which examines the rate and distribution of mental disorders in a population. This important type of research is used to determine the extent of mental disturbance found in a targeted population and the factors that influence the rate of mental disturbance. Two terms, *prevalence* and *incidence,* are used to describe the rates. The *prevalence rate* tells us the percentage of individuals in a targeted population who have a particular disorder during a specific period of time. For example, we might be interested in how many older adults had a spider phobia during the previous six months (six-month prevalence rate), during the previous year (one-year prevalence rate), or anytime during their lives (lifetime prevalence rate). In general, shorter time periods have lower prevalence rates. When we compare the prevalence rate of disorders cited in studies, it is important to identify the specified time periods. Determining the prevalence rate is vital for planning treatment services because mental health workers need to know the percentage of people who are likely to be afflicted with disorders.

The *incidence rate* tells us onset or occurrence—the number of *new* cases of a disorder that appear in an identified population within a specified time period. The incidence rate is likely to be lower than the prevalence rate because incidence involves only new cases, whereas prevalence includes new and existing cases during the specified time period. Incidence rates are important for examining hypotheses about the causes or origins of a disorder. For example, if we find that new cases of a disorder are more likely to appear in a population exposed to a particular stressor than in another population not exposed to the stressor, we can hypothesize that the stress causes the disorder.

Epidemiological research, then, is important not only in describing the distribution of disorders but also in analyzing the possible factors that contribute to disorders. The Mental Health and Society feature "Cultural Bias in Research" discusses some of the problems involved in conducting cross-cultural research.

Ethical Issues in Research

Although research is primarily a scientific endeavor, it also raises ethical issues. Consider the following examples:

1. To study the effects of a new drug in treating schizophrenia, a researcher needs an experimental group that receives the drug treatment and a control group that receives no treatment. Is it ethical to withhold treatment from a control group of people with schizophrenia who need treatment in order to test the effectiveness of the drug?

2. To study the ways in which depressed individuals respond to negative feedback, an investigator deceives people suffering from depression into believing they performed poorly on a task. Is the deception ethical?

3. A researcher is interested in developing a new assessment tool to uncover personal conflicts. The assessment tool asks people to disclose information about their sexual conduct and private thoughts and feelings—information that may cause embarrassment and discomfort. Does the assessment measure invade the participants' privacy?

4. A researcher hypothesizes that people with alcoholism cannot stop drinking after having one alcoholic drink. He arranges for patients with this disorder to have one drink and then examines how strongly they are motivated to have additional drinks. Is it unethical and detrimental for these patients to be given alcohol as a part of an experiment?

5. An investigator believes that people who are exposed to inescapable stress are likely to develop feelings of helplessness and depression. Because the investigator does not want to subject human beings to inescapable stress, the experiment is conducted with dogs, which are given painful and inescapable electric shocks. Is it ethical to cause pain to animals as part of a study?

These examples raise a number of ethical concerns about how research is conducted and whether it has, or should have, limits. How can the rights of human beings (or even of other animals) be protected without

MENTAL HEALTH AND SOCIETY
Cultural Bias in Research

In the past, "mentally healthy" African Americans were described as interested in servitude and being faithful to their masters.

In "Diseases and peculiarities of the Negro race," Dr. Samuel Cartwright (1851/1967) in the early 1800s described two mental disorders known specifically among slaves:

Drapetomania was a mental disorder with one symptom: the condition caused slaves to run away. Cartwright stated that with proper medical treatment (ministering to their needs, protecting them from abuse, and keeping them in servitude), the Negro would "become spell-bound and can not run away."

Dysaethesia Aethiopica (or as called by slave owners, "Rascality"): symptoms included destroying property, arguing, and creating disturbances with the overseers "without cause or motive." Cartwright argues that the condition was not due to slavery itself but exposure to "too much liberty."

Researchers have become more sophisticated in dealing with ethnic dif-ferences, but there are still indications that ethnic bias may exist in the diagnosis of mental disorders. African Americans are more likely to receive a diagnosis of schizophrenia than European Americans are (Trierweiler et al., 2000). Researchers (Iwamasa, Larrabee, & Merrit, 2000) wanted to determine whether college students exhibit preconceived ideas when asked to assign personality disorder characteristics to different ethnic groups. The diagnostic criteria for the different personality disorders were individually printed on 3 × 5 cards. The participants were told that the characteristics listed were those that people "sometimes have" and that they were to put each card in the box of the group they believed it described most often. The boxes were labeled "African American," "Asian American," "European American," "Latino," and "Native American." The participants were cautioned not to sort by "popular stereotypes" but according to their own beliefs.

The following personality disorders were disproportionately assigned to the following groups: antisocial and paranoid to African Americans; schizoid to Asian Americans; and schizotypal to Native Americans. Latinos did not receive a disproportionate assignment. One-fourth of the participants were African American. One ethnic difference was found. Although African Americans assigned anti-social personality characteristics equally to their own group and to European Americans, the latter were more likely to assign those characteristics to African Americans. These results can be interpreted several ways. First, a strong ethnic diagnostic bias exists that cannot be eliminated by instructions not to apply stereotypes. Second, personality disorders may actually be distributed differently among ethnic groups. A third point to consider is the possibility that the criteria for personality disorders may contain characteristics that are "culturally appropriate" rather than pathological in some ethnic groups. How might you determine which, if any, of these interpretations are accurate?

---

impeding valuable experimentation? There is no question that to understand psychopathology and to devise effective treatment and prevention interventions, experimenters occasionally may have to devise investigations that cause pain and involve deception. To study human behavior, pain may be inflicted (for example, surgical implants may cause pain, or shocks may be used to induce stress), and deception is sometimes necessary to conceal the true nature of a study. The research must be consistent with certain principles of conduct, however, and must be designed to protect participants, as well as to enable researchers to contribute to the long-term welfare of human beings (and other animals).

The American Psychological Association (APA, 2002) has adopted the principle that the prospective scientific, applied, or educational value of the proposed research must outweigh the risk or discomfort to research participants. APA guidelines state that participants should be fully informed of the procedures and risks involved in the research and should give their consent to participate. Researchers may use deception only when alternative means are not possible, and they should provide participants with a sufficient explanation of the study as soon as possible. Participants should be free to withdraw from a study at any time. Furthermore, all participants must be treated with dignity, and research procedures must minimize pain, discomfort, embarrassment, and so on. If undesirable consequences to participants are found, the researcher has the responsibility to detect the extent of these consequences and to remedy them. Finally, unless

Treating Animals Ethically
Research involving animals has yielded important information. The APA's ethical standards require that animals be treated "humanely" and that any procedure that subjects them to stress or pain be carefully evaluated. However, should we also determine whether the research can be "justified"? What problems would occur in attempting to develop standards?

otherwise agreed on in advance, information obtained from participants is confidential.

The American Psychological Association (1993) has also published guidelines for those working with culturally diverse populations. The guidelines indicate the need for researchers to (1) consider the impact of sociopolitical factors, (2) become aware of how their own cultural backgrounds might affect their perceptions, and (3) consider the validity of instruments used in research in a cross-cultural context.

SUMMARY

Should the scientific method be used to evaluate psychotherapy?

■ Our beliefs about the causes of and treatments for mental disorders are often inaccurate and need to be evaluated. The scientific method provides both for the systematic and controlled collection of data through controlled observation and for the testing of hypotheses.

■ Characteristics such as the potential for self-correction, the testing of hypotheses, the use of operational definitions, a consideration of reliability and validity, and an acknowledgment of base rates enable us to have greater faith in our findings.

How does the experimental design differ from other ways of investigating phenomena?

■ The experiment is the most powerful research tool we have for determining and testing cause-and-effect relationships. In its simplest form, an experiment involves an experimental hypothesis, an independent variable, and a dependent variable.

■ The investigator manipulates the independent variable and measures the effect on the dependent variable. The experimental group is the group subjected to the independent variable.

■ A control group is employed that is similar in every way to the experimental group except for the manipulation of the independent variable.

■ Additional concerns include expectancy effects on the part of the participants and the investigator and the extent to which an experiment has internal and external validity.

Child sexual abuse is relatively common and is correlated with a number of disorders and symptoms. Why can we not consider it the causal factor of these disorders?

■ A correlation is a measure of the degree to which two variables are related. It is expressed as a correlation coefficient, a numerical value between −1 and +1, symbolized by *r*.

- Correlational techniques provide less precision, control, and generality than experiments, and they cannot be taken to imply cause-and-effect relationships.

Can experimental findings obtained from college students with subclinical fears be applied to individuals with phobias?

- In the study of abnormal behavior, an analogue study is used to create a situation as close to real life as possible. It permits the study of phenomena under controlled conditions when such study might otherwise be ethically, morally, legally, or practically impossible.

- The generalizability of the findings to clinical populations has to be evaluated and cannot be automatically assumed.

If you were using a field study, what would you investigate in the aftermath of a tragedy such as the terrorist attack on the World Trade Center or the devastation produced by the tsunami in Indonesia and other countries?

- The field study relies primarily on naturalistic observations in the real-life situations. As opposed to analogue studies, events are observed as they naturally occur.

- However, a field study cannot determine causality, and it may be difficult to sort out all the variables involved.

How can you determine a cause-and-effect relationship using only one participant?

- Rather than studying large groups of people, many scientists study one individual in depth. Two types of single-participant techniques are the case study and the single-participant experiment.

- The case study is especially appropriate when a phenomenon is so rare that it is impractical to try to study more than a few instances.

- Single-participant experiments differ from case studies in that cause-and-effect relationships can be determined. They rely on experimental procedures; some aspect of the person's own behavior is taken as a control or baseline for comparison with future behaviors.

What are some of the advantages and shortcomings of the biological approach in abnormal psychology?

- Biological research strategies allow us to search for genetic factors involved in psychological disorders or to identify biological markers or indicators of a disorder.

- As with any approach, consideration of other factors may be minimized because the stress is on the biological model. Iatrogenic effects or side effects from antidepressant medication have been mistakenly interpreted as symptoms of Alzheimer's disease or organic conditions.

Obtaining the prevalence rate of mental disorders is important. Why do some surveys show large discrepancies in the rates for disorders?

- A particularly important type of research in abnormal psychology is epidemiological research, which examines the rate and distribution of mental disorders in a population. It can also provide insight into what groups are at risk for mental disturbance and what factors may influence disturbance.

- There is often confusion between prevalence and incidence rates. Prevalence rates are statements of new and existing cases during a specified time period. Incidence rates are statements of new cases only.

- Surveys may often differ in the threshhold needed to make a diagnosis for a specific disorder.

Is it ethical to withhold treatment from mentally ill individuals because they are part of the control group?

- Like other tools, the scientific method is subject to misuse and misunderstanding, both of which can give rise to moral and ethical concerns. Such concerns have led the American Psychological Association (APA) to develop guidelines for ethical conduct and to establish ways for dealing with violations within the mental health professions. The APA has also published guidelines for those working with culturally diverse populations.

- Employing control groups who do not receive treatment is an important aspect of experimental research. There needs to be a careful evaluation of potential benefits to the study and harm to the participants.

KEY TERMS

analogue study (p. 119)

base rate (p. 110)

biological marker (p. 123)

case study (p. 121)

correlation (p. 115)

dependent variable (p. 112)

epidemiological research
  (p. 125)

experiment (p. 112)

experimental hypothesis
  (p. 112)

external validity (p. 112)

field study (p. 119)

genetic linkage study
  (p. 123)

hypothesis (p. 107)

iatrogenic (p. 124)

independent variable (p. 112)

internal validity (p. 112)

operational definitions
  (p. 108)

scientific method (p. 107)

single-participant experiment
  (p. 121)

theory (p. 107)

MULTIMEDIA PREVIEW

For additional study aids, we invite you to explore our media resources accompanying *Understanding Abnormal Behavior,* Eighth Edition. The Student CD-ROM includes videos, quizzing, and critical thinking activities that help to reinforce key concepts in a fun and engaging manner. The Student Web Site provides additional interactive activities, chapter outlines, and research links that further support and complement the text. All Web resources may be accessed by logging onto the Web site at **http://psychology.college.hmco.com/students**.

CHAPTER 5
Anxiety Disorders

FOCUS QUESTIONS

- What are the different ways in which anxiety can be expressed, and under what conditions does it become so overwhelming that a panic attack occurs?

- In two anxiety disorders, the source of the fear cannot be clearly identified. What causes these reactions, and how can they be treated?

- Some people are housebound with fear, and others are afraid of public speaking or harmless insects. How do these irrational fears develop, and what is the best way of treating them?

- Intrusive thoughts, such as the desire to shout in a church, or behaviors that one is compelled to perform over and over again, such as checking to determine if the door is locked, are relatively common. When do they become a disorder, and how do you eliminate them?

- A large minority of individuals will face a traumatic incident sometime in their lives. Under what conditions will the trauma lead to a stress disorder such as PTSD, and how are these disorders best treated?

The disorders discussed in this chapter are all characterized by anxiety, or feelings of fear and apprehension. These disorders can produce seemingly illogical—and often restrictive—patterns of behavior, as illustrated in the following examples:

A woman reports, "For me, a panic attack is almost a violent experience. I feel disconnected with reality. ... I feel like I'm losing control. ... My heart pounds really hard, I feel like I can't get my breath, and there's an overwhelming feeling that things are crashing in on me." (National Institute of Mental Health [NIMH], 2000, p. 2)

A National Guardsman who had served in Iraq reports that even when driving on U.S. highways, "his eyes can't stop working the guardrails and curbs, the sewer grates and bridge overpasses, the guy changing the tire on the side of the road, and the dead animals—the road kill that could end everything in a heartbeat." (Lyke, 2004a, p. A8)

A male college student displayed extreme nervousness and anxiety in social situations with females. He would cross the street to avoid having to interact with female classmates. Thoughts of asking them out produced such

anxiety that he had only once tried to ask a woman for a date. (D. Sue, case files)

"Washing my hair would take about an hour. I would wash the back of my hair, the sides of my hair, the front of my hair, the very top of my hair. Washing the front of my forehead, I would scrub it sixty times; it could never be sixty-one. The arms would start with the shoulders, and I would scrub them to the point where I was scrubbing so hard on my collarbone and shoulder blades that it almost felt like the bone was piercing through the skin and touching the soap." (Strobeck, 2002, p. 79)

Anxiety is a fundamental human emotion that was recognized as long as five thousand years ago. Everyone has experienced it, and we will continue to experience it throughout our lives. Many observers regard anxiety as a basic condition of modern existence. Yet "reasonable doses" of anxiety act as a safeguard to keep us from ignoring danger, and anxiety appears to have an adaptive function. Something would be wrong if an individual did not feel some anxiety in facing day-to-day stressors. For example, many persons report anxiety in terms of overload at home, work, or school; family demands; financial concerns; and interpersonal conflicts. When facing these stressors, individuals who

FIGURE 5.1 Disorders Chart: Anxiety Disorders

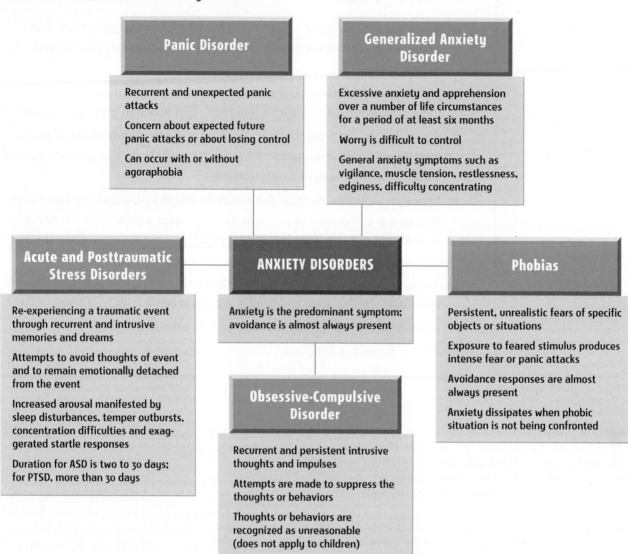

do not have a disorder are likely to handle the situation by facing it. They use strategies such as relaxation and problem solving to reduce stress. For others, however, overwhelming anxiety can disrupt social or occupational functioning or produce significant distress, as illustrated in the following case.

I've always been tense from as far back as I can remember. But lately it's getting worse. Sometimes I think I'm going crazy—especially at ... night. I can't sleep for fear of what has to be done the next day. Should I go to my psych class tomorrow, or skip it and study for my stat exam? If I skip it, maybe the prof will throw a pop quiz. He's known for that, you know. These attacks are frightful. I had another one last week. It was horrible. I thought I

would die. My roommate didn't know what to do. By the time it was over, my blouse was completely drenched. My roommate was so scared she called you. I was so embarrassed afterward. I think she [the roommate] wants to move out. I don't blame her. (D. Sue, case files)

The person describing herself here suffers from an **anxiety disorder,** which, according to the current definition, is a disorder that meets one of the following criteria:

- The anxiety itself is the major disturbance.

- The anxiety is manifested only in particular situations.

- The anxiety results from an attempt to master other symptoms.

FIGURE 5.1 Disorders Chart: Anxiety Disorders (continued)

ANXIETY DISORDERS	Lifetime Prevalence	Gender and Cultural Factors	Age of Onset	Course
Panic Disorder	2–3%	May involve intense fear of the supernatural in some cultures. 2–3 times more common in females.	Late adolescence and mid-30s	Chronic; waxes and wanes
Generalized Anxiety Disorder	5%	Up to 2 times more prevalent in females. May be over diagnosed in children.	Usually childhood or adolescence	Chronic; fluctuating; worsens during stress; over 2/3 have a comorbid disorder
Agoraphobia	Unknown; in clinical samples 95% met criteria for panic disorder or specific phobia	Far more prevalent in females.	20s to 40s	Little known
Social Phobias	3–13%; may depend on threshold used in study	More common in women. In certain Asian cultures may involve fear of offending others.	Mid-teens	Often continuous
Specific Phobia	7–13%	Approximately 2 times more common in females but depends on type of phobia. Fear of magic or spirits present in many cultures and only if reaction is excessive in context of culture would the diagnosis be considered.	Childhood or early adolescence but depends on type of phobia	Phobias that persist into childhood (about 20%) remit infrequently
Obsessive-Compulsive Disorder	1–2.5% depending on assessment tool	Equally common in males and females; less prevalent among African Americans, Asian Americans, and Hispanic Americans than White Americans.	Usually adolescence or early adulthood	Majority have chronic waxing and waning course
Post-Traumatic Stress Disorder	8%; elevated rates are found among refugees	More common in females, and in survivors of rape, military combat, and captivity.	Any age	Symptoms usually occur within 3 months after trauma, but may be delayed for some; approximately 50% recover within 3 months
Acute Stress Disorder	Currently not known; from 14–33% for specific traumas	Uncertain; probably more common in females.	Any age	Time limited to one month; if persists longer may meet criteria for PTSD

Source: Based on data from American Psychiatric Association (2000), NIMH (1999), Stein (2001).

Anxiety disorders can be quite debilitating for some individuals and quite costly for society. They account for over one-third of the costs of mental disorders (Rice & Miller, 1998). Anxiety can be manifested in three ways.

1. *Cognitive manifestations* of anxiety take place in a person's thoughts. They may range from mild worry to panic. Severe forms can bring a conviction of impending doom (the end of the world or death), a preoccupation with unknown dangers, or fears of losing control over bodily functions.

2. *Behavioral manifestations* of anxiety occur in a person's actions. They may take the form of avoiding anxiety-provoking situations. A student with an extreme fear of public speaking, for example, may avoid classes in which oral presentations are necessary. Individuals who experience extreme anxiety in public may stay at home rather than risk the possibility of experiencing an attack.

3. *Somatic manifestations* are changes in a person's physiological or biological reactions. They include shallow breathing, mouth dryness, cold hands and feet, diarrhea, frequent urination, fainting, heart palpitations, elevated blood pressure, increased perspiration, muscular tenseness (especially in the head, neck, shoulders, and chest), and indigestion.

The anxiety disorders do not involve a loss of contact with reality: people suffering from them can usually go about most of the day-to-day business of living. Although these people are aware of the illogical and self-defeating nature of some of their behaviors, they seem incapable of controlling them. In severe cases, the disturbed individuals may spend great amounts of time dealing with their debilitating fears—but to no avail. This preoccupation may, in turn, lead to emotional stress and turmoil, maladaptive behaviors, and disruptions in interpersonal relationships.

In this chapter, we discuss five major groups of anxiety disorders—panic disorder, generalized anxiety disorder, phobias, obsessive-compulsive disorder, and acute and posttraumatic stress disorders. These are shown in the disorders chart in Figure 5.1, along with comparative data on the prevalence, onset, and course of some anxiety disorders. It is estimated that more than 19 million adults in the United States suffer from an anxiety disorder (NIMH, 2000).

In each of the anxiety disorders, the person can experience *panic attacks,* intense fear accompanied by symptoms such as a pounding heart, trembling, shortness of breath, or fear of losing control or dying.

DSM-IV-TR (American Psychiatric Association, 2000) recognizes three types of panic attacks: (1) situationally bound—those that occur before or during exposure to the feared stimulus; (2) situationally predisposed—those that occur usually but not always in the presence of the feared stimulus; and (3) unexpected or uncued—those that occur "spontaneously" and without warning. Persons with obsessive-compulsive disorder and social and specific phobias generally report that their panic attacks are triggered by specific situations (situationally bound). An individual's panic when facing a feared situation—such as occurs in types 1 and 2—is not considered unusual. What has generated much controversy and research is the question of unexpected or "spontaneous" panic attacks. Why do some persons experience panic when no identifiable fearful stimulus is present? To gain insight into this question, we begin our discussion with a closer look at panic disorder. Individuals with panic disorder can have both unexpected and situation-specific panic attacks.

Panic Disorder and Generalized Anxiety Disorder

The predominant characteristic of both panic disorder and generalized anxiety disorder is unfocused, or *free-floating,* anxiety. That is, the affected individual is fearful and apprehensive but often does not know exactly what he or she is afraid of. Patients with panic disorder suffer episodes of intense fear accompanied by bodily sensations of heart palpitations, dyspnea (shortness of breath), and faintness, along with thoughts of dying, losing control, or going crazy while those with generalized anxiety disorder report milder anxiety-evoking thoughts dealing with themes such as misfortune, financial concerns, academic and social performance, and rejection. Individuals with either disorder report higher anxiety levels, are more sensitive to bodily changes, and exhibit higher physiological responses than controls (Hoehn-Saric, McLeod, Funderburk, & Kowalski, 2004).

Panic Disorder

Anxiety itself is the major disturbance in **panic disorder,** which is characterized by severe and frightening episodes of apprehension and feelings of impending doom. These episodes are often described as horrible and can last from a few minutes to several hours. The anxiety associated with panic disorder is much greater than that found in generalized anxiety disorder. According to DSM-IV-TR, a diagnosis of panic disorder includes recurrent unexpected panic attacks and at least one month of apprehension over having another attack or worrying about the consequences of an attack. Individuals with panic disorder report intense panic attacks alternating with periods of somewhat lower anxiety, during which they may be apprehensive about having another panic attack. One twenty-six-year-old Web designer described her feelings this way: "It happened so suddenly. Without warning I felt like I had been swept up in a tornado! … my pulse was pounding, my palms were drenched with sweat, and my throat was closing up, leaving me gasping for air. I felt paralyzed with fear, convinced I was going to die" (Kusek, 2001, p. 182). The attacks are especially feared because they often occur unpredictably and without warning. Individuals with panic disorder often have comorbid disorders involving other anxiety conditions or mood disturbances.

During the attacks, people report a variety of physical symptoms, such as breathlessness, sweating, choking, nausea, and heart palpitations. Many will go to emergency rooms with complaints of chest pain (Fleet et al., 2003). Some people also develop *agoraphobia,* or anxiety about leaving the home, which is caused by fear of having an attack in a public place. Such cases are diagnosed as panic disorder with agoraphobia. The following case seems typical:

At age thirty-eight, Eve Robinson of Oakland was sure she was losing her mind. While driving on the freeway one evening, she suddenly found she couldn't swallow. In panic, she pulled over to calm herself and slowly made her way home, vowing never to use the freeway again. A few months later, Robinson's heart started pounding as she boarded a plane to return home from her sister's wedding in Los Angeles. Convinced she was going to die, she begged a flight attendant to let her off and wrapped her hands around his neck when he refused. … Eve soon hit rock bottom when she found herself so fearful of having more attacks that she was unable to leave the house for four months. (Cash, 1998, p. 34)

Some factors seem to be associated with an increased risk of developing panic disorder. Many patients report a disturbed childhood environment that involved anxiety over separation from parents, family conflicts, or school problems (Laraia, Stuart, Frye, Lydiard, & Ballenger, 1994). Others indicate that they first experienced panic attacks after some form of separation, such as leaving home, or after the loss or threatened loss of a loved one (Mahoney, 2000; Wittchen, Zhao, Kessler, & Eaton, 1994). Exposure to

The Scream, by Edvard Munch The Scandinavian painter describes the scene this way: "I was walking along the road with two friends. The sun set. I felt a touch of melancholy. Suddenly the sky became a blood red. I stopped, leaned against a railing, dead tired (my friends looked at me and walked on), and I looked at the flaming clouds that hung like blood and a sword … over the blue-black fjord and the city. My friends walked on. I stood there trembling with fright. And I felt a loud unending scream piercing nature" (cited in Harris, 2004, p. 15).

stressors may also contribute. Individuals who report having panic attacks indicate that they faced more major life changes just before the attacks began (Pollard, Pollard, & Corn, 1989).

The *lifetime prevalence rate* (in a sample, the proportion of individuals who have ever had the disorder) for panic disorder is approximately 3.5 percent and is two times more common in women (Kessler et al., 1994; NIMH, 1999). The prevalence rate for Mexican Americans is somewhat lower than for the general population. In a survey on panic disorder conducted over the World Wide Web, more women (83.5 percent) than men (76.4 percent) reported "out of the blue" panic attacks (Stones & Perry, 1997). Women are also more likely than men to suffer a recurrence of panic symptoms after the remission of the disorder (Yonkers, Zlotnick, Allsworth, & Warshaw, 1998). One-third to one-half of individuals diagnosed with a panic disorder also have agoraphobia (American Psychiatric Association, 2000).

Although panic disorder is diagnosed in only a small percentage of individuals, panic attacks appear to be fairly common. Among college students, one-fourth to one-third reported having had a panic attack during a one-year period (Asmundson & Norton, 1993; Brown & Cash, 1990). Nearly 45 percent of college women had one panic attack or more within the previous year (Whittal, Suchday, & Goetsch, 1994). Similarly, 43 percent of adolescents in one sample reported having had a panic attack (N. King, Gullione, Tonge, & Ollendick, 1993). Most of these panic attacks are associated with an identifiable stimulus. However, in one study, more than 12 percent reported experiencing unexpected panic attacks (Telch, Lucas, & Nelson, 1989). Although panic attacks appear common, few persons who have them will develop a panic disorder.

Generalized Anxiety Disorder

Generalized anxiety disorder (GAD) is characterized by persistent high levels of anxiety and excessive worry over many life circumstances. These concerns are accompanied by physiological responses such as heart palpitations, muscle tension, restlessness, trembling, sleep difficulties, poor concentration, and persistent apprehension and nervousness. Afflicted people are easily startled and are continually "on edge." Most will present their problem as somatic complaints and "about 90 percent of those with GAD will say 'yes' to the question 'During the past 4 weeks, have you been bothered by feeling worried, tense, or anxious most of the time'" (Ballenger et al., 2000, p. 53). Because they are unable to discover the "real" source of their fears, they remain anxious and occasionally experience even more acute attacks of anxiety. Over two-third of cases of GAD have comorbid (co-occurring) disorders such as depression, substance abuse, or phobia. Of those with "pure" GAD, 28 percent indicated that the symptoms interfered with life activities versus 51 percent of those with comorbid GAD (Stein, 2001).

Individuals with GAD, in contrast to those with panic disorder, are as likely to worry over minor events as over major events. Children with GAD reported concern over taking tests, doing school work, being alone, hearing noises, being teased, experiencing personal harm, and going to hospitals. Somatic symptoms, such as headaches, stomachaches, and muscle tension, often accompanied their worries (Eisen & Silverman, 1998). Physiological reactions associated with GAD tend to be less extreme than those that accompany panic disorder but also tend to be more persistent (Gross & Eifert, 1990). Individuals with

GAD appear to have a lower threshold for uncertainty, which leads to worrying and to have erroneous beliefs such as "worry is an effective way to deal with problems" (Ladouceur et al., 2000). Some of the characteristics of GAD are evident in the following case:

> Joanne W. was known by her college friends as a worrier. She was apprehensive about anything and everything: failing in school, making friends, eating the right foods, maintaining her health, and being liked. Because of her concerns, Joanne was constantly tense. She often felt short of breath, which was accompanied by a fast heart rate and trembling. Joanne also had difficulty making decisions. Her insecurity was so great that even the most common decisions—what clothes to wear, what to order at a restaurant, which movies to see—became major problems. Every night Joanne reviewed and rereviewed every real and imaginary mistake she had made during the day or might make in the future. This produced another problem, sleeplessness.

To meet DSM-IV-TR's criteria for a diagnosis of generalized anxiety disorder, symptoms must be present for six months. In medical settings around the world, GAD is the most frequently diagnosed anxiety disorder (Goldberg, 1996; Stein, 2001). Some believe that GAD is not a distinct disorder but is actually a diagnosis made from the anxiety symptoms resulting from other disorders, such as panic disorder (Hettema, Prescott, & Kendler, 2004). The disorder is chronic, and it produces social and functional impairment. Fewer than half of the individuals with GAD seek treatment (Rickels & Schweizer, 1997). The lifetime prevalence rate for GAD is about 5.0 percent of the adult population, with women twice as likely to receive this diagnosis as men (NIMH, 2000). Among older adults, GAD is more common than major depression or severe cognitive impairment (Wetherell, Gatz, & Craske, 2003).

Etiology of Panic Disorder and Generalized Anxiety Disorder

In our discussions of the causes and origins of mental disorders in this chapter and ensuing chapters, we must distinguish among the viewpoints that derive from the various models of psychopathology. Here we examine the etiology of unfocused anxiety disorders from the psychodynamic, behavioral, and biological perspectives. Research has been directed toward explaining the reason for unexpected panic attacks.

Psychodynamic Perspective The psychodynamic view stresses the importance of internal conflicts (rather than external stimuli) in the origin of

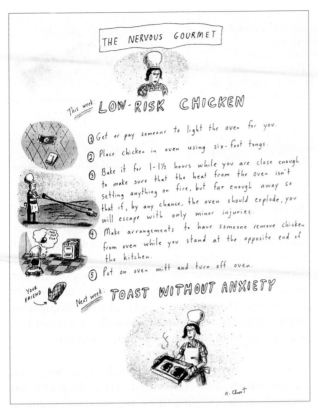

THE NERVOUS GOURMET

This week: LOW-RISK CHICKEN

① Get or pay someone to light the oven for you.

② Place chicken in oven using six-foot tongs.

③ Bake it for 1-1½ hours while you are close enough to make sure that the heat from the oven isn't setting anything on fire, but far enough away so that if, by any chance, the oven should explode, you will escape with only minor injuries.

④ Make arrangements to have someone remove chicken from oven while you stand at the opposite end of the kitchen.

⑤ Put on oven mitt and turn off oven.

YOUR FRIEND

Next week: TOAST WITHOUT ANXIETY

r. Chast

Learning to Use Coping Strategies For those who suffer from generalized anxiety disorder, identifying anxiety-evoking thoughts and developing coping strategies to deal with them is an important part of effective therapy.

panic disorder and GAD. In this theory, the disorders are hypothesized to originate in sexual and aggressive impulses that are seeking expression. When a forbidden impulse threatens to disturb the ego's integrity, an intense anxiety reaction occurs. Because this conflict is unconscious, the individual does not know the source of the anxiety.

A person's defense against unfocused anxiety is generally considered poorly organized and less effective than defenses mounted against other anxiety disorders. In a phobia, for example, the conflict between id impulses and ego is displaced onto a specific external stimulus that can be controlled simply through avoidance. But the person with generalized anxiety disorder has only one defense—to try to repress the impulses. When that defense weakens, panic attacks may occur.

Cognitive Behavioral Perspective Cognitive behavioral theorists emphasize that cognitions and conditioning are major factors in the development of anxiety disorders. Not everyone who experiences altered physical sensations develops anxiety attacks. McNally (1999) and Reiss and coworkers (1986) contended that people react differently to physical symp-

toms or sensations. They used the Anxiety Sensitivity Inventory (ASI) to investigate this phenomenon. The ASI measures a person's reaction to anxiety symptoms. People who score high on the test agreed with such statements as "When I notice that my heart is beating rapidly, I worry that I might be having a heart attack." People with low anxiety sensitivity interpreted the sensation as being only unpleasant. The *anxiety-sensitivity theory of panic* focuses on the cognitions or thoughts that individuals have in response to bodily sensations. People with high levels of anxiety sensitivity appear to have an overly active degree of bodily vigilance, along with intense fear of and worry about bodily sensations. They are likely to make "catastrophic" misinterpretations of bodily symptoms, seeing heart palpitations, sweaty palms, and shortness of breath as indicators of an impending heart attack, suffocation, or death. Those with low anxiety sensitivity interpret similar sensations as merely feeling anxious. Among adolescents, those with high anxiety sensitivity were more likely to experience a panic attack than those with low anxiety sensitivity. In the same study, Asian and Hispanic adolescents reported higher anxiety sensitivity than Caucasian adolescents but were less likely to have panic attacks (Weems, Hayward, Killen, & Taylor, 2002). However, anxiety sensitivity accounts for only a small amount of the variance in predicting panic attacks (Bouton, Mineka, & Barlow, 2001). Other factors may be more important in the cause of panic attacks.

The cognitive-behavioral model attributes panic attacks to the individual's interpretation of unpleasant bodily sensations as indicators of an impending disaster. Cognitions and somatic symptoms can best be viewed as a positive feedback loop that results in increasingly higher levels of anxiety (P. M. Clark, 1996; Ehlers, 1993). In other words, after an external or internal stressor, a person may become aware of a bodily sensation, such as a racing heart. Anxiety develops when the person interprets the sensation as a signal of a dreadful event. This belief then produces even greater physical reactions. Figure 5.2 illustrates this pattern. If the positive feedback loop continues, a panic attack may follow.

In one study that supports the positive feedback loop hypothesis, twenty-eight participants with panic disorder and twenty healthy controls wore portable electrocardiographs (ECGs) to record their heart rates during a twenty-four-hour period. Both groups noticed changes in cardiac activity. But after observing these changes, only the clients with panic disorder showed an acceleration of their heart rate and reported feelings of anxiety (Pauli et al., 1991). Although this study highlighted the importance of the perception of bodily sensations, some research has

FIGURE 5.2 Positive Feedback Loop Between Cognitions and Somatic Symptoms Leading to Panic Attacks

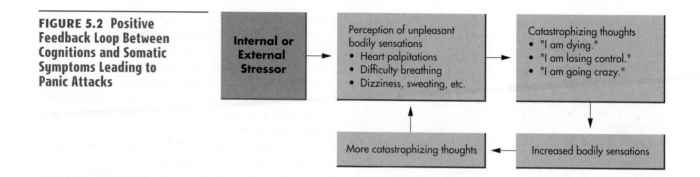

also suggested that panic attacks may begin with anxiety-provoking thoughts.

To support this hypothesized relationship between cognitions and anxiety, a researcher must be able, first, to find that thoughts precede or contribute to panic attacks and, second, to show that cognitions influence the severity of somatic symptoms. Some research supports the cognitive hypothesis. Anxiety producing cognitions such as thoughts of dying, passing out, or acting foolish have been found to precede or accompany panic attacks (Bakker, Spinhoven, Van Balkom, & Van Dyck, 2002; Schmidt, Lerew, & Trakowski, 1997; Whittal & Goetsch, 1995).

If disturbing thoughts can increase cardiovascular activity, can they precipitate a panic attack? The answer is yes, at least some of the time. In one study, a twenty-five-year-old woman with a nine-year history of panic attacks received two types of feedback, accurate and false. When she received accurate feedback of her resting heart rate, no changes were observed in her physiological functioning. Twenty seconds after the woman received inaccurate feedback showing that her heart rate had increased, however, her heart rate really did increase—to fifty beats per minute over baseline. During this period, the patient reported that she was having a severe panic attack (Margraf, Ehlers, & Roth, 1987). Similar results were found in another group of patients with panic disorder. Of particular interest is the finding that feedback falsely suggesting arousal produced significantly greater increases in physiological measures in people who had histories of panic attacks than in people who lacked such a history (Ehlers, Margraf, Roth, Taylor, & Birbaumer, 1988).

The search for cognitive factors, although promising, leaves some questions unanswered. First, although most individuals report that their panic attacks are accompanied by cognitions, a substantial percentage report they are not aware of any thoughts during these episodes. In India, panic attacks are associated with physiological symptoms such as tachycardia and shortness of breath more than with thoughts of losing control or of going crazy (Neerakal & Srinivasan,

2003). However, there is some evidence that catastrophic thoughts may occur so quickly and automatically that the individual is not consciously aware of them (Cloitre, Shear, Cancienne, & Zeitlin, 1994). Second, it is unclear why individuals with GAD and panic disorder are so prone to having thoughts of catastrophe. It must be remembered that the cognitive approach does not preclude the possible impact of biological factors in the cause of panic disorders.

Biological Perspective   Research on the biological factors involved in GAD and panic disorders has focused on neural structures and on neurochemical responses to stressful stimuli. The work is preliminary and has produced conflicting findings. Because benzodiazepines—a family of antianxiety drugs that includes Valium and Librium—have been successful in treating GAD, some researchers have hypothesized that GAD is associated with abnormalities of the benzodiazepine receptors in the brain; other lines of study focus on neural structures and neurotransmitter abnormalities (Brawman-Mintzer, Lydiard, Rickels, & Small, 1997).

Anxiety involves a number of interacting subsystems that include cognitive, physiological, affective, and behavioral components. Changes in one can lead to changes in the others (Ladouceur, Dugas, et al., 2000). For example, the amygdala plays a central role in emotions, interacts with the hippocampus and medial prefrontal cortex, and also has connections to the thalamus, hypothalamus, and other brainstem sites. Fear may result in the overactivity of these systems. These connections allow one to speculate about why medications and psychotherapy may both be effective in treating anxiety disorders. Each may operate on different levels of the brain. Cognitive approaches may reduce arousal by deconditioning fear at the hippocampus, which will strengthen the ability of the medial prefrontal cortex to inhibit the amygdala. Medication may directly influence or decrease activity in the amygdala and other brainstem structures (Gorman, Kent, Sullivan, & Coplan, 2000; see Figure 5.3).

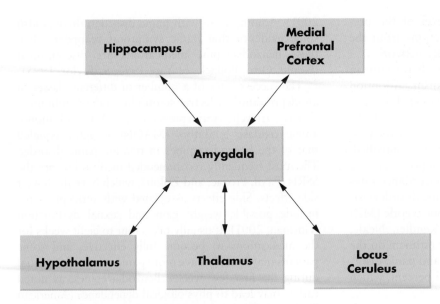

Source: From Gorman, Kent, Sullivan, & Coplan (2000).

FIGURE 5.3 Neuroanatomical Basis of Panic and Other Anxiety Reactions The fear network in the brain is centered in the amygdala and interacts with the hippocampus and medial prefrontal cortex. Projections from the amygdala to the hypothalamic and brainstem sites are associated with conditioned fear responses. Medication that influences the serotonin system desensitizes the fear network from the level of the amygdala through projections to the hypothalmus and brainstem. CBT or other psychotherapies reduce contextual fear and cognitive misattributions at the level of the prefrontal cortex and the hippocampus.

Several other biological explanations have been offered. Papp and colleagues (1993) believe that a specific biological dysfunction may predispose people to panic disorder. They hypothesize that the dysfunction involves receptors that monitor the amount of oxygen in the blood. The receptors give the incorrect message that oxygen is insufficient, triggering fears of suffocation and resulting in hyperventilation. M. S. George and Ballenger (1992) hypothesized that panic disorders may be associated with a dysfunction of the *locus ceruleus,* which is part of the central anxiety system in the brain. The increased sensitivity of the anxiety network can be activated by anything that increases anxiety, such as thoughts or such anxiogenic agents as cocaine and caffeine.

The search for biological factors that may contribute to panic disorder has taken several forms. Two of the most important are biological challenge tests and genetic studies. To determine whether some people have a predisposition to panic attacks, researchers have designed *biological challenge tests.* In these tests, researchers administer a biological agent such as sodium lactate or carbon dioxide to people who have panic attacks and to others who do not have such attacks. The assumption is that a biological sensitivity to lactate or carbon dioxide produces feelings of alarm and that only people who are biologically susceptible should show panic symptoms. Most people with panic disorder do have a panic attack when given sodium lactate (Papp et al., 1993) or carbon dioxide (Carter, Hollon, Carson, & Shelton, 1995). The same is true when panic-disordered patients are asked to hyperventilate (Nardi, Valenca, Nascimento, Mezzasalma, &

Zin, 2001). Antidepressants have been found to block both spontaneous and lactate-induced panic attacks (Aronson, 1987). Presumably, medication raises the threshold for attacks in individuals who are susceptible.

Although these results support a biological model, some findings are contradictory. For example, some "normal" participants also experience panic attacks during biological challenge tests (Balon, Pohl, Yeragani, Rainey, & Berchou, 1988; Kent et al., 2001). Individuals who have a panic attack after infusion of sodium lactate may no longer respond to the sodium lactate after going through desensitization treatment (Guttmacher & Nelles, 1984) or cognitive-behavioral therapy (Shear et al., 1991). An individual's expectations may also affect the results of biological challenge tests. For example, instructions given before lactate infusion seem to influence the way participants respond to the substance. Those who expect pleasant sensations show less anxiety than those who expect unpleasant bodily sensations (Van Der Molen, van den Hout, Vroemen, Lousberg, & Griez, 1986). Also, an individual's reactions can be influenced by the presence of another person with whom he or she feels safe. Panic disorder patients accompanied by a "safe" person reported fewer catastrophic thoughts and showed less physiological arousal when inhaling carbon dioxide than did those without a safe person present (Carter et al., 1995).

Thus, psychological factors may influence panic attacks by changing the threshold for this response. Although the research seems to support a biological mechanism in panic disorder, cognitive factors can also influence the emotional and physiological reactivity (Rapee, 1995). As mentioned earlier, it may be that cognitive factors occurring at the level of the prefrontal cortex can act to inhibit reactions from the amygdala and other parts of the anxiety network.

Genetic studies offer researchers another avenue in their search for a biological mechanism. Adoption studies have not been reported for anxiety disorders, so environmental influences cannot be eliminated. We must be careful in interpreting studies because the possible impact of modeling has not been controlled. Nevertheless, several studies seem to support a genetic influence for panic disorder. Higher concordance rates (percentages of relatives sharing the same disorder) for panic disorder have been found for monozygotic (MZ) twins versus dizygotic (DZ) twins (Kendler, Neale, Kessler, Heath, & Eaves, 1992). Their estimate on the degree of heritability for agoraphobia and panic disorder due to genetic factors was about 35 percent, which is a modest contribution.

Fewer genetic studies have been done on generalized anxiety disorder than on panic disorder. The strategy used to study GAD has been to examine the distribution of anxiety disorders among family members of people with the disorder and compare it with that of control group members. This strategy yields less support for the role of genetic factors in generalized anxiety disorder than in panic disorder. Still, there appears to be a small but significant heritability factor in GAD (Brawman-Mintzer et al., 1997; Gorman, 2001; Kendler et al., 1992).

Treatment of Panic Disorder and Generalized Anxiety Disorder

Treatments for panic disorder and GAD can generally take one of two approaches: biochemical (via medication) and psychotherapeutic. The latter are usually behavioral approaches, including cognitive behavioral therapy. See the Critical Thinking feature "Panic Disorder Treatment: Should We Focus on Internal Control?" regarding self-efficacy in treatment outcome.

Biochemical Treatment   Evaluating the efficacy of medical treatment for panic disorder can be difficult, given placebo response rates as high as 75 percent in clinical trials (American Psychiatric Association, 1998). Benzodiazepines have been successful in treating GAD, but these drugs can lead to tolerance and dependence (Nutt, 2001). They are not recommended for those who have a history of substance abuse, and, because of their sedating effect, they have been associated with an increase in falls and hip fractures in the elderly (Gorman, 2001; Wagner et al., 2004). Because GAD is a chronic condition, antidepressants rather than benzodiazepines are the medications of choice (Davidson,

2001). Among those with panic disorder, there is also some evidence that panic symptoms reappear when these benzodiazepine medications are discontinued (Gould, Otto, Pollack, & Yap, 1997; S. Taylor, 1995).

The success rates of a number of different classes of antidepressants—selective serotonin reuptake inhibitors (SSRIs), tricyclic antidepressants (TCAs), and monoamine oxidase inhibitors (MAOIs)—roughly equaled that of the benzodiazepines in treating panic disorder. The most frequently recommended medications are the SSRIs (Paxil, Prozac, and Zoloft), which have the fewest side effects. Side effects associated with antidepressants include possible weight gain and sexual dysfunction (Gorman, 2001). It usually takes four to eight weeks for the medications to become fully effective, and some patients may initially have more panic attacks than usual during the first few weeks. Benzodiazepines, as noted earlier, may lead to physiological dependence (American Psychiatric Association, 1998).

That so many different medications have been used successfully indicates the possibility that they operate on different neural structures that form the anxiety network. In general, medications have been useful in treating anxiety disorders. However, in one large-scale study, only 24 percent of patients with panic disorder were panic free one year after treatment with either imipramine or alprazolam (Katschnig & Amering, 1994). Relapse rates after cessation of drug therapy appear to be quite high, especially among clients who believed the remission of symptoms was due to the medication (Biondi et al., 2003).

Behavioral Treatment   Cognitive behavioral treatments, both in individual therapy (Barlow, Gorman, Shear, & Woods, 2000; Otto, Pollack, & Sabatino, 1996) and in group therapy (Penava, Otto, Maki, & Pollack, 1998), have been successful in treating panic disorder. Reviews of these treatments for panic disorder found that 80 percent or more of clients achieved and maintained panic-free status (Margraf, Barlow, Clark, & Telch, 1993; Fava, Zielezny, Savron, & Grandi, 1995).

In general, the cognitive behavioral treatment for panic disorders involves the following steps (American Psychiatric Association, 1998; B. J. Cox, Fergus, & Swinson, 1994; Öst & Westling, 1995; S. Taylor, Woody, Koch, McLean, & Anderson, 1996):

1. Educating the client about panic disorder and symptoms.

2. Training the client in muscle-relaxation techniques.

3. Performing symptom-induction tasks (such as voluntary hyperventilation or breathing through a straw) to reduce alarm about bodily sensations.

Panic Disorder Treatment: Should We Focus on Internal Control?

Imagine standing in the middle of a busy mall when suddenly your heart starts to pound, you begin to sweat, you become nauseated and can barely breathe, you can't move, and you are completely disoriented. You feel as though you will either pass out or die. What is happening to you? What brought on this terrifying experience? Will it happen again? When you regain composure, you think about what has just happened. If these panic attacks occur repeatedly, you will probably explore treatment options. Which techniques will you choose?

Figures 5.2 and 5.3 offer two explanations for panic attacks; Figure 5.2 illustrates the role of cognitions in interpreting unpleasant bodily sensations, whereas Figure 5.3 shows the interactions among neural structures in the brain's fear network. Are these models mutually exclusive, or do they interact? If excessive anxiety were caused by faulty cognitions (e.g., misinterpretation of bodily sensations and catastrophizing thoughts), then a cognitive approach to treatment would seem appropriate. If biological factors are responsible for overstimulating fear structures of the brain, then medications might be the best solution to treating the symptoms. If these systems interact, integrating psychotherapy and pharmacological interventions might best treat the panic disorders. What role do your beliefs play in treatment effectiveness?

Abraham Bakker and his colleagues (2002) compared outcomes of two groups of patients. In one group, the patients were treated with cognitive therapy (CT)—a therapy that included patients' accepting personal control for their panic reactions. In the other group, patients were given antidepressant medications without psychotherapy. Although more patients who received CT left the study than did patients receiving medication (15 of 65 CT patients left the study versus 5 of 64 of those receiving medication), those remaining in the CT group had lower relapse rates than those treated pharmacologically, and those in the CT group learned to view their symptoms *and* their gains as the result of their own efforts, not as a matter of luck, therapy, or medication.

Biondi and colleagues (2003) compared medication alone with a combination of medication and cognitive-behavioral therapy (CBT). Among the CBT strategies used was sharing information about panic disorders, challenging catastrophic misinterpretations and considering alternative explanations of bodily sensations, exposure to feared situations, relaxation training, and understanding what the disorder might mean in a patient's life. Before, during, and at the end of treatment, the researchers also assessed participants' beliefs concerning whether recovery would be based on medication. Almost twice as many medication-group patients left the study than did those in the CBT group, and relapse rate was 78.1

percent for the medication group compared with 14.3 percent for the CBT group. Long-term outcomes were significantly better for patients who came to attribute their anxiety and recovery to internal factors than for patients who attributed their improvement to medication.

Critical among the cognitive training strategies outlined here, and a common factor in both studies, is the enhancement of the patients' self-efficacy—learning that both recovery and the ability to manage anxiety are under their own control. Patients who believed (or who came to believe) that their success was in their own hands, thus demonstrating an internal locus of control over their bodies and their disorder, were significantly more likely to reduce their anxiety symptoms than patients who attributed their improvement to external factors, such as medications.

Do you attribute anxiety in your life to internal factors (e.g., how you interpret events) or to external elements (e.g., "things like this are always happening to me")? Do you believe medications are more likely to help you control your anxiety, or do you see yourself in control when it comes to understanding and dealing with anxiety-provoking events? Are there ways of altering medication practices or rationale that would also foster internal control over symptoms? Based on these studies, how would you structure an intervention for panic disorder?

4. Helping the client identify and change unrealistic thoughts—for example, the therapist might comment, "Maybe you are attributing danger to what is going on in your body," or "A panic attack will not stop your breathing."

5. Encouraging the client to face the symptoms, both within the session and in the outside world, using such statements as, "Allow your body to have its reactions and let the reactions pass."

6. Providing coping statements: "This feeling is not pleasant, but I can handle it."

7. Teaching the client to identify the antecedents of the panic: "What stresses are you under?"

8. Helping the client to learn to use coping strategies, such as relaxation and cognitive restructuring (interpreting events more positively), to handle stress.

Cognitive behavioral therapy appears to be successful in treating GAD as well, and it has the additional benefit of significantly reducing the depression that often accompanies GAD. It is the only consistently validated treatment for the disorder (Ballenger et al., 2000). The treatment strategies generally involve the following steps (Dugas & Ladouceur, 2000; Eisen & Silverman, 1998; Stanley et al., 2003): (1) identification and modification of the worrisome thoughts; (2) discriminating between worries about situations that are amenable to problem solving and those that are not; (3) evaluation of beliefs concerning worry; (4) discussion of and evidence for and against the distorted beliefs; (4) decatastrophizing worrisome thoughts; (5) development of self-control skills to monitor and challenge irrational thoughts and substitute more positive, coping thoughts; and (6) muscle relaxation to deal with somatic symptoms. In an evaluation of thirteen controlled clinical trials, cognitive behavioral strategies were effective in treating GAD and were associated with low dropout rates and long-term improvement (Borkovec & Ruscio, 2001).

Myth vs Reality

Myth: Because the metabolism rate in certain areas of the brain associated with anxiety disorders can be "normalized" with medication, biological explanations and treatments should predominate.

Reality: Psychotherapy is highly effective with anxiety disorders and may also affect brain metabolism by operating at a different pathway of the fear network. Medications appear to affect the fear network at the level of the amygdala, whereas cognitive behavior therapy has its effects at the prefrontal cortex and hippocampus.

Phobias

The word *phobia* comes from the Greek word that means "fear." A **phobia** is a strong, persistent, and unwarranted fear of some specific object or situation. An individual with a phobia often experiences extreme anxiety or panic attacks when he or she encounters the phobic stimulus. Attempts to avoid the object or situation notably interfere with the individual's life. Adults with this disorder realize that their fear is excessive, though children may not. Most people with a phobia have other anxiety, mood, or substance use disorders (Hofmann, Lehman, & Barlow, 1997).

Nearly anything can become the focus of intense fear. There is even a fear of phobias, called *phobophobia* (see Table 5.1). Phobias are the most common mental disorder in the United States. DSM-IV-TR includes three subcategories of phobias: agoraphobia, the social phobias, and the specific phobias.

Agoraphobia

Agoraphobia is an intense fear of being in public places where escape or help may not be readily available. It arises from a fear that panic-like symptoms will occur and incapacitate the person or cause him or her to behave in an embarrassing manner, such as fainting, losing control over bodily functions, or displaying excessive fear in public. Anxiety over showing these symptoms can prevent people from leaving their homes. If the individual has a history of unexpected panic attacks, a more appropriate diagnosis might be panic disorder with agoraphobia. Some researchers (Goisman, Warshaw, Steketee, & Fierman, 1995) believe that agoraphobia should be considered a variant of, or a secondary response to, panic disorder, not a separate entity. Agoraphobia occurs much more frequently in females than in males. Although this is not the most common phobia, it is the one seen most frequently among people who have phobias and who seek treatment for them.

Many people report having panic attacks before developing agoraphobia, as illustrated in the following case:

> The patient was a twenty-eight-year-old woman whose attacks of anxiety were triggered by the terrifying sensation of impending death. This feeling was so horrifying

TABLE 5.1 Phobias and Their Objects

Acrophobia: fear of heights	**Microphobia:** fear of germs
Agoraphobia: fear of open spaces	**Monophobia:** fear of being alone
Ailurophobia: fear of cats	**Mysophobia:** fear of contamination or germs
Algophobia: fear of pain	**Nyctophobia:** fear of the dark
Arachnophobia: fear of spiders	**Ochlophobia:** fear of crowds
Astrapophobia: fear of storms, thunder, and lightning	**Pathophobia:** fear of disease
Aviophobia: fear of airplanes	**Phobophobia:** fear of phobias
Brontophobia: fear of thunder	**Pyrophobia:** fear of fire
Claustrophobia: fear of closed spaces	**Syphilophobia:** fear of syphilis
Dementophobia: fear of insanity	**Topophobia:** fear of performing
Genitophobia: fear of genitals	**Xenophobia:** fear of strangers
Hematophobia: fear of blood	**Zoophobia:** fear of animals or some particular animal

that she would clutch passersby and beg them for help. These episodes were acutely embarrassing to her, because no physical illness could be found. In an interview, it was discovered that her anxiety attacks occurred in situations in which she felt trapped, such as in a crowded restaurant. Finally, her fear of experiencing these symptoms in public reached the point at which she was unwilling to leave her home unless accompanied by her husband.

Interest in examining the role of cognitions in agoraphobia is increasing. Eighty-one percent of individuals with agoraphobia reported catastrophic cognitions that involved "fear of doing something embarrassing," "fainting," "losing control," or "becoming ill" (Goisman et al., 1995). It is possible that people with this phobia misinterpret events or elevate them to catastrophes. In a study of sixty patients with agoraphobia, J. A. Franklin (1987) found the following pattern:

- Some physical or psychological stressor

- Altered physical sensations, such as increased heart rate and overbreathing

- Faulty appraisal, such as incorrectly interpreting the symptoms as representing a severe physical problem—a heart attack or loss of control

- Avoidance of the situation associated with the fear. The attacks were described as highly aversive, and the patients' belief that they represented a pathological outcome intensified the fear. This led to avoidance.

As with individuals who have panic attacks, those with agoraphobia may misinterpret and overreact to bodily sensations. In support of this view, Reiss and colleagues (1986) found that agoraphobics scored higher on the Anxiety Sensitivity Inventory (ASI) than did people with other anxiety disorders. Similar results were obtained by Asmundson and Norton (1993). It is too early to tell whether anxiety sensitivity or faulty appraisal act as predisposing factors in the development of panic disorders and agoraphobia or whether both are the result of having the disorders. However, there is increasing support for the role of cognitions in the cause of anxiety disorders.

Social Phobias

A **social phobia** is an intense, excessive fear of being scrutinized in one or more social or performance situations. An individual with a social phobia avoids or endures these situations, which often lead to intense anxiety reactions or panic attacks. The person's fear stems from anxiety that, when in the company of others, he or she will perform one or more activities in a way that is embarrassing or humiliating (Bruch, Fallon, & Heimberg, 2003). There is no such fear when the person engages in any of these activities in private. Examples of fearful thoughts by patients with social anxiety are shown in Table 5.2. The most common fears in social phobia involve public speaking and meeting new people (American Psychiatric Association, 2000). Individuals with social phobias will consume more alcohol on tasks that increase anxiety, such as speaking in front of an audience (Abrams, Kushner, Medina, & Voight, 2002). The following case example describes a typical fear:

TABLE 5.2   Thoughts Reported by Patients with Social Phobia During Social Situations

Patient	Age	Duration (in years)	Idiosyncratic Negative Belief
1	27	5	I'll shake constantly, and people will think that I'm an alcoholic.
2	29	7	I'll look anxious, and people will think that I'm stupid.
3	34	11	I'll babble a lot, and everyone will think that I'm nervous.
4	44	27	I'll blush, and people will think that I'm anxious.
5	22	2	I'll look very tense, and people around will stare at me.
6	18	4	I'll sweat heavily, and everyone will think that I'm nervous.
7	25	8	I'll go red, and people will think that I'm anxious.
8	43	24	I'll tremble uncontrollably, and people will think that I have Parkinson's disease.

Source: From Wells & Papageorgiou (1999).

In any social situation, I felt fear. I would be anxious before I even left the house, and it would escalate as I got closer to a college class, a party or whatever. When I would walk into a room full of people, I'd turn red and it would feel like everybody's eyes were on me. I was embarrassed to stand off in a corner by myself, but I couldn't think of anything to say. ... It was humiliating. ... I couldn't wait to get out. (NIMH, 2000, p. 5)

People with social phobias, like those with other phobias, usually realize that their behavior and fears are irrational, but this understanding does not reduce the distress they feel. Individuals with high social anxiety tend to be biased in the direction of perceiving other people's emotions toward them as negative (Winton, Clark, & Edelmann, 1995). Social phobias can be divided into three types: (1) *performance* (excessive anxiety over activities such as playing a musical instrument, public speaking, eating in a restaurant, using public restrooms); (2) *limited interactional* (excessive fear only in specific social situations, such as going out on a date or interacting with an authority figure); and (3) *generalized* (extreme anxiety displayed in most social situations). In a sample of individuals with generalized social phobia, multiple social fears were present, including fears of public speaking, using the toilet away from home, eating or drinking in public, and writing with someone watching (Kessler, Stein, & Berglund, 1998). Having generalized social phobia appears to affect the occupational status of women. They were more likely to be employed in noninterpersonally oriented jobs, to be underemployed, and to believe that their work supervisors would rate them lower in dependability than

women with more limited forms of social phobia (Bruch et al., 2003).

In a given year about 3.7 percent of adults have social phobia. Women are twice as likely as men to have this disorder; however, more men seek treatment (NIMH, 1999). Social phobias tend to begin during adolescence, and they appear to be more common in families who use shame as a method of control and who stress the importance of the opinions of others (Bruch & Heimberg, 1994). These are common child-rearing practices in Asian families, and social evaluative fears tend to be more common in Chinese children and adolescents than in Western comparison groups (Dong, Yang, & Ollendick, 1994). Other family characteristics, such as parental rejection, overprotectiveness, and a lack of emotional warmth, do not appear to be related to social anxiety in children (Bogels, van Oosten, Muris, & Smulders, 2001). Social fears and other anxiety disorders may be expressed differently in other cultures. The Mental Health and Society feature "Anxiety Disorders from a Cross-Cultural Perspective" discusses this issue.

Specific Phobias

A **specific phobia** is an extreme fear of a specific object (such as snakes) or situation (such as being in an enclosed place). Exposure to the stimulus nearly always produces intense anxiety or a panic attack. The specific phobias provide a catchall category for irrational fears that cannot be classified as either agoraphobia or social phobias. The only similarity among the various specific phobias is the existence of an irrational fear. To produce some organizational frame-

work, DSM-IV-TR divides specific phobias into five types:

1. Animal (such as spiders or snakes)

2. Natural environmental (such as earthquakes, thunder, water)

3. Blood/injections or injury; individuals with this type of phobia, as opposed to other phobias, are likely to have a history of fainting in the phobic situation

4. Situational (includes fear of traveling in cars, planes, and elevators and fear of heights, tunnels, and bridges)

5. Other (phobic avoidance of situations that may lead to choking, vomiting, or contracting an illness)

Unusual and uncommon specific phobias have involved bath water running down the drain (after pulling out the plug, the affected person would dash out of the bathroom with great anxiety); snow (the fear developed after the man got stuck in a snowstorm and arrived too late to talk to his dying father); and three-legged stools (Adler et al., 1984). As we mentioned in the chapter on the scientific method in abnormal psychology, one fourteen-year-old boy who displayed a phobia of dolls reacted with greatest fear to plastic dolls with mobile eyes or dolls with the roots of their hair visible on the scalp (Hatcher, 1989).

The following is a report of a fairly common specific phobia in a twenty-six-year-old public relations executive:

If I see a spider in my house, I get out! I start shaking, and I feel like I'm going to throw up. I get so scared, I have to bolt across the street to drag my neighbor over to get rid of the spider. Even after I know it's gone, I obsess for hours. I check between my sheets 10 times before getting in bed, and I'm so creeped out that I won't get up and go to the bathroom at night, even if my bladder feels like it's about to burst. (Kusek, 2001, p. 183)

Specific phobias are about twice as prevalent in women as in men (see Figure 5.1) and are rarely incapacitating. The degree to which they interfere with daily life depends on how easy it is to avoid the feared object or situation. These phobias often begin during childhood. In a study of 370 patients with phobias (Öst, 1987, 1992), retrospective data revealed that animal phobias tended to have the earliest onset age (seven years), followed by blood phobia (nine years), dental phobia (twelve years), and claustrophobia (twenty years). Figure 5.4 illustrates ages at which different phobias typically begin.

Specific Phobias The extreme fear of spiders is a specific phobia. Is this fear due to cognitions or belief that the spider is malevolent and has targeted him or her for attack, or is it due to feelings of disgust?

MENTAL HEALTH AND SOCIETY
Anxiety Disorders from a Cross-Cultural Perspective

Determining the prevalence of disorders in different countries is problematic. Diagnosis of such disorders usually relies on systems such as DSM-IV-TR, which were developed in Western countries, and the forms and patterns of abnormal behavior in non-Western cultures may not fit specifically within the DSM-IV categories. For example, the American Psychiatric Association (2000) describes a number of culture-bound syndromes that are not "universal" but are limited to specific cultures (see Table 3.3). Taijin Kyofusho, for instance, is a culturally distinctive phobia found in Japan. It is somewhat similar to social phobia as described in DSM-IV-TR. However, instead of a fear involving social or performance situations, Taijin Kyofusho is a fear of offending or embarrassing others, a concept consistent with Japanese cultural emphasis on maintaining interpersonal harmony (Okazaki, 1997; Suzuki, Takei, Kawai, Minabe, & Mori, 2003). Individuals with this disorder are fearful that their appearance, facial expression, eye contact, body parts, or odor are offensive to others. In one study of suburban high school students in Japan, 0.8 percent of boys and 0.2 percent of girls had a phobia involving their body odor; 0.3 percent of boys and 0.2 percent

of girls were fearful of offending others with eye contact (Yasumatsu, 1993). Even though rare, Taijin Kyofusho is considered to be a cultural syndrome and is included in the Japanese diagnostic system for mental disorders.

Although questions remain about the validity of using Western-devised diagnostic instruments with individuals from other cultures, some cross-cultural research on anxiety disorders has been accomplished. In one study of five European cities (Weiller, Bisserbe, Maier, & Lecrubier, 1998), the most prevalent anxiety disorder was generalized anxiety disorder (GAD), with an average current prevalence rate of 8.5 percent. GAD prevalence rates were higher in Paris and Berlin than in Mainz (Germany), Manchester (United Kingdom), and Groningen (Netherlands; Weiller et al., 1998). Similar symptom patterns emerged in a ten-country cross-national epidemiological study of panic disorders (Weissman et al., 1997). Prevalence rates for panic disorder ranged from 1.4 percent in Edmonton, Canada, to 2.9 percent in Florence, Italy. (The prevalence rate was only 0.4 percent in Taiwan, but all rates of mental disorder in that country are low.)

In all countries, women were more likely to be diagnosed with

panic disorder, but there was a large difference in the sex ratio from country to country, ranging from nearly 6 times more women than men in Korea to only 1.3 times more women in Puerto Rico. In another study (Davey et al., 1998), college students in seven Western and Asian countries responded similarly in their ratings of fear of animals. However, students in Hong Kong and Japan scored significantly higher mean fear ratings than in the other countries. In all seven countries, however, women indicated more fear of animals than did males.

Although cross-cultural investigations on anxiety disorders are useful, it is difficult to determine the meaning of differences. Taiwan's levels of reported mental disorders are very low compared with those of other countries. These low levels could reflect a social stigma attached to admitting having mental symptoms, or it could result from differences in the way questions are interpreted or understood. Whatever the explanation, interpretation of such findings remains problematic so long as cross-cultural studies apply Western diagnostic categories to other cultural groups. The very system of classification may obscure important culturally specific mental disorders.

The most common childhood fears are of spiders, the dark, frightening movies, and being teased (Muris, Merckelbach, & Collaris, 1997). Among a sample of 160 primary-school children, 17.6 percent met the criteria for a specific phobia (Muris & Merckelbach, 2000). The type of fears reported by adolescents change over time. A longitudinal study of the fears of individuals at the age of thirteen and again at age fifteen found that the number of fears the young women reported had doubled, whereas those of their male counterparts had decreased. For both males and

females, the most frequently reported fear was speaking in class, followed by speaking to strangers, heights, and animals. Most fears did not persist. Many individuals did, however, report new fears at age fifteen that had not been present earlier (Poulton et al., 1997).

Blood phobias differ from other phobias in being associated with a unique physiological response: fainting in the phobic situation. Fainting appears to result from an initial increase in autonomic arousal followed by a sudden drop in blood pressure and heart rate. Nearly 70 percent of those with blood phobias report a history of

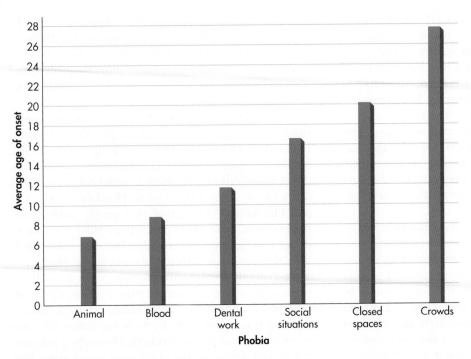

FIGURE 5.4 Phobia Onset
This graph illustrates the average ages at which 370 patients said their phobias began. Animal phobias began during childhood, whereas the onset of agoraphobia did not occur until the individuals were in their late twenties. What do you feel accounts for the differences reported in the age of onset?

Source: Data from Öst (1987, 1992).

fainting in the feared situation (Antony, Brown, & Barlow, 1997). Many are severely handicapped by the phobia. They may avoid medical examinations, caring for an injured child, or shopping at the meat counter in supermarkets (Hellstrom, Fellenius, & Öst, 1996).

Etiology of Phobias

How do such strong and "irrational" fears develop? Both psychological and biological explanations have been proposed. In this section, we examine the psychodynamic, behavioral, and biological views of the etiology of phobias. Although these perspectives are discussed separately, it is plausible that phobias may result from an interaction of biological, cognitive, and environmental factors.

Psychodynamic Perspective According to the psychodynamic viewpoint, phobias are "expressions of wishes, fears and fantasies that are unacceptable to the patient" (Barber & Luborsky, 1991). These unconscious conflicts are displaced (or shifted) from their original internal source to an external object or situation. The phobia is less threatening to the person than recognition of the underlying unconscious impulse. A fear of knives, for example, may represent castration fears produced by an unresolved Oedipus complex or aggressive conflicts. People with agoraphobia may develop their fear of leaving home because they unconsciously fear that they may act out unacceptable sexual desires. The presence of a friend or spouse lowers anxiety because it provides some protection against the agoraphobic impulses. In this sense, phobias represent a compromise between the ego and the impulses that seek gratification. The person blocks from consciousness the real source of anxiety and is able to avoid the dangerous impulse that the phobia represents.

Therapists in the psychodynamic tradition believe that the level of phobic fear shows the strength of the underlying conflict. This formulation, presented by Freud in 1909, was based on his analysis of a fear of horses displayed by a five-year-old boy named Hans (Freud, 1909/1959). Freud believed that the phobia represented a symptomatic or displaced fear arising from the Oedipus complex. The hypothesized factors involved were the boy's incestuous attraction to his mother, hostility toward his father because of the father's sexual privileges, and castration fear (fear of retribution by his father). Freud became convinced that these elements were present in the phobic boy.

At the age of three, Hans had displayed an interest in his penis (which he called his "widdler"); he would examine both animate and inanimate objects for the presence of a penis. One day as he was fondling himself, his mother threatened to have a physician cut off his penis. "And then what will you widdle with?" (Freud, 1909/1959, p. 151). Hans enjoyed having his mother bathe him and especially wanted her to touch his penis. Freud interpreted these events to suggest that Hans was aware of pleasurable sensations in his penis and that he knew it could be "cut off" if he did not behave. Wanting his mother to handle his genitals showed Hans's increasing sexual interest in her.

Hans's fear that horses would bite him developed after he saw a horse-drawn van overturn. According to Freud, little Hans's sexual jealousy of his father and the hostility it aroused produced anxiety. He believed that his father could retaliate by castrating him. This unconscious threat was so unbearable that the fear was displaced to the idea that horses "will bite me." Freud concluded that phobias were adaptive because they prevented the surfacing of traumatic unconscious conflicts.

Although Freud's formulation has clinical appeal, it has problems. According to the psychodynamic perspective, if the phobia is only a symptom of an underlying unconscious conflict, treatment directed to that symptom—the feared object or situation—should be ineffective, leaving the patient defenseless and subject to overwhelming anxiety or leading to the development of a new symptom. But the evidence does not support the view that eliminating the symptom is ineffective.

Behavioral Perspective Behaviorists have examined three possible processes—classical conditioning, modeling, and cognitive negative information—in their attempt to explain the etiology of phobias (N. King, Eleonora, & Ollendick, 1998). The specific process by which phobias develop may depend on the class of fear. Children report that animal fears, medical fears, and fear of failure or criticism develop from conditioning experiences, whereas fears of the unknown, danger, and death are due to information. In self-reports, children with strong fears chose conditioning experiences as the most frequent cause for the onset of fears (39.7 percent), followed by information (26.7 percent). Modeling accounted for only 0.8 percent of the causes of fears, and the origin of 32.8 percent of fears could not be identified (Muris, Merckelbach, & Collaris, 1997).

Classical Conditioning Perspective The view that phobias are conditioned responses is based primarily on Watson's conditioning experiment with Little Albert. Watson was able to produce a fear response in the infant to a white rat by pairing it with a loud sound (Watson & Rayner, 2000). Thus it appears that fears can result through classical conditioning or association. There is some evidence that emotional reactions can be conditioned. Before undergoing chemotherapy for breast cancer, women were given lemon-lime Kool-Aid in a container with a bright orange lid. After repeated pairings of the drink and the chemotherapy, the women indicated emotional distress and nausea when presented with the container (Jacobsen et al., 1995). Approximately 17 percent of individuals who were injured in traffic accidents developed travel phobia. Many show a reluctance to enter vehicles, stay home more frequently, and are intolerant of high or even moderate speeds in an automobile (DiGallo, Barton, & Parry-Jones, 1997).

Most children with severe phobias report conditioning experiences as the cause (N. King, Clowes-Hollins, & Ollendick, 1997; N. King et al., 1998). Similarly, more clients attributed their phobias to direct (classical) conditioning experiences than to any other factor (Öst, 1987; Öst & Hugdahl, 1981). Öst and Hugdahl (1981) found that people with agoraphobia were most likely to attribute their disorder to direct conditioning experiences; the next most likely were those with claustrophobia and dental phobia.

In general, retrospective reports seem to indicate that conditioning experiences play a role in the development of phobias for most clients seeking therapy and that this process may be more important for some types of phobias than for others. However, a substantial percentage of surveyed patients report something other than a direct conditioning experience as the "key" to their phobias. Also, the classical conditioning perspective does not explain why only some people exposed to potential conditioning experiences actually develop phobias.

Observational Learning Perspective Emotional conditioning can be developed through observational learning, or modeling. An observer who watched while a model exhibited pain cues in response to an auditory stimulus (a buzzer) gradually developed an emotional reaction to the sound (Bandura & Rosenthal, 1966). The buzzer, formerly a neutral stimulus, became a conditioned stimulus for the observer. In a clinical (rather than an experimental) example involving modeling, several people who had seen the horror film *The Exorcist* had to be treated for a variety of anxiety reactions (Bozzuto, 1975). A fear or phobia in children can result from the observation of fright displayed by a parent or friend or in media such as television or the movies.

The role of modeling may depend on the type of phobia. Among individuals with speech phobia, none attributed his or her fear to "observing others who are afraid of speaking" or "seeing someone else experience an extremely unpleasant event" (Hofmann, Ehlers, & Roth, 1995). The data from these studies, however, are based on patients' recollections of past events, and such data are subject to a variety of errors. The observational learning perspective seems to share a problem with the classical conditioning approach: neither, by itself, can explain why only some people develop phobias after exposure to a vicarious experience.

Negative Information Perspective To determine the influence of negative information on the acquisition of nighttime fears in children, researchers asked them questions such as, "Did you see frightening things on television about...?" (Muris, Merckelbach, Ollendick, King, & Bogie, 2001). The most common fears included concern with intruders, imaginary creatures, frightening dreams, animals, and frightening thoughts. Most (73.3 percent) of the children attributed their fears to negative information acquired largely from television. However, it is not clear whether negative information is sufficient to produce a phobia. Actual phobias may be more a product of conditioning and modeling experiences. About 24 percent of children were unable to specify the cause of their fear.

Cognitive-Behavioral Perspective Why do individuals with spider phobia react with such terror at the sight of a spider? Some researchers believe cognitive distortions and catastrophic thoughts may cause such strong fears to develop. For example, people with spider phobia believe that spiders single them out for attack and that they will move rapidly and aggressively toward them (Riskind, Moore, & Bowley, 1995). Others report thoughts that the spider "will attack me" or "will take revenge" (Mulkens, de Jong, & Merckelbach, 1996). Similar negative thoughts, such as "I will be trapped," "I will suffocate," or "I will lose control," have been reported by individuals with claustrophobia. Removal of these thoughts was associated with dramatic decreases in their fear (Shafran, Booth, & Rachman, 1993). Individuals with high social anxiety tend to engage in negative self-observation and monitoring and are alert to "threat" cues such as any sign of disapproval or criticism (Harvey, Clark, Ehlers, & Rapee, 2000; Mogg, Philippot, & Bradley, 2004). Studies also indicate that a person with a phobia is more likely to overestimate the odds of an unpleasant event occurring. Patients with acrophobia (fear of heights) overestimate not only the probability of falling but also the probability of being injured (Menzies & Clarke, 1995). Such studies seem to indicate that cognitions involving catastrophic or distorted thinking may be causal or contributing factors in phobias.

Biological Perspective Some researchers (Muris et al., 2001) believe that biological factors such as genetics or biological preparedness may explain why the origins of some fears or phobias cannot be identified. You may recall that genetic factors may be implicated in the development of a disorder if a higher-than-average prevalence of the disorder is found in close relatives or if identical twins (who share the same genetic makeup) show a higher concordance rate for the disorder than that found among fraternal twins (who have different genetic makeups). Studies on male and female twin pairs have supported a moderate contribution from a common genetic factor for all phobia subtypes (Hettema, Annas, Neale, Kendler, & Fredrikson, 2003; Kendler, Myers, Prescott, & Neale, 2001).

However, evidence for the direct genetic transmission of specific anxiety disorders is not strong. In a study of the influence of heredity on agoraphobia, social phobia, and specific phobias in women, Kendler and associates (1992) concluded that genetic influences are modest and that they vary among the subtypes of phobias. Specific phobias appear to be a result of a modest genetic vulnerability and conditioning experiences, whereas agoraphobia has a slightly stronger genetic influence. A higher rate of social phobia among the relatives of *probands* (individuals with the disorder under study) has been reported for generalized social phobia (Stein, Chartier, Hazen, & Kozak, 1998).

More support exists for the view that constitutional or physiological factors may *predispose* individuals to develop fear reactions. It is possible that a certain level of autonomic nervous system (ANS) reactivity is inherited; people born with high ANS reactivity respond more strongly to stimuli, and their chances of developing an anxiety disorder are increased.

A different biological approach to the development of fear reactions is that of *preparedness* (Ohman & Mineka, 2001; Poulton, Waldie, Craske, Menzies, & McGee, 2000; M. Seligman, 1971). Proponents of this position argue that fears do not develop randomly. In particular, they believe that it is easier for human beings to learn fears to which we are physiologically predisposed. Such quickly aroused (or "prepared") fears may have been necessary to the survival of pretechnological humanity. In fact, evolutionarily prepared fears may occur even without exposure to traumatic conditioning experiences. Several predictions can be made from the preparedness hypothesis (Ohman & Mineka, 2001):

1. A fear module or neural circuitry in the amygdala exists that is activated by fear-relevant stimuli (those dangerous to pretechnical humans, such as snakes and other animals).

2. In humans, the fear module is activated by fear-relevant stimuli even without conscious recognition.

3. Once the fear module is activated, it cannot be aborted through conscious control. (Understanding that the object such as a spider or snake is not dangerous will not terminate the fear).

4. Fear-irrelevant conditioning (involving fears that are not "prepared") is different from fear-relevant

conditioning in that the former is tied to expectancies about the stimuli and usually does not activate the fear module.

These predictions received some support from one study (Forsyth, Eifert, & Thompson, 1996). Participants inhaled a 20 percent concentration of carbon dioxide (unconditioned stimulus), which produced sensations of heart racing, breathlessness, faintness, and sweaty palms. They were then exposed to videos of fear-relevant stimuli (a snake moving toward the viewer, a human heart beating irregularly) or to fear-irrelevant stimuli (daisies swaying in the wind, a magnified view of human sperm). As the preparedness theory predicted, the conditioned responses to fear-relevant stimuli not only were more easily acquired but also were of a higher magnitude and more difficult to extinguish than the responses to fear-irrelevant stimuli.

Other researchers (Davey et al., 1998; de Jong, Vorage, & van den Hout, 2000) believe that the preparedness hypothesis is incomplete and that humans' fear of animals such as spiders and rats (normally physically harmless) is due instead to the disgust they evoke. These researchers attribute the avoidance reaction to an inherent fear of disease or contamination, not to a threat of physical danger. In an experiment to determine if disgust is involved in spider phobia, Mulkens and his colleagues (1996) had women with and without spider phobias indicate their willingness to eat a cookie. An assistant of the researchers then guided a "medium sized" spider (*Tegenaria Atrica*) across the cookie. An

associate then removed the spider from the room. The researchers reasoned that if disgust is a factor, those with a spider phobia should be more reluctant to eat the "contaminated" cookie. Results supported this idea: only 25 percent of women with spider phobia eventually ate some of the cookie, compared with 70 percent of the control group participants.

In another study, men and women with spider phobia were found to respond to spiders with a combination of fear and disgust, although fear appeared to predominate (Tolin, Lohr, Sawchuk, & Lee, 1997). Thorpe and Salkovskis (1998) also report that individuals with spider phobia associate the words *legs, hairy, creepy, black,* and *fast* with spiders. *Disgust* received seventh or eighth place in a list of adjectives used to describe spiders. The disease avoidance or disgust theory may be more appropriate for animals such as cockroaches, maggots, or slugs. It is also possible that some animals evoke both fear and disgust, whereas others evoke only one or the other emotion.

Although the combination of classical conditioning and prepared learning is a promising area for further research, it is difficult to believe that most phobias stem from prepared fears. Many simply do not fit into the prepared-fear model. It would be difficult, for example, to explain the survival value of social phobias such as the fear of using public restrooms and of eating in public, of agoraphobia, and of many specific phobias. In addition, prepared fears appear to have variable age of onset and are among the easiest to eliminate.

"Glad to hear your fear of contracting infectious diseases is under control."

Treatment of Phobias

Specific and social phobias have been successfully treated by both behavioral methods and medication. In some studies the two types of treatments have been combined, although the results from combination have been mixed. Individuals with generalized social phobia were treated with either cognitive behavioral therapy (CBT), fluoxetine, or both CBT and medication. The results indicated that both were equally effective and that the combination produced no improvement in outcome (Davidson et al., 2004). Other researchers have reported that medication combined with CBT is a more effective in treating anxiety disorders (Blomhoff et al., 2001).

Biochemical Treatments   Biochemical treatments are predicated on the view that anxiety disorders involve neurobiological abnormalities that can be normalized with medication. The most commonly identified neurotransmitters involved are norepinephrine, serotonin, and dopamine. In general, antidepressants can help reduce not only the extreme fear but also the depression that often accompanies anxiety disorders. In treating phobias, a number of medications appear to be effective. For agoraphobia, there is "clear evidence of clinical efficacy" for benzodiazepines (antianxiety medications), tricyclic antidepressants, and SSRIs (selective serotonin reuptake inhibitors). For social phobia, both benzodiazepines and SSRIs have shown "preliminary evidence of efficacy," and benzodiazepines have been used with some success in treating specific phobias (Lader & Bond, 1998). As with most medications, side or negative effects can occur. Benzodiazepines can produce dependence, withdrawal symptoms, and paradoxical reactions such as increased talkativeness, excessive movement, and even hostility and rage (Mancuso, Tanzi, & Gabay, 2004). SSRIs can result in diminished libido and decreased sexual arousal and functioning. In one study up to 53 percent of those on antidepressant medication reported a decrease in sexual interest or function and up to 22 percent reported weight gain ("Drugs and Talk Therapy," 2004). Some antidepressants can also result in weight gain, dry mouth, memory impairment, and other anticholinergic effects. The phobia symptoms often recur if the patient stops taking the medications (Sundel & Sundel, 1998).

Methodological flaws tend to hamper the evaluation of drugs in treating phobias for three reasons. First, most studies rely only on self-reports as measures of success. Second, few studies employ control groups. And third, the drug treatment condition often encourage patients to expose themselves to the fear-producing

situation while they receive medication. Having patients confront fear-producing situations in an attempt to reduce this fear is a basic part of behavioral therapy. When biochemical treatment studies do not control for this effect, results are difficult to interpret.

Behavioral Treatments   Phobias have been successfully treated with a variety of behavioral approaches. These approaches can include: exposure (gradually introducing the individual to the feared situation or object until the fear dissipates); desensitization (similar to exposure but with an additional response, such as relaxation, to help combat anxiety); modeling (demonstration of another person's successful interactions with the feared object or situation); cognitive restructuring (identifying irrational or anxiety-arousing thoughts associated with the phobia and changing them); and skills training (learning skills necessary to function in the phobic situation). Some behavioral programs rely primarily on one approach; others combine several techniques. A combined approach for social phobia using training in social skills, rehearsal in a group setting, cognitive restructuring, and skills practice in actual social situations was successful for nearly two-thirds of the participants (Salaberria & Echeburua, 1998).

Exposure Therapy   In **exposure therapy**, the patient is gradually introduced to increasingly difficult encounters with the feared situation. For example, in agoraphobia, which involves the fear of leaving the house, the therapist may first ask the patient only to visualize or imagine the anxiety-evoking situation. After completing this task, the person would be asked to actually take walks outside the home with the therapist until the fear has been eliminated. Exposure therapy has also been used successfully to treat specific phobias such as speech anxiety (Hofman et al., 2004), fear of spiders (Muris, Merckelbach, & de Jong, 1995; Carlin, Hoffman, & Weghorst, 1997), claustrophobia (Booth & Rachman, 1992), fear of flying (Rothbaum, Hodges, Watson, & Kessler, 1996), and fear of heights (W. Marshall, 1988). In one case, a thirty-one-year-old Asian man reported a fear of being in a falling elevator. The fear developed when he was trapped in an elevator on the seventh floor for about an hour. He became increasingly fearful that it would fall. His treatment involved confronting his fear by riding in elevators for a period of ninety minutes. After just one session, his phobia disappeared (L. Myers, 1997). A variant of exposure therapy has been developed for the treatment of blood-injection phobia, which is associated with fainting caused by a sudden drop in blood pressure and slowing of the heart rate. A procedure

MENTAL HEALTH AND SOCIETY
Virtual Reality Therapy

Mary Muppet (pseudonym) is a thirty-seven-year-old woman with a severe and incapacitating spider phobia that has lasted for twenty years. Encounters with a spider or spider web produce panic, waves of anxiety, and weeping over the restrictions to her life caused by the fear. She washes and vacuums her car every day and fumigates it with pesticides to eliminate spiders. While driving her car, she wears "spider gloves" to sweep out any spider webs she observes. In an attempt to prevent spiders from entering her bedroom, she seals her bedroom windows with duct tape every day. She places individual pieces of clothing in sealed plastic bags to prevent contact with spiders (Carlin, Hoffman, & Weghorst, 1997).

Because of the limited success of exposure techniques (looking at photos of spiders, handling models of spiders, and hanging a plastic spider on the rear-view mirror), Mary Muppet and her therapists agreed to try an experimental procedure, virtual reality, to eliminate her incapacitating phobia. The equipment included a helmet with video monitors that produced computer-generated three-dimensional images that immerse the participant in a realistic setting. The images are generated in response to the individual's head movements. When Mary raised her head, for example, she would see the ceiling. In addition, she had a cyber hand that moved in correspondence to her real hand. The virtual "spider world" was a kitchen in which Mary could reach out and open cupboards. The spider in this kitchen might climb walls, drop from the ceiling, or jump unpredictably from the cupboard.

Initially, Mary was allowed to control her interaction with the spider. Later, the therapists were in charge of the appearance of the spider. When Mary first began the sessions, her body shook uncontrollably. After twelve sessions, her twenty-year spider phobia was completely eliminated. In fact, when Mary now spots a spider in her home, she responds by saying, "I'm sorry, you came to the wrong house!" and squashes it (Salyer, 1997, p. C2).

Virtual reality has the potential to deal with a number of phobias and fears (Garcia-Palacios, Hoffman, Carlin, Furness, & Botella, 2002). Using this procedure, therapists can generate a variety of images (such as scenes from combat) that are not available in real life and can immerse the individual in a "real-life" experience. Virtual reality therapy has been used in the treatment of fear of flying (M. M. North, North, & Coble, 1997; Rothbaum, Anderson, Smith, Hodges, & Price, 2002)) and may even be appropriate for treating some social phobias (Glantz, Durlach, Barnett, & Aviles, 1996; Lubell, 2004). Computer programs and hardware are being developed to implement this promising technology more fully.

known as *applied tension,* combined with exposure, has proven effective (Hellstrom et al., 1996).

One patient, Mr. A., reported feeling faint when exposed to any stimuli involving blood, injections, injury, or surgery. Even hearing an instructor discuss the physiology of the heart caused Mr. A. to feel sweaty and faint. Mr. A. was first taught to recognize the first signs of a drop in blood pressure and then to combat this autonomic response by tightening (tensing) the muscles of his arms, chest, and legs until his face felt warm. Mr. A. was then taught to stop the tension for about fifteen to twenty seconds and then to reapply the tension, repeating the procedure about five times. (The rise in blood pressure that follows this process prevents fainting, and the fear becomes extinguished.) After going through this process, Mr. A. was able to watch a video of thoracic surgery, watch blood being drawn, listen to a talk about cardiovascular disease, and read an anatomy book—stimuli that in the past would have produced fainting (Anderson, Taylor, & McLean, 1996). This procedure involving muscle tension is specific for phobias in which fainting may occur.

Exposure therapies employing computer technology have recently been developed. The Mental Health and Society feature "Virtual Reality Therapy" discusses this approach.

Cognitive Strategies In this approach, unrealistic thoughts are altered, as they are believed to be responsible for phobias. Individuals with social phobias, for example, tend to be intensely self-focused and fearful that others will see them as anxious, incompetent, or weak. Their own self-criticism is the basis for their phobia (Harvey et al., 2000; Hofman, 2000). Cognitive strategies can help "normalize" social anxiety by encouraging patients to interpret emotional and physical tension as "normal anxiety" and by helping them redirect their attention from themselves to others in the social situations. This approach has been successful in treating individuals with public-speaking phobia, in which a strong relationship was found between a decrease in self-focus and a reduction in speech anxiety (Woody, Chambless, & Glass, 1997). Claustrophobic individuals have also been successfully treated by having them identify specific beliefs about danger and testing them when they are in an enclosed chamber (Kamphuis & Telch, 2000; Öst, Alm, Brandberg, & Breitholtz, 2000).

Systematic desensitization uses muscle relaxation to reduce the anxiety associated with specific and social phobias. Wolpe (1958, 1973), who introduced the treatment, first taught clients a muscle relaxation response that is incompatible with fear. Second, he had them visualize the feared stimuli (arranged from least to most anxiety provoking) while in the relaxed state. This was continued until the clients reported little or no anxiety with the stimuli. This procedure was adapted for Mr. B., who had a fear of urinating in restrooms when others were present. He was trained in muscle relaxation and, while relaxed, learned to urinate under the following conditions: no one in the bathroom, therapist in the stall, therapist washing hands, therapist at adjacent urinal, therapist waiting behind client. These conditions were arranged in ascending difficulty. The easier items were practiced first until Mr. B's anxiety was sufficiently reduced. Over a period of seventeen

weeks, the anxiety diminished completely, and the gains were maintained in a follow-up at seven and one-half months (McCracken & Larkin, 1991).

As was discussed earlier, some researchers believe that the fear of spiders is primarily due to the emotion of disgust. To determine if this is the case, de Jong and colleagues (2000) compared two treatments: (1) gradual exposure and (2) desensitization that involved gradual exposure with an anxiety-reducing stimulus (participants' favorite music played). The music was supposed to reduce the "disgusting" properties of the spider. Both treatments were effective and not significantly different from one another. Systematic desensitization has been shown to be effective with both specific and social phobias.

Modeling therapy procedures—which include filmed modeling, live modeling, and participant modeling—have also been highly effective in treating certain phobias. When modeling is used as therapy, the person with the phobia observes a model in the act of coping with, or responding appropriately in, the fear-producing situation (Ollendick & King, 1998). Some researchers believe that modeling is a unique therapeutic approach in its own right, whereas others believe that it is a type of exposure treatment.

Obsessive-Compulsive Disorder

Obsessive-compulsive disorder (OCD) is characterized by **obsessions** (intrusive, repetitive thoughts or images that produce anxiety) or **compulsions** (the need to

Modeling Therapy Watching a fear-producing act being performed successfully (like the man handling the snake) can help people overcome their fear. Modeling therapy has proven effective in treating both specific and social phobias. Why do you think modeling works?

perform acts or to dwell on thoughts to reduce anxiety). Although obsessions and compulsions can occur separately, they frequently occur together (Freeston & Ladouceur, 1997), as in the following case.

> A microbiology technician developed an obsession about becoming contaminated with the HIV virus. She began to wash her hands compulsively more than eight times after contact with bodily fluids. She washed and bleached her work clothes at home several times. And she would not allow her children to take a bath until she cleaned and disinfected the bathtub. (Kraus & Nicholson, 1996)

The symptoms of obsessive-compulsive disorder are described as *ego-dystonic*—that is, the afflicted individual considers the thoughts and actions alien and not subject to his or her voluntary control. The inability to resist or rid oneself of uncontrollable, alien, and often unacceptable thoughts or to keep from performing ritualistic acts over and over again arouses intense anxiety. In general, these thoughts and impulses are recognized as being unreasonable (this latter characteristic may not apply to children), although a minority of individuals with OCD will not recognize their symptoms as being senseless (Catapano, Sperandeo, Perris, Lanzaro, & Maj, 2001). Failure to engage in ritual acts often results in mounting anxiety and tension. Individuals with obsessive-compulsive disorder report that their problem interferes with their work, school, or homemaking roles and with interpersonal relationships (Koran, Thienemann, & Davenport, 1996).

Some features of obsessive-compulsive disorder are obvious, as in the following case involving a forty-five-year-old-woman:

> [W]hen I left any room in the house, or entered a room, I would have to touch a light switch, and I would have to touch a doorknob. If I could do something the first time … , and I did it perfectly—if it felt right to me—then I could go on to the next thing, move out of the room, or go to the next ritual. If it didn't feel right, then I would have to do it again. But I couldn't do it just 1 more time because then that would be 2 times, and 2 wasn't my good number, 5 was. So, automatically, if I didn't do it right the first time, I had to do it 5 times. If I didn't get it right in 5 times, then I would have to do it 25 times. So you can see why I ended up in my bed for the next 8 months. Because it was so out of control, it could take me an hour just to get out of my bedroom and into the bathroom. … The reason I do these kinds of rituals and obsessing is that I have a fear that some-

> one is going to die. This is not rational thinking to me. I know I can't prevent somebody from dying by putting 5 ice cubes in a glass instead of 4. (Jenike, 2001, p. 2122)

The woman was hospitalized for depression and did not realize that she had OCD until she saw a television program describing the disorder. She was treated with medication and cognitive behavioral therapy.

Obsessive-compulsive disorder was once thought to be relatively rare. However, the prevalence may be underestimated, because people may be secretive or lack insight about their problem (Jenike, 2004). In epidemiological studies of obsessive-compulsive disorder, the lifetime prevalence rate for the disorder is estimated to be 2.5 percent (American Psychiatric Association, 2000). The disorder is about equally common in males and females but is less common in African Americans and Mexican Americans (Zhang & Snowden, 1999). It is more common among the young and among individuals who are divorced, separated, or unemployed (Karno & Golding, 1991). Most have both obsessions and behavioral or mental compulsions (Foa & Kozak, 1995). Possibly because of the emotional distress associated with the symptoms of OCD, many with this disorder are depressed and may abuse substances. See Figure 5.5 for some of the more common obsessions and compulsions.

Obsessions

As mentioned earlier, an obsession is an intrusive and repetitive anxiety-arousing thought or image. The person may realize that the thought is irrational, but he or she cannot keep it from arising over and over again. One successful woman in her mid-twenties was tormented by thoughts of hurting children, even though she adores them, and of couples copulating on the altar when she attends Mass (Wen, 2001). Among a sample of children and adolescents, the most common obsessions involved dirt or germs, disease and death, or danger to self or loved ones (Swedo, Rapoport, Leonard, Lenane, & Cheslow, 1989). Obsessions common to adults involve bodily wastes or secretions, dirt or germs, and environmental contamination (George, Trimble, Ring, Sallee, & Robertson, 1993). To reduce the discomfort caused by obsessions, patients have used strategies such as changing their thoughts, focusing on something positive, listening to music, and taking a walk or reading (Freeston & Ladouceur, 1997). However, escape is only temporary, and the distressing thoughts return.

Although most of us have experienced persistent thoughts—for instance, a song or tune that keeps running through our minds—clinical forms are

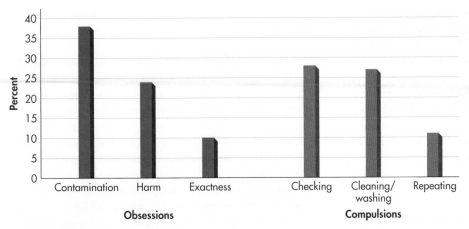

Source: Data from Foa & Kozak (1995).

FIGURE 5.5 Common Obsessions and Compulsions About half of the patients reported both obsessions and compulsions. Twenty-five percent believed that their symptoms were reasonable. How would a therapist work with a patient who believed his or her symptoms were appropriate?

stronger and more intrusive. They create great distress or interfere with social or occupational activities. Many people who suffer from this disorder become partially incapacitated. One man was upset by having sacrilegious mental images while in church. In addition, he was having obsessional problems during driving: when he felt a bump as his tire rolled over a little stone, he would think he might have accidentally run over a pedestrian. He would instantly check his rear-view mirror for the injured person he feared was lying on the road. Relieved not to see an injured person, he would start to drive forward. Obsessing that the injured person might have been flung entirely off the road by the impact, he would then stop, back up his car to the scene, and search the ditch and weeds. These obsessions and compulsions were taking over his life, but he was too embarrassed to tell anyone about them (National Anxiety Foundation, 2003, p. 1).

Do "normal" people have intrusive, unacceptable thoughts and impulses? Several studies (Edwards & Dickerson, 1987; Freeston & Ladouceur, 1993; Ladouceur, Freeston, et al., 2000) have found that more than 80 percent of normal samples report the existence of unpleasant intrusive thoughts and impulses. Apparently, a considerable majority of the "normal" population has obsessive symptoms. But are obsessions reported by patients different from those reported by normal individuals?

Rachman and DeSilva (1987) printed the obsessions of individuals with and without obsessive-compulsive disorder on cards, mixed them up, and gave them to six expert judges to resort into normal and clinical obsessional thoughts. On the whole, the judges were not very accurate in identifying the clinical obsessions. They were somewhat more successful in identifying "normal" obsessions or impulses (such as the impulse

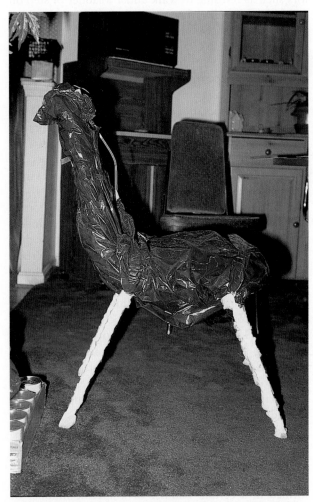

Contamination Obsession The individual who wrapped this chair had an obsessive fear of dust that reached psychotic proportions. What kinds of thoughts about dust can produce such anxiety?

to buy unwanted things). Obsessions reported by obsessive-compulsive patients and by normal populations overlap considerably. But Rachman and DeSilva (1987) did find some differences. Obsessive patients reported that their obsessions lasted longer, were more intense, produced more discomfort, and were more difficult to dismiss. The mere existence of obsessive-compulsive symptoms may not be very meaningful for diagnostic purposes because these symptoms are also reported in the general population.

Compulsions

A compulsion is the need to perform acts or to dwell on mental acts repetitively. Distress or anxiety occurs if the behavior is not performed or if it is not done "correctly." Compulsions are often, but not always, associated with obsessions. Mild forms include behaviors such as refusing to walk under a ladder or step on cracks in sidewalks, throwing salt over one's shoulder, and knocking on wood. The three most common compulsions among a sample of children and adolescents (Swedo et al., 1989) involved excessive or ritualized washing, repeating rituals (such as going in and out of a door and getting up and down from a chair), and checking behaviors (doors and appliances). Changes in patterns or type of compulsion were common. Compulsive hoarding, acquiring or failing to discard useless items, is relatively common. It accounts for about one-fourth of compulsions in obsessive-compulsive disorders (Frost et al., 1998).

Compulsions are also a common phenomenon in nonclinical populations. In one study of 150 undergraduates, nearly 55 percent acknowledged that they "have rituals or feel compelled to carry out certain behaviors in certain circumstances" (Muris, Merckelbach, & Clavan, 1997). The students reported having one or more of the following compulsions: checking (26.8 percent); washing, cleaning, or ordering items (15.9 percent); magical protective acts, such as saying particular numbers or touching a lucky object (10.5 percent); and avoiding particular objects (6.1 percent). A continuum appears to exist between "normal" rituals and "pathological" compulsions; in individuals with obsessive-compulsive disorder, the compulsions are more frequent and of greater intensity, and they produce more discomfort.

In the severe compulsive state, the behaviors become stereotyped and rigid; if they are not performed in a certain manner or a specific number of times, the compulsive individual is flooded with anxiety. To the person performing them, these compulsive behaviors often seem to have magical qualities, as though their correct performance wards off danger.

The following case, treated by one of the authors, is fairly typical:

A fifteen-year-old boy had a two-year history of compulsive behaviors involving sixteen repetitions of the following behaviors: opening and closing a door, touching glasses before drinking from them, and walking around each tree in front of his house before going to school. These compulsive acts produced much discomfort in the boy. His schoolmates ridiculed him, and his parents were upset because his rituals prevented him from reaching school at the appropriate time. An interview with the boy revealed that his compulsive behaviors were associated with the onset of masturbation, an act that the boy considered "dirty," although he was unable to refrain from it. It was when he began to masturbate that the first of his compulsive behaviors (touching a glass sixteen times before drinking from it) developed (case files).

Table 5.3 contains additional examples of obsessions and compulsions.

Etiology of Obsessive-Compulsive Disorder

The causes of obsessive-compulsive disorder remain speculative, although increased attention has recently been paid to biological explanations. We examine the cause of this disorder from the perspectives of the psychodynamic, behavioral, and biological models.

Psychodynamic Perspective   In the psychodynamic perspective, obsessive-compulsive behaviors are attempts to fend off anal sadistic (antisocial), anal libidinous (pleasurable soiling), and genital (masturbatory) impulses (Burgy, 2001). For example, Freud (1949) believed that obsessions represent the substitution or replacement of an original conflict, usually sexual in nature, with an associated idea that is less threatening. He found support for his notion in the case histories of some of his patients. One patient, a girl, had disturbing obsessions about stealing or counterfeiting money; these thoughts were absurd and untrue. During analysis, Freud discovered that these obsessions reflected anxiety that stemmed from guilt about masturbation. When the patient was kept under constant observation, which prevented her from masturbating, the obsessional thoughts (or, perhaps, the reports of the thoughts) ceased.

The dynamics of obsession have been described as involving "the intrusion of the unwelcome thought [that] 'seeks' to prevent anxiety by serving as a more tolerable substitute for a subjectively less welcome thought or impulse" (Laughlin, 1967, p. 311). Freud's patient found thoughts involving stealing less disturbing

TABLE 5.3 Clinical Examples of Obsessions and Compulsions

Patient Age	Gender	Duration of Obsession in Years	Content of Obsession
21	M	6	Teeth are decaying, particles between teeth
42	M	16	Women's buttocks, own eye movements
55	F	35	Fetuses lying in the street, killing babies, people buried alive
24	M	16	Worry about whether he has touched vomit
21	F	9	Strangling people
32	F	7	Contracting AIDS (acquired immunodeficiency syndrome)

Patient Age	Gender	Duration of Compulsion in Years	Content of Compulsion
42	F	17	Hand washing triggered by contamination by touching surfaces touched by other people
45	F	36	Touching doorknob and light switch in specific manner and number of times when leaving or entering a room; performing it correctly might take an hour before she could leave a room
21	M	2	Intense fear of contamination after touching library books, money; washes hands 25 times a day and ruminates about how people have handled the objects before him
7	M	4	Walking only on the edges of floor tiles
9	M	4	Going back and forth through doorways five hundred times

Source: Based on data from Jenike (2001); Kraus & Nicholson (1996); Rachman, Marks, & Hodgson (1973); Swedo et al. (1989); Williams, Chambless, & Steketee (1998).

than thoughts about masturbation. Her displacement of that feeling to a *substitute* action prevented her ego defenses from being overwhelmed.

Several other psychoanalytic defense mechanisms are considered prominent in obsessive-compulsive behaviors. For example, *undoing* is canceling or atoning for forbidden impulses by engaging in repetitive, ritualistic activities. Washing one's hands may symbolically represent cleansing oneself of unconscious wishes. Because the original conflict remains, however, one is compelled to perform the act of atonement over and over again. *Reaction formation* provides a degree of comfort because it counterbalances forbidden desires with diametrically opposed behaviors. To negate problems stemming from the anal psychosexual stage (characteristic of those with obsessive-compulsive

disorder), such as the impulse to be messy, patients tend toward excessive cleanliness and orderliness. Those with obsessive-compulsive disorder may also employ the defense of *isolation*, which allows the separation of a thought or action from its effect. Aloofness, intellectualization, and detachment reduce the anxiety produced by patently aggressive or sexual thoughts.

Behavioral and Cognitive Perspectives Proponents of the behavioral perspective maintain that obsessive-compulsive behaviors develop because they reduce anxiety. A distracting thought or action recurs more often if it reduces anxiety. For example, many college students may develop mild forms of compulsive behavior during intense exam periods, such as final examinations. During this stressful and anxiety-filled time, students may find themselves engaging in escape activities such as daydreaming, straightening up their rooms, or eating five or more times a day, all of which serve to shield them from thoughts of the upcoming tests. If the stress lasts a long time, a compulsive behavior may develop.

Researchers have also attempted to determine the cognitive factors that lead to severe doubts associated with compulsive behavior. It seems that OCD patients do not trust their own memory and judgment and make futile attempts to determine if they actually performed the behavior or performed it "correctly." The uncertainty leads to the rituals, and doubts may occur even in the face of unambiguous evidence. An "OC checker may turn the key in the lock over and over again without being able to convince himself or herself that the door has in fact been locked, even though he or she can plainly see that the key is in the proper position, hear it engaging, and feel the lock snapping" (Dar, Rish, Hermesh, Taub, & Fux, 2000, p. 673). Individuals with OCD may have a disconfirmatory bias—that is, they generate a search for evidence that undermines their confidence. The person checking the lock may develop thoughts of all the factors that may have prevented the door from staying locked. It is uncertain whether the lack of confidence leads to OCD or whether it is a result of having the disorder. Along with uncertainty, individuals with obsessive-compulsive disorders show two other cognitive characteristics: (1) probability bias, or the belief that having a thought, such as shouting obscenities in church, increases the chance that the action will occur; (2) morality bias, or the view that having an immoral thought, such as throwing a child in front of a car, is as bad as the actual behavior. Research has supported the view that these are important aspects in OCD and that therapy should address these cognitive biases (Rassin, Muris, Schmidt, & Merckelbach, 2000).

Biological Perspective   Biological explanations of obsessive-compulsive behaviors are based on data relating to brain structure, genetic studies, and biochemical abnormalities. Positron emission tomography (PET) has enabled us to observe metabolic reactions in the brain. These reactions have been found to differ among people with obsessive-compulsive disorder, those with severe depression, and control groups with no evidence of psychiatric disorders. Some people with obsessive-compulsive disorder show increased metabolic activity in the frontal lobe of the left hemisphere. Perhaps this area of the brain, the orbital frontal cortex, is associated with obsessive-compulsive behaviors (Blier, Szabo, Haddjeri, & Dong, 2000; see also Figure 5.6). Of special interest is the fact that when these individuals were given fluoxetine (a medication that

FIGURE 5.6 Orbital Frontal Cortex   Untreated patients with obsessive-compulsive disorder show a high metabolism rate in this area of the brain. This rate is reduced to "normal" levels by certain medications, which also produce a reduction in obsessive-compulsive symptoms. What would it mean if similar results are found with psychotherapy?

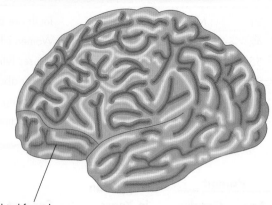

Orbital frontal cortex

increases the activity level of serotonin), the cerebral blood flow to the frontal lobes was decreased to values found in individuals without the disorder, and patients reported a reduction in symptoms (Hoehn-Saric, Pearlson, Harris, Machlin, & Camargo, 1991).

Other researchers believe that OCD should be viewed as comprising a number of different subgroups rather than as a single disorder (Mataix-Cols et al., 2004). Use of magnetic resonance imaging (MRI) has found that different brain areas are activated by different OCD symptoms such as hoarding and washing (Saxena et al., 2004). Additional support for the view that OCD is an etiologically diverse condition is the finding that certain symptom types show different responses to treatment (Hurley, Saxena, Rauch, Hoehn-Saric, & Taber, 2002). Behavior therapy seems to be more effective for OCD clients with aggressive-checking, contamination-cleaning, and symmetry-ordering symptoms than for those with sexual-religious obsessions (Mataix-Cols, Marks, Greist, Kobak, & Baer, 2002).

Medications such as clomipramine, Paxil, Prozac, and Zoloft increase the amount of available serotonin in the brain, and these medications have been effective in treating many individuals with obsessive-compulsive disorder. As a result, researchers have hypothesized that the disorder is the result of a serotonin deficiency (Greenberg, Altemus, & Murphy, 1997; Perse, Greist, Jefferson, Rosenfeld, & Dar, 1987; Tollefson et al., 1994). Drugs that have less effect on raising serotonin availability have been less effective in treating this disorder. Although most studies of medication have methodological flaws—including reliance on clinical reports, small sample size, failure to include control and placebo groups, and differences in dosage levels—a small body of methodologically sound literature supports the hypothesis that serotonin is involved in obsessive-compulsive disorder. However, Pigott (1996) describes our understanding of the disorder to be "fairly rudimentary." Even the most effective medications typically provide only partial relief from symptoms.

Some researchers (Bellodi et al., 2001; Hudziak et al., 2004) believe that some obsessive-compulsive behaviors are caused by genetic factors. Family and twin studies offer some support for this theory. First-degree relatives of individuals with obsessive-compulsive disorder are more likely to have an anxiety disorder than are first-degree relatives of psychiatrically normal controls (D. Black, Noyes, Goldstein, & Blum, 1992). In a carefully controlled study, McKeon and Murray (1987) found that the relatives of people with obsessive-compulsive disorder were twice as likely to have an anxiety or emotional disorder than were relatives of the matched control group. However, both groups had a similar number of relatives with obsessive-compulsive disorder. These studies seem to suggest that "overreactive tendency" or vulnerability to developing an anxiety disorder may be inherited and that the actual development of an obsessive-compulsive disorder may depend on life events or personality factors.

Treatment of Obsessive-Compulsive Disorder

The primary modes of treatment for obsessive-compulsive disorder are either biological or behavioral in nature. Behavioral therapies have been used successfully for many years, but treatment with medication has recently enjoyed increased attention. Cultural aspects of treatment must also be considered. African Americans and Hispanic Americans are less likely to receive a diagnosis of OCD than European Americans are (Zhang & Snowden, 1999). In treating two African American women with OCD, K. E. Williams, Chambless, and Steketee (1998) found that each had believed that she was the only black person to have this problem (neither had contact with one another). Their sense of isolation was increased when they found that the local OCD support group had no black members. Both declined to join the group. Although both women improved with cognitive behavior therapy, the therapists, who were European Americans, were concerned about the possible impact of therapist-client racial match. They stress the need to be sensitive to special issues involved in therapy with ethnic minorities and point out that African Americans with OCD have been underrepresented in clinical outcome studies.

Biological Treatments Because obsessive-compulsive disorder is classified as an anxiety disorder, benzodiazepines might be thought to be helpful. However, antianxiety medications are less effective with OCD symptoms than with other anxiety disorders (Huppert et al., 2004). For severe cases of OCD, effectiveness can be improved through the addition of cognitive behavioral therapy with medication (Bouvard, Milliery, & Cottraux, 2004).

As mentioned earlier, fluoxetine and clomipramine, which increase the serotonin level in the brain, have been reportedly successful in treating patients with obsessive-compulsive disorder (Lydiard, 1996; Pigott, 1996; Tollefson et al., 1994). However, only 60 to 80 percent of persons with obsessive-compulsive disorder respond to these medications, and often the relief is only partial (Pigott & Murphy, 1991; Pigott & Seay, 1997). Catapano and his colleagues (2001) found that those with poor insight were not responsive to SSRIs. Many clients also report adverse side reactions to medications and drop out of treatment (Clomipramine Collaborative Study Group, 1991). In addition, there is a rapid return of symptoms, and relapse occurs within months of stopping the medication (Jenike, 2001; Stanley & Turner, 1995). Some evidence does indicate that medication levels can be reduced without adverse effects (Mundo, Bareggi, Pirola, & Bellodi, 1997).

Behavioral Treatments The treatment of choice for obsessive-compulsive disorder is the combination of exposure and response prevention. The results of this two-stage approach have been consistently impressive, and fewer therapy sessions are typically required than in systematic desensitization (Abramowitz, Foa, & Franklin, 2003; Calamari, Faber, Hitsman, & Poppe, 1994). *Exposure* is a technique that involves continued actual or imagined exposure to the fear-arousing situations; it can be performed at high-anxiety level (**flooding**) or with more gradual exposure. The steps generally involve (Franklin, Abramowitz, Kozak, Levitt, & Foa, 2000): (1) educating the clients about OCD and the rationale for exposure and response prevention; (2) development of an exposure hierarchy (from moderately fearful to most feared situations); (3) exposure to feared situations until anxiety has diminished; and (4) refraining from rituals (response prevention).

Exposure and response prevention was used with a client who had contamination fears and washing compulsions. Exercises were employed to trigger obsessional fears. For instance, he was asked to refrain from showering for a few days during the week and was only allowed to wash in a "normalized" manner and then was recontaminated by having to use a soiled towel.

Once properly "contaminated," the response-prevention stage would begin, and the client would not be allowed to cleanse himself by engaging in his compulsive washing ritual. Instead, he would be required to remain "contaminated" until his anxiety had been extinguished. Exposure is used to extinguish contamination fears and response prevention further extinguishes anxiety and helps eliminate the avoidance behavior (Franklin, Abramowitz, Bux, Zoellner, & Feeny, 2002).

Follow-up studies that range from one to six years indicate that from 55 to 79 percent of individuals treated with behavior therapy maintain their improvement. Some, however, required additional treatments during the follow-up period (Stanley & Turner, 1995). A promising approach is cognitive therapy that attempts to identify and modify clients' irrational thoughts. This technique may be as effective as exposure alone in reducing symptoms of the disorder (Emmelkamp & Beens, 1991; Freeston et al., 1997; McLean et al., 2001; Van Oppen et al., 1995). Some therapists report success in combining cognitive strategies with exposure and response prevention, as in the following case:

> A twenty-four-year-old woman reported having intrusive thoughts of stabbing her mother and sister with a large knife. She was very fearful that she would harm them. These thoughts had first occurred at the age of sixteen after she read a murder mystery. Later, she also had obsessions about gouging out her own eyes, thrusting her face into an operating fan, and driving her car off a bridge. (O'Kearney, 1993)

To eliminate the obsessive-compulsive disorder, the woman's therapist employed both exposure with response prevention and cognitive therapy. The woman monitored the frequency of her obsessive thoughts, recorded them on tape, and listened to them at home. She also identified illogical and catastrophizing thoughts and generated new and more realistic thoughts. These approaches were successful in reducing the obsessive thoughts. She had one relapse when she observed a woman patient reacting hysterically to a blood test; during this relapse, thoughts of gouging out her own eyes returned. (Figure 5.7 shows the changes in the frequency of her obsessional thoughts.) This recurrence was successfully treated when therapy focused on the theme of loss of control. The addition of cognitive strategies to combined exposure and response prevention may be more effective than either treatment alone.

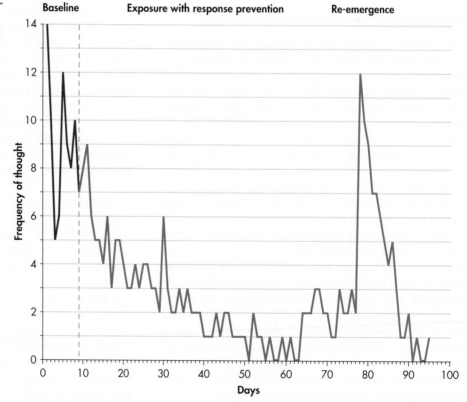

FIGURE 5.7 Frequency of Intrusive Eye-Gouging Thought
One patient's obsessive thought of gouging out her own eyes declined during cognitive therapy. One relapse occurred when she viewed another individual's reaction to a blood test, but the patient was able to recover from that situation when cognitive training focused on perceived loss of control. What might produce such an obsessive thought?

Acute and Posttraumatic Stress Disorders

> Ripping down an Iraqi road in a truck going 50 mph, the Guardsman spotted a dead goat on the highway with its head on the yellow line. Having prodded scores of carcasses looking for explosives, he realized something wasn't right. He screamed, "Brake left! Brake left!" Too late. The bomb inside the goat ... detonated about 10 feet from the truck, embedding shards of glass in his face (Lyke, 2004b, p. A8).

> A lone gunman crashed his pickup truck through a wall of a crowded lunchtime cafeteria in Killeen, Texas. ... He proceeded to hold more than one hundred patrons and employees of the restaurant captive as he walked around the dining room, shooting victims at point-blank range, for a period of about fifteen minutes. Once cornered by the police, he shot himself fatally. Twenty-three others lay dead in a scene of unprecedented carnage in this small town. (North, Smith, & Spitznagel, 1997, p. 1697)

Acute and posttraumatic stress disorders are anxiety disorders that develop in response to an extreme psychological or physical trauma. The reaction to the event must involve intense fear, evoked helplessness, or horror. Although stress disorders have many similarities to the other anxiety disorders, they have some unique symptoms, such as detachment from others, restricted range of affect, nightmares, and loss of interest in activities (Foa, Riggs, & Gershuny, 1995).

Acute stress disorder (ASD) involves the exposure to a traumatic stressor that results in dissociation, reliving the experience, and attempts to avoid reminders of the event; this disorder lasts for more than two and fewer than thirty days and occurs within four weeks of exposure to the stressor. In the shooting incident described earlier, 33 percent of the observers developed an acute stress disorder. Individuals with the stress disorders also have increased rates of other anxiety, mood, or substance use disorders.

Posttraumatic stress disorder (PTSD) lasts for more than thirty days, develops in response to a specific extreme stressor, and is characterized by intrusive memories of the traumatic event, emotional withdrawal, and heightened autonomic arousal. The events that trigger these disorders may involve a threat to one's life or to a spouse or family member. The prevalence of PTSD is as high as 19 percent for veterans serving in Iraq or Afghanistan who have engaged in firefights or have been wounded. Unfortunately, only a minority of veterans suffering from this disorder are seeking help, citing fears of stigmatization such as "I would be seen as weak," "My unit leadership might treat me differently," and "Members of my unit might have less confidence in me" (Hoge et al., 2004). Other situations that may lead to PTSD include school shootings (Curry, 2001); being abducted and threatened (Saigh, 1987); automobile accidents (DiGallo et al., 1997); natural disasters (Joseph, Brewin, Yule, & Williams, 1993); rape and incest (Faravelli, Giugni, Salvatori, & Ricca, 2004; Vernberg, LaGreca, Silverman, & Prinstein, 1996); concentration camp experiences (Kinzie, Frederickson, Ben, Fleck, & Karls, 1984; Yehuda & McFarlane, 1995); refugee status and torture (Van Ommeren, de Jong, & Komproe, 2001); child abuse (Graham-Bermann & Levendovsky, 1998); and the battered-woman syndrome (Astin, Ogland-Hand, Foy, & Coleman, 1995; Walker, 1991). Interestingly, the sexual assault of women military personnel by fellow soldiers during the Gulf War was more likely to produce PTSD than was combat exposure (Wolfe, Sharkansky, Read, & Dawson, 1998). These and similar events produce feelings of terror and helplessness. The following case illustrates the features and origin of PTSD.

> I was raped when I was twenty-five years old. For a long time, I spoke about the rape as though it was something that happened to someone else. I was very aware that it had happened to me, but there was just no feeling. Then I started having flashbacks. They kind of came over me like a splash of water. I would be terrified. Suddenly I was reliving the rape. Every instant was startling. I wasn't aware of anything around me, I was in a bubble, just kind of floating. And it was scary. Having a flashback can wring you out. (NIMH, 2000, p. 4)

Diagnosis of Acute and Posttraumatic Stress Disorders

The diagnostic criteria for acute stress disorder and posttraumatic stress disorder are similar. Both require exposure to an extreme stressor. They differ primarily in onset (ASD within four weeks and PTSD at any time) and duration (ASD two to twenty-eight days and PTSD longer than one month). An individual with an initial diagnosis of ASD is likely to receive a diagnosis of PTSD if the symptoms persist for more than four weeks (Classen, Koopman, Hales, & Spiegel, 1998). It may be possible to identify those who may be susceptible to a more chronic condition. In a study of survivors of automobile accidents, 13 percent received a diagnosis of ASD; six months later, 78 percent of those previously diagnosed with ASD met the criteria for PTSD (Harvey & Bryant, 1998). In one sample of hospitalized motor accident survivors who were diagnosed

One Possible Cause for Anxiety Disorders Involvement in the horrific events surrounding the death and injuries of victims involved in the terrorist attack on the World Trade Center on September 11, 2001, can result in anxiety disorders such as PTSD, phobias, and GAD. Why is it that only some survivors or observers develop an anxiety disorder, whereas others do not?

with ASD, those with higher resting heart rates were at high risk for a later diagnosis of PTSD (Bryant, Guthrie, Moulds, & Harvey, 2000). Most individuals will face a traumatic event in their lives, and up to 25 percent will develop a disorder. Some types of traumas are more likely to result in PTSD (Hidalgo & Davidson, 2000).

DSM-IV-TR Criteria As noted earlier, the following additional symptoms are necessary for the diagnosis. We examine them in more detail.

1. *Reexperiencing the event in disturbing dreams or intrusive memories.* One woman who had been forced to play Russian roulette described flashbacks and nightmares of the event: "Different scenes came back, replays of exactly what happened, only the time is drawn out. … It seems to take forever for the gun to reach my head" (Hudson, Manoach, Sabo, & Sternbach, 1991, p. 572). One veteran with PTSD reported continued disturbing thoughts of a Viet Cong soldier whom he had taken prisoner. Later, he saw the prisoner pushed out of a helicopter in flight. Because Mr. B. had captured the prisoner, he felt responsible for the death (Hendin, Pollenger, Singer, & Ullman, 1981) and continued to reexperience this episode. Many rape victims report intrusive memories of the attack (Vernberg et al., 1996).

2. *Emotional numbing, or avoiding stimuli associated with the trauma.* As a defense against intrusive thoughts, people may withdraw emotionally and may avoid anything that might remind them of the events.

Traffic accident survivors avoided thinking or talking about the incident (DiGallo et al., 1997). Concentration camp survivors who developed posttraumatic stress disorder often displayed emotional numbness and avoided talking about their experiences in the camp. One man said flatly, "What is there to say? There was just killing and death" (Kinzie et al., 1984, p. 646). Avoidance is only partially successful, however. Certain stimuli, such as the sound or sight of helicopters for combat veterans, can bring back the intrusive memories (Mooney, 1988).

3. *Heightened autonomic arousal.* This reaction can include symptoms such as sleep disturbance, hypervigilance, and loss of control over aggression. Veterans from the Iraq war can become "unglued" to the sound of a door slamming, a nail gun being used, or the click of a camera. One man also struggles with anger: "When friends say 'I know where you're coming from,' he burns. 'How could they? They didn't have to deal with insects, the heat, not knowing who is the enemy, not knowing where the bullet is coming from'" (Lyke, 2004b, A8). The veteran says his tolerance is gone, and he nearly attacked some men at a Mariners' baseball game.

In the National Comorbidity Survey, the lifetime prevalence of PTSD for Americans between the ages fifteen and fifty-four was 8 percent, with about twice as many women as men receiving the diagnosis (Kessler, Sonnega, Bromet, Hughes, & Nelson, 1995). As with many mental disorders, the diagnosis of PTSD depends on self-reports of the victims. In some cases, elevated percentages of the disorder have been found to be related to personal injury claims (Rosen, 1995). Among PTSD victims involved in traffic accidents who experienced delayed onset of the disorder, 71 percent were involved in litigation, compared with only 34 percent of accident victims without PTSD (Buckley, Blanchard, & Hickling, 1996).

Many patients with severe mental disorders have faced traumatic situations and developed PTSD. In a study of individuals with schizophrenia or bipolar disorder, 43 percent met the criteria for PTSD, but only 2 percent had this diagnosis on their charts. PTSD may be a common comorbid disorder in some forms of severe mental illness (Mueser et al., 1998). The experience of psychotic symptoms and the experience of hospitalization contributed significantly to the development of PTSD in approximately two-thirds of a sample of men and women undergoing a psychotic episode. These results indicate the importance of assessing for PTSD and reducing the distress of patients with psychosis (Frame & Morrison, 2001).

In both ASD and PTSD, the acute reactions can be considered normative responses to an overwhelming and traumatic stimulus. Symptoms such as numbing, detachment, depersonalization, and dissociation can help the individual minimize awareness of traumatic memories and subsequently alleviate discomfort (Harvey, Bryant, & Dang, 1998). Most victims show a marked decrease in symptoms with time (Shalev, Freedman, Peri, & Brandes, 1998). For example, among the 29.8 percent of children who developed severe or very severe levels of PTSD symptoms after Hurricane Andrew, only 12.5 per-

cent still had the disorder after ten months (LaGreca, Silverman, Vernberg, & Prinstein, 1996).

Several questions remain regarding the conceptualization of PTSD. First, if short-lived cases of PTSD are to be considered "normative reactions," how should chronic cases be conceptualized? Second, in many cases, emotional or mental breakdown after trauma is not determined entirely by the type or the intensity of the trauma. Research is needed on the risk factors associated with an increased risk of developing ASD or PTSD after exposure to trauma. Certainly the magnitude of the stressor may be very important in the development of PTSD. In a study of Cambodian refugees living in the United States for four to six years who had experienced multiple stressors, such as the deaths of family members, torture, extreme fear, and deprivation, during their escapes, 86 percent met the criteria for PTSD (E. B. Carlson & Rosser-Hogan, 1991). Rape is also clearly a traumatic event. Immediately after a sexual assault, 74 percent of the victims met the criteria for ASD, and, after three months, 35 percent of the sample met the criteria for PTSD (Valentiner, Foa, Riggs, & Gershuny, 1996). These data support the contention that some extreme stressors may produce PTSD in almost everyone (E. B. Carlson & Rosser-Hogan, 1991; see Table 5.4 for PTSD prevalence associated with specific stressors.)

The Individual's Perception of the Event There appears to be a strong correlation between the level of danger perceived from a trauma and the likelihood of developing PTSD. This may account for the finding that about two-thirds or more of those exposed to

TABLE 5.4   Lifetime Prevalence Exposure to Stressors by Gender and PTSD Risk

Trauma	Lifetime Prevalence (%)		PTSD Risk	
	Male	Female	Male	Female
Life-threatening accident	25.0	13.8	6.3	8.8
Natural disaster	18.9	15.2	3.7	5.4
Threatened with weapon	19.0	6.8	1.9	32.6
Physical attack	11.1	6.9	1.8	21.3
Rape	0.7	9.2	65.0	45.9

Note: Some traumas are more likely to result in PTSD than others. Significant gender differences were found in reactions to "being threatened with a weapon" or "physical attack." What accounts for the differences in risk for developing PTSD among the specific traumas and for the gender differences?

Source: From Ballenger et al. (2000).

severe trauma will display a "normal acute stress reaction," whereas the remainder may develop ASD or PTSD (Ballenger et al., 2000). In DSM-IV (American Psychiatric Association, 1994), little was said about the individual's subjective perception of the event. This has been remedied in DSM-IV-TR (American Psychiatric Association, 2000) through the addition of Criterion A2, which requires that the trauma be viewed with "intense fear, helplessness, or horror." However, there is also evidence that PTSD symptoms can develop in individuals faced with repeated sub-traumatic stressors, such as employment problems or marital distress (Astin et al., 1995; Scott & Stradling, 1994). If such cases fulfill all the criteria for PTSD with the exception of a specific traumatic stressor, how should they be diagnosed? More work needs to be done to define more clearly the nature of a traumatic stressor in PTSD and to determine its necessity in the diagnosis of the disorder. In addition, several researchers (Figley, 1985; Valentiner et al., 1996) have posed the following questions, which still have to be answered for PTSD:

- When people are exposed to a psychologically traumatic event, which ones will develop posttraumatic stress disorder?

- Should this condition be considered a "normative" response to trauma?

- Among those who develop PTSD, how many will show the reaction immediately and how many after a period of time?

- Can we determine who has PTSD and who is malingering?

PTSD and Battered Women Posttraumatic stress disorder is not isolated to combat situations. Women who have been battered or have suffered sexual assaults often report high rates of acute stress or posttraumatic stress disorder. Here, two women living in a shelter for battered women share their experiences in a counseling session.

Etiology and Treatment of Acute and Posttraumatic Stress Disorders

The development of acute or posttraumatic stress disorder appears to depend on the nature of the traumatic event, on a response that shows intense fear and horror, and on vulnerability factors involving past psychiatric history. This latter component probably plays a larger role with some traumatic events. In some cases, the nature of the specific traumas may predominate, such as in the case of rape or torture.

According to the model shown in Figure 5.8, the degree of trauma is one variable in developing PTSD, but the person's own coping style and a supportive recovery environment can reduce its effects. Attempts to identify predisposing factors have produced mixed results and may depend on the specific population being studied. As compared with individuals who have agoraphobia, patients with PTSD had significantly

fewer premorbid predisposing factors related to their disorder (McKenzie, Marks, & Liness, 2001). However, other studies have reported the importance of preexisting conditions, such as family or past history of mental illness. In general, factors operating during and immediately after the trauma (severity, dissociation, lack of social support, and additional life stressors) were more important than the more modest influences of family history, childhood abuse, and family history (Brewin, Andrews, & Valentine, 2000; Ozer, Best, Lipsey, & Weiss, 2003). Disaster survivors with a psychiatric history were more likely to develop PTSD than were those without a previous disorder (C. S. North et al., 1997). One study showed that war veterans who developed PTSD were more likely to have sustained injuries, engaged in firefights, come closer to their own deaths, and seen people who had died (Hoge et al., 2004). Negative childhood experiences (Bremner, Southwick, Johnson, Yehuda, & Charney, 1993) and being more withdrawn and inhibited (Schnurr, Friedman, & Rosenberg, 1993) are also associated with an increased risk of developing PTSD. Among the general population, people with less education, those who scored high on neuroticism, and those who are African American were more likely to be exposed to traumatic events and were therefore at a higher risk for developing PTSD (Breslau, Davis, & Andreski, 1995). A variety of individual experiences or characteristics of a supportive environment can apparently moderate the impact of a traumatic stressor. Along with specific vulnerabilities, both behavioral and biological explanations and treatment have been proposed for ASD and PTSD.

Behavioral Perspective Because a traumatic event precipitates the disorder, several researchers (Orr et al., 1995; Yehuda & McFarlane, 1995) believe that classical conditioning is involved. People who have PTSD often show reactions to stimuli present at the time of the trauma (darkness, time of day, smell of diesel fuel, propeller noises, and so on). According to this perspective, the reason extinction does not occur is that the individual avoids thinking about the situation. As we indicated in our discussion of phobias, however, the classical conditioning model falls short of a full explanation. Not everyone who is exposed to a traumatic event develops acute or posttraumatic stress disorder. Other factors—such as the person's individual characteristics, his or her perception of the event, and the existence of support groups—also have an influence.

Exposure to the cues associated with the trauma appears to be effective in treating PTSD (Basoglu, Livanou, & Salcioglu, 2003; Foa, 2000; Taylor et al., 2003), and, for veterans, brief outpatient treatment appears to be more effective than long-term inpatient hospital PTSD care (Fontana & Rosenheck, 1997). The process of exposure may involve asking the person to recreate the traumatic event in imagination. In one study of victims of sexual assault (Foa et al., 1999), the women were asked to repeatedly imagine and describe the assault "as if it were happening now." They verbalized the details of the assault, as well as

---

FIGURE 5.8 Processing a Catastrophic Event: A Working Model   Factors such as the coping style and characteristics of the individual, the way traumatic events are processed, and whether or not social supports are available have an impact on whether PTSD develops.

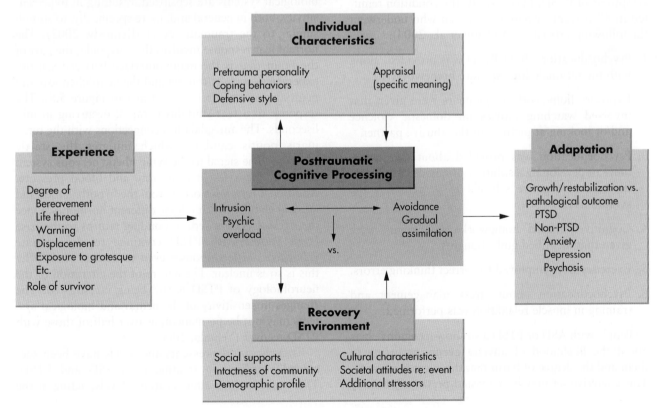

their thoughts and emotions regarding the incident. Their descriptions were recorded, and this process was repeated for about an hour. The women were then instructed to listen to the recordings once a day and, when doing so, to "imagine that the assault is happening now." This process allowed extinction to occur. It is believed that the more accurate the imagined details, the more effective the therapy will be. Exposure also appears to effectively correct erroneous cognitions associated with the traumatic event.

In dealing with PTSD in Vietnam veterans, therapists have used imagination, videos, movies, and even helicopter rides to provide images of combat. Recently, another tool, software based on videos of actual footage of the war, has become available. One combat program using "virtual reality" is so realistic that veterans can distinguish between the sounds of the AK-47 used by the North Vietnamese and the M-60s employed by the U.S. forces (Clothier, 1998). The simulation is much more realistic and intense than other procedures because the individual is immersed in the situation in a very vivid way. See the Mental Health and Society feature "Virtual Reality Therapy" for information on other virtual reality programs.

Cognitive factors may also account for some of the symptoms of PTSD. Battered women with this disorder have thoughts associated with guilt or self-blame. Cognitions such as "I could have prevented it," "I never should have," and "I'm so stupid" maintain the symptoms of PTSD. In one study, the condition remitted in 87 percent of battered women who underwent the following procedure (Kubany et al., 2004):

1. Psychoeducation about PTSD was provided, along with the rationale for exposure homework.

2. Exposure homework assignments were given that involved watching movies on domestic violence and/or looking at pictures of the abusive partner.

3. Psychoeducation was provided about the importance of developing a solution-oriented attitude and the role of negative self-talk in perpetuating the symptoms of PTSD.

4. Cognitively based homework assignments were given that identified guilt thoughts.

5. Exercises were employed to correct thinking errors.

6. Psychoeducation about stress management and training in muscle relaxation was performed.

People with ASD or PTSD also show a cognitive bias about the likelihood of adverse events occurring to them and the degree of harm that the event may cause. This cognitive set may have existed previously or may be a result of the traumatic event. As compared with controls, individuals who have ASD or PTSD overevaluate the probability of negative trauma-related events occurring and the adverse impact of these events (K. Smith & Bryant, 2000). Perhaps because of the higher level of threat involved in these disorders, cognitive bias appears to be activated in more circumstances than those displayed in other anxiety disorders.

A number of coping strategies can also be useful in treating PTSD. In one study (Valentiner et al., 1996), some sexual assault victims were able to obtain social support. Others used cognitive strategies, such as refusing to dwell on negative thoughts about the incidents and focusing on an optimistic outlook. Self-blame was associated with greater PTSD severity. One cognitive treatment for sexual assault victims who had chronic nightmares involved the use of strategies to change the previous disturbing dream content into pleasant imagery while in the waking stage and rehearsing the "new dream" several times. This procedure decreased nightmares, improved sleep quality, and decreased the severity of PTSD (Krakow et al., 2001).

Biological Perspective and Treatment   As compared with trauma-exposed individuals who do not have PTSD, those who have the disorder show a sensitized autonomic system (Orr et al., 2000). There is some evidence that PTSD is not a biologically normative stress response but one in which a number of neural and biological systems are sensitized, resulting in hypersensitivity, both in general and, more specifically, to stimuli similar to the traumatic event (Kennedy, 2002). The normal fear response involves the amygdala, the part of the brain that is the major interface between sensory experiences such as trauma and the neurochemical and neuroanatomical circuitry of fear (see Figure 5.8). The response to a fear stimulus is rapid, occurring in milliseconds. The amygdala has connections with the reticularis pontis caudalis, which initiates the startle response. The signal to the sympathetic nervous system produces increases in heart rate and blood pressure. Additional responses occur from the hypothalamus and adrenal glands, which release different hormones. Once the stressor is removed, responding returns to the base level. People with PTSD continue to demonstrate enhanced startle responses even to neutral cues. Why this is so is unclear. The nature of the alteration of the neurobiology of PTSD is still being investigated. The changes in sensitivity of the neural and biological systems may not be permanent, as over half of those with PTSD recover (Yehuda, 2000).

Tricyclic antidepressants and SSRIs have been successfully utilized in treating both ASD and PTSD. These medications alter serotonin levels, acting at the

Treating PTSD The intense terror and fear associated with combat may result in posttraumatic stress disorder. In this photo, veterans are attending a group counseling session at the VA Center in Fort Lauderdale, Florida. This session was held on March 25, 2003. Events such as the conflict with Iraq often result in an increase in the number of veterans seeking help.

level of the amygdala and its connections, and desensitizes the fear network. Depending on the specific medication, 50 percent to 85 percent report "very or much improved" in symptom relief, although from 17 percent to 62 percent of those on placebos also report the same degree of improvement (Davidson, 2000). SSRIs (Zoloft, Paxil, Prozac) are the treatment of choice for ASD and PTSD (Ballenger et al., 2000). However, they are associated with side effects such as insomnia, diarrhea, nausea, fatigue, and depressed appetite. Because of this, discontinuation rates are twice as high as those for behavioral treatments (Davidson, 2000; Foa, 2000).

SUMMARY

What are the different ways in which anxiety can be expressed, and under what conditions does it become so overwhelming that a panic attack occurs?

- Anxiety is an emotion we all experience. It appears in our cognitions or thoughts, in our behaviors, and in our physiological or biological reactions.
- When the anxiety becomes intense, panic attacks involving extreme fear may develop. In some cases these attacks will occur almost invariably when exposed to a specific stimulus (situationally bound); others will usually occur in certain circumstances (situationally predisposed).

- Panic attacks that seem to occur "out of the blue" (unexpected) have been the most difficult to explain.
- Panic attacks are relatively common and not always associated with an anxiety or any other disorder.

In two anxiety disorders, the source of the fear cannot be clearly identified. What causes these reactions, and how can they be treated?

- Panic disorder and generalized anxiety disorder (GAD) are characterized by direct and unfocused anxiety.
- Panic disorder is marked by episodes of extreme anxiety and feelings of impending doom.
- Generalized anxiety disorder involves chronically high levels of anxiety and excessive worry that is present for six months or more.

- Psychoanalysts believe that these disorders are unfocused because they stem from internal conflicts that remain in the person's unconscious.
- Cognitive behavioral theorists emphasize cognitions and conditioning in the development of these disorders. According to the biological perspective, a specific biological dysfunction may predispose some people to panic disorder.
- Drug therapy, behavioral therapies, and psychodynamic therapies have been used to treat these disorders.

Some people are housebound with fear, and others are afraid of public speaking or harmless insects. How do these irrational fears develop, and what is the best way of treating them?

- Phobias are strong fears that exceed the demands of the situation.
- Agoraphobia is an intense fear of being in public places; it can keep afflicted people from leaving home because attempts to do so may produce panic attacks.
- Social phobias are irrational fears about situations in which the person can be observed by others. The anxiety generally stems from the possibility of appearing foolish or making mistakes in public.
- Specific phobias include all the irrational fears that are not classed as social phobias or agoraphobia. Commonly feared objects in specific phobias include small animals, heights, and the dark.
- In the psychodynamic view, phobias represent unconscious conflicts that are displaced onto an external object.
- Behavioral explanations include the classical conditioning view, in which phobias are based on an association between some aversive event and a conditioned stimulus; conditioning through observational learning; the role of thoughts that are distorted and frightening; and reinforcement for fear behaviors.
- Biological explanations are based on studies of the influence of genetic, biochemical, and neurological factors or on the idea that humans are prepared to develop certain fears.
- The most effective treatments for phobias seem to be biochemical (via antidepressants) and, primarily, behavioral (via exposure and flooding, systematic desensitization, modeling, and graduated exposure).

Intrusive thoughts, such as the desire to shout in a church, or behaviors that one is compelled to perform over and over again, such as checking to determine if the door is locked, are relatively common. When do they become a disorder, and how do you eliminate them?

- Obsessive-compulsive disorder involves thoughts or actions that are involuntary, intrusive, repetitive, and uncontrollable. Most persons with obsessive-compulsive disorder are aware that their distressing behaviors are irrational.
- Obsessions (which involve thoughts or images) and compulsions (which involve actions or thoughts) may occur together or separately. The behaviors have to cause marked distress or significantly interfere with life activities before the diagnosis is given.
- Freud believed that this disorder represented the replacement of thoughts of a threatening conflict with a behavior or thought that was less threatening.
- According to the anxiety-reduction hypothesis, a behavioral explanation, obsessions and compulsions develop because they reduce anxiety.
- Proponents of operant conditioning suggest that the disorder stems from the chance association of a behavior with a reinforcer, but this view fails to explain some aspects of the disorder.
- Positron emission tomography has opened new avenues of research for those using the biological approach. The most commonly used treatments are either biological or behavioral.
- The treatment of choice is a combination of flooding and response prevention, sometimes combined with cognitive therapy.

A large minority of individuals will face a traumatic incident sometime in their lives. Under what conditions will the trauma lead to a stress disorder such as PTSD, and how are these disorders best treated?

- Posttraumatic and acute stress disorders involve exposure to a traumatic event, resulting in intrusive memories of the occurrence, attempts to forget or repress the memories, emotional withdrawal, and increased arousal.
- Exposure to extreme stress will result in a strong emotional reaction in most people.

■ A diagnosis of a stress disorder is given only when symptoms of distress are clinically significant and last for at least two days for ASD or one month for PTSD.

■ Classical conditioning, cognitive approaches, and biological principles have been used to both explain and treat the condition.

KEY TERMS

acute stress disorder (ASD) (p. 161)

agoraphobia (p. 142)

anxiety (p. 131)

anxiety disorder (p. 132)

compulsion (p. 153)

exposure therapy (p. 151)

flooding (p. 159)

generalized anxiety disorder (GAD) (p. 136)

modeling therapy (p. 153)

obsession (p. 153)

obsessive-compulsive disorder (OCD) (p. 153)

panic disorder (p. 134)

phobia (p. 142)

posttraumatic stress disorder (PTSD) (p. 161)

social phobia (p. 143)

specific phobia (p. 144)

systematic desensitization (p. 153)

MULTIMEDIA PREVIEW

For additional study aids, we invite you to explore our media resources accompanying *Understanding Abnormal Behavior*, Eighth Edition. The Student CD-ROM includes videos, quizzing, and critical thinking activities that help to reinforce key concepts in a fun and engaging manner. The Student Web Site provides additional interactive activities, chapter outlines, and research links that further support and complement the text. All Web resources may be accessed by logging onto the Web site at **http://psychology.college.hmco.com/students**.

CHAPTER 6
Dissociative Disorders and Somatoform Disorders

Dissociative Disorders
Dissociative Amnesia
Dissociative Fugue
Depersonalization Disorder
Dissociative Identity Disorder
   (Multiple-Personality Disorder)
Etiology of Dissociative Disorders
Treatment of Dissociative Disorders

Somatoform Disorders
Somatization Disorder
Conversion Disorder
Pain Disorder
Hypochondriasis
Body Dysmorphic Disorder
Etiology of Somatoform Disorders
Treatment of Somatoform Disorders

FOCUS QUESTIONS

■ What are dissociations? What forms can they take? How are they caused, and how are they treated?

■ When do physical complaints become a type of disorder? What are the causes and treatments of these conditions?

The following cases illustrate characteristics found in the **dissociative disorders**—mental disorders in which a person's identity, memory, and consciousness are altered or disrupted and the **somatoform disorders,** which involve physical symptoms or complaints that have no physiological basis. Both groups of disorders occur because of some psychological conflict or need.

Sam McNulty was found by the police sitting in a motel room in Houston two days after being reported missing. He had disappeared after just getting married and reported that he did not know who he was and had no memory of his life. Psychiatrists believed that McNulty was suffering from psychogenic fugue. (Lezon, 2002)

A boy of twelve was referred for investigation of gait disorder. ... He was noted to walk with a bizarre staggering gait which on close inspection could be seen to be carefully coordinated. ... Systematic detailed clinical examination showed no neurological abnormality. ... Shortly before the onset of his illness he had moved with his peer group to a secondary school with high academic expectations of pupils. He had not been able to achieve these and the teacher of his favourite subject had humiliated him by rejecting class work he had done and throwing his workbook on the floor. (Leary, 2003, p. 436)

The symptoms of the dissociative disorders and the somatoform disorders, such as memory disturbance or hysterical blindness, generally become known through self-reports. Thus the possibility of faking must be considered. Mr. Wadlh El-Hage, a defendant on charges of being a conspirator with Osama bin Laden in the attacks on the U.S. embassies in Kenya and Tanzania, claimed that he suffered from a loss of memory. The court-appointed experts voiced the opinion that he was "malingering and faking the symptoms of amnesia" (Weiser, 2000). Lee Malvo, the Washington, D.C., sniper, claimed to have a dissociative disorder (Jackson,

2003). In addition to the possibility of faking, other questions have been raised about several of the dissociative disorders. For example, some researchers are concerned about the sudden increases in reports of multiple personalities and dissociative amnesia. They believe that counselors and therapists or clients may be inadvertently "creating" these disorders.

Physical complaints from individuals with somatoform disorders are also difficult to evaluate when no biological basis seems to exist for the physical symptoms. Yet the fact remains that in genuine cases of dissociative and somatoform disorders, the symptoms are produced "involuntarily" or unconsciously. Affected individuals actually are puzzled by their memory loss and behavioral changes or suffer from their physical pain or disability. This situation leads to a paradox: a person *does* suffer memory disturbance in psychogenic (of psychological or emotional origin) amnesia, yet that memory must exist somewhere in the neurons and synapses of the brain. Similarly, a person *does* "lose" his or her sight in hysterical blindness, yet physiologically the eyes are perfectly capable of seeing. What exactly happens in these cases? The dissociative and somatoform disorders are among the most puzzling of all disorders.

Dissociative Disorders

The dissociative disorders—*dissociative amnesia, dissociative fugue, dissociative identity disorder (multiple personality),* and *depersonalization disorder*—are shown in Figure 6.1. Each disorder involves some sort of dissociation, or separation, of a part of the person's consciousness, memory, or identity. Figure 6.1 also summarizes the prevalence rates, age of onset, and course of dissociative disorders.

The dissociative disorders are highly publicized and sensationalized and, except for depersonalization disorder, were considered relatively rare. But reports of one of these disorders—dissociative identity disorder, or multiple-personality disorder, as it is commonly

FIGURE 6.1 Disorders Chart: Dissociative Disorders

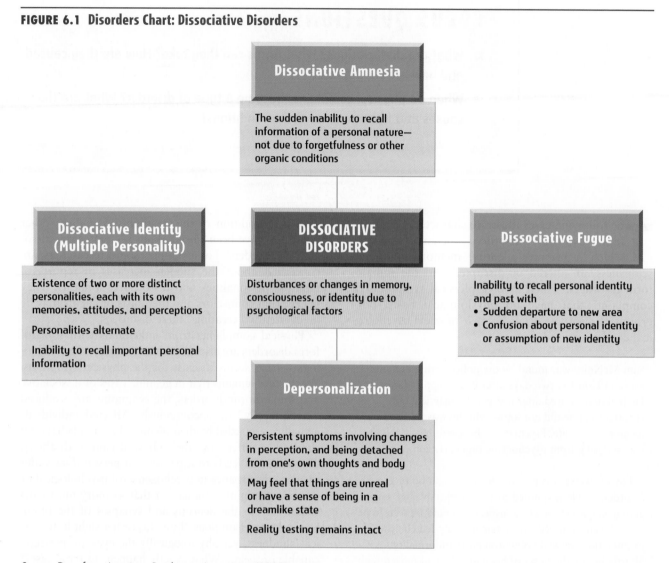

Dissociative Amnesia

The sudden inability to recall information of a personal nature—not due to forgetfulness or other organic conditions

DISSOCIATIVE DISORDERS

Disturbances or changes in memory, consciousness, or identity due to psychological factors

Dissociative Identity (Multiple Personality)

Existence of two or more distinct personalities, each with its own memories, attitudes, and perceptions

Personalities alternate

Inability to recall important personal information

Dissociative Fugue

Inability to recall personal identity and past with
- Sudden departure to new area
- Confusion about personal identity or assumption of new identity

Depersonalization

Persistent symptoms involving changes in perception, and being detached from one's own thoughts and body

May feel that things are unreal or have a sense of being in a dreamlike state

Reality testing remains intact

Source: Data from American Psychiatric Association (2000).

known—have increased dramatically (Reasons for this increase are discussed later in the chapter.) Interestingly, this disorder is rarely diagnosed in Japan or Britain (Merskey, 1992; Phelps, 2000).

Corresponding to this increase is a complex legal debate about acts that were committed but for which the individual is amnesic, as in the following:

- A therapist claimed that one of William Greene's twenty-four personalities kidnapped and took sexual liberties with her and that he (the main personality) was not responsible (Haley, 2003).

- A man was charged with the rape of a woman with multiple personalities when the nonconsenting personalities brought up the charge.

- A South Carolina woman with twenty-one personalities asked for alimony payments, claiming that

she did not commit adultery and that she had tried to stop the responsible personality, "Rosie." (In South Carolina, adultery is grounds for barring alimony payments.)

These issues raise troubling questions regarding responsibility in these disorders. Does a diagnosis of dissociative identity disorder or dissociative amnesia constitute mitigating circumstances and "diminished capacity"? (See the chapter on legal and ethical issues in abnormal psychology for a discussion of legal issues.)

Dissociative Amnesia

Dissociative amnesia is the partial or total loss of important personal information, sometimes occurring suddenly after a stressful or traumatic event. Several individuals listed as missing after the September 11

FIGURE 6.1 Disorders Chart: Dissociative Disorders (continued)

DISSOCIATIVE DISORDERS	Prevalence	Age of Onset	Course
Dissociative Amnesia	Recent increase involving forgotten early childhood trauma	Any age group	Acute forms may remit spontaneously—others are chronic; usually related to trauma or stress
Dissociative Fugue	0.2 percent; may increase during natural disasters or wartime	Usually adulthood	Related to stress or trauma; recovery is generally rapid
Depersonalization	Unknown; 50 percent of adults may experience brief episodes of stress-related depersonalization	Adolescence or adulthood	May be short lived or chronic
Dissociative Identity (Multiple Personality)	Sharp rise in recently reported cases; up to nine times more frequent in women	Childhood to adolescence, but misdiagnosis may result in late reporting	Fluctuates; tends to be chronic and recurrent

attacks on the World Trade Center had apparently developed amnesia (Tucker, 2002). The disturbed person may be unable to recall information such as his or her name, address, friends, and relatives but does remember the necessities of daily life—how to read, write, and drive. Individuals with this disorder often score high on tests measuring hypnotizability and may also report depression, anxiety, and trance states (American Psychiatric Association, 2000). Although amnesia can also be caused by strokes, substance abuse, or other medical conditions, dissociative amnesia is the result of psychological factors (Tikhonova et al., 2003).

There are five types of dissociative amnesia—localized, selective, generalized, systematized, and continuous—and they vary in terms of the degree and type of memory that is lost. The most common, **localized amnesia,** is a failure to recall all the events that happened in a specific short period, often centered on some highly painful or disturbing event. The following cases are typical of localized amnesia.

A thirty-eight-year-old mother had no memory of being molested by her father until she underwent therapy at the age of thirty-three.

An eighteen-year-old woman who survived a dramatic fire claimed not to remember it or the death of her child and husband in the fire. She claimed her relatives were lying about the fire. She became extremely agitated and emotional several hours later, when her memory abruptly returned.

Selective amnesia is an inability to remember certain details of an incident. For example, a man remembered having an automobile accident but could not recall that his child had died in the crash. Selective amnesia is often claimed by people accused of violent criminal offenses (Mendlowicz et al., 2002). Many murderers report that they remember arguments but do not remember killing anyone. According to one estimate, about 70 percent of criminals who say they have amnesia of the crime are feigning (Merryman, 1997).

Generalized amnesia is an inability to remember anything about one's past life. Because of the complete loss of memory of the individual's entire life, law enforcement agencies or hospitals often become involved. The following cases illustrate some of the psychological events associated with generalized amnesia:

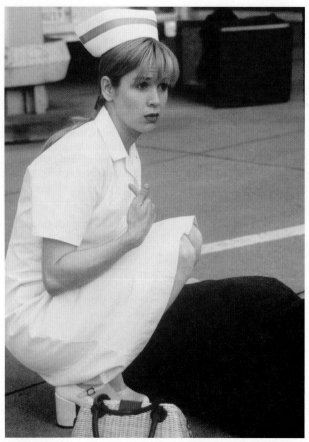

Fugue State, Delusion, or Both? In the film *Nurse Betty,* Renee Zellweger's character witnesses the killing of her husband and develops amnesia about the event and her identity. She then develops an identity based on her favorite soap opera and leaves for Los Angeles in search of a fictional character on the show. How would you diagnose her condition?

A twenty-nine-year old woman was brought into the psychiatric emergency room after being away from her home for four days and presenting a complete amnesia for that period upon her return. ... Each episode was preceded by an increase in stress and nervousness. ... In the last year, the patient had been subjected to chronic stress situations, and her husband had thrown her out of the house in the course of several arguments, during the last of which she threatened not to return. (O'Neill & Fernandez, 2000)

Mr. A, a seventy-four-year-old white man, was brought to the hospital emergency room after awakening on a park bench not knowing who or where he was. He reported having no memory of how he got to the park, nor did he know his name or where he was from (Ballew, Morgan, & Lippmann, 2003, p. 347). Mr. A was treated with diazepam, an antianxiety medication,

and recovered his memory. His family was contacted, and his sister reported that Mr. A. had disappeared on two other occasions when under stress.

Systematized amnesia involves the loss of memory for only selected types of information. Patients may lose the ability to recall all memories of their families or of a particular person. Finally, **continuous amnesia,** the fourth and least common form of dissociative amnesia, is an inability to recall any events that have occurred between a specific time in the past and the present time. The individual remains alert and attentive but forgets each successive event after it occurs. This cognitive problem may be transient and is more common in people age fifty and over (Sadovsky, 1998).

Psychologists are uncertain about the processes involved in dissociative amnesia. They believe it results from the person's repression of a traumatic event or from some process closely related to repression. For example, **posthypnotic amnesia,** in which the individual cannot recall events that occurred during hypnosis, is somewhat similar to dissociative amnesia. In both cases, the lost material can sometimes be retrieved with professional help. There is, however, one important difference. In posthypnotic amnesia, the hypnotist suggests what is to be forgotten, whereas in dissociative amnesia, both the source and the content of the amnesia are unknown. Because of this difference, experiments to study amnesia are difficult to design. Therefore, information on dissociative amnesia has been gathered primarily through case studies.

An increasing number of cases of dissociative amnesia involving sexual abuse have been reported (L. Shapiro, Rosenberg, Lauerman, & Sparkman, 1993). Some researchers now question whether the memories reported in some of these cases may be caused by therapists' suggestions and clients' attempts to explain their problems (see the Critical Thinking feature "How Valid Are Repressed Memories?").

Dissociative Fugue

Dissociative fugue (also called *fugue state*) is confusion over personal identity (often involving the partial or complete assumption of a new identity), accompanied by unexpected travel away from home. Most cases involve only short periods away from home and an incomplete change of identity. However, there are exceptions:

Jane Dee Williams says she remembers nothing before the day in May 1985 when she was found wandering and

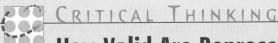

CRITICAL THINKING

How Valid Are Repressed Memories?

In May 1990, George Franklin was brought to trial for raping and killing a child twenty years previously. This case was one of the first to rely heavily on repressed memories. The man's daughter, twenty years after the incident, remembered the killing of her friend in flashes of memory. She was playing with her friend in the back of the family van when the attack took place. She also retrieved memories of being sexually abused by her father. Three of her sisters also related being sexually abused. George Franklin was convicted and sent to prison. (Questions about the testimony's validity led to his release.)

In the past few years, many individuals have reported repressed memories. For example, after her former husband related an instance of sexual abuse that he suffered as a child, television celebrity Roseanne remembered being abused by her father thirty-six years earlier. And in a sample of psychologists who had experienced childhood abuse, 40 percent reported a period of forgetting some or all of the abuse. In 56 percent of the cases, the memory returned during therapy (Feldman-Summers & Pope, 1994).

Although survey data show that childhood sexual abuse and incest are more prevalent than had previously been estimated, controversy arises over the accuracy and validity of repressed memories. Some clinicians would prefer to err on the side of the victim. Ellen Bass and Laura Davis (1988), authors of the book *The Courage to Heal,* which deals with sexual abuse, wrote, "If you are unable to remember any specific instances, but still have a feeling that something happened to you, it probably did." Psychologist Elizabeth Loftus, however, believes that for some individuals, the "memory" may be inaccurate and may result from imagination or suggestion or may function as a means of explaining unhappiness in life (Loftus, 1993). Determining the authenticity of the memories, especially those dating to very early ages, is difficult. One therapist indicated that some of his patients report that they remember incidents that occurred before speech had developed or even while in the womb (Laker, 1992).

Parents who believe that they have been falsely accused of child abuse have formed a nationwide support group, the False Memory Syndrome Foundation. They claim that the "memories" are often a product of the therapist's approach or their children's attempt to blame them for their problems. They also cite research findings that indicate that women who report repressed memory also score high on fantasy proneness (McNally, Clancy, Schacter, & Pitman, 2000). Although sexual abuse of children does exist and some victims do repress the memory of the event, controversy remains over the accuracy and acceptability of the reports.

As a scientist, how could you determine whether any "repressed memories" are accurate representations of the past? How could you separate "true" from "false" memories, knowing that information obtained through hypnosis may be unreliable? Can counselors inadvertently produce false memories in their clients? In cases of suspected sexual abuse, some clinicians say they will believe what the client says no matter how incredible the details. But, as Loftus, Garry, and Feldman (1994) have pointed out, people also forget automobile accidents, the deaths of family members, or being hospitalized. Have these memories been repressed or merely forgotten? How can you distinguish between these two processes? How might you interpret a statement from a client who says that she has no clear memory of her childhood before the age of five?

---

disoriented in an Aurora, Colorado, shopping mall, wearing a green coat and carrying a Toyota key, a copy of *Watership Down,* two green pens, and a notebook—but having no clue as to who she was. She went to Aurora police for help and ended up at the Colorado Mental Health Institute at Fort Logan with a diagnosis of psychogenic fugue. Jane Dee Williams was actually Jody Roberts, who had disappeared five days earlier from her home and job as a reporter in Tacoma. She was treated and released without recovering her memory. During the next twelve years she remained missing and amnesic. During that time she married and had two sets of twins. In 1997, a tip to the police from someone who recognized Roberts from photographs led to her discovery. She had no memory of her biological family (Merryman, 1997, A8). Although most people with dissociative fugue recover their memories after a short period, Jane Dee Williams still cannot remember her childhood. (Kremer, 1999)

Sometimes, a patient reports multiple fugue episodes, as in the following:

> E. F. was a forty-six-year-old man who described twelve to fifteen episodes of "going blank" during the previous five years. He said that these episodes lasted two to thirty-six hours, and that, in "coming round," his feet were often sore, he was a long way from home, and he had no idea of the time or what had been happening during the previous hours. For example, he found himself on one occasion near the Thames, ten miles from his home, with his clothes sopping wet. Marital and legal difficulties were believed to be contributing factors in the episodes of fugue. (Kopelman, 1987, p. 438)

As with dissociative amnesia, recovery from fugue state is often abrupt and complete, although the gradual return of bits of information may also occur. Kopelman (2002) believes that genuine cases are short lived. "Fugue states usually last only a few hours or days, if prolonged, suspicion of simulation must always arise" (p. 2171). However, DSM-IV-TR (American Psychiatric Association, 2000) indicates that some fugue states may last for months.

Depersonalization Disorder

Depersonalization disorder is perhaps the most common dissociative disorder. It is characterized by feelings of unreality concerning the self and the environment. Questions such as "Have you ever had the feeling recently that things around you were unreal?" or "Have you yourself felt unreal, that you were not a person, not living in the real world?" are used to screen for this disorder (Lambert et al., 2001). This diagnosis is given only when the feelings of unreality and detachment cause major impairment in social or occupational functioning. At one time or another, most young adults have experienced some symptoms typical of depersonalization disorder: perceptions that the body is distorted or that the environment has somehow changed, feelings of living out a dream, or feelings of detachment. In a sample of thirty individuals with depersonalization disorder, the illness started in mid-adolescence, with a waxing and waning of symptoms. Among these individuals, the disorder followed a chronic course and was resistant to treatment. One woman described her symptoms this way: "It is as if the real me is taken out and put on a shelf and stored somewhere inside of me. Whatever makes me me is not there" (Simeon et al., 1997, p. 1110). The condition tends to be chronic and is often accompanied by mood and anxiety disorders (Simeon et al., 2000).

Episodes of depersonalization can be fairly intense, and they can produce great anxiety because the people who suffer from them consider them unnatural, as the following case illustrates.

Depersonalization Disorder An individual may feel like an automaton—mechanical and robotlike—when suffering from depersonalization disorder. This painting, "The Subway" (ca. 1950), by George Tooker, captures this feeling.

A twenty-year-old college student became alarmed when she suddenly perceived subtle changes in her appearance. The reflection she saw in mirrors did not seem to be hers. She became even more disturbed when her room, her friends, and the campus also seemed to take on a slightly distorted appearance. The world around her felt unreal and was no longer predictable. During the day before the sudden appearance of the symptoms, the woman had been greatly distressed by the low grades she received on several important exams. When she finally sought help at the university clinic, her major concern was that she was going insane.

Like other dissociative disorders, depersonalization can be precipitated by physical or psychological stress. There is some evidence that emotional abuse, especially by parents, may be related to this disorder (Simeon, Guralnik, Schmeidler, Sirof, & Knutelska, 2001). See the Mental Health and Society feature "Culture and Somatoform and Dissociative Disorders" for culture-specific forms of dissociation or somatoform disorders.

Dissociative Identity Disorder (Multiple-Personality Disorder)

Dissociative identity disorder (DID), formerly known as *multiple-personality disorder*, is a dramatic condition in which two or more relatively independent personalities appear to exist in one person. The relationships among the personalities are often complex. Only one personality is evident at any one time, and the alternation of personalities usually produces periods of amnesia in the personality that has been displaced. However, one or several personalities may be aware of the existence of the others. The personalities usually differ from one another and sometimes are direct opposites, as the following cases illustrate.

"Little Judy" is a young child who laughs and giggles. "Gravelly Voice" is a man who speaks with a raspy voice. The "one who walks in darkness" is blind and trips over furniture. "Big Judy" is articulate, competent, and funny. These are four of the forty-four personalities that exist within Judy Castelli. She was initially diagnosed with schizophrenia but later told that dissociative identity disorder was the appropriate diagnosis. She has become a lay expert on mental health issues, a singer, a musician, an inventor, and an artist whose work appeared on the February 2000 cover of the American Psychological Association Monitor. (Woliver, 2000)

A twenty-eight-year-old female has a total of sixteen personalities. Three major personalities are usually present sometime during each day.

Margaret is the core personality and is described as having good social skills but tends not to be assertive. She has a good sense of humor and puts on a "good front" to prevent the detection of the other personalities. She is left-handed.

Rachel is sixteen years old. She engages in antisocial behaviors involving activities such as prostitution and aggression. She has a sarcastic sense of humor and appears when there is a need to fight back. She is right-handed.

Dee is eight years old. She speaks and behaves like a child. She appears to have "taken the pain" whenever the personalities have been abused. She holds the memories of sexual abuse. She is ambidextrous. (Dick-Barnes, Nelson, & Aine, 1987)

In cases in which one personality is that of a child (like Dee), that part of the personality may be aware only of events that took place at an early age. For example, one woman's "child" personality was confused about being in an adult body and had never heard of *Sesame Street*, Burger King, or Sprite, which did not exist when she was a child. She wanted to see her childhood friends and return to elementary school (Davidson, Allen, & Smith, 1987).

Dissociative identity disorder is much more prevalent in women, who often report having experienced childhood physical or sexual abuse (Boon & Draijer, 1993; Coons, 1994; Mulder, Beautrais, Joyce, & Fergusson, 1998). No gender differences in the prevalence of the disorder, however, were found in Switzerland (Modestin, 1992). *Conversion symptoms* (loss of physical or sensory function with no physical basis), depression, and anxiety are common in people with the disorder.

Dissociative identity disorder appears to originate in childhood, with most reporting their first alternate personality before the age of twelve (Richardson, 1998). In contrast to other diagnostic groups, females with dissociative identity disorder report more alterations in consciousness, have a history of trance states and sleepwalking, and have very high levels of substance abuse and very high rates of suicidality (Scroppo, Drob, Weinberger, & Eagle, 1998). Mothers with this disorder also report that it interferes with their child rearing. One stated, "Sometimes I forget that I'm her mother. I feel somebody dropped their kid off for me to babysit and never picked her up" (Benjamin, Benjamin, & Rind, 1998, p. 340). Another said, "If the angry part is in control, it causes friction and tension with the kids. It's hard to tell them that I didn't mean it" (p. 342).

The characteristics of this disorder have changed over time. Goff and Simms (1993) compared case reports from between the years 1800 and 1965 with those from the 1980s. The earlier cases involved fewer

MENTAL HEALTH AND SOCIETY
Culture and Somatoform and Dissociative Disorders

A fifty-six-year-old South American man requested an evaluation and treatment. He had the firm belief that his penis was retracting and entering his abdomen, and he was reacting with a great deal of anxiety. He attempted to pull on his penis to prevent the retraction. This procedure had been effective with a previous episode that occurred when he was nineteen. An evaluation of his mental state ruled out other psychiatric diagnoses such as obsessive-compulsive disorder or schizophrenia (Hallak, Crippa, & Zuardi, 2000).

Dibuk ak Suut, a Malaysian woman, goes into a trancelike state in which she will follow commands and blurt out offensive phrases and may mimic the actions of people around her. She displays profuse sweating and increased heart rate but claims to have no memory of what she did or said. This behavior is set off by being startled or suddenly frightened (Osbourne, 2001).

The symptoms of the first case fit the description of *koro*, a culture-bound syndrome listed in DSM-IV-TR (American Psychiatric Association, 2000) that has been reported primarily in South and East Asia. The symptoms involve an intense fear that the penis or, in a woman, the labia, nipples, or breasts are receding into the body. Koro may be related to body dysmorphic disorder, but it differs in that koro is usually of brief duration

and is responsive to positive reassurances. In the second case, the woman is displaying symptoms related to *latah*, a condition found in Malaysia and many other parts of the world that involves mimicking or following the instructions or behaviors of others and dissociation or trancelike states. Other culture-bound disorders may be related to either somatoform or dissociative disorders:

Brain fag Somatic symptoms involving a "fatigued" brain, neck or head pain, or blurring of vision due to difficult coursework or classes. It is found primarily in West Africa among high school and college students.

Dhat A term used in India to describe hypochondriacal concerns and severe anxiety over the discharge of semen. The condition produces feelings of weakness or exhaustion.

Nervios Commonly found in Hispanics residing in the United States and Latin America. The symptoms can include "brain aches," stomach disturbances, anxiety symptoms, and dizziness. Patterns of symptoms can resemble somatoform, anxiety, dissociative, or depressive disorders.

Pibloktoq A dissociative-like episode accompanied by

extreme excitement that may be followed by convulsions and coma. It is generally found in Inuit communities. The victim may perform aggressive and dangerous acts and report amnesia after the episode.

Zar A condition found in Middle Eastern or North African societies that involves the experience of being possessed by a spirit. The person may engage in bizarre behaviors that may include shouting or hitting his or her head against the wall. During this period the individual is in a dissociative state.

Culture-bound syndromes are interesting because they point to the existence of a pattern of symptoms that are associated primarily with specific societies or groups. These "disorders" do not fit easily into the DSM-IV-TR classification or into many of the biological and psychological models for dissociative and somatoform disorders. What does it mean when disorders are discovered that do not fit into Western-developed classification systems? Would we assume that the etiology and treatment would be similar to those developed for somatoform and dissociative disorders?

personalities (three versus twelve), a later age of onset of first dissociation (age twenty as opposed to age eleven in the 1980s), a greater proportion of males, and a much lower prevalence of child abuse (see Figure 6.2). Goff and Simms believe that these findings support the view that this disorder is a "culturally determined disorder that occurs in highly suggestible patients" (p. 598).

Psychological and physiological tests have been used to try to confirm the existence of distinct personalities in dissociative identity disorders. Current attempts to identify this disorder through the use of electroencephalograms, cerebral blood flow, galvanic skin response, and other physiological measures have produced contradictory and conflicting findings (Miller & Triggiano, 1992).

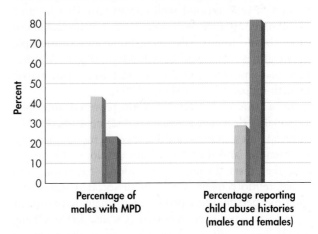

Dissociative Identity Disorder
Judy Castelli stands beside her stained glass artwork. The people in the art have no faces but are connected and touching each other. She considers her artistic endeavors a creative outlet for her continuing struggle with multiple personalities.

Diagnostic Controversy We noted earlier that dissociative identity disorder is among the less common dissociative disorders, but there is some question about how rare it really is. Before the case of Sybil (a patient who appeared to have sixteen different personalities) became popularized in a movie and book in the 1970s, there were fewer than two hundred reported cases of multiple personality worldwide. Now there are about six thousand new cases reported each year (Milstone, 1997). Some clinicians believe that dissociative identity disorder is relatively common but that the condition is underreported because of misdiagnosis. Richard Kluft and Brad Foote (1999) believe that up to 6 percent of psychiatric inpatients have undiagnosed DID. Others believe that the prevalence of DID is overestimated because of a reliance on questionable self-report measures. In a carefully controlled study involving the use of a semistructured interview instead of a self-rating screening instrument, only 1 percent of one hundred randomly selected women admitted to an acute psychiatric hospital was found to have dissociative identity disorder (Rifkin, Ghisalbert, Dimatou, Jin, & Sethi, 1998).

In a survey of psychologists (Cormier & Thelen, 1998), most believed dissociative identity disorder to be a rare but valid diagnosis. About half believed they had encountered a client with the disorder, and one-third believed one of their clients was feigning it. Over half (53 percent) said they did not think the disorder was due to *iatrogenic* factors (unintended effects of some action by the therapist), whereas one-third believed the "condition" was produced by the use of a technique

such as suggestion or hypnosis. In a survey of board-certified American psychiatrists (H. G. Pope, Oliva, Hudson, Bodkin, & Gruber, 1999), only one-third felt that dissociative disorders should be included in DSM-IV without reservation, more believed that they should be included only as "proposed diagnoses," and only

FIGURE 6.2 Comparison of Characteristics of Reported Cases of Dissociative Identity Disorder (Multiple-Personality Disorder) This graph illustrates characteristics of multiple-personality-disorder (MPD) cases reported in the 1980s versus those reported between 1800 and 1965. What could account for these differences?

Percentage of males with MPD | Percentage reporting child abuse histories (males and females)

Between 1800 and 1965
1980s

Source: Data from Goff & Simms (1993).

about one-fourth believed that the diagnoses were strongly supported by scientific research. The theoretical orientations of the psychiatrists also affected their opinions of dissociative disorders. Psychodynamic psychiatrists were more likely than biological psychiatrists to accept the validity of these disorders.

Gleaves (1996) believes it is highly unlikely that dissociative identity disorder is a result of clinician practices, noting that individuals with the disorder show a core set of symptoms, such as amnesia, lack of autobiographical memory for their childhood, chronic depersonalization, and alteration and alternation of identity. In addition, most individuals are not hypnotized before the diagnosis is made. Other researchers have suggested that the sudden increase in reports of dissociative identity disorder may be an artifact of the procedures used in investigating this disorder and that it is a "fashionable" diagnosis.

With the exception of the Netherlands and Turkey, dissociative identity or multiple-personality disorder is rarely diagnosed outside the United States and Canada (Merskey, 1995; Tutkun, Sar, Yargic, & Ozpulat, 1998). In a study of this disorder in Switzerland, Modestin (1992) concluded that it is relatively rare and estimated its prevalence rate to be 0.05 percent to 0.1 percent of patients. He also found that three psychiatrists accounted for more than 50 percent of the patients given this diagnosis. Why is it that some psychiatrists report treating many patients with multiple personalities, whereas the majority do not? One prominent psychiatrist indicated that in forty years of practice he had encountered only one "doubtful case" of the disorder and wondered why he and his colleagues had seen so few cases of multiple-personality disorder (Chodoff, 1987). The psychiatrists who treated "Eve," another well-known case that became popularized in a movie, received tens of thousands of referrals and found only one genuine case of multiple personalities (Thigpen & Cleckley, 1984). Another therapist characterized the disorder as a "psychiatric growth industry" (Weissberg, 1993).

In a study of patients with reported multiple-personality disorder, Merskey (1992) believed that the "personalities" represent differences in mood, memory, or attention and that "they" are developed by unwitting therapists through expectation, suggestion, and social reinforcement. Cases of dissociated states and multiple personalities produced through hypnosis or suggestion have been reported (Coons, 1988; Ofshe, 1992). Dissociation experiences such as alterations in memory, thoughts, and time and changes in reality and depersonalization (feeling detached or numb) are common in the face of stress (Freinkel, Koopman, &

Spiegel, 1994). Some clinicians could interpret these symptoms of stress as multiple personalities.

Because this disorder is difficult to diagnose, some clinicians have developed questionnaires to assess dissociation. The following questions are used to determine whether some type of dissociation is occurring in children (M. K. Shapiro, 1991):

"Do you ever kinda space out, and lose track of what's going on around you?" (decreased awareness of the environment)

"Do you have any problems with forgetting things?" (amnesia)

"Does it ever happen that time goes by, and then you can't really remember what you were doing during that time?" (fugue state)

"Does it ever seem like things aren't real, like everything is just a dream?" (feelings of unreality)

"Does it ever happen that you do things that surprise you, and afterward you stop and say to yourself, 'Why did I do that?'?" (multiple personalities)

These questions direct the clinician to investigate possible dissociation disorders. Some researchers, however, doubt the validity of scales purporting to measure this phenomenon (D. G. Fischer & Elnitsky, 1990). Many children, adolescents, and adults may answer yes to these questions without having a dissociative disorder. Interpretations are difficult to make without appropriate comparison groups. Whether the increase in cases of dissociative identity disorder is the result of more accurate diagnosis, false positives, an artifact, or an actual increase in the incidence of the disorder is still being debated.

Myth vs Reality

Myth: Dissociative identity disorder is relatively easy to diagnose; the category is accepted by most mental health professionals.

Reality: There are no objective measures from which a diagnosis can be made, and cases involving feigning the disorder have been reported. Those who question the category raise the possibility that the disorder is due to iatrogenic factors that are inadvertently produced through suggestion or hypnosis. In one study of board-certified psychiatrists, only one-third indicated that dissociative amnesia and dissociative identity disorder should be included in the DSM-IV without reservation.

Etiology of Dissociative Disorders

The diagnosis and causes of dissociative disorders are subject to much conjecture. Because diagnosis depends heavily on patients' self-reports, feigning or faking is always a possibility. Malingered (fabricated) amnesia, fugue, or dissociative identity disorder can be produced by individuals who "are attempting to flee a situation involving legal, financial, or personal difficulties, as well as in soldiers who are attempting to avoid combat or unpleasant military duties" (American Psychiatric Association, 2000, p. 525). However, true cases of these disorders may also result from these types of stressors. Differentiating between genuine cases of dissociative disorders and faked ones is difficult. Even expert judges cannot distinguish between genuine inability to recall and individuals who simulate amnesia (D. Schacter, 1986). Researchers have found that recollections obtained under hypnosis are often inaccurate and distorted and that the retrieved information can alter waking memories (Nash, Drake, Wiley, & Khalsa, 1986; Sheehan, Grigg, & McCann, 1984).

Some researchers hoped that objective measures such as electroencephalograph (EEG) readings could show the presence of multiple personalities. Researchers later concluded, however, that EEG differences among the different personalities in individuals with multiple-personality disorder reflected differences mainly in concentration, mood, and degree of muscle tension (Coons, Milstein, & Marley, 1982).

Although clinical evidence supports the existence of dissociative disorders, reliable methods of determining their validity do not currently exist.

We next examine the causes of dissociative disorders from the psychodynamic and learning perspectives, and we also examine the possible influence of the clinician. It is important to realize that none of these approaches provides completely satisfactory explanations. As we indicated earlier, the dissociative disorders are not well understood.

Psychodynamic Perspective Psychodynamic theory views the dissociative disorders as a result of the person's use of repression to block from consciousness unpleasant or traumatic events (Richardson, 1998). When complete repression of these impulses is not possible because of the strength of the impulses or the weakness of the ego, dissociation or separation of certain mental processes may occur. In dissociative amnesia and fugue, for example, large parts of the individual's personal identity are no longer available to conscious awareness. This process protects the individual from painful memories or conflicts (Gleaves, 1996).

A twenty-seven-year-old man found lying in the middle of a busy intersection was brought to a hospital. He appeared agitated and said, "I wanted to get run over." He claimed not to know his personal identity or anything about his past. He only remembered being

Cross-Cultural Factors and Dissociation Dissociative trance states can be entered voluntarily as part of certain cultural or religious practices, as demonstrated by this woman in Brazil. Can the study of such phenomena in another culture shed light on the process of dissociation in Western societies?

brought to the hospital by the police. The inability to remember was highly distressful to him. Psychological tests using the TAT (Thematic Apperception Test) and the Rorschach inkblot test revealed primarily anxiety-arousing, violent, and sexual themes. The clinician hypothesized that a violent incident involving sex might underlie the amnesia. Under hypnosis the patient's memory returned, and he remembered being severely assaulted. He had repressed the painful experience. (Kaszniak, Nussbaum, Berren, & Santiago, 1988)

The dissociation process is carried to an extreme in dissociative identity disorder. Here, the splits in mental processes become so extreme that more or less independent identities are formed, each with its own unique set of memories. Conflicts within the personality structure are responsible for this process. Equally strong and opposing personality components (stemming from the superego and the id) render the ego incapable of controlling all incompatible elements. A compromise solution is then reached in which the different parts of the personality are alternately allowed expression and repressed. Because intense anxiety and disorganization would occur if these personality factions were allowed to coexist, each is sealed off from the others.

The split in personality may develop because of traumatic early experiences combined with an inability to escape them. Some researchers believe that one or more personalities take on the "pain" to shield the other personalities (Shapiro, 1991). From case histories, we have learned that some conditions may produce a dissociative reaction. In the case of Sybil, for example, Sybil's mother severely abused her. Dr. Wilbur, Sybil's psychiatrist, speculated that "by dividing into different selves [which were] defenses against an intolerable and dangerous reality, Sybil had found a [design] for survival" (Schreiber, 1973, p. 158).

Most people with dissociative identity disorder do report a history of physical or sexual abuse during childhood (Boon & Draijer, 1993; Fagan & McMahon, 1984; Richardson, 1998). Besides traumatic childhood events, the person must have the capacity to dissociate—or separate—certain memories or mental processes. A person's susceptibility to hypnotism may be a characteristic of the dissociation process, and, in fact, people who have multiple personalities appear to be very receptive to hypnotic suggestion. Some researchers believe that pathological dissociation is a result of the interaction between auto- or self-hypnosis and acute traumatic stress (Butler, Duran, Jasiukaitis, Koopman, & Spiegel, 1996). Those people might escape unpleasant experiences through self-hypnosis—by entering a hypnotic

state. According to Kluft (1987), the four factors necessary in the development of multiple personalities are:

1. The capacity to dissociate (whether this is produced by traumatic events or is innate is not known)

2. Exposure to overwhelming stress, such as physical or sexual abuse

3. Encapsulating or walling off the experience

4. Developing different memory systems

If a supportive environment is not available or if the personality is not resilient, multiple personality results from these factors (H. J. Irwin, 1998; also see Figure 6.3).

Behavioral Perspective   Behavioral theorists suggest that the avoidance of stress by indirect means is the main factor to consider in explaining dissociative disorders. For example, patients with dissociative amnesia and fugue are often ill equipped to handle emotional conflicts. Their way of fleeing stressful situations is either to forget them or to block out the disturbing thoughts. These people typically have much to gain and little to lose from their dissociative symptoms. The causes of dissociative identity disorders

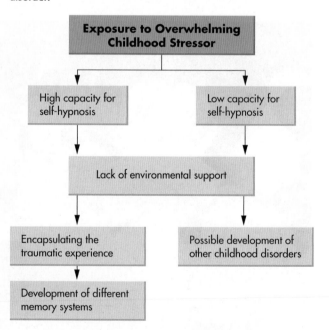

FIGURE 6.3 Psychodynamic Model for Dissociative Identity Disorder   Note the importance of the capacity for self-hypnosis in the development of dissociative identity disorder.

Source: Adapted from Kluft (1987); Loewenstein (1994).

have received much greater attention. One of the current approaches is the sociocognitive model of DID, developed by Spanos (1994) and further elaborated by Scott Lilienfeld and his colleagues (1999). In this perspective, the disorder is conceptualized as

a syndrome that consists of rule-governed and goal-directed experiences and displays of multiple role enactments that have been created, legitimized, and maintained by social reinforcement. Patients with DID synthesize these role enactments by drawing on a wide variety of sources of information, including the print and broadcast media, cues provided by therapists, personal experiences, and observations of individuals who have enacted multiple identities. (Lilienfeld et al., 1999, p. 507)

According to this model, patients learn the behaviors through a variety of means and produce these roles according to the demands of the situation. The "personalities" are displayed spontaneously and without conscious deception. Support for this perspective comes from the large increases shown in DID after mass media portrayal of this disorder and the possibility that procedures used to investigate the disorder may actually produce the condition.

As noted earlier, *iatrogenic* refers to an unintended effect of therapy—a condition or disorder produced by a physician or therapist through such mechanisms as selective attention, suggestion, reinforcement, and expectations that are placed on the client. Could some or even most cases of dissociative identity disorder be the result of these factors? A number of researchers and clinicians say yes. They believe that many of the "cases" of multiple personalities and of dissociative amnesia have unwittingly been produced by therapists, self-help books, and the mass media (Aldridge-Morris, 1989; Chodoff, 1987; Goff & Simms, 1993; Loftus, Garry, & Feldman, 1994; Merskey, 1995; Ofshe, 1992; Weissberg, 1993). Interestingly, Goff and Simms (1993) observed that early cases of multiple-personality disorder averaged about three different personalities. After the 1973 publication of *Sybil* (whose subject had sixteen personalities), the mean number of personalities rose to twelve.

The authenticity of this well-known case of multiple personality has recently been questioned (Borch-Jacobsen, 1997). Herbert Spiegel, a hypnotist, also worked with Sybil and used her to demonstrate hypnotic phenomena in his classes. He described her as a "Grade 5" or "hypnotic virtuoso," something found in only 5 percent of the population. Sybil told Spiegel that her psychiatrist, Cornelia Wilbur, had wanted her to be "Helen," a name given to a feeling she expressed during therapy. Spiegel later came to believe that Wilbur was using a technique in which different memories or emotions were converted into "personalities." Sybil also wrote a letter denying that she had multiple personalities and stating that the "extreme things" she told about her mother were not true. Recently, audiotapes of sessions between Wilbur and Sybil were found, and they indicate that Wilbur may have described personalities for Sybil (Associated Press, 1998).

Lynn and Nash (1994) point out that therapists hold implicit theories regarding the cause of mental disorders and that they may convey these theories to their clients. Therapists may insist, for example, that clients with eating disorders "remember" incidents of abuse and may treat clients' denials as indications of defense (Esman, 1994).

Although iatrogenic influences can be found in any disorder, dissociative disorders may be especially vulnerable, in part because of the high levels of hypnotizability and suggestibility found in people with dissociative disorders. As Goff (1993) states, it is "no coincidence that the field of [multiple-personality disorder] studies in the United States largely originated among practitioners of hypnosis" (p. 604). Hypnosis and other memory-retrieval methods may create rather than uncover personalities in suggestible clients. Nicholas Spanos, Weekes, and Bertrand (1985) found that suggestions and hypnosis could induce students to report having different personalities. Interestingly, the "personalities" showed different patterns of responses on personality tests. In a later study, Spanos, Menary, Gabora, DuBreuil, and Dewihirst (1991) found that the characteristics of the personalities and the reports of child abuse were also influenced by the instructions or expectations of the hypnotists. Although some cases of dissociative identity disorder probably are therapist produced, we do not know to what extent iatrogenic influences can account for this disorder. However, the sociocognitive model of DID does offer testable hypotheses.

Treatment of Dissociative Disorders

A variety of treatments for the dissociative disorders have been developed, including supportive counseling and the use of hypnosis and personality reconstruction. Currently, there are no specific medications for the dissociative identity disorders. Instead, medications are prescribed to treat the anxiety or depression that may accompany dissociative disorders. The Mental Health and Society feature "'Suspect' Techniques to Treat Dissociative Identity Disorder" discusses some controversial practices.

MENTAL HEALTH AND SOCIETY

"Suspect" Techniques to Treat Dissociative Identity Disorder

Bennett Braun, who founded the International Society for the Study of Dissociation and who trained many therapists to work with dissociative identity disorder, was brought up on charges by the Illinois Department of Professional Regulation. The charges stemmed from a former patient's claims that Braun used inappropriate techniques in therapy with her. The former patient, Patricia Burgess, claimed that Braun inappropriately used hypnotic and psychotic drugs, hypnosis, and leather strap restraints to stimulate "abuse" memories. Under repressed-memory therapy, Burgess became convinced that she possessed three hundred personalities, was a high priestess in a satanic cult, ate meatloaf made of human flesh, and sexually abused her children. Burgess later began to question her "memories." In November 1997, she won a $10.6 million lawsuit, alleging inappropriate treatment and emotional harm to both her and her children. The lawsuit named Braun, the hospital he is affiliated with, and another psychiatrist (Associated Press, 1998). In Braun's defense, Marlene Hunter, past president of the association he founded, described Braun as a dedicated psychiatrist who "has done the best he could according to what he thought

was right at the time" (p. A12). Bennett Braun lost his license to practice for two years and was placed on probation for an additional five years. While on probation, he must submit the judgment against him to prospective employers and will not be allowed to treat patients diagnosed with dissociative identity disorder. His former patient, Pat Burgess, said she was satisfied with the decision (Bloomberg, 2000). Another former patient, Elizabeth Gale, also won a $7 million settlement against Braun and other staff at the hospital. She became convinced she was raised as a "breeder" to produce babies for sexual abuse, and she is now seeking to reestablish relationships with family members whom she accused as being part of a cult (Dardick, 2004).

Such lawsuits create a quandary for mental health practitioners. Many feel intimidated by the threat of legal action if they attempt to treat adult survivors of childhood sexual abuse, especially those cases involving recovered memories. However, discounting the memory of patients may represent further abuse and condone the action of the perpetrator. But for those who take on such cases, the risks are high. In 1994, about 16 percent of all claims made against

clinicians involved repressed memories ("Repressed memory claims," 1995). Especially worrisome is the use of certain techniques such as hypnosis, as they may produce inaccurate "memories," resulting in legal action by either the client or family members (Benedict & Donaldson, 1996). One risk analysis (Knapp & VandeCreek, 1996) indicates that liability risks are greatest when therapists employ nonexperimentally supported techniques, such as trance work, body memories, or age regression, in cases of recovered memories. Encouraging the client to confront the "perpetrator" also increases malpractice risks.

What's your opinion? In the case of "repressed memories," should therapeutic techniques be restricted, and should clients be told that some techniques are experimental and may produce inaccurate information? Under what conditions, if any, should a therapist express doubt about information "remembered" by a client? Given the high prevalence of child sexual abuse and the indefinite nature of "repressed" memories, how should clinicians proceed if a client claims to remember early memories of abuse?

In working with a group of survivors of childhood sexual abuse who frequently dissociated, Janice Shaffer, Brown, and McWhirter (1998) found a three-part group format to be useful:

1. *Psychoeducation* Therapists informed members of the group about the effects of childhood sexual abuse and the use of dissociation as a survival mechanism. They then discussed appropriate techniques to cope with stress.

2. *Use of group resources* If therapists observed dissociation by a member of the group, they would call the individual by name, ask that person to identify the trigger for the episode, and discuss different ways of handling the stress. One participant, Sarah, appeared to be sitting higher than other group members and had glassy eyes. When called by name, Sarah described being high on the wall and looking down but not being part of the scene. The trigger for Sarah's episode was her memories of the

past, and she learned to separate past events from the present.

3. *Development of cognitive and social skills* Group members learned to use cognitive strategies to combat and challenge irrational ideas and to practice assertiveness and relationship skills.

Dissociative Amnesia and Dissociative Fugue

The symptoms of dissociative amnesia and fugue tend to remit, or abate, spontaneously. Moreover, patients typically complain of psychological symptoms other than the amnesia, perhaps because the amnesia interferes only minimally with their day-to-day functioning. As a result, therapeutic intervention is often not directed specifically toward the amnesia. Instead, therapists provide supportive counseling for clients with amnesia.

It has been noted, however, that depression is often associated with the fugue state and that severe stress is often associated with both fugue and dissociative amnesia (Kopelman, 2002). A reasonable therapeutic approach is then to treat these dissociative disorders indirectly by alleviating the depression (with antidepressants or cognitive behavior therapy) and the stress (through stress-management techniques).

Depersonalization Disorder

Depersonalization disorder is also subject to spontaneous remission, but at a much slower rate than that of dissociative amnesia and fugue. In common with other dissociative disorders, individuals with this disorder score high on dissociation (Simeon et al., 2001). Treatment generally concentrates on alleviating the feelings of anxiety or depression or the fear of going insane. Occasionally a behavioral approach has been tried. For example, behavior therapy was successfully used to treat depersonalization disorder in a fifteen-year-old girl who had blackouts that she described as "floating in and out." These episodes were associated with headaches and feelings of detachment, but neurological and physical examinations revealed no biological cause. Treatment involved getting increased attention from her family and reinforcement from them when the frequency of blackouts was reduced, training in appropriate responses to stressful situations, and self-reinforcement (Dollinger, 1983).

Dissociative Identity Disorder

The mental health literature contains more information on the treatment of dissociative identity (multiple-personality) disorder than on the other three dissociative disorders combined. Treatment for this disorder is not always successful. Chris Sizemore (who was the inspiration for *The Three Faces of Eve*) developed additional personalities after therapy but has now recovered. She is a writer, lecturer, and artist. Sybil also recovered—she became a college art professor and died in Lexington, Kentucky, in 1998 at the age of seventy-five (M. Miller & Kantrowitz, 1999). Success, however, may be difficult to achieve. Coons (1986) conducted a follow-up study of twenty patients with multiple personalities. Each patient was studied for about thirty-nine months after his or her initial assessment. Nine patients achieved partial or full recovery, but only five patients maintained it—the others dissociated

A Famous Case of Dissociative Identity Disorder Chris Sizemore, whose experiences with dissociative identity disorder inspired the book and movie *The Three Faces of Eve*, is an artist today and no longer shows any signs of her former disorder. How do individuals with DID reconcile having different identities?

again. More than one-third were unable to work because of their disorder. However, a more recent two-year follow-up study of fifty-four patients with dissociative identity disorder showed more optimistic results. Most showed improvement, especially those who had been able to integrate their separate personalities during therapy (Ellason & Ross, 1997).

The most widely reported approaches to treating dissociative identity disorder combine psychotherapy and hypnosis. One suggested procedure begins with hypnosis. With the patient in a hypnotic state, the different personalities are asked to emerge and introduce themselves to the patient, to make the patient aware of their existence. Then the personalities are asked to help the patient recall the traumatic experiences or memories that originally triggered the development of new personalities. An important part of this recalling step is to enable the patient to experience the emotions associated with the traumatic memories. The therapist then explains to the patient that these additional personalities used to serve a purpose but that alternative coping strategies are available now. The final steps involve piecing together the events and memories of the personalities, integrating them, and continuing therapy to help the patient adjust to the new self.

Although working through the traumatic material is still important in treating dissociative identity disorder, there is growing recognition that "remembered" events may be inaccurate, and greater emphasis is being placed on helping patients develop new coping skills. There are four main areas of progress in treatment (Kluft, 1996). The first is *better assessment*. Questionable signs, such as frequent blinking, eye rolling, changes in voice or posture, changes in clothing or jewelry, sudden laughter or emotional outbursts, and (in children) imaginary playmates, are receiving less attention as indicators of dissociative identity disorder (Milstone, 1997). Better questionnaires and structured interviews specifically designed to assess this disorder have now been developed, reducing the number of false diagnoses. Second, *greater understanding of the disorder* seems possible. In the past, much attention was placed on bringing forth and studying the different personalities. There is now increasing focus on the behavioral problems exhibited by individuals with this disorder. The third area of progress is in *handling controversial issues*. Even as they acknowledge the possibility of false memories involving child abuse or cult involvement, therapists are shifting attention from the accuracy of the memories to helping the individuals work through emotional issues. Finally, in the area of *treatment*, the strategy is on using research-based methods and approaches to achieve quick resolution of acute symptoms. This problem-focused therapy holds patients responsible for their own behaviors and involves the whole person rather than the separate personalities. The goal is to improve functioning early in treatment rather than waiting for personality integration. Greater effort has also been made to incorporate cognitive behavior strategies in treatment, even among psychodynamically oriented therapists (Fine, 1999; Shusta, 1999).

Somatoform Disorders

The somatoform disorders, shown in Figure 6.4, involve complaints of physical symptoms that closely mimic authentic medical conditions. Although no actual physiological basis exists for the complaints, the symptoms are not considered voluntary or under conscious control. The patient believes the symptoms are real and are indications of a physical problem. The somatoform disorders include somatization disorder, conversion disorder, pain disorder, hypochondriasis, and body dysmorphic disorder. Individuals with somatoform disorders are also likely to have comorbid (accompanying) disorders such as mood disorder, personality disorder, and substance use disorder (G. C. Smith, Clarke, Handrinos, Dunsis, & McKenzie, 2000; Noyes et al., 2001). Figure 6.4 summarizes the prevalence, onset, and course of somatoform disorders, and Table 6.1 shows some differences.

Depending on the particular primary care setting, from 10 to 50 percent of all patients report physically unexplained symptoms (Allen, Gara, Escobar, Waitzkin, & Silver, 2001; DeWaal, Arnold, Eekhof, & Van Hemert, 2004; Rief & Hiller, 2003). However, determining whether the proper diagnosis for these individuals is somatoform disorder can be difficult. As Peveler (1998) points out, "Somatoform disorder diagnoses are still mostly diagnoses of exclusion, rather than constructs with clinical utility" (p. 94). In some cases, physical or neurological factors that explain the symptoms have later been discovered (Moser, Wenzel-Abatzi, Stelzeneder, & Wenzel, 1998).

Before we discuss the somatoform disorders individually, we should note that they are wholly different from either **malingering**—faking a disorder to achieve some goal, such as an insurance settlement—or the factitious disorders. **Factitious disorders** are mental disorders in which the symptoms of physical or mental illnesses are deliberately induced or simulated with no apparent incentive (see the Mental Health and Society feature "Factitious Disorders"). In contrast to both of these conditions, individuals with somatoform disorders believe that a physical condition actually exists.

TABLE 6.1   Variables That Distinguish Subgroups of Confirmed Somatoform Disorder (n = 127)

	Conversion Disorder n = 30	Somatization Disorder n = 10	Somatoform Pain Disorder n = 60	Hypochondriasis n = 27
Demographic data				
Married	39.3%	30.0%	65.0%	61.5%
Serious physical illness in patient—past 12 months	57.7%	90.0%	74.6%	50.0%
Serious physical illness in family—past 12 months	36.0%	12.5%	13.6%	4.3%
Referral data				
Referred for strange behavior	33.3%	20.0%	10.0%	11.5%
Referred for pain	6.7%	30.0%	68.3%	26.9%
Referred for diagnosis—suspected psychological component	83.3%	80.0%	43.3%	65.4%
Interventions				
Increase physical activity	41.4%	10.0%	18.6%	3.7%
Anxiolytics recommendation	3.3%	0.0%	31.7%	7.7%
Antidepressant recommendation	20.0%	50.0%	51.7%	26.9%

Source: From Smith et al. (2000).

Cultural factors can influence the frequency, expression, and interpretation of somatic complaints. Physical complaints often occur in reaction to stress among Asian Americans (Sue & Sue, 1999). In fact, Asian Indian children who were referred for psychiatric services had three times as many somatoform disorders as their counterparts in a control sample of white children (Jawed, 1991). Among some African groups, somatic complaints (feelings of heat, peppery and crawling sensations, and numbness) differ from those expressed in Western cultures (Ohaeri & Odejide, 1994).

Differences such as those just described may reflect different cultural views of the relationship between mind and body. The dominant view in Western culture is the *psychosomatic* perspective, in which psychological conflicts are expressed in physical complaints. But many other cultures have a *somatopsychic* perspective, in which physical problems produce psychological and emotional symptoms. Although we probably believe that our psychosomatic view is the "correct" one, the somatopsychic view may be the dominant perspective in most cultures. As G. M. White (1982) claimed, "It is rather the more psychological and psychosomatic mode of reasoning found in Western cultures which appears unusual among the world's popular and traditional system of belief" (p. 1520). Physical complaints expressed by persons of ethnic minorities may have to be interpreted differently than similar complaints made by members of the majority culture.

Somatization Disorder

An individual with **somatization disorder** chronically complains of bodily symptoms that have no physical basis. According to DSM-IV-TR (American Psychiatric Association, 2000), the following are necessary for a diagnosis of somatization disorder:

- A history of complaints that involve at least four pain symptoms in different sites, such as the back, head, and extremities

- Two gastrointestinal symptoms, such as nausea, diarrhea, and bloating

- One sexual symptom, such as sexual indifference, irregular menses, or erectile dysfunction

FIGURE 6.4 Disorders Chart: Somatoform Disorders

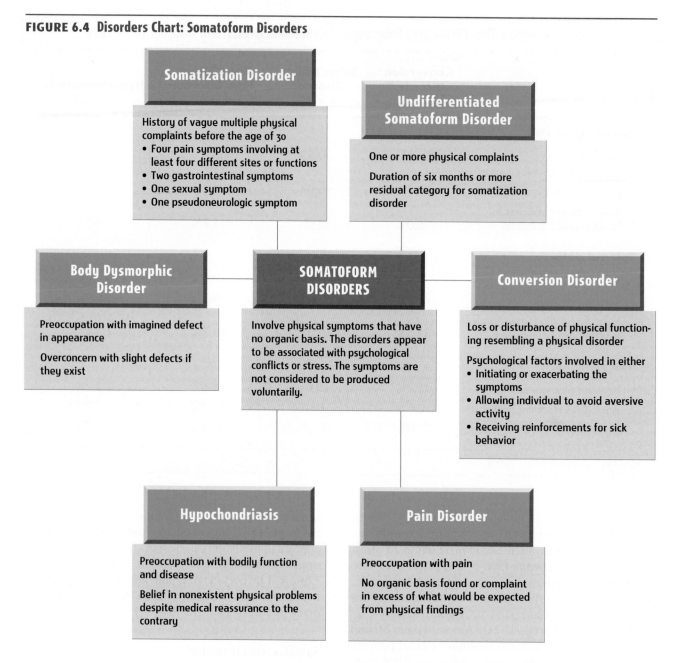

Somatization Disorder

History of vague multiple physical complaints before the age of 30
• Four pain symptoms involving at least four different sites or functions
• Two gastrointestinal symptoms
• One sexual symptom
• One pseudoneurologic symptom

Undifferentiated Somatoform Disorder

One or more physical complaints

Duration of six months or more residual category for somatization disorder

Body Dysmorphic Disorder

Preoccupation with imagined defect in appearance

Overconcern with slight defects if they exist

SOMATOFORM DISORDERS

Involve physical symptoms that have no organic basis. The disorders appear to be associated with psychological conflicts or stress. The symptoms are not considered to be produced voluntarily.

Conversion Disorder

Loss or disturbance of physical functioning resembling a physical disorder

Psychological factors involved in either
• Initiating or exacerbating the symptoms
• Allowing individual to avoid aversive activity
• Receiving reinforcements for sick behavior

Hypochondriasis

Preoccupation with bodily function and disease

Belief in nonexistent physical problems despite medical reassurance to the contrary

Pain Disorder

Preoccupation with pain

No organic basis found or complaint in excess of what would be expected from physical findings

Source: Data from K. Phillips et al. (1993); Swartz et al. (1991); American Psychiatric Association (2000).

■ One pseudoneurological symptom, such as conversion symptoms, amnesia, or breathing difficulties

If the individual does not fully meet these criteria but has at least one physical complaint of six months' duration, he or she would be given a diagnosis of **undifferentiated somatoform disorder.** The following case illustrates several of the characteristics involved in these disorders.

Cheryl was a thirty-eight-year-old, separated Italian American woman who was raising her ten-year-old daughter without much support. ... Cheryl suffered from vertigo and had a history of neck pain and other vague somatic complaints as well as a history of several abusive relationships and unresolved grief about the loss of her mother. ... Cheryl and Melanie described in rich detail an elaborate system of cues that Melanie had learned to respond to by comforting her mother, providing remedies such as back rubs and hot compresses or taking over activities such as grocery shopping if her mother felt dizzy in the store. (McDaniel & Speice, 2001)

FIGURE 6.4 Disorders Chart: Somatoform Disorders (continued)

SOMATOFORM DISORDERS	Prevalence	Age of Onset	Course
Somatization Disorder	Up to 2 percent; mostly women with less education; high rates also found among African Americans	Often by adolescence; menstrual complaints are frequently first symptom in women	Chronic and fluctuating; rarely remits completely
Undifferentiated Somatoform Disorder	Mostly women of low SES	Adolescence or early adulthood	Unpredictable
Conversion Disorder	Relatively rare; only 1 to 3 percent of referrals to mental health clinics; more women; lower socioeconomic status	Late childhood to early adulthood; onset usually acute	Mixed; if of sudden onset, with identifiable stressor, prognosis is better
Pain Disorder	Relatively common; gender ratio is unknown—depends on type of pain	Can occur at any age	Most resolve with treatment; poorer prognosis with more pain areas
Hypochondriasis	Equally common in males and females; from 2 to 7 percent of all medical-practice patients	Any age, but most often in early adulthood	Usually chronic; waxes and wanes
Body Dysmorphic Disorder	Equally common in males and females; from 5 to 15 percent depending upon setting	Early adolescence to 20s; onset may be sudden or gradual	Fairly continuous

In this case, the problem was treated by helping Cheryl and Melanie identify "nonhelpful behaviors" that may reinforce the symptoms and those that are useful in adapting to problem situations. Alternate ways of getting support were also discussed. However, in many cases the "cause" of the behavior is difficult to determine.

People who have somatization disorder tend to constantly "shop around" for doctors and often have unnecessary operations. Psychiatric interviews typically reveal psychological conflicts that may be involved in the disorder. Anxiety and depression and other psychiatric disorders are common complications of somatization disorder (Allen et al., 2001; Stern, Murphy, & Bass, 1993). Although somatization disorder is considered a chronic condition, in one large

study, only about one-third who were diagnosed with the disorder met the criteria twelve months later (Simon & Gureje, 1999).

Although physical complaints are common, the diagnosis of somatization disorder (or *hysteria*, as it was formerly called) is relatively rare, with an overall prevalence rate of 2 percent (see Table 6.1). It is much more prevalent in females and African Americans and twice as likely among those with less than a high school education (Swartz, Landerman, George, Blazer, & Escobar, 1991). Accurate data on its prevalence are difficult to obtain, however, because until DSM-III was published, somatization disorder and conversion disorder were combined in prevalence studies. Although this disorder is rarely diagnosed in men, more than one-third of men who had been referred because of multiple unexplained somatic

MENTAL HEALTH AND SOCIETY

Factitious Disorders

A most remarkable type of mental disorder is illustrated in the following cases:

> In a two-year period, four women presented for HIV-related care, claiming that they were HIV-seropositive, but repeated serologic testing revealed no evidence of HIV infection. In all cases, the women were either quite angry or appeared surprised when told they did not have HIV infection. A common denominator in all four women was a history of prolonged sexual, physical, or emotional abuse. Three of the four had been to other physicians, changing doctors as soon as the absence of HIV infection was established. (Mileno et al., 2001, p. 263)

> A hidden camera at a children's hospital captured the image of a mother suffocating the baby she had brought in for treatment of breathing problems. In another case, a child was brought in for treatment of ulcerations on his back; hospital staff discovered the mother had been rubbing oven cleaner on his skin. A "sick" infant had been fed laxatives for nearly four months (Wartik, 1994). In each of these cases, no apparent incentive was found other than the attention the parent received from the hospital staff that cared for the child's "illness."

> A thirty-two-year-old African American male had a superficial wound on his arm that would not heal. Different treatments were tried without success. Although a surgeon reopened the wound, discovered foreign material embedded in the deep tissue, and removed it, the infection continued. (A pathology examination revealed that the material was recently placed in the wound.) Because of an increasing suspicion that the patient was interfering with the healing process, the surgeon placed the arm in a cast. When the cast was removed several weeks later, the wound had healed nearly completely. Two days later, however, the patient returned with a reinfection. He sought other physicians over a four-year period. In the end, the only course was amputation. (Eisendrath, 1996)

These cases illustrate a group of mental disorders, termed *factitious disorders* in DSM-IV-TR, in which people voluntarily simulate physical or mental conditions or voluntarily induce an actual physical condition. The criteria include (1) intentional production or feigning of physical or psychological symptoms; (2) the only apparent motivation for the behavior is to assume the sick role or to be a patient; and (3) the purpose of this behavior is not for external incentives such as economic gain, avoiding legal responsibilities, and so forth. This practice differs from *malingering*, which involves simulating a disorder to achieve some goal—such as feigning sickness to collect insurance. The goals usually are apparent, and the individual can "turn off" the symptoms whenever they are no longer useful. In factitious disorders, the purpose of the simulated or induced illness is much less apparent, complex psychological variables are assumed to be involved, and the individual is usually aware of the motivation for the behaviors. The individual displays a compulsive quality in the need to simulate illness. Signs of a factitious disorder may include long unexplained illnesses with multiple surgical or complex treatments, "remarkable willingness" to undergo painful or dangerous treatments, tendency to anger if the illness is questioned, and the involvement of multiple doctors (Flaherty, Infante, Tinsley, & Black, 2001).

If an individual deliberately feigns or induces an illness in another person, the diagnosis is *factitious disorder by proxy*. In the preceding cases, the mothers produced symptoms in their children to indirectly assume the sick role. Because this diagnostic category is somewhat new, little information is available on prevalence, age of onset, or familial pattern. However, diagnosis of this condition is difficult. In Seattle, a pediatrician has been involved in over 100 purported cases during the past twenty-five years. He has been accused of being negligent by misdiagnosing factitious disorder by proxy that has resulted in children being removed from their families. One appeals court judge wrote that the pediatrician "apparently has a penchant for diagnosing (or misdiagnosing) MSBP (another term for this disorder is Munchausen syndrome by proxy), notwithstanding its rarity and his questioned qualification to make that diagnosis" (Smith, 2002, A.10). If factitious disorder by proxy becomes an official diagnosis, how would you balance the protection of the child with the possibility of making a false accusation against the parent?

complaints met the criteria for somatization disorder (Golding, Smith, & Kashner, 1991).

In a cross-cultural study on the prevalence of somatization disorder in fourteen countries, it was found to be relatively rare (average frequency of 0.9 percent). The highest frequency of somatic complaints was found in the cities of Rio de Janeiro, Santiago, Berlin, and Paris; the lowest were in Taiwan, Ibadân, Manchester, Nagasaki, and Verona (Gureje, Simon, Ustun, & Goldberg, 1997). Interestingly, somatoform disorders are not included in the revised edition of the *Chinese Classification of Mental Disorders,* the Chinese equivalent of DSM-IV. Sing Lee (1997), a psychiatrist in Hong Kong, argues that somatization is a Western construct.

Conversion Disorder

Conversion disorder is one of the more puzzling disorders. The term *conversion neurosis* comes from Freud, who believed that an unconscious sexual or aggressive conflict was "converted" into a physical problem. An individual with **conversion disorder** will complain of physical problems or impairments of sensory or motor functions controlled by the voluntary nervous system—such as paralysis, loss of feeling, and impairment in sight or hearing—all suggesting a neurological disorder but with no underlying organic cause. Although they are rare, complaints may also include memory loss or "cognitive or intellectual impairment" that resembles dementia but is reversible (Liberini, Faglia, Salvi, & Grant, 1993). Individuals with conversion disorder are not consciously faking symptoms, as are those who have a factitious disorder or who are malingering. A person with conversion disorder actually believes that there is a genuine physical problem, and it produces notable distress or impairment in social or occupational functioning. As discussed in the chapter on abnormal behavior, it was known earlier as *hysteria,* and Mesmer was able to effect cures using hypnosis. A case of a visual conversion disorder follows:

> D.B. was a thirty-three-year-old, single white male who was employed in a clerical job and who lived with his parents. ... D.B.'s visual disorder began ... when he was hit in the right eye with a rifle butt during military training. D.B. reported pain and impaired vision in his right eye and was hospitalized for three weeks. He reported seeing only "shapes and silhouettes of objects" and "cones of white rings" in his right eye. Toward the end of this period, D.B. reported that he could not see anything with his right eye. ... D.B. then received intensive ophthalmological and neuropsychological assessment. None of these assessments revealed any apparent physical basis for his visual disorder. (Bryant & McConkey, 1989, pp. 326–327)

Conversion Disorder Although there is nothing physically wrong with the eyes of this Cambodian woman, she claims to be blind. It is thought that trauma suffered in Cambodian prison camps due to the brutality of the Khmer Rouge produced such horror that her eyesight "shut down" psychologically. Hysterical blindness is a very rare conversion disorder in the United States but is quite high among Cambodian refugees. Approximately 150 individuals (mostly women) from a Cambodian community of 85,000 people in Long Beach, California, suffer from this disorder.

One intriguing factor in this case is D.B.'s clear use of visual information. Although he claimed to be unable to see, D.B. did do better on tasks in which visual cues were present than on those with no visual cues. Yet he was not aware of this ability. This finding produces a contradiction between the belief that conversion disorders are involuntary and the evidence that on some level, D.B. could "see." The dynamic underlying this process is not clear, although psychological factors are considered important in conversion disorder, in either the initiation or exacerbation of the problem, as illustrated in the following cases:

A forty-four-year-old woman was admitted to a psychiatric hospital from a neurology ward with "pseudo-seizures" and "functional hemiplegia" (paralysis of one side of the body). She was wheelchair-bound and lived in a specially adapted council bungalow with a female friend. ...

She described a disrupted childhood with a physically abusive, alcoholic father. She had two stormy and violent marriages. ... Although reluctant to accept a psychological origin of her symptoms, she agreed to undergo hypnosis. Under hypnosis, she walked and moved her paralyzed limbs normally. She received psychotherapy, exploring her childhood and relationship difficulties. Within six months she was using her right upper limb normally and walking with a frame. (Singh & Lee, 1997, pp. 426–427)

The boy was referred at age ten as a case of juvenile myasthenia gravis (weakening of the voluntary muscles). For five weeks he had been unable to open his eyes and the consequent "blindness" had stopped him from attending school. ... On detailed physical examination no other abnormalities were found. In the hospital ward it was noted he did not walk into furniture. ... He was the local village football star. ... he had been blamed for his team's defeat in a needle match and from that day he had been unable to open his eyes. (Leary, 2003, p. 436)

The most common conversion symptoms seen in neurological clinics involve psychogenic pain, disturbances of stance and gait, sensory symptoms, dizziness, and psychogenic seizures (Rechlin, Loew, & Joraschky, 1997). The occurrence of symptoms is often related to stress. Nearly 75 percent of respondents in one sample reported that their conversion symptoms developed after they had experienced a stressor. One man became "paralyzed" after finding his wife in bed with another man. One woman developed a speech disturbance after disclosing childhood sexual abuse (Singh & Lee, 1997). Individuals with a conversion disorder are also more likely to have other forms of psychopathology than are patients with

organic problems (Binzer, Andersen, & Kullgren, 1997). In a ten-year follow-up study of individuals diagnosed with conversion disorder, symptoms persisted in about 40 percent of the cases (Mace & Trimble, 1996). Sudden onset, shorter duration of symptoms, and a good premorbid (pre-illness) personality are associated with a positive outcome (Crimlisk, Bhatia, Cope, & David, 1998; Singh & Lee, 1997).

It is often difficult to distinguish between actual physical disorders and conversion reactions. In one sample of sixty patients with sudden onset of neurological symptoms, 50 percent had physical disorders, and the remainder received a diagnosis of conversion disorder (Binzer, Eisenmann, & Kullgren, 1998). Conversion disorder, however, usually involves either the senses or motor functions that are controlled by the voluntary (rather than the autonomic) nervous system, and there is seldom any actual physical damage. For example, a person with hysterical paralysis of the legs rarely shows the atrophy of the lower limbs that occurs when there is an underlying biological cause, although in some persistent cases, disuse *can* result in atrophy (Schonfeldt-Lecuona, Connemann, Spitzer, & Herwig, 2003).

Some symptoms, such as glove anesthesia (the loss of feeling in the hand, ending in a straight line at the

FIGURE 6.5 Glove Anesthesia   In glove anesthesia, the lack of feeling covers the hand in a glovelike shape. It does not correspond to the distribution of nerve pathways. This discrepancy leads to a diagnosis of conversion disorder.

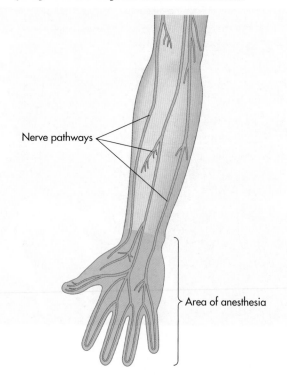

Nerve pathways

Area of anesthesia

wrist) are easily diagnosed as conversion disorder because the area of sensory loss does not correspond to the distribution of nerves in the body (see Figure 6.5). Other symptoms may require extensive neurological and physical examinations to rule out a true medical disorder before a diagnosis of conversion disorder can be made. Discriminating between people who are faking and those with conversion disorder is difficult. For example, participants asked to simulate a hearing loss can produce response patterns highly similar to those of individuals with hearing loss from conversion disorder (Aplin & Kane, 1985).

Pain Disorder

Pain disorder is characterized by reports of severe pain that may (1) have no physiological or neurological basis, (2) be greatly in excess of that expected with an existing physical condition, or (3) linger long after a physical injury has healed. As with the other somatoform disorders, psychological conflicts are involved. People who have pain disorder make frequent visits to physicians and may become drug or medication abusers. Most individuals with pain disorder have numerous physical complaints (see Figure 6.6). Compared with individuals who have an organic basis

for their pain, those with psychogenic pain are more vague in their description of the experience and are less able to clearly localize the area of pain (Adler et al., 1997). Unexplained physical pain involving the abdomen, head, and limbs is present in a considerable number of young children (Hunfeld et al., 2002).

But some researchers question the usefulness of a dichotomous organic-psychogenic model. Salvidge and Slade (1997) reviewed research on chronic pelvic pain, a common gynecological complaint in women. They were unable to draw any conclusions about the role of psychological factors in this disorder. For example, if women with "psychogenic" chronic pelvic pain had elevations on measures of psychopathology, we would not know whether this was the consequence of the chronic pain or its cause. Salvidge and Slade recommend the development of a biopsychological model of pain that considers how psychological and socioenvironmental factors can moderate the pain experience.

Hypochondriasis

The primary characteristic of **hypochondriasis** is a persistent preoccupation with one's health and physical condition, even in the face of physical evaluations that reveal no organic problems. The disorder is a complex

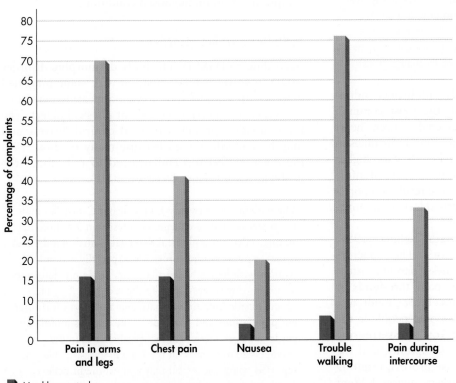

FIGURE 6.6 Physical Complaints: A Comparison of Individuals with Pain Disorder Versus Healthy Controls
Individuals with somatoform disorders have numerous physical complaints. This graph illustrates the percentage of complaints expressed by a group of individuals with pain disorders.

■ Healthy controls

■ Patients

Source: Data from Bacon, Bacon, Atkinson, & Slater (1994).

phenomenon that includes a fear of having a disease, fear of death or illness, a tendency toward self-observation, and oversensitivity to bodily sensations (Kellner, Hernandez, & Pathak, 1992; Leibbrand, Hiller, & Fichter, 2000). People with this disorder are hypersensitive to bodily functioning and processes. They regard symptoms such as chest pain or headaches as evidence of an underlying disease, and they seek repeated reassurance from medical professionals, friends, and family members. An estimated 2 to 7 percent of general medical patients have this disorder (American Psychiatric Association, 2000).

> Mr. X was a sixty-eight-year-old Chinese man who reported sleep disturbances, a loss of appetite, dizziness, and a sensation of tightness around his chest. Several episodes of chest pain led to admission and medical evaluation at the local hospital. All results, including tests for ischemic heart disease, were normal. He was referred to psychiatric consultation. Because traditional Chinese views of medicine recognize an interconnection between mind and body, the psychiatrist accepted and showed interest in the somatic symptoms, such as their onset, duration, and exacerbating and relieving factors. Medication was provided as a supportive treatment. Later the man was able to tell the psychiatrists that his physical symptoms became worse when his wife aggravated him. He reported that they argued frequently over decisions. Suggestions were made on how to improve communication, and the couple decided to take turns making decisions. Physical complaints decreased as the communication improved. (Yeung & Deguang, 2002)

In a study of twenty individuals with hypochondriasis (ten females and ten males), the most common health concerns involved undetected cancer, heart attack, and brain tumors. As opposed to individuals in a control group, they showed a bias toward higher estimates of negative outcomes in health-related information that was ambiguous. Thus the results support a cognitive model of hypochondriasis (Haenen, de Jong, Schmidt, Stevens, & Visser, 2000).

In his review of hypochondriacs, Kellner (1985) found several predisposing factors. These factors included a history of physical illness, parental attention to somatic symptoms, low pain threshold, or greater sensitivity to somatic cues. Hypochondriasis, therefore, might develop in predisposed people in the following manner: an anxiety- or stress-arousing event, the perception of somatic symptoms, and the fear that sensations reflect a disease process, resulting in even greater attention to somatic cues. Kellner (1985) believes that reassurance by physicians reduces anxiety only temporarily because the patients continue

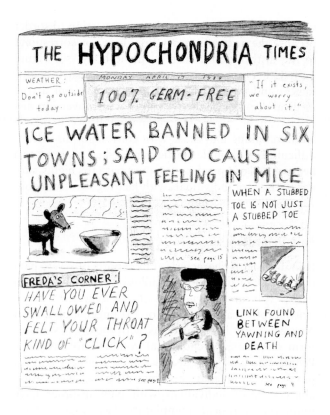

to experience bodily symptoms that they interpret as symptoms of an undiagnosed condition.

Body Dysmorphic Disorder

According to DSM-IV-TR, **body dysmorphic disorder (BDD)** involves a preoccupation with some imagined defect in appearance in a normal-appearing person or an excessive concern over a slight physical defect. The preoccupation produces marked clinical distress and may be underdiagnosed because many of those with the disorder feel too embarrassed to talk about the problem (Grant, Kim, & Crow, 2001).

> The patient was a twenty-four-year-old Caucasian male in his senior year of college. He presented at intake by stating, "I've got a physical deformity (small hands) and it makes me very uncomfortable, especially around women with hands bigger than mine. I see my deformity as a sign of weakness; it's like I'm a cripple." … He spent considerable time researching hand sizes for different populations and stated at intake that his middle finger is one and one-fourth inches smaller than the average size for a male in the United States. … He also reported being concerned that women might believe small hands are indicative of having a small penis. (Schmidt & Harrington, 1995, pp. 162–163)

Imagining Defects The individual with body dysmorphic disorder depicted in this illustration is preoccupied with an imagined "defect" in his appearance. What leads to such an inaccurate belief?

Concern commonly focuses on bodily features such as excessive hair or lack of hair and the size or shape of the nose, face, or eyes (see Figure 6.7). In DSM-IV-TR, body build or muscularity has been added as an area of body preoccupation in BDD. Individuals with this disorder often engage in frequent mirror checking, regard their "defect" with embarrassment and loathing, and are concerned that others may be looking at or thinking about their defect. People with body dysmorphic disorder show evidence of emotional problems, have a minimal degree of "disfigurement," and make frequent requests for additional operations despite the outcome of previous treatment. The degree of insight they have about their condition ranges from good to absent (K. Phillips, McElroy, Dwight, Eisen, & Rasmussen, 2001). They may have a body image disorder similar to that found in anorexia. Most have more than one concern (K. Phillips et al., 1993). As with the other somatoform disorders, individuals with body dysmorphic disorder seek medical attention— often from dermatologists or plastic surgeons. They are also likely to undergo multiple medical procedures (Phillips & Rasmussen, 2004). Persons with body dysmorphic disorder often suffer from functional impair-

ment. They may avoid social activities, work, and school and may become housebound and suicidal (Schmidt & Harrington, 1995). In one study of fifty patients with this disorder (Veale, Boocock, Gournay, & Dryden, 1996), the average age of onset was late adolescence. They were also likely to have a mood disorder or social phobia, and about 24 percent had attempted suicide (Veale et al., 1996). Some bodybuilders who show a pathological preoccupation with their muscularity may also suffer from body dysmorphic disorder. Researchers identified a subgroup of bodybuilders who scored high in body dissatisfaction, had low self-esteem, and mistakenly believed they were "small" even though they were large and very muscular (Choi, Pope, Olivardia, & Cash, 2002; Olivardia, Pope, & Hudson, 2000).

Some questions that may indicate the presence of BDD follow; the more a person agrees with these statements, the more likely he or she is to have characteristics of this disorder.

1. Do you believe that there is a "defect" in a part of your body or appearance?

2. Do you spend considerable time checking this "defect"?

3. Do you attempt to hide or cover up this "defect" or remedy it by exercising, dieting, or seeking surgery?

4. Does this belief cause you significant distress, embarrassment, or torment?

5. Does the "flaw" interfere with your ability to function at school, at social events, or at work?

6. Do friends or family members tell you that there is nothing wrong or that the "defect" is minor?

Researchers have raised several issues regarding body dysmorphic disorder. First, the other somatoform disorders deal with physical disease or dysfunction; does concern over appearance fit best in this category? Second, how easy is it to figure out where the boundary lies between individuals with the disorder and those who have "normal" concerns over their appearance or those who seek cosmetic surgery? Dissatisfaction and preoccupation with one's appearance is relatively common. In one study of American college students, 74.3 percent indicated body image concerns, 28.7 percent were preoccupied with them, and 4 percent appeared to meet the criteria for BDD (Bohne et al., 2002). Third, what is the relationship between body dysmorphic disorder and obsessive-compulsive disorder or delusional disorder, somatic type (a psychotic disorder characterized by delusions that the person has a physical defect)? The preoccupation with the imagined defect in body dysmorphic

FIGURE 6.7 Imagined Defects in Patients with Body Dysmorphic Disorder This graph illustrates the percentage of thirty patients who targeted different areas of their body as having "defects." Many of the patients selected more than one body region.

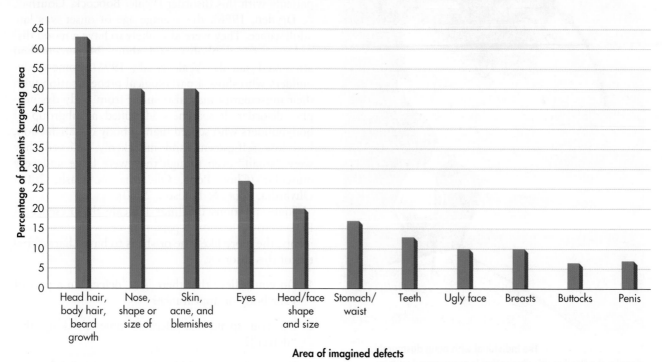

Source: From K. A. Phillips et al. (1993).

disorder is very similar to obsessive-compulsive disorder. Some researchers believe the disorders are related to one another or are variants of the same disorder (Saxena et al., 2001), although preliminary findings appear to indicate that the disorders involve different brain regions (van Heerden, Stein, Carey, Seedat, & Warwick, 2004). Some people with body dysmorphic disorder have been successfully treated with fluoxetine, a serotonin reuptake inhibitor, which is also used to treat obsessive-compulsive disorder (Lydiard, Brady, & Austin, 1994; K. A. Phillips & Rasmussen, 2004). The precise relationship between BDD, obsessive-compulsive disorder, and delusional disorder is still not known. If imagined defects qualify as delusions, then delusional disorder, somatic type, may be an extreme form of body dysmorphic disorder, as Phillips and others have suggested.

Etiology of Somatoform Disorders

Most etiological theories tend to focus on what they consider to be the "primary" cause of somatoform disorders. Diathesis-stress models, however, point to multiple contributing factors. For example, Barsky and Wyshak (1990) believe that a predisposition may develop through learning or may be "hard-wired" into

the central nervous system. They believe the predisposition involves (1) hypervigilance or exaggerated focus on bodily sensation, (2) increased sensitivity to weak bodily sensations, and (3) a disposition to react to somatic sensations with alarm. The predisposition becomes a fully developed disorder only when a trauma or stressor occurs that the individual cannot deal with. An even broader diathesis-stress model, shown in Figure 6.8, includes other variables, such as social and cultural components, personality, and maintaining factors (Gramling, Clawson, & McDonald, 1996; Kellner, 1985). As you read the following etiological theories, consider the possible advantages of a diathesis-stress model over the single-focus explanations.

Psychodynamic Perspective In psychodynamic theory, somatic symptoms are seen as a defense against the awareness of unconscious emotional issues (Dworkin, VonKorff, & LeResche, 1990). Sigmund Freud believed that hysterical reactions (biological complaints of pain, illness, or loss of physical function) were caused by the repression of some type of conflict, usually sexual in nature. To protect the individual from intense anxiety, this conflict is converted into some physical symptom (Breuer & Freud,

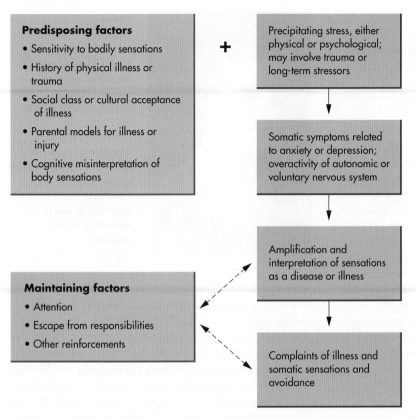

Predisposing factors

- Sensitivity to bodily sensations
- History of physical illness or trauma
- Social class or cultural acceptance of illness
- Parental models for illness or injury
- Cognitive misinterpretation of body sensations

+

Precipitating stress, either physical or psychological; may involve trauma or long-term stressors

Somatic symptoms related to anxiety or depression; overactivity of autonomic or voluntary nervous system

Amplification and interpretation of sensations as a disease or illness

Maintaining factors

- Attention
- Escape from responsibilities
- Other reinforcements

Complaints of illness and somatic sensations and avoidance

FIGURE 6.8 Diathesis-Stress Model for Somatoform Disorders   This chart illustrates a diathesis-stress model for somatoform disorders that considers a number of predisposing factors, stressors, and maintaining variables.

Source: Adapted from Kellner (1985); Gramling, Clawson, & McDonald (1996).

1895/1957). For example, in the case of a thirty-one-year-old woman who developed visual problems with no physical basis, therapy revealed that the woman had, as a child, witnessed her parents engaging in sexual intercourse. The severe anxiety associated with this traumatic scene was later converted into visual difficulties (Grinker & Robbins, 1954).

The psychodynamic view suggests that two mechanisms produce and then sustain somatoform symptoms. The first provides a *primary gain* for the person by protecting him or her from the anxiety associated with the unacceptable desire or conflict; the need for protection gives rise to the physical symptoms. This focus on the body keeps the patient from an awareness of the underlying conflict (Simon & VonKorff, 1991). Then a *secondary gain* accrues when the person's dependency needs are fulfilled through attention and sympathy. In a study of twenty-five patients with a somatoform disorder, all relied on family members and friends to complete domestic tasks and were receiving disability allowances (Allanson, Bass, & Wade, 2002).

Behavioral Perspective   Behavioral theorists have stressed the importance of reinforcement, modeling, cognitive styles, or a combination of these in the development of somatoform disorders. Some contend that

people with somatoform disorders assume the "sick role" because it is reinforcing and because it allows them to escape unpleasant circumstances or avoid responsibilities (L. Schwartz, Slater, & Birchler, 1994). Fordyce (1982, 1988) analyzed psychogenic pain from the operant perspective. He pointed out that the only available data concerning the pain (or any other somatoform symptoms) are the subjective reports from the afflicted people. Physicians and nurses are trained to be attentive and responsive to reports of pain, and medication is given quickly to patients suffering pain. In addition, exercise and physical therapy programs are set up so that exertion continues only until pain or fatigue is felt. These practices serve to reinforce reports of pain. The importance of reinforcement was shown in a study of male pain patients. Men with supportive wives (attentive to pain cues) reported significantly greater pain when their wives were present than when the wives were absent. The reverse was true of patients whose wives were nonsupportive: reports of pain were greater when their wives were absent (Williamson, Robinson, & Melamed, 1997).

Parental modeling and reinforcement of illness behaviors may also be influential in determining people's current reactions to illness. Individuals with somatoform disorders showed a background of parental models or family members with chronic physical illnesses (G. C. Smith et al., 2000), and they were also more likely to report having missed school for health reasons and having had childhood illnesses (Barsky, Wool, Barnett, & Cleary, 1995).

The most recent views of somatoform disorders from a behavioral model stress the importance of cognitive factors (Severeijns, Vlaeyen, van den Hout, & Picavet, 2004). Most people show a bias toward believing they are healthy and assess their risk of illness as lower than average, whereas those with hypochondriasis appear to have a strong bias toward believing they are unhealthy and seek out evidence that they have an illness (Lecci & Cohen, 2002). Because of this, individuals with these disorders are prone to making unrealistic interpretations of bodily sensations and to overestimating the dangerousness of bodily symptoms and the probability of negative health effects (Haenen et al., 2000). Believing such sensations to be abnormal then leads to a preoccupation that one has a serious disease. Thus common bodily sensations are amplified or misinterpreted.

Sociocultural Perspective   Hysteria, now known as conversion disorder, was originally perceived as a problem that afflicted only women; in fact, it derived its name from *hystera,* the ancient Greek word for uterus. Hippocrates believed that a shift or movement of the uterus resulted in complaints of breathing difficulties, anesthesia, and seizures. He presumed that the movement was due to the uterus "wanting a child." Although Freud was among the first to suggest that hysteria could also occur in men, most of his patients were women. Satow (1979) argued that hysteria was more prevalent in women when social mores did not provide them with appropriate channels for the expression of aggression or sexuality. Hollender (1980) also stressed the importance of societal restrictions in producing hysterical symptoms in women and suggested the case of Anna O. as an example.

Anna O., a patient of physician Josef Breuer, was a twenty-one-year-old woman who developed a variety of symptoms, including dissociation, muscle rigidity, and insensitivity to feeling. Freud and Breuer both believed that these symptoms were the result of intrapsychic conflicts. They did not consider the impact of social roles on abnormal behavior.

According to Hollender (1980), Anna O. was highly intelligent, but her educational and intellectual opportunities were severely restricted because she was a woman. Breuer described her as "bubbling over with intellectual vitality." As Hollender pointed out, "Not only was Anna O., as a female, relegated to an inferior position in her family with future prospects limited to

Conversion Disorder or Society's Victim? Anna O., whose real name was Bertha Pappenheim, was diagnosed as being severely disturbed, even though her later years were extremely productive. Was her condition a product of societal restrictions on the role of women or her inability to conform to that role? Or was it something totally different?

that of becoming a wife and mother, but at the age of twenty-one she was suddenly called on to assume the onerous chore of nursing her father" (Hollender, 1980, p. 798). It is possible that many of her symptoms were produced to relieve the guilt she felt because of her resentment of this duty—as well as to maintain her intellectually stimulating contact with Breuer. After treatment, Anna O. was supposedly cured. However, she in fact remained severely disturbed and received additional treatment at an institution. Later, she headed a home for orphans, was involved in social work, and became recognized as a feminist leader. Interestingly, Ellenberger (1972) believes that the cathartic treatment was unsuccessful and that Anna O. is a poor case study on which to build the psychoanalytic foundation.

Satow (1979) believes that, as societal restrictions on women are loosened, the incidence of somatoform disorders among women should decline. Yet the diagnostic criteria involved in some of these disorders tend to ensure the overrepresentation of women.

Biological Perspective   Some physical complaints may have more than a merely imaginary basis. Researchers have found that hypochondriacal patients were more sensitive to bodily sensations than other people (Barsky, Cleary, Sarnie, & Klerman, 1993); they were better at estimating their heart rates when exposed to short films than were individuals with phobias (Tyrer, Lee, & Alexander, 1980). In a test involving a physical stressor (foot placed in cold water), individuals with hypochondriasis demonstrated greater increases in heart rate, displayed a greater drop in temperature in the immersed limb, rated the experience as more unpleasant, and terminated the task more frequently relative to a control group (Gramling et al., 1996). It has been hypothesized that "people who continually report being bothered by pain and bodily sensations [hypochondriacs] may have a higher-than-normal arousal level, which results in increased perception of internal stimuli" (Hanback & Revelle, 1978, p. 523). College students who are predisposed to attending to somatic symptoms rate the sensations they experience more negatively than those who attend less to bodily symptoms (Ahles, Cassens, & Stalling, 1987). Innate factors may account for greater sensitivity to pain and bodily functions.

Treatment of Somatoform Disorders

Somatoform disorders have been treated with psychodynamic approaches, cognitive and operant techniques, and family therapy. The behavioral approaches have received the greatest amount of attention.

Psychodynamic Treatment The earliest treatment for somatoform disorders was psychoanalysis. Over the years Freud (1905) and Freud and Breuer (1895) reported many cases of "hysterical" patients who, like Anna O., would probably now be classified as showing a conversion reaction or a somatization disorder. Freud believed that the crucial element in treating hysterical patients with psychoanalysis was to help them *relive* the actual feelings associated with the repressed traumatic event—and not simply to help them remember the details of the experience. Once the emotions connected with the traumatic situation were experienced, the symptoms would disappear.

Although Freud eventually dropped hypnosis from his psychoanalytic repertoire, many of his disciples continued to find it beneficial, and variations of it became known as hypnotherapy. Bliss (1984) was a modern advocate of *hypnotherapy* as treatment for somatization disorder and conversion symptoms. Bliss argued that people afflicted with a somatoform disorder engage in involuntary self-hypnosis as a defense, in much the same way that patients with multiple-personality disorders do. Hypnotherapy involves bringing repressed conflicts to consciousness, mastering these traumas, and developing coping skills that are more adaptive than self-hypnosis.

Behavioral Treatment Although psychodynamic treatments are most often associated with certain somatoform disorders, several behavioral methods appear worth investigating. Individuals with hypochondriasis have been treated with a variety of approaches, including exposure and response prevention. The approach generally involves extinction and nonreinforcement of complaints of bodily symptoms.

Hypnosis as Therapy or Assessment Tool Some practitioners continue to use hypnosis to assess and treat somatoform disorders, based on the belief that these disorders may be induced by self-hypnosis. What kind of research evidence supports this orientation and what questions do you have regarding this approach?

For example, in one study, seventeen patients were forced to confront their health fears by visiting hospitals, reading literature about their feared illness, and writing down extensive information about the illness. Some were asked to try to "bring forth a heart attack." Reassurance seeking was banned, and relatives were taught not to reinforce the behavior. If a patient said, "My heart has a pain. I think it might be a heart attack," relatives were instructed to ignore the statements. Under this program, the patients improved significantly. However, seven of the patients were found to still have concerns about illness or disease at a five-year follow-up (Warwick & Marks, 1988).

Because many patients with somatoform disorders appear to have a cognitive distortion involving an exaggerated conviction of an increased vulnerability to disease, a cognitive-behavioral approach to correct these misinterpretations has been a successful treatment (Barsky & Ahern, 2004). In one program, individuals with hypochondriasis who had fears of having cancer, heart disease, or other fatal diseases underwent the following process. They were educated on the relationship between misinterpretations of bodily sensations and selective attention to illness themes. Six 2-hour group sessions were held that covered topics such as "what is hypochondriasis?" "the role of your thoughts," "attention and illness anxiety," "stress and bodily symptoms," and "your own vicious cycle." Homework assignments were given in monitoring and challenging hypochondriacal thoughts. After completing these sessions, most participants showed considerable improvement or no longer met the criteria for hypochondriasis, and the gains were maintained at a six-month follow-up (Hiller, Leibbrand, Rief, & Fichter, 2002). Similarly, a cognitive-behavioral program for individuals with somatic complaints was effective. It involved the following steps. First, a history was taken of physical and psychosocial problems. Second, a tentative explanation was given for the somatic problem by relating it to psychosocial or lifestyle factors. For example, a complaint of back pain would be attributed to workplace stress that resulted in tension in the muscles of the back. Third, intervention would be developed to lessen stress and increase relaxation (Morriss & Gask, 2002). Reattribution training also led to improvement among individuals with somatic complaints. Case studies indicate that systematic desensitization, exposure, and cognitive therapy are promising approaches in the treatment of body dysmorphic disorder (Neziroglu & Yaryura-Tobias, 1997; J. C. Rosen, Reiter, & Orosan, 1995).

Biological Treatment   Antidepressant medications have been prescribed for the somatoform disorders, primarily somatization and somatoform pain disorders. In addition, interventions involving an increase in physical activity have been recommended for conversion disorders (G. C. Smith et al., 2000). SSRIs such as fluvoxamine have proven useful in improving nearly two-thirds of individuals with body dysmorphic disorder (K. A. Phillips & Rasmussen, 2004; K. A. Phillips et al., 2001).

Family Systems Treatment   The role of the family in maintaining somatoform symptoms has also been recognized by promoters of family therapy for the disorder. Chronic pain is often used to gain rewards (such as attention) and to disclaim responsibility for certain behaviors (such as anger) within the family system. Thus family therapy can be an important part of the treatment for somatoform disorders.

Research indicates that, in families of patients with somatization disorder, a disproportionately high number of female relatives also have somatization disorder, and many male relatives are labeled either antisocial personalities or alcoholics (Bohman, Cloninger, von Knorring, & Sigvardsson, 1984). It is certainly not necessary to have multiple cases of psychiatric disorders in a family before considering family therapy, but these research findings strongly suggest that the entire family be drawn into the treatment process. The therapy could then be used to place the identified patient's disorder in proper perspective, to teach the family adaptive ways of supporting one another, and to prepare family members to deal with anticipated and predicted problems.

SUMMARY

What are dissociations? What forms can they take? How are they caused, and how are they treated?

- Dissociation involves a disruption in consciousness, memory, identity, or perception and may be transient or chronic.
- Dissociative amnesia and dissociative fugue involve a selective form of forgetting in which the person loses memory of information that is of personal significance.
- Depersonalization disorder is characterized by feelings of unreality—distorted perceptions of oneself and one's environment.
- Multiple personality involves the alternation of two or more relatively independent personalities in one individual.
- Psychoanalytic perspectives on the etiology of dissociative disorders attribute them to the repression of certain impulses that are seeking expression.
- Behavioral explanations suggest role enactment, reinforcement, and responding to the expectations of the situation.
- Dissociative amnesia and dissociative fugue tend to be short-lived and to remit spontaneously; behavioral therapy has also been used successfully.

- Dissociative identity disorder has most often been treated with a combination of psychotherapy and hypnosis, as well as with behavioral and family therapies. In most cases, the therapist attempts to fuse the several personalities.

When do physical complaints become a type of disorder? What are the causes and treatments of these conditions?

- Somatoform disorders involve complaints about physical symptoms that mimic actual medical conditions but that have no apparent organic basis. Instead, psychological factors are directly involved in the initiation and exacerbation of the problem.

- Somatization disorder is characterized by chronic multiple complaints and early onset.

- Conversion disorder involves such problems as the loss of sight, paralysis, or another physical impairment that has no organic cause.

- Pain disorder is a condition in which reported severe pain has a psychological rather than a physical basis. Hypochondriasis involves a persistent preoccupation with bodily functioning and disease.

- Body dysmorphic disorder is preoccupation with an imagined bodily defect in a normal-appearing individual.

- The psychoanalytic perspective holds that somatoform disorders are caused by the repression of sexual conflicts and their conversion into physical symptoms.

- Behavioral theorists contend that the role of "being sick" is reinforcing and allows the individual to escape from unpleasant circumstances or avoid responsibilities.

- Psychogenic pain is often reinforced by the external environment.

- In the sociocultural perspective, the somatoform disorders are seen to result from the societal restrictions placed on women, who are affected to a much greater degree than men by these disorders.

- Psychoanalytic treatment emphasizes reliving the emotions associated with the repressed traumatic event.

- Other treatment approaches involve reinforcing only "healthy" behaviors rather than the pain or disability. If possible, treatment is administered within the family system.

KEY TERMS

body dysmorphic disorder (BDD) (p. 194)

continuous amnesia (p. 174)

conversion disorder (p. 190)

depersonalization disorder (p. 176)

dissociative amnesia (p. 172)

dissociative disorder (p. 171)

dissociative fugue (p. 174)

dissociative identity disorder (DID) (p. 177)

factitious disorder (p. 186)

generalized amnesia (p. 173)

hypochondriasis (p. 193)

localized amnesia (p. 173)

malingering (p. 186)

pain disorder (p. 192)

posthypnotic amnesia (p. 174)

selective amnesia (p. 173)

somatization disorder (p. 188)

somatoform disorder (p. 171)

systematized amnesia (p. 174)

undifferentiated somatoform disorder (p. 188)

MULTIMEDIA PREVIEW

For additional study aids, we invite you to explore our media resources accompanying *Understanding Abnormal Behavior,* Eighth Edition. The Student CD-ROM includes videos, quizzing, and critical thinking activities that help to reinforce key concepts in a fun and engaging manner. The Student Web Site provides additional interactive activities, chapter outlines, and research links that further support and complement the text. All Web resources may be accessed by logging onto the Web site at **http://psychology.college.hmco.com/students.**

CHAPTER 7
Psychological Factors Affecting Medical Conditions

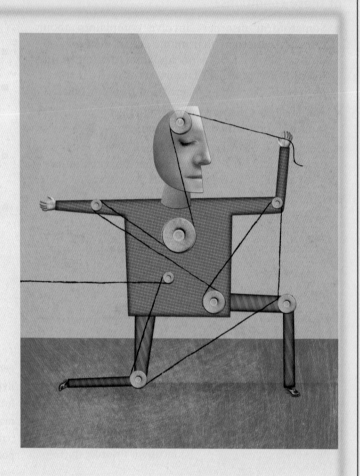

FOCUS QUESTIONS

■ What are psychophysiological disorders, and how do they differ from conversion disorders?

■ What kinds of stressors affect physical health, and why doesn't everyone develop an illness when exposed to them?

■ How do stressors (both physical and psychosocial) affect the immune system? How do factors such as personality and mood states influence the course of an illness such as AIDS or cancer?

■ What is the evidence that illnesses such as coronary heart disease, hypertension, headaches, and asthma are affected by emotional states, and how are the emotions involved?

■ What are possible causes of psychophysiological disorders?

■ What methods have been developed to treat the psychophysiological disorders?

On November 7, 1991, basketball star Magic Johnson announced to the world that he had tested positive for HIV. More than thirteen years later, Magic remains in good health and even briefly returned to playing professional basketball in 1996. He continues to be active in charitable and business ventures (Brown, 2004) and attributes his health to ten different medications taken daily and his positive attitude.

Another individual who contracted HIV believes that psychological states are associated with longevity. "I feel it all goes back to my attitude. ... I won't let this make me ill. I've watched quite a number of friends go from being relatively healthy to sick and dead in very short periods of time. In every case, they all bought into the idea that you have to die from AIDS if you have HIV. I just simply don't agree with that." (Associated Press, 1994)

The data from 200 patients who happened to have implanted defibrillators before the World Trade Center attack on September 11, 2001, provided interesting information regarding the impact of the stressful event. The defibrillators, which record serious arrhythmias, showed that the frequency of life-threatening tachyarrhythmias increased twofold for thirty days after 9/11. (Steinberg et al., 2004)

Why is it that some HIV-infected individuals succumb and develop AIDS (acquired immune deficiency syndrome) rapidly, whereas others, such as Magic Johnson, are able to resist the disease? It is possible that one's attitude may be related to survival. However, alternative explanations may be that these individuals are carrying a less virulent strain of HIV or that they have genetically superior immune systems. Such factors must be eliminated before we can assess the importance of a positive attitude in delaying the appearance of AIDS.

But in some cases, attitudes do appear to influence the course of an illness. What other biological effects might attitudes have? Can people "worry or scare themselves to death"? Medical evidence suggests that they can. Stress and anxiety appear to have at least some role in what is called the **sudden death syndrome**—unexpected, abrupt death that often seems to have no specific physical basis.

Sudden death is the leading cause of death in industrialized countries. Each year, about half a million people in the United States wake up feeling fine but collapse and die later in the day. Rates of sudden death are highest among African Americans and lowest among Hispanic Americans (Gillum, 1997). Some people who die this way are discovered to have coronary heart disease, such as narrowing of the arteries or evidence of past heart attacks, but many who succumb have normal hearts and cardiac vessels (Wren, 2002). Many professionals have called on the World Health Organization to recognize sudden unexplained death syndrome in adults as they have in children (sudden infant death syndrome, or SIDS; Watson, 2004). Sudden death may involve the physiological changes that occur with stress (Carels et al., 2003; Evans, 1997; Merz, 1997), which include the following:

1. Blood tends to clot more easily, thus increasing the risk of blockage in the coronary arteries.

2. Blood pressure rises and fat deposits may tear loose, blocking cardiac vessels.

3. Changes in heart rhythm occur, such as *ventricular fibrillation* (rapid, ineffective contractions of the heart), *bradycardia* (slowing of the heartbeat), *tachycardia* (speeding up of the heartbeat), or *arrhythmia* (irregular heartbeat). See an example of ventricular fibrillation in Figure 7.1.

Certainly, the sudden death syndrome is an extreme example of the power of anxiety and stress to affect physiological processes. (See the Mental Health and Society feature "The Hmong Sudden Death Syndrome" for another example of a similar phenomenon.) Most researchers now acknowledge that attitudes and emotional states can have an impact on physical well-being. In DSM-I and DSM-II, physical

disorders such as asthma, hypertension, and headaches that stem from psychological problems were called *psychosomatic disorders*. The use of this term was meant to distinguish disorders from conditions considered strictly organic in nature. Mental health professionals now recognize, however, that almost any physical disorder can have a strong psychological component or basis.

Although the psychosomatic disorders were previously considered a separate class of disorders, DSM-IV-TR (American Psychiatric Association, 2000) does not categorize them as such. Instead, it contains the category "Psychological Factors Affecting Medical Condition." The physical disorders themselves are listed on Axis III. This classification method acknowledges the belief that both physical and psychological factors are involved in all human processes (White & Moorey, 1997). And the term *psychosomatic disorder* has been replaced with **psychophysiological disorder,** meaning any physical disorder that has a strong psychological basis or component.

Characteristics of Psychophysiological Disorders

The psychophysiological disorders should not be confused with the conversion disorders discussed in the chapter on dissociative and somatoform disorders. The conversion disorders do involve reported physical symptoms, such as loss of feeling, blindness, and paralysis, but they do not involve any physical disorder or process. They are considered essentially psychological in nature. By contrast, most psychophysiological disorders involve actual tissue damage (such as coronary heart disease) or physiological dysfunction (as in asthma or migraine headaches). Both medical treatment and psychotherapy are usually required.

A DSM-IV-TR diagnosis of psychological factors affecting medical condition requires both the presence of a medical condition and the presence of one of the following (American Psychiatric Association, 2000):

■ A temporal relationship between psychological factors and the onset of, exacerbation of, or delay in recovery from a medical condition

■ A psychological factor that interferes with treatment

■ Psychological factors that constitute additional health-risk factors in the individual

The relative contributions of physical and psychological factors in a physical disorder may vary greatly. Although psychological events are often difficult to

FIGURE 7.1 Ventricular Defibrillation in Sudden Unexplained Death   A Thai man fitted with a defibrillator because of cardiac arrest during sleep showed ventricular episodes when asleep. The rapid spikes on the graph set off the defibrillator, which then slowed the heart rate to a normal pattern. Is this the explanation for sudden unexplained death syndrome? (Nademanee et al., 1997)

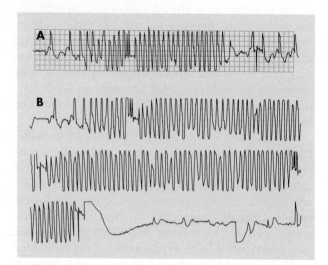

Source: Nademanee et al. (1997).

MENTAL HEALTH AND SOCIETY

The Hmong Sudden Death Syndrome

Vang Xiong is a former Hmong (Laotian) soldier who, with his wife and child, resettled in Chicago in 1980. The change from his familiar rural surroundings and farm life to an unfamiliar urban area must have produced a severe culture shock. In addition, Vang vividly remembered seeing people killed during his escape from Laos, and he expressed feelings of guilt about having to leave his brothers and sisters behind in that country. He reported having problems almost immediately.

[He] could not sleep the first night in the apartment, nor the second, nor the third. After three nights of sleeping very little, Vang came to see his resettlement worker, a bilingual Hmong man named Moua Lee. Vang told Moua that the first night he woke suddenly, short of breath, from a dream in which a cat was sitting on his chest. The second night, the room suddenly grew darker, and a figure, like a large black dog, came to his bed and sat on his chest. He could not push the dog off, and he grew quickly and dangerously short of breath. The third night, a tall, white-skinned female spirit came into his bedroom from the kitchen and lay on top of him. Her weight made it increasingly difficult for him to breathe, and as he

grew frantic and tried to call out he could manage but a whisper. He attempted to turn onto his side, but found he was pinned down. After fifteen minutes, the spirit left him, and he awoke, screaming. (Tobin & Friedman, 1983, p. 440)

As of 1993, 150 cases of sudden death among Southeast Asian refugees had been reported. Almost all were men, with the possible exception of one or two women; most occurred within the first two years of residence in the United States. Autopsies produced no identifiable cause for the deaths. Some cases of sudden unexplained deaths have also been reported in Asian countries. Although the number of cases is declining, these deaths remain a most puzzling phenomenon (Gib Parrish, Centers for Disease Control, personal communication, 1993). All the reports were the same: a person in apparently good health went to sleep and died in his or her sleep. Often, the victim displayed labored breathing, screams, and frantic movements just before death. Some consider the deaths to represent an extreme and very specific example of the impact of psychological stress on physical health.

Vang was one of the lucky victims of the syndrome—he survived it. He

went for treatment to a Hmong woman, Mrs. Thor, who is a highly respected shaman in Chicago's Hmong community. She interpreted his problem as being caused by unhappy spirits and performed the ceremonies that are required to release them. After that, Vang reported, he had no more problems with nightmares or with his breathing during sleep.

Aoki and his colleagues (2003) have studied the sudden unexplained death phenomenon among young Asian males and conjecture that some of these episodes might be related to ventricular fibrillation or the rapid, ineffective beating of the heart. That view is supported by one study (Nademanee et al., 1997) that monitored eight Thai men, who had survived a sudden death episode through resuscitation, with an ICD (implantable cardioverter-defibrillator). Three displayed ventricullar defibrillation when asleep. In one case the wife had reported that her husband had labored respiration and groaning before the ICD discharged and induced a regular heartbeat. Whether or not these episodes in the Thai men were stress related is unknown, but they certainly resemble the characteristics of the Hmong sudden death syndrome.

detect, repeated association between stressors and the disorder or its symptoms should increase the suspicion that a psychological component is involved.

Psychological factors can influence physical processes in three ways (Stone, Smyth, Kaell, & Hurewitz, 2000; White & Moorey, 1997). First, they can directly produce physiological changes in the immune system through the release of neurohormones (catecholamines, corticosteroids, and endorphins) or alter physical functioning. In individuals with irritable

bowel syndrome, for example, emotional stressors can produce painful spasms in the colon. Second, psychological conditions such as depression can influence behaviors that affect health. An individual who is depressed or is facing stress may sleep and exercise less, eat less healthy foods, and consume more caffeine, alcohol, or cigarettes. These behaviors may in turn increase the individual's susceptibility to disease or may prolong an existing illness. Third, an individual's beliefs about the causes, symptoms, duration, and curability of the disease may determine whether the person seeks help and follows the treatment program. Patients who strongly believe that an illness is controllable or treatable often recover more quickly than others who believe otherwise (Weinman & Petrie, 1997). Thus psychological factors can affect illness in many different ways.

In this chapter, we first consider three models that help explain the impact of stress on physical health. Second, we examine the evidence suggesting a connection between stress and some ways in which decreased immunological function can contribute to the onset and course of cancer. Third, we discuss several of the more prevalent psychophysiological disorders: coronary heart disease, hypertension (high blood pressure), headaches, and asthma.

Models for Understanding Stress

A **stressor** is an external event or situation that places a physical or psychological demand on a person. **Stress** is an internal response to a stressor. But something that disturbs one person doesn't necessarily disturb someone else, and two people who react to the same stressor may do so in different ways. Many people who are exposed to stressors, even traumatic ones, eventually get on with their lives. Other people show intense and somewhat long-lasting psychological symptoms.

This section discusses three stress models—the general adaptation, the life-change, and the transaction models—each seeking to explain this difference. To do so, they examine

1. the development and differential effects of stress

2. the apparent ability of relatively weak stressors to result in strong stress reactions

3. the ability some people have to cope more "easily" with stress

The General Adaptation Model

Florida was hit by four hurricanes within a six-week period. One woman was able to deal with the first, even though Hurricane Francis smashed her windows, flooded her carpets, and caused her to throw food away. Then Hurricane Jeanne hit her again, causing similar damage. She had to wait in the hot sun to get ice but was without food or water for her children. As she related, "The first one, I stayed strong. But this second one, I started crying and couldn't stop." (Barton, 2004, A3)

Being alive means that you are constantly exposed to stressors: relationship problems, illness, marriage,

divorce, the death of someone you love, job seeking, aging, retiring, even schoolwork. Most people can cope with the stressors they encounter, provided those stressors are not excessively severe and do not "gang up" on the individual. But when someone is confronted with excessive external demands, coping behaviors may fail, and he or she may resort to inappropriate means of dealing with them. The result may be psychophysiological symptoms, apathy, anxiety, panic, depression, violence, and even death.

There are, in general, three kinds of stressors:

- *Biological stressors* such as infection, physical trauma, disease, malnutrition, and fatigue

- *Psychological stressors* such as threats of physical harm, attacks on self-esteem, and guilt-inducing attacks on one's belief system

- *Social stressors* such as crowding, excessive noise, economic pressures, natural disasters, and war

Hans Selye (1956, 1982) proposed a helpful model for understanding the body's physical reaction to biological stressors. He put forth a three-stage model, which he called the **general adaptation syndrome (GAS),** for understanding the body's physical and psychological reaction to biological stressors. The stages are alarm, resistance, and exhaustion.

Selye describes the *alarm stage* as a "call to arms" of the body's defenses when it is invaded or assaulted biologically. During this first stage, the body reacts immediately to the assault, with rapid heartbeat, loss of muscle tone, and decreased temperature and blood pressure. A rebound reaction follows as the adrenal cortex enlarges and the adrenal glands secrete corticoid hormones.

If exposure to the stressor continues, the *adaptation* or *resistance stage* follows. Now the body mobilizes itself to defend, destroy, or coexist with the injury or disease. The symptoms of illness may disappear. With HIV, for example, the immune system reacts by producing nearly a billion lymphocytes a day to combat the virus. Over time, the immune system gradually weakens and is overcome (Ho et al., 1995). The decrease in the body's resistance increases its susceptibility to other infections or illnesses.

If the stressor continues to tax the body's finite resistive resources, the symptoms may reappear as exhaustion sets in (therefore the name *exhaustion stage*). If stress continues unabated, death may result.

Research does support the view that brief exposure to stressors enhances immune functioning, whereas long-lasting stress is associated with its deterioration (Segerstrom & Miller, 2004). Although Selye developed his model for describing physical responses to biological stressors, continuing research now suggests

How Much Stress Is Too Much? High pressure situations, such as juggling the demands of being a "working mom" or dealing with traffic after a long day's work, are likely to be stressful. But the amount of stress needed to negatively affect an individual varies from person to person. In fact, some people seem to deal efficiently with a great deal of stress, whereas others find it difficult to cope with even small amounts. Why do some people become ill when facing stressors, whereas others do not?

that psychological and social stressors have similar effects. In fact, sustained stress—resulting from psychological or social stressors—not only may make a person more susceptible to illness but also may actually alter the course of a disease. For example, it has been documented that recently bereaved widows are three to twelve times more likely to die than are married women, that tax accountants are most susceptible to heart attacks around April 15, that people living in high-noise areas near airports have more hypertension and medical complaints than other people, and that air traffic controllers suffer four times as much hypertension as the general population (Wilding, 1984). The common factor in these groups is stress.

For years scientists were skeptical about the supposed effects of stress on the body and dismissed any relationship between the two as folklore. We now know, however, that stress affects the immune system, heart function, hormone levels, nervous system, and metabolic rates. Bodily "wear and tear" owing to stress can contribute to diseases such as hypertension, chronic pain, heart attacks, cancer, and the common cold.

The Life-Change Model

As several researchers (de Jong, Timmerman, & Emmelkamp, 1996; Holmes & Holmes, 1970; Rahe, 1994) have noted, events that lead to stress reactions need not be of crisis proportions. Seemingly small, everyday events can also create stress, and any life change, even positive ones, can have a detrimental impact on health. These researchers' work led to the

formulation of the **life-change model,** which assumes that all changes in a person's life—large or small, desirable or undesirable—can act as stressors and that the accumulation of small changes can be as powerful as one major stressor. Consider the following case:

> Janet M., a college freshman, had always been a top-notch student in her small-town high school and had been valedictorian of her graduating class. Her SAT test scores placed her in the ninety-fifth percentile of all students taking the exam. Her social life was in high gear from the moment she arrived on the Berkeley campus. Yet Janet was suffering. It started with a cold that she seemed unable to shake. During her first quarter, she was hospitalized once with the "flu" and then three weeks later for "exhaustion." In high school Janet appeared vivacious, outgoing, and relaxed; at Berkeley she became increasingly tense, anxious, and depressed.

In Janet's case, all the classic symptoms of stress were present. No single stressor was responsible; rather, a series of life changes had a cumulative impact. An examination of Janet's intake interview notes at her university's counseling center revealed the following stressors:

1. Change from a somewhat conservative small-town environment to a more permissive atmosphere on a liberal campus

2. Change from being the top student in her high school class to being slightly above average at Berkeley

Life Change and Stress Changes such as leaving home to enter school, adjusting to a roommate, preparing for papers and exams, leaving your old network of friends, and eating dorm or self-prepared food can function as stressors. Why is it that some people will develop an illness as a reaction to the changes?

3. Change in living accommodations, from a home with a private room to a dormitory with a roommate

4. Change from being completely dependent on family finances to having to work part time for her education

5. Change from having a steady boyfriend in her home town to being unpaired

6. Change in family stability (her father recently lost his job, and her parents seemed headed for divorce)

7. Change in food intake from home-cooked meals to dormitory food and quick snacks

Although each of these changes may seem small, their cumulative impact was anything but insignificant. And what happened to Janet is seen, to various degrees, among many students entering college. Going

to college is a major life change. Most students can cope with the demands, but others need direct help dealing with stress.

To measure the impact of life changes, Holmes and Rahe (1967) devised the Social Readjustment Rating Scale (SRRS), in which they asked people to rate forty-three events in terms of the amount of readjustment that would be required. For example, participants rated the death of a spouse as requiring the greatest adjustment, whereas a minor law violation required the least. For each life event, researchers assigned a numerical value that corresponded to its strength as a stressor (Wyler, Masuda, & Holmes, 1971). These "stress potential" values are referred to as *life change units* (LCUs). The investigators found that 93 percent of health problems (infections, allergies, bone and muscle injuries, and psychosomatic illness) affected patients who, during the previous year, had been exposed to events whose LCU values totaled 150 or more. Although a minor life change was not sufficient to constitute a serious stressor, the cumulative impact of many events could be considered a crisis. Particularly revealing was the finding that exposure to a greater number of LCUs increased the chances of illness. Of those exposed to mild crises (150 to 199 LCUs), 37 percent reported illness; to moderate crises (200 to 299 LCUs), 51 percent; and to major crises (more than 300 LCUs), 79 percent.

Further research shows that different populations and cultures vary in the way they rank stressors. In one study, mainland Chinese people ranked divorce fourth in severity of impact, whereas American samples ranked it second. The Chinese participants gave death of and serious illness in a close family member second and third ratings. This may reflect the greater importance of the family of origin in Chinese culture. Both groups, however, rated the death of a spouse as the greatest stressor (Zheng & Lin, 1994). See Table 7.1 for ratings of stressors among U.S. undergraduates.

Clearly, stressful life events do play some part in producing physical and psychological illnesses for many people. Yet it is too soon to say that stress causes these illnesses. Most studies cited here are retrospective—they search for influences after the illness is diagnosed. And they are also correlational in nature, so no cause-and-effect relationship can be inferred. In addition, the data used in the studies depend on (1) people's perceptions of health and illness, (2) their recollections and reports of illness (both psychological and physical; sick individuals may recall more events than healthy ones), and (3) their health histories over a defined period (Levenstein et al., 1993). Furthermore, many people have illnesses that do not seem to be preceded by identifiable stressors, and some who undergo stress

TABLE 7.1   Sample Stressors Generated and Ranked by College Undergraduates

Item	Severity	Frequency
Death of family member or friend	3.97	1.89
Had lots of tests	3.62	4.39
Finals week	3.62	3.64
Breaking up a relationship	3.45	2.21
Property stolen	3.41	1.96
Having roommate conflicts	3.10	2.68
Lack of money	3.07	3.36
Arguments with friends	2.97	2.43
Trying to decide on a major	2.79	3.25
Sat through boring class	1.66	4.07

Note: Event severity was rated on a 4-point scale, ranging from "none" to "a lot." Event frequency was rated on a 5-point scale, ranging from "never" to "always."

Source: Data from Crandall, Preisler, & Aussprung (1992).

do not seem to get sick. Finally, evidence now shows that positive and negative life events do not have equal effects. Undesirable life changes seem to be more detrimental than positive life changes (Sarason, Johnson, & Siegel, 1978). Also, personal interpretations or characteristics modify the impact of life changes (Kobasa, Hilker, & Maddi, 1979; Lazarus, 1983; Sarason et al., 1978). Obviously, further investigation of the relationship between life changes and illness is needed.

The Transaction Model

The general adaptation syndrome model is concerned with the process by which the body reacts to stressors, and the life-change model is concerned with external events that cause stress as a response. But neither model considers the person's subjective definition or interpretation of stressful events or life changes. Several processes intervene between the stressor and the development of stress. In particular, the thoughts and interpretations we have about impending threats (stressors), the emotions we attach to them, and the actions we take to avoid them can either increase or decrease the impact of stressors.

In his classic book *Psychological Stress and the Coping Process* (1966), Richard Lazarus formulated a **transaction model of stress.** He noted that stress resides neither in the person alone nor in the situation alone, but rather in a transaction between the two. An example can illustrate this point:

On the morning of August 16, 2004, Mrs. Mavis C. discovered a small lump on her left breast. She immediately contacted her doctor and made an appointment to see him. After examining her, the physician stated that the lump could be either a cyst or a tumor and recommended a biopsy. The results revealed that the tumor was malignant.

Mrs. C. accepted the news with some trepidation but went about her life with minimal disruption. When she was questioned about the way in which she was handling the situation, she replied that there was no denying that this was a serious problem and that there was great ambiguity about the prognosis but that people are successfully treated for cancer. She planned to undergo treatment and would not give up.

Unlike Mrs. C., many patients would have been horrified at even the thought of having cancer. They might have viewed the news that the tumor was malignant as a catastrophe and focused on thoughts of dying, abandoning all hope. This reaction differs from Mrs. C.'s, who coped with the stressor through internal processes. The impact of stressors can be reduced or increased depending on the way the situation is interpreted. A person who can adapt cognitively may reduce susceptibility to illness or limit its course. They will make efforts to alter health-impairing habits and to adhere to treatment guidelines, whereas those who view the illness with a sense of hopelessness may give up (Gonzalez et al., 2004; Shnek, Irvine, Stewart, & Abbey, 2001).

Negative or Positive Stress—It Makes a Difference Research has found that undesirable life changes, such as the death of a loved one, are more likely to impact the physical health of people than are positive life changes, such as getting married.

One dominant theme threads its way through each of the models discussed: no one factor is enough to cause illness. Rather, illness results from a complex interaction of psychosocial, physiological, and cognitive stressors.

Myth vs Reality

Myth: Psychophysiological disorders are merely psychological in nature and can be treated with only psychotherapy. Real physical problems are not present.

Reality: Although psychophysiological disorders do have a psychological component, actual physical processes or conditions are involved. They differ from conversion reactions that are only psychological in nature. Any physical condition can be considered a psychophysiological disorder if psychological factors are implicated etiologically, make the condition worse, or delay improvement. In most cases, both medical and psychological treatments are utilized.

Stress and the Immune System

We have already suggested a relationship between stress and illness. How do emotional and psychological states influence the disease process? Consider the following case:

> Anne was an unhappy and passive individual who always acceded to the wishes and demands of her husband. She had difficulty expressing strong emotions, especially anger, and often repressed her feelings. She had

> few friends and, other than her husband, had no one to talk to. She was also depressed and felt a pervasive sense of hopelessness. During a routine physical exam, her doctor discovered a lump in her breast. The results of a biopsy revealed that the tumor was malignant.

Could Anne's personality or emotional state have contributed to the formation or the growth of the malignant tumor? If so, how? Could she now alter the course of her disease by changing her emotional state? That such questions are being asked represents a profound change in the way in which physical illness is now being conceptualized.

The view that diseases other than traditional psychophysiological disorders are strictly organic appears too simplistic. Many theorists (such as S. Cohen et al., 1998; S. Cohen & Rodriguez, 1995; White & Moorey, 1997) now believe that most diseases are caused by an interaction of social, psychological, and biological factors. This relationship has been found in many diseases. For example, chronic stress, especially, may create greater susceptibility to disease. Cohen and his associates (1998) had 276 volunteers complete a life stressor interview, after which they were evaluated to determine whether they were ill. Those who were healthy were then quarantined and given nasal drops containing cold viruses to determine whether they would develop a cold within five days. Of this group, 84 percent became infected with the virus, but only 40 percent developed cold symptoms. Types of life stressors varied for those who did and did not develop colds. Participants with acute stressful life events lasting less than one month tended not to develop colds. In contrast, those who suffered severe stress for one or more months were much more likely to develop colds. The types of chronic stressors most closely related to colds were long-term conflicts with family or friends and either unemployment or underemployment.

In other examples of the interaction of social, psychological, and biological factors in diseases, King and Wilson (1991) found that interpersonal stress and depression were significantly related to dermatitis. The researchers pointed out, however, that although it is possible to speculate that interpersonal stress caused the skin symptoms, it is also possible that increases in itchiness or unsightliness from the skin condition produced interpersonal stress. A study by McLarnon and Kaloupek (1988) appears to support the stress-causes-symptoms view. People with herpes reported their moods and thoughts daily on a questionnaire. New lesions developed in participants who had reported higher anxiety four days before lesions appeared. This held true even when physical symptoms such as tingling and itchiness were controlled. Here the emotional state clearly preceded the physical sensations. In general, research attempting to show a connection of emotional stress with other skin conditions or diseases has suffered from deficiencies in experimental designs (Abeni, 2001).

As mentioned earlier, the course or severity of a disease can be influenced through the following pathways: (1) *biological:* there may be a direct physiological reaction (blood pressure, heart rate, etc.) or changes in immune functioning following a stressor; (2) *behavioral:* the individual may respond by either engaging in poor health practices or by altering his or her lifestyle in a positive manner; (3) *cognitive:* feelings of either hopelessness or optimism could have an impact on health decisions in either a positive or negative manner; (4) *social:* the stressor or emotional state could cause either a deterioration or an increase in the social support system. Each pathway has received some experimental support in the progression of a disease. Research has tended to focus on only one of the pathways, whereas several may be involved. For example, the biological process of depression may directly produce a deterioration of the immune system, but poorer immune functioning could also be due to behavioral characteristics associated with depression, such as not eating appropriately or a lack of exercise.

Following treatment guidelines can also influence the course of a disease. In one study, nearly one-third of individuals with HIV had missed medication doses (a demanding and rigorous process involving taking up to twenty-two pills a day). Rates of adherence were related to levels of depression, self-efficacy, social support, and side effects of medication (Catz, Kelly, Bogart, Benotsch, & McAuliffe, 2000; Gonzalez et al., 2004). As you can

Coping with Stress The evidence supporting the importance of psychosocial stressors on the development and progress of AIDS may be mixed, but the reality for Michelle Lopez and her daughter, Raven, is clear. Several years ago, when Raven was diagnosed HIV-positive, Michelle was homeless and using drugs. Since then Michelle has quit drugs and found an apartment and a job educating women and children about AIDS. Both she and Raven are enrolled in a clinical trial to test a new drug for AIDS, and Raven is now symptom free.

see, immune functioning can be influenced through different pathways or affected by their interaction. Keep this in mind when you read research. We will consider some of these pathways in the following discussion of research on HIV and AIDS. It is estimated that 42 million people worldwide have been infected with HIV since its onset, and each day 16,000 more contract the disease (Steinbrook, 2004). Although AIDS cases and deaths in the United States have declined in recent years due to better treatments, HIV infection rates have not declined and actually have increased among women and people of color. In 2003, it was estimated that there were 950,000 people living with HIV in the United States (Steinbrook, 2004). There is some evidence that the speed at which HIV turns to AIDS may be the result of innate differences in immune system responsiveness or of weaker and less virulent strains of HIV (Susman, 2002). However, some researchers believe that psychological variables may also be involved (Solano et al., 1993; Szapocznik et al., 2004). In one study of HIV-infected gay men, the disease progressed more rapidly among those who showed emotional inhibition (concealed their sexual identity) than among those who openly professed their sexual identity (Cole, Kemeny, & Taylor, 1997). Those who concealed their sexual identity were also more likely to develop cancer, pneumonia, bronchitis, sinusitis, and tuberculosis over a five-year follow-up period (Cole, Kemeny, Taylor, & Visscher, 1996). Other researchers have found that having a negative view of oneself ("I'm responsible for the bad things that happen to me") was associated with decreased immune functioning in some HIV-infected men (Segerstrom, Taylor, Kemeny, Reed, & Visscher, 1996) and that positive self-efficacy (an ability to cope with stressors) was associated with a slower decline in immune functioning (Benight et al., 1997). Theorell and colleagues (1995) reported that individuals with HIV who had fewer sources of emotional support showed more rapid deterioration of immune functioning. If it is found that psychological states are associated with the progression of HIV, medical professionals could incorporate these findings in a larger treatment plan. Although the preceding research seems to indicate the importance of psychological variables in the disease progression of AIDS, it is not clear what is involved. Is greater longevity due to improved immune functions, improved health habits, social support, or greater adherence to treatment procedures? For example, depressed patients are three times more likely to fail to adhere to treatment recommendations as nondepressed patients (DiMatteo, Lepper, & Croghan, 2000).

Yet the evidence supporting the importance of psychosocial stressors on the development and progress of AIDS is mixed. In a review of studies examining the impact of psychosocial variables such as depression on the immune function of individuals with HIV, Stein, Miller, and Trestman (1991) concluded that "psychosocial factors, such as depression or stress, do not have a measurable or substantial effect on the immune system in relation to physical disorders, such as AIDS" (p. 171). Factors that may contribute to the contradictory findings include differences in the prior health of the individual, drug abuse history, age, gender, health behaviors, and the stage of the disease process (Kiecolt-Glaser & Glaser, 1995). At this point, it is still unclear how much impact psychological factors have on immune function in a disease such as AIDS. Nevertheless, psychological treatments can at the very least improve the mental well-being of clients.

The Immune System

We know that stress is related to illness, but what is the precise relationship between the two? How does stress affect health? Stress itself does not appear to

Under Attack This highly magnified photo shows the surface of a T-cell that is infected with the HIV virus. T-cells function as a part of the immune response to viruses and infections. In this case it is being compromised. Some believe that one's attitude can influence the susceptibility of components of the immune system such as T-cells, whereas others disagree.

cause infections, but it may decrease the immune system's efficiency, thereby increasing a person's susceptibility to disease (Koh, 1998; Luecken et al., 1997). This connection has received the greatest amount of attention.

The white blood cells in the immune system help maintain health by recognizing and destroying pathogens such as bacteria, viruses, fungi, and tumors. In an intact system, over 1,000 billion white blood cells are based in the lymph system or circulate through the bloodstream. Two major classes of white blood cells are lymphocytes and phagocytes. *Lymphocytes* comprise B-cells (which produce antibodies against invaders), T-cells (which detect and destroy foreign cells), and natural killer (NK) cells (which act as an early detection system to prevent the growth of tumors). *Phagocytes* are also attracted to and destroy invaders (S. Cohen & Herbert, 1996; Kiecolt-Glaser & Glaser, 1993).

As mentioned earlier, stress produces physiological changes in the body. Part of the stress response involves the release of several neurohormones that impair immune functioning. *Corticosteroids*, for example, have very strong immunosuppressive actions and are often used to suppress immunity caused by allergic reactions. *Endorphins* also appear to decrease natural killer cells' tumor-fighting ability. A deficient immune system may fail to detect invaders or to produce antibodies. Its killing ability may be impaired, or its blood cells may be unable to multiply. Because of the weakening in defenses, infections and diseases are more likely to develop or worsen.

Decreased Immunological Functioning as a Function of Stress   Impaired immunological functioning has been associated with a variety of social and psychological stressors (Dickerson & Kemeny, 2004; Pike et al., 1997). The spouses of dementia victims showed lower immune functioning than was found among controls, and spouses who reported lower levels of social support showed the greatest drop (Kiecolt-Glaser et al., 1991). Divorced or separated men tend to have poorer immunological functioning than their married counterparts. Happily married men tend to have stronger immune systems than men who are experiencing marital problems (Kiecolt-Glaser et al., 1987). And abrasive marital interactions between long-married men and women are associated with negative immunological changes (Kiecolt-Glaser et al., 1997). The quality of social relationships may affect our vulnerability to illnesses.

Bereavement (loss of a spouse) has also been found to weaken the immune system. The lymphocyte responsiveness of men married to women with terminal breast cancer was measured approximately one month before their wives' deaths and again afterward. The second measurement showed a drop in immune response. The decrease in efficiency continued for approximately two months, after which the immune functioning gradually increased (Schleifer, Keller, Camerino, Thornton, & Stein, 1983). Similar results have been reported in recently widowed women. Women whose husbands had died showed lower NK cell responsiveness than did a group of nonbereaved women (M. Irwin, Daniels, Smith, Bloom, & Weiner, 1987). Although these stressors are associated with a decrease in immune response, not everyone was equally affected. As indicated in our earlier discussion of the transaction stress model, the person's perception or interpretation of the event is important. Separated and divorced men who were preoccupied with thoughts of their former partners showed a lower level of immune functioning (Kiecolt-Glaser et al., 1987). How a person interprets an event can influence its impact.

Evidence suggests, however, that the reduction in immune system efficiency related to psychological factors is often relatively small and may account for only about 10 percent of the variance in predicting disease occurrence (Rabkin et al., 1991). Similarly, psychological interventions to improve immune functioning in humans have produced only modest results (Miller & Cohen, 2001). As Kiecolt-Glaser and Glaser (1992) point out, "It is sometimes erroneously assumed that changes in immune function translate directly into changes in health. In fact, whether interventions that produce relatively small immunological changes can actually affect the incidence, severity, or duration of infections or malignant disease is not known" (p. 573).

Although our discussion has focused on the direct impact of stress on the immune system, indirect pathways must also be considered. For example, the health care practices of an individual who is depressed or facing many different stressors may deteriorate (less sleep, less nutritious meals, greater alcohol consumption, and less attention to physical care). Such changes can also decrease immune functioning (Koh, 1998). Thus decreased resistance to disease might be due to changes in behavioral or nutritional patterns as a function of being depressed or stressed. Similarly, bereaved persons may show lowered immune functioning because of a decrease in health care practices. Research that attempts to link changes in immune functioning directly with stressors or psychological states must control for such variables.

Mediating the Effects of Stressors

As we have seen, not everyone who faces stressful events develops an illness. In this section, we explore some of the intervening factors that can mediate the effects of a stressor.

Helplessness or Control   Control and the perception of control over the environment and its stressors appear to mitigate the effects of stress. One study of nursing home residents examined the impact of control on the residents' health and emotional states (Langer & Rodin, 1976). In the "responsibility induced" group, residents were allowed to make certain decisions, such as how to arrange their rooms, when to see movies, whether to accept visitors, and whether to have plants in their rooms. The "traditional" group was not offered these choices. They saw movies when they were scheduled. In this group, the nurses arranged the rooms and chose the plants for the residents.

Within a short period, the nurses rated 71 percent of the traditional group as more debilitated and 93 percent of the responsibility-induced group as improved. Self-report questionnaires revealed that the responsibility-induced group rated themselves as more active and happier. Mortality rates also differed between the two groups. After eighteen months, 15 percent (7 of 47) of those in the responsibility-induced group had died versus 30 percent (13 of 44) in the traditional group. The reason for the differences in mortality rates is unclear. Some deaths, however, might be associated with a less efficient immune system.

A direct relationship between control and the immune system has been found in several studies. In one study, ten participants were placed in two stressful situations involving noise. In the first situation, participants could control the noise level by pressing buttons in a simple sequence. In the other, participants could

Control and Stress Although these assembly-line workers at Apple Computer would seem to have low-stress jobs, they may be highly vulnerable to stress-related illnesses. What seems to be most important is the perception of control over your work. How could you increase the feeling of control in assembly-line work?

not control the noise level. Blood samples were obtained and analyzed after each session. The level of epinephrine (a hormone released during stress) in the uncontrollable-stress situation was significantly higher than that found in the controllable-stress situation. The participants also reported a greater sense of helplessness, higher tension, anxiety, and depression while in the uncontrollable-stress situation (Breier et al., 1987). Although changes in physical functioning occur with stress, can we show experimentally that lack of control is related to disease?

One study that attempted to do so directly measured the effect of the ability to "control" immune functioning in rats injected with cancer cells. The rats were assigned to one of three groups: (1) a controllable-shock group (pressing a bar would end the shock),

(2) a yoked-control group (rats in this group would receive the same pattern of shocks as those in the escapable condition but would have no control over it), or (3) a no-shock control group. Sixty-five percent of the rats in the controllable-shock group rejected the cancer cells, as opposed to only 27 percent in the yoked-control group and 55 percent in the no-shock control group. The inability to control a stressor seems to decrease immune system efficiency (Laudenslager, Ryan, Drugan, Hyson, & Maier, 1983; Visintainer, Volpicelli, & Seligman, 1982).

Hardiness: Personality Characteristics and Mood State Maddi (1972) believes that "hardy" people are more resistant to illnesses. In a classic study, Kobasa and her colleagues (1979) conducted large-scale research on highly stressed executives in various occupations, seeking to identify the traits that distinguish those who handle stress well from those who do not. They found that high-stress executives who reported few illnesses showed three kinds of **hardiness,** or ability to deal well with stress. In their attitudes toward life, these stress-resistant executives showed an *openness to change,* a feeling of *involvement* or *commitment,* and a *sense of control* over their lives. The most important protective factor that was correlated with health was attitude toward change (or *challenge*). Those who are open to change seem likely to interpret events to their advantage and to reduce their levels of stress.

Suppose, for example, that two people lose their jobs. The person who is open to change may view this situation as an opportunity to find a new career better suited to his or her abilities. The person who is not open to change is likely to see the job loss as a devastating event and to suffer the emotional and physical consequences of this perception. Although the idea that hardiness may buffer the impact of stressors makes sense, the construct has been difficult to define and assess (Woodard, 2004).

Self-Efficacy and Optimism Another cognitive variable that appears to have an impact on illness is the belief in one's ability to take action to attain goals or to effect change. An individual with high self-efficacy may engage in more health-related activities when an illness occurs, whereas low self-efficacy would result in feelings of hopelessness. Self-efficacy has been related to recovery from orthopedic surgery; the stronger the belief in the ability to recover by participating in rehabilitation, the more successful the outcome (Waldrop, Lightsey, Ethington, Woemmel, & Coke, 2001). Similar findings were reported for individuals suffering from degenerative disk disease and low-back problems (Kaivanto, Estlander, Moneta, & Banharanta, 1995; Lackner, Carosella, & Feuerstein, 1996). Individuals with high self-efficacy are more likely to follow treatment guidelines, to exercise, and to develop a more healthy diet, thereby shortening the recovery period.

Optimism, another cognitive state, also appears to mediate the impact of a disease. Optimism or even illusory positive beliefs about serious illnesses may improve psychological and possibly mental health. In a study on psychosocial predictors of the course of illness in men with AIDS, Taylor and colleagues (2000) found that realistic acceptance of death was associated with longevity. Surprisingly, those with a high realistic acceptance died an average of nine months earlier than those with a low realistic acceptance. This result was found even when severity of illness, immune functioning, depression, health habits, and social support were controlled for. The researchers believe that "an optimistic, even unrealistically optimistic, view of the future, may reserve resources that not only help people manage the ebb and flow of everyday life but that assume special significance in helping people cope with intensely stressful and life-threatening events" (p. 106). The manner in which optimism influences the progression of a disease, the conditions under which it may be detrimental, and how to incorporate it in therapy are currently being investigated.

Personality, Mood States, and Cancer

Are certain emotions or personality characteristics involved in either the cause or the course of cancers? A number of researchers (Colon, Callies, Popkin, & McGlave, 1991; Greer, 1991; D. Phillips, Todd, & Wagner, 1993; Temoshok & Dreher, 1992) believe that certain emotional states—such as depression, hopelessness, or anger—or specific personality styles can cause or influence the course of cancer. Demonstrating such a link would have important implications in treatment and prevention.

In the United States, 1,334,100 new cancer cases were detected and 556,500 died of cancer in 2003 (American Cancer Society, 2004). About 9.6 million Americans are currently living with cancer or are cancer survivors (Earle & Neville, 2004). Rates of cancer vary by ethnic group; African Americans and native Hawaiians have the highest rates. Among African Americans, lung and prostate cancers are especially high, and their mortality rate for these diseases is much higher than that of white Americans (American Cancer Society, 2004). In general, Hispanic Americans, Native Americans, and Asian Americans have low rates of cancer (National Center for Health Statistics, 2003).

Greer (1991) believes that a "fighting spirit" can increase survival time in cancer patients. It is possible that stressful emotions can impair cellular functions, such as DNA repair, and that such emotions could contribute to cancer, whereas positive emotions improve immune functioning. However, the emotional state of an individual may also affect the course of cancer by producing altered health habits or adherence to treatment (Baum & Posluszny, 1999). Some early researchers (Bahnson, 1981; Simonton, Mathews-Simonton, & Creighton, 1978) argued that negative emotions and the inability to form lasting relationships increase an individual's chances of developing cancer. Such research led to the hypothesis that positive emotional states would enhance immune functioning, and some researchers (Meares, 1979) urged physicians to take "the big step of attempting to influence cancer growth by psychological means" (p. 978). See the Mental Health and Society feature "Can Laughter or Humor Influence the Course of a Disease?" for the possible impact of a positive emotion such as humor on the disease process.

Several problems exist in research that investigates the relationship between moods and personality on cancer (Honda & Goodwin, 2004). First, *cancer* is a general name for a variety of disease processes, each of which may have a varying susceptibility to emotions. Second, cancer develops over a relatively long period of time. Determining a temporal relationship between its occurrence and a specific mood or personality is not possible. Third, most studies examining the relationship between psychological variables and cancer have been retrospective—that is, personality or mood states were assessed after the cancer was diagnosed. The discovery that one has a life-threatening disease can produce a variety of emotions. People who receive the life-threatening diagnosis of cancer may respond with depression, anxiety, and confusion. Thus, instead of being a cause, negative emotions may be a result of the knowledge of having a life-threatening disease. Fourth, although it has been shown that injected malignant cells are more likely to grow in stressed versus unstressed mice, the findings do not address the development of "spontaneous" cancers. Would the stressed mice be more likely to develop cancer anyway, without being injected with malignant cells?

Specific emotional states have been suspected of influencing the onset and course of cancer. Depression (as measured by the Minnesota Multiphasic Personality Inventory [MMPI]) was positively associated with a twenty-year incidence of mortality from cancer (Persky,

MENTAL HEALTH AND SOCIETY

Can Laughter or Humor Influence the Course of a Disease?

It's hard not to feel a laugh bubbling to the surface at the sight of a grown man—a psychotherapist, no less— standing before a group of his sober-minded peers, holding a teddy bear that tells knock-knock jokes when you press its paw. Hard not to laugh when he talks about building a concept of personal "mindfoolness." Hard not to resist a smirk as he hands out finger traps, those venerable props from kidhood in which you stick one finger in each end and can't pull them out no matter how hard you tug (McGuire, 1999, p.1).

Clown noses, whoopee cushions, the antics of the Three Stooges can produce laughter. Can humor reduce the severity of a physical illness or even be curative? Norman Cousins, who suffered from rheumatoid disease, described how he recovered his health through laughter. He claimed that ten minutes of laughter would provide two hours of pain relief (Cousins, 1979). In 1999,

Patch Adams, a physician whose use of humor with his patients was made into a movie, received an award for "excellence in the field of therapeutic humor" at the American Association of Therapeutic Humor. Ohio psychologist Steve Wilson quit clinical practice in 1998 to found the World Laughter Tour and teach classes in therapeutic laughter. He believes humor can reduce the need for pain medication, possibly boost immune functioning, and lower blood pressure ("Psychosomatic Medicine," 2004).

How might humor influence the disease process? Several routes are possible. (1) Humor may have a direct impact on physiological functioning. (2) Humor may influence people's beliefs about their ability to carry out health-promoting behaviors and give them greater confidence that their actions can relieve the illness. (3) Humor may serve as a buffer between exposure to stressors

and the development of negative states, such as depression, which have been found to be related to the development or severity of physical conditions. (4) Humor may make an individual more likely to receive social support from friends and family. In two reviews of studies on the relationship between humor, laughter, and physical health (Martin, 2001; Salovey, Rothman, Detweiler, & Steward, 2000), limited support was found. There does appear to be an increase in immune functioning after exposure to humorous videotapes versus tapes that are neutral or sad. Humor can also increase the self-efficacy of individuals and reduce the impact of negative events. The relationship between humor and social support has not received adequate attention. A major problem in this area has been an accepted definition of humor. How would you determine what is funny?

Kempthorne-Rawson, & Shekelle, 1987). People with high depression scores were more than one-third more likely to develop cancer and almost twice as likely to die of cancer than were those rated low in depression. This was true even when risk factors such as age, smoking, alcohol intake, occupational status, family history of cancer, and serum cholesterol levels were considered. Because the study was prospective (begun before the cancer cases were diagnosed), the possibility that depression resulted from knowledge of having a cancer was eliminated. Depression was assessed only at the beginning of the study, however. To demonstrate a relationship of this emotion with cancer, we would have to show that it was a long-term disorder in these people. We would also have to demonstrate that emotions such as depression impair the immune system directly rather than indirectly through health care changes, such as a poorer diet, loss of sleep, increased use of substances,

and fewer recreational activities. Psychological factors may also function differently depending on such characteristics as the age of the individual. Consider pessimism, for example. Endorsement of a pessimistic life orientation is associated with increased mortality in younger cancer patients, but not in those age sixty or older. For these older individuals, pessimism may actually be a coping mechanism that helps them adjust to increasing poor health, whereas pessimism in younger cancer patients may reflect genuine despair and hopelessness (Schulz, Bookwala, Knapp, Scheier, & Williamson, 1996). Thus emotional factors may be influenced by other factors such as age, coping style, support system, and outlook on life.

Do stress, emotional difficulties, or personality characteristics increase the chance that a person will develop cancer or increase the cancer's severity if it does occur? Certain emotions and stressors have been

CFS: The Mystery Illness

When Sonya was four, she saw *The Nutcracker* ballet and determined to become a ballerina. At ten, she was dancing lead roles for a local ballet company; the next year she was accepted into the American Ballet School. By age twenty she was an internationally respected dancer. Eight months after having had the flu, she was still plagued with debilitating fatigue, muscle and joint pain, disturbed sleep, and difficulty remembering simple dance routines. Her doctors could not find a physical basis for her complaints, and psychologists said her distress was consistent with her limitations. Sonya went to a neurologist who gave a name to her illness: chronic fatigue syndrome, or CFS. Though her symptoms remained, she felt relief knowing that her disorder was real, not imagined, as many friends and family members had suggested.

CFS is a mysterious illness. It affects between 75 and 265 individuals per 100,000 in the United States, and, despite being called a "yuppie" disease, it actually crosses all demographic lines. The Centers for Disease Control and Prevention (CDC, 2003) says that CFS is diagnosed more often in middle- and upper-income white females because they are more likely to seek medical attention. Although CFS-like symptoms were diagnosed by nineteenth-century physician George Beard, researchers have still not determined its cause, diagnosis, course, or any universally effective treatment. Proposed causes include viral infec-

tions; immune system dysfunction; problems with the hypothalamic pituitary adrenal (HPA) axis that affects hormone production; low blood pressure; nutritional deficiency; low blood sugar; and allergies, none of which have been consistently supported by research. (A similar set of symptoms have been reported by some Gulf War veterans who show unexplained immunological changes; Vojdani & Thrasher, 2004.) No physical, psychological, or neuropsychological test leads to a diagnosis of CFS—diagnoses are made by evaluating symptoms and ruling out other possible disorders.

The primary symptom is persistent fatigue lasting at least six months that is not helped by bed rest, plus four or more other symptoms outlined by the CDC: "substantial impairment in short-term memory or concentration; sore throat; tender lymph nodes; muscle pain; multijoint pain without swelling or redness; headaches of a new type, pattern or severity; unrefreshing sleep; and post-exertional malaise lasting more than 24 hours" (CDC, 2003). Lacking objective evidence of a physical disorder, one might suspect a somatoform disorder as described in this chapter; however, the almost unrelenting fatigue of CFS is not a symptom of somatoform disorders.

The course of CFS is unpredictable. Some patients completely recover; many experience improvement with periodic recurrence of symptoms; and others are incapacitated in one or more areas of daily

living their whole lives. We cannot predict who recovers completely, partially, or not at all. Also unclear is what treatment is most effective. A combination of antidepressants and cognitive-behavioral therapy helps some patients, but not all. Other treatments include regular, gradually increasing exercise; treating the pain, allergy-like symptoms, or low blood pressure; and self-care strategies (stress reduction, developing good sleep habits, pacing oneself, proper nutrition, drinking enough fluids, engaging in fulfilling activities, and not smoking). Support groups help some patients learn to cope with the disorder, provide useful resources, and may reduce stress. Learning effective coping strategies, which vary for each individual, is important.

Who suffers from CFS? Florence Nightingale might have had it, and current diagnoses have been made for Olympic speed skater Amy Peterson; female athlete of the year Michelle Akers; Laura Hillenbrand, author of the book *Seabiscuit;* orchestra conductor Jackson Parkhurst; pianist Keith Jarrett; and Katharine, Duchess of Kent. Imagine the strength and courage these individuals have shown to succeed despite the heavy weight of fatigue, pain, and other impairments. Imagine, too, the relief to individuals suffering from unexplained physical fatigue, pain, and general unwellness once the mysteries of CFS are understood.

associated with a less efficient immune system, and under these conditions cancer might be more likely to gain a foothold. Nevertheless, the connection between stress and naturally occurring cancers remains to be shown (see the Critical Thinking feature "CFS: The

Mystery Illness" for another example of a possible stress-related physical condition). Maybe only certain cancers, at a certain level of development, are influenced by emotional states. Researchers are currently investigating this possibility.

Mood and Cancer Though research evidence is still mixed, many people believe that emotions can affect the onset and course of serious diseases such as cancer. In an effort to show emotional support for Sarah DeCristoforo, when she returned to school after receiving chemotherapy, her teacher and two friends shaved their heads.

Psychological Involvement in Specific Physical Disorders

Although most research that studies the impact of psychological factors on immune function is fairly recent, the mind-body connection between some physical disorders has been extensively studied. In many instances, a relationship has been found between psychological or social factors and the origin and exacerbation of these conditions.

Coronary Heart Disease

Coronary heart disease (CHD) is a narrowing of the arteries in or to the heart, resulting in the restriction or partial blockage of the flow of blood and oxygen to the heart. Symptoms of CHD may include chest pain (*angina pectoris*), heart attack, or, in severe cases, cardiac arrest. Approximately 400,000 Americans die of coronary heart disease each year, although the rate has been declining. In a longitudinal study, depression seems to be a risk factor for cardiac mortality, both in individuals who had or did not have cardiac disease at the beginning of the study. The risk was twice as high for those with major than with minor depression, although any depression was associated with increased mortality (Penninx et al., 2001; see Figure 7.2). Because women are much more likely to suffer from depression than men,

Schwartzman and Glaus (2000) believe that women should be educated about emotional factors and their involvement in CHD. For women, estrogen appears to offer some protection: women tend to develop coronary heart disease about ten years later than men do. However, because of the aging of the U.S. population, the number of women dying from coronary heart disease is now approaching that of men, and more women than men now die of cardiovascular disease each year (Torpy, 2002; Wenger, 1997). The fatality rate for women within the first year after a heart attack is twice as high as that for men (Legato, 1996; Marrugat et al., 1998).

The incidence of coronary heart disease has diminished in recent years because of changes in smoking, diet, and exercise behaviors and in treatment of hypertension. Although cigarette smoking, obesity, physical inactivity, hypertension, and elevated serum choles-

FIGURE 7.2 The Effect of Depression on Cardiac Death and Cardiac Heart Disease (CHD) Death Rates Data represent participants without cardiac disease (*n* = 2,397) (a) and participants with cardiac disease (*n* = 450) (b). Note that the scales for the upper and lower graphs are different, but the presence of depression, especially major depression, is associated with cardiac deaths in both conditions.

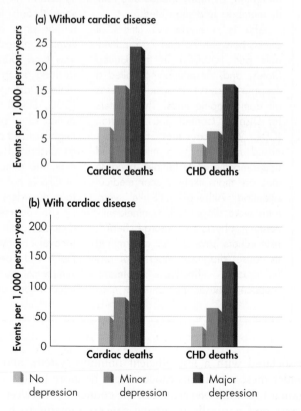

Source: Penninx et al. (2001).

TABLE 7.2   Anxiety Questionnaire Items That Correlated with Eventual Onset of Fatal Heart Attacks

Participants who checked yes for two or more of these questions were more than three times more likely to develop fatal coronary heart disease than were those who answered no.

- Do strange people or places make you afraid?
- Are you considered a nervous person?
- Are you constantly keyed up and jittery?
- Do you often become suddenly scared for no good reason?
- Do you often break out in a cold sweat?

Source: Kawachi et al. (1994).

---

terol are known to increase the risk of CHD, they do not by themselves seem to be sufficient to cause the disease. Studies suggest that psychological and social variables may be contributory factors that produce certain pathogenic physiological changes. Psychosocial factors can directly affect physiological processes that influence blood coagulation and increases in blood pressure, thereby increasing the thickness of artery walls and contributing to CHD (Harenstam, Theorell, & Kaijser, 2000; Karmarck et al., 2004).

For example, women who reported high job stress or who perceived their relationships with their bosses to be poor had higher fibrinogen levels than those found among other female employees. Fibrinogen, a blood-clotting compound, may contribute to coronary heart disease by contributing to atherosclerosis and by participating in the formation of blood clots (M. Davis, Mathews, Meilahn, & Kiss, 1995). Among older women, depression is significantly related to cardiovascular disease (Wassertheil-Smoller et al., 2004). Thus emotional states may increase susceptibility to developing CHD. Some evidence also exists that high levels of anxiety may be related to incidents of fatal heart attacks. In a thirty-two-year prospective study on 2,280 men with and without coronary heart disease, those with anxiety symptoms, as measured by a five-item questionnaire, were more than three times as likely as those without such symptoms to eventually die of sudden cardiac arrest. (See Table 7.2 for questions used in the anxiety questionnaire.) It is possible that anxiety may hasten the development of coronary heart disease and may produce coronary spasms or ventricular arrhythmias that lead to fatal cardiac arrest (Kawachi, Sparrow, Vonkonas, & Weiss, 1994). After the development of CHD, psychological states such as depression, self-efficacy, or optimism can influence the recovery process (Shnek et al., 2001).

Friedman and Rosenman (1974) identified a behavior pattern, called *Type A behavior,* that they believed was associated with increased risk of heart attack. The pattern involves aggressiveness, competitiveness, hostility, time pressure, and constant striving for achievement. Although evidence initially suggested that the Type A personality was related to coronary heart disease, recent research suggests something different. Researchers are reexamining the picture of a harried businessperson—competitive, hostile, under strict time constraints, and doing several things at once. Julkunen, Idanpaan-Heikkila, and Saarinen (1993) reviewed the qualities of the Type A personality that might be related to CHD and found that the only significant risk factor was irritability and hostility, either openly expressed or suppressed. A number of other researchers (Houston, Babyak, Chesney, Black, & Ragland, 1997; Mann & James, 1998; R. Williams et al., 1988; Wood, 1986) reached similar conclusions. The Type A behavior pattern apparently includes both benign factors and factors that place individuals at risk. If hostility is the important element, programs that focus on benign factors, such as helping people slow down and enjoy life, may not be helpful in averting the risk of CHD. The current emphasis is on the anger-hostility-aggression (AHA) syndrome in CHD (Richards, Alvarenga, & Hof, 2000).

Several possibilities exist that may explain the relationship between hostility and coronary heart disease. First, hostility may increase the hostile person's cardiovascular responsivity and physiology, subsequently increasing the risk of developing CHD. At least one study (Miller et al., 1998) supports this view. In that study, individuals who scored high on hostility showed exaggerated cardiovascular reactivity to a stressor (verbal harassment) compared with participants who were low on hostility. Thus hostility may lead to damaging

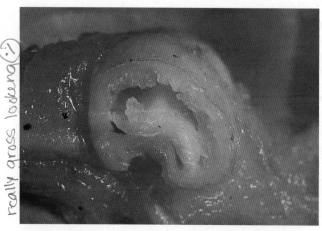

really gross looking ?

Stress and Coronary Heart Disease Stress may produce physiological changes that promote plaque buildup on the wall of the coronary artery, contributing to coronary heart disease. In this picture, the artery is almost entirely blocked.

physiological responses. The experience of strong anger in young healthy males when they were frustrated or treated unfairly was related to elevations in serum cholesterol and low-density lipoproteins, both of which have been found to increase the risk of developing CHD (Richards et al., 2000). Hostility in children and adolescents has also been related to elevated lipids and blood pressure (Raikkonen, Matthews, & Salomon, 2003).

A second possibility is that hostile individuals may have health-damaging lifestyles. They may sleep less, have less healthy diets, exercise less, or smoke and consume alcohol excessively. One sample of individuals with high hostility ratings consumed more salt than did those with low hostility ratings (Miller et al., 1998). A third possibility is that hostility could be an individual's reaction to having a particular disease rather than being a causal factor. Patient groups with serious diseases other than coronary heart disease have also scored higher on hostility (Ranchor, Sanderman, Bouma, Buunk, & van den Heuvel, 1997). One study has even found a relationship between hostility and other diseases, but not with coronary heart disease (Ranchor et al., 1997).

A final area of concern is that much of the research on hostility and CHD has been done on men. There is some evidence that hostility measures do not correlate with cardiovascular reactivity in women in the same way that they do in men. Whereas high hostility is associated with higher resting blood pressure in men, women high in hostility show a lower resting blood pressure than men do (K. Davidson, Hall, & MacGregor, 1997). Because of socialization differences, hostility may have different health implications for men and women.

Stress and Hypertension

On September 11, 2001, many survivors of the World Trade Center attack recounted the terror they felt during the attack and their fight for survival. Onlookers were also horrified to see people jump to their deaths in attempting to escape from the fire. The survivors and onlookers went through a traumatic event that produced severe physiological reactions. What was happening to them?

Although the following case does not compare to the trauma sustained by survivors and witnesses of the September 11 attacks, it does show how stress affects the human body dramatically when facing anxiety-provoking situations.

On October 19, 1987, the stock market drastically dropped 508 points. By chance, a forty-eight-year-old stockbroker was wearing a device measuring stress in the work environment on that day. The instrument measured his pulse every fifteen minutes. At the beginning of the day, his pulse was sixty-four beats per minute and his blood pressure was 132 over 87 (both rates within the normal range). As stock prices fell dramatically, the man's physiological system surged in the other direction. His heart rate increased to eighty-four beats per minute and his blood pressure hit a dangerous 181 over 105. His pulse was "pumping adrenaline, flooding his arteries, and maybe slowly killing himself in the process." (Tierney, 1988)

These events illustrate the impact of a stressor on blood pressure, the measurement of the force of blood against the walls of the arteries and veins. Many people who experienced the stock market plunge after the terrorist attacks on the World Trade Center or who survived the exploding and collapsing building may also have shown dangerously high levels of blood pressure. We all experience a transient physiological response to stressors, but in some people, it develops into a chronic condition called **essential hypertension,** or high blood pressure of 140 (systolic) over 90 (diastolic) or higher. Systolic blood pressure appears to be a better predictor of cardiovascular problems than diastolic blood pressure (Mallik, 2001). Essential hypertension is found in about 23 percent of the U.S. adult population. Over 50 million have high blood pressure that needs treatment. However, 30 percent are unaware of their hypertension, and more than 40 percent are not being treated (Chobanian et al., 2003). It is most prevalent in the African American population and the aged. Three-quarters of women and two-thirds of men over the age of seventy-five have hypertension (National Center for Health Statistics, 2001b). In older individuals, the disorder is often the result of the loss of elasticity in the aorta and large arteries. In other cases, no specific physiological cause can be determined. Figure 7.3 shows some gender and ethnic comparisons of hypertension among adults. Chronic hypertension may lead to arteriosclerosis (narrowing of arteries) and to increased risk of strokes and heart attacks (Everson et al., 1999; National Center for Health Statistics, 2001b).

A number of studies suggest that stressors, emotional states, and hypertension may be related. Individuals placed under stress experience significant increases in blood pressure (Bishop et al., 2003; Smith, Ruiz, & Uchino, 2000). Individuals with high blood pressure have exhibited exaggerated reactions to a stressor, compared with their counterparts with normal or borderline high blood pressure (Tuomisto, 1997). Living in crowded neighborhoods and being in a stressful occupation are associated with high blood pressure (Ely & Mostardi, 1986; Fleming, Baum, Davidson, Rectanus, & McArdle, 1987). A familial component may also be involved. Men who have both a family history of hypertension and normal blood pressure showed exaggerated cardiovascular responses to stressors (Semenchuk & Larkin, 1993). Hypertensive individuals with depression were more than twice as likely as nondepressed individuals to develop heart failure (8.1 percent versus 3.2 percent) during a five-year follow-up (Abramson, Berger, Krubholz, & Vaccarino, 2001).

In addition to studies that link the presence of stressors to the presence of hypertension, others have shown a connection between reducing stress and lowering blood pressure. Reducing stress by relaxing, both at home and at work, significantly lowers blood pressure. Having social support also reduces the impact of stressors (Christenfeld et al., 1997; Gerin, Milner, Chawla, & Pickering, 1995; Gerin, Pieper, Levy, & Pickering, 1992; Uchino & Garvey, 1997). Taken together, the two types of studies indicate that stress has a definite impact on blood pressure, and they support the contention that people who suffer from chronic stress may be at risk for developing hypertension.

Along with exposure to stressors, emotional reactions may also contribute to hypertension (Mann & James, 1998; Patterson, Matthews, Allen, & Owens, 1995). Blood pressure tends to be temporarily higher when people are angry or anxious than when they are relaxed and contented. Researchers are trying to identify emotional patterns that produce a chronic elevation. As with other disorders, there is evidence that angry cognitions or thoughts play a role in hypertension (Davison, Williams, Nezami, Bice, & DeQuattro, 1991).

Gender may also be involved in the development of hypertension. In a study by Lai and Linden (1992), men and women were evaluated on emotional expressiveness and classified as either "anger in" (suppressing anger) or "anger out" (expressing anger). They were then exposed to verbal harassment and either allowed to release their anger or inhibited from doing so. Men displayed greater cardiovascular reactivity to the harassment than did women. The opportunity to release anger facilitated heart rate and diastolic (blood pressure when the heart is at rest) recovery in men but not in women. Women with "anger in" tendencies showed better systolic (blood pressure when the heart

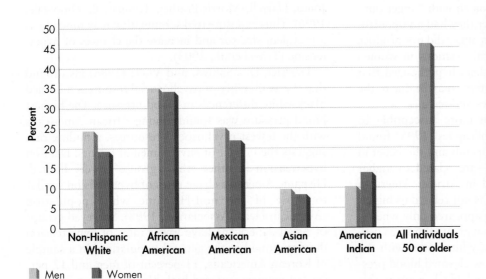

FIGURE 7.3 Gender and Ethnic Differences in Hypertension Among U.S. Adults The highest prevalence (percentage) of chronic high blood pressure occurs most frequently among African Americans and among all individuals over the age of fifty. Women tend to score somewhat lower than other groups. Biological, lifestyle, and psychological factors have been implicated in the gender and ethnic differences in hypertension.

Source: Data from Burt et al. (1995); American Heart Association (1998).

Stress and Hypertension On September 11, 2001, many survivors of the World Trade Center recounted the terror they felt during the attack and their fight for survival. Onlookers were also horrified to see people jump to their deaths; many people barely escaped the collapsing building. The survivors and observers went through a traumatic event that produced severe physiological reactions. What was happening to them?

is contracting) recovery than women with "anger out" tendencies, regardless of whether they had an opportunity to express anger. Holding in anger did not produce the strong negative physiological reactions in women that it did in men. The researchers hypothesized that these differences in recovery patterns may be due to the differential socialization of males and females.

Certain individuals may be more susceptible to stress on the job. Light and colleagues (1995) found that two variables—a high-status job and the belief in hard work to achieve success—are related to higher blood pressure in women and in African American men. A high-status job alone was not related to higher blood pressure. The correlation appeared only when it was combined with the belief that great effort was necessary for success. Interestingly, white males with the same characteristics did not show elevated blood pressure. It may be that women and black men in this

study believed that they had to overcome barriers and hostility to maintain their high-status positions.

Ethnic Factors in Hypertension African Americans have higher mean blood pressure levels and higher rates of hypertension than their white counterparts. Over a seven-year period, black youths in one study showed consistently greater systolic and diastolic blood pressure than their white counterparts (Murphy, Stoney, Alpert, & Walker, 1995). Black men also show greater increases in systolic and diastolic blood pressure in reaction to cold water than white men do. Such findings have been taken as evidence of possible genetic influences on the prevalence of hypertension in the two groups, possibly manifested as differences in sympathetic nervous system activity. But these studies are inconclusive, and the degree of genetic contribution to hypertension remains an unanswered question. We do know that increased awareness of the disorder and better treatment have substantially reduced hypertension among African Americans and have slightly reduced rates for white women. However, hypertension is still more prevalent among black Americans than among white Americans (National Center for Health Statistics, 2001b).

Although genetic and other biological explanations may explain the high rate of hypertension in African Americans, another line of research supports a psychological explanation. In one study, African Americans who reported experiencing and accepting discrimination had higher blood pressure than those who reported that they challenged discriminatory situations (Krieger & Sidney, 1996). In another study, African Americans who watched videotapes or imagined depictions of social situations involving racism showed increases in heart rate and blood pressure (Fang & Myers, 2001; D. Jones, Harrell, Morris-Prather, Thomas, & Omowale, 1996). Thus exposure to discrimination may function as a prevalent stressor and increase the chances of hypertension (Troxel et al., 2003).

Dressler, Dos Santos, and Viteri (1986) also found that the availability of psychosocial resources modified black-white differences in blood pressure. The highest blood pressure was found among African Americans with the fewest psychosocial resources, a finding that suggests the impact of environmental factors. Data on hypertension in other ethnic groups is very limited. Hispanic Americans have rates of hypertension similar to those of the non-Hispanic white population (American Heart Association, 1998). Surveyed groups of Asian Americans have lower rates of hypertension than are found in the general population. In a sample of Korean Americans, 11 percent of men and 12 percent of women reported high blood pressure (Kang et

accompanied by visual effects, such as sparklers flashing across her visual field. The symptoms would last for up to three days. (Adler & Rogers, 1999)

Frank Weeden describes his headaches in the following manner: "It feels like someone walked up to me, took a screwdriver and jammed it up in my right eye and kept digging it around for 20 minutes." (Linn, 2004, A1)

Headaches are among the most common psychophysiological complaints, accounting for more than 18 million visits to medical practitioners each year (J. Jones, 1995). The pain of a headache can vary in intensity from dull to excruciating. It is unclear whether the different forms of headaches (migraine, tension, and cluster) are produced by different psychophysiological mechanisms or whether they merely differ in severity. Compared with people who are headache free, individuals who have headaches show greater sensitivity to pain in body areas other than the head (Marlowe, 1992). Although we discuss migraine, tension, and cluster headaches separately, the same person can be susceptible to more than one type of headache. (Figure 7.4 illustrates some differences among the three types.) A number of conditions have been associated with the onset of headaches, including stress, negative emotions, sexual harassment, poor body posture, eyestrain, exercise, too much or too little sleep, exposure to smoke or strong odors, the weather, temperature changes, and changes in altitude (Goldenhar, Swanson, Hurrell, Ruder, & Deddens, 1998; P. Martin & Seneviratne, 1997; Silberstein, 1998).

In an experiment, Martin and Seneviratne (1997) attempted to verify that food deprivation and negative emotions can precipitate headaches. For nineteen hours, they either withheld food from thirty-eight women and eighteen men who suffered from migraine or tension headaches or exposed them to a stressor that produced negative emotions (difficult-to-solve anagrams). The findings supported the view that the two conditions can induce headaches. Individuals who had been deprived of food or subjected to stress reported both more headaches and headaches of greater intensity than individuals who had been allowed to eat or were not exposed to stress.

Migraine Headaches Constriction of cranial arteries, followed by dilation of the cerebral blood vessels resulting in moderate to severe pain, are the distinguishing features of **migraine headache**. Anything that affects the size of these blood vessels, which are connected to sensitive nerves, can produce a headache. Thus certain chemicals, such as sodium nitrate (found

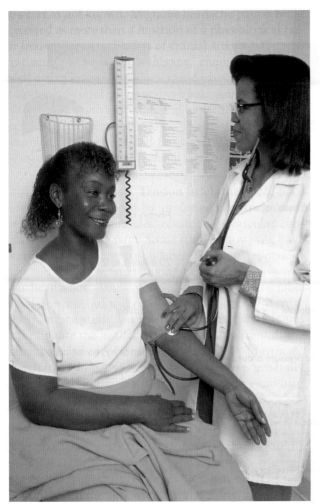

Ethnicity and Hypertension African Americans have much higher rates of hypertension than their white counterparts, whereas Asian Americans and American Indians have much lower rates. What factors may account for the large between-group differences?

al., 1997). Information is very sparse on the prevalence of hypertension among Pacific Islanders, American Indians, or Alaskan natives. Among the Navajo, 23 percent of men and 14 percent of women had hypertension (Mendlein et al., 1997). Because the incidence and prevalence of obesity are increasing in many ethnic groups, the rate of hypertension will probably also increase.

Migraine, Tension, and Cluster Headaches

A forty-two-year-old woman described her headache as a throbbing that pulsed with every heartbeat and occurred during every menstrual period. The pain was

FIGURE 7.5 An Asthma Attack   Asthma attacks and deaths have increased dramatically during the past fifteen years.

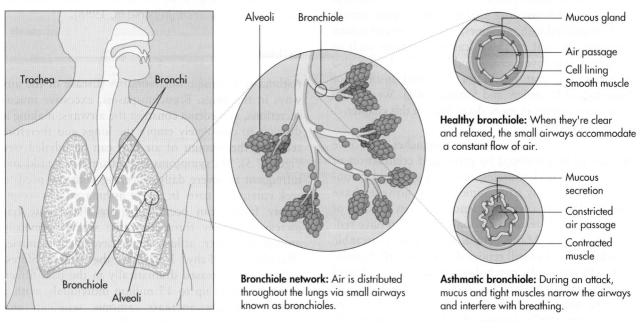

Alveoli   Bronchiole

Trachea

Bronchi

Bronchiole

Alveoli

Mucous gland
Air passage
Cell lining
Smooth muscle

Healthy bronchiole: When they're clear and relaxed, the small airways accommodate a constant flow of air.

Mucous secretion
Constricted air passage
Contracted muscle

Bronchiole network: Air is distributed throughout the lungs via small airways known as bronchioles.

Asthmatic bronchiole: During an attack, mucus and tight muscles narrow the airways and interfere with breathing.

When the respiratory system is working properly, the air we breathe passes in and out of the lungs through a network of airways (above, left). But for people with asthma, even a minor irritant will set off an immune response that can shut down the airways.

Source: Cowley & Underwood (1997, p. 61).

cockroaches) may be responsible. Rosenstreich, Eggleston, and Kattan (1997) examined 476 children with asthma who lived in inner cities. They found that 23 percent were allergic to pets, 35 percent to dust mites, and 37 percent to cockroaches. Allergy to cockroaches had the highest association with emergency room treatment, hospitalization, and school absences in these children. A program to reduce environmental allergens within the houses of children with asthma was associated with a reduction in symptoms (Morgan et al., 2004). Although early exposure to allergens may predispose a person to the development of asthma, it has also been proposed that decreased exposure to infectious diseases has lowered resistance to this disorder. There is a lower prevalence rate among those who have multiple siblings or who attend daycare, where there is an increased risk for infections (Woodruff & Fahy, 2001).

Although pollutants may be responsible for the increase in asthma cases, psychological factors seem to be important in producing attacks. Children who have parents with asthma are more likely to develop this condition if their family environment is characterized as being negative than children with asthmatic parents who did not provide poor or conflictual parenting (McCarthy, 2002). Emotional arousal has been found to be associated with decreased size of the airways of the lung (Isenberg, Lehrer, & Hochron, 1992) or feel-

ings of breathlessness in individuals with asthma (Rietveld, Everaerd, & van Beest, 2000). In one study (Fritz, Rubenstein, & Lewiston, 1987), psychological factors such as depression and family conflicts were found to be the main causes in 18 percent of individuals with this disorder. However, asthma in a child might be the cause of family conflict rather than being the result of family problems (Chen, Bloomberg, Fisher, & Strunk, 2003). Deaths among children with asthma have been associated with family dysfunction, poor adherence to medication, and poor self-care (Lehrer, Sargunaraj, & Hochron, 1992).

In most cases, however, physical and psychological causes interact. In the following case, a teenager with asthma used her attacks to influence family members in an intricate interplay of physical and psychological factors.

Kathy was a fifteen-year-old girl whose asthma was diagnosed at age six. ... Early on, emotional reactions were identified as important triggers to her episodes, along with exercise and infections. ... Her biologic parents had a stormy relationship that included the father's physical abuse of the mother during their frequent drinking bouts, numerous separations, and financial insecurity. ... Her asthma also served to interrupt

TABLE 7.3	A Psychodynamic Etiology: The Unconscious Correlates to Certain Physical Disorders
Disorder	**Unconscious Correlates**
Asthma	The person has an unresolved dependency on his or her mother, who is perceived as cold; fears separation; or needs to be protected. The person feels guilty about the dependency needs. Instead of crying, he or she develops a wheeze that can develop into respiratory disorder.
Hypertension	The person experiences a struggle against unconscious hostile impulses and fluctuates from excessive control to outbursts of aggression. Repressing these hostile feelings leads to chronic blood pressure elevation.
Arthritis	The person inhibits hostile impulses or has experienced parental restrictions of freedom of movement. Developing arthritis allows this individual to avoid physically expressing aggression.

Source: Adapted from Alexander (1950).

parental fights, and Kathy consciously used her asthma in her role as a peacemaker. ... The asthmatic symptoms were ... associated with helplessness and extreme anxiety. (Fritz et al., 1987, pp. 253–254)

Perspectives on Etiology

As we mentioned earlier, psychologists are becoming increasingly aware that single-cause models of psychophysiological illness are inadequate. Illness results from interactions at the cellular, organismic, interpersonal, group, and environmental levels (Drossman, 1998). However, different theoretical perspectives have offered a variety of insights in attempting to answer the following questions: Why does stress produce a physical disorder in some people but not in others? If a disorder does develop in someone experiencing emotional distress, what determines what the psychophysiological illness will be? Innate, developmental, and acquired characteristics certainly interact, but the nature and contribution of each are not well understood. In this section we discuss different perspectives on cause—none of which adequately accounts for all the factors involved.

Psychodynamic Perspective   Psychoanalysts have developed several formulations to explain physical disorders associated with psychological factors. According to these formulations, each type of psychophysiological disorder is produced by a specific form of unconscious conflict.

Alexander (1950) believed that an early unresolved childhood conflict produces an emotional response that is reactivated in adulthood. For example, the inhibition of aggressive feelings may produce hypertension or other cardiovascular disorders. According to this hypothesis, aggression and dependency needs are the basis for most of the psychophys-

iological disorders. The expression of dependency needs increases activity of the parasympathetic division of the autonomic nervous system. Chronic activation of this division produces such disorders as diarrhea and colitis. If feelings of anger predominate, the energy-expending sympathetic nervous system is activated, which may result in hypertension, migraine headaches, or arthritis.

A list of the unconscious complexes associated with a few disorders is given in Table 7.3. Although Alexander's theory is impressive in breadth and specificity, his propositions have not been experimentally supported. However, the idea that certain emotions or personality dynamics are related to specific disorders has received some support (Mann & James, 1998; P. Martin & Seneviratne, 1997; Ranchor et al., 1997; Schulz et al., 1996; Spiro, Aldwin, Ward, & Mroczek, 1995).

Biological Perspective   Some evidence points to a genetic base for the development of psychophysiological disorders. For example, migraine headaches appear to run in families and to have a genetic component (Silberstein, 1998). Additionally, African Americans as a group are at risk for hypertension. A modest significant correlation on cardiovascular reactivity has been found between monozygotic (identical) twins. Presumably a greater reactivity could contribute to the development of hypertension and coronary heart disease (T. Smith et al., 1987). Children with one asthmatic parent have a 20 percent chance of developing asthma. The probability increases to 50 percent with two asthmatic parents (Mrazek, 1993).

In addition, three other biological explanations for psychophysiological disorders have been suggested: somatic weakness, autonomic response specificity, and general adaptation syndrome.

The *somatic weakness hypothesis* is a commonsense explanation for the development of particular psychophysiological disorders. This view suggests that congenital factors or a vulnerability acquired through physical trauma or illness may predispose a particular organ to develop irregularities or to become weakened structurally by stressors. Therefore, the particular physiological disorder that develops is determined by whichever system is the "weakest link" in the body (Hovanitz & Wander, 1990). For example, 80 percent of people with asthma in one study had experienced previous respiratory infections, compared with only 30 percent of those in control groups (Rees, 1964). The infection may have weakened the respiratory system and made it more vulnerable to the development of asthma. Logical as it seems, the somatic weakness hypothesis is difficult to validate because it is not yet possible to measure the relative strengths of the different physical systems in the human body before an organ weakness appears.

Closely related to the somatic weakness hypothesis is the concept of *autonomic response specificity*—the hypothesis that some individuals respond to different stressors with the same physiological response. For example, an individual who constantly shows exaggerated cardiovascular reactions to a number of different situations may be more likely to develop hypertension. Tuomisto (1997) did find that, when exposed to different stressors, individuals with hypertension displayed an exaggerated reactivity in blood pressure compared with individuals without hypertension. The specific response an individual displays is believed to be largely inherited but may have been affected by a previously acquired vulnerability (Steptoe, 1991). Autonomic response specificity has been demonstrated experimentally. College students subjected to a variety of stressors (from cold water to tough mathematics problems) tended to show stable and consistent idiosyncratic patterns of autonomic activity in the different stress-producing conditions. That is, a person who showed a rise in blood pressure when reacting to one type of stressor showed a similar reaction to other types of stressors (Lacey, Bateman, & Van Lehn, 1953). Similar consistency was found in people who suffered migraine headaches, but not in a control group of people who did not get migraines (M. Cohen, Rickles, & McArthur, 1978). The suggestion that these physiological responses are innate is supported by researchers who observed that distinctive autonomic behavior patterns in infants tended to persist throughout early childhood (Thomas, Chess, & Birch, 1968).

The general adaptation syndrome, consisting of an alarm stage, a resistance stage, and an exhaustion stage, was discussed earlier in the chapter. According to

Selye (1956), continued stress after the final stage may result in diseases of adaptation such as hypertension. Unfortunately, this formulation is very general and does not explain why hypertension does not occur in all people who experience long-term stress. Nor does it specify which psychophysiological disorder will develop. Combining this theory with the somatic weakness or autonomic response specificity hypotheses may be one way to deal with such conceptual problems.

The Behavioral Perspective   As noted, classical conditioning may be involved in the psychophysiological disorders. The conditioning of neutral stimuli can elicit or activate a physiological response through generalization, as discussed in the chapter on assessment and classification of abnormal behavior. The greater the number of stimuli that can produce a specific physical reaction, the greater the probability that a chronic condition will develop.

Psychophysiological reactions can generalize to such stimuli as words, thoughts, and odors. Cough sensitivity of adolescents with asthma varied as a function of the situation they were in. The researchers hypothesized that patients with asthma cough more in situations that were associated with their condition (Rietveld, van Beest, & Everaerd, 2000). This view was supported in a study in which researchers used associative conditioning to evoke respiratory responses to different stimuli, such as odors (Van den Bergh, Stegen, & Van de Woestijne, 1997). In another study, the bronchial reactions of forty patients with asthma were compared with those of a normal control group. The patients were told they were being exposed to different concentrations of substances to which they were allergic; in fact, they were exposed only to neutral saline solution. Nearly half (nineteen) of the patients with asthma displayed bronchial constriction (a symptom of asthmatic attacks), and twelve developed full-blown asthma attacks. None of the participants in the control group showed any of these symptoms (Luparello, Lyons, Bleecker, & McFadden, 1968). The experimenters hypothesized that principles of classical conditioning could account for their finding. The thought of inhaling an allergic substance had become a conditioned stimulus capable of inducing asthmatic symptoms or attacks. In a review of twenty studies involving 427 persons with asthma, more than one-third of the persons with asthma were found to be "reactors," that is, they showed significant bronchial effects following suggestion (Isenberg et al., 1992).

The classical conditioning position alone cannot, however, account for the cause of the disorders discussed in this section. Physiological reactions must occur before other stimuli can be conditioned to them and before generalization can occur. Hence, classical conditioning may explain the continuation or increased severity of a disorder, but not its origin.

Although theorists first believed that the autonomic nervous system is not under operant control, later findings demonstrated that involuntary processes such as heart rate, blood pressure, and a variety of other functions can be influenced by reinforcement. These findings have important implications for the origin and treatment of psychophysiological disorders.

The precise role of operant conditioning in the cause of the disorders discussed here is still not clear. There is support for the contention that autonomic processes can be altered through reinforcement. But there is also controversy about the magnitude of the changes that are possible.

Sociocultural Perspectives Conflicts with cultural expectations appear also to result in physiological symptoms. Samoans, for example, have a culture that stresses rigid control of behaviors, including strict discipline for children, control of anger for females, and suppression of emotions in adults. Steele and McGarvey (1997) hypothesized that the Samoan traditional pattern in which women were expected to suppress their emotions could conflict with the expanded roles expected by modern young women, resulting in increases in blood pressure. In support of their hypothesis, the investigators found an interesting contrast: higher blood pressure was related to an inhibition of anger in young women but to an outward expression of anger in older women. The roles or behavior patterns the women were socialized to (modern or traditional) appears to influence whether the expression of anger increased blood pressure.

Cultural factors are also implicated in a study of Japanese persons living in Japan, Hawaii, and California, in which researchers found the highest mortality rate from coronary heart disease among those living in California and the lowest among those living in Japan. This difference was not accounted for by differences in the risk factors for CHD discussed earlier in this chapter. In trying to decide what was responsible for the variation in mortality rates, the researchers compared Japanese immigrants who had maintained a traditional lifestyle with those who had acculturated (adopted the habits and attitudes prevalent in their new home). The CHD rate for acculturated Japanese individuals was five times greater than that for those who had retained their traditional values (Marmot & Syme, 1976). Perhaps breaking close social and community ties, which is part of the acculturation process, promoted a greater vulnerability to the disease.

Treatment of Psychophysiological Disorders

Treatment programs for psychophysiological disorders generally consist of both medical treatment for the physical symptoms and psychological therapy to eliminate stress and anxiety. **Behavioral medicine** comprises a number of disciplines that study social, psychological, and lifestyle influences on health. This combined approach provides a wide array of approaches to these

Maintaining Tradition and Reducing Risk—It Works for Some Japanese Americans who maintain traditional lifestyles have a lower rate of coronary heart disease than those who have acculturated. The difference does not appear to be due to diet or other investigated risk factors. What reasons can you come up with to explain the findings?

disorders, with mainly positive results. Two of the dominant psychological approaches are stress management and anxiety management programs, which usually include either relaxation training or biofeedback. The concept of combined therapies is illustrated in the following case:

Jerry R. is a thirty-three-year-old male who has always taken pride in the vigor with which he attacks everything he does. He worries about keeping slim, so he exercises at a health spa three nights a week. He was shocked to discover, during a routine physical exam, that he has borderline high blood pressure.

His physician recommended that he take steps to lower his blood pressure by reducing his intake of salt, caffeine, and alcohol. Because coronary heart disease runs in Jerry's family, the physician also recommended that Jerry decrease his cholesterol intake by reducing the amount of eggs, saturated fats, and whole milk in his diet. He commended Jerry for having given up smoking five months previously.

Finally, Jerry was urged to become active in a stress management program geared toward lowering his blood pressure and preventing coronary heart disease. Although the effectiveness of these programs is somewhat controversial, Jerry's physician believes Jerry has more to gain than to lose by participating in a course of biofeedback and relaxation training.

The success of combined treatment programs suggests that the psychological approach to the treatment of certain physical disorders is receiving more attention. Relaxation training, biofeedback, and cognitive-behavioral interventions are emerging as the primary stress management techniques of behavioral medicine. They are used in treating all the psychophysiological disorders described in this chapter.

Relaxation Training

Relaxation training is a therapeutic technique in which a person acquires the ability to relax the muscles of the body in almost any circumstance. Current programs are typically modeled after Jacobson's (1938, 1967) progressive relaxation training. Imagine that you are a patient who is beginning the training. You are instructed to concentrate on one set of muscles at a time—first tensing them and then relaxing them. First you clench your fists as tightly as possible for approximately ten seconds, then you release them. As you release your tightened muscles, you are asked to focus on the sensation of warmth and looseness in your hands. You practice this tightening and relaxing cycle several times before proceeding to the next muscle

group, in your lower arms. After each muscle group has received individual attention in tensing and relaxing, the trainer asks you to tighten and then relax your entire body. The emphasis throughout the procedure is on the contrast between the feelings produced during tensing and those produced during relaxing. For a novice, the entire exercise lasts about thirty minutes.

With practice, you eventually learn to relax the muscles without first having to tense them. You can then use the technique to relax at almost any time during the day, even when only a few moments are available for the exercise. A relaxation-based treatment was found to be effective in producing "clinically significant" reductions in headache activity among recurrent headache sufferers. The program was unique in that it was conducted over the Internet and through e-mail. Participants received instructions for applied relaxation and its application in stressful situations. Although dropout rates were high, a large number of participants appeared to benefit from a minimal-therapist-contact and self-help-focused intervention (Strom, Pettersson, & Anderson, 2000).

Biofeedback

In **biofeedback training,** the client is taught to *voluntarily* control some physiological function, such as heart rate or blood pressure. During training, the client receives second-by-second information (feedback) regarding the activity of the organ or function of interest. For someone attempting to lower high blood pressure, for example, the feedback might be actual blood pressure readings, which might be presented visually on a screen or as some auditory signal transmitted through a set of headphones. The biofeedback device enables the patient to learn his or her own idiosyncratic method for controlling the particular physiological function. Eventually the patient learns to use that method without benefit of the feedback device.

A twenty-three-year-old male patient was found to have a resting heart rate that varied between 95 and 120 beats per minute. He reported that his symptoms first appeared during his last year in high school, when his episodes of tachycardia were associated with apprehension over exams. The patient came into treatment concerned that his high heart rate might lead to a serious cardiac condition.

The treatment consisted of eight sessions of biofeedback training. The patient's heart rate was monitored, and he was provided with both a visual and an auditory feedback signal. After the treatment period, his heart rate had stabilized and was within normal limits. One

Cognitive-Behavioral Interventions

Because hostility is associated with hypertension, cognitive-behavioral programs have been developed to reduce the expression of this emotion. In one study, individuals with hypertension participated in a six-week anger management program (Larkin & Zayfert, 1996). When initially exposed to confrontational role-playing situations, they experienced sharp rises in blood pressure. The participants learned to relax by using muscle relaxation techniques and to change their thoughts about confrontational situations. They also received assertiveness training to learn appropriate ways of expressing disagreements. After the various types of training, their blood pressure was significantly reduced when they again participated in confrontational role-playing scenes.

An increasing number of stress management programs are including a cognitive-behavioral component, often in the form of self-instructional techniques and cognitive restructuring. In one study (P. Bennett et al., 1991), Type A persons with hypertension were taught to evaluate and change the impact of stressors and to understand how their Type A behavior contributes to hypertension. They learned to change their thoughts to reduce their emotional reactions. This approach seems to augment the effectiveness of other components in stress management in dealing with hypertension (Davison et al., 1991).

The discovery or knowledge that one has a life-threatening disease can affect the individual's belief system. The world may be seen as unfair, leading to feelings of depression or avoidance and an inability to process the disease experience. Social-cognitive processing (SCP) approaches attempt to help the individual process and find validation and meaning in the experience. In a study of seventy women cancer survivors, the type of cognitive process was found to predict adjustment to cancer (Cordova, Cunningham, Carlson, & Andrykowski, 2001). Those who were unable to cognitively process their diseases because of invalidation ("When I talk about cancer, my husband tells me I'm living in the past") or because of discomfort ("It's difficult to share with those you love, as they are scared too"; p. 709) reported more depressive symptoms. In contrast, women who reported being able to talk about cancer were less depressed and better adjusted. Similar findings were reported in another study. Women with breast cancer who were able to discuss and manage the emotions associated with having the disease showed improved adjustment and health status. The women missed fewer appointments, were healthier, and reported less distress than women who did not employ emotional coping (Stanton et al., 2000). With many diseases, having the

Controlling Physiological Responses Meditation is associated with a relaxed bodily state produced by minimizing distractions and focusing on a positive image, mantra, or word. This process has been associated with the reduction in the level of stress hormones and the development of a sense of control. It has been found to be helpful in the treatment of hypertension and headaches.

year later, his heart rate averaged 73 beats per minute. The patient reported that he had learned to control his heart rate during stressful situations such as job interviews, by both relaxing and concentrating on reducing the heart rate. (Janssen, 1983)

Biofeedback is essentially an operant conditioning technique in which the feedback serves as reinforcement. It has been used to help people lower their heart rates and decrease their blood pressure during stressful situations (Nakao et al., 1997; Shahidi & Salmon, 1992), treat migraine and tension headaches (Holroyd, France, Cordingley, & Rockicki, 1995; Hovanitz & Wander, 1990), decrease the need for medication in asthma (Lehrer et al., 2004), reduce muscle tension (Gamble & Elder, 1983), and redirect blood flow (Reading & Mohr, 1976). Biofeedback and verbal reinforcement were used to help children with asthma control their respiratory functioning (Kahn, Staerk, & Bonk, 1974).

opportunity to express fears, to cognitively process beliefs, and to develop adaptive strategies appears to improve patients' feelings of well-being and physical health. Positive coping is related to health-promoting changes such as increases in physical activity, improvements in diet, and reduction of substance use among individuals diagnosed with HIV.

Cognitive strategies to improve coping skills and to manage stress have also been effective in improving both physiological functioning and psychological distress in HIV seropositive men (Cruess et al., 2000). Among patients with asthma, engaging in three sessions of writing about a trauma ("write about the most stressful experience in your life") significantly improved lung function as opposed to those who only wrote about time management (Stone et al., 2000).

Certainly, both psychological and biological processes are involved in all diseases. In some disorders and in some people, biological factors exert the primary influence, whereas in others, psychological factors predominate. Because so many variables are involved, science cannot predict which person will develop a psychophysiological disorder and under what conditions.

Although much is known about the psychophysiological disorders, a great deal is still to be learned. Psychologists in behavioral medicine are seeking to decrease a person's vulnerability to physical problems by suggesting changes in lifestyle, attitudes, and perceptions. Attention is also directed toward altering the course of an illness after it has occurred. The field of behavioral medicine will continue to receive greater attention from psychologists. We are only beginning to understand the relationship between psychological factors and physical illnesses.

SUMMARY

What are psychophysiological disorders, and how do they differ from conversion disorders?

- Psychophysiological disorders are any physical disorders that:
  - demonstrate a temporal relationship between psychological factors and the course of a physical illness
  - interfere with treatment
  - constitute additional health risk factors
- They are different from conversion disorders in that actual physical processes or conditions are involved.

What kinds of stressors affect physical health, and why doesn't everyone develop an illness when exposed to them?

- Stressors may be large or relatively weak.
- Several models have been created to explain the development of physical illness.
- The general adaptation model describes the body's reaction when exposed to stressors.
- If the stressors are long lasting, the body's defenses may be overwhelmed, and a disease will develop.
- The life-change model is based on the view that any changes, even positive ones, can produce illness if there are too many of them.
- Neither model explains why some people will not develop an illness even though they may be exposed to stressors.
- The transaction model emphasizes the subjective interpretation of stressors by an individual.

- The development of a disease is dependent on the way stressors are viewed.

How do stressors (both physical and psychosocial) affect the immune system? How do factors such as personality and mood states influence the course of an illness such as AIDS or cancer?

- Immunological functioning seems to be affected by physical and psychological stress, both short term and long term.
- A variety of factors, such as anxiety, divorce, and bereavement, can produce poor immunological responses. The causal direction of this relationship is unclear.
- Some research supports the suggestion that psychological stress can influence the initiation and course of certain infectious diseases through changes in immune functioning.
- Other research, particularly that focusing on AIDS, offers only limited support.
- Although stress decreases the ability of animals to reject injected cancer cells, whether psychological variables can influence the development of cancer in human beings is not known.
- Personality or mood states may also affect the course of a disease through changes in immune functioning, health habits, or amount of social support.
- *Cancer* is a term describing a variety of disease processes, which may vary in their susceptibility to emotions. Most studies are short term and retrospective, and they do not address the development of spontaneous cancer.

What is the evidence that illnesses such as coronary heart disease, hypertension, headaches, and asthma are affected by emotional states, and how are the emotions involved?

- Coronary heart disease (CHD) and essential hypertension are the most pervasive cardiovascular disorders.
- The incidence of CHD is influenced by social factors, personality, and lifestyle, as well as by such risk factors as smoking, obesity, inactivity, hypertension, and cholesterol levels.
- Hypertension is related to the emotions and how they are expressed, especially anger. There are gender and ethnic differences in the prevalence of hypertension.
- Headaches are among the most common psychophysiological complaints.
  - Migraine headaches involve the constriction and then the dilation of blood vessels in the brain.
  - Tension headaches are thought to be caused by contraction of the neck and scalp muscles, which results in vascular constriction. These headaches can also occur in the absence of detectable tension.
  - Cluster headaches are excruciating and occur on one side of the head near the eye.
- The onset of headaches may be preceded by emotional stress.
- Asthma attacks result from constriction of the airways in the lungs. Breathing is extremely difficult during the attacks, and acute anxiety may worsen the situation. In most cases, physical and psychological causes interact.

What are possible causes of psychophysiological disorders?

- Etiological theories must be able to explain why some people develop a physical disorder under stress, whereas others do not, and what determines which psychophysiological illness develops.
- None of the traditional perspectives does this in a satisfactory way.
- According to the psychodynamic perspective, the particular illness that is manifested depends on the stage of psychosexual development and the type of unresolved unconscious conflict involved.
- Biological explanations focus on somatic weakness and response specificity.
- The behavioral perspective emphasizes the importance of classical and operant conditioning in acquiring or maintaining these disorders.

What methods have been developed to treat the psychophysiological disorders?

- Behavioral medicine combines a number of approaches to psychophysiological disorders.
- These disorders are treated through stress management or anxiety management programs, combined with medical treatment for physical symptoms or conditions.
- Relaxation training and biofeedback training, which help the client learn to control muscular or organic functioning, are usually a part of such programs.
- Cognitive-behavioral interventions, which involve changing anxiety-arousing thoughts, have also been useful.

KEY TERMS

asthma (p. 225)
behavioral medicine (p. 229)
biofeedback training (p. 230)
cluster headache (p. 225)
coronary heart disease (CHD) (p. 218)

essential hypertension (p. 220)
general adaptation syndrome (GAS) (p. 206)
hardiness (p. 214)
life-change model (p. 207)

migraine headache (p. 223)
psychophysiological disorder (p. 204)
relaxation training (p. 230)
stress (p. 206)

stressor (p. 206)
sudden death syndrome (p. 203)
tension headache (p. 225)
transaction model of stress (p. 209)

MULTIMEDIA PREVIEW

For additional study aids, we invite you to explore our media resources accompanying *Understanding Abnormal Behavior*, Eighth Edition. The Student CD-ROM includes videos, quizzing, and critical thinking activities that help to reinforce key concepts in a fun and engaging manner. The Student Web Site provides additional interactive activities, chapter outlines, and research links that further support and complement the text. All Web resources may be accessed by logging onto the Web site at **http://psychology.college.hmco.com/students**.

CHAPTER 8
Personality Disorders and Impulse Control Disorders

- **What kinds of personality patterns are associated with mental disorders?**
- **Why do some people have a callous disregard for others and lack guilt and anxiety?**
- **In what ways can the failure to resist temptations lead to mental disorders?**

Although this chapter discusses both personality disorders and impulse control disorders, the two are separate and distinct categories in DSM-IV-TR. We discuss them together for convenience rather than because of any relationship between these two categories of disorders. As in other disorders, those involving personality or impulse control are associated with a person's subjective distress or impaired functioning. Some of these disorders (such as antisocial personality and pyromania) may have detrimental consequences for society.

The Personality Disorders

Personality disorders are characterized by inflexible, long-standing, and maladaptive personality traits that cause significant functional impairment or subjective distress for the individual. In addition to personal and social difficulties, these people also display temperamental deficiencies or aberrations, rigidity in dealing with life problems, and defective perceptions of self and others.

In spite of all these difficulties, people with personality disorders often function well enough to get along without aid from others. For this reason, and because these people rarely seek help from mental health professionals and because those who enter treatment often terminate prematurely (Clarkin & Levy, 2004), the incidence of personality disorders has been difficult to ascertain. Available statistics indicate that personality disorders account for 5 to 15 percent of admissions to hospitals and outpatient clinics. The overall lifetime prevalence of personality disorders is 10 to 13 percent, which indicates that the disorders are relatively common in the general population (Phillips & Gunderson, 1999; Weissman, 1993).

Gender distribution varies from one personality disorder to another. Men are more likely than women to be diagnosed as having paranoid, obsessive-compulsive, and antisocial personality disorders, whereas women more often receive diagnoses of borderline, dependent, or histrionic personality disorders (Reich, 1987; Widiger & Spitzer, 1991). The existence of gender differences in the diagnosis of certain personality disorders is widely accepted. The question being debated is whether these differences are attributable to biases in making diagnoses or to actual gender variations in disorders (Widiger & Coker, 2002), as discussed in the Critical Thinking feature "Is There Gender Bias in Diagnosing Mental Disorders?"

Similar issues arise in relation to culture and ethnicity. Not surprisingly, one's culture shapes habits, customs, values, and personality characteristics, so that expressions of personality in one culture may differ from those in another culture. Asians, for example, are more likely to exhibit shyness and collectivism, whereas Americans are more likely to show assertiveness and individualism. Japanese people and Asian Indians (South Asians) display the overt dependent behaviors characteristic of dependent personality more than Americans or Europeans display them (Bornstein, 1997). Does this mean that people in Japan and India are more likely to have this personality disorder? More likely, the high incidence of these behaviors reflects the influence of other factors, one of which may be cultural bias in the classification system. Anyone making judgments about personality functioning and disturbance must consider the individual's cultural, ethnic, and social background (American Psychiatric Association, 2000).

The signs of a personality disorder usually become evident during adolescence. In some cases, a person with a personality disorder may have had a similar childhood disorder. For example, it is common to find that a person diagnosed as having schizoid personality disorder was previously diagnosed as having schizoid disorder of childhood. When the features of certain

CRITICAL THINKING

Is There Gender Bias in Diagnosing Mental Disorders?

We know that gender differences exist in the diagnosed prevalence of mental disorders such as depression, which has been found to be higher among women than among men (see the chapter on mood disorders). Anorexia nervosa is found predominantly among women in our society (Griffith, Gonzalez, & Blue, 1999). For personality disorders, men have been found to have a higher rate of antisocial, paranoid, and obsessive personality disorders, whereas women have a higher rate of borderline, dependent, and histrionic personality disorders (Reich, 1987; Widiger & Spitzer, 1991). But are there real differences in the way these disorders affect men and women, or do the statistics reflect the influence of other factors, such as gender biases?

Gender bias in the diagnostic system occurs when diagnostic categories are not valid and when they have a different impact on men and women. Note that the mere fact that men and women have different prevalence rates for a particular disorder is not sufficient to prove gender bias. Rates may differ because of

actual biological conditions (for example, a genetic predisposition) or social conditions (stressors) that affect one gender more than another. For the diagnostic system itself to be biased, the differences must be attributable to errors or problems in the categories or diagnostic criteria. Widiger and Spitzer (1991) attempted to enumerate the sources of biases, in addition to biases in the diagnostic system. Try your hand at this task by examining the following sources of potential bias and indicating areas in which you believe bias can occur.

1. *In what ways can clinicians themselves be biased when evaluating others or when making a diagnosis?* For example, might a clinician evaluate the same behavior (for example, aggressiveness) differently, depending on whether a man or a woman displays it?
2. *How might a clinical assessment instrument be biased?* Can you think of characteristics that western culture considers desirable and healthy that are associated

more with one gender than the other and that could be used in a questionnaire? Tavris (1991) has argued that characteristics associated with women are more likely to be considered deviant or undesirable than are those associated with men. She attributed this to a male norm that tends to define characteristics found primarily in women as negative.

3. *Can you think of a situation in which sampling bias could distort the findings in a study of the prevalence of depression in women?* Sampling bias occurs in cases in which one gender with a particular disorder is more likely than the other gender to be present in a particular setting, in which the research is conducted.
4. *Given that gender bias can occur, what can a clinician do to guard against such bias in his or her work?* This final question is, perhaps, the most important to address.

---

childhood disorders persist into adulthood (that is, beyond age eighteen), the diagnosis may be changed to a personality disorder.

In the diagnostic scheme of DSM-IV-TR, personality disorders are recorded on Axis II. A person may receive diagnoses on both Axis I and Axis II. For example, a person with a personality disorder may also be diagnosed with schizophrenia or alcohol dependency (Axis I disorders). Usually, people with personality disorders are hospitalized only when a second, superimposed disorder so impairs social functioning that they require inpatient care. In fact, the treatment outcome for people with an Axis I disorder who also have a personality disorder is worse than for

those who have only an Axis I disorder (Benjamin & Karpiak, 2002; Clarkin & Levy, 2004). The rationale for having two axes for mental disorders is that Axis II disorders generally begin in childhood or adolescence and persist in a stable form into adulthood. Axis I disorders usually fail to show these characteristics.

Diagnosing personality disorders is difficult for three primary reasons. First, to varying degrees and at various times, we all exhibit some of the traits that characterize personality disorders—for example, suspiciousness, dependency, sensitivity to rejection, or compulsiveness. For this reason, many investigators (such as Livesley, Schroeder, Jackson, & Jang, 1994) prefer to view personality disorders as the extremes of underlying dimensions of normal personality traits. They argue that dimensions such as extraversion (sociability), agreeableness (nurturance), neuroticism, conscientiousness, and openness to experience may be used to describe personality disorders. Because people differ in the extent to which they possess a trait, a clinician may have trouble deciding when a client exhibits a trait to a degree that could be considered a symptom of a disorder (Millon, 1994). DSM-IV-TR criteria for diagnosing disorders are based on a categorical model in which a disorder is present if "enough of" certain symptoms or traits are exhibited and is not present if "not enough of" the symptoms are demonstrated (American Psychiatric Association, 2000). Thus, according to DSM, people are classified as either having or not having a disorder. In reality, people may "have" a personality disorder to varying degrees. Researchers are now using taxometric methods (analyzing data to discover the underlying data structure) to see which personality disorders better fit a categorical or continuous model. So far, based on these methods, schizotypal personality disorder appears to be categorical in nature (Haslam, 2003).

In addition, personality patterns may not be stable. Many investigators have consistently argued that personality characteristics exhibited in one situation may vary or be unstable across situations (Mischel, 1968).

Second, diagnosis is often difficult because symptoms of one personality disorder may also be symptoms of other disorders. Although diagnosticians show excellent reliability in diagnosing *whether* a particular client has a personality disorder, they show much lower reliability when they must classify clients as to the precise *type* of personality disorder (Bornstein, 1998). Morey (1988) found that many people diagnosed with one type of personality disorder also met the criteria for other personality disorders. Because people can have more than one type of personality disorder, the problems in diagnosing these disorders are formidable. Moreover, although the distinction between personality disorders and other disorders is valid, many individuals have symptoms that do not neatly characterize a particular disorder and that overlap with different disorders (Widiger & Shea, 1991).

The third reason that personality disorders are difficult to diagnose is that clinicians may not adhere to diagnostic criteria. In one study, clinicians were asked to indicate the symptoms exhibited by their clients who had been diagnosed with personality disorders. In many cases, the clinicians' diagnoses were incongruent with the symptom patterns DSM requires for diagnosing the personality disorders (Morey & Ochoa, 1989).

DSM-IV-TR asserts that a number of traits, not just one, must be considered in determining whether a disorder exists. For example, to diagnose dependent personality disorder, the clinician must find a constellation of characteristics (such as the inability to make decisions independently and the subordination of one's own needs). The clinician must also consider other criteria or factors. For example, the personality pattern (1) must characterize the person's current, as well as long-term, functioning, (2) must not be limited to episodes of illness, and (3) must either notably impair social or occupational functioning or cause subjective distress. Thus a person who is temporarily dependent because of an illness would not be diagnosed as having a dependent personality.

Etiological and Treatment Considerations for Personality Disorders

Although personality disorders have generated rich clinical examples and speculation, not much empirical research has been conducted to provide definitive insights into the causes of the disorders. Many researchers use the five-factor model (FFM) of personality, which describes personality patterns in terms of *neuroticism* (emotional adjustment and stability), *extraversion* (preference for interpersonal interactions, being fun-loving and active), *openness to experience* (curiosity, willingness to entertain new ideas and values, and emotional responsiveness), *agreeableness* (being good-natured, helpful, forgiving, and responsive), and *conscientiousness* (being organized, persistent, punctual, and self-directed). Individuals vary in the extent to which they exhibit any of these factors. One analysis (O'Connor & Dyce, 1998) of data from different studies with clinical and community samples determined that the five-factor model was among the best in accounting for personality disorders. Other researchers (Widiger, Trull, Clarkin, Sanderson, & Costa, 1994) found that personality disorders can be translated as extreme maladaptive variants of the five basic factors of personality. For example, in terms of deliberation (the factor of conscientiousness), antisocial personality disorder would score low, whereas obsessive-compulsive personality disorder would score high. The FFM allows researchers and clinicians to assess personality disorders as a particular set of personality characteristics and to compare different disorders. It also views the etiology of personality disorders as a matter of discovering determinants of personality in general.

Another interesting line of research has examined the role of heredity in personality development. Scarr, Webber, Weinberg, and Wittig (1981) studied the personality characteristics of biologically related and adoptive families. If heredity is important, biologically related parents, children, and siblings should show similar personality characteristics. If learning and environment are important, similarity should be shown between the adoptive family and those who were adopted. Although the results indicated that genetic, as well as environmental, factors are important in personality traits, neither could fully explain the development of personality characteristics. Individual differences between family members may be influential in personality. That is, certain genetic characteristics of individual children may determine much of the environment they experience, so that the contributions of heredity and environment may be quite complex. Genetic characteristics may affect environmental factors, which in turn influence personality (Saudino, 1997). For example, individuals who have inherited a disposition to be sociable may seek out certain social environments, joining social clubs and engaging in interpersonal activities. These environments may then further strengthen the personality's tendency toward sociability.

Twin studies have helped researchers to sort out the effects of genetic and environmental similarity on personality and to study them. One such study (Tellegen et al., 1988) examined the personality characteristics of monozygotic and dizygotic twins reared either apart or together. (Recall from the chapter on the scientific method in abnormal psychology that monozygotic twins are genetically identical and that dizygotic twins share about 50 percent of each other's genes.) The results indicated that heredity is important in personality development. Environment is also critical, but the investigators found that a shared environment—twin pairs living in the same family environment—was not strongly related to personality similarity. Environmental influences can be shared or unshared. Despite the popular belief that shared environmental influences explain personality similarity, a person's unique, unshared experiences may be crucial. All of these studies indicate the complexities researchers confront in trying to find determinants of personality in general and of personality disorders in particular.

The treatment approaches to personality disorders are as varied as the many different theories about how personality characteristics develop and change. Many of these approaches are illustrated in the discussion of antisocial personality, which is the most studied personality disorder, and which is covered in depth later in this chapter. Unfortunately, data are limited on the treatment of the full range of personality disorders (Sanderson & Clarkin, 1994). Many people with these disorders do not seek treatment and do not believe they need treatment. Many can function in society despite their adjustment problems, so their motivation

to change may be weak. Also, the long-term and inflexible personality traits that characterize these disorders are not easily modified. In fact, some therapists have targeted the inflexibility of individuals with personality disorders. They attempt to build resilience in their clients by teaching them to monitor their perceptions and reactions to events and to bounce back after setbacks (Dingfelder, 2004). Individuals with different personality traits may also respond differently to therapy and treatment (McCrae, 1994). Proponents of the five-factor model believe that delineating core personality characteristics in personality disorders can enhance treatment. MacKenzie (1994) has tried to outline ways of treating individuals with high or low five-factor-model characteristics. Although such approaches seem to make sense, research is needed to verify their efficacy.

As Figure 8.1 illustrates, DSM-IV-TR lists ten specific personality disorders and groups them into three clusters, depending on whether they are characterized by odd or eccentric behaviors; dramatic, emotional, or erratic behaviors; or anxious or fearful behaviors. The clustering of these disorders is based more on descriptive similarities than on similarities in etiology (Phillips & Gunderson, 1999). Clustering and categorizing the disorders also mask dimensional aspects. That is, the task of categorizing can conceal differences in the degree to which people possess certain characteristics. In any event, we begin by discussing each of the ten personality disorders rather briefly. Then we focus on one of them—*antisocial personality disorder*—in more detail, primarily because more information is available for this disorder.

Disorders Characterized by Odd or Eccentric Behaviors

Three personality disorders are included in this cluster: paranoid personality, schizoid personality, and schizotypal personality.

Paranoid Personality Disorder   People with **paranoid personality disorder** show unwarranted suspiciousness, hypersensitivity, and reluctance to trust others. They interpret others' motives as being malevolent, question their loyalty or trustworthiness, persistently bear grudges, or are suspicious of the fidelity of their spouses. They may demonstrate restricted affect (that is, aloofness and lack of emotion), and they tend to be rigid and preoccupied with unfounded beliefs that stem from their suspicions and sensitivity. These beliefs are extremely resistant to change. Many persons with this disorder fail to go for treatment because of their guardedness and mistrust (Meissner, 2001).

Certain groups, such as refugees and members of minority groups, may display guarded or defensive behaviors not because of a disorder but because of their minority group status or their unfamiliarity with the majority society. To avoid misinterpreting the clinical significance of such behaviors, clinicians assessing members of these groups must do so cautiously.

DSM-IV-TR estimates the prevalence of paranoid personality disorder to be about 0.5 to 2.5 percent of the population, and probably somewhat higher among males (see Figure 8.1). Here is an example of paranoid personality disorder:

Ralph and Ann married after knowing each other for two months. The first year of their marriage was relatively happy, although Ralph tended to be domineering and very protective of his wife. Ann had always known that Ralph was a jealous person who demanded a great deal of attention. She was initially pleased that her husband was concerned about how other men looked at her; she felt that it showed Ralph really cared for her. It soon became clear, however, that his jealousy was excessive. One day when she came home from shopping later than usual, Ralph exploded. He demanded an explanation but did not accept Ann's, which was that she stopped to talk with a neighbor. Ralph told her that he wanted her to be home when he returned from work—always. Believing him to be in a bad mood, Ann said nothing. Later, she found out that Ralph had called the neighbor to confirm her story.

The situation progressively worsened. Ralph began to leave work early to be with his wife. He said that business was slow and that they could spend more time together. Whenever the phone rang, Ralph insisted on answering it himself. Wrong numbers and male callers took on special significance for him; he felt they must be trying to call Ann. Ann found it difficult to discuss the matter with Ralph. He was always quick to take the offensive, and he expressed very little sympathy or understanding toward her. He thought she and her male friends must be playing him for a fool.

Ralph's suspicions regarding his wife's fidelity were obviously unjustified. Nothing that Ann did implicated her with other men. Yet Ralph persisted in his pathological jealousy and suspiciousness, and he took the offensive when she suggested that he was wrong in distrusting her. This behavior pattern, along with Ralph's absence of warmth and tenderness, indicates paranoid personality disorder.

Follow-up: After several weeks of treatment, Ann began to feel stronger in her relationship with Ralph. During one confrontation, in which Ralph objected to her seeing the therapist, Ann asserted that she would continue the treatment. She said that she had always been faithful to him and that his jealousy was driving them apart. In a rare moment, Ralph broke down and started crying. He said that he needed her and begged her not to leave him. At this time, Ralph and Ann are each seeing a counselor for marital therapy.

Some psychodynamic explanations propose that persons with paranoid personality disorder engage in the defense mechanism of projection, denying their unacceptable impulses and attributing them to others ("I am not hostile; they are"). Vaillant (1994) has shown that paranoid personality is associated with projection to a striking degree. In terms of treatment, psychotherapy is usually the treatment of choice. However, because clients are suspicious and have difficulty trusting others, rapport and intimacy in the therapeutic relationship are difficult to build.

Schizoid Personality Disorder Schizoid personality disorder is marked primarily by social isolation, emotional coldness, and indifference to others. People with this disorder have a long history of impairment of social functioning. They are often described as being reclusive and withdrawn (Siever, 1981). Many live alone in apartments or furnished rooms and engage in solitary recreational activities such as watching television, reading, or taking walks. They tend to neither desire nor enjoy close relationships; they have few activities that provide pleasure. Because of a lack of capacity or desire to form social relationships, people with schizoid disorder are perceived by others as peculiar and aloof and therefore inadequate as dating or marital partners. The disorder appears to be uncommon, and slightly more males are diagnosed with it, according to DSM-IV-TR. Members of different cultures vary in their social behaviors, and diagnosticians must consider the cultural background of individuals who show schizoid symptoms.

People with schizoid disorder may have to relate to others in the workplace and similar situations, but these relationships are superficial and frequently awkward. In such situations, people with this disorder tend to comply with the requests or feelings of others, perhaps in an attempt to avoid extensive involvement, conflicts, and expressions of hostility. They tend to prefer a hermit-like experience (Stone, 2001). Social isolation can be found even in their marital relationships. Spitzer, Skodol, Gibbon, and Williams (1981) describe the case of a man who had married primarily to please his parents. After a while, his wife literally forced him to see a therapist because he was unaffectionate, lacked interest in sex, and was unwilling to participate in family activities. He was as emotionally

FIGURE 8.1 Disorders Chart: Personality Disorders

Odd, Eccentric

Paranoid
Unwarranted suspiciousness, hypersensitivity, and reluctance to confide in others

Schizoid
Socially isolated, emotionally cold, indifferent to others

Schizotypal
Peculiar thoughts and behaviors, poor interpersonal relationships

PERSONALITY DISORDERS

Inflexible and maladaptive personality traits that cause significant functional impairment or subjective distress for the individual

Anxious, Fearful

Avoidant
Fear of rejection and humiliation, reluctance to enter into social relationships

Dependent
Reliance on others and inability to assume responsibilities

Obsessive-Compulsive
Perfectionism, interpersonally controlling, devotion to details, and rigidity

Dramatic, Emotional, Erratic

Histrionic
Self-dramatization, exaggerated emotional expressions, and attention-seeking behaviors

Narcissistic
Exaggerated sense of self-importance, exploitative, and lack of empathy

Antisocial
Failure to conform to social or legal codes, lack of anxiety and guilt, irresponsible behaviors

Borderline
Intense fluctuations in mood, self-image and interpersonal relationships

Linking Symptoms with Personality Disorders
Symptoms such as chronic distrust and suspiciousness must be evaluated within the context of an individual's life before making a judgment as to whether the symptoms the person is experiencing are indicative of paranoid personality. These illegal immigrants applying for amnesty at an Immigration and Naturalization Service office may be distrustful and suspicious but understandably so. What criteria would you use to distinguish between paranoid personality disorder and normal variations of distrust and suspiciousness?

FIGURE 8.1 (continued)

PERSONALITY DISORDERS	Prevalence (%)	Gender Differences	Age of Onset*	Course**
Paranoid	0.5 – 2.5	Higher in males	—	—
Schizoid	0.2 – 0.3	Higher in males	—	—
Schizotypal	2.5 – 3.0	Higher in males	—	—
Histrionic	0.7 – 3.0	None	—	—
Narcissistic	0.3 – 1.0	Higher in males	—	—
Antisocial	2.0	Higher in males	—	—
Borderline	1.0 – 2.0	Higher in females	—	—
Avoidant	0.3 – 1.0	None	—	—
Dependent	1.9 – 2.5	Unclear	—	—
Obsessive-Compulsive	1.0 – 1.9	Higher in males	—	—

* In all of the personality disorders, early symptoms appear in childhood or adolescence.
** Personality disorders tend to be stable and to endure over time, although symptoms of antisocial and borderline personality disorders tend to remit with age.

Source: Based on American Psychiatric Association (2000); Corbitt & Widiger (1995); Marmar (1988); Weissman (1993). Prevalence figures and gender differences have varied from study to study, and investigators may disagree on the rates.

men than women. Again, the evaluation of individuals must take into account their cultural milieu. Superstitious beliefs, delusions, and hallucinations may be condoned or encouraged in certain religious ceremonies or other cultures.

The peculiarities seen in schizotypal personality disorder stem from distortions or difficulties in cognition (Siever, 1981). That is, these people seem to have problems in thinking and perceiving. People with this disorder often show social isolation, hypersensitivity, and inappropriate affect (emotions). They seem to lack pleasure from social interactions (Blanchard, Gangestad, Brown, & Horan, 2000).

The prevailing belief is that the disorder is defined primarily by cognitive distortions, however, and that affective and interpersonal problems are secondary. Research has demonstrated some cognitive processing abnormalities in individuals with this disorder that help to explain many of the symptoms (Stone, 2001).

The man described in the following case was diagnosed as having schizotypal personality disorder:

A forty-one-year-old man was referred to a community mental health center's activities program for help in improving his social skills. He had a lifelong pattern of social isolation, with no real friends, and spent long hours worrying that his angry thoughts about his older brother would cause his brother harm. On interview, the patient was distant and somewhat distrustful. He described in elaborate and often irrelevant detail his rather uneventful and routine daily life. ... For two days he had studied the washing instructions on a new pair of jeans—Did "Wash before wearing" mean that the jeans were to be washed before wearing the first time, or did they need, for some reason, to be washed each time before they were worn? ... He asked the interviewer whether, if he joined the program, he would be required to participate in groups. He said that groups made him very nervous because he felt that if he revealed too much personal information, such as the amount of money that he had in the bank, people would take advantage of him or manipulate him for their own benefit. (Spitzer, Gibbon, Skodol, Williams, & First, 1994, pp. 289–290)

unresponsive to members of his family as he was to his colleagues at work.

The relationship between this disorder and schizophrenia (described in the chapter on schizophrenia) is unclear. One view is that schizoid personality disorder is a beginning stage of schizophrenia. Another is that schizophrenia may develop as a complication of the schizoid personality disorder. Some studies have shown that schizoid personality disorder is associated with a cold, unempathic, and emotionally impoverished childhood (Marmar, 1988). Whether there is a genetic predisposition to the disorder is not clear.

With respect to treatment, as with most personality disorders, individual psychotherapy is preferred. However, persons with this disorder usually seek treatment only if they are experiencing stress or a crisis. The intervention should then be directed at resolving the crisis.

Schizotypal Personality Disorder People who have **schizotypal personality disorder** manifest peculiar thoughts and behaviors and have poor interpersonal relationships. Many believe they possess magical thinking abilities or special powers ("I can predict what people will say before they say it"), and some are subject to recurrent illusions ("I feel that my dead father is watching me"). Speech oddities, such as frequent digression or vagueness in conversation, are often present. The disorder occurs in approximately 3 percent of the population (American Psychiatric Association, 2000), more frequently among

The man's symptoms included absence of close friends, magical thinking (worrying that his thoughts might harm his brother), being distant in the interview, and social anxiety. They are associated with schizotypal personality disorder.

As is true of schizoid personality disorder, many characteristics of schizotypal personality disorder resemble those of schizophrenia, although in less serious form. For example, people with schizophrenia exhibit problems in personality characteristics, psychophysiological responses, and information processing—deficits that have also been observed among persons with schizotypal personality disorder (Grove et al., 1991; Lenzenweger, 2001; Lenzenweger, Cornblatt, & Putnick, 1991). Some evidence is consistent with a genetic interpretation of the link between the two disorders. Kendler (1988) found a higher risk of schizotypal personality disorder among relatives of people diagnosed with schizophrenia than among members of a control group. In general, family, twin, and adoption studies support the genetic relationship between schizophrenia and schizotypal personality disorder. Despite the possibility of genetic influence in the disorder, early environmental enrichment for children (two years of enhanced nutrition, education, and physical exercise) has been found to reduce schizotypal personality disorder and symptoms compared with a nonenrichment group of children (Raine, Mellingen, Liu, Venables, & Mednick, 2003).

Various psychotherapies have been used to treat schizotypal personality disorder, such as dynamic therapy, supportive therapy, and cognitive behavioral approaches, as well as group psychotherapy. For clients who are experiencing a great deal of anxiety, small doses of anxiolytics may be used (Stone, 2001).

Disorders Characterized by Dramatic, Emotional, or Erratic Behaviors

The group of disorders characterized by dramatic, emotional, or erratic behaviors includes four personality disorders: histrionic, narcissistic, antisocial, and borderline.

Histrionic Personality Disorder People with **histrionic personality disorder** engage in self-dramatization, exaggerated expression of emotions, and attention-seeking behaviors. The desire for attention may lead to flamboyant acts or flirtatious behaviors (Phillips & Gunderson, 1999). Despite superficial warmth and charm, the histrionic person is typically shallow and egocentric. Individuals from different cultures vary in the extent to which they display their emotions, but the histrionic person goes well beyond cultural norms. In the United States, about 1 to 3 percent of the population may have this disorder. Gender differences are not evident (Corbitt & Widiger, 1995). Histrionic behaviors were evident in a woman client seen by one of the authors:

The woman was a thirty-three-year-old real estate agent who entered treatment for problems involving severe depression. Her boyfriend had recently told her that she was a self-centered and phony person. He found out that she had been dating other men, despite their understanding that neither would go out with others. The woman claimed that she never considered "going out with other men" as actual dating. Once their relationship was broken, her boyfriend refused to communicate with her. The woman then angrily called the boyfriend's employer and told him that unless the boyfriend contacted her, she would commit suicide. He never did call, but instead of attempting suicide, she decided to seek psychotherapy.

The woman was attractively dressed for her first therapy session. She wore a tight and clinging sweater. Several times during the session she raised her arms, supposedly to fix her hair, in a very seductive manner. Her conversation was animated and intense. When she was describing the breakup with her boyfriend, she was tearful. Later, she raged over the boyfriend's failure to call her and, at one point, called him a "son of a bitch." Near the end of the session, she seemed upbeat and cheerful, commenting that the best therapy might be for the therapist to arrange a date for her.

None of the behaviors exhibited by this client alone warrants a diagnosis of histrionic personality disorder. In combination, however, her self-dramatization, incessant drawing of attention to herself via seductive movements, angry outbursts, manipulative suicidal gesture, and lack of genuineness point to this disorder. Both biological factors, such as autonomic or emotional excitability, and environmental factors, such as parental reinforcement of a child's attention-seeking behaviors and the existence of histrionic parental models, may be important influences in the development of histrionic personality disorder (Millon & Everly, 1985).

The lack of research on the effectiveness of treatments with personality disorders in general makes it difficult to definitively designate a treatment of choice. As noted by Horowitz (2001), psychodynamic therapies have been aimed at establishing a therapeutic alliance with the client and providing insight into resistance to change. Cognitive-behavioral therapy has focused on changing the client's irrational cognitions and assumptions.

Narcissistic Personality Disorder The clinical characteristics of **narcissistic personality disorder** are an exaggerated sense of self-importance, an exploitative attitude, and a lack of empathy. People with this disorder require attention and admiration and have difficulty accepting personal criticism. In conversations, they talk mainly about themselves and show a lack of interest in

Histrionic Behavior In the film *Blue Sky*, Jessica Lange portrays a woman who brazenly seeks attention from others, which is a criterion of histrionic personality disorder. To warrant a diagnosis, however, the individual would also need to display additional characteristics, such as self-dramatization, exaggerated expression of emotions, shallowness, and egocentricity. Can you think of any cultures in which attention seeking is discouraged?

others. Many have fantasies about power or influence, and they constantly overestimate their talents and importance. Individuals diagnosed with this disorder show reflective responses and idealization involving unlimited success, a sense of entitlement, and a sense of self-importance (Hilsenroth, Fowler, Padawer, & Handler, 1997). Owing to their sense of self-importance, people with narcissistic personality disorder expect to be the superior participants in all relationships. For example, they may be impatient and irate if others arrive late for a meeting but may frequently be late themselves and think nothing of it.

One narcissistic client reported, "I was denied promotion to chief executive by my board of directors, although my work was good, because they felt I had poor relations with my employees. When I complained to my wife, she agreed with the board, saying my relations with her and the children were equally bad. I don't understand. I know I'm more competent than all these people" (Masterson, 1981, p. ix). The client was depressed and angry about not being promoted and about the suggestion that he had difficulty in forming social relationships. His wife's confirmation of his problems further enraged him. During therapy, he was competitive and sought to devalue the observations of the therapist. Many persons with this disorder exhibit arrogance and grandiosity (Groopman & Cooper, 2001).

In a study that evaluated the kinds of defense mechanisms used by individuals with different personality disorders, narcissistic personality disorder was strongly associated with the use of dissociation as a

defense mechanism (Vaillant, 1994). People with this disorder may use denial and dissociation to ward off feelings of inferiority developed from early childhood (Kernberg, 1975; Marmar, 1988), and they may attempt to maintain their inflated self-concept by devaluing others (Kernberg, 1975).

Narcissistic traits are common among adolescents and do not necessarily imply that a teenager has the disorder (American Psychiatric Association, 2000). The prevalence of narcissistic personality disorder is about 1 percent, although some studies have found lower rates. More males than females are given the diagnosis.

As in the case of most of the personality disorders, no controlled treatment studies for narcissistic personality disorder have been conducted, and treatment recommendations are therefore based on clinical experience (Groopman & Cooper, 2001). Individual psychotherapy and group therapy have been used and are generally recommended.

Antisocial Personality Disorder Chronic antisocial behavioral patterns, such as a failure to conform to social or legal codes, a lack of anxiety and guilt, and irresponsible behaviors, indicate **antisocial personality disorder**. People with this disorder show little guilt for their wrongdoing, which may include lying, using other people, and aggressive sexual acts. Their relationships with others are superficial and fleeting and involve little loyalty. Antisocial personality disorder, which is far more prevalent among men than among women, is discussed in greater detail later in this chapter.

Narcissistic Behavior Tim Robbins, starring in the film *The Player*, illustrates some of the symptoms of narcissistic personality disorder, including an exaggerated sense of self-importance, an excessive need for admiration, and an inability to accept criticism or rejection. Do you think that narcissistic personality disorder is increasing among young people?

Borderline Personality Disorder Borderline personality disorder is characterized by intense fluctuations in mood, self-image, and interpersonal relationships. Persons with this disorder are impulsive, have chronic feelings of emptiness, and form unstable and intense interpersonal relationships. They may be quite friendly one day and quite hostile the next. Many perceive their early childhoods as having malevolent others—others who were hostile or physically violent (Nigg, Lohr, Westen, Gold, & Silk, 1992). Many exhibit recurrent suicidal behaviors or gestures (Yen et al., 2003), and the probability of suicide is higher than average among those who have this disorder (Duberstein & Conwell, 1997). Self-destructive behaviors such as suicide attempts are often triggered by interpersonal conflicts and events (Welch, Shaw, & Linehan, 2002). Sexual difficulties, such as sexual preoccupation, dissatisfaction, and depression, have also been observed (Zanarini, Parachini, Frankenburg, & Holman, 2003). Although no single feature defines borderline personality disorder, its essence can be captured in the capriciousness of behaviors and the lability of moods (Millon & Everly, 1985).

According to DSM-IV-TR, the prevalence is about 2 percent of the population, with females three times more likely than males to receive the diagnosis. This is the most commonly diagnosed personality disorder in both inpatient and outpatient settings (Trull, 1995). Some researchers believe that the prevalence of the disorder is increasing because our society makes it difficult for people to maintain stable relationships and a sense of identity.

The following example illustrates some of the many facets of borderline personality disorder.

Bryan was a twenty-three-year-old graduate student majoring in sociology at a prestigious university. He was active in student government and was viewed as charismatic, articulate, and sociable. When he met other students for the first time, he could often persuade them to participate in the campus activities that interested him. Women were quite attracted to him because of his charm and self-disclosing nature. They described him as exciting, intense, and different from other men. Bryan could form close relationships with others very quickly.

Bryan could not, however, maintain his social relationships. Sometimes he would have a brief but intense affair with a woman and then abruptly and angrily ask himself what he ever saw in her. At other times, the woman would reject him after a few dates, because she thought Bryan was moody, self-centered, and demanding. He often called his friends after midnight because he felt lonesome, empty, and bored and wanted to talk. Several times he threatened to commit suicide. He gave little thought to the inconvenience he was causing. Once he organized a group of students to protest the inadequate student parking the university provided. The morning of the planned protest demonstration, he announced that he no longer supported the effort. He said he was not in the right mood for the protest, much to the consternation of his followers, who had spent weeks preparing for the event. Bryan's intense but brief relationships, the marked and continual shifts in moods, and boredom with others in spite of his need for social contacts all point to borderline personality disorder.

Masterson (1981) believes that many clients with borderline personality disorder lack purposefulness.

Borderline Personality Disorder In the film *Fatal Attraction*, the character Alex Forrest exhibits many traits of borderline personality disorder: impulsiveness, marked fluctuations in mood, chronic feelings of emptiness, and unstable and intense interpersonal relationships. Why do women receive this diagnosis far more frequently than do men?

For example, one of his clients reported, "I have such a poor self-image and so little confidence in myself that I can't decide what I want, and when I do decide, I have even more difficulty doing it" (p. ix). Masterson sees this lack as a deficiency in the borderline-personality-affected person's emotional investment in the self—a lack of directedness in long-term goals.

People who have borderline personality disorder may exhibit psychotic symptoms, such as auditory hallucinations (for example, hearing imaginary voices that tell them to commit suicide), but the symptoms are usually transient. They also have an ego-dystonic reaction to their hallucinations (Spitzer et al., 1981). That is, they recognize their imaginary voices or other hallucinations as being unacceptable, alien, and distressful. By contrast, a person with a psychotic disorder may not realize that his or her hallucinations are pathological. Some researchers (Trull, 1995; Trull, Useda, Conforti, & Doan, 1997) have found that individuals with borderline personality features are more likely to show dysfunctional moods, interpersonal problems, poor coping, and cognitive distortions than are people without borderline personality characteristics. However, it is important to note that, using taxometric methods, some researchers have found that borderline personality disorder may be better viewed as a continuous rather than a categorical disorder (Rothschild, Cleland, Haslam, & Zimmerman, 2003). That is, rather than either having or not having the disorder, people differ in the degree of borderline personality characteristics they exhibit.

Although diverse models have been used to conceptualize borderline personality disorder, most of the literature comes from researchers with psychodynamic perspectives. For example, Kernberg (1976) proposed the concept of object splitting—that people with borderline personality disorder perceive others as all good

or all bad at different times. This split results in emotional fluctuations toward others.

Another perspective looks at the disorder from a social learning viewpoint. One view (Millon, 1981) is that borderline personality is caused by a faulty self-identity, which affects the development of consistent goals and accomplishments. As a result, persons with this disorder have difficulty coping with their own emotions and with life in general. They then develop a conflict between the need to depend on others and the need to assert themselves. A similar model (Sable, 1997) views the conflict as a desire for proximity and attachment versus a dread and avoidance of engagement, but it attributes the conflict to traumatic attachment experiences that occurred early in life, not to a faulty self-identity. A third possibility is that the fluctuations in emotions or dysfunctions in emotional regulation are at the core of the disorder (Linehan, 1987). Such emotional dysregulations have been observed in different populations of people with this disorder, including adolescents (Santisteban, Muir, Mena, & Mitrani, 2003). An interesting aspect of this approach is the idea that biological factors may be responsible for the emotional dysregulation among individuals with borderline personality disorder.

Cognitive-oriented approaches have also been used. Westen (1991) defined two core aspects of borderline personality: difficulties in regulating emotions and unstable and intense interpersonal relationships. According to this approach, these two aspects are affected by distorted or inaccurate attributions (explanations for others' behaviors or attitudes). Westen's cognitive-behavioral therapy for borderline personality disorders, therefore, attempts to change the way clients think about and approach interpersonal situations. Another cognitive theorist, Aaron Beck, argued that an individual's basic assumptions (that is, thoughts) play a central role in influencing perceptions, interpretations, and behavioral and emotional responses (Beck et al., 1990). Individuals with borderline personality disorder seem to have three basic assumptions: (1) "The world is dangerous and malevolent," (2) "I am powerless and vulnerable," and (3) "I am inherently unacceptable." Believing in these assumptions, individuals with this disorder become fearful, vigilant, guarded, and defensive. For these reasons, they are difficult to treat. Regardless of therapeutic approach, most individual psychotherapies end with the borderline patient's dropping out of treatment (Gunderson & Links, 2001). Finally, Linehan (1993) has developed dialectical behavior therapy (DBT) specifically for clients with borderline personality disorder. Patients are taught skills that include emotional regulation, distress tolerance, and interpersonal effectiveness (Benjamin & Karpiak, 2002). Linehan's goals, in descending order of priority, are to change (1) suicidal behaviors, (2) behaviors that interfere with therapy, (3) behaviors that interfere with quality of life, (4) behavioral skills acquisition, (5) posttraumatic stress behavior, and (6) self-respect behaviors. Thus she targets as priorities possible suicidal behaviors in clients and the therapist-client relationship. Her treatment has been found to decrease dropping out and suicidal behaviors and to be generally effective (Emmelkamp, 2004). Because of positive treatment outcomes, DBT has been increasingly used as a treatment procedure.

These diverse theoretical perspectives on this disorder reflect the strong interest in borderline personality. In contrast to the theoretical contributions, empirical research is sparse. Some investigators have found that individuals with the disorder have a history of chaotic family environments, including physical and sexual abuse (Clarkin, Marziali, & Munroe-Blum, 1991; Golier et al., 2003; Phillips & Gunderson, 1999) and family history of mood and substance-use disorders (Morey & Zanarini, 2000). Such family experiences may affect perceptions of self and others. Benjamin and Wonderlich (1994) found in one study that individuals with borderline personality disorder viewed their mothers and others in their environment as more hostile than did a comparable group of people with mood disorders.

Again, mood changes, intense and unstable interpersonal relationships, identity problems, and other characteristics associated with borderline personality disorder can be observed in all persons to a greater or lesser extent. In fact, although borderline personality disorder is associated with relationship dysfunctions and problems, so are other personality disorders (Daley, Burge, & Hammen, 2000). As is the case with other personality disorders, diagnosis is difficult, and formulations about the causes of the disorder must rely on what we know about personality development in general. We return to that topic later in this chapter.

Disorders Characterized by Anxious or Fearful Behaviors

Another cluster of personality disorders is characterized by anxious or fearful behaviors. This category includes the avoidant, dependent, and obsessive-compulsive personality disorders.

Avoidant Personality Disorder The essential features of **avoidant personality disorder** are a fear of rejection and humiliation and a reluctance to enter into social relationships. Persons with this disorder tend to have low self-esteem and to avoid social relationships without a guarantee of uncritical acceptance

by others. Unlike persons with schizoid personalities, who avoid others because they lack interest, and unlike persons who are shy because of their cultural background, people with avoidant personality disorder do not desire to be alone. On the contrary, they crave affection and an active social life. They want—but fear—social contacts, and this ambivalence may be reflected in different ways. For example, many people with this disorder engage in intellectual pursuits, wear fine clothes, or are active in the artistic community (Millon, 1981). Their need for contact and relationships is often woven into their activities. Thus an avoidant person may write poems expressing the plight of the lonely or the need for human intimacy. A primary defense mechanism is fantasy, whereby wishes are fulfilled to an excessive degree in the person's imagination (Millon & Everly, 1985).

Avoidant personality disorder occurs in less than 1 percent of the population, and no gender differences are apparent (American Psychiatric Association, 2000). People with this disorder are caught in a vicious cycle: because they are preoccupied with rejection, they are constantly alert to signs of derogation or ridicule. This concern leads to many perceived instances of rejection, which cause them to avoid others. Their social skills may then become deficient and invite criticism from others. In other words, their very fear of criticism may lead to criticism. People with avoidant personality disorder often feel depressed, anxious, angry at themselves, inferior, and inadequate.

> Jenny L., an unmarried twenty-seven-year-old bank teller, shows several features of avoidant personality disorder. Although she functions adequately at work, Jenny is extremely shy, sensitive, and quiet with fellow employees. She perceives others as being insensitive and gross. If the bank manager jokes with other tellers, she feels that the manager prefers them to her. Although Jenny tries to be friendly, she does not interact much with anyone because of the possibility of them criticizing or rejecting her.
>
> Jenny has very few hobbies. A great deal of her time is spent watching television and eating chocolates. (As a result, she is about forty pounds overweight.) Television romances are her favorite programs; after watching one, she tends to daydream about having an intense romantic relationship. Jenny eventually sought treatment for her depression and loneliness.

Some researchers believe that the disorder is on a continuum with the Axis I disorder social phobia, whereas others see it as a distinct disorder that simply has features in common with social phobia (Sutherland, 2001). Little research has been conducted on the etiology of avoidant personality disorder. One suggestion (Marmar, 1988) is that a complex interaction of early childhood environmental experiences and innate temperament produce the disorder. Parental rejection and censure, reinforced by rejecting peers, have been proposed as factors in the disorder (Phillips & Gunderson, 1999).

Because of the fear of rejection and scrutiny, clients may be reluctant to disclose personal thoughts and feelings. It is important for the therapist to establish rapport and a therapeutic alliance, or the client may fail to return for treatment. A number of different therapies have been used, such as cognitive-behavioral, psychodynamic, interpersonal, and psychopharmacological treatments (Sutherland, 2001).

Dependent Personality Disorder People who rely on others and are unwilling to assume responsibility show **dependent personality disorder**. These people lack self-confidence, and they subordinate their needs to those of the people on whom they depend. Nevertheless, casual observers may fail to recognize or may misinterpret their dependency and inability to make decisions. Friends may perceive dependent personalities as understanding and tolerant, without realizing that they are fearful of taking the initiative because they are afraid of disrupting the relationship. In addition, a dependent personality may allow his or her spouse to be dominant or abusive for fear that the spouse will otherwise leave. Beck and associates (1990) believe that the dependency is not simply a matter of being passive and unassertive, problems that can be treated with assertiveness training. Rather, dependent personalities have two deeply ingrained assumptions that affect their thoughts, perceptions, and behaviors. First, they see themselves as inherently inadequate and unable to cope. Second, they conclude that their course of action should be to find someone who can take care of them. Depression, helplessness, and suppressed anger are often present in dependent personality disorder.

The individual's environment must be considered before rendering a diagnosis of dependent personality disorder. The socializing process that trains people to be independent, assertive, and individual rather than group oriented is not equally valued in all cultures. Nor do all people manifest dependency all the time in the cultures that do value it. Some individuals, such as hospitalized patients, typically develop some degree of dependency during confinement.

The prevalence of this disorder is about 2.5 percent. The prevalence by gender is unclear. Bornstein (1997) finds evidence that it is found more often among men than among women, but Corbitt and Widiger (1995)

believe there are no gender differences in this disorder. The following case illustrates a dependent personality disorder that cannot be attributed to cultural or situational factors.

> Jim was fifty-six, a single man who was living with his seventy-eight-year-old widowed mother. When his mother was recently hospitalized for cancer, Jim decided to see a therapist. He was distraught and depressed over his mother's condition. Jim indicated that he did not know what to do. His mother had always taken care of him, and, in his view, she always knew best. Even when he was young, his mother had "worn the pants" in the family. The only time that he was away from his family was during his six years of military service. He was wounded in the Korean War, was returned to the United States, and spent a few months in a Veterans Administration hospital. He then went to live with his mother. Because of his service-connected injury, Jim was unable to work full time. His mother welcomed him home, and she structured all his activities.
>
> At one point, Jim met and fell in love with a woman, but his mother disapproved of her. During a confrontation between the mother and Jim's woman friend, each demanded that Jim make a commitment to her. This was quite traumatic for Jim. His mother finally grabbed him and yelled that he must tell the other woman to go. Jim tearfully told the woman that he was sorry but she must go, and the woman angrily left.
>
> While Jim was relating his story, it was clear to the therapist that Jim harbored some anger toward his mother, though he overtly denied any feelings of hostility. Also clear were his dependency and his inability to take responsibility. His life had always been structured, first by his mother and then by the military. His mother's illness meant that his structured world might crumble.

People clearly differ in the degree to which they are dependent or submissive. How dependency is explained varies according to theoretical perspective. From the psychodynamic perspective, the disorder is a result of maternal deprivation, which causes fixation at the oral stage of development (Marmar, 1988). Behavioral learning theorists believe that a family or social environment that rewards dependent behaviors and punishes independence may promote dependency. Some cognitive theorists attribute dependent personality disorder to the development of distorted beliefs about one's inadequacies and helplessness that discourage independence. Research findings (Bornstein, 1997) show that dependency is associated with overprotective, authoritarian parenting styles. Presumably, these parenting styles prevent the child from developing

MENTAL HEALTH AND SOCIETY
OCPD or OCD?

Actor Jack Nicholson portrayed a person with obsessive-compulsive symptoms in the movie *As Good As It Gets*. Did he have an obsessive-compulsive personality disorder (OCPD) or an obsessive-compulsive disorder (OCD)? Unfortunately, his movie character had symptoms of both disorders. However, OCPD as presented in this chapter is distinct from OCD as discussed in the chapter on anxiety disorders. The two disorders have similar names, but the clinical manifestations of these disorders are quite different. OCPD is not characterized by the presence of obsessions (intrusive and repetitive anxiety-arousing thoughts) or compulsions (a need to perform acts or to dwell on mental acts repetitively). Rather, OCPD involves a preoccupation with orderliness, perfectionism, and control. Persons with OCD experience tremendous anxiety related to specific preoccupations, which are perceived as threatening. They usually recognize that their obsessions or compulsions are irrational or senseless. In OCPD, it is one's dysfunctional philosophy that produces anxiety, discomfort, and frustration. OCPD is a pervasive characterological disturbance. People with the disorder genuinely see their way of functioning as the "correct" way. Their overall style of relating to the world around them is processed through their own strict standards. In rare instances, an individual may manifest symptoms of both OCPD and OCD, in which case both diagnoses can be given.

As the following shows, the two conditions have distinct characteristics, although some overlap may exist.

Characteristic	OCPD	OCD
Rigidity in personality	Yes	Not usual
Preoccupation in thinking	Yes	Yes
Orderliness in general	Yes	Not usual
Control	Yes	Not usual
Perfectionism	Yes	Not usual
Indecisiveness	Yes	Not usual
Intrusive thoughts/behaviors	Not usual	Yes
Need to perform acts	Not usual	Yes
Recognition of irrationality	Not usual	Yes

a sense of autonomy and self-efficacy. Different forms of treatment (including individual and group) have been found to be beneficial, although research on the use of medications has not been well researched. In general, dependent personality disorder is successfully treated more often than other personality disorders, such as borderline or antisocial personality disorder (Perry, 2001).

Obsessive-Compulsive Personality Disorder The characteristics of **obsessive-compulsive personality disorder** are perfectionism, a tendency to be interpersonally controlling, devotion to details, and rigidity. Again, these traits are found in many normal people. Unlike normal people, however, individuals with obsessive-compulsive personality disorder show marked impairment in occupational or social functioning. Their relationships with others may be quite stiff, formal, and distant (McCullough & Maltsberger, 2001). Further, the extent of the character rigidity is greater among people who have this disorder (Weintraub, 1981). Unlike obsessive-compulsive disorder, in which there are specific recurrent thoughts or repetitive behaviors (see the Mental Health and Society feature "OCPD or OCD?"), obsessive-compulsive personality disorder involves general traits of perfectionism, inflex-ibility, and attention to details. Research also shows that obsessive-compulsive symptoms are related to anger and depression and that those with these symptoms are more prone to suppress their anger (Whiteside & Abramowitz, 2004).

The preoccupation with details, rules, and possible errors leads to indecision and an inability to see "the big picture." There is an overconcern with being in control, not only over the details of their lives but also over their emotions and other people (Phillips & Gunderson, 1999). Coworkers may find the individual with this disorder too demanding, inflexible, miserly, and perfectionistic. He or she may actually be ineffective on the job, despite long hours of devotion, as in the following case.

Cecil, a third-year medical student, was referred for therapy by his graduate adviser. The adviser told the therapist that Cecil was in danger of being expelled from medical school because of his inability to get along with patients and with other students. Cecil often berated patients for failing to follow his advice. In one instance, he told a patient with a lung condition to stop smoking. When the patient indicated he was unable to stop, Cecil angrily told the patient to go for medical treatment elsewhere—that the medical center had no place for such a "weak-willed fool." Cecil's relationships with others were similarly strained. He considered many members of the faculty to be "incompetent old deadwood," and he characterized fellow graduate students as "partygoers."

The graduate adviser told the therapist that Cecil had not been expelled only because several faculty members thought that he was brilliant. Cecil studied and worked sixteen hours a day. He was extremely well read and had an extensive knowledge of medical disorders. Although he was always able to provide a careful and detailed analysis of a patient's condition, it took him a great deal of time to do so. His diagnoses tended to cover every disorder that each patient could conceivably have, on the basis of all possible combinations of symptoms.

Obsessive-compulsive personality disorder occurs in about 1 percent of the population and is about twice as prevalent among males as females, according to DSM-IV-TR. Cognitive-behavioral therapy, as well as supportive forms of psychotherapy, have helped some clients (Barber, Morse, Krakauer, Chittams, & Crits-Christoph, 1997; Beck et al., 1990). No medications specific to obsessive-compulsive personality disorder are currently available (McCullough & Maltsberger, 2001).

We turn now to the etiology and treatment of antisocial personality disorder, which we lightly touched on earlier in this chapter. Research on the other personality disorders has been quite limited. By discussing antisocial personality disorder at greater length, we hope to give you a broader view and an appreciation of the wide range of explanatory views that can be proposed for the personality disorders in general.

Antisocial Personality Disorder

The following case presents an example of antisocial personality disorder:

Roy W. was an eighteen-year-old high school senior who was referred by juvenile court for diagnosis and evaluation. He was arrested for stealing an automobile, something he had done on several other occasions. The court agreed with Roy's mother that he needed evaluation and perhaps psychotherapy.

During his interview with the psychologist, Roy was articulate, relaxed, and even witty. He said that stealing was wrong but that none of the cars he stole was ever damaged. The last theft occurred because he needed transportation to a beer party (which was located only a mile from his home) and his leg was sore from playing basketball. When the psychologist asked Roy how he got along with young women, he grinned and said that he was very outgoing and could easily "hustle" them. He then related the following incident:

"About three months ago, I was pulling out of the school parking lot real fast and accidentally sideswiped this other car. The girl who was driving it started to scream at me. God, there was only a small dent on her fender! Anyway, we exchanged names and addresses and I apologized for the accident. When I filled out the accident report later, I said that it was her car that pulled out from the other side and hit my car. How do you like that? Anyway, when she heard about my claim that it was her fault, she had her old man call me. He said that his daughter had witnesses to the accident and that I could be arrested. Bull, he was just trying to bluff me. But I gave him a sob story—about how my parents were ready to get a divorce, how poor we were, and the trouble I would get into if they found out about the accident. I apologized for lying and told him I could fix the dent. Luckily he never checked with my folks for the real story. Anyway, I went over to look at the girl's car. I really didn't have any idea of how to fix that old heap so I said I had to wait a couple of weeks to get some tools for the repair job.

"Meanwhile, I started to talk to the girl. Gave her my sob story, told her how nice I thought her folks and home were. We started to date and I took her out three times. Then one night I laid her. The crummy thing was that she told her folks about it. Can you imagine that? Anyway, her old man called and told me never to get near his precious little thing again. She's actually a slut.

"At least I didn't have to fix her old heap. I know I shouldn't lie but can you blame me? People make such a big thing out of nothing."

The irresponsibility, disregard for others, and disregard for societal rules and morals evident in this interview indicated to the psychologist that Roy had antisocial personality disorder. Historically, the terms *moral insanity, moral imbecility, moral defect,* and *psychopathic inferiority* have been attached to this condition. An early nineteenth-century British psychiatrist, J. C. Prichard (1837), described it this way:

> The moral and active principles of the mind are strongly perverted or depraved; the power of self-government is lost or greatly impaired; and the individual is found to be incapable, not of talking or reasoning upon any subject proposed to him … but of conducting himself with decency and propriety in the business of life. (p. 15)

Prichard believed that the disorder was reflected not in a loss of intellectual skills but in gross violations of moral and ethical standards.

The diagnosis of antisocial personality (also referred to as *sociopathic* or *psychopathic* personality) has now lost some of its original moral overtones. Nevertheless, people with antisocial personalities do show a disregard for conventional societal rules and morals.

Cleckley's (1976) classic description of the disorder included the following characteristics:

1. *Superficial charm and good intelligence* Persons with antisocial personalities are often capable in social activities and adept at manipulating others.

2. *Shallow emotions and lack of empathy, guilt, or remorse* Absent are genuine feelings of love and loyalty toward others and of concern over the detrimental consequences of their behaviors.

3. *Behaviors indicative of little life plan or order* The actions of antisocial personalities are not well planned and are often difficult to understand or predict.

4. *Failure to learn from experiences and absence of anxiety* Although the behaviors may be punished, people with antisocial personality disorder may repeat the same behaviors, and they frequently show little anxiety.

5. *Unreliability, insincerity, and untruthfulness* Persons with antisocial personalities are irresponsible and may lie or feign emotional feelings to callously manipulate others; their social relationships are usually unstable and short-lived.

Some of these characteristics are apparent in Roy's case. For example, he felt no guilt for his actions or for manipulating the young woman and her family. In fact, he was quite proud of his ability to seduce her

Antisocial Personality Disorder Criminal behavior, irritability, aggressiveness, impulsivity, lack of remorse, and deceitfulness are all characterstics of antisocial personality disorder. Serial murderer Ted Bundy exhibited many of these characteristics. He is shown here in front of television cameras after his indictment for the murders of two Florida State University women. Bundy was executed for his crimes in 1989.

and avoid responsibility for the automobile repair. The ease with which Roy related his story to the psychologist demonstrated his lack of concern for those who were hurt by his behaviors. Roy showed no anxiety during the interview.

DSM-IV-TR criteria for the disorder differ somewhat from Cleckley's description, which is based on clinical observations of various cases. For example, DSM-IV-TR criteria do not include lack of anxiety, shallow emotions, failure to learn from past experiences, and superficial charm. They do include a history before age fifteen of failing to conform to social norms with respect to lawful behaviors, irritability and aggressiveness, impulsivity, lack of remorse, and deceitfulness. For the diagnosis to be made, the individual must be at least eighteen years old. DSM-IV-TR criteria, however, fail to convey the conceptual sense of the disorder that was conveyed in Cleckley's original description.

Hare and colleagues (Harpur, Hare, & Hakstian, 1989; Hart & Hare, 1989) constructed a measure, the Psychopathy Checklist—Revised (PCL-R), that captures some of the elements of Cleckley's description, as well as those of DSM-IV-TR. Initially, two factors were found underlying the measure (Hare, Hart, & Harpur, 1991). Some research now suggests that psychopathy is composed of three factors: arrogant and deceitful interpersonal style, deficient affective experience, and impulsive and irresponsible behavioral style (Cooke & Michie, 2001). Interestingly, a subscale of the PCL (i.e., the PCL-SV) was found to be a good predictor of violence. Skeem and Mulvey (2001) administered the PCL-SV to a large number of psychiatric patients with a variety of psychiatric disorders. Patients and collateral informants (e.g., family members) were asked whether the patients had engaged in a range of violent activities over a period of a year. Violent actions ranged from pushing or shoving to use of a weapon. Results indicated that, although only 8 percent of the patients were probably psychopathic, scores on the PCL-SV were a strong predictor of violence.

The distinction between Cleckley's conceptualization and DSM-IV-TR criteria is important because sole use of DSM-IV-TR may not capture the "personality" aspect or the underlying construct of the disorder. Because they overemphasize behavioral manifestations and criminality, the DSM-IV-TR criteria make it easier and more reliable to render a diagnosis, but they may fail to capture the essence of the disorder. Thus Cleckley's conceptualization and the research on psychopathy are more likely to emphasize personality components than is the description of antisocial personality disorder in DSM-IV-TR. Antisocial behaviors may arise from a multitude of causes, of which personality pathology is only one (Cooke & Michie, 2001). Furthermore, only a minority of patients with antisocial personality disorder have severe psychopathy (Meloy, 2001).

In the United States, the incidence of antisocial personality disorder is estimated to be about 2 percent overall; rates differ by gender, at 3 percent for men and less than 1 percent for women (American Psychiatric Association, 2000). Overall estimates vary from study to study, however, which may be due to differences in sampling, diagnostic, and methodological procedures. The disorder is much more frequent in urban environments than in rural ones and in lower socioeconomic groups than in higher ones. Rates of antisocial personality disorder appear comparable among whites, African Americans, and Latino Americans (Robins, Tipp, & Przybeck, 1991). Although African Americans had a higher rate of incarceration for crimes, their rate of antisocial personality disorder was no different from those of the other groups.

The behavior patterns associated with antisocial personality disorder are different and distinct from behaviors involving social protest or criminal lifestyles. People who engage in civil disobedience or violate the conventions of society or its laws as a form of protest are not, as a rule, persons with antisocial personalities. Such people can be quite capable of forming meaningful interpersonal relationships and of experiencing

guilt. They may perceive their violations of rules and norms as acts performed for the greater good. Similarly, engaging in delinquent or adult criminal behavior is not a necessary or sufficient condition for diagnosing antisocial personality. Although many convicted criminals have been found to have antisocial characteristics, many others do not. They may come from a subculture that encourages and reinforces criminal activity; hence in perpetrating such acts they are adhering to group mores and codes of conduct. As mentioned earlier, DSM-IV-TR criteria tend to emphasize criminality, but the appropriateness of this emphasis is being questioned.

People with antisocial personalities are a difficult population to study because they do not voluntarily seek treatment. Only one out of seven will ever discuss their problems with a doctor, and concurrent problems are the reason for their participation in treatment (Meloy, 2001). Consequently, investigators often seek research participants in prison populations, which presumably harbor a relatively large proportion of psychopaths. But now a different problem arises: researchers cannot know whether the psychopaths in prison are also representative of the psychopathic population not in prison.

Using an ingenious research approach, Widom (1977) tried to find a number of noninstitutionalized psychopaths to discover whether their characteristics matched those of psychopaths typically found in prison groups. She placed the following advertisement in a major Boston counterculture newspaper:

Are You Adventurous? Psychologist studying adventurous, carefree people who've led exciting, impulsive lives. If you're the kind of person who'd do almost anything for a dare and want to participate in a paid experiment, send name, address, phone, and short biography proving how interesting you are.

Widom reasoned that such an ad might appeal to individuals with antisocial personalities. Of the seventy-three people who responded, twenty-eight met her criteria for antisocial personality and were studied further. On the basis of psychological tests and interviews, Widom concluded that the noninstitutionalized people she studied did have characteristics similar to those associated with antisocial personality among prisoners. But her respondents tended to have a higher level of education and, although often arrested, they were infrequently convicted of crimes.

Explanations of Antisocial Personality Disorder

People with antisocial personality disorder are appar-ently unable to learn from past experience. They

Behavior Patterns, Context, and Diagnosis Individuals who engage in social protest or civil disobedience are rarely regarded as having an antisocial personality disorder. Although some may break the law, the other features of antisocial personality disorder—chronic lack of remorse and deceitfulness, for example—are usually absent. In this photo, a group of individuals demonstrate to rally support against the war in Iraq. Are social protests, as well as antisocial personality disorders, more common among young adults than older adults?

continue to engage in antisocial behaviors despite criticism and scorn from others, the disruption of close personal relationships, and frequent encounters with legal authorities. They often sincerely promise to change their lives and make amends, only to return to antisocial behavior soon after. A variety of theories emphasize the inability of persons with antisocial personalities to learn appropriate social and ethical behaviors. The reasons given for this defect, however, are quite diverse.

Theories of the etiology of this disorder vary with theoretical orientation and with the theorist's definition of *antisocial personality*. We examine a number of the most frequently cited constructs from the psychodynamic, family and socialization, biological, and anxiety-arousal-behavioral perspectives.

Psychodynamic Perspective According to one psychodynamic approach, the psychopath's absence of guilt and frequent violation of moral and ethical standards are the result of faulty superego development (Fenichel, 1945). Id impulses are more likely to be expressed when the weakened superego cannot exert very much influence. People exhibiting antisocial behavior patterns presumably did not adequately identify with their parents. Frustration, rejection, or inconsistent discipline resulted in fixation at an early stage of development.

Family and Socialization Perspectives Some early theorists believed that relationships within the family—the primary agent of socialization—are paramount in the development of antisocial patterns (McCord & McCord, 1964). In a review of factors that predict delinquency and

antisocial behaviors in children, Loeber (1990) found that a family's socioeconomic status was a weak predictor, whereas other family characteristics, such as poor parental supervision and involvement, were good predictors. Rejection or deprivation by one or both parents may mean that the child has little opportunity to learn socially appropriate behaviors or that the value of people as socially reinforcing agents is diminished. There is also evidence that family structure, predictability of expectations, and dependability of family roles are related to lower antisocial tendencies (Tolan, Gorman-Smith, Huesmann, & Zelli, 1997). Parental separation or absence and assaultive or inconsistent parenting are related to antisocial personality (Phillips & Gunderson, 1999). Children may have been traumatized or subjected to a hostile environment during the parental separation (Vaillant & Perry, 1985), or the hostility in such families may result in interpersonal hostility among the children (Millon & Everly, 1985). Such situations may lead to little satisfaction in close or meaningful relationships with others. Individuals with this disorder do show a significant amount of misperception about people in general (Widom, 1976). The inability to perceive another's viewpoint can create problems in personal interactions.

People with antisocial personality disorder can learn and use social skills very effectively (Ullmann & Krasner, 1975), as shown in their adeptness at manipulation, lying, and cheating and their ease at being charming and sociable. The difficulty is that, in many areas of learning, these individuals do not pay attention to social stimuli, and their schedules of reinforcement differ from those of most other people. Perhaps this relatively diminished attention stems from inconsistent reinforcement from parents or inadequate feedback for behaviors.

Another explanation is that the child may have modeled the behaviors of a parent who had antisocial tendencies. In one study, researchers examined the past records and statuses of nearly 500 adults who had been seen about thirty years earlier as children in a child guidance clinic. More than 90 of the adults exhibited antisocial tendencies. These persons were compared with a group of 100 adults who, as children, had lived in the same geographic area but had never been referred to the clinic. The researchers found the following (Robins, 1966):

1. There was little relationship between having antisocial personality disorder as an adult and participating in gangs as a youth.

2. Antisocial behavior (theft, aggression, juvenile delinquency, lying) in childhood was a predictor of antisocial behaviors in adults.

3. The adjustment level of fathers, but not that of mothers, was significant—having a father who was antisocial was related to adult antisocial characteristics.

4. Growing up in a single-parent home was not related to psychopathy.

The study seemed to indicate that antisocial behavior is probably influenced by the presence of an antisocial father who either serves as a model for such behavior or provides inadequate supervision, inconsistent discipline, or family conflict. The father's influence on antisocial behaviors in children may be a result of traditional gender role training. Males have traditionally received more encouragement to engage in aggressive behaviors than females have, and antisocial patterns are more prevalent among men than among women. As traditional gender roles change, one might reasonably expect that antisocial tendencies will increase among females and that mothers will play a greater role in the development of antisocial behaviors in children.

Another study also found that parental antisocial patterns, especially among fathers, were strongly associated with child conduct disorder (Lahey et al., 1988). Interestingly, results also indicated that divorce among parents was not related to having children with conduct disorder, once parental antisocial background was controlled. That is, although some researchers have speculated that divorce of parents is associated with antisocial conduct problems among children, this study found that the association was caused primarily by the fact that divorced parents were more likely to be antisocial than were married parents. It is unclear,

however, whether the effects of having a psychopathic parent are genetic (parents transmitting a certain genetic makeup to children) or environmental (parents providing an antisocial role model).

A disturbed family background or disturbed parental model is neither a necessary nor a sufficient condition for the development of antisocial personality. Indeed, antisocial personality probably has multiple causes.

Genetic Influences Throughout history, many people have speculated that some individuals are "born to raise hell." These speculations are difficult to test because of the problems involved in distinguishing between the influences of environment and heredity on behavior. For example, antisocial personality disorder is five times more common among first-degree biological relatives of males and ten times more common among first-degree biological relatives of females with this disorder than among the general population (American Psychiatric Association, 1987, 2000). These findings can be used to support either an environmental or a genetic hypothesis. Within the past decade, however, some interesting research has been conducted on genetic influences in antisocial personality disorder.

One strategy has been to compare concordance rates for identical, or monozygotic (MZ), twins with those for fraternal, or dizygotic (DZ), twins. Although MZ twins share exactly the same genes, DZ twins, with about 50 percent of the same genes, are genetically no more alike than any two siblings. Most studies show that MZ twins do tend to have a higher concordance rate than DZ twins for antisocial tendencies, delinquency, and criminality (Mednick & Christiansen, 1977); this finding tends to support a genetic basis for these behavior patterns. Nevertheless, some caution must be exercised in drawing firm conclusions. Twin pairs can influence each other's behavior, and if MZ twins influence each other more than do DZ twins, the higher concordance rate may be caused at least in part by this influence. G. Carey (1992) found that twin interaction is important and believes that both heredity and sibling interaction contribute to antisocial behavior.

Another strategy for studying genetic influence is to note the rate of antisocial personality disorder among adopted people with antisocial biological parents. Because these adoptees were separated from their biological parents early in life, learning antisocial behaviors from those parents would have been difficult. Results have generally shown that adoptees whose biological parents exhibited antisocial behaviors have a higher rate of antisocial characteristics than that found among adoptees whose biological parents did *not* exhibit antisocial behaviors (Cadoret & Cain, 1981). Even Robins's study (1966), in which the development of antisocial personality was associated with having antisocial fathers, revealed that the association existed even when the people were not raised in the presence of their fathers.

Do adoptive parents' antisocial patterns influence adopted individuals who develop antisocial behavior patterns? If so, this would be evidence of environmental influence. Research results show, however, that the rate of criminality or antisocial tendencies is higher among the biological parents than among the adoptive parents of such individuals (Hutchings & Mednick, 1977; Mednick & Kandel, 1988). Again the evidence suggests that antisocial personality patterns are influenced by heredity (Goodwin & Guze, 1984).

Although this body of evidence seems to show a strong causal pattern, it should be examined carefully, for several reasons. First, many of the studies fail to clearly distinguish between antisocial personalities and criminals; as we noted earlier, they may draw research participants only from criminal populations. Truly representative samples of people with antisocial personality disorder should be investigated.

The second reason for caution is that evidence supporting a genetic basis for antisocial tendencies does not preclude the environment as a factor. Antisocial personality is undoubtedly caused by environmental, as well as genetic, influences (Slutske et al., 1997). The fact that crime has increased fivefold or more in most industrialized western countries over the past fifty years has to be attributed to environmental influences, because gene pools cannot change that quickly (Rutter, 1997). One way to try to sort out genetic and environmental influences is to study family members who vary in genetic relatedness and who share or do not share environmental factors. One such study (O'Connor, McGuire, Reiss, Hetherington, & Plomin, 1998) investigated these variations with MZ twins, DZ twins, full siblings, half siblings, and unrelated siblings. Heredity accounted for 56 percent of the variance in antisocial behavior, and shared environmental experiences (for example, those that are common to both siblings) explained about 25 percent of the variance. Research by Wootton, Frick, Shelton, and Silverthorn (1997) suggests that heredity and environment may interact in complex ways. They found that ineffective parenting was unrelated to conduct problems in children with antisocial temperamental characteristics, but for children without such characteristics, ineffective parenting increased conduct disorders.

There is a third reason for caution: studies indicating that genetic factors are important do not provide much insight into how antisocial personality is inherited. What exactly is transmitted genetically? Rutter (1997) suggests that genetic factors do not influence crime and antisocial behavior directly but rather that they affect the probability that such behavior will occur. Hence there is no specific "gene for crime."

Myth vs Reality

Myth: Antisocial personality problems are primarily caused by genetic factors. Some people seem born to "raise hell."

Reality: Although genetic factors are related to antisocial personality disorder, a wide range of family patterns can influence the development of the disorder. For example, dysfunctional aspects of family life, such as severe parental discord, a parent's maladjustment or criminality, overcrowding, and even large family size, can predispose a child to antisocial personality disorder, especially if the child does not have a loving relationship with at least one parent (U.S. Surgeon General, 1999).

Central Nervous System Abnormality Some early investigators suggested that people with antisocial personalities tend to have abnormal brain wave activity (Hill & Watterson, 1942; Knott, Platt, Ashley, & Gottlieb, 1953). In these studies, the measurement of the brain waves, or electroencephalograms (EEGs), of psychopaths were sometimes found to be similar to those of normal young children. According to one survey, most studies revealed that between 31 and 58 percent of people with antisocial personality showed some EEG abnormality, frequently in the form of slow-wave, theta activity (Ellingson, 1954). Perhaps these abnormalities indicate brain pathology. Such pathology could inhibit the capacity of those with antisocial personalities to learn how to avoid punishment and could render them unable to learn from experience (Hare, 1970). This explanation is plausible, but there simply is not enough evidence to support its acceptance. Many persons diagnosed with antisocial personality disorder do not show EEG abnormalities, and individuals who do not have the disorder may also exhibit theta-wave activity (Milstein, 1988). In addition, the EEG is an imprecise diagnostic device, and abnormal brain wave activity in people with antisocial personalities may simply be correlated with, rather than a cause of, disturbed behavior. For example, these individuals could simply be less anxious or more bored than other people, which may account for the slow-wave EEGs.

Autonomic Nervous System Abnormalities Other interesting research points to the involvement of the autonomic nervous system (ANS) in the prominent features of antisocial personality disorder: the inability to learn from experience, the absence of anxiety, and the tendency to engage in thrill-seeking behaviors. Two lines of investigation can be identified, both based on the assumption that people with antisocial personality disorder have ANS deficiencies or abnormalities. The first is based on the premise that ANS abnormalities make antisocial personalities less susceptible to anxiety and therefore less likely to learn from their experiences in situations in which aversive stimuli (or punishment) are involved. The second line of research focuses on the premise that ANS abnormalities could keep antisocial people emotionally underaroused. To achieve an optimal level of arousal or to avoid boredom, underaroused individuals might seek excitement and thrills and fail to conform to conventional behavioral standards. The two premises—lack of anxiety and underarousal—may, of course, be related, because underarousal could include underaroused anxiety.

Fearlessness or Lack of Anxiety Lykken (1982) maintained that because of genetic predisposition, people vary in their levels of fearlessness. Antisocial personality develops because of fearlessness or low anxiety levels. People who have high levels of fear avoid risks, stress, and strong stimulation; relatively fearless people seek thrills and adventures. Fearlessness is associated with heroes (such as those who volunteer for dangerous military action or who risk their lives to save others), as well as with individuals with antisocial personalities who may engage in risky criminal activities or impulsively violate norms and rules (see the Mental Health and Society feature "Heroes and Psychopaths").

Lykken's (1957) classic research suggested that, because psychopaths do not become conditioned to aversive stimuli as readily as nonpsychopaths do, they fail to acquire avoidance behaviors, experience little anticipatory anxiety, and consequently have fewer inhibitions about engaging in antisocial behavior. More recent studies have also demonstrated that low anxiety among psychopaths is associated with more errors in learning tasks (Newman & Schmitt, 1998).

Arousal, Sensation-Seeking, and Behavioral Perspectives These studies by Lykken and others suggest that individuals with antisocial personalities may have deficiencies in learning because of lower anxiety. Another line of research proposes that antisocial personalities simply have lower levels of ANS reactivity and are underaroused. According to this view, the sensitivity of individuals' reticular cortical

systems varies, although there is an optimal level for each person. The system regulates the tonic level of arousal in the cortex, so that some people have high and some have low levels of arousal. Those with low sensitivity need more stimulation to reach an optimal level of arousal (Goma, Perez, & Torrubia, 1988). If psychopaths are underaroused, it may take a more intense stimulus to elicit a reaction in them than in nonpsychopaths. The lowered levels of reactivity may cause psychopaths to show impulsive, stimulus-seeking behaviors to avoid boredom (Quay, 1965).

Zuckerman (1996) believes that a trait he calls *impulsive unsocialized sensation seeking* can help explain not only antisocial personality disorder but also other disorders. Those with this trait want to seek adventures and thrills, are disinhibited, and are susceptible to boredom. Psychopaths score high for this trait. Similarly, Farley (1986) proposed that people vary in their degree of thrill-seeking behaviors. At one end of the thrill-seeking continuum are the "Big T's"—the risk takers and adventurers who seek excitement and stimulation. Because of their low levels of CNS or ANS arousal, Big T's need stimulation to maintain an optimal level of arousal. On the other end of the continuum are "Little t's"—people with high arousal who seek low levels of stimulation to calm their hyped-up nervous systems. In contrast to Big T's, Little t's prefer certainty, predictability, low risk, familiarity, clarity, simplicity, low conflict, and low intensity.

Farley speculated that Big T characteristics can lead to either constructive or destructive behaviors, which can occur in either mental or physical domains. In the constructive-mental domain, Big T's include artists, scientists, and entertainers, who channel their thrill-seeking tendencies into creative mental contributions. In the destructive-mental domain, criminal masterminds, schemers, and con artists are Big T's whose actions in society are harmful. In the constructive-physical domain, Big T's become adventurers and physical risk takers. Their destructive-physical domain counterparts are violent delinquents and criminals whose Big T characteristics result in antisocial, destructive behaviors. Farley (1986) reported that juvenile delinquents are more likely than nondelinquents to be Big T's. In a study of delinquents in prison, Big T's were more likely than Little t's to fight, disobey supervisors, and attempt to escape. Farley believes that we need to direct stimulation-hungry Big T's into constructive, rather than destructive, mental and physical activities.

Other researchers have found evidence of underarousal, as well as lowered levels of anxiety, among those with antisocial personality disorder. A study by Hare (1968) focused on the intensity of the stimulus needed to elicit a reaction in psychopaths and in

●●● MENTAL HEALTH AND SOCIETY
●●● Heroes and Psychopaths

Lykken (1982) argued that heroes and psychopaths are two sides of the same coin. For example, Lykken noted that Chuck Yeager, a heroic test pilot, once concealed broken ribs that he had suffered in a wild midnight horseback ride so that he could go aloft in the belly of a B-29, wedge himself in the tiny cockpit of the X-1 rocket plane, and let himself be jettisoned at an altitude of 26,000 feet to become the first person to travel faster than the speed of sound. And Ted Bundy was a charming, intelligent, and articulate psychopath who left a coast-to-coast trail of brutal and sadistic murders of young women. Lykken believes that heroes and psychopaths share one characteristic—namely, fearlessness. In an attempt to measure fearlessness, he developed the Activity Preference Questionnaire. The questionnaire instructs respondents to pretend that one or the other situation described must occur and asks respondents to choose the situation that is the lesser of two evils. Here are some of the items:

1. a. Cleaning up your house after floodwaters have left it filled with mud
   b. Making a parachute jump
2. a. Spending hours fixing a fancy barbecue for some guests, who then eat very little and seem not to like it
   b. Distributing 1,000 handbills in mailboxes from door to door
3. a. Having to walk around all day on a blistered foot
   b. Sleeping out on a camping trip in an area where rattlesnakes have been reported
4. a. Washing a car
   b. Driving a car at 95 miles an hour

The questionnaire items present a frightening or embarrassing situation paired with a situation that is merely onerous. People who are relatively fearless, such as heroes and psychopaths, may have a greater tendency to choose the frightening or embarrassing alternative than do fearful people.

What factors influence the probability of becoming a hero rather than a psychopath among those who are relatively fearless? Although very fearless children are difficult to bring up, circumstances and family environment may play crucial roles. Those who have the opportunity to channel their fearlessness into socially approved activities (such as being a test pilot) and who are socialized in families that emphasize warm and loving relationships rather than punishment techniques may be less likely to become psychopaths.

nonpsychopaths. The study assessed the resting state reactivity and the stress-produced reactivity of psychopaths and nonpsychopaths using cardiac, galvanic skin response, and respiratory measures. Hare found that psychopaths required a more intense stimulus, in both the resting state and in response to stressors, than did nonpsychopaths. Quay's hypothesis (1965) that psychopaths' lowered levels of reactivity led them to engage in impulsive, stimulus-seeking behaviors to avoid boredom was supported by another study. Investigators found that antisocial preadolescent children did show stimulus-seeking behaviors (Whitehill, DeMeyer-Gapin, & Scott, 1976).

If learning deficiencies among individuals with antisocial personality disorder are caused by the absence of anxiety and by lowered autonomic reactivity, is it possible to improve their learning by increasing their anxiety or arousal ability? To test this idea, researchers designed two conditions in which psychopaths, a mixed group, and nonpsychopaths would perform an avoidance learning task, with electric shock as the unconditioned stimulus. Under one condition, participants were injected with adrenaline, which presumably increases arousal; under the other, they were injected with a placebo. Psychopaths receiving the placebo made more errors in avoiding the shocks than did nonpsychopaths; psychopaths receiving adrenaline, however, tended to perform better than nonpsychopaths (see Figure 8.2). These findings imply that psychopaths do not react to the same amount of anxiety as do nonpsychopaths and that their learning improves when their anxiety is increased (S. Schachter & Latané, 1964).

The *kind* of punishment used in avoidance learning is also an important consideration in evaluating psychopaths' learning deficiencies (Schmauk, 1970). Whereas psychopaths may show learning deficits when faced with physical (electric shock) or social (verbal feedback) punishments, they learn as well as nonpsychopaths when the punishment is monetary loss. Figure 8.3 shows the effects of the three types of punishment for incorrect responses in Schmauk's study of convicted psychopaths.

The *certainty* of punishment may also influence the responsiveness of those with antisocial personality

Sensation Seeking and Antisocial Personality Lykken theorized that people with low anxiety levels are often thrill seekers. The difference between the psychopath who takes risks and the adventurer may largely be a matter of whether the thrill-seeking behaviors are channeled into destructive or constructive acts. Are there gender differences in thrill-seeking behaviors? If so, what can account for the gender differences?

FIGURE 8.2 Anxiety and Avoidance Learning Among Psychopaths and Others   When psychopaths, a group with mixed characteristics, and a control group were injected with a placebo, the psychopathic group performed least well on an avoidance learning task. However, when injected with adrenaline, which increases arousal, the psychopaths outperformed the mixed group, indicating that arousal may facilitate learning in psychopaths.

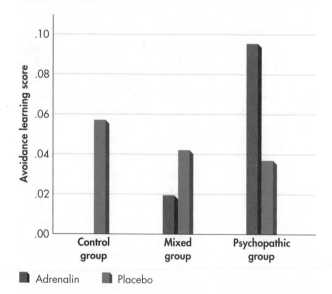

Source: Schachter & Latané (1964).

disorder to punishment. Psychopaths and nonpsychopaths do not seem to differ in responding when punishment is a near certainty (R. Siegel, 1978). When the probability of punishment is highly uncertain, however, psychopaths do not suppress their behaviors. Threats of punishment by themselves do not seem to be sufficient to discourage psychopaths.

Normal people respond to physical, social, or material punishment, and they are influenced by uncertain, as well as certain, punishment. The work of Schmauk and Siegel suggested that psychopaths do not respond to the same range of aversive conditions. Hare (1975) proposed a psychophysiological model to account for the lack of anxiety that makes learning difficult for psychopaths. He speculated that this lack of anxiety results from a defensive mechanism—a psychophysiological ability psychopaths develop to reduce the emotional impact (or anxiety-producing effect) of aversive situations and thus defend themselves against anxiety and pain.

Taking a somewhat different perspective, Patrick, Cuthbert, and Lang (1994) argue that psychopaths may have an emotional imagery deficit. This deficit takes the form of a weak or absent association between perceptual or semantic elements in memory and responding. That is, antisocial personality disorder may be characterized by a deficiency in the ability to respond physiologically to fear stimuli because the association between perception and responding is weakened. The investigators compared two groups—

FIGURE 8.3 Effect of Type of Punishment on Psychopaths and Others The effects of three different types of punishment on an avoidance learning task are shown for three groups of participants. Although physical or social punishment had little impact on psychopaths' learning, monetary punishment was quite effective.

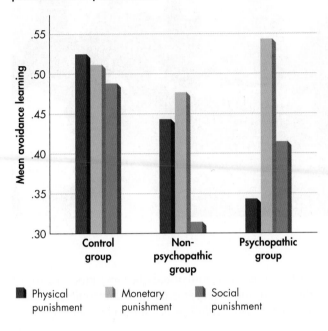

Source: Schmauk (1970).

one of individuals who scored high on psychopathy and another who scored low on psychopathy. Even though both groups had similar ratings of fearfulness, the high-psychopathy group did not respond physiologically as strongly as did the other group. There has also been speculation that the weaker responses are caused by defensive reactions among psychopaths (Levenston, Patrick, Bradley, & Lang, 2000). The study further demonstrates the consistency of the findings of reduced-anxiety responses among psychopaths, even though researchers continue to debate the reasons for the findings.

Reid (1981) agreed that psychophysiological factors may be involved in antisocial personality disorder. He viewed the disorder as a heterogeneous condition with many causes. Familial, biological, social, and developmental factors may converge and provide a coherent picture in explaining the disorder. Brinkley, Newman, Widiger, and Lynam (2004) also view antisocial personality disorder as having different etiological causes and suggest that effective treatment of the disorder requires an understanding of particular causes.

Treatment of Antisocial Personality Disorder

As you have seen, evidence is growing that low anxiety and low autonomic reactivity characterize individuals with antisocial personality disorder. But we still do not know whether these characteristics are products of inherited temperament, of an acquired congenital defect, or of social and environmental experiences during childhood. The theory that psychopaths have developed a defense against anxiety is intriguing, but the factors behind the development of such a defense have not been pinpointed. Because people with antisocial personality disorder feel little anxiety, they are poorly motivated to change themselves; they are also unlikely to see their behaviors as "bad" and may try to manipulate or "con" therapists. Thus traditional treatment approaches, which require the genuine cooperation of the client, may be ineffective for antisocial personality disorder. Few treatment outcome studies have been conducted for this disorder (L. Simon, 1998). In some studies, drugs with tranquilizing effects (phenothiazines and Dilantin) have been helpful in reducing antisocial behavior (R. Meyer & Osborne, 1982). People with antisocial personality disorder, however, are not likely to follow through with self-medication. Moreover, drug treatment is effective in only a few cases, and it can result in side effects such as blurred vision, lethargy, and neurological disorders.

It may be that successful treatment can occur only in a setting in which behavior can be controlled (Vaillant, 1975). That is, treatment programs may need to provide enough control so that those with antisocial personalities cannot avoid confronting their inability to form close and intimate relationships and the effect of their behaviors on others. Such control is sometimes possible for psychopaths who are imprisoned for crimes or who, for one reason or another, are hospitalized. Intensive group therapy may then be initiated to help clients with antisocial personalities in the required confrontation.

Some behavior modification programs have been tried, especially with delinquents who behave in antisocial ways. The most useful treatments are skill based and behavioral (Meloy, 2001). Money and tokens that can be used to purchase items have been given as rewards to young people who show appropriate behaviors (discussion of personal problems, good study habits, punctuality, and prosocial and nondisruptive behaviors). This use of material rewards has been fairly effective in changing antisocial behaviors (Van Evra, 1983). Once the young people leave the treatment programs, however, they are likely to revert to antisocial behavior unless their families and peers help them maintain the appropriate behaviors.

Treating Antisocial Behaviors
Peers and family are critically important in the treatment of antisocial youths and in maintaining progress made in treatment. Here, a group led by a peer counselor is exploring some of the issues troubling these young people. What would you do as a peer counselor to help these youths to open up and talk about their own problems?

Cognitive approaches have also been used. Because individuals with antisocial personalities may be influenced by dysfunctional beliefs about themselves, the world, and the future, they vary in skills for anticipating and acting on possible negative outcomes of their behaviors. Beck and colleagues (1990) have advocated that the therapist build rapport with the client, attempting to guide the patient away from thinking only in terms of self-interest and immediate gratification and toward higher levels of thinking. These higher levels would include, for example, recognizing the effects of one's behaviors on others and developing a sense of responsibility. Because cognitive and behavioral approaches assume that antisocial behaviors are learned, treatment programs may target these behaviors by setting rules and enforcing consequences for rule violations, substituting new behaviors for undesirable ones, and learning to anticipate consequences for behaviors (Meloy, 2001).

Kazdin (1987) noted that, because current treatment programs do not seem very effective, new strategies must be used. These strategies should focus on antisocial youths who seem amenable to treatment, and treatment programs should broaden the base of intervention to involve not only the young clients but also their families and peers. Farley (1986) believes that because people with antisocial personality disorder may seek thrills (Big T's), they may respond to intervention programs that provide the physical and mental stimulation they need. Longitudinal studies show that the prevalence of this disorder diminishes with age as these individuals become more aware of the social and interpersonal maladaptiveness of their social behaviors (Phillips & Gunderson, 1999).

Disorders of Impulse Control

Most people have seen films and television programs that depict pathological gamblers, fire setters, or impulsive thieves. Such behaviors are characteristic of **impulse control disorders.** People with impulse control disorders tend to share three characteristics. First, they fail to resist an impulse or temptation to perform some act, although they know the act is considered wrong by society or is harmful to them. Second, they experience tension or arousal before the act. Third, after committing the act, they feel a sense of excitement, gratification, or release. Guilt or regret may or may not follow. The core feature of the disorder is the repeated expression of impulsive acts that lead to physical or financial damage to the individual or another person, often resulting in a sense of relief or release of tension (Fauman, 1994).

This category does not include impulse control behaviors related to sexual conduct or compulsive ingestion of drugs or alcohol, for example, which are usually classified under the paraphilias and substance-use disorders, respectively. Disorders in this category, including intermittent explosive disorder, kleptomania, pathological gambling, pyromania, and trichotillomania, are not classified elsewhere (see Figure 8.4).

Intermittent Explosive Disorder

People with **intermittent explosive disorder** experience separate and discrete episodes of loss of control over their aggressive impulses, resulting in serious assaults on others or the destruction of property. The aggressiveness is grossly out of proportion to any precipitating stress that may have occurred. People with this disorder show no signs of general aggressiveness between episodes and may genuinely feel remorse for their actions. However, some believe that individuals with this disorder harbor a good deal of suppressed anger (R. Meyer, 1989). The disorder is apparently rare and believed to be much more common among males than females. It often co-occurs with other disorders, especially mood, anxiety, and substance use disorders (McElroy & Arnold, 2001). A patient diagnosed with intermittent explosive disorder described the following incident:

> I'm usually a good and safe driver. I'm married and a very successful businessman. My colleagues say that I am a kind and happy-go-lucky person. That's why it's so strange that I lose control of my temper while driving my car. Last week an elderly woman was driving her car very slowly in front of me. I wanted her to speed up so I honked at her. She kept on moving slowly. I became so irritated that I rammed the back of her car and then drove off. Her car was severely damaged—and so was mine—and I could have killed her. After driving for several miles, I was overwhelmed with guilt and disgust with myself. I tried to find the woman, to apologize and pay for damages. But I couldn't find her. There's something wrong with me. Why do I do these things? I've run several people off the road and tried to ram others if they honk or cut in front of my car. I get so overwhelmed with rage I become a different person. Maybe I should turn myself in to the police.

Kleptomania

Kleptomania is characterized by a recurrent failure to resist impulses to steal objects. People with this disorder do not need the objects for personal use and do not steal them for their monetary value; indeed, they usually have enough money to buy the objects and typically discard, give away, or surreptitiously return them. The individual feels irresistible urges and tension before stealing or shoplifting and then an intense feeling of relief or gratification after the theft. The stealing is not committed to express anger or vengeance and is not in response to a delusion or hallucination. Although theft is common, only a small percentage of thieves (perhaps fewer than 5 percent) fit the criteria for kleptomania, which is

believed to be a rare disorder (American Psychiatric Association, 2000). Some researchers have found depression to be associated with kleptomania (Wise & Tierney, 1999). The disorder appears to be more common among females than among males (Spitzer et al., 1994). The man in the following case relates feelings and behaviors that are typical for this disorder.

> Harold was stopped as he was leaving a grocery store with three cans of lobster hidden in his pockets. He was charged with shoplifting ... he had no prior criminal record and no particular need for the food he had stolen. ... He describes how he entered the store impulsively, experienced an increasing sense of tension ... then he had a desire to take the cans of lobster. ... The tension increased until he could no longer resist it. He took the cans and stuffed them in his pockets, after which he experienced a sense of relief. ... He and his wife have excellent jobs and no financial problems. (Spitzer et al., 1994, p. 61)

Pathological Gambling

The essential feature of **pathological gambling** is a chronic and progressive failure to resist impulses to gamble. The gambling occurs despite the detrimental consequences that often accompany the behavior, such as financial ruin, turning to illegal activities to support gambling, disruptions of family or interpersonal relationships, and sacrificing obligations and responsibilities. Gambling is big business. About $166.5 billion was legally wagered in 1986, and about 80 percent of the U.S. population gambles (Lesieur, 1989). Those afflicted with pathological gambling constitute about 1 to 3 percent of adults, with the disorder more common among men than among women (American Psychiatric Association, 2000). Higher rates of gambling are also found among adolescents and college students. However, a longitudinal study of gambling among college students revealed that for them problem gambling was episodic rather than chronic, with most of the students recovering from gambling problems (Slutske, Jackson, & Sher, 2003).

Unlike social gamblers, who may place limits on the amount of money that may be lost or who can avoid gambling, a pathological gambler is preoccupied with gambling for its own sake and usually feels tension or restlessness when unable to gamble. There is a tendency to gamble with increasing amounts of money to achieve the desired excitement and, at times, to use gambling as a way to relieve dysphoric moods. The person may constantly borrow money or engage in illegal activities (such as forgery or theft) to continue. Interestingly, many individuals with histories of pathological gambling also have

FIGURE 8.4 Disorders Chart: Impulse Control Disorders

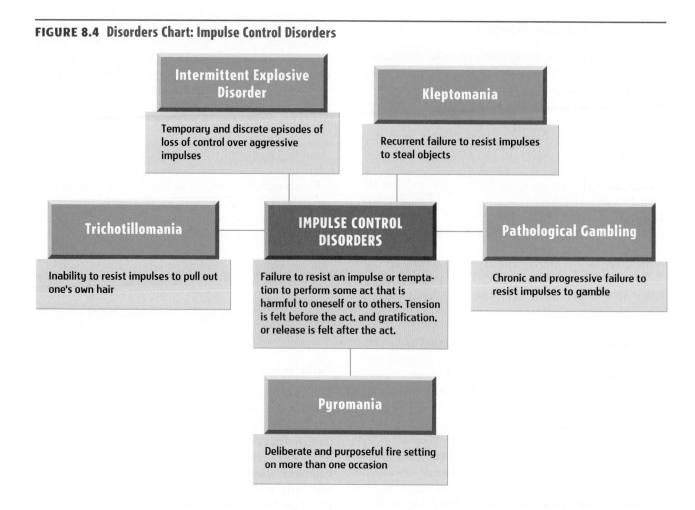

histories of engaging in antisocial behaviors. There is evidence that this association between pathological gambling and antisocial behaviors is more the result of sharing a genetic vulnerability to both characteristics than the result of gambling (e.g., need for money) causing antisocial behaviors (Slutske et al., 2001).

Winning streaks are often occasions for manic behaviors and a heightened sense of excitement, but depression usually follows the frequent gambling losses. At such times, the person may try to borrow more money, rationalizing that the "big win" is about to happen, as in the following case:

Jason L. was a twenty-nine-year-old married salesman. His wife of two years came from a well-to-do family, and Jason increasingly asked his wife's family to help subsidize his business ventures. She was initially impressed with Jason's dreams to "make it big" in his business ventures. Unknown to his wife, however, Jason actually needed the money to continue his habit of gambling at a local card house. He was unable to stay away from gambling. When he won, he was ecstatic and

would tell his wife that his business ventures were succeeding. Jason would then celebrate by taking her out to the finest restaurants. Unfortunately, he lost money most of the time. He would then beg his wife and her family for more money.

After a while, Jason's wife found out that he had no business ventures and that he was simply using the money to continue gambling. She threatened to divorce him if he did not stop gambling. At this point, Jason became infuriated. He claimed that her family looked down on him, so he was gambling in an attempt to get one big win that would let them live in luxury. He also said that he owed thousands of dollars in debts to the card house. Jason's wife indicated that she would take care of the debts but that he must stop gambling. After she gave him the money, Jason promptly lost the money playing cards. His wife again threatened to divorce him unless he entered psychotherapy and ceased his gambling habit. The therapist who saw Jason diagnosed him as a pathological gambler. Although Jason showed some antisocial behaviors, they were confined to his gambling and attempts to get money for gambling.

FIGURE 8.4 Continued

IMPULSE CONTROL DISORDERS	Prevalence (%)	Gender Differences	Age of Onset	Course
Intermittent Explosive	Rare	Higher in males	17 – 30	Unclear
Kleptomania	Rare	Higher in females	Unclear	May continue for years
Pathological Gambling	1.0 – 3.0	Higher in males	Adolescence	Chronic
Pyromania	Rare	Higher in males	Unclear	Unclear
Trichotillomania	1.0 – 2.0*	Higher in females	Childhood	Chronic or episodic

*Rate is among college students.
Source: Based on American Psychiatric Association (2000).

Cognitive-behavioral approaches to this disorder focus on the erroneous beliefs pathological gamblers may have about their ability to influence outcomes that are governed by chance. For example, they may exhibit superstitious beliefs about the relationship between behaviors and outcomes, such as blowing on dice before rolling them or wearing certain clothes in order to win. Cognitive-behavioral treatment intended to correct these erroneous beliefs and to provide better problem-solving and social skills has been extremely helpful in treating some pathological gamblers (Sylvain, Ladouceur, & Boisvert, 1997). Hodgins, Currie, and El-Guebaly (2001) have shown that brief treatments (motivational messages over the telephone and a self-help workbook for problem gamblers) can be effective. The group receiving the brief treatments showed more decreased gambling behaviors than a no-treatment control group, and the reduction in gambling persisted over a follow-up period of one year.

Pyromania

Pyromania is characterized by deliberate and purposeful fire setting on more than one occasion. Fire and burning objects fascinate people with this disorder, who get intense pleasure or relief from setting the fires, watching things burn, or observing firefighters and their efforts to put out fires. Their fire-setting impulses are driven by this fascination rather than by motives involving revenge, sabotage, or financial gains. Fire setters have been reported to have high rates of mood and substance use disorders (McElroy & Arnold, 2001).

The history of fire setting usually begins in childhood. Gaynor and Hatcher (1987) believe that many children first start fires out of curiosity, exploration, or accident. The persistence of fire-setting behavior is associated with certain individual characteristics (being a young male, experiencing overwhelming anger, and having a conduct or personality disorder),

Feeding the Urge In *Hard Eight*, actor John C. Reilly (on the left) stars as a person consumed with gambling. In pathological gambling, a person is unable to resist urges to gamble, despite financial and interpersonal conflicts that may result. While gambling, the person may demonstrate hyperactive and manic behaviors, and later, experience depression because they have lost money and now need to find more money to support his or her gambling urge. Why do people gamble when most of them lose money?

social circumstances (poor family environment and interpersonal maladjustment), and environmental conditions (stressful life events). Others have also found that children who set fires have higher levels of behavioral dysfunction, hostility, and impulsivity than are found among other children (Kolko & Kazdin, 1991). Although many children may play with fire, they do so without the intense pleasure, lack of concern over the destruction caused by fires, and inability to control the impulse that is seen among people with pyromania.

The prevalence of pyromania is unknown, although it is probably rare and is diagnosed far more frequently among males than among females. Interestingly, whereas pyromania is a rare disorder, fire-setting behavior among children and adults with psychiatric

disorders is not (Wise & Tierney, 1999). The case of Kevin, a fourteen-year-old boy, illustrates some of the characteristics associated with this disorder.

> Kevin was arrested for the crime of arson. He had allegedly set a fire that resulted in the destruction of some houses being constructed. Kevin was watching the fire when a witness told firefighters that she had seen Kevin with a gasoline can at the construction site just before the nighttime fire. After arson investigators found the gasoline can (which was later found to have Kevin's fingerprints) and questioned Kevin and his parents, he confessed to the crime. Kevin had a long history of setting fires. When he was about six years of age, he used his father's lighter to burn his sister's doll, which then ignited the window curtain. At age eight, he burned some bushes while he was camping with his family. Kevin was always playing with matches and lighters. He was also caught setting off a fire alarm at an office building. Kevin's parents reported that he always became quite excited when hearing the sirens of fire engines. He often asked his parents to follow the fire engines just to see the fires. Although the parents had punished Kevin for playing with fire, he continued, without his parents' knowledge, to burn items. Outside of setting fires, Kevin had few problems. He was an average student who was quiet and fairly well behaved.

Trichotillomania

Trichotillomania is a disorder characterized by an inability to resist impulses to pull out one's own hair. Although trichotillomania principally involves the hairs in the scalp, a person with this disorder may pull hair from other parts of the body, such as eyelashes, beard, or eyebrows. Skin inflammation, itch, or other physical conditions do not provoke the hair pulling. Rather, the person simply cannot resist the impulse, which begins with a feeling of tension that is replaced by a feeling of release or gratification after the act. Initially, the hair pulling may not disturb the follicles, and new hair will grow. In severe cases, new growth is compromised and permanent balding results. In some cases, extracted hair may be chewed or swallowed (McElroy & Arnold, 2001). A thirty-five-year-old woman who entered therapy with one of the authors said that she had a compulsion to pull the hairs from her head. When asked to reveal the extent of her hair pulling, she removed her wig—she was completely bald except for a few strands of hair at the back of her head.

There is no information on the prevalence of trichotillomania, although it is probably more common than currently believed and more common among women than men (Meyer, 1989). About 1 percent of

Going Down in Smoke Though most people watching a fire experience fear, sadness, and perhaps even shock over the loss, pyromaniacs feel intense pleasure or a sense of relief from setting fires, seeing burning objects or structures, or watching firefighters extinguish fires. Do you think that most individuals like to see fires? Why?

college students appear to have a past or current history of this disorder (American Psychiatric Association, 2000). Trichotillomania has been found to differ from obsessive-compulsive disorders in that hair pulling is usually associated with pleasure and that persons with trichotillomania have few associated obsessive-compulsive symptoms (Wise & Tierney, 1999).

Etiology and Treatment of Impulse Control Disorders

Although some of the impulse control disorders, such as pathological gambling and pyromania, have gained much public attention, we know very little about their specific causes. Furthermore, the characteristics of impulse control disorders seem similar to those found in other disorders in at least three ways. First, the disorders have an obsessive-compulsive quality in that the person feels a compulsion to perform certain acts. In obsessive-compulsive disorders, however, the repetitive behaviors seem more purposeful and serve to prevent or produce some future event or situation. Second, the impulse control disorders also have a compulsive feature that is found in substance abusers or addicts who must maintain their habits. Substance use, however, has more clear physiological involvement. Third, to some extent, the behaviors of people with impulse control disorders resemble those of people with sexual disorders (such as exhibitionism and fetishism) in that tension, fascination, and release may precede or follow the acts. Indeed, some psychoanalysts link pyromania to sexual release and gratifica-

tion. The problem is that orgasm and many sexual activities are intrinsically pleasurable or reinforcing, whereas trichotillomania and fire setting are not. Interestingly, the five impulse control disorders are so different from one another that it is impossible to confuse them diagnostically (Fauman, 1994).

Given the diverse disorders included in the impulse control category, it is not surprising that psychodynamic explanations for impulse control disorders have been quite varied (see Booth, 1988). Pathological gambling has been likened to masturbation in that built-up tension and a need to release the tension drive both behaviors. Alternatively, gambling has been attributed to an unconscious need to lose because of underlying guilt. Kleptomania has been seen as an attempt to gain esteem, nourishment, or sexual gratification through stealing. Pyromania has been associated with sexual gratification, attempts to overcome feelings of impotence and inferiority, or unconscious anger toward a parental figure. And trichotillomania has been described as a response to unhealthy parent-child relationships. These formulations have been based primarily on clinical case studies rather than on empirical research.

Behaviorists tend to explain impulse control disorders through learning principles such as operant conditioning, classical conditioning, and modeling. For example, pathological gambling has been viewed as being influenced by reinforcement schedules. Researchers know that high rates of responding occur when a positive reinforcement schedule is variable rather than continuous. In the context of gambling, this could mean that initial wins may attract the person to gamble; as wins become less frequent and quite variable, a high rate of responding is likely. Learning principles can also be used to conceptualize the other disorders.

Some researchers have even speculated on the role of physiological factors. Roy and colleagues (1988) found that compulsive gamblers were more likely than nongamblers to have abnormalities in their noradrenergic systems (affecting heart rate and blood pressure), which may indicate a greater sensation-seeking or thrill-seeking drive among pathological gamblers. Some promising research has also found a relationship between impulsivity, a characteristic found in impulse control disorders, and the neurotransmitter serotonin and selective serotonin reuptake inhibitors (Wise & Tierney, 1999).

Lesieur (1989) noted the existence of two explanatory "camps." (Although he applied his analysis to pathological gambling, the same analysis can be applied to other impulse control disorders.) The first camp holds that impulse control ranges on a continuum from problem free to troubled. Behavioral, cognitive, and sociological perspectives would probably be included in this first camp. The second camp holds that impulse control disorders are diseaselike—one either has the disorder or does not. Psychodynamic and physiologically based theories could, perhaps, fall into this second orientation. The diversity of explanations and the lack of empirical research on impulse control disorders reflect the fact that, although these disorders have fascinated mental health professionals, their prevalence is sufficiently low that researchers have difficulty studying them. Furthermore, it is likely that impulse control disorders may share similar symptoms (inability to resist an impulse, for example) but lack a common specific cause. That is, different types of disorders, such as intermittent explosive disorder and kleptomania, may be influenced by quite different factors.

There is no established psychological or medical treatment for any of the impulse control disorders, and little systematic research is available (McElroy & Arnold, 2001). Booth (1988) has noted the wide variety of treatment approaches used for impulse control disorders. In many of the disorders, behavioral and cognitive behavioral methods have been moderately successful. Some patients have been taught to recognize tension states that lead to the unacceptable behavior and to make self-statements, such as "I feel like stealing the item but I'd better not." Some therapists have patients rehearse alternative responses, such as having a person with intermittent explosive disorder take a deep breath and relax when tension exists. Other patients have been taught to associate their behavior with aversive consequences through aversive conditioning.

Changing the cognitive styles of people with impulse control problems may be beneficial. In a study of pathological gamblers undergoing treatment (McCormick & Taber, 1988), attributional style (that is, their ways of thinking about the causes of negative experiences; see the chapter on mood disorders) was related to failure to abstain from gambling after treatment. These findings imply that a cognitive approach in treatment might help change the way gamblers think about events. Some insight-oriented approaches have been helpful in treating kleptomania, especially with people who feel guilty over the theft. In treating intermittent explosive disorder, Meyer (1989) recommended awareness techniques, such as those found in gestalt therapy, which attempt to put clients in touch with their anger. Teaching ways to deal with anger in a productive fashion is also recommended. Multimodal approaches (combining techniques) involving family and friends and even organizations (such as Gamblers Anonymous for pathological gamblers) may also be beneficial.

SUMMARY

What kinds of personality patterns are associated with mental disorders?

- The personality disorders include a diversity of behavioral patterns in people who are typically perceived as being odd or eccentric; dramatic, emotional, and erratic; or anxious and fearful.

- DSM-IV-TR lists ten specific personality disorders; each causes notable impairment of social or occupational functioning or subjective distress for the person. They are usually manifested in adolescence, continue into adulthood, and involve disturbances in personality characteristics.

- Because personality is at the core of the disorders, etiological explanations focus on factors that influence personality, such as heredity, family environment, self-identity, and others.

- The five-factor model of personality has been used to conceptualize personality disorders.

Why do some people have a callous disregard for others and lack guilt and anxiety?

- The main characteristics of antisocial (or psychopathic) personality are selfishness, irresponsibility, lack of guilt and anxiety, failure to learn from experience, superficiality, and impulsiveness.
- People with antisocial personalities frequently violate the rules, conventions, or laws of society. Most explanations of antisocial personality attribute its development to family and socialization factors, heredity, or autonomic nervous system abnormalities that result in lowered anxiety or underarousal.
- Traditional treatment approaches are not particularly effective with antisocial personalities.

In what ways can the failure to resist temptations lead to mental disorders?

- The impulse control disorders involve the person's failure to resist a temptation to perform an act. People with such disorders experience tension before the act and a sense of gratification or release afterward.
- DSM-IV-TR lists five impulse control disorders: intermittent explosive disorder, kleptomania, pathological gambling, pyromania, and trichotillomania.
- Although little is known about cause and effective treatment, these disorders have gained much public attention through mass media dramatizations.

KEY TERMS

antisocial personality disorder (p. 245)

avoidant personality disorder (p. 247)

borderline personality disorder (p. 245)

dependent personality disorder (p. 248)

histrionic personality disorder (p. 243)

impulse control disorder (p. 260)

intermittent explosive disorder (p. 261)

kleptomania (p. 261)

narcissistic personality disorder (p. 243)

obsessive-compulsive personality disorder (p. 249)

paranoid personality disorder (p. 238)

pathological gambling (p. 261)

personality disorder (p. 235)

pyromania (p. 263)

schizoid personality disorder (p. 239)

schizotypal personality disorder (p. 242)

trichotillomania (p. 264)

MULTIMEDIA PREVIEW

For additional study aids, we invite you to explore our media resources accompanying *Understanding Abnormal Behavior*, Eighth Edition. The Student CD-ROM includes videos, quizzing, and critical thinking activities that help to reinforce key concepts in a fun and engaging manner. The Student Web Site provides additional interactive activities, chapter outlines, and research links that further support and complement the text. All Web resources may be accessed by logging onto the Web site at **http://psychology.college.hmco.com/students**.

CHAPTER 9
Substance-Related Disorders

■ **What are substance-use disorders?**

■ **Why do people become addicted to drugs?**

■ **How can we successfully help people to overcome substance abuse and addiction?**

Throughout history, people have swallowed, sniffed, smoked, or otherwise taken into their bodies a variety of chemical substances for the purpose of altering their moods, levels of consciousness, or behaviors. The widespread use of drugs in our society today is readily apparent in our vast consumption of alcohol, tobacco, coffee, medically prescribed tranquilizers, and illegal drugs such as cocaine, marijuana, and heroin. Compared with other societies, our society is generally permissive with regard to the use of these substances. As indicated in Figure 9.1, many people have tried substances, especially alcohol, at some time in their lives. The substances or drugs are psychoactive in that they alter moods, thought processes, or other psychological states.

Our society becomes less permissive and more concerned when a person's ingestion of drugs results in

■ impairment of social or occupational functioning;

■ an inability to abstain from using the drug despite its harmful effects on the body;

■ the user's becoming a danger to others;

■ criminal activities, such as the sale of illegal drugs or robbery, to support a drug habit.

The first two of these problems are directly involved in **substance-related disorders,** which result from the use of psychoactive substances that affect the central nervous system, causing significant social, occupational, psychological, or physical problems, and that sometimes result in abuse or dependence. The other two problems arise in connection with such use.

Yet another concern is that use of one substance may lead to use of other substances. In a longitudinal study of drug use among youths, Ellickson, Hays, and Bell (1992) found that involvement with "legal" drugs such as alcohol and cigarettes tended to precede the use of illicit drugs such as marijuana and "hard" drugs. Furthermore, alcohol or drug-related disorders are often part of a dual diagnosis, in which the individual has some other mental disorder, such as depression, antisocial personality, mania, or schizophrenia

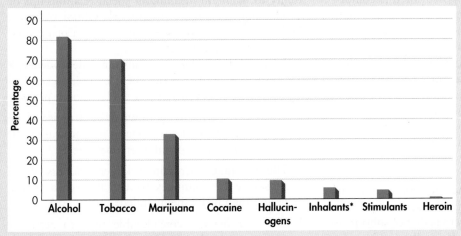

FIGURE 9.1 Percentage of Persons Who Reported Using Specific Illicit Substances at Any Time During Their Lives (Age 12 and Over) As you can see, the vast majority of Americans have used psychoactive substances, particularly alcohol and tobacco.

*Substances that are inhaled, such as glue.

Source: Data from Substance Abuse and Mental Health Services Administration (2004).

FIGURE 9.2 Disorders Chart: Substance-Related Disorders

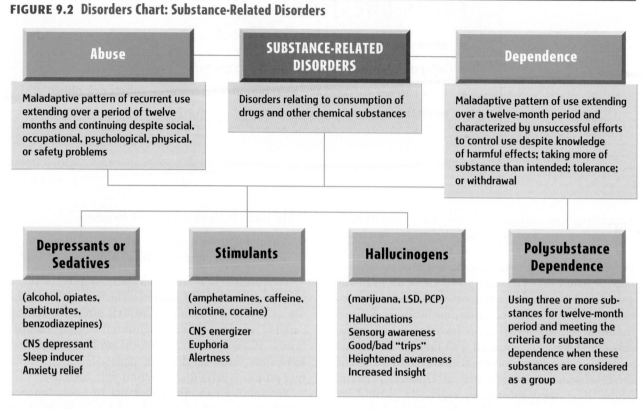

Source: Data from DSM-IV-TR.

(Emmelkamp, 2004). For instance, cigarette smoking and nicotine dependence are associated with depression (Windle & Windle, 2001). Finally, as many as half of people with severe mental disorders develop alcohol or other substance abuse problems at some point in their lives (U.S. Surgeon General, 1999). Although a number of explanations (biological as well as psychosocial) have been proposed for this comorbidity or dual diagnosis (the presence of more than one disorder), the cause is unknown.

DSM-IV-TR divides substance-related disorders into two categories: (1) substance-use disorders that involve dependence and abuse and (2) substance-induced disorders, such as withdrawal and substance-induced delirium. The discussion in this chapter focuses primarily on the substance-use disorders represented in Figure 9.2. Substance-induced cognitive disorders are discussed in the chapter on cognitive disorders.

DSM-IV-TR differentiates the substance-use disorders in two ways: (1) by the actual substance used and (2) by whether the disorder pattern is that of substance abuse or substance dependence. Regardless of the substance involved, the general characteristics of the abuse or dependence are the same. **Substance abuse** is a maladaptive pattern of recurrent use that extends over a period of twelve months, that leads to notable impairment or distress, and that continues despite social, occupational, psychological, physical, or safety problems. The abuse may cause legal problems or jeopardize the safety of the user or others (such as driving while intoxicated). It may impair the user's ability to maintain meaningful social relationships or fulfill major role obligations at work, school, or home. And need for the substance may lead to a preoccupation with its acquisition and use.

To make the diagnosis of **substance dependence**, a therapist must find that the client exhibits several of the following symptoms over a twelve-month period:

1. The user is unable to cut down or control use of the substance, despite knowledge of its harmful physical, psychological, or interpersonal effects.

2. The user takes increasingly larger amounts of the substance or continues to use it over a longer period than he or she intended.

3. The user devotes considerable time to activities necessary to obtain the substance, even though those activities mean that important social, occupational, and recreational activities must be sacrificed.

FIGURE 9.2 Disorders Chart: Substance-Related Disorders (continued)

SUBSTANCE-RELATED DISORDERS	Prevalence of Abuse/ Dependence (%)	Gender Differences	Age of Onset	Course
Depressants or Sedatives	1.2	Higher in females for certain sedatives	Variable	May become dependent from recreational use or from prescribed medications
Alcohol	14.0	5 times higher in males	First drink in mid-teens; peak drinking in 20s and 30s	Periods of remission and relapse; prognosis favorable for some
Opiates	0.7	3–4 times higher in males	Any age but usually in late teens or early 20s	Once dependent, continues over period of years; brief periods of abstinence are common
Stimulants	1.7	3–4 times higher in males	Teens or young adult	Dependency can occur rapidly; tendency to decrease or stop after 8–10 years
Cocaine	0.2	No gender differences observed	Young adult	Use can be episodic or daily; long-term course unclear
Hallucinogens	0.4	3 times higher in males	Teens or young adult	Use can be brief and episodic or chronic
Marijuana	4.4	Higher in males	Teens to young adult	Develops over extended period of time; may gradually become dependent

4. The user exhibits evidence of **tolerance**: increasing doses of the substance are necessary to achieve the desired effect, such as a "high."

5. The user shows evidence of **withdrawal**: distress or impairment in social, occupational, or other areas of functioning or physical or emotional symptoms such as shaking, irritability, and inability to concentrate after reducing or ceasing intake of the substance.

In diagnosing substance dependence, the clinician also specifies whether the dependence is physiological; evidence of either tolerance or withdrawal indicates physiological dependence.

Although intoxication and withdrawal are considered substance-induced disorders, and therefore outside the primary topic of this chapter, we discuss them here because they are necessary for an understanding of the substance-use disorders. **Intoxication** is a condition in which a substance affecting the central nervous system has been ingested and certain maladaptive behaviors or psychological changes, such as belligerence and impaired judgment and functioning, are evident. The effects of intoxication and withdrawal vary according to the substance, but they generally cause significant distress or impairment in social, occupational, or other important areas of functioning.

As can be readily noted, the criteria for substance dependence include those for abuse and withdrawal. Because dependence is considered the more severe disorder, people who meet the criteria for both dependence and abuse for a particular substance are diagnosed only as dependent, not as abusing. Although the two categories have some overlap in criteria and both have biopsychosocial effects, research has indicated that distinguishing between dependence and abuse is meaningful and can differentially predict severity of disorder and treatment outcome (Nathan, 1991). Diagnosis of withdrawal or intoxication may be made when the major symptoms at the time of diagnosis are those of withdrawal or intoxication. In cases such as these, the client may also be dependent on the substance. Finally, some clients may be dependent on substances or may be abusing them, but they may not show certain psychological characteristics, such as intentional drug use. These persons may have substance-induced conditions as a result of unintentional exposure to substances or of side effects of medication.

The progression from drug experimentation to abuse or dependence often follows a typical pattern (Walter, 2001). First, adolescents may decide to experiment with drugs, especially with peers. Tobacco, alcohol, and marijuana are often the first drugs of choice. Second, early regular use may then ensue. The adolescents now actively seek the substances and the drug-induced perceptions and feeling states. They may begin to lose interest in previous activities or hobbies and become rebellious or withdrawn. Third, at a later stage, they plan daily activities around opportunities to use drugs. As use increases, unpleasant states may worsen, leading to more drug use. Self-destructiveness, risk-taking behaviors, and poor functioning may occur. Finally, drugs are now needed to avoid constant dysphoria, and more potent substances may be used. Physical and mental deterioration becomes obvious. Although many adolescents may not go beyond the first stage of experimentation or may cease using drugs as they mature, others progress to the later stages.

In this chapter, we first examine substance-use disorders, including the effects of the abuse of alcohol and various drugs. We also examine the degree to which different theories may increase our understanding of the causes and treatment of the abuse of alcohol and other substances.

Substance-Use Disorders

A number of substances can result in abuse, dependence, intoxication, and withdrawal. Among them are prescription drugs such as Valium; legal substances such as alcohol and cigarettes; and illegal substances such as LSD (lysergic acid diethylamide), cocaine, and heroin. Alcohol and substance abuse is the second leading cause of disability in the United States, Canada, and western Europe, ahead of physical diseases and second only to mental illness (President's New Freedom Commission on Mental Health, 2003).

Substance-related disorders are most prevalent among youths and young adults. In 2003, an estimated 19.5 million Americans, or 8.2 percent of the population age 12 or older, were current illicit drug users (Substance Abuse and Mental Health Services Administration, 2004). There are nine different categories of illicit drug use: marijuana (including hashish), cocaine (including crack), heroin, hallucinogens (including LSD, PCP, peyote, mescaline, mushrooms, and "Ecstasy" or MDMA), inhalants (including a variety of substances, such as amyl nitrite, cleaning fluids, gasoline, paint, and glue), and nonmedical use of prescription-type pain relievers, tranquilizers, stimulants, and sedatives. The four categories of prescription-type drugs (pain relievers, tranquilizers, stimulants, and sedatives) cover numerous drugs available through prescriptions and sometimes illegally "on the street." Respondents are asked to report only uses of drugs that were not prescribed for them or drugs they took only for the experience or feeling they caused. Over-the-counter drugs and legitimate uses of prescription drugs are not included. Abuse/dependence was greatest for marijuana. Note that a person may abuse or be dependent on more than one drug.

Figure 9.3 shows the prevalence of illicit drug use among various ethnic groups. These drugs include the nine categories mentioned in the preceding paragraph. As can be seen in the figure, use varies considerably among the different groups. Incidentally, in terms of prescription, as well as over-the-counter, drugs, it is anticipated that abuse will increase among the elderly as the baby boomers age (U.S. Surgeon General, 1999).

Each of the drugs discussed in this chapter can create an abuse or dependence disorder. Many are also associated with legal problems, because their use is expressly prohibited except under strict medical supervision. We discuss general categories of substances—depressants, stimulants, and hallucinogens—that contain many specific drugs, such as alcohol, narcotics, barbiturates, benzodiazepines, amphetamines, caffeine, nicotine, cocaine and crack, marijuana, LSD, and phencyclidine (PCP). Table 9.1 lists these substances, their effects, and their potential for dependency. In practice, some substances are not easily classified because they may have multiple effects.

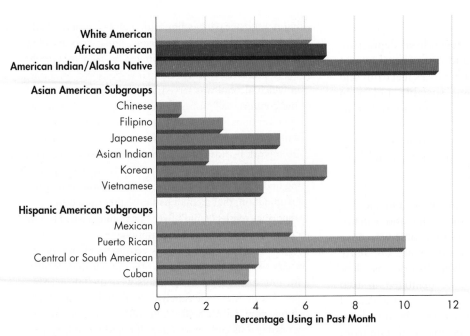

FIGURE 9.3 Past-Month Illicit Drug Use Among Persons Aged 12 and Older, by Race/Ethnicity

Source: http://www.samhsa.gov/oas/NHSDA/2KNHSDA/chapter2.htm.

TABLE 9.1   Characteristics of Various Psychoactive Substances

Drugs	Short-Term Effects[a]	Potential for Dependency
Sedatives		
Alcohol	Central nervous system (CNS) depressant, loss of inhibitions	Moderate
Narcotics (codeine, morphine, heroin, opium, methadone)	CNS depressant, pain relief	High
Barbiturates (amytal, nembutal, seconal)	CNS depressant, sleep inducer	Moderate to high
Benzodiazepines (Valium)	CNS depressant, anxiety relief	Low
Stimulants		
Amphetamines (Benzedrine, Dexedrine, Methedrine)	CNS energizer, euphoria	High
Caffeine	CNS energizer, alertness	Low
Nicotine	CNS energizer	High
Cocaine and crack	CNS energizer, euphoria	High
Hallucinogens		
Marijuana, hashish	Relaxant, euphoria	Moderate
LSD	Hallucinatory agent	Low
PCP	Hallucinatory agent	Moderate

[a] Specific effects often depend on the quality and dosage of the drug, as well as on the experience, expectancy, personality, and situation of the person using the drug.

Depressants or Sedatives

Depressants or *sedatives* cause generalized depression of the central nervous system and a slowing down of responses. People taking such substances feel calm and relaxed. They may also become sociable and open because of lowered interpersonal inhibitions. Let us examine in more detail one of the most widely used depressants—alcohol—and then discuss other depressants, such as narcotics, barbiturates, and benzodiazepines.

Alcohol-Use Disorders   Alcohol abuse and alcohol dependence are, of course, substance abuse and dependence in which the substance is alcohol. People who have either of these alcohol-related disorders are popularly referred to as **alcoholics**, and their disorder as **alcoholism.** Drinking problems can be exhibited in two major ways. First, the person may need to use alcohol daily to function; that is, he or she may be unable to abstain. Second, the person may be able to abstain from consuming alcohol for certain periods of time but be unable to control or moderate intake once he or she resumes drinking. This person is a "binge" drinker. Both patterns of drinking can result in deteriorating relationships, job loss, family conflicts, and violent behavior while intoxicated. The following case is typical.

Jim was a fifty-four-year-old alcoholic. He was well educated, having received a bachelor's degree in engineering and a master's degree in management. Until recently, he was employed as a middle manager in an aerospace firm. Because of federal defense industry budget cuts and because of his absenteeism from work caused by drinking, Jim lost his job. He decided to enter treatment.

His drinking history was long. Jim clearly recalled the first time that he drank. At age fifteen, he attended a party at his friend's house. Alcohol was freely served. Jim took a drink, and despite the fact that alcohol "tasted so bad," he forced himself to continue drinking. Indeed, he became drunk and had a terrible hangover the next day. He swore that he would never drink again, but two weeks later he drank again at his friend's house. Over the next several years, Jim acquired the ability to consume large amounts of alcohol and was proud of his drinking capacity. At social gatherings, he was uninhibited and the "life of the party." His drinking continued during college, but it was confined primarily to his fraternity weekend parties. He was considered a very heavy drinker in the fraternity, but the drinking did not seem to affect his academic performance. He frequently drove his car during weekend binges, however, and was once caught and convicted of drunken driving.

After graduate school, he got married and took a position in an aerospace firm. Katie, Jim's wife, also drank but never as heavily as Jim. Although his drinking had been largely confined to weekends, Jim started drinking throughout the week. He attributed his increased drinking to pressures at work, company-sponsored receptions in which alcohol was served, and a desire to feel "free and comfortable" in front of company executives during the receptions. Over time, Jim was unable to complete work assignments on time and was frequently absent from work because of his drinking. The drinking continued despite frequent arguments with Katie over his drinking and a physician's warning, after a routine physical examination, that alcohol had probably caused the abnormal results of Jim's liver-functioning tests. He could not control his alcohol consumption.

Katie noticed that Jim was getting more and more angry over his work assignments. Jim felt that deadlines for him to complete assignments were unrealistic. She felt that he was increasingly difficult to be around. He drank now daily, usually in his office at the end of the workday. His colleagues knew Jim had a drinking problem but because he was still functioning well at work, they kidded him about drinking rather than counseling him against consuming alcohol. They were, however, concerned about his absenteeism, frequent tardiness, and inability to get started in the morning, which were caused by his drinking.

Over the years, Katie simply fell out of love with Jim. The arguments, Jim's drinking, and his unwillingness to communicate with her finally led to a divorce. He was quite bitter over the divorce, although Katie could not see how he was getting anything out of the marriage.

When awards for defense contracts had diminished, Jim's company started to lay off workers. Jim was among the first to be asked to leave.

Problem drinking can develop in many different ways and can begin at almost any age. However, Jim's history is typical in several respects. First, as is true of most people, he initially found the taste of alcohol unpleasant, and, after his first bout of drunkenness, he swore that he would never drink again. Nevertheless, Jim did return to drinking. Second, heavy drinking served a purpose: it reduced his anxiety, particularly at work. Third, consumption continued despite the obvious negative consequences. Fourth and finally, a preoccupation with alcohol consumption and the deterioration of social and occupational functioning are also characteristic of the problem drinker.

Alcohol Consumption in the United States   People drink considerable amounts of alcohol in the United States. About 11 percent of adults consume one ounce or more of alcohol a day, 55 percent drink fewer than three alcoholic drinks a week, and 35 percent abstain completely (American Psychiatric Association, 1987).

Patterns of Alcohol Consumption Societies differ not only in the extent to which alcohol is consumed but also in the pattern of use. In many European countries, alcohol is freely used with meals throughout the day. Wine drinking is relatively high. Are rates of alcoholism likely to be higher in these countries?

The per-person average annual consumption is 2.43 gallons of absolute alcohol (alcohol containing no more than 1 percent water) by individuals age fifteen and older (Franklin & Frances, 1999). Most of the alcohol is consumed by a small percentage of people; 50 percent of the total alcohol consumed is drunk by only 10 percent of drinkers. Drinking is widespread among young people. Heavy drinking is most common among those between eighteen and twenty-five years of age (National Institute on Drug Abuse, 1991). One national survey found that approximately 10.9 million persons ages twelve to twenty (29.0 percent of this age group) reported drinking alcohol in the previous month (Substance Abuse and Mental Health Services Administration, 2004). About 14 million American adults suffer from alcohol abuse or dependence (Nitzkin & Smith, 2004). Early use of alcohol has been found to be a strong predictor of progression into serious problem drinking (C. Nelson, Heath, & Kessler, 1998). Men drink two to five times as much as women, although gender differences in the use of alcohol are decreasing (C. Nelson et al., 1998). Jackson, Sher, Gotham, and Wood (2001) examined the drinking habits of college students from their first year in college to six years later. Interestingly, they found that over time, many drank as frequently as before but reduced the amount consumed (e.g., they did not drink to drunkenness). However, those with a history of family alcoholism did not show this reduction in amount consumed.

Alcohol consumption varies according to the cultural traditions of various societies. In Italy and some other countries, wine is a traditional accompaniment to meals, and individuals drink freely throughout the day.

In most societies, females tend to consume less alcohol than do males, and in Asian countries, the male-to-female rate of consumption is particularly high. In general, drinking alcohol is less common in some Asian countries than in Europe or the United States. The low prevalence rates among Asians may be caused by a deficiency, in perhaps 50 percent of Japanese, Chinese, and Korean individuals, of the form of aldehyde dehydrogenase that eliminates low levels of the first breakdown product of alcohol, acetaldehyde. This leads to the accumulation of acetaldehyde, which accounts for dysphoria, a flushed face, and palpitations among many Asians (American Psychiatric Association, 2000). Within the United States, alcohol consumption varies according to gender, ethnicity, and age. Some rates for selected groups are shown in Figure 9.4, which graphs self-reports of alcohol use during a one-month period, as reported by the Office of National Drug Control Policy (1998). Rates for non-Hispanic whites were higher than those for either African Americans or Hispanic Americans. In all groups, males consume more alcohol than females (Office of National Drug Control Policy, 1998).

Problems associated with alcohol consumption in the United States are apparent in terms of social, medical, physical, and financial costs. Alcohol consumption and alcoholism are associated with serious health-care costs; lowered productivity on the job; shortened life expectancy (by about ten to twelve years); and high rates of suicide, automobile accidents, spousal abuse, and divorce. One hundred thousand deaths per year are alcohol related (Franklin & Frances, 1999; Office for Substance Abuse Prevention,

FIGURE 9.4 Gender, Ethnic, and Age Differences in Self-Reports of Alcohol Use During a One-Month Period Important gender, ethnic, and age differences are shown in the self-reports of alcohol use during "the past month." Men, whites, and individuals ages eighteen to thirty-four reported relatively greater consumption than other groups.

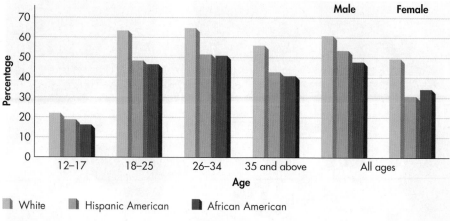

Source: Data from Office of National Drug Control Policy (1998).

1990). Concern has also developed over the children of alcoholic parents, who are at risk for social maladjustment, self-depreciation, lower self-esteem, and alcoholism (Berkowitz & Perkins, 1988; Cooper & McCormack, 1992).

In view of the problems associated with alcohol use, why do people continue drinking? Particularly ironic is the fact that, like Jim in the earlier case, most people consuming alcoholic beverages for the first time find the taste unpleasant. To better understand this puzzle, let's consider the physiological and psychological effects of alcohol.

The Effects of Alcohol Alcohol has both physiological and psychological effects, which can be further broken down into short-term and long-term effects. We consider short-term effects first. Once swallowed, alcohol is absorbed into the blood without digestion. When it reaches the brain, its short-term physiological effect is to depress central nervous system functioning. When the alcohol content in the bloodstream (the blood alcohol level) is about 0.1 percent (the equivalent of drinking five ounces of whiskey or five glasses of beer), muscular coordination is impaired. The drinker may have trouble walking a straight line or pronouncing certain words. At the 0.5 percent blood alcohol level, the person may lose consciousness or even die.

The short-term physiological effects of alcohol on a specific person are determined by the individual's body weight, the amount of food present in the stomach, the drinking rate over time, prior drinking experience, heredity, personality factors, and the individual's environment and culture. Table 9.2 shows the effect of alcohol intake on blood alcohol level as a function of body weight.

The short-term psychological effects of alcohol often include feelings of happiness, loss of inhibitions (because alcohol depresses the inhibitory brain centers), poor judgment, and reduced concentration. Depending on the situation or context in which drinking occurs, other effects, such as negative moods and anger, may also be experienced. Reactions also depend on the expectancy that individuals have developed with respect to alcohol (Hull & Bond, 1986). Some people behave differently in the presence of others simply because of their perception that they have been drinking, not because of the effects of the alcohol (as, for example, when an individual has only a few sips of beer and begins to act hostile). Heavy and prolonged drinking often impairs sexual performance and produces a hangover. Ironically, because of the loss of inhibitions, people mistakenly believe that alcohol is a stimulant rather than a depressant.

The long-term psychological effects of heavy drinking are more serious. Although there is no single type of alcoholic, Jellinek (1971) observed certain patterns in the course of individuals who develop alcohol dependence. Most people begin to drink in social situations. Because the alcohol relieves tension, the drinkers tend to drink more and to drink more frequently. Tolerance levels may increase over a period of months or years.

Because of stress, inability to adequately cope, or biological predisposition to alcoholism, some drinkers become preoccupied with thoughts of alcohol. They may worry about whether there will be enough alcohol at a party; they may try to drink inconspicuously or furtively. They begin to consume large amounts and may "gulp" their drinks. Such drinkers frequently feel guilty; they are somewhat aware that their drinking is excessive. Heavy, sustained drinking may lead to blackouts, periods of time for which drinkers have no memory of their activities. Jellinek believed that sustained drinking could then lead to a loss of control

TABLE 9.2   Blood Alcohol Level as a Function of Number of Drinks Consumed and Body Weight

Body Weight, Pounds	Number of Drinks Consumed[a]						
	1	2	3	4	5	6	7
100	.020	.055	.095	.130	.165	.200	.245
120	.015	.045	.075	.105	.135	.165	.195
140	.010	.035	.060	.085	.115	.140	.165
160	.005	.030	.050	.075	.095	.120	.145
180	.0	.025	.045	.065	.085	.105	.125
200	.0	.020	.040	.055	.075	.085	.110
220	.0	.020	.035	.050	.065	.085	.100
240	.0	.015	.035	.045	.060	.075	.090

[a]The given blood alcohol levels are those that would exist 1 hour after the start of drinking. Because alcohol is metabolized over time, subtract 0.015 from the given level for each additional hour. For example, a 100-pound person consuming two drinks would, after 2 hours, have a blood alcohol level of 0.055 minus 0.015, or 0.040. One drink equals 12 ounces of beer, 4 ounces of wine, or 1.25 ounces of liquor.

Source: Adapted from Vogler & Bartz (1983).

over alcohol intake and to frequent periods of intoxication. Individuals may then drink only to become intoxicated.

It should be noted that most theories of alcoholism are based on research with male alcoholics because relatively few studies have examined female alcoholics. The available evidence suggests, however, that gender differences do exist. For example, alcoholic women report more childhood problems—such as alcoholic parents, unhappy childhoods, and broken homes—than do alcoholic men. Furthermore, women become problem drinkers at a later age than men (Perodeau, 1984). Such findings suggest that perspectives based on research with alcoholic men should be carefully scrutinized for their applicability to women.

The long-term physiological effects of alcohol consumption include an increase in tolerance as the person becomes used to alcohol, physical discomfort, anxiety, and hallucinations. Chronic alcoholism destroys brain cells and is often accompanied by poor nutritional habits and physical deterioration. Thus the left brain hemispheres of alcoholics have been found to be less dense than those of a control group of nonalcoholics (Golden et al., 1981). Other direct or indirect consequences generally attributed to chronic alcoholism are liver diseases such as cirrhosis, in which an excessive amount of fibrous tissue develops and impedes the circulation of blood; heart failure; hemor-

rhages of capillaries, particularly those on the sides of the nose; and cancers of the mouth and throat. Alcohol consumption in pregnant women may affect their unborn children: children who suffer *fetal alcohol syndrome* are born mentally retarded and physically deformed.

Interestingly, the moderate use of alcohol (one or two drinks a day) in adults has been associated in some studies with lowered risk of heart disease. The precise reasons for this effect are unknown. What is clear, though, is that chronic heavy consumption has serious negative consequences, both for the drinker and sometimes for society at large, as the Mental Health and Society feature "MADD (Mothers Against Drunk Driving" points out.

Narcotics (Opiates)   Like alcohol, the organic **narcotics**, which include opium and its derivatives morphine, heroin, and codeine, depress the central nervous system; act as sedatives to provide relief from pain, anxiety, and tension; and are addictive. Feelings of euphoria and well-being (and sometimes negative reactions such as nausea) often accompany narcotics use. Opium and its derivatives (especially heroin) result in dependency. Tolerance for narcotics builds rapidly, and withdrawal symptoms are severe. Opiates such as heroin are usually administered intravenously, causing puncture marks on the extremities of the body and spreading

MENTAL HEALTH AND SOCIETY

MADD (Mothers Against Drunk Driving)

On May 3, 1980, a thirteen-year-old girl was walking to a church carnival in Fair Oaks, California. A car suddenly swerved out of control and killed her. Police arrested the vehicle's driver, who was intoxicated. A check of the driver's record revealed that he had a long history of arrests for drunk driving. Only the week before, he had been bailed out of jail after being charged with hit-and-run drunk driving.

Candy Lightner, the mother of the girl, was furious over the death of her daughter and concerned that the driver might not be sent to prison for the crime. At that time the penalties for drunk driving were frequently light, even when someone was injured or killed. Lightner wanted to find ways to keep drunk people from driving and to help the victims of drunk drivers and victims' families. She decided to form an organization called Mothers Against Drunk Driving (MADD).

Initially Lightner was unsuccessful. She wanted to meet with Jerry Brown, who was then governor of California, to find a means of dealing with drunk drivers, but he declined to see her. Finally, after Lightner began to show up at his office day after day and succeeded in obtaining newspaper publicity for her crusade, Brown took action. He appointed a task force to deal with drunk driving and named her a member.

As a result of the efforts of Lightner and the task force, California eventually passed tough new laws against drunk driving. Lightner's organization has grown as well; MADD now has 600 chapters and offices nationwide. They have persuaded most states to enact more severe penalties for drunk driving.

Incidentally, the driver who was responsible for the death of Lightner's daughter did eventually serve twenty-one months in jail (Friedrich, 1985).

In view of the dangers associated with drunken driving, every person should address several questions: Have you ever driven after having several drinks? If so, did you feel that you were proficient as a driver? At a party at which there is alcohol consumption, do you encourage others to drink to intoxication? What should you do if a friend who has driven to the party has had too much to drink? These questions are important to address ahead of time. After consuming alcohol, a person's judgment may be impaired so that he or she may believe that safe driving is simply a matter of being careful. Safe driving is also a matter of being sober, and we must all plan strategies for handling situations in which we or others become intoxicated.

Fighting Mad Mothers Against Drunk Driving (MADD) is an organization started by Candy Lightner, a mother whose daughter was killed by a drunk driver. MADD's goal is to prevent drunk people from driving and to assist the victims of drunk drivers and victims' families. Well over one-half million individuals are involved in MADD. Has MADD had a beneficial impact in reducing drinking and driving?

diseases such as AIDS, which can be transmitted through needle sharing (D. Smith & Landry, 1988). Twenty-five percent of AIDS cases involve persons who abuse intravenous drugs (Franklin & Frances, 1999).

About 0.7 percent of the adult population has shown opioid abuse or dependence at some time during their lives. The prevalence of addiction decreases with age, and males are more affected than females, by a ratio of 1.5:1 for opioids other than heroin (i.e., those available by prescription) and 3:1 for heroin. (American Psychiatric Association, 2000).

Because dependency is likely to occur after repeated use, narcotics addicts are usually unable to maintain normal relationships with family and friends or to pursue legitimate careers. They live to obtain the drug through any possible means. Nonmedical use of narcotics is illegal, and many addicts have little choice but to turn to criminal activities to obtain the drug and to support their expensive habits.

Barbiturates   Synthetic **barbiturates**, or "downers," are powerful depressants of the central nervous

system and are commonly used to induce relaxation and sleep. Next to the narcotics, they represent the largest category of illegal drugs, and they are quite dangerous for several reasons. First, psychological and physical dependence can develop. Second, although their legal use is severely restricted, their widespread availability makes it difficult to control misuse or abuse. More than 1 million individuals—primarily middle-aged and older people—are now estimated to be barbiturate addicts. Third, users often experience harmful physical effects. Excessive use of either barbiturates or heroin can be fatal, but barbiturates are the more lethal. Constant heroin use increases the amount of the drug required for a lethal dosage. The lethal dosage of barbiturates does not increase with prolonged use, so accidental overdose and death can easily occur. And combining alcohol with barbiturates can be especially dangerous because alcohol compounds the depressant effects of the barbiturates, as it did in the following case.

Kelly M., a seventeen-year-old girl from an upper-middle-class background, lived with her divorced mother. Kelly was hospitalized after her mother found her unconscious from an overdose of barbiturates consumed together with alcohol. She survived the overdose and later told the therapist that she had regularly used barbiturates for the previous year and a half. The overdose was apparently accidental and not suicidal.

For several weeks following the overdose, Kelly openly discussed her use of barbiturates with the therapist. She had been introduced to the drugs by a boy in school who told her they would help her relax. Kelly was apparently unhappy over her parents' divorce. She felt that her mother did not want her, especially because her mother spent a lot of time away from home building a real estate agency. And, although she enjoyed her occasional visits with her father, Kelly felt extremely uncomfortable in the presence of the woman who lived with him. The barbiturates helped her relax and relieved her tensions. Arguments with her mother would precipitate heavy use of the drugs. Eventually she became dependent on barbiturates and always spent her allowance to buy them. Her mother reported that she had no knowledge of her daughter's drug use. She did notice, though, that Kelly was increasingly isolated and sleepy.

The therapist informed Kelly of the dangers of barbiturates and of combining them with alcohol. Kelly agreed to undergo treatment, which included the gradual reduction of barbiturate use and psychotherapy with her mother.

Kelly's practice of *polysubstance use,* or the use of more than one chemical substance at the same time, can be extremely dangerous. For example, heavy smokers who consume a great deal of alcohol run an increased risk of esophageal cancer. Chemicals taken simultaneously may exhibit a synergistic effect, interacting to multiply one another's effects. For example, when a large dose of barbiturates is taken along with alcohol, death may occur because of a synergistic effect that depresses the central nervous system. Furthermore, one of the substances (such as alcohol) may reduce the person's judgment, resulting in excessive (or lethal) use of the other drug. Equally dangerous is the use of one drug to counteract the effect of another. For instance, a person who has taken a stimulant to feel euphoric may later take an excessive amount of a depressant (such as a barbiturate) in an attempt to get some sleep. The result can be an exceedingly harmful physiological reaction.

According to DSM-IV-TR, **polysubstance dependence** may be diagnosed if (1) a person has used at least three substances (not including nicotine and caffeine) for a period of twelve months and (2) during this period, the person meets the criteria for substance dependence for the substances considered as a group but not for any single specific substance.

Benzodiazepines   One member of this category of drugs is Valium, which is one of the most widely prescribed drugs in the United States today. Like other sedatives, Valium is a central nervous system depressant; it is often used to reduce anxiety and muscle tension. People who take the drug seem less concerned with and less affected by their problems. Some side effects may occur, such as drowsiness, skin rash, nausea, and depression, but the greatest danger in using Valium is in abusing it. Because life stressors are unavoidable, many people use Valium as their sole means of dealing with stress; then, as tolerance develops, dependence on the drug may also grow. The female-to-male and white-to-African-American use ratios are about 3:1 (Franklin & Frances, 1999). Benzodiazepines are more likely to be prescribed for older adults, so there is special concern for this population (U.S. Surgeon General, 1999).

Stimulants

A **stimulant** is a substance that is a central nervous system energizer, inducing elation, grandiosity, hyperactivity, agitation, and appetite suppression. Commonly used stimulants are the amphetamines, caffeine, nicotine, and cocaine and crack.

Amphetamines   The **amphetamines,** also known as "uppers," speed up central nervous system activity and bestow on users increased alertness, energy, and sometimes feelings of euphoria and confidence. They increase the concentration of the neurotransmitter dopamine in synapses, which exposes the postsynaptic cells to high levels of dopamine. Increased concentration of dopamine may amplify nerve impulses in the brain that are associated with pleasure (Wise, 1988). Amphetamines inhibit appetite and sleep, and some are used as appetite suppressants or diet pills. These stimulants may be physically addictive and become habit forming with a rapid increase in tolerance. They are taken orally, intravenously, or nasally ("snorting").

"Speed freaks" inject amphetamines into their blood vessels and become extremely hyperactive and euphoric for days. Another immediate and powerful effect is obtained by smoking a pure, crystalline form ("ice") of the substance (American Psychiatric Association, 2000). Assaultive, homicidal, and suicidal behaviors can occur during this time. Heavy doses may trigger delusions of persecution, similar to those seen among paranoid schizophrenics. Overdoses are fatal, and brain damage has been observed among chronic abusers.

About 2 percent of U.S. adults have suffered from amphetamine abuse or dependence at some time during their lives. It is more common among persons from lower socioeconomic groups and among men than women by a ratio of three or four to one (American Psychiatric Association, 2000).

Caffeine   *Caffeine* is a widely used legal stimulant ingested primarily in coffee, chocolate, tea, and cola drinks. The average American consumes approximately 200 milligrams (mg) of caffeine per day (Larson & Carey, 1998). Caffeine is considered intoxicating when, after the recent ingestion of 250 mg (about two cups of coffee) or more, a person shows several of the following symptoms: restlessness, nervousness, excitement, insomnia, flushed face, gastrointestinal disturbance, rambling speech, and cardiac arrhythmia. The consequences of caffeine intoxication are usually transitory and relatively minor. In some cases, however, the intoxication is chronic and seriously affects the gastrointestinal or circulatory system.

Nicotine   *Nicotine* is another widely used legal stimulant, and dependence on it is most commonly associated with cigarette smoking. Media campaigns periodically immerse the public in warnings that cigarette smoking is harmful to the body. A U.S. surgeon general's report (U.S. Surgeon General, 1999) has indicated that cigarette smoking accounts for one-sixth of the deaths in the United States and is the single most preventable cause of death. The prevalence of smoking is decreasing slightly in most industrialized nations, but it is rising in developing areas. According to the Substance Abuse and Mental Health Services Administration (2004), an estimated 70.8 million Americans (29.8 percent of the population age 12 or older) reported current use of a tobacco product. There were 60.4 million (25.4 percent) who had smoked cigarettes in the past month, 12.8 million (5.4 percent) who had smoked cigars, 7.7 million (3.3 percent) who had used smokeless tobacco, and 1.6 million (0.7 percent) who had smoked tobacco in pipes. Some, of course, used more than one type of tobacco. The highest rate of use was reported by young adults

The pictures say it all.

Healthy lung

Smoker's lung
(Emphysema)

AMERICAN
CANCER
SOCIETY

A Not So Pretty Picture Ad campaigns like this one by the American Cancer Society use fear appeals to encourage people to stop smoking or to discourage them from ever starting. Do you think these ad campaigns help to decrease smoking? How do these ads make you feel?

ages 18 to 25 (40.2 percent). In terms of gender, among those age 12 or older, a higher proportion of males than females smoked cigarettes (28.1 vs. 23.0 percent). Among youths ages 12 to 17, however, girls (12.5 percent) were as likely as boys (11.9 percent) to smoke. As it is estimated that between 80 percent and 90 percent of regular smokers are nicotine dependent, up to 25 percent of the U.S. population may be nicotine dependent (American Psychiatric Association, 2000). Many cigarette manufacturers have been sued by smokers and government officials for the health problems caused by smoking and for failing to adequately warn the public about the dangers of smoking.

The following symptoms are characteristic of nicotine dependence:

- Attempts to stop or reduce tobacco use on a permanent basis have been unsuccessful.

- Attempts to stop smoking have led to withdrawal symptoms, such as a craving for tobacco, irritability, difficulty in concentrating, sleep difficulties, and restlessness.

- Tobacco use continues despite a serious physical disorder, such as emphysema, that the smoker knows is exacerbated by tobacco use.

Cocaine and Crack A great deal of publicity and concern have been devoted to the use of **cocaine**, a substance that is extracted from the coca plant and that induces feelings of euphoria and self-confidence in users. A number of professional athletes, film stars, political figures, and other notables use this drug regularly. Cocaine is a fashionable drug, especially among middle-class and upper-class professionals, and its use is equally distributed between males and females. From 1 to 3 million cocaine abusers are in need of treatment, a number many times higher than the number of heroin addicts (Gawin, 1991).

In the late 1800s, cocaine was heralded as a wonder drug for remedying depression, indigestion, headaches, pain, and other ailments. It was often included in medicines, tonics, and wines; it was even used in cola drinks such as Coca-Cola. In the early 1900s, however, its use was controlled, and the possession of cocaine is now illegal.

Cocaine can be eaten, injected intravenously, or smoked, but it is usually "snorted" (inhaled). Eating does not produce rapid effects, and intravenous use requires injection with a needle, which leaves needle marks and introduces the possibility of infection. When cocaine is inhaled into the nasal cavity, however, the person quickly feels euphoric, stimulated, and confident. Heart rate and blood pressure increase, and (according to users) fatigue and appetite are reduced. As in the case of amphetamines, cocaine appears to increase synaptic dopamine levels in the brain by inhibiting the reuptake of the dopamine. Wise (1988) believes that these actions make the drug reinforcing and stimulating.

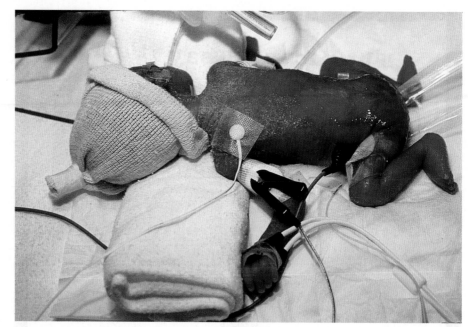

Cocaine Addiction from Mother to Child Women who use drugs during pregnancy are likely to have drug-addicted, underweight babies at risk for serious development problems. Pictured here is a newborn "crack baby" being monitored as it goes through cocaine withdrawal symptoms.

Users may become dependent on cocaine. That is, a user can develop an addiction and be unable to stop using it, sometimes after only a short period of time (American Psychiatric Association, 2000). Although users do not show gross physiological withdrawal symptoms, Gawin (1991) noted that the distinction between psychological and physical addiction is difficult to make and that chronic abuse of cocaine can produce neurophysiological changes in the central nervous system. The constant desire for cocaine can impair social and occupational functioning, and the high cost of the substance can cause users to resort to crime to feed their habit. In addition, side effects can occur. Feelings of depression and gloom may be produced when a cocaine high wears off. Heavy users sometimes report weight loss, paranoia, nervousness, fatigue, and hallucinations. Because cocaine stimulates the sympathetic nervous system, premature ventricular heartbeats and death may occur.

Crack is a purified and potent form of cocaine produced by heating cocaine with ether ("freebasing"). Crack is sold as small, solid pieces or "rocks." When smoked, crack produces swift and marked euphoria, followed by depression. About 3 percent of young adults between the ages of eighteen and twenty-five reported having used crack during a twelve-month period (Office of National Drug Control Policy, 1998).

Crack is a major concern to society for four reasons. First, it is relatively inexpensive and readily obtainable, so large segments of the population have easy access to the substance. Second, the euphoria of the high from crack is quite intense and immediate compared with sniffing cocaine. Thus many people

prefer crack. Third, users appear to develop a relatively rapid addiction to crack, and they continually seek the substance. Fourth, because of the increasing popularity of the drug and the crimes associated with crack, law enforcement resources have been expanded in the attempt to control its sale, distribution, and use.

Hallucinogens

Hallucinogens are substances that produce hallucinations, vivid sensory awareness, heightened alertness, or perceptions of increased insight. Their use does not typically lead to physical dependence (that is, to increased tolerance or withdrawal reaction), although psychological dependency may occur. Common hallucinogens are marijuana, LSD, and PCP.

Marijuana   The mildest and most commonly used hallucinogen is **marijuana,** also known as "pot" or "grass." Although DSM-IV-TR does not technically consider marijuana a hallucinogen, it does have many of the same effects as hallucinogens. This substance is generally smoked in a cigarette, or "joint." About 40 percent of the U.S. population over age twelve have used marijuana, although it is an illegal substance (Substance Abuse and Mental Health Services Administration, 2004). Marijuana use is most common in the age range of eighteen to thirty years and in the male population. As in the case of cigarettes, chronic smoking of marijuana can lead to lung cancer.

The subjective effects of marijuana include feelings of euphoria, tranquility, and passivity. Once the drug

●●● MENTAL HEALTH AND SOCIETY
●●● Club Drugs

"Club drugs" is a term that comes from the popular use of certain drugs at dance clubs and "raves." At these clubs, groups of young people dance to rapid, electronically synthesized music. As many as 70 percent of the attendees may be using drugs (McDowell, 2001). Among the commonly used club drugs are: Ecstasy or MDMA (methylenedioxymethamphetamine), LSD (d-lysergic acid diethylamide), GHB (gamma hydroxybutyrate), Ketamine, methamphetamine, and Roofies or Rohypnol (flunitrazepam). Of these six drugs, methamphetamine accounts for the largest number of emergency room visits (Clay, 2001). Many young people at raves take multiple substances, which may include alcohol, marijuana, and cocaine.

Two of the better known club drugs are Ecstasy and Rohypnol. Ecstasy is a synthetic type of amphet-amine with stimulant properties. Although recreational use is illegal in the United States, its use has sky-rocketed (McDowell, 2001). It tends to induce feelings of well-being and connection with others and one's environment. After it is ingested, the effects of well-being may last for hours. The aftereffects may last for twenty-four hours or more, and users may experience lethargy, low motivation, and fatigue. Some experience severe effects, such as depression and anxiety, as well as physical changes in blood pressure, convulsions, and even death. Users tend not to increase use over time because highs usually diminish while undesirable effects increase. One reason for the rapid rise in the drug's popularity is that many young people believe that Ecstasy is a new safe drug. But the drug is far from benign. Ecstasy can cause a dangerous increase in body temperature that can lead to cardiovascular failure. It can also increase heart rate, blood pressure, and heart wall stress. Although the research is not conclusive at this time, a number of studies show that long-term heavy Ecstasy users suffer cognitive deficits, including problems with memory (National Institute on Drug Abuse, 2004).

Roofies are short-acting benzodiazepines that interfere with short-term memory. It is known as the "date-rape" drug because unsuspecting individuals who are given the drug may feel uninhibited and not remember recent activities. It is a tasteless and odorless drug that dissolves easily in beverages. Because of psychological, cognitive, and biological dangers associated with their use, club drugs are considered unsafe.

has taken effect, subjective time passes slowly, and some users report increased sensory experiences, as well as mild perceptual distortions. Individual reactions vary according to prior experience with marijuana, expectancy of its effects, and the setting in which it is used. J. Simons, Correia, Carey, and Borsari (1998) found that the enhancement of perceptual and cognitive experiences was an important motive in marijuana use.

Although much controversy has raged over the effects of marijuana, many states have now decriminalized the possession of small quantities of this substance. Marijuana has been helpful in treating some physical ailments, such as certain forms of glaucoma (an eye disorder), and in reducing the nausea of patients being treated with chemotherapy for cancer.

Lysergic Acid Diethylamide (LSD)   LSD or "acid" gained notoriety as a hallucinogen in the mid-1960s. Praised by users as a potent psychedelic consciousness-expanding drug, LSD produces distortions of reality and hallucinations. "Good trips" are experiences of sharpened visual and auditory perception, heightened sensation, convictions that one has achieved profound philosophical insights, and feelings of ecstasy. "Bad trips" include fear and panic from distortions of sensory experiences, severe depression, marked confusion and disorientation, and delusions. Some users report "flashbacks," the recurrence of hallucinations or other sensations days or weeks after taking LSD. Fatigue, stress, or the use of another drug may trigger a "flashback."

LSD is considered a *psychotomimetic* drug because, in some cases, it produces reactions that mimic those seen in acute psychotic reactions. It does not produce physical dependence, even in users who have taken the drug hundreds of times. Aside from its psychological effects, no substantial evidence supports the belief that LSD is dangerous in and of itself. Large doses do not cause death, although there are reports of people who have unwittingly committed suicide while under the influence of LSD. Initially researchers believed that LSD caused chromosomal damage and spontaneous abortions, but such events are probably attributable to impurities in the drug, the use of other drugs, or the unhealthy lifestyles of many users.

A Joint for What Ails You
Although marijuana can be abused as a recreational drug, the evidence of its effectiveness in treating patients with certain problems—such as glaucoma, AIDS-related loss of appetite, nausea due to chemotherapy, and symptoms of epilepsy and multiple sclerosis—continues to grow. Still, marijuana is not readily available for medicinal purposes. Until the federal government lifts the ban on the medical use of marijuana, patients will continue to rely on operations like Oakland's Cannabis Buyers Club (shown here), an underground network that supplies marijuana to the sick. Do you believe marijuana should be freely available to patients with these problems?

Phencyclidine (PCP)   Phencyclidine, also known as PCP, "angel dust," "crystal," "superweed," and "rocket fuel," has emerged as one of the most dangerous of the so-called street drugs. Originally developed for its pain-killing properties, PCP is a hallucinatory drug that causes perceptual distortions, euphoria, nausea, confusion, delusions, and violent psychotic behavior. Reactions to the drug are influenced by dosage, the individual user, and the circumstances in which it is taken. One thing is clear: PCP has in many cases caused aggressive behavior, violence, or death from the taker's recklessness or delusions of invincibility. The drug is illegal, but it is still widely used, often sprinkled on marijuana and smoked.

Spitzer and coworkers (1994, pp. 121–122) described the effects of PCP on a chronic user. As you will see, one long-term effect may have been a personality change.

The patient was a twenty-year-old male who was brought to the hospital, trussed in ropes, by his four brothers. This was his seventh hospitalization in the past two years, each for similar behavior. One of his brothers reported that he "came home crazy" late one night, threw a chair through a window, tore a gas heater off the wall, and ran into the street. The family called the police, who apprehended him shortly thereafter as he stood, naked, directing traffic at a busy intersection. He assaulted the arresting officers, escaped them, and ran home screaming threats at his family. There his brothers were able to subdue him.

On admission the patient was observed to be agitated, his mood fluctuating between anger and fear. His speech was slurred, and he staggered when he walked. He remained extremely violent and disorganized for the first several days of his hospitalization, then began having longer and longer lucid intervals, still interspersed with sudden, unpredictable periods in which he displayed great suspiciousness, a fierce expression, slurred speech, and clenched fists.

After calming down, the patient denied ever having been violent or acting in an unusual way ("I'm a peaceable man") and said he could not remember how he got to the hospital. He admitted to using alcohol and marijuana socially but denied phencyclidine (PCP) use except for once, experimentally, three years previously. Nevertheless, blood and urine tests were positive for phencyclidine, and his brother believed "he gets dusted every day."

DSM-IV-TR includes a category for other substance-related disorders. Maladaptive use of substances such as anabolic steroids and nitrous oxide ("laughing gas") are included in this category.

Myth vs Reality

Myth: Smoking marijuana or taking one drug does not lead to the use of more serious drugs.

Reality: Although some individuals can abuse or become dependent on only one drug, others are sus-

In advertising, they say one of the surest ways to get your message across is to put celebrities in your ad.

DRUG-FREE SOUTHERN CALIFORNIA A member of the Partnership for a Drug-Free California and America!

Polysubstance Abuse Using one psychoactive drug can be dangerous in itself, but mixing two or more chemical substances at the same time can be deadly. Each of these talented performers—Jim Morrison, Janis Joplin, John Belushi, and River Phoenix—died from polydrug use. How common is polydrug use?

ceptible to polysubstance use. This pattern of use seriously increases risks for mental and physical deterioration. For example, in emergency medical visits for club drug use, over 70 percent of the cases involved more than one drug. Alcohol was the most frequent substance associated with most club drugs, and marijuana was frequently found in combination with LSD (Clay, 2001).

Etiology of Substance-Use Disorders

Why do people abuse substances, despite the knowledge that alcohol and drugs can have devastating consequences in their lives? The answer to this question is complicated by the number of different kinds of substances that are used and the number of factors that interact to account for the use of any one substance. Many theories have been proposed in the attempt to answer the question. Of these, the major types have been either biological in perspective (involving genetic or physiological factors) or psychological and cultural (involving psychodynamic, personality, sociocultural, or behavioral and cognitive factors). Both perspectives offer valid insights into addiction. The first focuses on dependence, or the bodily need for alcohol or drugs. The second attempts to explain how abuse patterns develop before actual dependence and why addicts who try to stop their habit may relapse and return to substance use. In the case of alcohol, for example, drinking behavior was traditionally believed to be the result of psychological factors, whereas the maintenance of heavy drinking resulted from physical dependence on alcohol. According to this viewpoint, one first drinks because of curiosity; because of exposure to

drinking models such as parents, peers, or television characters; and because of the tension-reducing properties of alcohol. After prolonged consumption, however, the person becomes physically dependent and drinks heavily to satisfy bodily needs.

As these statements indicate, traditional theories often assumed that the acquisition and maintenance of substances were largely distinct processes in which psychological factors influenced acquisition and biological factors were responsible for maintenance. This assumption is overly simplistic. As you will see shortly, both the acquisition and maintenance of drinking behavior are influenced by a complex interaction of psychological and physical factors. Recent theories have attempted to integrate the two approaches.

Because of alcohol's widespread use, availability, and consequences to society, more research has been conducted on alcohol than on other substances. Most of our discussion therefore centers on alcohol, although we comment on the relevance of different theories to the use of substances other than alcohol.

Biological Explanations

Because alcohol affects metabolic processes and the central nervous system, investigators have explored the possibility that heredity or congenital factors increase susceptibility to addiction. Alcoholism "runs in families" (Azar, 1995). The incidence of alcoholism is four times higher among male biological offspring of alcoholic fathers than among offspring of nonalcoholic fathers (Franklin & Frances, 1999). Because children share both genetic and environmental influences with their parents, researchers face the challenge of somehow separating the contributions of these two sets of factors. The role of in utero and neonatal influences must also be determined. Many investigators have attempted to isolate genetic and environmental factors through the use of adoption studies and twin studies.

Several studies have indicated that children whose biological parents were alcoholics but who were adopted and raised by nonrelatives are more likely to develop drinking problems than are adopted children whose biological parents were not alcoholics (Franklin & Frances, 1999; Goodwin, 1979; Kanas, 1988). In one study of alcohol abuse among adopted individuals, Cadoret and Wesner (1990) found clear-cut evidence of a genetic factor operating from biological parent to adopted child. However, they also found evidence of environmental influences: having an alcoholic in the adoptive home also increases the risk of alcohol problems in the adopted person.

Investigators studying the concordance rates for alcoholism among identical and fraternal twins have reported similar findings. Concordance rates indicate the likelihood that both twins have a disorder. Although identical twins have higher concordance rates, fraternal twins also have high rates (Rosenthal, 1971).

Collectively, these two sets of findings suggest that both heredity and environmental factors are important. Two types of alcoholism may exist: familial and nonfamilial (Goodwin, 1985). *Familial alcoholism* shows a family history of alcoholism, suggesting genetic predisposition. This type of alcoholism develops at an early age (usually by the late twenties), is severe, and is associated with an increased risk of alcoholism (but not other mental disorders) among blood relatives (Emmelkamp, 2004). Genetic factors appear to be important both for males and females (Slutske et al., 1998). *Nonfamilial alcoholism* does not show these characteristics and is presumably influenced more by environment.

The Search for Specific Genes   The consensus among experts studying alcoholism is that this disorder has a genetic component. Sophisticated new techniques and strategies are being used to localize the responsible genes and to understand how those genes operate (Wijsman, 1990). A great deal of interest has focused on quantitative trait loci (QTL) analysis (Azar, 1995). QTL analysis attempts to identify the genes that contribute to complex traits such as alcoholism. It involves the selective breeding of animals for certain traits. For example, if the trait being studied were aggression, aggressive rats would be inbred over many generations to produce an extremely aggressive rat. The same sort of inbreeding would take place for pas-

Family Ties   Today, Drew Barrymore's life seems filled with successes. But it hasn't always been so: in 1988, at the young age of thirteen, Drew entered rehabilitation to deal with her addiction to drugs and alcohol. Although it is difficult to separate out environmental and genetic influences in cases of alcohol and substance abuse, it is likely that both were operating in Drew's case. Not only did she experience the stress of being thrust into the limelight of an acting career at a very young age, but she also had a family history filled with problems of alcohol abuse— her grandfather, John Barrymore, drank himself to death, and her father had long abused both alcohol and drugs. Does this mean that drug abuse is inherited?

sive rats. Investigators would then try to find markers and sites on the rats' DNA that distinguish the aggressive and passive rats. The genes within the sites would be tested and analyzed to determine whether they are responsible for the traits. If similar human genes exist, researchers then could check to see if the genes differ in aggressive and passive human beings. Using this technique, researchers have identified genes that may be responsible for certain traits in alcoholism, such as a preference for alcohol (Azar, 1995).

The Search for Risk Factors   Other researchers have attempted to find risk factors or markers for alcoholism. Risk factors are variables related to, or etiologically significant in, alcoholism. Biological markers involving neurotransmitters in the brain have been found to be related to alcoholism (Kranzler & Anton,

1994; Tabakoff, Whelan, & Hoffman, 1990). Another risk factor appears to be sensitivity or responsiveness to alcohol (Schuckit, 1990). Individuals who are not sensitive to alcohol may be able to consume large amounts of it before feeling its effects, and they may therefore be more susceptible to alcoholism.

Being a child of an alcoholic and coming from a family with a history of alcoholism also seem to be risk factors. Noble (1990) compared two groups: high-risk sons of alcoholic fathers and low-risk sons of social drinking fathers. The boys in the two groups were matched for demographic background, and at the start of the study none had ever consumed alcohol or used drugs. The researchers compared central nervous system functioning, using behavioral, neuropsychological, and electrophysiological measures. The central nervous system functioning of both the high-risk boys and their alcoholic fathers differed from that of the low-risk boys and their fathers. Furthermore, the high-risk boys were more likely than low-risk boys to begin drinking. Noble also studied family environments to see if high-risk boys had disturbed family backgrounds. No differences in family background and environment were found. Noble concluded that hereditary factors may be important in alcoholism.

A final area of investigation of the cause of alcoholism has attempted to implicate nutritional or vitamin deficiencies, hormonal imbalances, or abnormal bodily processes. There is no clear-cut evidence to indicate that these congenital factors are important in human alcoholism.

With respect to other substances such as opiates, tobacco, and LSD, research on the hereditary basis for dependence has not been as extensive as it has for alcohol. Nevertheless, it is conceivable that genetic differences may be a factor in addiction. Some researchers have found racial (and presumably genetic) differences in responses to certain drugs (Lin, Cheung, Smith, & Poland, 1997). Compared with their white counterparts, Asian American clients appear to require smaller dosages of psychotropic medication to achieve the same clinical effects for mental disorders.

Psychodynamic Explanations

A number of psychodynamic explanations have been proposed for alcoholism. Most hold that childhood traumas (such as an overprotecting mother, maternal neglect, or frustration of dependency needs), especially during the oral stage of development, result in the repression of painful conflicts involving dependency needs (Kanas, 1988). During stress or encounters with situations reminiscent of the original conflicts, symptoms such as anxiety, depression, and hostility begin to occur. Alcohol is seen as (1) releasing inhibitions and allowing the repressed conflicts to be expressed or (2) enabling people to obtain oral gratification and to satisfy dependency needs. Most of the psychoanalytic formulations are based on retrospective clinical case studies rather than empirical data, so their validity is open to question.

Explanations Based on Personality Characteristics

Some researchers believe that certain personality characteristics function as a predisposition, making people vulnerable to alcoholism. Alcoholism has been found to be associated with high activity level, emotionality, goal impersistence, and sociability. Causality cannot be determined from correlational data, but these characteristics may interact with one's social environment to increase the risk of alcoholism (Tarter & Vanyukov, 1994).

Life transitions or maturational events, such as changing from a student to a working-adult role, may also affect drinking patterns. In one study of the stability of alcohol consumption from college years and beyond (Gotham, Sher, & Wood, 1997), researchers identified young adults who drank heavily during their years in college and who significantly decreased their drinking after college. The investigators found that entering the work force full time, being male, and being less open to experiences were important predictors of the change in consumption.

In reviews of research on personality and alcoholism, Nathan (1988), Franklin and Frances (1999), and Sher and Trull (1994) have concluded that there is no single alcoholic personality. Nathan found only two personality characteristics—antisocial behavior and depression—associated with drinking problems. Particularly consistent is the relationship between a childhood or adolescent history of antisocial behavior (such as rejection of societal rules) and alcoholism. Nathan warned, however, that the role of personality characteristics, including antisocial tendencies and depression, as causal factors in alcoholism cannot be uncritically accepted. Many alcohol abusers do not show antisocial histories, and many antisocial people do not drink excessively. Furthermore, depression may well be a consequence rather than an antecedent of alcohol abuse (that is, problem drinking may cause people to feel depressed). Tarter and Vanyukov (1994) and other researchers who have found personality characteristics (such as emotionality and sociability) associated with alcoholism believe that the effects, if any, of such characteristics are complex and indirect. Some evidence exists that the link between personality characteristics and alcohol use is influenced by heredity (Mustanski, Viken, Kaprio, & Rose, 2003).

CRITICAL THINKING

Is Drug Use an Indicator of Disturbance?

Many individuals believe that drug users are maladapted and have higher rates of emotional disturbance than nondrug users. Indeed, antisocial personality characteristics are associated with drug use. Does this mean that drug use causes a person to become antisocial or maladjusted? Or is a person maladjusted and therefore prone to drug use? When two characteristics—such as drug use and antisocial personality patterns—are related, what kinds of causal inferences can be made?

One way of examining these issues is to conduct a longitudinal study. As mentioned in the chapter on the scientific method in abnormal psychology, longitudinal research evaluates the behaviors of individuals over a period of time. If longitudinal research shows that a characteristic or behavior occurs *before* drug use, we can be certain that drug use did not cause the behaviors. For example, Sher, Bartholow, and Wood (2000) evaluated the personality characteristics of students and then determined their subsequent degree of substance use. They found that sensation seeking or behavioral disinhibition predicts substance-use disorders. Because the

sensation-seeking behaviors occurred before substance use, we are confident that substance use did not cause sensation seeking. In practice, however, interpreting cause and effect is not easy.

In another longitudinal study, psychological evaluations (including personality, adjustment, and parent-child assessments) were made of boys and girls at different ages, beginning at age three and continuing to age eighteen. At age eighteen, they were interviewed about the frequency of drug use. The investigators, Shedler and Block (1990), wanted to see if certain psychological characteristics were associated with drug use—characteristics that were present before drug use and therefore could not be caused by drug use. The results were quite striking: those who frequently used marijuana and had tried at least one other drug were maladjusted, demonstrating alienation, poor control over impulses, and emotional distress. These psychological characteristics were present before and during drug use. Do the results also imply that adolescents who do not use drugs are better adjusted than those who do?

In addition to studying frequent users, the investigators also examined abstainers—adolescents who had never tried marijuana or other drugs—and they studied experimenters, those who had used drugs only a few times. Interestingly, the abstainers were relatively anxious, emotionally constricted, and lacking in social skills. Those who had experimented with drugs occasionally were better adjusted than either the adolescents who used drugs frequently or those who had never used drugs! Parents of abstainers and frequent users also exhibited greater personality problems.

Given the finding that those who experiment with drugs are the best adjusted, should we advocate that adolescents occasionally try drugs? Such a position would be inconsistent with the results. Recall from the data that adjustment patterns preceded drug use, so experimenting with drugs will not necessarily cause one to be better adjusted. The point is that we often make mistakes in drawing inferences about cause and effect, and we must be careful not to base practices or policies on these erroneous inferences.

Nathan's (1988) warning is also pertinent to attempts to find a relationship between personality characteristics and the use of drugs other than alcohol. In the 1960s and 1970s, some researchers hoped to identify a cluster of personality traits that would account for addiction to substances. No such clusters were found, and attempts to find a common pattern of personality traits underlying addiction have failed (Platt, 1986). However, some general personality tendencies, such as impulsive sensation seeking or behavioral disinhibition (undercontrol), have been found to be related to substance-use disorders (Sher, Bartholow, & Wood, 2000). It is highly unlikely that addiction is

caused by a single personality type. (See the Critical Thinking feature "Is Drug Use an Indicator of Disturbance?" for a discussion of some of the problems inherent in drawing inferences about drug use and personality characteristics.)

Sociocultural Explanations

Drinking varies according to sociocultural factors such as gender, age, socioeconomic status, ethnicity, religion, and country (American Psychiatric Association, 2000). As mentioned previously, males and young adults consume more alcohol than females and older adults, respectively. Interestingly, consumption tends to increase with socioeconomic status, although alcoholism is more frequent in the middle socioeconomic classes (Kanas, 1988). In terms of religious affiliation, heavier drinking is found among Catholics than among Protestants or Jews. Furthermore, drinking behavior varies from country to country. In wine-producing countries such as France and Italy, alcohol consumption is high (Goodwin, 1985). Relative to France and Italy, consumption is low in Israel and mainland China, with the United States being moderate in consumption.

Rates of alcoholism may not correspond to per capita consumption of alcohol. For example, in Portugal and Italy, where per capita consumption is high, the incidence of alcoholism is relatively low (Kanas, 1988). In the United States and the Soviet Union, alcoholism is high relative to overall consumption levels. Among ethnic groups within the United States, American Indians and Irish Americans are far more likely to become alcoholics than are Americans of Italian, Hispanic, or Asian backgrounds (S. Sue & Nakamura, 1984). France has high rates of both alcohol consumption and alcoholism. Drinking patterns in France are characterized by moderate alcoholic intake throughout the day, and drunkenness is more permissible there than in Italy. In Italy, drinking wine at meals is common, but drinking to become intoxicated is discouraged.

These findings suggest that cultural values play an important role in drinking patterns. The values affect not only the amount consumed and the occasions on which drinking takes place but also the given culture's tolerance of alcohol abuse.

Cultural values and behaviors are usually learned within the family and community. A review of the literature on adolescent drinking led researchers to conclude that teenage problem drinkers are exposed first to parents who are themselves heavy drinkers and then to peers who act as models for heavy consumption (Braucht, 1982). The parents not only consumed a great deal of alcohol but also showed inappropriate behaviors, such as antisocial tendencies and rejection of their children. When such children loosened their parental ties, they tended to be strongly influenced by peers who may be heavy drinkers (Bray, Adams, Getz, & McQueen, 2003). In addition to acting as role models, parents who consume a great deal of alcohol have been shown to exhibit reduced parental monitoring of the activities of adolescent children and to produce stress and negative affect. These, in turn, make the adolescent more likely to associate with alcohol and drug-using peers and to increase substance usage (Chassin, Pillow, Curran, Molina, & Berrera, 1993). There is evidence to indicate that adolescents who are exposed to peer and adult drinkers tend to develop positive expectancies over the use of alcohol (e.g., believing that drinking alcohol makes it easier to be part of a group; Cumsille, Sayer, & Graham, 2000).

Studies also indicate that both peer selection and peer socialization influence drug-use patterns. Frequency of alcohol and drug use reported by African American adolescents was significantly related to both peer

Drinking and Driving In California, posters sponsored by Mothers Against Drunk Driving (MADD) were intended to remind people of the dangers of drunken driving. Why do people drink and drive even when they are aware of the inherent dangers of doing so?

pressure and peer drug use in one study (Farrell & White, 1998). In another study of adolescents who did not initially smoke, those who had more friends who smoked were subsequently more likely to smoke (Killen et al., 1997). Sussman and his colleagues (1994) also found that a good predictor of subsequent smoking in adolescents was their identification with groups in which members smoked. However, smoking did not predict subsequent group identification. Curran, Stice, and Chassin (1997) note that the association between peer use and self-use of drugs appears to be a two-way street: a drug user tends to choose friends who are users, and friends who use drugs tend to influence one to take drugs.

As in the case of alcohol, use of other psychoactive substances varies widely, and these variations reflect sociocultural influences. For example, in the United States, lifetime prevalence of drug abuse and dependence is higher among white Americans than among African and Hispanic Americans, although white Americans have lower rates of alcoholism than do the other two groups (Robins & Regier, 1991). Similarly, although white Americans are less likely than African or Hispanic Americans to have used heroin during their lifetimes, they are more likely to have used hallucinogens and PCP (National Institute on Drug Abuse, 1991).

Behavioral Explanations

Early behavioral explanations for alcohol abuse and dependence were based on two assumptions: (1) alcohol temporarily reduces anxiety and tension, and (2) drinking behavior is learned.

Anxiety Reduction   In a classic experiment, researchers induced an "experimental neurosis" in cats (Masserman, Yum, Nicholson, & Lee, 1944). After the cats were trained to approach and eat food at a food box, they were given an aversive stimulus (an air blast to the face or an electric shock) whenever they approached the food. The cats stopped eating and exhibited "neurotic" symptoms—anxiety, psychophysiological disturbances, and peculiar behaviors. When the cats were given alcohol, however, their symptoms disappeared, and they started to eat. As the effects of the alcohol wore off, the symptoms began to reappear.

The experimenters also found that these cats now preferred "spiked" milk (milk mixed with alcohol) to milk alone. Once the stressful shocks were terminated and the fear responses extinguished, however, the cats no longer preferred spiked milk. Alcohol apparently reduced the cats' anxieties and was used as long as the anxieties were present. (Note that the cats were placed

in an *approach-avoidance conflict;* that is, their desire to approach the food box and eat was in conflict with their desire to avoid the air blast or shock.)

Later, another experimenter wanted to test the hypothesis that alcohol reduces the anxiety of conflict—that it resolves conflicts by increasing approach behaviors or by decreasing avoidance behaviors. He placed rats in a conflict situation and measured the strengths of approach behaviors and avoidance behaviors before and after the use of alcohol (Conger, 1951). He found that the main effect of alcohol was to reduce avoidance behaviors, and he concluded that alcohol helps resolve conflicts by reducing fear of unpleasant or aversive elements. Many theorists believe that the anxiety-reducing properties of alcohol are reinforcing and therefore largely responsible for maintaining the drinking behavior of the alcoholic.

Learned Expectations   A group of researchers (Marlatt, Demming, & Reid, 1973) provided evidence that learned expectations also affect consumption. In the process, they challenged the notion that alcoholism is a disease in which drinking small amounts of alcohol leads, in an alcoholic, to involuntary consumption to the point of intoxication. In their study, alcoholics and social drinkers were recruited to participate in what was described as a "tasting experiment." Both the alcoholics and the social drinkers were divided into four groups:

1. Members of the "told alcohol, given alcohol" group were told that they would be given a drink of alcohol and tonic, and they were actually given such a drink.

2. Members of the "told alcohol, given tonic" group were told that they would receive a drink of alcohol and tonic, but they were actually given only tonic.

3. Members of the "told tonic, given alcohol" group were told that they would receive a drink of tonic, but they were actually given an alcohol-and-tonic drink.

4. Members of the "told tonic, given tonic" group were told that they would be given tonic, and they were actually given tonic.

The proportions of the alcohol-and-tonic drink (five parts tonic and one part vodka) made it difficult to tell whether the drink contained alcohol.

At the beginning of the experiment, the participants were "primed" with an initial drink—either alcohol and tonic or tonic only, depending on which group they were in. (That is, the "given alcohol" groups were primed with alcohol, and the "given tonic" groups were primed with tonic.) After the primer drink, participants were told what kind of drink they would next receive. They were free to sample as much of the drink as they wished, alone and uninterrupted. If alcoholism is a condition in which alcoholics lose control of drinking (a disease model), then those given an alcohol primer should drink more alcohol. Alternatively, if alcoholics learn or expect that alcohol reduces anxiety or enhances feelings of well-being, then those told that they would receive alcohol (whether or not alcohol was actually given) would drink more because they expected alcohol.

The results suggested that alcoholism is not simply a disease in which a person loses control over drinking. Participants who were told that they would receive alcohol drank more than those who were told that they would receive tonic, and those who actually consumed alcohol did not drink more than those who consumed tonic (Marlatt, Demming, & Reid, 1973). The participants' expectancy had a stronger effect than the actual content of their drinks on how much they consumed. In fact, several people who were given tonic when they believed they were imbibing alcohol acted as though they were "tipsy" from the drinks!

The importance of expectancy was also demonstrated in a study of adolescents over a two-year period (G. Smith, Goldman, Greenbaum, & Christiansen, 1995). Their drinking pattern was best characterized by a positive feedback model: those who expected social benefits (such as feelings of confidence and comfort) from drinking drank more. They then endorsed even more positive social benefits, which made even greater consumption more likely. This and other experiments on drinking behavior imply that psychological factors, such as tension reduction and expectancy, are important in maintaining drinking behavior.

Cognitive Influences   The *tension-reducing model*, which assumes that alcohol reduces tension and anxiety and that the relief of tension reinforces the drinking response, is difficult to test, and research with alcoholics has produced conflicting findings. In fact, prolonged drinking is often associated with increased anxiety and depression (McNamee, Mello, & Mendelson, 1968). Although alcoholics who have high blood alcohol levels after drinking may show low muscular tension, they tend to report a high degree of distress (Steffen, Nathan, & Taylor, 1974). Alcohol is a sedative that can reduce anxiety, and, ironically, it is possible that the knowledge that one is drinking alcohol can increase one's level of anxiety (Polivy, Schueneman, & Carlson, 1976).

Other evidence supports the idea that the tension-reducing model is too simplistic. Steele and Josephs (1988, 1990) found that alcohol can either increase or decrease anxiety, depending on the way alcohol affects perception and thought. When confronted with a stressful situation, people who drank alcohol in the experiment experienced anxiety reduction if they were allowed to engage in a distracting activity. When faced with a stressor, however, those who drank and did not have a distracting activity experienced an increase in anxiety. The investigators argued that the distracting activity allowed drinkers to divert attention from the stressor. Without the distraction, drinkers' attention may have focused on the stressor, which served to magnify their anxiety.

Another study found that different types of tension (electric shock versus social evaluation) produced different results (Marlatt, 1978). When a group of people expected to receive a painful shock, their consumption of alcohol was no greater than that of a control group who expected to receive a nonpainful shock. When a social, rather than a physical, source of tension or anxiety was anticipated (for example, when men were told that a group of women would rate them on their personal attractiveness), however, the men tended to consume more alcohol than did a control group who did not expect to be evaluated by others.

Coping responses and expectancy may exert a combined effect. M. L. Cooper, Russell, and George (1988) found that stress is related to drinking when individuals expect positive effects from drinking and have coping styles that avoid dealing with anger. In contrast, stress and drinking were negatively correlated among those with little positive expectancy for alcohol and a tendency to actively deal with their anger. Other investigators (Stacy, Newcomb, & Bentler, 1991) found that expectancy is also predictive of drug use.

Both the expectancy and tension-reduction models have difficulty accounting for the two phases of alcohol effects, in which blood alcohol levels initially rise and then fall. Giancola and Zeichner (1997) found that increases in aggression tended to occur during the ascending phase (when blood alcohol level is increasing) rather than the descending phase (when blood alcohol level is decreasing) of blood alcohol levels. That is, despite having similar blood alcohol levels, individuals exhibited more aggression during the ascending rather than during the descending phase. The expectancy and tension-reduction models have a problem explaining this two-phase effect because the blood alcohol levels, tensions, and expectations are presumably similar regardless of the phase. This research raises the possibility that the concepts of expectancy and tension reduction are too simple to explain the effects of alcohol.

Currently, tension-reduction models are being revised to try to take into account some of the conflicting findings. For example, Hussong, Hicks, Levy, and Curran (2001) have found that young adults with less intimate and supportive friendships, as compared with their peers, showed risk for greater drinking following emotional states such as sadness and hostility. Thus they propose that individual differences are important to consider. Some, though not all, individuals may act in accordance with a tension-reduction model. In another study, Carney, Armeli, Tennen, Affleck, and O'Neil (2000) were interested in the relationship between experiences with negative or positive events and alcohol consumption. Rather than asking individuals if they drank when experiencing negative events, the investigators had them record in a daily diary for sixty days their daily experiences, perceived stress, alcohol consumption, and desire to drink. Experiences were divided into work and nonwork events. Interestingly, there was a tendency to drink more and to desire drinking when experiencing negative nonwork events. However, with negative work events, although there was a stronger desire to drink, actual alcohol consumption did not increase. The tensions from work did not result in greater alcohol consumption. Perhaps negative work events add pressures to do more work, thereby reducing the opportunities to drink. In any event, tensions are related to alcohol consumption in complex ways.

Relapse: A Source of Evidence For persons attempting to abstain from using substances after addiction, relapse is common. Factors associated with relapse include younger age at onset of drug use, more extensive involvement with substances, antisocial behavior, comorbid psychiatric disorder, less involvement in school or work, and less support from drug-

free family and peers (Walter, 2001). In terms of relapse, Marlatt (1978) suggested that the type of stressor, the loss of a sense of personal control over situations, and the lack of alternative coping responses influence drinking and resumption of drinking after abstinence.

Relapse is the resumption of drinking after a period of voluntary abstinence. A fairly consistent relationship has been found between relapse and time elapsed since last use of a substance for alcohol, heroin, tobacco, and other substances (Woody & Cacciola, 1994). Risk of relapse is greatest during the first three months following treatment, becoming less and less likely over time. By the end of three years, relapse is unlikely. Negative emotional states (such as depression, interpersonal conflict, and anxiety) are highly associated with relapse (Cooney, Litt, Morse, Bauer, & Gaupp, 1997). They account for 53 percent of relapses among alcoholics trying to quit drinking (Hodgins, El-Guebaly, & Armstrong, 1995). Negative emotional states tended to play a role in major relapse (substantial use of the substance), whereas social pressure led to minor relapse (taking just a beer). Negative physical states, urges and temptations, and positive emotional states did not strongly predict relapse. Interestingly, there was a gender difference in the states reported. Women were more likely than men to cite interpersonal conflict and less likely to report emotional states such as depression. This suggests that women may be more vulnerable to social influences than men are in the context of alcohol use and relapse.

In 1985, Marlatt and Gordon developed a comprehensive relapse and relapse-prevention model. In their view, negative emotional feelings (for example,

Can't Wait In *Leaving Las Vegas*, actor Nicholas Cage's character Ben Sanderson is an alcoholic who, after losing his job and becoming estranged from his family, has moved to Las Vegas to drink himself to death. Is the inability of an alcoholic to refrain from alcohol caused by having a disease or by a lack of will power?

frustration or anger), social pressure to drink, or temptations (such as walking by a bar) are "high-risk" situations that make a person vulnerable to resumption of drinking. Coping responses (various means of resisting social pressure—for instance, by insisting on a soft drink) can provide an alternative to drinking in such situations. Coping responses include assertion (such as saying no when pressured by others to drink), avoidance (such as not walking near a favorite bar), and more satisfactory means of dealing with anger or anxiety. Those who have coping responses can feel they can control their drinking and continue their abstinence. People who lack a coping response to the high-risk situation, however, may take that first drink.

A person can obviously stop drinking after one drink. To explain the full-blown resumption of drinking that so often follows an alcoholic's first drink, Marlatt (1978) proposed the notion of an *abstinence violation effect*. That is, once drinking begins, the person senses a loss of personal control. He or she feels weak-willed and guilty and gives up trying to abstain (see Figure 9.5). The abstinence violation effect may also apply to other relapse behaviors, such as overeating, masturbating, and smoking. Treatment to overcome the abstinence violation effect focuses on giving people coping responses for situations in which there is also a high risk of relapse. Rohsenow, Monti, Martin, and their colleagues (2000) found that training cocaine users to cope with high-risk situations was beneficial not only in lowering cocaine use but also in lowering the amount of cocaine used during a relapse.

In a test of the abstinence violation effect, Shiffman and his colleagues (1996) asked participants in a smoking-cessation program to record any instances of relapse (smoking) and their reactions. The investigators then followed the participants' progress for three months to assess their subsequent smoking after an instance of relapse. Interestingly, the investigators found little evidence that self-efficacy, attributions, and affective reactions were important predictors of

FIGURE 9.5 The Relapse Process   Shown here is Marlatt's model illustrating why some recovering alcoholics or drug abusers either remain abstinent or relapse. Those who encounter high-risk situations (ones that encourage consumption) and have good coping skills develop feelings of self-efficacy and confidence in their ability to avoid consumption and, therefore, have a decreased probability of relapse. On the other hand, those without good coping responses lose confidence and feelings of self-efficacy, which could lead to a relapse. Once this occurs, Marlatt suggests, they feel weak, powerless, or guilty and give up trying to abstain.

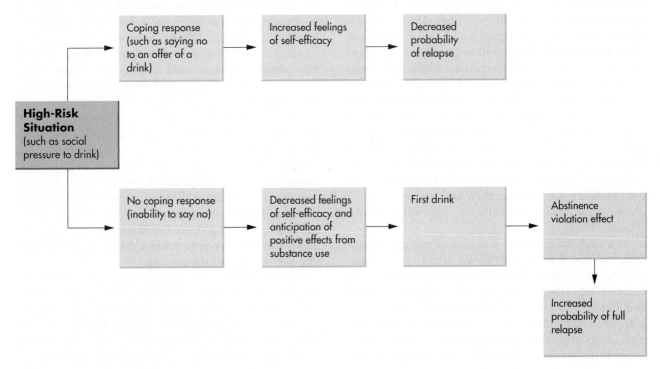

Source: Based on Marlatt & Gordon (1985), Marlatt (1978).

subsequent relapse. They did find that psychological demoralization after an initial instance of relapse played a role in progression to another relapse. Thus only certain aspects of the relapse model of Marlatt and Gordon (1985) may be valid. In addition, individual reactions to smoking cessation have been found to be quite variable, so that the severity and length of withdrawal distress cannot be easily characterized (Piasecki, Jorenby, Smith, Fiore, & Baker, 2003). Substantial research evidence points to the effectiveness of relapse prevention, and the relapse model was revised by Witkiewitz and Marlatt (2004) in order to account for more recent research findings. Although the revised model is still based on the factors found in the original model, it now proposes that the factors are part of a dynamic system in which the factors interact in a complex fashion. For example, many different factors may trigger and operate within high-risk situations. Furthermore, there may be reciprocal causation (coping skills influence drinking behavior and, in turn, drinking behavior may influence coping).

Many researchers and clinicians formerly believed that addiction to other substances, such as heroin, could be best explained by biological factors such as physical dependence and the attempt to avoid withdrawal symptoms. However, we now know that drug use is a complex phenomenon and that explanatory models must also incorporate the role of learning, expectancy, and situational factors. Consider heroin withdrawal, for example. Some have characterized heroin withdrawal reactions as no more agonizing than a bad case of the flu (Ausubel, 1961). Heroin addicts who enter a hospital and receive no heroin while hospitalized will stop having withdrawal symptoms in a week or two. Nevertheless, these statements about the addicts' physiological responses do not explain why the vast majority who have lost their bodily need for the drug resume heroin use after hospitalization. Further evidence of the influence of cognitive and behavioral factors comes from the behavior of Vietnam servicemen who were addicted to heroin. When they returned to the United States, many discontinued its use because they had easier access to alcohol and great difficulty in procuring heroin (Pilisuk, 1975).

In a study of marijuana and cocaine use among college students, Schafer and Brown (1991) showed the importance of expectancies. Their survey of positive and negative expectancies (for example, relaxation, social facilitation, and cognitive impairment) for the use of marijuana and cocaine showed that students who used these drugs also expected strong positive experiences.

Such studies show that there are many factors that maintain drug use and drug dependence.

Overall Theories of the Addiction Process

So far in our discussion, we have cited biological, psychodynamic, personality trait, sociocultural, and behavioral approaches to explain alcohol consumption. In the process, we have briefly mentioned how these approaches also explain the development of drug dependence. Some investigators have proposed broad theories that focus on the addiction process rather than on a particular substance. In this section, we examine three of these theories.

Solomon's Opponent Process Theory
R. L. Solomon (1977) argued that the conditions that cause a person to try a drug have not been identified. The best predictor of drug sampling is drug availability, but drug use is too widespread and drug addiction too rare for the mere sampling of a drug to be a major cause of subsequent addiction. Solomon suggested that the initial reasons for using drugs are complex, varied, and obscure. Most drug use is probably reinforcing at the outset—an attempt to solve some social problem, to respond to peer group influences, to relieve unpleasant emotional states, or to become "high." Then, after continued use, the motivation for drug use changes. The user now must cope with drug craving, a fear of withdrawal, and other acquired motivations. The addict's desire to maintain social relationships and a certain lifestyle may also be a motivating factor.

In other words, Solomon believes that addiction is an acquired motivation, much like other acquired motivations such as love or attachment. To explain the process, Solomon (1980) proposed the *opponent process theory of acquired motivation*. Consider first the person who has used a drug only a few times: before taking the drug again, that person, who is not yet addicted, is in a resting state. Then, while ingesting the drug, the person experiences a peak state (the rush) and euphoria; in other words, the psychopharmacological properties of the drug make the user feel "high." After the effects subside, there may be mild discomfort ("coming down" from the drug). The person may start to crave the drug to combat the discomfort, but the discomfort soon subsides and the person returns to a resting state. For this occasional user, the motivation for use is to achieve the high and to avoid the aversiveness of the craving.

Now consider the chronic user, for whom the process is somewhat different. During the period before the drug is consumed, this person experiences a *craving* for the drug. Then, during ingestion of the drug, the experienced user feels only *contentment* rather than a rush and intense euphoria. And, once the effects of the drug wear off, he or she experiences *withdrawal* reactions and intense physiological or psychological craving (or both), which do not subside until he or she again uses the drug. In essence, the motivation for drug use has changed with experience, from positive to aversive control. A new motivation for drug use has been acquired.

Wise's Two-Factor Model

Wise (1988) also agreed that a single-factor explanation is insufficient. He believes that a two-factor model, involving positive and negative reinforcement, may explain addiction. He theorized that drugs have *positive* reinforcing effects (pleasure or euphoria) through a common biological mechanism. In addition, drugs can independently act as a *negative* reinforcer in that taking the drug can terminate distress or feelings of dysphoria. This theory suggests that either reinforcer results in cravings for the drug. Simply treating the withdrawal symptoms of a drug addict—the negative reinforcement component—is therefore inadequate because the positive reinforcing properties of drug use are not addressed. Wise's theory combines both a behavioral perspective involving learning and reinforcement and a biological approach in that the learning is rooted in neural mechanisms. There is some evidence that drugs of abuse boost the brain's reward system and change certain brain neurons and structures, effects that may last for months or years. Over time, these changes dampen the pleasurable effects of the substance so that more and more is needed (that is, increased craving) in order to achieve the effects (Nestler & Malenka, 2004).

The theories posited by Solomon (1980) and by Wise (1988) are considerably different. For Solomon, motivation for drug use changes with repeated consumption. In Wise's model, two separate processes help maintain addiction. Nevertheless, each theory points to the problems in conceptualizing addiction as simply one process with one main cause. Another common assumption is that addiction involves both psychological and biological components. Future research will probably shed more light on the adequacy of each.

Tiffany's Theory of Automatic Processes

Although Solomon and Wise agreed that the motivation and urge to use drugs are complex, Tiffany (1990) took issue with the role of urges and cravings in drug use. Most theories argued that urges, based on the positive aspects of drug use or on the avoidance of withdrawal, are important in drug-use behavior and in relapse. Research has, however, found only a modest relationship between self-reported urges to use drugs and actual drug use. Furthermore, self-reports of urges have been found to be unrelated to physiological reactions (Drobes & Tiffany, 1997). These findings have led Tiffany to reconceptualize the role of urges. In Tiffany's view, drug-use behaviors are largely controlled by "automatic" processes. Over the course of drug use, addicts develop skills involving drug acquisition and use. The skills are invoked rather automatically so that drug-use behaviors tend to be relatively fast and efficient, repeated without much cognitive attention or effort, and initiated by the presence of certain stimuli. For example, a smoker can quickly and without thought or clumsiness pull out a cigarette, light it, and start smoking. These automatic processes are likely to occur in certain situations or in the presence of certain stimuli that have in the past been the occasions for smoking (for example, at a party with friends).

Although drug-use behavior is an automatic cognitive process, urges are a nonautomatic process and may not be necessary to explain drug use. They may occur when drug-use plans are hindered (for example, when an alcoholic finds the supply of alcohol has been depleted). To overcome this hindrance, the person must engage in nonautomatic processes that require attention, time, and effort (the alcoholic who no longer has any drinks must find ways of obtaining alcohol). The implications of Tiffany's theory are that urges are not necessary to explain consumption and that once drug-use behaviors become automated, they are highly resistant to change. Thus the theory emphasizes the maintenance of behavior rather than the acquisition of drug use before the development of automatic processes.

These three theories have general relevance for treatment. Clinicians should attend to the course of addiction to understand the motives for addicts, according to Solomon's theory. From the perspective of Wise, clinicians should address the positive *and* negative reinforcement that addicts receive. And according to Tiffany's theory, automatic processes involving abstinence should be inculcated in addicts. Let us now turn to more specific treatment approaches to substance-use disorders.

Intervention and Treatment of Substance-Use Disorders

Treatment of substance abusers and addicts depends on both the individual user and the type of drug being used. Most alcohol and drug treatment programs have two phases: first, the removal of the abusive substance, and second, long-term maintenance without it. In the first phase, which is also referred to as **detoxification,** the user is immediately or eventually prevented from consuming the substance. The removal of the substance may trigger withdrawal symptoms that are opposite in effect to the reactions produced by the drug. For instance, a person who is physically addicted to a central nervous system depressant such as a barbiturate will experience drowsiness, decreased respiration, and reduced anxiety when taking the drug. When the depressant is withdrawn, the user experiences symptoms that resemble the effects of a stimulant—agitation, restlessness, increased respiration, and insomnia. Helping someone successfully cope during withdrawal has been a concern of many treatment strategies dealing with various drugs, particularly in treating heroin addicts. Sometimes, addicts are given medication to alleviate some of the withdrawal symptoms. For example, tranquilizers may be helpful to alcoholics experiencing withdrawal.

In the second phase, intervention programs attempt to prevent the person from returning to the substance (in some rare cases, controlling or limiting the use of the substance). These programs may be community programs, which include sending alcoholics or addicts to a hospital, residential treatment facility, or halfway house, where support and guidance are available in a community setting. Family therapy has consistently been successful in treating adolescent substance abusers (Sexton, Alexander, & Mease, 2004). Whatever the setting, the treatment approach may be chemical, cognitive or behavioral, or multimodal. In this section, we discuss these approaches to the treatment of various substance-use disorders and review

their effectiveness. We also take a quick look at prevention programs.

Self-Help Groups

Alcoholics Anonymous (AA) is a self-help organization composed of alcoholics who want to stop drinking. Perhaps a million or more alcoholics worldwide participate in the AA program, which is completely voluntary. There are no fees, and the only membership requirement is the desire to stop drinking. AA assumes that once a person is an alcoholic, he or she is always an alcoholic—an assumption based on the disease model of alcoholism. Members must recognize that they can never drink again and must concentrate on abstinence, one day at a time. As a means of helping members abstain, each may be assigned a sponsor who provides individual support, attention, and help. Group meetings encourage fellowship, spiritual awareness, and public self-revelations about past wrongdoings because of alcohol.

Some people believe that membership in AA is one of the most effective treatments for alcoholism. A few studies with methodological limitations have found an association between AA attendance and positive treatment outcome (McCrady, 1994), although the success rate of AA is not as high as AA members claim it is (Brandsma, 1979). Approximately one-half of the alcoholics who stay in the organization are still abstinent after two years (Alford, 1980), but many drop out of the program and are not counted as failures. In

"I Am an Alcoholic." At an Alcoholics Anonymous (AA) meeting, a woman is recounting her experiences as an alcoholic. AA assumes that once an alcoholic, always an alcoholic. Thus, AA members are taught that they must never drink again. However, some researchers believe that it is possible for alcoholics to become "social drinkers" and to learn to control their drinking. What do you think of this controversy over total abstinence versus controlled drinking for alcoholics?

one of the most rigorous studies of AA, Morgenstern, Labouvie, McCrady, Kahler, and Frey (1997) investigated the effects of affiliation with AA among individuals who had undergone treatment for alcoholism. Greater affiliation with AA did predict better treatment outcomes. However, the involvement with AA was associated with increased feelings of self-efficacy, active coping, and motivation to stop drinking, which were, in turn, predictors of outcome. Spinoffs of AA such as Al-Anon and Alateen have been helpful in providing support for adults and teenagers living with alcoholics (Kanas, 1988). There are similar self-help groups for drug abuse (Narcotics Anonymous), although they have not gained the widespread attention and participation seen in AA.

Pharmacological Approach

To keep addicts from using certain substances, some treatment programs dispense other chemical substances. For example, alcohol treatment programs may include the chemical *Antabuse* (disulfiram) to produce an aversion to alcohol. A person who consumes alcohol one to two days after taking Antabuse suffers a severe reaction, including nausea, vomiting, and discomfort. Antabuse has the effect of blocking the progressive breakdown of alcohol so that excessive acetaldehyde accumulates in the body; acetaldehyde causes dysphoria (depression or distress). Most alcoholics will not consume alcohol after ingesting Antabuse. Those who do risk not only discomfort but also, in some cases, death.

While clients are taking Antabuse and are typically abstinent, as demonstrated in several studies (see Gallant, 2001), psychotherapy and other forms of treatment may be used to help them develop coping skills or alternative life patterns. The families of patients may also be encouraged to work at solving the problems created by the drinking. Knowing that alcohol consumption is unlikely during Antabuse treatment, families do not have to rely solely on the alcoholic's promise to stop drinking—a promise that alcoholics often make but are rarely able to keep.

The problem with Antabuse treatment is that alcoholic patients may stop taking the drug once they leave the hospital or are no longer being monitored. And some may drink anyway because they believe the effects of Antabuse have dissipated, because they have forgotten when they last took it, or because they are tempted to drink in spite of the Antabuse. Naltrexone has been used to reduce craving or the reinforcing effects of alcohol. The reduced craving appears specific to alcohol, not to just any drink (e.g., fruit juices), as found in a study by Rohsenow, Monti, Hutchinson, and colleagues (2000).

Pharmacological agents such as clonidine and naltrexone have allowed some heroin addicts to be detoxified as outpatients (Franklin & Frances, 1999). Chemical treatment may also be used to reduce the intensity of withdrawal symptoms in heroin addicts who are trying to break the drug habit. The drug methadone is prescribed to decrease the intensity of withdrawal symptoms. *Methadone* is a synthetic narcotic chemical that reduces the craving for heroin without producing euphoria (the "high"). It was originally believed that reformed heroin addicts could then quite easily discontinue the methadone at a later date. Although methadone initially seemed to be a simple solution to a major problem, it has an important drawback: it can itself become addicting. The following case illustrates this problem, as well as other facets of the typical two-phase treatment program for heroin addiction.

After several months of denying the seriousness of his heroin habit, Gary B. finally enrolled in a residential treatment program that featured methadone maintenance, peer support, confrontational therapy, and job retraining. Although at first Gary responded well to the residential program, he soon began to feel depressed. He was reassured by the staff that recovering heroin addicts frequently experience depression and that several treatment options existed. A fairly low dose of tricyclic antidepressant medication was prescribed, and Gary also began supportive-expressive (psychodynamic) therapy.

Psychotherapy helped Gary identify the difficult relationships in his life. His dependence on these relationships and his dependence on drugs were examined for parallels. His tendency to deny problems and to turn to drugs as an escape was pointed out. The therapy then focused on the generation of suitable alternatives to drugs. He worked hard during his therapy sessions and made commendable progress.

For the next three months Gary enjoyed his life in a way that previously had been foreign to him. He was hired by a small restaurant to train as a cook. He was entirely satisfied with the direction in which his life was going until the day he realized that he was eagerly looking forward to his daily methadone dose. Gary knew of people who had become addicted to methadone, but it was still a shock when it happened to him. He decided almost immediately to terminate his methadone maintenance program. The withdrawal process was physically and mentally painful, and Gary often doubted his ability to function without methadone. But by joining a support group composed of others who were trying to discontinue methadone, he was eventually able to complete methadone withdrawal. Gary had never imagined that the most difficult part of his heroin treatment would be giving up methadone.

It is clear that the use of chemical substances, such as Antabuse or methadone, has not had a dramatic impact in the treatment of addiction. Side effects and potential addiction to chemical treatments are major problems that have to be considered.

In smoking cessation programs, however, one tactic has been the use of nicotine replacement strategy, especially in the application of transdermal nicotine patches, as discussed in the Mental Health and Society feature "Smoking: Can the Body 'Kick the Habit'?" A patch is applied to the arm, and the nicotine in the patch is absorbed through the skin. Researchers are also studying the effectiveness of directly inhaling nicotine.

Cognitive and Behavioral Approaches

Cognitive and behavioral therapists have devised several strategies for treating alcoholism and other substance-use disorders. Aversion therapy, which is based on classical conditioning principles, has been used for many years. **Aversion therapy** is a conditioning procedure in which the response to a stimulus is decreased by pairing the stimulus with an aversive stimulus. For example, alcoholics may be given painful electric shocks while drinking alcohol, or they may be given *emetics* (agents that induce vomiting) after smelling or tasting alcohol or when they get the urge to drink. After several sessions in which the emetic is used, alcoholics may vomit or feel nauseated when they smell, taste, or think about alcohol.

Imagery has been used as part of **covert sensitization**, an aversive conditioning technique in which the individual imagines a noxious stimulus in the presence of a behavior. Alcoholic patients, for example, are trained to imagine nausea and vomiting in the presence of alcoholic beverages (Cautela, 1966). Covert sensitization has also been used for drug addicts. One difficulty with this technique is the inability of some patients to generalize the treatment—that is, to pair the learned aversive reaction (nausea and vomiting) with the stimulus (taking a particular drug) outside the clinic or hospital setting.

Skills training has also been used in drug-cessation programs. These skills may involve techniques for refusing to give in to peer pressures or temptations, for resolving emotional conflicts or problems, and for more effective communication. J. Smith, Meyers, and Delaney (1998) found that skills training was effective in reducing alcohol consumption among homeless alcohol-dependent individuals. Bickel, Amass, Higgins, Badger, and Esch (1997) found that **reinforcing abstinence** was effective for opioid-dependent individuals. The individuals received either reinforcement (such as vouchers for cash) for being abstinent, as

Puffing So Fast Your Stomach Churns   This fifteen-year-old is undergoing aversive conditioning in an attempt to help her stop smoking. The technique involves having the person puff their cigarettes at a very rapid pace, which usually brings on nausea. Repeated pairing of rapid smoking and feelings of nausea may result in an aversion to smoking.

measured by urinalysis, or standard forms of counseling used in methadone clinics. Results indicated that the behavioral method was more effective than the counseling method in promoting abstinence.

Behavioral Treatment for Cigarette Smoking People who wish to end their addiction to cigarette smoking have used behavioral techniques almost exclusively. Most aversive procedures (such as covert sensitization and shock) have yielded rather disappointing results, but "rapid smoking" has achieved some positive outcomes. This technique requires the client to puff a cigarette once every six seconds, until he or she absolutely cannot continue any longer. Its purpose is to pair a highly aversive situation (the feeling of illness that results from extremely rapid smoking) with the act of smoking. This is expected to eliminate or reduce the person's desire to smoke. Although rapid smoking has been reasonably effective over both the short and the long term, it is somewhat controversial. Some early studies suggested the technique may increase heart rate and blood pressure (Lichtenstein & Glasgow, 1977; Lichtenstein & Rodrigues, 1977). Other studies of smokers with cardiopulmonary disease who engaged in rapid smoking, however, showed that the treatment was effective and did not produce any cardiac complications (R. G. Hall, Sachs, Hall, & Benowitz, 1984).

Another treatment for cigarette smoking is *nicotine fading* (Foxx & Brown, 1979). In this method, the client attempts to withdraw gradually from nicotine by progressively smoking cigarette brands that contain less and less nicotine. When clients reach the stage at which they are smoking cigarettes that contain only 0.1 milligrams of nicotine, their reduced dependence should enable them to stop altogether (Lichtenstein & Danaher, 1976). However, some individuals who smoke low-nicotine cigarettes may simply inhale more deeply or smoke more rapidly, thus defeating the purpose of smoking low-nicotine cigarettes. A more familiar method is simply to smoke less and less—increasing the interval between cigarettes. Cinciripini and his colleagues (1995) found that systematically increasing the amount of time between using cigarettes was a more effective way of achieving abstinence one year later than were other methods, such as going "cold turkey" (abruptly ceasing smoking) or gradually reducing smoking without any fixed and systematic plan. The scheduled interval method also appeared to be superior in decreasing tension and withdrawal symptoms. The investigators suggest that individuals using this method could plan and bring to bear coping mechanisms to deal with urges to smoke.

In general, multicomponent behavioral therapy programs that incorporate relapse-prevention techniques appear to be very effective for quitting smoking (Compas, Haaga, Keefe, Leitenberg, & Williams, 1998). These programs combine behavioral strategies, such as relaxation and gradual reduction of nicotine intake, with relapse-prevention skills, such as learning how to refuse peer pressures to smoke. Because smoking cessation is related to body-weight increase (Klesges et al., 1997), some attention must also be paid to smokers' concerns over gaining weight after quitting smoking.

Other Cognitive-Behavioral Treatments   Relaxation and systematic desensitization may be useful in reducing anxiety. Almost any aversive conditioning procedure may be effective in treating alcoholism if there is also a focus on enhanced social functioning, resistance to stress, and reduction of anxiety (Nathan, 1976). Some programs incorporate social learning techniques.

Cox and Klinger (1988) developed a motivational approach in which alcoholics set important and realis-

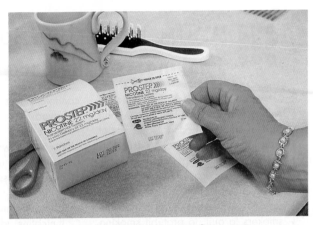

Kicking the Habit with Nicotine Replacement
Transdermal nicotine patches such as the ones shown are usually applied to the arm. They deliver nicotine, which is absorbed through the skin. The patches are intended to help smokers quit smoking by fulfilling the need for nicotine without the use of tobacco. What is the effectiveness of such patches?

tic goals they would like to accomplish. The therapist helps alcoholics achieve these goals and develop a satisfying life without alcohol. Cooper et al. (1988) found that drinking to cope with emotional problems was a strong factor in alcohol abuse. They suggested that alcoholics should find more adaptive ways of coping with negative emotions and stress through techniques such as stress management and cognitive restructuring.

Cognitive-behavioral treatments, based on analyses of why addicts experience relapse, have also been tried. Niaura and colleagues (1988) believe that certain cues are strongly associated with substance use (smoking while having coffee, drinking alcohol at a party, and so forth). They suggested that addicts be placed in these situations or in the presence of the cues and prevented from using the substance. In this way, the consumption response to these cues is extinguished. To prevent relapse, some treatment programs help addicts restructure their thoughts about the pleasant effects of drug use (Cooper et al., 1988). Addicts are taught to substitute negative thoughts for positive ones when tempted to drink. For example, instead of focusing on the euphoria felt from taking cocaine, a person might be taught to say, "I feel an urge to take the substance, but I know that I will feel depressed later on, that many of my friends want me to stop taking it, and that I may get arrested."

The Controlled-Drinking Controversy   A great deal of debate has been generated by the suggestion that it is possible for alcoholics to control their intake and learn to become social drinkers. Proponents of controlled drinking assume that, under the right conditions, alcoholics can learn to limit their drinking to appropriate

MENTAL HEALTH AND SOCIETY

Smoking: Can the Body "Kick the Habit"?

Many people assume that sufficient will power and motivation on the part of smokers or legal and social sanctions from nonsmokers (such as prohibiting smoking in public facilities) can reduce or eliminate the smoking habit. Judging from current statistics, however, efforts to motivate smokers to quit, to prohibit smoking in certain areas, and to regulate advertising by the tobacco industry have not been successful in achieving that goal. About 60 million Americans smoke (Franklin & Frances, 1999). Why do smokers continue to smoke? The answer may lie in the physiological effects of smoking. Even though smokers report feeling more relaxed during smoking, cigarettes act as a stimulant. Heart rate, for instance, increases during smoking. These effects point to the fact that nicotine is a drug. Nicotine is both an addictive agent and a pleasure enhancer.

Stanley Schachter, a noted psychologist, argued that people smoke because they are physically addicted to nicotine. In a series of experiments, Schachter (1977) drew two conclusions. First, chronic smokers need their "normal" constant intake of nicotine. When heavy smokers are given low-nicotine cigarettes, they smoke more cigarettes and puff more frequently. Withdrawal symptoms, such as irritability and increased eating, appear when smokers do not receive their "dose" of nicotine. Second, smoking does not reduce anxiety or calm the nerves. But not smoking increases anxiety and produces withdrawal reactions. Smokers

can tolerate less stress when they are deprived of cigarettes than when they are able to smoke. Even with cigarettes, however, smokers do not perform better under stress than nonsmokers. Stress seems to deplete body nicotine, so that smoking is necessary to maintain the nicotine level.

If nicotine addiction maintains cigarette smoking, then supplying smokers with nicotine in a nontobacco product may reduce the need to smoke. Some researchers (S. M. Hall, Tunstall, Ginsberg, Benowitz, & Jones, 1987) found that giving smokers a nicotine gum was more effective than giving a placebo gum in a stop-smoking program, even if the smokers were not told what substance was in the gum. Fortmann and Killen (1995) also found that smokers who used nicotine gum were more likely to be abstinent and to have lower relapse rates after a one-year follow-up period than were those treated without the gum. Gottlieb, Killen, Marlatt, and Taylor (1987), however, found that when smokers were led to believe that they had received nicotine gum (whether or not they actually had received it) in a treatment program, they reported fewer withdrawal symptoms and lower cigarette consumption in a two-week period than did those who were told they had received no nicotine. Smokers' belief about the presence of nicotine was more important in treatment than their actual ingestion of nicotine. This study seemed to negate the role of nicotine in treatment and, perhaps, in smoking. The study followed the smokers for only

two weeks, however, so the long-term effects of nicotine versus expectancy are unclear.

In a review of the research on nicotine replacement therapy, Lichtenstein and Glasgow (1992) concluded that nicotine gum helps alleviate withdrawal and prevent short-term relapse. Behavioral treatment is most useful in warding off longer term relapse. However, nicotine gum is not the most effective method of delivering nicotine. The levels of nicotine in the blood can vary considerably depending on the way the gum is chewed, the number of pieces of gum used, and the ingestion of drinks such as coffee, which may alter the effects of nicotine.

If the treatments involving nicotine gum are limited, are there more effective ways of delivering the nicotine? There has recently been a great deal of interest in nicotine transdermal patches. In this treatment, an adhesive patch, which delivers a standard dose of nicotine during the day, is placed on the upper arm. This method minimizes problems in delivering a consistent dosage level. Studies comparing the nicotine patch with a placebo patch, in which neither the smokers nor the experimenters knew who had nicotine or placebo patches during treatment (a double-blind study), showed that the nicotine patch is more effective than the placebo patch in smoking cessation (Lichtenstein & Glasgow, 1992). More recently, inhaling nicotine or using a nicotine nasal spray have been tried as a form of treatment, although research findings on the efficacy of these methods are not yet conclusive. In general, nicotine replacement interventions have been very helpful in smoking cessation programs, especially in conjunction with psychosocial interventions (Wetter et al., 1998). Nicotine replacement has been considered by some as being the state-of-the-art treatment for nicotine dependence (Killen et al., 2000). However, other drugs appear to be helpful. In 1997, the FDA approved the use of Wellbutrin (Zyban) sustained-release capsules, a non-nicotine alternative for smoking cessation (Franklin & Frances, 1999), which seems to help some individuals to quit smoking.

Without denying the role of nicotine in physical dependence, Lichtenstein (1982) sees the develop-ment and maintenance of smoking as a complex process involving a variety of factors. For example, factors such as the availability of cigarettes, curiosity, and smoking models influ-ence the initial use of cigarettes. Then physiological and psychosocial factors, such as nicotine addiction and positive consequences, maintain smoking. For psychosocial reasons, including health and the expense of smoking materials, the person may try to stop smoking. Withdrawal symptoms and alcohol consumption (former smokers who drink are often tempted to smoke while consuming alcohol), however, are powerful fac-tors motivating the resumption of smoking. Lichtenstein's analysis emphasized the value of multicompo-nent programs for the treatment and prevention of smoking. His factors are listed in the accompanying table.

A recent view is that the nicotine from smoking may bind to the trans-mitting end of neurons and release glutamate, one of the key neurotrans-mitters involved in the pleasure response in the brain ("Nicotine: Powerful Grip on the Brain," 1995). By binding at the transmitter, nico-tine's effects may be multiplied in the limbic system of the brain, thereby enhancing the pleasure associated with reproduction, eating, and satis-fying the basic drives. Whether smoking is maintained because of addiction or because of pleasure enhancement, quitting smoking through the exercise of will power is no simple matter.

Factors Involved in Smoking Behaviors

Starting (psychological factors)	Continuing (psychological and psychosocial factors)	Stopping (psychosocial factors)	Resuming (psychosocial and physiological factors)
Availability	Nicotine	Health	Withdrawal symptoms
Curiosity	Immediate positive conse-quences	Expense	Stress and frustration
Rebelliousness		Social support	Social pressure
Anticipation of adulthood	Signals (cues) in environs	Self-mastery	Alcohol consumption
Social confidence	Avoiding negative effects (withdrawal)	Aesthetics	Abstinence violation effect
Social pressure/modeling: peers, siblings, parents, media		Example to others	

Source: Lichtenstein (1982).

levels. The finding that alcoholics tend to gulp drinks rather than sip them (as social or moderate drinkers do), to consume straight rather than mixed drinks, and to drink many rather than a few drinks gave investigators clues to behaviors that require modification. Alcoholics were then trained to drink appropriately. In a setting resembling a bar, they were permitted to order and drink alcohol, but they were administered an aversive stimulus for each inappropriate behavior. For example, alcoholics who gulped drinks or ordered too many were given painful electric shocks.

There is evidence that controlled drinking may work for some alcohol abusers (Emmelkamp, 2004). However, one problem with this technique is that patients need to receive periodic retraining or to learn alternative responses to drinking. Otherwise, they tend to revert to their old patterns of consumption on leaving the treatment program (Marlatt, 1983). The major task is to discover the conditions under which controlled drinking or abstinence interventions work.

Opponents of controlled drinking generally believe that total abstinence should be the goal of treatment, that controlled drinking cannot be maintained over a period of time, and that alcoholism is a genetic-physiological problem. Furthermore, by trying to teach alcoholics that they can resume and control drinking, proponents are unwittingly contributing to the alcoholics' problems. There have even been questions about the validity of the findings in controlled drinking programs (Pendery, Maltzman, & West, 1982).

Multimodal Treatment

In view of the many factors that maintain drug-use disorders, some treatment programs make systematic use of combinations of approaches. For example, alcoholics may be detoxified through Antabuse treatment and simultaneously receive behavioral training (via aversion therapy, biofeedback, or stress management), as well as other forms of therapy. In one outpatient treatment program, alcohol-dependent men were given standard care (life-skills training, relapse prevention and coping skills, after-care meetings, and counseling). A group of these men was randomly assigned to another condition, the contingency management group. In this group, the men were given the opportunity to win prizes (ranging from small gift certificates to larger gifts, such as a television) if they tested negative for alcohol consumption on a Breathalyzer. Those patients who had the combined treatment involving contingency management and standard care were more likely to be abstinent than patients who were exposed solely to standard care (Petry, Martin, Cooney, & Kranzler, 2000).

Other therapies may include combinations of Alcoholics Anonymous, educational training, family therapy, group therapy, and individual psychotherapy. For example, opioid-dependent patients have been helped by the use of behaviorally oriented family counseling, individual psychotherapy, and daily ingestion of naltrexone, an opioid antagonist that blocks the subjective reinforcing properties of opioid-based drugs (Fals-Stewart & O'Farrell, 2003). Proponents of multimodal approaches recognize that no single kind of treatment is likely to be totally effective and that successful outcomes often require major changes in the lives of alcoholics. The combination of therapies that works best for a particular person in his or her particular circumstances is obviously the most effective treatment.

In the case of an amphetamine abuser, the individual may initially be admitted to an inpatient facility for approximately thirty days. There he or she receives individual and group therapy, takes part in occupational and recreational therapy and stress management counseling, and perhaps is introduced to a support group modeled after Alcoholics Anonymous. The patient's spouse may also be asked to participate in the group sessions.

Once the patient has successfully completed this inpatient phase, he or she is scheduled for outpatient treatment. As part of this treatment, the patient is asked to agree to unannounced urine screenings to test for the presence of drugs. The patient is encouraged to continue attending the support group, along with his or her spouse, and to become involved in individual outpatient therapy. Family therapy is the treatment of choice for adolescent substance users (Haley, 1980; Reilly, 1984; Rueger & Liberman, 1984), and it is highly recommended for adults as well. The outpatient program typically continues for about two years.

One recent multimodal project involved 600 youths being treated for marijuana use, the largest experiment ever conducted on outpatient adolescent treatment (Clay, 2001). The youths were exposed to a number of different treatments that included the adolescents, their families, schools, and other systems. Preliminary results showed dramatic changes in the adolescents' drug use. For example, the percentage of youths reporting no marijuana abuse or dependence in the previous month increased from 19 percent before treatment to 61 percent six months after treatment. Problems with the criminal justice system, their families, and schools also decreased.

Prevention Programs

Prevention programs have been initiated to discourage drug and alcohol use before it begins. Campaigns to educate the public about the detrimental consequences

dents was not involved in the training program. The participants received three initial training sessions and a booster training session given a year later. Two years after the initial three sessions, the students exposed to the training were generally less likely to show increases in smoking or in trying smoking than were students not exposed to the training. The investigators warn that longer term success may depend on additional training in high school or at some other future time.

Attitudes toward drug use can be altered. Cruz and Dunn (2003) exposed fourth-grade students to one-session alcohol prevention presentations that emphasized the sedating effects of alcohol, challenged the positive effects of alcohol, or alerted them to the dangerous consequences of consumption. Compared with students assigned to a no-prevention group, those who participated in the alcohol presentations had less favorable attitudes toward alcohol use. Because of the public's constant exposure to television, radio, and newspapers, some researchers have used these media as a means to prevent drug use, as noted earlier. Jason (1998) has found that media programs to prevent or reduce drug use and to maintain abstinence have been very successful.

Effectiveness of Treatment

Research evidence indicates that treatment programs are effective in reducing substance abuse and dependence (McLellan et al., 1994), although outcomes have been quite modest (Woody & Cacciola, 1994) and estimates vary from study to study. Currently, approximately half a million Americans are under treatment for alcoholism (Nitzkin & Smith, 2004). About one-third of alcoholic clients remain abstinent one year after treatment. Most opiate-dependent clients and heroin addicts become readdicted within the first year following treatment. The majority of treated smokers return to smoking within one year. Again, relapse occurs most frequently during the first several months of abstinence, and the type of substance is important to consider. Part of the problem in delivering effective treatment is that many individuals with substance-use disorders do not continue treatment (Stark, 1992). However, some individuals recover on their own, without treatment. Other individuals who relapse after treatment subsequently undergo treatment again and become abstinent or develop an ability to control their intake.

Interestingly, McLellan and his colleagues (1994) believe that treatment of substance abuse is effective and find that the same factors predict outcome regardless of the substance used. They examined the outcomes for male and female clients in twenty-two inpatient and outpatient treatment programs for

of substance use, to reestablish norms against drug use, and to give coping skills to others who are tempted by drug use are waged in the media. Other prevention programs take place in schools, places of worship, youth groups, and families.

Such programs are having some effect. For example, Marlatt and others (1998) assigned heavy-drinking college students to a brief intervention group or to a no-intervention control group for three months of the first year of college. The intervention consisted of providing students with feedback on the extent of their drinking and on possible consequences, without confrontation or direct advice. The investigators conducted one-year and two-year follow-up assessments of drinking, which indicated that the intervention was successful. Students receiving the intervention reported lower alcohol consumption and fewer problems resulting from drinking, and the self-reports from students were consistent with those of friends of the students who were also asked to provide ratings of the students.

In another study, Dent and his colleagues (1995) evaluated the outcome of a junior high school smoking-prevention program. One group of students received training focused on (1) resistance to social influence (for example, resisting peer pressure to smoke), (2) information (such as correcting misperceptions of the social image of smokers), (3) the physical consequences of smoking, or (4) a combination of the three other approaches. A control group of stu-

opiate, alcohol, and cocaine dependency. Outcome was assessed six months after treatment, and demographic background, severity of problems, and type of treatment were examined as predictors of outcome. Although a no-treatment control group was not available for comparison purposes, all groups showed significant and pervasive improvements in reduced substance use, family relations, and adjustment six months after treatment, and the same factors predicted outcomes regardless of the type of drug problem. The findings suggest that treatment can be helpful and that outcomes are governed by the same client and treat-ment factors. In a review of the treatment outcomes for adolescents, Williams and Chang (2000) found that treatment for substance abuse was generally beneficial, especially if the adolescents completed treatment and if parental and peer support for nonuse was available. Read, Kahler, and Stevenson (2001) conclude that there is probably no single "best" treatment for substance use disorders, although a number of different treatment approaches exist and are helpful. The task is to find the best combination of treatments for particular individuals with substance use disorders.

SUMMARY

Substance abuse and dependence are widespread problems. Substance abuse is defined as a maladaptive pattern of recurrent use over a twelve-month period, during which the person is unable to reduce or cease intake of a harmful substance, despite knowledge that its use causes social, occupational, psychological, medical, or safety problems. Substance dependence is a more serious disorder, involving not only excessive use but also tolerance and withdrawal in many cases.

What are substance-use disorders?

- Substance-use disorders vary according to age, gender, and ethnic group. Major categories of substances are depressants, stimulants, and hallucinogens.
- A large proportion of the U.S. population consumes alcohol, one of the depressants. Alcohol is associated with traffic accidents, absenteeism from work, accidents, violence, and family problems. The consumption of alcohol results in both long-term and short-term psychological and physiological effects.
- Other depressants, such as narcotics, barbiturates, and benzodiazepines, can also cause psychological, physiological, or legal problems.
- Other categories of psychoactive substances include stimulants and hallucinogens. Stimulants energize the central nervous system, often inducing elation, grandiosity, hyperactivity, agitation, and appetite suppression.
- Amphetamines and cocaine/crack cocaine, as well as widely used substances such as caffeine and nicotine, are considered stimulants.

- Abuse and dependency often occur after regular use of stimulants.
- Hallucinogens, another category of psychoactive substances, often produce hallucinations, altered states of consciousness, and perceptual distortions.
- Included in this category are marijuana, LSD, and PCP.
- Drug dependency with these substances is relatively rare, although abuse may occur.
- PCP in many cases causes delusions, perceptual distortions, and violent behaviors.

Why do people become addicted to drugs?

- There appears to be no single factor that can account for drug abuse or for dependence on other substances such as depressants, stimulants, and hallucinogens. In all likelihood, heredity and environmental factors are important.
- With respect to alcoholism, some research has indicated that heredity, along with environmental factors, plays an important role.
- Recent experiments have demonstrated the importance of cognitive factors in drinking behavior.
- The tension-reducing hypothesis alone is inadequate to account for alcoholism because alcohol consumption sometimes results in increased feelings of depression or anxiety.
- Drinking and alcoholism may be closely related to the type of stress anticipated, the perceived benefits of alcohol, the availability of alternative coping responses in a particular situation, and the drinker's genetic or physiological makeup.
- For narcotic addiction, both physical and psychological factors are important.

- Overall theories of addiction have been proposed that emphasize changes in motivation for drug use with chronic consumption, the positive and negative reinforcing effects of drugs, and cognitive factors in maintaining drug use.

How can we successfully help people to overcome substance abuse and addiction?

- A variety of treatment approaches have been used, including detoxification, drug therapies, psychotherapy, and behavior modification.
- Multimodal approaches (the use of several treatment techniques) are probably the most effective.
- Many alcoholics are helped by treatment, and some achieve abstinence by themselves.
- The treatment prescribed for other drug users depends on the type of drug and on the user.

- Heroin addicts usually undergo detoxification followed by methadone maintenance and forms of treatment such as residential treatment programs, psychotherapy, cognitive or behavior therapy, and group therapy. Detoxification and occupational, recreational, and family therapies may be suggested for users of other drugs.
- For addiction to cigarette smoking, aversive procedures such as "rapid smoking," nicotine fading (the use of brands containing less and less nicotine), and transdermal nicotine patches have had some success.
- Prevention programs have also been extensively used in an attempt to discourage substance use.
- Treatment for substance-use disorders has not been overwhelmingly successful. Evidence indicates that relapse is particularly likely during the first three months after treatment. The risk of relapse decreases as a function of time.

KEY TERMS

alcoholic (p. 274)
alcoholism (p. 274)
amphetamine (p. 280)
aversion therapy (p. 298)
barbiturate (p. 278)
cocaine (p. 281)

covert sensitization (p. 298)
depressant (p. 274)
detoxification (p. 295)
hallucinogen (p. 282)
intoxication (p. 271)
marijuana (p. 282)

narcotic (p. 277)
polysubstance dependence (p. 280)
reinforcing abstinence (p. 298)
skills training (p. 298)
stimulant (p. 280)

substance abuse (p. 270)
substance dependence (p. 270)
substance-related disorder (p. 269)
tolerance (p. 271)
withdrawal (p. 271)

MULTIMEDIA PREVIEW

For additional study aids, we invite you to explore our media resources accompanying *Understanding Abnormal Behavior*, Eighth Edition. The Student CD-ROM includes videos, quizzing, and critical thinking activities that help to reinforce key concepts in a fun and engaging manner. The Student Web Site provides additional interactive activities, chapter outlines, and research links that further support and complement the text. All Web resources may be accessed by logging onto the Web site at **http://psychology.college.hmco.com/students**.

CHAPTER 10
Sexual and Gender Identity Disorders

FOCUS QUESTIONS

■ **What are normal and abnormal sexual behaviors?**

■ **What does the normal sexual response cycle tell us about sexual dysfunctions?**

■ **What causes gender identity disorders?**

■ **What are the paraphilias?**

■ **Are rape and incest acts of aggression?**

Sexual and gender identity disorders encompass a wide range of behaviors. Consider the following cases:

I just don't know what to do. I think my husband is losing interest in me. I can't fake it anymore. It's tiring to pretend that I enjoy sex and that I'm having orgasms. After twelve years of marriage, I've never once had an orgasm with him. I think he suspects, that's why he never asks me whether I like it anymore. I've read sex manuals on sexual pleasuring and tried to masturbate, but nothing happens. When I was fourteen or fifteen, I had sex with this boy and think I had a mild orgasm, but I can't even remember now what it was like. I mean, it's not like I don't like men. I'm not a lesbian, but why can't I be like everyone else? All I know is that I really feel lousy about myself. Why am I frigid? What's wrong with me?

Roger recalls that, as a young child, he always seemed more interested in "girly things" and activities. He often believed he was a girl, played like a girl, and had no interest in boys' games. Roger often got in trouble for using the women's restroom (because he needed to sit while urinating), dressing in his sister's clothes, and wearing his mother's makeup. As he became older, Roger could not help believing that nature had played a cruel hoax on him, that he was a woman trapped in a man's body. After much counseling and exploration, Roger became "Rosie" via sex-reassignment surgery. Although Rosie eventually married, she regrets not being able to conceive a child.

From early childhood, Peter F., a forty-one-year-old man, had fantasies of being mistreated, humiliated, and beaten. He recalls how he would become sexually excited when envisioning such activities. As he grew older, he experienced difficulty achieving an orgasm unless he was able to experience pain from his sexual partners. He was obsessed with masochistic sexual acts, which made it difficult for him to concentrate on other matters. He had been married and divorced three times because of his proclivity for demanding that his wives engage in "sex games" that involved having them hurt him. These games involved being bound spread-eagled on his bed and tortured by whippings, biting his upper thighs, the sticking of pins into his legs, and other forms of torture. During these sessions, he could ejaculate.

These cases illustrate some of the disorders we present in this chapter. We discuss the following categories listed in DSM-IV-TR (American Psychiatric Association, 2000):

■ *Sexual dysfunctions,* which involve problems of inhibited sexual desire, arousal, and response. The woman who is unable to have an orgasm and wonders whether she is frigid falls into this category.

■ *Gender-identity disorders,* which involve an incongruity or conflict between one's anatomical sex and one's psychological feeling of being male or female. Roger/Rosie had such a conflict.

■ *Paraphilias,* which involve sexual urges and fantasies about situations, objects, or people that are not part of the usual arousal pattern leading to reciprocal and affectionate sexual activity. Peter F.'s activities place him in this category.

In addition to these three dysfunctions and disorders, we also discuss sexual aggression. Although it is not considered a DSM-IV-TR disorder, we believe that the magnitude and seriousness of problems related to sexual aggression in our society warrant such discussion. Public awareness of these problems has heightened in the wake of highly publicized allegations of assault or sexual harassment made against such public figures as basketball player Kobe Bryant, boxer Mike Tyson, conservative talk show host Bill O'Reilly, Supreme Court Justice Clarence Thomas, and former President Bill Clinton. Although Paula Jones and Clinton reached an out-of-court settlement in 1998 without any admission of guilt, it marked the first time a sexual harassment lawsuit had ever been filed against a sitting U.S. president.

Before we begin these discussions, however, let's consider another question: How do we decide what constitutes "normal" sexual functioning?

What Is "Normal" Sexual Behavior?

It was an affair that shocked the country. Under investigation by Kenneth Starr and the Office of the Independent Counsel, former President Clinton admitted to a sixteen-month affair with a young female intern. The Starr Report, as it came to be known, provided excruciating and graphic descriptions of the sexual activity—including oral sex, phone sex, and use of a cigar—that took place between Clinton and Monica Lewinsky. The public discussions that ensued focused not only on legal and constitutional issues but also on whether the described sexual behaviors were normal or abnormal.

■ Is oral sex normal? Many consider oral sex offensive, but it is not an uncommon practice. One survey (Andersen & Cyranowski, 1995) indicates that 70 percent of sexually active college-age women have orally stimulated the genitals of their partners and that the same percentage have had their genitals orally stimulated in return.

■ Does oral sex constitute "sex" if no intercourse has occurred? Clinton's attorneys argued that the president did not lie under oath when he testified in the Paula Jones case that he had not had sex with Monica Lewinsky. According to Clinton's attorneys, the president believed that as long as penetration (intercourse) had not taken place, he was telling the truth. He stated that "most ordinary Americans would embrace this distinction." Polls showed that many Americans agreed with Clinton's view. A 1991 survey conducted by the Kinsey Institute and a 1996 survey conducted by *Playboy* magazine both revealed that a slight majority of respondents believed that oral sex without intercourse did not constitute "real sex" (Marine, 1998).

■ Does Clinton's use of a "cigar" in sex play constitute perversion? Many men and women use sex toys (such as vibrators and dildos) and engage in sex games (phone sex, "talking dirty," and verbally creating sexual fantasies).

■ Is the former president oversexed, and is he a "sex addict"? DSM-IV-TR does not recognize the existence of a "sex addiction" disorder, nor does it classify "oversexed" as a sexual desire disorder. As you will see later in this chapter, sexual desire and frequency of sexual intercourse vary widely. Slightly over 2 percent of married men and 1 percent of married women have intercourse more than once a day (Laumann, Gagnon, Michael, & Michaels, 1994; LoPiccolo & Friedman, 1988). By statistical standards, would these people be considered abnormal? (See the Mental Health & Society feature "Is Compulsive Sexual Behavior [CSB] an Addiction?")

Of all the psychological or psychiatric disorders discussed in this text, sexual and gender identity disorders present the greatest difficulty for those attempting to distinguish between "abnormal" (maladaptive) behavior and nonharmful variations that reflect personal values and tastes markedly different from social norms. The definitions of normal sexual behavior vary widely and are influenced by both moral and legal judgments. For example, the laws of some states define oral-genital sex as a "crime against nature." This view is reflected in a California statute that was repealed as late as 1976:

Oral Sex Perversion—Any person participating in an act of copulating the mouth of one person with the sexual organ of another is punishable by incarceration in the state prison for a period not exceeding fifteen years, or by imprisonment in the county jail not to exceed one year.

It would be difficult today to justify the classification of oral sex as a "perversion." The pioneering work of Kinsey and colleagues revealed that oral sex is widespread, especially among the more highly educated part of the population (Kinsey, Pomeroy, Martin, & Gebhard, 1953). And, as noted earlier, surveys (Young, 1980; Andersen & Cyranowski, 1995) have found that most sexually experienced college men and women have engaged in this behavior. As you can see, legal decisions on sexuality sometimes reflect past moods and morals or questionable and idiosyncratic views. Consider the 1943 ruling of the Minnesota Supreme Court in the case of *Dittrick* v. *Brown County*. The court upheld the conviction of a father of six as a sexual psychopath because he had an "uncontrollable craving for sexual intercourse with his wife." This "craving" amounted to three or four times a week. If he were tried today, Mr. Dittrick could base

Cultural Influences and Sexuality Sexuality is influenced by how it is viewed in different cultures. Some societies have very rigid social, cultural, and religious taboos associated with exposure of the human body, whereas other societies are more open. Note the contrast between the teens from Muslim and American societies shown here.

his defense on the views of some current researchers who believe that not having sex often *enough* indicates a sexual desire disorder.

Shifting perspectives on sexual conduct challenge legal definitions of normal and abnormal. One area currently being challenged involves relations between individuals of the same sex. In 1998, two men were arrested in Houston, Texas, for violating the state's 119-year-old law against sodomy. Six states consider consensual oral and anal sex between homosexual couples a crime even if it occurs in private ("Houston Case," 1998). Such laws may be struck down as they are tested.

Classification of normal and abnormal behavior becomes especially difficult when one compares Western and non-Western cultures or different time periods within a particular culture (Rathus, Nevid, & Fichner-Rathus, 2005). For example, in ancient Greece, homosexuality was not only accepted but encouraged (Arndt, 1991). In many countries, sex with animals is fairly common among rural youths but is rare among urban boys. And in many parts of Southeast Asia, individuals are afflicted by a disorder called *koro*, characterized by a sudden and intense anxiety that the penis will recede into the body (American Psychiatric Association, 2000). Thus it is clear that definitions of sexual disorders are also strongly influenced by cultural norms and values.

If legal, moral, and statistical models fall short of the viable definition of normal sexual behavior that is needed, can we resolve the controversy by simply stating that sexual behavior is deviant if it is a threat to society, causes distress to participants, or impairs social

or occupational functioning? Using this definition, there would be no objection to our considering rape as deviant behavior; it includes the elements of nonconsent, force, and victimization. But what about sexual arousal to an inanimate object (fetishism), or low sexual drive, or gender identity conflict? These conditions are not threats to society, they may not cause distress to people who experience them, and they may not result in impaired social or occupational functioning. They are deviant simply because they do not fall within "normal arousal and activity patterns." And they are considered deviant even though what constitutes a normal sexual pattern is the subject of controversy (Nevid, Fichner-Rathus, & Rathus, 1995).

In short, ambiguities surround all the classification systems, and the controversies will become more obvious as we discuss the three groups of sexual disorders and sexual aggression in the remainder of this chapter. Nevertheless, the *Merck Manual of Diagnosis and Therapy* (Beers & Berkow, 1999) provides a three-phase process of judging whether something constitutes a sexual problem: (1) it is persistent and recurrent over a long period of time; (2) it causes personal distress; and (3) it negatively affects one's relationship with one's sexual partner. Our journey begins with a brief look at the study of human sexuality and the human sexual response cycle.

The Study of Human Sexuality

Because sexual behavior is such an important part of our lives and because so many taboos and myths surround it, people have great difficulty dealing with the

Understanding Sexuality Through their clinical research and well-known publications, *Human Sexual Response* (1966) and *Human Sexual Inadequacy* (1970), William Masters and Virginia Johnson, shown here, have done much to further understanding and dispel myths of human sexuality.

eventual release of sexual tension. In the man, muscles at the base of the penis contract, propelling semen through the penis. In the woman, the outer third of the vagina contracts rhythmically. Following orgasm, men enter a refractory period during which they are unresponsive to sexual stimulation for a period of time. However, women are capable of multiple orgasms with continued stimulation.

4. The *resolution phase* is characterized by relaxation of the body after orgasm. Heart rate, blood pressure, and respiration return to normal.

Problems may occur in any of the four phases of the sexual response cycle, although they are rare in the resolution phase. If problems related to arousal, desire, or orgasm are recurrent and persistent, they may be diagnosed as dysfunctions. We cover this topic in detail later in this chapter in the section on sexual dysfunctions.

Homosexuality

Although the American Psychiatric Association and the American Psychological Association no longer consider homosexuality to be a mental disorder, some individuals still harbor this belief. In 1998 Trent Lott, then the U.S. Senate majority leader, described homosexuality as a disorder akin to alcoholism and kleptomania—a condition that should be treated (Mitchell, 1998). Jerry Falwell, on the Pat Robertson program, stated that the September 11, 2001, terrorist attack that took thousands of lives was punishment for the growing influence of gay and lesbian groups. Falwell was forced to later apologize for his remarks. It is clear from the tone of these statements that *homophobia*—

FIGURE 10.1 Human Sexual Response Cycle The studies of Masters and Johnson reveal similar normal sexual response cycles for men and women. Note that women may experience more than one orgasm. Sexual disorders may occur at any of the phases, but seldom at the resolution phase.

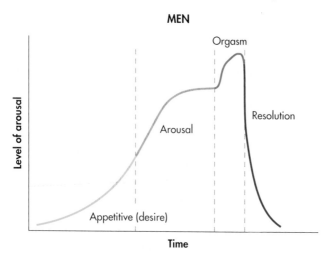

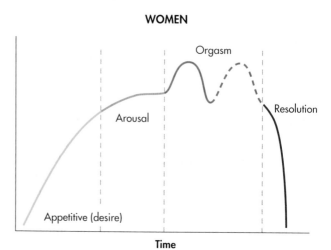

FIGURE 10.2 Genital Changes Associated with Stages of the Human Male Sexual Response Cycle Although we often focus on the differences between men and women, Masters and Johnson found that the physiological responses of both to sexual stimulation are quite similar (compare this figure to Figure 10.3).

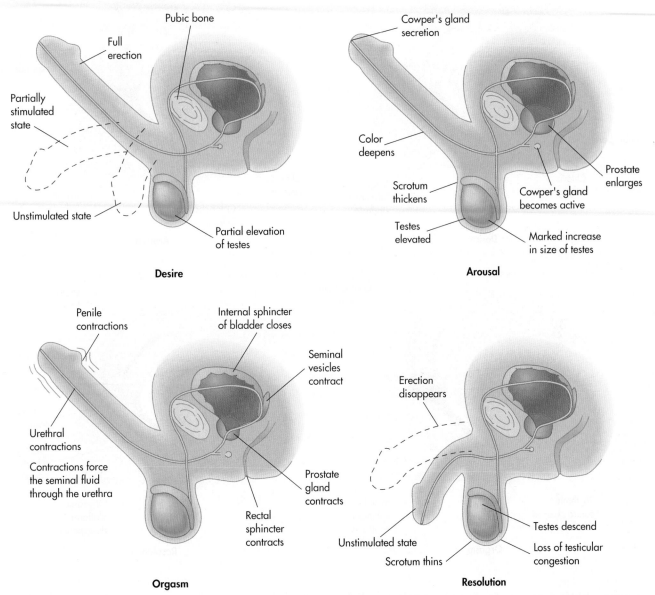

the irrational fear of homosexuality—continues to be a major part of these objections.

Given the level of public misunderstanding and misinformation, we believe it is important to discuss briefly what homosexuality is *not*. Is homosexuality a mental disorder? The answer is no. The American Psychiatric Association did not include homosexuality as a disorder beginning with DSM-III-R or any future editions.

DSM-I and DSM-II classified homosexuality as sexual deviance because sexual behavior was considered normal only if it occurred between two consenting adults of opposite sexes. The changing view of homosexuality has been influenced by two main objections (Halderman, 2002; Yarhouse & Burkett, 2002). First, many clinicians felt that heterosexual sexuality should not be the standard by which other sexual behaviors are judged. Second, many homosexual people argued that they are mentally healthy and that their sexual preference reflects a normal variant of sexual expression. Research supports these views. Studies on male and female homosexuals suggest that most accepted their sexual orientation and indicated no regrets at being homosexual (Croteau, Lark, Lidderdale, &

FIGURE 10.3 Genital Changes Associated with Stages of the Human Female Sexual Response Cycle

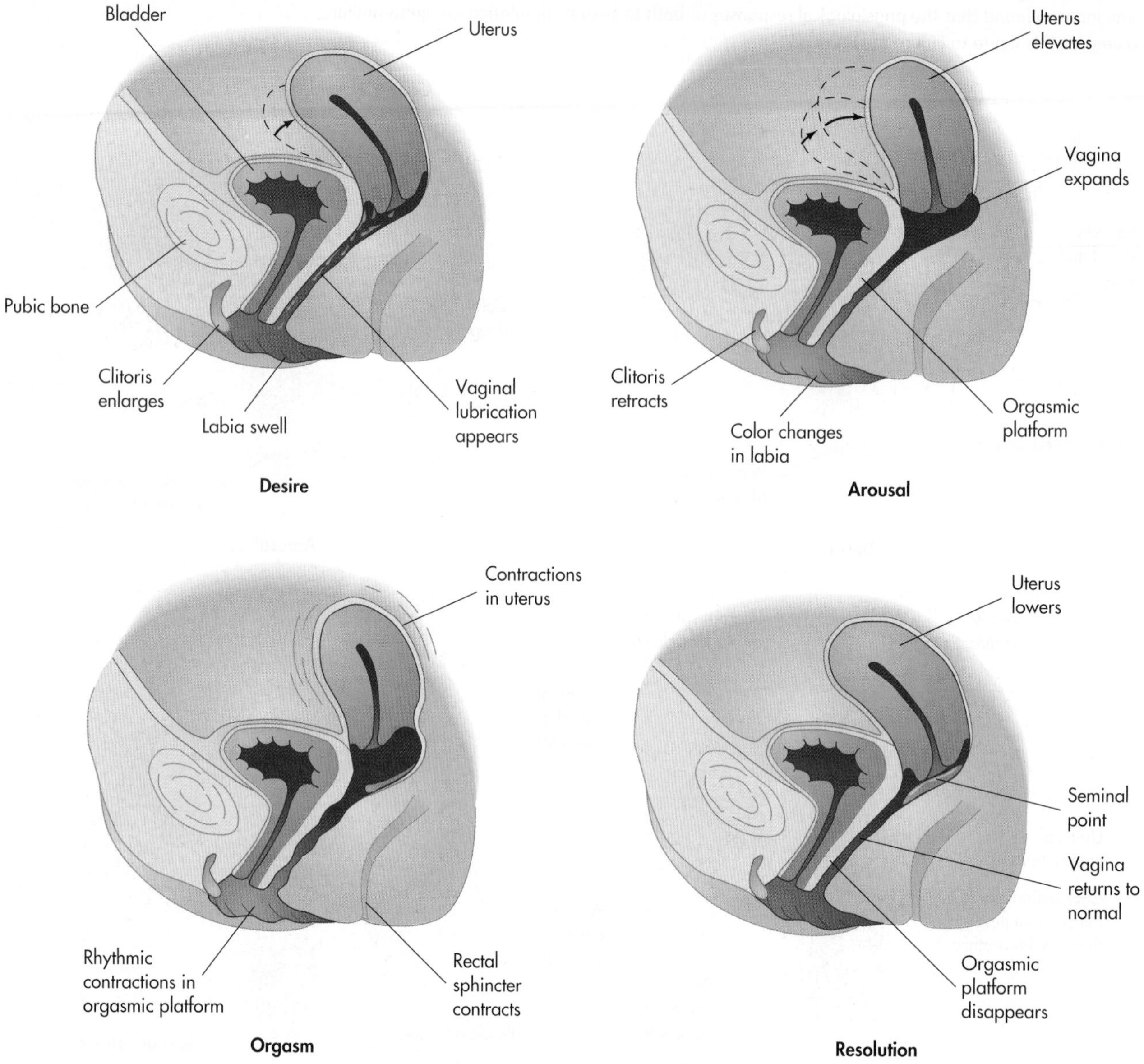

Desire

Bladder
Uterus
Pubic bone
Clitoris enlarges
Labia swell
Vaginal lubrication appears

Arousal

Uterus elevates
Vagina expands
Clitoris retracts
Color changes in labia
Orgasmic platform

Orgasm

Contractions in uterus
Rhythmic contractions in orgasmic platform
Rectal sphincter contracts

Resolution

Uterus lowers
Seminal point
Vagina returns to normal
Orgasmic platform disappears

Chung, 2005; Greenan & Tunnell, 2003; Laird & Green, 1996). In a move indicative of changing international views of homosexuality, as of March 2001, the Chinese Psychological Association no longer considers it an illness. This move is even more meaningful because China has always been conservative toward sexual orientation matters, and its recognition that homosexuality is not an illness may mean that the estimated 30 million gays and lesbians may become increasingly visible in Chinese society.

It is also important to note that although the human sexual response cycle appears equally applicable to a homosexual population, the sexual issues may differ quite dramatically. For example, problems among heterosexuals most often focus on sexual intercourse, whereas gay and lesbian sexual concerns focus on other behaviors (aversion toward anal eroticism and cunnilingus). Lesbians and gay men must also deal with societal or internalized homophobia, which often inhibits open expression of their affection toward one another (Schneider, Brown, & Glassgold, 2002). Finally, gay men are forced to deal with the association between sexual activity and HIV infection. These broader contextual issues may create diminished sexual desire, sexual aversion, and negative feelings toward sexual activity.

Helen Singer Kaplan In her book, *The Disorders of Sexual Desire* (1979), renowned sexuality researcher Dr. Helen Singer Kaplan proposed an alternative to the Masters and Johnson model of human sexual response, employing a three-stage psychophysical model: (1) desire, (2) excitement, and (3) orgasm. By including desire as the first stage, Dr. Kaplan broadened our understanding of the role emotions play in the sexual experience.

In summary, the available studies (Croteau, Lark, Lidderdale, & Chung, 2005; Green, Mandel, Hotvedt, Gray, & Smith, 1986; Greenan & Tunnell, 2003; Hu, Pattatucci, & Patterson, 1995; Laird & Green, 1996; Masters & Johnson, 1979; Strong & DeVault, 1994; W. Turner, 1995; Wilson, 1984) on homosexuals and heterosexuals lead to the following conclusions:

- There are no physiological differences in sexual arousal and response between homosexuals and heterosexuals.

- On measures of psychological disturbance, homosexuals and heterosexuals do not differ significantly from each other.

- Homosexuals do not suffer from gender identity confusions; rather, any gender conflicts they experience are due to societal intolerance to their lifestyles.

- Because of the societal context in which they live (homophobia, health concerns, and other such issues), the sexual concerns of homosexuals may differ significantly from those of heterosexuals.

- Research suggests that homosexuality is not simply a lifestyle choice but is rather a naturally occurring phenomenon linked to a biological disposition.

The Origins of Homosexuality Debate about whether homosexuality is a life choice or a biologically determined orientation has often been intense and emotional. Recent research, however, seems to support biological determination. Pictured here are Drs. Dean Hamer and Victoria Magnuson as they examine DNA markers trying to locate a possible "gay" gene.

Nothing more need be said. Homosexuality is not a psychological disorder.

Aging and Sexual Activity

It is important to understand how the aging process can affect sexuality. When women reach menopause, estrogen levels drop, and women may experience vaginal dryness and thinning of the vaginal wall. This may result in discomfort during sexual activity. Likewise, older men are at higher risk for prostate problems that may increase the risk of erectile dysfunction. Both sexes are also at higher risk for illnesses that affect sexual performance and interest (diabetes, high blood pressure, rheumatism, and heart disease). Hormone replacement therapy, drugs (Cialis, Levitra, and Viagra), and other medical procedures may help

Sexual Behavior Among Seniors Contrary to the belief that the elderly lose their sexual desire, studies reveal that sexual desire, activity, and enjoyment remain high in the older population.

minimize the effects of these organic problems on sexual activity. Nevertheless, our society continues to perpetuate the myth that aging is associated with sexual difficulties and unhappiness. A recent survey of 1,384 adults aged forty-five and older shed much light on the sexual behaviors and attitudes of a segment of the population (American Association of Retired Persons [AARP], 1999):

- Although most men and women report that satisfying sex is important in their lives, they found relationships to be more important than sex.

- Sexual activity is affected by the "partner gap." Whereas 80 percent of those surveyed between the ages of forty-five and fifty-nine have partners, only 58 percent of men and 21 percent of women seventy-five and older do.

- Both men and women report that sexual activity declines with advancing age due to health problems; yet 64 percent of men and 68 percent of women with sexual partners report being satisfied with their sex lives.

Sexuality during old age is an area of intolerance in our youth-oriented society, in which sexual activity is simply not associated with aging. Nevertheless, a large percentage of older Americans clearly have active sex lives. In one study (Diokno, Brown, & Herzog, 1990) investigators found a clear relationship between the reported frequency of intercourse at younger ages and at the present time among sixty- to seventy-nine-year-old married men. The most active respondents reported a present frequency that was 61 percent of their frequency between ages forty and fifty-nine, whereas the least active reported a present frequency of only 6 percent of that between ages forty and fifty-nine. The most active also indicated that they became aroused on seeing women in public situations and in response to visual stimuli. The vast majority (69 percent) felt that sex was important for good health, and most (63 percent) looked on masturbation as an acceptable outlet. Sexual dysfunctions were also more prevalent in the older groups than in younger ones, and the prevalence was affected by the individuals' prior and present sexual activity levels. Of the least active, 21 percent suffered from premature ejaculation, and 75 percent were either impotent or had erectile difficulties. For the most active group, the corresponding percentages were 8 and 19 percent. (The results of this study are summarized in Figures 10.4 and 10.5.)

A comprehensive survey (Janus & Janus, 1993) suggested that sexual activity and enjoyment among the older population remains surprisingly high. The Januses' survey found that (1) the sexual activity of people age sixty-five and older declined little from that of their thirty- to forty-year-old counterparts, (2) their ability to reach orgasm and have sex diminished very little from their early years, and (3) their desire to continue a relatively active sex life was unchanged. These findings are supported by a recent poll of 1,292 Americans (534 men and 758 women) age sixty or older who reported that their interest in sex remains high, that over half engage in sexual activity at least once a month, and that half rated their sexual activity to be physically better now than in their youth (National Council on the Aging, 1998).

Aside from sexual outlook and behavior, physiologically based changes in patterns of sexual arousal and orgasm have been found in people over age sixty-five (Masters & Johnson, 1966). For both men and women, sexual arousal takes longer (McAnulty & Burnette, 2003). Erection and vaginal lubrication are slower to occur, and the urgency for orgasm is reduced. Both men and women are fully capable of sexual satisfaction if no physiological conditions interfere. Many elderly individuals felt that such changes allowed them to experience sex more fully. They reported that they had more time to spend on a seductive buildup, felt positively about their ability to experience unhurried sex-for-joy, and experienced more warmth and intimacy after the sex act (Janus & Janus, 1993).

Sexual Dysfunctions

A **sexual dysfunction** is a disruption of any part of the normal sexual response cycle. Problems in sexual functioning, such as premature ejaculation, low sexual desire, and difficulties in achieving orgasm, are quite common in our society. For example, lifetime prevalence of sexual problems in young adults at some time in their lives is summarized in the following list (Haas & Haas, 1993):

Women

- Reduced libido: 40 percent

- Arousal difficulties: 60 percent

- Reaching orgasm too soon: 10 percent

- Inability to have orgasm: 35 percent

- Dyspareunia: 15 percent

Men

- Reduced libido: 30 percent

- Arousal difficulties: 50 percent

- Reaching orgasm too soon: 15 percent

- Inability to have orgasm: 2 percent

- Dyspareunia: 5 percent

To be diagnosed as a dysfunction, the disruption must be recurrent and persistent. DSM-IV-TR also requires that such factors as frequency, chronicity, subjective distress, and effect on other areas of functioning be considered in the diagnosis. As indicated in Figure 10.6, the DSM-IV-TR categories for sexual dysfunctions are sexual desire disorders, sexual arousal disorders, orgasmic disorders, and sexual pain disorders. Prevalence of the sexual dysfunctions is summarized here as well.

FIGURE 10.4 Percentage of Men with Erectile Problems, Ages 60 and Older   It is clear that erectile problems increase with age. This increase is most likely attributed to biological rather than psychological factors.

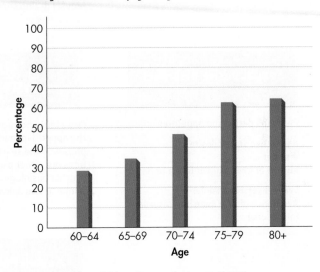

Source: Data from Diokno, Brown, & Herzog (1990, pp. 197–200).

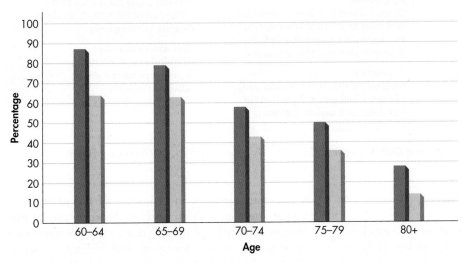

■ Male   ■ Female

Source: Data from Diokno, Brown, & Herzog (1990, pp. 197–200).

FIGURE 10.5 Percentages of Men and Women Remaining Sexually Active, Ages 60 and Older   Contrary to many myths about aging and reduced sexual activity, studies reveal that elderly people are surprisingly active. At all age levels, however, men continue to be more sexually active than women. What explanations might account for this difference?

FIGURE 10.6 Disorders Chart: Sexual Dysfunctions

Sexual Arousal Disorders

Problems involving feelings of sexual pleasure or physiological changes associated with sexual excitement

Male erectile disorder
Inability to attain or maintain an erection sufficient for sexual intercourse and/or psychological arousal during sexual activity

Female sexual arousal disorder
Inability to attain or maintain physiological response and/or psychological arousal during sexual activity

Sexual Desire Disorders

Problems during the appetitive phase

Hypoactive sexual desire disorder
Absent or low sexual interest or desire

Sexual aversion disorder
Avoidance of and aversion to sexual intercourse

SEXUAL DYSFUNCTIONS

Persistent and recurrent problems in the appetitive, excitement, and orgasm phases of the sexual cycle. Dysfunctions are either psychological or psychophysiological in origin (never primarily physiological)

Orgasmic Disorders

Problems with the orgasm phase of the sexual cycle

Female orgasmic disorder
Persistent delay or inability to achieve an orgasm after the excitement phase has been reached. The sexual activity must be adequate in focus, intensity, and duration

Male orgasmic disorder
Persistent delay or inability to achieve an orgasm after the excitement phase has been reached and the sexual activity has been adequate in focus, intensity, and duration. Usually restricted to the inability to reach orgasm introvaginally

Premature ejaculation
Ejaculation with minimal sexual stimulation before, during, or shortly after penetration

Sexual Pain Disorders

Dyspareunia
Genital pain in a man or woman that is not due to a lack of lubrication in the vagina. It occurs either before, during or after sexual intercourse

Vaginismus
Involuntary spasm of the outer third of the vaginal wall that prevents or interferes with sexual intercourse

Source: Data from American Psychiatric Association (2000); Spector & Carey (1990); LoPiccolo (1995, 1997); Hooper (1998).

Sexual Desire Disorders

Sexual desire disorders are related to the appetitive phase and are characterized by a lack of sexual desire. There are two types: *hypoactive sexual desire disorder,* characterized by little or no interest in sexual activities, either actual or fantasized, and *sexual aversion disor-*

der, characterized by an avoidance of and aversion to sexual intercourse. Both of these disorders can be lifelong or acquired and may be due to psychological or a combination of psychological and biological factors (Rathus, Nevid, & Fichner-Rathus, 2005). Some people may report low sexual desire because of inexperience. Many of these people may not have learned to

FIGURE 10.6 Disorders Chart: Sexual Dysfunctions (continued)

SEXUAL DYSFUNCTIONS	Prevalence	Age of Onset	Course
Sexual Desire Disorders	Affects 20% of adult population; women have higher rates (20–35%) than men (15%)	Usually noticed in adulthood by a partner who complains	May be lifelong or acquired; treatment may help, but person may not perceive lower desire as a problem
Sexual Arousal Disorders	10% of men report erectile dysfunction, but some 50% have experienced "transient" conditions; estimated 10–50% of women suffer from arousal lubrication problems	Can occur at age of sexual maturity, but increases with age, especially in men	Most can be helped by psychological or medical treatment
Orgasmic Disorders	Estimates of premature ejaculation range from 30–50% in men; 3–10% of nonclinical population suffer from inhibited male orgasm; 10% of women have primary orgasmic dysfunction (never experienced an orgasm)	At age of sexual maturity	In men, often related to performance anxiety; in women, lack of foreplay is the most frequent reason
Sexual Pain Disorders	Dyspareunia is considered relatively rare in men but more common in women (10–15%); vaginismus in women occurs in less than 1% of the female population	Can occur because of medical problems (such as infections or injury to the pelvis) or because of a traumatic event	Most have physical causes and can be treated appropriately

label or identify their own arousal levels, may not know how to increase their arousal, and may have a limited expectation for their ability to be aroused (LoPiccolo, 1995).

About 20 percent of the adult population (20 to 35 percent of women and 15 percent of men) are believed to be suffering from hypoactive sexual desire disorder (American Psychiatric Association, 1994; LoPiccolo, 1995; Rosen & Leiblum, 1995; Spector & Carey, 1990). Some clinicians estimate that 40 to 50 percent of all sexual dysfunctions involve deficits in desire (Stuart, Hammond, & Pett, 1987), and it is now the most common complaint of couples seeking sex therapy (McAnulty & Burnette, 2004; Spector & Carey, 1990). Although people with sexual desire disorders are often capable of experiencing orgasm, they claim to have little interest in, or to derive no pleasure from, sexual activity (LoPiccolo, 1995; Rosen & Leiblum, 1995). In the following case, relationship problems contributed to the sexual dysfunction:

A thirty-six-year-old woman and her thirty-eight-year-old husband were referred by her psychotherapist for sex therapy. The couple had had little or no sexual contact over the preceding three years, and the sexual relationship had been troubled and unsatisfactory since the day they met. Kissing and gentle fondling were enjoyable to both of them, but as their relationship progressed to genital caressing, she became more anxious, despite her being easily orgasmic. ... She explained the difficulty as being due to conflict in the relationship. She saw him as angry, controlling, and demanding and very critical of her. Naturally, she did not feel loving or sexually receptive. Correspondingly, he felt angry, resentful, and cheated of a "normal sex life." (J. Golden, 1988, p. 304)

In this case, the woman was diagnosed as having inhibited sexual desire. According to DSM-IV-TR, a sexual dysfunction should be diagnosed in such cases because the interpersonal problem is the primary cause of the disturbed functioning. Many people question the legitimacy of these criteria and of the categories themselves, however. They challenge the idea that sexual problems stemming from a troubled relationship or from job or academic stress are sufficient to indicate a disorder.

TABLE 10.1 Frequency of Thoughts About Sex			
	Once or Several Times a Day	Weekly or Monthly	Less Than Once a Month or Never
Men	54%	43%	4%
Women	19%	67%	14%

Source: Adapted from Michael, Gagnon, Laumann, & Kolata (1994).

There is an even larger issue in diagnosing these problems. As noted earlier in this chapter, we do not really know what constitutes "normal" sexual desire, and we know little about what frequency of sexual fantasies or what activities are "normal." Kinsey and colleagues (1948) found tremendous variation in reported total sexual outlet, or release. One man reported that he had ejaculated only once in thirty years; another claimed to have averaged thirty orgasms per week for thirty years. After analyzing mean frequencies of orgasm from sex surveys, a group of researchers noted that "a total orgasmic outlet of less than once every two weeks is considered one

marker of low desire ... unless extenuating circumstances such as a lack of privacy occur" (Schover, Friedman, Weiler, Heiman, & LoPiccolo, 1982, p. 616). However, using some average frequency of sexual activity does not seem appropriate for categorizing people as having inhibited sexual desire. One person may have a high sex drive but not engage in sexual activities; another may not have sexual interest or fantasies but may engage in frequent sexual behaviors for the sake of his or her partner (Rosen & Leiblum, 1987). Tables 10.1 and 10.2 summarize two surveys concerning how often people think about sex and their desired and actual frequencies of sexual intercourse.

Furthermore, using number of orgasms (intercourse or masturbation) or desire for orgasms may introduce gender bias into the definition of "normal" sexual desire. The *Janus Report* indicated that, for all age groups, men masturbate and experience orgasms more than women do (Janus & Janus, 1993). Does this mean that women's sexual desire is less than that of men? Until we can decide on a normal range of sexual desire, we can hardly discover the causes of sexual desire disorders or develop treatment programs for them.

Sexual Arousal Disorders

Sexual arousal disorders are problems that occur during the excitement phase and that relate to difficulties with feelings of sexual pleasure or with the physiological

TABLE 10.2 Desired Versus Actual Frequency of Sexual Intercourse in 93 Happily Married Couples				
	Males		Females	
Frequency	Desired	Actual	Desired	Actual
More than once a day	12.2	2.2	3.3	1.1
Once a day	28.9	2.2	19.8	1.1
Three to four times a week	42.4	35.6	50.6	39.6
Twice a week	12.2	30.0	16.5	24.2
Once a week	4.4	15.6	9.9	20.9
Once every two weeks	0	8.9	0	8.8
Once a month	0	2.2	0	2.2
Less than once a month	0	3.3	0	0
None	0	0	0	0

Source: LoPiccolo & Friedman (1988).

"To you it was fast."

changes associated with sexual excitement. In men, inhibited sexual excitement takes the form of **male erectile disorder,** an inability to attain or maintain an erection sufficient for sexual intercourse and/or psychological arousal during sexual activity. The man may feel fully aroused, but he cannot finish the sex act. In the past, such a dysfunction has been attributed primarily to psychological reasons ("it's all in the head"). Masters and Johnson (1970), for example, estimated that only about 5 percent of erectile dysfunctions were due to physical conditions. Recent studies now indicate that from 30 percent (Segraves, Schoenberg, & Ivanoff, 1983) to as many as 70 percent (Hooper, 1998) of erectile dysfunctions are caused by some form of vascular insufficiency, such as diabetes, atherosclerosis, or traumatic groin injury, or by other physiological factors. A primary reason that DSM-IV-TR includes general medical conditions as a factor in sexual dysfunctions is that a man may also have a minor organic impairment that "makes his erection more vulnerable to being disrupted by psychological, biological, and sexual technique factors" (LoPiccolo & Stock, 1986). The technology does not yet exist, however, to accurately assess a "minor" organic impairment.

Distinguishing between erectile dysfunctions that are primarily biological and those that are primarily psychological has been difficult (see Table 10.3). For example, one procedure involves recording nocturnal penile tumescence (NPT). During sleep men have frequent erections. If, however, they suffer from an organic problem, they are not able to have erections during the waking state of sleep. Psychological distress is minimized during sleep and should not impair erec-

tions. Thus men who do not display adequate spontaneous erections during sleep suffer from an organic impairment, and psychological causes are thought to predominate in men who have such erections. Unfortunately, considerable overlap in NPT scores has been found between samples of diabetic men with erectile difficulties and normally functioning men in control groups (LoPiccolo & Stock, 1986). Therefore, some people diagnosed with organic impotence may actually have a psychologically based impotence. The reverse could also be true.

Primary erectile dysfunction is the diagnosis for a man who has never been able to engage successfully in sexual intercourse. This difficulty often has a clear psychological origin, because many men with this dysfunction can get an erection and reach orgasm during masturbation and can show erection during the REM (rapid eye movement) phase of sleep. In *secondary erectile dysfunction,* the man has had at least one successful instance of sexual intercourse but is currently unable to achieve an erection and penetration in 25 percent or more of his sexual attempts (Masters & Johnson, 1970).

A twenty-year-old college student was suffering from secondary erectile dysfunction. His first episode of erectile difficulty occurred when he attempted sexual intercourse after drinking heavily. Although to a certain extent he attributed the failure to alcohol, he also began to have doubts about his sexual ability. During a subsequent sexual encounter, his anxiety and worry increased. When he failed in this next coital encounter, even though he had not been drinking, his anxiety level rose even more. The client sought therapy after the discovery that he was unable to have an erection even during petting.

The prevalence rate of erectile dysfunction is difficult to determine because it is often unreported. Clinicians estimate that approximately 50 percent of men have experienced transient impotence (Feldman, Goldstein, Hatzichristou, Krane, & McKinlay, 1994). Of 448 men with sexual dysfunctions treated at the Masters and Johnson sex clinic, 32 were suffering from primary erectile dysfunction and 213 from secondary erectile dysfunction. Prior to the introduction of drugs such as Levitra and Viagra, the generally accepted figure of erectile dysfunction among men was between 10 million and 15 million (Leary, 1992). Current estimates of erectile problems place the figure at approximately 30 million (Hooper, 1998). Several factors may be contributing to this increase in the number of reported cases: (1) an increasing acceptance that the dysfunction may be caused by some physical

TABLE 10.3   Some Possible Physical Causes of Erectile Disorder and Dyspareunia

Erectile Disorder

- Alcoholism (neuropathy)
- Diabetes mellitus
- Arterial disease (e.g., Leriche syndrome)
- Renal failure
- Carcinomatosis
- Neurosyphilis
- Hypothalamo-pituitary dysfunction
- Liver failure
- Multiple sclerosis
- Many others

Dyspareunia

Female

- Failure of vaginal lubrication
- Failure of vasocongestion
- Failure of uterine elevation and vaginal ballooning during arousal
- Estrogen deficiency leading to atrophic vaginitis
- Radiotherapy for malignancy
- Vaginal infection (e.g., Trichomonas or herpes)
- Vaginal irritation (e.g., sensitivity to creams or deodorants)
- Abnormal tone of pelvic floor muscles
- Scarring after episiotomy or surgery
- Bartholin's gland cysts or abscess
- Rigid hymen, small introitus

Male

- Painful retraction of the foreskin
- Herpetic and other infections
- Asymmetrical erection due to fibrosis or Peyronie's disease
- Hypersensitivity of the glans penis

Source: Haas & Haas (1993).

condition and not by feelings of "psychological inadequacy"; (2) the availability of drugs such as Viagra as a nonintrusive successful treatment; (3) an increasing willingness among men to talk about this problem; and (4) a greater acceptance of women's right to expect satisfaction in sexual relationships.

Female sexual arousal disorder is an inability to attain or maintain physiological response and/or psychological arousal during sexual activity. It is characterized by a lack of physical signs of excitement, such as vaginal lubrication or erection of the nipples, or complaints of a lack of pleasure during sexual interactions (American Psychiatric Association, 1994). As with other sexual dysfunctions, this disorder may be lifelong or acquired and is often the result of negative attitudes about sex or early sexual experiences. Receiving negative information about sex, having been sexually assaulted or molested, and having conflicts with a sexual partner can contribute to the disorder (Rathus, Nevid, & Fichner-Rathus, 2005).

A thirty-eight-year-old woman had a satisfying sexual relationship with her husband for many years. Then her husband developed a drinking problem, which created conflict between them. Sexual intercourse started to become aversive to her, and she eventually lost all interest in sex. After her divorce, the woman was disturbed to discover that she was unable to become sexually aroused with other men. A desensitization procedure was used to eliminate her conditioned anxiety toward sexual intercourse. (Wolpe, 1982)

Estimates of this disorder vary widely, from 10 to 50 percent of the female population; accurate numbers are difficult to obtain because it is extremely difficult to distinguish this condition from other sexual disorders (Laumann et al., 1994; LoPiccolo, 1997). Indeed, female sexual arousal disorder is rarely diagnosed alone and usually is accompanied by or submerged with other desire or orgasmic disorders.

Orgasmic Disorders

An *orgasmic disorder* is an inability to achieve an orgasm after entering the excitement phase and receiving adequate sexual stimulation.

Female Orgasmic Disorder (Inhibited Female Orgasm)

A woman with **female orgasmic disorder,** or *inhibited female orgasm,* experiences persistent delay or inability to achieve an orgasm with stimulation that is "adequate in focus, intensity, and duration" after entering the excitement phase. Whether the lack of orgasm is categorized as a dysfunction or as a "normal variant" is left to the judgment of the clinician. Again, the criteria that define adequate functioning during sexual intercourse are quite controversial.

Inhibited female orgasm may be termed *primary*, to indicate that orgasm has never been experienced, or *secondary*, to show that orgasm has been experienced. Primary orgasmic dysfunction is considered relatively common in women: approximately 10 percent of all women have never achieved an orgasm (Rosen & Lieblum, 1995; Spector & Carey, 1990). This disorder is not equivalent to primary orgasmic dysfunction in males, who often can achieve orgasm through masturbation or by some other means.

Wakefield (1988) argued that inhibited female orgasm actually is rare and exists in less than 1 percent of women. He pointed out that many women do not reach orgasm during initial sexual encounters. In addition, they may not have engaged in masturbation. Wakefield believes that the diagnosis of inhibited orgasm should be made only if the woman has had experiences conducive to eliciting orgasmic responses but still has not had an orgasm.

Male Orgasmic Disorder (Inhibited Male Orgasm) Male orgasmic disorder, or *inhibited male orgasm*, is the persistent delay or inability to achieve an orgasm after the excitement phase has been reached and sexual activity has been adequate in focus, intensity, and duration. The term is usually restricted to the inability to ejaculate within the vagina, even with full arousal and penile erection. As noted, men who have this dysfunction can usually ejaculate when masturbating. Inhibited orgasm in males is relatively rare, and little is known about it (Dekker, 1993; McAnulty & Burnette, 2004). Treatment is often urged by the wife, who may want to conceive or who may feel (because of the husband's lack of orgasm) that she is unattractive.

An examination of the backgrounds of men with this disorder may reveal either the occurrence of some traumatic event or a severely restrictive religious background in which sex is considered evil. Masters and Johnson (1970) gave an example of a man who discovered that his wife had engaged in sexual intercourse with another man. Although they remained married, he could no longer ejaculate during intercourse.

Premature Ejaculation The inability to satisfy a sexual partner is a source of anguish for many men. **Premature ejaculation** is ejaculation with minimal sexual stimulation before, during, or shortly after penetration. It is a relatively common problem, but sex researchers and therapists differ in their criteria for prematurity. Kaplan (1974) defined *prematurity* as the inability of a man to tolerate high (plateau) levels of sexual excitement without ejaculating reflexively. Kilmann and Auerbach (1979) suggested that ejaculation less than five minutes after coital entry is a suitable criterion of prematurity. Masters and Johnson (1970) contended that a man who is unable to delay ejaculation long enough during sexual intercourse to produce an orgasm in the woman 50 percent of the time is a premature ejaculator. The difficulty with the latter definition is the possibility that a man may be "premature" with one partner but entirely adequate for another. From the perspective of males, however, surveys suggest that slightly more than one in three men admit to occasional premature ejaculation problems (Spector & Carey, 1990).

Some support has been found for Kaplan's definition. The sexual responsiveness of ten premature ejaculators was compared with that of fourteen normally functioning men, and no differences were found in rate, degree, or amount of arousal, either subjectively or physiologically. The premature ejaculators, however, did ejaculate at lower levels of arousal (Spiess, Geer, & O'Donohue, 1984).

Sexual Pain Disorders

Sexual pain disorders can be manifested in both males and females in a condition termed **dyspareunia,** which is a recurrent or persistent pain in the genitals before, during, or after sexual intercourse. Dyspareunia is not caused exclusively by lack of lubrication or by **vaginismus,** which is an involuntary spasm of the outer third of the vaginal wall, preventing or interfering with sexual intercourse. The incidence of vaginismus is not known, but it is considered very rare. Several causal factors have been identified in vaginismus. Masters and Johnson (1970) found one or more of the following conditions among many women with this dysfunction: (1) a husband or partner who was impotent; (2) rigid religious beliefs about sex; (3) prior sexual trauma, such as rape; (4) prior homosexual identification; and (5) painful intercourse. A history of incestuous molestation is often found in women with this disorder (LoPiccolo & Stock, 1986).

DSM-IV-TR also recognizes the diagnoses of sexual dysfunction due to a general medical condition and substance-induced sexual dysfunction. For example, a man may suffer from an erectile disorder caused by a general medical condition, such as diabetes, as noted earlier, or by a substance-induced condition, such as alcohol abuse.

Etiology and Treatment of Sexual Dysfunctions

Sexual dysfunctions may be due to psychological factors alone or to a combination of psychological and biological factors. They may be mild and transient or lifelong and chronic. Masters and Johnson (1970) identified some psychological elements in sexual dysfunctions, but they deemphasized physical factors. Later studies indicate that neurological, vascular, and hormonal factors are important in many cases of sexual dysfunctions (Blakeslee, 1993; Sakheim, Barlow, Abrahamson, & Beck, 1987). Such factors may play a major role in most cases of some sexual disorders (LoPiccolo, 1985, 1991). Although some of these physical problems may be relatively minor (such as vaginal infections, which cause itching and burning), they may render sexual functioning more susceptible to psychological or social stresses.

Biological Factors and Medical Treatment

Lower levels of testosterone or higher levels of estrogens such as prolactin (or both) have been associated with lower sexual interest in both men and women and with erectile difficulties in men (Kresin, 1993; Spark, 1991). Drugs that suppress testosterone levels appear to decrease sexual desire in men (Schiavi & Segraves, 1995). Conversely, the administration of androgens is associated with reports of increased sexual desire in both men and women. However, the relationship between hormones and sexual behavior is complex and difficult to understand. Many people with sexual dysfunctions have normal testosterone levels (Spark, 1991).

Medications given to treat ulcers, glaucoma, allergies, and convulsions have also been found to affect the sex drive. Drugs such as hypertensive medication and alcohol are also associated with sexual dysfunctions, as are illnesses and other physical conditions (McAnulty & Burnette, 2003, 2004; Schiavi, 1990; Schiavi & Segraves, 1995). But again, not everyone who takes hypertensive drugs, consumes alcohol, or is ill has a sexual dysfunction. In some people, these factors may combine with a predisposing personal history or current stress to produce problems in sexual function. A complete physical workup—including a medical history, physical exam, and a laboratory evaluation—is a necessary first step in assessment before treatment decisions are made.

For some, a lack of sexual desire may be physiological. One group of women reported no feelings of anxiety about, or aversion to, sexual intercourse. However, they showed significantly lower sexual arousal during exposure to erotic stimuli than did sexually active women and no increase in responsiveness

after participation in therapy (Wincze, Hoon, & Hoon, 1978). The researchers concluded that the absence of sexual arousal in these women is biological and that the appropriate treatment for this condition is unknown. Hypersensitivity to physical stimulation may also affect sexual functioning (Assalian, 1988). Men who ejaculate prematurely may have difficulty determining when ejaculation is inevitable once the sympathetic nervous system is triggered.

The amount of blood flowing into the genital area is also associated with orgasmic potential in women and erectile functioning in men. In women, masturbation training and Kegel exercises (tightening muscles in the vagina) may increase vascularization of labia, clitoris, and vagina. In men, vascular surgery to increase blood flow to the penis is successful when used appropriately. Unfortunately, if the problem is due to arteriosclerosis, which affects a number of the small blood vessels, vascular surgery meets with little success (LoPiccolo & Stock, 1986; Hooper, 1998).

If hormone replacement and sex therapy do not appear beneficial, men with organic erectile dysfunction may be treated with vacuum pumps, suppositories, or penile implants (Blakeslee, 1993). The penile prosthesis is an inflatable or semirigid device that, once inflated, produces an erection sufficient for intercourse and ejaculation (see Table 10.4). One study of men with penile implants found that 90 percent would choose it again (Steege, Stout, & Carson, 1986). As indicated in the following case, however, a significant number of men report dissatisfaction with the procedure and minimal improvement in their desire for sex.

> Mr. F. was a fifty-four-year-old recovered alcoholic who had received a surgical implant (Scott prosthesis) following a diagnosis of organic impotence. Despite the patient's newfound ability to perform intercourse at will, in the two years following surgery he made infrequent use of the prosthesis. His wife became increasingly distressed by his disinclination to either initiate or respond with any enthusiasm to her overtures for sexual contact. In reviewing the history, it became apparent that Mr. F.'s loss of sexual desire had preceded the erectile failure and that the absence of desire appeared to be the primary problem for treatment. Unfortunately, both the urologist and the patient's wife had assumed that once the capacity for intercourse was restored, sexual interest would reemerge unassisted. (Rosen & Leiblum, 1987, p. 153)

Another form of medical treatment for erectile problems is the injection of substances into the penis (Mohr & Beutler, 1990). Within a very short time the man will obtain a very stiff erection, which may last

TABLE 10.4   Treating Impotence: Medical Interventions

Treatment	Primary Agent	Effects	Drawbacks
Oral Medication	Viagra (sildenafil)	Taken as a pill. Some 70 to 80 percent of users achieve erections normal for their ages. Viagra enhances blood flow and retention by blocking an enzyme found primarily in the penis. The drug must be taken an hour before sex, and stimulation is needed for an erection.	Possible headaches and diarrhea. A drop in blood pressure. Temporary blue-green-tinted vision.
Surgery	Vascular surgery	Corrects venous leak from a groin injury by repairing arteries to boost blood supply in the penis. Restores the ability to have a normal erection.	Minimal problems when used appropriately with diagnosed condition.
Suppository	Muse (alprotadil)	A tiny pellet is inserted into the penis by means of an applicator 5 to 10 minutes before sex. Erections can last an hour. Some 65 percent of users show some tumescence.	Penile aching, minor urethral bleeding or spotting, dizziness, and leg-vein swelling.
Injection Therapy	Vasodilating drugs, including Caverject (alprotadil), Edex (alprostadil), and Invicorp (VIP and phentolamine)	Drug is injected directly into the base of the penis 10 minutes to 2 hours before sex, depending on the drug. The drug helps relax smooth-muscle tissues and creates an erection in up to 90 percent of patients. Erection lasts about an hour.	Pain, bleeding, and scar-tissue formation. Erections may not readily subside.
Devices	Vacuum pump	Creates negative air pressure around the penis to induce the flow of blood, which is then trapped by an elastic band encircling the shaft. Pump is used just before sex. Erection lasts until band is removed.	Some difficulty in ejaculation. Penis can become cool and appear constricted in color. Apparatus can be clumsy to use.
	Penile implants	Considered a court of last resort. A penile prosthesis is implanted in the penis, enabling men to literally "pump themselves up" by pulling blood into it.	Destruction of spongy tissue inside the penis.

from one to four hours. Although men and their mates have reported general satisfaction with the method (Althof et al., 1987), it does have some side effects. There is often bruising of the penis and the development of nodules. Some men find the prolonged erection disturbing in the absence of sexual stimulation.

Oral medications such as Viagra, Levitra, and Cialis have been found to be an attractive alternative in minimizing the negative effects of injection therapy. Viagra made headlines in 1998 as a "miracle cure" for the 30 million men suffering from erectile dysfunctions. This was followed in 2002 by other, similar drugs, such as Levitra and Cialis. According to the nonstop hype surrounding these drugs, they can make aging baby boomers as virile as teenagers; increase fertility, libido, or orgasms; and offer sexual insurance even to normally functioning men (Tuller, 2004). No more enduring needles or pellets inserted into the shaft of the penis; men can now simply "pop a pill" and make love continuously. The early clinical trials on 4,500 men indicated between 50 and 80 percent effectiveness; users' testimony of its "instantaneous success" has added to the hype (Leland, 1997; Hooper, 1998). Former presidential candidate Robert Dole and his wife, Elizabeth, and former Chicago Bears football coach Mike Ditka have also made sly pronouncements of its ability to improve their sex lives. There have even been reports that, by increasing blood flow to the genital areas, the pill can increase sexual desire in women. Recently, Pfizer reported that Viagra has not proven effective for women.

What is the truth about these miracle "sex drugs"? Is it a new virility solution for men, the end of man's search for the ultimate aphrodisiac, the key to sexual paradise? Or does it simply reflect our runaway fantasies of effortlessly possessing a superhuman sexual appetite and capacity? Unlike injectables, Viagra and its competitors do not produce an automatic erection in the absence of sexual stimuli. If a man becomes aroused, the drugs enable the body to follow through the sexual response cycle to completion. Urologists claim that for individuals with no sexual dysfunction, taking Viagra, for example, will not improve their erections; in other words, Viagra will not provide physiological help that will enable normally functioning men to improve their sexual functioning, nor will it lead to a stiffer erection. These drugs may aid sexual arousal and performance by stimulating men's expectations and fantasies; this psychological boost may then lead to subjective feelings of enhanced pleasure. Eager to capitalize on the economic implications of the demand for drugs such as Viagra, however, drug companies have tried to redefine erectile dysfunction as a quality-of-life issue rather than a medical one (Tuller, 2004). Thus the appeal is increasingly directed at younger men who have only moderate to minimal symptoms of erectile difficulties—a normal consequence of aging.

Table 10.4 describes five forms of medical interventions for erectile dysfunctions, along with their potential drawbacks.

Psychological Factors and Behavioral Therapy
Psychological causes for sexual dysfunctions may

include predisposing or historical factors, as well as more current problems and concerns.

Predisposing or Historical Factors Early experiences can interact with current problems to produce sexual dysfunctions. Traditional psychoanalysts have stressed the role of unconscious conflicts. For example, erectile difficulties and premature ejaculation represent male hostility to women due to unresolved early developmental conflicts involving the parents. Psychodynamic treatment is directed toward uncovering and resolving the unconscious hostility. The results of this approach have been disappointing (Kaplan, 1974; Kilmann & Auerbach, 1979). It seems plausible, however, that the attitudes that parents display toward sex and affection and toward each other can influence their children's attitudes. For example, women with sexual desire disorders rated their parents' attitudes toward sex more negatively than did women without sexual desire disorders (Stuart et al., 1987). Being raised in a strict religious environment is also associated with sexual dysfunctions in both men and women (Masters & Johnson, 1970). Traumatic sexual experiences involving incestuous molestations during childhood or adolescence or rape are also factors to consider (Burgess & Holmstrom, 1979; LoPiccolo & Stock, 1986).

Current Factors As we saw in the case study featured in the section on sexual desire disorders, current problems may interfere with sexual function. A relationship problem is often a contributing factor, even in the apparent absence of predisposing factors. In a study of fifty-nine women with sexual desire disorders, only eleven had had the problem before marriage; the other forty-eight developed it gradually after being married. The women voiced dissatisfaction about their relationships with their husbands, complaining that their spouses did not listen to them. Marital dissatisfaction may have caused them to lose their attraction toward their husbands (Leiblum & Rosen, 1991).

Situational or coital anxiety can interrupt sexual functioning in both men and women. A group of men with psychological erectile dysfunction reported anxieties over sexual overtures, including a fear of failing sexually, a fear of being seen as sexually inferior, and anxiety over the size of their genitals. These patients also reported marked increases in subjective anxiety and displayed somatic symptoms, such as sweating, trembling, muscle tension, and heart palpitations, when asked to imagine engaging in sexual intercourse (Cooper, 1969). In a sample of 275 college men, sexual pressure from a partner was associated with sexual dysfunction (Spencer & Zeiss, 1987). The men most

affected were those who identified most heavily with the traditional masculine role.

Factors associated with orgasmic dysfunction in women include having a sexually inexperienced or dysfunctional partner; a crippling fear of performance failure, of never being able to attain orgasm, of pregnancy, or of venereal disease; an inability to accept the partner, either emotionally or physically; and misinformation or ignorance about sexuality or sexual techniques.

Therapy Many approaches have been used to treat sexual dysfunctions, including desensitization, graded exercises, masturbation, sex education training, and the modification of sexual expectations. Most general treatment approaches include the following components:

- *Education* The therapist replaces sexual myths and misconceptions with accurate information about sexual anatomy and functioning.

- *Anxiety reduction* The therapist uses procedures such as desensitization or graded approaches to keep anxiety at a minimum. The therapist explains that constantly "observing and evaluating" one's performance can interfere with sexual functioning.

- *Structured behavioral exercises* The therapist gives a series of graded tasks that gradually increase the amount of sexual interaction between the partners. Each partner takes turns touching and being touched over different parts of the body except for the genital regions. Later the partners fondle the body and genital regions, without making demands for sexual arousal or orgasm. Successful sexual intercourse and orgasm is the final stage of the structured exercises.

- *Communication training* The therapist teaches the partners appropriate ways of communicating their sexual wishes to each other and also teaches them conflict resolution.

Some specific nonmedical treatments for other dysfunctions are as follows:

1. *Female orgasmic dysfunction* The general approach just described has been successful in treating sexual arousal disorders in women and erectile disorders in men. Masturbation appears to be the most effective way for orgasmically dysfunctional women to have an orgasm. The procedure involves education about sexual anatomy, visual and tactile self-exploration, using sexual fantasies and images, and masturbation, both individually and with a partner. Success rates of 95 percent have been reported with this procedure for women with

primary orgasmic dysfunction (LoPiccolo & Stock, 1986). This approach does not necessarily lead to the woman's ability to achieve orgasm during sexual intercourse.

2. *Premature ejaculation* In one technique, the partner stimulates the penis while it is outside the vagina until the man feels the sensation of impending ejaculation. At this point, the partner stops the stimulation for a short period of time and then continues it again. This pattern is repeated until the man can tolerate increasingly greater periods of stimulation before ejaculation (Semans, 1956). Masters and Johnson (1970) and Kaplan (1974) used a similar procedure, called the "squeeze technique." They reported a success rate of nearly 100 percent. The treatment is easily learned.

   Although the short-term success rate for treating premature ejaculation is very high, a follow-up study of men after six years of treatment found that relapses were very common (Hawton, Catalan, Martin, & Fagg, 1986). More long-term follow-ups of all treatments for the sexual dysfunctions are necessary to judge treatment effectiveness.

3. *Vaginismus* The results of treatment for vaginismus have been uniformly positive (Kaplan, 1974; LoPiccolo & Stock, 1986). The involuntary spasms or closure of the vaginal muscle can be deconditioned by first training the woman to relax, and by then inserting successively larger dilators while she is relaxed, until insertion of the penis can occur.

Evaluation of Behavior Therapy   Although early reports on behavioral treatment for sexual dysfunctions were highly positive, later studies have questioned the reports' high success rates (LoPiccolo & Stock, 1986; Malatesta & Adams, 1984). Other researchers have found lower reversal (success) rates than those reported by Masters and Johnson (LoPiccolo, 1985).

One study (Hawton et al., 1986) of the results of sexual therapy for 140 couples with a variety of sexual disorders assessed long-term outcome as follows: vaginismus, very good; erectile dysfunction, good; premature ejaculation, surprisingly poor; and sexual desire disorders among women, very poor. Recurrence of the problem during the follow-up period was common; 75 percent of the sample had relapses. Some couples were able to eliminate the problem themselves. Discussing the problem with one's partner, practicing exercises learned during therapy, and reading books on human sexuality were reported to be effective strategies. Ignoring the problem or not having sex

were ineffective. The results of this study indicated that relapse-prevention procedures (strategies to be employed when problems recur) should be incorporated in sex therapy programs and that new treatment strategies, especially for the sexual desire disorders, should be developed.

Gender Identity Disorders

In a milestone legislative act, the San Francisco Board of Supervisors voted on April 30, 2001, to extend sex-change health coverage to its city employees who were suffering from gender identity disorders. By doing so, it became the only government employer to pay for such benefits. The approved procedures include hormone treatment, surgery, and psychotherapy. The move brought howls of protest from many in the community who viewed the actions as "political correctness" and providing special benefits to a select group of citizens. Despite the controversy, much of the debate and discussion centered around attempts to explain the definitions and causes of transsexualism, gender dysphoria, and gender identity problems.

In contrast to the sexual dysfunctions, which involve any disruption of the normal sexual response cycle, the **gender identity disorders** are characterized by conflict between a person's anatomical sex and his or her gender identity, or self-identification as male or female. These disorders, which are shown in Figure 10.7, are relatively rare, and they may appear in both adults and children.

DSM-IV-TR groups these disorders into two categories: specified gender identity disorder and gender identity disorder, not otherwise specified. In the specified category of gender identity disorder—often called **transsexualism**—the person experiences strong and persistent cross-gender identification and persistent discomfort with his or her anatomical sex, creating significant impairment in social, occupational, or other important areas of functioning. People with this disorder hold a lifelong conviction that nature has played a cruel hoax by placing them in a body of the wrong gender. This feeling produces a preoccupation with eliminating the "natural" physical and behavioral sexual characteristics and acquiring those of the opposite sex.

People with gender identity disorders tend to exhibit gender-role conflicts at an early age and to report transsexual feelings in childhood, some as early as two years (Beers & Berkow, 1999; McAnulty & Burnette, 2004; Tsoi, 1993). It is important to note that most children with gender identity conflicts do not develop gender identity disorders as adults. As a result, a diagnosis of

FIGURE 10.7 Disorders Chart: Gender Identity Disorders

Gender Identity Disorder	GENDER IDENTITY DISORDERS	Gender Identity Disorder Not Otherwise Specified
Strong and persistent cross-gender identification (e.g., desire to be the other gender) and persistent discomfort with one's anatomical sex, which cause significant distress or impairment in social, occupational, or other important areas of functioning (also known as transsexualism)	Disorders involving conflicts between a person's anatomical sex and gender identity, or self-identification as male or female	Disorders in gender identity not classifiable as gender identity disorder, such as adults with transient stress-related cross-dressing behavior or individuals who have a persistent preoccupation with castration without a desire to acquire the sex characteristics of the other sex

GENDER IDENTITY DISORDERS	Prevalence	Age of Onset	Course
Gender Identity Disorder	Relatively rare; more common in males (1 in 37,000–100,000) than in females (1 in 100,000–400,000)	Early manifestation; noticeable gender role conflicts in childhood; lifelong	Person adopts anatomically opposite gender role; may seek sexual conversion via hormones or surgery
Gender Identity Disorder Not Otherwise Specified	Unknown because it includes multiple gender-related disorders that are not specific	Varies	Varies

Source: Data from American Psychiatric Association (2000); Arndt (1991); Laumann et al. (1994).

this disorder should not be made until much later in life. A boy may claim that he will grow up to be a woman, may demonstrate disgust with his penis, and may be exclusively preoccupied with interests and activities considered "feminine." Table 10.5 lists some typical behaviors. Boys with this disorder are frequently labeled "sissies" by their male peers. They prefer playing with girls and generally avoid the rough-and-tumble activities in which boys are traditionally encouraged to participate. They are more likely than normal boys to play with "feminine" toys.

Girls with a gender identity disorder may insist that they have a penis or will grow one and may exhibit an avid interest in rough-and-tumble play. Female transsexuals report being labeled "tomboys" during their childhoods. Although it is not uncommon for girls to be considered tomboys, the strength, pervasiveness, and persistence of the cross-gender identification among those with a gender identity disorder are the distinguishing features.

Transsexuals may report little interest in homosexual, heterosexual, or bisexual activities before the diagnosis of transsexualism (R. Blanchard, 1988). Those who are attracted to members of the same sex do not consider themselves to be homosexuals because they believe they actually *are* members of the opposite sex. Gender identity disorders are in no way related to homosexuality (Selvin, 1993).

Transsexualism is more common in males than in females. According to various estimates, the prevalence rate of the disorder ranges from 1 in 100,000 to 1 in 30,000 among males and from 1 in 400,000 to 1 in 100,000 among females (Arndt, 1991; Beers & Berkow, 1999).

TABLE 10.5   Frequency of Symptoms in 55 Boys with Cross-Gender Preferences (Elicited as Part of a Structured Interview)

Symptom	Number of Boys			
	Present	*Absent*	*Uncertain*	*No Data*
Feminine dressing	50	2	2	1
Aversion to boys' games	50	1	3	1
Desire to be female	43	6	2	4
Girl playmate preference	42	5	3	5
Doll playing	41	5	4	5
Feminine gestures	40	5	5	5
Wearing lipstick	34	12	3	6

Source: Zuger (1984).

The not-otherwise-specified gender identity category includes disorders that are not classifiable as a specific gender identity disorder. Examples include children with persistent cross-dressing behavior without the other criteria for gender identity disorder; adults with transient, stress-related cross-dressing behavior; and individuals who have a persistent preoccupation with castration without a desire to acquire the sex characteristics of the other sex.

Etiology of Gender Identity Disorders

The etiology of gender identity disorders is unclear. Because the disorder is quite rare (R. Green & Blanchard, 1995; Zucker, 1990), investigators have focused more attention on other sexual disorders. In all likelihood, a number of variables interact to produce gender identity disorders.

Biological Perspective   Are sexual orientation and sex-typed behaviors substantially determined by neurohormonal factors? Reviewing the research in this area, Ellis and Ames (1987) found some support for this view. In their study, male rats were castrated perinatally. This procedure reduces the production of testosterone, which appears to influence the organization of brain centers that govern sexual orientation. The male rats subsequently displayed femalelike gender behaviors. In human females, early exposure to male hormones has resulted in a more masculine behavior pattern. Thus it does appear that gender orientation can be influenced by a lack or excess of sex

hormones. In a review of the research, Bancroft (1989) also noted other biological differences in persons with gender identity disorder: female transsexuals have been found in some studies to show raised testosterone levels or menstrual irregularities.

Not all research supports the biological perspective. Arndt's (1991) review of the biological basis of transsexualism did not yield clear support for the role of neuroendocrine or chromosomal involvement. Some researchers believe that gender identity is malleable. Because many transsexual children have normal hormone levels, their ability to adopt an opposite-sex orientation raises doubt that biology alone determines male-female behaviors. Neurohormonal factors are important, but their degree of influence on sexual orientation in human beings may be minor (Hurtig & Rosenthal, 1987).

Psychodynamic Perspective   Psychoanalysts have written more about other sexual disorders than about transsexualism. In psychodynamic theory, all sexual deviations symbolically represent unconscious conflicts that began in early childhood (Meyers, 1991). They occur, say psychoanalysts, because the Oedipus complex is not fully resolved. The male or female child has a basic conflict between the wish for and the dread of maternal reengulfment (W. Meyer & Keith, 1991). The conflict results from a failure to deal successfully with separation-individuation phases of life, which creates a gender identity problem. Inability to resolve the Oedipus complex is important in gender identity disorder, according to this view.

A Case of Sex Reassignment Before sex-reassignment surgery, Renee Richards (right), a top-ranked tennis player and now coach, was Dr. Richard Raskin (left), a successful ophthalmologist.

Behavioral Perspective Some researchers have hypothesized that childhood experiences influence the development of gender identity disorders (Bernstein, Steiner, Glaisler, & Muir, 1981; Green, 1987). Factors thought to contribute to these disorders in boys include parental encouragement of feminine behavior, discouragement of the development of autonomy, excessive attention and overprotection by the mother, the absence of an older male as a model, a relatively powerless or absent father figure, a lack of exposure to male playmates, and encouragement to cross-dress (Marantz & Coates, 1991). Such factors may result not only in cross-gender behavior but also in ostracism and rejection by one's peers. Given that isolation, the boy may view complete adoption of the already familiar feminine role as the only available course. Not all males with gender identity disorders describe their fathers as weak or passive, however, nor do they all have excessively attentive mothers (Sugar, 1995).

Treatment of Gender Identity Disorders

Most treatment programs for children identified as having a gender identity disorder include separate components for the child and for his or her parents. The child's treatment begins with sex education. The therapist highlights favorable aspects of the child's physical gender and discusses the child's reasons for avidly pursuing cross-gender activities. The therapist attempts to correct stereotypes regarding certain roles that are "accepted" for one gender and not for the other. Young boys are always assigned to male therapists, which facilitates positive male identification.

Meanwhile, the child's parents receive instruction in the behavior modification practice of reinforcing appropriate gender behavior and extinguishing "inappropriate" behavior (Roberto, 1983). Some therapists help children deal with the peer-group ostracism that frequently occurs when a child exhibits strong cross-gender identities and behaviors (Zucker, 1990).

Some success has been reported for behavioral programs that incorporate strategies for modifying sex-typed behavior through modeling and rehearsal. The therapist demonstrates appropriate masculine behavior and mannerisms (modeling) in a number of different situations, and then patients practice (rehearse) their own versions of these behaviors. This is followed by a behavioral procedure that reinforces heterosexual fantasies:

electric shock is applied whenever the person reports transsexual fantasies (Barlow, Abel, & Blanchard, 1979; Khanna, Desai, & Channabasavanna, 1987).

In spite of such gains with psychotherapy and behavioral procedures, sex-change operations are indicated for some transsexuals. Prior to surgery, patients may be required to pass the "real-life" test, in which they try to live as completely as possible as members of the opposite gender (Clemmensen, 1990). This requires changing names, clothing, roles, and so on. Almost all patients must deal with reactions from employers, coworkers, friends, and relatives. Successfully "passing" the test paves the way for actual surgical change.

For men, the sex conversion operation begins with removal of the penis and testes. Then plastic surgery constructs female genitalia, including a vagina, cervix, and clitoris. The skin of the penis is used in this construction because the sensory nerve endings that are preserved enable some transsexuals to experience orgasm. The male-to-female operation is nearly perfected and, sometimes, it even fools gynecologists (Stripling, 1986). Research suggests that genital surgery can produce happier lives, especially in highly motivated and carefully screened transsexuals who have a stable work record and a network of social support (Beers & Berkow, 1999). In some cases, accompanying treatment includes teaching patients how to "pass" in public, using sex-role gestures and voice modulation.

Women who want to become men generally request operations to remove their breasts, uterus, and ovaries; some ask for an artificial penis to be constructed. This procedure is much more complicated and expensive than the male-to-female conversion (Fleming, Baum, Davidson, Rectanus, & McArdle, 1982). Hormonal treatments to accentuate desired physical and psychological effects (inducing more masculine muscle and fat distribution and altering the voice) can be used instead of, or in conjunction with, surgery (Dickey & Steiner, 1990).

Society often has difficulty in accepting and understanding people who undergo such extreme operations. One twenty-one-year-old male transsexual who was charged with carrying a concealed weapon was placed in a maximum security prison with several thousand men. This person had already had breast implants and was taking hormones (Blank, 1981). The partners of transsexuals also go through self-doubt. One woman, married to a female transsexual scheduled to undergo the woman-to-man operation, wondered if she might be a lesbian and if her three-year-old son (through artificial insemination) would have gender confusion. Because others react negatively, few transsexuals make their condition public (Stripling, 1986).

Some studies of transsexuals indicate positive outcomes for sex-conversion surgery (Bradley, 1995). Most females who "changed" to males express satisfaction over the outcome of surgery, although males who "changed" to females are less likely to feel satisfied (Arndt, 1991). Perhaps adjusting to life as a man is easier than adjusting to life as a woman, or perhaps others may react less negatively to woman-to-man changes than man-to-woman changes.

Many transsexuals remain depressed and suicidal after surgery (Hershkowitz & Dickes, 1978; Meyer & Peter, 1979). In one study (Kockott & Fahrner, 1987), more than one-half of the people who were offered sex-conversion surgery later changed their minds or became ambivalent about having the operations. Psychotherapy is typically recommended for patients who discover that their problems have not disappeared as a result of the operation (McCauly & Ehrhardt, 1984).

Doubts about the benefits of sex-conversion surgery have resulted in a decrease in these procedures. Although some psychologists believe it to be a humane solution, others argue that it is a radical and drastic action akin to lobotomies. Their contention is that gender identity disorders are psychological problems that should be corrected through psychotherapy, not surgery. Because some patients seem to benefit from the procedure and others do not, the controversy is likely to continue.

Paraphilias

Paraphilias are sexual disorders of at least six months' duration in which the person has either acted on or is severely distressed by recurrent urges or fantasies involving any of the following three categories (see Figure 10.8): (1) nonhuman objects, as in fetishism and transvestic fetishism; (2) nonconsenting others, as in exhibitionism, voyeurism, frotteurism (rubbing against others for sexual arousal), and pedophilia; and (3) real or simulated suffering or humiliation, as in sadism and masochism. A person who is highly distressed by paraphiliac urges or fantasies but has not acted on them would be diagnosed as having a mild case of the paraphilia. All of these acts are considered deviant because they are obligatory for sexual functioning (erection, for example, cannot occur without the stimulus).

People in this category may possess multiple paraphilias (Abel & Osborn, 1992). In one study of sex offenders (Rosenfield, 1985), researchers found that nearly 50 percent had engaged in a variety of sexually deviant behaviors, averaging between three and four paraphilias, and had committed more than 500 deviant acts. For example, a substantial number of men who had committed incest had also molested nonrelatives, exposed themselves, raped adult women, and engaged in voyeurism and frotteurism. In most cultures, paraphilias seem to be much more prevalent in males than in females (Beers & Berkow, 1999). This finding has led some to speculate that biological reasons may account for the unequal distribution.

Paraphilias Involving Nonhuman Objects

Fetishism Fetishism comprises an extremely strong sexual attraction to and fantasies involving inanimate objects such as female undergarments. The fetish is often used as a sexual stimulus during masturbation or sexual intercourse. The disorder is rare among women.

> Mr. M. met his wife at a local church. Some kissing and petting took place but never any other sexual contact. He had not masturbated before marriage. Although he and his wife loved each other very much, he was unable to have sexual intercourse with her because he could not obtain an erection. However, he had fantasies involving an apron and was able to get an erection while wearing an apron. His wife was described as upset over this discovery but was persuaded to accept it. The apron was kept hanging somewhere in the bedroom and it allowed him to consummate the marriage. He remembers being forced to wear an apron by his mother during his childhood years. (Kohon, 1987)

Most males find the sight of female undergarments sexually arousing and stimulating; this does not constitute a fetish. An interest in such inanimate objects as panties, stockings, bras, and shoes becomes a sexual disorder when the person is often sexually aroused to the point of erection in the presence of the fetish item, needs this item for sexual arousal during intercourse, chooses sexual partners on the basis of their having the item, or collects these items (Jones, Shainberg, & Byer, 1977). In many cases, the fetish item is enough by itself for complete sexual satisfaction through masturbation, and the person does not seek contact with a partner. Common fetishes include aprons, shoes, undergarments, and leather or latex items. As a group, people diagnosed with fetishism are not dangerous, nor do they tend to commit serious crimes.

Transvestic Fetishism A diagnosis of fetishism is not made if the inanimate object is an article of clothing used only in cross-dressing. In such cases, the appropriate diagnosis would be **transvestic fetishism**—intense sexual arousal obtained through cross-dressing

Not Necessarily What You Might Think The etiology and behavioral symptoms of gender identity disorder go far beyond enjoying dressing as the opposite sex; more important is persistent cross-gender identification and discomfort with one's own anatomical sex.

(wearing clothes appropriate to the opposite gender). This disorder should not be confused with *transsexualism,* which is a gender identity disorder in which one *identifies* with the opposite gender. Although some transsexuals and homosexuals cross-dress, most transvestites are exclusively heterosexual and married. Some research, however, suggests that transvestites may be fairly hostile and self-centered, with high levels of marital discord and a limited capacity for intimacy (Wise, Fagan, Schmidt, & Ponticas, 1991). Several aspects of transvestism are illustrated in the following case study:

> A twenty-six-year-old graduate student referred himself for treatment following an examination failure. He had been cross-dressing since the age of ten and attributed

FIGURE 10.8 Disorders Chart: Paraphilias

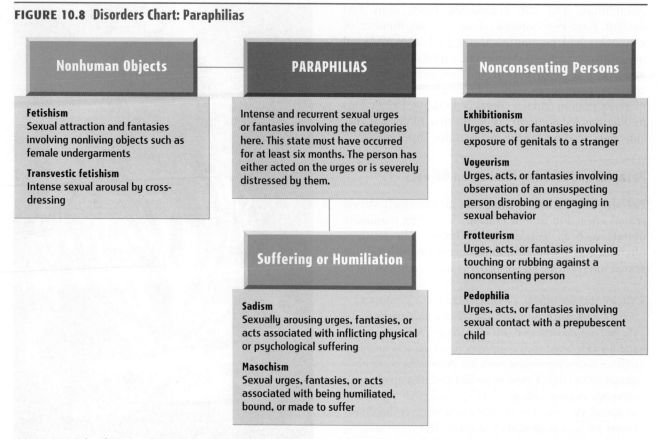

Source: Data taken from American Psychiatric Association (2000); Tsoi (1993); Kinsey et al. (1953); Spector & Carey (1990); Allgeier & Allgeier (1998).

his exam failure to the excessive amount of time that he spent doing so (four times a week). When he was younger, his cross-dressing had taken the form of masturbating while wearing his mother's high-heeled shoes, but it had gradually expanded to the present stage, in which he dressed completely as a woman, masturbating in front of a mirror. At no time had he experienced a desire to obtain a sex-change operation. He had neither homosexual experiences nor homosexual fantasies. Heterosexual contact had been restricted to heavy petting with occasional girlfriends. (Lambley, 1974, p. 101)

Sexual arousal while cross-dressing is an important criterion in the diagnosis of transvestic fetishism. If arousal is not present or has disappeared over time, a more appropriate diagnosis may be gender identity disorder. This distinction, however, may be difficult to make. Some transsexuals show penile erections to descriptions of cross-dressing (Blanchard, Racansky, & Steiner, 1986). Whether sexual arousal occurs in cross-dressing, therefore, may not serve as a valid distinction between transsexualism and transvestic fetishism. If the cross-dressing occurs only during the course of a gender identity disorder, the person is not considered in the category of transvestic fetishism.

Male transvestites often wear feminine garments or undergarments during sexual intercourse with their wives, as described by Newman and Stoller (1974, p. 438):

> He continued to have sexual intercourse (while clad in a woman's nightgown) with his wife, while imagining that they were no longer man and wife but rather two women engaged in a lesbian relationship. He especially enjoyed it when she cooperated with his idea and referred to him by his chosen feminine name.

Many transvestites believe that they have alternating masculine and feminine personalities. In a feminine role, they can play out such behavior patterns as buying nightgowns and trying on fashionable clothes. They may introduce their wives to their female personalities and urge them to go on shopping trips together as women. Other transvestites cross-dress only for the purposes of sexual arousal and masturbation and do not fantasize themselves as members of the opposite sex.

FIGURE 10.8 Disorders Chart: Paraphilias (continued)

PARAPHILIAS	Prevalence	Age of Onset	Course
Fetishism	Primarily a male disorder; rare in women; exact figures unavailable	Usually begins in adolescence	Causes of fetishism are difficult to pinpoint; conditioning and learning seem likely
Transvestic Fetishism	Exact figures difficult to obtain because cross-dressing often goes unreported and is acceptable in many societies	Begins as early as puberty	Cross-dressing is not usually associated with major psychiatric problems
Exhibitionism	Almost exclusively a male activity; exact figures lacking	Begins in teenage years, but the exhibitionist is most likely to be in his 20s	Most likely to have doubts about his masculinity; likes to shock; many have an erection during the act; most masturbate after the exposure
Voyeurism	Difficult to determine; most are men	Begins at the age of 15 and tends to be chronic	Voyeurs tend to be young and male; they become sexually aroused and may masturbate during or after the "peeping" episode
Frotteurism	Difficult to determine; most are men	Begins in adolescence or earlier	Usually decreases after age 25
Pedophilia	Primarily men; exact figures not available	Must be at least 16 years of age; contrary to the "dirty old man" image, pedophiles tend to be in their late 20s and 30s	Prefer children who are at least 5 years younger than they are and usually less than 13 years old; most are friends, relatives, or acquaintances of the victim; pedophiles often have very poor social skills
Sadism	Usually male, rates unknown, however, 22% of men and 12% of women in one study report some sexual arousal from sadistic stories	Begins in early childhood with sexual fantasies	While fantasies begin in childhood, sadistic acts usually develop in adulthood and can stay at the same level of cruelty or, more rarely, increase to problematic proportions
Masochism	Precise figures difficult to obtain; most information comes from questionnaires and/or sadomasochistic magazines	Males report first interests around 15 years and women at age 22	Not all suffering arouses; usually it must be produced in a specific way; classical conditioning strongly implicated as causal

Paraphilias Involving Nonconsenting Persons

This category of disorders involves persistent and powerful sexual fantasies about unsuspecting strangers or acquaintances. The victims are nonconsenting in that they do not choose to be the objects of the attention or sexual behavior.

Exhibitionism   Exhibitionism is characterized by urges, acts, or fantasies of exposing one's genitals to a stranger, often with the intent of shocking the unsuspecting victim:

> A nineteen-year-old single white college man reported that he had daily fantasies of exposing and had exposed himself on three occasions. The first occurred when he masturbated in front of the window of his dormitory room, when women would be passing by. The other two acts occurred in his car; in each case he asked young women for directions, and then exposed his penis and masturbated when they approached. He felt a great deal of anxiety in the presence of women and dated infrequently. (Hayes, Brownell, & Barlow, 1983)

Exhibitionism is relatively common. The exhibitionist is most often male and the victim female. Surveys of selected groups of young women in the United States have indicated that between one-third and one-half have been victims of exhibitionists (Cox & McMahon, 1978). Although most women did not report any psychological traumas associated with the episodes, about 40 percent indicated being moderately to severely distressed, and 11 percent believed the incident had negatively affected their attitude toward men (Cox & McMahon, 1978).

One study (Kolarsky & Madlatfousek, 1983) demonstrated that exhibitionists, unlike normal male participants in a control group, were sexually aroused by sexually neutral scenes such as women knitting, ironing, or sweeping. Similar findings were obtained by Fedora, Reddon, and Yeudall (1986), who monitored sexual arousal in exhibitionists, normal controls, and nonexhibitionist sex offenders. Only the exhibitionists responded sexually to scenes of fully clothed erotically neutral women. Fedora hypothesized that exhibitionists may be aroused by female uncooperativeness or neutrality.

The main goal of the exhibitionist seems to be the sexual arousal he gets by exposing himself; most exhibitionists want no further contact. However, there may be two types of exhibitionists—those who engage in criminal behavior and those who do not. The former tend to be sociopathic and impulsive, and they may be more likely to show aggression (Forgac & Michaels, 1982; Forgac, Cassel, & Michaels, 1984).

Exhibitionists may expect to produce surprise, sexual arousal, or disgust in the victim. The act may involve exposing a limp penis or masturbating an erect penis. In a study of ninety-six exhibitionists, only 50 percent reported that they "almost always" or "always" had erections when exposing, although a large percentage of the men wanted the women to be impressed with the size of their penises. Fantasies about being watched and admired by female observers were common among exhibitionists. More than two-thirds reported that they would not have sex with the victim even if she were receptive (Langevin et al., 1979).

Most exhibitionists are in their twenties—far from being the "dirty old men" of popular myth. Most are married. Their exhibiting has a compulsive quality to it, and they report that they feel a great deal of anxiety about the act. A typical exposure sequence involves the person first entertaining sexually arousing memories of previous exposures and then returning to the area where previous exposures took place. Next, the person locates a suitable victim, rehearses the exposure mentally, and finally exposes himself. As the person moves through his sequence, his self-control weakens and disappears. Many men use alcohol before exposing themselves, perhaps to reduce inhibitions (Arndt, 1991).

Voyeurism   Voyeurism comprises urges, acts, or fantasies of observing an unsuspecting person disrobing or engaging in sexual activity. "Peeping," as voyeurism is sometimes termed, is considered deviant when it includes serious risk, is done in socially unacceptable circumstances, or is preferred to coitus. The typical voyeur is not interested in looking at his wife or girlfriend; about 95 percent of the cases of voyeurism involve strangers. Observation alone produces sexual arousal and excitement, and the voyeur often masturbates during this surreptitious activity.

The voyeur is like the exhibitionist in that sexual contact is not the goal; viewing an undressed body is the primary motive. However, a voyeur may also exhibit or use other indirect forms of sexual expression (American Psychiatric Association, 1994). Because the act is repetitive, arrest is predictable. Usually an accidental witness or a victim notifies the police. Potential rapists or burglars who behave suspiciously are often arrested as voyeurs.

The proliferation of sexually oriented television programs, "romance" paperbacks, explicit sexual magazines, and NC17-rated movies all point to the voyeuristic nature of our society. The growing number of "night clubs" featuring male exotic dancers and

Jerry Lee Lewis: Pedophiliac or Something Else? When rock 'n' roll star Jerry Lee Lewis married a thirteen-year-old girl in the 1950s, it created a furor in Great Britain, where many considered him a pedophiliac. The public's outrage resulted in the cancellation of many of his concerts, forcing him to return to New York. Lewis was twenty-two at the time of this marriage and not yet divorced from his second wife.

attended by women may indicate women's increasing interest in men's bodies and their acknowledgment that it is all right to be sexual.

Frotteurism   Whereas physical contact is not the goal of voyeurism, contact is the primary motive in frotteurism. **Frotteurism** involves recurrent and intense sexual urges, acts, or fantasies of touching or rubbing against a nonconsenting person. The touching, not the coercive nature of the act, is the sexually exciting feature. As in the case of the other paraphilias, the diagnosis is made when the person has acted on the urges or is markedly distressed by them.

Pedophilia   Pedophilia is a disorder in which an adult obtains erotic gratification through urges, acts, or fantasies of sexual contact with a prepubescent child. According to DSM-IV-TR, to be diagnosed with this disorder, the person must be at least sixteen years

of age and at least five years older than the victim. Pedophiles may victimize their own children (incest), stepchildren, or those outside the family. Most pedophiles prefer girls, although a few choose prepubertal boys.

Sexual abuse of children is common (Phillips & Daniluk, 2004). Between 20 and 30 percent of women report having had a childhood sexual encounter with an adult man. And, contrary to the popular view of the child molester as a stranger, most pedophiles are relatives, friends, or casual acquaintances of their victims (Morenz & Becker, 1995; Zverina, Lachman, Pondelickova, & Vanek, 1987).

In most cases of abuse, only one adult and one child are involved, but cases involving several adults or groups of children have been reported. For example, a fifty-four-year-old man, a person who had won a community award for his work with youths, was arrested for child molestation involving boys as young as ten years old. The man encouraged and photographed sexual acts between the boys, including mutual masturbation and oral and anal sex. He then would have sex with one of them (Burgess, Hartman, McCausland, & Powers, 1984).

A study of 229 convicted child molesters (Erickson, Walbek, & Seely, 1988) revealed the following information. Nearly one-fourth of the victims were younger than six years of age. Another 25 percent were ages six to ten, and about 50 percent were ages eleven to thirteen. Fondling the child was the most common sexual behavior, followed by vaginal and oral-genital contact. Bribery was often used to gain the cooperation of the victims. Pedophiles have a relapse rate of approximately 35 percent, the highest among sex offenders (Erickson, Luxenberg, Walbek, & Seeley, 1987).

Child victims of sexual abuse show a variety of physical symptoms, such as urinary tract infections, poor appetite, and headaches. Reported psychological symptoms include nightmares, difficulty in sleeping, a decline in school performance, acting-out behaviors, and sexually focused behavior. One boy was overheard asking another to take down his pants, which was the request made by the person who had molested him (Burgess, Groth, & McCausland, 1981). Some child victims show the symptoms of posttraumatic stress disorder. In a sample of sixty-six victims, forty-five reported experiencing flashbacks of the molestation. They also demonstrated diminished responsiveness to their environment, hyperalertness, and jumpiness (Burgess et al., 1984). The effects of sexual abuse can become lifelong. One study of women who were victims of childhood sexual abuse revealed a "contaminated identity" characterized by self-loathing, shame, and powerlessness (Phillips & Daniluk, 2004).

On psychological tests such as the Minnesota Multiphasic Personality Inventory (MMPI), child molesters tend to have profiles indicating passive-dependent personality, discomfort in social situations, impulsiveness, and alcoholism (Erickson et al., 1987). Compared with control group members, child molesters are deficient in social skills. They also display a significantly higher fear of negative evaluation (Overholser & Beck, 1986). Some studies found that pedophiles tend to score on the low end of normal on intelligence tests, and some show left hemispheric problems in brain functioning (Langevin, 1990), although brain dysfunction as a cause of the disorder is still speculative. Pedophiles display sexual arousal to slides of young children and report having fantasies involving children during masturbation (Alford, Morin, Atkins, & Schuen, 1987). More than 50 percent of one sample of child molesters reported using "hard core" pornography to excite themselves in preparing to commit an offense (Marshall, 1988).

Some cases of child abuse are also incestuous. We cover that topic in more detail at the end of this chapter.

Paraphilias Involving Pain or Humiliation

Pain and humiliation do not appear to be related to normal sexual arousal. In sadism and masochism, however, they play a prominent role. **Sadism** is a form of paraphilia in which sexually arousing urges, fantasies, or acts are associated with inflicting physical or psychological suffering on others. The word *sadism* was coined from the name of the Marquis de Sade (1740–1814), a French nobleman who wrote extensively about the sexual pleasure he received by inflicting pain on women. The marquis himself was so cruel to his sexual victims that he was declared insane and jailed for twenty-seven years.

Masochism is a paraphilia in which sexual urges, fantasies, or acts are associated with being humiliated, bound, or made to suffer. The word *masochism* is derived from the name of a nineteenth-century Austrian novelist Leopold von Sacher-Masoch, whose fictional characters obtained sexual satisfaction only when pain was inflicted on them.

Sadistic behavior may range from the pretended or fantasized infliction of pain through mild to severe cruelty toward partners to an extremely dangerous pathological form of sadism that may involve mutilation or murder. Because of their passive roles, masochists are not considered dangerous. For some sadists and masochists, coitus becomes unnecessary; pain or humiliation alone is sufficient to produce sexual pleasure. As with other paraphilias, DSM-IV-TR specifies that to receive the diagnosis the person must have acted on the urges or must be markedly distressed by them.

In a study of 178 sadomasochists (47 women and 131 men), most reported engaging in and enjoying both submissive and dominant roles. Only 16 percent were exclusively dominant or submissive. Many engaged in spanking, whipping, and bondage (see Table 10.6). Approximately 40 percent engaged in behaviors that caused minor pain using ice, hot wax, biting, or face slapping. Fewer than 18 percent engaged in more harmful procedures, such as burning or piercing. Nearly all respondents reported sadomasochistic (S&M) activities to be more satisfying than "straight" sex (Moser & Levitt, 1987). Most sadomasochists who have been studied report that they do not seek harm or injury but that they find the sensation of utter helplessness appealing (Baumeister, 1988). S&M activities are often carefully scripted and involve role playing and mutual consent by the participants (Weinberg, 1987). In addition, fantasies involving sexual abuse, rejection, and forced sex are not uncommon among both male and female college students (D. Sue, 1979). Most sadomasochistic behavior among college students involves very mild forms of pain (such as in biting or pinching) that are accepted in our society.

Sadomasochistic behavior is considered deviant when pain, either inflicted or received, is necessary for sexual arousal and orgasm. According to Kinsey and his associates (1953), 22 percent of men and 12 percent of

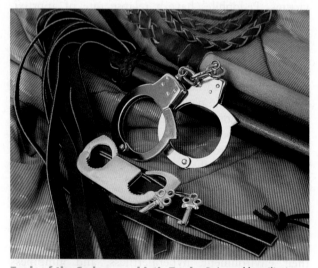

Tools of the Sadomasochistic Trade Pain and humiliation are associated with sexual satisfaction in sadism and masochism. Sadism involves inflicting pain on others; masochism involves receiving pain. Instruments used in sadomasochistic activities include handcuffs, whips, chains, and sharp objects.

TABLE 10.6 Sadomasochistic Activities, Ranked by Selected Samples of Male and Female Participants

Activity	Male	Female
Spanking	79	80
Master-slave relationships	79	76
Oral sex	77	90
Bondage	67	88
Humiliation	65	61
Restraint	60	83
Anal sex	58	51
Pain	51	34
Whipping	47	39
Use of rubber or leather	42	42
Enemas	33	22
Torture	32	32
Golden showers (urination)	30	37

Note: These sadomasochistic sexual preferences were reported by both male and female respondents. Many more men express a preference for S&M activities, but women who do so are likely to engage in this form of sexual behavior more frequently and with many more partners.

Source: Data from Brewslow, Evans, & Langley (1986).

women reported at least some sexual response to sadomasochistic stories. Janus and Janus (1993) reported that 14 percent of men and 11 percent of women have had at least some sadomasochistic experiences.

Some cases of sadomasochism appear to be the result of an early experience associating sexual arousal with pain. One masochistic man reported that as a child he was often "caned" on the buttocks by a school headmaster as his "attractive" wife looked on (Money, 1987). He reported, "I got sexual feelings from around the age of twelve, especially if she was watching" (p. 273). He and some of his schoolmates later hired prostitutes to spank them. Later yet, he engaged in self-whipping.

Although the association of pain and sexual arousal can account for some cases of sadomasochistic behaviors, 80 percent of a sample of sadomasochists did not remember a link between physical punishment during childhood and erotic sensations (Weinberg, 1987). Langevin (1990) and Langevin and associates (1988) found that sadists were more likely than nonsadistic

but sexually aggressive men and nonsexual offenders (controls) to have anomalies in the right temporal portions of the brain—brain areas that play a role in sexual behavior. They speculate that brain pathology and life experiences may underlie sadism.

In addition to the paraphilias covered here, DSM-IV-TR lists many others under the category of "not otherwise specified" paraphilias. They include *telephone scatalogia* (making obscene telephone calls) and sexual urges involving corpses *(necrophilia)*, animals *(zoophilia)*, or feces *(coprophilia)*.

Etiology and Treatment of Paraphilias

All etiological theories for the paraphilias must answer three questions (Finkelhor & Araji, 1986): (1) What produced the deviant arousal pattern? (2) Why doesn't the person develop a more appropriate outlet for his or her sexual drive? (3) Why is the behavior not deterred by normative and legal prohibitions? So far, biological, psychodynamic, and behavioral perspectives have provided only partial answers, and a number of behavioral strategies have emerged for treating the paraphilias.

Biological Perspective Earlier, we noted that investigators have attempted to find genetic, neurohormonal, and brain anomalies that might be associated with sexual disorders. Some of the research findings conflict; others need replication and confirmation (Nevid et al., 1995). In any event, researchers need to continue applying advanced technology in the study of the biological influences on sexual disorders. Even if biological factors are found to be important in the causes of these disorders, psychological factors are also likely to contribute in important ways.

Psychodynamic Perspective In psychodynamic theory, all sexual deviations symbolically represent unconscious conflicts that began in early childhood. Castration anxiety is hypothesized to be an important etiological factor underlying transvestic fetishism and exhibitionism, sadism, and masochism. It occurs, say psychoanalysts, when the Oedipus complex is not fully resolved. Because the boy's incestuous desires are only partially repressed, he fears retribution from his father in the form of castration. If this is the case, many sexual deviations can be seen as attempts to protect the person from castration anxiety. For example, in transvestic fetishism, acknowledging that women lack a penis raises the fear of castration. To refute this possibility, the male transvestite "restores" the penis to women through cross-dressing. In this manner, he unconsciously represents a "woman who has a penis" and therefore reduces the fear of castration (Shave, 1976). An item of clothing or a particular fetish is selected because it represents a phallic symbol (Arndt, 1991).

Similarly, an exhibitionist exposes to reassure himself that castration has not occurred. The shock that registers on the faces of others assures him that he still has a penis. A sadist may protect himself from castration anxiety by inflicting pain (power equals penis). A masochist may engage in self-castration through the acceptance of pain, thereby limiting the power of others to castrate him. Because castration anxiety stems from an unconscious source, the fear is never completely allayed, however, and so the person feels compelled to repeat deviant sexual acts.

The psychodynamic treatment of sexual deviations involves helping the patient understand the relationship between the deviation and the unconscious conflict that produced it. To treat the man whose fetish was wearing an apron before he could engage in sexual intercourse, the therapist used dream analysis and free association. These techniques helped him and the patient understand the "roots" of his behavior, which they interpreted as follows: the apron was made by his mother from a boiler suit that belonged to his father's mother. Because the patient's relationship with his mother produced castration anxiety, the fetish accomplished two purposes. First, it allowed him to reduce castration anxiety by denying that women do not have penises (the apron symbolized a "penis" that was cut out of the body of another woman). Second, a "penis" (the apron) was returned to him (Kohon, 1987). The psychoanalyst helped the patient bring the conflicts into conscious awareness through interpretation. After this, the patient gained insight into his behavior and was able to work through his problem.

Behavioral Perspective   Learning theorists stress the importance of early conditioning experiences in the etiology of sexually deviant behaviors. One such conditioning experience is masturbating while engaged in sexually deviant fantasies combined with inadequate social skills that hamper the development of normal sexual patterns. For example, one boy developed a fetish for women's panties at age twelve after he became sexually excited watching girls come down a slide with their underpants exposed. He began to masturbate to fantasies of girls with their panties showing and had this fetish for twenty-one years before seeking treatment (Kushner, 1965). In another example, two young men became sexually aroused when female passersby surprised them as they were urinating in a semiprivate area. The accidental association between sexual arousal and exposure resulted in exhibitionism (McGuire, Carlisle, & Young, 1965).

These reports, however, must be interpreted carefully because they are extracted from case studies and do not originate from controlled research.

Another researcher (Rachman, 1966), however, did use controlled research to demonstrate the possible role of conditioning in the development of a fetish. The investigators showed three men a picture of a pair of women's black boots, followed by slides of nude women, which produced sexual arousal (as measured by penile volume). Initially, the picture of boots did not elicit any increases in penile volume. But after slides of boots and nude women were paired several times (classical conditioning), all three participants developed conditioned sexual arousal at the sight of the boots alone. Although the conditioned responses were weak, they could have been strengthened if the participants had masturbated while the boots were shown.

The conditioning process may involve the concept of "preparedness" (Laws & Marshall, 1990). Unconditioned and conditioned stimuli, as well as responses and reinforcers, are not associated with equal ease. Organisms appear to be prepared to learn to associate some stimuli with some reinforcers rather than with others. For example, rats can learn to avoid the *taste* of a certain food if they experienced nausea after eating the food. However, they could not learn to associate the *sight* of food (in the absence of tasting it) with nausea when the sight of food was paired with nausea (Garcia, McGowan, & Green, 1972). Thus stimuli may vary in the extent to which they can be conditioned (that is, preparedness). Preparedness may depend on the survival value of the elements to be learned. Under this theory, human beings are more prepared to condition to, or find sexually attractive, an opposite-sex person than a neutral object, such as women's boots. Nevertheless, such conditioning may occur in some people.

Learning approaches to treating sexual deviations have generally involved one or more of the following elements: (1) weakening or eliminating the sexually inappropriate behaviors through processes such as extinction or aversive conditioning; (2) acquiring or strengthening sexually appropriate behaviors; and (3) developing appropriate social skills. The following case illustrates this multiple approach:

A twenty-seven-year-old man with a three-year history of pedophilic activities (fondling and cunnilingus) with four- to seven-year-old girls was treated through the following procedure. The man first masturbated to orgasm while exposed to stimuli involving adult females. He then masturbated to orgasm while listening to a relaxation tape, and then masturbated (but not to orgasm) to deviant stimuli. The procedure allowed the strengthening of normal arousal patterns and lessened the ability to achieve an orgasm while exposed to deviant stimuli (extinction). Measurement of penile tumescence when exposed to the stimuli indicated a sharp decrease to pedophilic stimuli and high arousal to heterosexual stimuli. These changes were maintained over a twelve-month follow-up period. (Alford et al., 1987)

One of the more unique treatments for exhibitionism is the *aversive behavior rehearsal* (ABR) program (Wickramasekera, 1976), in which shame or humiliation is the aversive stimulus. The technique requires that the patient exhibit himself in his usual manner to a preselected audience of women. During the exhibiting act, the patient must verbalize a conversation between himself and his penis. He must talk about what he is feeling emotionally and physically and must explain his fantasies regarding what he supposes the female observers are thinking about him.

One premise of the ABR program is that exhibitionism often occurs during a hypnoticlike state, when the exhibitionist's fantasies are extremely active and his judgment is impaired. The ABR method forces him to experience and examine his act while being fully aware of what he is doing (Kilmann, Sabalis, Gearing, Bukstel, & Scovern, 1982).

The results of behavioral treatment have been generally positive, but the majority of the studies involved single participants. Few control groups were included. Another problem in interpreting the results of these studies becomes apparent when we examine the approaches that were employed. For the most part, several different behavioral techniques were used within each study, so evaluation of a particular technique is impossible.

Sexual Aggression

Sexual aggression refers to a specific class of actions, such as rape, incest, and any type of *sexual activity* (petting, oral-genital sex, anal intercourse, and sexual intercourse) performed against a person's will through the use of force, argument, pressure, alcohol or drugs, or authority (McAnulty & Burnette, 2004; Strong & DeVault, 1994). *Sexual coercion* is a broader term (Rathus, Nevid, & Fichner-Rathus, 2005) used to encompass any or all forms of *sexual pressure* (pleading, arguing, cajoling, or force or threat of force). In this section, we discuss two forms of sexual aggression: rape and incest.

Myth vs Reality

Myth: Male rapists generally have higher than average sexual desire with low inhibitions. They have been found to arouse quickly to sexual cues and to act impulsively, to the detriment of their potential victims.

Reality: Rape is an act of aggression and control, not sex. Most rapists are quite deliberate and often plan their attacks in advance.

Rape

Rape is an act surrounded by many myths and misconceptions (see Table 10.7). Considerable controversy

---

TABLE 10.7   What Have You Been Told About Rape? Was It This?

1. Anyone can be raped. This includes women, men, girls, boys, infants, grandmothers, and teenagers.

2. Rape is an act of violence. It is not about sex but about the abuse of power.

3. Rape is never the fault of the victim. It is painful, humiliating, and hurtful. No one ever enjoys being raped.

4. Most rapes happen between people of the same race.

5. You are more likely to be raped by someone you know than by a stranger.

6. You can be raped by someone you've had sex with before. Each time you are asked to have sex, you have the right to say no, even if you've said yes before.

7. Most rapists do not use weapons to force someone into having sex. Threats or emotional and physical force are more commonly used.

8. If you say no and someone forces you to have sex, it's rape.

9. Most rapists plan their attacks and test their victim's tolerance of abuse over a period of time. This includes husbands, someone you're dating, and family members, as well as strangers.

10. Not only is rape always wrong; it's also a crime. Rape is against the law.

Source: San Francisco Women Against Rape, 3543 18th Street, San Francisco, CA 94110, (415) 861-2024.

exists over whether rape is primarily a crime of violence or of sex (J. Marsh, 1988). Feminists have challenged the belief that rape is an act of sexual deviance; they make a good case that it is truly an act of violence and aggression against women. The principal motive, they believe, is that of power, not sex. **Rape** is an act of intercourse accomplished through force or threat of force (McAnulty & Burnette, 2004). The Federal Bureau of Investigation (FBI) uses a more limited definition: "Carnal knowledge of a female forcibly and against her consent." This definition fails to include behavior between individuals of the same sex and with males as victim, which certainly does occur. Most states extend their definition of rape to include statutory rape—sexual intercourse with a child younger than a certain age.

FBI statistics reveal that the number of rapes in the United States has risen dramatically: more than 102,000 cases were reported in 1990, and there was one reported rape for every 270 women in 1995 and an average of one rape every five minutes (Federal Bureau of Investigation [FBI], 1991, 1996; U.S. Senate Committee on the Judiciary, 1991). However, in past decades, only about 16 percent of the reported cases resulted in a conviction for rape, with another 4 percent of those cases producing convictions for lesser offenses. This low conviction rate and the humiliation and shame of a rape trial keep many women from reporting rapes, so the actual incidence of the crime is probably much higher than reported. Some experts believe that unreported rapes range from two to ten times the official numbers (Beers & Berkow, 1999; Gibbs, 1991) and that the number of unreported rapes is rising faster than that of reported rapes (U.S. Senate Committee on the Judiciary, 1991).

Some police officers still believe that rape victims are partly to blame because of their manner of dress or behavior, and these officers endorse such statements as "Most charges of rape are unfounded" and "Nice women do not get raped" (LeDoux & Hazelwood, 1985). Estimates based on surveys indicate that as many as one of every five women will be a rape victim at some time during her life (Sorenson & Siegel, 1992). Most rape victims are young women in their teens or twenties, although infants and extremely elderly victims have been reported. In approximately one-half of all rape cases, the victim is at least acquainted with the rapist and is attacked in the home or in an automobile. About 90 percent of rapists attack persons of the same race; most rapes are planned and not impulsive; and more than half of the attacks involve a weapon, usually a knife (Beers & Berkow, 1999). The most frequent form of rape reported is "acquaintance" or "date" rape, as in the following case:

> Colleen, twenty-seven, a San Francisco office manager, had been involved with her boyfriend for about a year when it happened. After a cozy dinner at her apartment, he suggested that she go to bed while he did the dishes. But a few moments later he stalked into Colleen's bedroom with a peculiar look on his face, brandishing a butcher knife and strips of cloth. After tying her, spread-eagled, to the bed, the formerly tender lover raped her brutally for three hours. When it was all over, he fell soundly asleep. (Seligman et al., 1984, p. 91)

Date rape may account for the majority of all rapes. Many victims may be reluctant to report such an attack; they feel responsible—at least in part—because they made a date with their attacker. Statistics vary as to the incidence of date rapes. Between 8 and 25 percent of female college students have reported that they had "unwanted sexual intercourse," and studies have generally found that most college women had experienced some unwanted sexual activity (Craig, 1990). Estimates vary from study to study because of different definitions of rape and intercourse as presented by the researchers, as well as the willingness or unwillingness of women to participate in surveys or to accurately report their experiences.

Men who try to coerce women into intercourse share certain characteristics (Craig, 1990; Hall, 1996; Hall, Windover, & Maramba, 1998; Marshall & Barbaree, 1990). They tend to (1) actively create the situation in which sexual encounters may occur; (2) interpret women's friendliness as provocation or their protests as insincerity; (3) try to manipulate women into sexual favors by using alcohol (some 70 percent of rapes are associated with alcohol intoxication) or "date rape drugs" such as rohypnol and GHB (see the Mental Health and Society feature "Warning: Date Rape Drugs"); (4) attribute failed attempts at sexual encounters to perceived negative features of the woman, thereby protecting their egos; (5) come from environments of parental neglect or physical or sexual abuse; (6) initiate coitus earlier than men who are not sexually aggressive; and (7) have more sexual partners than males who are not sexually aggressive. Many men who do not rape may also have these characteristics. Indeed, when asked to indicate the likelihood that they would rape if assured that they would not be caught and punished, about 35 percent of college males reported some likelihood and 20 percent indicated fairly high likelihood (Malamuth, 1981).

Should intercourse between a couple be considered rape if the woman did not want to engage in that activity? One police official, in reacting to the high number of rapes reported in his community, noted, "We definitely do not have a serious rape problem in

Educating Against Violence Across the country, efforts are being made to educate people young and old, male and female, to the fact that rape is an act of violence and aggression. Shown here, the Clothesline Project, a series of shirts depicting violence against women, is one effort to empower women to speak out against such violence.

Preventing Sexual Aggression through Education Todd Denny, M.S.W., is a nationally recognized speaker who has given over 1,000 presentations to colleges, public schools, and community organizations. His program, Sexual Aggression 101, combines music, theater, storytelling, and audience participation to educate students across the nation about all forms of sexual aggression.

this city. The problem is in the classification. If you took all our rapes one by one, you'd see that nine of ten are a girlfriend-boyfriend thing. These people are known to each other" (Girard, 1984, p. 12). The erroneous assumption made by that police official is that forced intercourse between acquaintances should not be considered rape. Unfortunately, sexual aggression by men is quite common. Fifteen percent of a sample of college men reported that they did force intercourse at least once or twice. Only 39 percent of the men did not admit to any coerced sex (Rapaport & Burkhart, 1984). In a survey (Koss, Gidycz, & Wisniewski, 1987) of 6,159 male and female students enrolled in thirty-two universities in the United States, more than 50 percent of the women reported being the victims of sexual aggression, and 8 percent of men admitted to committing sexual acts that met the legal definition of rape. Women seldom reported episodes of date rape (Hall, 1996; Koss et al., 1987). Many universities are conducting workshops for students to help them understand that intercourse without consent during a date or other social activity is rape.

Effects of Rape   More than two-thirds of rape victims were not physically injured, 20 percent incurred minor physical injuries, and 4 percent suffered serious injuries (National Victim Center, 1992). However, the psychological scars from rape are often more devastating than the physical damage. Needless to say, rape is highly traumatic. Victims may experience a cluster of emotional reactions known as the **rape trauma syndrome;** they include psychological distress, phobic reactions, and sexual dysfunction (Calhoun & Atkeson, 1991; Koss, 1993). These reactions are consistent with *posttraumatic stress disorder* (*PTSD*; Bownes, O'Gorman, & Sayers, 1991; Hall et al., 1998; Kimerling & Calhoun, 1994). Two phases have been identified in rape trauma syndrome:

1. *Acute Phase: Disorganization* During this period of several or more weeks, the rape victim may have feelings of self-blame, fear, and depression. The victim may believe she was responsible for the rape (for example, by not locking the door or wearing provocative clothing or by being overly friendly

MENTAL HEALTH AND SOCIETY

Warning: Date Rape Drugs

On January 16, 1999, fifteen-year-olds Samantha Reid and Melanie Sindone were secretly given GHB (gamma-hydroxybutyrate), a date-rape drug, in their soft drinks. Samantha died the next day, but her friend survived after a brief coma. Both had attended a party with several young men. The men were alleged to have purposely spiked the girls' drinks for the purpose of raping them. Three of the men were convicted of involuntary manslaughter charges, and a fourth was convicted of a lesser charge (Associated Press, 1999).

Reports such as this have become increasingly frequent in the news media, and several news-magazine programs have brought the issue of date rape drugs to the attention of the American public. Reports have surfaced of the use of date rape drugs on high school and college campuses, at private parties, and in social situations in which women claimed their drinks were spiked before they were raped. A **date rape drug** is any substance, such as alcohol and/or sedating drugs such as GHB or Rohypnol, that is used to weaken or incapacitate a victim, making her susceptible to a sexual assault. The latter two have become the drug of choice in date rapes because they are tasteless, colorless, and odorless and because they can be quickly placed into the drinks of unsuspecting victims. In most cases, the drugs take effect in twenty to thirty minutes, leaving the victims drowsy, dizzy, confused, and with impaired judgment and memory. Often, the symptoms are mistaken as intoxication. Higher doses may induce amnesia, resulting in the victim being unable to recall whether a sexual assault had occurred. Even when the victims suspect that they have been drugged, they are often unable to remember events and details necessary to prosecute the perpetrator.

What Are Rohypnol and GHB?

Rohypnol is the brand name for the drug flunitrazepam, which belongs to a class of drugs known as benzodiazepines. It belongs to the family of medications that include Valium, Librium, and Xanax. It is important to note that Rohypnol is seven to ten times more potent than Valium. Smaller than an aspirin, this white tablet comes in 1-milligram doses and is marked on one side with the name "Roche" and an encircled 1 or 2; the reverse side is marked with either a cross or single horizontal groove. The common street names are roachies, la rocha, rope, roofies, ruffies, Mexican Valium, rib, R-2, and Roach-2.

GHB, or gamma-hydroxybutyrate, is a central nervous system depressant that comes in a capsule form or as a grainy, white to sandy-colored powder. It is often taken for its intoxicating effects, but it can be easily dissolved in liquids such as alcohol, soft drinks, or water. Street names

---

toward the attacker). The victim may have a strange fear that the attacker will return and anxiety that she may again be raped or even killed. She may express these emotional reactions and beliefs directly as anger, fear, rage, anxiety, and/or depression, or she may conceal them, appearing amazingly calm. Beneath this exterior, however, are signs of tension, including headaches, irritability, restlessness, sleeplessness, and jumpiness (Nevid et al., 1995).

2. *Long-Term Phase: Reorganization* This second phase may last for several years. The victim begins to deal directly with her feelings and attempts to reorganize her life. Lingering fears and phobic reactions continue, especially to situations or events that remind the victim of the traumatic incident. A host of reactions may be present. Many women report one or more sexual dysfunctions as the result of the rape; fear of sex and lack of desire or arousal appear most common. Some women recover quickly, but others report problems years after the rape. Victims may experience selective fears involving things such as darkness and enclosed places—conditions likely to be associated with rape. Duration and intensity of fear also appear to be related to perceptions of danger. Many women drastically alter their feelings of safety and personal vulnerability; they feel unsafe in many situations and over an extended period of time.

Rape victims often report that they cannot resume sexual activity for some time after the attack and that their sexual enjoyment is strongly affected. One victim described it this way:

It depends how I relate to the man. If I'm in a position to enjoy it—a 50-50 thing—then I'm OK. But if I'm feeling that I'm only doing this for him and not for my own enjoyment, then I feel like the incident again. ... Then sex is bad.

include grievous bodily harm, easy lay, gook, gamma 10, soap, scoop, salty water, and zonked.

The original use of these drugs was to treat sleep disorders. Although Rohypnol and GHB are illegal in the United States, they are relatively inexpensive and can be purchased for between $2 and $5 per tablet on the streets.

What Are the Effects of These Drugs?

The effects of these drugs depend on dosage, body weight, interactions with other substances such as alcohol, and individual drug sensitivity. For Rohypnol, the effects can be felt to occur some fifteen to twenty minutes after ingestion. It produces an intoxicated state. Other reported effects include blackouts, amnesia, convulsions, hallucinations, muscle pain, and confusion. It is potentially dangerous when mixed with alcoholic beverages and is noted to impair judgment and motor skills, to slur speech, and to cause dizziness. The effects can last up to eight hours.

It is generally undetectable in the body after twenty-four hours. GHB produces intoxication, deep sedation, and a number of other symptoms similar to those of Rohypnol. Its effects occur faster, however, and it lasts one to three hours. Both Rohypnol and GHB have been implicated in deaths.

How Do I Defend Myself Against Date Rape Drugs?

The best defenses are acquiring knowledge about date rape drugs, using precautions to ensure your safety, and maintaining constant awareness of your surroundings.

1. When in social situations such as a party or bar, monitor how your drink is being prepared.
2. Avoid drinking from a common container such as a punch bowl. Although it is probably safe, it can be easily spiked.
3. Don't accept drinks from an open container.
4. Never leave your drinks unattended. If you must do so, refresh the drink rather than continue drinking it.
5. Never share or exchange drinks.
6. At a bar, restaurant, club, or social place, accept drinks only from the bartender, waiter, waitress, or designated host.
7. When in the company of people you don't know well, don't accept drinks from them.
8. Look out for your friends and have them look out for you. If, for example, one of your friends appears especially intoxicated after drinking a beverage or shows signs of confusion, make sure you take steps to ensure her safety.
9. If you see someone dosing a drink, don't hesitate to warn potential victims and the appropriate authorities.
10. Avoid high-risk places and situations in which drug use is known.

Sexually active victims often report flashbacks, such as fleeting memories that cannot be repressed, reliving the experience, and associating a current sex partner with the rapist. Sympathetic understanding, nondemanding affection, and a positive attitude from the partner have been found beneficial. Hugging and gentle caressing are generally satisfying to the victim even if sexual approaches are aversive.

In light of the severe sexual and psychological problems that rape victims can experience, the availability of multiple support systems and counseling become very important. Most large cities now have rape crisis centers that provide counseling, as well as medical and legal information, to victims. Trained volunteers often accompany the victim to the hospital and to the police station. Women's organizations have made many hospital personnel and police officers more aware of the trauma of rape and have taught them to behave more sensitively when dealing with victims.

Etiology of Rape   Rape is not specifically listed in DSM-IV-TR as a mental disorder because the act can have a variety of motivations. In an influential study of 133 rapists, Groth, Burgess, and Holstrom (1977) distinguished the three motivational types:

- The *power rapist*, comprising 55 percent of those studied, is primarily attempting to compensate for feelings of personal or sexual inadequacy by trying to intimidate his victims.

- The *anger rapist*, comprising 40 percent of those studied, is angry at women in general; the victim is merely a convenient target.

- The *sadistic rapist*, comprising only 5 percent of those studied, derives satisfaction from inflicting pain and may torture or mutilate the victim.

These findings tend to support the contention that rape has more to do with power, aggression, and

CRITICAL THINKING

Why Do Men Rape Women?

In 1995, former world heavyweight boxing champ Mike Tyson was released from prison after serving a sentence for raping a beauty contestant in his hotel room. Here was a man who made his living via physical dominance and force. During his trial, "talk radio" and the print media were filled with speculations about his motives and responsibility for the event. Some claimed that Tyson was only minimally responsible because the woman had willingly gone to his hotel room. (This reasoning was also offered to excuse Kobe Bryant of the alleged rape of a young hotel worker.) Others placed the blame on certain sports such as boxing, saying the activity condones aggression, even sexual aggression. Still others speculated that Tyson was over-sexed, that his testosterone levels were high, or that he acted out because of steroid use.

In science, as in the media, many explanations and theories attempt to explain why men rape women. As a useful and interesting class exercise,

we invite you to engage in a mock trial based on the Tyson case. There are two major perspectives on rape. After reading about them, divide yourselves into two camps to argue the two viewpoints.

Sociocultural Perspective

A variety of views of the causes of rape have been proposed (Sorenson & White, 1992). Some researchers theorized that rape was committed by mentally disturbed men, and studies were initiated to find personality characteristics that might be associated with rape. When Malamuth (1981) published survey results indicating that a significant proportion of men would consider rape if they could get away with it, the view that rapists were simply mentally disturbed individuals began to change.

Sociocultural views then gained favor. Many argued that rape was a means of control and dominance, whereby men keep women in a perpetual state of intimidation. This view emphasized a "culture" of male dom-

inance rather than a sexual motive as a primary reason for sexual assault (McAnulty & Burnette, 2004). For example, a permissive attitude toward violence (L. Baron, Straus, & Jaffee, 1988) or rigid gender roles and women's forced dependency on men by society (Lisak, 1991) may be factors in rape.

Other theorists believe that social myths embedded in our culture reinforce themes that underlie rape: (1) that women have an unconscious desire to be overpowered and raped; (2) that women "ask for it" by dressing in provocative clothing, visiting a man's room, or going where they should not go; (3) that women could avoid rape if they wanted to; (4) that only "bad girls" get raped; and (5) that women only "cry rape" for revenge (Byers & Enos, 1991; Lisak, 1991; Stock, 1991).

Can you give examples that support or disprove the sociocultural perspective? Does the sociocultural perspective seem accurate to you?

violence than with sex. In fact, a study of more than 100 rapists indicated that 58 percent showed some sexual dysfunction, such as erectile difficulties, during the attack (Groth et al., 1977).

Although these distinctions are of interest, little empirical research was done on the importance of aggressive cues in the sexual arousal of rapists until a study performed by Abel, Barlow, Blanchard, and Guild (1977). These investigators recorded the degree of penile erection of rapists and nonrapists in response to two-minute audiotapes describing violent and nonviolent sexual scenes. The nonviolent tape described an incident of mutually enjoyable sexual intercourse. The violent tape described a rape in which the man forced himself on an unwilling woman. The rapists were aroused by both tape descriptions, whereas the nonrapists displayed a significantly lesser degree of erection in response to the portrayal of violent sex,

preferring the scene involving mutually enjoyable sex. Some rapists in the study also showed strong sexual arousal in response to another tape that was entirely aggressive in content.

Later studies have shown that certain groups of men who are not rapists also respond sexually to aggressive cues. In addition, a portrayal of the woman as taking physical pleasure in the attack also increases sexual response in some men. Here are the results of some of these studies:

1. College men with sadistic tendencies rated slides of women displaying emotional distress (fear, anger, disgust, sadness) as more sexually arousing than did nonsadistic men (Heilbrun & Loftus, 1986).

2. Men who admitted to being more likely to commit rape showed more erections when listening to audiotapes of dramatized sex between nonconsent-

Sociobiological Perspective

There are different sociobiological models for sexual aggression and rape. One is that sexual aggression has an evolutionary basis, although no unequivocal proof of biochemical differences between sex offenders and the general population has been found (Hall & Hirschman, 1991). One view (Ellis, 1991) is that sex differences have evolved as a means of maximizing the reproduction of the human species: men have much more to gain in reproductive terms by being able to pass on their genes rapidly to a large number of women, which increases their chances of having offspring. Men's advantage is women's disadvantage, however. Because women must bear much more of the investment in each offspring before and after birth, natural selection would favor women whose mates are likely to supply a greater share of the investment in offspring. Therefore, it would be advantageous for women to avoid multiple partners and to seek male commitment. Ellis also argued that men's sex drive is stronger than women's, and cited as evidence these three points:

- Men in all societies have higher self-reported desires for copulation and other forms of sexual experiences.
- Males (including males in other species of primates) masturbate more, especially in the absence of sex partners.
- Women are more likely than men to report having sexual intercourse for reasons other than sexual gratification.

Ellis took issue with the view that rape is not a sexual crime. He agreed that rapists often try to obtain sex by actions such as getting women drunk and falsely pledging love; that they use physical force only after these other tactics fail; and that fewer men than women believe rape is motivated by power and anger. Nevertheless, sociobiological theories have difficulty explaining differences in rates of rape in different societies or changes in rates of rape over time without references to cultural conditions or experiential factors. Ellis believes that the motivation for sexual assault is unlearned but that the behavior surrounding sexual assault is learned. Thus sexual motivation (including the drive to rape) is innate. If sexual aggression is reinforced (or not punished), forced copulatory attempts will persist.

Do you think punishment is an effective deterrent to rape? Does the sociobiological perspective seem accurate to you?

Isolating and testing different propositions concerning sexual assault have been difficult. Even so, no one—not even those who believe that men have a stronger biological sexual drive—can excuse or condone such behavior. Research findings suggest that changes in the way men and women relate to one another, attitudes toward violence, and cultural practices can reduce the incidence of rape.

---

ing participants than when listening to scenes between consenting participants. Men who reported that they were not very likely to rape anyone showed the opposite pattern (Malamuth & Check, 1983).

3. When exposed to a situation in which a woman is portrayed as being initially repelled but later responds sexually to rape, male students (but not female students) became less sensitive to rape victims. They viewed the rapist as less responsible for the act and as deserving less punishment. They also showed desensitization to violent sex and were more likely to accept rape myths (Donnerstein & Linz, 1986).

Because of these findings, researchers are raising questions about the effect that media portrayals of violent sex, especially in pornography, have on rape rates. Exposure to such material may affect attitudes and thoughts and influence patterns of sexual arousal (Allgeier & Allgeier, 1998; Laumann et al., 1994; Malamuth & Briere, 1986). These media portrayals may reflect and affect societal values concerning violence and women.

Baron, Straus, and Jaffee (1988) proposed a "cultural spillover" theory—namely, that rape tends to be high in cultures or environments that encourage violence. The investigators studied the relationship between cultural support for violence, as well as demographic characteristics and rates of rapes in all fifty states. They also measured rates of rape and cultural support for violence for each state. Their ratings of support for violence were determined by (1) the proportion of individuals who chose magazines and television programs involving violence; (2) the amount of legislation permitting corporal punishment in schools, the number of prisoners sentenced to death, and the number of executions for crimes; (3) National Guard enrollments; and (4) public opinion on such issues as favoring the death penalty, opposing the requirement that gun owners obtain mandatory gun permits, and approving the punching of a stranger in a variety of situations. The researchers also examined demographic variables that could be related to rates of rape in each state, such as percentage of divorced or single males, percentage of women, age of individuals, social class, and race. Results indicated that cultural support for violence was significantly related to the rate of rape, independent of the effects of demographic variables. Having a high proportion of divorced and single men was also related to increased rates of rape. The results suggested that when violence is generally encouraged or condoned, there is a "spillover" effect on rape.

Researchers are turning their attention to variables other than personality characteristics of rapists (Hall, 1996; Hall et al., 1998). The role of sociocultural variables is gaining increasing attention, particularly among those who see rape as a manifestation of male dominance and control of women (Sorenson & White, 1992). Other researchers have proposed integrative models that incorporate many different factors (Barbaree & Marshall, 1991; Hall & Hirschman, 1991; Malamuth, Sockloskie, Koss, & Tanaka, 1991). See the Critical Thinking feature "Why Do Men Rape Women?" for a discussion of controversial explanations for rape.

Incest

Incest may be defined as sexual relations between people too closely related to marry legally; it is nearly universally taboo in human society. Estimates of the incidence of incest range from 48,000 to 250,000 cases per year (Stark, 1984). The cases of incest most frequently reported to law enforcement agencies are those between a father and his daughter or stepdaughter. However, the most common incestuous relationship is brother-sister incest, not parent-child incest, according to one study (Waterman & Lusk, 1986). Less than 0.5 percent of the women in this study reported sexual contact with their fathers. Mother-son incest seems to be rare. In another study (Finkelhor, 1980), sexual activities between siblings were again found to be relatively frequent: 15 percent of the women and 10 percent of the men reported that they had had sexual involvement with their siblings. In 75 percent of these cases, mutual consent was involved. About half considered the experience positive; the other half, negative.

Although brother-sister incest is more common, most research has focused on father-daughter incest (Masters, Johnson, & Kolodny, 1992). This type of incestuous relationship generally begins when the daughter is between six and eleven years old, and it continues for at least two years (Stark, 1984). Unlike sex between siblings, father-daughter incest is always exploitative. The girl is especially vulnerable because she depends on her father for emotional support. As a result, the victims often feel guilty and powerless. Their problems continue into adulthood and are reflected in their high rates of drug abuse, sexual dysfunction, and psychiatric problems (Emslie & Rosenfeld, 1983; Gartner & Gartner, 1988; McAnulty & Burnette, 2003). Incest victims often have difficulty establishing trusting relationships with men. Incestuous relationships that were forceful, intrusive, or of a long duration are more likely to result in long-lasting negative effects (Herman, Russell, & Trocki, 1986).

Studies suggest that incestuous fathers are lower in intelligence than other fathers (Williams & Finkelhor, 1990) and often shy (Masters et al., 1992). Three types of incestuous fathers have been described (Herman & Hirschman, 1981). The first is a socially isolated man who is highly dependent on his family for interpersonal relationships; his emotional dependency gradually evolves (and expands) into a sexual relationship with his daughter. The second type of incestuous father has a psychopathic personality and is completely indiscriminate in choosing sexual partners. The third type has pedophilic tendencies and is sexually involved with several children, including his daughter. In addition, incest victims have reported family patterns in which the father is violent and the mother is unusually powerless. Williams and Finkelhor (1990) noted that some studies have shown that incestuous fathers were more likely than nonincestuous fathers to have experienced childhood sexual abuse themselves, although such abuse is absent in many cases. They also found that incestuous fathers tend to have difficulties in empathy, nurturance, caretaking, social skills, and masculine identification.

Treatment for Sex Offenders

Conventional Treatment   Imprisonment has been the main form of treatment for incest offenders and for rapists. However, it is more accurate to describe it as punishment, as the majority of convicts receive little or no treatment in prison (Goleman, 1992). In some cases of incest, an effort is made to keep the family intact for the benefit of the child. Behavioral treatment for sexual aggressors (rapists and pedophiles) generally involves the following steps:

1. Assessing sexual preferences through self-report and measuring erectile responses to different sexual stimuli

2. Reducing deviant interests through aversion therapy (the man receives electric shock when deviant stimuli are presented)

3. Orgasmic reconditioning or masturbation training to increase sexual arousal to appropriate stimuli

4. Social skills training to increase interpersonal competence

5. Assessment after treatment

Treatments for sex offenders are becoming increasingly sophisticated. They involve identifying risk factors and attempting to develop intervention strategies directly attuned to them. These risk factors include: (1) *dispositional*, such as psychopathic or antisocial personality characteristics; (2) *historical*, such as prior history of crime and violence and developmental trauma; (3) *criminogenic*, such as deviant social networks and lack of positive social supports; and (4) *clinical*, such as indicators of substance abuse, psychiatric problems, and poor social functioning (Ward & Stewart, 2003). Treatment as outlined above attempts to use the most empirically sound strategies to alter or minimize the risk factors (Polaschek, 2003). For example, if a person has a deviant social network, attempts are made to remove the person from such an environment.

Although treatment is becoming more sophisticated, questions remain about the effectiveness of these programs. Some treatment programs have been effective with child molesters and exhibitionists, but treatment outcomes have tended to be poor for rapists (Marshall, Jones, Ward, Johnston, & Barbaree, 1991).

Public revulsion and outrage against incest offenders, pedophiles, and rapists have resulted in calls for severe punishment, although there is no agreement as to what this should entail. In one case, a judge ordered a man who had had a seven-year incestuous relationship with his stepdaughter to receive injections of the hormone progesterone to control his sex drive. This judicial ruling caused an uproar. Some groups believed the punishment was inadequate, some believed it would not work, and others indicated it was "cruel and unusual."

Controversial Treatments   Surgical castration has been used to treat sexual offenders in many European countries, and results indicate that rates of relapse have been low (Marshall et al., 1991). An investigation of sex offenders (rapists, heterosexual pedophiles, homosexual pedophiles, bisexual pedophiles, and a sexual murderer) who were surgically castrated reported a decrease in sexual intercourse, masturbation, and frequency of sexual fantasies. However, twelve of the thirty-nine were still able to engage in sexual intercourse several years after being castrated. The rapists constituted the group whose members were most likely to remain sexually active.

Chemical therapy, usually involving the hormone Depo-Provera, reduces self-reports of sexual urges in pedophiles but not the ability to show genital arousal. Drugs appear to reduce psychological desire more than actual erection capabilities (Wincze, Bansal, & Malamud, 1986). The effectiveness of biological treatment such as surgery and chemotherapy is not known, and controversy obviously continues over the appropriate treatment for incest offenders, pedophiles, and rapists.

SUMMARY

What are normal and abnormal sexual behaviors?

- One of the difficulties in diagnosing abnormal sexual behavior is measuring it against a standard of normal sexual behavior. No attempt to establish such criteria has been completely successful, but these attempts have produced a better understanding of the normal human sexual response cycle.

- That cycle has four stages: the appetitive, arousal, orgasm, and resolution phases. Each may be characterized by problems, which may be diagnosed as disorders if they are recurrent and persistent.

- Many myths and misunderstandings continue to surround homosexuality. The belief that homosexuality is deviant seems to relate more to homophobia than to scientific findings. DSM-IV-TR no longer considers homosexuality to be a psychological disorder.

- Despite myths to the contrary, sexuality extends into old age. However, sexual dysfunction becomes increasingly prevalent with aging, and the frequency of sexual activity typically declines.

What does the normal sexual response cycle tell us about sexual dysfunctions?

- Sexual dysfunctions are disruptions of the normal sexual response cycle. They are fairly common in the general population and may affect a person's ability to become sexually aroused or to engage in intercourse. Many result from fear or anxiety regarding sexual activities; the various treatment programs are generally successful.

What causes gender identity disorders?

- Specified gender identity disorder involves a strong and persistent cross-gender identification.
- Transsexuals feel a severe psychological conflict between their sexual self-concepts and their genders. Some transsexuals seek sex-conversion surgery, although behavioral therapies are increasingly being used. Gender identity disorder can also occur in childhood.
- Children with this problem identify with members of the opposite gender, deny their own physical attributes, and often cross-dress. Treatment generally includes the parents and is behavioral in nature.
- Other disorders in this group are classified as gender identity disorder, not otherwise specified.

What are the paraphilias?

- The paraphilias are of three types, characterized by (1) a preference for nonhuman objects for sexual arousal, (2) repetitive sexual activity with nonconsenting partners, or (3) the association of real or simulated suffering with sexual activity.
- Suggested causes of the paraphilias are unconscious conflicts (the psychodynamic perspective) and conditioning, generally during childhood.
- Biological factors such as hormonal or brain processes have also been studied, but the results have not been consistent enough to permit strong conclusions about the role of biological factors in the paraphilias.
- Treatments are usually behavioral and are aimed at eliminating the deviant behavior while teaching more appropriate behaviors.

Are rape and incest acts of aggression?

- Sexually aggressive behaviors such as rape and incest are not listed in DSM-IV-TR, but they are serious problems. There appears to be no single cause for these deviations, and rapists seem to have different motivations and personalities.
- Some researchers feel that sociocultural factors can encourage rape and violence against women; others believe that biological factors coupled with sociocultural factors are important in explaining rape.
- Most research on incest, which involves sexual relations between close relatives, has examined father-daughter incest. Several types of incestuous fathers have been identified, which points again to the likelihood that incest is caused by different factors.

KEY TERMS

compulsive sexual behavior (p. 310)

date rape drug (p. 344)

dyspareunia (p. 323)

exhibitionism (p. 336)

female orgasmic disorder (p. 322)

female sexual arousal disorder (p. 322)

fetishism (p. 333)

frotteurism (p. 337)

gender identity disorder (p. 328)

incest (p. 348)

male erectile disorder (p. 321)

male orgasmic disorder (p. 323)

masochism (p. 338)

paraphilia (p. 332)

pedophilia (p. 337)

premature ejaculation (p. 323)

rape (p. 342)

rape trauma syndrome (p. 343)

sadism (p. 338)

sexual addiction (p. 310)

sexual arousal disorder (p. 320)

sexual desire disorder (p. 318)

sexual dysfunction (p. 317)

transsexualism (p. 328)

transvestic fetishism (p. 333)

vaginismus (p. 323)

voyeurism (p. 336)

MULTIMEDIA PREVIEW

For additional study aids, we invite you to explore our media resources accompanying *Understanding Abnormal Behavior*, Eighth Edition. The Student CD-ROM includes videos, quizzing, and critical thinking activities that help to reinforce key concepts in a fun and engaging manner. The Student Web Site provides additional interactive activities, chapter outlines, and research links that further support and complement the text. All Web resources may be accessed by logging onto the Web site at **http://psychology.college.hmco.com/students**.

CHAPTER 11
Mood Disorders

- What are the symptoms of mood disorders?
- How are mood disorders classified in the APA diagnostic scheme?
- Why do people develop depression and mania?
- What kinds of treatment are available for people with mood disorders, and how effective are the therapies?

We have all felt depressed or elated at some time during our lives. The loss of a job or the death of a loved one may result in depression; good news may make us manic (for example, ecstatic, hyperactive, and brazen). How do we know whether these moods are normal reactions or manifestations of a serious mental disorder? In general, we should be concerned if the reaction pervades every aspect of our lives, if it persists over a long period of time, if it occurs for no apparent reason, or if a depressive reaction is markedly out of proportion to a stressful or depressing situation, for these are signs of a mood disorder.

Mood disorders are disturbances in emotions that cause subjective discomfort, hinder a person's ability to function, or both. They rank among the top ten causes of worldwide disability and are a leading cause of absenteeism and diminished productivity in the workplace (U.S. Surgeon General, 1999). Depression and mania are central to these disorders. **Depression** is characterized by intense sadness, feelings of futility and worthlessness, and withdrawal from others. **Mania** is characterized by elevated mood, expansiveness, or irritability, often resulting in hyperactivity.

The prevalence of depression has been found to be eight times higher than that of mania (Robins, Locke & Regier 1991). Depression is quite prevalent in the general population, and it is the most common complaint of individuals seeking mental health care (Gotlib, 1992; Strickland, 1992). Some 10 million Americans, and more than 100 million people worldwide, will experience clinical depression this year. In the large-scale Epidemiologic Catchment Area (ECA) survey, Weissman, Bruce, Leaf, Florio, and Holzer (1991) found that 2.3 percent of the adult male population and 5 percent of the adult female population in the United States had experienced a mood disorder over a one-year period. Slight ethnic differences were found, but regardless of ethnicity, women were far more likely than men to experience a mood disorder.

Lifetime prevalence (the proportion of people who develop severe depression at some point in their lives) ranges from 10 to 25 percent for women and from 5 to 12 percent for men (American Psychiatric Association, 2000). A large-scale study has found even higher overall lifetime prevalence rates for all mood disorders—reaching almost 15 percent for adult males and almost 24 percent for adult females, as indicated in Figure 11.1 (Kessler et al., 1994). Prevalence rates can be expected to differ from study to study because of methodological and conceptual variations; the important point is that depression is relatively common. There are indications that it may be a continuous phenomenon that waxes and wanes. After one episode of depression, the likelihood of another is 50 percent; after two episodes, 70 percent; and after three episodes, 90 percent (Munoz et al., 1995). Moreover, depression has been found to be associated with the risk of having a heart attack and a shortened life expectancy (President's New Freedom Commission on Mental Health, 2003). In one large-scale study, individuals with depression were more than four times as likely to suffer a heart attack over a twelve- to thirteen-year follow-up period than were people with no history of the disorder (Spearing & Hendrix, 1998). Among college students, one survey found that over half indicated that they had experienced depression, 9 percent had thought of suicide, and 1 percent had attempted suicide since the beginning of college (Furr, Westefeld, McConnell, & Jenkins, 2001). Depression shortens life expectancy and increases the risk of dying from heart disease by as much as threefold (President's New Freedom Commission on Mental Health, 2003). It is also very costly. About $43 billion annually is spent on health care services and lost work days (Nitzkin & Smith, 2004).

Severe depression may afflict rich or poor, successful or unsuccessful, highly educated or uneducated. The following case illustrates one woman's experience:

FIGURE 11.1 One-Year and Lifetime Prevalence Rates of Mood Disorders in the United States

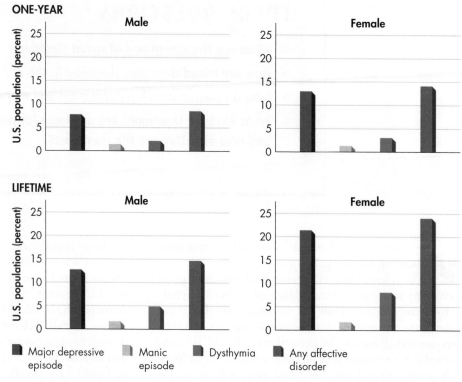

Source: Adapted from Kessler et al. (1994).

Amanda was a thirty-nine-year-old homemaker with three children, ages nine, eleven, and fourteen. Her husband, Jim, was the sales manager for an auto agency, and the family did well financially and lived comfortably. For years, family life was stable and no serious problems existed between family members. The family could be described as cohesive and loving. However, Jim began to notice that his wife was becoming more and more unhappy and depressed. She constantly said that her life lacked purpose. Jim would try to reassure her, pointing out that they had a nice home and that she had no reason to be unhappy. He suggested that she find some hobbies or socialize more with their neighbors and friends. But Amanda became progressively more absorbed in her belief that her life was meaningless.

After a while, Amanda no longer bothered to keep the house clean, to cook, or to take care of the children. At first Jim thought she was merely in a "bad mood" and that it would pass, but as her lethargy deepened, he became increasingly worried. He thought his wife was either sick or no longer loved him and the children. Amanda told him that she was tired and that simple household chores took too much energy. She said that she still loved Jim and the children but no longer had strong feelings for anything. Amanda did show some guilt about her inability to take care of the children and

to be a wife, but everything was simply too depressing. Life was no longer important, and she just wanted to be left alone. At that point she began to cry uncontrollably. Nothing Jim said could bring her out of the depression or stop her from crying. He decided that she had to see a physician, and he made an appointment for her. Amanda is currently receiving medication and psychotherapy to treat her depression.

In this chapter, we first describe the clinical symptoms of depression and mania and the two major types of mental disorders—depressive disorders and bipolar disorders. Then we discuss their causes and treatment. In the chapter on suicide, we examine a very serious problem that has been strongly linked to depression.

The Symptoms of Depression and Mania

Depression and mania, the two extremes of mood or affect, can be considered the opposite ends of a continuum that extends from deep sadness to wild elation. As noted earlier, depression is eight times more prevalent than mania. Depression appears in 90 percent of all diagnosed cases of mood disorders, and it would be expected to show up in the other 10 percent if they should remain untreated.

Symptoms of Depression

Certain core characteristics are often seen among people with depression. These characteristics may be organized within the four psychological domains used to describe anxiety: the affective domain, the cognitive domain, the behavioral domain, and the physiological domain. Table 11.1 shows this organization and compares the core group symptoms for depression and mania.

Affective Symptoms The most striking affective symptom of depression is depressed mood, with feelings of sadness, dejection, and an excessive and prolonged mourning. Feelings of worthlessness and of having lost the joy of living are common. Wild weeping may occur as a general reaction to frustration or anger. Such crying spells do not seem to be directly correlated with a specific situation. Anxiety frequently accompanies depression, with a correlation typically in the range of 0.45 to 0.75 (Watson et al., 1995).

To illustrate these affective characteristics, we present the following statements, made by a severely depressed patient who had markedly improved after treatment:

> It's hard to describe the state I was in several months ago. The depression was total—it was as if everything that happened to me passed through this filter which colored all experiences. Nothing was exciting to me. I felt I was no good, completely worthless, and deserving of nothing. The people who tried to cheer me up were just living in a different world.

We should note that severe depressive symptoms often occur as a normal reaction to the death of a loved one. This intensive mourning seems to have a positive psychological function in helping one to adjust. An excessively long period of bereavement, accompanied by a preoccupation with feelings of worthlessness, marked functional impairment, and serious psychomotor retardation, however, can indicate a major mood disorder. Cultures vary in the normal duration of bereavement, but severe incapacitating depression rarely continues beyond the first three months.

Cognitive Symptoms Besides general feelings of futility, emptiness, and hopelessness, certain thoughts and ideas, or cognitive symptoms, are clearly related to depressive reactions. For example, the person has profoundly pessimistic beliefs about the future. Lack of interest, decreased energy, and loss of motivation make it difficult for the depressed person to cope with everyday situations. Work responsibilities become monumental tasks, and the person avoids them. Self-accusations of incompetence and general self-denigration are common, as are thoughts of suicide. The suicide risk of depressed persons is at least eight times higher than that of the general population (Nitzkin & Smith, 2004). Other symptoms include difficulty in concentrating and in making decisions.

As noted in Table 11.2, depression may be reflected in faulty thinking. A cognitive triad develops with negative views of the self, of the outside world, and of the future (Beck, 1974). The person has pessimistic beliefs about what he or she can do, about what others can do to help, and about prospects for the future. Some of the elements of this triad can be seen in the following self-description of the thoughts and feelings of someone with severe depression:

> The gradual progression to this state of semicognizance and quiescence was steady; it is hard to trace. People and things counted less. I ceased to wonder. I asked a member of my family where I was and, having received

TABLE 11.1 Symptoms of Depression and Mania

Domain	Depression	Mania
Affective	Sadness, unhappiness, apathy, anxiety, brooding	Elation, grandiosity, irritability
Cognitive	Pessimism, guilt, inability to concentrate, negative thinking, loss of interest and motivation, suicidal thoughts	Flighty and pressured thoughts, lack of focus and attention, poor judgment
Behavioral	Low energy, neglect of personal appearance, crying, psychomotor retardation, agitation	Overactive, speech difficult to understand, talkative
Physiological	Poor or increased appetite, constipation, sleep disturbance, disruption of the menstrual cycle in women, loss of sex drive	High levels of arousal, decreased need for sleep

an answer, accepted it. And usually I remembered it, when I was in a state to remember anything objective. The days dragged; there was no "motive," no drive of any kind. A dull acceptance settled upon me. Nothing interested me. I was very tired and heavy. I refused to do most of the things that were asked of me, and to avoid further disturbance I was put to bed again. (Hillyer, 1964, pp. 158–159)

Ezra Pound, one of the most brilliant poets of the twentieth century, suffered a severe depression when he was in his seventies. He told an interviewer bitterly, "I have lived all my life believing that I knew something. And then a strange day came and I realized that I knew nothing, nothing at all. And so words have become empty of meaning. Everything that I touch, I spoil. I have blundered always" (Darrach, 1976, p. 81). Pound stopped writing for years; for days on end, he ceased to speak. For both Hillyer and Pound, motivation, activity, vitality, and optimism had declined drastically.

Behavioral Symptoms   A person with depression often shows behavioral symptoms such as social withdrawal and lowered work productivity. This low energy level is one of the dominant behavioral symptoms of depression, and it has been found to distinguish depressed individuals from nondepressed individuals (Christensen & Duncan, 1995). Depressed persons often show little motivation and exhibit anhedonia, or a loss in the capacity to derive pleasure from normally pleasant experiences. Other symptoms include sloppy or dirty clothing, unkempt hair, and lack of concern for personal cleanliness. A dull, mask-like facial expression may become characteristic, and the person tends to move slowly and does not initiate new activities. Speech is similarly reduced and slow, and responses may be limited to short phrases. This slowing down of all bodily movements, expressive ges-

Depression Slows a Muse Ezra Pound (1885–1972). American poet and expatriate, developed severe depression later in life and at one point was institutionalized. During his depression, he became extremely pessimistic and derogated much of his own work. For a time, he even stopped speaking and writing. Is creativity related to mood disorders?

TABLE 11.2 Beck's Six Types of Faulty Thinking

Arbitrary inference   Drawing conclusions about oneself or the world without sufficient and relevant information. Example: A man not hired by a potential employer perceives himself as "totally worthless" and believes he probably will never find employment of any sort.

Selective abstraction   Drawing conclusions from very isolated details and events without considering the larger context or picture. Example: A student who receives a C on an exam becomes depressed and stops attending classes even though he has A's and B's in his other courses. The student measures his worth by failures, errors, and weaknesses rather than by successes or strengths.

Overgeneralization   Holding extreme beliefs on the basis of a single incident and applying it to a different or dissimilar and inappropriate situation. Example: A depressed woman who has relationship problems with her boss may believe she is a failure in all other types of relationships.

Magnification and exaggeration   The process of overestimating the significance of negative events. Example: A runner experiences shortness of breath and interprets it as a major health problem, possibly even an indication of imminent death.

Personalization   Relating external events to one another when no objective basis for such a connection is apparent. Example: A student who raises his hand in class and is not called on by the professor believes that the instructor dislikes or is biased against him.

Polarized thinking   An "all-or-nothing," "good or bad," and "either-or" approach to viewing the world. Example: At one extreme, a woman who perceives herself as "perfect" and immune from making mistakes; at the other extreme, a woman who believes she is totally incompetent.

tures, and spontaneous responses is called *psychomotor retardation*. Although psychomotor retardation is typical, some people suffering from depression manifest an agitated state and symptoms of restlessness.

Physiological Symptoms   The following somatic and related symptoms frequently accompany depression:

1. *Appetite and weight changes* During depression, some people may experience either increased or decreased eating and weight. Those who constantly eat may do so even if they are not hungry. For

others, a loss of appetite often stems from the person's disinterest in eating; food seems tasteless. In severe depression, weight loss can become life threatening.

2. *Constipation* The person may not have bowel movements for days at a time.

3. *Sleep disturbance* Difficulty in falling asleep, waking up early, waking up erratically during the night, insomnia, and nightmares leave the person exhausted and tired during the day. Many dread the arrival of night because it represents a major fatigue-producing battle to fall asleep. Some depressed people, however, show hypersomnia, or excessive sleep. They often feel continually tired despite excessive sleep.

4. *Disruption of the normal menstrual cycle in women* The disruption is usually a lengthening of the cycle, and the woman may skip one or several periods. The volume of menstrual flow may decrease.

5. *Aversion to sexual activity* Many people report that their sexual arousal dramatically declines.

Culture influences the experience and expression of symptoms of depression. In some cultures, depression may be experienced largely in somatic or bodily complaints, rather than in sadness or guilt. Complaints of "nerves" and headaches (in Latino and Mediterranean cultures), of weakness, tiredness, or "imbalance" (in Chinese and Asian cultures), of problems of the "heart" (in Middle Eastern cultures), or of being "heartbroken" (among Hopi) may reveal the depressive experience (American Psychiatric Association, 2000).

The core symptoms of a major depressive episode are the same for children and adolescents, although the prominence of characteristic symptoms may change with age. In a longitudinal study of adolescents who experienced major depressive disorder, as they progressed into adulthood depressive symptoms were found to vary considerably (Lewinsohn, Pettit, Joiner, & Seeley, 2003). However, certain symptoms such as somatic complaints, irritability, and social withdrawal are particularly common in children, whereas psychomotor retardation, hypersomnia, and delusions are more common in adolescence and adulthood (American Psychiatric Association, 2000).

Symptoms of Mania

Affective Symptoms In mania, affective symptoms include elevated, expansive, or irritable mood (see Table 11.1). Social and occupational functioning is impaired, as shown in the following case:

Alan was a forty-three-year-old unmarried computer programmer who had led a relatively quiet life until two weeks before, when he returned to work after a short absence for illness. Alan seemed to be in a particularly good mood. Others in the office noticed that he was unusually happy and energetic, greeting everyone at work. A few days later, during the lunch hour, Alan bought a huge cake and insisted that his fellow workers eat some of it. At first everyone was surprised and amused by his antics. But two colleagues working with him on a special project became increasingly irritated because Alan didn't put any time into their project. He just insisted that he would finish his part in a few days.

On the day the manager had decided to tell Alan of his colleagues' concern, Alan behaved in a delirious, manic way. When he came to work, he immediately jumped onto a desk and yelled, "Listen, listen! We aren't working on the most important aspects of our data! I know, since I've debugged my mind. Erase, reprogram, you know what I mean. We've got to examine the total picture based on the input!" Alan then spouted profanities and made obscene remarks to several of the secretaries. Onlookers thought that he must have taken drugs. Attempts to calm him down brought angry and vicious denunciations. The manager, who had been summoned, also couldn't calm him. Finally the manager threatened to fire Alan. At this point, Alan called the manager an incompetent fool and stated that he could not be fired. His speech was so rapid and disjointed that it was difficult to understand him. Alan then picked up a chair and said he was going to smash the computers. Several coworkers grabbed him and held him on the floor. Alan was yelling so loud that his voice was quite hoarse, but he continued to shout and struggle. Two police officers were called, and they had to handcuff him to restrain his movements. Within hours, he was taken to a psychiatric hospital for observation.

People with mania, like Alan, show boundless energy, enthusiasm, and self-assertion. If frustrated, they may become profane and quite belligerent, as he did.

Cognitive Symptoms Some of the cognitive symptoms of mania include flightiness, pressured thoughts, lack of focus and attention, and poor judgment. The verbal processes of patients with mania reflect their cognitive state. For example, their speech is usually quite accelerated and pressured. They may change topics in midsentence or utter irrelevant and idiosyncratic phrases. Although much of what they say is understandable to others, the accelerated and disjointed nature of their speech makes it difficult to follow their train of thought. They seem incapable of controlling their attention, as though they are constantly distracted by new and more exciting thoughts and ideas.

Behavioral Symptoms   In terms of behavioral symptoms, individuals with mania are often uninhibited, engaging impulsively in sexual activity or abusive discourse. Two levels of manic intensity have been recognized—hypomania and mania (American Psychiatric Association, 2000). In the milder form, *hypomania,* affected people seem to be "high" in mood and overactive in behavior. Their judgment is usually poor, although delusions are rare. They start many projects but complete few, if any. When they interact with others, people with hypomania dominate the conversation and are often grandiose.

People who suffer from *mania* display more disruptive behaviors, including pronounced overactivity, grandiosity, and irritability. Their speech may be incoherent, and they do not tolerate criticisms or restraints imposed by others. In the more severe form of mania, the person is wildly excited, rants, raves (the stereotype of a wild "maniac"), and is constantly agitated and on the move. Hallucinations and delusions may appear. Because these individuals may be uncontrollable and are frequently dangerous to themselves or to others, physical restraint and medication are often necessary.

Physiological Symptoms   The most prominent physiological or somatic characteristic is a decreased need for sleep, accompanied by high levels of arousal. The energy and excitement these patients show may cause them to lose weight or to go without sleep for long periods. Whereas hypomania is not severe enough to cause marked impairment or hospitalization, the mood disturbance in mania is sufficiently severe to cause marked impairment in social or occupational functioning.

Classification of Mood Disorders

Mood disorders are largely divided into two major categories in DSM-IV-TR (American Psychiatric

"Either cheer up or take off the hat."

Association, 2000): depressive disorders (often referred to as *unipolar disorder*) and bipolar disorder. Once a depressive or manic episode occurs, the disorder is classified into both a category and a subcategory (see Figure 11.2). Let us examine the major categories and subcategories, as well as other aspects of the classification scheme.

Depressive Disorders

Depressive disorders in DSM-IV-TR include major depressive disorders, dysthymic disorder, and depressive disorders, not otherwise specified. In all of these disorder classifications there is no history of a manic episode. People who experience a major depressive episode are given the diagnosis of **major depression**. Symptoms should have been present for at least two weeks and should represent a change from the individual's previous functioning. The symptoms of major depression include a depressed mood or a loss of interest or pleasure, weight loss or gain, sleep difficulties, fatigue, feelings of worthlessness, inability to concentrate, and recurrent thoughts of death. If the episode is the person's first, it is classified as a single episode. For people who have had previous episodes, the disorder is considered a recurrent one. About one-half of those who experience a depressive episode eventually have another episode. In general, the earlier the age of onset, the more likely is a recurrence (Reus, 1988).

If a disorder is characterized by depressed mood but does not meet the criteria for major depression, dysthymic disorder may be diagnosed. In **dysthymic disorder,** the depressed mood is chronic and relatively continual. Typical symptoms include pessimism or guilt, loss of interest, poor appetite or overeating, low self-esteem, chronic fatigue, social withdrawal, or concentration difficulties. Unlike major depression, dysthymia may last for years, although the symptoms are often not as severe (Klein et al., 1998). Each year, about 10 percent of individuals with dysthymia go on to have a first major depressive episode. In dysthymia, the depressive symptoms are present most of the day and for more days than not during a two-year period (or, for children and adolescents, a one-year period). One study (Myers et al., 1984) found the prevalence of dysthymia to be higher among women than men. Overall, the lifetime prevalence is about 6 percent (American Psychiatric Association, 2000).

Bipolar Disorders

The essential feature of **bipolar disorders** is the occurrence of one or more manic or hypomanic episodes; the term *bipolar* is used because the disorders are usually accompanied by one or more depressive episodes. Symptoms of manic episodes include abnormally and persistently elevated, expansive, or irritable moods lasting at least one week in the case of mania and four days in the case of hypomania. Grandiosity, decreased need for sleep, flight of ideas, distractibility, and impairment in occupational or social functioning are often observed in persons with the disorder.

As indicated in the disorders chart, bipolar disorders include subcategories that describe the nature of the disorder. Bipolar I disorders include *single manic episode, most recent episode hypomanic, most recent episode manic, most recent episode mixed, most recent episode depressed,* and *most recent episode unspecified.* Bipolar II disorder includes *recurrent major depressive episodes with hypomania.* Persons in whom manic but not depressive episodes have occurred are extremely rare; in such cases, a depressive episode will presumably appear at some time. Interestingly, mood disorders, especially bipolar conditions, have occasionally been associated with artistic talent (Jamison, 1996). For example, Michelangelo, Van Gogh, Tchaikovsky, F. Scott Fitzgerald, Ernest Hemingway, and Walt Whitman experienced such disorders. We do not know why this association occurs, although it should be noted that most people with mood disorders are not especially creative. Perhaps the elevated energy, expansiveness, and uninhibited mood may contribute to productivity and novel ideas.

In contrast to the much higher lifetime prevalence rates for depressive disorders, the lifetime prevalence rates for bipolar I and II hover around 0.8 and 0.5 percent, respectively (Weissman et al., 1991). Unlike depression, there appear to be no major gender differences in the prevalence of bipolar disorders (Dubovsky & Buzan, 1999). Some people have hypomanic episodes and depressed moods that do not meet the criteria for major depressive episode. If the symptoms are present for at least two years, the individuals are diagnosed with cyclothymic disorder. (For children and adolescents, one year rather than two years is the criterion.) As in the case of dysthymia, **cyclothymic disorder** is a chronic and relatively continual mood disorder in which the person is never symptom free for more than two months. With lifetime prevalence between 0.4 and 1 percent, cyclothymia is less common than dysthymia. The risk that a person with cyclothymia will subsequently develop a bipolar disorder is 15 to 50 percent (American Psychiatric Association, 2000).

Other Mood Disorders

Mood disorder due to a general medical condition is a disturbance characterized by either (or both) depressed mood or elevated or irritable mood as a direct result of a general medical condition. (For example, patients with serious medical conditions may exhibit insomnia, weight loss, and depression.) This disorder is diagnosed when the symptoms are serious enough to cause significant impairment in social or occupational functioning or marked distress. *Substance-induced mood disorder* is a prominent and persistent disturbance of mood (depression, mania, or both) attributable to the use of a substance or to the cessation of the substance use. Again, it is diagnosed when notable distress and impairment occur.

Symptom Features and Specifiers

To be more precise about the nature of the mood disorders, DSM-IV-TR has listed certain characteristics that may be associated with these disorders (American Psychiatric Association, 2000). They are important symptom features that may accompany the disorders, but they are not criteria used to determine diagnosis. *Specifiers* may be used to more precisely describe the major depressive episode. Certain features, such as severity, presence or absence of psychotic symptoms, and remission status may be noted. For example, psychotic features include delusions, hallucinations, and gross impairment in reality testing (an inability to accurately perceive and deal with reality). Their presence tends to predict a relatively poor diagnosis, more chronicity, and impairment. If a person who is diagnosed with a major depressive episode has psychotic symptoms, the person would receive the diagnosis of major depressive episode with psychotic features. Similarly, major depressive episodes for some of the mood disorders may include (1) *melancholia* (loss of pleasure, lack of reactivity to pleasurable stimuli, depression that is worse in the morning, early morning awakening, excessive guilt, weight loss) and (2) *catatonia,* which is motoric immobility (taking a posture and not moving), extreme agitation (excessive motor activity), negativism (resistance to changing positions), or mutism.

Course Specifiers Course specifiers indicate the cyclic, seasonal, postpartum, or longitudinal pattern of mood disorders. For example, in the *rapid cycling* type, which is applicable to bipolar disorders, the manic or depressive episodes have occurred four or more times during the previous twelve months. The episodes may also appear with periods of relative normality in between. In some cases, there may be only partial remission in between the episodes. One patient was reported to demonstrate manic behaviors for almost exactly twenty-four hours, immediately followed by depressive behaviors for twenty-four hours. At the manic extreme, the patient was agitated, demanding, and constantly shouting; the next day, he was almost mute and inactive. The alternating nature of the disorder lasted eleven years (Jenner et al., 1967). Typical manic episodes appear suddenly and last from a few days to months. Depressive episodes tend to last longer.

FIGURE 11.2 Disorders Chart: Mood Disorders

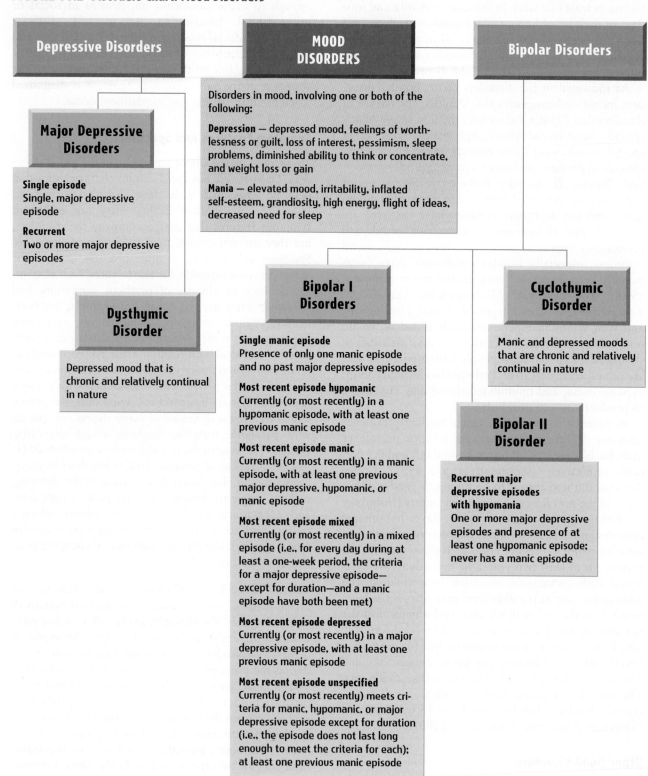

Source: American Psychiatric Association (2000).

FIGURE 11.2 Disorders Chart: Mood Disorders (continued)

MOOD DISORDERS	Lifetime Prevalence (%)	Gender Differences	Age of Onset	Course
Major Depressive Disorder	8.0 – 19.0	Much higher in females	Any age; average age in 20s	May last 6 or more months; may end or may recur frequently
Dysthymia	6.0	Much higher in females	Often starts in childhood or adolescence	Chronic depression, which may precede major depression
Bipolar I Disorder	0.4 – 1.6	No major difference	Any age; usually in early 20s	Manic episode, usually recurrent; may occur before or after depressive episode
Bipolar II Disorder	0.5	Higher in females	Any age	Hypomanic episode usually occurs before or after depressive episode
Cyclothymia	0.4 – 1.0	No difference	Often starts during adolescence	Chronic hypomanic condition with a risk for developing bipolar disorder

Postpartum Psychosis
Depression is sometimes associated with certain life events or changes. Specifiers are used to more precisely describe the mood disorder. One course specifier indicates whether the depression or mania in women occurs within four weeks of childbirth. If it does, the mood disorder has the specifier "postpartum onset." It occurs in about 13 percent of mothers (O'Hara, 2003), and Andrea Yates, who drowned her five children, built her defense case on this mood disorder. Why do you think that postpartum depression occurs?

One of the more interesting course specifiers involves a *seasonal pattern*. For some people, moods are accentuated during certain times. Lehmann (1985) noted that many depressed people find the morning more depressing than the evening. Many individuals also find winter, when days are shorter and darker, more depressing than summer. In seasonal affective disorder (SAD), serious cases of depression fluctuate according to the season, although the precise reasons for this fluctuation are unclear. Proposed explanations include the possibility that SAD is an abnormal body response to seasonal changes in the length of the day, that the dark days of winter may bring about hormonal changes in the body that somehow affect depression levels, and that disruption of the body's circadian rhythm produces mood fluctuations (Lee et al., 1998). SAD appears to be related to the photoperiod (hours from sunrise to sunset) rather than to daily hours of sunshine, mean daily temperature, or total daily radiation (Young, Meaden, Fogg, Cherin, & Eastman, 1997). Interestingly, "light therapy" (exposure to bright light) for several hours a day, especially during winter, appears to be helpful for many individuals with SAD (Oren & Rosenthal, 2001), as may vacations to sunny parts of the country. In some cases of recurrent major depression and bipolar disorder, the onset, end, or change of an episode coincides with a particular time of the year. For example, one man regularly became depressed after Christmas.

Other course specifiers include *postpartum onset* (if depression or mania in women occurs within four weeks of childbirth) and longitudinal specifiers that indicate the nature of the recurrence and the status of individuals between episodes.

Comparison Between Depressive and Bipolar Disorders

Several types of evidence seem to support the distinction between depressive (unipolar) and bipolar disorders (Dubovsky & Buzan, 1999; Goodwin & Guze, 1984; Research Task Force of the National Institute of Mental Health, 1975). First, genetic studies have revealed that blood relatives of patients with bipolar disorders have a higher incidence of manic disturbances than do relatives of patients with unipolar disorders. In addition, stronger evidence of genetic or psychophysiological influences exists for bipolar disorders than for unipolar disorders. Second, the age of onset is somewhat earlier for bipolar disorders (the early twenties) than for unipolar disorders (the late twenties). Third, individuals with bipolar disorder display psychomotor retardation and a greater tendency to attempt suicide than do individuals with unipolar disorder, whose depressive symptoms often include anxiety. And fourth, bipolar disorders respond to lithium, whereas the drug has little effect on unipolar disorders. However, there is some evidence that the two are not entirely distinct. Relatives of those with unipolar disorders have an increased probability of having unipolar disorders. On the other hand, relatives of those with bipolar disorders have an increased chance of having not only bipolar disorders but also unipolar disorders (Faraone, Kremen, & Tsuang, 1990).

As mentioned earlier, only 1 to 2 percent of the adult population has experienced bipolar disorder, whereas about 8 to 19 percent have at some time experienced a major depressive episode. Unlike major depression, which seems to be more common in females than in

Seasonal Patterns of Depression In seasonal affective disorder (SAD), depressive symptoms vary with the seasons. One theory for this is that during winter, reduced daylight affects hormone levels, which in turn may induce depression. The man in this photo is receiving light therapy, which involves exposure to bright light. The treatment appears to be helpful in some cases of SAD. Do you believe that most people feel happier during the summer than winter?

males, no major overall gender difference exists in the frequency of bipolar I disorders, although bipolar II disorder appears to be more common among women (American Psychiatric Association, 2000). Both unipolar and bipolar mood disorders often coexist with other mental disorders and medical illnesses, such as anxiety, substance use, posttraumatic stress disorder, and hypertension and arthritis (Erickson, Wolfe, King, King, & Sharkansky, 2001; U.S. Surgeon General, 1999).

The Etiology of Mood Disorders

Despite increasing evidence for a unipolar-bipolar distinction, little is known about what causes the extreme mood changes in the bipolar disorders. Perhaps the regulatory mechanism for maintaining *homeostasis*, or stability of mood, no longer works. Maybe the apparent euphoria, irritability, and overactivity seen in mania are attempts to deny or ward off depression. Simoneau, Miklowitz, and Saleem (1998) have found that families of bipolar patients who are high in expressed emotions (such as critical, hostile, or emotionally overinvolved attitudes) create stressful family interaction patterns. These researchers recommend examining ways to avoid these patterns. Other research findings raise the possibility that manic symptoms in bipolar disorder are manifestations of dysregulation in the brain activation system, which corresponds to neural pathways in the brain. Consistent with a dysregulation model, Johnson and her colleagues (2000) found that individuals with bipolar disorders show elevated manic symptoms after experiencing goal-attainment life events (but not just any positive life events). They speculate that bipolar individuals cannot regulate motivation and that goal-attainment events trigger manic symptoms. In contrast, persons without the disorder tend to "coast" or decrease activation after these events. In any case, much more is known about what causes unipolar depression than about what causes the bipolar disorders, and psychological-sociocultural perspectives focus primarily on depression rather than on mania. As indicated earlier, biological factors may play a more prominent role in the etiology of bipolar disorders than in unipolar disorders. Another possibility is that the category of unipolar disorders is more heterogeneous and that some of these disorders are caused by internal conditions within the organism, whereas others are caused by external precipitating events. In any case, we focus our discussion of psychological or sociocultural explanations primarily on depression. The later section on biological explanations covers both unipolar and bipolar disorders, leading into treatment approaches based on those explanations.

Psychological or Sociocultural Approaches to Depression

Over the years, a number of different explanations have been proposed to account for depression. Some of the major theories discussed in this section are the psychodynamic, behavioral, cognitive, cognitive-learning, and sociocultural viewpoints.

Psychodynamic Explanations   The psychodynamic explanation of depression focuses mainly on two concepts: separation and anger. Separation may occur when a spouse, lover, child, parent, or significant other person dies or leaves for one reason or another. But depression cannot always be correlated with the immediate loss of a loved one, and for those instances, Freud used the construct of "symbolic loss." That is to say, the depressed person may perceive any form of rejection or reproach as symbolic of an earlier loss. For example, the withdrawal of affection or support or a rejection can induce depression.

Freud (1917) believed that depressed people are excessively dependent because they are fixated in the oral stage. As we discussed in the chapter on models of abnormal behavior, he viewed the mouth as the primary mechanism by which infants relate to the world, so being fixated at this stage fosters dependency. Being passive and having others fill one's needs (being fed, bathed, clothed, cuddled, and so forth) results in emotional dependency that continues into adult life. Thus, for people fixated in the oral stage, self-esteem depends on other important people in the environment. When a significant loss occurs, the mourner's self-esteem plummets.

Freud also believed that a person in depression fails to follow through the normal process of mourning, which he called "grief or mourning work." In this process, the mourner consciously recalls and expresses memories about the lost person in an attempt to undo the loss. In addition, the mourner is flooded with two strong sets of feelings: anger and guilt. The anger, which arises from the sense of being deserted, can be very strong. The mourner may also be flooded with guilt feelings about real or imagined sins committed against the lost person.

Psychodynamic explanations of depression have strongly emphasized the dynamics of anger. Many patients in depression have strong hostile or angry feelings, and some clinicians believe that getting clients to express their anger reduces their depression. Such a belief has led some to speculate that depression is really anger turned against the self (Freud, 1917). Freud suggested that, when a person experiences a loss (symbolic or otherwise), he or she may harbor feelings of resentment and hostility toward the lost person, in addition to feelings of love and affection.

There have been relatively few empirical tests of psychodynamic ideas. One longitudinal study (Stroebe & Stroebe, 1991) examined whether persons whose spouses had died were less depressed if they directly confronted the loss (that is, performed grief work) rather than avoided dealing with it. Results were equivocal in that performing grief work was inversely related to adjustment for widowers but not for widows. Other studies (such as Paykel, 1982) have shown that loss (death or separation) of significant others in one's life can precipitate depression. However, stressors other than the loss of a significant other may bring about depression, and the loss of a significant other can lead to disorders other than depression, such as anxiety and substance abuse.

Behavioral Explanations   Behaviorists also see the separation or loss of a significant other as important in depression. However, behaviorists tend to see reduced reinforcement as the cause, rather than fixation or symbolic grief, which they view as untestable concepts. When a loved one is lost, an accustomed level of reinforcement (whether affection, companionship, pleasure, material goods, or services) is immediately withdrawn. The survivor can no longer obtain the support or encouragement of the lost person, and the survivor's level of activity (talking, expressing ideas, working, joking, engaging in sports, going out on the town) diminishes markedly in the absence of this reinforcement. Thus many behaviorists view depression as a product of inadequate or insufficient reinforcers in a

person's life, leading to a reduced frequency of behavior that previously was positively reinforced (Lewinsohn, 1974; Wells, Sturm, Sherbourne, & Meredith, 1996).

As the period of reduced activity continues, the person labels himself or herself "depressed." If the new lower level of activity causes others to show sympathy, the depressed person may remain inactive and become chronically "depressed." By being sympathetic about the incident (loss), friends, relatives, and even strangers may be reinforcing the person's current state of inactivity. (This reinforcement for a lower activity level is known as *secondary gain*.) Thus the depression continues to deepen, and the person disengages still further from the environment and further reduces the chance of obtaining positive reinforcement from normal activity.

Depression has been associated both with low levels of self-reinforcement and with reductions in environmental reinforcements (Heiby, 1983). In other words, when people get less reinforcement from the environment (such as after the death of a loved one) and do not give themselves reinforcement, they are prone to become depressed. Depressed people may lack the skills required to replace lost environmental reinforcements.

This behavioral concept of depression can be elaborated to cover many situations that may elicit depression (such as failure, loss, change in job status, rejection, and desertion). Lewinsohn's model of depression, illustrated in Figure 11.3, is perhaps the most comprehensive behavioral explanation of depression (Lewinsohn, 1974; Lewinsohn, Hoberman, Teri, & Hautzinger, 1985). Along with the reinforcement

Loss as a Source of Depression
Mourning over the death of a loved one occurs in all cultures and societies, as illustrated by these women mourning at the funerals of 75 victims of the Celina Massacre in Kosovo. However, in most cultures, severe and incapacitating depression rarely continues after the first three months. If it does continue longer, then a depressive disorder may have developed. What other characteristics or symptoms would help one to distinguish between "normal" grief and a depressive disorder?

Separation as a Cause of Depression Harry and Margaret Harlow (1962) found that infant monkeys reacted with fear and despair when separated from their mothers. Even monkeys raised with surrogate mothers (in this case, a wire frame covered with terrycloth) exhibited anxiety and despair when separated from them. The psychodynamic perspective asserts that separation can be a cause of depression. Do you think separation anxiety and depression are genetically determined?

view of depression, Lewinsohn suggested three sets of variables that may enhance or hinder a person's access to positive reinforcement.

1. *The number of events and activities that are potentially reinforcing to the person.* This number depends very much on individual differences and varies with the biological traits and experiential history of the person. For example, age, gender, or physical attributes may determine the availability of reinforcers. Handsome people are more likely to receive positive attention than are nondescript people. Young people are likely to have more social interaction than retirees are. A task-oriented person who values intellectual pursuits may not respond to interpersonal or affiliative forms of reinforcement as readily as other people would. To such a person, a compliment such as "I like you" may be less effective than "I see you as an extremely competent person."

2. *The availability of reinforcements in the environment.* Harsh environments, such as regimented institutions or remote isolated places, reduce reinforcements.

3. *The instrumental behavior of the individual.* The number of social skills a person can exercise to bring about reinforcement is important. People in depression lack social behaviors that can elicit positive reinforcements. They interact with fewer people, respond less, have very few positive reactions, and initiate less conversation. They also feel more uncomfortable in social situations (Youngren & Lewinsohn, 1980), and they elicit depression in others (Hammen & Peters, 1978). Further, people in depression seem to be preoccupied with themselves; they tend to talk about themselves (more so than other people do) without being asked to do so (Jacobson & Anderson, 1982). For this reason or others, family, friends, and acquaintances may not enjoy talking to people in depression and may provide little positive reinforcement to them during social interactions. By creating conditions that further their depression or drive others away, these individuals thereby lose any social reinforcement that others could provide (Coyne, 1976).

A low rate of positive reinforcement in any of these three situations can lead to depression, as Figure 11.3 illustrates. A beautiful person who begins to age may notice declining interest from possible lovers. A person who has recently lost a loved one through divorce or death and has no other friends or family may receive little or no support. And a young student who lacks social skills in sexual relationships may be denied the pleasures of such interactions. Behavioral approaches to treating depression might attempt to intervene in any of these conditions.

Lewinsohn also recognized the important role of other factors in depression. For example, Lewinsohn, Hoberman, and Rosenbaum (1988) found that having a prior depressed mood, encountering stress, and being female (as mentioned previously, women are more likely than men to suffer depression) are associated with the occurrence of depressive episodes. Although a low rate of positive reinforcement is a critical feature of his theory, Lewinsohn and colleagues (1985) adopted a more comprehensive view of depression. They believe that an antecedent event such as stress disrupts the predictable and well-established behavior patterns of people's lives. Such disruptions then reduce the rate of positive reinforcements or increase aversive experiences. If individuals are unable to reverse the impact of the stress, they begin to have a heightened state of self-awareness (for example, self-criticism, negative expectancies, and loss of self-confidence) and to

FIGURE 11.3 Lewinsohn's Behavioral Theory of Depression If reinforcing events, availability of reinforcement, and instrumental behaviors are limited, the person experiences a low rate of positive reinforcement and may become depressed. In turn, depression leads to a low rate of positive reinforcement by reducing reinforcing events, availability, and so on.

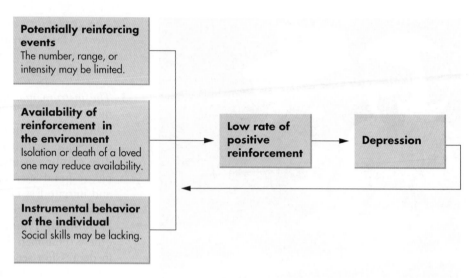

Potentially reinforcing events
The number, range, or intensity may be limited.

Availability of reinforcement in the environment
Isolation or death of a loved one may reduce availability.

Instrumental behavior of the individual
Social skills may be lacking.

Low rate of positive reinforcement

Depression

Source: Based on Lewinsohn (1974).

experience depressed affect. With depressed moods, persons then have a more difficult time functioning appropriately, which makes them further vulnerable to depression. Thus Lewinsohn's model attempts to cover not only behavioral elements but also cognitive and emotional consequences.

Behaviorists have made major contributions to the understanding of depression, but, as noted earlier, they and many other theorists have not really given much attention to mania. While acknowledging that biological factors may be important in bipolar disorders, Staats and Heiby (1985) also believe that learning principles contribute to mania. They believe that individuals may receive praise and admiration because of some behavior (such as performing well using social or interpersonal skills). The euphoria from receiving the praise may elicit further use of the skills, resulting in even more positive consequences. The behaviors then become accelerated and euphoria increases even more—as in a manic state. At some point, however, the behaviors elicit negative reactions, which set up conditions for depression.

Cognitive Explanations Some psychologists believe that low self-esteem is the key to depressive reactions. All of us have both negative and positive feelings about what we see as our "self." We like or value certain things about ourselves, and we dislike other things. Cognitively oriented psychologists have proposed that the way people think, rather than low rates of positive reinforcement, can cause depression. In their view, depressed persons have negative thoughts and specific errors in thinking that result in pessimism, negative views of self, feelings of hopelessness, and depression (Emmelkamp, 2004). Some people, especially people in depression, have a generally negative

The Reinforcement Factor Learning theory suggests that depression may be a product of reduced reinforcement in a person's life, which may lead to reduced activity levels. Ironically, consolation and sympathy from others may sometimes serve to reinforce and maintain depressive behaviors. In such cases, should you withhold sympathy? Would this be beneficial?

self-concept, perceiving themselves as inept, unworthy, and incompetent, regardless of reality. If they do succeed at anything, they are likely to dismiss it as pure luck or to forecast eventual failure. Hence a cognitive interpretation of oneself as unworthy may lead to thinking patterns that reflect self-blame, self-criticism, and exaggerated ideas of duty and responsibility. Such beliefs are often exaggerated and irrational and are interpreted in a catastrophic manner (Ellis, 1989).

Beck (1976) proposed one major cognitive theory that views depression as a primary disturbance in *thinking* rather than a basic disturbance in *mood*. How persons structure and interpret their experiences determines their affective states. If individuals see a situation as unpleasant, they will feel an unpleasant mood. Patients with depression are said to have **schemas** that set them up for depression. In one study, for example, Crowson and Cromwell (1995) offered research participants the choice of listening to positive or negative tape-recorded messages. The researchers found that the group not suffering from depression was more likely to choose positive messages, whereas the group with depression showed little preference in the messages. Perhaps depression involves schemas that perpetuate negative outlooks and attention to negative messages.

According to this theory, people in depression operate from a "primary triad" of negative self-views, present experiences, and future expectations. Four characteristic errors in logic typify this negative schema (see also Table 11.2):

1. *Arbitrary inference* The person with depression tends to draw conclusions that are not supported by evidence. For example, a woman may conclude that "people dislike me" just because no one speaks to her on the bus or in the elevator. A man who invites a woman to dinner and finds the restaurant closed that evening may see this as evidence of his own unworthiness. In both cases, the person draws erroneous conclusions from the available evidence. People with depression are apparently unwilling or unable to see other, more probable, explanations.

2. *Selected abstraction* The individual takes a minor incident or detail out of context and focuses on it, and these incidents tend to be trivial. A person corrected for a minor aspect of his or her work may take the correction as a sign of incompetence or inadequacy—even when the supervisor's overall feedback is highly positive.

3. *Overgeneralization* The individual tends to draw a sweeping conclusion about his or her ability, performance, or worth from one single experience or incident. A woman laid off from a job because of

budgetary cuts may conclude that she is worthless. The comments of a student seen by one of the authors at a university psychology clinic provide another illustration of overgeneralization: when he missed breakfast at the dormitory because his alarm clock didn't ring, the student concluded, "I don't deserve my own body because I don't take care of it." Later, when he showed up late for class through no fault of his own, he thought, "What a miserable excuse for a student I am." When a former classmate passed by and smiled, he thought, "I must look awful today or she wouldn't be laughing at me."

4. *Magnification and minimization* The individual tends to exaggerate (magnify) limitations and difficulties and play down (minimize) accomplishments, achievements, and capabilities. Asked to evaluate personal strengths and weaknesses, the person lists many shortcomings or unsuccessful efforts but finds it almost impossible to name any achievements.

All four of these cognitive processes can be seen as either results or causes of low self-esteem, which makes the person expect failure and engage in self-criticism that is unrelated to reality. People with low self-esteem may have experienced much disapproval in the past from significant others, such as parents. Their parents or significant others may have responded to them by punishing failures and not rewarding successes or by holding unrealistically high expectations or standards, as in the following case:

Paul was a twenty-year-old college senior majoring in chemistry. He first came to the student psychiatric clinic complaining of headaches and a vague assortment of somatic problems. Throughout the interview, Paul seemed severely depressed and unable to work up enough energy to talk with the therapist. Even though he had maintained a B+ average, he felt like a failure and was uncertain about his future. His parents had always had high expectations for Paul, their eldest son, and had transmitted these feelings to him from his earliest childhood. His father, a successful thoracic surgeon, had his heart set on Paul's becoming a doctor. The parents saw academic success as very important, and Paul did exceptionally well in school. Although his teachers praised him for being an outstanding student, his parents seemed to take his successes for granted. In fact, they often made statements such as "You can do better."

When Paul failed at something, his parents would make it obvious to him that they not only were disappointed but also felt disgraced. This pattern of punishment for failures without recognition of successes, combined with his parents' high expectations, led to the development of Paul's extremely negative self-concept.

Some studies have demonstrated a relationship between cognition and depression. Dent and Teasdale (1988) studied the depression levels and self-schemas (self-descriptions) of the same women at two different periods of time. Women who made negative self-descriptions tended subsequently to have higher levels of depression and to recover more slowly than did women who made less negative self-descriptions. The investigators concluded that although two individuals may have equal levels of depression, the one who has negative self-schemas may turn out to have a more serious and longer-lasting depressive episode.

Further evidence of a link between cognition and depression comes from studies of memory bias. When people with depression are given lists of words that vary in emotional content, they tend to recall more negative words than do their control group counterparts. This may indicate a tendency to attend to, and remember, negative and depressing events (Mineka & Sutton, 1992). Even individuals who have recovered from depression show a greater tendency toward negative cognitive styles than is found among individuals who have never been depressed (Hedlund & Rude, 1995). They presumably have developed negative schemas.

Although the cognitive explanation of depression has merit, it seems too simple. At times, negative cognitions may be the result, rather than the cause, of depressed moods, as noted by Hammen (1985). That is, one may first feel depressed and then, as a result, have negative or pessimistic thoughts about the world. Hammen also found that a person's schema tends to mediate the relationship between stress and depression. Stress can lead to depression if a person has developed a predisposing schema. Another criticism of cognitive explanations is that many people get depressed, but they do not feel depressed all the time. Yet negative cognitive styles are often hypothesized to be stable or enduring.

Cognitive-Learning Approaches: Learned Helplessness and Attributional Style

Martin Seligman (1975; Nolen-Hoeksema, Girgus, & Seligman, 1992) proposed a unique and interesting view of depression based on cognitive learning theory. The basic assumption of this approach is that both cognitions and feelings of helplessness are learned and that depression is **learned helplessness**—an acquired belief that one is helpless and unable to affect the outcomes in one's life. A person who sees that his or her actions continually have very little effect on the environment develops an expectation of being helpless. When this expectation is borne out in settings that may not be controllable, passivity and depression may result.

A person's susceptibility to depression, then, depends on his or her experience with controlling the

Learned Helplessness and Depression According to Seligman, feelings of helplessness can lead to depression. However, if people can learn to control their environment and believe in their ability to succeed, despite difficulties, they can overcome their feelings of helplessness and despair and begin to lead productive lives again. California Angels' pitcher Jim Abbott fought feelings of helplessness and won his battle with depression. In Seligman's theory, what can be done to alter feelings of helplessness?

environment. In his study of helplessness, Seligman discovered strong parallels between the symptoms and causes of helplessness and those of depression (see Table 11.3). He also noticed similarities in cures; one could say that depression is cured when the person no longer believes he or she is helpless.

Seligman described depression as a *belief in one's own helplessness*. Many other investigators have described depression in terms of hopelessness, powerlessness, and helplessness. For example, "The severely depressed patient believes that his skills and plans of action are no longer effective for reaching the goals he has set" (Melges & Bowlby, 1969, p. 693). And, according to Seligman (1975, pp. 55–56), "The expectation that an outcome is independent of responding (1) reduces the motivation to control the outcome; (2) interferes with learning that responding controls the outcome; (3) produces fear for as long as the subject is uncertain of the uncontrollability of the outcome, and then produces depression." In general, research has shown that depression is associated with an external

TABLE 11.3   Similarities Between Learned Helplessness and Depression

	Learned Helplessness	Depression
Symptoms	Passivity	Passivity
	Difficulty learning that response produces relief	Negative cognitive set
	Dissipates in time	Time course
	Lack of aggression	Introjected hostility
	Weight loss, appetite loss	Weight loss, appetite loss
	Social and sexual deficits	Social and sexual deficits
Cause	Learning that responding and reinforcement are independent	Feelings of helplessness
		Belief that responding is useless

Source: Adapted from Seligman (1975).

locus of control—persons with depression tend to perceive events as being uncontrollable (Benassi, Sweeney, & Dufour, 1988).

Attributional Style   Seligman's theory of learned helplessness was first published in 1975. Three years later, he and his coworkers revised the model to include more cognitive elements (Abramson, Seligman, & Teasdale, 1978). The essential idea is that people who feel helpless make *causal attributions,* or speculations about why they are helpless. These attributions can be internal or external, stable or unstable, and global or specific. For instance, suppose that a student in a math course receives the same low grades regardless of how much he has studied. The student may attribute the low grades to internal or personal factors ("I don't do well in math because *I'm* scared of math") or to external factors ("The *teacher* doesn't like me, so I can't get a good grade"). The attribution can also be stable ("I'm the type of person who can never do well in math") or unstable ("My poor performance is due to my heavy work load"). Additionally, the attribution can be global or specific. A global attribution ("I'm a poor student") has broader implications for performance than a specific one ("I'm poor at math but good in other subjects"). Abramson and coworkers believe that a person whose attributions for helplessness are internal, stable, and global is likely to have more pervasive feelings of depression than someone whose attributions are external, unstable, and specific (see Figure 11.4). Attributions have been found to be associated with many aspects of life.

Some people tend to have a pessimistic attributional style, explaining bad events (such as failure to pass an examination) in global, stable, and internal terms (such as believing that "I fail in many courses, it always happens to me, and I am stupid"). Attributional style is related to a number of characteristics.

People who have pessimistic attributional styles receive lower grades in universities, perform worse as sales agents, and have poorer health (Seligman, 1987).

To assess attributional style, Seligman and his colleagues developed the Attributional Style Questionnaire, which asks the individual to indicate the cause of a number of hypothetical situations. Attributional style can also be reliably determined from a content analysis of verbatim explanations (CAVE), in which the content of an explanation is rated on attributional style. For example, a baseball player who says, "Once in a while I play poorly because of bad breaks, but I always know I'll get my good share of hits," is far more optimistic than one who says, "I'm getting old—my reactions to a pitch have slowed." In an analysis of newspaper quotes from Baseball Hall of Fame players who played between 1900 and 1950, Seligman found that players who had an optimistic attributional style outlived those who were more pessimistic. Zullow, Oettingen, Peterson, and Seligman (1988) also noted that when President Lyndon Johnson's press conferences contained optimistic phrases, bold presidential actions were taken in the Vietnam War; when he used more pessimistic phrases, the actions were passive.

The implications are that (1) people vary in their attributional styles, (2) attributional style can be assessed, and (3) attributional style may be related to achievements, health, and other behaviors. Obviously, a causal relationship between attributional style and behavior has not been clearly established. But the research suggests that how we explain things may be quite important in our lives.

Both the learned helplessness model and the attributional style approach have generated a great deal of research. There is evidence that people with depression make "depressive" attributions and feel that their lives are less controllable than others do (Raps, Peterson,

FIGURE 11.4 Attributional Styles As this figure indicates, attributional styles vary according to whether they are internal or external, stable or unstable, and global or specific. People with depression tend to explain failures in terms of internal, global, and stable factors. In the example illustrated here, a student attributes a failure to get a date as the direct result of such factors: "I have a rotten personality."

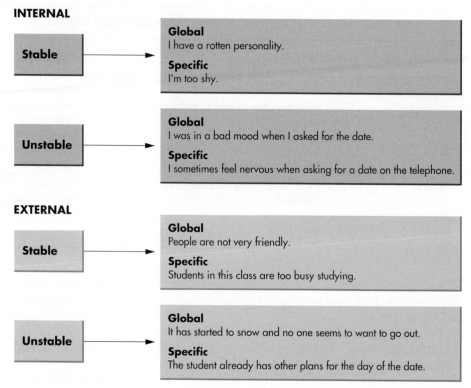

INTERNAL

Stable
> **Global**
> I have a rotten personality.
>
> **Specific**
> I'm too shy.

Unstable
> **Global**
> I was in a bad mood when I asked for the date.
>
> **Specific**
> I sometimes feel nervous when asking for a date on the telephone.

EXTERNAL

Stable
> **Global**
> People are not very friendly.
>
> **Specific**
> Students in this class are too busy studying.

Unstable
> **Global**
> It has started to snow and no one seems to want to go out.
>
> **Specific**
> The student already has other plans for the day of the date.

Reinhard, Abramson, & Seligman, 1982). One study has also shown that negative self-appraisals by children can predict subsequent changes in level of depression (Hoffman, Cole, Martin, Tram, & Seroczynski, 2000). As with cognitive theory, however, researchers question whether the learned helplessness model, even with its attributional components, can adequately explain depression, and they also question whether attributions result from depression or are caused by it. Cognitions and attributions may be important factors in depression, but the disorder is complex; current models tend to include or explain only particular facets of depression (Dubovsky & Buzan, 1999; Hammen, 1985). Helplessness theory (which some investigators have reformulated as the "hopelessness" theory) and attributions may explain only a certain type of depression (Abramson, Metalsky, & Alloy, 1989; DeVellis & Blalock, 1992). As we mentioned earlier, many researchers believe that an external locus of control is associated with depression, yet Seligman believes that internal attributions are important in depression. Benassi and colleagues (1988) raise the possibility that internality and externality may be related to different types of depression. Depression may be a heterogeneous disorder that can be caused by genetic, biochemical, or social factors.

Interestingly, Seligman and his colleagues (Seligman, Reivich, Jaycox, & Gillham, 1995) combine their theory with a cultural analysis. They note that depression in Western countries has dramatically increased over the last several decades. The rapid increase in depression occurred over too short a time to be explained by a genetic theory, and no biological or biochemical changes among human beings have been observed over this time period. They argue that changes in the rate of depression were affected by two major cultural shifts during the 1960s and 1970s. The first shift was a movement to achieve higher levels of personal self-satisfaction and individual freedom (e.g., the "me" generation). The second was a movement away from an allegiance to causes greater than the self (e.g., principles, parenthood, community, nation, and God). As the self became more important, failure to enhance self, achieve, or succeed was devastating. Furthermore, meaning in life was difficult to find because many people no longer believed in larger causes or spirituality. The consequence is that individuals have difficulty perceiving meaning in their existence and consequently become more prone to depression.

Response Styles   Another theory of depression is that individuals have consistent styles of responding to depressed moods and that these responses affect the course of depression (Nolen-Hoeksema, 1991). In particular, ruminative responses—in which one dwells on why one feels bad, considers the possible consequences of one's symptoms, and expresses to others how badly one feels—are believed to prolong and intensify depressive moods and to possibly bring about the onset of depressive episodes (Just & Alloy, 1997). Ruminative response style has been found to be predictive of later depression and more pronounced depressive moods. Both the notions of response styles and of attributional styles propose that one's thoughts (whether ruminative or pessimistic in nature) can affect depressive moods.

Interestingly, Lewinsohn, Joiner, and Rohde (2001) have comparatively tested the cognitive theories of Beck and Seligman. Both theories propose a diathesis-stress process. The diathesis involves a vulnerability because of negative cognitions (Beck) or pessimistic attributional styles (Seligman). The vulnerability in the presence of stress (negative life events) results in depression, according to each theory. In a longitudinal study of adolescents, the investigators assessed (at Time 1) dysfunctional attitudes and negative attributional styles, as well as depressive symptoms, stressful life events, nondepressive diagnoses, past and family history of depression, and gender. Another assessment was conducted a year later (Time 2). The researchers wanted to find out which cognitive theory could better predict the onset of depression from Time 1 to Time 2. They wanted to control for initial level of depression (Time 1), family history of depression, and gender, because these three factors have been found to be related to the subsequent development of depression. Furthermore, it was important to assess nondepressive diagnosis because, according to both theories, the cognitive diathesis and stress should influence depression specifically, not just any disorder. Results tended to support Beck's theory over that of Seligman. High levels of negative cognitions coupled with stress predicted subsequent depression. Negative attributional style did not result in greater depression at high levels of stress. Only at low levels of stress did negative attributional styles predict depression (which is somewhat counterintuitive). The diathesis-stress models did not predict nondepressive disorders. Because this was a first comparative test of the two theories, further tests are necessary, using different measures and participant samples.

Sociocultural Explanations   Cross-cultural studies of mood disorders have found that prevalence rates and manifestation of symptoms vary considerably among different cultural groups and societies (Goodwin & Guze, 1984). For example, American Indians and Southeast Asians living in the United States appear to have higher rates of depression than are found among other Americans (Chung & Okazaki, 1991; Vega & Rumbaut, 1991). In China, Chinese patients with depression commonly present somatic (bodily) complaints rather than dysphoria (depression, anxiety, or restlessness), which indicates that the expression of symptoms for a particular disorder may differ from culture to culture (Kleinman, 1991). These findings suggest that factors such as culture, social experiences, and psychosocial stressors play an important role in mood disorders. We focus on the role of stressors and resources in mood disorders and then address the issue of the apparent higher rates of depression among women than men.

Stress and Depression   Conceptualizations of the role of stress in psychopathology in general and in depression in particular have typically proposed that stress is one of three broad factors that are important to consider: diathesis, stress, and resources or social supports. (See the discussion of stress in the chapter on psychological factors affecting medical conditions.)

Diathesis refers to the fact that because of genetic or constitutional or social conditions, certain individuals may have a predisposition or vulnerability to developing depression (Monroe & Simons, 1991). Stress may act as a trigger to activate this predisposition, especially when individuals lack resources to adjust to the stress. Presumably, individuals with low predisposition (compared with those with high predisposition) require greater levels of stress to become depressed.

The importance of stress in depression has been demonstrated. In a study of individuals' self-reports of daily stress and depressive moods, stressors such as dependency (e.g., having to depend on others) and interpersonal problems (e.g., having an argument with someone) tended to occur just before the onset of depressive symptoms (Stader & Hokanson, 1998). Other studies have shown that severe psychosocial stress, such as the death of a loved one, a life-threatening medical condition, and frustration of major life goals, often precedes the onset of major depression (Brown & Harris, 1989; Lewinsohn et al., 1988; Mazure, 1998; Paykel, 1982). This finding has led investigators to ask what kinds of stress lead to depression. Brown and Harris (1989) concluded that one severe stressor is more likely to cause depression than several minor stressors. In other words, several minor stressors do not seem to have the same effect as one very serious stressor. Moreover, in a survey of respondents in a study of stress and depressive symptoms, McGonagle and Kessler (1990) classified stress according to chronicity. *Chronic* stress was defined as beginning more than twelve months before the study; *acute* stress was defined as stress beginning within twelve months of the study. The investigators found that chronic stress was more highly related to depression than was acute stress, even though respondents rated both types of stress as equally severe. Perhaps stress that persists for a long time is viewed as being uncontrollable and stable. Stress also appears to be important in *relapse*—the recurrence of depression after treatment (Krantz & Moos, 1988; Lewinsohn, Zeiss, &

Cultural Differences in Symptoms and Treatment People from different cultures differ in the extent to which they display the symptoms listed in DSM-IV-TR for disorders. Chinese people with depression often exhibit somatic or bodily complaints instead of depressive symptoms, such as sadness and depression. Chinese medicine and acupuncture, not psychotherapy, are often the preferred forms of treatment for this disorder. Are such treatments effective?

Duncan, 1989). Finally, the particular type of stress is important to consider. For example, stressors such as loss and humiliation are associated with depression, whereas others, such as exposure to dangerous events, are more likely to be associated with anxiety (Kendler, Hettema, Butera, Gardner, & Prescott, 2003).

Cross-cultural studies have provided insight into culture-specific or more universal aspects of stress. Greenberger, Chen, Tally, and Dong (2000) compared the correlates of depressed mood among adolescents in China and the United States. In both cultures, "culture general" stressors such as parents' illness and family economic losses had similar effects on depressed mood. Cultural differences emerged for other variables. For instance, the correlations between depressed mood and poor relationships with parents, as well as poorer academic achievement, were higher for Chinese than for Americans, perhaps reflecting the Chinese cultural emphasis on family and achievements.

Why do some people who encounter stress develop depression, whereas others do not? People may differ in their degrees of vulnerability to depression. The vulnerability may be caused by biological factors (discussed later), psychosocial factors, or both. Hammen, Davilla, Brown, Ellicott, and Gitlin (1992) argued that the relationship between stress and depression is complex and interactive. In a longitudinal study of people with unipolar depression, the investigators found evidence that having dysfunctional parents who create stressful conditions in the family may influence an individual's vulnerability to stress. Individuals from such families may fail to acquire adaptive skills and positive self-images, which in turn brings on more

stress, which can trigger depression. (See the Mental Health and Society feature "Depression as a Cause of Depression?" for a further discussion of Hammen's ideas.) There is also evidence that harsh discipline in childhood is associated with levels of depression among people who experience a major depressive episode (Lara, Klein, & Kasch, 2000). Thus vulnerability may arise from early experiences in the family. And not only does stress cause depression, but depression can also cause stress (Pianta & Egeland, 1994). Cronkite, Moos, Twohey, Cohen, and Swindle (1998) found that people with depression have greater stress, more limited personal resources (are less easygoing), and fewer social resources (e.g., confidants). Thus the research suggests that stress and depression are bidirectional.

Adequate social support or resources may act as a buffer against depression when we are exposed to stress. To study the role of social resources in stress and depression, Holahan and Moos (1991) collected data on individuals at the beginning and end of a four-year period. Information was included on personality characteristics, family support (such as helpfulness of family members), stress, and depression. At the end of the four-year period, persons with positive personality traits and family support had less depression than those without these characteristics, even when initial level of depression (during year one) was controlled. The researchers speculated that personal or family resources help individuals cope and adjust to stress. A ten-year follow-up of clients with depression (Moos, Cronkite, & Moos, 1998) showed that social resources (such as more helpful friends, fewer family

MENTAL HEALTH AND SOCIETY
Depression as a Cause of Depression?

Research has shown that stress can trigger a depressive episode. There is increasing evidence that persons experiencing depression may seek or bring about conditions that tend to maintain their depression. College students who were diagnosed with depression were found to choose interaction with partners who perceived them unfavorably over those who perceived them favorably. Compared with other students, they also preferred friends and dating partners who had negative appraisals of them, and they were inclined to seek negative feedback from their roommates (Swann, Wenzlaff, Krull, & Pelham, 1992). People experiencing depression have also been found to be consistently rejected by others (Segrin & Abramson, 1994). Investigators raised the possibility that these individuals view themselves negatively. By choosing others who give negative feedback, they verify, stabi-

lize, and make predictable their unfavorable self-images.

In addition to seeking negative feedback, persons in depression may also create stress for themselves. Hammen (1991) conducted a one-year, longitudinal study of women with unipolar depression, bipolar disorder, chronic medical illness, or no illness or disorder. The purpose was to ascertain the relationship between stress and depression. Women with unipolar depression, bipolar depression, and medical illnesses had similar levels of stress, which were greater than those encountered by their healthy counterparts. An evaluation of the stressors determined the degree to which their occurrence either was certainly or almost certainly independent of the women's behaviors or characteristics or was likely to be caused by them. For example, some stressors (such as being robbed) were considered independent of the women's

behaviors, whereas others (such as initiating an argument with another person) were judged to be dependent on the women's behaviors. Women with unipolar depression were more likely than other women to have experienced stressors in which they were contributors and also to have stressors involving interpersonal interactions. Hammen (1991) speculated that these individuals may help contribute to the stress they encounter, which, in turn, provokes further depression!

This research should not be interpreted as demonstrating that individuals in depression purposely want to further their depressive states. Rather, depressive episodes and the associated negative self-images and cognitions may reduce coping skills, which then lead to situations (such as seeking negative feedback or creating stress for themselves) that in turn lead to further depression.

---

arguments, and sharing activities with friends) were important in remission. Further evidence of the effects of social support was found in a study of gay men at risk for AIDS (Hays, Turner, & Coates, 1992), which assessed their levels of depression, social supports, and HIV-related symptoms over a one-year period. Results indicated that men who were more satisfied with their social supports were subsequently less likely to suffer from depression.

The research on stress and depression has been impressive. Longitudinal research designs and prospective studies (studies of individuals before their depressive episodes occur) have helped decipher cause-and-effect relationships between stress and depression. The work has also moved from the study of broad variables (for example, stress) to more specific ones (for example, types of stress).

Gender and Depression Depression is far more common among women than among men regardless of region of the world, race and ethnicity, or social class

(Strickland, 1992). Although men and women have about the same rate of bipolar disorder, women's rates of major depression are twice as high as those for men (Kessler, 2003). Women are more likely than men to be seen in treatment and to be diagnosed with depression, but this may not necessarily mean that women are more prone to depression. Other explanations for this finding are noted in Table 11.4. First, women may simply be more likely than men to seek treatment when depressed; this tendency would make the reported depression rate for women higher, even if the actual male and female rates were equal. Second, women may be more willing to report their depression to other people. That is, the gender differences may occur in self-report behaviors rather than in actual depression rates. Third, diagnosticians or the diagnostic system may be biased toward finding depression among women (Caplan, 1995). And fourth, depression in men may take other forms and thus be given other diagnoses, such as substance dependency.

Some clinicians believe that these four possibilities account for only part of the gender difference in

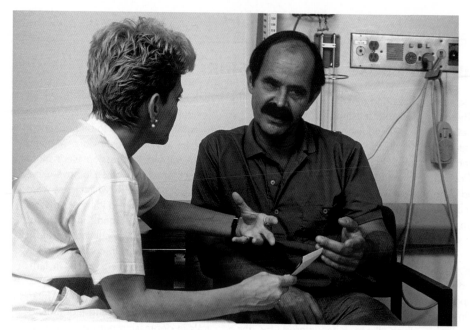

Vulnerability to Depression
Threatening medical conditions can serve as stressors that may elicit depression in vulnerable individuals. In working with an AIDS patient, the counselor is shown discussing treatment options and the value of gaining assistance from others. In cases of stress such as this, social support can serve as a buffer against depression. Why are social supports important in preventing depression?

depression and that women really do have much higher rates of depression (Radloff & Rae, 1981). Attempts to explain these differences have focused on physiological or social psychological factors.

Although biological factors, such as genetic or hormonal differences between the sexes, may account for the gender differences in depression, relatively little research has been conducted on these factors. Moreover, available findings are inconsistent with respect to hormonal changes and depression. This fact has led researchers to propose social or psychological

factors, one of which is women's traditional gender role. Women have been encouraged to present themselves as attractive, sensitive to other people, and passive in relationships (Strickland, 1992). This subservience to men, combined with a lack of occupational opportunities, may have produced more depression in women (Bernard, 1976). Women who fulfill the gender-role expectations may be more likely than men to experience lack of control in life situations. They may then attribute their "helplessness" to an imagined lack of personal worth. Interestingly, women who are

---

TABLE 11.4 Explaining the Findings That Rates of Depression Are Higher Among Women Than Among Men

The Gender Differences Only Appear to Be Real Because

- Women may be more likely to seek treatment.
- Women may be more willing to report their depression to other people.
- Diagnosticians or the diagnostic system may be gender biased.
- Men may exhibit depression in different ways and may be given other diagnoses.

The Gender Differences Are Real Because

- Genetic or hormonal differences between genders may account for higher depression levels among women.
- Women are subjected to gender roles that may be unfulfilling and that limit occupational opportunities.
- Gender roles may lead to feelings of helplessness.
- Traditional feminine roles may be less successful at eliciting positive reinforcement from others, compared with traditional male roles, which foster assertive and forceful behavior.

Gender and Depression Among the Amish, men and women appear to have similar rates of depression. Egeland and Hostetter (1983) believe that gender roles may affect depression rates. Gender roles, such as working together in the fields, are similar for Amish men and women and may account for the lack of gender differences in rates of depression. What are the implications of the findings for a genetic or environmental explanation of depression?

not employed outside the home and who are raising children are particularly vulnerable to depression (Gotlib, 1992). Finally, the traditional feminine gender role behaviors (gentleness, emotionality, and self-subordination) may not be so successful in eliciting reinforcement from others as the assertive and more forceful responses typically associated with males.

In a review of different explanations for the gender differences in rates of depression, Nolen-Hoeksema (1987) concluded that none truly accounts for the observed differences. She hypothesized that the way a person responds to depressed moods contributes to the severity, chronicity, and recurrence of depressive episodes. In her view, women tend to ruminate and amplify their depressive moods, and men tend to dampen or find means to minimize dysphoria. Nolen-Hoeksema (1991) found that when individuals tracked their depressed moods and responses to these moods for one month, women were more likely than men to ruminate in response to depressed moods. Those who tended to ruminate had longer periods of depressed moods, and when tendency to ruminate was statistically controlled, gender differences in duration of depressed moods disappeared.

Egeland and Hostetter (1983) also speculated that responses to depressive moods may affect observed rates of depression. In their study of an Amish religious community in Pennsylvania, they found that males and females have the same rates for depression. The researchers noted that because Amish men do not show alcoholism or antisocial behaviors, their depression cannot be masked. Additionally, Amish women,

like the men, must work outside the home, so engaging in a sick (depressed) role is discouraged. Although role behavior may help explain some of the differences in rates of depression between women and men, it is not clear whether the explanation is enough to account for the vast differences that have been recorded. The findings suggest that some aspect of the environment may interact with a woman's biology to account for the disproportionate incidence of depression among women (U.S. Surgeon General, 1999).

The work on sociocultural or psychosocial influences provides a perspective on how cultural, institutional, and environmental conditions affect depression. Now let us turn to theories that are primarily biological in nature.

Biological Perspectives on Mood Disorders

Biological approaches to the causes of mood or affective disorders generally focus on genetic predisposition, physiological dysfunction, or combinations of the two.

The Role of Heredity Mood disorders tend to run in families, and the same type of disorder is generally found among members of the same family (American Psychiatric Association, 2000; Perris, 1966; Winokur, Clayton, & Reich, 1969). As we have noted in earlier chapters, one way to assess the role of heredity is to compare the incidence of disorders among the biological and adoptive families of people who were adopted early in life and who had the disorders. If heredity is more important, then biological families (which contributed the genetic makeup) should show a high incidence of the disorders. If environment is more important, then adoptive families (which provided the early environment) should show a high incidence. The results of such a comparison indicated that the incidence of mood disorders was higher among the biological families than among the adoptive families; the latter showed an incidence similar to that of the general population (American Psychiatric Association, 2000).

Another way to study the possible genetic transmission of mood disorders is to compare identical and fraternal twins. Nine such studies of twins have been reported. The concordance rate (the probability of one twin having the same disorder as the other twin) for bipolar disorders was 72 percent for identical (monozygotic—MZ) twins and 14 percent for fraternal (dizygotic—DZ) twins. A study of MZ and DZ twins seventy-five years of age or older also revealed a higher concordance rate for depressive symptoms among MZ than among DZ twins (McGue & Christensen, 1997). The studies suggest that the genetic component is extremely important, although nongenetic factors also appear to be influential (Baron, 1991). By contrast, the concordance rate for unipolar mood disorders was only 40 percent for MZ twins and 11 percent for DZ twins (Goodwin & Guze, 1984).

Both of these research approaches (and others) consistently turn up evidence of genetic influence on mood disorders. Moreover, the bulk of the research suggests that heredity is a stronger factor in bipolar mood disorders than in unipolar disorders (Reus, 1988). Nevertheless, the rate of bipolar disorders in the families of patients with unipolar depression is three to four times the rate in controls (Dubovsky & Buzan, 1999). This suggests that the two disorders are somehow related or under the influence of common factors.

Egeland and colleagues (1987) also provided some evidence of genetic involvement in bipolar disorders. Again studying the Amish religious community in Pennsylvania, these investigators found a number of people with bipolar disorders, many of whom had the same ancestors. Using sophisticated techniques, they found that a gene located on a specific region of a chromosome was associated with mood disorders among the Amish. Gershon, Berrettini, Nurnberger, and Goldin (1989) could not replicate the findings in other populations, although the discrepancy in findings could be a result of the different populations studied. They noted that technological advancements in instrumentation, statistical genetic techniques, and molecular biology have allowed researchers to become increasingly sophisticated in the study of biological aspects of mood disorders.

Although heredity appears to be important, especially in bipolar disorders, researchers show little consensus on the appropriate model for the transmission of affective disorders. Some researchers have proposed that depression is caused by one primary gene rather than many genes; most favor a polygenetic theory over a monogenetic theory (Gershon et al., 1989).

Neurotransmitters and Mood Disorders   But how is heredity involved in the major mood disorders? A growing number of researchers believe that genetic factors influence the amounts of *catecholamines*—a group of substances, including norepinephrine, dopamine, and serotonin—that are found at specific sites in the brain. These substances, called **neurotransmitters,** help transmit nerve impulses from one neuron to another. They may mediate between active motor behavior and emotions.

Nerve impulses are transmitted from neuron to neuron across *synapses,* which are small gaps between the axon (or transmitting end) of one neuron and the dendrites (or receiving end) of a receptor neuron. In Figure 11.5, Neuron A is the transmitting neuron, and Neuron B is the receptor neuron. For a nerve impulse to travel from A to B, the axon at A must release a neurotransmitter into the synaptic gap, thereby stimulating B to fire, or transmit the impulse. According to the *catecholamine hypothesis,* depression is caused by a deficit of specific neurotransmitters at brain synapses; similarly, mania is presumed to be caused by an oversupply of these substances (Bunney, Pert, Rosenblatt, Pert, & Gallaper, 1979).

As in other areas, most research has focused on the study of depression. Figure 11.5 illustrates two mechanisms, either of which could cause the amount of neurotransmitters in the synapses to be insufficient: (1) neurotransmitters are broken down or chemically depleted by the enzyme monoamine oxidase (MAO), which is normally found in the body; (2) neurotransmitters are reabsorbed by the releasing neuron in the process of *reuptake.*

Support for the catecholamine hypothesis comes from two lines of research. In the first, researchers have established a connection between levels of neurotransmitters and motor activity. In one study, researchers put rats in stressful situations—for example, a series of inescapable shocks—and found that the level of norepinephrine in the rats' brains was reduced. The animals with these low levels showed "depressive" behaviors, such as motor passivity and an inability to learn avoidance-escape responses. Giving rats a drug that depletes brain norepinephrine also results in motor passivity and an inability to learn (Weiss, Glazer, & Pohorecky, 1975).

The second line of support for the catecholamine hypothesis comes from studies of the effects of antidepressant medication on neurotransmitters and on

FIGURE 11.5 The Catecholamine Hypothesis: A Proposed Connection Between Neurotransmitters and Depression   On the left is a representation of the production of neurotransmitter substances at a synapse between two neurons in the brain of a person with no depression. Some of the neurotransmitter is reabsorbed by the transmitting neuron in a process known as *reuptake*. Neurotransmitters are also broken down or chemically depleted by the enzyme monoamine oxidase (MAO), which is normally found in the body. In people with depression, either or both of these two processes may reduce neurotransmitters to a level that is insufficient for normal functioning.

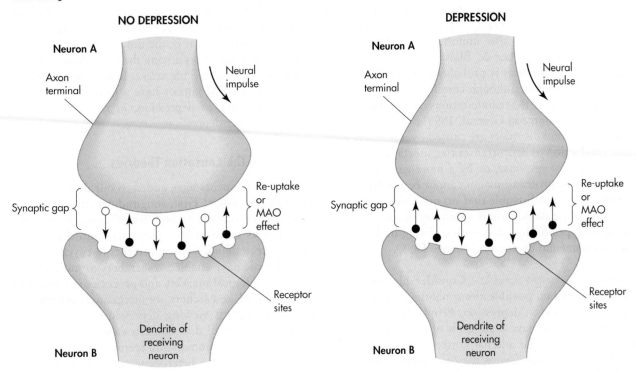

mood changes. Antidepressant medications appear to increase the level of neurotransmitters. One group, the MAOIs, blocks the effects of MAO in breaking down the neurotransmitters. Another group, the tricyclic drugs, blocks the reuptake of certain transmitter substances. Fluoxetine (Prozac) seems to block the reuptake of serotonin in particular.

Further support comes from the study in which rats were subjected to inescapable shocks. If the rats are given a drug that protects against the depletion of norepinephrine, and if this drug is administered before an experience with inescapable shock, the rats become immunized against passivity and poor learning (Weiss et al., 1975). Clearly, these findings suggest the importance of norepinephrine in depressive behaviors. In addition, they also show that environmental stressors produce biochemical and behavioral changes and, conversely, that biochemical changes can produce behavioral effects similar to those of environmental stressors. Even so, no matter how similar laboratory animals and people may be in various respects, the behavior of animals is not the same as the behavior of

human beings. Investigators therefore need more evidence of a direct link between the role of neurotransmitters and depressive behaviors in human beings.

Some evidence implicating neurotransmitters in human depression and mania has been obtained accidentally. For example, it was discovered that when the drug reserpine was used in treating hypertension, many patients became depressed. (*Reserpine* depletes the level of neurotransmitters in the brain.) Similarly, the drug iproniazid, given to tubercular patients, elevated the mood of those who were depressed. (*Iproniazid* inhibits the destruction of neurotransmitters.) Thus mood levels in human beings were found to vary with the level of neurotransmitters or of neurotransmitter activity in the brain. These variations are consistent with the catecholamine hypothesis.

Some researchers have suggested that the level, or amount, of neurotransmitters present is not the primary factor. They noted that, to travel from one neuron to another, an electrical impulse must release neurotransmitters that stimulate the receiving neuron. The problem may not be the amount of neurotransmitter made available by the sending neuron but rather a dysfunction in the reception of the neurotransmitter by the receiving neuron (Sulser, 1979). Other researchers suggest that the catecholamine hypothesis may be simplistic. They note, for example, that drugs that raise the level of neurotransmitters in the synapse trigger such increases immediately, yet the alleviation of depressive symptoms may be delayed for several weeks after this increase. This delay may indicate that other factors, such as longer term membrane responses to changes in neurotransmitters, are also important in alleviating depression (Rivas-Vazquez & Blais, 1997). Thus the catecholamine hypothesis is probably too simplistic in explaining depression, although catecholamine impairment may be one of the manifestations or correlates of depression (U.S. Surgeon General, 1999).

Whether mood disorders are caused by a deficiency in the production of neurotransmitter substances, by a blunted receptor response, or by a more general dysregulation in neurotransmission cannot be resolved at this time. It is also possible that no one cause will be isolated because depression is a heterogeneous collection of subtypes of disorders with differing biological and environmental precursors (Mann, 1989).

Abnormal Cortisol Levels   Considerable interest has also focused on possible abnormalities in neuroendocrine regulation in depression. People experiencing depression tend to have high levels of *cortisol*, a hormone secreted by the adrenal cortex. Cortisol levels are measured by the *dexamethasone suppression test (DST)*. In this test, patients are given dexamethasone, which normally suppresses the cortisol secretion. Studies in different countries have shown that people with depression register higher blood levels of cortisol than are found in nondepressed people (World Health Organization, 1987) and that prognosis for recovery is poorer when these levels are not suppressed (Reus, 1988). Whether cortisol helps cause depression or is produced by depression, however, is still unclear. Furthermore, measuring cortisol levels accurately has been difficult, and patients with other disorders often exhibit responses similar to those of individuals with depression (Free & Oei, 1989). Although the DST may eventually provide some insight into the physiology of mood disorders, its use as a screening or diagnostic tool is questionable (Dubovsky & Buzan, 1999).

REM Sleep Disturbances   Findings of a different sort have also aroused interest in the biological or physiological processes of depression. For example, the sleep patterns of adults with depression differ from those of other people, particularly during rapid eye movement

(REM) sleep. (There are several stages of sleep; during REM sleep the eyes move rapidly, and dreaming occurs.) Depression is linked with a relatively rapid onset of, and an increase in, REM sleep (Goodwin & Guze, 1984). Moreover, reducing the REM sleep of persons with depression seems to help (Vogel, Vogel, McAbee, & Thurmond, 1980). Why sleep patterns are linked to depression is unclear. Monroe, Thase, and Simons (1992) found that some patients in depression experienced severe, acute life stress, whereas others did not. REM latency (that is, the time before REM occurs during sleep) was short among the individuals who did not experience severe life stress. It may be that those with reduced REM latency have a lower threshold for the development of depression, in that less stress is needed to affect depression.

Evaluating the Causation Theories

Three developments have added to our understanding of mood disorders. First, longitudinal or prospective studies have allowed greater insights into the possible causal links between life experiences and depression. Second, technological advancements in psychophysiological tools have enabled researchers to more clearly identify biological markers and processes in mood disorders. Third, researchers are increasingly attentive to the possibility of viewing depression as a heterogeneous collection of disorders. In view of the fact that depression is so common and seemingly influenced by so many factors, the heterogeneous view of the disorder is not surprising. There is even evidence that different cognitive models of depression (such as ones proposed by Beck and by Abramson) may describe cognitive processes accurately but for different kinds of depressive disorders (Spangler et al., 1997).

The theories of depression presented in this chapter explain certain aspects of the disturbance, but all have weaknesses. According to the psychodynamic perspective, loss and separation provoke a depressive reaction. But what determines the extent and severity of depression? Fixation at the oral stage, dependency, and symbolic loss are psychodynamic concepts that are difficult to test. The psychodynamic assumption that depression may simply be hostility turned inward on the self also seems open to question. When some patients with depression experienced success on experimental tasks, their self-esteem and optimism increased. If depression is hostility turned inward, why would success alleviate some of its symptoms?

As we have noted, Beck's idea is that the tendency to think in negative terms helps produce depression. His theory has, over time, become increasingly complex. To

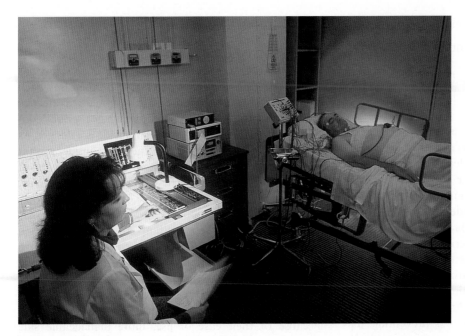

Sleep Disturbances and Depression Sleep patterns have been linked to depression. For example, rapid eye movement during sleep occurs more often among those who have depression than among those who do not. The reasons for this are unclear. Here, a researcher is monitoring a man's sleep. Can you find reasons for depression being associated with sleep disturbances?

what extent is depression caused by negative thoughts and to what extent is it the effect of them? Aren't cognitive aspects of depression overemphasized relative to environmental stressors that evoke depression? Lewinsohn's behavioral theory and Seligman's learned helplessness theory are well grounded in research findings. Lewinsohn's work has mainly shown a relationship between depression and inadequate positive reinforcement. But do these low rates of reinforcement actually cause depression? Seligman has shown that learned helplessness and certain attributions can lead to depressive behaviors. However, this model explains only certain kinds of depression—mainly reactions to stress. How can behavioral and cognitive theorists present a more convincing account of the development of manic behaviors?

Endogenous (congenital) factors seem to play a crucial role in mood disorders. The precise genetic mechanisms are not known, but research into biochemical factors or neurotransmitters seems quite promising.

One good way to think about mood disorders is to see them as a range of mood states resulting from an interaction between environmental and biological factors (U.S. Surgeon General, 1999). On one end of the range is mild sadness, then normal grief and the specific affective disorders, and, at the other end of the range, the major mood disorders. The causes of milder instances of depression (or, for that matter, mania) may tend to be more external. In mood disorders in the middle of the spectrum, both external and internal factors may be important. In severe disorders, includ-

ing psychotic forms of the major mood disorders, endogenous factors may become more prominent.

The Treatment of Mood Disorders

Biological approaches to the treatment of mood disorders are generally based on the catecholamine hypothesis. That is, treatment consists primarily of controlling the level of neurotransmitters at brain synapses. Psychological treatment also seems to offer promise for persons with depression.

Myth vs Reality

Myth: Saint John's Wort has been proven to be effective in alleviating depression.

Reality: Saint John's Wort (*Hypericum perforatum* plant) has been popularly used by consumers to treat depression. It can be found in the herbal supplement section of most pharmacies in the United States. Despite its popularity, little rigorous research has been conducted to establish its effectiveness or possible side effects. Research, primarily in Germany, has obtained positive results in alleviating mild to moderate depression with only mild gastrointestinal side effects. However, most of these studies have had methodological weaknesses, and basic questions concerning the mechanisms of action of the substance remain (U.S. Surgeon General, 1999).

Biomedical Treatments for Depressive Disorders

Biomedical treatments are interventions that alter the physical or biochemical state of the patient. They include the use of medication and electroconvulsive therapy.

Medication   According to the U.S. Surgeon General (1999), antidepressant medications are effective across the full range of severity of depressive episodes, although effectiveness is greater with less severe depressive episodes. There are four kinds of antidepressant medication: tricyclic antidepressants (TCAs), heterocyclic antidepressants (HCAs), monoamine oxidase inhibitors (MAOIs), and selective serotonin reuptake inhibitors (SSRIs). Each medication is designed to heighten the level of a target neurotransmitter at the neuronal synapse. This heightening can be accomplished by (1) boosting the neurotransmitter's synthesis, (2) blocking its degradation, (3) preventing its reuptake from the synapse, or (4) mimicking its binding to postsynaptic receptors. For example, TCAs seem to block the reuptake of norepinephrine, thereby leaving more norepinephrine at the synapses. These higher levels of residual norepinephrine seem to be linked with reduced depressive symptoms. The tricyclics, however, may cause side effects. Reactions include drowsiness, insomnia, agitation, fine tremors, blurred vision, dry mouth, and reduced sexual ability.

MAOIs also work by increasing the level of norepinephrine at the brain synapses. Rather than blocking reuptake as the tricyclics do, the MAOIs prevent the MAO enzyme (which is normally found in the body) from breaking down norepinephrine that is already available at the synapse. Both MAOIs and tricyclic antidepressants may act in ways more complicated than previously believed. There is growing suspicion that the drugs may affect not only the levels of neurotransmitters at synapses but also the sensitivity of receptors on the receiving (postsynaptic) neurons.

MAOIs are currently prescribed for patients with depression who have not responded well to treatment with tricyclics. But MAOIs also have many side effects, including insomnia, irritability, dizziness, constipation, and impotence. The most serious side effect, however, is tyramine-cheese incompatibility. One normal function of the MAO enzyme is to break down tyramine, a substance found in many cheeses, as well as in some beers, wines, pickled products, and chocolate. Because the MAOIs interfere with this function, people using these drugs must severely restrict their intake of tyramine. Failure to do so triggers the tyramine-cheese reaction, which begins with increased blood pressure, vomiting, and muscle twitching and can, if untreated, result in intracranial bleeding, followed by death.

Such side effects are a major drawback of the antidepressant drugs, and careful monitoring of the patient's reactions is thus absolutely necessary. Another drawback is that the antidepressant drugs are essentially ineffective during the first two weeks of use, which is a serious concern, particularly in cases in which suicide is a danger. As mentioned earlier, the effectiveness of antidepressant drugs may be caused by changes in the sensitivity of postsynaptic receptors. These changes in sensitivity, however, seem to require a couple of weeks to develop.

SSRIs block the reuptake of serotonin. The SSRIs include the drugs Prozac (fluoxetine hydrochloride), Paxil (paroxetine), and Zoloft (sertraline). They have become quite popular in the treatment of depression because they seem to have fewer side effects and to be at least as effective as the other tricyclics. In fact, SSRIs are "favored" as the first-line medication for depression because of their ease of use, more manageable side effects, safety in overdose, and cost (U.S. Surgeon General, 1999). Many patients report much relief after taking the medication. However, it should be noted that SSRIs, as well as other drugs used to treat mood disorders, restore functioning of patients but may not halt the disease process (Delgado & Gelenberg, 2001). One issue that has recently arisen over the use of certain SSRIs is whether suicide risk, especially among young people who take the drugs, is increased. Under investigation by the Federal Drug Administration is the charge that Paxil and other SSRIs can contribute to young people committing suicide (Lemonick, 2004). At this point, the side effects of SSRIs are unclear (Mears, 2004), and the drugs are widely prescribed for depression.

Sometimes effectiveness can be improved by the application of systematic procedures. The Texas Medication Algorithm Project is an evidence-based practice in which a flow chart is used to help clinicians make the best choice of medications. The systematic application of the procedures has been found to be more effective than treatment as usual for depression and bipolar disorders (President's New Freedom Commission on Mental Health, 2003).

Electroconvulsive Therapy   Electroconvulsive therapy (ECT) is generally reserved for patients with severe unipolar depression who have not responded to antidepressant medications. The procedure is also described in the chapter on therapeutic interventions; in essence, it consists of applying a moderate electrical voltage to the person's brain for up to half a second. The patient's response to the voltage is a convulsion (seizure) lasting thirty to forty seconds, followed by a five- to thirty-minute coma.

Most patients with serious depression show at least a temporary improvement after about four ECT treatments (Campbell, 1981). The ECT mechanism is not fully understood; it may operate on neurotransmitters at the synapses, as do antidepressants. Some of the decrease in symptoms may also be due to the amnesia that develops for a short time after the treatment. One major advantage of ECT is that the response to treatment is relatively fast (Gangadhar, Kapur, & Kalyanasundaram, 1982). However, common side effects include headaches, confusion, and memory loss. And many patients are terrified of ECT. In about 1 of every 1,000 cases, serious medical complications occur (Goldman, 1988). The Mental Health and Society feature "I Am Suffering from Depression" describes a case in which medication was used in combination with ECT to treat a bipolar affective disorder. Many clinicians believe that ECT is the most rapid and effective treatment for major depressive episodes (Weiner & Krystal, 2001). The U.S. Surgeon General (U.S. Surgeon General, 1999) considers ECT as among those treatments that are effective for severe depression. Still, ECT is controversial, and critics have urged that it be banned as a form of treatment (see the Critical Thinking feature "Should Electroconvulsive Shock Treatment for Depression Be Banned?" for more on this idea).

Psychotherapy and Behavioral Treatments for Depressive Disorders

Because the use of antidepressant medication or ECT involves a number of disadvantages, clinicians have sought other approaches to either supplement or replace medical treatment of depression. A variety of psychological forms of treatment have been used, such as psychoanalysis, behavior therapy, group psychotherapy, and family therapies—all with some success (Hirschfield & Shea, 1985; McDermut, Miller, & Brown, 2001).

Treatment strategies reflect the theoretical orientation of the therapists. For example, psychodynamic therapists attempt to help their clients gain insight into unconscious and unresolved feelings of separation or anger. To this end, the therapist interprets the client's free associations, reports of dreams, resistances, and transferences (see the chapter on therapeutic interventions). Psychodynamic therapies of depression have not been rigorously studied, but some investigations suggest that brief dynamic therapy appears to be effective in reducing the depressive symptoms of patients (Gabbard, 2001). In contrast to psychodynamic therapists, behavioral therapists may believe that reduced reinforcement is responsible for depression. They would attempt to teach clients to increase their exposure to pleasurable events and activities and to improve their social skills and interactions.

Two types of treatment—interpersonal psychotherapy and cognitive-behavioral therapy—have been intensively examined for their effectiveness in depressive disorders. There is evidence that the two treatments are effective (and in some studies, just as effective as antidepressant medications), particularly in the treatment of less severe cases of unipolar depression (Cardemil & Barber, 2001; Dubovsky & Buzan, 1999; President's New Freedom Commission on Mental Health, 2003).

Interpersonal Psychotherapy Interpersonal psychotherapy is a short-term, psychodynamic-eclectic type of treatment for depression. It targets the client's interpersonal relationships and uses strategies found in psychodynamic, cognitive-behavioral, and other forms of therapy (Klerman, Weissman, Rounsavelle, & Chevron, 1984). The assumptions underlying interpersonal psychotherapy are that depression occurs within an interpersonal context and, accordingly, that interpersonal relationship issues must be addressed. The focus is on conflicts and problems that occur in these relationships. Clients gain insight into conflicts in social relationships and strive to change these relationships. For example, by improving communications with others, by identifying role conflicts, and by increasing social skills, clients come to find relationships more satisfying and pleasant. Although interpersonal psychotherapy resembles psychoanalysis and psychodynamic approaches in acknowledging the role of early life experiences and traumas, it is oriented primarily toward present, not past, relationships. As we discuss later, interpersonal psychotherapy has been found to be effective in the treatment of depression.

Cognitive-Behavioral Therapy As its name implies, cognitive-behavioral therapy combines cognitive and behavioral strategies. The cognitive component involves teaching the patient the following (Beck, Rush, Shaw, & Emery, 1979):

- to identify negative, self-critical thoughts (cognitions) that occur automatically,

- to note the connection between negative thoughts and the resulting depression,

- to carefully examine each negative thought and decide whether it can be supported,

- to try to replace distorted negative thoughts with realistic interpretations of each situation.

Cognitive therapists believe that distorted thoughts cause psychological problems such as depression and

MENTAL HEALTH AND SOCIETY

I Am Suffering from Depression

Dr. Norman Endler, a prominent psychologist, stable family man, and chairman of the psychology department at York University, wrote:

I honestly felt subhuman, lower than the lowest vermin. Furthermore, I was self-deprecatory and could not understand why anyone would want to associate with me, let alone love me. ...

I was also positive that I was going to be fired from the university because of incompetence and that we could become destitute—that we would go broke.

... I was positive that I was a fraud and phony and that I didn't deserve my Ph.D. I didn't deserve to have tenure; I didn't deserve to be a full professor; I didn't deserve to be chairman of the psychology department.

... I couldn't understand how I had written the books and journal articles that I had and how they had been accepted for publication. (Endler, 1982, pp. 45–48)

These comments are from a poignant and very explicit book in which Endler described his experiences with bipolar disorder and his reactions to treatment. Until the spring of 1977, Endler felt fine. He was at the height of his successful career. He was active in sports and was constantly on the move. In retrospect, Endler realized that he was showing evidence of hypomania as early as the fall of 1976, but not until the following April did he became aware that something was wrong. He had difficulty sleeping and had lost his sex drive. "I had gone from being a winner to feeling like a loser. Depression had turned it around for me. From being on top of the world in the fall, I suddenly felt useless, inept, sad, and anxious in the spring" (p. 11).

Endler sought treatment and was administered several drugs that did not prove effective. He was then given electroconvulsive therapy (ECT). Endler described his reaction to ECT, as well as the way the treatment was administered.

I was asked to lie down on a cot and was wheeled into the ECT room proper. It was about eight o'clock. A needle was injected into my arm and I was told to count back from 100. I got about as far as 91. The next thing I knew I was in the recovery room and it was about eight-fifteen. I was slightly groggy and tired but not confused. (Endler, 1982, p. 81)

After about seven ECT sessions, his depression lifted dramatically: "My holiday of darkness was over and fall arrived with a bang!" (p. 83).

The next few months were free of depression, and Endler enjoyed everything he did. Later, he realized that he was again experiencing hypomania during this period. He was a bit euphoric, energetic, and active; he talked incessantly. Then depression struck again. He recognized that he was experiencing the initial signs of depression and again underwent drug treatment and ECT. This time, however, the treatments were ineffective. Slowly, over the course of about two years, he improved with the aid of medication.

Endler concludes by offering some advice. First, when people think they are depressed, they should seek treatment immediately. Second, some combinations of treatments, such as psychotherapy, antidepressant drugs, and ECT, may be effective. Third, the person's family can have an important effect on recovery: when a family member has severe depression, existing family conflicts may become exacerbated. A supportive and understanding family can help a person survive this disorder.

Depression is a common pervasive illness affecting all social classes, but it is eminently treatable. A great deal of heartbreak can be avoided by early detection and treatment. There is nothing to be ashamed of. There is no stigma attached to having an affective disorder. It is unwise to try to hide it and not seek help. I lived to tell and to write about it. ...

As of this writing ... I have been symptom-free for almost three years. ... I am not experiencing an emotional crisis and I hope I never do again. ... I am reminded of a telephone conversation I had with my wife. ... I mentioned that I had to do a lot of work to finish the first draft of [his] book, before I left Stanford at the end of the month. Beatty said to me, "What's so terrible if you don't finish?" That put it all in perspective for me. I intend to live life to the fullest, but carefully. The sun will rise and shine whether or not I finish things today. But it's nice knowing that I did finish the first draft ... before I left Stanford! (Endler, 1982, pp. 167–169)

Source: Endler (1982).

CRITICAL THINKING

Should Electroconvulsive Shock Treatment for Depression Be Banned?

I completed three ECT sessions. ... I could not account for the activities of several days, and I made uncharacteristic mistakes in writing. I had trouble with vocabulary. ... I do recommend ECT ... when medications have failed. ... But I do not recommend it lightly. I tell them this can help, maybe quickly, maybe dramatically. I warn them about short-term memory problems and the possibility for subtler cognitive changes. (Mahler, 2004, p. 99)

On the editorial page of *USA Today*, two views of electroconvulsive therapy (ECT) were presented:

Shock therapy is gaining new respectability these days. ... But ... this drastic, potentially deadly treatment is still far too poorly understood. ... Even proponents disagree on how the jolts work, and the cheery benefits are short-lived. ... Meanwhile, the long-term effects can be devastating. They include confusion, memory loss, heart failure, and in some patients, death. ("Patients, public need full story on shock therapy," *USA Today*, December 8, 1995, p. 12A)

I am astounded at *USA Today's* use of inaccuracies and half-truths

this week to malign electroconvulsive therapy, an often lifesaving medical treatment. Thousands of psychiatrists and neuroscientists agree: ECT is a safe and effective treatment for certain serious illnesses. Thousands of patients are living proof. (William Reid, "Don't malign treatment," *USA Today*, December 8, 1995, p. 12A)

These opposing viewpoints are not unusual. Testimonies can be obtained from patients and therapists wholeheartedly supporting either the use or the abolition of ECT. Proponents argue that convulsive spasms of the body from ECT have been controlled by muscle relaxants and, although the reasons are unclear, ECT seems to work. In fact, Weiner and Krystal (2001) believe that because of the negative portrayals of ECT in the media, which often cast ECT as a crude and inhumane means of behavioral control, advances have been made in ECT methodology. Modern techniques have reduced side effects, and the treatment has been found to be effective with severe depression (U.S. Surgeon General, 1999). The United Kingdom government funded a comprehensive literature review to identify all randomized trials involv-

ing ECT in patients with depression over the past forty years (Geddes, 2003). The review revealed that ECT was effective, in some cases more effective than medication, in treating depression. The main adverse effect was impaired cognitive ability, especially memory loss. The investigator concluded that ECT remains an important treatment option for the management of severe depression. Critics are concerned with confusion, memory loss, and other side effects that may occur, as well as the troublesome inability to explain why ECT works. Why is the controversy over ECT so strong? And how do we decide when to ban a certain form of treatment? Clearly, effectiveness is only one factor to consider in evaluations of treatment. What other kinds of information do we need to make a decision? After reading about ECT in this chapter, do you feel it should be banned? (Before answering, you might want to take a quick look at the chapter on therapeutic interventions, which also discusses ECT, as well as the Mental Health and Society feature in this chapter.)

that changing the distorted thoughts can eliminate the depression.

At the outset of the cognitive therapy, the client is usually asked to begin monitoring his or her negative thoughts and to list them on a chart. It is important for the client to include all the thoughts and emotions associated with each distressing event that takes place each day (see Figure 11.6).

The client brings the chart to the session each week, and the therapist uses it to demonstrate that the client's

distress is being caused by his or her own unnecessarily negative thoughts. The client's own rational alternatives to these thoughts are discussed, and the client makes a conscious effort to adopt those alternatives that seem plausible. The goal of the cognitive part of the therapy is to train the client to automatically substitute logical interpretations for self-denigrating thoughts. Cognitive therapists maintain that when a patient's thoughts about himself or herself become more consistently positive, the emotions follow suit.

FIGURE 11.6 Daily Cognition Chart for a Typical Client with Depression Cognitive-behavioral therapists use such charts to demonstrate to clients that they are causing their own negative thoughts and that they can substitute more positive thoughts instead.

Date	Situation	Automatic Thoughts	Emotions	Rational Alternative	Emotion
2/9	I sat home all alone on a Fri. night.	Nobody likes me or I would have been asked out.	Depressed	Most people know that I usually work Fri. nights. Maybe nobody knew I had the night off.	Relief, contentment
2/10	I had trouble understanding my reading assignment.	I must be an idiot. This should be an easy subject.	Depressed, anxious	If I don't understand the material, I bet a number of others don't either.	Calm, determined

Some therapists also assign reading materials that help teach clients to think positively and to overcome negative cognitions (*bibliotherapy*). The beneficial impact of such procedures has remained even three years after treatment (Smith, Floyd, Scogin, & Jamison, 1997).

The second part of the cognitive-behavioral approach is behavior therapy, which is usually indicated in cases of severe depression in which the patient is virtually inactive. One primary assumption underlying this approach is that the patient is not doing enough pleasant, rewarding activities. During depression, people tend to belittle themselves and to withdraw from others; they then interpret their self-imposed social isolation as a sign of being unpopular and inadequate (Lewinsohn, 1977).

To address this problem, the therapist asks the patient to keep a daily activity schedule, listing life events hour by hour and rating the "pleasantness" of each event. When a person is asked to monitor and rate events or activities, activities generally increase in frequency. This in itself is a worthwhile strategy for people with severe depression; simply getting them to engage in more activities increases the chance that they will become involved in some pleasant, reinforcing events. The patient's chart of this information also helps the therapist spot specific patterns of activity. For instance, a client who insists that he or she does not enjoy anything may rate as "slightly pleasant" time spent outdoors. The therapist would point out this pattern to the client and encourage that person to spend more time outdoors (Beck, Rush, et al., 1979).

Once the client becomes more active, the therapist may ask the person to attend a social skills training program. Improvements in social skills generally help clients become more socially involved and can make that involvement rewarding (Hersen, Bellack, & Himmelhoch, 1980).

Both interpersonal psychotherapy and cognitive-behavioral therapy have been found to be effective treatments for depression. In an intensive study, clients suffering from depression were randomly assigned to one of four treatment conditions for four months: interpersonal psychotherapy, cognitive-behavioral therapy, imipramine plus clinical management, and pill-placebo plus clinical management (Elkin, 1994; Elkin et al., 1995). Imipramine, a tricyclic drug, was included in the design because its effectiveness has been studied and the other treatments could be compared with it. The imipramine and pill-placebo conditions were paired with clinical management (in which minimal supportive therapy was provided) because of the ethical need to provide some therapy for clients in the pill-placebo and imipramine conditions. Results indicated that, in general, the interpersonal psychotherapy, cognitive-behavioral, and imipramine treatments were equally effective in reducing depression. All were significantly more effective than the pill-placebo condition. However, specific effects were influenced by the initial severity of disturbance. In addition, many of the clients who showed major improvement at the end of treatment (regardless of treatment condition) had relapsed and were suffering from depression again eighteen months following treatment. Thus interpersonal psychotherapy, cognitive-behavioral therapy, and imipramine appear to be effective, although some of the effects diminish over time.

Hollon, DeRubeis, and Seligman (1992) found that cognitive therapy may reduce the risk of episodes of depression occurring after treatment. Clients treated with cognitive therapy were less likely to develop subsequent symptoms of depression than were clients treated pharmacologically. The researchers believe that cognitive changes in explanatory styles and attributions among the clients in cognitive therapy may help prevent depressive symptoms. In fact, cognitive-behavioral techniques have been used in prevention programs. Munoz and his colleagues (1995) found that teaching cognitive-behavioral skills can be helpful in preventing depression. Indeed, the majority of programs that attempt to prevent depression have been cognitive-behavioral in orientation. The reason is not that other approaches cannot be effective. Rather, cognitive-behavioral orientations have been shown to be effective and can be used as an intervention for many people at the same time (Cardemil & Barber, 2001). In a review of depression-focused psychotherapies, Thase (2001) notes that behavioral, cognitive, and interpersonal therapies share common features: they are nontraditional (the focus is not on the unconscious) and short term in nature (two to four months of treatment), and their theoretical models of depression are linked with intervention tactics. These three therapies have demonstrated their effectiveness and practicality in the treatment of mild to moderately severe depressive disorders.

Both psychotherapy and drug therapy are effective, with some evidence that antidepressant medications may be particularly advantageous with severe cases of depression (Lambert & Ogles, 2004). However, there appear to be advantages in combined treatments that involve medication and psychotherapy. Medication tends to produce rapid and reliable reductions in symptoms among chronic or severely depressed patients, and psychotherapy can enhance social functioning or reduce subsequent risk and relapse (Friedman et al., 2004; Hollon & Fawcett, 2001).

Treatment for Bipolar Disorders

Although the forms of psychotherapy and behavior therapy used for depressive disorders are also used for bipolar disorders (e.g., MAOIs and SSRIs), drugs (especially lithium) are typically given to bipolar clients. Since it was introduced to the United States in 1969, lithium (in the form of lithium carbonate) has been the treatment of choice for bipolar and manic disorders. Response rates with lithium range from 60 percent to 80 percent in "classic" bipolar disorder (Delgado & Gelenberg, 2001). Lithium is also used as a mood-stabilizing drug to prevent or reduce future episodes of bipolar disorder (National Institute of Mental Health, 1985). As noted, the manic phase of bipolar disorder may be caused by too much neurotransmitter (primarily norepinephrine) at brain synapses or by neurotransmitter dysfunction. Lithium decreases the total level of neurotransmitters in the synaptic areas by increasing the reuptake of norepinephrine into the nerve cells.

The generally positive results achieved with lithium have been overshadowed somewhat by reports of distressing side effects (Dubovsky, Franks, Lifschitz, & Coen, 1982). The earliest danger signals are gastrointestinal complications (such as vomiting and diarrhea), fine tremors, muscular weakness, and frequent urination. The more serious side effects, associated with excessive lithium in the blood, are loss of bladder control, slurred speech, blurred vision, seizures, and abnormal heart rate. Fortunately, accurate measurements of

Overcoming Depression Few people know that television host Jane Pauley from NBC's *Jane Pauley Show* suffered for years with depression and bipolar disorder but leads a very productive life. Actor Ben Stiller suffered from bipolar disorder, as did other members of his family. Comedian Robin Williams—who makes others laugh— also suffered from bouts of depression.

lithium blood levels are easily obtained, and dosages can be adjusted accordingly.

Another problem associated with lithium is lack of patient compliance with the treatment program. For some reason, this problem is consistently worse with bipolar patients taking lithium than with any other group of patients taking any other drug. Bipolar patients often report that they have tried to adjust their lithium dosage by themselves so that they will experience the mania but not the depression of bipolar disorder. Unfortunately, lithium levels cannot be manipulated in this manner. When the dosage is decreased, the initial slightly manic state quickly develops into either a severe manic state or depression.

Some initial positive results have been reported with anticonvulsant drugs such as carbamazepine, valproate, lamotrigine, and gabapentin in the treatment of bipolar disorders (Dubovsky & Buzan, 1999). Further testing of the effectiveness of these drugs is essential.

Although pharmacological treatments have often been used in the treatment of bipolar disorders, psychotherapy and family therapy have also been helpful. For example, family-focused treatment involving psychosocial education about bipolar disorders, communication training, and problem-solving skills training, was found to be a useful adjunct to pharmacotherapy

"More lithium."

in decreasing the risk of of relapse and hospitalization in patients with a bipolar disorder (Rea et al., 2003).

SUMMARY

What are the symptoms of mood disorders?

- Severe depression is a major component of the mood disorders; it involves affective, cognitive, behavioral, and physiological symptoms, such as sadness, pessimism, low energy, and sleep disturbances.
- Mania, which may accompany depression, is characterized by elation, lack of focus, impulsive actions, and almost boundless energy. DSM-IV-TR recognizes hypomania and mania.

How are mood disorders classified in the APA diagnostic scheme?

- In bipolar mood disorders, manic episodes occur or alternate with depressive episodes.
- Depressive disorders (major depression and dysthymic disorder) involve only depression.
- Psychotic and other features may also appear in persons with severe mood disorders.

- The depressive disorders are the most common mood disorders; some evidence suggests that they are fairly distinct from the bipolar disorders.

Why do people develop depression and mania?

- Psychological theories of depression have been proposed by adherents of the psychodynamic, behavioral, cognitive, cognitive-learning, and sociocultural viewpoints, but each has certain weaknesses.
- Psychodynamic explanations focus on separation and anger.
- Behavioral explanations focus on reduced reinforcement following losses.
- Cognitive explanations see low self-esteem as an important factor.
- According to the learned helplessness theory of depression, susceptibility to depression depends on the person's experience with controlling the environment. The person's attributional style—speculations about why he or she is helpless—is also important.
- Sociocultural explanations have focused on cultural factors that influence the rates and symptoms of

mood disorders and the role of stress and of social supports.

- Some people may be more vulnerable to depression, perhaps because of biological or psychosocial factors.
- Social supports may provide a buffer against depression.
- Sociocultural factors have also been used to explain the higher observed rates of depression among women. They include gender role differences that make women more likely than men to amplify depressive symptoms.
- Genetic and biochemical research has demonstrated that heredity plays a role in depression and mania, probably by affecting neurotransmitter activity or levels in the brain.
- For example, according to the catecholamine hypothesis, a decrease in the amount of norepinephrine causes depression. Sensitivity of neurotransmitter receptors may also be a factor.

What kinds of treatment are available for people with mood disorders, and how effective are the therapies?

- Biomedical approaches to treating depression focus on increasing the amounts of neurotransmitters available at brain synapses or affecting the sensitivity of postsynaptic receptors through either medication or electroconvulsive therapy.
- Different forms of psychological and behavioral treatments have been found to be effective with mood disorders such as cognitive-behavioral treatment, which seeks to replace negative thoughts with more realistic (or positive) cognitions, and interpersonal therapy, which is a short-term treatment focused on interpersonal issues.
- The most effective treatment for bipolar and manic disorders is lithium, a drug that lowers the level of neurotransmitters at synapses by increasing the reuptake of norepinephrine, although other drugs are being tested for use in these disorders.

KEY TERMS

bipolar disorder (p. 358)	depression (p. 353)	learned helplessness (p. 368)	mood disorder (p. 353)
cyclothymic disorder (p. 359)	depressive disorder (p. 358)	major depression (p. 358)	neurotransmitter (p. 376)
	dysthymic disorder (p. 358)	mania (p. 353)	schema (p. 367)

MULTIMEDIA PREVIEW

For additional study aids, we invite you to explore our media resources accompanying *Understanding Abnormal Behavior*, Eighth Edition. The Student CD-ROM includes videos, quizzing, and critical thinking activities that help to reinforce key concepts in a fun and engaging manner. The Student Web Site provides additional interactive activities, chapter outlines, and research links that further support and complement the text. All Web resources may be accessed by logging onto the Web site at **http://psychology.college.hmco.com/students**.

CHAPTER 12
Suicide

FOCUS QUESTIONS

■ What do we know about suicide?

■ Why do people decide to end their lives?

■ Who are the victims of suicide?

■ How can we intervene or prevent suicides?

■ Are there times and situations in which suicide should be an option?

Cleopatra, Nirvana's Kurt Cobain, Bruno Bettelheim (psychiatrist), Ernest Hemingway, Adolf Hitler, Jim Jones (People's Temple leader), David Koresh (Branch Davidian sect leader), Marshal Herff Applewhite (leader of the cult Heaven's Gate), Marilyn Monroe, Freddie Prinze (comedian), King Saul, Samson, and Virginia Woolf.

What do these individuals have in common? As you may have guessed, they all committed suicide—the intentional, direct, and conscious taking of one's own life. As the following cases reveal, people commit suicide for any number of reasons.

Late one evening Carl Johnson, M.D., left his downtown office, got into his Mercedes 500 SL, and drove toward his expensive suburban home. He was in no particular hurry because the house would be empty anyway; the year before, his wife had divorced him and, with their two children, had moved back east to her parents' home. Carl was deeply affected. Although he had been drinking heavily for two years before the divorce, he had always been able to function at work. For the past several months, however, his private practice had declined dramatically. He used to find his work rewarding, but now he found people boring and irritating. The future looked bleak and hopeless. Carl knew he had all the classic symptoms of depression—he was, after all, a psychiatrist. The garage door opened automatically as he rolled up the driveway. Carl parked carelessly, not even bothering to press the switch that closed the door. Once in the house, he headed directly for the bar in his den; there he got out a bottle of bourbon and three glasses, filled the glasses, and lined them up along the bar. He drank them down, one after the other, in rapid succession. For a good half hour, he stood at the window staring out into the night. Then Carl sat down at his mahogany desk and unlocked one of the drawers. Taking a loaded .38-caliber revolver from the desk

drawer, Dr. Carl Johnson held it to his temple and pulled the trigger. *Possible reasons for suicide:* Recent divorce; loss of family life; subsequent depression.

Elizabeth Shin, a nineteen-year-old sophomore biology major, seemed to have it all. To her parents she was a giggly, busy, and overachieving daughter who was an accomplished clarinetist and high school salutatorian, and had been admitted to the Massachusetts Institute of Technology (MIT) and Yale. Others have described her as brilliant, beautiful, and very trustworthy. By external standards, Elizabeth had done well academically while attending MIT.

On April 10, 2000, Elizabeth locked the door of her dorm room, lit some candles, and failed to open the door for students who reported smelling smoke and hearing her moan and cry while in the room. Because of the heavy smoke, the campus police were called, and the dispatcher told students to pull the fire alarm and leave the building immediately. When the campus police arrived, they kicked in her door and reported a large fireball in the middle of the room and Elizabeth flailing about while engulfed in flames. When the flames were put out, they rushed her to Massachusetts General Hospital. The doctor said Elizabeth had suffered third-degree burns over 65 percent of her body. She died on April 14, 2000.

The death was subsequently ruled a suicide because of her two-year history of suicidal gestures and attempts to hurt herself while attending MIT. It was only after the death of their daughter that Elizabeth's parents learned that she had suffered from feelings of depression, inadequacy, and a sense of failure in school. While at MIT, she had multiple contacts with mental health professionals and administrators, who were concerned about her mental state. There were speculations that her perfectionistic character and the "pressure cooker" atmosphere at MIT proved too much for Elizabeth. The

A Tragic Act Although some suicidologists believe that there are commonalities among those who choose to die, it is also true that people take their lives for many different reasons. We can never be sure of the exact reasons for their suicides, but we do know that Ernest Hemingway (left) had become increasingly despondent over growing physical problems, and Kurt Cobain (right) was finding it difficult dealing with the fame and fortune of being lead singer in the popular group Nirvana.

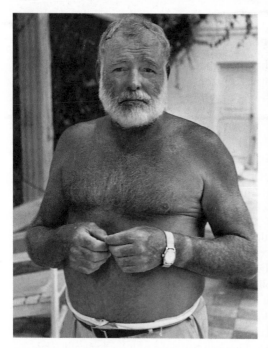

case has earned high national visibility because it has major legal implications for university mental health care that will be discussed in the chapter on legal and ethical issues in abnormal psychology. *Possible reasons for suicide:* Could not live up to own high standards; felt pressured to excel; felt a failure.

In 1990 the psychology community was shocked by the suicide of one of their very own, Bruno Bettelheim. Bettelheim was a renowned psychologist whose work on infant and childhood autism had influenced the field of mental health and treatment immensely. In his personal and professional lives he had dedicated himself to helping others and improving the quality of their lives, but he began to experience declining health. In a very personal interview with a reporter, Bettelheim expressed his thoughts on death and suicide. He stated that he did not fear death but was frightened at the prospect of suffering. At eighty-six years, he had lived a productive and enjoyable life and was fearful he would be kept alive without a purpose. Bettelheim had recently suffered a stroke, was fearful that he would suffer another, did not want to be a burden to his family or friends, and could no longer take part in many of the activities that had brought joy and meaning to

his life. He believed that he was living on borrowed time and met with a doctor in the Netherlands who was willing to give him a lethal injection. *Possible reasons for suicide:* Avoidance of further or anticipated suffering; declining physical health; inability to take part in activities that brought him joy; unwillingness to be a burden to others.

Ten-year-old Tammy Jimenez was the youngest of three children—a loner who had attempted suicide at least twice in the previous two years. Tammy's parents always seemed to be bickering about one thing or another and threatening divorce. She and her sisters were constantly abused by their alcoholic father. Finally, in February 1986, Tammy was struck and killed by a truck when she darted out into the highway that passed by her home. The incident was listed as an accident, but her older sister said Tammy had deliberately killed herself. On the morning of her death, an argument with her father had upset and angered her. Her sister said that, seconds before Tammy ran out onto the highway, she had said that she was unwanted and would end her own life. *Possible reasons for suicide:* Unhappy family life; child abuse; feelings of being unwanted and unloved.

On September 11, 2001, terrorists hijacked four planes; two of them destroyed the twin towers of the World Trade Center in New York City, one struck the Pentagon, and another crashed in Pennsylvania. Thousands of innocent lives were lost. All the terrorists also perished and were praised as martyrs by al-Qaeda leader Osama Bin Laden. In televised gloating, Bin Laden indicated that the Islamic extremists willingly gave their lives for a greater good, to combat the evil of the United States. He stated that those responsible for the heinous act were destined for an idyllic afterlife. *Possible reason for suicide:* Belief in killing oneself for a greater good or cause.

Suicide is now recognized as a serious threat to public health. To emphasize this point, the White House, in conjunction with the Surgeon General's office, called a major press conference to unveil the *Surgeon General's Call to Action to Prevent Suicide* (United States Public Health Service [USPHS], 1999). In that report, the devastating toll of suicide and steps needed to prevent it were outlined for public health officials,

educators, and the general public. Suicide is not only a tragic act; it is a baffling and confusing one as well. Although we have provided possible reasons for the deaths of the aforementioned individuals, we can never be entirely certain why people knowingly and deliberately end their own lives (Rudd, Joiner, & Rajab, 2004). The easy and most frequent explanation is that people who kill themselves are suffering from a mental disorder. For example, suicide is usually discussed in conjunction with mood disorders in most abnormal psychology texts. Yet our increasing understanding of suicide suggests that a single explanation is simplistic. Suicide has many causes, and people kill themselves for many different reasons (Rosenfeld, 2004). Our discussion of suicide follows the course charted in Figure 12.1.

We have chosen to provide a separate chapter on suicide for several reasons. First, although suicide is not classified as a mental disorder in DSM-IV-TR, the suicidal person usually has clear psychiatric symptoms. Many persons who suffer from depression, alcohol dependence, and schizophrenia exhibit suicidal

FIGURE 12.1 Suicide

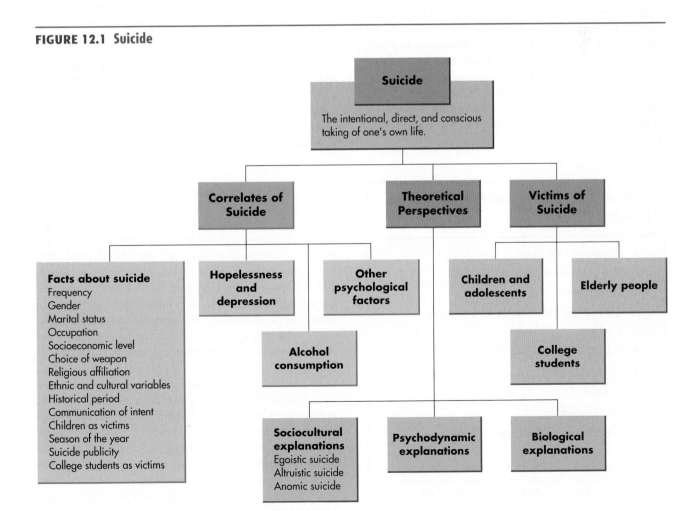

thoughts or behavior (Sanchez, 2001). Yet suicide does not fall neatly into one of the recognized psychiatric disorders. There is evidence that suicide and **suicidal ideation**—thoughts about suicide—may represent a separate clinical entity. Few, for example, would argue that the topic is not an important domain of the study of abnormal psychology.

The second reason for treating suicide as a separate topic is that increasing interest in suicide and the fact that it is the eighth leading cause of death for all Americans (see Table 12.1) appears to warrant study of this phenomenon in its own right. Every year, there have been more deaths due to suicide than to homicide! Throughout history, suicide has remained a hidden and mysterious act. People have traditionally avoided discussing it and have participated in a "conspiracy of silence" because of the shame and stigma involved in taking one's life (Maris, Berman, & Silverman, 2000; Rudd et al., 2004). Even some mental health professionals find the topic uncomfortable and personally disturbing (Shea, 2002; Friedman, 2004). Over the past several decades, we have learned much about suicide.

Third, we are witnessing increased openness in discussing issues of death and dying, the meaning of suicide, and the right to take one's own life. Some prominent individuals have even gone so far as to advocate a "right to suicide" and the legalization of "assisted suicide." Although the American Psychological Association has not taken a pro or con stand on this question, its Board for the Advancement of Psychology in the Public Interest is exploring the issue. Regardless of its decision, however, a federal court in May 2004 upheld the only law in the nation (Oregon) authorizing doctors to aid their terminally ill patients to commit suicide (Hastings & Robbennolt, 2004).

And, finally, we need to recognize that suicide is an irreversible act. Once the action has been taken, there is no going back, no reconsideration, and no reprieve. Regardless of the moral stand one takes on this position, the decision to commit suicide is often an ambivalent one, clouded by many personal and social stressors. Many mental health professionals believe that the suicidal person, if taught how to deal with personal and social crises, would not consciously take his or her own life. As a result, understanding the causes of suicide and what can be done to prevent such an act becomes extremely important to psychologists (Klott & Jongsma, 2004).

Myth vs Reality

Myth: People who attempt suicide are not serious about ending their lives. They are usually manipulative, attention seeking, and have little intent to complete the act.

Reality: Although this statement may hold some truth, it is dangerous to assume that people who attempt suicide are not serious. Indeed, most people who are successful have made attempts in the past. A suicide attempt is a danger signal that should not be taken lightly.

Correlates of Suicide

People who commit suicide—who complete their suicide attempts—can no longer inform us about their motives, frames of mind, and emotional states. We have only indirect information, such as case records and reports by others, to help us understand what led them to their tragic act. The systematic examination of existing information for the purpose of understanding and explaining a person's behavior before his or her death is called a **psychological autopsy** (Jacobs & Klein, 1993; Roberts, 1995; Robins & Kulbok, 1988). It is patterned on the *medical autopsy*, which is an examination of a dead body to determine the cause or nature of the biological death. The psychological autopsy attempts to make psychological sense of a suicide or homicide by compiling and analyzing case histories of victims, recollections of therapists, interviews with relatives and friends, information obtained from crisis phone calls, and messages left in suicide notes. Unfortunately, these sources are not always available

---

TABLE 12.1   Leading Causes of Death in the United States

1. Diseases of the heart
2. Malignant neoplasms
3. Cerebrovascular diseases
4. Chronic obstructive pulmonary diseases
5. Accidents
6. Pneumonia and influenza
7. Diabetes mellitus
8. SUICIDE
9. HIV infection
10. Chronic liver disease and cirrhosis

Source: Adapted from Centers for Disease Control and Prevention (1999). Surveillance for injuries and violence among older adults. *MMWR 48* (No. SS-8), 27–34.

or reliable. Only 12 to 34 percent of victims leave suicide notes (Black, 1993; Leenaars, 1992), and many people who commit suicide have never undergone psychotherapy (Fleer & Pasewark, 1982). Explanations from relatives or friends are often distorted because of the emotional impact of the loved one's death.

Another strategy involves studying those who survive a suicide attempt. The problem with this method is that it assumes that people who attempt suicide (attempters) are no different from those who succeed. Studies suggest that these two populations differ on many important dimensions (Diekstra, Kienhorst, & de Wilde, 1995; Furr, Westefeld, McConnell, & Jenkins, 2001; Lester, 1994). In general, attempters are more likely to be white females, housewives in their twenties and thirties, who are experiencing marital difficulties, and who attempt suicide with barbiturates. Those who succeed are likely to be white males, in their forties or older, who suffer from ill health or depression, and who shoot or hang themselves (Fremouw, Perczel, & Ellis, 1990; Shea, 2002).

Despite difficulties in compiling information, the psychological autopsy and the study of attempters continue to be used, not only because they represent the only limited avenues open to us but also because they serve a broad and important need. If psychologists can isolate the events and circumstances that lead to suicide and can identify the characteristics of potential suicide victims, they may be able to prevent other people from performing this irreversible act (Klott & Jongsma, 2004).

Facts About Suicide

No single explanation is sufficient to account for all types of suicide. Considering the examples at the beginning of this chapter, common sense alone leads to the conclusion that Bruno Bettelheim's reasons for taking his life differ from those of Tammy Jimenez, the September 11th terrorists, or Elizabeth Shin. In seeking to understand suicide, researchers have focused on events, characteristics, and demographic variables that recur in psychological autopsies and that are highly correlated with the act (Maris et al., 2000). Our first example, Carl Johnson, fits a particular profile. Higher suicide rates are associated with divorce (National Center for Health Statistics [NCHS], 1988, 1994; USPHS, 1999; Rudd et al., 2004) and with certain professions (psychiatry in particular). Alcohol is frequently implicated (Canapary, Bongar, & Cleary, 2002; Cornelius et al., 1995; Rogers, 1992), and men are more likely to kill themselves using firearms than by other means (Kushner, 1995; NCHS, 1988).

Profiles such as these, as well as others described later in this chapter, emerge from our increasing knowledge of facts that are correlated with suicide

(Berman & Jobes, 1991, 1995; Bongar, 1991; Canetto & Lester, 1995; Diekstra, 1990; Li, 1995; McIntosh, 1991; NCHS, 1988; Rogers, 1990; Shneidman, 1993; Staal & Hughes, 2002; Stillion & McDowell, 1996; U.S. Bureau of the Census, 1988; USPHS, 1999). Let's examine some of them in greater detail. But first, look at Table 12.2, which examines some of the characteristics shared by suicidal individuals.

Frequency   Every twenty minutes or so, someone in the United States takes his or her own life. Approximately 31,000 persons kill themselves each year. Suicide is among the top ten causes of death in the industrialized parts of the world; it is the eighth leading cause of death among American adults and the third leading cause of death among young people ages fifteen to twenty-four (Beers & Berkow, 1999; USPHS, 1999). Some evidence shows that the number of actual suicides is probably 25 to 30 percent higher than that recorded. Many deaths that are officially recorded as accidental—such as single-auto crashes, drownings, or falls from great heights—are actually suicides. According to some estimates, eight to ten persons attempt suicide for every one person who completes the act.

Children and Young People as Victims   Persons under age twenty-five accounted for 15 percent of all suicides in 1997. Recent reports suggest that about 12,000 children between the ages of five and fourteen are admitted to psychiatric hospitals for suicidal behavior every year, and it is believed that twenty times that number actually attempt suicide. Suicides among young people ages fifteen to twenty-four have increased by more than 40 percent in the past decade (50 percent for males and 12 percent for females); suicide is now the second leading cause of death for whites in this age group. For all groups between the ages of fifteen and nineteen, suicide increased by 11 percent, and for those aged ten through fourteen, it increased by 109 percent from 1980 to 1996 (USPHS, 1999). College students appear less at risk for suicide than their age-matched noncollege peers (see the Mental Health and Society feature "College Student Suicides"), although the recent rash of highly visible suicides on the MIT and New York University campuses may seem to contradict these statistics (Sontag, 2002; Swindler, 2004).

Suicide Publicity and Identification with Victims   Media reports of suicides, especially of celebrities, seem to spark an increase in suicide (Bailey, 2003). The twelve-month period following Marilyn Monroe's suicide saw a 12 percent increase. Suicides by young people in small communities or schools seem to evoke copycat suicides in some students. Publicized murder-suicides also seem to be correlated with an increase in

TABLE 12.2 Ten Common Characteristics of Suicide

1. *The common purpose is to seek a solution.* People may believe that suicide represents a solution to an insoluble problem. To the suicidal person, taking one's life is not a pointless or accidental occurrence.

2. *The cessation of consciousness is a common goal.* Consciousness represents constant psychological pain, but suicide represents a termination of distressing thoughts and feelings.

3. *The stimulus for suicide is generally intolerable psychological pain.* Depression, hopelessness, guilt, shame, and other negative emotions are frequently the basis of a suicide.

4. *The common stressor in suicide is frustrated psychological need.* The inability to attain high standards or expectations may lead to feelings of frustration, failure, and worthlessness. When progress toward goals is blocked, some individuals become vulnerable to suicide.

5. *A common emotion in suicide is hopelessness-helplessness.* Pessimism about the future and a conviction that nothing can be done to improve one's life situation may predispose a person to suicide.

6. *The cognitive state is one of ambivalence.* Although the suicidal person may be strongly motivated to end his or her life, there is usually a desire (in varying degrees) to live as well.

7. *The cognitive state is also characterized by "tunnel vision."* Vision is constricted: the person has great difficulty seeing "the larger picture" and can be characterized as suffering from tunnel vision. People intent on suicide seem unable to consider other options or alternatives. Death is the only way out.

8. *The common action in suicide is escape.* The goal is eggression—escape from an intolerable situation.

9. *The common interpersonal act in suicide is communication of intention.* At least 80 percent of suicides are preceded by either verbal or nonverbal behavioral cues indicating their intentions.

10. *The common consistency is in the area of life-long coping patterns.* Patterns or habits developed in coping with crisis generally are the same response patterns that are used throughout life. Some patterns may predispose one to suicide.

Source: Shneidman (1992).

transportation accidents. It is hypothesized that group suicides involving two or more individuals represent an extreme form of personal identification with others. Studies suggest that group suicides are characterized by highly emotional involvements or settings that overcome the desire for self-preservation. Interestingly, publicized natural deaths of celebrities do not produce similar increases.

Gender   The completed suicide rate for men is about three to four times that for women, although recent findings suggest that many more women are now incurring a higher risk. Further, women are more likely to make attempts, but it appears that men are more successful because they use more lethal means. Among people older than sixty-five, the rate for men is ten times that for women. However, women attempt suicide three times as often as men. The age group beginning at age sixty-five has the highest suicide rate of all, but men continue to lead in deaths. Even at younger ages, males commit the majority of suicides among adolescents. For example, among the fifteen to twenty-four age category, over 70 percent of suicides are men.

Marital Status   As Figure 12.2 indicates, the lowest incidence of suicide is found among people who are married and the highest among those who are divorced. The suicide rates for single and widowed or divorced men are about twice those for women of similar marital status. Attempted and completed suicide rates are higher among those who are separated, divorced, or widowed. It is especially high among single adolescent girls and single men in their thirties.

Occupation   Physicians, lawyers, law enforcement personnel, and dentists have higher than average rates

---

FIGURE 12.2 Marital Status and Suicide per 100,000
Divorced persons are nearly three times more likely to commit suicide. Does a stable marriage somehow tend to immunize people against killing themselves? What other reasons might explain these differences?

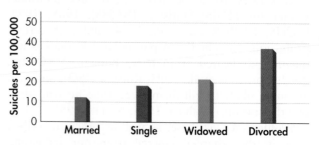

Source: Data from McIntosh (1991).

MENTAL HEALTH AND SOCIETY
College Student Suicides

Contrary to what college students might believe, suicide rates among their peers are no higher than among a matched noncollege group (Furr et al., 2001). Indeed, in a study conducted over a sixty-year period of twelve colleges and universities, it was found that the rate was nearly half that of a nonstudent group (Schwartz & Whittaker, 1990).

Nevertheless, as many as 20 percent of college students have entertained suicidal thoughts during their college careers. Suicide is the second leading cause of death among students. In October 2004, President Bush signed the Garrett Lee Smith Memorial Act, named after the twenty-one-year-old son of Oregon Republican Senator Gordon Smith, who committed suicide while attending college. The new law authorizes $82 million in grants aimed at preventing suicide among young people.

When you consider how well endowed college students as a group are—with youth, intelligence, and boundless opportunity—you might wonder why this would be so.

Characteristics of Student Suicides

One of the oldest but most comprehensive studies undertaken, a ten-year study at the University of California at Berkeley, found that, compared with nonsuicidal students, students who committed suicide

- Tended to be older than the average student by almost four years.
- Were significantly overrepresented among postgraduate students.
- Were more likely to be men, although the proportion of women suicides was higher than among the general population.
- Were more likely to be international students and language or literature majors.
- Tended to have better than average academic records as undergraduates but as postgraduates were below the graduate grade point average.

In addition, more suicides occurred in February and October (near the beginning of each semester) than in the other months of the year. Thus the notion that suicides occur in response to anxiety over final examinations was not supported by the results. In fact, the danger period appeared to be the start, not the finish, of the school semester. Most of the students committed suicide at their campus residences. Suicides seemed more frequent at larger universities than at smaller ones, such as community colleges and small liberal arts colleges. Firearms were the most common

means of committing suicide; ingestion of drugs was next. In later studies on other campuses, however, drug overdose was found to be more frequently used than firearms (Klagsbrun, 1976).

Reasons for Student Suicides

In a study of 1,455 students at four different colleges and universities, researchers (Furr et al., 2001) found the following to be contributing factors to suicidal ideation and behavior among the students surveyed:

- Hopelessness (49 percent)
- Loneliness (47 percent)
- Helplessness (37 percent)
- Relationship problems with girlfriends or boyfriends (27 percent)
- Unspecified depression (26 percent)
- Money problems (27 percent)
- Parental problems (20 percent)

It is clear that many of the same dynamics related to suicide in the general population hold for college students as well. Many colleges and universities would be well served to develop programs and resources to (1) identify warning signs related to suicide, (2) have well-established procedures for counselors, faculty, and staff about how to handle such cases, and (3) clearly identify campus and community services with expertise in a suicidal crisis.

---

of suicide. Among medical professionals, psychiatrists have the highest rate and pediatricians the lowest. Because medical personnel have easy access to drugs and know what constitutes a fatal dose, they may be more likely to complete a suicide. Interestingly, the suicide rate of women physicians is four times higher than that of a matched general population. Such marked differences raise the question of whether the specialty influences susceptibility or whether a suicide-prone person is attracted to certain specialties.

Socioeconomic Level   Suicide is represented proportionately among all socioeconomic levels. Level of wealth does not seem to affect the suicide rate as much as do changes in that level. In the Great Depression of the 1930s, suicide was higher among the suddenly impoverished than among those who had always been poor.

Choice of Weapon   Over 60 percent of suicides are committed by firearms, and 70 percent of attempts are

Religion and Suicide   Many religions have strong taboos and sanctions against suicide. In countries in which Catholicism and Islam are strong, for example, the rates of suicide tend to be lower than in countries in which religious sanctions against suicide are not as deeply held.

accounted for by drug overdose. Men most frequently choose firearms as the means of suicide; poisoning and asphyxiation via barbiturates are the preferred means for women. The violent means (which men are more likely to choose) are more certain to complete the act; this partially explains the disproportionately greater number of incomplete attempts by women. Recent studies indicate, however, that women are increasingly choosing firearms and explosives as methods (55.9 percent increase). Some have speculated that this change may be related to a change in role definitions of women in society. Among children younger than fifteen years, the most common suicide method tends to be jumping from buildings and running into traffic. Older children try hanging or drug overdoses. Younger children attempt suicide impulsively and thus use more readily available means.

Religious Affiliation   Religious affiliation is correlated with suicide rates. Although the U.S. rate is 12.2 per 100,000, in countries in which Catholic Church influences are strong—Latin America, Ireland, Spain, and Italy—the suicide rate is relatively low (less than 10 per 100,000). Islam, too, condemns suicide, and the suicide rates in Arab countries are correspondingly low. Where religious sanctions against suicide are absent or weaker—for example, where church authority is weaker, as it is in Scandinavian countries, in the former Czechoslovakia, and in Hungary—higher rates are observed. Indeed, Hungary has the highest recorded rate of suicide, at 40.7 per 100,000, and the former Czechoslovakia's rate was 22.4 per 100,000.

Ethnic and Cultural Variables   Suicide rates vary among ethnic minority groups in the United States. American Indian groups have the highest rate, followed by white Americans, Mexican Americans, African Americans, Japanese Americans, and Chinese Americans. American Indian youngsters have frighteningly high rates (26 per 100,000) as compared with white youths (14 per 100,000). High rates of alcoholism, a low standard of living, and an invalidation of their cultural lifestyles may all contribute to this tragedy.

Jails and Prisons   As might be expected, suicide is the most frequent cause of death in U.S. jails. A suicide number that ranges from 90 to 230 per 100,000 population means that the suicide rate in prisons is 16 times higher than in the general population. The most frequent means in jails was hanging. Most victims were arrested for nonviolent crimes, and nearly half were intoxicated with drugs or alcohol at the time of death.

Historical Period   Suicide rates tend to decline during times of war and natural disasters, but they increase during periods of shifting norms and values or social unrest, when traditional expectations no longer apply. Sociologists speculate that during wars, people "pull together" and are less concerned with their own difficulties and conflicts.

Native American and Proud of It Suicide rates among American Indian youth are extremely high, due perhaps to a lack of validation of their cultural lifestyle. One effort to replenish native pride, shown here, is Camp Walakota, a "spiritual boot camp" for troubled teens from the Cheyenne River Sioux Tribe in South Dakota. Here teens are reacquainted with their cultural heritage as they bond with their elders, who offer many valuable life lessons.

Communication of Intent   More than two-thirds of the people who commit suicide communicate their intent to do so within three months of the fatal act. The belief that people who threaten suicide are not serious about it, or will not actually make such an attempt, is ill founded. It is estimated that 20 percent of persons who attempt suicide try again within one year and that 10 percent finally succeed. Most people who attempt suicide appear to have been ambivalent about death until the suicide. It has been estimated that fewer than 5 percent unequivocally wish to end their lives.

Other Important Facts   The time of year is correlated with suicides. Spring and summer months have the highest incidence. About one in six persons who complete the act leave suicide notes. Western mountain states seem to have higher rates, with Nevada being the highest. The average physician encounters six or more potentially suicidal persons in his or her practice per year.

Hopelessness and Depression

A survey of facts correlated with suicide allows us to learn much about it, but the factors that are probably most closely linked with suicide are hopelessness and depression.

Although it is dangerous to assume that depression causes suicide, a number of studies indicate that the two are very highly correlated (Kienhorst, de Wilde, Diekstra, & Wolters, 1995; Shneidman, 1992). Depression is involved in more than half of attempted suicides (USPHS, 1999) and is often related to unhappiness over a broken or unhappy love affair, marital discord, disputes with parents, and recent bereavements (Rudd et al., 2004). For example, interest in suicide usually develops gradually, as a result of pleasure loss and fatigue accompanying a serious depressed mood (Hamilton, 1982). Shneidman (1993) has described it as a "psychache," an intolerable pain created from an absence of joy. Studies indicate that 50 to 67 percent of all suicides are related to a primary mood disorder (Whybrow, Akiskal, & McKinney, 1984) and that 15 percent of patients suffering mood disorders will eventually kill themselves (Sainsbury, 1982). More recent findings continue to support these statistics (Clark & Fawcett, 1992; Hawton, 1987). Among both children and adolescents, depression seems to be highly correlated with suicidal behavior (Garland & Zigler, 1993; Kosky, 1983; Rosenthal & Rosenthal, 1984).

Such data can lead to the conclusion that depression plays an important role in suicide. Yet other studies indicate that the way this role is manifested is far from simple. For example, patients seldom commit suicide while severely depressed. Such patients generally show motor retardation and low energy, which keep them from reaching the level of activity required for suicide. The danger period often comes after some treatment, when the depression begins to lift. Energy and motivation increase, and patients are more likely to carry out the act. Most suicide attempts occur during weekend furloughs from hospitals or soon after discharge, a fact that supports this contention. The risk of suicide seems to be only about 1 percent during the year in which a depressive episode occurs, but it is about 15 percent in subsequent years (Klerman, 1982).

Although depression is undeniably correlated with suicidal thoughts and behavior, the relationship seems very complex. Why do some people with depression commit suicide, whereas others do not? The answer may be found in the characteristics of depression and in the factors that contribute to it.

For example, it has been found that an increase in sadness is a frequent mood indicator of suicide, but heightened feelings of anxiety, anger, and shame are also associated (Kienhorst et al., 1995). Some researchers believe that hopelessness, or negative expectations about the future, may be the major catalyst in suicide and, possibly, an even more important factor than depression and other moods (Hewitt, Newton, Flett, & Callander, 1997; Weishaar & Beck, 1992). Beck, Emery, and Greenberg (1985) conducted a ten-year study of 207 psychiatric patients who had suicidal thoughts but no recent history of suicide attempts. Within seventy-two hours after hospital admission, each patient was measured on three variables: hopelessness, depression, and suicidal ideation (thoughts about suicide). During the ten-year period, fourteen patients committed suicide, and the test scores of these people were compared with those of the others. The investigators found that the two groups did not differ in terms of depression and suicidal ideation, but they did differ in terms of hopelessness. Those who died were more pessimistic about the future than were those who survived. Although the overall results obtained by the scale did not predict suicide risk, the hopelessness item within the measure did. Some sample statements indicative of hopelessness are "My future seems dark for me"; "I might as well give up because there's nothing I can do about making things better for myself"; "I never get anything I want, so it's foolish to want anything." These findings suggest that therapists should assess all depressed patients' attitudes toward their futures to determine how hopeless they feel.

Alcohol Consumption

One of the most consistently reported correlates of suicidal behavior is alcohol consumption (Canapary et al., 2002; Schuckit, 1994; Shea, 2002). As many as 60 percent of suicide attempters drink alcohol before the act, and autopsies of suicide victims suggest that 25 percent are legally intoxicated (Flavin, Franklin, & Frances, 1990; Suokas & Lonnqvist, 1995). Indeed, a successful suicide unconnected to alcohol abuse is a rare event. Alcohol-implicated suicide rates may be as high as 270 per 100,000, which is an astounding 27 times higher than the rate found in the general popu-

lation (Stillion, McDowell, & May, 1989). Heavy alcohol consumption, like binge drinking, also seems to deepen feelings of remorse during dry periods, and the person may be at risk even when sober (Beers & Berkow, 1999). Many theorists have traditionally argued that alcohol may lower inhibitions related to the fear of death and make it easier to carry out the fatal act. Recent formulations, however, suggest a cognitive link between alcohol use and suicide.

J. R. Rogers (1992) argued that the strength of the relationship between alcohol and suicide is the result of alcohol-induced myopia (a constriction of cognitive and perceptual processes). This line of reasoning relies heavily on the cognitive characteristics of people who attempt suicide: they are more rigid in their line of thinking, less flexible in problem solving, and more prone to dichotomous thinking (Shneidman, 1987, 1993). They generally perceive solutions as all or none (life or death) and are myopically incapable of coming up with alternative solutions. Alcohol use by an individual in psychological conflict may increase rather than decrease personal distress. Steele and Josephs (1990) found that alcohol constricts cognitive and perceptual processes. Although alcohol-induced myopia may relieve depression and anxiety by distracting the person from the problem, it is equally likely to intensify the conflict and distress by narrowing the person's focus on the problem. Thus the link between alcohol and suicide may be the result of the myopic qualities of alcohol exaggerating a previously existing constrictive state. If this is true, alcohol is most likely to increase the probability of a suicide in an already suicidal person. Rogers (1992) stated, "The most efficacious and ethically sound intervention in this area would be to promote abstinence by providing information to clients regarding the potential dangers involved in alcohol consumption" (p. 542).

Other Psychological Factors

Although the correlations are not as strong as those with hopelessness and depression, many other psychological factors have been found to be associated with suicide (Maris et al., 2000). Findings have consistently revealed that many individuals who commit suicide suffer from a DSM-IV-TR disorder (Harris & Barraclough, 1997; Litman, 1987; Moscicki, 1995; Sanchez, 2001). Conversely, approximately 15 percent of individuals diagnosed with mood disorders, schizophrenia, and substance abuse attempt to kill themselves (Brent, Perper, & Allman, 1987; Rossow & Amundsen, 1995). Those suffering from schizophrenia are most likely to be experiencing an episode of depression, and their suicide methods are usually violent and bizarre; those with personality disorders are usually the emotionally immature with low frustration tolerance (borderline and antisocial personalities). A review of the literature on suicide also reveals a number of other contributing factors, including such experiences as separation and divorce (Garfinkel & Golumbek, 1983), academic pressures (Priester & Clum, 1992), shame (Shreve & Kunkel, 1991), serious illness (Mackenzie & Popkin, 1987), loss of a job, and other life stressors (Rosenfeld, 2004).

Theoretical Perspectives

Some clinicians believe that everyone, at one time or another, has wished to end his or her life. Fortunately, most of us do not act on such wishes, even during extreme distress. But why do some people do so? Even though suicide is closely linked to hopelessness and depression, and even though many theories of depression apply to suicide as well, the question cannot be answered easily. We have already discussed how difficult it is to know what causes a person to take his or her life. Generally, such people seem to share a common motive: to gain relief from a life situation that is unbearable. In the search for a more detailed answer, leading explanations have taken sociocultural, psychodynamic, or biological perspectives.

Sociocultural Explanations

Early explanations of suicide emphasized its relationship to various social factors. As we saw earlier, rates of suicide vary with age, gender, marital status, occupation, socioeconomic level, religion, and ethnic group. Higher rates are associated with high- and low-status (as opposed to middle-status) occupations, urban living, middle-aged men, single or divorced status, and upper and lower socioeconomic classes (Fremouw et al., 1990; NCHS, 1988). In a pioneering work, the French sociologist Emile Durkheim related differences in suicide rates to the impact of social forces on the person (Durkheim, 1897/1951). From his detailed study of suicides in different countries and across different periods, he proposed three categories of suicide: egoistic, altruistic, and anomic.

Egoistic Suicide   In Durkheim's view, **egoistic suicide** results from an inability to integrate oneself with society. Failing to maintain close ties with the community deprives the person of the support systems that are necessary for adaptive functioning. Without such support, and unable to function adaptively, the person becomes isolated and alienated from other people. Some suicidologists believe that modern, mobile, and highly technological society has deemphasized the

importance of extended families and the sense of community. The result, even among young people, has been an increase in suicide rates.

Altruistic Suicide   **Altruistic suicide** is motivated by the person's desire to further group goals or to achieve some greater good. Someone may give up his or her life for a higher cause (in a religious sacrifice or the ultimate political protest, for example). Group pressures may make such an act highly acceptable and honored. During World War II, Japanese kamikaze pilots voluntarily dove their airplanes into enemy warships "for the Emperor and the glory of Japan." The self-immolation of Buddhist monks during the Vietnam War are likewise in this category. Although likely to arouse considerable disagreement, a strong case can be made that the suicide bombings now so

An Altruistic Suicide During the Vietnam War, people were horrified by scenes of self-immolation by Buddhist monks as a form of protest against the government. This altruistic suicide in 1963 was witnessed by passersby in the central market of Saigon.

Suicide Bombing In the aftermath of a Palestinian suicide bomb attack in Jerusalem, Israel, Jewish rescue volunteers collect victim's remains from a passenger bus shortly after it is blown apart. Does continual media coverage of these escalating attacks heighten our fear of such attacks or, instead, desensitize us to the horrors of terrorism?

prevalent in the Middle East and in Iraq against Israeli citizens and U.S. troops qualify for this category. From the perspective of those who condone such acts, the perpetrators do not perceive themselves as terrorists but as freedom fighters who willingly give their lives for a greater good.

Anomic Suicide   Durkheim's third category, **anomic suicide,** results when a person's relationship to society is unbalanced in some dramatic fashion. When a person's horizons are suddenly broadened or constricted by unstable conditions, he or she may not be able to handle the change or cope with the new status and may choose suicide as a way out. The suicides of people who lost their personal wealth during the Great Depression or who killed themselves after being freed from concentration camps at the end of World War II are of this type. Similarly, a person who suddenly and unexpectedly acquires great wealth may be prone to suicide.

Durkheim's theory suggests an important dimension of suicide: social or societal factors that operate to separate people or to make them somehow less connected to other people or to their families, religious institutions, or community can increase susceptibility to suicide. Suicide prevention measures, therefore, should be vastly more effective when social support and connectedness are increased and when social isolation is decreased. Conversely, we would expect rates to be higher among the elderly, as their loved ones and friends die off and as they begin to disengage from their work and other activities through retirement. We would also expect that in the divorced, separated, or widowed population, suicide rates would be higher than among those

who are married. As we have seen, the research literature supports all of these expectations.

Durkheim's theory also can be used to make sense of the differential suicide rates among the various racial and ethnic minority groups. As mentioned previously, American Indians have much higher rates of suicide than are found among all other groups in American society, including European Americans. One in six American Indian teenagers has attempted suicide, a rate four times higher than that of the general teenage population (Resnick, Yehnuda, & Pitts, 1992). Among fifteen- to twenty-four-year-old American Indian youths, the suicide rate (not attempts) is twice that for white youngsters. Asian American and Hispanic American rates are significantly lower than that of the white group (U.S. Department of Health and Human Services [USDHHS], 1991). Although rates for African American youngsters have also been traditionally lower than for their white counterparts, a recent report reveals a dramatic increase over the past two decades (USPHS, 1999). The federal Centers for Disease Control and Prevention found that the suicide rate for black youths from fifteen to eighteen has doubled, from 3.6 per 100,000 in 1980 to 8.1 per 100,000 in 1995.

Rates among these groups are consistent with Durkheim's belief that social change and disorganization, which leads to a breakup in integration with one's community, in turn predisposes one to suicide. Suicidologists point to the disorganization imposed on American Indians by Western society: deprived of their lands, forced to live on reservations, and trapped between the margins of two different cultural traditions, many American Indians become alienated and isolated from both their own communities and the larger society. Similarly, the increased suicide rate among African American youths may be due to movement to middle-class life, "accompanied by a splintering of community and family support networks, a weakening of bonds to religion and the pressure of trying to compete in historically white-dominated professions and social circles" ("Suicide Rate Climbing for Black Teens," 1998, p. A17).

Sociocultural explanations may be valid to an extent, but attributing suicide to a single sociological factor (economic depression, residence, or occupation) is too simplistic and mechanistic. As we have noted throughout this text, correlations do not imply cause-and-effect relationships. Thus Durkheim's three categories are more descriptive than explanatory. Moreover, purely sociological explanations that take into account only one sociocultural factor—group cohesion, for example—omit the psychological dimension of the person's struggles. They fail to explain why only certain members of a group commit suicide and others do not.

Psychodynamic Explanations

Early psychological explanations of suicide tended to ignore social factors in favor of psychological ones. In the classical Freudian approach, for example, self-destruction was seen as the result of hostility that is directed inward against the introjected love object (the loved one with whom the person has identified). That is, people who kill themselves are really directing anger and the suicidal act against others whom they have incorporated within themselves. If the angry feelings reach murderous proportions, a suicide attempt is the result. Later in his career, Freud suffered from failing health (jaw cancer), faced his own mortality, and continued to be perplexed about the existence of war, violence, and suicide. During this period, he posited the existence of *thanatos*, a death instinct that is antagonistic to the life instinct. According to Freud, the function of the death instinct is to return the organism to its most stable (inorganic) state through death. Thanatos, he believed, was the fuel of death, which could be manifested in suicide.

Biological Explanations

Neither a purely sociocultural nor a purely psychological perspective seems to adequately explain the causes of suicide. Both sociological and psychological factors are probably involved, but other factors seem to be operating as well. Two sets of findings—from biochemistry and from genetics—suggest that suicide may have a biological component. For example, you may recall that there is strong evidence that chemical neurotransmitters are associated with depression and

mania. Similar evidence shows that suicide is influenced by low serotonin levels in the brain.

Evidence of this link began to accumulate in the mid-1970s, when researchers identified a chemical called *5-hydroxyindoleacetic acid* (5HIAA; Asberg, Traskman, & Thoren, 1976; Stanley & Mann, 1983; Van Praag, 1983). This chemical is produced when serotonin, a neurotransmitter that affects mood and emotions, is broken down in the body. Moreover, some evidence indicates that the serotonin receptors in the brainstem and frontal cortex may be impaired. The spinal fluid of some depressed and suicidal patients has been found to contain abnormally low amounts of 5HIAA (Bongar, 1991).

Statistics on patients with low levels of 5HIAA indicated that they are more likely than others to commit suicide, more likely to select violent methods of killing themselves, and more likely to have a history of violence, aggression, and impulsiveness (Edman, Asberg, Levander, & Schalling, 1986; Roy, 1992). Researchers believe that the tendency toward suicide is not a simple link to depression. We already know that patients suffering from depression also exhibit low levels of 5HIAA. What is startling is that low levels of 5HIAA have been discovered in suicidal people without a history of depression and in suicidal individuals suffering from other mental disorders (Brown et al., 1982; Volavka, 1995).

This discovery may lead to a chemical means of detecting people who are at high risk for attempting suicide. However, researchers in this area caution that social and psychological factors also play a role. If, in the future, cerebral serotonin can be detected easily in blood tests, it can be used as a biological marker (a warning sign) of suicide risk (Hawton, 1987). Researchers believe that low 5HIAA content does not cause suicide, but it may make people more vulnerable to environmental stressors (Pines, 1983). And still another caution is in order: this evidence is correlational in nature; it does not indicate whether low levels of 5HIAA are a cause or a result of particular moods and emotions—or even whether the two are directly related.

There is also evidence to implicate genetics in suicidal behavior, but the relationship is far from clear. There appears to be a higher rate of suicide and suicide attempts among parents and close relatives of people who attempt or commit suicide than among nonsuicidal people (Brent, Bridge, Johnson, & Connolly, 1996; Roy, 1992). As always, great care must be used in drawing conclusions because it can be argued that modeling by a close member of the family might make a family relative more prone to find suicide an acceptable alternative. Some researchers are hopeful that the Human Genome Project might provide a means of clarifying the genetic markers that may help identify those individuals at risk for suicide.

Victims of Suicide

In this section we briefly discuss two groups of people who are especially victimized by suicide: the very young and the elderly. It is important, however, to realize that those who are left behind may be considered victims as well.

Children and Adolescents

Suicide among the young is an unmentioned tragedy in our society. We have traditionally avoided the idea that some of our young people find life so painful that they consciously and deliberately take their own lives. As in the case of Tammy Jimenez, it may feel easier to call a suicide "an accident." The suicide rate for children younger than fourteen is increasing at an alarming rate, and the rate for adolescents is rising even faster. Among the fifteen- to twenty-four-year-olds, 73 percent of suicides are committed by white males, but the rise in suicides is most rapid among black males. Suicide is now second only to automobile accidents as the leading cause of death among teenagers, and some automobile "accidents" may also really be suicides (Rudd et al., 2004).

In one Gallup poll of teenage respondents, 6 percent admitted to a suicide attempt, and another 15 percent said they had come close to trying (Freiberg, 1991). Experts on adolescent suicide, however, believe these to be gross underestimates (Berman & Jobes, 1991). The Gallup Organization polled middle-class families (median family income of $41,500) and thus missed certain high-risk groups, such as school dropouts. The Gallup study suggested that between 8 and 9 percent of teenagers have engaged in self-harm behavior. Figures reveal that officially recorded suicides for young people between the ages of fifteen and twenty-four are more than triple the rate in 1957 (Freiberg, 1991; Maris et al., 2000).

Characteristics of Childhood Suicides   A lack of research on childhood suicides has generally hindered our understanding of why such acts occur (Cytryn & McKnew, 1996; Kovacs, Goldston, & Gatsonis, 1993). Recent research, for example, has now established a link between antidepressant medication and increased suicidal risk for children. As a result, the Food and Drug Administration issued a warning in October 2004 (see the chapter on disorders of childhood and adolescence). Two studies, however, have helped identify characteristics of suicidal children and have helped form the foundation for other work in this area.

In a retrospective study of admissions to a pediatric hospital emergency room over a seven-year period, researchers identified 505 children and adolescents who had attempted suicide (Garfinkel, Froese, & Hood, 1982). This group was compared with a control group of children who were similar in age, gender, and date of admission. The researchers did not, however,

Teens and Suicide As more and more teens like those shown here find themselves attending the funerals of their peers, it is becoming clear that suicide among high school students is reaching epidemic proportions. One of the dangers parents and teachers need to guard against is copycat suicides, a phenomenon in which other students take their lives. To prevent more suicides, schools sometimes initiate programs to help students and faculty cope with their feelings of loss and anger.

compare these children with those who had successfully completed the suicidal act. Some would suggest that unsuccessful attempters differ from successful ones. Nevertheless, children in the group that attempted suicide had the following characteristics:

1. There were three times as many girls as boys, and the boys who attempted suicide were significantly younger than the girls. The gender rates are consistent with adult rates, but the younger age of the boys is not.

2. The clinical symptoms most often shown by both the children and the adolescents were changes in mood and aggressiveness, hostility, or both.

3. Most of the suicide attempts (73 percent) occurred at home, 12 percent in public areas, 7 percent at school, and 5 percent at a friend's house. In 87 percent of the suicide attempts, someone else was nearby—generally parents. The fact that most suicide attempts occur at home implies that parents are in the best position to recognize and prevent suicidal behavior.

4. Most of the attempts were made during the winter months, in the evening or afternoon.

5. Drug overdose was the primary means of attempted suicide, accounting for 88 percent of the attempts. Next, in order, were wrist laceration, hanging, and jumping from heights or in front of moving vehicles.

6. More than 77 percent of the attempts were judged to be of low probability of completion; 21 percent were moderately probable; and slightly more than 1 percent were highly probable. Most attempts were judged to have been made in a way that ensured a high likelihood of rescue. These figures lend credence to the belief that most children who attempt suicide do not really want to end their lives.

The researchers found that the families of the suicidal children were under greater economic stress than were the families of the control group. The former had twice the rate of paternal unemployment. Maybe parents who are preoccupied with economic concerns are less readily available to support their children in time of need. Furthermore, fewer than half the families of those who attempted suicide were two-parent families. The families of suicide attempters also had higher rates of medical problems, psychiatric illness, and suicide than did the control group families. The dominant psychiatric problem was alcohol or drug abuse.

The second study that sheds light on the characteristics of suicidal children also found that family instability and stress and a chaotic family atmosphere were correlated with suicide attempts (Cosand, Bourque, & Kraus, 1982). Suicidal children seemed to have experienced unpredictable traumatic events and to have suffered the loss of a significant parenting figure before age twelve. Their parents tended to be alcohol or drug abusers who provided poor role models for coping with stress. As in the first study, the child's self-destructive behavior seemed to be a last-ditch attempt to influence or coerce those who threatened his or her psychological well-being. The suicidal children showed considerable anger.

Because such children are at great risk of committing suicide when their problems remain unrecognized and untreated, early detection of their distress signals is vital. Intensive family therapy, including the education of parents with regard to parenting roles, can help. Parents can be taught to recognize the signs of depression, to become aware of their children's afterschool activities, and to be cognizant of the role and accessibility of drugs. In some cases the child may need to be removed from the family.

Despite the fact that these two studies (Garfinkel et al., 1982; Cosand et al., 1982) were conducted over two decades ago, their conclusions remain amazingly stable (USPHS, 1999). Mental health professionals and the public need to be aware that the complexion of adolescent suicides is changing at a rapid pace. For example, since the publication of these two studies, two trends are notable. First, the ratio of male to female suicides in 1987 was about 5:1, a change from the previous decade's 3:1 ratio. Second, youngsters are now selecting more lethal methods of killing themselves (Berman & Jobes, 1991; Cytryn & McKnew, 1996).

Copycat Suicides Considerable attention has been directed at multiple or so-called copycat suicides, in which youngsters in a particular school or community seem to mimic a previous suicide (Phillips, Van Voorhees, & Ruth, 1992). For example, within a three-month period in 1985, nine youths ages fourteen to twenty-five killed themselves, all by hanging. All were members of the Shoshone tribe, and all lived in Wind River, Wyoming. In another incident in Omaha, Nebraska, seven high school students attempted suicide within a very short span of time; three were successful. Likewise, the Bergenfield suicides grabbed headlines in 1987, when two male and two female students killed themselves by inhaling fumes from their car. Their deaths followed that of a friend who had also committed suicide. This event was unusual because the four signed a suicide pact on a brown paper bag. Tragically, their deaths were in turn followed by those of two other young women, who used the same method of death ("Suicide Belt," 1986). More recently, New York University student Joanne Michelle Leavy leaped to her death from a twelve-story building on

September 6, 2004. This would not have been noticed on a national level were it not that it represented the sixth fatal fall by students leaping to their deaths in the preceding year (Swindler, 2004).

Although many events, beliefs, and feelings may have contributed to these tragic deaths, suggestion and imitation seem to have played an especially powerful role. Young people may be especially vulnerable, but studies indicate that highly publicized suicides—such as those of a celebrity, close friend, relative, coworker, or other well-known person—can increase the number of subsequent suicide attempts (Bandura, 1985; Stack, 1987). In the months following Marilyn Monroe's death, for example, suicides increased by some 12 percent. When Nirvana's Kurt Cobain committed suicide in 1994, many youth counselors warned about potential imitations by fans. Thus it appears that grief, depression, and mourning are not the culprits that induce copycat behaviors.

Although imitative suicides may not be as common as the media suggest, research has indicated that publicizing the event may have the effect of glorifying and drawing attention to it. Thus depressed people may identify with a colorful portrayal, increasing the risk of even more suicides. This pattern appears to be especially true for youngsters who may already be thinking about killing themselves. The stable, well-adjusted teenager does not seem to be at risk in these situations.

Adolescence and young adulthood are often periods of confusing emotions, identity formation, and questioning. It is a difficult and turbulent time for most teenagers, and suicide may seem to be a logical response to the pain and stress of growing up. A suicide that occurs in school brings increased risk of other suicides because of its proximity to students' daily lives. In such instances, a suicide prevention program should be implemented to let students vent their feelings in an environment equipped to respond appropriately and perhaps even to save their lives. Encouragingly, the Gallup survey (Freiberg, 1991) discussed earlier in this chapter reported that 41 percent of schools had programs aimed at suicide prevention (professional counseling services, peer counseling, and special seminars). It is no longer unusual to hear about school programs that are immediately implemented when a tragedy strikes (student suicide, violent death of a student or teacher, natural disaster, for example). One such program is discussed later in this chapter.

Elderly People

Aging inevitably results in generally unwelcome physical changes, such as wrinkling and thickening skin, graying hair, and diminishing physical strength. In addition, we all encounter a succession of stressful life changes as we grow older. Friends and relatives die, social isolation may increase, and the prospect of death becomes more real. Mandatory retirement rules may lead to the need for financial assistance and the difficulties of living on a fixed and inadequate income. Such conditions make depression one of the most common psychiatric complaints of elderly people. And their depression seems to be involved more with "feeling old" than with their actual age or poor physical health (Rosenfeld, 2004).

Suicide seems to accompany depression for older people. Their suicide rates (especially rates for elderly white American men) are higher than those for the general population (McIntosh, 1992); indeed, suicide rates for elderly white men are the highest for any age group (National Center for Health Statistics, 1989). From 1980 through 1997, the largest relative increases in suicide rates occurred among those eighty to eighty-four years of age. Firearms were the most common method of suicide for both men and women sixty-five years or older. The elderly make fewer attempts per completed suicide, being among the most likely to succeed in taking their lives. In one study comparing rates of suicide among different ethnic groups, it was found that elderly white Americans committed almost 18 percent of all suicides although they composed only about 11 percent of the population. Suicide rates for Chinese Americans, Japanese Americans, and Filipino Americans are even higher than the rate for elderly white Americans. American Indians and African Americans show the lowest rates of suicide among older adults (although both groups are at high risk for suicide during young adulthood).

Of the Asian American groups, first-generation immigrants were at greatest risk of suicide. One possible explanation for this finding is that the newly arrived Asian immigrants had intended to earn money and then return to their native countries. When they found they were unable to earn enough either to return home or to bring their families to the United States, they developed feelings of isolation that increased their risk of suicide. This risk has decreased among subsequent generations of Asian Americans (and, probably, among other immigrant groups as well) because of acculturation and the creation of strong family ties.

Preventing Suicide

In almost every case of suicide, there are hints that the act is about to occur. Suicide is irreversible, of course, so preventing it depends very much on early detection and successful intervention (Bongar, 1992; Shea, 2002; Klott & Jongsma, 2004). Mental health professionals involved in suicide prevention efforts operate under the

A Matter of Respect Suicide is less likely to occur among the elderly in cultures that revere, respect, and esteem people of increasing age. In Asian and African countries increasing age is equated with greater privilege and status, such as that shown (right) for an elderly Ghanian chief; in contrast, in the United States, growing old is often associated with declining worth and social isolation, as appears to be the case for this elderly resident (below) in a U.S. nursing home.

assumption that potential victims are ambivalent about the act. That is, the wish to die is strong, but there is also a wish to live. Potential rescuers are trained to exert their efforts to preserve life. Part of their success in the prevention process is the ability to assess a client's suicide **lethality**—the probability that a person will choose to end his or her life (Rudd et al., 2004). The Mental Health and Society feature "A Clinical Approach to Suicide Intervention" discusses suicide intervention from the point of view of one of the authors.

Working with a potentially suicidal individual is a three-step process that involves (1) knowing what factors are highly correlated with suicide; (2) determining whether there is high, moderate, or low probability that the person will act on the suicide wish; and (3) implementing appropriate actions (Canapary et al., 2002; see Table 12.3). People trained in working with suicidal clients often attempt to quantify the "seriousness" of each factor. For example, a person with a *clear suicidal plan* who has *the means* (e.g., a gun) to carry

out a suicide threat is considered to be in a more lethal state than a recently *divorced* and *depressed* person.

Clues to Suicidal Intent

The prevention of suicide depends very much on the therapist's ability to recognize its signs. Clues to suicidal intent may be demographic or specific. We have already discussed a number of demographic factors, such as the fact that men are three times more likely to kill themselves than are women and that increased age is associated with an increased probability of suicide (Maris et al., 2000). And, although the popular notion is that frequent suicidal gestures are associated with less serious intent, most suicides do have a history of making suicide threats; to ignore them is extremely dangerous. Any suicidal threat or intent must be taken seriously (Rudd et al., 2004).

General characteristics often help detect potential suicides, but individual cases vary from statistical norms. What does one look for in specific instances? The amount of detail involved in a suicide threat can indicate its seriousness. A person who provides specific details, such as method, time, and place, is more at risk than one who describes these factors vaguely. Suicidal potential increases if the person has direct access to the means of suicide, such as a loaded pistol. Also, sometimes a suicide may be preceded by a precipitating event. The loss of a loved one, family discord, or chronic or terminal illness may contribute to a person's decision to end his or her life.

A person contemplating suicide may verbally communicate the intent. Some people make very direct statements: "I'm going to kill myself," "I want to die," or "If such and such happens, I'll kill myself." Others make indirect threats: "Goodbye," "I've had it," "You'd be better off without me," and "It's too much to put up with." On the other hand, cues are frequently very subtle:

MENTAL HEALTH AND SOCIETY
A Clinical Approach to Suicide Intervention

As a practicing clinician, I have had the stressful experience of working with suicidal clients; indeed, one of my patients on a psychiatric ward committed suicide when I was serving my internship in 1968. Since that time, I have had to deal with many feelings related to this tragic act, and I have conscientiously kept up with both the literature and the clinical work on suicide intervention. Notice that I prefer the word *intervention* rather than *prevention*. I believe that, under certain conditions, individuals have a right to take their own lives. I may intervene in helping them understand their decision, but I do not necessarily view my role as one of prevention.

Despite this philosophical stand, my clinical experience has led me to conclude that, overwhelmingly, the majority of suicidal people do not truly wish to end their lives. When helped to understand the sources of their distress and the resources and options available to them, they inevitably choose life over death. My purpose in discussing this topic is not to debate the ethical merits of suicide or to discuss how one arrives at such a conclusion, but to explain how I, as a mental health professional, approach working with a potentially

suicidal client. The setting I am most familiar with is our public schools, where I train and supervise school counselors. Increasingly, many of my trainees are encountering students who express suicidal ideation and threats. Following are some of the clinical thoughts and suggestions that I attempt to impart to them. Interestingly, many of these suggestions are equally valid when applied to friends or relatives who may be contemplating suicide.

1. *Be comfortable discussing suicide.* Many beginning counselors are not comfortable openly and directly discussing suicide with their clients or students. They are afraid that, if they open the door to this topic, they will inadvertently encourage a suicidal gesture or that their actions will result in a suicide. Nothing could be further from the truth. My experience has taught me that those who are serious about suicide have entertained those thoughts for some time. Indeed, reluctance to discuss or indirectly allude to possible suicide can have a most devastating effect: it prevents the student from examining himself

or herself objectively and reinforces the belief that "only crazy people" entertain these thoughts. Thus the psychological distress for the student may become even more heightened. Furthermore, it also prevents the mental health professional from quickly and accurately ascertaining suicidal risk. Asking direct questions such as the following progression is a necessity:

"Are you feeling unhappy and down most of the time?" (If yes …)
"Do you feel so unhappy that you sometimes wish you were dead?" (If yes …)
"Have you ever thought about taking your own life?" (If yes …)
"What methods have you thought about using to kill yourself?" (If the client specifies a method …)
"When do you plan to do this?"

Contrary to fears that such an approach will adversely affect the student, I have found that directness diminishes students' distress. Many students are relieved to be able to discuss a taboo topic openly and honestly.

A patient says to Nurse Jones, who is leaving on vacation, "Goodbye, Miss Jones, I won't be here when you come back." If some time afterward Nurse Jones, knowing that the patient is not scheduled to be transferred or discharged prior to her return, thinks about that conversation, she may do well to telephone her hospital. (Danto, 1971, p. 20)

As this example illustrates, verbal expressions must be judged within the larger context of recent events and behavioral cues. We have all, at one time or another, made or heard such statements.

Behavioral clues can be communicated directly or indirectly. The most direct clue is a "practice run," an

actual suicide attempt. Even if the act is not completed, *it should be taken seriously;* it often communicates deep suicidal intent that may be carried out in the future. Indirect behavioral clues can include actions such as putting one's affairs in order, taking a lengthy trip, giving away prized possessions, buying a casket, or making out a will, depending on the circumstances. In other words, the more unusual or peculiar the situation, the more likely it is that the action is a cue to suicide. Clinicians often divide up warning signs into two categories: (1) early signs, such as depression, statements or expressions of guilt feelings, tension or anxiety, nervousness, insomnia, loss of

2. *Use the natural barrier against suicide.* Studies reveal that almost all people who commit suicide have made attempts in the past. Most of us have a trained-in barrier against hurting ourselves or taking our own lives. Once a person crosses that barrier, it becomes easier to act against one's moral, ethical, and religious upbringing. Even in students who have made a suicidal gesture, the barrier is never completely gone. When students have never attempted to kill themselves but have thought about ending their lives, the counselor should immediately and forcefully reinforce the barrier to prevent it from being crossed. This can be done in a number of different ways, but generally it involves concrete actions on the part of the counselor.

3. *Take action to affect the client's immediate environment.* If your assessment leads you to believe that you are dealing with a high-risk student, no amount of talk or philosophical debate will help. Although acting in an autocratic manner may be unappealing, a counselor is often required to make decisions and take actions against the wishes of the student. High-risk students should not be allowed to leave the school office without a clear-cut treatment plan and the involvement of responsible parties. Parents may need to be notified immediately, and if they are not cooperative, the school should have specific procedures for involving civil authorities. I tell my students that it is always better to err on the conservative side than to gamble with a person's life.

If, however, your assessment leads you to conclude that you are dealing with a low-risk client, other, more democratic and less severe actions are possible. For example, two options are involving the student in counseling (within the school) or referring the student to a private practitioner in the community. If you decide to continue a counseling relationship with the student, you may use yourself to reinforce the barrier. I have found, for example, that obtaining an agreement with the student can be a powerful means of blocking suicidal attempts. It may be as simple as extracting a verbal promise that the student will not make any attempt at suicide that week or as formal as actually signing a behavioral contract, such as this one:

1. I agree not to attempt to kill myself or harm myself from _____ to _____.
2. I agree to get rid of any or all things that may be used to kill myself, such as knives, guns, or pills.
3. I agree to immediately call my counselor at or the Suicide Prevention Center should I feel like hurting myself.
4. I agree to these conditions as a part of my counseling with _____.

Signed _____
Witnessed _____
Dated _____

Suicide intervention, in some respects, goes against the traditional therapeutic training of most mental health professionals. A potential suicide crisis does not allow the mental health professional either the luxury of time to explore the client's problems or the ease of simply sitting back and behaving in a passive, democratic manner. The actions we choose to take or not take can have major effects on the final outcome for our suicidal clients.

appetite, loss of weight, and impulsiveness; and (2) critical signs, such as sudden changes in behavior (calmness after a period of anxiety), giving away belongings or putting affairs in order, direct or indirect threats, and actual attempts.

Crisis Intervention

Suicide prevention can occur at several levels, and the mental health profession has now begun to move in several coordinated directions to establish prevention efforts. At the clinical level, attempts are being made to educate staff at mental health institutions and even at schools to recognize conditions and symptoms that indicate potential suicides (Kneisel & Richards, 1988; Kaslow & Aronson, 2004). For example, a single man older than fifty years of age suffering from a sudden acute onset of depression and expressing hopelessness should be recognized by mental health professionals as being at high risk.

When a psychiatric facility encounters someone who fits a particular risk profile for suicide, crisis intervention strategies will most likely be used to abort or ameliorate the processes that could lead to a suicide attempt. Crisis intervention is aimed at providing intensive short-term help to a patient in resolving an

TABLE 12.3   Risk and Protective Factors in Suicide Assessment and Intervention
Risk Factors
■ Previous suicide attempt
■ Mental disorders, such as depression and bipolar disorder
■ Co-occurring mental and alcohol and substance abuse disorders
■ Family history of suicide
■ Hopelessness
■ Impulsive and/or aggressive tendencies
■ Barriers to accessing mental health treatment
■ Relational, social, work, or financial loss
■ Physical illness
■ Easy access to lethal methods, especially guns
■ Unwillingness to seek help because of social stigma
■ Family members, peers, or celebrities who have died from suicide
■ Cultural or religious beliefs that suicide is a noble resolution
■ Local epidemics of suicide that have a contagious influence
■ Isolation
Protective Factors
■ Effective resources for clinical care for mental, physical, and substance abuse disorders
■ Easy access to a variety of clinical interventions and support for seeking help
■ Restricted access to lethal means of suicide
■ Family and community support
■ Good skills in problem solving, conflict resolution, and nonviolent means of handling disputes
■ Cultural and religious beliefs that discourage suicide and support self-preservation instincts
Source: USPHS (1999).

team for two to four hours every day until the person is stabilized and the immediate crisis has passed. In these sessions, the team is very active not only in working with the patient but also in taking charge of the person's personal, social, and professional life outside of the psychiatric facility. Many suicide intervention strategies have been developed through clinical work rather than research because the nature of suicide demands immediate action. Waiting for empirical studies is not a luxury the clinician can afford. Figure 12.3 summarizes the process of assessing risk and determining lethality.

After patients return to a more stable emotional state and the immediate risk of suicide has passed, they are then given more traditional forms of treatment, either on an inpatient or outpatient basis. In addition to the intense therapy they receive from the psychiatric team, relatives and friends may be enlisted to help monitor patients when they leave the hospital. In these cases, the responsible relatives or friends are provided with specific guidelines about how to deal with the patient between treatment team contacts, whom to notify should problems arise outside of the hospital, and so forth.

Suicide Prevention Centers

Crisis intervention can be highly successful if a potentially suicidal patient is either already being treated by a therapist or has come to the attention of one through the efforts of concerned family or friends. Many people in acute distress, however, are not formally being treated. Although contact with a mental health agency may be highly desirable, many people are unaware of the services available to them. Recognizing that suicidal crises may occur at any time and that preventive assistance on a much larger scale may be needed, a number of communities have established suicide prevention centers.

The first suicide prevention center was established in Los Angeles in 1958 by psychologists Norman L. Farberow and Edwin S. Shneidman. The center first sought patients from the wards of hospitals. Soon, however, its reputation grew, and in little more than a decade, 99 percent of its contacts were by phone (Farberow, 1970). In the past forty years, hundreds of suicide prevention centers patterned after the first one have sprung up throughout the United States. These centers are generally adapted to the particular needs of the communities they serve, but they all share certain operational procedures and goals.

Telephone Crisis Intervention   Suicide prevention centers typically operate twenty-four hours a day, seven days a week. Because most suicide contacts are

immediate life crisis. Unlike traditional psychotherapy, in which sessions are spaced out and treatment is provided on a more leisurely long-term basis, crisis intervention recognizes the immediacy of the patient's state of mind. The patient may be immediately hospitalized, given medical treatment, and seen by a psychiatric

FIGURE 12.3 The Process of Preventing Suicide   Suicide prevention involves the careful assessment of risk factors to determine lethality—the probability that a person will choose to end his or her life. Working with a potentially suicidal individual is a three-step process that involves (1) knowing what factors are highly correlated with suicide; (2) determining whether there is high, moderate, or low probability that the person will act on the wish; and (3) implementing appropriate actions.

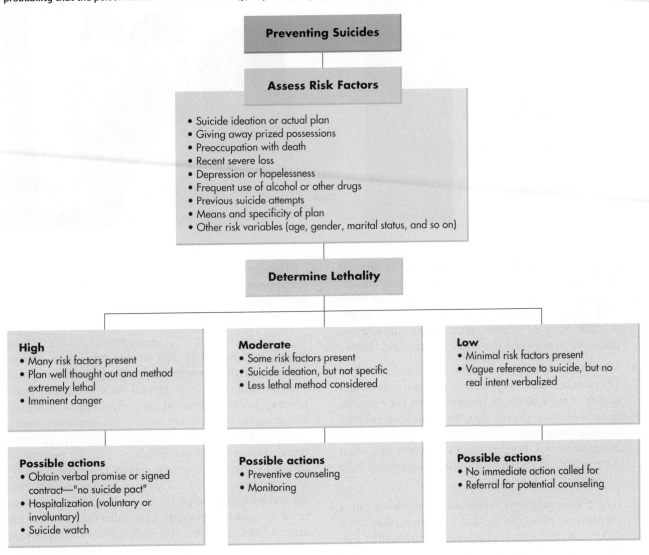

by phone, a well-publicized telephone number is made available throughout the community for calls at any time of the day or night. Furthermore, many centers provide inpatient or outpatient crisis treatment. Those that lack such resources develop cooperative programs with other community mental health facilities. Most telephone hot lines are staffed by paraprofessionals. All workers have been exposed to crisis situations under supervision and have been trained in crisis intervention techniques such as the following:

1. *Maintain contact and establish a relationship.* The skilled worker who establishes a good relationship with the suicidal caller not only increases the caller's chances of working out an alternative solution but also can exert more influence. Thus it is important for the worker to show interest, concern, and self-assurance.

2. *Obtain necessary information.* The worker elicits demographic data and the caller's name and address. This information is very valuable in case an urgent need arises to locate the caller.

3. *Evaluate suicidal potential.* The staff person taking the call must quickly determine the seriousness of the caller's self-destructive intent. Most centers use lethality rating scales to help the worker determine suicide potential. These usually contain questions

Intervening Before It's Too Late Suicide prevention centers (SPCs) operate twenty-four hours a day, seven days a week, and have well-publicized telephone numbers because most contacts are made by phone. Even though there is controversy about SPC effectiveness, the mental health profession continues to support these centers.

on age, gender, onset of symptoms, situational plight, prior suicidal behavior, and the communication qualities of the caller. Staffers also elicit other demographic and specific information that might provide clues to lethality, such as the information discussed in the section on clues to suicidal intent.

4. *Clarify the nature of the stress and focal problem.* The worker must help callers to clarify the exact nature of their stress, to recognize that they may be under so much duress that their thinking may be confused and impaired, and to realize that there are other solutions besides suicide. Callers are often disoriented, so the worker must be specific to help bring them back to reality.

5. *Assess strengths and resources.* In working out a therapeutic plan, the worker can often mobilize a caller's strengths or available resources. In their agitation, suicidal people tend to forget their own strengths. Their feelings of helplessness are so overwhelming that helping them recognize what they can do about a situation is important. The worker explores the caller's personal resources (family, friends, coworkers), professional resources (doctors, clergy, therapists, lawyers), and community resources (clinics, hospitals, social agencies).

6. *Recommend and initiate an action plan.* Besides being supportive, the worker is highly directive in recommending a course of action. Whether the recommendation entails immediately seeing the person, calling the person's family, or referring the person to a social agency the next day, the worker presents a plan of action and outlines it step by step.

This list implies a rigid sequence, but in fact both the approach and the order of the steps are adjusted to fit the needs of the individual caller.

The Effectiveness of Suicide Prevention Centers

Today, approximately 200 suicide prevention centers function in the United States, along with numerous "suicide hot lines" in mental health clinics. Little research has been done on their effectiveness, however, and many of their clients want to remain anonymous.

Nevertheless, some data are available, although dated. One early study indicates that 95 percent of callers to suicide prevention centers never use the service again (Speer, 1971). This finding may indicate that the service was so helpful that no further treatment was needed or, just as possibly, that callers do not find the centers helpful and feel it is useless to call again. Worse yet, they may have killed themselves after the contact. Another study has shown that potential suicides do not perceive contact with a prevention center as more helpful than discussion with friends (Speer, 1972). And if the justification for such centers is based on their ability to offer services to a large number of clients, then the fact that only 2 percent of the people who kill themselves ever contact such a service is disturbing (Weiner, 1969). Furthermore, studies on cities with hot line services provide mixed findings (Lester, 1989, 1991). Some studies found that suicides decreased in a community with hot line services (Miller, Coombs, & Leeper, 1984), some found no change (Barraclough, Jennings, & Moss, 1977), and others found an increase (Weiner, 1969). However, in cities without prevention centers, the rates increased even more (Lester, 1991).

Before you jump to the conclusion that suicide prevention centers are ineffective, however, note that the studies cited could have been influenced by several factors. For example, cities with and cities without such centers may differ so much that they are not comparable. Additionally, clients may contact these centers only when they are in such great distress that they despair of asking friends for help. They may later perceive their contacts with friends as being more beneficial relative to the distress they feel. Finally, despite the lack of convincing evidence, there is always the possibility that suicide prevention centers do help. Because life is precious, the mental health profession continues to support them.

Community Prevention Programs

Suicide prevention programs also are found at work sites and schools. Increasingly, community leaders have recognized that the suicide of a worker or student has dramatic and stressful emotional effects on fellow workers and students who may have known the victim. When a school experiences a suicide, the staff and students quickly learn of the event. This is often followed by emotional upheaval, anxiety, guilt, and severe grieving. Educational institutions now routinely consult mental health professionals after a suicide to help facilitate the natural grieving process; to reduce the secrecy, confusion, and rumors surrounding a suicide; and to prevent possible copycat suicides.

One interesting and effective form of intervention was developed in response to a particularly violent suicide (Kneisel & Richards, 1988). A fifth- and sixth-grade teacher took her own life by dousing herself with gasoline and igniting herself. Local media coverage was quite intense, and little else was discussed. In responding to this terrible event and to the emotional needs of the students, the school assembled a mental health consulting team comprising two child psychologists trained in crisis intervention and one representative each of the fire department and mayoral task force. The fire department representative was included because of concern about possible increased risk of fire setting among students. The team worked directly with the school psychologist, who already knew the students and staff. The primary goal of the program was to mitigate the effects of the tragedy by providing survivors with an opportunity to express and understand their reactions to the event. To accomplish this goal, the team scheduled the following activities:

1. A faculty meeting was called to give teachers a forum in which they could share feelings and information with one another. This session was only partially successful. It gave the team insight into student concerns, but it failed to meet the needs of the faculty.

2. In a classroom discussion, children were given an opportunity to express their feelings and concerns, especially those dealing with fears of death, suicide, and fire. They were reassured that the teacher's decision to kill herself was not based on their behavior and that her death was not their fault. All questions were answered truthfully and in a straightforward manner.

3. Throughout this period of intervention, the school psychologist was available for individual sessions with teachers, staff, and students. Some sought individual sessions because they had an especially close relationship to the victim; others sought help because they were already dealing with personal issues of loss, separation, and abandonment. Some students were referred because they were excessively tearful, withdrawn, or distraught; others were seen because they denied the suicide. Many of these individuals were referred for ongoing follow-up treatment.

After all these meetings, the team met with the principal to plan follow-up actions. A memorial service was held. Parents were sent letters telling them about the suicide and informing them about mental health resources in the community. Written guidelines for suicide prevention were developed and distributed in the school.

Kneisel and Richards (1988) concluded that such an institutional response to a suicide minimizes mental health problems among the survivors, restores equilibrium in the school and community, and represents an effective suicide prevention program.

The Surgeon General's Call to Action to Prevent Suicide

In response to the suicide crisis, Surgeon General David Satcher (USPHS, 1999) issued a call to arms to combat what has been labeled a public health problem. In one of the largest collaborative efforts ever undertaken between the public and private sectors, agencies in the U.S. Department of Health and Human Services and many community groups sought to develop a national strategy for the United States. The outcome of this partnership was published in *The Surgeon General's Call to Action to Prevent Suicide* (USPHS, 1999). The blueprint for reducing suicide can be summarized under three categories: awareness, intervention, and methodology, or AIM. Following is a list of goals:

1. *Awareness* aims at broadening the public's awareness of suicide and its risk factors.

- Promote public awareness that suicide is a public health problem and many suicides are preventable.

- Expand awareness, enhance and develop community resources for suicide prevention programs.

- Develop strategies to reduce the stigma associated with mental illness, substance abuse, and suicidal behavior so help seeking is not avoided.

2. *Intervention* aims at enhancing services and programs for community and clinical care.

- Build collaboration with and among public and private sectors to complete a national strategy for suicide prevention.

- Improve the ability of primary care providers to recognize and treat depression and mental disorders associated with suicide.

- Eliminate barriers in public and private insurance programs for quality mental and substance-abuse disorder treatments and create incentives to treatment.

- Institute training of health, mental health, and human service professionals, teachers, and others in recognition, treatment, management, and after-care interventions.

- Develop and implement effective training programs for family members of those at risk and for natural community helpers on how to recognize, respond to, and refer people showing suicidal risk.

- Develop and implement safe and effective programs in educational settings that address adolescent distress and crisis intervention.

- Enhance community care resources by using schools and workplaces as access and referral points.

- Promote private/public collaboration with the media to ensure that entertainment and news coverage represent balanced and informed portrayals of suicide and its associated risk factors.

3. *Methodology* is aimed at advancing the science of suicide prevention.

- Enhance research to understand the risk and protective factors related to suicide. Increase research on effective suicide prevention programs and culture-specific interventions.

- Develop additional scientific strategies for evaluating suicide prevention interventions.

- Establish mechanisms for federal, regional, and state interagency public health collaboration toward improving monitoring systems for suicide potential and develop standard terminology in these systems.

- Encourage the development and evaluation of new prevention technologies, including firearm safety measures, to reduce easy access to lethal means of suicide.

The Right to Suicide: Moral, Ethical, and Legal Implications

The following letter captured worldwide attention when a twenty-one-year-old paraplegic, Vincent Humbert, wrote a special appeal to French President Jacques Chirac asking to end his own life:

Mr. Chirac,

My respects to you, Mr. President.

My name is Vincent Humbert, I am 21. I was in a traffic accident on 24 September 2000. I spent nine months in a coma. I am currently in Helio-Marins hospital in Berck, in the Pas-de-Calais region.

All my vital organs were affected, except for my hearing and my brain, which allows me a little comfort.

I can move my right hand very slightly, putting pressure with my thumb on each letter of the alphabet. These letters make up words and the words form sentences. This is my only method of communication. I currently have a nurse beside me, who spells me the alphabet separating vowels and consonants.

This is how I have decided to write you. The doctors have decided to send me to a specialised clinic. You have the right of pardon and I am asking you for the right to die.

I would like to do this clearly for myself but especially for my mother; she has left her old life to be by my side, here in Berck, working morning and evening after visiting me, seven days out of seven, without a day of rest. And all this to be able to pay the rent for her miserable studio flat.

For the moment she is still young. But in a few years, she will not be able to keep up such a pace of work, that is to say she will not be able to pay her rent and so will be obliged to go back to her apartment in Normandy.

But it is impossible to imagine my remaining here without her by my side, and I think that all patients who are sound of mind are responsible for their actions and have the right to want to continue to live or to die.

I would like you to know that you are my last chance. You should also know that I was a fellow citizen without a history, without any judicial record, a sportsman and a volunteer fireman.

I do not deserve a scenario as terrible as this and I hope that you will read this letter, which is specially addressed to you.

Please accept, Mr. President, my warmest compliments.

In September 2003, after the release of his book *I Ask the Right to Die*, Vincent Humbert's mother administered an overdose of sedatives into his intravenous line, causing his death (Smith, 2003). The case of Vincent Humbert set off a national debate about the morality and legality of euthanasia.

Do people have the right to end their own lives if their continued existence would result in psychological and physical deterioration? Surveys of the American public indicate that a majority believe terminally ill individuals should be allowed to take their own lives; in a 1995 survey of physicians working with AIDS patients, over half indicated that they have prescribed lethal doses of narcotics to suicidal patients (Clay, 1997; Drane, 1995). Advocates contend that people should be allowed the choice of dying in a dignified manner, particularly if they suffer from a terminal or severely incapacitating illness that would cause misery for their families and friends (Rosenfeld, 2004).

The act of suicide seems to violate much of what we have been taught regarding the sanctity of life. Many segments of the population consider it immoral and provide strong religious sanctions against it. Suicide is both a sin in the canonical law of the Catholic Church and an illegal act according to the secular laws of most countries. Within the United States, many states have laws against suicide, and some consider it illegal. Of course, such laws are difficult to enforce because the victims are not around to prosecute. Many are beginning to question the legitimacy of such sanctions, however, and are openly advocating a person's right to suicide. In 1976 the California State Assembly became one of the first state legislatures to provide that right to people with terminal illnesses. Since then, many other states have passed "living will" laws that offer protection against dehumanized dying and confer immunity on physicians and hospital personnel who comply with a patient's wishes. In November 1998,

Oregon voters passed a physician-assisted suicide act granting physicians the legal right to help end the lives of terminally ill patients. In 2001, however, U.S. Attorney General John Ashcroft issued a directive intended to overturn the law. In May 2004, the United States Court of Appeals for the Ninth Circuit upheld Oregon's law, ruling that the attorney general had overstepped his authority in trying to punish doctors who prescribed suicide drugs.

One of the most outspoken critics of suicide prevention programs is Thomas Szasz (1986). He argues that suicide is an act of a moral agent who is ultimately responsible. Szasz opposes coercive methods (such as depriving clients access to the means of suicide and involuntary hospitalization) that mental health professionals use to prevent suicide. By taking such actions against a client's wishes, practitioners have allied themselves with the police power of the state and have identified themselves as foes of individual liberty and responsibility. Szasz does not claim that suicide is always good or morally legitimate. Rather, he maintains that we must abstain from empowering agents of the state to use coercion to prevent suicide.

Recent legislation has intensified the debate over whether it is morally, ethically, and legally permissible to allow relatives, friends, or physicians to provide support, means, and actions to carry out a suicide (Rosenfeld, 2004). Two high-profile individuals have fueled the debate by virtue of their actions. Derek Humphrey, former director of the Hemlock Society (an organization that advocates people's right to end their lives), published a best-selling book, *Final Exit* (1991). It is a manual that provides practical information, such as drug dosages needed to end one's life; when published, it created a national stir. Another individual who has become a household name is Dr. Jack Kevorkian, a physician who has helped nearly 130 people to end their own lives using a device he calls a "suicide machine." Those who see Kevorkian as a courageous physician willing to help others in their search for a dignified death call him a savior; those who oppose his actions refer to him as "Dr. Death" (see the Critical Thinking feature "Do People Have a Right to Die?").

Ironically, the success of medical science has added fuel to the right-to-die movement. As a part of our remarkably successful efforts to prolong life, this society has also begun to prolong the process of dying. And this prolongation has caused many elderly or terminally ill people to fear the medical decision maker who is intent only on keeping them alive, giving no thought to their desires or dignity. They and many others find it abhorrent to impose on a dying patient a horrifying array of respirators, breathing tubes, feeding tubes, and repeated violent cardiopulmonary

CRITICAL THINKING

Do People Have a Right to Die?

On November 22, 1998, over 15 million viewers of *60 Minutes* watched in either horror or sadness the death by lethal injection of fifty-two-year-old Thomas Youk. This was not, however, a death sentence carried out for a murder conviction but the enactment of a conscious desire and decision of a man suffering from the latter stages of Lou Gehrig's disease. Youk's wife stated she was "so grateful to know that someone would relieve him of his suffering. ... I consider it the way things should be done." The man who videotaped the event was Dr. Jack Kevorkian, a retired physician, who has carried on a ten-year battle with the U.S. legal system and society over the right to die.

It is estimated that, since 1989, Kevorkian has assisted in the suicides of nearly 130 people (most of them women) with chronic debilitating diseases. The means of death was Kevorkian's "suicide machine," composed of bottles containing chemicals that could be fed intravenously into the arm of the person. The solution could bring instantaneous unconsciousness and quick painless death. His first client, Mrs. J. Adkins, suffered from Alzheimer's disease. She did not want to put her family through the agony of the disease, believed that she had a right to choose death, stated that her act was that of a rational mind, and had the consent of her husband. Many others whom Kevorkian helped commit suicide did not have diseases that threatened to kill them in the immediate future.

Before the CBS taping, charges of homicide had been brought against Kevorkian four previous times, and in each case either the charges were ultimately dropped or he was found innocent. Because of his actions, a Michigan law outlawing "physician-assisted suicides" was passed and used to charge him with manslaughter. Prosecutors contended that Kevorkian's actions in the death of Youk went far beyond what many consider "assistance." Because Thomas Youk was too weak to administer the dose himself, Kevorkian administered it for him. For that act, in 1999, the retired physician was charged with and convicted of second-degree murder, criminal assistance to a suicide, and delivery of a controlled substance. Ironically, Kevorkian welcomed the trial because he believed that the case would finally force some resolution of the issue of whether euthanasia is legal in the United States. Unfortunately, because he acted as his own attorney against the advice of the court, the verdict may be more a reflection of his lack of expertise in the courtroom.

What reactions do you have to these events? Did Thomas Youk have a right to end his own life? What reasons led you to your answer? Does a doctor—or, for that matter, anyone—have a right to help others terminate their lives? What might motivate someone like Dr. Kevorkian to risk censure and imprisonment in helping others to die? Would you be in favor of legislation that would legalize physician-assisted suicides? Why or

why not? To this day, only the state of Oregon has legalized physician-assisted suicide. These questions do not have easy answers. Although we may pride ourselves on being social scientists concerned with objective facts in helping provide answers, the topic of suicide raises unavoidable moral, legal, and ethical issues. It is certainly possible for us to study suicide in an academic fashion, but what if we encounter a friend, classmate, neighbor, or relative who is contemplating suicide? In these situations neither we nor the practicing mental health professional can be mere observers, for our actions or decisions not to act will reflect our beliefs and values about suicide. And consider this question: might there ever come a time in your life when you would contemplate suicide? Imagine yourself, like Thomas Youk, faced with losing control of your bodily functions, your ability to move about or to read or to feed yourself, and anticipating future suffocation from choking on your own saliva? Would you want to be kept alive?

We would like to have you, perhaps with other classmates, consider these questions. Can you build a case in favor of the right to die? Can you build a case against the right to take one's own life? We hope that you and your classmates will be able to clarify your thoughts and values about suicide. Remember: allowing, respecting, and understanding the diversity of views on this controversial topic are important.

resuscitations—procedures that are often futile and against the wishes of the patient and his or her family. Humane and sensitive physicians, who believe that the resulting quality of life will not merit such heroic measures but whose training impels them to sustain

life, are caught in the middle of this conflict. A civil or criminal lawsuit may be brought against the physician who agrees to allow a patient to die.

Proponents of the right to suicide believe that it can be a rational act and that mental health and medical

Fighting for the Right to Choose Dr. Jack Kevorkian, a Michigan physician, has been a lifelong advocate fighting for the repeal of laws against assisted suicide. He poses here with Marcella Lawrence and Marguerit Tate, two women he helped to die hours before Michigan's governor signed a law officially banning assisted suicides. Since then Kevorkian was actually convicted in 1999 of second-degree murder in connection with an assisted suicide of a fifty-two-year-old man suffering from Lou Gehrig's disease, which he videotaped and then aired on *60 Minutes*.

professionals should be allowed to help such patients without fear of legal or professional repercussions (Corey, 2001; Rosenfeld, 2004; Werth, 1996). Others argue, however, that suicide is not rational or that determining rationality is fraught with hazards. They cite studies indicating that suicide is a symptom of mental illness and that allowing this final act may result in "a duty to die" (Hendin, 1995; Seale & Addington-Hall, 1995). Some are voicing the fear that one result of legalizing suicide may be that patients will fall victim to coercion from relatives intent either on collecting inheritances or on convincing patients that they will overburden their loved ones and friends or become a financial drain on them. Other critics of assisted suicide fear that in this time of medical cost control, medical professionals might encourage the terminally ill to choose to die and that those who are poor and disadvantaged would receive the most encouragement (Werth, 1996).

Major problems also exist in defining the subjective terms *quality of life* and *quality of humanness* as the criteria for deciding between life and death. At what point do we consider the quality of life sufficiently poor to justify terminating it? Should people who have been severely injured or scarred (through loss of limbs, paralysis, blindness, or brain injury) be allowed to end their own lives? What about mentally retarded or emotionally disturbed people? Could it be argued that their quality of life is equally poor? Moreover, who will decide whether a person is or is not terminally ill? There are many recorded cases of

"incurable" patients who recovered when new medical techniques or treatments arrested, remitted, or cured their illnesses.

Such questions deal with ethics and human values, and they cannot be answered easily. Yet the mental health practitioner cannot avoid these questions. Like their medical counterparts, clinicians are trained to save people's lives. They have accepted the philosophical assumption that life is better than death and that no one has a right to take his or her own life. Strong social, religious, and legal sanctions support this belief. Therapists work not only with terminally ill clients who wish to take their own lives but also with disturbed clients who may have suicidal tendencies. These latter clients are not terminally ill but may be suffering severe emotional or physical pain; their deaths would bring immense pain and suffering to their loved ones. Moreover, most people who attempt suicide do not want to die, are ambivalent about the act, or find that their suicidal urge passes when their life situation improves (Bongar, 1991, 1992; Clay, 1997).

In his book, *Rational Suicide? Implications for Mental Health Professionals*, Werth (1996) summarizes several basic criteria that mental health professionals should use in making a decision to help terminate a life. First, the patient should have a hopeless condition (includes low quality of life and intense psychological or physical pain). Second, the person should be free of coercion from relatives, friends, medical professionals, and others. Third, the patient should be of sound mind and engaged in rational

Derek Humphrey Derek Humphrey, author of the bestselling book *Final Exit* (1991), helped his cancer-stricken first wife die in 1975, violating British law in the process. The authorities learned about the illegal assistance in suicide when his book *Jean's Way* appeared in 1978 but, after a police investigation, chose not to bring a prosecution. For more information, visit www.finalexit.org.

decision making. In other words, the person should be mentally competent, should have considered other options (such as psychotherapy, assisted living, and medication), and should be aware of the negative impact suicide will have on significant others. Fourth, the decision to commit suicide should be consistent with the patient's values. According to Werth, mental health professionals who have a long-term relationship with their clients have plenty of time to assess these factors. They should not prevent a client from taking his or her own life if the client has adequately addressed these four factors.

Of course, these criteria do not address the legal implications of suicide. According to one observer, no clear constitutional or legal statement gives a person the right to choose death, but the Constitution does seem to provide a basis for the right to refuse treatment, even lifesaving treatment (Powell, 1982). Despite this apparent contradiction, therapists have a responsibility to prevent suicide if they can reasonably anticipate the possibility of self-destruction. Failure to do so can result in legal liability.

Clearly, suicide and suicide prevention involve a number of important social and legal issues, as well as the personal value systems of clients and their families, mental health professionals, and those who devise and enforce our laws (Rosenfeld, 2004). And just as clearly, we need to know much more about the causes of suicide and the detection of people who are at high risk for suicide, as well as the most effective means of intervention (Rudd et al., 2004). Life is precious, and we need to do everything possible, within reason, to protect it.

SUMMARY

What do we know about suicide?

- Suicide is both a tragic and a puzzling act. In the past, it has often been kept hidden, and relatives and friends of the victim did not speak of it. Mental health professionals now realize that understanding the causes of suicide is extremely important.
- Much is known about the *facts* of suicide, but little about the reasons is understood. Although studies indicate that depression, hopelessness, and excessive alcohol consumption are highly correlated with suicide, the complex relationship between these variables and suicide is not simply one of cause and effect.

Why do people decide to end their lives?

- Early explanations of suicide were based on either a sociocultural or a psychodynamic view.
- Durkheim identified three categories of suicide on the basis of the nature of the person's relationship to a group. Egoistic suicide results from an inability to integrate oneself with society. Altruistic suicide is motivated by the need to further the goals of the group or to achieve a "higher good." Anomic suicide results when a person's relationship to the group becomes unbalanced in some dramatic fashion.
- In the psychodynamic view, self-destruction results when hostility toward another person turns inward.
- More recent evidence has indicated that biological factors may be important, but no single explanation seems sufficient to clarify the many facets of suicide.

Who are the victims of suicide?

- In recent years, childhood and adolescent suicides have increased at an alarming rate. A lack of research has limited our understanding of why children take their own lives. However, the available studies have indicated that those who attempt suicide come from families characterized by psychiatric illness (primarily drug and alcohol abuse), medical problems, suicide, paternal unemployment, and the absence of one parent. Most childhood suicide attempts occur in the home, and drug overdose is the primary means.

- Many people tend to become depressed about "feeling old" as they age, and depressed elderly people often think about suicide.

How can we intervene or prevent suicides?

- Perhaps the best way to prevent suicide is to recognize its signs and intervene before it occurs. People are more likely to commit suicide if they are older, male, have a history of attempts, describe in detail how the act will be accomplished, and give verbal hints that they are planning self-destruction.

- Crisis intervention concepts and techniques have been used successfully to treat clients who contemplate suicide. Intensive short-term therapy is used to stabilize the immediate crisis.

- Suicide prevention centers operate twenty-four hours a day to provide intervention services to all potential suicides, especially those not undergoing treatment. Telephone hot lines are staffed by well-trained paraprofessionals who will work with anyone who is contemplating suicide. In addition, these centers provide preventive education to the public.

- More and more community intervention programs are directed at organizations that may have experienced a suicide. The focus is not only on preventing future suicides but also on helping friends, family, workers, and others affected by the tragedy.

- The U.S. Surgeon General has declared suicide to be a serious public health problem and, in 1999, issued a call to develop a national blueprint to address its devastating consequences through recommendations in his *Call to Action to Prevent Suicide*.

Are there times and situations in which suicide should be an option?

- Do people have a right to take their own lives? This question is difficult to answer, particularly when the person is terminally ill and wishes to end his or her suffering. Nevertheless, therapists, like physicians, have been trained to preserve life, and they have a legal obligation to do so.

KEY TERMS

altruistic suicide (p. 399)

anomic suicide (p. 400)

egoistic suicide (p. 399)

lethality (p. 405)

psychological autopsy (p. 392)

suicidal ideation (p. 392)

suicide (p. 389)

MULTIMEDIA PREVIEW

For additional study aids, we invite you to explore our media resources accompanying *Understanding Abnormal Behavior*, Eighth Edition. The Student CD-ROM includes videos, quizzing, and critical thinking activities that help to reinforce key concepts in a fun and engaging manner. The Student Web Site provides additional interactive activities, chapter outlines, and research links that further support and complement the text. All Web resources may be accessed by logging onto the Web site at **http://psychology.college.hmco.com/students**.

CHAPTER 13
Schizophrenia: Diagnosis and Etiology

- How have our views of schizophrenia changed over time?
- What kinds of symptoms are found in this disorder?
- How do the specific types of schizophrenia differ from one another?
- Is there much chance of recovery from schizophrenia?
- What causes schizophrenia?
- Is schizophrenia an inherited condition?
- What supports the view that schizophrenia is a result of brain abnormalities?
- Can psychological factors "cause" schizophrenia?
- What is the best etiological model for schizophrenia?
- What kinds of treatments are currently available, and are they effective?

Schizophrenia is a severely disabling disorder that has a profound impact both on the victim and on family members and friends. Eric Sundstrom presents a personal perspective on the older sister who had helped to raise him and later developed schizophrenia. His early memory of her was activated when he spotted a small set of clogs:

> My family spent 3 years in Holland when my sister was in middle school. I think she was truly happy then, forming friendships and teaching me about the things she loved. It seems incredible she was once an ordinary girl, full of vibrant personality. I still remember how she taught me to read, using a now-ancient copy of *The Cat in the Hat*. When our family returned to America, all of her friends signed the clogs for her to remember them by. The clogs and a few memories are my only window into who she was then and who she should be now. (Sundstrom, 2004, p. 191)

Eric recounts how his sister developed delusions and violent behavior during her sophomore year in high school. Auditory hallucinations insulted her and commanded her to break things. One day, after a change of medication resulted in an intensification of symptoms, his sister destroyed items around the house and had to be hospitalized. After he and his brother cleaned up the broken glass, they ate dinner in silence and realized that their sister had baked quiche for them; one side filled with vegetables for his brother

and the other side plain for him. "The girl with the clogs is the same girl who cooked us dinner; she is the same girl who fought her way through college. That is who my sister is, and that is why I can love her now more than ever" (p. 192).

For the relatives of individuals with schizophrenia, the psychotic symptoms shown by their loved ones can be confusing, frightening, and heart wrenching. At times, reality becomes so distorted that affected people cannot trust their perceptions and thoughts.

Eric's sister showed some of the features of the schizophrenic disorders, which involve disorders of thought, perception, behavior, and emotional states. In this chapter we discuss the diagnosis, etiology, and treatment of schizophrenia.

Schizophrenia

Schizophrenia is a group of disorders characterized by severely impaired cognitive processes, personality disintegration, affective disturbances, and social withdrawal. People thus affected may lose contact with reality, may see or hear things that are not actually occurring, or may develop false beliefs about themselves or others.

Schizophrenia receives a great deal of attention for several reasons. First, the disorders are severely disabling and frequently require hospitalization. The financial costs of hospitalization and the psychological costs to patients, families, and friends can be enormous.

Second, the lifetime prevalence rate of schizophrenia in the United States is about 1 percent, so it affects millions of people directly and males and females equally (National Institute of Mental Health [NIMH], 2001). And third, the causes of these disorders are not well known, and it has been difficult to find effective treatments. Although DSM-IV-TR tries to present schizophrenia as a distinct disorder, evidence suggests that it is a heterogeneous clinical syndrome with different etiologies and outcomes (Roth, Flashman, Saykin, McAllister, & Vidaver, 2004; Heinrichs, 1993).

The age of onset for schizophrenia occurs earlier in males than in females. The gender ratio shifts by the mid-forties, when the percentage of women receiving this diagnosis is greater than that of men. This trend is especially pronounced in the mid-sixties and later (Castle & Murray, 1993; Howard, Rabins, Seeman, & Jeste, 2000). The reason for the gender differences in age of onset appears to be due to the presence of estrogen, which diminishes after menopause (Goldstein, 1997; Hafner et al., 1998). Estrogen may affect either dopamine levels or dopamine sensitivity, which have been associated with schizophrenia. Besides the possible protective function, higher estrogen levels also are associated with better cognitive functioning among women with schizophrenia (Hoff et al., 2001). The lifetime prevalence rate for schizophrenia is higher among African Americans (2.1 percent) and lower among Hispanic Americans (0.8 percent). The higher rate among African Americans can be accounted for by their lower socioeconomic status and higher divorce rates, which are independently related to higher rates of schizophrenia (Keith, Regier, & Rae, 1991). The lower rate among Hispanic Americans may be due both to the underreporting of symptomatology and to a lower level of help seeking (Dassori, Miller, & Saldana, 1995).

History of the Diagnostic Category and DSM-IV-TR

What is schizophrenia? Most clinicians agree that the symptoms shown by Eric Sundstrom's sister (delusional thoughts and auditory hallucinations) are consistent with a diagnosis of schizophrenia. The criteria that define this disorder, however, have changed over time. Some people who were diagnosed with schizophrenia under criteria used in the past might not receive that diagnosis today.

In 1896 Emil Kraepelin recognized that symptoms such as hallucinations, delusions, and intellectual deterioration were characteristic of a particular disorder whose onset began at an early age. He called this disorder *dementia praecox* (insanity at an early age). Because he believed that the disorder involved some

form of organic deterioration, its outcome was considered to be poor. People who recovered from dementia praecox were thought to have been misdiagnosed.

A Swiss psychiatrist, Eugen Bleuler (1911/1950), disagreed with Kraepelin's theory for several reasons. He did not believe that all or even most cases of schizophrenia developed at an early age. In his view, the symptoms of schizophrenia were the result of disordered thought processes affecting the four *As*: autism (complete self-focus), associations (unconnected ideas), affect (inappropriate emotions), and ambivalence (uncertainty over actions). He argued that the outcome of schizophrenia did not always involve progressive deterioration, and he believed that dementia praecox represented a group of disorders that have different causes. Bleuler also theorized that environmental factors interacting with a genetic predisposition produced the disorder.

Bleuler's definition of schizophrenia was broader than Kraepelin's in that age of onset and the course of the disorder were more variable. DSM-I and DSM-II incorporated the broader definition of schizophrenia and focused on Bleuler's four *As* as the criteria. Several international studies (Cooper et al., 1972; World Health Organization, 1973) revealed that other countries used a stricter definition for schizophrenia. When patients diagnosed with schizophrenia in the United States were rediagnosed according to the international standards, approximately 50 percent were placed into other categories, such as mood, personality disorders, or other psychotic disorders.

This discrepancy with other diagnostic systems forced researchers to reexamine the criteria used to define schizophrenia, and this reexamination resulted in changes in DSM-III and DSM-III-R. "The DSM-III concept is more restrictive in order to identify a group that is more homogeneous in regard to differential response to somatic therapy, presence of a familial pattern, a tendency toward onset in early adult life, recurrence, and severe functional impairment" (American Psychiatric Assocation, 1980, p. 373). DSM-IV-TR (American Psychiatric Association, 2000) continues to use the more restrictive definition. Although these changes are thought to increase diagnostic reliability and validity of research on schizophrenia, they also create difficulties in comparing earlier studies done in the United States under different diagnostic criteria.

According to the DSM-IV-TR criteria, a diagnosis of schizophrenic disorder should be given only if delusions, auditory hallucinations, or marked disturbances in thinking, affect, or speech are shown. The patient must also have deteriorated from a previous level of functioning concerning work, interpersonal relationships, self-care, and the like. Evidence should show that the disorder has lasted at least six months and that the symptoms have been present most of the time for at least one month. Organic mental disorders and affective disorders must be ruled out as causes of the patient's symptoms. (See Table 13.1 for DSM-IV-TR criteria for schizophrenia.)

The Symptoms of Schizophrenia

Symptoms of schizophrenia include delusions, hallucinations, thought disorder (shifting and unrelated ideas that produce incoherent communication), and bizarre behavior. There appear to be three uncorrelated dimensions in schizophrenia (Andreasen, Arndt, Alliger, Miller, & Flaum, 1995; Arndt, Andreasen, Flaum, Miller, & Nopoulous, 1995). The first two—psychoticism, represented by hallucinations and delusions, and disorganization, which includes disorganized speech and behavior, inappropriate affect, motor disturbances,

Eugen Bleuler (1857–1939) Bleuler was a Swiss psychiatrist who believed that the age of onset and the outcomes for schizophrenia were variable. He was the first to use the term "schizophrenia."

and disordered thought—are often described as **positive symptoms.** They appear to reflect an excess or distortion of normal functions. These symptoms are present during the active phase of the disorder and tend to disappear with treatment. **Negative symptoms,** the third dimension, are associated with inferior premorbid (before the onset of illness) social functioning and carry a poorer prognosis. One such symptom is **flat affect**—little or no emotion in situations in which strong reactions are expected. Others include *alogia* (a lack of meaningful speech) and *avolition* (an inability to take action or to become goal oriented). Positive symptoms may indicate a reversible condition, whereas negative symptoms may represent irreversible neuronal loss in a structurally abnormal brain.

Individuals with schizophrenia often become quite distressed and confused over their symptoms. One woman had terrifying hallucinations and delusions, which included seeing her nephew's head sitting on top of her VCR laughing at her and believing that flying saucers were beaming obscene words into her head and that she was being raped by the devil (Gerhardt, 1998). It is a private struggle in which some of the unusual behaviors—such as shaving or cutting off one's hair, wearing redundant clothing, or drastically changing makeup—may represent attempts to maintain identity or to deal with anxieties before a psychotic break (Campo, Frederikx, Nijman, & Merckelback, 1998).

Others may deal with the turmoil by withdrawing into themselves to obtain some peace. "I wait for time to go by. … I want calmness, to be with myself, then to evolve internally" (Corin, 1998, p. 139). Most display a feeling of personal failure and sense of inadequacy. "A normal woman will not go out with a guy who has been in a psychiatric hospital. … Will I end up alone, without a wife, without children, alone in the street?"

TABLE 13.1 DSM-IV-TR Criteria for Schizophrenia

A. At least two of the following symptoms lasting for at least one month in the active phase (exception: only one symptom if it involves bizarre delusions or if hallucinations involve a running commentary on the person or two or more voices talking with each other).

1. Delusions

2. Hallucinations

3. Disorganized speech (incoherence or frequent derailment)

4. Grossly disorganized or catatonic behavior

5. Negative symptoms (flat affect, avolition, alogia, or anhedonia)

B. During the course of the disturbance, functioning in one or more areas such as work, social relations, and self-care has deteriorated markedly from premorbid levels (in the case of a child or adolescent, failure to reach expected level of social or academic development).

C. Signs of the disorder must be present for at least six months.

D. Schizoaffective and mood disorders with psychotic features must be ruled out.

E. The disturbance is not substance-induced or caused by organic factors.

A Beautiful Mind John Nash, a Princeton University professor whose struggles with schizophrenia were portrayed in a film, addresses a news conference on October 11, 1994, after winning the Nobel Prize for economics. He struggled with his psychotic symptoms and learned to ignore hallucinations. Even today, he occasionally hears voices.

(p. 142). The despair felt by an individual with schizophrenia takes a severe toll—up to 11 percent commit suicide (Wiersma, Nienhuis, Slooff, & Giel, 1998).

Positive Symptoms

Positive symptoms represent distortions or excesses of normal functioning; with treatment, they diminish in intensity. These symptoms include delusions, hallucinations, disorganized communication and thought disturbances, and motor disturbances.

Myth vs Reality

Myth: Individuals experiencing delusions or hallucinations steadfastly accept them as reality.

Reality: The strength of hallucinations and delusions among individuals with schizophrenia varies during the course of the illness and among specific individuals. Some believe in them 100 percent, wheras others acknowledge being less certain. Even without treatment, many attempt to develop means of reestablishing contact with reality or testing out their disturbances in thought. Some individuals with schizophrenia, such as mathematician John Nash, who was portrayed in the movie *A Beautiful Mind,* are able to struggle with their illness through will power and medication. However, most need to supplement medica-

tions with specific cognitive training to develop the skills necessary to question their own hallucinations and delusions.

Delusions   The disordered thinking of schizophrenics may be exhibited in **delusions,** which are false personal beliefs that are firmly and consistently held despite disconfirming evidence or logic. Delusions reflect a loss of distinction between one's private thoughts and external reality. Individuals with schizophrenia are often terrified that their inner world has been completely exposed and that others can see into their minds and even "hear" them engaging in activities such as reading a paper. They may believe that the entire world is audience to their most private thoughts and behaviors (Leferink, 1998). Delusions may vary from those that are plausible, such as being followed or spied on, to those that are bizarre (internal organs have been removed or thoughts are being placed in their minds).

Studies have suggested that delusions may differ in their strength and their effects on the person's life. In one study (Harrow et al., 2004), nearly half of individuals with delusions had some questions regarding their beliefs, and 21 percent were fully aware that others might view their beliefs as atypical. An example of a delusion follows:

Ms. A., an 83-year-old widow who had lived alone for fifteen years, complained that the occupant of an upstairs flat was excessively noisy and that he moved furniture around late at night to disturb her. Over a period of six months, she developed delusional persecutory ideas about this man. He wanted to frighten her from her home and had started to transmit "violet rays" through the ceiling to harm her and her ten-year-old female mongrel dog. ... For protection, she placed her mattress under the kitchen table and slept there at night. She constructed what she called an "air raid shelter" for her dog from a small table and a pile of suitcases and insisted that the dog sleep in it. When I visited Ms. A. at her home, it was apparent that the dog's behavior had become so conditioned by that of its owner that upon hearing any sound from the flat upstairs, such as a door closing, it would immediately go to the kitchen and enter the shelter. (Howard, 1992, p. 414)

Ms. A. absolutely believed in her delusion and had little insight into her behavior. Hers was a delusion of persecution, which is one of several types, as listed here.

■ *Delusions of grandeur* A person's belief that he or she is a famous or powerful person (from the present or past). Individuals with schizophrenia may assume the identities of these other people.

■ *Delusions of control* A person's belief that other people, animals, or objects are trying to influence or take control of him or her.

■ *Delusions of thought broadcasting* A belief that others can hear the individual's thoughts.

■ *Delusions of persecution* A person's belief that others are plotting against, mistreating, or even trying to kill him or her.

■ *Delusions of reference* A person's belief that he or she is always the center of attention or that all happenings revolve about him- or herself—for instance, that others are always whispering behind his or her back.

■ *Thought withdrawal* A person's belief that his or her thoughts are being removed from his or her mind.

A rare delusion is *Capgras's syndrome* (named after the person who first reported it). It is the belief in the existence of identical "doubles" who may coexist with or replace significant others or the patient. One daughter, for example, would phone her mother asking questions such as what she wore as a Halloween costume at the age of twelve or about the children who came to one of her birthday parties. "She was testing me because she didn't think I was her mother. ... No matter what question I answered, she was just sobbing" (Stark, 2004, p. A1). The daughter believed that her mother had been replaced by an imposter in a body suit and that her real mother had been kidnapped.

Individuals with schizophrenia may reach a conclusion on little information, which may be related to the development of unusual beliefs. Delusional individuals appear to make errors during the stages of hypothesis formation and evaluation. They develop unlikely hypotheses and then overestimate the probability that the hypotheses are true. In one study, delusional individuals demonstrated a reasoning bias when rating narratives of twenty-five actual delusions involving themes of grandiosity, persecution, thought broadcasting, or thought insertion as "more likely to be true" than nondelusional patients. Interestingly, they did not display this reasoning bias when presented with neutral narratives (themes that involved the probability that red or black balls could be picked blindly from a bag with differing proportions of colored balls). To account for these differences, the researchers hypothesized that delusional individuals may have an attentional bias for emotionally salient or threat-related information (McGuire et al., 2001).

People with schizophrenia can be trained to challenge their delusions. One fifty-one-year-old patient believed—with almost 100 percent certainty—that she

Delusions of Grandeur Assuming the identity of another, powerful person can be a sign that an individual suffering from schizophrenia is experiencing delusions of grandeur.

was younger than twenty and that she was the daughter of Princess Anne. Her therapist asked her to view her delusion as only one possible interpretation of the event. Then they discussed evidence for her belief, and the therapist presented the inconsistencies and irrationality of the belief, as well as alternative explanations. After this procedure, the patient reported a large drop in the conviction of her beliefs, stating "I look 50 and I tire more quickly than I used to; I must be 50" (Lowe & Chadwick, 1990, p. 471). She agreed that she was probably older than Princess Anne and therefore could not be her daughter. Belief modification appears to be a helpful procedure for some individuals with schizophrenia, though there is some controversy surrounding this approach, as the Mental Health and Society feature "Should We Challenge Delusions and Hallucinations?" illustrates.

Perceptual Distortion Those with schizophrenia often report **hallucinations,** which are sensory perceptions that are not directly attributable to environmental

MENTAL HEALTH AND SOCIETY

Should We Challenge Delusions and Hallucinations?

The doctor asked of a patient who insisted that he was dead: "Look. Dead men don't bleed, right?" When the man agreed, the doctor pricked the man's finger, and showed him the blood. The patient said, "What do you know, dead men do bleed after all." (Walkup, 1995, p. 323)

Clinicians have often been unsure about whether to challenge psychotic symptoms. Some believe that the delusions and hallucinations serve an adaptive function and that any attempt to change them would be useless or even dangerous. The previous example is supposed to illustrate the futility of using logic in treating people with schizophrenia. However, Walkup and other clinicians (Beck & Rector, 2000; Chadwick et al., 2000; Chadwick & Birchwood, 1994; Kuipers et al., 1997) have found that some clients respond well to challenges to their hallucinations and delusions.

The approach has two phases. In the first, hypothetical contradictions are used to assess how open the patients are to conflicting information.

During this phase, patients are introduced to information that might contradict their beliefs, and it is here that their delusions are often weakened.

- A woman, H. J., with auditory hallucinations was asked if her belief in the "voices" would change if it could be determined that they were coming from her. She agreed. She was given a set of industrial earmuffs, which she wore. She still reported hearing voices.
- A woman believed that God was commanding her to kill. She was asked if her belief would be lessened if a priest informed her that God would not ask anyone to kill another person.

In the second phase the therapist issues a verbal challenge, asking clients to give evidence for their beliefs and to develop alternative interpretations. For example, one client claimed that voices were accurate in telling her when her spouse would return. The therapist asked how she might determine her husband's return if the voices were

unable to foretell the future. Another patient who claimed he would be killed if he did not comply with auditory commands was told that he could resist the voices and would not die.

Alternative explanations are proposed for the hallucinations, such as the possibility that the voices are "self-talk" or thoughts. After cognitive behavioral treatment, most patients report a decrease in the strength of their beliefs in their psychotic symptoms. In H. J.'s case (presented earlier), her degree of certainty about her auditory hallucinations dropped from 100 percent to 20 percent. Although she still heard voices telling her she would die, she learned to disregard them and attributed them as "coming from her head."

Should we challenge psychotic symptoms? We are beginning to find that the development of active coping responses to symptoms is better than "getting along with them" (Bak et al., 2003).

stimuli. They may claim to see people or objects, to hear voices, or to smell peculiar odors that are not really present. (Note the distinction between hallucinations and delusions: hallucinations are false sensory experiences, whereas delusions are false intellectual experiences.) Hallucinations are not **pathognomonic**—that is, they are not specifically distinctive to this disorder. Persons with certain mood disorders, brief reactive psychoses, and schizophreniform disorders also report hallucinations. But it does appear that individuals with schizophrenia are more likely to report bizarre hallucinations than are persons with other disorders.

Hallucinations may involve a single sensory modality or a combination of modalities: hearing (*auditory* hallucinations), seeing (*visual* hallucinations), smelling (*olfactory* hallucinations), feeling (*tactile* hallucina-

tions), and tasting (*gustatory* hallucinations). Auditory hallucinations are the most common and can range from being malevolent to being benevolent to having qualities of both (Copolov, Mackinnon, & Trauer, 2004). The greatest distress is expressed when the voices are dominant and insulting and the patient has a lack of communication with the voice (Vaughan & Fowler, 2004). Auditory hallucinations appear to be "real" to the individual experiencing them. In one study, 61 percent reported that the voices had a distinct gender, 46 percent believed that the voice was that of a friend, family member, or acquaintance, and 80 percent reported having back-and-forth conversations with the voices. The voices, in some cases, introduced themselves to the patients and acted like real persons. As one individual responded, "They are not imaginary. They see what I do. They tell me that I'm baking a cake. They must be there. How would they know what I'm doing?" (Garrett & Silva, 2003, p. 447). Most believed the voices were independent entities, and some had conducted "research" to test the reality of the voices. One had said she initially thought that the voice might be her own but rejected it when her voice called her "mommy," something she would not call herself.

As noted earlier, delusions and hallucinations can be extremely distressing to people with schizophrenia, as they respond to their internal realities. One college student who suffered auditory hallucinations involving messages from radio and television programs asked, "How can I tell when the radio is really on and when it is my imagination?" This question obviously reflects an attempt to discriminate between reality and hallucinations. Some people have developed ways of coping with their hallucinations. Romme, Honig, Noorthoorn, and Escher (1992) studied 186 individuals with schizophrenia and found that approximately one-third had developed coping strategies to reduce or even prevent psychotic symptoms. These strategies included:

1. *Distraction* Taking a shower, jogging, watching a video, meditating, and so on.

2. *Ignoring* One woman had auditory hallucinations telling her to injure herself. Her husband asked if she would harm herself if their neighbor told her to. She said no and has learned to ignore the voices.

3. *Selective listening* A woman was able to select positive aspects from the voices.

4. *Setting limits* One patient indicated that she had made a deal with the voices: they were allowed expression after 8 P.M., but not during the day. This was successful in removing the impact of the voices.

During acute stages (in which the symptoms are most prominent), the person may be so involved in hallucinations that he or she cannot do anything but respond as though they were real. This may be true concerning delusions as well.

Disorganized Thought and Speech

Interviewer: ALL POLICE WORLD DISAPPEAR. ... WHAT HAPPENS?

Patient: WHEN WORLD c.e.l.l. c.e.l.l. GROW SPREAD SPREAD LATER YOU KNOW d.o.n.o.s.a.u.r. WALK SIDEWAYS MONKEY RISE UP SLOW (Thacker, 1994, p. 821).

Disordered thinking is a primary characteristic of schizophrenia, as illustrated in the preceding example. Interestingly, the response was obtained from a deaf individual with schizophrenia. Disturbances in thought and communication were demonstrated during the interview through the use of sign language. During communication, the individual may jump from one topic to another, speak in an unintelligible manner, or reply tangentially to questions. The **loosening of associations,** or *cognitive slippage,* is the continual shifting from topic to topic without any apparent logical or meaningful connection between thoughts. It may be shown by incoherent speech and bizarre and idiosyncratic responses, as indicated in the following example (Thomas, 1995):

Interviewer: "You just must be an emotional person, that's all."

Patient (1): "Well, not very much I mean, what if I were dead. It's a funeral age. Well I um. Now I had my toenails operated on. They got infected and I wasn't able to do it. But they wouldn't let me at my tools." (p. 289)

The beginning phrase in the first sentence appears appropriate to the interviewer's comment. However, the reference to death is not. Slippage appears in the comments referring to a funeral age, having toenails operated on, and getting tools. None of these thoughts are related to the interviewer's observation, and they have no hierarchical structure or organization. People with schizophrenia may also respond to words or phrases in a very concrete manner and demonstrate difficulty with abstractions. A saying such as "a rolling stone gathers no moss" might be interpreted as "moss can't grow on a rock that is rolling." Part of their communication problem appears to be an inability to inhibit contextually irrelevant information (Titone, Levy, & Holzman, 2000). For example, the word "pen" has several meanings depending on the context (animal enclosure, writing instrument, etc.) and might be related to other words such as "paper" and "pig." Both control participants and individuals with schizophrenia are able to respond to the dominant meaning of the words, but the latter also responds as strongly to related words. Thus the word "pen" might generate an equally strong response of "paper" or "pig." Why individuals with schizophrenia are unable to inhibit secondary or related meanings of words or display disordered thinking is unknown.

Disorganized Motor Disturbances

The symptoms of schizophrenia that involve motor functions can be quite bizarre. The person may show extreme activity levels (either unusually high or unusually low), peculiar body movements or postures, strange gestures and grimaces, or a combination of these. Like hallucinations, a patient's motoric behaviors may be related to his or her delusions. For example, during a clinical interview one

Painting the Symptoms of Schizophrenia The inner turmoil and private fantasies of schizophrenics are often revealed in their artwork. The paintings you see here were created in the 1930s and 1940s by psychiatric patients in European hospitals. They are part of the Prinzhorn collection. What do you think the paintings represent?

the *catatonic* type of schizophrenia (to be discussed shortly). A catatonic patient may stand for hours at a time, perhaps with one arm stretched out to the side, or may lie on the floor or sit awkwardly on a chair, staring, aware of what is going on around, but not responding or moving. If a hospital attendant tries to change the patient's position, the patient may either resist stubbornly or may simply assume and maintain the new position. Catatonic symptoms are not specific to schizophrenia and may also occur with mood disorders or medical conditions.

Negative Symptoms

Negative symptoms have been associated with a poor prognosis and may be the result of structural abnormalities in the brain. Clinicians must be careful to distinguish between *primary symptoms* (symptoms that arise from the disease itself) and *secondary symptoms* (symptoms that may develop as a response to medication and institutionalization). It is the former that researchers are primarily interested in. You may recall from our earlier discussion that the negative symptoms include *avolition* (an inability to take action or become goal-oriented), *alogia* (a lack of meaningful speech), and *flat affect* (little or no emotion in situations in which strong reactions are expected; a delusional patient, for instance, might explain in detail how parts of his or her body are rotting away but show absolutely no concern or worry through voice tone or facial expression). Most are unaware or only somewhat aware of negative symptoms (Selten, Gernaat, Nolen, Wiersma, & van den Bosch, 1998). Beiser, Fleming, Iacono, and Lin (1988) reported that, of the patients with schizophrenia whom they had studied, more than one-half showed restricted

patient with schizophrenia kept lowering his chin to his chest and then raising his head again. Asked why he lowered his head in that way, the patient replied that the atmospheric pressure often became too great to bear, and it forced his head down.

Some individuals with this disorder may display extremely high levels of motor activity, moving about quickly, swinging their arms wildly, talking rapidly and unendingly, or pacing constantly. At the other extreme, others hardly move at all, staring out into space (or perhaps into themselves) for long periods of time. The inactive patients also tend to show little interest in others, to respond only minimally, and to have few friends. During periods of withdrawal, they are frequently preoccupied with personal fantasies and daydreams.

The assumption and maintenance of an unusual (and often awkward) body position is characteristic of

affect ("expressionless face and voice") regardless of the topic of discussion. However, flat affect may not be a symptom of the disorder but rather the result of institutionalization, depression, or antipsychotic medications (Lieberman, 1995; Tremeau et al., 2005). If negative symptoms are a result of medication, institutionalization, or a mood disorder, they must not be used in making the diagnosis of schizophrenia.

Associated Features and Mental Disorders

Several other characteristics are relatively common in individuals with schizophrenia. Anhedonia (an inability to feel pleasure) is often present. Social anhedonia, or the decreased ability to derive pleasure from interactions with others, is also observed in depression but appears to be an enduring characteristic of individuals with schizophrenia (Blanchard, Horan, & Brown, 2001). Another common associated symptom of schizophrenia is lack of insight. In one study (Amador et al., 1994), more than 57 percent of the participants were either "unaware" or "moderately unaware" of their symptoms (see Figure 13.1). During the active phase of their disorder, people with schizophrenia often cannot recognize that their thinking is disturbed. As one individual wrote, "I had always been proud of my academic achievements, and now my mind was literally grinding to a halt and my thought processes had become irrational. ... Electricity was constantly arcing across from electrical appliances to my temple. Associated irrational behavior was that I took a metal tray outside to try to triangulate the source of the electricity" (Tolton, 2004, p. 470). A person who had obtained a Ph.D. could not understand the bizarre nature of her hallucinations and delusions, such as being controlled by the television station, having the power to make dogs bark by using mind rays, and receiving brain waves from alien creatures (Payne, 1992). Lack of insight is not, by itself, enough to justify a diagnosis of schizophrenia, for it is also displayed in other disorders. Individuals with schizophrenia often suffer from other mental disorders, such as PTSD, phobias, depersonalization, depression, and substance abuse (Muenzenmaier et al., 2005). A large percentage suffer from a severe level of social anxiety (Pallanti, Quercioli, & Hollander, 2004) and approximately 11 percent of individuals with this disorder commit suicide. Factors associated with the highest risk of suicide include severe depression, younger age, and the experience of traumatic stress (Schwartz & Cohen, 2001).

Cultural Issues

Culture may affect how symptoms are displayed or interpreted. In Japan schizophrenia is highly stigmatized. Part of the problem is that the condition is called *seishin-bunretsu-byou*, which roughly translates as a split in mind or spirit. The term conjured up an irreversible condition. Because of this connotation, the Japanese Society of Psychiatry and Neurology is considering finding a less negative term (Sugiura, Sakamoto, Tanaka, Tomada, & Kitamura, 2001). In Western countries, individuals with schizophrenia tend to show more depressive symptoms and to report thought broadcasting and insertion, whereas those in non-Western countries tend to report more visual and directed auditory hallucinations (Jilek, 2001). The content of delusions also seems to be influenced by culture and society. During the social and political upheavals of the period known as the Cultural Revolution in China in the 1960s, a number of different delusions appeared among Chinese patients with schizophrenia (Yu-Fen & Neng, 1981). These include the delusion of leadership lineage, in which patients insist that their

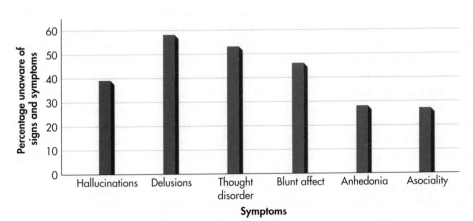

FIGURE 13.1 Lack of Awareness of Psychotic Symptoms in Patients with Schizophrenia Most individuals with schizophrenia are unaware or only moderately aware that they have symptoms of the disorder. The symptoms they were most unaware of having were delusions, thought disorder, and blunt or flat affect.

Source: Amador et al. (1994, p. 830).

FIGURE 13.2 Disorders Chart: Schizophrenia

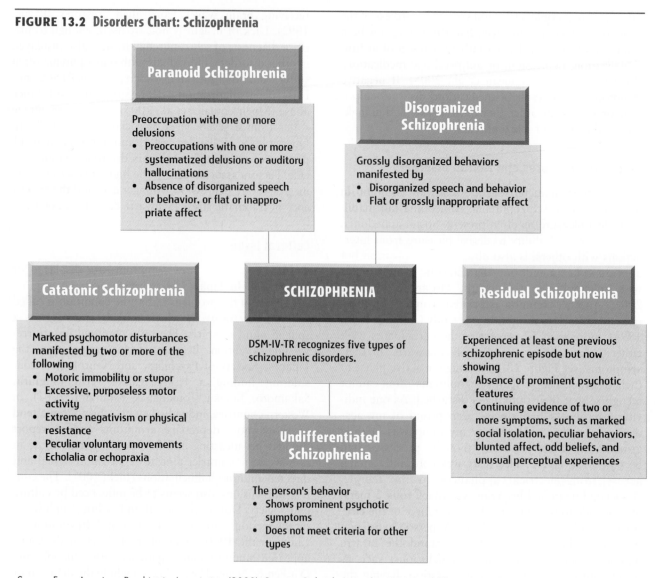

Paranoid Schizophrenia

Preoccupation with one or more delusions
- Preoccupations with one or more systematized delusions or auditory hallucinations
- Absence of disorganized speech or behavior, or flat or inappropriate affect

Disorganized Schizophrenia

Grossly disorganized behaviors manifested by
- Disorganized speech and behavior
- Flat or grossly inappropriate affect

Catatonic Schizophrenia

Marked psychomotor disturbances manifested by two or more of the following
- Motoric immobility or stupor
- Excessive, purposeless motor activity
- Extreme negativism or physical resistance
- Peculiar voluntary movements
- Echolalia or echopraxia

SCHIZOPHRENIA

DSM-IV-TR recognizes five types of schizophrenic disorders.

Residual Schizophrenia

Experienced at least one previous schizophrenic episode but now showing
- Absence of prominent psychotic features
- Continuing evidence of two or more symptoms, such as marked social isolation, peculiar behaviors, blunted affect, odd beliefs, and unusual perceptual experiences

Undifferentiated Schizophrenia

The person's behavior
- Shows prominent psychotic symptoms
- Does not meet criteria for other types

Source: From American Psychiatric Association (2000); Beratis, Gabriel, & Hoidas (1994); Pfuhlmann & Stober (1997).

parents are people in authority; the delusion of being tested, in which patients believe that their superiors are assessing them to determine whether they are suitable for promotion; the delusion of impending arrest, in which patients assume that they are about to be arrested by authorities; and the delusion of being married, in which a female patient insists that she has a husband even though she is unmarried.

Ethnic group differences have also been found. A comparison of the symptoms of Americans of Irish and Italian descent who were hospitalized for schizophrenia found that Irish Americans tended to show less hostility and acting out but more fixed delusions than did Italian Americans. These differences have been attributed to cultural-familial backgrounds: in

Irish families, mothers played a very dominant role, were quite strict, and prohibited strong emotional displays; in Italian families, mothers showed the opposite pattern (Opler, 1967). Similarly, Japanese patients hospitalized for schizophrenia are often described as rigid, compulsive, withdrawn, and passive—symptoms that reflect the Japanese cultural values of conformity within the community and reserve within the family (S. Sue & Morishima, 1982). In a study of 273 patients with schizophrenia admitted to hospitals and mental health centers in Missouri over a three-and-one-half-year period, researchers found that African-American patients exhibited more severe symptoms than white patients: angry outbursts, impulsiveness, and strongly antisocial behavior. They also showed

FIGURE 13.2 Disorders Chart: Schizophrenia (continued)

SCHIZOPHRENIA	Prevalence	Age of Onset	Course
Paranoid Schizophrenia	Most common type, found equally in men and women	In the 30s; later in life than other types; later onset in women	Prognosis better than with other types; often little impairment in occupational functioning
Disorganized Schizophrenia	Somewhat common type; more common in females	Mid to late teens; earlier in females than in males	Prognosis poor; continuous course without significant remission
Catatonic Schizophrenia	Rare in United States but more prevalent in non-Western countries	Late teens to early 20s	Course may be intermittent or insidious and chronic
Undifferentiated Schizophrenia	Relatively common type; found equally in men and women	Early 20s or somewhat earlier	Uncertain; depends on specific symptom patterns
Residual Schizophrenia	Somewhat common type	Early 20s for both males and females	Course may be time-limited, representing a transition between psychotic episodes

greater disorientation and confusion and more severe hallucinatory behaviors compared with white patients (Abebimpe, Chu, Klein, & Lange, 1982).

However, between-group differences are difficult to interpret. As DSM-IV-TR notes, "There is some evidence that clinicians may have a tendency to overdiagnose Schizophrenia in some ethnic groups. Studies conducted in the United Kingdom and the United States suggest that Schizophrenia may be diagnosed more often in individuals who are African American and Asian American than in other racial groups" (American Psychiatric Association, 2000, p. 307). It is not clear whether these differences in rates are actual or whether they represent clinician bias. Cultural differences between patient and clinician may also produce diagnostic errors—the greater the difference, the greater the likelihood of error. Finally, misdiagnosis can result from racial stereotyping or bias or from applying diagnostic systems based on white middle-class norms to other racial groups.

Types of Schizophrenia

Five types of schizophrenic disorders are traditionally recognized: paranoid, disorganized, catatonic, undifferentiated, and residual (see Figure 13.2).

Paranoid Schizophrenia

The most common form of schizophrenia is the paranoid type. **Paranoid schizophrenia** is characterized by one or more systematized delusions or auditory hallucinations and by the absence of such symptoms as disorganized speech and behavior or flat affect. Some delusions may function to protect the self-concept by turning personal problems into an accusation that "others are responsible for the bad things that are happening to me." Several studies have found that individuals with paranoid delusions externalize their problems (Kinderman & Bentall, 1996, 1997). Delusions of persecution are the most common symptom. The deluded individuals believe that others are plotting against them, are talking about them, or are out to harm them in some way. They are constantly suspicious, and their interpretations of the behavior and motives of others are distorted. A friendly, smiling bus driver is seen as someone who is laughing at them derisively. A busy clerk who fails to offer help is part of a plot to mistreat them. A telephone call that was a wrong number is an act of harassment or an attempt to monitor their comings and goings. Interestingly, as compared with non-paranoid schizophrenic patients and control participants, paranoid schizophrenic patients were more accurate in recognizing genuine nonverbal expressions of emotions (Davis & Gibson, 2000).

> Mr. A., a thirty-seven-year-old Mexican-American Vietnam veteran previously treated at several Veterans Administration hospitals with the diagnosis of paranoid schizophrenia, came to the emergency room stating, "My life is in danger."... Mr. A. told a semicoherent story of international spy intrigue that was built around the release of soldiers still missing in action or held as prisoners of war in Vietnam. He believed he was hunted by Vietnamese agents. ... Mr. A. reported hearing the voices of the men from his company who died. ... These voices tended to severely criticize and chastise him. He had become so disturbed by these beliefs and auditory hallucinations that he made suicidal efforts to escape the torment. (Glassman, Magulac, & Darko, 1987, pp. 658–659)

Individuals with paranoid schizophrenia may be prone to anger, as many feel persecuted. The prognosis for the paranoid type tends to be more positive than for other types of schizophrenia. A similar disorder, **delusional disorder,** is characterized by persistent, non-bizarre delusions that are not accompanied by other unusual or odd behaviors. It is not a form of schizophrenia, although it is often confused with paranoid schizophrenia. Delusional disorder is described in the Mental Health and Society feature "Delusional Disorder."

Disorganized Schizophrenia

Disorganized schizophrenia (formerly called *hebephrenic schizophrenia*) is characterized by grossly disorganized behaviors manifested in disorganized speech and behavior and flat or grossly inappropriate affect. Behaviors may begin at an early age. People with this disorder act in an absurd, incoherent, or very odd manner that conforms to the stereotype of "crazy" behavior. Their emotional responses to real-life situations are typically flat, but a silly smile and

childish giggle may appear at inappropriate times (Kumperscak et al., 2005). The hallucinations and delusions of patients with disorganized schizophrenia tend to shift from theme to theme rather than remain centered on a single idea, such as persecution or sin. Because of the severity of the disorder, many people affected with disorganized schizophrenia are unable to care for themselves and are institutionalized. People with this disorder usually exhibit extremely bizarre and seemingly childish behaviors, such as masturbating in public or fantasizing aloud.

Catatonic Schizophrenia

Marked disturbance in motor activity—either extreme excitement or motoric immobility—is the prime characteristic of **catatonic schizophrenia.** Diagnostic criteria include two or more of the following symptoms: motoric immobility or stupor; excessive, purposeless motor activity; extreme negativism (resisting direction) or physical resistance; peculiar voluntary posturing or movements; or echolalia (repetition of other people's speech) or echopraxia (repetition of other people's movements; American Psychiatric Association, 2000). This disorder is quite rare but somewhat more prevalent in non-Western countries.

People with *excited catatonia* are agitated and hyperactive. They may talk and shout constantly, while moving or running until they drop from exhaustion. They sleep little and are continually "on the go." Their behavior can become dangerous, however, and violent acts are not uncommon. People in *withdrawn catatonia* are extremely unresponsive with respect to motor activity. They show prolonged periods of stupor and mutism, despite their awareness of all that is going on around them. Some may adopt and maintain strange postures and refuse to move or change position. Others exhibit a *waxy flexibility,* allowing themselves to be "arranged" in almost any position and then remaining in that position for long periods of time. During periods of extreme withdrawal, people with catatonic schizophrenia may not eat or control their bladder or bowel functions. Alternating periods of excited motor activity and withdrawal may occur in this disorder.

Undifferentiated and Residual Schizophrenia

Undifferentiated schizophrenia is diagnosed when the person's behavior shows prominent psychotic symptoms that do not meet the criteria for the paranoid, disorganized, or catatonic categories. These symptoms may include thought disturbances, delusions, hallucinations, incoherence, and severely impaired behavior.

MENTAL HEALTH AND SOCIETY

Delusional Disorder

Delusional disorder is often confused with schizophrenia. In both, thought processes are disturbed. Nevertheless, some differences do exist. Delusional disorder involves "nonbizarre beliefs" (situations that could actually occur) that have lasted for at least one month. Also, except for the delusion, the person's behavior is not odd. In schizophrenia, additional disturbances in thoughts and perceptions are involved. People with delusional disorder behave normally when their delusional ideas are not being discussed. Common themes in delusional disorders involve

- *Erotomania*—the belief that someone is in love with you; usually the love is romanticized rather than sexual.
- *Grandiosity*—the conviction that you have great, unrecognized talent or have some special ability or relationship with an important individual.
- *Jealousy*—the conviction that your spouse or partner is being unfaithful.
- *Persecution*—the belief in being conspired or plotted against.
- *Somatic complaints*—convictions of having body odor,

being malformed, or being infested by insects or parasites.

The following case illustrates some features of delusional disorders:

Mr. A, a fifty-five-year-old single man, was remanded to the Regional Psychiatric Centre. ... For over twenty-one years he had pursued a famous female entertainer... He met the entertainer for the first time twenty-one years ago when she invited him to join her fan club. Since then he has bombarded her with thousands of phone calls, many letters and gifts. ... Notwithstanding her public denials, he has maintained the belief that she loves him, approves and encourages their relationship. ... Several things were responsible for "reinforcing" his behaviour. In particular, she had never returned any of his letters or gifts. He implied that she communicated with him through her songs but would not elaborate. ... His identical twin brother still lived at home and also had problems of an emotional nature with a woman. She had to resort to calling the police, but according to Mr. A's

mother, "at least he knew when to quit." (Menzies, Fedoroff, Green, & Isaacson, 1995, p. 530)

Erotomania occurs more commonly in females, but most who come to the attention of the law are males. One homeless man was arrested after lounging naked by a swimming pool he believed to belong to former tennis pro Anna Kournikova. He explained to the police that Anna loved him and had left the door unlocked and laid out clothing for him ("Man Accused," 2005). Lack of feedback may play a role in the development of delusional disorder (Zayas & Grossberg, 1998). In a study of people with this disorder, most were characterized as socially isolated, and nearly half had a physical impairment such as deafness or visual problems (Holden, 1987). A decreased ability to obtain corrective feedback, combined with a preexisting personality type that tends toward suspiciousness, may increase the susceptibility of developing delusional beliefs.

Sometimes undifferentiated schizophrenia turns out to be an early stage of another subtype.

The diagnosis of **residual schizophrenia** is reserved for people who have had at least one previous schizophrenic episode but who are now showing an absence of prominent psychotic features. There is continuing evidence of two or more symptoms, such as marked social isolation, peculiar behaviors, blunted affect, odd beliefs, or unusual perceptual experiences. The disorder may be in remission. In any case, the person's symptoms are neither strong enough nor prominent enough to warrant classification as one of the other types of schizophrenia.

Psychotic Disorders That Were Once Considered Schizophrenia

Brief psychotic episodes were considered to represent acute forms of schizophrenia in DSM-II. With DSM-III-R and DSM-IV-TR, people who have "schizophrenic" episodes that last fewer than six months are now diagnosed as having either **brief psychotic disorder** (duration of at least one day but less than one month) or **schizophreniform disorder** (duration of at least one month but less than six months). In contrast to schizophrenia, a diagnosis of schizophreniform disorder does not require impairment in social or occupational functioning.

Characteristics of Disorganized Schizophrenia Grossly disorganized behavior in which an individual dresses or behaves in an unusual manner is displayed in some people with schizophrenia. Here, a hospitalized patient showers in her clothes. Would the woman understand that this behavior is odd?

Differences between these disorders and schizophrenia are shown in Table 13.2. Although they appear to be distinct, the disorders are often highly similar in characteristics. DSM-IV-TR recommends that the diagnoses of brief psychotic disorder and schizophreniform disorder be "provisional." For example, an initial diagnosis of brief psychotic disorder should change to schizophreniform disorder if it lasts longer than one month and to schizophrenia if it lasts longer than six months. (Approximately two-thirds of those with schizophreniform disorder will later receive a diagnosis of schizophrenia or schizoaffective disorder; see the next section.) Because duration is the only accurate means of distinguishing among the disorders, questions about the validity of categories have been raised.

Characteristics of Catatonic Schizophrenia Individuals with catatonic schizophrenia experience a variety of disturbances in motor activity. Those who are excited exhibit great agitation and hyperactivity; those who are withdrawn (like the woman shown in this picture) may exhibit extreme unresponsiveness or adopt strange postures.

Other Psychotic Disorders

Other psychotic disorders include delusional disorder, shared psychotic disorder, and schizoaffective disorder (American Psychiatric Association, 2000). Delusional disorder was discussed more fully in the Mental Health and Society feature earlier in this chapter. In shared psychotic disorder, a person with a close relationship with an individual with delusional or psychotic beliefs comes to accept those beliefs (Wehmeier, Barth, & Remschmidt, 2003). In one case, seven members of a family shared the same delusional belief of being poisoned by government forces. They all exhibited the same pattern of physical complaints due to the "poisoning" (Bryant, 1997). Shared psychotic disorder is relatively rare and is more prevalent among those who are socially isolated. The pattern generally involves a family member or partner acquiring the delusional

TABLE 13.2   Comparison of Brief Psychotic Disorder, Schizophreniform Disorders, and Schizophrenia

	Brief Psychotic Disorder	Schizophreniform Disorders	Schizophrenia
Duration	Less than one month	Less than six months	Six months or more
Psychosocial Stressor	Always present	Usually present	May or may not be present
Symptoms	Emotional turmoil; psychotic symptoms	Emotional turmoil; vivid psychotic symptoms	Emotional reactions variable; hallucinations
Outcome	Return to premorbid level of functioning	Possible return to earlier, higher level of functioning	Return to earlier, higher level of functioning is uncommon
Familial pattern	No information; possible relationship to mood disorder	Possible increased risk of schizophrenia among family members	Higher prevalence of schizophrenia among family members

belief from the dominant individual (Neagoe, 2000). In many cases, an individual who shares another person's delusional or psychotic beliefs loses faith in those beliefs when the two individuals are separated. Schizoaffective disorder includes both a mood disorder (major depression or bipolar disorder) and the presence of psychotic symptoms "for at least two weeks in the absence of prominent mood symptoms" (American Psychiatric Association, 2000, p. 323). The prognosis appears to be more positive for this disorder than for schizophrenia.

The Course of Schizophrenia

It is popularly believed that overwhelming stress can cause a well-adjusted and relatively normal person to experience a schizophrenic breakdown. There are, in fact, recorded instances of the sudden onset of psychotic behaviors in previously well-functioning people. Soldiers have been reported to develop auditory, visual, and tactile hallucinations under combat conditions (Spivak, Trottern, Mark, Bleich, & Weizman, 1992). In most cases, however, the person's *premorbid personality* (personality before the onset of major symptoms) shows some impairment. Similarly, most people with schizophrenia recover gradually rather than suddenly. The typical course of schizophrenia consists of three phases: prodromal, active, and residual.

The *prodromal phase* includes the onset and buildup of schizophrenic symptoms. Social withdrawal and isolation, peculiar behaviors, inappropriate affect, poor communication patterns, and neglect of personal grooming may become evident during this phase. Of eleven patients who were interviewed in one

study (Campo et al., 1998), nine indicated that they had drastically changed their appearances (cutting or changing hairstyles, wearing multiples of the same type of clothing) just before the onset of the schizophrenic episode. They said the changes were an attempt to maintain their identities. Friends and relatives often considered such behavior odd or peculiar.

Often, psychosocial stressors or excessive demands on an individual with schizophrenia in the prodromal phase result in the onset of prominent psychotic symptoms, or the *active phase* of schizophrenia. In this phase, the person shows the full-blown symptoms of schizophrenia, including severe disturbances in thinking, deterioration in social relationships, and flat or markedly inappropriate affect.

At some later time, the person may enter the *residual phase,* in which the symptoms are no longer prominent. The severity of the symptoms declines, and the individual may show the milder impairment found in the prodromal phase. (At this point, the diagnosis would be residual schizophrenia.) Complete recovery is rare, although long-term studies have shown that many people with schizophrenia can lead productive lives (see Figure 13.3 for different courses of the disease). For whatever reason, recovery rates appear higher in developing countries. (See the Critical Thinking feature "Schizophrenia in Developing Countries" for a discussion of this phenomenon.)

Long-Term Outcome Studies

What are the chances for recovery or improvement from schizophrenia? Kraepelin believed that the disorder follows a deteriorating course. He would have

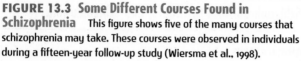

FIGURE 13.3 Some Different Courses Found in Schizophrenia This figure shows five of the many courses that schizophrenia may take. These courses were observed in individuals during a fifteen-year follow-up study (Wiersma et al., 1998).

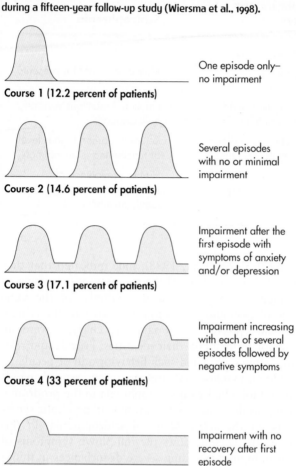

Course 1 (12.2 percent of patients)   One episode only—no impairment

Course 2 (14.6 percent of patients)   Several episodes with no or minimal impairment

Course 3 (17.1 percent of patients)   Impairment after the first episode with symptoms of anxiety and/or depression

Course 4 (33 percent of patients)   Impairment increasing with each of several episodes followed by negative symptoms

Course 5 (11 percent of patients)   Impairment with no recovery after first episode

than 26 percent showed complete remission of symptoms, although about half of this group had had more than one psychotic episode. About 50 percent showed partial remission of symptoms that were either accompanied by anxiety and depression or negative symptoms, and 11 percent showed no recovery after the initial psychotic episode. Relapses occurred in two-thirds of this sample, after which about one of six showed no remission of symptoms (Wiersma et al., 1998). "Full recovery" for about half the individuals diagnosed with schizophrenia may take the form of time-limited remissions (Torgalsboen & Rund, 1998).

The long-term outcome for people with schizophrenia may be more positive than that portrayed by Kraepelin, DSM-III, or DSM-IV-TR. One researcher who reviewed the prognosis of schizophrenia believes there is a "wide spectrum of possible courses that patients follow," many of them being quite positive (Harding, Zubin, & Strauss, 1992). The cognitive decline in schizophrenia appears to occur within the first five years of the illness, after which stability and even improvement can occur (Goldberg, Hyde, Kleinman, & Weinberger, 1993). Bleuler might have been correct in indicating a variable outcome for the disorder.

Etiology of Schizophrenia

A thirteen-year-old boy who was having behavioral and academic problems in school was taking part in a series of family therapy sessions. Family communication was negative in tone, with a great deal of blaming. Near the end of one session, the boy suddenly broke down and cried out, "I don't want to be like her." He was referring to his mother, who had been receiving treatment for schizophrenia and was taking antipsychotic medication. He had often been frightened by her bizarre behavior, and he was concerned that his friends would "find out" about her condition. But his greatest fear was that he would inherit the disorder. Sobbing, he turned to the therapist and asked, "Am I going to be crazy, too?"

agreed with the following statement concerning the prognosis for schizophrenia: "Complete remission (i.e., a return to full premorbid functioning) is probably not common in this disorder" (American Psychiatric Association, 2000, p. 309). The chances for improvement or recovery are difficult to evaluate because of the changing definitions for schizophrenia. Before DSM-III, the United States had a very broad definition of schizophrenia. DSM-III and DSM-IV-TR provided a narrower definition. Symptoms of the disorder have to be present for six months for its diagnosis. It makes sense that an individual who does not recover within six months has a more severe condition than one who recovers sooner. We have, therefore, now defined schizophrenia as a chronic condition.

In a fifteen-year follow-up study of eighty-two individuals diagnosed with schizophrenia, a number of different courses were found (see Figure 13.3). More

If you were the therapist, how would you respond? We are constantly exposed to news articles indicating that schizophrenia is produced by an "unfortunate" combination of genes or is due to physical problems in the brain. Does this mean that schizophrenia is only a biological disorder? Some evidence also exists that family communication patterns can influence relapse in individuals with schizophrenia. Can the way we interact in a family also precipitate a schizophrenic episode? If so, how? Researchers generally agree that this boy's chances of developing schizophrenia are greater than those of the average person. Why this is

CRITICAL THINKING

Schizophrenia in Developing Countries

The following observation appears in DSM-IV-TR: "Individuals with schizophrenia in developing nations tend to have a more acute course and a better outcome than do individuals in industrialized nations" (American Psychiatric Asociation, 2000, p. 307). Do people in developing countries who have schizophrenia recover more quickly and fully than individuals in developed countries? If so, why? The World Health Organization examined these questions in a cross-cultural study (Sartorius et al., 1986). The study applied standardized and reliable sets of criteria and found similar prevalence rates for schizophrenia in ten different countries. However, a follow-up of 1,379 persons diagnosed with schizophrenia and described as "remarkably similar in their symptom profiles" in the ten countries revealed that patients in India, Colombia, and Nigeria showed more rapid and more complete recovery than those in London, Moscow, or Washington. Fifty-six percent of people diagnosed with this disorder in developing countries had only one schizophrenic episode, compared with 39 percent in developed

countries. Severe chronic course was found in 40 percent of those from developed countries, compared with 24 percent in developing countries. Sartorius and colleagues hypothesized that some cultural factor might be responsible for the observed difference in outcome. Why should patients from developing countries who have less access to modern treatment recover so quickly? Some have speculated that in developing countries, recovered patients are quickly reintegrated into society. In India, for example, patients with schizophrenia are more likely to be living with their families and to be employed than are similar patients in England (Sharma et al., 1998). In fact, researchers in another study reported difficulty in interviewing recovered patients because they were working in the fields (Warner, 1986). Returning to work and being socially integrated may help prevent relapses.

Stevens (1987) believes that the higher recovery rate for schizophrenia found in developing countries is due to misdiagnosis. To support her view, she pointed out that in the WHO study, 36 percent of patients

in Nigeria and 27 percent in India recovered in less than one month. She conjectured that the illnesses were in actuality either brief psychotic disorders or schizophreniform disorders and not schizophrenia. Although this explanation is certainly plausible, the WHO investigation had found an approximately equal frequency of schizophrenia among the different countries. If misdiagnosis did occur, it must mean that brief psychotic disorders and schizophreniform disorders are more prevalent in developing countries and that schizophrenia occurs less frequently in these countries. This possibility must be examined.

If we define schizophrenia as a "chronic" condition, how can we account for the fact that more than 50 percent of people diagnosed with schizophrenia in developing countries recover after one episode? If schizophrenia is a brain disorder, why is the outcome so different between developing and developed countries? If "culture" is responsible for the more positive outcome in developing countries, how does it influence the course of this disorder?

so is a subject of controversy. Researchers who favor a biological paradigm tend to favor genetic, brain-structure, and biochemical explanations. Other researchers focus primarily on the impact of psychological and social factors in the development of the disorder. We will consider the strengths and weaknesses of the different approaches. At the end of the section on genetics, you should reach your own conclusion about what to tell the thirteen-year-old boy.

Heredity and Schizophrenia

"That genetic factors are involved in the etiology in schizophrenia is no longer a matter of controversy" is

a conclusion that has been reached by many researchers (Cannon, Kaprio, Lonnqvist, Huttunen, & Koskenvuo, 1998, p. 67). What remains controversial, however, is the degree and the nature of the contribution. About forty years ago, one researcher posed the following challenge to his colleagues:

You [are] required to write down a procedure for selecting an individual from the population who would be diagnosed as schizophrenic by a psychiatric staff; you have to wager $1,000 on being right. You may not include in your selection procedure any behavioral fact, such as a symptom or trait, manifested by the individual. (Meehl, 1962, p. 827)

According to Meehl, your best chance of winning this wager is to look for someone whose identical twin has already been diagnosed with schizophrenia. This solution reflects the belief that heredity is an important cause in the development of this disorder—a belief supported by research (Cannon et al., 1998; Erlenmeyer-Kimling et al., 1997; Gottesman, 1991; Heinrichs, 1993; Roberts, 1991).

Problems in Interpreting Genetic Studies

Obtaining a clear picture of the genetic contribution to schizophrenia is not an easy task. To demonstrate a clear link between heredity and schizophrenia, research studies must overcome several major complications, some of which inflate the degree of genetic influence.

1. *Several types of schizophrenia may exist, with different sets of causes and varying degrees of genetic influence.* For example, the risk of developing schizophrenia and related disorders is higher for a child whose parent has been diagnosed with schizophrenia and has not responded to antipsychotic medication than for the child of a parent with schizophrenia who does respond to such medication.

2. *The psychological condition of both parents must be considered.* If only one parent has schizophrenia, but the other parent has a similar or related disorder, this spousal contribution could increase genetic risk. One study (Parnas, 1987) found that the mates of people with schizophrenia were more likely to have functional psychoses and schizoid, paranoid, or borderline personality disorders before marriage than were mates of individuals who did not have schizophrenia. If spousal contributions are not considered, genetic influences based only on one parent's diagnosis of schizophrenia may be overestimated.

3. *Studies based on patients with severe and chronic cases of schizophrenia may inflate estimates of genetic influence.* The **concordance rate**—the likelihood that both members of a twin pair will show the same characteristic—for schizophrenia was nearly three times higher among identical twins hospitalized for more than two years than for those hospitalized less than two years (Gottesman, 1991).

4. *Researchers may use differing definitions of concordance.* Some investigators define schizophrenia very narrowly and use the same definition to determine concordance, which would result in lower estimates of genetic influence. Other investigators believe that a number of disorders (such as schizoid and borderline personality disorders and schizo-

phreniform disorders) are genetically related to schizophrenia. Considering the concordance rate as including a diagnosis of schizophrenia or of these other disorders would produce higher estimates of genetic influence.

5. *An interviewer who knows that he or she is interviewing relatives of a person with schizophrenia might be more likely to find pathology.* Raters involved in genetic studies are often aware of the diagnosis and status (nonblind) of the patients, controls, and the relatives. Studies that use nonblind raters report higher rates of psychopathology among relatives with disorders than studies that use blind ratings (Gottesman & Shields, 1982).

In this section, we discuss several kinds of research that link heredity to the schizophrenic disorders. Many of them have one or more of the methodological problems we just discussed.

Studies Involving Blood Relatives

Close blood relatives are genetically more similar than distant blood relatives. For example, first-degree relatives (parents, siblings, child) share 50 percent of their genes with the individual who has schizophrenia. Second-degree relatives (grandparents, uncles, aunts, nephews) share only 25 percent of their genes. If schizophrenia has a genetic basis, researchers should find the disorder more often among close relatives of people diagnosed with schizophrenia than among more distant relatives.

Figure 13.4 suggests that this situation is indeed the case. The data are summarized from several major studies on the prevalence of schizophrenia (Gottesman, 1978, 1991). They show that closer blood relatives of people diagnosed with schizophrenia run a greater risk of developing the disorder. Thus the boy described earlier has a 16 percent chance of being diagnosed with schizophrenia, but his mother's nieces or nephews have only a 4 percent chance. (It should be noted that the risk for the general population is 1 percent.)

Even if well-designed studies pointed to a relationship between degree of genetic relatedness and schizophrenia, however, they still do not clearly demonstrate the role of heredity. Why? Simply because closer blood relatives are more likely to share the same environmental factors or stressors, as well as the same genes. To confirm a genetic basis for schizophrenia, research must separate genetic influences from environmental influences.

Twin Studies

Throughout this book we have described the use of twin studies by researchers who seek to differentiate

A Sure Sign of Genetic Influence The Genain quadruplets, shown here at age sixty-three, all developed schizophrenia, which is unusual because the concordance rate for the disorder in identical twins is only 50 percent. Still, the sisters differed in terms of symptoms, level of recovery, and age of onset, all of which suggest that environmental influences were at work as well. Pictured from left to right are Edna, Wilma, Sarah, and Helen.

between the effects of heredity and those of environment. You may recall that identical, or monozygotic (MZ), twins are genetically identical, so differences between MZ twins are presumably caused by differences in their environments. If reared together, MZ twins share the same general environment, as well as the same hereditary makeup. But fraternal, or dizygotic (DZ), twins, though born at about the same time,

are not genetically more similar than any other two siblings, and they may be of different sexes. If DZ twins are reared together, they share the same general environment, but their genetic makeup is, on the average, only 50 percent identical.

In a twin study, concordance rates for a particular disorder are measured among groups of MZ and DZ twins. (Recall that a concordance rate is the likelihood

FIGURE 13.4 Morbidity Risk Among Blood Relatives of People with Schizophrenia
This figure reflects the estimate of the lifetime risk of developing schizophrenia—a risk that is strongly correlated with the degree of genetic influence.

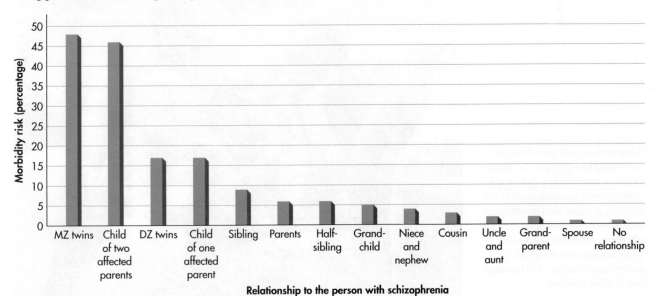

Source: Data from Gottesman (1978, 1991).

that both members of a twin pair will show the same characteristic—in this case, the disorder being studied.) If environmental factors are of major importance, the concordance rates for MZ twins and for DZ twins should not differ much. If genetic factors are of prime importance, however, MZ twins should show a higher concordance rate than DZ twins.

In general, concordance rates for schizophrenia among MZ twins are two to four times higher than among DZ twins. This seems to point to a strong genetic basis for the disorder. However, early studies reported concordance rates as high as 86 percent (Weiner, 1975). This high rate is probably due to methodological differences in what is considered "concordant." Many early twin studies of schizophrenia not only considered schizophrenia but also included disorders such as "latent or borderline" schizophrenia, acute schizophrenic reactions, and schizoid and inadequate personality as concordant. These disorders are part of the **schizophrenia spectrum**—that is, they are considered to be genetically related to schizophrenia.

The broader definition of schizophrenia was used in most studies that reported high concordance rates. Unfortunately, this breadth decreases the diagnostic reliability and validity of twin studies as a whole. The twin study by Onstad, Skre, Edvardsen, Torgersen, and Kringlen (1991) used a narrow definition of schizophrenia and reported a concordance rate of 48 percent among MZ twins.

Even though the high concordance rates reported in many earlier studies have been inflated by using the broad definition of schizophrenia, we can conclude that there is clearly moderate genetic influence in the disorders. This is true whether a strict definition is employed or whether the schizophrenia spectrum is included. Moreover, it appears that the spectrum disorders are more likely to be found in families with diagnosed schizophrenic members (Hans, Auerbach, Styr, & Marcus, 2004).

Adoption Studies

Even with twin studies, it is difficult to separate the effects of heredity from the effects of environment because twins are usually raised together. Thus when the child of a parent with schizophrenia develops the disorder, three explanations are possible:

1. The mother or father with schizophrenia may have genetically transmitted schizophrenia to the child.

2. The parent, being disturbed, may have provided a stressful environment for the child.

3. The child's schizophrenia may have resulted from a combination of genetic factors and a stressful environment.

In what has become a classic effort to sort out the effects of heredity and environment, researchers determined the incidence of schizophrenia and other disorders in a group of people who were born to mothers with schizophrenia but who had had no contact with their mothers and had left the maternity hospital

Separating the Effects of Heredity and Environment
These monozygotic twin boys are genetically identical but also share the same environment. One of the problems with studying twins is the difficulty of separating heredity factors from environmental influences. Adoption studies are useful because heredity and environmental factors can be more clearly differentiated.

within three days of birth (Heston, 1966; Heston & Denny, 1968). This condition eliminated the possibility that contact with the mother increased the chance of developing the disorder. The lives of these people were traced through the records of child-care institutions; all had been adopted by two-parent families. A control group, consisting of people who were born to mothers who did not have schizophrenia and who were adopted through the same child-care institutions, was selected and matched. Information regarding both the at-risk and control groups was collected from many sources (including school records, court records, and interviews). The people themselves were interviewed and given psychological tests. Five individuals in the at-risk group (mothers with schizophrenia) were later diagnosed with schizophrenia, compared with none in the control group. These results are highly significant and support a genetic explanation for schizophrenia.

The study seems to have been well designed. Its only weaknesses involve the diagnostic criteria, which were described as being based on "generally accepted standards" for schizophrenia, and the fact that the mothers with schizophrenia "as a group were biased in the direction of severe, chronic disease." (As discussed earlier, genetic factors seem to play a greater role in the more severe cases of schizophrenia.)

Two additional criticisms have been raised, however. First, the mothers with schizophrenia received antipsychotic medication during pregnancy, and such drugs present a potential risk to the fetus (Physician's Desk Reference, 2003). Second, most families who adopted the child of a mother with schizophrenia knew about the mother's disorder. This knowledge could have influenced the adoptive parents' attitudes toward the child (Shean, 1987).

Of special interest is the finding that nearly one-half of those in the at-risk group were "notably successful adults":

> The twenty-one experimental subjects who exhibited no significant psychosocial impairment were not only successful adults but in comparison to the control group were more spontaneous when interviewed and had more colorful life histories. They held the more creative jobs: musician, teacher, home-designer; and followed the more imaginative hobbies: oil painting, music, antique aircraft. Within the experimental group there was much more variability of personality and behavior in all social dimensions. (Heston, 1966, p. 825)

Sohlberg (1985) reported similar findings. Approximately 50 percent of "high-risk" children have "healthy personalities" and are "remarkably invulnerable" to schizophrenia. Being "at risk" does not necessarily (or even usually) lead to a negative outcome. Why do some children who have poor familial or environmental backgrounds develop so successfully? Perhaps studies of "stress resistant" children will one day answer this question.

In another study designed to separate hereditary and environmental influences, investigators identified adults who were diagnosed with schizophrenia and who had been adopted in infancy. Then they located both the adoptive parents (the families who had raised the children who developed schizophrenia) and the biological parents, who had minimal contact with their children. If environmental factors play the major role in schizophrenia, the adoptive families should be more disturbed than the biological parents. Conversely, if heredity is more important, biological families should show more disturbance than adoptive families. Schizophrenia and spectrum disorders (4.7 percent and 8.2 percent, respectively) were found only among the biological relatives, thus supporting the importance of heredity (Kety et al., 1994). Similar results were reported in another adoption study by Tienari and others (1994).

Another line of evidence comes from a study of children who had normal biological parents but who were adopted and raised by a parent later diagnosed with schizophrenia (Wender, Rosenthal, Rainer, Greenbill, & Sarlan, 1977). If environmental factors are of primary importance, these children should be more likely than others to develop schizophrenia. The researchers found no such difference. Thus various adoption studies do indicate that heredity plays a major role in the transmission of schizophrenia.

Studies of High-Risk Populations

Perhaps the most comprehensive way to study the etiology of schizophrenia is to monitor a large group of children over a long time to watch the differences between those who eventually develop schizophrenia and those who do not. This sort of developmental study allows the investigator to see how the disorders develop. But because the prevalence of schizophrenia in the general population is only 1 percent, a prohibitively large group would have to be monitored if a random sample of children were chosen. Instead, investigators have chosen participants from "high-risk" populations; this procedure increases the probability that a smaller group of participants will include some who develop schizophrenia. In one study (Erlenmeyer-Kimling et al., 1997), for example, children ages seven to twelve years of parents with schizophrenia (a high-risk group) and without schizophrenia were studied twenty-five years later. Those who had developed schizophrenia (13.1 percent) were all in the high-risk group. This percentage is much higher than would have been predicted from the general population.

Mednick's Study   The best known developmental studies are those conducted by Mednick and colleagues (Mednick, 1970; Mednick, Cannon, Parnas, & Schulsinger, 1989), who are still studying about 200 persons whose mothers had schizophrenia (the high-risk group) and about 100 persons whose mothers did not have schizophrenia (the low-risk control group). The researchers have followed these people for more than thirty years. On the basis of existing data, they have predicted the eventual outcome for both high-risk and low-risk persons. Their prediction was that approximately one-half of the high-risk group may eventually display some form of psychopathology, including but not limited to schizophrenia.

At this time, fifteen of the high-risk individuals have developed schizophrenia; the researchers estimate that another fifteen will later receive this diagnosis. Comparisons of the characteristics of the high-risk individuals who developed schizophrenia with those of high-risk individuals who did not develop the disorder revealed that the individuals with schizophrenia were more likely to:

■ Have had mothers who displayed more severe symptoms of schizophrenia.

■ Have been separated from their parents and placed in children's homes early in their lives.

■ Have had mothers who had more serious pregnancy or birth complications.

■ Have been characterized by their teachers as extremely aggressive and disruptive.

■ Have a slower autonomic recovery rate (habituate more slowly when exposed to certain stimuli).

It appears that both environmental and biological factors may influence the development of schizophrenia in the high-risk group.

The Israeli Study   Are high-risk children more likely to develop schizophrenia or related disorders if they live with their parent who has schizophrenia, or might they do better when raised in a "healthier" environment? In an attempt to answer this question, an Israeli research team (Ayalon & Mercom, 1985; Marcus et al., 1987; Nagler, Marcus, Sohlberg, Lifshitz, & Silberman, 1985; Shotten, 1985; Sohlberg, 1985) conducted a **prospective study**, a long-term study of a group of people, beginning before the onset of a disorder, to allow investigators to see how the disorder

develops. The study followed fifty high-risk children (children who had parents with schizophrenia). Twenty-five of the children were born and raised in a kibbutz (a collective farm), and the other twenty-five were living in a suburban area with their mentally ill parents. In the kibbutz, all the children lived together. They had regular contact with their parents, but they were raised by child-care workers.

The researchers also included a control group, comprising fifty low-risk children of mentally healthy parents—twenty-five living in the kibbutz and the other twenty-five living in town. Neurophysiological, observational, perceptual-motor, psychophysiological, and behavioral measures were taken at regular intervals.

By the time the high-risk groups reached their thirties, four had received a diagnosis of schizophrenia—two each in the kibbutz and the town groups (Ingraham, Kugelmass, Frenkel, Nathan, & Mirsky, 1995). High-risk individuals in the kibbutz were more likely than any other participants to have a major affective disorder, and personality disorders were more frequent in the high-risk groups. No one in the control group was diagnosed with schizophrenia, which again would indicate the importance of a genetic predisposition.

During the twenty-five-year follow-up assessment, most participants who were diagnosed with affective disorder and one who was diagnosed with schizophrenia no longer showed symptoms of these disorders. As Ingraham and colleagues observed, however, "The most striking finding is the relative absence of severe psychopathology evident at present in most of the subjects" (1995, p. 186). Most of the participants currently do not meet the criteria for affective disorders, and most show good adjustment. Living in town or in the kibbutz did not seem to be related to risk factors in developing schizophrenia but may have influenced the expression of major affective disorder.

A number of differences were found in the development of high-risk and control children. High-risk children were more likely to be described as withdrawn, poorer in social relationships, behaving in antisocial ways, uncooperative and incapable of relating to the interviewers, poor at schoolwork, having problems with mood, accident prone, and functioning at lower perceptual-motor levels. Social withdrawal seemed to be the characteristic most related to the risk of developing schizophrenia in the high-risk children (Hans, Marcus, Henson, Auerbach, & Mirsky, 1992; Mirsky, Kugelmass, Ingraham, Frenkel, & Nathan, 1995). Nevertheless, the two groups of children overlapped considerably. Deficiencies were shown by only about one-half of the high-risk children. The other half appeared to show "healthy" development.

Environmental factors also appear to be important in schizophrenia. None of the high-risk children who had received "adequate" parenting developed schizophrenia. Approximately 60 percent of the parents with schizophrenia provided adequate care for their children.

Conclusions and Methodological Problems

What can we conclude from the high-risk studies? First, there is reasonably strong support for the involvement of heredity in schizophrenia and its associated spectrum disorders. Second, childhood and adolescence may be especially vulnerable periods. Third, schizophrenia seems to result from interaction between the predisposition and environmental factors. Fourth, most high-risk children do not develop the disorder, and most show good adjustment. With this information in mind, what would you tell the thirteen-year-old boy from the preceding case study about his chances of developing schizophrenia?

Studies of high-risk individuals are a promising line of research. However, some methodological problems have already been pointed out. First, it may not be possible to generalize results of a study that takes as participants the offspring of parents with schizophrenia. The majority of people who receive this diagnosis do not have a parent with schizophrenia (Gottesman, 1991; Sanders & Gejman, 2001). Additionally, differences have been found between patients with familial schizophrenia (in which a first-degree relative has the disorder) and patients with no schizophrenia in the family (Kendler & Hays, 1982). Second, the studies do not include control groups with other psychopathologies; it therefore is hard to decide whether the characteristics found are specific to schizophrenia. For example, some characteristics listed by Mednick and colleagues (1989)—such as pregnancy and birth complications, separation from parents, and problems in school—are also reported for other disorders. Third, there is uncertainty about whether the most relevant variables are being measured. For example, because Mednick and colleagues (1989) believe that autonomic reactivity (measured by galvanic skin response) is an important factor in schizophrenia, they have assessed this variable carefully. But they did not assess parent-child interaction, which they considered less important. Fourth, the parents with schizophrenia in both high-risk studies were diagnosed according to the criteria used at that time; they might not meet the DSM-IV-TR criteria.

Physiological Factors in Schizophrenia

Two important areas of research into the causes of schizophrenia focus on brain chemistry and brain pathology. Logically, either could serve as a vehicle for the genetic transmission of schizophrenia, but no substantive evidence to that effect has yet been found. Currently, researchers have found no physiological sign or symptom that leads solely to an invariant diagnosis of schizophrenia. Nonetheless, research in these areas has implications for treatment, as well as etiology.

Biochemistry: The Dopamine Hypothesis

Biochemical explanations of schizophrenia have a long history. A century ago, for example, Emil Kraepelin suggested that these disorders result from a chemical imbalance caused by abnormal sex gland secretion. Since then, a number of researchers have tried to show that body chemistry is involved in schizophrenia. Most have failed to do so.

What generally happens is that a researcher finds a particular substance in the biochemical makeup of people with schizophrenia and does not find it in "normal" controls, but other researchers cannot replicate those findings. In addition, patients with schizophrenia differ from normal persons in lifestyle and in food and medication intake, all of which affect body chemistry and tend to confound research results. Table 13.3 summarizes some of the problems associated with current biological research findings.

One line of biochemical research has focused on the neurotransmitter dopamine and its involvement in schizophrenia (Davis, Kahn, & Ko, 1991). According to the **dopamine hypothesis** (discussed briefly in the chapter on models of abnormal behavior), schizophrenia may result from excess dopamine activity at certain synaptic sites. Support for the dopamine hypothesis has come from research with three types of drugs: phenothiazines, L-dopa, and the amphetamines.

- *Phenothiazines* are antipsychotic drugs that decrease the severity of thought disorders, alleviate withdrawal and hallucinations, and improve the mood of patients with schizophrenia. Evidence shows that the phenothiazines reduce dopamine activity in the brain by blocking dopamine receptor sites in postsynaptic neurons.

- *L-dopa* is generally used to treat symptoms of Parkinson's disease, such as muscle and limb rigidity and tremors. The body converts L-dopa to dopamine, and the drug sometimes produces schizophrenic-like symptoms. By contrast, the phenothiazines, which reduce dopamine activity, can produce side effects that resemble Parkinson's disease.

- Amphetamines are stimulants that increase the availability of dopamine and norepinephrine

TABLE 13.3   Biological Findings in Schizophrenia and Some Problems Associated with Them

Biological Finding	Problem
Disturbed functioning in dopamine system	A large minority of people with schizophrenia are not responsive to antipsychotic medications affecting dopamine.
	Other effective medications (clozapine) work primarily on the serotonin, rather than the dopamine, system.
	Neuroleptics block dopamine receptors quickly, but relief from symptoms is not seen for weeks.
Ventricular enlargement	Differences are relatively small compared with control groups.
	Reported in only 6 to 40 percent of patients with schizophrenia in a variety of studies.
	Also reported in some patients with mood disorders.
Diminished volume of frontal or temporal lobes	Differences are relatively small, compared with control groups.
	About 50 percent of patients with schizophrenia fall within range of control groups on this measure.
Low relative glucose metabolism in frontal areas	Participants are generally chronic patients on heavy neuroleptic medications.
	Some evidence indicates that neuroleptics influence cerebral blood flow even in patients who are currently medication free.
Cognitive dysfunctions (visual processing, attention problems, recall memory problems)	Some members of control groups also have such dysfunctions.
	May be a result of medication, hospitalization, or other such variables.
	Validity of measures is questionable.

Source: Compiled from Chua & McKenna (1995); Faraone et al. (1995); Kane & Freeman (1994); Vita et al. (1995); Wiesel (1994).

Note: Although differences have been found in the functioning and structure of the brain in many people with schizophrenia, the findings are subject to different interpretations.

(another neurotransmitter) in the brain. When individuals not diagnosed with schizophrenia are given continual doses of amphetamines, they show symptoms very much like those of acute paranoid schizophrenia. And very small doses may increase the severity of symptoms in patients diagnosed with schizophrenia. Other stimulants, such as caffeine, do not produce these effects.

Thus a drug that is believed to block dopamine reception has the effect of reducing the severity of schizophrenic symptoms, whereas two drugs that increase dopamine availability either produce or worsen these symptoms. Such evidence obviously supports the idea that excess dopamine may cause schizophrenic symptoms.

The evidence is not all positive, however. For example, the dopamine hypothesis might lead us to expect that treating schizophrenia with phenothiazines would be effective in almost all cases. Yet about one-fourth of patients with schizophrenia responded very little or not at all to antipsychotic medication (Kane & Freeman, 1994). In a review of studies on dopamine and schizophrenia, Davis and colleagues (1991) argued that the dopamine hypothesis has to be modified to explain the discrepant findings. They believe that specific brain areas have to be identified that may be sensitive to either an excess or a deficiency of dopamine. The effectiveness of clozapine, which acts more on the serotonin than on the dopamine system, indicates that other neurotransmitters may be important in schizophrenia (Tamminga & Frost, 2001).

As noted earlier, schizophrenia may very well be a group of disorders with different causes; this explanation could account for the variable course of the disorders and the uneven responses to phenothiazines. Moreover, researchers may be looking for an oversimplified explanation by focusing on dopamine alone, without considering the interactive functioning of the brain and the biochemical system as a whole. Or perhaps dopamine blockers can influence the symptoms of schizophrenia but not the course of the illness. Obviously, much more remains to be discovered.

Neurological Findings

Abnormal Neurological Findings   Do the symptoms of schizophrenia indicate neurological impairment? This is certainly a possibility. Anywhere from 20 to 75 percent of patients with schizophrenia show some signs of neurological abnormalities (Coursey, Alford, & Safarjan, 1997; Crespo-Facorro et al., 2001; Kim, Ha, & Kwon, 2004). Again, the wide differences in estimates may indicate problems in the reliability of assessment techniques or may reflect the possibility that different subgroups of people with schizophrenia were assessed.

Some researchers (Arango, Kirkpatrick, & Buchanan, 2000) believe that the three symptom complexes found in schizophrenia—hallucinations/delusions, disorganization of thought, and negative symptoms—are the result of neurobiological differences. Other researchers (Roth et al., 2004) feel that those who show predominantly negative symptoms—such as flat affect, poverty of speech, and loss of drive—display characteristics associated with neuronal loss or deterioration in a structurally abnormal brain. These patients would be expected to show less responsiveness to antipsychotic medication and to have a poorer prognosis. In contrast, with positive symptoms of schizophrenia—such as hallucinations and delusions—patients do not show brain deterioration but have reversible biochemical abnormalities.

The search for abnormal neurological factors in schizophrenia has intensified as increasingly sophisticated brain-imaging techniques for studying the living brain have been developed. Using these procedures, researchers have found that, compared with members of control groups, people with schizophrenia are more likely to show ventricular enlargement (enlarged spaces in areas of the brain), cerebral atrophy, and a decrease in the size of the thalamus (Andreasen et al., 1994; Nakamura et al., 2004; Staal et al., 2001; Vita et al., 1991; Wolkin, Rusinek, Vaid, & Arena, 1998). But decreased cerebral volume is also found in patients newly diagnosed with schizophrenia, so it probably precedes the development of the disorder and cannot be attributed to the effects of antipsychotic medication (Andreasen, O'Leary, Flaum, & Nopoulous, 1997; Zipursky, Lambe, Kapur, & Mikulis, 1998). Ventricular enlargement may indicate only an increased

susceptibility to schizophrenia, because healthy siblings of patients with schizophrenia also show ventricle enlargement (Staal et al., 2001). Poor outcome is especially associated with gray matter volume loss in the frontal lobes and ventricular enlargement, whereas smaller thalamic volumes may reflect a greater susceptibility to schizophrenia (Staal et al., 2001).

In an interesting longitudinal study of brain changes among youths with and without schizophrenia, those with the disorder showed a striking loss of gray brain matter over a period of six years. The loss was so rapid that it was likened to a "forest fire" (Thompson et al., 2001.) The areas of brain loss were related to the symptoms associated with the disorder. It is not clear how generalizable the findings are because the sample involved adolescents with early-onset schizophrenia. Interpreting the data is complicated by the fact that a reduction in brain volume over time is found among individuals with schizophrenia (Jacobsen et al., 1998), and higher doses of medication are also associated with reduction in frontal and temporal lobe volumes (Gur et al., 1998).

Decreased functioning in the frontal lobes and other cerebral areas has also been observed using brain scans (Andreasen et al., 1992; Buchsbaum, 1990). Cerebral glucose metabolism is significantly lower in patients with schizophrenia than in their control group counterparts, especially during cognitive tasks (Andreasen et al., 1992; Kircher et al., 2001; Wolkin et al., 1992). Thus areas of the brain involved in attention, planning, and volition seem to be impaired in patients with this disorder. Interestingly, studies comparing identical twins not concordant for schizophrenia have found that the affected twins had larger ventricles than their cotwins (Suddath, Christison, Torrey, & Weinberger, 1990). One study comparing cerebral blood flow in identical twins (discordant and concordant for schizophrenia) found decreased blood flow only in those with schizophrenia (Berman, Torrey, Daniel, & Weinberger, 1992). These studies illustrate some of the subtle differences in brain structure and cerebral functioning that have been found in some individuals with schizophrenia. The finding that unaffected twins may not show these anatomical or metabolic differences may indicate the impact of environmental factors.

Conclusions   What can we conclude from studies of brain structure and functioning in schizophrenia? Neurological abnormalities tend to be reported more often in people with schizophrenia than in other individuals and more often in patients with negative symptoms of schizophrenia. The observations are intriguing because they highlight the possibility that some subtypes of schizophrenia may be caused by structural

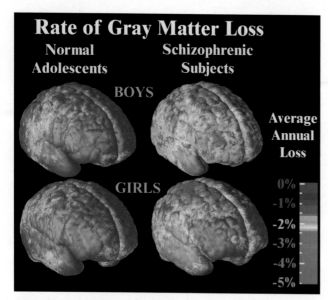

Rate of Gray Matter Loss

Normal Adolescents	Schizophrenic Subjects	
		Average Annual Loss

BOYS

GIRLS

0%
-1%
-2%
-3%
-4%
-5%

Rate of Gray Matter Loss in Teenagers with Schizophrenia
Male and female adolescents with schizophrenia show progressive loss of gray matter in the parietal, frontal, and temporal areas of the brain that is much greater than that found in "normal" adolescents. A similar pattern of gray matter loss in the different brain regions is found among both boys and girls with schizophrenia. How would you interpret this finding?

brain pathology. Findings that abnormalities in the prefrontal cortex may be a factor are especially interesting because this area is involved with some of the intellectual symptoms associated with schizophrenia.

Interpreting the findings is problematic, however. These neurological abnormalities do not seem to be specific to schizophrenia. They are also found in some healthy individuals and in persons with mood disorders, alcohol and substance abuse, and organic impairment (Alanen, 1997; Shelton et al., 1988; Syvalahti, 1994). After reviewing thirty-nine studies on ventricular size, Van Horn and McManus (1992) concluded, "It [the size difference] is probably too small to be of practical significance in diagnosis" (p. 6). Other problems in interpreting the results of neurophysiological studies include small sample sizes, outdated diagnostic criteria, unreliable assessment techniques, and the potential effects of medication (Bogerts, 1993; Heinrichs, 1993). The search for neurological abnormalities in people with schizophrenia nevertheless is promising.

The research evidence has clearly indicated that schizophrenia is a brain disorder. However, the underlying structure(s) or neuropathological processes have not been identified. Heinrichs (1993) pointed out the many contradictions in the disorder:

1. The presentation of the disorder and its course are varied. Some patients have hallucinations; some have only delusions.

2. Some patients show poor premorbid adjustment in their histories, and others seem fine until the disorder strikes.

3. Some patients respond positively to antipsychotic medications, whereas others do not.

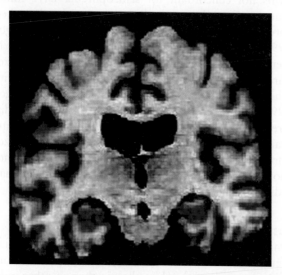

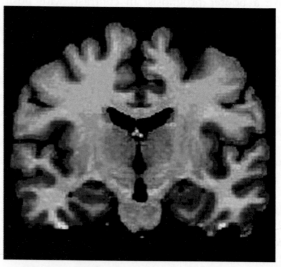

Coronal Sections of the Brain in a Patient with Schizophrenia   Structural brain abnormalities have been found in most individuals with schizophrenia. The degree and extent of the abnormalities appear to be related to outcome. Patients with poor outcome (represented by the left photo) show significantly greater loss of cerebral gray matter and greater enlargement of the ventricles than patients with a good outcome (represented by the photo on the right) (Staal et al., 2001).

4. Neuroanatomical abnormalities are found in some patients but not in others.

5. Genetic factors are important, but they do not seem sufficient for the expression of the disorder.

6. Information-processing deficits are found in most patients with schizophrenia, but they are also found in other psychiatric patients.

7. Individuals with brain lesions in the areas of the brain associated with schizophrenia show performance patterns different from those found in people with schizophrenia.

What does this conflicting information mean? Heinrichs believes that "schizophrenia is a heterogeneous illness that, paradoxically, resists subdivision." Another group of researchers (Kendler, Karkowski-Shuman, O'Neill, & Straub, 1997) concluded that "schizophrenia as currently defined may be etiologically heterogeneous" (p. 171). We need to identify and subdivide the disorder so that we can study the different etiological types. So far, attempts to do so have been largely unsuccessful.

Environmental Factors in Schizophrenia

Obviously, genetic and biological research has not yet clarified the cause of the various schizophrenic disorders. Because the concordance rate is less than 50 percent when one identical twin has the disorder, nonshared environmental influences must also play a role. Most of these may be physical in nature, such as damage to a susceptible individual from prenatal infections, obstetric complications, or early trauma (Jablensky et al., 2005; Sanders & Gejman, 2001). Retroviruses have also been found in some cases of recent-onset schizophrenia (Karlsson et al., 2001). Although these findings may be coincidences, they illustrate the attempt to identify early environmental factors, such as infections during fetal or perinatal development, which could be related to schizophrenia.

Another theory proposes that some forms of schizophrenia may result from a disruption of normal brain development during the fetal or perinatal periods through infection or injury. Patients with schizophrenia often have records of pregnancy and birth complications that might have produced structural brain abnormalities (Ohman & Hultman, 1998). Several studies have reported that individuals whose mothers were exposed to the influenza virus during the second trimester of pregnancy have higher-than-expected rates of schizophrenia (Machon, Mednick, & Huttunen, 1997).

Psychological stressors that may trigger this disorder have also been considered. There are reports of stress-induced hallucinations among individuals facing highly anxiety-arousing circumstances (Spivak et al., 1992), but these episodes were temporary and did not result in diagnoses of schizophrenia. Stressors do appear to be related to probability of relapse. As with the biological theories, environmental explanations are not sufficient to explain the etiology of schizophrenia. In this section we consider some of the more developed of these theories—those concerning the role of family dynamics, social class, and cultural differences.

Measuring Abstract Thinking in Individuals with Schizophrenia This participant is connected to a device that records the activation of specific areas of the brain during a card sorting task—a measure of abstract thinking. Researchers believe that schizophrenic people do poorly on this task because they may be deficient in the ability to activate the prefrontal cortex.

Family Influences

It was once strongly believed that exposure to specific dysfunctional family patterns was enough to produce schizophrenia in nearly everyone (Wahlberg, Wynne, Oja, & Keskitalo, 1997). However, as Lehman and Steinwachs (1998) note, "Research has failed to substantiate hypothesized causal links between family dysfunction and the etiology of schizophrenia. ... The presumption that family interaction causes schizophrenia ... has led to serious disruptions in clinician/family trust" (p. 8). These researchers believe that unless a person has a genetic predisposition toward schizophrenia, environmental factors have little impact on the development of the disorder. Others strongly disagree. In this section, we consider theories that support psychological factors as either the cause of or a contributor to schizophrenia.

Theoretical Constructs   Studies of high-risk children have found that those who developed schizophrenia had negative family environments (Marcus et al., 1987; Tienari et al., 1994). Several theories have attempted to pinpoint patterns of family interaction that could produce such a disorder. The first was proposed by psychodynamic theorists, who believed that certain behavioral patterns among parents could inhibit appropriate ego development in the child (Alanen, 1994). This, in turn, would make the child vulnerable to the severe regression characteristic of schizophrenia. Attention was focused mainly on the mother, who usually has a great deal of contact with the child. These theorists characterized the **schizophrenogenic** (or schizophrenia-producing) mother as being simultaneously or alternately cold and overprotecting, rejecting and dominating. This behavior pattern led to the development of schizophrenia in the child.

The second theory involving family interaction asked another question: can some kind of communication pattern produce schizophrenia? This is the **double-bind theory** (Bateson, Jackson, Haley, & Weakland, 1956)—the suggestion that schizophrenia develops as a result of repeated experiences that a child has with one or more family members (usually the mother and father) in which the child receives contradictory messages. The child cannot discern the parent's meaning and cannot escape the situation. This conflict eventually leads the person to develop difficulty in interpreting other people's communications and inaccuracy in conveying his or her own thoughts and feelings to others. To survive, children in such situations may resort to self-deception, falsely interpreting their own thoughts, as well as those communicated by others. They may develop a false concept of reality, an inability to communicate effectively, withdrawal, and other symptoms of schizophrenia.

Problems with Earlier Research   Most studies conducted before the mid-1970s supported the view that communications were much more dysfunctional in families in which a member had schizophrenia than in other families. Methodological shortcomings, however, kept researchers from generalizing these results to a relationship between schizophrenia and family dynamics. Two flaws were most common: a family's interactions were studied only after one of its members had been diagnosed with schizophrenia, and studies generally lacked control groups. Thus even if negative family interaction was correlated with schizophrenia, researchers could not tell which was the cause and which the effect or whether the correlation was unique to schizophrenia.

Some researchers continue to believe that the family environment may be involved in the onset and course of the disorder. Several prospective studies have found that high-risk children who develop schizophrenia are more likely to have negative family relationships than are high-risk children who do not develop the disorder (Burman, Mednick, Machon, Parnas, & Schulsinger, 1987; Marcus et al., 1987; Tienari et al., 1994). The importance of parenting was indicated in the Israeli high-risk study discussed earlier in this chapter. Among the high-risk group, none who had received "good parenting" from a parent with schizophrenia developed schizophrenia or a spectrum disorder. However, parenting style may also be a result of how "sick" the child is, a possibility we consider later in the chapter.

Expressed Emotion   Current research is directed toward a specific behavior pattern called **expressed emotion** (EE), a negative communication pattern that is found among some relatives of individuals with schizophrenia and that is associated with higher relapse rates. The EE index is determined by the number of critical comments made by a relative (criticism); the number of statements of dislike or resentment directed toward the patient by family members (hostility); and the number of statements reflecting emotional overinvolvement, overconcern, or overprotectiveness made about the patient. For example, high-EE relatives are likely to make a greater number of statements such as "You are a lazy person" or "You've caused our family a lot of trouble" (Rosenfarb, Goldstein, Mintz, & Nuechterlein, 1995). High-EE relatives may be more critical because they are more likely than low-EE relatives to believe that the psychotic symptoms are under the personal control of the patients (Weisman, Nuechterlein, Goldstein, & Snyder, 2000). The EE construct strongly predicts the course of the disorder (Karno et al., 1987; Miklowitz, 1994; Mintz, Mintz, & Goldstein, 1987). A review of twenty-six studies (Kavanagh, 1992) indicated that the median relapse rate for patients living with high-EE relatives was 48 percent, compared with 21 percent for those living with low-EE relatives. The fact that more than twice as many people suffer relapses in a high-EE environment than in a low-EE environment indicates the strength of this variable. However, family criticism scores were not associated with relapse for Mexican Americans with schizophrenia. This may be due to the fact that the role of the family differs for Mexican American and Anglo American families; communication patterns such as emotional overprotection or overinvolvement may be interpreted differently by the two groups. Family warmth was found to be related to fewer psychotic exacerbations in Mexican American patients but not for European Americans. Lopez and his associates (2004) concluded that family communication processes among ethnic minority members with schizophrenia must be examined according to a sociocultural perspective.

Although these studies are better designed than those discussed earlier, they are still correlational in nature and are therefore subject to different interpretations. Figure 13.5 indicates three possible interpretations.

1. A high-EE environment is stressful, and it may lead directly to relapse in the family member who has schizophrenia. Patients whose parents are rated high in EE are more likely to recount negative and stressful memories involving their parents than those whose parents are low on EE (Cutting & Docherty, 2000). Most of the family-communication theories of schizophrenia are based on the view that negative parent-child interactions increase vulnerability to relapse.

2. A more severely ill individual may produce high-EE communication patterns in relatives. The severity of the illness means that the chances of relapse are high. Schreiber, Breier, and Pickar (1995) found some support for this pattern. They examined the parental emotional response in families who had both children with schizophrenia and children without. The parents reacted differently, with more EE communication, to the sick child. The researchers hypothesize that expressed emotions may be a response of parents to the "chronic disabling aspect of this illness, and a belief by the parents that increased involvement would facilitate increased functioning of the child" (p. 649).

3. In the bidirectional model, the patient's odd behaviors or symptoms may cause family members to attempt to exert control and to react with frustration, which in turn produce more psychotic symptoms in the patient. An examination of communication patterns in families of patients with schizophrenia also shows some support for this view (Rosenfarb et al., 1995).

High-EE communication does not appear to be peculiar to schizophrenia. These patterns have also been found in the families of patients with depression, bipolar disorder, and eating disorders (Butzlaff & Hooley, 1998; Kavanagh, 1992). And although EE has

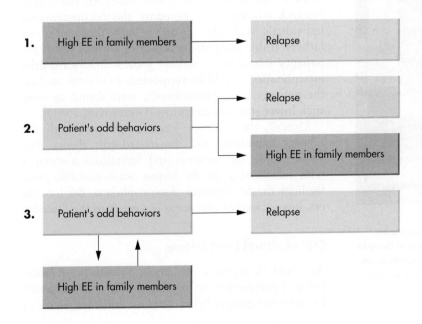

FIGURE 13.5 Possible Relationships Between High Rates of Expressed Emotion and Relapse Rates in Patients with Schizophrenia Although some researchers believe that high expressed emotions among family members are related to relapse rates in schizophrenic patients, the precise relationship has not been determined. This figure shows several ways in which expressed emotions and relapse rates can be related.

been found to be related to relapse, little evidence supports the idea that deviant family communication patterns are, by themselves, sufficient to produce schizophrenia. However, they may function as stressors on an individual with a biological predisposition for the disorder (Wahlberg et al., 1997). These findings also support the view that expressed emotions may, in part, be a reaction of family members to severe illnesses. High-EE communication appears to be more prevalent in Western families. Studies of the families of patients living in India show much lower levels of expressed emotion than are found in American families (Leff et al., 1990).

Not all studies have supported the EE hypothesis, and some researchers are voicing concern that the EE hypothesis may be used to blame families for the dis-

Some Neighborhoods May Nurture Schizophrenia
Schizophrenia is much more prevalent at lower socioeconomic levels. Some believe this is due to the increased stress of living in poverty; others believe that individuals with schizophrenia move into poor neighborhoods due to their inability to function fully. How would you determine which view is correct?

order. Miklowitz (1994) points out that terms such as "high expressed emotions" seem to imply that the relatives are excessively emotional or disturbed in some way. He recommends substituting a term such as "negative affective relationships" to indicate the bidirectional nature of interactions.

Effect of Social Class

Schizophrenia is most common at the lower socioeconomic levels, regardless of whether prevalence is measured relative to patient populations or to general populations. One of the most consistent research findings is that the disorder is disproportionately concentrated among people in the poorest areas of large cities and in the occupations with the lowest status. It is five times more common at the lowest socioeconomic level than at the highest (Keith et al., 1991).

This correlation between social class and schizophrenia has two possible explanations. First, low socioeconomic status is itself stressful. Physical and psychological stressors associated with poverty, a lack of education, menial employment, and the like, increase the chance that schizophrenia will develop (*breeder hypothesis*). Second, just prior to, or at the onset of, the disorder, people with schizophrenia tend to drift to the poorest urban areas and the lowest socioeconomic levels because they cannot function effectively elsewhere in society (*downward-drift theory*).

Although one way to test downward-drift theory is to determine whether individuals with schizophrenia do actually move downward in occupational status, the results of such studies have been inconclusive. Some researchers have found evidence of downward mobility, but others have found none. An alternative research strategy is to compare the occupations of individuals with this disorder with those of their fathers. If this comparison indicates a lower status for patients' jobs than for fathers' jobs, a downward-drift interpretation would be supported. In several studies, the patients with schizophrenia were found to have such lower status occupations (Gottesman, 1991).

Overall, the evidence seems to support both the breeder hypothesis and downward-drift theory. For some people, the stressors and limitations associated with membership in the lowest socioeconomic class facilitate the development of schizophrenia. But for others, low socioeconomic status is a result of the disorder.

Cross-Cultural Comparisons

As noted throughout this book, the study of cross-cultural perspectives on psychopathology is important because indigenous belief systems influence views of

FIGURE 13.6 Members of Two Cultures Explain the Causes of Auditory Hallucinations   A study of 281 individuals in Saudi Arabia and England had very different beliefs about the causes of auditory hallucinations. These differences in beliefs also influenced the respondents' recommendations for treatment.

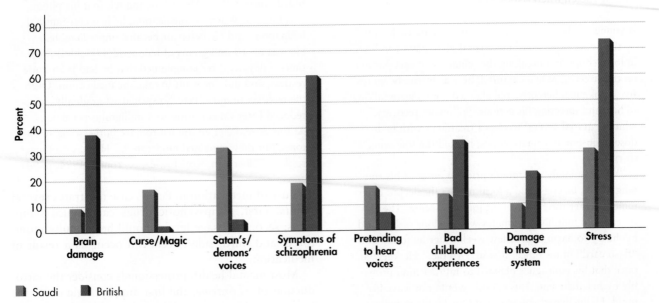

Source: From Wahass & Kent (1997).

etiology and treatment. In India, for example, the belief in the supernatural causation of schizophrenia is very widespread, and it leads to consultation and treatment by indigenous healers (Banerjee & Roy, 1998). In a study of 281 individuals in Saudi Arabia and England, the researchers (Wahass & Kent, 1997) found that the Saudis were likely to believe that auditory hallucinations were due to Satanic or demonic powers (32.7 percent) or to a curse or magic (16.7 percent). Only 18.7 percent believed these "voices" to be a symptom of schizophrenia. Most English respondents attributed auditory hallucinations to symptoms of schizophrenia (60.5 percent) or some form of brain damage (38 percent). Figure 13.6 lists other comparisons from this study. Not surprisingly, beliefs influenced treatment choices. About two-thirds of the Saudi sample believed that the most appropriate intervention would be religious assistance, whereas nearly two-thirds of the English sample believed that medication and psychological therapies would be treatments of choice.

Cultural considerations also were evident in the case of a thirteen-year-old child of a Tongan mother and Caucasian father living in the United States. The girl appeared to have visual hallucinations, had become isolative, exhibited echolalia, would be observed conversing with herself, and reported hear-

ing voices of a woman who sounded like her mother and a man who sounded like her dead grandfather. Although some improvement was observed with antipsychotic medication, the girl still reported being disturbed by ghosts and reported ideas of reference—that people were talking about her. The mother decided that her daughter suffered from "fakamahaki" (a culture-bound syndrome in which deceased relatives can inflict illness or possess the living when customs have been neglected) and took her daughter to Tonga to be treated. For five days, a traditional healer ("witch doctor") treated the girl with herbal potions. Vomiting was induced to remove toxins from the body. She also visited her grandfather's grave site to allow proper mourning. The girl returned to the United States and was reevaluated. No symptoms of psychosis could be found. Follow-up contacts revealed that the girl was continuing to do well. This case is interesting because medication had only limited success, whereas traditional healing seemed to be effective. Again, it might have been just that the disorder was time-limited, but how can we account for the seemingly successful treatment of severe mental disorders through folk medicine (Takeuchi, 2000)?

Cultural differences are not confined solely to explanations of symptoms, however. Less developed countries seem to have a greater percentage of "hysterical psychoses," "possession syndromes," and other brief psychotic disorders. These psychoses tend to be rapid in onset and short in duration; they have a good prognosis. The following case from Zimbabwe illustrates some of the characteristics:

> A young teacher was brought to the psychiatric hospital by the police after smashing several plate-glass windows in local shops and breaking the windows of cars parked on the street. ...When captured, he was intensely aggressive, spoke incoherently, and claimed voices were talking to him and directing his actions. Following recovery, which required several weeks of treatment with high-dose, high-potency neuroleptics, he told the following story.
>
> Approximately one month prior to onset of his running amok, he consulted a local n'anga [healer] to determine whether the future of his job was secure. The n'anga told him his workmates were jealous of him and might try to harm him. A few weeks later he found a "flash card" in his office. It read, "To die." He knew at once that his colleagues planned to murder him, probably by bewitchment. This episode would not leave his mind. Hallucinated voices began to echo his thoughts, and his state of wild excitement ensued. (Stevens, 1987, p. 394)

Cases of psychotic reactions after hearing a negative prediction from a healer have been reported in some less developed countries.

The Treatment of Schizophrenia

Through the years, schizophrenia has been "treated" by a variety of means, including "warehousing" severely disturbed patients in overcrowded asylums and prefrontal lobotomy, a surgical procedure in which the frontal lobes are disconnected from the remainder of the patient's brain. Such radical procedures were generally abandoned in the 1950s, when the beneficial effects of antipsychotic drugs were discovered. Today schizophrenia is typically treated with antipsychotic medication, along with some type of psychosocial therapy. In recent years, the research and clinical perspective on people with schizophrenia has shifted from a focus on disease and deficit to one promoting health, competencies, independence, and self-determination (Coursey et al., 1997). This change of focus is affecting therapists' roles, their views of clients and their families, and appropriate treatments. (The Mental Health and Society feature "Families of the Mentally Ill" discusses some of the ways therapists are now addressing the needs of these families.)

Antipsychotic Medication

> Peter was a twenty-nine-year-old man with chronic paranoid schizophrenia. ... When on medication, he heard voices talking about him and felt that his phone was bugged. When off medication, he had constant hallucinations and his behavior became unpredictable. ... He was on 10 milligrams of haloperidol (Haldol) three times a day. ... Peter complained that he had been quite restless, and did not want to take the medication. Over the next six months, Peter's psychiatrist gradually reduced Peter's medication to 4 milligrams per day. ... At this dose, Peter continued to have bothersome symptoms, but they remained moderate. ... He was no longer restless. (Liberman, Kopelowicz, & Young, 1994, p. 94)

The use of medication in Peter's case illustrates several points. First, antipsychotic drugs can reduce symptoms; second, dosage levels should be carefully monitored; and third, side effects can occur as a result of medication.

Most mental health professionals consider the introduction of *Thorazine,* the first antipsychotic drug, the beginning of a new era in treating schizophrenia. For the first time, a medication was available that sufficiently relaxed even violent patients with schizophrenia and helped organize their thoughts to the point at which straitjackets were no longer needed to restrain the individuals. Three decades later, the phenothiazines, which are variations of Thorazine, are still viewed as the most effective drug treatment for schizophrenia. They are not, however, a "cure" for the condition.

The antipsychotic medications (also called **neuroleptics**) are, however, far from perfect and can produce a number of extremely unwelcome side effects that resemble neurological conditions. They quite effectively reduce the severity of the positive symptoms of schizophrenia, such as hallucinations, delusions, bizarre speech, and thought disorders. Most, however, offer little relief from the negative symptoms of social withdrawal, apathy, and impaired personal hygiene (Carpenter, Conley, Buchanan, Breier, & Tamminga, 1995; Strous et al., 2004). Moreover, a "relatively large group" of people with schizophrenia do not benefit at all from antipsychotic medication (Wiesel, 1994; Silverman et al., 1987). In addition, about up to 40 percent of individuals on antipsychotic medications show poor adherence. This is especially true among African American and younger patients (Valenstein et al., 2004).

Some new antipsychotic drugs (including clozapine, risperidone, quetiapine, and olanzapine) were released for use in the United States in the 1990s. Over 50 percent of new prescriptions for treating schizophrenia

MENTAL HEALTH AND SOCIETY
Families of the Mentally Ill

A serious mental illness such as schizophrenia can have a powerful effect on the patient's family members, who may feel stigmatized or responsible for the disorder (Phelan, Bromet, & Link, 1998). As one woman stated,

All family members are affected by a loved one's mental illness. The entire family system needs to be addressed. To assure us that we are not to blame and the situation is not hopeless. To point us to the people and places that can help our loved one. The impact still lingers on. (Marsh & Johnson, 1997)

Siblings without the disorder also display a variety of emotional reactions to their sick brother or sister—from love ("She's really kind and loves me so very much it's never been a problem"); loss ("Somehow I've lost my sister the way she was before and I think I won't get her back"); anger ("Yes, it's hell. ... She's incredibly mean to our mother and she sure as hell doesn't deserve that"), guilt and shame ("Yes, you can think about how he got ill and I didn't"), and fear ("You worry a lot about getting it yourself") (Stalberg, Ekerwald, & Hultman, 2004, p. 450).

In the past, the health care system did not address the needs of the families of the mentally ill. In many cases, parents or other family members were blamed as causing mental illness in the afflicted individual. After a review of the research on schizophrenia, Lehman and Steinwachs (1998) concluded that there is little evidence of any causal link between family dysfunction and the disorder. Such a belief, they warn, is not only inaccurate but also undermines the trusting relationship between therapist and family.

There is currently a move toward collaborative family therapy in which therapists work with families of mentally ill individuals to identify their needs, such as financial difficulties, restricted social activities, and diminished physical and psychological health as a consequence of their caregiving activities (Fadden, 1998). For example, family members may grieve the loss of a relative to mental illness. Some may also have to face a life or family that is no longer "normal." Expectations about childhood and parenting may be severely disrupted. As one man noted about his childhood experience:

My father's paranoid schizophrenia meant that we moved frequently because he felt the conspiracy was closing in on him. ... I couldn't have friendships with my peers because my father felt they might "poison" my mind against him. (Marsh & Johnson, 1997, p. 230)

By addressing the needs of both the family and the mentally ill member, collaborative family therapy offers new hope and support. With this kind of assistance, some families have been surprisingly resilient and able to view the experience in a constructive way:

I have become much more tolerant of imperfection in myself and others. ... I have learned to appreciate the strengths of other people who appear to be different or are handicapped in some way. ... My husband and I are closer and more honest with each other as a result of our shared grief and stress. ... We are proud that our family has remained intact and strong. (Marsh et al., 1996, p. 10)

---

are for the new atypical antipsychotics (Meltzer, 2000). These medications have fewer side effects than some older neuroleptics and are effective with up to 50 percent of patients who do not respond to traditional medications (Jackson, Covell, & Essock, 2004; Reid & Mason, 1998; Tollefson, Beasley, Tran, & Street, 1997). Some have also shown some success in reducing negative symptoms (Rivas-Vazquez, Blais, Rey, & Rivas-Vazquez, 2000). For those who can tolerate clozapine, the medication appears to have superior efficacy for positive symptoms and is associated with long-term improvement in social and occupational functioning (Buchanan, Breier, Kirkpatrick, Ball, & Carpenter, 1998). Clozapine also appears to have

lower risk of extrapyramidal (unwanted movement) symptoms than risperidone (Azorin et al., 2001). Its use is carefully monitored because one of its side effects is potentially fatal lesions of the mucous membranes or gastrointestinal system. There is also concern that abrupt discontinuation of the drug will cause more symptom rebound than occurs with other antipsychotic medications (Shore, Matthews, Cott, & Lieberman, 1995).

Regulation and monitoring of antipsychotic drugs is especially important, and using the minimum effective dose is recommended (Lehman, Kreyenbuhl, Buchanan, & Dickerson, 2004). However, a study of 719 patients diagnosed with schizophrenia revealed that the dosage levels of their antipsychotic medications were often outside the recommended treatment ranges and that minority patients were more likely to be on higher levels than white patients (Lehman & Steinwachs, 1998). Similarly, 38 percent of patients in another sample received "poor" medication management (Young, Sullivan, Burnam, & Brook, 1998). And a third study showed that women were given higher doses of antipsychotic medication than their male counterparts and that women's medication was seldom reduced to a maintenance level after the acute stage passed (Zito, Craig, Wanderling, & Siegel, 1987). This may be problematic because women, especially those with late-onset schizophrenia, are more likely to develop tardive dyskinesia (Lindamer, Lohr, Caligiuri, & Jeste, 2001). Segal, Cohen, and Marder (1992) found that psychiatrists tended to administer higher and higher doses of antipsychotic medications to patients living in halfway houses and other sheltered-care facilities. Nearly one-half received increases in medication during a twelve-year period, and 10 percent received "extreme doses."

Equally disturbing, clinicians are often unaware of possible reactions to the drugs, which include tremors, motor restlessness, anxiety, agitation, extreme terror, and even impulsive suicide attempts (Drake & Ehrlich, 1985; Hirose, 2003; Lehman & Steinwachs, 1998). In one study (Weiden, Mann, Haas, Mattson, & Frances, 1987) clinicians did not identify motor symptoms such as restlessness, rigidity, and tremors produced by medications. Clinicians identified only one of ten patients showing tardive dyskinesia (involuntary movement disorder). The inability to recognize these symptoms in patients who are medicated is disturbing. The Critical Thinking feature "Should Patients Have the Right to Refuse Medication?" examines the issue of patients' rights in taking medication.

Because of the severity of some side effects, researchers are trying to identify the groups of patients with schizophrenia who do not need maintenance medication. One approach is to reduce medication and watch for a relapse. Those who function well on a lower dosage might later undergo a trial period in which medication is totally eliminated. In one study conducted over a twelve-month period, reducing dosage levels by 50 percent tripled the relapse rate (32 percent, as opposed to 10 percent on maintenance medication). A tradeoff, however, is that reduced-dose patients showed decreased risk of tardive dyskinesia (Johnson, Ludlow, Street, & Taylor, 1987). Although a higher relapse rate was associated with a lower level of medication (10 percent of the standard dose), the families of these patients expressed more satisfaction with their adjustment than did the families of patients taking a standard dose. On the lower dose, patients showed greater social competence and adjustment. More than 50 percent remained stable. Researchers also found that negative family attitudes toward the patient were associated with relapse. So dosage reduction, together with careful monitoring, may be useful with some people, but standard dosage levels may be needed for patients in nonsupportive families.

Psychosocial Therapy

> Philip's psychotic symptoms were reduced with medication. However, he was unable to obtain employment. The counselor suggested that his attire (sweatshirt, exercise pants, head band, and worn sneakers) might be inappropriate for a job interview. In addition, his first impression skills for interviews were lacking. Field trips allowed Philip to observe attire worn by individuals in different businesses. He was also trained in conversational topics and practiced job interviews with his counselor. Philip decided to apply for landscape work, wore a work shirt, blue jeans, and construction boots, and was hired by a landscaping contractor. (Heinssen & Cuthbert, 2001)

Many individuals with schizophrenia behave "strangely" and do not have positive conversational skills (Nisenson, Berenbaum, & Good, 2001), Heinssen and Cuthbert (2001) found that eccentricities in appearance, attire, communication patterns, and lack of discretion in discussing their illness can impede employment or the establishment of social networks; these problems can also be addressed through the use of psychotherapeutic interventions. With appropriate interventions, many individuals with schizophrenia can acquire competitive employment.

Most clinicians today agree that the most beneficial treatment for schizophrenia is some combination of antipsychotic medication and therapy. This attitude is fairly new, and strict advocates of a medical approach resisted the idea of psychotherapy for many years. But even as scientists continued to introduce drugs that effectively reduced or eliminated many symptoms of schizophrenia, one vital fact became clear: medicated and adequately functioning people with schizophrenia who were discharged from protective hospital environments were returning to stressful home or work situations. The typical result was repeated rehospitalizations; medication alone was not enough to help these individuals function in their natural environments. Clinicians soon realized that antipsychotic medication had to be supplemented with outpatient therapy.

CRITICAL THINKING

Should Patients Have the Right to Refuse Medication?

Should individuals with schizophrenia have the right to refuse antipsychotic medications that produce potentially hazardous side effects? Patients in many state hospitals do not have this right. Before you respond to this question, consider that there is no known effective treatment for tardive dyskinesia. Tardive dyskinesia is characterized by involuntary and rhythmic movements of the protruding tongue; chewing, lip smacking, and other facial movements; and jerking movements of the limbs. At risk for this disorder are people who have been treated with antipsychotic medications—also known as neuroleptics—over a long period of time. The elderly appear to be especially vulnerable to neuroleptic side effects (Meltzer, 2000; Zayas & Grossberg, 1998). Women tend to have more severe tardive dyskinesia and a higher prevalence than men do (American Psychiatric Association, 1997; Yassa & Jeste, 1992). However, this syndrome is appearing increasingly more often in younger patients and nonpsychotic patients because neuroleptics are now being prescribed to treat anxiety, hyperactivity in children, aggression, and mood disorders. Legal and ethical issues are becoming involved, as the "cure may be worse than the illness."

In one large prospective study, nearly 20 percent of the sample developed tardive dyskinesia after being on the medication for four years. After eight years, 40 percent had tardive dyskinesia (Kane, Woerner, Borenstein, Wegner, & Lieberman, 1986). As Kane and Freeman (1994) have observed, "In patients who are already socially disabled by negative and deficit symptoms, bizarre behavior, and impaired social skills, the addition of embarrassing and stigmatizing involuntary movements of [tardive dyskinesia] is certainly an added obstacle to optimal adjustment in the community" (p. 28). In most cases, the symptoms persist and cannot be eliminated (Glazer, Morgenstern, & Doucette, 1991). The use of antipsychotic medications during pregnancy has been associated with symptoms such as tremors, abnormal movement, and problems with voluntary movement in infants (Collins & Comer, 2003).

The antipsychotic medications may also have some side effects that are reversible. Approximately 60 percent of patients on antipsychotic medications develop extrapyramidal side effects such as *Parkinsonism* (muscle tremors, shakiness, and immobility), *dystonia* (slow and continued contrasting movements of the limbs and tongue), *akathesis* (motor restlessness), and *neuroleptic malignant syndrome* (muscle rigidity and autonomic instability), the latter of which can be fatal if untreated (American Psychiatric Association, 1997). Other symptoms may involve the loss of facial expression, immobility, shuffling gait, tremors of the hand, rigidity of the body, and poor postural stability; these symptoms are usually reversible (Lehman & Steinwachs, 1998).

Patients have described a variety of reactions to the medication: "I feel restless; I cannot keep still; my nerves are jumpy; I feel like jumping out of my skin; my legs just want to keep moving; it's like having ants in my pants" (Sachdev & Loneragan, 1991, p. 383). Other side effects include drowsiness, skin rashes, blurred vision, dry mouth, nausea, and rapid heartbeat.

Groups that support the concept of patients' rights argue that forced administration of drugs violates a person's basic freedoms. Yet hospital staff members fear that violent patients may be dangerous to themselves, other patients, and staff if they are not medicated. As the funding of state mental institutions has decreased, the use of medication has increased.

Should patients who admit themselves voluntarily for treatment be able to refuse antipsychotic medications? What about those who are involuntarily committed? Should the state, institution, or psychiatrist be liable for the development of permanent side effects among patients? Can an individual who is currently undergoing a psychotic episode give "consent" to being treated with antipsychotic medications? States and the mental health profession are wrestling with these issues. Additional controversies over the right of patients to refuse medications continue to have to be addressed. In several cases, individuals have refused to take antipsychotic medications to allow them to be competent to stand trial for murders. Not only have these individuals refused, but some psychiatrists also feel conflicted in giving medication under these conditions.

How do patients with severe mental disorders feel about their experiences with psychotherapy? A random sample of 212 patients from different clinics in Maryland responded to a questionnaire. Nearly three-fourths of patients with schizophrenia believed that individual psychotherapy brought about positive changes in their lives. Although the remaining 28 percent reported that it produced no change or had a negative effect, most patients felt that the best treatment was a combination of talking therapy with medication. The study (Coursey, Keller, & Farrell, 1995) found that the following aspects of individual therapy were considered most useful. (The numbers in parentheses represent the percentage of patients who agreed with the statement.)

- Therapist gave me practical advice (52 percent)

- Getting in touch with my feelings (45 percent)

- Understanding how I affect other people and how they affect me (25 percent)

- Looking at the ways I usually act and feel and why (24 percent)

- Understanding the impact of my past on what I do now (24 percent)

Most patients felt that the most important quality of a therapist was friendship. It appears that patients with schizophrenia do value psychotherapy. Another former patient offers suggestions to psychotherapists that may be helpful in working with the severely mentally ill (Bassman, 2000): (1) see the patient as a whole person with a unique history, (2) decrease the power imbalance in the therapeutic relationship, (3) be honest and engage in genuine interaction with the patient, (4) work in collaboration and develop a trusting relationship, (5) help the patient identify and rediscover lost dreams, (6) identify the individual's strengths and abilities, not just the deficits, and (7) explore possibilities of transformation, new identity, and meaning. As all of us do, individuals with schizophrenia desire the opportunities to work, have social contacts and friends, and be independent in living (Angermeyer, Holzinger, Kilian, & Matschinger, 2001).

Institutional Approaches Traditional institutional treatments providing custodial care and medication for patients with schizophrenia have yielded poor results, although milieu therapy and behavioral therapy have been found to be more effective. In **milieu therapy,** the hospital environment operates as a community, and patients exercise a wide range of responsibilities, helping to make decisions and to manage the wards. This type of therapy sharply contrasts with the

passive role patients with schizophrenia have had in traditional settings. Social learning programs focus on increasing appropriate self-care behaviors, conversational skills, and role skills, such as job training and ward activities. Undesirable behaviors such as "crazy talk" or social isolation are decreased through reinforcement and modeling techniques. Both approaches have been shown to be effective in helping many people with schizophrenia achieve independent living (Falloon, Boyd, & McGill, 1984). Living in community homes also has produced positive results. In a study of nearly 100 patients with chronic schizophrenia placed in community facilities, almost all improved. They reported more friendships and fewer symptoms than those who remained institutionalized (Leff, 1994).

Cognitive-Behavioral Therapy Major advances have been made in the use of cognitive and behavioral strategies in treating the symptoms of schizophrenia, especially among those who have not been fully helped through medications. The therapeutic interventions tend to share the same format. Positive and negative symptoms are targeted with the goal of reducing their frequency and severity and the associated distress. Coping skills are enhanced to allow the patient to manage both positive and negative symptoms (Beck & Rector, 2000).

Individuals with auditory hallucinations are often terrified; the voices are viewed as omnipotent, producing feelings of helplessness. Using a cognitive-behavioral format, Chadwick, Sambrooke, Rasch, and Davies (2000) were able to weaken beliefs about omnipotence and increase a sense of personal control among individuals with schizophrenia. The initial sessions focused on exploring when the voices began, why they thought the voices occurred, and how the voices affected their lives. Later, the beliefs about the voices' omnipotence were subjected to empirical testing by demonstrating that certain behaviors could reduce the voices. They also evaluated the possibility that the voice was internally generated. This process was effective in reducing the perceived power and control of the voices. In another study (Jenner et al., 2004), techniques such as the reduction of psychotic symptoms through the use of a destigmatizing explanation and providing patients with analytical skills were effective. False beliefs were challenged through reasoning and empirical testing. Auditory hallucinations were monitored and triggering events were identified. The focus was on having the patients regain control and command of their thoughts.

Individuals with this disorder have also learned to employ coping strategies such as reading aloud to combat auditory hallucinations. After trying out this approach, they are asked to report their success in using it. They also experiment with other strategies, such as asking for increased medication, seeking help or distraction, or relaxing when they feel their symptoms are worsening. Through such experimentation, patients learn to evaluate and develop different strategies for dealing with psychotic symptoms (Kuipers, Garety, Fowler, & Dunn, 1997).

Because people with schizophrenia typically lack social skills, training in these skills is almost always a part—sometimes the major part—of behavioral therapy. The training emphasizes communication skills and assertiveness (Sotillo, Rodriguez, & Salazar, 1998). The patient is repeatedly placed in social situations that he or she tends to avoid. Experience with such situations eventually decreases the patient's anxiety concerning them to the point at which he or she will seek out, rather than avoid, these situations. This is a crucially important contribution of social-skills training, because social withdrawal is a major schizophrenic symptom that is untouched by antipsychotic medication. Social-skills training has been found to be helpful for patients with chronic schizophrenia (Liberman & Green, 1992; Sovani & Thatte, 1998; Wallace, 1998).

Social-skills training has also been successfully adapted for patients who have schizophrenia and come from different cultural groups (Nilsson, Grawe, Levander, & Lovaas, 1998). In modifying social-skills training for Latinos with schizophrenia, Kopelowicz (1998) set goals that encouraged the functional interdependence of the client with relatives (85 to 90 percent of Latinos with schizophrenia live with their families). Family members participated in training sessions in social skills. In line with cultural expectations, therapists formed a personal relationship with the clients and the family members by engaging in small talk and self-disclosures and by making the event a festive occasion by sharing food during breaks.

Interventions Focusing on Family Communication and Education

More than 50 percent of recovering patients now return to live with their families, and new psychological interventions address this fact. Family intervention programs have not only reduced relapse rates but have also lowered the cost of care (Fadden, 1998). They have been beneficial for families with and without communication patterns such as EE (Lehman & Steinwachs, 1998). Most programs include the following components (Marsh & Johnson, 1997; Mueser et al., 2001):

1. normalizing the family experience

Creative Endeavors by Individuals with Schizophrenia
Dr. Nancy Clayton (right) and Ms. Paula Mayence (left) are Co-Chairs of the "Brushes with Life" program, part of STEP (Schizophrenia Treatment and Evaluation Program). By displaying artwork and poetry by inpatients and clinic outpatients from the UNC STEP program, the STEP gallery hopes to decrease the stigma associated with mental illness by demonstrating its patients' creative talents.

2. educating family members about schizophrenia

3. identifying the strengths and competencies of the patient and family members

4. developing skills in problem solving and managing stress

5. learning to cope with the symptoms of mental illness and its repercussions on the family

6. recognizing early signs of relapse (One study, by Stenberg, Jaaskelainen, and Royks [1998], found that simply teaching family members to recognize early signs of relapse resulted in earlier treatment and shorter hospital stays.)

7. creating a supportive family environment

8. understanding and meeting the needs of all family members

In one program, high-EE and low-EE family members meet in a group to talk about specific themes, such as problems faced by families of patients recovering from schizophrenia, methods of reducing guilt and responsibility for these patients, and healthy ways of dealing with the stress and frustrations of living with the patients. Vaughn and Leff (1981) and Kavanagh (1992) found that the group format successfully reduced EE levels and also reduced patients' relapse rates. Falloon (1992) found these procedures even more useful when individuals first show symptoms suggestive of a schizophrenic episode. Family intervention approaches based on this model also successfully reduced the rehospitalization rate of men with schizophrenia in China (Zhang, Wang, & Phillips, 1994).

Family approaches and social skills training have been shown to be much more effective in preventing relapse than is drug treatment alone. Combining cognitive behavioral strategies, family counseling, and social skills training seems to produce the most positive result (Penn et al., 2004).

The combination of medication and the new psychological interventions has provided hope for many patients with schizophrenia; continuing research points to an even more promising future.

SUMMARY

How have our views of schizophrenia changed over time?

- Kraepelin believed the onset of schizophrenia was early, a result of organic deterioration, the outcome of which is poor. Bleuler believed that both the age of onset and the course were variable.
- DSM-I and II used Bleuler's broader definition. In DSM-III and through DSM-IV-TR, a stricter definition more in line with Kraepelin's view has been adopted.

What kinds of symptoms are found in this disorder?

- Positive symptoms of schizophrenia include delusions; perceptual distortion, as in hallucinations; disorganized communications; and thought disturbances, including loosening of associations, attention problems, and disorganized motor disturbances.
- Negative symptoms in schizophrenia include avolition, alogia, anhedonia, and flat affect.

How do the specific types of schizophrenia differ from one another?

- DSM-IV-TR distinguishes five types of schizophrenia.
- Paranoid schizophrenia is characterized by persecutory delusions or frequent auditory hallucinations.
- Disorganized schizophrenia is characterized by disorganized speech and behavior and inappropriate affect. Extreme social impairment and severe regressive behaviors are often seen.
- Catatonic schizophrenia's major feature is disturbance of motor activity. Patients show excessive excitement, agitation and hyperactivity, or withdrawn behavior patterns.
- The undifferentiated type includes schizophrenic behavior that cannot be classified as one of the other types.
- Residual schizophrenia is a category for people who have had at least one episode of schizophrenia but are not now showing prominent symptoms. In addition, other severe disorders may include schizophrenic-like symptoms.

Is there much chance of recovery from schizophrenia?

- The degree of recovery from schizophrenia is difficult to evaluate, in part because of changing definitions. Although most people assume that the prognosis for individuals with schizophrenia is not good, research is beginning to show that that may not be the case. Many of these individuals experience minimal or no lasting impairment. Most individuals with schizophrenia recover enough to lead relatively productive lives.

What causes schizophrenia?

- Much research and theorizing has focused on the etiology of schizophrenia, but methodological flaws and research design limitations restrict the kinds of conclusions that can be drawn. The best conclusion is that genetics, along with some type of environmental factors, combine to cause the disorder.

Is schizophrenia an inherited condition?

- Using research strategies such as twin studies and adoption studies, investigators have shown that heredity does influence this group of disorders. The degree of influence is open to question, however; when methodological problems are taken into account, it appears lower than previously reported.

Heredity is a major factor but not sufficient to cause schizophrenia; environmental factors are also involved.

What supports the view that schizophrenia is a result of brain abnormalities?

■ The process by which genetic influences are transmitted has not been explained. Brain structure and neurotransmitter differences have been found between individuals with and without schizophrenia. However, some of the findings report only small differences and are difficult to interpret.

Can psychological factors "cause" schizophrenia?

■ The search for an environmental basis for schizophrenia has met with no more success than has the search for genetic influences.
■ Certain negative family patterns, involving parental characteristics or intrafamilial communication processes, have been hypothesized to result in schizophrenia.
■ High expressed emotions (negative comments), or high EE, from family members may be related to relapse in people with schizophrenia.
■ There is little evidence that psychological factors in and of themselves can cause the condition.

What is the best etiological model for schizophrenia?

■ The research on the etiology of schizophrenia has suggested an interaction between genetic and environmental factors. When the vulnerable person is exposed to strong environmental stressors but does not have the resources to cope with them, a schizophrenic episode may result.

What kinds of treatments are currently available, and are they effective?

■ Schizophrenia seems to involve both biological and physiological factors, and treatment programs that combine drugs with psychotherapy appear to hold the most promise.
■ Drug therapy usually involves the phenothiazines, or antipsychotics.
■ The accompanying psychosocial therapy consists of either supportive counseling or behavior therapy, with an emphasis on social-skills training and changing communication patterns among patients and family members.

KEY TERMS

brief psychotic disorder (p. 431)
catatonic schizophrenia (p. 430)
concordance rate (p. 436)
delusional disorder (p. 430)
delusion (p. 422)
disorganized schizophrenia (p. 430)

dopamine hypothesis (p. 441)
double-bind theory (p. 446)
expressed emotion (EE) (p. 446)
flat affect (p. 421)
hallucination (p. 423)
loosening of associations (p. 425)
milieu therapy (p. 454)

negative symptom (p. 426)
neuroleptics (p. 450)
paranoid schizophrenia (p. 429)
pathognomonic (p. 424)
positive symptom (p. 422)
prospective study (p. 440)
residual schizophrenia (p. 431)

schizophrenia (p. 419)
schizophrenia spectrum (p. 438)
schizophreniform disorder (p. 431)
schizophrenogenic (p. 446)
undifferentiated schizophrenia (p. 430)

MULTIMEDIA PREVIEW

For additional study aids, we invite you to explore our media resources accompanying *Understanding Abnormal Behavior,* Eighth Edition. The Student CD-ROM includes videos, quizzing, and critical thinking activities that help to reinforce key concepts in a fun and engaging manner. The Student Web Site provides additional interactive activities, chapter outlines, and research links that further support and complement the text. All Web resources may be accessed by logging onto the Web site at **http://psychology.college.hmco.com/students**.

CHAPTER 14
Cognitive Disorders

FOCUS QUESTIONS

■ How can we determine whether someone has brain damage or a cognitive disorder?

■ What are the different types of cognitive disorders?

■ Why do people develop cognitive disorders?

■ What kinds of interventions can be used to treat people with cognitive disorders?

■ What is mental retardation?

I n the ring, Muhammad Ali was able to "float like a butterfly, sting like a bee" as he won, lost, and twice regained the world heavyweight boxing championship. Outside the ring he was known for his ego, his wit and rapid-fire speech, and his never-ending rhyming. But it was a different Muhammad Ali who, at age fifty-four and retired from boxing, visited Cuba to donate medicine and supplies on behalf of two American relief organizations. His hands trembled and he could barely speak. He tended to shuffle when he walked; he often seemed remote and expressionless, constantly felt tired, and suffered occasional lapses of memory. Ali often spoke through hand signals that were translated by his wife.

Ali's symptoms resemble those of Parkinson's disease, a brain disorder, but his doctors ruled out that possibility. His disorder was diagnosed as Parkinson's syndrome, meaning that he has many symptoms of Parkinson's disease although he does not have the disorder. Ali's symptoms are probably due to some sort of brain trauma. Anti-Parkinson's medication has reduced the severity of some of the symptoms, but the prognosis is vague.

> As his health has declined, Ali, fifty-four, has been described as a sad figure, a man swallowed up by the body that once challenged the world like a piece of beautiful, controversial art. In fact, he has never been more heroic. All that is left is his humanity as he travels 250 days a year to promote good causes, Islam, and peace. (Fainaru, 1996, p. 2)

Like many other individuals, Ali suffers from a *cognitive disorder*—a behavioral disturbance that results from transient or permanent damage to the brain. DSM-IV-TR (American Psychiatric Association, 2000) characterizes **cognitive disorders** as disorders that

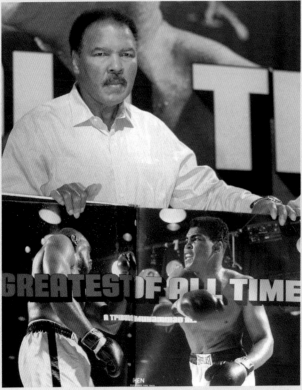

Still a Champion but at What a Cost Muhammad Ali, one of the greatest heavyweight champion boxers ever, suffers Parkinson-like symptoms, such as slurred speech, shuffling when walking, expressionless facial appearance, and occasional memory lapses. These symptoms are believed to be caused by the repeated blows to the head suffered by Ali during his boxing career. What cognitive symptoms are associated with this disease?

affect thinking processes, memory, consciousness, perception, and so on and that are caused by brain dysfunction. Psychiatric conditions with associated cognitive symptoms (such as schizophrenia) are not

FIGURE 14.1 Disorders Chart: Cognitive Disorders

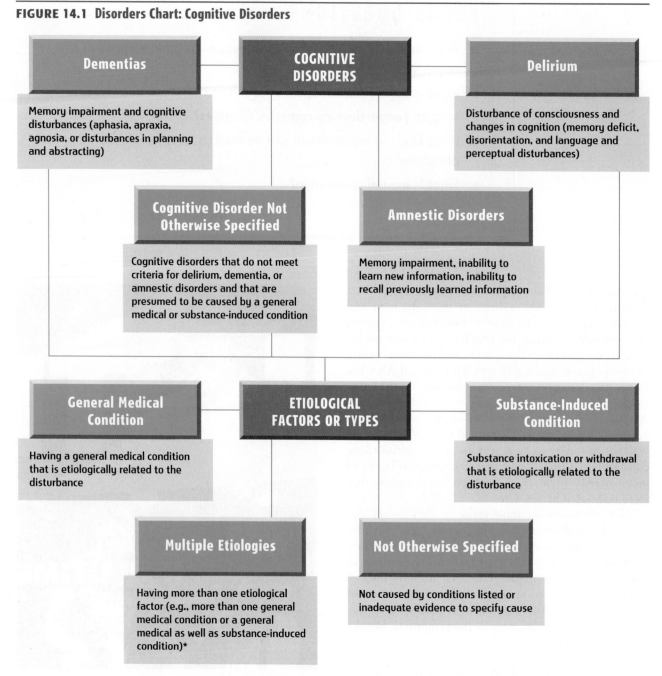

*In the case of amnestic disorders, the category of multiple etiologies is not used.

considered in this category or in this chapter. We also discuss mental retardation. Although mental retardation is considered within the DSM-IV-TR category of disorders usually first diagnosed in infancy, childhood, or adolescence, we consider it in this chapter because it deals with cognitive and intellectual functioning. Strictly speaking, however, mental retardation is not considered a cognitive disorder.

DSM-IV-TR classifies cognitive disorders into four major categories: (1) dementia, (2) delirium, (3) amnestic disorders, and (4) cognitive disorders not otherwise specified (see Figure 14.1). DSM-IV-TR also attempts to specify the etiological agent for each disorder.

To some extent, the diagnosis of a cognitive disorder is a process of elimination. For example, delirium is a syndrome in which someone shows a disturbance

FIGURE 14.1 Disorders Chart: Cognitive Disorders (continued)

COGNITIVE DISORDERS	Prevalence*	Gender Differences	Age of Onset	Course
Dementia	—	Usually none; depends on type of dementia	Depends on type; usually highest rates found among elderly	Depends on type; onset frequently gradual; may be temporary or progressively deteriorating
Delirium	—	Usually none; depends on type of delirium	Any age; but some variation, depending on type	Develops over hours to days; may persist for weeks; if underlying etiology is promptly corrected or is self-limiting, recovery is more likely to be complete
Amnestic Disorder	—	Usually none; depends on type of disorder	Variable	Variable; depends on type or etiology

*Prevalence for all cognitive disorders in the United States is about 6 percent.

Source: Based on American Psychiatric Association (2000).

of consciousness, an inability to maintain attention, memory problems, disorientation, and so on. When the delirium cannot be attributed to another mental disorder (such as a mood disorder) and there is evidence that a general medical condition such as disease or brain trauma is related to the disturbance, it is considered a cognitive disorder. The category of cognitive disorders is somewhat arbitrary because other mental disorders may be associated with cognitive dysfunction and organic involvement. As you will see, it is often difficult to measure and assess, as well as to discern, the exact causes of the cognitive disorders.

Possible causes of cognitive disorders include aging, trauma, infection, loss of blood supply, substance abuse, and various biochemical imbalances. These may result in cognitive, emotional, and behavioral symptoms that can resemble the symptoms of the mental disorders (Abeles & Victor, 2003).

The overall prevalence of cognitive disorders as found by the Epidemiologic Catchment Area (ECA) study (George, Landerman, Blazer, & Anthony, 1991), the largest epidemiological study conducted in the United States, is about 1 percent for severe disorders and 6 percent for mild disorders. The study also indicated that prevalence increases with age—for example, the severe cognitive impairment rate for persons age seventy-five and older is about twenty-two times

higher than that for persons between the ages of eighteen and thirty-four. Gender differences were not meaningful, but one ethnic difference was—African Americans have a higher rate of severe cognitive disorders than is found among either white or Hispanic Americans (see Figure 14.2).

Although behavioral disturbance stems from brain pathology, it is influenced by social and psychological factors, as well as by the specific pathology. People with similar types of brain damage may behave quite differently, depending on their premorbid personalities, their coping skills, and the availability of such resources as family support systems. Furthermore, people with cognitive impairments often are treated with insensitivity by other people, so they experience a lot of stress. This stress may add to or modify the symptoms that stem from the disorder.

Thus, physical, social, and psychological factors interact in complicated ways to produce the behaviors of people who have cognitive disorders (Binder, 1988). Treatment, too, often requires some combination of physical, medicinal, and psychological therapy; it may include behavior modification and skills training. For some patients who have severe and irreversible brain damage, the only available options may be rehabilitation, modified skills training, and the creation of a supportive environment.

FIGURE 14.2 Prevalence of Cognitive Impairment by Demographic Characteristics

Results indicate the prevalence of mild or severe cognitive impairment according to age, gender, race/ethnicity, and educational level. As can be seen, older, as compared with younger, individuals are far more likely to suffer from severe, as well as mild, cognitive impairment. Whites have lower rates of impairment than do other ethnic groups, and more highly educated persons have lower rates than do less educated persons. Gender appears to be largely unrelated to the prevalence of cognitive impairment. Respondents were administered a cognitive examination as part of the ECA study of adult Americans. Impairment was calculated on the basis of errors occurring during the examination or refusal to answer items on the examination.

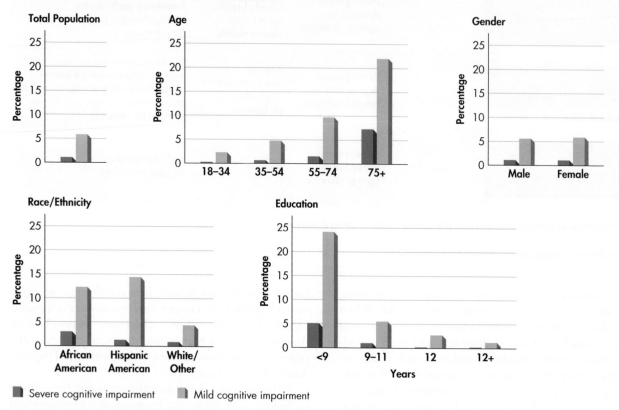

Source: Data from George et al. (1991).

We discussed the structure of the human brain in the chapter on models of abnormal behavior; here we focus primarily on the assessment, types, major causes, and treatment of cognitive disorders.

The Assessment of Brain Damage

Two types of techniques are used to assess brain damage, and both were discussed in the chapter on assessment and classification of abnormal behavior. The first consists of psychological tests and inventories that require behavioral responses from the patient and that assess functions such as memory and manual dexterity. These tests have become quite sophisticated, in that theories from neuropsychological science and quantitative methods are being applied to find a means to assess brain pathology (Meier, 1992).

Myth vs Reality

Myth: Mild head injuries among children and adolescents are a "silent epidemic" in terms of seriousness of cognitive, psychosocial, and academic consequences.

Reality: Although a great deal of concern has been raised over the frequency and consequence of mild head injuries among children, there is no compelling evidence that these injuries have the kinds of serious consequences as was initially believed. A thorough review of the research on children with mild head injuries revealed that most studies did not find major negative consequences (Satz, 2001). (A mild head injury is defined as one in which the period of unconsciousness is less than 20 minutes, which shows no evidence of hematoma, in which a patient is not hospitalized for more than two days, and in which the patient achieves nonserious scores on the Glasgow Coma Scale.) Of course, any head injury should be of concern. However, it is also important to place such injuries in proper perspective.

The second type of assessment tool is neurological tests, which permit more direct monitoring of brain functioning and structure. These tools increase diagnostic accuracy by letting researchers and diagnosticians "look into" the living brain and see evidence of its functions. For example, the **electroencephalograph (EEG)** measures electrical activity of brain cells. **Computerized axial tomography (CAT)** scanning assesses brain damage by means of x-rays and computer technology. Two additional techniques monitor a radioactive substance as it moves through the brain (Boller, Kim, & Detre, 1984). In **cerebral blood flow measurement,** the patient inhales a radioactive gas, and a gamma ray camera tracks the gas—and thus the flow of blood—as it moves throughout the brain. In **positron emission tomography (PET),** the patient is injected with radioactive glucose, and the metabolism of glucose in the patient's brain is monitored. This method provides a very accurate means of assessing brain function. A fifth technique produces snapshots of brain anatomy that have striking resolution, almost like a photograph with the skull removed—except that it is accomplished without surgery, exposure to x-rays (as in CAT scans), or ingesting radioactive materials (as in PET scans). In **magnetic resonance imaging (MRI),** the patient is placed in a magnetic field, and radio waves are used to produce pictures of the brain. Anatomical areas of the brain are not obscured by bone because bone does not show in the MRI (Frumkin, Palumbo, & Naeser, 1994). Continuing advances in neuroimaging, especially with MRI, have resulted in new functional brain imaging approaches such as the dynamic functional MRI (Morihisa, Rosse, Cross, Balkoski, & Ingraham, 1999). Each of these techniques has strengths and weaknesses in terms of costs, benefits, and possible side effects (Margolin, 1991). For example, compared with MRI, CAT scanning is less expensive, faster to operate, and can be used with patients who have metal in their heads (e.g., surgical clips, metal skull plates, etc.). On the other hand, MRI does not require use of x-rays and is better at detecting neoplasms, brain abnormalities related to seizures, and lesions in certain parts of the brain (Morihisa et al., 1999).

In initial screening for cognitive disorders, clinicians may evaluate cognitive functioning by using the mental status examination (see the chapter on assessment and classification of abnormal behavior) or by simply asking a patient to give his or her name and place of birth and to repeat phrases or write sentences that the clinician says aloud (Othmer & Othmer, 1994). At that time, and equally important, the clinician assesses the patient's general functioning, personality characteristics, and coping skills, as well as his or her behaviors and emotional reactions, particularly those that differ from reported premorbid functioning. Such an assessment can provide crucial information about brain dysfunction, and it is of utmost importance in planning treatment and rehabilitation.

Localization of Brain Damage

Neurological techniques such as CAT and PET scans and MRI help determine the location and extent of brain damage. But can the location of a damaged or disrupted area of the brain be determined from the type of functional loss the patient shows? Neuropsychologists have debated this question for a number of years and have made many attempts to relate functions to specific areas of the brain.

In one study, researchers used CAT scans to examine eighty-seven patients, each of whom had a brain lesion (brain damage) that was localized within one of eight areas of the brain (Golden, Graber, et al., 1981). Each area was then matched with the particular affected functions. The brain lobes (four in the cerebral cortex) are shown in Figure 14.3; the functions that they seemed to control are listed in Table 14.1. It should be noted that Table 14.1 is not intended to

FIGURE 14.3 The Major Areas of the Brain The frontal lobe is located in the front part of the brain. The parietal lobe is found behind the frontal lobe, with the temporal lobe located below the parietal lobe. The occipital lobe lies in the back of the brain. In general, different functions are localized in different areas of the brain (see Table 14.1).

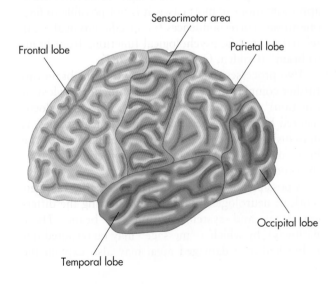

TABLE 14.1   Brain Areas and the Functions They Control

Left Frontal Area	Right Frontal Area
Expression via speech	Motor
Mathematics	Rhythm
Reception of speech	Mathematics
Left Sensorimotor Area	**Right Sensorimotor Area**
Expression via speech	Motor
Mathematics	Tactile
Left Parietal, Occipital Area	**Right Parietal, Occipital Area**
Mathematics	Tactile
Expression via speech	Motor
Writing	
Reading	
Left Temporal Lobe	**Right Temporal Lobe**
Reception of speech	Rhythm
Expression via speech	Motor
Memory	Tactile
Intelligence	

Source: Golden et al. (1981).

---

imply a simple one-to-one correspondence between a particular brain area and function.

Note the extensive overlapping of functions, which complicates the assessment of brain damage by determining functional losses. Moreover, as the researchers noted, "no two human brains are identical in appearance or in distribution of the functional organization of psychological skills. Although there are close approximations in most cases, it is not possible to find one-to-one correspondences for specific physical areas related to specific psychological functions from brain to brain" (Golden, Graber, et al., 1981).

Two processes that may occur within the brain can further complicate the matching of function (or loss of function) with specific brain areas. The first, documented by many experimental and clinical studies, is **diaschisis,** in which a lesion in a specific area of the brain disrupts other intact areas, sometimes even in the other hemisphere.

A possible mechanism for diaschisis is the vast network of neurological pathways connecting the different areas and systems within the brain. These pathways, by which a "message" may be rerouted if it is blocked at a damaged area, may also explain the

second process—the recovery of function after an area of the brain has been damaged. Other explanations for this recovery stress *redundancy,* in which an "unused" portion of the brain takes up the function of the damaged area, or *plasticity,* in which an undeveloped portion of the brain substitutes for the damaged portion. This plasticity would account for the development of language in young children who have left-hemisphere damage. For example, a five-year-old boy whose left hemisphere was removed (to stop his seizures) later developed superior language and intellectual abilities. Because the right hemisphere had not yet become fully specialized, it could develop the structure necessary to support language and intellectual ability (Smith & Sugar, 1975). Plasticity and compensatory reorganization appear to be greater in younger than in older individuals (Stiles, 1998).

Nevertheless, some evidence shows that such a shift of function from one hemisphere to the other may decrease the functional space available for the development of other skills. One person who had left-hemisphere damage at birth did develop normal language ability, but his visual-spatial memory was impaired. The development of language may have

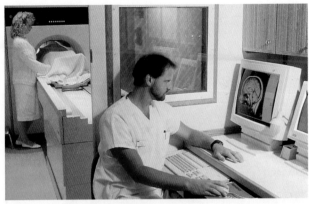

MRI Scans A technician observing the MRI scan of a patient. In MRI, radio waves produce pictures of the brain that are not obscured by bone. With striking resolution, they can reveal detailed anatomical areas of the brain. However, the procedure is expensive and requires patients to remain perfectly still while the imaging is taking place. What advantages do you see in using the MRI over other procedures, such as PET or CAT scans?

required functional space normally devoted to visual-spatial ability (Bullard-Bates & Satz, 1983).

The Dimensions of Brain Damage

Brain damage can be evaluated along a continuum of degree, from mild to moderate to severe. In addition, clinicians often use three sets of distinctions in their evaluations: endogenous versus exogenous causes, diffuse versus specific damage, and acute versus chronic conditions.

Endogenous brain damage is caused by something within the person; for example, by loss of blood flow to the brain, which deprives neural tissue of vital oxygen. *Exogenous* brain damage is caused by an external factor, such as a severe blow to the head or poisoning.

The diffuse-specific distinction helps indicate the extent of the brain damage. *Diffuse* damage is rather generalized; it typically involves widespread impairment of functioning, including disorientation, poor memory and judgment, and emotional instability. *Specific* brain damage is fairly localized, usually causing impairment or behavioral consequences that correspond only to the psychological or physiological function of the injured area.

An *acute* brain disorder is not accompanied by significant and permanent brain damage. A high fever or a severe bout of alcoholic intoxication can result in acute but reversible and temporary brain changes. (Note, however, that the ability of the central nervous system to repair itself when damaged is extremely limited.) A *chronic* disorder involves permanent and irreversible brain damage—for example, as a result of the severe lead poisoning caused by a child's eating paint that contains lead.

People with chronic brain disorders may display similar symptoms as those in acute disorders, but impaired memory is usually the first noticeable sign of a chronic condition. Over time, the person may learn to compensate for many of the other symptoms.

Diagnostic Problems

As noted earlier, diagnosing cognitive disorders is problematic. People who have not suffered brain damage may be misdiagnosed as having a cognitive disorder. People with deep depression often show characteristics similar to those of individuals with cognitive disorders; in particular, the neuropsychological tests used to assess a wide range of functions (including language, cognition, motor functions, and visual-motor functions) were found to be subject to the effects of depression (Sweet, 1983). Neuropsychological tests may not provide clear distinctions between patients with brain damage and those with schizophrenia (Portnoff, Golden, Wood, & Gustavson, 1983). If a client has symptoms of a mental disorder such as marked depression and if a general medical condition is related to the mood disturbance, the client may be classified as having a mood disorder due to a general medical condition. Finally, some individuals with head injuries are seeking litigation or compensation and are motivated to show impairment on neurospsychological tests, which adds to the problems in making valid assessments (Inman et al., 1998).

Older people are particularly vulnerable to misdiagnoses of brain damage. They are more likely to perform poorly during assessment testing because of reduced sensory acuity, performance anxiety, fatigue, or failure to understand test instructions. Thus tests that differentiate between normal and brain-damaged young adults cannot be assumed to apply to older people. In a study of fifty retired teachers, many scored in the brain-damaged range on the Halstead-Reitan Neuropsychological Test Battery (discussed in the chapter on assessment and classification of abnormal behavior), even though they scored in the superior range on the Wechsler Adult Intelligence Scale (WAIS) and functioned very well in their daily lives (Price, Fein, & Feinberg, 1980). These findings also reveal another problem—namely, the often-observed lack of agreement between different measures of cognitive functioning (Clark, 1997).

To be sure that particular symptoms indicate a cognitive disorder, clinicians usually try to determine whether the central nervous system has been damaged or whether a causal agent (such as a poison) is responsible for the symptoms. In some cases, support for a diagnosis of cognitive disorder can come from a patient's positive response to a treatment known to be effective against a particular disorder. For example, a diagnosis of Parkinson's disease is supported by the patient's response to treatment with L-dopa.

Another diagnostic problem is opposite in effect: people who have suffered brain damage may be diagnosed as having a psychological disorder (Clarkin, Hurt, & Mattis, 1999). The following case is an example:

> Larry D., age thirty-eight, was an energetic community college teacher and athletic coach and the happily married father of four children. During a particularly busy period, he suffered an apparent seizure while attending a professional conference. Just prior to the seizure, he reported smelling an unusual odor; he then temporarily lost consciousness. Medical evaluations following the episode revealed no obvious cause for Larry's loss of consciousness, and it was assumed to be due to a lack of sleep and general fatigue.
>
> Although he did not pass out again, Larry began to show such symptoms as loss of appetite, difficulty in sleeping, fatigue, and some mental confusion. He became increasingly withdrawn, both from his family and from his professional activities, and he mentioned suicide several times. His family and colleagues became extremely concerned about his behavior. A mental health professional was consulted, and psychiatric hospitalization was recommended. But Larry's condition continued to deteriorate.
>
> At this point, Larry's wife sought a second opinion from the neuropsychology clinic at a local university. The results of neuropsychological testing suggested brain dysfunction. A CAT scan was performed, and a brain tumor was located.

Joint neuropsychological and medical assessments were able to pinpoint the cause of Larry's disorder. Naturally, the course of treatment changed markedly after the brain tumor was discovered. In many cases, as here, an initial neuropsychological assessment or even the initial use of techniques such as CAT scanning may not yield information that clearly points to a brain impairment. For this reason, follow-up testing at regular intervals is often recommended. Such tests also allow the clinician to measure the patient's performance against a base rate to detect significant patterns of deterioration.

Types of Cognitive Disorders

Four major cognitive disorder categories are listed in DSM-IV-TR: dementia, delirium, amnestic disorders,

Pet Therapy in a Nursing Home   Caring for pets has been found to be beneficial, often reducing the levels of depression and boredom of individuals. Increasingly, in nursing homes and other settings people are allowed to play with and care for pets. Thus, pet therapy can be beneficial to both patients and pets. Why do you think that having pets can be therapeutic for elderly patients?

and cognitive disorders not otherwise specified. In each, clinicians categorize the disorder according to its cause. In general, the causes are classified as due to a general medical condition, a substance-induced condition, multiple etiologies, or conditions not otherwise specified. For example, a client may be given the diagnosis of delirium. If the delirium is caused by the use of psychoactive substances, it is considered to be a case of substance-induced delirium. If the type of substance is identified, it is also specified (see Figure 14.1).

In some cases, individuals also have symptoms of other mental disorders (such as a mood, psychotic, or anxiety disorder) in which there is evidence that the disorder is due to a general medical condition. In this case, DSM-IV-TR lists the disorder within a category appropriate for the symptom pattern. For example, a mood disorder due to a general medical condition is classified under mood disorders, and an anxiety disorder due to a general medical condition is found under the category of anxiety disorders. Neither would be diagnosed as a cognitive disorder.

Dementia

Dementia is characterized by memory impairment and cognitive disturbances, such as *aphasia* (language disturbance), *apraxia* (inability to carry out motor activities despite intact comprehension and motor function), *agnosia* (failure to recognize or identify objects despite intact sensory function), or disturbances in planning and abstracting in thought processes. The multiple cognitive deficits are severe enough to hinder social and occupational activities and represent a significant decline from a previous level of functioning. People

●●● MENTAL HEALTH AND SOCIETY
●●● Aphasia: At a Loss for Words

The loss of motor or sensory functions that are associated with language is known as aphasia. People who have aphasia and motor disturbances may have trouble expressing themselves via verbal language (speech aphasia), may be unable to recall the names of familiar objects (nominal aphasia), or may have problems in writing words (manual aphasia). Sensory aphasias include the inability to understand spoken words (auditory aphasia) and the inability to understand written words (visual aphasia or alexia). Aphasic problems may be extremely specific. For example, persons with visual aphasia lose the ability to understand written words, although they have no difficulty in reading the words aloud or in understanding spoken words. Thus impairment is manifested in listening, speaking, reading, and writing—although not necessarily to the same extent in each area (Chapey, 1994).

Two primary problems in aphasia are the loss of access to words and

their meanings and the inability to retain words and their meanings (Schuell, 1974). Persons with aphasia may become quite emotional and frustrated over their deficits, and this, in turn, can impede efforts at rehabilitation.

The following dialogue illustrates some of the problems involved in aphasia. Albert Harris is a sixty-seven-year-old man who suffered a stroke. In addition to physical therapy for his partially paralyzed right side, an effort was made to rehabilitate his speech. Mr. Harris was unable to communicate fully and expressed himself almost exclusively with the words "Mrs. Harris," his wife's name.

Psychologist: Hello, Mr. Harris.
Mr. Harris (responding to psychologist): Hello, Mrs. Harris. Hello, Mrs. Harris.
Psychologist: You look pretty cheerful today.
Mr. Harris: Yes, Mrs. Harris. Ah … Ah … Ah [apparently trying

to elaborate on his response] … Yes, Mrs. Harris. Ah … Ah (looking disappointed and frustrated).
Psychologist: I know it's hard to say what you want to say.
Mr. Harris: Yes, Mrs. Harris, yes. Things will get better, Mrs. Harris.
Psychologist: You've already shown improvement, don't you think?
Mr. Harris: Mrs. Harris a little bit better, yes. Slow but sure, Mrs. Harris.

Speech therapy and skills training are frequently used to treat aphasia. Although many patients recover from the problem, the reasons for recovery are not well understood. It is possible that other areas of the brain can be trained to compensate for the damaged areas.

---

with dementia may forget to finish tasks, the names of significant others, and past events. (The Mental Health and Society feature "Aphasia: At a Loss for Words" presents the case of an individual with aphasia.) Some people who exhibit dementia also display impulse control problems. They may, for example, disrobe in public or make sexual advances to strangers. Dementia is characterized by gradual onset and continuing cognitive decline. It should be noted that memory decline in normal aging is distinct from that found in dementia. In age-associated memory impairment, patients experience a gradual loss of memory in daily life activities (e.g., remembering names, misplacing objects, or forgetting phone numbers) but retain intact global intellectual functioning. This normal-aging memory loss does not represent early stages of Alzheimer's disease (Wise, Gray, & Seltzer, 1999).

Dementia can occur for numerous reasons. DSM-IV-TR lists the major etiological categories for dementia as

(1) general medical conditions (such as Alzheimer's disease, cerebrovascular disease, Parkinson's disease, brain trauma); (2) substance-induced persisting dementia, in which the symptoms are associated with substance use; (3) multiple etiologies, in which more than one factor has caused the disorder (such as a general medical condition and substance use); and (4) dementia not otherwise specified, in which there is insufficient evidence to establish a specific etiology.

About 1.5 million Americans suffer from severe dementia, and an additional 1 million to 5 million have mild to moderate forms of the disorder (Read, 1991). Although dementia is most often encountered in older people, only a small proportion of them actually develop this syndrome. Among people over age sixty-five, about 5 to 7 percent have dementia (APA Working Group on the Older Adult, 1998), and 2 to 4 percent have dementia of the Alzheimer's type. (Alzheimer's disease is discussed in detail later in this chapter.) Other types of dementia are even less common. The prevalence of dementia increases with age, with a prevalence of over 20 percent or more in people over the age of eighty-five (American Psychiatric Association, 2000).

Dementia can also occur with delusions, hallucinations, disturbances in perception and communication, and delirium. If these features are predominant, they are noted in the DSM-IV-TR classification.

Dementia is, in fact, associated with a range of disorders. C. E. Wells (1978) analyzed the records of 222 patients who displayed dementia as the primary sign, rather than a secondary sign, of a diagnosed disorder. The disorders associated with dementia included Alzheimer's disease, vascular disease, normal pressure hydrocephalus (the accumulation of an abnormal amount of cerebrospinal fluid in the cranium, which can damage brain tissues), dementia in alcoholics, intracranial masses, and Huntington's disease. These findings have important implications for diagnosis because such problems as depression, drug toxicity, normal pressure hydrocephalus, and benign intracranial masses can be corrected. Identifying noncorrectable causes of dementia is also important because specific therapeutic intervention may reduce or limit symptoms in some cases.

Delirium

Delirium is characterized by disturbance of consciousness and changes in cognition (memory deficit, disorientation, and language and perceptual disturbances). These impairments and changes are not attributable to dementia. The disorder develops rather rapidly over a course of hours or days. The patient often shows a reduced ability to focus, sustain, or shift attention and exhibits disorganized patterns of thinking, as manifested by rambling, irrelevant, or incoherent speech. At times patients show a reduced level of consciousness and disturbances in the cycle of sleep and waking. The following describes a case of a student who was treated for amphetamine-induced delirium:

An eighteen-year-old high school senior was brought to the emergency room by police after being picked up wandering in traffic on the Triborough Bridge [in New York City]. He was angry, agitated, and aggressive and talked of various people who were deliberately trying to "confuse" him by giving him misleading directions. His story was rambling and disjointed, but he admitted to the police officer that he had been using "speed." In the emergency room he had difficulty focusing his attention and had to ask that questions be repeated. He was disoriented as to time and place and was unable to repeat

the names of three objects after five minutes. The family gave a history of the patient's regular use of "pep pills" over the past two years, during which time he was frequently "high" and did very poorly in school. (Spitzer et al., 1994, p. 162)

Among individuals over age sixty-five who are hospitalized for a general medical condition, about 10 percent exhibit delirium on admission (American Psychiatric Association, 2000). Certain groups of patients are at risk for developing delirium (Wise et al., 1999). They include the elderly, individuals recovering from surgery, patients with preexisting brain dysfunction (e.g., stroke), patients in the withdrawal phase of drug dependency, patients with AIDS, and those with high illness burden (e.g., burn patients and elderly patients). Obviously, some patients have multiple risk factors, as found in those who are elderly, who have suffered a stroke, and who are recovering from surgery. When people grow older, they have less cerebral reserve and are more likely to develop delirium with medical illness, stress conditions, or surgical procedures (Wise, Hilty, & Cerda, 2001). As in the case of dementia, delirium is classified according to its cause: general medical condition, substance-induced condition, multiple etiologies, and not otherwise specified.

Amnestic Disorders

Amnestic disorders are characterized by memory impairment as manifested by an inability to learn new information and an inability to recall previously learned knowledge or past events. As a result, confusion and disorientation occur. The memory disturbance causes major problems in social or occupational functioning and does not occur exclusively during the course of dementia or delirium. As in the case of dementia and delirium, the etiology is specified. The memory impairment is not the result of a developmental process but rather the result of some insult to the central nervous system (Burke & Bohac, 2001). The most common causes of amnestic disorders include head trauma, stroke, and Wernicke's encephalopathy, which is an alcohol-induced organic mental disorder probably involving thiamine deficiency (Wise et al., 1999).

All three conditions—dementia, delirium, and amnestic disorders—have overlapping symptoms, especially those involving memory deficits. Some important differences distinguish the three, however. In dementia, there is not only memory impairment but also conditions such as aphasia, apraxia, or agnosia. In contrast, the memory dysfunctions that occur in delirium happen relatively quickly, unlike those of dementia, in

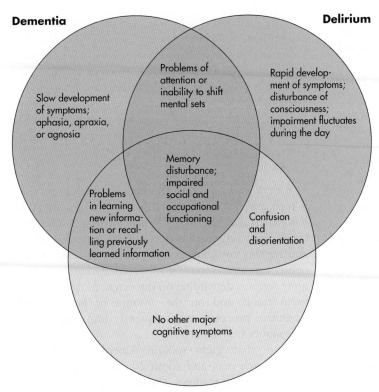

Dementia

Slow development of symptoms; aphasia, apraxia, or agnosia

Problems of attention or inability to shift mental sets

Delirium

Rapid development of symptoms; disturbance of consciousness; impairment fluctuates during the day

Problems in learning new information or recalling previously learned information

Memory disturbance; impaired social and occupational functioning

Confusion and disorientation

No other major cognitive symptoms

Amnestic Disorders

FIGURE 14.4 Unique and Overlapping Symptoms in Dementia, Delirium, and Amnestic Disorders Dementia, delirium, and amnestic disorders share some symptoms. The three overlapping circles show the unique and the overlapping areas. The symptoms that occur in all three include memory disturbance and impaired functioning. Where the circles do not overlap, symptoms are largely unique. For example, aphasia and apraxia are exhibited in dementia but not in delirium or amnestic disorders. Confusion and disorientation are more likely to occur in delirium and amnestic disorders than in dementia.

which functioning gradually declines. In delirium, there is also an impairment of consciousness. In amnestic disorders, the primary symptom involves memory. Figure 14.4 shows the unique characteristics, as well as the overlap in cognitive symptoms, of the three conditions.

Cognitive disorders that do not meet the criteria for dementia, delirium, or amnestic disorders would be classified as cognitive disorders not otherwise specified.

Etiology of Cognitive Disorders

Cognitive disorders can be caused by many different factors, and the same factor can result in dementia, delirium, or amnestic disorder. The sources of cognitive disorders discussed here are brain trauma; processes associated with aging, disease, and infection; tumors; epilepsy; and psychoactive substance-induced disorders. Toxic substances, malnutrition, and even brain surgery may also produce cognitive disorders.

Brain Trauma

On September 13, 1848, at Cavendish, Vermont, Phineas Gage was working as foreman of a railroad excavation crew. A premature explosion of a blast sent a tamping iron—a three-foot rod about an inch in diameter—through the lower side of Gage's face and out of the top of his head. Exhibiting some convulsions and bleeding profusely, Gage soon regained speech. He was taken to his hotel, where he walked up a flight of stairs to get to his room. Remarkably, Gage survived the trauma, even though there must have been extensive damage to his brain tissue. Later, he appeared to have completely recovered from the accident with no physical aftereffects. However, Gage began to complain that he had a strange feeling, which he could not describe. Soon, his employers and others noticed a marked personality change in him. Although he had been a very capable employee prior to the accident and was known for his affable disposition, Gage now became moody, irritable, profane, impatient, and obstinate. So radically changed was Gage that his friends said that he was "no longer Gage." (Adapted from J. M. Harlow, 1868)

A **brain trauma** is a physical wound or injury to the brain, as in the case of Phineas Gage. Each year, an estimated 1.9 million Americans experience a traumatic injury to the brain (Schalock, 1998). The severity, duration, and symptoms may differ widely, depending on the person's premorbid personality and on the extent and location of the neural damage.

Generally, the greater the tissue damage, the more impaired the functioning. In some cases, however, interactions among various parts of the brain, coupled with brain redundancy, in which different parts of the brain can control a specific function, may compensate for some loss of tissue.

Head injuries are usually classified as concussions, contusions, or lacerations. A *concussion* is a mild brain injury, typically caused by a blow to the head. Blood vessels in the brain are often ruptured, and circulatory and other brain functions may be disrupted temporarily. The person may become dazed or even lose consciousness and, on regaining consciousness, may experience postconcussion headaches, disorientation, confusion, and memory loss. The symptoms are usually temporary, lasting no longer than a few weeks. In some cases, symptoms may persist for months or years, for unknown reasons, without neurological signs of impairment (Binder, 1986).

In a *contusion*, the brain is forced to shift slightly and press against the side of the skull. The cortex of the brain may be bruised (that is, blood vessels may rupture) on impact with the skull. As in concussion, the person may lose consciousness for a few hours or even for days. Postcontusion symptoms often include headaches, nausea, an inability to concentrate, and irritability. Although the symptoms are similar to those of concussion, they are generally more severe and last longer.

Thirteen-year-old Ron G. was a catcher for his school baseball team. During a game, a player on the other team lost his grip on the bat as he swung at a pitch, and the bat hit Ron on the forehead. Although his catcher's mask absorbed some of the force, the blow knocked Ron out. An hour elapsed before he regained consciousness at a nearby hospital, where he was diagnosed as having a cerebral contusion. Headaches, muscle weakness, and nausea continued for two weeks.

Lacerations are brain traumas in which brain tissue is torn, pierced, or ruptured, usually by an object that has penetrated the skull. When an object also penetrates the brain, death may result. If the person survives and regains consciousness, a variety of temporary or permanent effects may be observed. Symptoms may be quite serious, depending on the extent of damage to the brain tissue and on the amount of hemorrhaging. Cognitive processes are frequently impaired, and the personality may change.

More than eight million Americans suffer head injuries each year, and about 20 percent of these result in serious brain trauma. The majority show deficits in attention and poor concentration, are easily fatigued, and tend to be irritable. Brain injuries are often inflicted on abused women by their partners, and cognitive functioning is affected (Valera & Berenbaum, 2003). Personality characteristics may undergo change in the

Danger Just a Tumble Away
More than 8 million Americans suffer head injuries each year, such as concussions, contusions, and lacerations. In order to reduce the risk of head injuries, individuals are well advised to wear helmets while skateboarding, rollerblading, and bicycling. If you engage in these activities, do you wear a helmet?

areas of motivation, subjective emotional experiences, or emotional expressions (Stuss, Gow, & Hetherington, 1992). One study examined twenty-three patients with severe traumatic brain injuries (seventeen closed-head injuries, three penetrating missile wounds, two cerebral contusions, and one brainstem contusion) who had spent an average of twenty days in a coma. Every one displayed a distress syndrome characterized by depression, anxiety, tension, and nervousness—yet they all denied having these feelings (Sbordone & Jennison, 1983). It is, in fact, common for patients with severe traumatic injuries to deny emotional reactions and physical dysfunctions until they begin to recover from their injuries.

Closed-head injuries are the most common form of brain trauma and the most common reason that physicians refer patients younger than age forty to neurologists (Golden, Moses, Coffman, Miller, & Strider, 1983). They usually result from a blow that causes damage at the site of the impact and at the opposite side of the head. If the victim's head was in motion before the impact (as is generally the case in automobile accidents), the blow produces a forward-and-back movement of the brain, accompanied by tearing and hemorrhaging of brain tissue. Epilepsy develops in about 5 percent of closed-head injuries and in more than 30 percent of open-head injuries in which the brain tissue is penetrated. Damage to brain tissues in the left hemisphere often results in intellectual disorders, and affective problems more frequently result from damage to brain tissues in the right hemisphere. The cumulative impact of traumas to the head may also affect brain functioning. In one study, boxers who suffered severe blows to the head (e.g., so severe that the referee stopped the bout) exhibited changes in cognitive abilities (Moriarity et al., 2004).

Severe brain trauma has long-term negative consequences. Many young adults who are comatose for at least twenty-four hours later experience residual cognitive deficits that interfere with employment and psychosocial adjustment. Recovery from the trauma often does not ensure a return to the victim's premorbid level of functioning. Along with any physical or mental disabilities produced by the brain damage, motivational and emotional disturbances result from the frustration of coping with these physical or mental deficits. As a consequence, only one-third of patients with severe closed-head injuries can return to gainful employment after traditional rehabilitative therapy (Prigatano et al., 1984).

In one treatment approach, intensive cognitive retraining is combined with psychotherapeutic intervention. This program provides patients with increased awareness and acceptance of their injuries and residual deficits, cognitive retraining to counter selected residual deficits, a repertoire of compensatory skills, and understanding of their emotional and motivational disturbance. When patients in this program were compared with patients in a traditional rehabilitation program, the former showed better neuropsychological functioning, greater improvement in personality traits, and greater success at work (Prigatano et al., 1984).

Aging and Disorders Associated with Aging

Before discussing the cognitive disorders often associated with aging, it seems appropriate to describe the nature of the older population. A growing proportion of the U.S. population, as well as that of the world, is sixty-five years of age or older (Powell & Whitla, 1994). This group, which numbered only 3.1 million in 1900, has increased more than tenfold, to 34.7 million of the U.S. population (Takamura, 1998); by 2030, that number is expected to double to 20 percent of the population (Dittmann, 2003). The increase is attributable both to longer life expectancy and to the relatively large numbers of people from the "baby-boom" generation who were born in the 1940s and who will be elderly by 2010.

The cognitive disorders most common among the elderly are strokes, Alzheimer's disease, and memory loss. These conditions are correlated with aging, but they also occur among younger people. Unfortunately, the elderly are less likely than younger individuals to seek help from mental health professionals (Clarkin & Levy, 2004). Because assessment of the cognitive functioning of the older adult has taken on increased importance, there have been calls to establish practical guidelines for this assessment (Baker, Lichtenberg, & Moye, 1998).

Cerebrovascular Accidents or Strokes Although the brain represents only 2 percent of the body's weight, it requires 15 percent of the blood flow and 20 percent of the oxygen (Oliver, Shaller, Majovski, & Jacques, 1982). A *stroke* or **cerebrovascular accident** is a sudden stoppage of blood flow to a portion of the brain, leading to a loss of brain function. Stroke risk factors include hypertension, heart disease, cigarette smoking, diabetes mellitus, and excessive alcohol consumption. Vascular problems are the second leading cause of dementia, right behind Alzheimer's disease (Wise et al., 1999).

Strokes are the third major cause of death in the United States, afflicting more than 400,000 persons annually. Only about 50 to 60 percent of stroke victims survive, and they generally require long-term care

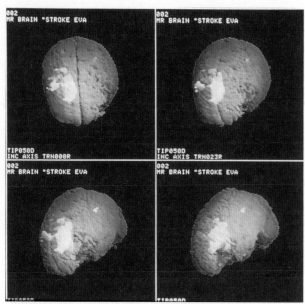

Losing Brain Function Due to a Stroke A stroke is a condition in which brain functioning is lost because blood flow to an area of the brain slows or stops. This stoppage is caused by burst or obstructed blood vessels. Shown are three-dimensional images of a brain stroke from four different angles.

while suffering from a variety of mental and sensory-motor disabilities (Oliver et al., 1982). Stroke victims are often frustrated and depressed by their handicaps, and they show greater depression and interpersonal sensitivity than other groups of patients. At least one-fourth of stroke victims appear to develop major depression (Conn, 1991), which in many cases tends to deepen with time (Magni & Schifano, 1984). Their depression, pessimism, and anxiety about their disabilities occasionally leads to further disability (Burruss, Travella, & Robinson, 2001).

The bursting of blood vessels (and the attendant intracranial hemorrhaging) causes 25 percent of all strokes and often occurs during exertion. Victims report feeling that something is wrong within the head, along with headaches and nausea. Confusion, paralysis, and loss of consciousness follow rapidly. Mortality rates for this type of stroke are extremely high.

Strokes may also be caused by the narrowing of blood vessels owing to a buildup of fatty material on interior walls *(atherosclerosis)* or by the blockage of blood vessels. In either case, the result is **cerebral infarction,** the death of brain tissue from a decrease in the supply of blood. These strokes often occur during sleep, and the person is paralyzed when he or she awakens. Approximately 20 percent die, 20 percent exhibit full to nearly full recovery, and 60 percent suffer residual disabilities (Lishman, 1978).

The residual loss of function after a stroke usually involves only one side of the body, most often the left. Interestingly, one residual symptom of stroke is a "lack of acknowledgment" of various stimuli on one side of the body. For example, a patient who is asked to copy a pattern may draw half the pattern and may ignore the left side of his or her body (Golden et al., 1983).

Some functional reorganization of the brain may occur after a stroke to compensate for the loss of function. Three months after suffering a stroke owing to cerebral infarction, one patient showed significantly reduced cerebral blood flow in one area. An examination performed one year later showed no abnormalities. The pattern of blood flow, however, suggested increased activation in brain areas surrounding the affected area. It is possible that the patient's clinical improvement was due to brain reorganization, in which the function of the destroyed area was taken over by other areas.

A series of infarctions may lead to a syndrome known as **vascular dementia,** which is characterized by the uneven deterioration of intellectual abilities (although some mental functions may remain intact). The specific symptoms of this disruption depend on the area and extent of the brain damage. Both physical and intellectual functioning are usually impaired. The patient may show gradual improvement in intellectual functioning, but repeated episodes of infarction can occur, producing additional disability.

Memory Loss in Older People Memory loss occurs for a variety of reasons. It is one of the most obvious symptoms of Alzheimer's disease, which we discuss in depth in the next section. Memory loss may be part of a severe loss of intellectual functioning produced by brain cell deterioration as a result of aging, usually after age seventy-five. Research indicates, however, that age-related decreases in certain cognitive functions can be mitigated in cognitively active persons, such as professors who maintain intellectual activities (Shimamura, Berry, Mangels, Rusting, & Jurica, 1995). Loss of memory may also be shown by elderly people suffering vascular dementia. And finally, occasional loss of memory, as well as an overall slowing of the speed of mental processing, is part of the normal aging process (Bashore, Ridderinkhof, & Van der Molen, 1997) and is not indicative of dementia (Wise et al., 1999).

Because memory loss is associated with so many disorders, as well as with normal aging, it is of concern to older adults and yet difficult for clinicians to assess. Occasional lapses of memory are not necessarily a sign of senility. Smyer (1984) points out that complaints of memory loss must be examined in light of the person's perception of the event, concurrent factors such as

Aging Well The proportion of elderly Americans in the U.S. population is growing rapidly. Increasingly, older Americans are staying active and healthy longer than previous generations did. These men are competing in the 100-yard dash at the Senior Olympics. What skills are maintained or enhanced and what skills decline as a function of aging?

depression or anxiety that might contribute to memory problems, and actual memory behavior. Gallagher and Frankel (1980) have stated their belief that if the Halstead-Reitan Neuropsychological Battery were employed, most normal elderly participants would be incorrectly identified as brain damaged because no normative standards are established for their age group.

One of the most common reasons for memory loss and confusion in older patients is therapeutic drug intoxication. People may take several medications that can interact with one another to produce negative side effects (Butler, 1984). Medication often has a stronger effect on older people and takes longer to be cleared from their bodies, yet dosages are often determined by testing on young adults only. In addition, cardiac, metabolic, and endocrine disorders and nutritional deficiencies can produce symptoms resembling dementias.

Losing cognitive and mental capabilities is the symptom of aging most feared by elderly people. One eighty-two-year-old man commented, "It's not the physical decline I fear so much. It's becoming a mental vegetable inside of a healthy body. It is a shame that we can rehabilitate or treat so much of the physical ills, but when your mind goes, there's nothing you can do" (Gatz, Smyer, & Lawton, 1980, p. 12). Age-related declines in cognitive functioning can be relatively large. The declines may not be noticed because cognitive ability is only one factor in the success of one's functioning, because very few situations require maximum levels of performance, because people may adapt to age-related changes by somehow compensating for these changes, and because greater knowledge and experience may also make up for the changes (Salthouse, 2004).

Although tests of intellectual functioning indicate that performance abilities generally start to decline with advancing age, verbal fluency and cognitive skills are relatively stable over time. Intellectual performance on knowledge acquired over the course of the socialization process is fairly stable, whereas fluid abilities (those abilities involving solutions to novel problems or requiring creativity) tend to decline with age (Poon & Siegler, 1991). Ivnik, Smith, Malec, Petersen, and Tangalos (1995) have also found that stability depends on the particular cognitive ability being examined. About 75 percent of older people retain sharp mental functioning, and an additional 10 to 15 percent experience only mild to moderate memory loss (Butler, 1984). (See the Mental Health and Society feature "Am I Losing It as I Get Older?" for a further discussion of memory loss.)

Myth vs Reality

Myth: As we become older, cognitive changes are negative or undesirable.

Reality: With age, adults experience less negative emotion, attend less to negative than to positive emotional stimuli, and decrease their memory of negative versus positive emotional materials. They tend to show reduced reactivity to negative information while maintaining or even increasing reactivity to positive information. By using functional magnetic resonance imaging to assess amygdala activation, Mather and her colleagues (2004) found that for older adults, seeing positive pictures led to greater amygdala activation

MENTAL HEALTH AND SOCIETY

"Am I Losing It as I Get Older?"

Do you worry about memory loss in elderly individuals that you know or about your own possible memory loss as you become older? Concerns over memory loss as one becomes older are not simply negative stereotypes that younger people have about older people (Craik, 1994). Although age-related declines have often been exaggerated, cognitive performance does diminish with age, and many older individuals are afraid of memory loss. We know some things with certainty. Some cognitive and memory tasks are more likely to decline than others. Some individuals are more affected than others, and age-associated memory impairment does not represent the early stages of a dementing illness (Wise et al., 1999). Engaging in intellectual activities reduces the risk of cognitive decline. And the observed memory loss is a matter of degree—individuals can be placed on a continuum ranging from excellent memory to extremely poor memory, as in the advanced stages of Alzheimer's disease.

An important task is to determine whether memory loss is a "normal" part of aging or whether it is caused by Alzheimer's disease. In other words, how can we measure and interpret memory loss that is associated with aging? Powell and Whitla (1994) have discussed assessment issues, citing the case of a sixty-nine-year-old professor who was concerned that her memory had deteriorated and that she was "losing it." She had difficulty recalling the names of new faculty, could not remember the room number of her classroom, and could not think of the name for the "thing you turn over eggs with." Has her memory deteriorated? How do we know? Some of the strategies to assess cognitive aging include:

1. *Population normative*—comparing a person's cognitive performance with that of the general population. In the case presented, we would compare the sixty-nine-year-old professor's performance with that of the general population, young and old.
2. *Age-group normative*—comparing a person's cognitive performance with that of others of the same age. Using this approach, we would compare the professor's performance with that of other sixty-nine-year-olds.
3. *Reference-group normative*—comparing a person's cognitive performance with that of others of the same group. Using this tactic, we would compare the professor's performance with that of other faculty members.
4. *Previous functioning*—comparing a person's current cognitive performance with his or her past performance to see if changes have occurred. In this case, we would measure the professor's present performance against her past performance.

What advantages and disadvantages do you see in each strategy? Is one particular method preferable to the others in trying to determine whether memory changes have taken place? If you were being tested for a cognitive or memory deficit, which would you prefer, and why would you prefer it?

---

than seeing negative pictures, whereas this was not the case with younger adults. With age, the amygdala may show decreased reactivity to negative information while maintaining or increasing its reactivity to positive information. Perhaps this is one advantage that comes with age.

Alzheimer's Disease

The disorder perhaps most often associated with aging is **Alzheimer's disease,** in which brain tissue atrophies, leading to marked deterioration of intellectual and emotional functioning. It is one of the most prevalent forms of dementia, accounting for almost 80 percent of dementia in older persons (Teri & Wagner, 1992). The risk for the disease increases with age. The incidence

(new cases) each year is 0.6 percent for ages sixty-five to sixty-nine, 1 percent for ages seventy to seventy-four, 2 percent for ages seventy-five to seventy-nine, 3.3 percent for ages eighty to eighty-four, and 8.4 percent for ages eighty-five and older (Wise et al., 1999). About 4 million Americans suffer from the disease (Nash, 1997). The disease affects about 8 to 15 percent of those above the age of sixty-five (Department of Health and Human Services [DHHS], 1999). We have become increasingly aware of the disease because public figures such as former president Ronald Reagan have candidly discussed their condition.

Characteristics of Alzheimer's Disease   As noted, patients with Alzheimer's disease show marked deterioration of intellectual and emotional functioning.

Early symptoms—memory dysfunction, irritability, and cognitive impairment—gradually worsen, and other symptoms, such as social withdrawal, depression, apathy, delusions, impulsive behaviors, and neglect of personal hygiene may eventually appear. At present, no curative or disease-reversing interventions exist for Alzheimer's disease (Rivas-Vazquez, 2001). Death usually occurs within five years of the onset of the disorder, which is the fourth leading cause of death in the United States (Francis & Bowen, 1994).

> Elizabeth R., a forty-six-year-old woman diagnosed as suffering from Alzheimer's disease, is trying to cope with her increasing problems with memory. She writes notes to herself and tries to compensate for her difficulties by rehearsing conversations with herself, anticipating what might be said. However, she is gradually losing the battle and has had to retire from her job. She quickly forgets what she has just read, and she loses the meaning of an article after reading only a few sentences. She sometimes has to ask where the bathroom is in her own house and is depressed by the realization that she is a burden to her family. (Clark et al., 1984, p. 60)

The deterioration of memory seems to be the most poignant and disturbing symptom for those who have Alzheimer's disease. They may at first forget appointments, phone numbers, and addresses. As the disorder progresses, they may lose track of the time of day, have trouble remembering recent and past events, and forget who they are (Reisberg, Ferris, & Crook, 1982). But even when memory is almost gone, contact with loved ones is still important.

> I believe the emotional memory of relationships is the last to go. You can see daughters or sons come to visit, for example, and the mother will respond. She doesn't know who they are, but you can tell by her expression that she knows they're persons to whom she is devoted. (Materka, 1984, p. 13)

Alzheimer's Disease and the Brain   Persons with this disease have an atrophy of cortical tissue within the brain. Autopsies performed on the brains of Alzheimer's victims reveal *neurofibrillary tangles* (abnormal fibers that appear to be tangles of brain tissue filaments) and *senile plaques* (patches of degenerated nerve endings). Both conditions are believed to disrupt the transmission of impulses among brain cells, thereby producing the symptoms of the disorder. Alzheimer's disease is generally considered a disease of the elderly, and its incidence does increase with increasing age. However, it also can attack people in their forties or fifties. It occurs more frequently in women.

Etiology of Alzheimer's Disease   The etiology of Alzheimer's disease is unknown, although it is thought to be a product of hereditary and environmental factors

The Tragedy of Alzheimer's Disease Jack Guren, an Alzheimer's patient living in a nursing home, is being visited by his son Peter. Alzheimer's disease is responsible for most cases of dementia among the elderly. Dementia is characterized by multiple and severe cognitive deficits, especially impairment of memory. Is Alzheimer's disease hereditary?

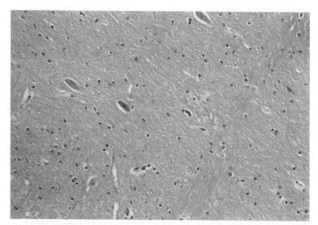 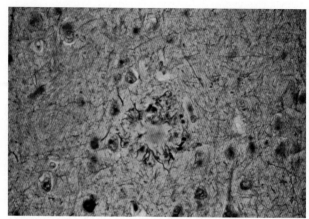

On the Physical Trail of Alzheimer's The photo on the left shows a magnified sample of healthy brain tissue. The diseased brain tissue (on the right) from an Alzheimer's patient shows senile plaques (patches of degenerated nerve endings) located in the gray matter. Some researchers believe that the plaques may interfere with transmission of nerve impulses in the brain, thereby causing the disease's symptoms.

(Hendrie, 2001). Many different explanations have been proposed. They include reduced levels of the neurotransmitter acetylcholine in the brain; repeated head injuries; infections and viruses; decreased blood flow in the brain; and the effect of plaques and tangles in disrupting cellular metabolism or in reducing glucose absorption from the bloodstream (Nash, 1997; Read, 1991). Some researchers believe that aluminum is the primary cause, because high concentrations of the substance have been found in the brains of Alzheimer's patients, because increased concentration of aluminum in drinking water is associated with higher incidence of the disease, and because aluminum has been experimentally found to pass through the blood-brain barrier, resulting in severe impairment of nerve cells (Yumoto et al., 1995). For a subgroup, heredity appears to be important. Approximately 50 percent of individuals with a family history of the disease, if followed into their eighties and nineties, develop the disease (DHHS, 1999). The gene that appears to be responsible for senile plaques and neurofibrillary tangles found in Alzheimer's disease is located on chromosome 21 (Clarke & Clarke, 1987). Furthermore, early-onset cases of Alzheimer's disease—those that occur before age sixty-five—may be caused by genetic anomalies (Mullan & Brown, 1994). Some researchers have found that genetic predisposition to Alzheimer's disease coupled with low levels of two B vitamins (B-12 and folate) may affect memory performance, again suggesting that heredity and diet may be important (Bunce, Kivipelto, & Wahlin, 2004).

Although abnormalities are found in the brains of affected individuals, it is not clear whether the abnormalities are the cause, the effect, or an accompanying condition of Alzheimer's disease. Snowden and his colleagues (1997) studied two groups of individuals: those with and without neurofibrillary tangles and senile plaques. Presumably, those with the tangles and plaques met the neuropathological criteria for Alzheimer's disease. The investigators found that among individuals having Alzheimer's disease, those who also suffered brain infarcts exhibited poorer cognitive functioning and a higher prevalence of dementia than those without brain infarcts. However, individuals who suffered brain infarcts but did not have Alzheimer's disease exhibited better cognitive functioning than those suffering from both infarcts and Alzheimer's disease. The findings point to the possible interaction of other conditions with Alzheimer's disease in producing cognitive deficits.

Several protective factors have been identified that may delay the onset of Alzheimer's disease. These include genetic endowment with the ApoE-e2 allele, which decreases the risk for the disease; higher education and occupational attainments; use of nonsteroidal anti-inflammatory drugs or estrogen replacement therapy; and taking vitamin E. The reasons that these factors may provide protection are unclear, but they may reduce the deleterious action of oxidative stress (via antioxidants such as vitamin E or estrogen) or the action of inflammatory mediators associated with plaque formation (DHHS, 1999). In the case of education and occupation, it may be that increased cognitive activity associated with education and occupational status helps to reduce the incidence of the disease (Wilson & Bennett, 2003).

Other Diseases and Infections of the Brain

A variety of diseases and infections result in brain damage that leads to behavioral, cognitive, and emotional changes, including the development of cognitive disorders.

Parkinson's Disease   Parkinson's disease is a progressively worsening disorder characterized by muscle tremors; a stiff, shuffling gait; a lack of facial expression; social withdrawal; and, in some cases, dementia and depression. The disease affects about one person out of a thousand, slightly more men than women (Rao, Huber, & Bornstein, 1992). Parkinson's disease is usually first diagnosed in people between the ages of fifty and sixty, and about 1 to 2 percent of individuals over the age of sixty-five are afflicted (Pfeiffer & Ebadi, 1994). In some persons, the disorder stems from causes such as infections of the brain, cerebrovascular disorders, brain trauma, and poisoning with carbon monoxide; in other persons, no specific origin can be determined. Genetic predisposition may play a role in the disease (Kurth & Kurth, 1994), but evidence for that view is not strong. Death generally follows within ten years of the onset of Parkinson's disease, although some patients have survived for twenty years or longer.

Parkinson's disease seems to be associated with lesions in the motor area of the brainstem and with a diminished level of dopamine in the brain. Some researchers have also found degeneration in the dopaminergic neurons (Tassin, Trovero, Blanc, Herve, & Glowinski, 1994). Reasons for this degeneration are unclear, but some researchers speculate that an inflammatory process may be involved. Lower rates of Parkinson's disease have been found among people who regularly used nonsteroidal anti-inflammatory drugs such as ibuprofen (Chen et al., 2003). Individuals with the disease are often treated with L-dopa, which increases dopamine levels and relieves most of its symptoms (Lishman, 1978), although the improvement in symptoms is not maintained as the disease progresses (Arciniegas & Dubovsky, 2001). Muhammad Ali's Parkinson-like condition has been treated with Sinemet and Symmetrel, which have the same effect. For some patients, high-technology surgical procedures on the brain or the implantation of electrodes to continuously stimulate areas of the brain have been helpful (Hartman-Stein, 2004).

AIDS (Acquired Immunodeficiency Syndrome)   The general public knows about the disastrous consequences of AIDS, or acquired immunodeficiency syndrome—the susceptibility to diseases, the physical deterioration, and death, often within several years of infection. Relatively few people, however, know that dementia may be the first sign of AIDS, as one person described in the following:

> It was frightening. It was terrifying. It was terrible headaches, months when I could only stand or lie down. I lost control of one side of my body. I couldn't write. I had lost fine motor control. I also had memory lapses. One time I was in a supermarket and suddenly I couldn't remember how I got there. (Joyce, 1988, p. 38)

Joyce (1988) noted that the vast majority of AIDS patients suffer from some form of dementia. The symptoms involve an inability to concentrate and to perform complex sequential mental tasks. The person may be unable to follow television or movie plots, may miss appointments, and may have hand tremors. Other symptoms include forgetfulness, impaired judgment, and personality disturbances such as anxiety and depression. After initial cognitive symptoms, progression to global cognitive impairment is rather rapid, usually within two months (Tross & Hirsch, 1988).

The dementia can be attributed to three factors. First, the AIDS virus itself reaches the brain at some phase of the infection and may lie dormant for a period of time (Baum & Nesselhof, 1988). When it becomes active, the virus can affect mental, as well as physical, processes. Second, because AIDS affects the immune system, AIDS-related infections may cause neuropsychological problems. A variety of chemical factors secreted during the course of an immune response may also cause changes in brain-controlled physiological processes (Hall, 1988). Some degree of cerebral atrophy is present in almost all HIV patients with dementia (Wise et al., 1999). Third, depression, anxiety, and confusion can arise from simply knowing that one has AIDS, and experiencing negative reactions from others increases stress for AIDS victims (Kelly & Murphy, 1992). Medication to combat AIDS and its symptoms may also bring about side effects that influence cognitive functioning. Thus people with AIDS are at high risk for cognitive disorders.

Neurosyphilis (General Paresis)   Syphilis is caused by the spirochete *Treponema pallidum,* which enters the body through contact with an infected person. This microorganism is most commonly transmitted from infected to uninfected people through intercourse or oral-genital contact. A pregnant woman can also transmit the disease to her fetus, and the spirochete can enter the body through direct contact with mucous

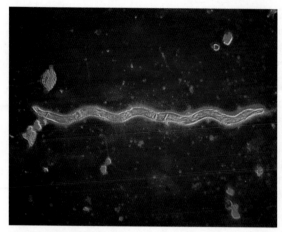
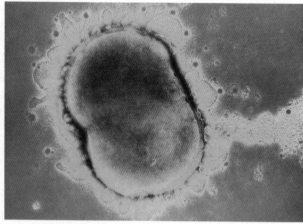

Taming Potential Killers Through Research   Shown at left is the syphilis spirochete *Treponema pallidum*, the bacterium responsible for the development of syphilis and, if untreated, general paresis; shown at right is the spherical bacterium *Neisseria meningitidis*, which causes bacterial meningitis in humans. Both can cause destruction of brain tissue, seizures, and ultimately death, but they can now be treated with antibiotics.

membranes or breaks in the skin. Within a few weeks, the exposed person develops a chancre, a small sore at the point of infection, as well as a copper-colored rash. If untreated, the infection spreads throughout the body. There may be no noticeable symptoms for ten to fifteen years after the initial infection, but eventually the body's organs are permanently damaged. In about 10 percent of persons with syphilis who are untreated, the spirochete directly damages the brain or nervous system, causing general paresis (muscular weakness, mental deterioration, and speech problems).

The most commonly described form of paresis, which includes approximately 18 percent of all cases, has grandiose characteristics: people display expansive and euphoric symptoms, along with delusions of power or wealth. A depressive form has also been described, in which the affected person displays all the classic symptoms of depression.

The most frequent course for the illness begins with simple dementia, including memory impairment and early loss of insight. If the disorder remains untreated, the dementia increases, the occasional delusions fade, and the patient becomes quiet, apathetic, and incoherent. Paralysis, epileptic seizures, and death usually occur within five years of the onset of the disease's symptoms.

If syphilis is treated early, however, clinical remission occurs, and the patient often can return to work. After five years of treatment, more than one-half of the patients with disorientation, convulsions, tremors, and euphoria generally lose their symptoms.

Encephalitis   Encephalitis, or sleeping sickness, is a brain inflammation that is caused by a viral infection and that produces symptoms of lethargy, fever, delirium, and long periods of stupor and sleep. Numerous different viruses can lead to encephalitis (Stacy & Roeltgen, 1991). It is not known whether the virus enters the central nervous system directly or whether the brain is hypersensitive to a viral infection at some other site in the body. One form, *epidemic encephalitis*, was widespread during World War I, but the disease is now very rare in the United States. It is still a problem, however, in certain areas of Africa and Asia.

Most cases follow a rapidly developing course that begins with headache, prostration (having to lie down), and diminished consciousness. Epileptic seizures are common in children with encephalitis, and these seizures may be the most obvious symptom. Acute symptoms, as noted earlier, include lethargy, fever, delirium, and long periods of sleep and stupor. When wakeful, the victim may show markedly different symptoms: hyperactivity, irritability, agitation, and seizures. In contrast to past behaviors, a child may become restless, irritable, cruel, and antisocial. A coma, if there is one, may end abruptly. Usually a long period of physical and mental recuperation is necessary, and the prognosis can vary from no residual effects to profound brain damage (Golden et al., 1983).

Meningitis   Meningitis is an inflammation of the *meninges*, the membrane that surrounds the brain and spinal cord, and it can result in the localized destruction of brain tissue and seizures. Research on meningitis is complicated because the disorder has three major forms: bacterial, viral, and fungal. In the United States, approximately 400,000 persons develop *bacterial meningitis* annually (Wasserman & Gromisch, 1981).

This form generally begins with a localized infection that spreads, via the bloodstream, first to the meninges and then into the cerebrospinal fluid. Some government panels have recommended that youths be vaccinated against bacterial meningitis because it can be spread in school or college campuses (Yee, 2005). *Viral meningitis*, which produces symptoms much less serious than those of the bacterial type, is associated with a variety of diseases, including mumps, herpes simplex, toxoplasmosis, syphilis, and rubella. *Fungal meningitis* usually occurs in children with immunological deficiencies, such as leukemia.

The symptoms of meningitis vary with the age of the patient. In neonates and young infants, the symptoms are nonspecific (fever, lethargy, poor eating, and irritability), which makes diagnosis difficult. In patients older than one year, symptoms may include stiffness of the neck, headache, and cognitive and sensory impairment. All three forms can result in the localized destruction of brain tissue and in seizures, but their incidence is much greater in the bacterial form than in the others (Edwards & Baker, 1981). The outcome is most serious when meningitis is contracted during the neonatal period.

Residual effects of the disorder may include partial or complete hearing loss as a result of tissue destruction (Berlow, Caldarelli, Matz, Meyer, & Harsch, 1981), mental retardation, and seizures (Snyder, Stovring, Cushing, Davis, & Hardy, 1981). Meningitis also seems to attack the abstract thinking ability of some of its victims.

Huntington's Disease Huntington's disease is a rare, genetically transmitted degenerative disease characterized by involuntary twitching movements and eventual dementia. Because the disorder is transmitted from parent to child through an abnormal gene, approximately 50 percent of the offspring of an affected person develop it. Scientists have identified the gene that causes the disease, so they are now able to better detect whether a person has inherited the disorder (Saltus, 1993). At this time, Huntington's disease cannot be treated, so genetic counseling is extremely important in preventing transmission of the disease. However, with technological and scientific advances, researchers hope that the precise nature of the genetic defect can be discovered, leading to prevention and treatment of the disorder (Craufurd, 1994).

The prevalence of the disease is 5 to 7 per 100,000 population (Wise et al., 1999). The first symptoms usually occur as behavioral disturbances when the person is between the ages of twenty-five and fifty, although some are afflicted before age twenty (Brooks, Murphy, Janota, & Lishman, 1987). The first physical symptoms are generally twitches in the

Tracking Down a Deadly Gene The gene for Huntington's disease was discovered by a team of researchers headed by Nancy Wexler. This discovery increases the likelihood that the disease can, sometime in the future, be prevented or treated. Wexler (on the left) is shown here with Mary Lasker in 1993 after receiving the Albert Lasker Medical Research Award for outstanding public service and achievement in research. Because the disease is genetically transmitted, how can genetic counseling be helpful to affected families?

fingers or facial grimaces. As the disorder progresses, these symptoms become more widespread and abrupt, involving jerky, rapid, and repetitive movements. Changes in personality and emotional stability also occur. For example, individuals with Huntington's disease may become moody and quarrelsome. They may develop a peculiar manner of walking and find it difficult to speak normally. Before they are diagnosed, their inability to control their movements may even be blamed on alcoholism. Huntington's disease always ends in death, on the average from thirteen to sixteen years after the onset of symptoms. Early misdiagnoses are given in many of the cases; schizophrenia is a common misdiagnosis.

Cerebral Tumors

A **cerebral tumor** is a mass of abnormal tissue growing within the brain. The symptoms depend on the area affected and on the amount of intracranial pressure exerted by the tumor. Fast-growing tumors generally produce severe mental symptoms, whereas slow growth may result in few symptoms. Unfortunately, in the latter case, the tumor is often not discovered until death has occurred in a psychiatric hospital. Tumors that affect the temporal area produce the highest frequency of psychological symptoms (Golden et al., 1983).

The most common symptoms of cerebral tumors are disturbances of consciousness, which can range from diminished attention and drowsiness to coma. People with tumors may also show mild dementia and other problems of thinking. Mood changes may also result from either the direct physical impact of the tumor or the patient's reaction to the problem. Removing a cerebral tumor can produce dramatic results.

The woman was admitted to a mental hospital, exhibiting dementia and confusion. She responded little to questioning by staff, or to attempts at therapy, even after twelve years of hospitalization. She would simply sit blindly, with her tongue protruding to the right, making repetitive movements of her right arm and leg. She also showed partial paralysis of the left side of her face. This "left-side, right-side" pattern of symptoms suggested that her condition might be due to a physical problem. Surgery was performed, and a massive brain tumor was discovered and removed. After the operation, the patient improved remarkably. She regained her speech and sight and was able to recognize and converse with her relatives for the first time in twelve years. (Hunter, Blackwood, & Bull, 1968)

Epilepsy

Epilepsy is a general term that refers to a set of symptoms rather than to a specific etiology. In particular, **epilepsy** includes any disorder characterized by intermittent and brief periods of altered consciousness—often accompanied by seizures—and by excessive electrical discharge from brain cells. It is the most common of the neurological disorders; 1 to 2 percent of the population has epileptic seizures at some time during their lives. About 2.5 million children and adults in the United States live with epilepsy or other seizure disorders (McLin, 1992). It also seems to be one of the earliest recognized cognitive disorders: Julius Caesar, Napoleon, Dostoevsky, and Van Gogh are among those who presumably had this disorder.

Epilepsy is most frequently diagnosed during childhood. It can be symptomatic of some primary disorder of the brain without apparent etiology, or it can arise from such causes as hereditary factors, brain tumors, injury, degenerative diseases, and drugs (Lishman, 1978). Epileptic seizures and unconsciousness may last from a few seconds to several hours; they may occur only a few times during the patient's entire life or many times in one day. And they may produce only a

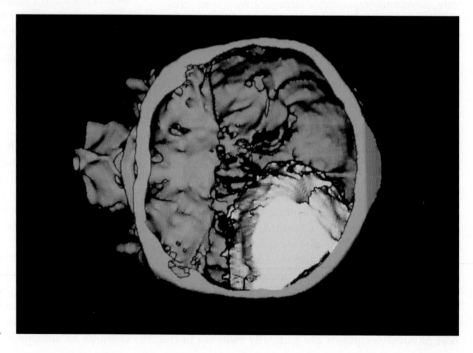

A Cerebral Tumor Symptoms of cerebral tumor, an abnormal tissue growing within the brain, depend on the size and location of the tumor. Some are fairly large, such as the one shown in this CAT scan. The most common effects of tumors involve disturbances in consciousness.

The Most Common Neurological Disorder Epilepsy refers to any disorder that is characterized by intermittent and brief periods of altered consciousness, often accompanied by seizures. It also seems to be one of the earliest recognized organic brain syndromes. Among those who suffered from the disease was Vincent van Gogh, shown here in a self-portrait painted sometime after he had cut off his ear.

momentary disturbance of consciousness or a complete loss of consciousness—in which case they can be accompanied by violent convulsions and a coma lasting for hours. Alcohol, lack of sleep, fever, a low blood-sugar level, hyperventilation, a brain lesion or injury, or general fatigue can all induce an epileptic seizure. Particular musical notes, flickering lights, and emotionally charged situations have also been known to provoke epileptic attacks. Even everyday stress can bring on a seizure (Devinsky, 1994).

Epilepsy can often be controlled, but it cannot be cured. Although people with epilepsy usually behave and function quite normally between attacks, their chronic, long-term illness is still regarded with suspicion and repugnance by much of society. An attack can be frightening to the afflicted person and observers alike. They face their own anxiety and other people's fear resulting from the unpredictable and dramatic nature of their seizures. They are embarrassed by their seeming lack of control over their illness and must deal with society's negative stereotypes concerning epilepsy. Perhaps as a result of these stereotypes concerning

epilepsy, approximately 30 to 50 percent of people with epilepsy have accompanying psychological problems (Golden et al., 1983). The following description highlights a common problem among those suffering from brief and minor epileptic episodes.

Jack D. is a sixteen-year-old student who was admitted to the outpatient psychiatric service of a large hospital to receive treatment for epilepsy. Jack and his parents explained that the seizures lasted only a few seconds each but occurred twenty to thirty times a day. His parents were especially concerned because Jack was very eager to get a driver's license; driving a car would be quite dangerous if he were subject to momentary losses of consciousness. Jack was interviewed at a case conference at which a group of mental health professionals, medical students, and paraprofessionals discussed his symptoms, the etiology of the disorder, the prognosis, and treatment. During the fifteen-minute interview, Jack experienced two petit mal or minor seizures. The first occurred while he was answering a question. A psychiatrist had asked Jack whether his seizures significantly handicapped him in school. Jack replied, "It really hasn't been that bad. Sometimes I lose track of what the teacher is." At that point, Jack paused. He had a blank stare on his face, and his mouth was slightly opened. After about four seconds, he resumed speaking and said, "Uh, writing on the blackboard." A psychologist then asked Jack if he had noticed that he had paused in midsentence. Jack answered that he was not aware of the pause or the brief seizure. Interestingly, several of those present at the case conference later admitted that they, too, were unaware that a seizure had occurred at that time. They thought Jack's pause was due to an attempt to find the right words.

Later Jack had another seizure that went unnoticed by most of the interviewers. While the resident psychiatrist was elaborating on a question, Jack appeared to be listening. But when the psychiatrist finished, Jack had a puzzled look on his face. He said, "It [a seizure] happened again. I was listening to what you were saying and suddenly you were all finished. I must have blanked out. Could you repeat the question?"

As you can see, such brief interruptions of consciousness may go unnoticed by people interacting with individuals undergoing a seizure—and sometimes by the individual also. Fortunately the prognosis for Jack was good. This type of seizure usually disappears with age and can be controlled with proper medication and treatment.

The most common and dramatic type of epileptic seizure is the *tonic-clonic seizure*. Although this type usually lasts no longer than a few minutes, it typically consists of four distinct phases, beginning with an *aura,* an unusual sensory experience that lasts only a few seconds and signals the onset of a seizure. During this first phase, the person feels physical or sensory sensations such as headaches, hallucinations, mood changes, dizziness, or feelings of unreality. During the *tonic* phase, the individual becomes unconscious and falls to the ground. The muscles become rigid and the eyes remain open. During the third or *clonic* phase, body muscles rapidly contract and relax, producing jerking movements, which may be so violent that the persons bruise their heads on the ground, bite their tongues, or vomit. Fourth and finally, the muscles relax and a *coma* ensues, lasting from a few minutes to several hours. Upon awakening, the individual may feel exhausted, confused, and sore. Some people report that they feel relieved and refreshed.

Tonic-clonic attacks may occur daily or be limited to only once or twice during an entire lifetime. In rare cases, they occur in rapid succession without return of consciousness between attacks—a condition known as *status epilepticus* (Cummings, Trimble, & Hales, 1999)—and can result in death if untreated.

Etiological Factors   As we have noted, epilepsy has been attributed to a wide range of factors, including brain tumors, head injuries, biochemical imbalances, physical illness, and stress. These somehow result in excessive neuronal discharge within the brain. Sometimes the discharge appears to be quite localized, producing focal seizures or twitching in isolated parts of the body. Generalized seizures are presumably caused by general cortical discharge, and the effects involve the whole body.

Some researchers have investigated the hypothesis that genetic or personality factors predispose people to epilepsy. The concordance rate for epilepsy is greater among identical than among fraternal twins, and seizures are much more frequent among family members of a person with epilepsy than among unrelated people (Devinsky, 1994). However, heredity may not be a necessary or sufficient condition for the onset of epilepsy.

Nor has any single type of personality been associated with epilepsy. Although personality disturbances are correlated with some cases of epilepsy, it is unclear whether personality factors predispose people to epilepsy or whether epilepsy influences personality development. Another possibility is that the person is under great stress because of the condition and because of the stigma attached to the disorder. This stress, rather than either the disorder or its causes, may affect the personalities of those who have epilepsy.

Use of Psychoactive Substances

Using psychoactive substances (see the chapter on substance-related disorders) can result in cognitive disorders (dementia, delirium, or amnestic disorder). The substances have effects on the nervous system. Most people diagnosed as having a cognitive disorder involving psychoactive substances also have problems concerning substance use. The most common psychoactive substances that can lead to cognitive disorders are alcohol, amphetamines, caffeine, marijuana, cocaine, hallucinogens, inhalants, nicotine, opioids, PCP, and sedatives.

Treatment Considerations

Because cognitive disorders can be caused by many different factors and are associated with different symptoms and dysfunctions, treatment approaches have varied widely. The major interventions have been surgical, medical, psychological, and environmental. Most treatment programs are comprehensive in nature, providing patients with medication, rehabilitation, therapy, and environmental modifications (see Cohen & Weiner, 1994).

Neuropsychologists are often asked to provide assessment of the cognitive problems and determine longitudinal progress of patients (Nelson & Adams, 1997). Surgical procedures may be used to remove cerebral tumors, relieve the pressure caused by tumors, or restore ruptured blood vessels. Psychotherapy may help patients deal with the emotional aspects of these disorders. And some patients who have lost motor skills can be retrained to compensate for their deficiencies or can be retaught these skills. Sometimes, patients with cognitive disorders need complete hospital care. We'll examine the use of medication and cognitive and behavioral approaches in more detail.

Medication

Drugs can prevent, control, or reduce the symptoms of brain disorders, as in the use of L-dopa in Parkinson's disease. Medication is of the most benefit in controlling some symptoms of cognitive disorders. For example, more than 50 percent of the people with epilepsy can control their seizures with medication such as Dilantin; another 30 percent can reduce the frequency of seizures. However, side effects can occur, such as a decrease in the speed of motor responding, tremors, weight gain, and swollen gums (Dodrill & Matthews, 1992; Hauser, 1994). Only 20 percent of patients with epilepsy fail to improve on the medications (Epilepsy Foundation of America, 1983).

Sometimes medication is used to control emotional problems that may accompany cognitive impairment. Antidepressant drugs, for example, can alleviate the depression found in many patients with Alzheimer's disease (Teri & Wagner, 1992). Alzheimer's disease has also been treated using acetylcholinesterase inhibitors that increase the availability of acetylcholine in the synaptic clefts of the brain (DHHS, 1999). Interestingly, the regular use of some anti-inflammatory medications such as ibuprofen may cut the risk of developing the disease by as much as one-half (Nash, 1997). The goals of current treatment approaches have been to delay the onset of symptoms, slow the progression of the disease, improve symptoms and reduce disease morbidity, modify risk factors, and prevent the disease (Masterman & Cummings, 2001).

Cognitive and Behavioral Approaches

The cognitive therapeutic approaches also appear to be particularly promising. Memory-improvement techniques and other strategies have been used (Schalock, 1998). Researchers have hypothesized, for example, that the impaired attention and concentration shown by head-injured people result from the disruption of private speech, which regulates behavior and thought processes (Luria, 1982). One therapeutic program uses self-instructional training to enhance the self-regulation of speech and behavior (Webster & Scott, 1983). The program was used to treat a twenty-four-year-old construction worker who had been in a coma for four days as a result of a car accident. Tests showed him to have poor recall, poor concentration, and attentional difficulties; he couldn't concentrate on any task for a long period of time. He also complained that intrusive nonsexual thoughts kept him from maintaining an erection during intercourse.

The patient was told to repeat the following self-instructions aloud before doing anything:

1. "To really concentrate, I must look at the person speaking to me."

2. "I also must focus on what is being said, not on other thoughts which want to intrude."

3. "I must concentrate on what I am hearing at any moment by repeating each word in my head as the person speaks."

4. "Although it is not horrible if I lose track of conversation, I must tell the person to repeat the information if I have not attended to it." (Webster & Scott, 1983, p. 71)

After he had learned to use these vocalized instructions, rephrased in his own words, he was taught to repeat them subvocally before each task. His concentration and attention soon improved greatly, and he returned to his former job. He also successfully blocked intrusive thoughts during sexual intercourse by focusing on his partner. Such self-vocalizations often increase a person's effectiveness at the task at hand (Kohlenberg & Tsai, 1991).

A similar program was developed to eliminate the anger response brain-injured people sometimes display, either as a result of the brain damage or in reaction to their deficits. One twenty-two-year-old patient had suffered a severe head trauma in a motorcycle accident at age sixteen. After two months of intensive medical treatment, he had returned home to live with his parents. There he showed outbursts of anger toward people and objects, a low frustration level, and impulsiveness. These behaviors led to many failures in a vocational rehabilitation program. Medication did not help control his outbursts.

A stress inoculation program was developed for this patient. Twelve 30-minute sessions, spread over three weeks, focused on the following areas:

1. *Cognitive preparation* The function and appropriateness of anger were explained, as were alternatives to being destructive. The situations that produced anger were identified, and appropriate responses were demonstrated.

2. *Skills acquisition* The patient was taught to stop himself from becoming angry, to reevaluate anger-evoking situations, and to use self-verbalizations that were incompatible with the expression of anger.

3. *Application training* A hierarchy of situations evoking anger was developed. The patient role-played and practiced the use of cognitive and behavioral skills to cope with progressively greater anger-evoking stimuli. He also used these techniques in the hospital setting and received feedback about his performance.

Before treatment, the patient had averaged about three outbursts each week. No outbursts at all were recorded immediately after treatment, and a follow-up five months later indicated that the gain had been maintained. He found a part-time job as a clerk and was living independently.

In an early seizure-prevention program using classical conditioning (Efron, 1956, 1957), one woman who suffered from tonic-clonic seizures learned to prevent the occurrence of the tonic (body extended and stiff) and clonic (rapid alternation of muscle contraction and relaxation) phases by sniffing an unpleasant odor during the initial stage of an attack. Researchers first

Help For People Who Experience Memory Problems
Memory loss can be extremely frustrating. Affected individuals may require constant attention and aid from others in locating items. With labels, those with memory problems are able to function more independently. What other strategies can be used to assist those with memory difficulties?

presented the odor to the woman while she stared at a bracelet, then paired the smell with the bracelet over a period of several days. At that point, the bracelet alone was enough to elicit thoughts of the unpleasant odor, and the patient could stop a seizure by staring at it when she felt an attack starting. Eventually she could cut an attack short by just thinking about the bracelet. Other behavior modification and biofeedback techniques have also been helpful in reducing seizure activity (Devinsky, 1994).

Environmental Interventions and Caregiver Support

The effects of many cognitive disorders are largely irreversible. This raises the issue of how family and friends can assist those with cognitive disorders. There are a variety of means by which people with these disorders may be helped to live comfortably and with dignity while making use of those abilities that remain. The following interventions have been proposed by Butler (1984):

1. To preserve the patient's sense of independence and control over his or her life, the environment must be modified to make it safer. Rails can be installed to allow the patient to move freely in the house. A chair that is easy to get into and out of, a remote-control device for the television set, and guard rails

for the bathtub will help the patient do things for himself or herself. The patient should be encouraged to make as many personal decisions as possible—to choose which clothing to wear and which activities to take part in—even if the choices are not always perfect.

2. Continued social contacts are important, but visits by friends and relatives should be kept short so that the patient does not feel pressured to continue the social interaction. Visits should not involve large groups of individuals, which could overwhelm the patient.

3. Diversions, such as going out for a walk, are important. It is better to stroll through a calm and peaceful area than to visit a crowded shopping mall, where the environment tends to be unpredictable.

4. Tasks should be assigned to the patient to increase his or her sense of self-worth. These tasks may not be completed to perfection, but they will provide a very important sense of having contributed. In addition, older people can be taught to use memory aids and other strategies to facilitate remembering.

The family and friends who provide care may, themselves, need support. They often feel overwhelmed, helpless, frustrated, anxious, or even angry at having to take care of someone with a cognitive impairment. They may worry about how to take proper care of a loved one who has a cognitive disorder or feel guilty if the loved one is injured or deteriorates under their care. Role relationships may change, as the child becomes the primary caregiver for a parent with a disability (Feldman, Mosbach, Thomas, & Perry, 1994). In all of these circumstances, caregivers should learn as much as possible about the disorder and the means of taking care of loved ones, realize that the role of a caregiver is stressful, and seek out personal support (such as through self-help groups composed of other caregivers).

Mental Retardation

A teenager with mental retardation told his fellow students, during a high school assembly, how he felt about his handicap:

> My name is Tim Frederick. ... I would like to tell you what it is like to be retarded. ... I am doing this so that you might be able to understand people like me. I do chores at home. I have to take care of all the animals—twelve chickens, three cats, a dog, three goldfish, and a horse. That's a lot of mouths to feed. ... After I graduate

TABLE 14.2   Mental Retardation: Prevalence, Onset, and Course

Disorder	Prevalence	Gender Differences	Age of Onset	Course
Mental retardation	1 to 3%	1.5 to 1 (male to female)	Before age eighteen; precise age of onset depends on etiology and severity	Depends on severity; with appropriate training, many individuals learn good adaptive skills

Source: Based on American Psychiatric Association (2000).

from school, I hope to live in an apartment. ... The hardest thing is when people make fun of me. I went to a dance a few weeks ago, and no girl would dance with me. Can you guys imagine how you would feel if that happened to you? Well, I feel the same way. (K. Smith, 1988, pp. 118–119)

The perception of mental retardation, formerly considered a hopeless condition that required institutionalization, is undergoing a fundamental change. Tim Frederick's mother was told that her son's development would be delayed and that he might never be able to walk or talk. We now know that the effects of mental retardation are variable and that with training, even people with severe retardation can make intellectual and social gains (see Table 14.2).

The Association for Retarded Citizens, an advocacy organization, has estimated that 75 percent of children with mental retardation can become completely self-supporting adults if given appropriate education and training. Another 10 to 15 percent have the potential to be self-supporting. The challenge is to develop appropriate programs to ensure the greatest success. The movement away from institutionalization will continue to increase contact between people with mental retardation and the general population. In 1967, more than 200,000 people with mental retardation lived in public institutions. By 1984, this number had decreased to 110,000 (Landesman & Butterfield, 1987). It is now widely accepted that these people should have the opportunity to live, work, learn, and develop relationships with the general population in integrated settings. People are beginning to question assumptions about what individuals with mental retardation can do. A dance troupe called "Images in Motion," composed of individuals with IQ scores between 30 and 60, has won rave reviews (Walker, 1991). The next frontier will be fuller integration of people into the social fabric (Wolfensberger, 1988).

Diagnosing Mental Retardation

About 7 million or more persons in the United States have IQ scores of about 70 or less (Madle, 1990). Prevalence figures for the United States are 1–3 percent, depending primarily on the definition of adaptive functioning (Popper & West, 1999). As mentioned earlier, mental retardation is categorized by DSM-IV-TR as one of the disorders usually first diagnosed in infancy, childhood, or adolescence. It is not considered a cognitive disorder, although we have included it in this chapter simply because mental retardation affects cognitive functioning. The definition of **mental retardation** in DSM-IV-TR includes the following criteria:

1. *Significant subaverage general intellectual functioning* (ordinarily interpreted as an IQ score of 70 or less on an individually administered IQ test)

2. *Concurrent deficiencies in adaptive behavior* (social and daily living skills, degree of independence lower than would be expected by age or cultural group)

3. *Onset before age eighteen* (subaverage intellectual functioning arising after age eighteen is typically categorized as dementia)

Common characteristics that accompany mental retardation are dependency, passivity, low self-esteem, low tolerance of frustration, depression, and self-injurious behavior (American Psychiatric Association, 2000). Relative to the general population, persons with mental retardation are much more likely to suffer from psychiatric problems (Dykens & Hodapp, 1997). The problems include a higher incidence of aggression, self-injurious behavior, tantrums, and stereotyped behaviors (Phelps, Brown, & Power, 2002). The more severe levels of mental retardation are associated with speech difficulties, neurological disorders, cerebral palsy, and vision and hearing problems (McQueen, Spence, Garner, Pereira, & Winson, 1987). Individuals with autism may also exhibit cognitive deficits, but mental retardation has been distinguished from autism on various mental and perceptual tasks (Shulman, Yirmiya, & Greenbaum, 1995).

Issues Involved in Diagnosing Mental Retardation

Arguments have been raised against the use of IQ scores to determine mental retardation, especially among members of ethnic minority groups. The validity of IQ scores is questionable, especially when they are used to test members of minority groups. This controversy resurfaced with the publication of *The Bell Curve* (Herrnstein & Murray, 1994), which attributes African Americans' poorer performance on IQ tests to genetic factors. Frisby (1995), however, points out that alternative explanations for IQ performance can be made (see Table 14.3). IQ tests also may measure familiarity with mainstream middle-class culture, not intelligence. Jane Mercer (1988) argued that the IQ test has been inappropriately used and that it is unfair to attempt to "measure" intel-

ligence by using items drawn from one culture to test individuals from a different cultural group. In addition, IQ tests do not acknowledge the positive coping characteristics of persons from various ethnic minority groups.

In a 1979 ruling in the *Larry P. v. Riles* case, Judge Robert Peckham of the Federal District Court for the Northern District of California held that IQ tests were culturally biased and were not to be used in decisions regarding the placement of African Americans in classes for children with mental retardation. He broadened his decision in 1986 by saying that IQ tests could not be used—even with parental consent—to determine the educational needs of African American children as part of a comprehensive educational program. His decision was challenged by the mother of an African American child who requested IQ testing. She argued that this was a case of reverse discrimination, as IQ tests can be administered for special education services to European Americans, Hispanic Americans, Asian Americans, and American Indians. On September 1, 1992, Judge

---

TABLE 14.3   Alternative Explanations for Lower Performance by African Americans on IQ Tests

Disadvantage/Oppression Explanations

Legacy of slavery

Teacher racism/prejudice

Inadequate schools
- Lack of funds, resources
- Lack of parental involvement

Inadequate home environment
- Poverty
- Lack of opportunities to learn
- Deficient mother-child interactions
- Lack of parental support
- Lack of academic role models

Cultural Difference Explanations

Cultural bias in tests
- Lack of African Americans in standardization samples
- Preference for "dynamic" vs. "static" testing
- Item loading on white middle-class culture
- Different race of the examiner from test taker

- Lack of "test-wiseness"

Afrocentric home/Eurocentric school mismatch
- Active opposition to "white" cultural values
- Lack of cultural competence in teachers
- Lack of multicultural curricula
- Preference for cooperative vs. competitive learning
- Preference for African American English vs. standard English
- African American behavioral/learning style

Psychological Maladjustment Explanations

Expectancy of failure due to low teacher expectations

Low self-esteem (negative self-concept)
- Caused by segregation from whites
- Caused by integration with whites

Lack of motivation to achieve

Test/performance anxiety

Learned helplessness

Negative peer pressure (burden of acting white)

Source: Adapted from Frisby (1995).

TABLE 14.4   Estimated Number of Mentally Retarded People by Level of Retardation

Level	Range Wechsler IQ	Percentage of All Mentally Retarded	Number
Mild	50–70	85	7,926,000
Moderate	35–49	10	933,000
Severe	20–34	3–4	326,700
Profound	0–19	1–2	140,000

Note: Estimates based on percentages from the American Psychiatric Association (2000) and applied to the normal probability distribution of intelligence based on a U.S. population of 274 million.

Peckham reversed his 1986 ruling. IQ tests can again be used with African American children as part of a special education assessment. However, the 1979 ruling still holds. They cannot be used to place African American children in classes for those with mental retardation.

Levels of Retardation   DSM-IV-TR specifies four different levels of mental retardation, which are based on IQ score ranges, as measured on the revised Wechsler scales (WISC-R and WAIS-R): (1) mild (IQ score 50–55 to 70), (2) moderate (IQ score 35–40 to 50–55), (3) severe (IQ score 20–25 to 35–40), and (4) profound (IQ score below 20 or 25). Social and vocational skills and degree of adaptability may vary greatly within each category. Table 14.4 contains estimates of the number of people within each level in the United States.

It should be noted that the American Association on Mental Retardation (AAMR) does not use a classification of mental retardation based on levels of intellectual functioning as revealed in IQ scores. Instead, AAMR considers concurrent limitations in both the intellectual and adaptive skills of the individual (Kanaya, Scullin, & Ceci, 2003). Adaptive skills include those required in communication, self-care, social interactions, health and safety, work, and leisure. Furthermore, the skills are placed in the context of one's culture and community. Mental retardation is diagnosed only if low intelligence is accompanied by impaired adaptive functioning. Low intelligence alone, or deficits in adaptive behaviors alone, do not result in a diagnosis of mental retardation according to AAMR (Popper & West, 1999). Although DSM-IV-TR and AAMR use intellectual and adaptive functioning as criteria in the diagnosis of mental retardation, AAMR focuses more on adaptive functioning and specifies the type and nature of psychosocial supports needed in adaptive functioning (Harris, 2001).

Etiology of Mental Retardation

Mental retardation is thought to be produced by environmental factors (such as poor living conditions), biological factors, or some combination of the two (see Table 14.5). It can be caused by injury, disease, or a brain abnormality. The etiology is dependent to some extent on the level of mental retardation. Mild retardation is generally idiopathic (having no known cause) and familial, whereas severe retardation is typically related to genetic factors or to brain damage (Popper & West, 1999).

Environmental Factors   Certain features of the environment may contribute to retardation. Among these are the absence of stimulating factors or situations, a lack of attention and reinforcement from parents or significant others, and chronic stress and frustration. In addition, poverty, lack of adequate health care, poor nutrition, and inadequate education place children at a disadvantage. A lower socioeconomic status generally implies a lower mean group IQ score (Ardizzone & Scholl, 1985).

Genetic Factors   Genetic factors in mental retardation include genetic variations and genetic abnormalities (Thapar, Gottesman, Owen, O'Donovan, & McGuffin, 1994). Mental retardation caused by normal genetic variation simply reflects the fact that in a normal distribution of traits, some individuals will fall in the upper range and some in the lower. Researchers have suggested that the normal range of intelligence lies between the IQ scores of 50 and 150, and that some individuals simply lie on the lower end of this normal range (Zigler, 1967). No organic or physiological anomaly associated with mental retardation is usually found in this type of retardation. Most people

TABLE 14.5   Predisposing Factors Associated with Mental Retardation

Factor	Percentage of Cases	Examples
Heredity	5	Errors of metabolism (Tay-Sachs), single gene abnormalities (tuberous sclerosis), chromosome aberrations (translocation Down syndrome, fragile X syndrome)
Alteration of embryonic development	30	Chromosomal changes (Down syndrome, trisomy 21), prenatal damage due to toxins (fetal alcohol syndrome), infections
Pregnancy and perinatal complications	10	Malnutrition, prematurity, hypoxia, traumas, infections
Infancy or childhood medical conditions	5	Traumas, infections, lead ingestion
Environmental influences and other mental conditions	15–20	Social, linguistic, and nurturance deprivation; severe mental disorders (autistic disorder)
Etiology unknown	30–40	Etiological factors cannot be identified

Source: Based on DSM-IV-TR.

classified with mild retardation have normal health, appearance, and physical abilities.

The most common inherited form of mental retardation that is caused by genetic anomalies is called the *fragile X syndrome* because an abnormal gene is present on the bottom end of the X chromosome (Hagerman, 1996). It occurs in 1 of every 2,000 to 5,000 live births (Hessl et al., 2001). Affected by the abnormal gene are the higher control processes of attention, such as executive functioning. The executive cognitive functions include cognitive flexibility, planning, initiation, behavioral and attentional regulation, feedback utilization, and self-perception (Loesch et al., 2003). Although impairment in functioning varies among those with inherited forms of mental retardation, many affected persons have severe deficits. Those with profound retardation (about 1 to 2 percent of those with the disorder) may be so intellectually deficient that they require constant and total care and supervision. Many also have significant sensorimotor impairment (Irwin & Gross, 1990) and are confined to a bed or wheelchair by the congenital defects that produced the retardation. Even with teaching, there is minimal, if any, acquisition of self-help skills among these individuals. Their mortality rate during childhood is extremely high, with more than one-half dying before age twenty (Ramer & Miller, 1992). Associated physical problems such as neuromuscular disorders, impairment of vision or hearing, and seizures may coexist (Irwin & Gross, 1990).

Down syndrome is a condition produced by the presence of an extra chromosome (trisomy 21, an autosomal, or nonsex, chromosome) and resulting in mental retardation and distinctive physical characteristics. It may occur as often as once in every thousand live births (Thapar et al., 1994). About 10 percent of children with severe or moderate retardation show this genetic anomaly. As Figure 14.5 illustrates, the prevalence rate increases dramatically with the age at which the mother gives birth (U.S. Department of Health and Human Services, 1995a).

The well-known physical characteristics of Down syndrome are short incurving fingers, short broad hands, slanted eyes, furrowed protruding tongue, flat and broad face, harsh voice, and incomplete or delayed sexual development. Some Down syndrome children receive cosmetic surgery (consisting mostly of modifying tongue size) to make their physical appearance more nearly normal and to allow them to speak more clearly and to eat more normally. The procedure is intended to enable Down syndrome people to fit in as much as possible with their peers to enhance their social interactions and communication abilities (May & Turnbull, 1992).

People with Down syndrome who live past age forty are at high risk for developing early-onset dementia of the Alzheimer type (Bush & Beail, 2004), discussed earlier in this chapter. The gene responsible for the amyloid plaques and neurofibrillary tangles found in Alzheimer's disease is located on chromosome 21, indicating a possible relationship between Down syndrome

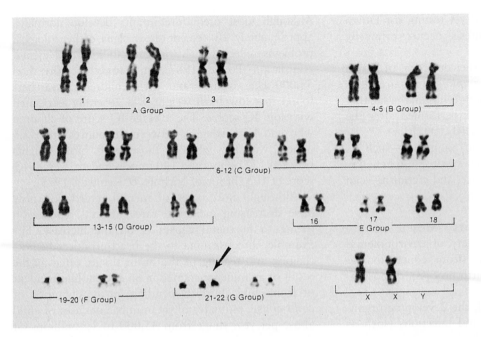

The Trisomy of Down Syndrome Three chromosomes in the number 21 chromosome set (trisomy 21) can be seen in this photograph. The extra chromosome is responsible for Down syndrome.

and Alzheimer's disease (Clarke & Clarke, 1987). People who have Down syndrome show a greater intellectual decline after the age of thirty-five than do other individuals with mental retardation (Young & Kramer, 1991). Congenital heart abnormalities are also common in people with Down syndrome, causing a high mortality rate. Surgical procedures have improved the probability of surviving these heart defects and have resulted in both a longer life expectancy and a healthier life (Carr, 1994).

Prenatal detection of Down syndrome is possible through **amniocentesis**, a screening procedure in which a hollow needle is inserted through the pregnant woman's abdominal wall and the amniotic fluid is withdrawn from the fetal sac. This procedure is performed during the fourteenth or fifteenth week of pregnancy. The fetal cells from the fluid are cultivated and, within three weeks, can be tested to determine whether Down syndrome is present. This procedure involves some risk for both mother and fetus, so it is employed only when the chance of finding Down syndrome is high—as, for example, with women older than age thirty-five. Remember, however, that the greater percentage of babies with Down syndrome are

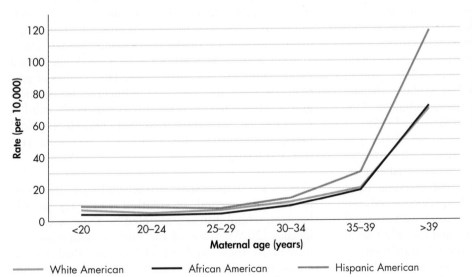

FIGURE 14.5 Rate of Down Syndrome Births This figure shows the rate of live Down syndrome births by mothers' ethnicity and age. For all groups, the rate of Down syndrome births increases after the maternal age of thirty.

Source: Data from U.S. Department of Health and Human Services, Centers for Disease Control (1995a).

born to younger mothers, and yet testing for Down syndrome through amniocentesis occurs primarily among older women.

A procedure that allows earlier detection of Down syndrome is *chorionic villus sampling*. Tests are made of cells on the hairlike projections (villi) on the sac that surrounds the fetus and can be performed after the ninth week of pregnancy (Pueschel, 1991).

Other, less common genetic anomalies—such as Turner's syndrome, Klinefelter's syndrome, phenylketonuria (PKU), Tay-Sachs disease, and cretinism—can also produce mental retardation.

Nongenetic Biological Factors Mental retardation may be caused by a variety of environmental mishaps during the prenatal (from conception to birth), perinatal (during the birth process), or postnatal (after birth) period.

During the prenatal period, the developing organism is susceptible to viruses and infections (such as German measles), drugs, radiation, poor nutrition, and other nongenetic influences.

Increasing attention is being focused on the problem of mental deficits related to alcohol consumption during pregnancy. Some children born to alcoholic mothers have **fetal alcohol syndrome (FAS)**, a group of congenital physical and mental defects including small body size and *microcephaly*, an anomaly whose most distinguishing feature is an unusually small brain. Such children are generally mildly retarded, but many are either moderately retarded or of average intelligence. Those with normal intelligence seem to have significant academic and attentional difficulties, however, as well as a history of hyperactivity and behavioral deficits (Streissguth, 1994). Smoking and poor nutrition may increase the likelihood that an alcoholic mother will have FAS offspring. Available information suggests that one case of FAS occurs in each 750 live births, which places alcohol among the most common causes of retardation for which an etiology can be determined (Streissguth, Landesman-Dwyer, Martin, & Smith, 1980). Among the different ethnic groups in the United States, the rate of FAS is especially high among American Indians (U.S. Department of Health and Human Services, 1995b).

During the perinatal period, mental retardation can result from birth trauma, prematurity, or asphyxiation. After birth or during the postnatal period, head injuries, infections, tumors, malnutrition, and ingesting toxic substances such as lead can cause brain damage and consequent mental retardation. Compared with prenatal factors, however, these hazards account for only a small proportion of organically caused mental retardation.

The most common birth condition associated with mental retardation is prematurity and low birth weight.

Although most premature infants develop normally, approximately 20 percent show signs of neurological problems reflected in learning disabilities and mental retardation (Pound, 1987). In a study of more than 53,000 U.S. women and their children, researchers found that low birth weight was generally associated with low IQ scores. The average IQ score of children who had birth weights between 26 ounces and 52.5 ounces was 86, whereas those with birth weights between 122 ounces and 140 ounces had an average IQ score of 105 (Broman, Nichols, & Kennedy, 1975).

Although most types of mental retardation now have decreasing incidence rates, mental retardation owing to postnatal causes is on the increase. For example, direct trauma to the head produces hemorrhaging and tearing of the brain tissue, often as the result of an injury sustained in an automobile accident or from child abuse. Depending on the definition of *child abuse,* estimates of the number of cases of child abuse per year range from 35,000 to 1.9 million. Of this group, a large percentage are subjected to violent abuse that could cause serious injury (Gelard & Sanford, 1987). Other postnatal causes include brain infections, neurological disease, toxic exposure, and even extreme malnutrition (Popper & West, 1999).

Programs for People with Mental Retardation

Early Intervention Programs such as Head Start have not produced dramatic increases in intellectual ability among at-risk children (those from low-income families). But long-term follow-up studies have found that they do produce positive results (Royce, Lazar, & Darlington, 1983; Zigler & Bergman, 1983). Children who participated in early intervention programs were found to perform better in school than nonparticipants, and the difference between the two groups continued to widen until the twelfth grade. In addition, a greater proportion of the participants in early intervention finished high school, which no doubt helped them obtain and hold better jobs. The families of participants were also positively influenced by the programs. They rated the programs as personally helpful, spent more time working with their children on school tasks, and perceived their children as becoming happier and healthier.

School Services Services received by children diagnosed with mental retardation can vary greatly between school districts, as noted by Kanaya and colleagues (2003). Some of the more common services offered to these students include modified regular classroom assignments (e.g., making the assignments shorter and/or easier) and direct instructions that explicitly teach the skills necessary to complete assignments (e.g., organizing materials for the student or showing the student exactly where the necessary information is in the text). Special education services may include removal from regular classrooms for all or part of the day to receive instruction from special education specialists, paid aides, and volunteers.

Employment Programs People with mental retardation can achieve more than was previously thought. The parents of one teenage boy, for example, were told that he would always be childlike and that the only job he would ever be fit for was stringing beads. Another person with moderate retardation, who spent most of his time staring at his hands and rubbing his face, also appeared to have a dismal future. Both of these men now have paying jobs, one as a janitor and the other as a dishwasher. Programs designed to help people with mental retardation learn occupational skills are largely responsible for the improved outcome of these men and others like them (McLeod, 1985). Gains made in social and vocational skills appear to be maintained or increased in follow-up studies (Foxx & Faw, 1992).

Living Arrangements Institutionalization of people with mental retardation is declining, as more individuals are placed in group homes or in situations in which they can live independently or semi-independently within the community. The idea is to provide the "least restrictive environment" that is consistent with their condition and that will give them the opportunity to develop more fully. Although the implication seems to

A Blind Adoptive Parent with Son Who Has Brain Damage from Fetal Alcohol Syndrome Our society is becoming increasingly aware of the importance and necessity of helping each other. There is also growing recognition of the roles that people can play in helping others regardless of physical challenges or disabilities.

Early Intervention and Training Can Make a Difference Many mentally retarded individuals can lead productive and satisfying lives, especially if they have access to programs designed to help them learn occupational skills. Here, mentally challenged women work in a kitchen in Vocational Visions in Mission Viejo, California. Do you feel people often stereotype individuals with mental retardation? What kinds of stereotypes exist?

be that institutions are bad places, they do not have uniformly negative effects. Nor do group homes always provide positive experiences. What seems to be most important are program goals; programs that promote social interaction and the development of competence have positive effects on the residents of either institutions or group homes (Tjosvold & Tjosvold, 1983).

Nontraditional group arrangements, in which a small number of people live together in a home, sharing meals and chores, provide increased opportunity for social interactions. These "normalized" living arrangements were found to produce benefits such as increased adaptive functioning, improved language development, and socialization (Kleinberg & Galligan, 1983; MacEachron, 1983). Many of these positive behaviors, however, were already part of the residents' repertoires; what they need are systematic programs that will teach them additional living skills (Kleinberg & Galligan, 1983). Merely moving people with mental retardation from one environment to another does not by itself guarantee that they will be taught the skills they need.

Nonetheless, properly planned and supported deinstitutionalization does provide these individuals an opportunity to experience a more "normal" life. Finally, it should be noted that living arrangements, environmental supports, and interventions should be tailored to the type of retardation and severity of limitations found among the individuals (Dykens & Hodapp, 1997). Research has found that customized or consumer-directed services are more effective than traditional agency-directed services (President's New Freedom Commission on Mental Health, 2003).

As mentioned earlier, parents and family members often serve as caregivers for a significant period of time. When this occurs, the family members may need education and training in dealing with someone who has mental retardation. Overcoming myths about the disorder, finding out how to deal with the affected family member, identifying supports and resources, and handling emotional problems (e.g., anxiety, guilt, and anger) within the family are important tasks for caregivers (Harris, 2001).

SUMMARY

How can we determine whether someone has brain damage or a cognitive disorder?

- Cognitive disorders are behavioral disturbances that result from transient or permanent damage to the brain. The effects of brain damage vary greatly.
- The most common symptoms include impaired consciousness and memory, impaired judgment, orientation difficulties, and attentional deficits.
- The effects can be acute (often temporary) or chronic (long term); the causes can be endogenous (internal) or exogenous (external); and the tissue damage can be diffuse or specific (localized).
- Assessing brain damage is complicated because its symptoms are often similar to those of functional disorders.

What are the different types of cognitive disorders?

- DSM-IV-TR lists four major types of cognitive disorders: dementia, delirium, amnestic disorders, and other cognitive disorders.
- In dementia, memory is impaired and cognitive functioning declines, as revealed by aphasia (language disturbance), apraxia (inability to carry out motor activities despite intact comprehension and motor function), agnosia (failure to recognize or identify objects despite intact sensory function), or disturbances in planning, organizing, and abstracting in thought processes.
- Delirium is a condition in which there is an impairment in consciousness with reduced ability to focus, sustain, or shift attention. Changes in cognition (memory deficit, disorientation, and language or perceptual disturbance) are observed, and the disorder develops rather rapidly over a course of hours or days.
- Amnestic disorders are characterized by memory impairment, as manifested by the inability to learn new information and the inability to recall previously learned knowledge or past events.
- Cognitive impairments that do not meet the criteria for the other three are classified as other cognitive disorders.

Why do people develop cognitive disorders?

- Many different agents can cause cognitive disorders; among these are physical wounds or injuries to the brain, processes of aging, diseases that destroy brain tissue (such as neurosyphilis and encephalitis), and brain tumors.
- Epilepsy is characterized by intermittent and brief periods of altered consciousness, frequently accompanied by seizures, and excessive electrical

discharge by neurons. Psychoactive substances can also cause cognitive disorders.

What kinds of interventions can be used to treat people with cognitive disorders?

- Treatment strategies include corrective surgery and cognitive and behavioral training. Medication is often used, either alone or with other therapies, to decrease or control the symptoms of the various cognitive disorders. Caregivers can learn to provide assistance to loved ones with cognitive disorders.

What is mental retardation?

- DSM-IV-TR identifies four different levels of mental retardation, which are based only on IQ scores: mild (IQ score 50 to 70), moderate (IQ score 35 to 49), severe (IQ score 20 to 34), and profound (IQ score below 20).

- Causes of retardation include environmental factors, normal genetic processes, genetic anomalies, and other biological abnormalities such as physiological or anatomical defects.
- Most mental retardation does not have an identifiable organic cause and is associated with only mild intellectual impairment.
- The vast majority of those with mental retardation can become completely self-supporting with appropriate education and training.
- Public schools provide special programs for children and adolescents; even people with severe retardation are given instruction and training in practical self-help skills.
- Various approaches—behavioral therapy in particular—are used successfully to help people with mental retardation acquire needed "living" skills.

KEY TERMS

Alzheimer's disease (p. 474)

amnestic disorder (p. 468)

amniocentesis (p. 489)

brain trauma (p. 469)

cerebral blood flow measurement (p. 463)

cerebral infarction (p. 472)

cerebral tumor (p. 480)

cerebrovascular accident (p. 471)

cognitive disorder (p. 459)

computerized axial tomography (CAT) (p. 463)

delirium (p. 468)

dementia (p. 466)

diaschisis (p. 464)

Down syndrome (p. 488)

electroencephalograph (EEG) (p. 463)

encephalitis (p. 478)

epilepsy (p. 480)

fetal alcohol syndrome (FAS) (p. 490)

Huntington's disease (p. 479)

magnetic resonance imaging (MRI) (p. 463)

meningitis (p. 478)

mental retardation (p. 485)

Parkinson's disease (p. 477)

positron emission tomography (PET) (p. 463)

vascular dementia (p. 472)

MULTIMEDIA PREVIEW

For additional study aids, we invite you to explore our media resources accompanying *Understanding Abnormal Behavior*, Eighth Edition. The Student CD-ROM includes videos, quizzing, and critical thinking activities that help to reinforce key concepts in a fun and engaging manner. The Student Web Site provides additional interactive activities, chapter outlines, and research links that further support and complement the text. All Web resources may be accessed by logging onto the Web site at **http://psychology.college.hmco.com/students**.

CHAPTER 15
Disorders of Childhood and Adolescence

- Which disorders fall under the category of pervasive developmental disorders?
- What are some of the characteristics of attention deficit/hyperactivity disorder, and what are the subtypes of this disorder?
- What is the difference between conduct disorder and oppositional defiant disorder?
- What is the general prognosis for children with anxiety disorders?
- What are some of the characteristics of reactive attachment disorder, and what circumstances lead to the development of this disorder?
- Which adult mood disorders are also seen in children and adolescents?
- What is the difference between Tourette's disorder and other tic disorders?
- What are elimination disorders, and what is their prognosis?

In this chapter, we discuss problems that arise primarily during childhood and adolescence. Much of the public continues to cling to the popular notion that childhood is a period relatively free of stress and that it represents a carefree and happy existence. Because children are less able to express unhappiness or fears verbally, their problems often go unnoticed unless they become glaringly extreme, as in the following cases:

"Leave Me Alone"
The five-and-one-half-year-old preschooler sat apart from the other children. In his hand, Ahmed held a toy truck, and he was spinning its wheels and humming aloud as if to mimic the sound. He then stood and placed the truck in the corner of the room before moving to the window. Peering out, he ran his right forefinger along the sill exactly five times. He then returned to the corner, picked up the truck, and repeated the entire sequence again, as he had been doing all morning. If by chance one of the other children accidentally moved or handled the truck, Ahmed seemed panic stricken and filled with rage. Caretakers' attempts to comfort him were unsuccessful. He showed no response when they talked to him, and he seldom looked in their eyes. Ahmed seemed to live in a world of his own, and he treated people as if they were inanimate objects that stood in his way. Diagnosis: autistic disorder

"Sit Still and Pay Attention"
The mother sat in the psychiatrist's office, watching apprehensively as her ten-year-old son fidgeted in his seat and played with the ornaments hanging from the nearby Christmas tree. The mother explained to the psychiatrist that Adam had been expelled from school twice for disruptive classroom behavior. He had difficulty concentrating in class, and he was failing. The school psychologist had said Adam was "hyperactive" and recommended that they seek professional help. Throughout the interview, the mother admonished the child, saying, "Sit still," "Don't play with those," and "Pay attention." Each time, the child appeared remorseful and his behavior abated briefly. But remaining still seemed impossible for Adam, and he was soon fidgeting again. By the end of the session, he had been in and out of his seat some half dozen times and had accidentally broken two ornaments. Diagnosis: attention deficit/hyperactivity disorder

"No, I Won't"
The father had never struck Kim before, but he was on the verge of doing so now. He was enraged and incensed at his fourteen-year-old son's defiance and argumentative nature. Standing before his father with a scowl on his face and both hands clenched in fists, Kim refused to come out of his room to meet friends and relatives attending his mother's surprise birthday party. Just

hours before, he and his father had had a heated encounter over picking up his room and helping with chores around the house. Kim had steadfastly refused. Even when he was threatened with being "grounded," Kim only stated, "You can't make me do anything." Diagnosis: oppositional defiant disorder

"Please Don't Leave Me Alone"

At eight years of age, Nina was suffering from multiple anxieties. During the day, she could not tolerate having her mother out of sight, and at night she was tormented by unrealistic fears and nightmares. Leaving her at school was becoming increasingly difficult because Nina would cling to her mother and often refused to leave the car. Even when her mother walked her to the classroom, Nina fussed and cried in front of the other children. The child's problem seemed to be worsening: She was complaining of stomachaches and headaches in school, and she had exaggerated fears that the school would burn down. Nina was now frequently sent to the school nurse for her physical symptoms. Diagnosis: separation anxiety disorder

Although it is easy for us to dismiss such childhood disorders as rare and unusual, it is estimated that almost 21 percent of the children in the United States between the ages of nine and seventeen have a diagnosable mental or addictive disorder associated with at least a minimal level of impairment, with 11 percent having significant impairment and 5 percent having an extreme degree of impairment (Schaffer et al., 1996). Children and adolescents are subject not only to childhood disorders but also to many of the "adult" disorders discussed in previous chapters. Unless effective intervention takes place early in the child's life, an untreated disorder may develop into a lifelong pattern that creates problems in future years.

Myth vs Reality

Myth: Childhood psychiatric disorders are easy to diagnose because symptoms in childhood and adolescence parallel characteristics of adult disorders.

Reality: It is generally more complex to diagnose psychiatric disorders in children and adolescents: first because of variations in the presentation of symptoms of disorders between childhood and adulthood; and second because characteristics that signify mental illness in adults may occur in normally developing children. Accurate diagnosis and treatment of psychiatric disorders requires a thorough understanding of normal child development and issues of child tempera-

ment, as well as an understanding of risk factors for and the symptoms of psychiatric disorders in children and adolescents.

Only recently has our understanding of developmental psychopathology (disorders of childhood and adolescence) shifted from an adult perspective to that of the child. Prior to the twentieth century, children were often seen as "miniature adults." And even though Freud recognized the importance of childhood experiences, his descriptions of early life were based on the recollections of his adult patients, not on direct observation of children. As a result, early explanations of children's problems were based on biased memories, and little effort was devoted toward understanding the normal developmental milestones and associated stressors from the perspective of the child. Developmental psychologists today realize that there is a profound difference between "the remembered child" and "the real child." Contemporary psychologists now believe the object of study must be the child, and direct, systematic, and empirical studies and/or clinical observations become the tools for describing the many forms of childhood disorders.

The disorders of childhood and adolescence encompass a wide variety of behavioral problems, ranging from severe disturbances affecting many aspects of behavior to those that are less severe. One of the most disturbing is a cluster of impairments called *pervasive developmental disorders*. Autistic disorder (the case called "Leave Me Alone") is a particularly baffling and debilitating condition that all too often dooms a child to constant dependent care. We also discuss disorders that involve attention deficits and/or hyperactivity that become especially pronounced during the school years, such as in the case "Sit Still and Pay Attention." Attention deficit/hyperactivity disorder (ADHD) has become a controversial diagnosis because of the criticisms leveled at the frequent use of Ritalin to control the problem (see the Mental Health and Society feature "Are We Overmedicating Children?"). The case called "No, I Won't" is a typical example of the class of problems called disruptive behavior disorders. In this case, the son can be described as suffering from an oppositional defiant disorder. Children can also suffer from excessive anxieties, as in the case "Please Don't Leave Me Alone," or from other forms of mood problems.

The numbers of childhood and adolescent disorders are plentiful, and we have chosen to concentrate on representative disorders that fall under the following classifications: pervasive developmental disorders (especially autism), attention deficit/hyperactivity disorders (ADHD), disruptive behavior disorders (oppositional defiant disorder and conduct disorder), anxiety

MENTAL HEALTH AND SOCIETY
Are We Overmedicating Children?

A large number of medications are being prescribed to treat childhood disorders. They include tranquilizers, stimulants, and antipsychotic medications. As with adults, the use of medications with children and adolescents has been increasing dramatically. Drug companies are now advertising directly to the public via television and magazines. They point out that up to 10 percent of all American children suffer from some mental illness (Kluger, 2003). Ritalin production increased ninefold from 1985 to 1995 (Guttman, 1995).

Controversy continues over the "quick fix" nature of medication, the large number of children for whom medications are prescribed, and the need to carefully determine whether medication, therapy, or intervention that focuses on other factors affecting the child (such as bullying at school or domestic violence within the home) is the best course of action for children experiencing difficulties (Marsa, 2000). Concerns about the overprescription of psychoactive drugs for children, especially stimulant medication, have resulted in recent legislative efforts to prohibit schools from recommending, requiring, or, in some cases, even discussing the idea of a child being evaluated for possible ADHD.

Others suggest that the increased use of stimulant medication is related to better diagnosis and public awareness of the disorder and increased participation in ADHD treatment by females and adolescents, previously underdiagnosed groups (DHHS, 1999). Additionally, ADHD is now diagnosed at earlier ages and, subsequently, medication therapy begins earlier, resulting in more prescriptions being given (Zito et al., 2000). In fact, recent reports have shown that only 2–3 percent of school-age children receive medication for ADHD, suggesting that reports that ADHD is overdiagnosed or that stimulant medications are overprescribed may not be accurate (Goldman, Genel, Bezman, & Slanetz, 1998; Jensen et al., 1999). Unfortunately, apart from the more extensively researched stimulant medications used for ADHD, concerns remain regarding the "off-label" use of medication and the paucity of controlled studies on the safety and efficacy of specific medications being prescribed. It is particularly important for physicians to receive information on the effects of specific drug concentrations, frequency of dose, and the use of medication combined with other therapies (Schaffer et al., 1996).

Several questions are raised. Are medications being used with children safe and effective in treating the specific disorders? Are medications being prescribed too freely? Is there adequate assessment or evaluation to determine whether medication is appropriate? Is there adequate monitoring of the effects of the drug and identification of possible side effects? Is there adequate information on the use of the specific medication with children? For example, clinicians recommend that Ritalin be prescribed only after a comprehensive diagnostic and evaluation procedure. The particular symptom or symptoms to be treated should be identified and the dosage modified if necessary. Prescribing any medication also necessitates the communication of possible side effects and contraindications to the patient and parent. Unfortunately, a large percentage of physicians and psychiatrists do not follow these guidelines (DuPaul & Barkley, 1993), and there is very limited research on some medications used with children, particularly mood stabilizers and newer antipsychotic medications (DHHS, 1999).

---

disorders, reactive attachment disorder, mood disorders, tic disorders, and elimination disorders. Mental retardation and other forms of learning problems were covered in the chapter on cognitive disorders.

Pervasive Developmental Disorders

The **pervasive developmental disorders,** also known as *autism spectrum disorders,* involve severe childhood impairment in areas such as social interaction and communication skills and the display of stereotyped interests and behaviors (Ozonoff & Rogers, 2003).

They include autistic disorder, Rett's disorder, childhood disintegrative disorder, Asperger's disorder, and pervasive developmental disorders not otherwise specified. The prevalence of these disorders is about 28 per 10,000 children (Fombonne, 2003). The pervasive developmental disorders differ distinctly from the psychotic conditions observed in adolescents and adults; they do not include symptoms such as hallucinations, delusions, loosening of associations, or incoherence. A child showing these symptoms probably would be diagnosed with schizophrenia.

The impairments shown in the pervasive developmental disorders are not simply delays in development but are distortions that would not be normal at any developmental stage (Kabot, Masi, & Segal, 2003). We begin our discussion with autistic disorder.

Autistic Disorder

Jim, currently twenty-nine years old, received a diagnosis of autism during his preschool years. His parents reported that Jim was not "cuddly." He would stiffen when touched and preferred being alone. Jim found touching aversive because it produced soundlike sensations, as well as tactile sensations. This was confusing to him. In talking about his reactions, Jim found it difficult to discuss sensations because he believed that his sensory and perceptual sensations were different from those of others. On responding to external stimuli, he replied, "Sometimes the channels get confused, as when sounds come through as color. Sometimes I know that something is coming in somewhere, but I can't tell right away what sense it's coming through" (Cesaroni & Garber, 1991, p. 305). Jim engaged in stereotyped movements involving rocking and twirling. He can now consciously control these behaviors, but they still occur when he is tired and not consciously aware. Any environmental change was very distressing to him. He strongly responded to the sale of the family car as the "loss of a family member." Jim feels different from others and is unable to understand social signals. He describes himself as "communication impaired." He is most comfortable when communication is concrete but not when different subjects or informal conversation occurs. Relationships are enormously difficult to form because of the communication problems.

In 1943 Leo Kanner, a child psychiatrist, identified a triad of behaviors that have come to define the essential features of autism: an extreme isolation and inability to relate to people; a psychological need for sameness; and significant difficulties with communication. Kanner called the syndrome *infantile autism,* from the Greek *autos* ("self"), to reflect the profound aloneness and detachment of these children. A typical characteristic of autistic children is their extreme lack of responsiveness to adults: "The child is aware of people ... but considers them not differently from the way he (or she) considers the desk, bookshelf, or filing cabinet" (Kanner & Lesser, 1958, p. 659).

The puzzling symptoms displayed by the children Kanner described (see opening case, "Leave Me Alone") fit the diagnostic criteria for **autistic disorder** in DSM-IV-TR—qualitative impairment in social interaction and/or communication; restricted, stereotyped interest and activities; and delays or abnormal functioning in a major area before the age of three. Figure

15.1 illustrates some characteristics of children with autism. Autistic disorder is rare—about 10 in every 10,000 children (Fombonne, 2003). The prevalence of autism has not been found to vary across socioeconomic classes, nor are there any significant racial or ethnic variations (Bristol et al., 1996). Autistic disorder occurs four to five times more frequently in boys than in girls (American Psychiatric Association, 2000). Unfortunately, only one-third of children with autism are able to lead even partially independent lives as adults (American Psychiatric Association, 2000).

Impairments   The impairments found with this disorder occur in three major areas: social interactions, verbal and nonverbal communication, and activities and interests (American Psychiatric Association, 2000; Gillberg, 1992; Klin, Volkmar, & Sparrow, 1992).

■ *Social Interactions* Unusual lack of interest in others is a primary aspect of this disorder. Individuals with autism interact as though other people were unimportant objects, and they show little interest in establishing friendships, imitating behaviors, or playing games (Stone & Lemanek, 1990). As a result, children with autistic disorder often fail to develop peer relationships. Disturbances may be displayed in body postures, gestures, facial expressions, and eye contact.

Autistic children appear to be unaware of other people's identity and emotions. They appear not to need physical contact with or emotional responses

FIGURE 15.1 Some Characteristics of Individuals with Autism/Autism Spectrum Disorders   Biological factors appear to be implicated by the unique characteristics shown in autism. For seizures, rates have varied from 3 percent to over 30 percent.

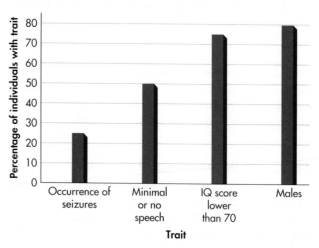

Source: Based on Dawson & Castelloe (1992); Ozonoff & Rogers (2003); Tharp (2003).

from their caretakers. For example, although children with autistic disorder are as likely as other children to smile when they successfully complete a task, they are much less likely to look at an adult to convey this feeling (Kasari, Sigman, Baumgartner, & Stipek, 1993). The social interactive component is missing. One study (Klin, 1991) divided participants into three groups, based on the characteristics of autism, mental retardation, and normal development. The children could choose to listen to their mothers' speech or to the buzz of conversation in a cafeteria. The children in the two comparison groups all showed a strong preference for their mothers' voices. Children with autism were more likely either to prefer the buzzing conversation tape or to show no preference for either selection. Infants with autism are usually content to be left alone and do not show an anticipatory response to being picked up.

■ *Verbal and Nonverbal Communication* About 50 percent of autistic children do not develop meaningful speech. Those who do generally show oddities such as echolalia (echoing what has previously been said). One child constantly repeated the words "How do you spell relief?" without any apparent reason. In addition, the child may reverse pronouns. For example, "you" might be used for "I," and "I" for "me." Even when they can speak, such children may be unable or unwilling to initiate conversations. Children with this disorder also use more nonsensical and idiosyncratic language than that of matched controls (Volden & Lord, 1991).

■ *Activities and Interests* Children with autistic disorder engage in few activities. They often have unusual repetitive habits such as spinning objects, whirling themselves, or fluttering or flapping their arms. They may show intense interest in self-induced sounds or in staring at their hands and fingers. They may stare into space and be totally self-absorbed. Minor changes in the environment may produce rages and tantrums. Children with this disorder also show a lack of imaginary activities.

As many as three-fourths of children with autistic disorder have IQ scores lower than 70. High-functioning individuals such as Jim or the person played by Dustin Hoffman in the movie *Rain Man* account for only a minority of people with this disorder—about 20 percent—who have average to above-average intelligence (Freeman, 1993; Gillberg, 1988). In the past, some theorists, including Kanner, believed that children with autism were unusually bright. They based their beliefs on two phenomena. First, some of them display *splinter skills*—that is, they often do well on one or more isolated tasks such as drawings, puzzle construction, and rote memory but perform poorly on verbal tasks and tasks requiring language skills and symbolic thinking. Second, they sometimes display unusual abilities and are referred to as "autistic savants." One Chinese boy with autism could identify the day of the week for different dates and convert the Gregorian calendar to the Chinese calendar. He also knew the lottery numbers and their drawing dates for the previous three months; the titles of songs in the popular charts for the previous ten years and their dates of release; and the numbers and routes of buses throughout the city (Ho, Tsang, & Ho, 1991). Miller (1999) discussed the association between the symptoms of autistic disorder and the emergence of savant skills, including music, drawing, and calendar calculations, and concluded that it is difficult to know whether autistic savants have particular cognitive strengths or whether the unusual skills are due to their perseverative attention to selected tasks.

Diagnosis Autism, which almost always occurs before age three, might seem to be easy to diagnose,

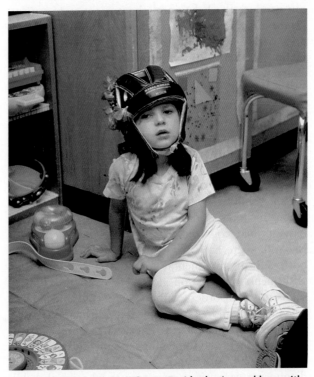

Autistic Girl Wearing Helmet Besides having problems with social interactions and communication, autistic children can show a variety of symptoms, such as impulsivity, temper tantrums, and self-injurious behavior. Here a child is wearing a helmet to prevent damage from head banging. How do self-injurious behaviors arise?

Therapist Signs to Autistic Boy Autistic individuals often benefit from the use of sign language to enhance their receptive and expressive communication skills. Can you think of additional means of communication that might be useful in working with autistic individuals?

given its unique characteristics (Ozonoff & Rogers, 2003). Yet questions have been raised about whether it is a distinct entity. Gillberg (1992) pointed out three problems in diagnosis: (1) different medical conditions can produce the behavioral characteristics of autism, (2) the autistic symptom profile has been found in children with and without signs of neurological impairments, and (3) autistic disorder shares several characteristics with other disorders that involve social and communication impairment. In addition, symptoms can vary widely from child to child, especially with regard to developmental age and level of functioning. Due to the fact that no specific etiological factor has been identified, and because symptoms of the disorder overlap with other pervasive developmental disorders, there is confusion over when to use the term *autism*. Children with autism are often diagnosed as having mental retardation, but their autistic symptoms may not be recognized. The two disorders often coexist. Still, there are ways to distinguish children with both autism and mental retardation from children with mental retardation alone. For example, children with autistic disorder exhibit splinter skills much more often than children with mental retardation. Also, children with mental retardation are more likely to relate to others and to be more socially aware than are children with both autism and mental retardation. In diagnosing cases, it is necessary to observe the children, as well as to interview parents about the children's early development and symptoms (Goodlin-Jones & Solomon, 2003).

Research on Autism   Research on social unresponsiveness and the unusual communication patterns of

autism tends to confirm clinical observations in some limited areas. For example, normal infants can distinguish between male and female and between child and adult, an ability that suggests responsiveness and attention to social cues. In contrast, children with autistic disorder have been described as more interested in inanimate objects than in human beings. Autistic infants fail to socially gaze at parents or others, nor do they engage in pretend play, even when prompted (Charman et al., 1997). Hobson (1987) was interested in this social unresponsiveness and wanted to find out if such children noticed people's age and gender. The researcher matched seventeen children with autism and seventeen control children. Both groups saw videotapes of nonhuman stimuli (bird, dog, train, and car) and videotapes of people (boy, girl, man, and woman), presented one at a time. Before, during, and after the videotaped presentations, the children were asked to match the object or person with five schematic drawings. The children in both groups correctly matched videotapes of nonhuman stimuli with the schematic drawings at least 75 percent of the time. Yet on the videotapes involving people, children in the autism group were highly inaccurate in choosing the correct face, whereas control-group children continued to achieve 75 percent accuracy. Another study found similar results: children with autism did a better job of discriminating between pictures of buildings than between faces (Boucher & Lewis, 1992). They also had difficulty responding to people according to qualities, such as age or gender. Hobson cited an example of a middle-aged man with autism who talked to babies, children, and elderly people with the same style of speech.

As mentioned earlier, some theorists (Baron-Cohen, Leslie, & Frith, 1985; Tager-Flusberg & Sullivan, 1994; Frith, 1991) believe that individuals with autism lack a "theory of mind," that they are unable to attribute mental states to others or to understand that others think and have feelings. As Cowley (1995) described it, "Their worlds are peopled not by fellow beings with thoughts, feelings and agendas but by skin-covered bags that approach and withdraw unpredictably" (p. 67). Their inability to apply mental states to others results in a corresponding inability to lie, deceive, or understand jokes. Parents have said their child "[is] embarrassingly honest," "wouldn't know what a white lie was," "tells jokes but they don't make any sense," and "knows you laugh at the end of [a joke]" (Leekham& Prior, 1994).

Individuals with autistic disorder seem unable to understand that others think and have beliefs. This inability to appreciate other people's mental states appears to be long lasting. Children who showed this deficit displayed unchanged performance seven years later, even though their experience had increased (S. Holroyd & Baron-Cohen, 1993). Even when children with autism "pass" tests in identifying thoughts in others, they do not demonstrate the ability to apply this skill in real-life situations (Leekham& Prior, 1994).

Although we are learning more about the symptoms of autism, many questions remain. What causes the bizarre and puzzling abnormalities that are seen in children with autism? Why do they lack social responsiveness? After a brief discussion of other pervasive developmental disorders, we consider the causes, prognosis, and treatment of autism.

Other Pervasive Developmental Disorders

About 22 in 10,000 children show some but not all of the characteristics of autistic disorder, and they also show severe social impairment (Brook & Bowler, 1992). These children would receive a diagnosis from one of the other categories of the pervasive developmental disorders. The diagnosis may be Rett's disorder, childhood disintegrative disorder, Asperger's disorder, or pervasive developmental disorder not otherwise specified. Characteristics of these disorders often overlap with autistic disorder (see Figure 15.2) to such a degree that some psychologists question whether they should be considered distinctive disorders. Some researchers believe that the various disorders are actually variations and partial expressions of a more primary disorder. They categorize all of the disorders as autism spectrum disorder (Jensen, 2003). Manjiviona and Prior (1995) believe, for example, that people diagnosed with Asperger's disorder are

actually high-functioning individuals with autism. Gillberg (1994) argues that Rett's syndrome is a neurological condition, that although there are autistic symptoms it should not be listed as a pervasive developmental disorder.

Little research exists on children with these diagnoses. To see the difficult diagnostic issues involved, consider the following case of a girl who was videotaped by her parents several times from birth to two years and seven months (Ericksson & de Chateau, 1992).

During the first year of her life the girl showed normal development (smiled, laughed, babbled, waved bye-bye to parents, and played peek-a-boo). During the second year she spoke few words. She sat on the floor and played with a book in a stereotyped manner and showed little response to her parents. After two years of age, she was withdrawn, spoke no words except meaningless phrases from songs. She was preoccupied with rocking or spinning her mother's hair. Computerized axial tomography scans, magnetic resonance imaging, and electroencephalogram readings were normal. No physical disorder was found to be associated with her condition.

Would you diagnose this child as suffering from autistic disorder or one of the following pervasive developmental disorders?

1. *Asperger's disorder* Children with this disorder have significant impairment in social interaction skills, limited and repetitive interests and activities, and lack of emotional reciprocity. They show no

Communicating Through Art
Tito Mukhopadhyay is a 15-year-old boy who is severely autistic but can communicate his thoughts and feelings through prose and poetry. He is pictured here with his mother Soma, who gave up a career in chemistry to devote her life to teaching her son.

FIGURE 15.2 Disorders Chart: Pervasive Developmental Disorders

Asperger's Disorder

Qualitative impairment in social interaction

Repetitive, stereotyped interest and activities

No significant delay in language

No delay in cognitive development (appropriate self-help skills, adaptive behaviors, and curiosity)

Pervasive Developmental Disorder Not Otherwise Specified

Severe and pervasive impairment in reciprocal social interaction or restricted, stereotyped interests

Does not fully meet onset age, specific behavior pattern, or other criteria for any specific pervasive developmental disorder

Autistic Disorder

Qualitative impairment in social interaction (lack of eye contact, failure to develop peer relationships, lack of social empathy or reciprocity)

Qualitative impairment in communication (delay or lack of spoken language, inability to converse, idiosyncratic language, lack of play)

Restricted, stereotyped interest and activities (stereotyped movements, compulsive adherence to rituals, preoccupation with parts of objects)

Delays or abnormal functioning in one of the above major areas before the age of three

PERVASIVE DEVELOPMENTAL DISORDERS

Qualitative impairment in verbal and nonverbal communication and social interaction are primary symptoms.

Rett's Disorder

Normal development for at least five months

Onset between 5 and 48 months
• Deceleration of head growth
• Loss of previously acquired movements and development of stereotyped hand movements
• Loss of social engagement
• Appearance of poorly coordinated movements
• Marked delay and impairment in language
• Diagnosed only in females

Childhood Disintegrative Disorder

Normal development for at least two years

Loss of previously acquired skills in two or more of
• Language
• Social skills
• Bowel or bladder control
• Play
• Motor skills

Qualitative impairment in social interaction

Qualitative impairment in communication

Restricted, stereotyped interest and activities

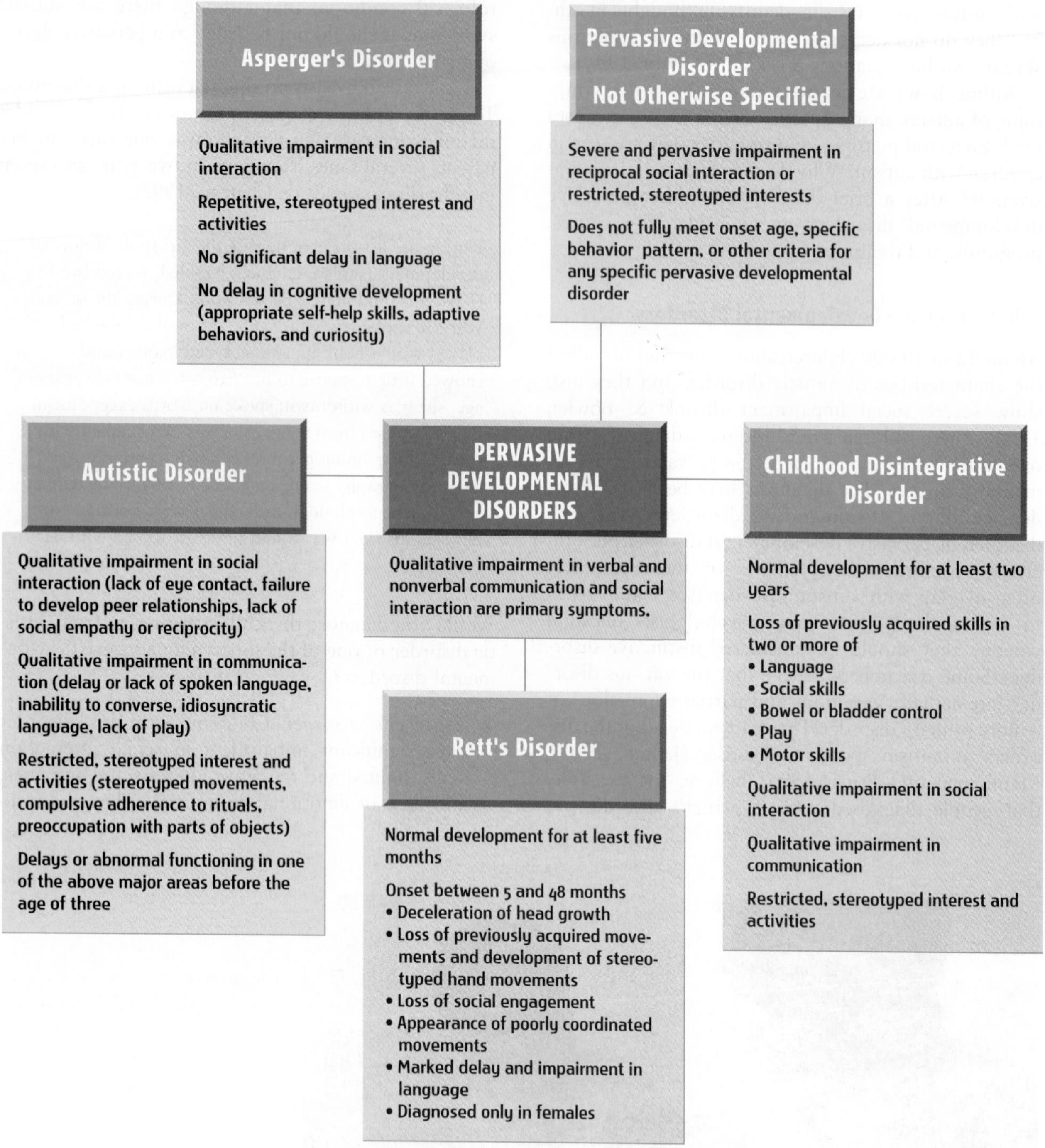

significant delay in cognitive development, and difficulties with communication skills tend to be subtle. An individual may not be diagnosed with Asperger's disorder if, at any time, they have met the diagnostic criteria for autistic disorder. Asperger's disorder is diagnosed five times more frequently in males than females (American

Psychiatric Association, 2000). Individuals with Asperger's disorder do not display the severe communication difficulties seen in those with autistic disorder, although they tend to demonstrate communication difficulties at the social level, such as failure to understand and abide by unspoken rules of conversation, or the tendency to take words

FIGURE 15.2 Disorders Chart: Pervasive Developmental Disorders (continued)

PERVASIVE DEVELOPMENTAL DISORDERS	Prevalence	Age of Onset	Course
Autistic Disorder	Rare; about 0.1% of children; affects many more boys than girls	Early childhood; may be evident during the first few weeks of birth	As many as 75 percent have low IQs; lack of speech and/or social withdrawal quite common; prognosis is poor
Pervasive Developmental Disorder Not Otherwise Specified	0.15% of children	Varies in childhood	Varies depending on uniqueness of the disorder
Rett's Disorder	Rare; diagnosed only in females; often classified as a form of autism	Between 5 and 48 months	Generally lifelong, with marked delay in cognitive, language, and social skills
Childhood Disintegrative Disorder	Rare; often classified as form of autism	Normal development for at least two years; loss occurs between 2–10 years	Normal development during first two years of life, followed by disintegration of social, verbal, and motor skills
Asperger's Disorder	Rare; about 0.025% of children; affects many more boys than girls	Early childhood	Impairment in social skills and emotional reciprocity; does not seem to affect language and cognitive development

Source: Data from DSM-IV-TR; Fombonne, 2004; Harris (1995); Manjiviona & Prior (1995).

literally (Perner, 2001). Individuals with Asperger's disorder exhibit an "eccentric and one-sided social approach to others rather than the social or emotional indifference seen in autistic disorder" and may even be seen as intellectually precocious in their early years due to an adult-like vocabulary, particularly in an area where they have obsessive interest (American Psychiatric Association, 2000). In fact, due to the outwardly sophisticated language skills of some children with Asperger's disorder, it may be at first assumed that their social difficulties are due to negativism rather than a lack of understanding of social interactions (Volkmar, Klin, Schultz, Rubin, & Bronen, 2000).

Although Asperger's disorder was not an official diagnosis until DSM-IV (American Psychiatric Association, 1994), the constellation of symptoms was first described by an Austrian physician, Hans Asperger, in 1944 shortly after Kanner first described autism. In fact, Asperger referred to the group of children he described as having an "autistic personality disorder." Wing (1981) renewed interest in the syndrome described by Asperger with a resultant introduction of the topic to the current literature. In view of the symptoms of social isolation, interpersonal relationship difficulties, communication abnormalities, desire for sameness, and narrow interests that are so similar to autistic disorder, there is continuing controversy as to whether or not Asperger's disorder is, in fact, a separate disorder or simply a description of high-functioning individuals with autistic disorder, particularly because the neuropsychological profiles of the two groups are quite similar (Miller & Ozonoff, 2000).

2. *Childhood disintegrative disorder* This disorder is characterized by at least two years of normal development in social relationships, verbal and nonverbal communication, motor skills, play, and bowel or bladder control, with subsequent severe impairment and deterioration in two or more of these skills beginning between two and ten years of age. The child also develops autistic-like symptoms, including impairment in social interaction, communication, and repetitive or stereotyped behaviors and interests.

3. *Rett's disorder* This disorder is characterized by normal development for at least five months and an onset of symptoms between five and forty-eight months, including deceleration of head growth, a loss of purposeful hand skills replaced by stereotyped hand movements, severely impaired language development, and a loss of social interaction skills. This condition has been diagnosed only in females. The discovery in 1999 of the gene for Rett's disorder has resulted in ongoing research into ways to slow, reverse, or even prevent the disorder in affected girls (National Institute of Child Health and Human Development, 1999).

4. *Pervasive developmental disorder not otherwise specified.* This category is for cases that are not typical in terms of age of onset or specific behavior pattern. Pervasive and severe impairment in reciprocal social interactions occurs, as do communication abnormalities and limited interests and activities. These children do not, however, meet the full criteria for autistic disorder.

Did you have trouble choosing a diagnosis? Based on the information given (approximately one year of normal development, severe isolation and communication difficulties, repetitive behaviors, no mention of deceleration of head growth), you may have correctly concluded that autistic disorder would be the most likely diagnosis. However, diagnosis involving the specific pervasive developmental disorders is difficult, and the appropriate criteria for each are still evolving.

Etiology

Limited research has been done on Rett's disorder, childhood disintegrative disorder, and Asperger's disorder, as they were new to the DSM-IV (American Psychiatric Association, 1994). Our discussion of etiology will therefore be confined to autistic disorder. There are four major etiological groupings in autism

(Gillberg, 1992): (1) familial autism, (2) autism related to a medical condition, (3) autism associated with nonspecific brain dysfunction, and (4) autism without a family history or associated brain dysfunction. One very puzzling aspect of this disorder is that different factors are associated with different cases (Folstein & Rutter, 1988; Gillberg, 1992; Volkmar et al., 1988). How the syndrome of autism can develop from so many different conditions is not known. One important implication of the four sets of conditions is that no single cause for autism is likely to be found. Because of the early lack of normal development and distinct social and cognitive deficits, researchers increasingly believe that autism results from biological rather than psychosocial factors. However, the early explanations for autism, evolving from psychodynamic theory, involved parent-child relationships.

Psychodynamic Theories Early psychodynamic theories of autism stressed the importance of deviant parent-child interactions in producing this condition. Kanner (1943), who named the syndrome, concluded that cold and unresponsive parenting is responsible for the development of autism. He described the parents as "successfully autistic," "cold, humorless perfectionists who preferred reading, writing, playing music, or thinking" (p. 663). These individuals "happened to defrost long enough to produce a child" (Steffenburg & Gillberg, 1989). Kanner has since changed his position and now believes the disorder is "innate."

Psychological factors are implicated in many disorders, but they do not seem to be involved in autism. Unfortunately, many mental health professionals continue to inflict guilt on parents who already bear the burden of raising a child with this disorder. Parents of children with autism show much stress and are particularly concerned about the well-being of their children after they can no longer take care of them (Koegel et al., 1992). In light of current research, no justification exists for allowing parents to think they caused their child's autism.

Family and Genetic Studies Current research is continuing to focus on genetics and the understanding of brain abnormalities underlying autistic disorder (National Institute of Neurological Disorders and Stroke, 2001). About 2 to 9 percent of siblings of children with autism also have this disorder; this rate is 100 to 200 times greater than that of the general population (American Psychiatric Association, 2000; Bolton et al., 1994; Ritvo et al., 1989; Smalley & Asarnow, 1990). These findings are supportive of genetic influences. E. H. Cook (1998) reported much greater concordance in identical than in fraternal twins.

A well-controlled twin study was performed by Folstein and Rutter (1977). They recruited fraternal and identical twins, some of whom were discordant and some concordant. (That is, in some pairs both twins had autism; in others only one twin had the disorder.) Identification as identical or fraternal was determined through blood analysis, and diagnoses were made without knowing who the twins' siblings were or whether the twins were fraternal or identical. The concordance rate for twenty-one pairs of twins was 36 percent for identical twins and 0 percent for fraternal twins. An interesting finding of the Folstein and Rutter study is that seven of the discordant identical twins showed some language impairment—one characteristic of autism. Folstein and Rutter also believe that the diathesis-stress model could account for some of their findings. In twelve of the seventeen discordant twin pairs, the twin with autism had suffered some birth complication. So a predisposition interacting with an environmental stressor may result in the disorder.

Central Nervous System Impairment Autistic disorder appears to be a neurodevelopmental disorder involving some form of inherited brain dysfunction (Rutter, 1994). However, what is confusing is that autistic disorder seems to be associated with many organic conditions (Bolton, Rutter, Butler, & Summers, 1989; Ghaziuddin, Tsai, Eilers, & Ghaziuddin, 1992), none of which are specific only to autism. Conditions such as the fragile X chromosome (malformation of the X chromosome), tuberous sclerosis (a congenital hereditary disease associated with brain tumors), neurofibromatosis (tumors of the peripheral nerves), phenylketonuria (PKU), and intrauterine rubella (measles) have been reported among children with autistic disorder. These diseases affect the central nervous system, but most people undergo them without developing autism. It is estimated that between one-fourth to one-third of those diagnosed with a pervasive developmental disorder eventually demonstrate seizures (American Psychiatric Association, 2000; National Institute of Neurological Disorders and Stroke, 2001).

That so many organic conditions are associated with autism has caused some researchers to search for central nervous system impairment—possibly in the left hemisphere, which is associated with cognition and language. Results have been mixed. Researchers have reported some differences in brain structure between autistic and nonautistic individuals (Courchesne, Yeung-Courchesne, Press, Hesselink, & Jernigan, 1988; Courchesne, 1995). For example, Hashimoto and his colleagues (1995) found that certain parts of the brainstem and cerebellum are significantly smaller in individuals with autism than in members of control

groups. However, other researchers found no difference in similar comparisons (Garber & Ritvo, 1992).

No consistent pattern of impairment has yet been found, which is perhaps to be expected, given the different subgroups of autism. Rutter and colleagues (Rutter, MacDonald, et al. 1990) believe that some of the confusion is due to including samples of "atypical" autism and other pervasive developmental disorders in studies of autism. Each of these may have etiological components that differ from those of "true" autism. The etiological picture may become clearer once the distinctions among the different pervasive developmental disorders are accepted.

Biochemical Studies Researchers are also interested in the role that neurotransmitters may play in autistic disorder. But the studies are difficult to interpret because they often use different intellectual and behavioral measures and because they may study different subgroups of people with autism (DuVerglas, Banks, & Guyer, 1988). Nevertheless, some children with this disorder do have elevated serotonin and dopamine levels. Ritvo and colleagues (1984) reported elevated blood serotonin levels in a minority of such patients. The significance of this elevation is still not clear, but it suggests a promising line of research. Nelson et al. (2001) report that, based on a study involving the archiving and later study of blood samples taken at birth, children who later developed mental retardation or autistic disorder showed elevated levels of neural growth factors, a protein important in the prenatal formation of the central nervous system.

Prognosis

The prognosis for children with pervasive developmental disorders is mixed. Approximately 25 percent are able to function in a supported environment, and another 25 percent will be able to live independently although social impairment continues (Ratey, Grandin, & Miller, 1992). The prognosis is somewhat better for those who are considered high functioning with good verbal skills. For example, Temple Grandin overcame the symptoms of autistic disorder to earn a doctorate in animal science and is now a recognized leader in the field of livestock handling (Ratey et al., 1992). The prognosis for those with Asperger's disorder tends to be the most promising. Many individuals with the disorder are self-sufficient and successfully employed. There are reports of significant intellectual success for some with Asperger's disorder; in fact, it is reported that compelling evidence exists that Albert Einstein exhibited symptoms consistent with Asperger's disorder or high-functioning autism (Perner, 2001).

Treatment

Because patients with these disorders have communication or social impairments, pervasive developmental disorders are very difficult to treat. Therapy with the parents, family therapy, drug therapy, and behavior modification techniques are all currently being used, with some success (Ozonoff & Rogers, 2003). Intensive behavior modification programs seem the most promising treatment. Interventions for those with Asperger's disorder can include verbally mediated therapies, such as structured problem-solving therapy, due to the higher level of language development demonstrated by this group compared with those with other pervasive developmental disorders (Volkmar et al., 2000).

Drug Therapy   The antipsychotic medication haloperidol can produce modest reductions in withdrawal, stereotypical movements, and fidgetiness. However, long-term use produces movement problems and other side effects in many children (Gadow, 1991). Other medications, such as selective serotonin reuptake inhibitors, have also been used to decrease anxiety and repetitive behaviors and to improve expressive language skills.

There has been significant interest in ongoing research on the use of secretin, a hormone that controls digestion, which is routinely administered during diagnostic gastrointestinal procedures. Interest in this hormone began when Victoria Beck made the connection between her son's infusion with secretin during a GI endoscopy procedure and the subsequent reduction of his autistic symptoms (Autism Society of Wisconsin, 2001; Paulson, 1999). Similar improvement in symptoms following secretin use has been reported in other children (Hovarth et al., 1998). However, many of the treatments have been initially encouraging but then disappointing once experimental studies have been conducted that control for placebo effects (des Portes, Hagerman, & Hendren, 2003).

Behavior Modification   Behavior modification procedures have been used effectively to eliminate echolalia, self-mutilation, and self-stimulation. They also have effectively increased attending behaviors, verbalizations, and social play through social interaction training (Oke & Schreibman, 1990; Plienis et al., 1987; Harris, 1995). Shiver, Allen, and Mathews (1999) indicate that applied behavior analysis has by far the strongest empirical support in the treatment of autistic disorder.

Comprehensive early childhood treatment programs have shown positive results, particularly with respect to measured IQ. Effective programs involve a curriculum focused extensively on social and communication skills, a structured teaching environment, a predictable routine, and use of choices to prevent problem behaviors, Family involvement and a carefully planned transition into the elementary school environment are also important factors. Research is still needed regarding the optimal intensity of intervention (Gresham, Beebe-Frankenberger, & MacMillan, 1999).

Even with intervention, certain symptoms of social impairment generally remain (Siegel, 2003). Even high-functioning adults with autistic disorder display problem behaviors involving inappropriate communication and poor interpersonal skills. One group of high-functioning autistic adults had problems obtaining employment because of behaviors such as rudely terminating or interrupting conversations, walking sideways, or waving arms in a robotlike fashion. Through behavioral interventions, these adults were able to become competitively employed, although some oddities of behavior remained (Burt, Fuller, & Lewis, 1991; Estrada & Pinsof, 1995).

Other Developmental Disorders

How do we know whether a child has a childhood disorder? Such decisions are often based on vague and arbitrary interpretations of the extent to which a given child deviates from some "acceptable" norm. And, as some critics have observed, the decision frequently depends on the tolerance of the referring agent. Cultural factors also play a role in the types of problems identified. In Thailand, where aggression is discouraged and values such as peacefulness, politeness, and deference are encouraged, clinic referrals are primarily for overcontrolled behaviors (fearfulness, sleep problems, somatization). In the United States, where independence and competitiveness are emphasized, problems generally involve undercontrolled behaviors (disobedience, fighting, arguing; Tharp, 1991). Table 15.1 compares some problem behaviors reported by teachers in four different countries.

The less severe childhood and adolescent disturbances cover a wide range of problems. In this section we discuss some of the more common disorders: attention deficit/hyperactivity disorders, disruptive disorders, separation-anxiety disorders, tic disorders, reactive attachment disorder, and elimination disorders.

Problems with Diagnosis

Has DSM-IV-TR done much to improve the reliability and validity of the diagnosis of childhood disorders? Unfortunately, criticisms remain. The difference between what is abnormal and what is a normal

TABLE 15.1   Behavioral Symptoms Reported by Teachers of Children in Four Countries (in Percent)

	Rutter et al. (1974)				Minde (1977)	McGee et al. (1985)		Ekblad (1990)	
Year	1974				1977	1982		1984	
Place	England				Uganda	New Zealand		China	
Informant	Teacher				Teacher	Teacher		Teacher	
Age group (years)	10				7–15	7		11–13	
Population	Nonimmigrant		West Indian		Ugandan	New Zealand		Chinese	
Gender	Boys	Girls	Boys	Girls	Both	Boys	Girls	Boys	Girls
Number	873	816	172	182	577	491	449	139	127
Behavioral disturbances									
Hyperactivity	30.5	17.9	49.5	32.4	15.0	33.0	17.4	13.7	2.4
Tics, twitches	8.3	3.6	7.0	5.5	6.7	5.5	4.9	0.7	0.0
Nailbiting	17.5	14.7	13.9	10.4	7.2	3.9	6.4	7.9	1.6
Thumbsucking	5.1	6.4	2.9	8.2	3.8	4.9	7.4	7.9	0.0
Stuttering	8.2	2.4	10.5	1.1	5.8	5.3	2.7	2.9	2.4
Aggressiveness	24.3	13.9	51.7	34.1	12.8	22.4	14.9	19.4	3.9
Depression	18.5	15.5	26.2	31.8	19.4	11.8	15.6	6.5	2.4
Anxiety	32.5	30.0	32.0	25.3	17.2	36.0	31.6	5.0	0.8
Phobias	28.5	26.1	32.0	35.7	9.9	27.5	28.3	7.2	6.3
Lying	12.5	6.3	30.2	25.3	10.1	11.8	8.7	16.6	2.4
Theft	3.4	1.7	13.4	13.2	4.4	5.3	4.2	1.4	0.8
Truancy	5.6	1.9	5.2	1.6	7.3	1.2	0.4	4.3	0.0

Note: Reports of behavioral symptoms vary according to country. Teachers of West Indian children reported the most aggression in their students, whereas teachers of Chinese students reported students to have few problems with anxiety.
Source: Ekblad (1990).

developmental process is often a matter of degree of the particular behavior, such as the noncompliant behavior that can typify an adolescent's search for independence compared with the parallel, yet more severe, behavior that may be seen in mood disorders or oppositional defiant disorder. At times, behavior that may look abnormal may actually be the child's adaptation to adverse home or social environments. It is therefore essential for mental health professionals to have a complete understanding of the child's social and developmental history and past experiences (including the magnitude and timing of any significant stressors), because they all may interact with the biological, as well as the personality, characteristics of the child. Unfortunately, guidelines for assessing the type of behavior and the degree of deviation necessary for a given diagnosis remain vague and often depend on "clinical judgment." Controversy exists over the number or types of behaviors that are needed for a diagnosis. If the diagnosis is too easy to make, false positives will occur, and children will be stigmatized. If the diagnosis is too difficult, individuals who need help will not be identified. The correct balance has been difficult to determine for many childhood disorders. The clinician must decide whether problem behaviors are present and then whether they are "excessive," "maladaptive," or "inappropriate" for the developmental level. Even mental health professionals have difficulty making such judgments. Whether a problem exists is often "in the eye of the beholder."

Attention Deficit/Hyperactivity Disorders and Disruptive Behavior Disorders

Attention deficit/hyperactivity disorders and disruptive behavior disorders involve symptoms that are often socially disruptive and distressing to others (see Figure 15.3). They include attention deficit/hyperactivity disorders (ADHD), conduct disorder, and oppositional defiant disorder (see the opening cases "Sit Still and Pay Attention" and "No, I Won't"). These disorders often occur together and have overlapping symptoms. Without intervention, these disorders tend to persist (Farmer, 1995; Fergusson, Horwood, & Lynskey, 1995; Root & Resnick, 2003). In a longitudinal study of "hard to manage" preschoolers followed from age three until school entry and then to age nine, 67 percent showed clinically significant problems at age six and met the criteria for one of the disorders in this category (Campbell & Ewing, 1990). The children displayed problem behaviors such as inattention, overactivity, and aggression, and they required supervision. Early identification and intervention are necessary to interrupt the negative course of these disorders.

Raising a child with a disruptive behavior disorder is difficult. Parents report more negative feelings about parenting, higher stress levels, and a more negative impact on their social lives than do parents of normally developing children (Donenberg & Baker, 1993).

Attention Deficit/Hyperactivity Disorders

Ron, an only child, was always on the go as a toddler and preschooler. He had many accidents because of his continual climbing and risk taking. Temper outbursts were frequent. In kindergarten Ron had much difficulty staying seated for group work and in completing projects. The quality of his work was poor. In the first grade, Ron was referred to the school psychologist for evaluation. Although his high activity level and lack of concentration were not so pronounced in this one-on-one situation, his impulsive approach to tasks and short attention span were evident throughout the interview. Ron was referred to a local pediatrician who specializes in attention deficit disorders. The pediatrician prescribed Ritalin, which helped reduce Ron's activity level.

Attention deficit/hyperactivity disorder (ADHD) is characterized by socially disruptive behaviors—either attentional problems or hyperactivity—that are present before age seven and persist for at least six months. *Hyperactivity* is a confusing term because it refers to both a diagnostic category and behavioral characteristics. Children who are "overactive" or who have "short attention spans" are often referred to as "hyperactive," even though they may not meet the diagnostic criteria for this disorder. Whether a child is merely overactive or has ADHD is often difficult to determine.

Three types of attention deficit/hyperactivity disorders are recognized:

- *ADHD, predominantly hyperactive-impulsive type,* is characterized by behaviors such as heightened motoric activity (fidgeting and squirming), short attention span, distractibility, impulsiveness, and lack of self-control. Children with this type of ADHD tend to have a pattern of being rejected by peers and more accidental injuries (American Psychiatric Association, 2000).

- *ADHD, predominantly inattentive type,* is characterized by problems such as distractibility, difficulty with sustained attention, inattention to detail, and difficulty completing tasks. Children with attentional deficits tend to have less severe conduct problems and impulsivity than children with the hyperactive form of ADHD. Instead, they are more likely to be described as sluggish, daydreamers, anxious, and shy; they respond to lower doses of stimulants than do children with hyperactivity (Frick & Lahey, 1991). This type of ADHD affects approximately the same number of boys as girls and tends to have the greatest impact on academic performance (American Psychiatric Association, 2000).

- *ADHD, combined type,* is probably the most common form of the disorder. In this case, the criteria for both the hyperactive and inattentive types are met.

A confusing aspect of attention deficit/hyperactivity disorder is the apparent inconsistency. Attentional deficit and excessive motor activity are not necessarily observed in all settings. Boys with ADHD, for example, may show greater motor activity during academic tasks but may not differ from normally functioning children during lunch, recess, and physical education activities. Thus a child might be identified as hyperactive in one situation but not in others. To receive a diagnosis of ADHD, the individual must display these characteristics in two or more situations (American Psychiatric Association, 2000).

ADHD is relatively common. Estimates of its prevalence range from 3 to 7 percent of school-age children, with boys much more likely to receive this diagnosis than girls, especially the hyperactive-impulsive subtype (American Psychiatric Association, 2000). ADHD is

FIGURE 15.3 Disorders Chart: Attention Deficit and Disruptive Behavior Disorders

Attention Deficit/Hyperactive Disorder

Symptoms are present before age seven

Disruptive behavior in either one or both of the following:
• Attentional problems (distractible, inattentive, not completing tasks)
• Hyperactivity (impulsive, heightened motor activity, interrupts)

Symptoms are present in two or more settings

Clear evidence of interference with social or academic functioning

ATTENTION DEFICIT AND DISRUPTIVE BEHAVIOR DISORDERS

These disorders involve socially disruptive behaviors that distress others. Disruptive behavior pattern must be present for at least six months.

Oppositional Defiant Disorder

Pattern of negativistic, hostile, and defiant behavior

Often loses temper, argues with adults, and defies or refuses adult requests

Does not take responsibility for actions

Angry and resentful

Often blames others

Often spiteful and vindictive

Conduct Disorder

Often bullies or threatens others

Lying and cheating common

Deliberately destroys property

Steals

Often truant from school

May be physically cruel to people and animals

Often initiates physical fights

Serious violations of rules

ATTENTION DEFICIT AND DISRUPTIVE BEHAVIOR DISORDERS	Prevalence	Age of Onset	Course
Attention Deficit/Hyperactive Disorder	3–7 percent of the school population; males are more likely to have this diagnosis	Usually diagnosed in elementary school but probably begins earlier	Marked improvement usually becomes noticeable at 18–24 years of age; in some cases, continues to affect the person as an adult
Oppositional Defiant Disorder	1–3 percent; found more often in males; difficult to estimate since determining normal and pathological defiance is a relative judgment	Generally before age 8	May be lifelong or situational
Conduct Disorder	1–10 percent of children; mostly males; more common in urban settings	May be childhood-onset type or adolescent-onset type	Prognosis poor; often leads to criminal behaviors, antisocial acts, and problems in adult adjustment to relationships and occupational responsibilities

Source: Data from American Psychiatric Association (2000); Gaub & Carlson (1997); Lewinsohn et al. (1993).

particularly difficult to diagnose in preschool-age children because there is such variability in their attentional skills and activity levels, in addition to the fact that preschoolers have fewer demands for sustained attention. ADHD is a persistent disorder. Children with ADHD continue to show problems with impulsivity, family conflicts, and attention during adolescence (Gaub & Carlson, 1997). This is especially likely if a disruptive disorder is also present (Barkley, Fischer, Edelbrock, & Smallish, 1991). Follow-up studies suggest that between 30 and 50 percent of children diagnosed with ADHD continue to experience symptoms such as inattention, fidgeting, difficulty sitting still, and impulsive actions throughout adulthood (Jackson & Farrugia, 1997). These difficulties may affect social relationships and occupational functioning.

The prognosis for children with only attentional problems is more promising. Forty percent of children display attentional problems at some point in their lives, but they persist in only about 5 percent of cases (Palfrey, Levine, Walker, & Sullivan, 1985).

ADHD is associated with many behavioral and academic problems. Children with this disorder are more likely to need to attend special classes or schools, to drop out of school, and to misbehave, become delinquent, or have problems with the law (Greene, Biederman, Faraone, & Ouellette, 1996; Lambert, 1988; Mariani & Barkley, 1997). Boys with ADHD have more difficulty in less structured situations or in activities demanding sustained attention. Based on parent reports, boys with ADHD show more sadness, anger, and guilt than those without ADHD (Braaten & Rosen, 2000). It is crucial to understand ADHD within the psychosocial context of the individual child (Johnston, Fine, Weiss, & Weiss, 2000).

Etiology   Many researchers believe that the symptoms of overactivity, short attention span, and impulsiveness suggest central nervous system involvement. In fact, many conditions thought to cause neurological impairment—such as lead poisoning, chromosomal abnormalities, neurotransmitter deficits, oxygen deprivation during birth, and fetal alcohol syndrome—have been associated with ADHD (Hynd, Hern, Voeller, & Marshall, 1991; Department of Health and Human Services [DHHS], 1999). The affected areas of the brain are thought to be the reticular activating system (attention), frontal lobes (voluntary control of attention and inhibition of inappropriate emotional or behavioral responses), and the temporal-parietal regions (involuntary attention). It has been suggested that because stimulant medications increase the availability of dopamine (a neurotransmitter that affects alertness, purposeful movement, and motivation), ADHD may be caused by inadequate dopamine in the central nervous system; this possibility has led to genetic research involving the dopamine-receptor genes on chromosomes 5 and 11 (DHHS, 1999). Researchers are continuing to examine the neuroanatomy of the brain and the relationship of differences or dysfunction to the symptoms seen in the various subtypes of ADHD (Castellanos, Giedd, Berquin, & Walter, 2001; Erk, 2000). The recent use of ionizing radiation using a SPECT (single-photon emission computed tomography) scan has led to many questions about how to interpret the findings due to the lack of comparative data from nonsymptomatic controls. It has been recommended (Giedd, 2001) that before using any kind of imaging procedure it is important to answer the question, Will the outcome of this procedure influence the course of treatment for this child? Neuroimaging studies are providing insight into the psychophysiology of disorders; however, given the lack of control data and the wide range of normal findings, they have limited use as a diagnostic tool other than ruling out obvious problems such as brain tumors (Giedd, 2001).

Some researchers believe that certain foods or food additives produce physiological changes in the brain or other parts of the body, resulting in hyperactive behaviors. This view was promoted by Feingold (1977), who developed a diet excluding these substances. Sugar has also been suspected as a causal factor in ADHD (Chollar, 1988). Approximately 45 percent of physicians have recommended low-sugar diets for children with ADHD (Bennett & Sherman, 1983). Many parents have tried the recommended diets for their children, and many claim that their children's behavior improved. But parental expectations or treating the children differently (e.g., going shopping with them to buy only certain foods) might result in behavioral changes. In one study (Hoover & Milich, 1994), mothers were told that their "sugar-sensitive" sons had just received a drink that contained sugar or a sugar substitute (placebo). All children received only the sugar substitute. The mothers were asked to rate the behavior of their sons as viewed during a videotaped play session. The mothers who believed their sons ingested sugar rated the sons as significantly more hyperactive, even though the videotapes recorded no increases in motor activity in the sons. Clearly, expectations can also result in misperceptions.

To determine whether certain chemicals or sugars are implicated in hyperactivity, carefully controlled double-blind studies have also been conducted. Some of these studies involved a "biological challenge test." In this design, the diets of the children were alternated

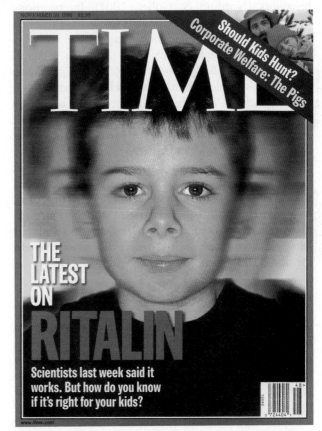

What Is the Effect of Eating Candy? Many parents and professionals believe that the ingestion of sugar or certain food additives can lead to hyperactivity in children and adults. Why does this belief remain even though most well-designed studies do not find this link?

so that some of the time they ate food with the additive and other times without. The parents were not aware of the type of food they were giving their children. Reviews of such studies showed that eliminating food additives or certain chemicals from the diets of hyperactive children had little effect on their behavior (Consensus Development Panel, 1982; Milich & Pelham, 1986; Wolraich, Wilson, & White, 1995).

Family variables also seem related to ADHD, although it is not clear whether genetic or environmental factors or some combination of the two is involved. Evidence supporting the hypothesis of genetic transmission includes higher prevalence rates for the disorder in the first- and second-degree relatives of children with ADHD and higher concordance rates for this disorder among identical twins (Gillis, Gilger, Pennington, & DeFries, 1992; Knopf, 1984). Recent twin and sibling pair studies in Australia also support the idea that ADHD symptoms are highly heritable in both boys and girls (Rhee, Waldman, Hay, & Levy, 1999).

Treatment Many children with ADHD have been treated with drug therapy. Approximately 75–90 percent of children with ADHD respond positively to stimulant medication (DHHS, 1999). The drugs seem to treat the symptoms of ADHD (particularly hyperactivity, impulsivity, and inattention) rather than its causes, so drug therapy alone does not produce any long-term benefits. Direct effects on the school achievement of ADHD children are seldom seen (Cantwell, 1996).

Satterfield, Hoppe, and Schell (1982) believe that using medication alone may be harmful because drug

A Partial Solution As is evident in this cover story for *Time* magazine, medication is a widely used treatment for attention deficit/hyperactivity disorders. Medication alone can be harmful, however, because it treats only the symptoms of the disorder and not the causes. Behavior therapy may be needed as well to overcome antisocial behavior, poor peer relationships, and learning difficulties.

therapy fails to address such problems as antisocial behavior, poor peer relationships, and learning difficulties. In fact, some studies that compared medication and behavior therapy in treating ADHD report that combining the two treatments produces the most positive results (Carlson, Pelham, Milich, & Dixon, 1992; DuPaul & Barkley, 1993). Other clinicians have suggested that both physicians and therapists should pay more attention to family dynamics and child management problems rather than rely solely on pharmacological intervention. Self-instructional procedures, modeling, role playing, classroom contingency management programs, and parent training programs have been useful in dealing with the problems of children with ADHD (Abramowitz & O'Leary, 1991; Whalen & Henker, 1991). It has been strongly suggested that mental health professionals working with children with suspected ADHD use systematic observation and data gathering to look for environmental factors that may be overtly or inadvertently encouraging problem behaviors (Northup & Gulley, 2001). Interventions based on functional behavior assessment have resulted in almost complete elimination of aggressive behavior in children with high activity levels (Boyajian, DuPaul, Handler, Eckert, & McGoey, 2001). Simply providing recesses to schoolchildren with ADHD has been found to be beneficial in reducing inappropriate behaviors (Ridgway, Northup, Pellegrin, LaRue, & Hightshoe, 2003). The National Institute of Mental Health instituted the NIMH Multimodal Study of ADHD with the goal of obtaining information regarding best practices in the use of medication with ADHD; it was concluded that, even when used without other interventions, carefully managed and monitored use of stimulant medication is effective in reducing ADHD symptoms and that behavioral treatment seems to have the greatest benefit for non-ADHD symptoms (Greenhill et al., 1998).

Oppositional Defiant Disorder

Oppositional defiant disorder (ODD) is characterized by a negativistic, argumentative, and hostile behavior pattern. Children with this disorder often lose their temper, argue with adults, and defy or refuse adult requests. They may refuse to do chores and refuse to take responsibility for their actions. The defiant behavior is directed primarily toward parents, teachers, and other people in authority. Anger, resentment, blaming others, and spiteful and vindictive behaviors are common. Although confrontation often occurs, it does not involve the more serious violations of the rights of others that are involved in conduct disorders. Before puberty more males than females meet the criterion for this disorder, with closer to equal numbers after

puberty (American Psychiatric Association, 2000).

Oppositional defiant disorder is a relatively new category and is certainly one of the more controversial childhood disorders. It is often difficult to separate this disorder from milder forms of conduct disorder and from normal developmental difficulties in children and adolescents (Paternite, Loney, & Roberts, 1995). Most children and adolescents go through a period or several periods of defiant behaviors. In DSM-IV-TR, a criterion indicating that the problem causes "significant impairment in social or academic functioning" was added to try to discriminate between "normal" and "pathological" defiance. ODD tends to be associated with parent-child conflict, the espousing of unreasonable beliefs, and negative family interactions (Barkley, Anastopoulos, Guevremont, & Fletcher, 1992). Because DSM-IV attempted to raise the threshold for the diagnosis of ODD, it is not clear how this will affect conclusions of studies using a lower threshold.

Conduct Disorders

Charles was well known to school officials for his many fights with peers. After a stabbing incident at school, he was put on probation and then transferred to another junior high school. Two months later, at age fourteen, Charles was charged with armed robbery and placed in a juvenile detention facility. He had few positive peer contacts at the juvenile facility and seemed unwilling or unable to form close relationships. Some progress was achieved with a behavioral contract program that involved positive reinforcement from adults and praise for refraining from aggression in handling conflicts. He was transferred to a maximum-security juvenile facility when he seriously injured two of his peers, whose teasing had angered him. Charles completed a vocational training program in this second facility, but he couldn't hold a regular job. He was sent to prison following a conviction for armed robbery.

Conduct disorders are characterized by a persistent pattern of antisocial behaviors that violate the rights of others. Many children and adolescents display isolated instances of antisocial behavior, but this diagnosis is given only when the behavior is repetitive and persistent. Conduct disorders may include behaviors such as bullying, lying, cheating, fighting, destruction of property, stealing, setting fires, cruelty to people and animals, assaults, rape, and truant behavior. The pattern of misconduct must last for at least twelve months to warrant this diagnosis (American Psychiatric Association, 2000). The diagnosis of conduct disorder applies only when the behaviors reflect dysfunction in the individual rather than a reaction to the individual's social and economic environment. Males with this disorder tend to display confrontational aggressiveness such as fighting, stealing, and vandalism, whereas females are more likely to display truancy, running away, substance abuse, prostitution, or chronic lying. Estimates of prevalence range from 1 to 10 percent of the population. It is more common in males and in urban settings (American Psychiatric Association, 2000). Two types of conduct disorder are recognized: (1) childhood-onset type (at least one conduct problem occurs before age ten) and (2) adolescent-onset type (conduct problem occurs after age ten). Early onset for both boys and girls is related to more chronic and more serious offenses. Less serious behavior limited to the adolescent years is associated with later onset (Tolan & Thomas, 1995). Early-onset conduct disorder is related to a greater risk of adult antisocial personality disorder, with between 25 and 50 percent of highly antisocial children becoming antisocial adults (DHHS, 1999).

Conduct disorders in adolescence represent a serious societal problem. In the United States, approximately 83,000 juveniles are housed in correctional institutions for antisocial behaviors, and 1.75 million were arrested in 1990 (Zigler, Taussig, & Black, 1992). Parents often report the following pattern in the development of the disorder: early arguments, stubbornness, and tantrums, oppositional behaviors leading to fire setting and stealing and then truancy, vandalism, and substance abuse (Robins, 1991). Children and adolescents with conduct disorders have a greater tendency to seek novel situations and are less concerned about avoiding risk or harm (Schmeck & Poustka, 2001). Although oppositional-defiant disorder frequently precedes childhood-onset conduct disorder, it is important to note that many children with oppositional-defiant disorder do not later exhibit a conduct disorder. Although many childhood disorders remit over time, children are less likely to outgrow conduct disorders. Lambert, Wahler, Andrade, and Bickman (2001) emphasize the global nature of the difficulties experienced by children with conduct disorder. Children with this disorder not only have the externalizing aggressive behaviors that define the disorder but many also display internalizing symptoms, such as withdrawal and major depression, perhaps due to the social alienation created by their behaviors. It is interesting to note that childhood depression has been found to be a strong predictor of personality disorder in adulthood, including antisocial personality, although it is not clear if the relationship is related to genetics or to the psychological outcomes of depressed mood (Harrington, 2001). Barry et al. (2000) found that subgroups of children with severe conduct disorder who also show callous, unemotional personality traits do not show much distress about their behavioral difficulties, a pattern consistent with adults who have antisocial personality traits. It may be that the group of children who show conduct-disordered behavioral symptoms but who do not have callous, unemotional personalities are, in fact, distressed by the lack of social connectedness that results from their behavior.

As noted, prognosis for conduct disorders is poor; they often lead to criminal behavior, antisocial personality, and problems in marital and occupational adjustment during adulthood (Kazdin, Siegel, & Bass, 1992). Many people with these disorders show early involvement with alcohol and illegal drugs (Lynskey & Fergusson, 1995). Many delinquent adolescents later become adult criminals. Nearly all adult offenders have a history of repeated antisocial behavior as children, and about 25 percent develop an antisocial personality disorder (Robins, 1991). The key factor associated with negative outcome is aggression. Highly aggressive children tend to remain aggressive over time, whereas other childhood adjustment problems show much less stability (Lerner, Hertzog, Hooker, Hassibi, & Thomas, 1988). A particularly negative sign is sexually aggressive behavior. Individuals who engage in sexual assaults are more likely to show subsequent violence (both sexual and nonsexual) than are individuals who commit nonsexual violence (Rubinstein, Yaeger, Goodstein, & Lewis, 1993). Prognosis is better for males who have higher IQ scores and whose parents do not have antisocial personalities (Lahey et al., 1995). Females also have a better prognosis. (See the Critical Thinking feature "School Violence: A Sign of the Times?")

Etiology From a psychodynamic perspective, antisocial and delinquent behaviors in children are symptoms of an underlying anxiety conflict in the child. This conflict results from an inadequate relationship with the parents; the problem behaviors can be produced by either emotional deprivation or overindulgence. In the first case, the parents offer the child little affection or concern, so childhood conflicts are not resolved and the superego does not develop adequately. The lack of a strong conscience increases the likelihood of aggressive and antisocial behaviors. The child becomes unable to form close personal relationships with others.

From a biological perspective, genetic factors may be important. Boys with conduct disorders are more likely than other boys to have antisocial parents (Edelbrock, Rende, Plomin, & Thompson, 1995; Hinshaw, 1987; Rutter, Bolton, Harrington, & Couteur, 1990), but this higher rate could result from either genetic or social factors (Hendren & Mullen, 1997). Very little is actually known about genetic influences for conduct disorder.

●●● MENTAL HEALTH AND SOCIETY
●●● Child Abuse

Because the three-and-one-half-year-old boy had defecated in his pants once too often, the mother forced him to sit for two whole days on the toilet. She told her son that he would not be allowed to get up or eat unless he evacuated his stools. When the son became constipated and did not respond appropriately, the mother pulled him from the toilet seat and lashed his buttocks. She did this every hour on the hour, until they were raw and bleeding. Despite the son's pleading, the mother became so enraged that she gave him an enema with scalding water. The youngster lost consciousness and had to be hospitalized.

"Children are our most precious resource." "The future of society depends upon the youths of today." "Caring and nurturance of children are important responsibilities of a civilized society." These statements are repeated often by parents, teachers, social scientists, and politicians. Yet the maltreatment of children remains a significant national problem (Dogden, 2000). The following statistics present a shameful and dismal picture of how we value and care for our children:

■ The U.S. Advisory Board on Child Abuse and Neglect (1995) conservatively estimates that nearly 2,000 infants and young children die from abuse and neglect by parents or caretakers each year; that's an average of 5 children each day.

■ Abuse and neglect kills 5.4 children out of every 100,000 who are age four and under (McClain, 1995).

■ Approximately 1 child in 10 is the victim of severe physical abuse each year; 1 in 5 lives below the poverty line (McClain, 1995).

■ An estimated 1 million or more youngsters run away from home (at an average age of fifteen); many do so to escape an intolerable home situation of physical or sexual abuse (Famularo, Kinscherff, Fenton, & Bolduc, 1990; Feitel, Margetson, Chamas, & Lipman, 1992).

■ Abuse of children results in tens of thousands of victims who are overwhelmed with lifelong psychological trauma and who continue to bear physical and psychological scars as adults; 18,000 children a year are left permanently disabled (Baladerian, 1991).

The Abused

Since the 1960s, when child abuse was recognized as a major social problem, reports of abuse have increased. Whether that increase reflects better reporting or an actual rise in abusive practices by parents is unclear. We do know, however, that children who are abused are more prone to exhibit significant direct and indirect physical and psychological problems. The physical consequences of abuse range from mild bruises and lacerations to quite severe long-term damage, including brain damage, mental retardation, and cerebral palsy. Orthopedic injuries such as broken bones are not uncommon. X-rays of children who have been abused frequently reveal evidence of multiple old fractures and breaks that have healed.

Psychological effects of abuse include impaired memory, depression, self-destructive behavior, low self-esteem, and aggressive impulsivity (Alessandri, 1991; Sternberg, Lamb, Greenbaum, & Cicchetti, 1992; Toth, Manly, & Cicchetti, 1992). Abused children may show excessive anxiety, which can lead to bedwetting, nightmares, eating and sleeping disorders, and—in the teenage years—conduct disorders. Although physical and mental abuse can by itself be devastating, the impact of abuse is even more complex when it involves sexual molestation, incest, or rape (Kendall-Tackett, Williams, & Finkelhor, 1993). There is no one symptom or cohesive syndrome that characterizes children

---

Approximately 15 to 23 percent of children have single, transient tics; their occurrence usually peaks at age seven. Diagnoses of tic disorders can be made only in retrospect because there is no way of determining whether a tic will disappear or develop into a chronic tic disorder or Tourette's disorder (Gadow, 1986; Golden, 1987).

Tourette's Disorder

Saul Lubaroff, a disc jockey in Iowa City, is able to deliver smooth news reports on the weather, news, and sports.

However, whenever he turns off his microphone, an explosive, involuntary stream of obscenities follows. In high school, his classmates would mock and threaten him. Even today, his outbursts are highly embarrassing to him. He has shouted "HEY" and "I MASTURBATE" in a fancy restaurant. However, Saul does have control while he is on the air. He indicates that "I have no problem announcing. I can turn off my 'noises' for 20 to 25 seconds, sometimes up to two minutes." (Dutton, 1986, p. c1)

Saul Lubaroff has a severe form of Tourette's disorder. According to DSM-IV-TR, a diagnosis of **Tourette's**

who have been abused (Saywitz, Mannarino, Berliner, & Cohen, 2000), nor does DSM-IV-TR include child abuse as a disorder under the category disorders usually first diagnosed in infancy, childhood, or adolescence. However, children who have experienced the trauma of sexual or physical abuse may show symptoms, either in childhood or later in life, of posttraumatic stress disorder (see the chapter on anxiety disorders) with experiences such as flashbacks, nightmares, feelings of alienation, or high levels of anxiety. Men who were sexually abused as children make up 2 to 5 percent of the general population. These individuals are themselves more prone to substance abuse and to lifelong sexual problems, such as exhibitionism, homophobic behavior, and sexual dysfunctions, than is the general population. Women who were abused as children tend to have poorer social and sexual relationships than do other women (Watkins & Bentovim, 1992; Jackson, Calhoun, Amick, Maddever, & Habif, 1990). Those who have been sexually abused tend to engage in sexual acting-out behaviors (Margolin & Gordis, 2004).

The Abuser

Why would parents abuse their own children? This is a very difficult question to answer. We know, for example, that most people who abuse were themselves abused as children.

Most are under the age of thirty, are more likely to come from lower socioeconomic levels, are rarely psychotic, may show personality disorders, and often abuse alcohol and drugs (Peterson & Brown, 1994; Whipple & Webster-Stratton, 1991). Some studies indicate that abusive parents experience greater stressors (marital discord, unemployment, and poverty), tend to have low levels of tolerance for frustration, are more aggressive and selfish, and exhibit lower impulse control than their nonabusing counterparts (Hillson & Kuiper, 1994). It is clear that many factors contribute to abuse. Some, such as poverty, are situational; others, such as immaturity and lack of parenting skills, are more related to individual temperament.

Prevention and Public Policy

Federal and state laws require all mental health professionals, teachers, and doctors to report child abuse or neglect if they suspect such a situation exists. Despite the fact that all fifty states have enacted such legislation, child abuse persists. There is a need for more consistency in defining child abuse, particularly child sexual abuse, because definitions differ among professional groups, complicating policy decisions, legal reactions, and therapeutic interventions (Haugaard, 2000). Although it may seem easy to define abusive

behavior, the context in which a behavior occurs can affect whether the behavior is seen as sexually abusive and who might see it as such. For example, at what age does it become inappropriate, or even sexually abusive, for a father to bathe his daughter? Would legal authorities and mental health professionals answer this question in the same way?

There have been efforts to increase public awareness of the problem of child abuse through educational campaigns on television and other media concerning the prevalence and impact of child abuse. An area of ongoing debate in the field of child protection is the balance between child safety and maintaining the family (Dogden, 2000). Many communities now run parent education and support groups, especially for families identified as "at risk." One very promising development is the parent education movement, which focuses on helping mothers improve their parenting skills, monitor their own reactions to everyday stressors, and learn other coping skills that ward off potential child abuse. Studies show that parents who receive parenting education can become more emotionally supportive and show more warmth toward their children (Sleek, 1998).

disorder requires that the individual has demonstrated multiple motor tics and one or more vocal tics; tics must begin before age eighteen and have been apparent for at least one year (American Psychiatric Association, 2000). Although there have been reports of Tourette's disorder in children as young as age two, the median age of onset is age seven, with a single tic (often eye-blinking) presenting as the first symptom. Vocal tics may include grunting and barking sounds or, on rare occasions, may involve explosive coprolalia, the compulsion to shout obscenities. Stress increases the severity of tic symptoms (Silva, Munoz, Barickman, &

Friedhoff, 1995). Tourette's disorder is relatively rare, with a prevalence of 5 to 30 cases per 10,000 children; it occurs three to five times more frequently in males than in females in clinic samples and twice as often in community samples. (Approximately 1 to 2 children per 10,000 continue to demonstrate symptoms in adulthood.) The course of Tourette's disorder varies greatly from individual to individual. It is common for the frequency, complexity, and severity of a tic and the location of a tic to change over time. Tourette's disorder often involves only mild symptoms, with vocal tics taking the form of throat clearing or involuntary sniffing or

Loss as a Potential Source of Depression The expression shown by the girl in this painting, *The Dead Mother and the Little Girl*, by Edvard Munch, illustrates the overwhelming distress a child feels when a parent dies. Loss of a major attachment figure can result in depression in children.

snorting; in fact, a high percentage of individuals with Tourette's disorder suffer no significant distress or impairment from their tics and never even seek treatment (American Psychiatric Association, 2000).

Etiology and Treatment

Anxiety and stress seem to be primary factors in producing, maintaining, and exacerbating tic disorders. In the psychodynamic view, tics represent underlying aggressive or sexual conflicts. For example, eye blinking may represent attempts to block out thoughts of the "primal scene" (intercourse between the child's parents) or other anxiety-evoking stimuli. Although tics do appear early in life (when the fixation of sexual or aggressive impulses is most likely to occur), little support has been found for this explanation.

According to the learning theorists, tics are conditioned avoidance responses initially evoked by stress. These responses become habitual through reinforcement when they reduce anxiety. The therapeutic technique of negative practice or massed practice is based on this viewpoint. The technique requires that the person perform the tic intentionally, over and over again. This forced practice of the behavior produces fatigue, which inhibits the response. The tic gradually acquires aversive properties, so not performing the tic becomes reinforcing. Behavioral approaches, including habit reversal (recognizing their tic symptoms and then practicing behaviors that are incompatible with the tic behavior) and self-modeling (watching videotapes of themselves when no tics are present), were found to significantly decrease tic symptoms in a small school-age sample of children with Tourette's disorder (Clarke, Bray, Kehle, & Truscott, 2001).

Both chronic tics and Tourette's disorder appear to be transmitted in families. If a parent has a tic disorder, there is a 50 percent risk that the children will also have the disorder; genetic researchers are studying large multigenerational families affected by Tourette's disorder (Rutter, MacDonald, et al., 1990; Tourette Syndrome Association, 2001). Neurological studies involving MRI (magnetic resonance imaging) results have confirmed cortical differences in both children and adults with Tourette's disorder compared with controls; differences in various regions of the brain were also reported within the Tourette's disorder group, with those with the most severe symptoms showing the greatest variations from the control group (Peterson, Pine, Cohen, & Brook, 2001).

As many as 50 percent of children with Tourette's disorder also meet the criteria for attention deficit/hyperactivity disorder, which might reflect a genetic link between the two disorders (American Psychiatric Association, 2000). Researchers (Shucard, Benedict, Tekok-Kilic, & Lichter, 1997) have reported that children with Tourette's disorder show a slower reaction time than controls on a continuous performance test of attention, with those with the most complex vocal tics showing the slowest reaction time. Although individuals with ADHD are at greater risk for tic disorders, the tic disorders in individuals with ADHD do not appear to be related to the use of stimulant medications, nor do they relate to the overall outcome for ADHD symptoms across the lifespan (Spencer, Biederman, Faraone, & Mick, 2001). The interrelatedness between Tourette's disorder and obsessive-compulsive disorder and ADHD has been confirmed not only in clinic samples but also in epidemiological studies (Peterson et al., 2001).

Several investigators believe that Tourette's disorder may stem from an impairment of the central nervous system involving the dopamine system (Malison et al., 1995). Reported therapeutic success with the drug haloperidol, which acts on the dopamine receptors, supports this view (Gadow, 1991). However, haloperidol produces some negative side effects in children and can lead to motor dysfunctions such as tardive dyskinesia. Clonodine, an antihypertensive medication, has also been successful, particularly with motor tics (Tourette Syndrome Association, 2001). Psychosurgical intervention with severe forms of Tourette's disorder has occurred since the 1970s, generally resulting in the long-term reduction of tic severity, particularly vocal tics, although not without the risk of long-term side effects (Babel et al., 2001).

Elimination Disorders

Eight-year-old Billy did not want to go to school anymore. He was embarrassed about his inability to control his bladder, he frequently wet his pants while in class, and he had to put up with merciless teasing by classmates. Billy had been continent by age five, but he started wetting the bed again around the age of seven. His father was especially irate about his son's problem. He constantly berated Billy for being "a baby" and said he "should wear diapers again." The problem had become so severe that it disrupted the family's travel plans. On long outings by automobile, Billy—fearful that he would wet his pants—requested restroom stops every thirty minutes. For the first time, the family canceled their annual visit to their families on the East Coast. The trip would require traveling by plane, and both parents felt that the number of times Billy would visit the restroom on the plane and his tendency to wet his pants at the most inopportune times would ruin their pleasure in the vacation.

Most psychologists would agree with Freud that toilet training represents a major source of potential conflict for the child. It is one of the first times that demands for control of normal biological urges (urinating and defecating) are placed on the child. Most children handle this developmental milestone well, with no resulting problems. A small percentage of children like Billy experience elimination disorders—problems of bladder or bowel control.

Enuresis

According to DSM-IV-TR, **enuresis** is the habitual voiding of urine during the day or night into one's clothes, bed, or floor. The behavior is generally involuntary, but in rare situations it may be intentional. Enuresis is most likely to occur during sleep, but it is not uncommon during the daytime. To be diagnosed with enuresis, the child must be at least five years old and must void inappropriately at least twice per week for at least three months. Enuresis is also associated with clinically significant distress and with impairment in social, academic, or other areas of functioning. It is a fairly common disorder, experienced by 5 to 10 percent of five-year-olds and 3 to 5 percent of ten-year-olds. Most children have outgrown the disorder by adolescence, although 1 percent of individuals with enuresis continue to have symptoms in adulthood (American Psychiatric Association, 2000).

Many children with enuresis experience significant distress or impairment in their social, academic, or everyday lives, and the disorder can also drastically affect their families. Children tend to be fearful and apprehensive about not being able to control their bladders, sensitive to imagined or real parental disappointment and disapproval, and frightened of peer ridicule. They may withdraw from peer relationships or may be ostracized by other children. Unsympathetic or impatient parents can exacerbate the problem by putting greater pressures on the child, producing further anxiety and a sense of failure. A vicious cycle may ensue: the child wets the bed, which leads to condemnation by one or both parents, which causes the child to feel intense guilt and anxiety about causing the problem, which fosters the child's belief in being unable to control the urge to urinate, which only reinforces the child's continued enuresis. Studies evaluating self-esteem in enuretic children show lowered self-esteem prior to treatment but increased self-esteem following treatment, even when the treatment was not successful (Longstaffe, Moffatt, & Whalen, 2000).

Both psychological and biological explanations have been associated with enuresis. Psychological stressors—unrealistic toilet training demands placed on the child, delayed or lax toilet training, a stressful life situation (such as death of a parent or birth of a new sibling), disturbed family patterns, or the presence of other emotional problems—can all be predisposing factors (Haug Schnabel, 1992; Olmos de Paz, 1990). Biological determinants may include delayed maturation of the urinary tract, delays in the development of normal rhythms of urine production, or a hypersensitive or small bladder. Seventy-five percent of all children with enuresis have a first-degree relative who had the condition; a child whose parent was enuretic has a five to seven times greater likelihood of having enuresis (American Psychiatric Association, 2000).

Interventions often involve using medications that decrease the depth of sleep (allowing the child to recognize the bladder urges) or that decrease urine volume (thereby decreasing enuretic events; Dahl, 1992). The most successful psychological procedures involve behavioral methods (Herschell et al., 2004), such as parents giving constant reinforcement to the child, awakening the child to use the toilet, and giving the child responsibility for making up his or her own bed should an accident occur. A bedtime urine alarm treatment is particularly effective (Schulman, Collish, von Zuben, & Kodman-Jones, 2000).

Encopresis

Although less common than enuresis, **encopresis** may be more disturbing because it involves repeated defecating onto one's clothes, the floor, or other inappropriate places. To be diagnosed with this disorder, the child must be at least four years old and must have defecated inappropriately at least once a month for at least three months. The incidents must not be due to the use of laxatives. Estimates of the prevalence of encopresis vary, but it appears to occur in 1 percent of children in the grade school years, with boys far outnumbering girls. Intermittent episodes of encopresis can persist for years. Encopresis is most commonly seen with functional constipation. The typical pattern for children with encopresis is a history of constipation, resulting in painful defecation and subsequent withholding of bowel movements, leading to additional constipation and involuntary soiling (Issenman,

Filmer, & Gorski, 1999). In rare situations in which encopresis is deliberate, other features of oppositional defiant disorder or conduct disorder may be present. In cases of encopresis in which constipation is not a primary factor, it is important to identify the reason for the resistance to using the toilet and to assess possible medical, developmental, or behavioral contributors to the problem, to understand the toilet refusal behavior, to ensure appropriate stools through diet and medication, and to develop a schedule for toileting (Kuhn, Marcus, & Pitner, 1999; Loening-Baucke, 2000).

According to DSM-IV-TR, the amount of psychological impairment associated with encopresis is in direct proportion to its effects on the child's self-esteem. Intense social problems can arise through shame, embarrassment, and attempts to conceal the disorder. Ostracism by peers, anger on the part of significant caregivers, and overall rejection can compound the problem. Apart from their reactions to the encopresis itself, most children with encopresis do not have serious psychological or behavior problems (Isserman et al., 1999). The most common means of treatment include proper medical evaluation (especially when constipation is present) and the use of behavioral and family forms of therapy. Parent and child education about toileting regimens and a well-organized bowel management program can produce dramatic results (Loening-Bauke, 2000).

SUMMARY

Which disorders fall under the category of pervasive developmental disorders?

- Pervasive developmental disorders include autistic disorder, Rett's disorder, childhood disintegrative disorder, Asperger's disorder, and pervasive developmental disorder not otherwise specified.

What are some of the characteristics of attention deficit/hyperactivity disorder, and what are the subtypes of this disorder?

- Attention deficit/hyperactivity disorder, or ADHD, is characterized by overactivity, restlessness, distractibility, short attention span, and impulsiveness.

- Three types of ADHD are recognized: predominantly hyperactive-impulsive, predominantly inattentive, and combined.

What is the difference between conduct disorder and oppositional defiant disorder?

- Oppositional defiant disorder (ODD) is characterized by a pattern of hostile, defiant behavior toward authority figures. Children with ODD do not display the more serious violations of others' rights that are symptomatic of conduct disorders. Conduct disorders, especially those that have an early onset, show a clear continuity with adult problems.

What is the general prognosis for children with anxiety disorders?

- Children's anxiety reactions are usually transitory and disappear with age.

What are some of the characteristics of reactive attachment disorder, and what circumstances lead to the development of this disorder?

- Children with reactive attachment disorder display either symptoms of withdrawal and avoidance of attachment or symptoms of excessive friendliness and indiscriminate efforts to attach to those with whom they come in contact, even strangers.
- Children with this disorder have experienced a severe, early disruption in attachment with primary caregivers due to such factors as having lived in an institutional setting, such as an orphanage, or due to severe abuse or neglect.

Which adult mood disorders are also seen in children and adolescents?

- Depression, dysthymic disorder, and bipolar disorder can occur in childhood; these disorders become even more prevalent during adolescence.

What is the difference between Tourette's disorder and other tic disorders?

- Tics and other stereotyped movements often occur in children and adolescents. In most cases, tics are transient and disappear with or without treatment. Tics that last longer than a year are diagnosed as chronic tic disorders.
- A more complex problem is Tourette's disorder, which involves both vocal and motor tics.

What are elimination disorders, and what is their prognosis?

- Enuresis and encopresis are elimination disorders that are diagnosed when children pass an age in which bladder or bowel control should normally exist.
- Enuresis is the usually involuntary voiding of urine into one's own clothes or bed.
- Encopresis is the usually involuntary expulsion of feces into one's own clothes or bed.
- Although they cause considerable distress to the child, both elimination disorders usually abate with increasing age.

KEY TERMS

attention deficit/
  hyperactivity disorder
  (ADHD) (p. 508)
autistic disorder (p. 498)
chronic tic disorder (p. 519)

conduct disorder (p. 512)
encopresis (p. 524)
enuresis (p. 523)
oppositional defiant disorder
  (ODD) (p. 512)

pervasive developmental
  disorder (p. 497)
reactive attachment disorder
  (p. 518)

separation anxiety disorder
  (SAD) (p. 516)
tic (p. 519)
Tourette's disorder (p. 520)
transient tic disorder (p. 519)

MULTIMEDIA PREVIEW

For additional study aids, we invite you to explore our media resources accompanying *Understanding Abnormal Behavior*, Eighth Edition. The Student CD-ROM includes videos, quizzing, and critical thinking activities that help to reinforce key concepts in a fun and engaging manner. The Student Web Site provides additional interactive activities, chapter outlines, and research links that further support and complement the text. All Web resources may be accessed by logging onto the Web site at **http://psychology.college.hmco.com/students**.

CHAPTER 16
Eating Disorders and Sleep Disorders

- How can people with anorexia nervosa not realize that they are starving themselves to death?

- How does bulimia nervosa differ from anorexia?

- When do food binges turn into binge-eating disorder?

- What other kinds of eating disorders are there?

- Why has there been such an increase in disordered eating?

- How can we treat eating disorders?

- Among primary sleep disorders, what are dyssomnias?

- What are parasomnias and how do they differ from dyssomnias?

- What is the etiology and treatment of sleep disorders?

Two types of health-related activities, eating and sleeping, can become seriously disturbed, producing profound detrimental effects on the psychological and physical functioning of individuals. In this chapter, we will consider how eating patterns and problems with sleep can develop into one of the eating or sleep disorders.

Eating Disorders

> I'm so weak ... last night I almost passed out. I'm scared about this ... but I love the control I have over food. It's like ... even though I'm so hungry I can not psychically bring myself to make/eat the food ... that would be an impossible task. I just don't know what to do. ... I'm about to go exercise (run my 3 miles, weights and crunches) but I'm so weak ... any tips on what I can do to get me more energized and not so weak? (Livejournal.com, 2004)

> I would eat crazy amounts of food. ... I'd eat ten pieces of bread and butter, a box of crackers, two bowls of cereal, and anything else that was sitting around in the kitchen. It was like I was in an alcoholic trance and I couldn't stop myself. In the morning I'd wake up thinking, I am so stupid. How can I be so stupid? (Jacobson & Alex, 2001, p. 1)

Eating disorders are becoming more prevalent in the United States, especially among young people. At some colleges, "vomit" signs are posted around women's bathrooms in the vicinity of dining halls urging women to clean up after themselves after vomiting. Cleaning equipment such as buckets, gloves, cleaning solutions, and sponges are often supplied (Palmer, 2001). The concern over body shape and weight is reflected in national surveys indicating that nearly 50 percent of adolescent females and 20 percent of adolescent males report dieting to control their weight. Weight concerns are so great that a reported 13.4 percent of girls and 7.1 percent of boys have engaged in disordered eating patterns (see Table 16.1). Factors associated with disordered eating patterns included being overweight, low self-esteem, depression, substance use, and suicidal ideation (Neumark-Sztainer, Hannan, & Stat, 2000). It is unclear whether these factors are the result or the cause of the binge-purge cycle of dieting.

Eating problems may be a result of the availability of many attractive high-calorie foods, sociocultural factors, mass media, family, and peer influences, and the American pursuit of thinness (Tiggemann & Kuring, 2004). Paradoxically, the increasing emphasis on thinness, especially for women, is occurring as the population of the United States is becoming heavier. Forty-one states have obesity rates higher than 20 percent (Zwillich, 2004). Studies indicate that from 30 to 67 percent of normal-weight adolescent girls and college females believe that they are overweight. Adolescent boys and college males also show weight dissatisfaction, but their goal is to be heavier and more muscular (Ricciardelli & McCabe, 2004). This differential response to weight was also found in ratings of attractiveness and satisfaction. Men who were overweight

TABLE 16.1   Prevalence of Weight Concerns of Youth in Grades 5–12

	Females	Males
Very important not to be overweight	68.5%	54.3%
Ever been on a diet	45.4%	20.2%
Diet recommended by parent	14.5%	13.6%
Diet to "look better"	88.5%	62.2%
Engage in binge/purge behaviors	13.4%	7.1%
Binge/purge at least once a day	8.9%	4.1%

Source: Data from national survey of 6,728 adolescents (Neumark-Sztainer Hannan & Stat, 2000).

rated themselves as more attractive and healthier than overweight women rated themselves, whereas underweight women felt more attractive and healthier than underweight men did (McCreary & Sadava, 2001). Similar findings about weight were reported with college men in Germany, France, and the United States. In the study (Pope et al., 2000), images of men with different degrees of fatness and muscularity were shown to a group of research participants. The males were asked to choose images that represented their own bodies, the bodies they would like to have, the body of an average man their age, and the male body they thought women preferred. In all three countries, the men picked an ideal body that was about twenty-eight pounds more muscular than they themselves were. The participants also believed that women preferred a male body thirty pounds more muscular than their current body. In actuality, women indicated a preference for an ordinary male body without added muscle. Thus it would appear that both men and women suffer from body dissatisfaction.

Weight and body shape concerns exist not only among young white females but also among older women and minorities (Andersen, 2001; Gilbert, 2003). Rates of eating disorders are high among Hispanic American and Native American females and are increasing among immigrant Asian females (Gilbert, 2003; Sherwood, Harnack, & Story, 2000; Story, Neumark-Sztainer, Sherwood, Stang, & Murray, 1998; Wax, 2000). Although African American women are less likely than white women to have eating disorders, there is some indication that prevalence rates are increasing.

With the exception of binge-eating disorder, males are much less likely than females to be diagnosed with an eating disorder. However, in certain areas, such as the sport of wrestling, males have been found to have high rates of eating disorders; in addition, the sociocultural emphasis on bodybuilding may underlie the fact that some men are also exhibiting an extreme fear of becoming fat (Holbrook & Weltzin, 1998). Although overeating and being overweight are more acceptable for men than for women, there is evidence of increasing body dissatisfaction in males. Women's magazines have shown a dramatic increase in the number of ads displaying the male body. During the 1970s photos exhibited men in bathing suits on beaches; ads today, however, show undressed male bodies with electronics, telephones, furniture, and beverage products in which the display of the male body had no direct relevance (Pope, Olivardia, Borowiecki, & Cohane, 2001). Perhaps the emphasis on the male body is responsible for the finding that between 6 and 7 percent of boys between the ages of fifteen and eighteen have taken anabolic steroids to gain more muscle mass (Kanayama, Pope, & Hudson, 2001).

Disordered eating patterns because of preoccupation with weight and body dimensions sometimes become so extreme that they may develop into one of the eating disorders—anorexia nervosa, bulimia nervosa, or binge-eating disorder (see Figure 16.1). About 7 million women and 1 million men in America suffer from an eating disorder. An additional 15 percent of young women have "substantially disordered" eating attitudes and behaviors (National Association of Anorexia Nervosa and Associated Disorders, 2004). Unfortunately, disordered eating attitudes and behaviors are becoming more common and are occurring even in children (Jones, Bennett, Olmsted, Lawson, & Rodin, 2001). In this chapter we attempt to determine the reason for the increase in eating disorders. In doing so, we consider the characteristics, associated features, etiology, and

FIGURE 16.1 Disorders Chart: Eating Disorders

Anorexia Nervosa	EATING DISORDERS	Binge-Eating Disorder

EATING DISORDERS

Characterized by physically and/or psychologically harmful eating patterns

Anorexia Nervosa

Types: restricting; binge eating/purging

Refusal to maintain a body weight above the minimum normal weight for one's age and height (is more than 15 percent below expected weight)

Intense fear of becoming obese, which does not diminish even with weight loss

Body image distortion (not recognizing one's thinness)

In females, absence of at least three consecutive menstrual cycles otherwise expected to occur

Bulimia Nervosa

Types: purging/nonpurging

Recurrent episodes of binge eating

Loses control of eating behavior when bingeing

Uses vomiting, exercise, laxatives, or dieting to control weight

Two or more eating binges a week, occurring for three or more months

Overconcern with body weight and shape

Binge-Eating Disorder

Proposed category

Recurrent episodes of binge eating

Loses control of eating when bingeing

No regular use of inappropriate compensatory activities to control weight

Binge eating occurs two or more times a week for six months

Concern about the effect of bingeing on body shape and weight

Marked distress over binge eating

EATING DISORDERS	Lifetime Prevalence and Sex Ratio	Age of Onset	Course
Anorexia Nervosa	Over 90 percent are white females; 0.5 percent prevalence	Usually after puberty or late adolescence	Highly variable; some recover completely; majority continue to be of low weight; 10 percent continue to meet diagnostic criteria 10 years after treatment
Bulimia Nervosa	Over 90 percent are white females; 1–3 percent prevalence rate	Late adolescence or early adulthood	Frequently begins after dieting; usually persists for at least several years; may be chronic or intermittent
Binge-Eating Disorder	0.7–4 percent; 1.5 times more prevalent in females than males; about 30 percent in weight control clinics have this disorder	Late adolescence or early 20s	Unknown; may be chronic among individuals seeking treatment

Source: Data from American Psychiatric Association (2000); Hoffman (1998); Sullivan, Bulik, Fear, & Pickering (1998); Walsh & Devlin (1998).

treatment of anorexia nervosa and bulimia nervosa, as well as binge-eating disorder, which was proposed as a category for inclusion in DSM-IV-TR (American Psychiatric Association, 2000; see Table 16.2).

Myth vs Reality

Myth: Females and males attempt to attain the body shape preferred by the group that they are attracted to.

Reality: Female heterosexuals desire a thinner body than those preferred by heterosexual males. Male heterosexuals desire to have a more muscular body than the ones chosen by heterosexual females. Lesbian females appear to have fewer body image problems than heterosexual females, whereas gay males have higher body image concerns than heterosexual males. However, studies have not been done to determine the actual body preferences of gay or lesbian individuals.

TABLE 16.2   Do You Have an Eating Disorder?

Questions for Possible Anorexia Nervosa

1. Are you considered to be underweight by others? (What is your weight?)
   (Screening question. If yes, continue to next questions.)
2. Are you intensely fearful of gaining weight or becoming fat even though you are underweight?
3. Do you feel that your body or a part of your body is too fat?
4. If you had periods previously, have they stopped?

Questions for Possible Bulimia Nervosa

1. Do you have binges in which you eat a lot of food?
   (Screening question. If yes, continue to next questions.)
2. When you binge, do you feel a lack of control over eating?
3. Do you make yourself vomit, take laxatives, or exercise excessively because of overeating?
4. Are you very dissatisfied with your body shape or weight?

Questions for Possible Binge Eating Disorder

1. Do you have binges in which you eat a lot of food?
2. When you binge, do you feel a lack of control over eating?
3. When you binge, do three or more of the following apply?
   a. You eat more rapidly than usual.
   b. You eat until uncomfortably full.
   c. You eat large amounts even when not hungry.
   d. You eat alone because of embarrassment from overeating.
   e. You feel disgusted, depressed, or guilty about binge eating.
4. Do you feel great distress regarding your binge eating?

Note: These questions are derived from the diagnostic criteria for DSM-IV-TR (APA, 2000). For anorexia nervosa, the individual's weight is 85 percent less than expected for age and height; for bulimia nervosa the binges must occur, on average, about twice a week for three months; and for binge eating the binges must occur, on average, at least two days a week for six months. If the full criteria for these disorders are not met and disturbed eating patterns exist, they may represent subclinical forms of the eating disorders or be diagnosed as eating disorder not otherwise specified.

Anorexia Nervosa

Marya Hornbacher is an award-winning writer who fights a continuing battle with anorexia nervosa. She has written a book, *Wasted,* that chronicles the influences of socio-cultural factors in the development of her eating disorder. At the age of eighteen, she weighed only fifty-two pounds and was so thin that she got bruises from lying in bed. As a fourth grader, Marya had become concerned about being "chubby," and she experimented with vomiting to control her weight. She ate highly colored foods so that she could identify them after throwing up. Marya is healthier now but still underweight—and she continues to struggle with eating. Her anorexia has left her with a variety of physical ailments: her heart muscle has been weakened, her stomach and esophagus are lacerated, her bones are brittle, and her immune system has been weakened. The disease has probably shortened her lifespan. Although fighting anorexia is difficult, Marya still believes that "it's your choice. ... We are not just victims of external disease—we have choices." (Marshall, 1998, p. D2)

Although anorexia nervosa has been known for more than 100 years, it is receiving increased attention owing to greater public knowledge of the disorder and the apparent increase in its incidence. The disorder occurs primarily in adolescent girls and young women. Estimates of its prevalence range from 0.5 to 1 percent of the female population. The rate peaks among fifteen- to nineteen-year-olds (American Psychiatric Association, 2000; Walsh & Devlin, 1998). Although some men also develop this eating disorder (less than 10 percent of those with this diagnosis are males), they are more likely to display "reverse anorexia"—they believe they are "too small." In one study, some bodybuilders displayed body dissatisfaction, preoccupation with food and disturbed patterns of eating and exercising, but their goal was to gain weight or muscle mass (Mangweth et al., 2001). Among men who develop anorexia nervosa, clinical symptoms are similar to those of women with the disorder (Woodside et al., 2001). A major concern with anorexia nervosa is that it is associated with serious medical complications. The mortality rate is the highest of any major psychiatric disorder, with many deaths occurring suddenly, usually from ventricular arrhythmias (Panagiotopoulos, McCrindle, Hick, & Katzman, 2000).

Anorexia nervosa is characterized by a refusal to maintain a body weight above the minimum normal weight for one's age and height; an intense fear of becoming obese, which does not diminish with weight loss; body image distortion; and, in girls, the absence of at least three consecutive menstrual cycles otherwise expected to occur. A person with this bizarre and puzzling disorder literally engages in self-starvation.

A very frightening characteristic of anorexia nervosa is that, even when they are clearly emaciated, most people with this disorder continue to insist they are overweight. Others will acknowledge that they are thin but claim that some parts of their bodies are "too fat." They may measure or estimate their body size frequently and believe that weight loss is a sign of achievement and that gaining weight is a failure of self-control (American Psychiatric Association, 2000). One eighteen-year-old woman with anorexia nervosa vomited up to ten times daily, took laxatives, and exercised four hours each day. Yet when her friends said, "You look sick," or "You need to eat," she viewed their comments as a sign of jealousy (Tarkan, 1998). Other times, peers will inadvertently provide reinforcement by expressing admiration for thinness. One woman, Rachel, hid her thin starving body under layers of bulky clothing. Some of her friends commented positively on her figure, which increased her determination to starve (Holahan, 2001a). In most cases, the body image disturbance is profound. As one researcher (Bruch, 1978, p. 209) noted more than twenty years ago, people with this disorder "vigorously defend their often gruesome emaciation as not being too thin. ... They identify with the skeleton-like appearance, actively maintain it, and deny its abnormality."

Some patients may have incorporated the eating disorder characteristics into their identities and are reluctant to give up the drive for thinness. At times, competition develops in treatment settings, with patients competing in terms of who is the thinnest, ate the least, or exercised the most (Bulik & Kendler, 2000). During the early part of the disorder, individuals with anorexia nervosa generally have only limited recognition of their disorder and may consider their symptoms as ego-syntonic—that is, their symptoms seem normal to them (American Psychiatric Association, 2000).

Subtypes of Anorexia Nervosa   There are two subgroups (restricting type and binge-eating/purging type) of patients with anorexia nervosa. The restricting type accomplishes weight loss through dieting or exercising. The binge-eating/purging type loses weight through the use of self-induced vomiting, laxatives, or diuretics. Most, but not all, binge eat. In one study of 105 patients hospitalized with this disorder, 53 percent had lost weight through constant fasting (restricting type); the remainder had periodically resorted to binge eating followed by purging or vomiting (binge-eating/purging type). Although both groups vigorously pursued thinness, they differed in some aspects. Those with restricting anorexia were more introverted and

Anorexia Claims a Victim Karen Carpenter of the award-winning musical duo The Carpenters is shown at a healthy weight in 1974 (left). In 1981, Karen showed visible signs of her illness (right). She died two years later of heart failure due to an anorexia-related complication. How can such individuals not realize they are starving themselves?

tended to deny that they suffered hunger and psychological distress. Those with the binge-eating/purging type were more extroverted. They reported more anxiety, depression, and guilt; admitted more frequently to having a strong appetite; and tended to be older (Halmi et al., 2000).

Physical Complications Self-starvation produces a variety of physical complications along with weight loss. Patients with anorexia often exhibit cardiac arrhythmias because of electrolyte imbalance; most have low blood pressure and slow heart rates. They may be lethargic, have dry skin and brittle hair, show hypertrophy of the parotid glands (from purging) that results in a chipmunk-like face, and exhibit hypothermia. For example, one woman had to wear heavy clothing even when the temperature was over ninety degrees (Bryant, 2001). Irreversible osteoporosis, vertebra contraction, and stress fractures are also significant complications of the disorder. Males with the bulimic type of anorexia are also prone to osteoporosis and are more likely than women to have comorbid substance

use disorder and antisocial personality (American Psychiatric Association, 2000). In addition, the heart muscle is often damaged and weakened because the body may use it as a source of protein during starvation. One result of such complications is a mortality rate of up to 20 percent, according to long-term follow-up studies (American Psychiatric Association, 2000; Hoffman, 1998). Unfortunately, even with the severe health and emotional damage associated with the disorder, support groups advocating anorexia as a lifestyle choice have appeared on the Internet. See the Mental Health and Society feature "Anorexia's Web" for the controversy over these Web sites.

Associated Characteristics A number of associated characteristics or mental disorders are comorbid (coexist) with anorexia nervosa. Obsessive-compulsive behaviors and thoughts that may or may not involve food or exercise are often reported (Rogers & Petrie, 2001). One woman developed obsessive thoughts and behaviors about food. She feared that touching or even breathing around food would cause her to gain weight

MENTAL HEALTH AND SOCIETY
Anorexia's Web

One individual writes, "Starvation is fulfilling. Colors become brighter, sounds sharper, odors so much more savory and penetrating. ... The greatest enjoyment of food is actually found when never a morsel passes the lips" (Irizarry, 2004). Another wrote, "I only had three olives, two cookies and some chicken curry today and puked it up so I'm starting to get back into the swing of things" (Hellmich, 2001, p. 2). On the Web, anorexia support groups write that Mary-Kate Olsen was fine at her weight and did not need to be treated for an eating disorder. Some of the names used in online discussion groups include "thinspiration," "puking pals," "disappearing acts," "anorexiangel," and "chunkeee monkeee."

Although anorexia nervosa has been associated with negative medical consequences and unhappiness for its victims, as many as 400 pro-eating-disorder Web sites have recently appeared. The Web sites include pictures of ultra-thin models, tips for dieting, and ways to conceal the thinness from family members and friends. They provide a circle of friends and encouragement. In response to before and after (thinner) pictures on the Web, one person wrote: "You're my thinspiration! How did you do it?" Another responded, "Your collar bones are beautiful—nice job" (Hayley, 2004, p. 01). Participants on the Anorexic Nation Web site talk about how it is important to have friends that are like them and argue that anorexia is a lifestyle

choice and not an illness. A woman on one site writes, "I am very much for anorexia and this webpage is a reflection of that. If you are recovered or recovering from an eating disorder, please, please, PLEASE do not visit my site. I can almost guarantee it will trigger you! But if you are like me and your eating disorder is your best friend and you aren't ready to give it up, please continue" (Hellmich, 2001, p. 3). These Web sites are visited by thousands of people each day, and medical experts are deeply concerned that the sites will produce a surge in eating-disorder cases, especially among susceptible individuals. Judy Sargent, who is recovering from the disorder, says, "These sites don't tell you that you're going to die if you don't get treatment" ("Anorexia's Web," 2001, p. 2). Eating-disorder organizations have been alarmed by these sites and have petitioned Yahoo! and other hosts to remove the forums. Initially the response they received was "no," because the issue involved freedom of speech. In August 2001, Yahoo! did agree to remove the pro-eating-disorder Web site; however, many sites have switched to other

servers, and there has been a flood of e-mail, some expressing suicidal feelings for being denied access to their "community" (Holahan, 2001b). However, Anorexic Nation responds on its Web site by writing, "We are not going anywhere. We will not let anybody chase us off the Internet so easily. The pro-ana witch hunts must end. Society must deal with us now, and on our own terms."

Helpful resources for individuals with body dissatisfaction do exist online, such as www.mirror-mirror .org/college.htm, the American Anorexia/Bulimia Association, Eating Disorders Awareness and Prevention, Anorexia Nervosa and Related Eating Disorders, and the Eating Disorder Referral and Information Center. In addition, Web sites also exist that focus on helping people feel comfortable with their bodies. Bodypositive.com is an online magazine that offers different perspectives on larger body sizes. About-face.com addresses positive body esteem in women and delves into the impact of mass media on women's physical, mental, and emotional well-being (Maltais, 2001).

(Bulik & Kendler, 2000). The manner in which these symptoms are related to anorexia nervosa is unclear because of the possibility that malnutrition or starvation may cause or exacerbate obsessive symptoms. Some researchers believe that anorexia nervosa is a variant of obsessive-compulsive disorder. In one study, a somewhat higher frequency of obsessive-compulsive

disorder was found among first-degree relatives of anorexia probands than in a group of comparison participants (Bellodi et al., 2001). Some investigators also believe that a characteristic of anorexia nervosa involves control. One individual noted that "Nothing could prevent my will from controlling my body" (Segall, 2001, p. 22). Personality disorders and other characteristics have also been linked to anorexia nervosa, although the restricting and binge-eating/purging types may differ in the characteristics with which they are linked. The restricting type is more likely to be linked to traits of introversion, conformity, perfectionism, and rigidity, whereas the bingeing/purging type is more likely to be associated with extroverted, histrionic, emotionally volatile personalities, impulse control problems, and substance abuse. Interpreting these relationships has been difficult, as they could (1) represent the misfortune of having two or more disorders by chance, (2) indicate that anorexia is an expression of a personality disorder, or (3) be the result of common environmental or genetic factors that underlie both anorexia and the personality disorder (Westen & Harnden-Fischer, 2001).

Course and Outcome   Anorexia nervosa tends to develop during adolescence, and the course is highly variable. Individuals with the binge/purging type may have a better outcome and may fit the profile of a high-functioning but chronically self-critical and perfectionistic person. However, the course and outcome of anorexia nervosa may also be influenced by the reason for the behavior. People with anorexia may form a heterogeneous group, with some developing the disorder because they fear their impulses and want to attempt to prove they can regulate them; others as an act of competitiveness or out of a sense of achievement; others as a form of self-punishment or a means of demonstrating control over one aspect of their lives. A difficulty in attempting to determine outcome by anorexia nervosa type is that many patients who have the restricting type later develop the binge-eating/purging subtype.

Approximately 44 percent of individuals treated for anorexia recover completely (remain within 15 percent of their recommended weight; menstruation is restored in women), another 28 percent show some weight gain but remain underweight, and the outcome for 24 percent is poor (weight is never reached within 15 percent of the recommended weight). About two-thirds continue to have weight and body image preoccupations, and up to 40 percent have bulimic symptoms. Depending on the length of the follow-up period, mortality primarily from cardiac arrest or suicide ranged from 5 percent to 20 percent (American Psychiatric Association, 2000). In a recent five-year follow-up study of ninety-five women patients age fifteen years and older with anorexia, 59 percent of the patients had initially had the restricting type, and 41 percent had had the binge-eating/purging type. At follow-up, over 50 percent no longer had a diagnosable eating disorder, but three had died within the five-year period. Most still showed disturbed eating patterns,

poor body image, and psychosocial difficulties (Ben-Tovim et al., 2001). For the most part, these follow-up studies do not include patients for whom a family therapy approach was included with medical treatment and individual psychotherapy; expectations are that the addition of family therapy would improve overall therapeutic results.

Bulimia Nervosa

"At first, after eating too much, I would just go to the toilet and make myself sick. I hadn't heard of bulimia. ... I started eating based on how I was feeling about myself. If my hair looked bad, I'd stuff down loads of candy. After a while, I started exercising excessively because I felt so guilty about eating. I'd run for miles and miles and go to the gym for three hours" (Dirmann, 2003, p. 60). Ex-Spice Girl Geri Halliwell struggled with bulimia nervosa for almost ten years. The anguish over losing control of her eating caused her to research the problem over the Internet and then to seek treatment.

Bulimia nervosa is an eating disorder characterized by recurrent episodes of binge eating (the rapid consumption of large quantities of food) at least twice a week for three months, during which the person loses control over eating. Two subtypes exist: the purging type, in which the individual regularly vomits or uses laxatives, diuretics, or enemas; and the nonpurging type, in which excessive exercise or fasting are used in an attempt to compensate for binges. A persistent overconcern with body image and weight also characterizes this disorder. Eating episodes may be stopped when abdominal pain develops or when vomiting is induced.

Individuals with bulimia nervosa evaluate themselves critically in terms of body shape and weight. They overestimate their body size. Compared with women at similar weight levels but without the disorder, women with bulimia exhibited more psychopathology, a greater external locus of control, lower self-esteem, and a lower sense of personal effectiveness on questionnaires (Shisslak, Pazda, & Crago, 1990; Williams, Taylor, & Ricciardelli, 2000). They also have a negative self-image, feelings of inadequacy, dissatisfaction with their bodies, and a tendency to perceive events as more stressful than most people would (Vanderlinden, Norre, & Vandereycken, 1992). These characteristics of patients diagnosed with bulimia may be a result of their loss of control over eating patterns, however, rather than the cause of the disorder.

People with bulimia realize that their eating patterns are not normal, and they are frustrated by that knowledge. They become disgusted and ashamed of their eating and hide it from others. The binges characterized by rapid consumption of foods, typically occur in private. Some eat nothing during the day but lose control and binge in late afternoon or evening. The loss of self-control over eating is characteristic of this disorder, and the individual feels difficulty stopping once a binge has begun. Consequences of binge eating are controlled through vomiting or the use of laxatives, which produce feelings of relief from physical discomfort and the fear of gaining weight. Those with the nonpurging type of bulimia often follow overeating episodes with a commitment to a severely restrictive diet, fasting, or engaging in excessive exercising or physical activity.

Bulimia is much more prevalent than anorexia. Up to 3 percent of women may suffer from bulimia nervosa (Gordon, 2001; Walsh & Devlin, 1998). An additional 10 percent of women report some symptoms but do not meet all the criteria for the diagnosis. The incidence of bulimia appears to be increasing in women and is especially prevalent in urban areas. Few males exhibit the disorder, presumably because there is less cultural pressure for them to remain thin, although it is estimated that about 10 percent of those affected by this disorder are males.

A person's weight seems to have little to do with whether or not the individual develops bulimia. Most are within the normal weight range (Mehler, 2003). Of a sample of forty women with the disorder, twenty-five were of normal weight, two were overweight, one was obese, and twelve were underweight. These women averaged about twelve binges per week, and the estimated calories consumed in a binge could be as high as 11,500. Typical binge foods were ice cream, candy, bread or toast, and donuts (Gordon, 2001).

Physical Complications People with this disorder use a variety of measures—fasting, self-induced vomiting, diet pills, laxatives, and exercise—to control the weight gain that accompanies binge eating. More than 75 percent of patients with this disorder practice self-induced vomiting (McGilley & Prior, 1998). Side effects and complications may result from this practice or from the excessive use of laxatives. The effects of vomiting include erosion of tooth enamel from vomited stomach acid; dehydration; swollen parotid glands, which produces a puffy facial appearance; and lowered potassium, which can weaken the heart and cause arrhythmia and cardiac arrest (American Dietetic Association, 2001; Mehler, 2003). In rare cases, binge eating can cause the stomach to rupture. Other possible gastrointestinal disturbances include esophagitis and gastric and rectal irritation.

Associated Features Some evidence has shown that individuals with bulimia eat not only out of hunger but also as an emotionally soothing response to distressing thoughts or external stressors. As noted earlier, women with this disorder tend to perceive events as more stressful than most people would. Such difficulties may lead them to consume food for gratification. In one study, eating and emotional states were monitored over a six-day period using handheld computers as recorders. Among the women, binges were preceded by poor mood, feelings of poor eating control, and the craving for sweets. Interestingly, a control sample of women without the disorder also reported frequent binges due to emotional states. There appears to be a close relationship between emotional states and disturbed eating patterns. As one woman stated, "Purging was the biggest part of my day. ... It was my release from the stress and monotony of my life" (Erdely, 2004, p. 117). Weight preoccupation is also related to the type of coping response an individual shows to life stressors. In a nonclinical sample of university women, those who responded emotionally when facing stressful situations ("Get angry," "Wish I could change what happened") were more preoccupied with weight than women who responded in a task-oriented style ("Outline my priorities," "Think about how I solved problems"; Denisoff & Endler, 2000). A task-oriented approach may diminish stress and, therefore, reduce the need to use food to control one's emotional state.

A number of mental disorders and features are comorbid with bulimia nervosa. Mood disorders are common, and rates of seasonal affective disorder, a syndrome characterized by depression during the dark winter months followed by remission during the spring and summer months, are higher among those with bulimia nervosa than in the general population (Lam, Lee, Tam, Grewal, & Yatham, 2001). Characteristics of borderline personality, such as impulsivity, substance abuse, and affective instability, are also found in individuals with bulimia nervosa. However, these relationships are difficult to interpret because in some cases depression and borderline characteristics precede the eating disorder, in some cases they coexist, and in others they appear to be the consequence of the eating disorder.

Course and Outcome Bulimia nervosa has a somewhat later onset than anorexia nervosa, beginning in late adolescence or early adult life. Outcome studies have shown a mixed course, although the prognosis is more positive than for anorexia nervosa. In a five-year community study of 102 participants with bulimia nervosa, only a minority still met the criteria for the disorder at the end of the study period. However, each year about one-third would remit, and another one-third would relapse. Most continued to show disturbed eating patterns and low self-esteem, and 40 percent met the criteria for a major depressive disorder (Fairburn, Cooper, Doll, Norman, & O'Connor, 2000). Another five-year study of individuals with bulimia nervosa reported a more positive outcome. Almost three-fourths had no diagnosable eating disorder at the end of the study (Ben-Tovim et al., 2001). The findings of a longer follow-up study (ten years) also reported generally positive outcomes. About 70 percent were in either partial or full remission, 11 percent met the full criteria for bulimia nervosa, 0.6 percent for anorexia nervosa, and 18.5 percent for eating disorder not otherwise specified. A history of substance use and a longer duration before treatment were associated with a poorer outcome (Keel, Mitchell, Miller, Davis, & Crow, 1999).

Binge-Eating Disorder

Ms. A was a thirty-eight-year-old African American woman who was single, lived alone, and was employed as a personnel manager ... she weighed 292 lb. ... Her chief reason for coming to the clinic was that she felt her eating was out of control and, as a result, she had gained approximately 80 lb over the previous year. ... A typical binge episode consisted of the ingestion of two pieces of chicken, one small bowl of salad, two servings of mashed potatoes, one hamburger, one large serving of french fries, one large chocolate shake, one large bag of potato chips, and 15 to 20 small cookies—all within a 2-hour period ... she was embarrassed by how much she was eating, and felt disgusted with herself and very guilty after eating. (Goldfein, Devlin, & Spitzer, 2000, p. 1052)

Binge-eating disorder (BED) is a diagnostic category that has been "provided for further study" in DSM-IV-TR (American Psychiatric Association, 2000). Further research will be conducted to determine if BED should be adopted as a distinct diagnostic category in DSM-V. The disorder is similar to bulimia nervosa in that they both involve the consumption of large amounts of food over a short period of time, an accompanying feeling of loss of control, and "marked distress" over eating during the episodes. However, in BED, the episodes are not generally followed by "the regular use of compensatory behaviors" such as vomiting, excessive exercise, or fasting. As in the case of bulimia nervosa, the individual with this disordered eating pattern eats large amounts of food, is secretive about this activity, and may eat large amounts even when not hungry. To be diagnosed with BED, an individual must have a history of binge-eating episodes at least two days a week for six months. Females are one and one-half times more likely to have this disorder than males, and a prevalence range from 0.7 percent to 4 percent in the general community has

been reported (American Psychiatric Association, 2000; Stice, Telch, & Rizvi, 2000). White women make up the vast majority of clinical cases, whereas in community samples, the percentages of African American and white women with BED are roughly equal (Wilfley, Pike, Dohm, Striegel-Moore, & Fairburn, 2001). Differences have been found between African American and white American women with BED. The former are less likely to have been treated for eating problems, are more likely to be obese, and show lower levels of eating, shape, and weight concerns and psychiatric distress (Pike, Dohm, Striegel-Moore, Wilfley, & Fairburn, 2001). African American women are as likely to have BED as white women, but they appear to have fewer attitudinal concerns (see Figure 16.2). American Indian women also appear to be at higher risk for BED, with a 10 percent prevalence rate reported in one study (Sherwood, Harnack, & Story, 2000).

Associated Characteristics   In contrast to those with bulimia nervosa, individuals suffering from binge-eating disorder are likely to be overweight (Bull, 2004). Most have a history of weight fluctuation. It is estimated that from 20 to 40 percent of individuals in weight-control programs have BED. In the general population, its prevalence ranges from 2 to 5 percent (Telch & Stice, 1998). The risk factors associated with this disorder include adverse childhood experiences, parental depression, vulnerability to obesity, and repeated exposure to negative comments from family members about body shape, weight, or eating (Fairburn et al., 1998). The binges are often preceded by poor mood, low alertness, feelings of poor eating control, and cravings for sweets (Greeno, Wing, & Shiffman, 2000). The complications from this disorder are due to medical conditions associated with obesity, such as high blood pressure, high cholesterol level, and diabetes. People with BED are also likely to suffer from depression (Hoffman, 1998).

As with the other eating disorders, comorbid features and mental disorders are associated with BED. In one study comparing 162 individuals with BED with other psychiatric samples, the lifetime rate for major depressive disorder, obsessive-compulsive personality disorder, and avoidant personality disorder was higher among those with BED. The presence of personality disorders was related to more severe binge eating and those with avoidant or obsessive-compulsive personality disorders reported higher rates of binge eating one year after treatment (Wilfley et al., 2000).

Course and Outcome   The onset for binge-eating disorder is similar to that of bulimia nervosa in that it typically begins in late adolescence or early adulthood.

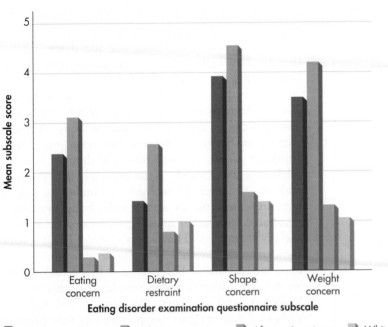

FIGURE 16.2 Binge-Eating Disorder Scores on subscales of the Eating Disorder Questionnaire by African American and white women with or without binge-eating disorder.

Source: Pike et al. (2001).

The natural course of BED in young women appears to be relatively positive in comparison with the other eating disorders. Over a five-year period, most individuals with BED made a full recovery even without treatment. They showed improved self-esteem and higher social functioning. Only 18 percent had an eating disorder of clinical severity versus 51 percent of the bulimia nervosa cohort. However, their weight remained high, and 39 percent eventually met the criteria for obesity (Fairburn et al., 2000). The finding of a different course between binge-eating disorder and bulimia nervosa supports the inclusion of BED as a separate diagnostic category within the eating disorders classification.

Eating Disorder Not Otherwise Specified

According to DSM-IV-TR (American Psychiatric Association, 2000), this category is for eating disorders that do not meet all the criteria for anorexia or bulimia nervosa. It currently includes the proposed category of binge-eating disorder. Examples of disordered eating that would fit in this category are:

1. A female who meets all the criteria for anorexia nervosa but has regular menses.

2. An individual who meets all the criteria for anorexia nervosa and has lost a significant amount of weight but is in the normal weight range.

3. An individual who engages in binge eating and compensatory activities less than twice a week or who has engaged in these behaviors for less than three months.

4. An individual of normal weight who uses compensatory behaviors even after ingesting small amounts of food (vomiting after eating a candy bar).

5. A person who chews or spits out large amounts of food without ingesting the food.

6. A person with binge-eating disorder (proposed category discussed earlier).

Etiology of Eating Disorders

The etiology of eating disorders is believed to be determined by social, gender, psychological, familial, biological, and cultural factors (Tylka & Subich, 2004). See Table 16.3 for some of the risk factors in eating disorders. In this section we present some of the etiological factors involved. Usually it is a combination of variables rather than one factor that produces eating disorders, and this combination may differ for specific individuals.

TABLE 16.3   Overview of Major Risk Factors for Eating Disorders

Biological

- Dieting
- Obesity/overweight/pubertal weight gain

Psychological

- Body image/dissatisfaction/distortions
- Low self-esteem
- Premorbid OCD or anorexia nervosa (for bulimia nervosa)
- Childhood sexual abuse

Family

- Parental attitudes and behaviors
- Parental comments regarding appearance
- Eating-disordered mothers
- Misinformation about ideal weight

Sociocultural

- Peer pressure regarding weight/eating
- Media: TV, magazines
- Distorted images: Toys
- Objectification: female and male bodies evaluated through appearance

Source: Tylka & Subich (2004); White (2000).

Societal Influences

In the United States physical appearance is a very important attribute, especially for females. The average American woman is five feet four inches tall and weighs 162 pounds, but teenage girls describe their ideal body as five feet seven inches, weighing 110 pounds, and fitting into a size five dress. Although this ideal is far from the actual statistics for body size among American women, it is consistent with the image portrayed in mass media. It is estimated that only about 5 percent of American women can achieve the size required for fashion models (Irving, 2001; see the height and weight table in Table 16.4).

Women are socialized to be conscious of their body shape and weight. As a result, many researchers believe that eating disorders result from the sociocultural demand for thinness in females, which produces a preoccupation with body image (Stice, Shaw, & Nemeroff, 1998). Society's increasing emphasis on thinness over the past twenty years has been accompanied by an increasing incidence of eating disorders. This standard of thinness results in the belief that approval and self-worth are dependent on body size and shape, a belief that develops early in life. By fifth grade, over 31 percent of girls are already dieting, and 11.3 percent are engaging in disordered eating (Neumark-Sztainer et al., 2000). The mass media are one route by which these messages can be delivered. Unrealistic body images of women are shown in movies, television, magazines, computer games, and even toys. The thinness of many celebrities and models is unattainable for the vast majority of American women. A number of studies have indicated that in mass media, body slimness is associated with social rewards, whereas a fat body is socially stigmatized (Harrison & Cantor, 1997; Spitzer, Henderson, & Zivian, 1999). The result of this type of mass media portrayal of women is that female bodies are sexually objectified and considered as objects to be looked at and evaluated. As women and girls are socialized according to this perspective, they begin to evaluate themselves on the basis of appearance. A process called "self-objectification," a form of self-consciousness that produces habitual monitoring of one's external appearance, is hypothesized to occur. This process leads to an increase in anxiety or shame about the body, resulting in disturbed eating patterns and depression (Tiggemann & Kuring, 2004).

Adolescent girls gave the following reasons for dieting and concern over their bodies: mass media (magazines, television, advertising, fashions), peer influences (wanting to fit in), and criticisms by family members about their weight (Wertheim, Paxton, Schutz, & Muir, 1997). The beginning of dating and mixed-gender social activities is also related to dieting and disordered eating, especially for young women who have recently experienced menarche (Cauffman & Steinberg, 1996). Unfortunately, high school and college females may not be aware of the psychologically harmful effect of the super-slim standard for women. When asked to examine forty magazine ads featuring potentially harmful female stereotypes, they picked out ones that portray women as helpless or dumb, as sex objects, or as using alcohol or cigarettes. They appeared to overlook the ultra-thin models, possibly because they were accustomed to seeing this or have accepted it as a social-cultural norm (Gustafson, Popovich, & Thomsen, 2001).

Body dissatisfaction was studied by Forbes, Adams-Curtis, Rade, and Jaberg (2001). Both male and female college students were asked to choose from drawings the figure that was closest to their own, the one that they would most like to have, the one that their gender would like, and the one that the opposite sex would like best (see Figure 16.3). From the drawings of male figures, males perceived the one "closest to their own"

TABLE 16.4	Height and Weight Table for Women and Men 20 to 74 Years for 1980–2002		
	1980	**1994**	**2000**
Women			
Height (inches)	63.7	63.9	64.0
Weight (pounds)	145.4	153.0	162.9
Men			
Height (inches)	69.1	69.2	69.4
Weight (pounds)	173.8	181.3	189.8
Average weight by ethnicity and gender			
White women		151.4	161.7
African American women		169.7	182.4
Mexican American women		152.6	157.1
White men		183.7	193.1
African American men		181.2	189.2
Mexican American men		172.3	177.3

Source: Ogden, Fryar, Carroll, & Flegal (2004).

as smaller than the one that most men or most women would prefer. Female participants perceived the figure "closest to their own" as much larger than the one they would like to have and that most women or men would prefer. Although society's emphasis on body types for males and especially for females may lead to general body dissatisfaction, it is important to identify individuals who are most influenced by the standard. The researchers found that among both males and females, those with low self-esteem of either gender displayed the greatest degree of body dissatisfaction.

Women in their twenties have a much higher standard of thinness than girls do. This might indicate that a need to be increasingly thin begins to develop in adolescence and becomes deeply ingrained when the young woman reaches full adulthood. Especially intriguing is the finding that 27 percent of adolescent girls who rate themselves as being at the "right weight" are still trying to lose weight (Walsh & Devlin, 1998). In fact, one study of 288 girls between the ages of ten and fifteen found that girls wanted thinner bodies than they thought boys found attractive. They did not consider themselves overweight, however, and displayed less body dissatisfaction than did older women (Cohn et al., 1987). Variables other than a desire to be attractive to men must be involved. An independent standard of thinness might be one fac-

tor. Some support for this view was found by Silverstein and Perdue (1988). They found that women equated thinness with attractiveness and with professional success and intelligence.

Mass media portrayals of lean, muscular male bodies are also increasing. There appears to be a gradual shift away from traditional measures of masculinity that include wealth and power to physical appearance. If this is true, there may be dramatic increases in eating disorders among men in the near future (Pope et al., 2001). The gay male subculture places a great deal of value on physical attractiveness, resulting in more concern over body size and appearance, and a greater prevalence of disturbed eating patterns than found among heterosexual males (Strong, Williamson, Netemeyer, & Geer, 2000). Some studies estimate that gay males constitute 30 percent of males with eating disorders (Carlat, Camargo, & Herzog, 1997; Heffernan, 1994). Subcultural influences on attractiveness are also apparent in the fact that lesbians appear to be less concerned about physical appearance and report that they are less influenced by the media (Pope et al., 2001).

What kind of predisposition or characteristic leads some people to interpret images of thinness in the media as evidence of their own inadequacy? Are people who develop eating disorders chronically self-conscious to begin with, or do they develop eating

FIGURE 16.3 Preferences for Female Body Types by Female and Male College Students

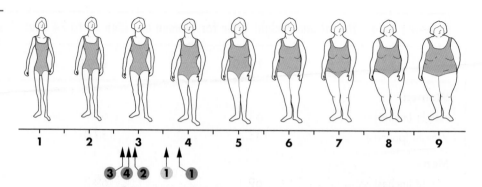

For Female Participants	Mean Rating
1 Which body type closely matches your own?	3.85
2 Which body type would you most like to have?	2.99
3 Which body type would most women like to have?	2.69
4 Which body type do you believe men like best?	2.85

For Male Participants	Mean Rating
1 Which body type do you find most attractive?	3.52

Source: Forbes et al. (2001).

Idealized Image? The Barbie doll illustrates some of the unrealistic physical standards that girls are exposed to. If the proportions of Barbie were applied to the woman on the left, she would have to be a foot taller, increase her breast size by four inches, and reduce her waist by five inches. Does exposure to the Barbie doll affect the body image of young girls?

disorders because agents in their social environment make them chronically self-conscious? How does exposure to mass media portrayals of thinness influence the values and norms of young people? The development of disordered eating and preoccupation with body image may involve multiple processes (Harrison, 2001; Tylka & Subich, 2004; see Figure 16.4): First, exposure to ultra-thin media models can lead to thin-body-image internalization, which could lead to patterns of eating intended to bring about this ideal. Second, exposure to a thin ideal could increase negative affect, which then triggers dieting. Third, exposure to the thin ideal can promote social comparison, which can lead to disordered eating to meet external standards of comparison. Although societal emphasis on thinness is related to an increase in disordered eating, it is not a sufficient explanation. Only a relatively small percentage of individuals in our media-conscious society develop eating disorders.

Family and Peer Influences

Interpersonal interaction patterns with parents and peers have also been put forth as explanations of eating disorders. The early psychodynamic formulation, which was based primarily on anorexia nervosa, hypothesized the following family characteristics. The

Can Ballerinas Be of Normal Weight? We expect ballerinas to be thin and tall. What is your reaction to these students in a ballet class? If they plan to be successful ballerinas, will they be exposed to pressure to become unusually thin?

Ideal Male Bodies? Most males prefer to be heavier and more muscular. Will the exposure in the media of physically powerful men produce body image distortion and dissatisfaction among men?

girl with the disorder has problems with maturation. She is afraid of having to grow up, which would lead to having to separate from her family and develop her own identity. By staying thin and not menstruating, she fulfills the unconscious desire to remain a child (Bruch, 1978; Halmi et al., 2000; Sands, 2003).

Other family characteristics are believed by some to be important in eating disorders. In the book *Psychosomatic Families: Anorexia in Context* (Minuchin, Rosman, & Baker, 1978), the typical family's communication pattern is described as "interactions between family members that are characterized by parental control, emotional enmeshment, and conflicts and tensions that are not openly expressed." This pattern of family relationships is believed to contribute to the development of anorexia. Additional family patterns that are thought to be important etiological factors are maternal overprotectiveness, parental

rejection, and absent or minimal paternal affection (Leung, Thomas, & Waller, 2000).

Unfortunately, the reported findings are difficult to interpret. Most are based on case studies, family systems theory, or depend on the perception of family members regarding their relationships. Also, family patterns may change as a result of dealing with an eating disorder. Parents may become more "controlling" in an attempt to force the person with the eating disorder to gain weight or to establish a healthier eating pattern. (In one family-based therapy, the adolescent with anorexia nervosa is seen as no longer capable of making sound choices regarding his or her health. This responsibility is taken over by the parents [Sim, Sadowski, Whiteside, & Wells, 2004].) Few empirical studies involving the observation of families with an eating-disordered member exist. We need to test the different theories or observations to determine if any

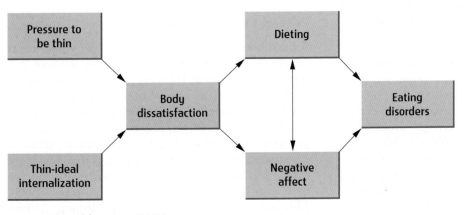

FIGURE 16.4 Route to Eating Disorders The route to the development of eating disorders.

Source: Adapted from Stice (2001).

Healthy or Overweight? In high school, Jamie-Lynn DiScala, who plays Meadow on "The Sopranos," would get up at 4 A.M. to exercise for two hours. Her dinner consisted merely of fat-free yogurt. She was so thin that size 0 clothing was too large for her. Now recovered, she has received criticisms from some fans that she is overweight and fat!

of the actual or perceived characteristics related to eating disorders are accurate. At this point we don't know if the described "family characteristics should be considered cause, consequence, or means of coping with an eating disorder" (Herzog, Kronmuller, Hartmann, Bergmann, & Kroger, 2000, p. 360).

Stice and Bearman (2001) believe that socialization agents such as peers or family members can produce pressure to be thin by engaging in criticism of weight, encouragement to diet, and the glorification of ultra-slim models. Perceived pressure from family, friends,

dating partners, or the media to have a slender figure was associated with the thin-ideal internalization and feelings of depression. Part of the depressive reaction arises from the view that "one should be able to diet or exercise to lose weight"—in other words, obtaining a slim figure is under voluntary control. Later, eating "too much," unsuccessful dieting, and guilt from purging or loss of control contributes to depressive feelings. One woman with an eating disorder remembers being teased about her weight by her family. Her nickname was "Checker." It was not until she was a teenager that her mother told her the name came from Chubby Checker (Goldfein et al., 2000). This revelation increased the young woman's sensitivity about her weight. Teasing and criticism about body weight or shape by family members has been found to predict ideal-body internalization, body dissatisfaction, dieting, and eating problems (Vincent & McCabe, 2000).

Other family and peer relationships are associated with eating disorders. Peer relationships can either serve as a buffer to eating disorders or produce pressure to lose weight. Girls exist in a subculture in which thinness is emphasized and weight issues are frequently discussed. Nearly 50 percent of adolescent girls in one study reported being encouraged to lose weight by their mothers, friends, or sisters (Mukai, 1996). Mothers who dieted also indirectly transmitted the message of the importance of slimness and the thin ideal to their daughters. Class differences have also been found. Adolescent girls from higher socioeconomic status families had a greater awareness and acceptance of societal ideals of slimness (Wardle et al., 2004). For boys, peer and father encouragement to lose weight was related to more severe disordered eating patterns. In general, it was the direct influences of family and peers rather than the quality of these relationships that predicted body dissatisfaction and disordered eating in both adolescent boys and girls (Vincent & McCabe, 2000).

Cultural Factors

Some observers believe that eating disorders are a culture-bound syndrome found only in Western cultures (see the Critical Thinking feature "Is Our Society Creating Eating Disorders?"). Few reports of eating disorders are found in Latin America, South America, and Asia, whereas they appear to be high or increasing in European countries, Israel, and Australia (Miller & Pumariega, 2001). Countries or groups that have been exposed to Western values show an increasing concern over eating (Srinivasan, Suresh, & Jayaram, 1998). Although the standard of beauty among African American women in South Africa is based on fuller

CRITICAL THINKING

Is Our Society Creating Eating Disorders?

There appears to have been a dramatic increase in eating disorders over the past twenty years, which is correlated with our society's emphasis on thinness and attractiveness. Even fourth-grade girls are beginning to diet, and 31 percent of nine-year-old girls are worried about being fat. About 80 percent of American girls report having dieted by the age of thirteen (Gardner, 1998). Liposuction is the leading cosmetic surgical procedure; 384,626 (women comprise 84 percent and men 16 percent of this figure) individuals had this procedure performed in 2003, more than double the rate for 1997 (American Society for Aesthetic Plastic Surgery, 2004). Equating thinness with success and attractiveness has taken a toll, especially among women. As many as 64 percent of women exhibit symptoms of eating disorders, and even more are dissatisfied with their body shapes (National Association of Anorexia Nervosa and Associated Disorders, 2004).

What role has society played in eating disorders, and why do they appear primarily in Western societies? Eating disorders are rare in China, Singapore, Malaysia, and Hong Kong (Lee, Hsu, & Wing, 1992; Tsai & Gray, 2000) and in other non-Western cultures (Bhadrinath, 1990; Miller & Pumariega, 2001). Root (1990) believes that thinness represents success and control in Western societies. Other societies do not place such emphasis on thinness. Is it possible that eating disorders are culture-bound syndromes and are attempts by women to resolve identity issues?

As psychologists, we are interested in the etiology or causes of problems. What do you think about the opinion that the "pursuit of thinness" is a culture-bound phenomenon? Do contemporary women gain status or identity through their physical appearance? Why have Western cultures been so susceptible to eating disorders? Do you think eating disorders will increase in the future in other societies? If society continues to equate desirable characteristics with thinness, how can we change its message? How have African Americans been somewhat able to insulate themselves from this standard? The women's movement stressed the importance of ability over appearance. Why, given the greater freedom and power that women have gained, is there an increase in the importance of appearance?

We are also beginning to see more physically attractive men in the mass media. (In one study of twenty-five college men with an eating disorder, they expressed dissatisfaction with their body images and used vomiting, laxatives, and exercise to control their weight [Olivardia, Pope, Mangweth, & Hudson, 1995].) Are such attitudes an early warning sign for a dramatic increase in eating disorders in men?

figures, black teenage girls are being drawn to Western standards of thinness, resulting in a dramatic increase in eating disorders among this group (Simmons, 2002). Asian female adolescents born in Britain also have concerns over body shape and eating (Hill & Bhatti, 1995). Among Pakistani adolescent girls, those who were the most exposed to Western culture had the highest rates of abnormal eating attitudes (Mumford, Whitehouse, & Choudry, 1992). In a shocking discovery, Becker (1995) found a large increase in dieting and disordered eating among Fijian girls during a three-year exposure to Western media. Prior to this period, these behaviors were virtually unknown. The girls reported that television influenced their beliefs regarding the thin body ideal. What is more impressive is that in Fiji the norm for an attractive woman is one who is of larger size with a good appetite (Irving, 2001).

Interestingly, African Americans appear to be somewhat insulated from the thinness standard. African American girls and women are more satisfied with their body size, weight, and appearance than are white females, even though they tend to be heavier than their white counterparts. They also have a lower level of negative attitudes toward body size and weight and less motivation for thinness (Gilbert, 2003; Lovejoy, 2001). Black adolescent females appear to be less concerned about their body size and shape than their white counterparts. Findings from a national survey of adolescents on dieting and disordered eating appear to support this view (Neumark-Sztainer et al., 2000). Ethnic comparisons revealed that dieting was lowest among African American girls (37.6 percent) and highest among white girls (51.3 percent). Disordered eating patterns (bingeing and purging) were highest among Hispanic American girls (19.1 percent) and lowest among African American girls (11.4 percent). Although the results may indicate that African American girls appear to experience lower levels of body dissatisfaction than girls from other ethnic groups, a substantial percentage of them also diet and binge or purge. The impact of ethnicity and dieting or disordered eating was more difficult to interpret in the case of boys. No relationship was found between ethnicity and dieting, but 13.9 percent of African American and 13.1 percent of Hispanic American boys engaged in disordered eating compared with only 4.4 percent of white boys. Why nonwhite boys in the study were more likely to report bingeing and purging is unclear (Story et al., 1998).

Fewer African American women appear to have either anorexia nervosa or bulimia nervosa but are as likely as other groups of women to have binge-eating disorder (Lovejoy, 2001; Striegel-Moore et al., 2003). African American female university students expressed less concern about weight, felt less social pressure to be thin, and chose a significantly heavier ideal body size than white women, and African American men were more willing than white men to date heavier women (Powell & Kahn, 1995). African American women are less distressed by their weight gain and change in shape during pregnancy than their white counterparts are (Cameron et al., 1996). African Americans appear to be able to ignore the white media messages that equate thinness with beauty. Table 16.5

compares some differences in body image and weight concerns among African American and white women. It is possible that African American girls and women are protected by several cultural factors. First, because they do not identify with white women, media messages of thinness have less impact. Second, their definition of attractiveness is broad, encompassing dress, personality, and confidence, and does not focus just on external characteristics such as body shape and weight. Third, African American women have roles that include being assertive and egalitarian in relationships that allow them to have important roles in the community. In this way, they are less influenced by gender-restrictive messages than white women are.

However, not all African American women are protected from majority-culture messages. Many engage in binge eating and attempt to diet. As with white American women, self-esteem and body dissatisfaction among African American women is related to bulimic symptoms. This relationship is greatest among those who have internalized U.S. societal values concerning attractiveness (Lester & Petrie, 1998). The prevalence among African American women of eating disorder not otherwise specified appears to be equivalent to that found in European American women (Mulholland & Mintz, 2001). In a study of African American and

TABLE 16.5 Differences in Body Image and Weight Concerns Among African American and White Females

Concern	African American Females	White American Females
Satisfied with current weight or body shape	70 percent	11 percent
Body image	Perceive selves to be thinner than they actually are.	Perceive selves to be heavier than they actually are.
Attitude toward dieting	Better to be a little overweight than underweight (65 percent of respondents in a survey).	Need to diet to produce a slender body. Fear of being overweight.
Definition of beauty	Well groomed, "style," and overall attractiveness. Beauty is the right "attitude and personality."	Slim; 5'7''; 100 to 110 pounds. Perfect body can lead to success and the good life.
Being overweight	Of those who were overweight, 40 percent considered their figures attractive or very attractive.	Those who considered selves as not having a weight problem were 6 to 14 pounds under the lower limit of the "ideal" weight range.
Age and beauty	Believed they would get more beautiful with age (65 percent chose this response).	Beauty is fleeting and decreases with age.

Source: Desmond, Price, Hallinan, Smith (1989); Kumanyika, Wilson, & Guilford-Davenport (1993); Lovejoy (2001); Parker, Nichter, Vuckovic, Sims, & Ritenbaugh (1995); Rand & Kuldau (1990).

white women with or without binge-eating disorder, certain differences were found (Pike et al., 2001). African American women had higher body weight than white women and had fewer weight and shape concerns, regardless of whether or not they had the disorder. Among those with binge-eating disorder, African Americans had significantly lower scores on eating concerns, dietary restraints, and shape and weight concerns (see Table 16.5). Thus African American women with binge-eating disorder differed in certain eating disorder characteristics from their white counterparts. The drive for thinness may be less an etiological factor for African Americans than it is for white Americans. Among Hispanic American female college students, weight and adherence to mainstream values were positively related to bulimic symptoms (Lester & Petrie, 1998). Some studies show that American Indian, Asian American, and Hispanic American girls show greater body image dissatisfaction than white females, possibly due to attempts to fit into the societal definition of beauty (Gilbert, 2003). Thus it appears that ethnic minorities are becoming increasingly vulnerable to societal messages regarding attractiveness and may be at especially high risk for developing eating disorders, as a greater percentage of ethnic minority children and adults, especially females, are overweight (Ogden, Fryar, Carroll, & Flegal, 2004).

Other Suggested Etiological Factors in Eating Disorders

Additional research has focused on personality characteristics, negative emotional moods, and sexual abuse as causal factors in eating disorders. Individuals with eating disorders often display low self-esteem and feelings of helplessness, resulting in the use of food or weight control as a means of handling stress or anxieties (Walsh & Devlin, 1998). Individuals with anorexia have been described as perfectionistic, obedient, good students, excellent athletes, and model children. It is hypothesized that the emphasis on weight allows them to have control over an aspect of their lives. Dieting and weight loss are individual activities over which one has nearly total control (Hoffman, 1998). Perfectionism has also been found to be a predictor of bulimic symptoms among women who perceived themselves as being overweight (Joiner, Heatherton, Rudd, & Schmidt, 1997). Among African American college women, body mass, body dissatisfaction, and low self-esteem were related to bulimic symptoms (Lester & Petrie, 1998). For both men and women, higher scores on characteristics such as passivity, low self-esteem, dependence, and nonassertiveness are associated with higher scores on disordered eating. Dieting may be used to demonstrate

self-control and improve self-esteem and body image (Lakkis, Ricciardelli, & Williams, 1999). Another line of inquiry has interested some researchers. Rates of affective disorders are higher in the relatives of individuals with eating disorders than in control relatives, and some investigators believe that eating disorders represent an expression of an affective disorder (Rutter, MacDonald, et al., 1990). Depression often accompanies eating disorders. One interesting finding is that binge eating, purging, and mood varied seasonally among patients with bulimia nervosa (Blouin et al., 1992). The researchers hypothesize that for some people, a relationship between bulimia and seasonal affective disorder may exist. The cycle of bingeing and purging may be associated with light availability. At this point, we still do not know the precise relationship between affective disorders and eating disorders. Some therapists believe that depression is the result, not the cause, of anorexia or bulimia (Vanderlinden et al., 1992).

Although it is widely believed that sexual abuse is a causal factor in eating disorders, several studies have failed to find such a connection (Conners & Morse, 1993; Pope & Hudson, 1992; Pope et al., 1994). Sexual abuse may be indirectly related to eating disorders in that it produces body disparagement or bodily shame, which affects body image (Tripp & Petrie, 2001).

Genetic Influences

Genetic influences may also contribute to eating disorders, which appear to run in families, especially among female relatives (Hoffman, 1998). Strober and colleagues (2000) examined the lifetime rates of full or partial anorexia nervosa and bulimia nervosa among first-degree relatives of patients with these eating disorders. The rate was compared with that of relatives of matched, never-ill comparison participants. Support was found for a genetic contribution to the disorders. Whereas anorexia nervosa and bulimia nervosa were relatively rare among the relatives of the never-ill group, these disorders occurred at significantly high levels among the first-degree relatives of those with eating disorders (see Table 16.6). Subclinical forms of the two eating disorders also aggregated around the relatives of the individual with anorexia or bulimia. Interestingly, in this study, the relatives of those with anorexia nervosa were as likely to develop bulimia as anorexia. The reverse was also true. There may be a shared familial factor between the two eating disorders. Kendler and associates (1991) examined identical and fraternal twins to estimate the role of genetics in bulimia nervosa. They reported concordance rates of 22.9 percent and 8.7 percent, respectively, which suggested a modest

TABLE 16.6   Lifetime Rates of Illness in Female First-Degree Relatives of Probands with Anorexia Nervosa, or No Psychiatric Illness

Proband Diagnosis	Number of Female Relatives	Female Relatives with Diagnosis									
		Anorexia Nervosa		Partial Anorexia Nervosa		Bulimia Nervosa		Partial Bulimia Nervosa		Total and Partial Illness	
		n	%	n	%	n	%	n	%	n	%
Anorexia nervosa	290	10	3.4	10	3.4	11	3.8	10	3.4	41	14.4
Bulima nervosa	297	11	3.7	10	3.4	12	4.0	11	3.7	44	14.8
Never ill	318	1	0.3	2	0.6	3	0.9	4	1.3	10	3.1

Source: Strober et al. (2000).

genetic influence. Wade, Bulik, Sullivan, Neale, and Kendler (2000) also believe that some common genetic factors exist for binge eating and bulimia among female twins.

How do we interpret the findings? There is strong support for the view that familial factors are implicated in the eating disorders. However, it is still not clear whether the influences are primarily genetic or environmental. To get a more conclusive answer, we would have to eliminate the possibility that the elevation of eating disorders among relatives of those with anorexia and bulimia was due to environmental influences such as modeling or exposure to disordered eating patterns.

Treatment of Eating Disorders

Prevention programs have been developed in schools to reduce the incidence of eating disorders and disordered eating patterns. A school-based group intervention program was developed for adolescent girls who were showing some problems with eating, body image, and self-esteem (Daigneault, 2000). The goals for the girls involved (1) learning to develop a more positive attitude toward their bodies, (2) becoming aware of societal messages of "what it means to be female," (3) developing healthier eating and exercise habits, (4) increasing their comfort in expressing their feelings to peers, family members, and significant others, (5) developing healthy strategies to deal with stress and pressures, and (6) increasing assertiveness skills. These points were addressed through group discussions and the use of videos, magazines, and examples from mass media. Similarly, Sands (1998) believes that the social

context for eating disorders needs to be acknowledged in any type of treatment. She recommends including a gender analysis by identifying sex role messages such as "girls must be thin, pretty, and sexy," identifying the consequences of the gender-related messages ("I'm going to starve myself to be thin"), choosing a statement of change and implementing it ("Being healthy is important to me so I will eat and exercise sensibly"), and developing assertiveness skills to combat patterns of helplessness and submissiveness. Both of these approaches focus on teaching girls and women to reexamine the consequences of gender messages and on the necessity of institutional awareness of the problem. These elements have been included in most of the treatments for anorexia nervosa, bulimia nervosa, and binge-eating disorder. Programs that are the most effective are those that involve an interactive versus a lecturing format, that are designed specifically for women, and that have multiple sessions (Stice & Shaw, 2004).

Anorexia Nervosa

A female undergoing treatment for anorexia nervosa—who was 5 feet, 3 inches tall and weighed 81 pounds and still felt fat—reported, "I did gain 25 pounds, the target weight of my therapist and nutritionist. But everyday was really difficult. I would go and cry. A big part of anorexia is fear. Fear of fat, fear of eating. But (my therapist) taught me about societal pressures to be ultra-thin comes from the media, TV, advertising. ... She talked me through what I was thinking and how I had completely dissociated my mind from my body. ... I'm slowly reintroducing foods one thing at a time. I'd like to think I am completely better, but I'm not. I'm still extremely self-conscious about my appearance. But I now know I have a problem and my family and I are finding ways to cope with it." (Bryant, 2001, p. B4)

As you have seen, eating disorders, especially anorexia nervosa, can be life threatening. Treatment for anorexia nervosa can be delivered on either an outpatient or an inpatient basis, depending on the weight and health of the individual. Because it is a complex disorder, there is a need for teamwork between physicians, psychiatrists, and psychotherapists. A dental exam should also be given to assess for damage from purging. Because the individual is starving, the initial goal is to restore weight. During the refeeding process, the patient's feelings of apathy may begin to fade. Restoration of weight should not be attempted without psychological support. Typically, the individual with anorexia nervosa will become terrified of gaining weight and need the opportunity to discuss her or his reactions. During the weight restoration period, new foods have to be introduced, because the individual's choices are not sufficiently high in calories. The physical condition of the person has to be carefully monitored because sudden and severe physiological reactions can occur during refeeding. Psychological interventions are used to help the patient (1) understand and cooperate with nutritional and physical rehabilitation, (2) identify and understand the dysfunctional attitudes related to the eating disorder, (3) improve interpersonal and social functioning, and (4) address comorbid psychopathology and psychological conflicts that reinforce eating disorder behavior (American Dietetic Association, 2001; American Psychiatric Association, 2000; Walsh & Devlin, 1998). The behavioral approach is designed to correct irrational preoccupation with weight and to encourage weight gain through the use of such positive reinforcers as television or telephone privileges, visits from family and friends, mail, and access to street clothes. The particular reinforcers used to reward weight gain depend, of course, on the likes and dislikes of the patient. Weight-gain plans are generally aimed at increases of about two pounds per week (Wilson & Shafran, 2005). Once the patient has gained sufficient weight to become an outpatient, family therapy sessions may be implemented. Experience has shown that this approach helps maintain the treatment gains achieved in the hospital.

The family of an eighteen-year-old girl who was unsuccessfully treated by inpatient treatment, dietary training, and cognitive behavioral therapy was enlisted in a new form of family therapy. The therapy involved (1) having the parents help re-feed the adolescent through the planning of meals, (2) reducing parental criticism by understanding anorexia nervosa as a serious disease, (3) negotiating a new pattern of family relationships, and (4) assisting the family with the developmental process of separation and individuation. Parents were encouraged to understand and help their daughter develop the skills, attitudes, and activities appropriate to this developmental stage. This form of family therapy resulted in the girl gaining over twenty-two pounds (Sim et al., 2004).

Bulimia Nervosa

During the initial assessment of patients with bulimia nervosa, conditions that might contribute to purging, such as esophageal reflux disease, should be identified. Physical conditions resulting from purging include muscle weakness, cardiac arrhythmias, dehydration, and electrolyte imbalance, as well as gastrointestinal problems involving the stomach or esophagus. In many patients, dental erosion can be quite serious. As with anorexia nervosa, bulimia nervosa should involve an interdisciplinary team that includes a physician and psychotherapist. One important goal in treatment is to normalize the eating pattern and to eliminate the binge-purge cycle. A routine of eating three meals a day with one to three snacks a day is used to break up the disordered eating pattern. Cognitive behavioral therapy and the use of antidepressant medication such as SSRIs have been helpful in treating this condition (American Psychiatric Association, 2000; Wilson & Shafran, 2005). Cognitive-behavioral approaches have also been effective in helping individuals with bulimia and binge-eating disorder develop a sense of self-control (Parrott, 1998). Common components of cognitive-behavioral treatment plans are encouraging the consumption of three or more balanced meals a day, reducing rigid food rules and body image concerns, and developing cognitive and behavioral strategies. This approach was as successful as antidepressant medication in treating bulimia nervosa, although combined treatment was the most effective (Agras et al., 1992). Even with these approaches, only about 50 percent of those with the disorder fully recover. Certain characteristics associated with treatment failure included poorer social adjustment and a reduction in purging of less than 70 percent by the sixth treatment session. For these individuals, different treatment strategies need to be developed (Agras et al., 2000).

Binge-Eating Disorder

Treatments for binge-eating disorder are similar to those for bulimia nervosa, although BED presents fewer physical complications because of a lack of purging. Individuals with BED do differ in some ways from those with bulimia nervosa. Most are overweight and have to deal with stereotypes of overweight individuals. Because of the health consequences of weight problems, some therapy programs also attempt to help the individual lose weight. In general, treatment follows three phases (Ricca, Mannucci, Zucchi, Rotella, & Faravelli, 2000). First, cognitive factors underlying the eating disorder are determined. The clients also are taught to use strategies that reduce eating binges. One patient, Mrs. A., had very rigid rules concerning eating that, when violated, would result in her "going the whole nine yards." Two types of triggers were identified for binges—emotional distress involving anger, anxiety, sadness, or frustration and work stressors (long hours, deadlines). Interventions were applied to help her develop more flexible rules regarding eating and to deal with her stressors. In many of these programs, body weight is recorded weekly, and a healthy pattern of three meals and two snacks a day is implemented. Food diaries may be utilized to determine type and amount of the food consumed and the psychological states preceding eating. Information about obesity, proper nutrition, and physical exercise is provided. These steps comprise the first part of the program. Second, cognitive strategies are employed regarding distorted beliefs about eating. The thoughts are identified and eliminated by changing the individual's thought patterns. The client is asked to prepare a list of "forbidden" foods and to rank them in order of "dangerousness." Gradually, the foods are introduced into normal eating, first beginning with those perceived as being less dangerous. The clients are asked observe their own bodies in a mirror to help reduce or eliminate cognitive distortions associated with their bodies. The prejudices of society about body size are discussed, and realistic expectations about the amount of change are addressed. The clients may also be asked to observe attractive individuals with a larger body size to help them consider positive qualities other than focusing on the body. After performing this "homework," Mrs. A. discovered that overweight women can look attractive, and she bought more fashionable clothes for herself. She was astonished at the positive reactions and comments from friends and coworkers. Although she had lost twelve pounds, she attributed the attention to her confidence and improved body image (Goldfein et al., 2000). Cognitive behavior therapy can produce significant reductions in binge eating but is successful in reducing weight (Carter & Fairburn, 1998; Ricca et al. 2000).

Primary Sleep Disorders

The performance of medical interns who worked more than eighty hours a week and who had some work shifts of twenty-four hours, a traditional schedule for physicians in training, was compared with their performance on a more restricted schedule of less than eighty hours a week and with no shifts longer than sixteen hours. When working the traditional shift, they made 5.6 times more serious diagnostic errors, 17.1 percent more serious medication errors, and over twice as many nonintercepted serious errors (Landrigan et al., 2004).

Most adults require eight hours of sleep or more to function at their optimal level. As you can see from the poll in the Mental Health and Society feature "Sleeplessness in America," obtaining restful and adequate sleep is difficult for many Americans. When people do not get enough sleep, attention, vigilance, and performance deteriorate. Five distinct stages of sleep are recognized. Stages 1, 2, 3, and 4 represent non-rapid-eye-movement sleep (NREM). In adults, approximately 5 percent of the time asleep is spent in Stage 1, the transition from wakefulness to sleep, 50 percent in Stage 2 sleep, and 10–20 percent in Stages 3 and 4, the deepest level of sleep. Rapid-eye-movement sleep (REM), which is associated with dream reports, occupies about 20–25 percent of sleep and usually alternates with NREM sleep every ninety minutes (American Psychiatric Association, 2000).

Generally, complaints regarding sleep are of two varieties (see Figure 16.5). The first involves the inability to initiate or maintain sleep at night (i.e., insomnia), and the second, excessive daytime sleepiness, or an inability to maintain wakefulness during the day. When initiating sleep, maintaining sleep, or excessive sleepiness becomes severe, the individual may meet the criteria for one of the sleep disorders. In this section, we present the primary sleep disorders that are due to physiological abnormalities in "sleep-wake generating or timing mechanisms" or conditioning factors. Problems with sleep due to other etiological factors, such as those that are directly related to a diagnosable mental disorder (e.g., major depression or generalized anxiety disorder), a general medical condition, or the influence of a substance, are not covered in this section. The primary sleep disorders are subdivided into dyssomnias which are abnormalities in the quality, amount, or timing of sleep and the parasomnias which are problems occurring during sleep, the different stages of sleep, or in the sleep-wake transition (American Psychiatric Association, 2000)

Dyssomnias

Dyssomnias involve difficulties in getting to sleep and maintaining sleep or complaints of excessive sleepiness during the day. They include primary insomnia, primary hypersomnia, narcolepsy, breathing-related sleep

MENTAL HEALTH AND SOCIETY

Sleeplessness in America

A national poll by the National Sleep Foundation (2002) found that, although a minimum of eight hours of sleep per night is recommended, most Americans sleep much less, and this contributes to attention span problems, accidents, and decreased work productivity. Symptoms related to sleep disorders were also prevalent among the respondents.

Sleep Deprivation and Its Impact

- 37 percent of adults report that excessive sleepiness interferes with their job performance.
- 68 percent of adults indicate that sleepiness interferes with their concentration.
- 68 percent of shift workers have problems sleeping.
- 51 percent of adults report driving while drowsy during the past year, and 21 percent reported that they dozed off at the wheel during the past year.

Problems with Sleep Quality

The inability to obtain quality sleep is more prevalent in women, younger and middle- aged adults, and shift workers. Seventy-four percent of the respondents had one or more of the following symptoms of a sleep disorder a few nights a week or more:

- Insomnia: 58 percent of adults report having insomnia a few nights a week, and 35 percent experience symptoms of insomnia every or almost every night. Specifically, 40 percent report waking up feeling unrefreshed; 36 percent being awake a lot during the night; 25 percent having difficulty in falling asleep; and 24 percent waking up too early and not being able to go back to sleep.
- Snoring (possible sleep apnea): Reported in 42 percent of men and 31 percent of women.
- Pauses in breathing (symptom of sleep apnea): Reported in

11 percent of men and 7 percent of women.

- Unpleasant, tingling feelings in legs (possible restless leg syndrome): Reported by 16 percent of adults.

Factors Associated with Sleep Disruption

- Stress: 26 percent of women and 16 percent of men
- Working night shifts: 35 percent versus 19 percent of regular day workers
- Pain: 20 percent of adults
- Noise, light, temperature, or other environmental factors: 16 percent
- Partner snoring: 22 percent of women; 7 percent of men
- Nasal congestion: 12 percent
- Allergies: 8 percent
- Concerns about pauses in partner's breathing: 11 percent of women; 2 percent of men

---

disorders, circadian-rhythm sleep disorder, and dyssomnia not otherwise specified.

Primary Insomnia

> It happens two or three times a week. I get in bed, turn off the light and wait to fall asleep ... and wait ... and wait. It might be two or three hours before I drop off. And even then, I might wake up a couple of hours later to go through the whole thing again. (Lemonick, 2004, p. 100)

Primary insomnia is defined in DSM-IV-TR as difficulty getting to sleep, maintaining sleep or having nonrestorative sleep for at least one month, which causes clinically significant distress in social, occupational, or other areas of functioning. The insomnia must not be the result of another sleep disorder, such as narcolepsy or restless leg syndrome. In a sample of older adults who complained of insomnia, up to 43 percent actually had undiagnosed sleep apnea or restless leg

movement instead (Lichstein, Riedel, Lester, & Aguillard, 1999). Insomnia can be the result of a wide range of causes, such as subclinical worry, anxiety, or conditioned arousal to the bedroom setting. Certain behaviors such as the consumption of caffeine, alcohol, or heavy meals or exercising within two hours of sleep can also interfere with the quality of sleep (Lichstein, Wilson, & Johnson, 2000). Individuals with insomnia may report intrusive and uncontrollable cognitive activity that interferes with sleep. Changes in sleep habits, such as naps, early bedtimes, overly long periods spent in bed, or stressors involving work or relationships, can prevent adequate sleep (Libman, Creti, Ansel, Brender, & Fichten, 1997). Excessive daytime sleepiness is a very common result of insomnia and may impair cognitive functioning and alertness, performance at work, and enjoyment of family and recreational activities.

Older adults show the highest rate of sleeping problems, with 52 percent reporting problems with inadequate sleep and excessive daytime sleepiness (Stepanski,

FIGURE 16.5 Disorders Chart (DSM-IV-TR): Sleep Disorders

Dyssomnias	PRIMARY SLEEP DISORDERS	Parasomnias
Disorders involving difficulty in initiating or maintaining sleep or excessive sleepiness	Endogenous abnormalities in sleep-wake mechanism that may be result of conditioning factors. Not included are sleep problems related to mental disorders, substance use, or a general medical condition.	Disorders involving abnormal behaviors or physiological reactions during sleep, specific sleep stages, or in the transition from sleep to wakefulness. These involve the activation of the autonomic nervous system, motor system, or cognitive process at inappropriate times during sleep or sleep to wakeful transitions.
Primary insomnia Difficulty initiating or maintaining sleep or nonrestful sleep for a minimum of one month		
Primary hypersomnia Excessive sleepiness for at least one month or prolonged sleep episodes occurring daily		**Nightmare Disorder** Repeated awakenings from sleep with vivid, recallable, and frightening dreams; on awakening, rapidly becomes oriented and alert
Narcolepsy Irresistible refreshing sleep occurring daily for at least 3 months; presence of cataplexy (sudden loss of muscle tone); and/or recurrent intrusions of REM sleep in transition from wakefulness to sleep		**Sleep Terror Disorder** Recurrent awakenings from sleep with panicky scream; intense fear and signs of autonomic arousal; unresponsive to attempts to comfort; amnesia for the episode
Breathing-Related Sleep Disorder Sleep disruption producing excessive sleepiness due to breathing condition during sleep		**Sleepwalking Disorder** Repeated episodes of rising from bed and walking; relatively unresponsive with blank face; on awakening, amnesia for the episode; within minutes of awakening, becomes alert
Circadian Rhythm Sleep Disorder Recurrent pattern of sleep disruption producing excessive sleepiness due to mismatch between sleep-wake schedule and circadian sleep-wake pattern		**Parasomnias Not Otherwise Specified** REM behavior disorder and sleep paralysis
Dyssomnia Not Otherwise Specified Other problems with sleep due to environmental factors, restless leg syndrome, periodic limb movements		

Source: American Psychiatric Association (2000).

Rybarczyk, Lopez, & Stevens, 2003). Ethnic and gender differences regarding insomnia have been found. Among older Americans, African Americans are less likely to report restless sleep than white Americans, and women have more sleep complaints than men (Kutner, Bliwise, & Zhang, 2004).

Primary Hypersomnia

A 27-year-old carpenter presented with a complaint that he "was always hard to wake up." ... Persistent excessive daytime sleepiness began at the age of 15–16 years, when he had to "sleep for the rest of the day" after school, and worsened over the next several years. He was able to resist sleepiness in important situations but he had a few car accidents related to sleepiness. ... Involuntary naps lasted 15 min to 2 h, were always unrefreshing. (Bassetti & Aldrich, 1997, p. 1428)

Primary hypersomnia is characterized by excessive daytime sleepiness or prolonged nighttime sleep for at least one month that causes significant distress or impairment in social, occupational, or other important areas of functioning. An individual with primary

FIGURE 16.5 Disorders Chart (DSM-IV-TR): Sleep Disorders (continued)

SLEEP DISORDERS	Prevalence	Age of Onset	Course
Primary Insomnia	From 1–10% of adults; up to 25% in elderly; more prevalent in women	Usually young adulthood or middle age	Often has sudden onset associated with psychological, social, or medical stressors; course variable
Primary Hypersomnia	Not known; incidence over 4-year period is about 8%	Typically begins between ages of 15–30	Usually chronic and stable, unless treated
Narcolepsy	Rare, from 0.02–0.16% in adult population; equal rates for men and women	Usually during adolescence, although symptoms may be present even during preschool	Has a stable course; in minority, symptoms improve
Breathing-Related Sleep Disorder	Approximately 1–10% of adults; may be higher in older adults; in adults, more prevalent in males	Seen in young children and adults; more common in middle aged, overweight males	Gradual, progressive course
Circadian Rhythm Sleep Disorder	Varies widely depending on type of disorder; delayed sleep in 7% of adolescents; shift work at night up to 60%	Delayed sleep type more often late childhood to early adulthood; shift work more in older adults	Delayed sleep type may be chronic; shift work type may be as long as on night schedule
Nightmare Disorder	Unknown; nightmares in up to 50% of children; more females than males	Children exposed to stressors; usually between 3 and 6 years	Most outgrow it; in minority, may persist
Sleep Terror Disorder	Between 1–6% among children and less than 1% in adults; in children more males; sex ratio even in adults	Usually between 4 and 12 years; in adults, between 20 and 30 years	Most resolve without treatment; in adults, may be chronic
Sleepwalking Disorder	Up to 30% of children have at least one sleepwalking episode; 1–5% have the disorder with more females in children, but more males during adulthood	Usually between 4 and 8 years; peaks at age 12	In children, it resolves by adolescence; less common, recurrence in adulthood

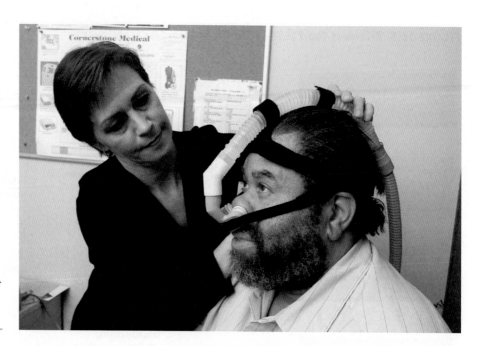

Insomnia This man with sleep apnea is being fitted with a nasal mask that will provide continuous air pressure and allow him to breathe normally during sleep.

hypersomnia feels compelled to nap during the day yet usually gains no relief from sleepiness. He or she may show difficulty waking up after sleeping (National Institute of Neurological Disorders and Stroke, 2004). The diagnosis of primary hypersomnia is not made if the cause of this condition is another sleep disorder, such as narcolepsy or sleep apnea, or a physical condition such as a tumor or brain injury.

In a study of forty-two patients with primary hypersomnia, almost all had problems with driving, work performance, or social functioning, and 60 percent had to take involuntary naps during the day, which were described as "unrefreshing." For these patients, the episodes of hypersomnia began during young adulthood and tended to worsen over several years (Bassetti & Aldrich, 1997).

Narcolepsy

For most of my early childhood, no one could understand why I fell asleep so often. I also remember waking up at night and not being able to move. ... I would find myself desperately trying to shake my head to wake myself up. ... Whenever I thought something was extremely funny and tried to laugh, I would lose all control of the muscles in my legs and neck. ("Sleepy in Florida," 2004, p. 2)

Narcolepsy is a sleep disorder with no known cause that is characterized by an overwhelming need for sleep in the daytime even when adequate sleep occurs during the night. Drowsiness or actually falling asleep can occur without warning and can be irresistible.

Other symptoms that may or may not occur are as follows (National Institutes of Health, 2004):

- Cataplexy (i.e., the sudden loss of muscle function) ranging from a slight weakness of the body to complete collapse. This may be triggered by emotional states such as anger, laughter, or fear and may last for seconds or minutes with the individual remaining conscious.

- Sleep paralysis involving the temporary inability to talk or move during wakefulness that may last from seconds to minutes.

- Hypnogogic hallucinations (i.e., vivid, dreamlike experiences) that occur just before falling asleep.

The sleep attacks must occur daily for at least three months and be accompanied by two or more of the preceding symptoms. Excessive sleepiness or unintended sleep occurs first, with cataplexy or other symptoms developing years later. Most individuals with narcolepsy go to sleep within five minutes and often go immediately into REM sleep (American Psychiatric Association, 2000). The regions of the brain that are involved in narcolepsy appear to be those associated with REM sleep (i.e., the dream state). Normal sleep has two phases. NREM sleep is a quiet sleep state in which the muscles are relaxed and loss of consciousness occurs. The second phase is REM sleep, in which breathing and heart rate are irregular, dreams occur, and muscle tone is greatly reduced. The sleep cycle of most individuals begins with NREM sleep followed by REM sleep approximately ninety minutes later. Individuals with narcolepsy often go immediately into REM sleep. The loss of muscle tone and dreamlike hypnogogic hallucinations are thought to be the triggering of some of the mechanisms involved in REM sleep (Siegel, 2000).

Breathing-Related Sleep Disorder

> My wife would tell me that I stopped breathing during the night and that she would lie awake counting the seconds until I started to breathe again. I thought I was sleeping through the night, so I never really gave it a lot of thought. Anyway, what's the big deal? So I snore and stop breathing. At least I'm getting some sleep. (American Sleep Apnea Association, 2004, p. 1)

"Bill" did undergo an assessment at a sleep clinic, which revealed that during one night, he had experienced arousal 592 times in order to resume breathing. Thus he was getting only about forty-five seconds of sleep before he would rouse himself by gasping for air. **Breathing-related sleep disorder** involves excessive sleepiness caused by sleep disruption due to abnormalities of breathing during sleep. The individual with this condition has disturbed sleep as a result of increased arousal when oxygen goes below a certain level due to a cessation of breathing. The most common form of breathing-related sleep disorder is *obstructive sleep apnea,* which is characterized by upper-airway obstruction during sleep. Two other forms of breathing-related sleep disorder are recognized: (1) central sleep apnea syndrome is the periodic cessation of breathing without airway obstruction and is the result of cardiac or neurological conditions; (2) central alveolar hypoventilation syndrome is more prevalent in extremely overweight individuals and involves the impairment of the ventilatory controls (American Psychiatric Association, 2000). In this section, we focus on obstructive sleep apnea.

Obstructive sleep apnea (OSA) is a relatively common condition that remains undiagnosed in about 75 percent of treatable cases (Young, Skatrud, & Peppard, 2004). Symptoms of OSA include disruptive snoring, breathing pauses, gasping, and excessive daytime sleepiness. It is produced by the obstruction of the airway through the collapse of the soft tissue in the rear of the throat. Being overweight can also contribute to this condition by increasing the amount of tissue around the airway (National Sleep Foundation, 2004). The obstruction repeatedly prevents the sleeper from breathing during sleep. The individual is aroused by a signal from the brain to resume breathing, which often occurs as snoring or gasping for breath. It is estimated that up to 10 million individuals suffer from unrecognized sleep apnea. This condition results in excessive daytime sleepiness, high blood pressure, cardiovascular disease, and weight gain (American Sleep Apnea Association, 2004). This form of sleep apnea can occur at any age but is usually evaluated in individuals between the ages of forty and sixty. It has a gradual onset and is considered to be a chronic condition found in two to four times as many males as females (American Psychiatric Association, 2000). There appears to be an increased risk of the disorder among family members (Young, Skatrud, & Peppard, 2004).

Circadian Rhythm Sleep Disorder Circadian rhythms are changes in bodily and mental characteristics that occur during the course of a day and that are controlled by the body's biological clock. This "clock" operates on a twenty-five-hour cycle for most individuals but is affected by sunlight. Our circadian rhythms can be reset by light, which switches off the production of the hormone melatonin. This hormone increases with darkness, causing drowsiness. **Circadian rhythm sleep disorder** is a pattern of recurrent sleep disruption caused by a disruption of the biological sleep-wake cycle or a mismatch between the internal "clock" for sleeping and waking and environmental demands. For example, in jet lag, the body has not adjusted to the time changes in traveling from one time zone to another. Adjustment usually takes several days. Shift work can also produce problems with the circadian rhythm, because the schedule of work is in opposition to sleep-regulating cues associated with sunlight. Problems with drowsiness or inattention can occur during nighttime duties when the body is biologically prepared for sleep and have been implicated in major disasters such as the Exxon *Valdez* oil spill and the Three Mile Island and Chernobyl nuclear power plant accidents (NIH, 2004a).

Dyssomnias Not Otherwise Specified In this category, sleep disorders that do not meet the criteria for a specific dyssomnia but that produce significant impairment include:

- Environmental factors such as noise or light that produce clinically significant insomnia.

- Excessive sleepiness produced by sleep deprivation.

- Restless leg syndrome (RLS), which is the sensation of unpleasant tingling, crawling, or pricking sensations in the legs and feet with an urge to move them for relief. This syndrome is common especially among older adults and affects as many as 12 million Americans (NIH, 2004a). The need to move the legs produces insomnia at night.

- Periodic limb movement disorder (PLMD) is a condition characterized by repetitive jerking movements of the limbs that interfere with sleep. It is found more frequently among older adults and considered to be a chronic condition (American Psychiatric Association, 2000).

Parasomnias

A husband remembers kissing his wife goodnight. His next memory was being awakened by the police. He was unaware that his wife was dead or that he had stabbed her 44 times while asleep. He had instances of sleepwalking earlier in his life. (Cartwright, 2004)

Parasomnias involve the activation of behavioral or physiological systems at inappropriate times during specific sleep stages or the sleep-wake transition. In sleepwalking, for example, some areas of the brain appear to be functioning in a waking state while others remain in sleep. Parasomnias are usually accompanied by complaints of unusual behaviors during sleep or the sleep-wake transition rather than excessive sleepiness during the day or the inability to obtain restful sleep as with the dyssomnias. The parasomnias include nightmare disorder, sleep terror disorder, sleepwalking disorder, and parasomnias not otherwise specified (American Psychiatric Association, 2000).

Nightmare Disorder　Approximately 3 percent of preschoolers and school-age children have nightmares several times a week (National Sleep Foundation, 2004b). **Nightmare disorder** involves dreams with themes of danger that are frightening enough to produce awakening. The individual becomes alert when awakened and may have difficulty going back to sleep because of the distress from the dream content. These episodes occur almost exclusively during REM sleep. Nightmares are common in children, are more prevalent in females, and are rare in adults, but the prevalence of nightmare disorder is unknown (American Psychiatric Association, 2000).

Sleep Terror Disorder　**Sleep terror disorder** involves vivid nightmares that occur during the first third of the night in deep sleep. The child usually screams with terror, is not fully aroused, and does not remember what happened. During this time, the child may be inconsolable. Because the child is not fully awake, he or she will do best when allowed to go back to sleep rather than be awakened (Townsley, 2004). In general, there is little or no memory of the episode the next day (National Sleep Foundation, 2004c). Sleep terrors are different from nightmares in that sleep terrors occur during NREM sleep. The prevalence of sleep terror disorder is unknown, but sleep terror episodes occur in up to 6 percent of children. It usually disappears spontaneously during adolescence. In adults it usually begins between the ages of twenty and thirty and generally follows a chronic course (American Psychiatric Association, 2000).

Nightmares　Nightmares are frightening or terrifying dreams that usually involve themes of imminent danger to the dreamer. They typically occur during REM sleep. Repeated occurrences can lead to a diagnosis of nightmare disorder. This painting by Louis Janmot is titled *The Poem of the Soul: Nightmare.*

Sleepwalking Disorder Sleepwalking disorder involves motor activity that ranges from sitting up to getting out of bed and walking about while still asleep. During these episodes the individual is in a state of reduced alertness and performs behaviors requiring little complexity, although some cases have been reported of individuals operating machinery while sleepwalking. According to the National Sleep Foundation (2004b), about 2 percent of school-age children sleepwalk "at least a few nights a week." The prevalence of sleepwalking disorder ranges from 1 percent to 5 percent, although up to 30 percent of children have at least one episode of sleepwalking. This disorder tends to disappear during early adolescence, but when it occurs in adults, it tends to follow a chronic waxing and waning course (American Psychiatric Association, 2000).

Parasomnias Not Otherwise Specified There are two types of parasomnias that are not otherwise specified. *REM sleep behavior disorder* usually involves motor behavior often of a violent nature during REM sleep. The individual may scream or hit his or her sleeping partner. Most with this disorder are male, and treatment using clonazepam, a benzodiazepine, has been effective (National Sleep Foundation, 2004a). *Sleep paralysis* is the inability to move during the transition from wakefulness to sleep. During this time the individual may have extreme anxiety and the fear of impending death.

Etiology and Treatment of Sleep Disorders

Problems in sleep can result from factors such as subclinical anxiety and depression, environmental changes due to noise, light or other stimuli, and health and behavioral habits. In many cases the etiology is unknown (Cohen, Nehring, & Cloninger, 1996). The assessment of dyssomnias should include the age of onset, predisposing characteristics (being a light sleeper, family history of sleep problems, current stressors, illnesses, or medications), lifestyle and daily activity patterns, and input from the bed partner about snoring, breathing pattern changes, or unusual leg or body movements.

Some etiological factors in sleep disorders involve the following (Libman, Creti, Amsel, Brender, & Fichten, 1997):

- Cognitions or intrusive, uncontrollable thoughts associated with worry, anxiety, or depression

- Personality and psychological adjustment problems that can predispose individuals to the development of sleep disorders

- Lifestyle factors, such as irregular schedules as a result of jobs, retirement, napping, early bedtimes, overly long periods spent in bed, and major stressors such as the death or illness of a loved one

- Nocturnal activities that interfere with sleep, such as the consumption of caffeine or alcohol or exercising in the evening

Excessive sleepiness, as in hypersomnia or narcolepsy, can be treated through the use of stimulants such as amphetamines and methylphenidate or with antidepressants. The treatment of narcolepsy with stimulant medications has met with only modest success (Cohen, Nehring, & Cloninger, 1996). For insomnia, sleep pills may be prescribed. However, they tend to lose their effectiveness after weeks of use and may actually interfere with good sleep over the long term (National Institute of Neurological Disorders and Stroke, 2004). The use of stimulants was effective in treating 72 percent of individuals with primary hypersomnia—some showed a spontaneous improvement over a period of three years without medication (Bassetti & Aldrich, 1997). Treatment for dyssomnias are similar in that the following are recommended (Lichstein, Wilson, & Johnson, 2000):

- Relaxation or focusing procedures that reduce arousal. These are particularly effective for those with problems falling asleep.

- Emphasizing relaxed attitude or frame of mind when going to bed

- Taking five slow, deep breaths, including a softly spoken "relax" with each exhale; slowly reviewing the body in sequential parts while focusing on relaxed sensations; repeating slowing and silently the autogenic phrase "I am at peace; my arms and legs are heavy and warm"

- Stimulus control, or the process of eliminating distractions and competing behaviors from the bedroom so that it becomes a sleep-conducive environment. This is particularly effective in regard to awakening at night and strengthens the association between the bedroom and sleep. This process includes:

1. Going to sleep only when sleepy

2. Not using the bed for anything except sleep (and sex)

3. After fifteen to twenty minutes of attempting sleep, getting up and going into another room, returning only when sleepy

4. Repeat step 3 if there is continued difficulty falling asleep. Do this as often as necessary throughout the night.

- Other suggestions include not taking a nap during the day, avoiding caffeine in the late afternoon, and avoiding heavy meals, exercise, or alcohol and nicotine within two hours of sleep.

For mild sleep apnea, recommendations include avoiding medications, alcohol, or other substances that make you sleepy, as they make it harder for the throat to remain open during sleep; losing weight (if overweight); and sleeping on the side rather than the back, as this position is more likely to keep the throat open. People with moderate to severe sleep apnea can also benefit from these recommendations, but they may also need to use a continuous positive airway pressure mask during sleep. This device forces air through the nasal passages to prevent the throat from collapsing during sleep. Restless leg syndrome can be relieved by medications that affect the neurotransmitter dopamine (NIH, 2004b). Behavioral treatment for Restless Leg Syndrome and Periodic Limb Movement Disorder include stretching the leg muscles and soaking the legs in warm water before bedtime (Stepanski, Rybarczyk, Lopez, & Stevens, 2003).

The etiology of parasomnias such as nightmare disorder, sleep terrors, and sleepwalking disorder is unknown. In most cases, they remit spontaneously during early adolescence. Sleepwalking disorder and sleep terror disorder may have some genetic contribution, as a family history involving these conditions has been found (American Psychiatric Association, 2000).

SUMMARY

How can people with anorexia nervosa not realize that they are starving themselves to death?

- Individuals with anorexia nervosa suffer from body image distortion. They feel fat no matter how thin they get. They weigh less than 85 percent of their expected weight and suffer from effects of starvation but are still deathly afraid of getting fat.

How does bulimia nervosa differ from anorexia?

- An individual with bulimia nervosa is generally of normal weight, engages in binge eating, feels a loss of control over eating during these periods, and uses vomiting, exercise, or laxatives to attempt to control weight. Some people with anorexia nervosa also engage in binge/purge eating but weigh less than 85 percent of their expected weight.

When do food binges turn into binge-eating disorder?

- Although many people have engaged in binge eating, the diagnosis for the disorder is given only when the individual has regularly recurrent episodes in which she or he feels a loss of control over eating and shows marked distress about the activity. Most of these individuals are overweight.

What other kinds of eating disorders are there?

- Individuals who show atypical patterns of severely disordered eating that do not fully meet the criteria for anorexia nervosa, bulimia nervosa, or binge-eating disorder would be given the diagnosis of eating disorder not otherwise specified. Currently, binge-eating disorders are subsumed under this category.

Why has there been such an increase in disordered eating?

- It is believed that the societal emphasis on thinness as being attractive may contribute to the increasing incidence of eating disorder. This is believed to lead to an internalized thin ideal that girls and women aspire to achieve.
- Most women suffer from some body image distortion in that they believe they weigh more than they actually do.
- Males also appear to be influenced by mass media presentation of muscular male bodies. Most prefer to be more heavily muscled.
- Countries that are influenced by Western standards are also reporting an increased incidence of eating disorders in women.

How can we treat eating disorders?

- Many of the therapies attempt to teach the clients to identify the impact of societal messages regarding thinness and encourage them to develop healthier goals and values.
- For individuals with anorexia nervosa, medical, as well as psychological, treatment is necessary because the body is in a starvation mode. The goal is to help them gain weight, normalize their eating patterns, understand and alter their thoughts related to body image, and develop more healthy methods of dealing with stress.

- With bulimia nervosa, medical assistance may also be required because of the physiological changes associated with purging.
- Because many people with binge-eating disorder are overweight or obese, weight reduction strategies are also included in treatment.
- With both bulimia nervosa and binge-eating disorder, the therapy involves normalizing eating patterns, developing a more positive body image, and dealing with stress in a healthier fashion.

Among primary sleep disorders, what are dyssomnias?

- Dyssomnias can involve the following problems: initiating sleep, staying asleep, or excessive daytime sleepiness. These problems are associated with obtaining the necessary quality or timing of sleep. In primary insomnia, the individual has difficulty falling or staying alseep. With primary hypersomnia, the symptom involved is excessive sleepiness. Narcolepsy involves repeated irresistible sleep episodes that are refreshing. Breathing-related sleep disorder is produced by sleep disruption because of obstruction of the airway. Circadian rhythm sleep disorder is produced by the body's cycle mismatch with environmental stimuli. Dyssomnias can also be produced by sleep deprivation or limb sensations of movement.

What are parasomnias and how do they differ from dyssomnias?

- Parasomnias are the activation of physiological systems at inappropriate times during the sleep-wake cycle. They do not involve problems in going to sleep or maintaining sleep, as do dyssomnias. They are represented by nightmare disorder, in which frightening dreams during REM sleep produce awakening; sleep terror disorder—abrupt awakening from sleep during NREM sleep—which is accompanied by extreme fear and unresponsiveness; and sleepwalking disorder, which involves rising from bed and walking during sleep, as well as a general unresponsiveness.

What is the etiology and treatment of sleep disorders?

- Dyssomnias can be the result of a variety of factors, such as subclinical anxiety, worry, or depression. Environmental factors such as exposure to light, noise, or changes in the work schedule can also be involved. Habits such as the consumption of alcohol or caffeine or exercising before sleeping can also result in a sleep disorder. Treatments for dyssomnias can involve stimulant medications to combat excessive sleepiness or psychological techniques such as relaxation or stimulus control and change in habits. Parasomnias tend to resolve in adolescence or early adulthood. The etiology is unknown.

KEY TERMS

anorexia nervosa (p. 531)

binge-eating disorder (p. 536)

breathing-related sleep disorder (p. 553)

bulimia nervosa (p. 534)

circadian rhythm sleep disorder (p. 553)

dyssomnia (p. 548)

narcolepsy (p. 552)

nightmare disorder (p. 554)

parasomnia (p. 554)

primary hypersomnia (p. 550)

primary insomnia (p. 549)

sleep terror disorder (p. 554)

sleepwalking disorder (p. 555)

MULTIMEDIA PREVIEW

For additional study aids, we invite you to explore our media resources accompanying *Understanding Abnormal Behavior,* Eighth Edition. The Student CD-ROM includes videos, quizzing, and critical thinking activities that help to reinforce key concepts in a fun and engaging manner. The Student Web Site provides additional interactive activities, chapter outlines, and research links that further support and complement the text. All Web resources may be accessed by logging onto the Web site at **http://psychology.college.hmco.com/students**.

CHAPTER 17
Therapeutic Interventions

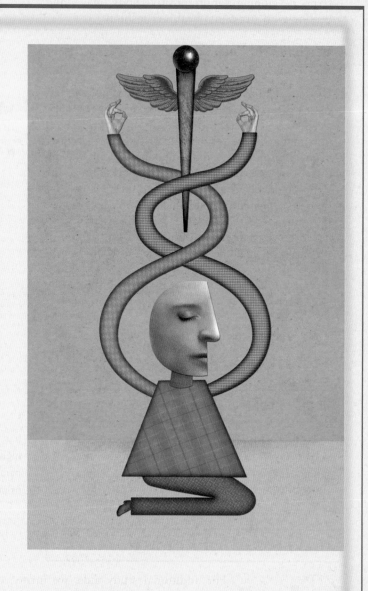

FOCUS QUESTIONS

- What forms of medical treatment have been found to be successful in treating mental disorders?
- What is psychotherapy?
- What are the different approaches to psychotherapy?
- How successful is therapy in treating mental disorders?
- How are group forms of therapy different from individual ones?
- Is there a way to combine or integrate the best features of effective therapies?
- Is therapy with racial/ethnic minority groups different from working with European American groups?
- What can society do to make the social environment a healthy place to live?

At some time in our lives, all of us have experienced personal, social, and emotionally distressing problems. Although many of us have been fortunate enough to handle such difficulties on our own, others have been greatly helped by discussing them with someone who could reassure and advise them. People have always relied on friends, relatives, members of the clergy, teachers, and even strangers for advice, emotional and social support, approval, and validation. In our society, however, this function has been increasingly taken over by psychotherapists.

In preceding chapters, we have examined a wide variety of disorders, ranging from personality disturbances to schizophrenia. We have also examined the treatment approaches that seem to help people suffering from these disorders. In this chapter, we provide a more rounded view of the various techniques used to treat psychopathology: biology-based approaches, individual psychotherapy (both insight and action approaches), and group, family, and couples therapies. We also provide insights into therapeutic approaches in working with four major racial/ethnic minority groups: African Americans, Asian Americans/Pacific Islanders, Latino or Hispanic Americans, and Native Americans. We end the chapter with a brief examination of community psychology.

Biology-Based Treatment Techniques

Biological or somatic treatment techniques use physical means to alter the patient's physiological state and hence his or her psychological state (Kolb, Gibb, & Robinson, 2003; Lickey & Gordon, 1991; Miller & Keller, 2000). The basic philosophy underlying this approach can be traced to ancient times, beginning with the practices of trephining (see the chapter on abnormal behavior) and bleeding and purging (laxatives and emetics) unwanted substances from the body. These primitive and barbaric methods of treatment have given way to more enlightened and benign forms. As our understanding of human physiology and brain functioning has increased, so has our ability to provide more effective biologically based therapies for the mentally ill (Department of Health and Human Services [DHHS], 1999). Three such techniques are examined here: electroconvulsive therapy, psychosurgery, and psychopharmacology (medication or drug therapy).

Electroconvulsive Therapy

Many people consider physically shocking the patient's body an abhorrent form of treatment. But electroconvulsive therapy (ECT) can be used successfully to treat certain mental disorders. This is especially true for severe depressive reactions, in which it can effect quite dramatic improvements (National Institute of Mental Health, 1985; Sackheim, Prudic, & Devanand, 1990). But how ECT acts to improve depression is still unclear. Whatever the mechanism, ECT seems to be effective against severe depression. Indeed, psychologist Norman Endler (1990) wrote a biography about his own struggle with depression and how ECT greatly helped his recovery. Evidence suggests that the treatment is particularly useful for endogenous cases of depression—those in which some internal cause can be determined (Klerman et al., 1994; see also the chapter on mood disorders).

The first therapeutic use of shock was *insulin shock treatment,* introduced in the 1930s by psychiatrist Manfred Sakel. Insulin was injected into the patient's body, drastically reducing the blood sugar level. The patient then went into convulsions and coma. The behavior of some patients with schizophrenia improved after awakening from this shock treatment.

Also in the 1930s, another psychiatrist, Lazlo von Meduna, hypothesized that schizophrenia and epileptic seizures are antagonistic (seizures seem to prevent schizophrenic symptoms) and that by inducing convulsions in people with schizophrenia he could eliminate their bizarre behaviors. Meduna injected patients with the drug *metrazol* to induce the seizures. Neither insulin nor metrazol shock treatment was very effective, however, and their use declined with the advent of electroconvulsive therapy.

In 1938, two Italian psychiatrists, Ugo Cerletti and Lucio Bini, introduced **electroconvulsive therapy (ECT)**, or electroshock treatment. ECT is the application of electric voltage to the brain to induce convulsions. The patient lies on a padded bed or couch and is first injected with a muscle relaxant to minimize the chance of self-injury during the later convulsions. Then 65 to 140 volts of electricity are applied to the temporal region of the patient's skull, through electrodes, for 0.1 to 0.5 seconds. Convulsions occur, followed by coma. On regaining consciousness, the patient is often confused and suffers a memory loss for events immediately before and after the ECT. Research indicates that unilateral shock (applying shock to only one hemisphere) causes less confusion and memory loss and is just as effective as bilateral shock (Abrams & Essman, 1982; Horne, Pettinati, Sugerman, & Varga, 1985).

For several reasons, the use of ECT declined in the 1960s and 1970s, despite its success. The first reason was concern that ECT might cause permanent damage to important parts of the brain. Indeed, animals that have undergone ECT treatment show brain damage. Would it be unreasonable to expect similar damage in human beings? Second, a small percentage of patients fracture or dislocate bones during treatment. Although modern techniques have reduced pain and side effects (the convulsions are now almost unnoticeable), many patients anticipate a very unpleasant experience. Third, clinicians often argue that the "beneficial changes" initially observed in patients after ECT do not persist over the long term. Fourth, the abuses and side effects of ECT have been dramatized—often sensationally—in the mass media. In the movie *One Flew*

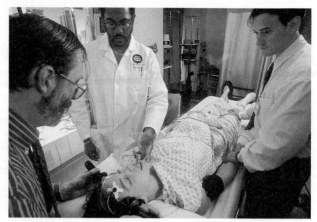

Shocking the Brain Electroconvulsive therapy involves the administration of electric shock to the brain. The treatment appears to be effective, especially with severe depression, although the precise reasons for its effectiveness are unclear.

Over the Cuckoo's Nest, for instance, ECT was administered repeatedly to the protagonist because he would not conform to regulations while in a mental hospital (such use of ECT is now illegal and probably nonexistent). Fifth, and most important, recent advances in medication have diminished the need for ECT, except in the treatment of people with profound depression for whom medications act too slowly.

Psychosurgery

As noted in the chapter on cognitive disorders, damage to brain tissue can dramatically alter a person's emotional characteristics and intellectual functioning. In the 1930s, the Portuguese neurologist Egas Moniz theorized that destroying certain connections in the brain, particularly in the frontal lobes, could disrupt psychotic thought patterns and behaviors. During the 1940s and 1950s, **psychosurgery**—brain surgery performed for the purpose of correcting a severe mental disorder—became increasingly popular. The treatment was used most often with patients suffering from schizophrenia and severe depression, although many who had personality and anxiety disorders also underwent psychosurgery.

Psychosurgery is a term applied to several procedures or techniques. In a *prefrontal lobotomy* holes are drilled in the skull, and a leukotome (a hollow tube that extrudes a cutting wire) is inserted through the holes to cut nerve fibers between the frontal lobes and the thalamus or hypothalamus. In *transorbital lobotomy,* the instrument is inserted through the eye socket, eliminating the need to drill holes in the skull. In a *lobectomy,* some or all of the frontal lobe is removed (to treat such disorders as brain tumors). Parts of the brain may also be subjected to electrical *cauterization* (searing or burning), which destroys selected brain tissue. Psychosurgical techniques have been refined to the point at which it is possible to operate on extremely small and contained areas of the brain. For example, videolaserscopy allows the surgeon to use a video camera in making extremely small incisions with a laser (Cowley, 1990).

Critics of psychosurgical procedures have raised both scientific and ethical objections. In the case of lobotomies, for example, initial reports of results were enthusiastic, but later evaluations indicated that the patient's improvement or lack of improvement was independent of the psychosurgical treatment. In addition, serious negative and irreversible side effects were frequently observed. Although postlobotomy patients often became quite manageable, calm, and less anxious, many emerged from surgery with impaired cognitive and intellectual functioning, were listless (even vegetative), or showed uninhibited impulsive behavior. Some such patients were described as "robots" or "zombies." A small number suffered from continuing seizures and, in rare cases, some died from the surgery. Finally, because psychosurgery always produces permanent brain damage, some critics called for a halt to this form of treatment on humanitarian grounds. On the whole, restriction and regulation of its use seem wise.

Psychopharmacology

Psychopharmacology is the study of the effects of drugs on the mind and on behavior; it is also known as *medication* or *drug therapy*. The use of medications has generally replaced shock treatment and psychosurgery for treating serious behavior disorders. Since the 1950s medication has been a major factor in allowing the early discharge of hospitalized mental patients and permitting them to function in the community. Medication is now widely used throughout the United States: more mental patients receive drug therapy than receive all other forms of therapy combined (Levinthal, 2005).

Table 17.1 lists the generic and brand names of the drugs most frequently prescribed to treat psychological disorders. The rise in the use of minor tranquilizers has become a concern to society because of possible abuses and because of their addictive qualities. Some researchers have also noted that gender bias may operate in the extent to which they are prescribed for women. Studies indicate that women receive twice as many antianxiety medication prescriptions than are given to men; that although women make up only slightly more than one-half of the patients seen by psychiatrists, they receive 73 percent of all prescriptions;

and that male psychiatrists prescribe medication twice as often as their female counterparts (Cypress, 1980; Hohmann, Larson, Thompson, & Beardsley, 1988; Rossiter, 1983). These issues will become even more prominent because many psychologists are advocating for the right to prescribe medication to their psychiatric patients, a right that has been largely limited to physicians (Gutierrez & Silk, 1998; Norfleet, 2003).

We discuss four major categories of medication in this section. These are the antianxiety drugs (or minor tranquilizers), the antipsychotic drugs (or major tranquilizers), the antidepressant drugs (which relieve depression by elevating one's mood), and antimanic drugs (such as lithium). Many of these will be familiar to you from our earlier discussions in the context of specific disorders.

Antianxiety Drugs (Minor Tranquilizers)   Before the 1950s, barbiturates were often prescribed to relieve anxiety. *Barbiturates* are sedatives that have a calming effect but that are also highly addictive. Many people who take barbiturates develop a physical tolerance to these medications and require increasing doses to obtain the same effects. An overdose can result in death, and discontinuing the medication can produce agonizing withdrawal symptoms. Moreover, physical and mental disturbances, such as muscular incoordination and mental confusion, can result even from normal dosages. For these reasons, the barbiturates were replaced with antianxiety drugs almost as soon as the latter became available.

During the 1940s and 1950s, the propanediols (meprobamate compounds) and benzodiazepines took over as the preferred medications. Researchers first developed *meprobamate* (the generic name of Miltown and Equanil) for use as a muscle relaxant and anxiety reducer. Within a few years, it was being prescribed for patients who complained of anxiety and nervousness or who had psychosomatic problems. Soon other antianxiety drugs, the benzodiazepines (Librium and Valium), also entered the market. Studies suggest that the benzodiazepines work by binding to specific receptor sites at the synapses and blocking transmission, which is another piece of evidence that supports the hypothesis that anxiety, like many other mental conditions, is linked to brain structure and physiology (Hayward, Wardie, & Higgitt, 1989).

The antianxiety medications can be addictive and can impair psychomotor skills; discontinuing them after prolonged usage at high doses can result in withdrawal symptoms (DHHS, 1999). But they are considered safer than barbiturates, and there is little doubt that they effectively reduce anxiety and the behavioral symptoms of anxiety disorder.

TABLE 17.1   Drugs Most Commonly Used in Drug Therapy

Category	Generic Name	Brand Name	Examples of Clinical Use
Antianxiety	alprazolam	Xanax	Anxiety
	meprobamate	Miltown and Equanil	
	chlordiazepoxide	Librium	
	diazepam	Valium	
Antipsychotic drugs	chlorpromazine	Thorazine	Schizophrenia, psychosis
	trifluoperazine	Stelazine	
	fluphenazine	Prolixin	
	haloperidol	Haldol	
	clozapine	Clozaril	
Antidepressants	phenelzine	Nardil	Depression, anxiety
	tranylcypromine	Parnate	
	imipramine	Tofranil	
	doxepin	Sinequan	
	amitriptyline	Elavil	
	fluoxetine	Prozac	
	paroxetine	Paxil	
	sertraline	Zoloft	
Antimanic drugs	lithium carbonate	Eskalith	Mania
	carbamazapine	Tegretol	
Stimulants	methylphenadate	Ritalin	Attention deficit/hyperactivity disorder
	pemoline	Cylert	

The major problem with the minor tranquilizers is the great potential for overuse and overreliance. Because of its selective ability to diminish anxiety and leave adaptive behavior intact, Valium has been widely prescribed in the past. In addition, antianxiety drugs have gained in popularity among the general public, and they are widely used in relieving psychological problems. Almost everyone feels anxious at one time or another, and the antianxiety drugs are effective, readily available, low in cost, and easy to administer. They are a quick, easy alternative to developing personal coping skills. As a result, people tend to choose the short-term relief offered by these medications over the long-term but more gradual gains of developing the ability to manage stress and to learn to solve one's own problems.

Antipsychotic Drugs (Major Tranquilizers)

Although the antianxiety medications seem to relax and reduce anxiety in patients, they have minimal impact on the hallucinations and distorted thinking of highly agitated patients and patients with schizophrenia. In 1950 a synthetic sedative was developed in France. This medication, *chlorpromazine* (the generic name of Thorazine), had an unexpected tranquilizing effect that decreased patients' interest in the events taking place around them. Within less than a year after its introduction, some 2 million patients used Thorazine. Chlorpromazine also seemed to reduce psychotic symptoms (believed to be a biochemical effect of blocking dopamine receptors). Thereafter, a number of other major tranquilizers were developed, mainly for administration to patients with schizophrenia. (The chapter on schizophrenia discusses use of medication as a treatment for this disorder.)

Several experimental studies have demonstrated the efficacy of antipsychotic drugs in treating schizophrenia (Klerman et al., 1994). A review of many large-scale controlled studies indicates that the beneficial effects of Thorazine, Stelazine, Prolixin, and other antipsychotic drugs have allowed institutions to release thousands of chronic "incurable" mental patients throughout the country (Lickey & Gordon, 1991; Wender & Klein, 1981). When patients hospitalized with schizophrenia were given *phenothiazines* (a class of major tranquilizers), they showed more social interaction with others, better self-management, and less agitation and excitement than when they were given placebos.

Despite their recognized effectiveness, antipsychotic drugs do not always reduce anxiety, and they can produce side effects. Patients may develop psychomotor symptoms resembling those of Parkinson's disease, sensitivity to light, dryness of the mouth, drowsiness, or liver disease. After an extended period of continuous treatment with antipsychotic drugs, some patients (usually patients older than forty years of age) develop tardive dyskinesia—a disorder characterized by involuntary movement of the head, tongue, and extremities.

Patients discharged from hospitals typically show only marginal adjustments to community life, and psychotic symptoms usually return when the medication is discontinued. As a result, the rehospitalization rate is high. Nevertheless, medication or drug therapy is very important in treating schizophrenia, and nearly all psychiatric institutions use it. Antipsychotic drugs have dramatically increased the proportion of patients with this disorder who can return to and function in the community, even though they may show residual symptoms.

"This next one is a sad little blues tune about love and pain that I wrote before I started taking Celexa."

Antidepressant Drugs   As in the case of antipsychotic drugs, the development of antidepressants was aided by a fortunate coincidence. During the 1950s, clinicians noticed that patients treated with the antituberculosis medication *iproniazid* became happier and more optimistic. When tested on people diagnosed with depression, the medication was found to be effective as an antidepressant. Unfortunately, liver damage and fatalities caused by the medication were relatively high. Continued interest in antidepressants has led to the identification of three large classes of the compounds: monoamine oxidase inhibitors, tricyclics, and selective serotonin reuptake inhibitors (a type of tricyclic).

Monoamine oxidase (MAO) inhibitors are antidepressant compounds that are believed to correct the balance of neurotransmitters in the brain. A number of the MAO inhibitors, such as *phenelzine,* were found to be less dangerous but similar in effect to iproniazid. It is hypothesized that the MAO inhibitors work primarily to correct a deficiency in concentrations of neurotransmitters in the brain. They block the action of monoamine oxidase, thereby preventing the breakdown of norepinephrine and serotonin. As you may recall from the chapters on abnormal behavior and on mood disorders, the lack of these neurotransmitters at pertinent synaptic sites has been implicated in depression. Although the MAO inhibitors relieve depression, they produce certain toxic effects and require careful dietary monitoring. (Certain foods and other drugs, when taken with an MAO inhibitor, could cause severe illness.)

More frequently used in cases of depression are the **tricyclics,** antidepressant compounds that relieve symptoms of depression and seem to work like the MAO inhibitors but produce fewer of the side effects associated with prolonged drug use. The medication *imipramine,* a tricyclic, has been at least as effective as psychotherapy in relieving the symptoms of depression (Elkin et al., 1995).

Until recently, the tricyclics were the most widely used medication in treating depression. Medications that may replace tricyclics as the preferred medication for treating depression are **selective serotonin reuptake inhibitors (SSRIs).** They work by inhibiting the central nervous system's neuronal uptake of serotonin—a mechanism that appears to be the treatment of choice for unipolar depression (Seligman & Levant, 1998). SSRIs include the drugs Prozac (fluoxetine hydrochloride), Paxil (paroxetine), and Zoloft (sertraline). The use of SSRIs has increased dramatically. These drugs affect serotonin but not other neurotransmitters, take effect in a shorter period of time than other antidepressants, have fewer side effects than the tricyclics, and are less likely to result in overdosing. However, reported side effects include feeling jittery and having stomach irritation.

In October 2004, the Food and Drug Administration issued a "black box" warning on the use of antidepressants with children and adolescents. Ironically, it was shown that the use of many popular antidepressants increased the risk of children's suicidal thinking and/or behaviors. Research is being conducted to determine which antidepressants have this unfortunate effect and what would explain susceptibility to suicidal ideation and behavior.

Antimanic Drugs   *Lithium* is another mood-controlling (antimanic) medication that has been very effective in treating bipolar disorders, especially mania (Klerman et al., 1994). About 70 to 80 percent of manic states can be controlled by lithium, and it also controls depressive episodes. How lithium works remains highly speculative. One hypothesis is that it somehow limits the availability of serotonin and norepinephrine at the synapses and produces an effect opposite from that of the antidepressants. Yet lithium's ability to relieve depression appears to contradict this explanation. Other speculations involve electrolyte changes in the body, which alter neurotransmission in some manner.

Strangely enough, lithium, which is administered as a salt, has no known physiological function. Yet with proper administration of lithium—a single tablet in the morning and another in the evening—patients' manic and depressive cycles can be modulated or prevented. However, cautions limit its use in treating bipolar disorders. First, it is largely preventive and must be taken before symptoms appear. Once a manic or depressive state occurs, lithium's effect is minimal. Second, it is often extremely difficult to determine a patient's appropriate dosage. The effective dosage level often borders on toxicity, which can cause convulsions, delirium, and other bad effects. Careful and constant monitoring of the lithium level in a patient's blood is very important.

Psychopharmacological Considerations   A major issue in psychopharmacology is deciding which medication to use with which kind of patient under what circumstances (Grilly, 2002). For example, although imipramine is more effective with long-standing and severe depressions without specific situational causes, antidepressants often do not begin to help patients until two to three weeks after treatment begins. The SSRI drugs appear to work more quickly. If very rapid improvement is necessary, ECT may be used as a last resort to treat a patient with severe depression or suicidal ideation.

The use of antidepressant, antianxiety, and antipsychotic drugs has greatly changed therapy. Patients who take them report that they feel better, that symptoms decline, and that overall functioning improves. Long periods of hospitalization are no longer needed in most cases, and patients are more amenable to other forms of treatment, such as psychotherapy. Remember, however, that medications do not cure mental disorders. Some would characterize their use as "control measures," somewhat better than traditional hospitalization, "straitjackets," or "padded cells." Furthermore, medications seem to be most effective in treating "active" symptoms such as delusions, hallucinations, and aggression and much less effective with "passive" symptoms such as withdrawal, poor interpersonal relationships, and feelings of alienation. Medication does not help patients improve their living skills. A large number of patients discharged from mental hospitals require continuing medication to function even minimally in the community. Unfortunately, many of them do not continue to take their medication after leaving the hospital. Some do not realize the importance of continued and timely medication. Others are unable to pay for medication, either individually or through an insurance plan. Others' lifestyles are not conducive to taking the medications. Once they discontinue their medications, patients may again experience the same disorder that led to their hospitalization. Finally, both medication and psychotherapy (administered together or alone) appear to be of benefit to clients (Gould, Buckminster, Pollack, Otto, & Yap, 1997).

Psychotherapy

In most cases, biological treatments such as medication are used as an adjunct to psychotherapy. But beyond general agreement that psychotherapy is an internal approach to treating psychopathology, involving interaction between one or more clients and a therapist, there is little consensus on exactly what else it is. Psychotherapy has been called "a conversation with a therapeutic purpose"; it has also been called "the talking cure" or the "purchase of friendship" (Sue & Sue, 2003).

For our purposes, **psychotherapy** may be defined as the systematic application, by a trained and experienced professional therapist, of techniques derived from psychological principles, for the purpose of helping psychologically troubled people (Day, 2004; Sommers-Flanagan & Sommers-Flanagan, 2004). We cannot be more succinct or precise without getting involved in specific types of therapy. Depending on their perspective and theoretical orientation, therapists may seek to modify attitudes, thoughts, feelings, or

Psychotherapy relies on the systematic use of techniques based on psychological principles to provide the client with an opportunity not only for catharsis but also for the acquisition of new behaviors and expectancies to help overcome psychological problems.

behaviors; to facilitate the patient's self-insight and rational control of his or her own life; to cure mental illness; to enhance mental health and self-actualization; to make clients "feel better"; to remove a cause of a disorder; to change a self-concept; or to encourage adaptation (Corey, 2005). Psychotherapy is practiced by many different kinds of people in many different ways—a fact that seems to preclude establishing a single set of standard therapeutic procedures. And—despite our emphasis on the scientific basis of therapy—in practice it is often more art than science.

Diverse psychotherapies do seem to share some common therapeutic factors. In one study the investigators examined fifty publications on psychotherapy and found that the characteristics common to most of them were (1) development of a therapeutic alliance, (2) opportunity for catharsis, (3) acquisition and practice of new behaviors, and (4) the clients' positive expectancies (Grencavage & Norcross, 1990). These characteristics are very consistent with those first proposed by Korchin (1976) nearly thirty years ago:

■ *Psychotherapy is a chance for the client to relearn.* Many people say to their psychotherapists, "I know I shouldn't feel or act this way, but I just can't help it." Psychotherapy provides a chance to unlearn, relearn, develop, or change certain behaviors or levels of functioning.

■ *Psychotherapy helps generate the development of new, emotionally important experiences.* A person questioning the value of psychotherapy may ask,

"If I talk about my problems, how will that cause me to change, even though I may understand myself better? I talk things over now, with friends." But psychotherapy is not merely a "talking cure." It involves the reexperiencing of emotions that clients may have avoided, along with the painful and helpless feelings fostered by these emotions. This experiencing allows relearning, as well as emotional and intellectual insight into problems and conflicts.

■ *A therapeutic relationship exists.* Therapists have been trained to listen, to show empathic concern, to be objective, to value the client's integrity, to communicate understanding, and to use their professional knowledge and skills. Therapists may provide reassurance, interpretations, self-disclosures, reflections of the client's feelings, or information, each at appropriate times. As a team, therapist and client are better prepared to venture into frightening areas that the client would not have faced alone.

■ *Clients in psychotherapy have certain motivations and expectations.* Most people enter therapy with both anxiety and hope. They are frightened by their emotional difficulties and by the prospect of treatment, but they expect or hope that therapy will be helpful.

The goals and general characteristics of psychotherapy as described seem admirable, and most people consider them so. Nevertheless, psychotherapy itself has been criticized as being biased and inappropriate to the lifestyles of many clients, including members of minority groups. Indeed, many psychologists have called for psychotherapy approaches that can better relate to the cultures of different ethnic groups (Carter & McGoldrick, 2005; Ivey, D'Andrea, Ivey, & Simek-Morgan, 2002; Sue & Sue, 2003). As we shall shortly see, racial/ethnic minority status must be considered in the provision of psychological services to these populations.

In the next two sections we discuss individual psychotherapy, in which one therapist treats one client at a time. We also distinguish between insight- and action-oriented approaches to individual therapy. This distinction separates approaches that stress awareness, understanding, and consciousness of one's own motivations (that is, insight) from those approaches that stress actions, such as changing one's behavior or thoughts. The first set includes the psychoanalytic and humanistic-existential therapies, whereas the second set involves mainly behavioral therapies. Following those two discussions, we turn to group, family, and couples therapy. Despite this variety of approaches, many therapists use similar treatment strategies. And, as noted in the chapter on abnormal behavior, many therapists choose relevant techniques from all the various "pure" approaches to develop the most effective integrative approach for each particular client.

Insight-Oriented Approaches to Individual Psychotherapy

The theoretical bases of the major insight-oriented psychotherapies were discussed in the chapter on models of abnormal behavior. Here we briefly review these theoretical bases and then discuss the most common treatment techniques.

Psychoanalysis

According to Freud's theory of personality, people are born with certain instinctual drives, urges that constantly seek to discharge or express themselves. As the personality structure develops, conflicts occur among the id, ego, and superego. If conflicts remain unresolved, they will resurface during adulthood. The relative importance of such an unresolved conflict depends on the psychosexual stage (oral, anal, phallic, or genital) in which it occurs. The earlier the stage in which an unresolved conflict arises, the greater the conflict's effect on subsequent behaviors. Repressing unacceptable thoughts and impulses (within the unconscious) is the primary way that people defend themselves against such thoughts.

Psychoanalytic therapy, or psychoanalysis, seeks to overcome defenses so that (1) repressed material can be uncovered, (2) the client can achieve insight into his or her inner motivations and desires, and (3) unresolved childhood conflicts can be controlled. Traditional psychoanalysis requires many sessions of therapy over a long period of time. It may not be appropriate for certain types of people, such as nonverbal adults, young children who cannot be verbally articulate or reasonable, people with schizoid disorders, those with urgent problems requiring immediate reduction of symptoms, and people with mental retardation.

Psychoanalysts traditionally use four methods to achieve their therapeutic goals: free association and dream analysis, analysis of resistance, transference, and interpretation.

Free Association and Dream Analysis In **free association** the patient says whatever comes to mind, regardless of how illogical or embarrassing it may seem, for the purpose of revealing the contents of the patient's unconscious. Psychoanalysts believe the material that surfaces in this process is determined by the patient's psychic makeup and that it can provide some understanding of the patient's conflicts, unconscious processes, and personality dynamics. Simply asking patients to talk about their conflicts is fruitless, because they have repressed the most important material from their consciousness. Instead, reports of dreams, feelings, thoughts, and fantasies reflect a patient's psychodynamics; the therapist's tasks are to encourage continuous free association of thoughts and to interpret the results.

Similarly, dream analysis is a very important therapeutic tool that depends on psychoanalytic interpretation of hidden meanings in dreams. Freud is often credited with referring to dreams as "the royal road to the unconscious." According to psychoanalytic theory, when people sleep, defenses and inhibitions of the ego weaken, allowing unacceptable motives and feelings to surface. This material comes out in the disguised and symbolic form of a dream. The portion we remember is called the *manifest content,* and the deeper, unacceptable impulse is the *latent content.* The therapist's job is to uncover the disguised symbolic meanings and let the patient achieve insight into the anxiety-provoking implications.

Analysis of Resistance Throughout the course of psychoanalytic therapy, the patient's unconscious may try to impede the analysis, in a process known as **resistance,** by preventing the exposure of repressed material. In free association, for example, the patient may suddenly change the subject, lose the train of thought, go blank, or become silent. Such resistance may also show up in a patient's late arrival or failure to keep an appointment. A trained analyst is alert to telltale signs of resistance because they indicate that a sensitive area is being approached. The therapist can make therapeutic use of properly interpreted instances of resistance to show the patient that repressed material is coming close to the surface and to suggest means of uncovering it.

Transference   When a patient begins to perceive, or behave toward, the analyst as though the analyst were an important person in the patient's past, the process of transference is occurring. In **transference** the patient reenacts early conflicts by carrying over and applying to the analyst feelings and attitudes that the patient had toward significant others—primarily parents—in the past. These feelings and attitudes then become accessible to understanding. They may be positive, involving feelings of love for the analyst, or negative, involving feelings of anger and hostility.

Part of the psychoanalyst's strategy is to remain "unknown" or ambiguous, so that the client can freely develop whatever kind of transference is required. The patient is allowed, even encouraged, to develop unrealistic expectations and attitudes regarding the analyst. These expectations and attitudes are used as a basis for helping the patient deal realistically with painful early experiences. In essence, a miniature neurosis is re-created; its resolution is considered crucial to the therapy.

At the same time, the analyst must be careful to recognize and control any instances of *countertransference*. In this process, the analyst—who is also a human being with feelings and fears—transfers those feelings to the patient. This is one reason that Freud believed so strongly that all psychoanalysts need to undergo psychoanalysis themselves.

Interpretation   Through interpretation—the explanation of a patient's free associations, reports of dreams, and the like—a sensitive analyst can help the patient gain insight (both intellectual and emotional) into his or her repressed conflicts. By pointing out the symbolic attributes of a transference relationship or by noting the peculiar timing of symptoms, the analyst can direct the patient toward conscious control of unconscious conflicts.

The following example shows the timely interpretation of an important instance of transference:

Sandy (the patient): John [her ex-husband] was just like my father. Always condemning me, always making me feel like an idiot! Strange, the two of them—the most important men in my life—they did the most to screw me up. When I would have fun with my friends and come home at night, he would be sitting there—waiting—to disapprove.

Therapist (male): Who would be waiting for you?

Sandy: Huh?

Therapist: Who's the "he" who'd be waiting?

Sandy: John—I mean, my father—you're confusing me now. ... My father would sit there—smoking his pipe. I knew what he was thinking, though—he didn't have to say it—he was thinking I was a slut! Someone—who, who was a slut! So what if I stayed up late and had some fun? What business was it of his? He never took any interest in any of us. [Begins to weep.] It was my mother—rest her soul—who loved us, not our father. He worked her to death. Lord, I miss her. [Weeps uncontrollably]—I must sound angry at my father. Don't you think I have a right to be angry?

Therapist: Do you think you have a right to be angry?

Sandy: Of course, I do! Why are you questioning me? You don't believe me, do you?

Therapist: You want me to believe you.

Sandy: I don't care whether you believe me or not. As far as I'm concerned, you're just a wall that I'm talking to—I don't know why I pay for this rotten therapy.—Don't you have any thoughts or feelings at all? I know what you're thinking—you think I'm crazy—you must be laughing at me—I'll probably be a case in your next book! You're just sitting there—smirking—making me feel like a bad person—thinking I'm wrong for being mad, that I have no right to be mad.

Therapist: Just like your father.

Sandy: Yes, you're just like my father.—Oh my God! Just now—I—I—thought I was talking to him.

Therapist: You mean your father.

Sandy: Yes—I'm really scared now—how could I have—can this really be happening to me?

Therapist: I know it must be awfully scary to realize what just happened—but don't run away now, Sandy. Could it be that your relationship with your father has affected many of the relationships you've had with other men? It seems that your reaction to me just now, and your tendency to sometimes refer to your ex-husband as your father—

Sandy: God!—I don't know—what should I do about it?—Is it real?

Modern Psychodynamic Therapy   In the chapter on models of abnormal behavior, we noted the contemporary changes in theoretical formulations of psychodynamic theory, especially the increased importance of the ego (ego autonomy theorists) and past interpersonal relationships (object relations theorists). Among the ego autonomy theorists were people such as Anna Freud,

Heinz Hartmann, and Erik Erikson, who believed that cognitive processes of the ego were often constructive, creative, and productive (independent from the id). Likewise, object relations theorists such as Melanie Klein, Margaret Mahler, Otto Kernberg, and Heinz Kohut stressed the importance of interpersonal relationships and the child's separation from the mother as important in one's psychological growth. The contributions of these theorists and practitioners expanded and loosened the rigid therapeutic techniques of traditional psychoanalysis (James & Gilliland, 2003). Today, very few psychodynamic therapists practice traditional psychoanalysis. Most are more active in their sessions, restrict the number of sessions they have with clients, place greater emphasis on current rather than past factors, and seem to have adopted a number of client-centered techniques in their practice (Nystul, 2003).

The Effectiveness of Psychoanalysis Psychoanalysis has been criticized for a number of reasons. Psychoanalysts tend to select certain kinds of clients for treatment, usually those who are young, white, and highly educated (Garfield, 1994). This means that psychoanalysis has been limited in addressing the needs of a larger population. Providing operational definitions for such constructs as the *unconscious* and the *libido* has been problematic, making it extremely difficult to confirm the various aspects of the theory. For example, psychoanalytic theory suggests that neurotic or anxiety symptoms are caused by underlying emotional conflicts. (DSM in the past had a diagnostic category for "neurotic disorders," which is no longer used. Psychoanalysts often refer to neuroses or neurotic disorders because the disorders have played an important role in conceptualizing psychoanalytic views.) When these symptoms are eliminated without removing the conflict, the person merely expresses the neurosis in other ways and shows other symptoms—a phenomenon known as *symptom substitution*. Many researchers, particularly behavior therapists, assert that it is possible to eliminate neurotic or anxiety symptoms without symptom substitution occurring. Furthermore, they contend that when the symptoms are eliminated, the neurosis or anxiety disorder is cured. Thus psychoanalysis has encountered many problems despite its vast influence in the field of psychotherapy. Although it is still widely practiced, many therapists do not strictly follow all psychoanalytic procedures, preferring psychodynamic or ego psychological modifications. Many psychotherapists predict that the use of psychoanalysis will decline in the future (Norcross & Freedheim, 1992).

Humanistic-Existential Therapies

In contrast to the psychic determinism implicit in psychoanalysis, the humanistic-existential therapies stress the importance of self-actualization, self-concept, free will, responsibility, and the understanding of the client's phenomenological world. The focus of therapy is on qualities of "humanness"; human beings cannot be understood without reference to their personal uniqueness and wholeness. Among the several humanistic-existential therapies are person-centered therapy, existential analysis, and gestalt therapy.

Person-Centered Therapy Carl Rogers, the founder of person-centered therapy, believed that people could develop better self-concepts and move toward self-actualization if the therapist provided certain therapeutic conditions. These are the conditions in which clients use their own innate tendencies to grow, to actively negotiate with their environment, and to realize their potential. Therefore, therapists must accept clients as people, show empathy and respect, and provide unconditional positive regard for them. A therapist should not control, inhibit, threaten, or interpret a client's behaviors. These actions are manipulative, and they undermine the client's ability to find his or her own direction.

Person-centered therapy thus emphasizes the kind of person the therapist should be in the therapeutic relationship rather than the precise techniques to use in therapy. Particular details of this therapeutic approach were discussed in the chapter on models of abnormal behavior.

Existential Analysis **Existential analysis** follows no single theory or group of therapeutic techniques. Instead, it is concerned with the person's experience and involvement in the world as a being with consciousness and self-consciousness. Existential therapists believe that the inability to accept death or nonbeing as a reality restricts self-actualization. In contemporary society, many people feel lonely and alienated; they lose a sense of the meaning of life, of self-responsibility, and of free will. This state of mind is popularly called "existential crisis." The task of the therapist is to engage clients in an encounter in which they can experience their own existence as being real. The encounter should involve genuine sharing between partners, in which the therapist, too, may grow and be influenced. When clients can experience their existence and nonexistence, then feelings of responsibility, choice, and meaning reemerge. (Again, see the chapter on models of abnormal behavior for additional details.)

Existential approaches to therapy are strongly philosophical in nature. They have not received any research scrutiny because many existential concepts and methods are difficult to define operationally for research purposes. Furthermore, existential therapists point out that therapist and client are engaged in a complex encounter that cannot be broken down into components for empirical observation, so research studies are incapable of assessing the impact of therapy. Although impressive case histories indicate its effectiveness, little empirical support for existential analysis exists.

Gestalt Therapy   The German word *gestalt* means "whole." As conceptualized by Fritz Perls in 1969, **gestalt therapy** emphasizes the importance of a person's total experience, which should not be fragmented or separated. Perls believed that when affective and cognitive experiences are isolated, people lack full awareness of their complete experience.

In gestalt therapy, clients are asked to discuss the totality of the here and now. Only experiences, feelings, and behaviors occurring in the present are stressed. Past experiences or anticipated future experiences are brought up only in relation to current feelings. Interestingly, Perls was originally trained as a psychoanalyst, but he later rejected Freudian theory. He did, however, incorporate dream analysis in his work. Dreams, too, are interpreted in relation to the here and now in gestalt therapy. As a means of opening clients to their experiences, therapists encourage clients to:

1. Make personalized and unqualified statements that help them "act out" their emotions. For example, instead of hedging by saying, "It is sometimes upsetting when your boss yells at you," a client is encouraged to say, "I get scared when my boss yells at me."

2. Exaggerate the feelings associated with behaviors to gain greater awareness of their experiences and to eliminate intellectual explanations for them.

3. Role-play situations and then focus on what was experienced during the role playing.

Like existential analysis, gestalt therapy has generated little research. Thus it is difficult to evaluate its effectiveness. Proponents of gestalt therapy are convinced that clients are helped, but sufficient empirical support has never emerged. (You might be interested in reading Perls's remarkable book *Gestalt Therapy Verbatim,* 1969, for a fuller explanation of this approach.)

Action-Oriented Approaches to Individual Psychotherapy

The principles underlying the action-oriented or behaviorist approaches to abnormal behavior were discussed in depth in the chapter on models of abnor-

mal behavior. Treatment based on classical conditioning, operant conditioning, observational learning, and cognitive-behavioral processes has gained widespread popularity (DHHS, 1999; Norcross & Freedheim, 1992). Behavior therapists typically use a variety of techniques, many of which were discussed in preceding chapters. This section presents a selection of the most important behavioral techniques.

Classical Conditioning Techniques

Using the classical conditioning principles described in the chapter on models of abnormal behavior, Joseph Wolpe (1973) used *systematic desensitization* as treatment for anxiety. This technique attempts to reduce anxiety in response to a stimulus situation by eliciting in the given situation an alternative response that is incompatible with anxiety. For example, if a woman is afraid of flying in a jet plane, her anxiety response could be reduced by training her to relax while in airplanes.

Systematic desensitization typically includes training in relaxation, the construction of a fear hierarchy, and the combination of relaxation and imagined scenes from the fear hierarchy. This process is described in detail in the chapter on anxiety disorders, but we can illustrate the process using the example of the woman who wants to overcome her fear of flying. The therapist would first train her to relax, probably employing a progressive relaxation method in which she learns to alternately tense and relax her muscles. Working with the therapist, the client would construct a fear hierarchy for flying, rating the level of fear in various scenarios on a scale of 1 to 100, as in Table 17.2. Notice that self-reported anxiety increases as the task approaches, and a high level of fear occurs in response to a scene in which the plane is shaking due to turbulence while flying. If there are large increases in anxiety from one consecutive scene to the next, other scenes may be constructed that occupy an intermediate position. For example, a 20-point difference occurs in Table 17.2 between scenes 5 and 6 (and between scenes 6 and 7). The client and therapist may find another scene that the client rates as 50 on the hierarchy—for example, she might imagine getting a boarding pass and checking in her luggage. The client is then asked to *imagine* herself in each of these situations. Most clients experience anxiety when they imagine such situations, and it is obviously more convenient to imagine them than to actually go through them. If the client is actually present in the fear-provoking situations, the approach is known as an in vivo approach. The development of a fear hierarchy is important in systematic desensitization when an in vivo approach is not used.

Once the person is able to relax, the therapist asks the client first to imagine a low-anxiety scene (such as making flight reservations) and to relax at the same time. The client then proceeds up the fear hierarchy, imagining each situation in order. If a particular situation elicits too much anxiety, the client is told to return to a less anxiety-provoking one. This procedure is repeated until the client can imagine the entire hierarchy without anxiety.

Behavior therapists believe that systematic desensitization is more effective than psychotherapy for certain kinds of problems such as simple phobias; it certainly requires fewer sessions to achieve desired results (Wolpe, 1973). Systematic desensitization has stimulated a great deal of research, and its efficacy in reducing fears has been well documented. Some researchers question the need for certain procedural aspects of the treatment approach. For example, Wolpe's rather rigid format for desensitization may be unnecessary, and alternatives to relaxation, such as talking about the fear or listening to soothing music, may be used in the process.

Flooding and Implosion   Two other techniques that use the classical conditioning principles of extinction are flooding and implosion (Sommers-Flanagan & Sommers-Flanagan, 2004). The two are very similar. **Flooding** attempts to extinguish fear by placing the client in a real-life anxiety-provoking situation at full intensity. **Implosion** attempts to extinguish fear by having the client imagine the anxiety-provoking situation at full intensity. The difference between systematic desensitization and flooding and implosion lies in the speed with which the fearful situation is introduced to the client. Systematic desensitization introduces it more slowly. Flooding and implosion require the client to immediately confront the feared situation in its full intensity. The belief is that the client's fears will be extinguished if he or she is not allowed to avoid or escape the situation. In flooding, for example, a client who is afraid of heights may be taken to the top of a tall building, mountain, or bridge and physically prevented from leaving. Some studies have indicated that flooding effectively eliminates

TABLE 17.2   A Systematic Desensitization Fear Hierarchy for a Client with a Fear of Flying

Scene	Fear Rating
1. Encountering turbulence while flying	99
2. Flying at 35,000 feet	95
3. Taking off	90
4. Fastening the seatbelt	85
5. Boarding the plane	80
6. Waiting to board the plane	60
7. Taking a taxi to the airport	40
8. Packing for a trip	25
9. Making airline reservations	20
10. Thinking about a trip involving flying	10

Facing the Problem Head-On Fear of snakes is not uncommon in the general population. Some people, however, have such intense fears that they are considered phobic. In such cases, desensitization procedures may be used to help reduce or eradicate the emotional reaction. In this session, a client is helped by the therapist to overcome her fear. The technique being used is flooding, which uses a real snake. According to classical conditioning principles, the anxiety and fear should be extinguished in the absence of any negative consequences happening.

specific fears such as phobias (Bornas, Fullana, Tortella-Feliu, Llabres, & de la Banda, 2001; Garcia-Palacios, Hoffman, Carlin, Furness, & Botella, 2002). In implosion therapy, the client is forced to imagine a feared situation. For example, a therapist might ask a client who is afraid of flying to close her eyes and imagine the following:

> You are flying in an airplane. Suddenly the plane hits an air pocket and begins to shake violently from side to side. Meal trays fly around, and passengers who do not have their seatbelts fastened are thrown from their seats. People start to scream. As you look out the window, the plane's wing is flying by. The pilot's frantic voice over the loudspeaker is shouting: "Prepare to crash, prepare to crash!" Your seatbelt breaks and you must hang on for dear life, while the plane is spinning around and careening. You can tell that the plane is falling rapidly. The ground is coming up toward you. The situation is hopeless—all will die.

Presumably the client feels intense anxiety, after which she is told to "wake up." Repeated exposure to such a high level of anxiety eventually causes the stimulus to lose its power to elicit anxiety and leads to extinction.

The developers of implosion and flooding believe that they can be effective, though some clients find the procedures too traumatic and discontinue treatment. In general, these methods have not been scrutinized as carefully as systematic desensitization has been, but they appear to be equally effective with clients with phobias (Emmelkamp, 1994).

Aversive Conditioning   In **aversive conditioning**, a widely used classical conditioning technique, the undesirable behavior is paired with an unpleasant stimulus to suppress the undesirable behavior. For example, aversive conditioning has been used to modify the smoking behaviors of heavy smokers. In the rapid smoking technique, smokers who are trying to quit are asked to puff cigarettes at a fast rate (perhaps a puff every six or seven seconds). Puffing at this rate usually brings on nausea, so the nausea from puffing is associated with smoking behaviors. After repeated pairings, many smokers find cigarette smoke aversive and are more motivated to quit.

Aversive conditioning has also been used in therapy with people who have drug or alcohol addictions or sexual disorders, again with varying degrees of success. The noxious stimuli have included electric shock, drugs, odors, verbal censure, and reprimands. Some aversive conditioning programs also provide positive reinforcement for alternative behaviors that are deemed appropriate (Emmelkamp, 1994).

Several problems have been encountered in the use of aversive conditioning. First, because noxious stimuli are used, many people in treatment discontinue therapy, as in the smoking-reduction program just described. Second, aversive methods often suppress the undesirable behavior only temporarily, especially when punishment for those behaviors is applied solely in a laboratory situation that bears little resemblance to real life. Third, the client may become anxious and hostile. And some critics argue that punishment is unethical or has the potential for misuse and abuse. Partially as a response to these criticisms, as well as for practical reasons, some therapists advocate the use of *covert sensitization*. Like implosion, it requires imagining the aversive situation, along with the behavior one is trying to eliminate. A person who wants to stop smoking may be asked to imagine a smoke-filled room, becoming nauseated, suffocating, and dying slowly of lung cancer and emphysema.

Operant Conditioning Techniques

Behavior modification using operant methods has flourished, and many ingenious programs have been developed. As in the case of classical conditioning, only a few important examples are presented here.

Token Economies   Treatment programs that reward patients with tokens for appropriate behaviors are known as **token economies**. The tokens may be exchanged for hospital privileges, food, or weekend passes. The goal is to modify patient behaviors using a secondary reinforcer (the tokens). In much the same way, money operates as a secondary reinforcer for people who work.

Three elements are necessary to a token economy: (1) the designation by hospital staff of certain patient behaviors as desirable and reinforceable; (2) a medium of exchange, such as coinlike tokens or tallies on a piece of paper; and (3) goods, services, or privileges that the tokens can buy (Christophersen & Mortweet, 2001; Watson & Tharp, 1999). It is up to the hospital staff to dispense the tokens for desirable patient behaviors. For example, tokens can be exchanged for hospital passes, cigarettes, food, television viewing, and the choice of dining room tablemates. Patients can be given tokens for good grooming and neat physical appearance or for washing dishes and performing other chores.

Token economy programs are used in a variety of settings, with such different types of people as juvenile delinquents, schoolchildren, people with mental retardation, and patients in residential community homes (Kazdin, 1994). Although such programs have been extremely successful in modifying behaviors in institutional settings, problems remain. Some patients do not respond to token economies. Complex behaviors, such as those involving language, are difficult to modify with this technique. A final criticism is that desirable patient behaviors that are exhibited in a hospital may not be continued outside the hospital setting.

Punishment   When less drastic methods are ineffective, punishment is sometimes used in treating children with autism and schizophrenia (Prochaska & Norcross, 2003). In an early study, Lovaas (Lovaas, 1977; Lovaas, Schaeffer, & Simmons, 1965) attempted to modify the behaviors of five-year-old identical twins, both diagnosed with schizophrenia. The children had shown no response to conventional treatment and were largely unresponsive in everyday interpersonal situations. They showed no reaction to speech and did not themselves speak. They did not recognize adults or each other, and they engaged in temper tantrums, self-destructive behaviors, and inappropriate handling of objects. The experimenters decided to use electric shock as a punishment for the purpose of modifying the children's behaviors. A floor gridded with metal tape was constructed so that a painful but not physically damaging shock could be administered to their bare feet. By turning the shock on and off, the experimenters were able to condition desired behaviors in the children. Affectionate responses such as kissing and hugging were developed, and tantrum behaviors were eliminated—all via the use of shock as an aversive stimulus. Lovaas (1987) has also used a loud "No," as well as a slap to the thigh of a child, to reduce undesirable or self-destructive behaviors.

Lovaas's work has shown that operant conditioning is a powerful technique for changing the behavior of children who have autism and have failed to respond to other forms of treatment. Because of the ethical issues raised by the use of electric shocks, however, use of this punishment technique has declined in recent years.

Observational Learning Techniques

As discussed in the chapter on models of abnormal behavior, *observational learning* is the acquisition of new behaviors by watching them being performed. The process of demonstrating these behaviors to a person or an audience is called *modeling*. Modeling has been shown to be effective in helping people acquire more appropriate behaviors. In one experiment, young adults who showed an intense fear of snakes were assigned to four groups:

1. The *live modeling with participation* group watched a live model who initiated progressively more fear-evoking activities with the snake. Participants were then guided to imitate the model and were encouraged to touch the snake, first with a gloved hand and then with a bare hand.

2. The *symbolic modeling* group underwent relaxation training and then viewed a film in which children and adults were seen handling snakes in progressively more fear-evoking circumstances.

3. The *systematic desensitization* group received systematic desensitization treatment for snake phobias.

4. The *control group* received no treatment.

Before treatment, the approach behaviors of all four groups of participants toward snakes were equally few. After treatment, the ability to approach and touch snakes had increased for members of all treated groups, who performed better than individuals in the control group. Group 1, in which treatment involved live modeling with participation, showed the greatest change: nearly all its members voluntarily touched the snake (Bandura, Blanchard, & Ritter, 1969).

Observation of models who verbalize how to perform a task and who make a few mistakes while completing the task has been found to be more effective than viewing models who do not verbalize or who perform with no anxiety or mistakes (Braswell & Kendall, 1988).

The modeling of behaviors shown in films has been successfully used in medical and dental practices to reduce fears of medical procedures (Wilson & O'Leary, 1980), in teaching social and problem-solving skills (Bellack, Hersen, & Himmelhoch, 1983; Braswell & Kendall, 1988), and in reducing compulsions and phobias (Rachman & Hodgson, 1980).

Cognitive-Behavioral Therapy

In the chapter on models of abnormal behavior, we discussed in some detail how cognitive-behavioral approaches rest on the belief that psychopathology stems from irrational, faulty, negative, and distorted thinking or self-statements that a person makes to himself or herself. As a result, most cognitive approaches share several elements. First, cognitive restructuring is used to change a client's irrational, self-defeating, and distorted thoughts and attitudes to more rational, positive, and appropriate ones. Second, skills training is used to help clients learn to manage and overcome stress. Third, problem solving provides clients with strategies for dealing with specific problems in living.

Initially, Albert Ellis's rational-emotive therapy, or RET (Ellis, 1962), was not well received by therapists. Attitudes soon changed, however, when the behaviorists became increasingly interested in mediating cognitive processes. In addition, RET and the behavioral strategies are similar in a number of ways. For example, RET incorporates cognitive restructuring, skills training, and problem-solving skills (Corey, 2005). Cognitive restructuring specifically is used to help clients deal with their irrational thoughts and beliefs. For example, a client's belief that he or she should be loved by everyone is attacked directly by the therapist: "What is so awful about not being loved by everyone? If your father doesn't love you, that's his problem!" Once the client begins to restructure his or her thoughts, the therapist begins the task of helping the client learn new ways to appraise and evaluate situations. Finally, homework assignments (behavioral rehearsal) are given to help the client learn new strategies to deal with situations.

Aaron Beck (1976, 1985; Beck & Weishaar, 1989) has also been a major contributor to cognitive-behavioral therapy. Originally using this approach to treat depression, he extended his treatment to other disorders such as anxiety and phobias. Beck holds that emotional disorders are primarily caused by negative patterns of thought, which he labels the "cognitive triad"—errors in how we think about ourselves (such as "I'm worthless"), our world ("Everything bad happens to me"), and our future ("Nothing is ever going to change") (see Table 17.3). Whereas RET engages the client in a rational or Socratic "debate," Beck's approach emphasizes the client's capacity for self-discovery. Less hurried and confrontative, the therapist and client work as a team to uncover underlying assumptions, to test them in the client's everyday life situations, and to determine by logical means whether they are valid. As in systematic desensitization, smaller challenges are assigned first, and more difficult ones are tackled as successes are experienced.

Other variations of cognitive-behavioral methods have been developed, and all are based on similar assumptions. For example, stress inoculation therapy was developed by Meichenbaum (Meichenbaum, 1985; Meichenbaum & Cameron, 1982). The assumption behind stress inoculation training is that people can be taught better ways to handle life stresses. Meichenbaum uses cognitive preparation and skill acquisition, rehearsal, application, and practice.

TABLE 17.3 Beck's Cognitive Triad of Depression
Negative View of Self—"I'm Worthless"
Believing that one is worthless, defective, inadequate, and undesirable. A person with depression may interpret negative events as being caused by personal inadequacies and failures.
Negative View of the World—"Everything Bad Happens to Me"
Perceiving the world and one's environment as being unreceptive, frustrating, and demanding. A person with depression may see the world in the most pessimistic and cynical manner.
Negative View of the Future—"Nothing Is Ever Going to Change"
Perceiving the future as hopeless and believing that negative events will continue to occur. The person with depression believes that one is helpless and powerless to improve the situation in the future.

Albert Ellis (left) (b. 1913) and Aaron Beck (right) (b. 1921) Ellis's rational-emotive therapy (RET) and Beck's cognitive triad have been widely used in promoting the cognitive restructuring that is the foundation of cognitive-behavioral therapies.

Cognitive-behavioral therapy shows much promise. Studies have indicated successful use of rational-emotive therapy, of Beck's approach, and of stress inoculation therapy (Chambless et al., 1998; Foa, Rothbaum, & Furr, 2003). Furthermore, some evidence suggests that the approaches may be at least as effective as medication or drug therapy for certain situational and specific depressions (Hollon & Beck, 1994; Lipman & Kendall, 1992). In one survey of psychotherapists, cognitive-behavioral approaches were rated as a therapeutic orientation that will continue to grow in popularity (Norcross & Freedheim, 1992).

Health Psychology

Health psychology integrates behavioral and biomedical science (Lewis, 2001). The two fields merged because people realized that psychological factors were often related to the cause and treatment of physical illnesses (Chiles, Lambert, & Hatch, 1999). The term psychobiology has also been used to address the importance of viewing the totality of the human condition (both biology and experience) in explaining and understanding behavior (Dewsbury, 1991). The goal of clinical health psychology is to help people change their lifestyles to prevent illness or to enhance the quality of their lives (Belar & Deardorff, 1995). As discussed in the chapter on psychological factors affecting medical conditions, heart disease, strokes, and cancer have been correlated with lack of exercise, diet, smoking, alcohol consumption, and other behaviors of a particular lifestyle. Health psychology makes people aware of the effects of these behaviors and helps them to develop healthier patterns of living.

One way to do this is through **biofeedback therapy**, which combines physiological and behavioral approaches. A patient receives information, or feedback, regarding particular autonomic functions, such as heart rate, blood pressure, and brain wave activity, and is rewarded for influencing those functions in a desired direction. Monitoring devices supply the information; the rewards vary, depending on the patient and the situation. Studies have found that biofeedback therapy can help reduce high blood pressure (Blanchard, 1992).

In an early study, researchers attempted to help patients with essential hypertension (elevated blood pressure) lower their systolic pressure. They used an operant conditioning feedback system in which patients saw a flash of light and heard a tone whenever their systolic blood pressure decreased. They were told that the light and tone were desirable and were given rewards—slides of pleasant scenes and money—for achieving a certain number of light flashes and tones. The patients gradually reduced their blood pressure at succeeding

biofeedback sessions. When they reached the point at which they were unable to reduce their pressure further for five consecutive sessions, the experiment was discontinued (Benson, Shapiro, Tursky, & Schwartz, 1971).

Meyer Friedman (1984) reported a study in which coronary patients who changed their lifestyles drastically reduced their recurrence of heart attacks. The investigation discovered that 95 percent of patients who suffer heart attacks exhibit what is called "Type A" behavior (discussed in the chapter on psychological factors affecting medical conditions), which is characterized by time urgency (the compulsion to finish tasks early, to be early for appointments, and to always race against the clock), attempts to perform several tasks at once, a propensity to anger quickly when others do not perform as expected, and rapid speech and body movements. The patients in Friedman's Recurrent Coronary Prevention Project learned, through counseling and practice drills, to control and change their Type A behaviors. Although the Type A hypothesis has proven to have a number of shortcomings (H. S. Friedman & Booth-Kewley, 1988), health psychology techniques, which focus on lifestyle changes, have proven very beneficial. Some of these are listed here:

1. *Establish priorities.* It is important for each of us to determine where to put our time and energies. Establishing a daily or weekly priority list, including everything that must be done, is a helpful strategy. If time is limited, learn to postpone the low-priority items without feeling guilty.

2. *Avoid stressful situations.* Do not put yourself in situations that involve unnecessary stress. For example, if you know that a particular traffic route involves constant tie-ups, consider another time for your commuting or take another route. Remember, we can and do have control over much of our lives.

3. *Take time out for yourself.* We all need to engage in activities that bring pleasure and gratification. Whether they involve going fishing, playing cards, talking to friends, or taking a vacation, they are necessary for physical and mental health. And they give the body time to recover from the stresses of everyday life.

4. *Exercise regularly.* Exercise is effective in reducing anxiety and increasing tolerance for stress. Furthermore, a healthy body gives us greater energy to cope with stress and greater ability to recover from a stressful situation.

5. *Eat right.* You have heard this advice before, but it happens to be excellent advice: eat well-balanced meals that are high in fiber and protein but low in

fat and cholesterol. Nutritional deficiencies can lower our resistance to stress.

6. *Make friends.* Good friends share our problems, accept us as we are, and laugh and cry with us. Their very presence enables us to reduce or eliminate much of the stress we may be experiencing.

7. *Learn to relax.* A major finding of stress management research is that tense, "uptight" people are more likely to react negatively to stress than are relaxed people. Relaxation can do much to combat the autonomic effects of anxiety and stress; thus the various relaxation techniques are helpful in eliminating stress.

Health psychology approaches have also been used to address a wide range of problems, including chronic pain, recurring headaches, and insomnia.

Evaluating Individual Psychotherapy

Both insight- and action-oriented approaches have attracted firm followers and loud critics (Kottler, 2002). Behavioral therapists, for example, believe that their action-oriented approach has solid theoretical support and empirical justification; that it provides a rapid means of changing behaviors; and that (unlike the insight-oriented approaches) it includes specific goals, procedures, and means of assessing its effectiveness. Critics have argued that behavioral therapy is dehumanizing, mechanical, and manipulative; that its relationship to learning theory is more apparent than real; and that it is applicable only to a narrow range of problems.

Whether one argues for either insight- or action-oriented therapies depends largely on whether one believes that human behavior is determined primarily by internal or external factors. Interestingly, Norcross and Freedheim (1992) surveyed a group of prominent psychotherapists and psychotherapy researchers about which therapeutic orientations would grow or decline in use during the next decade. As indicated in Figure 17.1, the respondents predicted that theoretical integration, eclecticism, and cognitive orientations would gain popularity, whereas psychoanalysis and transactional analysis would decrease in use.

More than fifty years ago, Hans Eysenck (1952) concluded that there was *no evidence that psychotherapy facilitates recovery* from what were then classified as neurotic disorders. According to the criteria he used, patients receiving no formal psychotherapy recovered at least as well as those who were treated! Since that time, others have also claimed that psychotherapy's success has been oversold and that both its practitioners and its clients are wasting time, money, and effort (Masson, 1998; Carey, 2004). Some opponents feel so strongly that they advocate a "truth in packaging" policy: prospective clients should be warned that "psychotherapy will probably not help you very much."

In a thought-provoking article, Persons (1991) pointed out that past outcome studies showing no

Laugh and the World Laughs with You A basic premise of behavioral medicine and health psychology is getting individuals to reduce stress. The Laughing Club of India reflects an interesting way to do this. According to the club's founder, Dr. Madan Kataria, laughter reduces stress. Shown here, the members breathe yoga-like, reach for the sky to reduce inhibitions, and then force a "ho, ho, ha, ha" until the laughter becomes contagious.

FIGURE 17.1 Predictions of the Theoretical Orientations of the Future   These ratings are averages compiled from the responses of prominent psychotherapists and psychotherapy researchers who were asked to predict the use of various psychotherapeutic orientations in the next decade. The ratings were made on a scale ranging from 1 (representing great decrease) to 7 (representing great increase).

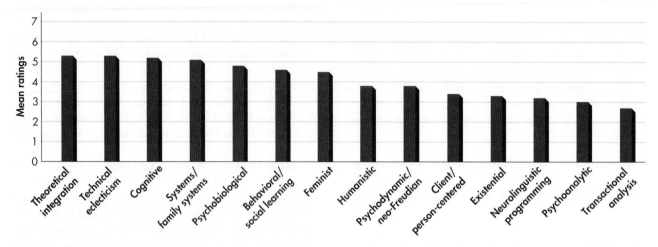

Source: Data from Norcross & Freedheim (1992).

Hans Eysenck (b. 1916)   Hans Eysenck started a controversy by asserting in 1952 that there was no evidence that psychotherapy was effective. Research, however, indicates that psychotherapy *is* effective and that the real issues concern types of treatment and their suitability for clients and their particular circumstances.

positive effects from psychotherapy or no difference in outcome in the use of different therapies suffered from major methodological flaws. They were based on poorly controlled studies, issues of diagnostic severity were not addressed, and the improvement measures were simplistic or poor. Taken together, these three points led Persons (1991) to conclude that contemporary outcome studies did not accurately represent psychotherapy. Furthermore, attempts to study psychotherapy and treatment outcomes often simplify human interactions, which are ongoing, context bound, and difficult to measure.

There is now an increasing distinction between efficacy research and effectiveness research (Seligman, 1995, 1998). An *efficacy study* is a laboratory distillation of treatment. It consists of a brief, well-controlled, and well-designed research investigation into the outcome of a treatment—a "laboratory" study of treatment. In contrast, an *effectiveness study* examines the outcome of treatment as it is actually delivered in real life, without the rigorous controls and designs found in efficacy studies. Importantly, in contrast to efficacy studies, effectiveness research demonstrates greater patient improvement and improvements across different kinds of therapies.

Meta-analysis and Effect Size

A form of statistical analysis (*meta-analysis*) has been found to be an extremely useful tool in analyzing therapy outcome studies. Meta-analysis allows us to analyze a large number of different studies by looking at *effect size,* a term that refers to treatment-produced change. To determine effect size, researchers subtract the mean of the control group from the mean of the treatment group. The difference is then divided by the standard deviation of the control group. The larger the numerical figure obtained, the larger is the effect of the treatment. Ideally, this comparison of effect size in many studies allows us to determine the effectiveness of different treatment approaches. It is important to note that meta-analysis is controversial; it has both staunch supporters (Shapiro & Shapiro, 1983; Smith, Glass, & Miller, 1980) and detractors (Erwin, 1986; Paul, 1985).

Meta-analytic studies strongly support the conclusion that psychotherapy is effective, and they allow researchers to estimate how large the effect is. Figure 17.2 graphically displays the effect of treatment based on two meta-analytic studies (Lambert & Bergin, 1994). As can be seen, individuals who receive psychotherapy are better off than 79 percent of individuals who receive no treatment. Those receiving minimal treatment (for example, a placebo) are better off than 66 percent of the people in no-treatment control groups.

Many reviews of outcome research have indicated that psychotherapy is effective and that people who are treated show more desirable and larger changes than those who do not receive formal psychotherapy (Garfield & Bergin, 1994; Shadish et al., 1997; Sloane et al., 1975; Smith & Glass, 1977; Smith et al., 1980). In addition, the largest gains in treatment tend to occur within the first few months and tend to endure (Lambert, Shapiro, & Bergin, 1986; Nicholson & Berman, 1983; Smith et al., 1980). Howard (1994) argues that psychotherapy is one of the best documented and most studied treatment interventions and that research clearly attests to its beneficial impact in people's lives.

One recent trend in psychotherapy research is the designation of *empirically supported treatments (ESTs),* clearly specified psychological treatments shown to be efficacious in controlled research with a delineated population (Chambless & Hollon, 1998). In other words, ESTs are those treatments for which rigorously designed research has demonstrated effectiveness in benefiting clients. Among the many ESTs are cognitive-behavioral treatment for anxiety and depression, interpersonal therapy for depression and bulimia, and behavioral therapy for sexual dysfunctions. Obviously, other forms of treatment may be effective, but they are not designated as ESTs because they have not yet been rigorously studied. This distinction has provoked some controversy. Critics of EST note that those treatments that are empirically supported tend to be either behavioral in nature or narrowly defined

FIGURE 17.2 Effect Sizes for Psychotherapy, Placebo, and No-Treatment Groups   Effect size is the result of calculations that reflect the changes produced by treatment. The effect size of psychotherapy is much higher than that of the placebo condition, which in turn is higher than the no-treatment condition. In terms of percentage improved, the figure can be interpreted as follows: the average client undergoing a placebo treatment is better off than 66 percent of the no-treatment controls; the average client undergoing psychotherapy appears to be better off than 79 percent of the no-treatment controls.

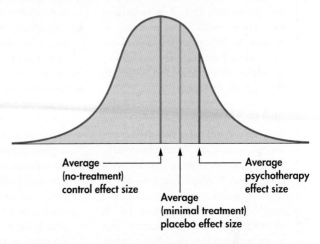

Source: Based on Lambert & Bergin (1994).

kinds of treatment, implying that other forms of treatment are being ignored and are not the focus of research attention (Carey, 2004; Nathan, 1998).

The controversy has resulted in a polarization between those who emphasize the common therapeutic factors that exist across all therapies and those who emphasize empirically supported therapies (Day, 2004). The "common factors" advocates identify four common dimensions of curative influence in therapy (Lambert, 1992). First, improvement is influenced by extra-therapeutic variables such as degree of psychopathology, motivation, ego strength, psychological-mindedness, and support in the environment. Second, the therapeutic change is affected by the relationship with the therapist, or the therapeutic alliance. Third, expectancy effects (hope for change) seem to play a role. Last, techniques, or the theoretical orientation, seem to play a role as well. In an empirical analysis of the contributions of common factors to therapeutic improvement, it was concluded that extratherapeutic variables accounted for 40 percent of the change, the therapeutic relationship for 30 percent, expectancy or placebo effects for 15 percent, and techniques for 15 percent (Lambert, 1992).

Regardless of the debate over the common factors approach versus the ESTs approach, we believe that

What Kind of Therapist Do You Want?

In general, people who experience emotional and behavioral problems benefit from psychotherapy. Yet benefits often vary according to client, therapist, and treatment characteristics. Given this fact, it is surprising that many individuals in need of therapy do little prior thinking about the kind of therapist they would like to see or about how and where to find "good" therapists.

If you were depressed or anxious, what kind of therapist would you like to find? What characteristics are important to you? What characteristics do you consider to be relatively unimportant? Why? The answers to these questions are complex and vary from person to person. Let us examine some of the factors that might be important and then provide an example of the kind of issues that can be raised.

- *Demographic characteristics of the therapist*   These include age, gender, educational and experiential background, ethnicity, and other similar characteristics. For example, would you mind seeing a therapist who had just recently completed training in psychotherapy?
- *Overall reputation and professional standing*   How can you determine how effective or successful a therapist is?
- *Experience with clients having problems similar to yours*   Does it matter whether the therapist specializes in your problem or is a general practitioner?
- *Therapeutic orientation (such as psychodynamic, behavioral, spiritual, and so on)*   Would you want to work with a therapist who believes that meditation is the primary tool to use against mental disorders?
- *Interpersonal style (such as humorous, serious, formal, informal, dominant, and submissive)*   Would you like a therapist who provides only minimal verbal responses in order to allow you all the time to talk?
- *Values and beliefs*   If you were a Christian fundamentalist, how comfortable would you feel working with an agnostic therapist?

Undoubtedly, many other important factors and issues can be listed. Your preferences will reflect your culture, feelings, beliefs, and needs.

In "A Buyer's Guide to Psychotherapy," psychotherapist Frank Pittman (1994) considers the client as a consumer who should not be afraid to ask questions of therapists in order to ascertain if they seem suitable. He recommends that the consumer should hire a therapist who has worked effectively with people the consumer knows, who leads a life that seems desirable to the consumer, and who treats a consumer with respect. In other words, Pittman argues that clients should become informed and selective in choosing a therapist.

---

psychotherapy *is* valuable and would best be served by emphasizing an integration of both views (Prochaska & Norcross, 1999). Increasingly, research now supports the effectiveness of psychotherapy (Ahn & Wampold, 2001; Hubble, Duncan, & Miller, 1999; Seligman, 1995). We also believe its maximal value is attained not by unreservedly accepting or rejecting any group of treatments, either behavioral or insight-oriented, but by using research to find the best match that can be made among therapist, client, and situational variables. The Critical Thinking feature discusses some options that should be considered in choosing a therapist.

Group, Family, and Couples Therapy

The classic form of psychotherapy is a one-to-one relationship between one therapist and one client. **Group, family,** and **couples therapies** are forms of treatment that involve the simultaneous treatment of two or more clients and may involve more than one therapist

Corey, 2004). Their increasing popularity stems from certain economic and therapeutic advantages: because the therapist sees several clients at each session, he or she can provide much more mental health service to the community. And, because several clients participate in the sessions, the cost to each person is noticeably reduced. Saving time and money is important, but the increasing use of group therapy seems also to be related to the fact that many psychological difficulties are basically interpersonal in nature—they involve relationships with others, and these problems are best treated within a group rather than individually.

Most of the techniques of individual psychotherapy are also used in group forms of treatment. Rather than repeat them here, we first discuss some general features of group therapy, family therapy, and couples therapy.

Group Therapy

There is now a great variety of group therapies, reflecting the many dimensions along which a therapeutic group may be characterized (Corey, 2004). One obvious dimension is the type of people who make up the group. In couples (which includes marital) and family therapy, they are related; in most other groups, they are initially strangers. Group members may share various characteristics. Groups may be formed to treat older clients, unemployed workers, or pregnant women; to treat clients with similar psychological disturbances; or to treat people with similar therapeutic goals.

Therapeutic groups also differ with regard to psychological orientation and treatment techniques, number of members, frequency and duration of meetings, and the role of the therapist or group leader. Some groups work without a leader. Others have leaders who play active or passive roles within the group. Moreover, the group may focus either on interrelationships and the dynamics of interaction or on the individual members. And groups may be organized to *prevent* problems, as well as to solve them; for example, group therapy has been suggested for divorced people who are likely to encounter stress.

Despite their wide diversity, successful groups and group approaches share several features that promote beneficial change in clients (Corey, 2004; Kottler & Brown, 1992; Yalom, 1970):

1. The group experience allows each client to become involved in a social situation and to see how his or her behavior affects others. An underlying assumption of group therapy is that problems are most likely manifested in interpersonal interactions with others. Once the group member can view his or her interactions realistically, problems can be identified and then resolved.

2. In group therapy the therapist can see how clients respond in a real-life social and interpersonal context. In individual therapy, the therapist either must rely on what clients say about their social relationships or must assess those relationships on the basis of client-therapist interactions. But data gathered thus are often unrepresentative or inaccurate. In the group context, response patterns are observed rather than communicated or inferred.

3. Group members can develop new communication skills, social skills, and insights. (This is one of the most powerful mechanisms of group therapy.) The group provides an environment for imitative learning and practice.

4. Groups often help their members feel less isolated and fearful about their problems. Many clients enter therapy because they believe that their problems are unique: no one else could possibly be burdened with such awful impulses, evil or frightening thoughts, and unacceptable ways. The fear of having others find out how "sick" they are may be as problematic to clients as their actual disorders. But when they suddenly realize that their problems are common, that others also experience them, and that others have similar fears, their sense of isolation is eased. This realization allows group members to be more open about their thoughts and feelings.

5. Groups can provide their members with strong social and emotional support. The feelings of intimacy, belonging, protection, and trust (which members may not be able to experience outside the group) can be a powerful motivation to confront

Sharing the Problems and Solutions Group therapy may be used in place of, or in conjunction with, individual therapy. In a group setting, participants often gain a sense of connection with others, achieve feelings of mutual support and assistance, and experience a decreased sense of isolation as they work toward solutions as part of a collective.

one's problems and actively seek to overcome them. The group can be a safe environment in which to share one's innermost thoughts and to try new adaptive behaviors without fear of ridicule or rejection.

Evaluating Group Therapy   Clients are sometimes treated in group and individual psychotherapy simultaneously. There are no simple rules for determining when one or the other, or both, should be employed. The decision is usually based on the therapist's judgment, the client's wishes, and the availability (or unavailability) of one treatment or the other. Of course, people who are likely to be disruptive are generally excluded from group therapy.

As desirable as it would be to base decisions regarding treatment techniques on the observed effectiveness of group therapy, little substantial research has been done on that topic. Reviews of studies have suggested that group therapy results in improvement, compared with no treatment or placebo treatment (Bednar & Kaul, 1978, 1994; Kaul & Bednar, 1986). The problems encountered in evaluating the success of group therapy include all those problems involved in assessing individual therapy, compounded by group variables and the behaviors of group members. Indeed, some have even questioned whether group therapy is really any different from individual therapy because the same therapeutic variables are involved (Hills, 1990).

Group therapy also has some disadvantages. For example, groups cannot give intensive and sustained attention to the problems of individual clients. Moreover, clients may not want to share some of their problems with a large group, and the sense of intimacy with one's therapist is often lost in a group. Group pressures may prove too strong for some members, or the group may adopt values or behaviors that are themselves deviant. And, in leaderless groups, the group members may not recognize or be able to treat people with psychotic or suicidal impulses.

Family Therapy

Family therapy may be broadly defined as group therapy that seeks to modify relationships within a family to achieve harmony. We use this definition to include all forms of therapy that involve more than one family member in joint sessions, including marital therapy and parent-child therapy. The important point is that the focus is not on an individual but on the family as a whole (Nichols & Schwartz, 2005). Family therapy is based on three assumptions: (1) it is logical and economical to treat together all those who exist and operate within a system of relationships (here, the primary nuclear family); (2) the problems of the "identified patient" are only symptoms, and the family itself is the client; and (3) the task of the therapist is to modify relationships within the family system (Corey, 2004; Day, 2004).

Two general classes of family therapy have been identified: the *communications approach* and the *systems approach* (Foley, 1989). Let us look briefly at each of them.

The Communications Approach   The communications approach to family therapy is based on the

Treating the Family Not Just the Individual Family therapy is a group approach that works with the family as a unit, not just one individual, to modify behaviors within the family system. In this photo, a family meets with a therapist to discuss issues regarding disagreements and miscommunications between the parents and their teenaged daughter. The therapist must be well versed in family counseling strategies and be aware of multicultural issues that may alter her conceptualization of the family.

assumption that family problems arise from communication difficulties. Many family communication problems are both subtle and complex. Family therapists may have to concentrate on improving not only faulty communications but also interactions and relationships among family members (Satir, 1967). The ways in which rules, agreements, and perceptions are communicated among members may also be important (Haley, 1963).

The therapist's role in repairing faulty family communications is active but not dominating. He or she must seek to show family members how they are now communicating with one another; to prod them into revealing what they feel and think about themselves and other family members and what they want from the family relationship; and to persuade them to practice new ways of responding.

The Systems Approach   People who favor the systems approach to family therapy also consider communication important, but they especially emphasize the interlocking roles of family members (Minuchin, 1974). Their basic assumption is that the family system itself contributes to pathological behavior in the family. A family member becomes "sick" because the family system requires a sick member. Treating that person outside the system may result in transitory improvement, but once the client returns to the family system, he or she will be forced into the "sick role" again. Thus family systems therapy is directed at the organization of the family. It stresses accurate assessment of family roles and dynamics and intervention strategies to create more flexible or changed roles that foster positive interrelationships.

Couples Therapy

Although the term *marital therapy* is often used in the mental health field, we prefer to use the more inclusive term *couples therapy* because it includes both marital relationships and intimate relationships between unmarried partners. It is a treatment aimed at helping couples understand and clarify their communications, role relationships, unfulfilled needs, and unrealistic or unmet expectations. Couples therapy has become an increasingly popular treatment for those who find that the quality of their relationship needs improvement (Nichols & Schwartz, 2005). Indeed, seeing only one partner has proven less effective in resolving interpersonal problems than seeing both together (Gurman & Kniskern, 1978). Couples therapists work on the assumption that it is normal for partners in an intense long-term relationship to experience conflicts. For example, the husband may find it difficult to express affectionate feelings toward his wife, who may have a

THE FAR SIDE® By GARY LARSON

© 1993 FarWorks, Inc. All Rights Reserved/Dist. by Creators Syndicate

"The problem, as I see it, is that you both are extremely adept at pushing each other's buttons."

strong need to be nurtured and loved. Or the couple may be locked in a power struggle involving financial decisions. Or the wife may resent a husband who shows any sign of weakness, because the man she married was supposed to be "strong and invulnerable." In all these cases, couples therapy attempts to clarify and improve the communications, interactions, and role relationships between the couple. Note that it is not the purpose of couples therapy to "save a relationship or marriage," as many couples believe when they first enter treatment. The decision to remain together, to separate, or to leave or divorce is a decision that must be made by the couple. The role of the therapist is to help the couple understand the nature of their relationship, how it may be contributing to conflicts and unhappiness, their available options, and, if they want, how to work toward a healthier and happier relationship.

Research on the effects of family and couples therapy has been consistent in pointing to the value of therapy compared with no-treatment and alternative-treatment control groups. However, research studies have generally not been rigorous in design; they often lacked appropriate control groups, follow-up periods of outcome, or good measures of outcome (Alexander, Holtzworth-Munroe, & Jameson, 1994). As a result, no strong conclusions are warranted at this time.

Systematic Integration and Eclecticism

The therapies discussed in this chapter share the common goal of relieving human suffering. Yet as we have seen, they differ considerably in their basic conceptions of psychopathology and in the methods they use to treat mental disorders. Many theories and techniques seem almost diametrically opposed to one another. For example, early criticisms of psychoanalysis concentrated on the mystical and unscientific nature of its explanation and treatment of behavioral pathology. Most of these criticisms came from behaviorists, who were likewise attacked by psychoanalysts as being superficial and concerned with "symptom removal" rather than with the cure of "deeper conflicts in the psyche." There have been attempts at rapprochement between psychodynamic therapy and behavior therapy (Davis, 1983; Goldfried, Greenberg, & Marmar, 1990; Marmor & Woods, 1980; Murray, 1983; Wachtel, 1982). But even these sophisticated attempts have come under fire as being empirically and theoretically inconsistent.

As we stated in the chapter on abnormal behavior, most practicing clinicians consider themselves eclectics (Garfield & Bergin, 1994). Relying on a single theory and a few techniques appears to be correlated with inexperience; the more experienced the clinician, the greater the diversity and resourcefulness used in a session (Norcross & Prochaska, 1988). *Therapeutic eclecticism* has been defined as the "process of selecting concepts, methods, and strategies from a variety of current theories which work" (Brammer & Shostrom, 1982, p. 35). An example is the early "technical eclecticism" of Arnold Lazarus (1967), which has been refined into a theoretical model called *multimodal behavior therapy* (Lazarus, 1967, 1984). Although behavioral in basis, this approach embraces many cognitive and affective concepts as well.

The eclectic model calls for openness and flexibility, but it can also encourage the indiscriminate, haphazard, and inconsistent use of therapeutic techniques and concepts. As a result, therapists who call themselves eclectic have been severely criticized as confused, inconsistent, contradictory, lazy, and unsystematic (Goldfried & Safran, 1986; Patterson, 1980). The resulting negative reception of the term *eclecticism* has led to other terms (including *creative synthesis, masterful integration,* and *systematic eclecticism*) that are more positively associated with attempts to integrate, to be consistent, to validate, and to create a unique and personalized theoretical position. Indeed, evidence indicates that practitioners prefer the term *integrative* to *eclectic* (Norcross & Prochaska, 1988).

There is, of course, no single integrative theory or position. Rather, an integrative approach recognizes that no one theory or approach is sufficient to explain and treat the complex human organism (Sommers-Flanagan & Sommers-Flanagan, 2004). All the therapies that we have discussed have both strengths and weaknesses; no one of them can claim to tell "the whole truth." The goal of the eclectic approach is to integrate those therapies that work best with specific clients who show specific problems under specific conditions (Corey, 2005). Thus in one sense, all therapists are eclectics—that is, each has his or her own personal and unique approach to therapy.

Culturally Diverse Populations and Psychotherapy

Just as the European American worldview is reflected throughout our society, Western psychology and mental health concepts are often characterized by an assumption that they are universal and that the human condition is governed by universal principles (Ridley, 1995; Sue et al., 1998). For example, cultural components of psychotherapy encompass the following characteristics: (1) healthy functioning is equated with individualism and independence, (2) clients can and should master and control their own lives and the universe, (3) self-awareness and personal growth are goals of the therapeutic process (DHHS, 1999). Many racial/ethnic minority groups possess values and beliefs that are at odds with these culture-bound traits: interdependence and collectivism are valued over individualism, concern is with group rather than self-development, and being in harmony with the universe is preferred over mastering it.

The *Surgeon General's Report on Mental Health* (DHHS, 1999) makes it explicitly clear that using European American standards to judge normality and abnormality is fraught with dangers; that it may result in denying appropriate treatment to minority groups; that it may oppress rather than help culturally different clients; and that it is important for mental health practitioners to recognize and respond to cultural concerns of African Americans, Asian Americans/Pacific Islanders, Latino or Hispanic Americans, and Native Americans (Boyd-Franklin, 2003; Flores & Carey, 2000; Ridley, 1995). Further, many ethnic minority researchers (Takeuchi & Uehara, 1996; Sue & Sue, 2003) have pointed out the appalling lack of research on the effectiveness of therapy for minority groups; few studies exist on empirically supported treatments with minority populations. Many minority mental health professionals have advocated the development of culture-specific treatments that recognize the cultural values, life experiences, and minority status of these populations in the United States (Ivey et al., 2002).

Myth vs Reality

Myth: Psychotherapy is equally effective across all populations and problems. There is no major need to adapt the techniques and strategies when working with different racial/ethnic minority groups.

Reality: There is considerable truth to this statement, but current clinical work and research reveal that the most effective forms of therapy are those that adapt to the clients' cultural values, lifestyles, and experiences. It is important to note that all therapy arises from a particular cultural context and that it is culture bound. Thus therapy techniques developed for one group may not be applicable to another.

African Americans

African Americans number between 34 and 35 million, or 13 percent of the population. The prevalence of mental disorders among African Americans is believed to be higher than that of the general population (DHHS, 1999). Further, they are underrepresented in privately financed care but overrepresented in public inpatient psychiatric care in relation to whites (Snowden & Cheung, 1990; Sue & Sue, 2003).

These differences do not appear to be the result of intrinsic differences between racial groups but a function of socioeconomic, cultural, and stress factors such as racism. The poverty rate for African Americans, for example, remains nearly three times higher than that of white Americans, and unemployment rates are twice as high (U.S. Bureau of the Census, 1995). Black Americans have also been subjected to continual prejudice and discrimination in society, making it understandable that these forces may cause greater personal distress and health problems (DHHS, 1999).

African Americans who seek therapy often have a negative view of mental health services and possess "historical hostility," triggering mistrust of the white therapist. Some minority therapists believe that it is important for the therapist to acknowledge the existence of historical hostility if effective psychotherapy is to be conducted with African Americans (Parham, White, & Ajamu, 1999; Vontress & Epps, 1997). In addition, these researchers believe that white therapists who work with minority populations must become aware of their own stereotypes, biases, and preconceived notions concerning African Americans. In one study, for example, African American and European American psychologists were presented a photograph and case information on an African American female and asked to rate the client on her attractiveness and ability to benefit from therapy (Atkinson et al., 1996).

White psychologists were more likely to rate the black female as less attractive, suffering from a more severe disorder, and less likely to be helped in therapy.

Another barrier to providing effective treatment for African Americans lies in the belief that therapies developed on European American populations are equally applicable across racial groups. Most forms of treatment are insight oriented, focus on individual development, are intrapsychic in orientation, and occur in the office on a one-to-one basis. As a group, African Americans tend to be more group centered and sensitive to interpersonal matters, to have strong kinship bonds, to be work and education oriented, and to have a strong commitment to religious values and church participation (Parham et al., 1999). They are more likely to believe that their problems are not internal but external: they live with discrimination, prejudice, racism, poverty, and other environmental concerns. Effective therapy for African Americans may mean understanding conflicting values in the therapeutic process and being able to play a more active role in helping African American clients deal with external problems rather than internal ones (Ridley, 1995).

Some guidelines in working with African American clients have been suggested by a number of multicultural specialists (Boyd-Franklin, 2003; Carter & McGoldrick, 2005; Nwachuku & Ivey, 1991; Parham 2002; Sue & Sue, 2003):

- During the first session, it may be beneficial for the white therapist to bring up the issue of racial difference between the two.

- Try to understand the worldview of African American clients before making an interpretation; determine how they view the problem and the possible solutions.

- Do not pathologize or prejudge the client's initial suspiciousness and reluctance to self-disclose. See it as a survival mechanism developed by the client to deal with issues of racism.

- Many African Americans have experienced racism as part of their life experiences. Don't be afraid to freely discuss issues of prejudice and discrimination.

- Assess the positive assets of the client, such as family (including relatives and nonrelated friends), community resources, and the church.

- Consider external factors related to the problem. This may involve contact with outside agencies and not dismissing issues of racism as "just an excuse."

- Use problem-solving approaches to deal with external issues.

- Above all, know that these are guidelines and should not be rigidly applied to all African Americans.

Cultural Diversity The increasing diversification of the United States has introduced many new customs, celebrations, and cultural events. In these photos, teenagers participate in a Dragon Dance in Chinatown (immediate right); a Latino family celebrates Christmas; an African American family celebrates Kwanzaa (a cultural rather than a religious holiday) (below, left and right); and a group of American Indians perform the Buffalo Dance during New Mexico's American Indian Day (far right).

Asian Americans/Pacific Islanders

Between 10 and 12 million people in the United States are Asian Americans (including Chinese, Filipinos, Koreans, Asian Indians, Vietnamese, Laotians, Japanese) and between 345,000 and 750,000 are Pacific Islanders (including Hawaiians, Guamanians, Samoans), forming a combined 4.1 percent of the population. Asian Americans are among the fastest growing minority groups in the United States (U.S. Bureau of the Census, 2001). Although they are generally lumped together, their population comprises at least forty distinct subgroups that differ in language, religion, and values (Sandhu, 1997). The contemporary image of Asian Americans is that of a highly successful minority who have "made it" in society. Indeed, a close analysis of census figures (U.S. Bureau of the Census, 1995) seems to support this contention. Mental health

statistics, for example, reinforce the belief that Asians in America are relatively well adjusted, function effectively in society, and experience few difficulties. Studies consistently reveal that they have low official rates of juvenile delinquency, divorce, psychiatric contact, and hospitalization (Sue & Sue, 2003).

Whether Asian Americans' underutilization of mental health facilities, however, is due to low rates of mental disorders, to discriminatory mental health practices, and/or to cultural values that inhibit self-referral is not known. It is becoming clear that many of the mental disorders, adjustment problems, and character disorders among Asians are hidden. Increasing evidence suggests that the discrepancy between official and real rates may be due to such cultural factors as the shame and disgrace associated with admitting to emotional problems, the desire to handle problems within the family rather than relying on outside resources, and the

manner of symptom formation, such as a low prevalence of acting-out disorders (DHHS, 1999; Sue & Sue, 2003). Many Southeast Asian refugees show psychiatric symptoms associated with past traumas and current resettlement problems. Very high levels of posttraumatic stress disorder and depression have been identified among this population.

Further, to believe that the issue of racism is not central to the life experiences of Asian Americans and Pacific Islanders is to deny social reality. Yet this appears to be a belief held by many mental health practitioners in our society. This belief is ironic in light of the historical and continuing bias directed at Asians. Denied the rights of citizenship and ownership of land and interned during World War II, Asians in America have been subjected to some of the most appalling forms of discrimination ever perpetrated against any immigrant group (Ina, 1997). Even more disturbing was a recent study indicating that 25 percent of the American public harbor negative attitudes toward and stereotypes about Chinese Americans, that 23 percent would be uncomfortable supporting an Asian American presidential candidate (as opposed to 15 percent who would be uncomfortable with an African American candidate), and that the public did not distinguish between Chinese Americans and other Asian American/Pacific Islander groups ("Asian Americans seen negatively," 2001). Like their African American counterparts, Asian Americans and Pacific Islanders may also approach mental health services with considerable suspiciousness.

Another potential barrier to effective therapeutic services for Asian Americans and Pacific Islanders lies in both the process and the goals of therapy that may prove antagonistic to their cultural values. First, mental health and psychotherapy are foreign concepts in Asian countries. Many refugees and immigrants have limited faith in talking about problems. Second, therapy often asks the clients to self-disclose their most intimate thoughts and feelings. Yet Asian cultural values make it clear that talking about one's personal life and family concerns to a stranger is inappropriate. Third, traditional Asian values regarding restraint of strong feelings contrast sharply with the more open and free expression of feelings in therapy. In light of these factors, several suggestions have been offered for working with Asian American populations (Ina, 1997; Sandhu, 1997; Sue & Sue, 2003):

■ Therapists should be aware of potential social stigma attached to seeking mental health services; issues of confidentiality should be strongly stressed.

■ Be aware that Asian Americans and Pacific Islanders are more likely to express psychological conflicts via somatic complaints and/or other socially acceptable issues (educational and vocational problems).

■ Consider the possibility that client reluctance to self-disclose and to freely express feelings and/or lower levels of verbalization in the therapy session may be due to cultural factors and not indicative of pathology.

■ The therapist should consider explaining the purpose of therapy, the expectations, and the process itself.

■ A more action-oriented problem-solving approach may be more consistent with the therapeutic expectations of the client.

Latino or Hispanic Americans

More than 35 million people, approximately 13 percent of the population, are Latino or Hispanic Americans. In physical characteristics, the appearance of Latinos varies greatly and may include resemblance to North American Indians, Blacks, Asians, or Latins and Europeans, depending on their country of origin. The U.S. Census classifies Hispanics not as a racial but as an ethnic group. As such, they can be members of any racial group. Latinos are overrepresented among the poor, they have lower levels of education and high unemployment, and they often live in substandard housing. They have lower annual incomes, higher rates of poverty, greater rates of medical problems, and less access to adequate health care than whites (DHHS, 1999; Flack et al., 1995; U.S. Bureau of Census, 1995).

For Hispanic Americans, family unity is seen as very important, as is respect for and loyalty to the family. For many Hispanic Americans, the extended family includes not only relatives but also "relatives" (though not by blood) such as the best man (*padrino*), maid of honor (*madrina*), and godparents (*compadre* and *comadre*). Each member of the family has a role: grandparents (wisdom), father (responsibility), children (obedience), and godparents (resourcefulness; Ruiz, 1995). Because of these relationships and resources, they generally do not seek outside help until after they obtain advice from the extended family and close friends (Flores & Carey, 2000; Paniagua, 1998; Santiago-Rivera, Arredondo, & Gallardo-Cooper, 2002; Sue & Sue, 2003). Epidemiological studies indicate that the lifetime rates of mental illness of whites and Latino Americans are no different (DHHS, 1999; Robins & Regier, 1991). Nevertheless, there do appear to be differences in the stressors experienced by Latinos, cultural differences that must be considered and unique problems related to mental health care access.

First, because many Hispanics suffer from external factors such as prejudice, discrimination, and poverty, some professionals have argued for social change (Paniagua, 1998). The role of therapists should be to help Hispanic clients become more aware of the oppression they face and to attain personal and collective liberation. As a result, it is important for therapists to understand the psychosocial, economic, and political needs of the Hispanic client (Flores & Carey, 2000).

Second, the most appropriate therapist to work with traditional Hispanic clients would be bilingual and bicultural. Yet the lack of bilingual therapists poses communication problems with Hispanics who are not conversant in English. It has been found, for example, that Mexican American clients are seen as suffering from greater pathology when they are interviewed in English rather than in Spanish (Sue & Sue, 2003). Further, the use of interpreters causes as many problems as it cures. Interpreters often misinterpret or distort the communication, become embarrassed with the topics discussed, fail to understand the therapeutic need for confidentiality, lack adequate psychiatric knowledge to work effectively, and may form an unhealthy alliance with the therapist or the client.

Third, the family structure of the traditional Hispanic family tends to be patriarchal, and sex roles are clearly defined. In working with Hispanic Americans, the therapist will often face problems dealing with conflicts over sex roles. In dealing with sex-role conflicts, the therapist faces a dilemma and a potential value conflict of his or her own. If therapists believe in equal relationships, should they move clients in this direction, or should they respect the cultural values of the group? Doing the former may be imposing one's view on the culturally different client. Doing the latter raises the question of whether the culture justifies a practice. Clear answers to these questions are difficult to find. Nevertheless, some suggestions can be given when working with Hispanic clients (Munoz & Sanchez, 1996; Paniagua, 1998; Sue & Sue, 2003; Vazquez, 1997):

■ Because interpersonal relationships are so valued in Hispanic culture (*personalismo*), it is important for the therapist to engage the client in a warm and respectful manner while maintaining a more formal persona.

■ The therapist must be sensitive to the possibility of linguistic misunderstandings, especially if the client speaks limited English. Determine whether a translator is needed.

■ Explaining therapy goals to the client is important.

■ Guard against misinterpretations. Lack of eye contact, silences, and other nonverbal behaviors may be an indicator of respect for the therapist rather than depression or cognitive dysfunction.

■ Determine the positive assets and resources available to the client and his or her family. Remember that the extended family system of the Hispanic family is often a source of help for the client.

Native Americans

Native Americans, with a population of approximately 3.5 million, make up slightly less than 1 percent of the U.S. population. They form a highly heterogeneous group composed of more than 550 distinct tribes. The population is young, with 39 percent under twenty-nine years of age, as compared with 29 percent of the total U.S. population. It is difficult to describe the Indian family, because tribes vary from matriarchal structures (Navajo) to patriarchal ones. Nevertheless, we know that as a group they have higher rates of poverty than their white counterparts, die at younger ages, have less education, and suffer from high unemployment rates. Although their diversity is great, certain generalizations can be made about their values: (1) honor and respect in a tribe is gained from sharing and giving, (2) cooperation to achieve mutually shared goals is valued over individual competition, (3) the concept of noninterference is valued over action and taking charge, (4) present time rather than the future is valued—punctuality or planning for the future is less important than experiencing the current moment, (5) the extended family is the unit of operation, and (6) harmony with nature is stressed (Carter & McGoldrick, 2005; Herring, 1999). These value differences can produce problems, especially when interpreted from a non-Indian perspective.

Wars and diseases that resulted from contact with Europeans decimated the Native American population so that by the end of the eighteenth century their population had decreased to only 10 percent of its original numbers. The experience of Native Americans in the United States is not comparable to that of any other ethnic group. They were the original people who lived on this land until it was taken from them due to federal and state policies (Johnson et al., 1995). During the 1930s, over 125,000 Native Americans from different tribes were forced from their homes in many different states to reservations. The move was and continues to be a traumatic one for Native American families, in many cases, disrupting their cultural traditions, forcing them into English-speaking schools, and removing children from their homes until the Child Welfare Act was passed in 1978. No wonder Native Americans are very suspicious of the motives of the majority culture and almost expect to be treated unfairly by non–Native American agencies (Johnson et al., 1995).

Many multicultural psychologists believe that the oppressive acts of the United States government toward Native Americans have resulted in the many mental health disorders in this group. The suicide epidemic among Native Americans is thought to be the result of poverty, a breakdown in family values caused by the disruption of the family, and prejudice and discrimination. American Indians have twice the rate of attempted and completed suicide as other youths (DHHS, 1999). Substance abuse is one of the greatest problems faced by Native Americans; they are more likely to die of alcohol-related causes than the general U.S. population (Penn, Kar, Kramer, Skinner, & Zambrana, 1995).

In working with Native Americans, some therapists have recommended the following guidelines (Carter & McGoldrick, 2005; DHHS, 1999; Herring, 1999; Sue & Sue, 2003):

- The therapist must be patient. Expectations that the client will rapidly and easily talk about sensitive materials may be unrealistic; it may take longer for clients to open up, because trust must be established first.

- Basic needs should be addressed first. Problems related to nourishment, health care, poverty, shelter, child care, and employment should receive top priority in the sessions, and appropriate action should be taken.

- The value of noninterference and the reality that problems reside in the client's environment may mean that the therapist should use a combination of therapeutic approaches. For example, person-centered strategies of respect and acceptance of the client and allowing the client to develop his or her solutions to the problem must be balanced with more behavioral/cognitive approaches to dealing with systemic issues.

- The therapist should be aware that communication style differences (eye contact, silences, and the expression of affect) are culturally determined. Making unwarranted psychiatric interpretations should be guarded against.

- Finally, the therapist might benefit from seeking counsel with indigenous healers in the Native American community.

Community Psychology

It is difficult to discuss psychotherapy and intervention without reference to the context in which services are provided. The context involves people living in families and communities and functioning within social, economic, educational, political, religious, cultural, and health institutions. **Community psychology** is an approach to mental health that takes into account the influence of environmental factors and that encourages

A Shameful Past, a Hope for the Future In the past, patients with mental disorders were often kept in mental hospitals under substandard living conditions, like those shown here. Today, community psychologists work to improve both community resources for people with disorders and the effectiveness of the services provided.

the use of community resources and agencies to eliminate conditions that produce psychological problems. It is concerned with the promotion of well-being and the prevention of mental disturbance. Pertinent issues include managed health care and the prevention of psychopathology.

Managed Health Care

The delivery of mental health services is headed for major changes. Concerns have been expressed over the rising costs of medical and mental health care, the uncertainty of treatment outcome, and the inadequacies in the delivery of treatment to certain segments of the population, such as older individuals and members of ethnic minority groups (Holloway, 2004). As Figure 17.3 indicates, only a small proportion of individuals with mental disorders seek care from the mental health system, and changes are needed to make services accessible, available, and affordable.

Reform is occurring in several ways. The following are among the most important. First, mental health care is shifting to health maintenance organizations (HMOs), which operate to reduce costs as much as possible. At the same time, traditional fee-for-service financing of services is diminishing. Many HMOs are turning to managed-care companies to administer their mental health benefit plans. Second, care providers tend to emphasize short-term treatment, intended to enable the client to function, rather than long-term treatment that attempts to "cure" the client. Third, individuals with master's degrees and others who do not have doctorates are increasingly providing services formerly provided by therapists with M.D.'s, Ph.D.'s or Psy.D.'s. Because doctoral providers' services cost more, they will be less in demand. Fourth, the effectiveness and cost efficiency of treatments and of clinicians must be continually assessed to reduce cost and inefficiency. Accountability and quality assurance are emphasized to an even greater degree than in the past.

Although there is general consensus that problems have existed in the mental health system, managed care has not been enthusiastically embraced by many mental health professionals. For example, there are concerns that health maintenance organizations may

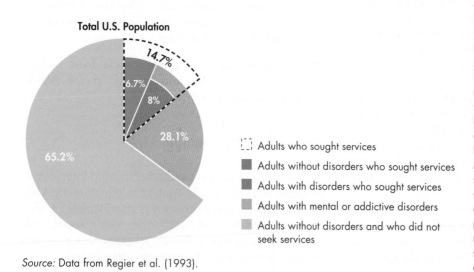

Total U.S. Population

14.7%
6.7%
8%
28.1%
65.2%

⌐¬ Adults who sought services
■ Adults without disorders who sought services
▨ Adults with disorders who sought services
▤ Adults with mental or addictive disorders
▢ Adults without disorders and who did not seek services

Source: Data from Regier et al. (1993).

FIGURE 17.3 Use of Mental Health Services Among Individuals with Mental or Addictive Disorders In the Epidemiologic Catchment Area survey of adult Americans, 28.1 percent of the sample said they were experiencing or had experienced a mental or addictive disorder during the previous year. During that year, 14.7 percent of Americans sought mental health services. Because many of those who sought services did not meet the criteria for a mental disorder, only 8 percent of the population had both a mental or addictive disorder and sought services. Thus only 28.5 percent of those with mental or addictive disorders used services (8 percent divided by 28.1 percent).

attempt to reduce costs simply by reducing the quality or extent of services, expending little effort on preventing problems, hiring providers to give cheap services, and gaining a much stronger voice than providers of services in determining treatment for clients (Holloway, 2004; Karon, 1995; Seligman & Levant, 1998). Clients may have a difficult time obtaining more long-term care. In adapting to the reforms in mental health care, some have pointed out the need for focused training of mental health care providers. These reforms could ensure that clinical health psychologists' educational background includes behavioral medicine and health psychology, as well as clinical psychology. Other skills in health assessment and intervention and outcome assessment are also needed (Belar, 1995).

Reform is also taking place in other ways. For example, the American Psychological Association has endorsed the principle that clinical psychologists with proper training should be able to prescribe medication for patients with mental disorders (Martin, 1995), although some psychologists oppose such a move (Hayes, 1995). Another facet of the reform movement is a systematic attempt that is being made to identify those treatments that have been empirically supported as being effective (Task Force on Promotion and Dissemination of Psychological Procedures, 1995). It is hoped that the effort will make it possible to establish standards for client and therapist treatment decisions based on scientific research.

"Manualized" treatment programs are also gaining popularity (Addis, 1997; Woody & Sanderson, 1998). These programs have manuals that instruct therapists (particularly those using cognitive and cognitive-behavioral approaches) to conduct treatment in a planned, systematic, and guided fashion. The assumption is that following treatment manuals will reduce possible ineffective discretionary practices that therapists use when they base procedures largely on their own judgment. The use of manuals in treatment, however, has generated some controversy, especially among those clinicians who believe that discretionary practices are necessary in psychotherapy (see Kazdin, 1998).

Finally, the increasing use of computer programs to provide psychotherapy to clients is evident (Marks, Shaw, & Parkin, 1998). Clients describe their problems on a computer and then receive programmed information and advice on the problems and how to deal with them. Proponents see advantages to computer-aided treatments, such as low cost and easy accessibility. Opponents believe that clients need the human contact of a therapist and that a computer cannot consider factors for which it was not programmed. Thus the field of clinical psychology, as well as the other fields

Reaching Out Before It's Too Late Groups and organizations often use the media to reach out to people with emotional problems. These communications reinforce the idea that problems can be prevented and offer help in how to go about it. This billboard is intended to not only reach people suffering from schizophrenia but also to educate the public about the need to provide appropriate treatment.

involved in mental health, is changing, and with this change come both opportunities and conflicts.

Prevention of Psychopathology

Preventing psychopathology is one of the most innovative functions of community psychology. Prevention programs are attempts to maintain health rather than to treat sickness. The main emphasis is on reducing the number of new cases of mental disorders, the duration of disorders among afflicted people, and the disabling effects of disorders. These three areas of prevention have been called *primary, secondary,* and *tertiary* prevention.

Primary Prevention **Primary prevention** is an effort to lower the incidence of new cases of behavioral disorders by strengthening or adding to resources that promote mental health and by eliminating community characteristics that threaten mental health. As an example of the former, Project Head Start was initiated in 1964 with the goal of setting up a new and massive preschool program to help neglected or deprived children develop social, emotional, and intellectual skills. Examples of the latter are efforts to eliminate discrimination against members of minority groups to help them fulfill their potential. Both techniques—introducing new resources and eliminating causal factors—can be directed toward specific groups of people or toward the community as a whole.

Munoz and colleagues (Munoz, Glish, Soo-Hoo, & Robertson, 1982; Munoz et al., 1995) have been systematically attempting to prevent depression in a

Raising Awareness Heather Irish is founder and CEO of Mental Illness Needs Discussion Sessions (MINDS™), a free program that works in urban, suburban, and rural middle and high schools to encourage awareness of and de-stigmatize mental disorders. During the seminars, students are given two brochures. One describes the symptoms of mental illness, and the other provides a guide to local, state, and national help lines; referral agencies; organizations; and other services.

community-wide project and in primary care patients. The project was particularly interesting. During a two-week period, nine televised programs intended to prevent depression were broadcast in San Francisco. Each program lasted for four minutes and showed viewers some coping skills, such as how to think positively, engage in rewarding activities, and deal with depression. Telephone interviews were conducted with 294 San Francisco residents. Some respondents were interviewed one week before the television segments were shown; others were interviewed one week after; and still others were interviewed both before and after the segments. Information about respondents' depression levels was collected during the interviews. (For those who were interviewed before and after the segments, the depression measure was administered twice.) Respondents who were interviewed after the televised segments were also asked to indicate whether they had watched any of the segments. Results indicated that those who saw the segments exhibited a significantly lower level of depression than that found among the nonviewers. The results, however, held only for respondents who had some symptoms of depression to begin with. Watching the television programs did not change the depression levels of those who initially (before the segments) reported little depression.

The results indicated that a community-wide prevention program could be beneficial. A large proportion (approximately one-third) of the viewers had some symptoms of depression, and this group showed fewer symptoms after viewing the programs. The long-term

effects of the programs were not assessed. Another problem in the study was that those who benefited from the programs had exhibited some initial symptoms. If they were clinically diagnosable as being depressed, the intervention might be considered secondary rather than primary prevention. (Secondary prevention is discussed in the next section.) Nevertheless, the San Francisco study demonstrated the effects of large-scale interventions that may help disorders.

Evidence also exists that early, primary prevention efforts can be successful in reducing the incidence of juvenile delinquency. Zigler, Taussig, and Black (1992) noted that few treatment and rehabilitation programs for juvenile delinquents have had much effect. In their review of early intervention programs aimed at children, they found evidence that these programs, intended to promote social and intellectual competence, have had an expected positive effect on preventing delinquency. The investigators speculated that gaining competence may snowball to generate further success in other aspects of life and prevent delinquency.

Although interest in primary prevention continues to grow, resistance to prevention is also strong. First, only through prospective and longitudinal research can developmental processes in primary prevention be uncovered (Lorion, 1990). Primary prevention is future-oriented, in that the benefits of the effort are not immediately apparent. Second, primary prevention competes with traditional programs aimed at treating people who already show emotional disturbances. Third, prevention may require social and environmental changes so that stresses can be reduced or resources can be enhanced. Most mental health workers are either unable or unwilling to initiate such changes; many others doubt that people have the ability to modify social structures. Fourth, funding for mental health programs has traditionally been earmarked for treatment. Prevention efforts constitute a new demand on the funding system. And fifth, primary prevention requires a great deal of planning, work, and long-term evaluation. This effort alone discourages many from becoming involved.

Secondary Prevention   **Secondary prevention** is an attempt to shorten the duration of mental disorders and to reduce their impact. If the presence of a disorder can be detected early and an effective treatment can be found, it is possible to minimize the impact of the disorder or to prevent its developing into a more serious and debilitating form. For example, classroom teachers can play an important role in secondary prevention by identifying children who are not adjusting to the school environment. Once identified, such children can be helped by teachers, parents, or school counselors.

In practice, there are a number of problems associated with secondary prevention. First, traditional diagnostic methods are often unreliable and provide little insight into which treatment procedures to use. It has been suggested that more specialized diagnostic techniques be used, perhaps focusing on certain behaviors or on demographic characteristics that may be related to psychopathology. Second, once a disorder is detected, it is often difficult to decide what form of treatment will be most effective with a particular patient. Third, prompt treatment is frequently unavailable because of the shortage of mental health personnel and the inaccessibility of services. Indeed, many mental health facilities have long lists of would-be patients who must wait months before receiving treatment. "Walk-in" clinics, crisis intervention facilities, and emergency telephone lines have been established in an attempt to provide immediate treatment.

Tertiary Prevention   The goal of **tertiary prevention** is to facilitate the readjustment of the person to community life after hospital treatment for a mental disorder. Tertiary prevention focuses on reversing the effects of institutionalization and on providing a smooth transition to a productive life in the community. Several programs have been developed to accomplish this goal. One involves the use of "passes," whereby hospitalized patients are encouraged to leave the hospital for short periods of time. By spending gradually increasing periods of time in the community (and then returning each time to the hospital), the patient can slowly readjust to life away from the hospital while still benefiting from therapy.

Psychologists can also ease readjustment to the community by educating the public about mental disorders. Public attitudes toward mental patients are often based on fears and stereotypes. Factual information can help modify these attitudes so that patients will be more graciously accepted. This help is especially important for

Serving Those in Need Because of client demand, some mental health clinics have waiting lists. Clients, therefore, may not receive immediate treatment unless it is an emergency. Walk-in clinics and drop-in centers like this one allow individuals easy and quick access to services.

the family, friends, and business associates of patients, who must interact frequently with them. A more difficult problem to deal with is the growing backlash against the discharge of former mental patients into nursing homes or rooming houses in the community. Many community members feel threatened when such patients live in their neighborhoods. Again, education programs may help dispel community members' fears and stereotypes.

SUMMARY

What forms of medical treatment have been found to be successful in treating mental disorders?

- Biological (or somatic) treatments use physical means to alter the physiological and psychological states of patients. The use of electroconvulsive therapy (ECT), or electroshock, has diminished, but it is still used for some patients with severe depression.
- Because psychosurgery permanently destroys brain tissue, it is now rarely used and strictly regulated.
- One reason for the declining use of both ECT and psychosurgery is a correspondingly greater reliance on medication or drug therapy. Antianxiety drugs reduce anxiety, antipsychotic drugs help control or eliminate psychotic symptoms, antimanic drugs reduce mania, and antidepressants effectively reduce depression. Medication has enabled many patients to function in the community and to be more amenable to other forms of treatment, particularly insight-oriented and behavioral therapy.

What is psychotherapy?

- Psychotherapy is the application of techniques derived from psychological principles to help disturbed clients. Clients, who usually have certain hopes and anxiety on entering therapy, have an opportunity to develop a therapeutic relationship with a therapist and, in the process, to learn new ways of dealing with problems and to experience or reexperience important emotions. The techniques therapists use vary widely and depend on the therapist's theoretical orientation.

What are the different approaches to psychotherapy?

- The insight-oriented therapeutic approaches include psychodynamic therapy, person-centered therapy, existential analysis, and gestalt therapy. These approaches provide the patient with an opportunity to develop better levels of functioning, to undergo new and emotionally important experiences, to develop a therapeutic relationship with a professional, and to relate personal thoughts and feelings.
- Action-oriented or behavior therapies (based on classical conditioning, operant conditioning, modeling, and cognitive restructuring) have been applied to a variety of disorders. Behavioral assessment, procedures, goals, and outcome measures are more clearly defined and more easily subjected to empirical investigation than are insight-oriented approaches. Two promising approaches are behavioral medicine and stress resistance training, which combine behavioral, cognitive, medical, and social knowledge.

How successful is therapy in treating mental disorders?

- Some critics claim that the effectiveness of psychotherapy—of whatever orientation—has not been demonstrated.
- Results from numerous studies and meta-analyses of these studies have pointed to the beneficial impact of treatment. The real issue, however, may be one of finding the best combination of therapies and situational variables for each client.
- Although critics argue that behavior therapy is dehumanizing, limited to a narrow range of human problems, and mechanical, proponents consider behavior modification both effective and efficient.

How are group forms of therapy different from individual ones?

- Group therapy involves the simultaneous treatment of more than one person.
- Many psychological difficulties are interpersonal in nature, and the group format allows the therapist and clients to work in an interpersonal context.
- Family and couples therapies consider psychological problems as residing within the family or couple rather than in one individual.
- The communications approach to family therapy concentrates on improving family communications, whereas the systems approach stresses the understanding and restructuring of family roles and dynamics.

Is there a way to combine or integrate the best features of effective therapies?

- Most practicing therapists are eclectic or integrative in perspective. They try to select therapeutic methods, concepts, and strategies from a variety of current theories that work.
- Being eclectic is sometimes criticized as being haphazard and inconsistent, but every therapist who fits the therapy to the client is, in fact, eclectic.

Is therapy with racial/ethnic minority groups different from working with European American groups?

- There is increasing awareness that psychotherapy is a western European construction that may not be applicable to various racial/ethnic minority groups.
- Culture-specific strategies in working with African Americans, Asian Americans/Pacific Islanders, Hispanic Americans, and Native Americans seem to require that the therapist take into consideration several important factors in therapy: (1) historical and continuing oppression in the form of prejudice and discrimination, (2) the cultural values and assumptions of the minority group, and (3) recognition that the process and goals of therapy may be antagonistic to the life experiences of the minority group.

What can society do to make the social environment a healthy place to live?

- In discussing therapeutic intervention, it is also important to be aware of broader mental health efforts involving community psychology or community mental health. Several developments are necessary to consider.
  - First, a growing trend in the delivery of mental health services is managed health care. Under managed health care, consideration will be given to cost effectiveness of services and short-term care. Although many mental health providers are critical of managed care, others have called for changes in the role of and services given by providers.
  - Second, the mental health field is also grappling with issues involving prescription privileges for psychologists, using empirically supported treatments as a guideline for delivery services, and employing treatment manuals in the practice of psychotherapy and behavioral modification.
  - Third, in addition to treatment, primary, secondary, and tertiary forms of prevention are important in our efforts to enhance mental health and well-being.

KEY TERMS

aversive conditioning (p. 571)

biofeedback therapy (p. 574)

community psychology (p. 587)

couples therapy (p. 578)

electroconvulsive therapy (ECT) (p. 560)

existential analysis (p. 568)

family therapy (p. 578)

flooding (p. 570)

free association (p. 566)

gestalt therapy (p. 569)

group therapy (p. 578)

implosion (p. 570)

monoamine oxidase (MAO) inhibitor (p. 563)

person-centered therapy (p. 568)

primary prevention (p. 589)

psychopharmacology (p. 561)

psychosurgery (p. 560)

psychotherapy (p. 564)

resistance (p. 566)

secondary prevention (p. 591)

selective serotonin reuptake inhibitor (SSRI) (p. 563)

tertiary prevention (p. 591)

token economy (p. 571)

transference (p. 567)

tricyclic (p. 563)

MULTIMEDIA PREVIEW

For additional study aids, we invite you to explore our media resources accompanying *Understanding Abnormal Behavior,* Eighth Edition. The Student CD-ROM includes videos, quizzing, and critical thinking activities that help to reinforce key concepts in a fun and engaging manner. The Student Web Site provides additional interactive activities, chapter outlines, and research links that further support and complement the text. All Web resources may be accessed by logging onto the Web site at **http://psychology.college.hmco.com/students**.

CHAPTER 18
Legal and Ethical Issues in Abnormal Psychology

- Does insanity mean the same thing as being mentally disturbed?

- What legal means are available for hospitalizing or committing someone to a mental institution?

- What is deinstitutionalization?

- Is everything confidential in a therapy session? What are the exceptions?

- What impact have the changing racial-cultural demographics had on the mental health profession?

Public interest in the workings of the legal system has never been more pronounced than it has been since the impeachment hearings of President Clinton and the O. J. Simpson trial. These high-profile cases introduced millions of Americans to such legal terminology as *high crimes and misdemeanors, perjury, obstruction of justice, inadmissible evidence, sidebar conference, presumption of innocence, Fifth Amendment rights, due process,* and *beyond a reasonable doubt.* Sitting as a mass-media jury, Americans speculated not only about the guilt or innocence of these two individuals but also about their states of mind. What would make President Clinton act so recklessly? Was he addicted to sex? If Simpson did kill his ex-wife, Nicole Brown Simpson, and her friend, Ronald Goldman, what could have motivated him to do so? Jealousy? Need for control? An ultimate extension of his wife-battering behaviors? And were these acts premeditated or impulsive, born of extreme and uncontrollable rage?

Increasingly, psychologists and other mental health professionals are being asked to answer such questions. They are playing an important role in determining the state of mind of defendants and are participating in decisions and actions of the legal system that affect human relationships, such as custody issues and jury selection (Tolman & Mullendore, 2003; Stromberg, Lindberg, & Schneider, 1995). In the past, psychologists dealt primarily with evaluation of competency and issues related to criminal cases. Now, however, their expanded roles include giving expert opinions on child custody, organic brain functioning, traumatic injury, suicide, and even deprogramming activities (see Table 18.1). And just as psychologists have influenced decisions in the legal system, they have also been influenced by mental health laws passed at local, state, and federal levels (Shuman, Cunningham, Connell, & Reid, 2003). The following case examples illustrate the complex relationship between mental health issues and the law.

On July 24, 1998, Russell Weston, Jr., carried a concealed gun into the nation's Capitol building as literally hundreds of tourists crowded through the security machines. Setting off an alarm as he passed through, Weston was confronted by Capitol guards and exchanged volleys of gunfire with them. Tourists ran panic stricken throughout the hallways as Weston killed two police officers and wounded a tourist.

Weston was subsequently captured, arrested, and charged with murder. Prosecutors offered no motive for the killings, but court papers revealed that the early investigation focused on Weston's alleged belief that federal agents had placed land mines on his Montana property. Family members testified that Weston had a twenty-year history of mental illness, suffered from paranoid schizophrenia, and believed government agents were out to get him. A government psychiatrist concluded that Weston "suffers from a mental disease or defect rendering him mentally incapable of assisting in his defense" and that he should be hospitalized indefinitely, until he is capable of understanding the proceedings. To improve his condition and render him competent, psychiatrists attempted to administer antipsychotic drugs. When consent forms for the medication were presented to Weston, he refused to sign. His attorneys had successfully fought for his right to refuse treatment until January 2002, when a judge allowed forced medication of Weston. In July 2004, another judge extended the medication ruling for another six months because Weston's mental state had improved. However, Weston still has not been tried for the murders of two Capitol police officers.

TABLE 18.1   The Intersection of Psychology and the Law

Increasingly, psychologists are finding that their expertise is either being sought in the legal system or being influenced by the law. Only a few of these roles and activities are described here:

Assessing dangerousness   This is a primary function that undergirds many of the other activities. The psychologist engaged in assessing dangerousness—suicide and homicide potential, child endangerment, civil commitment, and so on—must be knowledgeable about the clinical and research findings affecting such determinations.

Child custody evaluations in divorce proceedings   Psychologists often use their expertise to help courts and social service agencies to determine the "best interests of the child" in custody cases involving parenting arrangements, termination of parental rights, and issues of neglect and abuse.

Psychological evaluations in child protection matters   When a child is at risk for harm, courts may ask a psychologist to become involved. While being mindful of the parents' civil and constitutional rights, the psychologist will attempt to determine whether abuse or neglect has occurred, whether the child is at risk for harm, and what, if any, corrective action should be recommended.

Repressed/recovered or false memory determinations   One of the most controversial situations a psychologist faces is determining the accuracy and validity of repressed memories—claims by adults that they have recovered repressed memories of childhood abuse. Although psychologists are usually called as expert witnesses by the lawyers defending or prosecuting the alleged abuser, they sometimes play another role: suits have also been filed against mental health professionals for promoting the recall of false memories.

Civil commitment determination   Psychologists are asked to become involved in the civil commitment of an individual or the discharge of a person who has been so confined. They must determine whether the person is at risk of harm to self or others, is too mentally disturbed to take care of himself or herself, or lacks the appropriate resources for care if left alone.

Determination of sanity or insanity   Mental health professionals are often asked by the court, prosecution, or defense to determine the sanity or insanity of someone accused of a crime. The results are usually presented via a private hearing in the judge's chamber or expert testimony in front of a jury.

Determination of competency to stand trial   Psychologists may be asked to determine whether an individual is competent to stand trial. Is the accused sufficiently rational to aid in his or her own defense? Note that competence does not refer to the state of mind during the alleged crime.

Jury selection   A new breed of psychologists called *jury specialists* helps attorneys determine whether prospective jurors might favor one side or the other. Jury specialists use clinical knowledge in an attempt to screen out individuals who might be biased against their clients.

Profiling of serial killers, mass murderers, or specific criminals   In the field of forensic psychology, law enforcement officers now work hand in hand with psychologists and psychiatrists in developing profiles of criminals. The Unabomber Theodore Kaczynski, for example, was profiled with amazing accuracy.

Testifying in malpractice suits   A psychologist may be called in a civil suit to give expert testimony on whether another practicing clinician failed to follow the "standards of the profession" and is thus guilty of negligence or malpractice and/or on whether the client bringing the suit suffered psychological harm or damage as a result of the clinician's actions.

Protection of patient rights   Psychologists may become involved in seeing that patients are not grievously wronged by the loss of their civil liberties on the grounds of mental health treatment. Some of these valued liberties are the right to receive treatment, to refuse treatment, and to live in the least restrictive environment.

On August 20, 1989, two brothers, Erik and Lyle Menendez, killed their parents, entertainment executive José Menendez and Mary Louise (Kitty) Menendez. The brothers, then eighteen and twenty-one, admitted emptying their two pump-action Mossberg shotguns into their parents. Prosecutors claimed that the brothers killed their millionaire parents to inherit the family's fortune; indeed, just days after the slayings, the brothers went on a shopping spree, charging purchases on their credit cards. As support for their case, the prosecution played tapes of the Menendez brothers' therapy sessions in which they confessed to the killings.

The defense, however, argued that the killings were due to (1) an irrational fear that their lives were in danger, (2) years of sexual molestation by the father, (3) constant physical abuse and intimidation, and (4) threats that they would be killed if the "family secret" was ever exposed. The defense portrayed the brothers as "the victims" who endured years of sexual, psychological, and physical abuse and who, as a result, killed out of "mind-numbing, adrenaline-pumping fear." The prosecution argued for a first-degree murder conviction and sought the death penalty. The brothers were tried separately, and in each case the jury was deadlocked, unable to reach a verdict. The brothers were retried, and a second jury convicted them of first-degree murder in March 1996. They were sentenced to life in prison without possibility of parole.

Known as the "Wild Man of West 96th Street," Larry Hogue is a homeless Vietnam veteran who lives in the alleyways and doorways of Manhattan. He sleeps on park benches or in cardboard boxes, constantly forages for food from garbage cans, urinates and defecates on public streets, and wanders through the neighborhood talking to himself. But Hogue's notoriety and visibility go beyond these dimensions. He has been reported to harass passersby, threaten and stalk people in the area, smoke crack, and even become physically violent.

In and out of the criminal justice and mental health systems, Hogue has come to symbolize the multiple deficiencies of American society. When his behavior has been perceived as a threat to others, he has been committed and treated. With psychiatric help and medication, Hogue usually improves and is discharged. Without family or friends, financial resources, or a place to live, however, he returns to his former haunts, where his behavior once again deteriorates. Although Hogue is generally not violent when on prescribed medications, he is noted to be unreliable in taking them. According to official records, Hogue has been in and out of confinement some forty times.

In 1968, Prosenjit Poddar, a graduate student from India studying at the University of California at Berkeley,

sought therapy from the student health services for depression. Poddar was apparently upset over what he perceived to be a rebuff from a female student, Tatiana Tarasoff, whom he claimed to love. During the course of treatment, Poddar informed his therapist that he intended to purchase a gun and kill the woman. Judging Poddar to be dangerous, the psychologist breached the confidentiality of the professional relationship by informing the campus police. The police detained Poddar briefly but freed him because he agreed to stay away from Tarasoff. On October 27, Poddar went to Tarasoff's home and killed her, first wounding her with a gun and then stabbing her repeatedly with a knife.

In the chapter on abnormal behavior, we defined *abnormal psychology* as the scientific and objective approach to describing, explaining, predicting, and treating behaviors that are considered strange and unusual. All four of the preceding examples of behavior fit this definition well, and we can clearly see their clinical implications. What is less clear to many is that clinical or mental health issues can often become legal and ethical ones as well. This is evident in the Capitol Hill shooting of two police officers, for which the court psychiatrist ruled that Russell Weston, Jr., is not competent to stand trial. Yet how do we determine whether a person is competent to stand trial or whether he or she is insane or sane? What criteria do we use? If we call on experts, we find that professionals often disagree with one another (Shuman & Greenberg, 2003; Tolman & Mullendore, 2003). Might defendants in criminal trials attempt to fake mental disturbances to escape guilty verdicts?

An Abuse and Mental Illness Claim that Almost Worked Erik (right) and Lyle Menendez (left) killed their parents in August 1989. The defense argued that the brothers killed because of fear of their father and trauma suffered from years of sexual and physical abuse by him. The brothers were tried separately, and both cases resulted in hung juries. After a second trial, the brothers were found guilty.

MENTAL HEALTH AND SOCIETY

Was Lorena Bobbitt Insane When She Cut Off Her Husband's Penis?

The Presenting Facts

On June 23, 1993, Lorena Bobbitt approached her sleeping husband, cut off his penis with a twelve-inch carving knife, jumped into her car, drove some distance from the house, and threw the penis into some bushes. She was subsequently arrested and charged with malicious wounding. On January 21, 1994, the twenty-four-year-old woman was aquitted by reason of insanity of severing her husband's penis. After being incarcerated in a state mental hospital for five weeks, Lorena Bobbitt was freed because mental health professionals pronounced her "sane and no longer a threat."

The nature of Bobbitt's crime drew national attention, and the verdict produced jubilation from some advocates of women's groups fighting marital abuse. Others viewed the verdict as an outrage, especially since John Bobbitt, twenty-six, had been acquitted two months earlier of charges of assaulting his wife and has denied that he ever abused her. His penis has been surgically reattached but full functioning has not returned.

Defense Arguments in Favor of an Insanity Finding

In Lorena Bobbitt's trial, the defense presented evidence and an overall theory that she had experienced such intense fear and emotional conflict that she was overcome by an irresistible urge to protect herself and escape. Her ability to control her actions was diminished, and her ability to determine reality was also significantly impaired (temporary insanity). The defense

argued that she "snapped" and said her act was that of "an irresistible impulse" in which she did not have the power to control her behavior. To explain Bobbitt's state of mind, they presented the following points.

Bobbitt's action was evoked by years of abuse, beatings, rapes, and emotional torture at the hands of her husband, John. The defense constantly introduced the battered-woman concept in describing Lorena Bobbitt's behavior. During the trial, she testified that John had arrived home drunk that evening and raped her; that she had been subjected to years of beatings and rapes throughout their relationship; that John openly flaunted his unfaithful behavior to humiliate her; and that she felt trapped, with no way out. Lorena Bobbitt recounted her husband's especially barbarous treatment of her on the evening of the alleged rape and the extreme terror and anger she experienced. When he passed out after "the assault," she said, she recalled moving to the kitchen and seeing the knife. This was followed by flashbacks to years of other abuse and threats she had been

---

Or consider the issues raised by the case of the Menendez brothers. If their claim that they suffered from years of excessive abuse is true, do such reasons excuse them from the moral or legal obligations of a wrongful act? Increasingly, lawyers are using clients' claims of child abuse, domestic violence, and other psychological traumas to explain the criminal actions of their clients. In 1994, a jury found Lorena Bobbitt not guilty of charges related to cutting off her husband's penis because she had suffered physical and sexual abuse throughout her married life (see the Mental Health and Society feature "Was Lorena Bobbitt Insane When She Cut Off Her Husband's Penis?"). Should people like the Menendez brothers and Lorena Bobbitt be held responsible for their actions?

The example of Larry Hogue leads us into the area of criminal commitment and legal rulings that force mental health practitioners to go beyond clinical concepts defined in DSM-IV-TR (American Psychiatric Association, 2000). Some of Hogue's behaviors are extreme, but should a person who has committed no crime be institutionalized because he appears severely disturbed? Certainly, defecating and urinating in public are disgusting to most people and are truly unusual behaviors, but are they enough to deprive someone of his civil liberties? Does being a nuisance or a "potential danger" to self or others constitute grounds for commitment? What are the procedures for civil commitment? What happens to people once they are committed?

forced to endure. She states that she "blacked out" and could not recall severing John's penis, driving away in her car, or throwing his penis into some bushes. A psychiatrist testified that Lorena Bobbitt was under extreme stress at the time of the crime and that she suffered from a DSM-IV disorder—brief reactive psychosis—following the crime.

Prosecution Arguments in Favor of a Sanity Finding

The prosecution pointed out that Lorena Bobbitt did not act like an insane person. Her behavior leading up to her actions appeared planned and deliberate. She had the ability to distinguish right from wrong and chose the latter course. The prosecution presented some powerful evidence indicating that Bobbitt knew precisely what she was doing. She acted from hatred and revenge and, in a premeditated manner, carried out a spiteful plan, intended to take away John Bobbitt's manhood. A friend of John testified that Lorena had entertained the thought of cutting off her husband's penis before and had often threatened to do so if she ever caught him cheating on her. Several mental health professionals

testified that Bobbitt may have been under duress, but that her actions were purposeful and goal-directed.

Discussion Questions and Group Exercise

With other students from your class, form small groups and address this question: Was Bobbitt sane or insane? Present arguments in favor of your verdict and against it. Can your group come to a consensus? An enlightening exercise is to use a chart (similar to the one below) and to apply the four legal tests of insanity to this case. Remember, the defense used the irresistible impulse test, which in Virginia was grounds for acquittal. Would your verdict (guilty or not guilty by reason of insanity) on Lorena Bobbitt differ or remain the same using the other three standards? Why?

Verdict	M'Naghten Rule	Irresistible Impulse	Durham Rule	ALI Guidelines
Guilty				
Not Guilty				

After reading the rest of the chapter, indicate your response to each test by checking the guilty or not guilty verdict.

In the first three examples, the focus of legal and ethical issues tends to be on the individual or defendant. Mental health issues become legal ones (1) when competence to stand trial is in doubt, (2) when an accused person bases his or her criminal defense on insanity or diminished mental capacity, (3) when decisions must be made about involuntary commitment to mental hospitals, and (4) when the rights of mental patients are legally tested.

In the *Tarasoff* case, the focus of legal and ethical concern shifts to the therapist. When is a therapist legally and ethically obligated to breach patient-therapist confidentiality? In this case, had the therapist done enough to prevent a potentially dangerous situation from occurring? According to all previous codes of conduct issued by professional organizations such as the American Psychological Association, and according to accepted practice in the field, many would answer yes. Yet in 1976 the California Supreme Court ruled that the therapist should have warned not only the police but also the likely victim.

The ruling has major implications for therapists in the conduct of therapy. One implication is also related to the earlier cases. How does a therapist predict that another person is dangerous (to self, to others, or to society)? To protect himself or herself from being sued, does the therapist report all threats of homicide or suicide? Should a psychologist warn clients that not everything they say is privileged or confidential? How will this affect the clinical relationship?

Should This Man Be Committed? Between 1986 and 1993, Larry Hogue, known to some as the "Wild Man of West 96th Street" in New York City, frightened and intimidated residents in the neighborhood. Living in alleys and doorways of Manhattan, he would talk to himself, walk barefoot in winter, threaten to eat pets, and generally behave in bizarre ways. He has been arrested numerous times for threatening people and damaging property, but he has never been permanently confined.

We cover these and other topics in this chapter, and we begin by examining some of the issues of criminal and civil commitment. Then we look at patients' rights and deinstitutionalization. We end by exploring the legal and ethical parameters of the therapist-client relationship, taking a final look at ethical issues related to cultural competence in mental health.

Myth vs Reality

Myth: Because psychologists are specialists in understanding the human condition, they can predict the dangerousness of their clients well. We should rely on them to determine whether clients, inmates, and others are in danger of violence to others or of harm to themselves.

Reality: It would be wonderful if psychologists could predict dangerousness well. They appear to be no better than other citizens in predicting dangerousness, and some believe they are poorer; most mental health professionals overpredict dangerousness, thus lowering their accuracy. This seems to make sense, as they

may be inclined to "play it safe." Some believe that peace officers do a better job of ascertaining potential violence in people.

Criminal Commitment

A basic premise of criminal law is that all of us are responsible beings who exercise free will and are capable of choices. If we do something wrong, we are responsible for our actions and should suffer the consequences. **Criminal commitment** is the incarceration of an individual for having committed a crime. Abnormal psychology accepts different perspectives on free will; criminal law does not. Yet criminal law does recognize that some people lack the ability to discern the ramifications of their actions because they are mentally disturbed. Although they may be technically guilty of a crime, their mental state at the time of the offense exempts them from legal responsibility. Let us explore the landmark cases that have influenced this concept's evolution and application. Standards arising from these cases and some other important guidelines are summarized in Figure 18.1.

The Insanity Defense

For five months between 1977 and 1978, Los Angeles was terrorized by a series of murders of young women whose bodies were left on hillsides. All the women had been raped and strangled; some had been brutally tortured. The public and press dubbed the culprit the Hillside Strangler, and a massive hunt for the killer ensued. A major break occurred one year after the Los Angeles murders, when twenty-seven-year-old Kenneth Bianchi was arrested for two unrelated murders of college students in Bellingham, Washington. His fingerprints matched those found at the scene of the Hillside murders.

Bianchi was an unlikely murder suspect because many who knew him described him as dependable and conscientious—"the boy next door." Furthermore, despite the strong evidence against Bianchi, he insisted he was innocent. Police noticed that he was unable to remember much of his past life. During interviews in which hypnosis was used, a startling development occurred: Bianchi exhibited another personality (Steve). Steve freely admitted to killing the women, calling Ken a "turkey," and laughing at Ken's ignorance of his existence.

The concept of "innocent by reason of insanity" has provoked much controversy among legal scholars, mental health practitioners, and the general public. The **insanity defense** is a legal argument used by

FIGURE 18.1 Legal Standards That Address the Mental State of Defendants

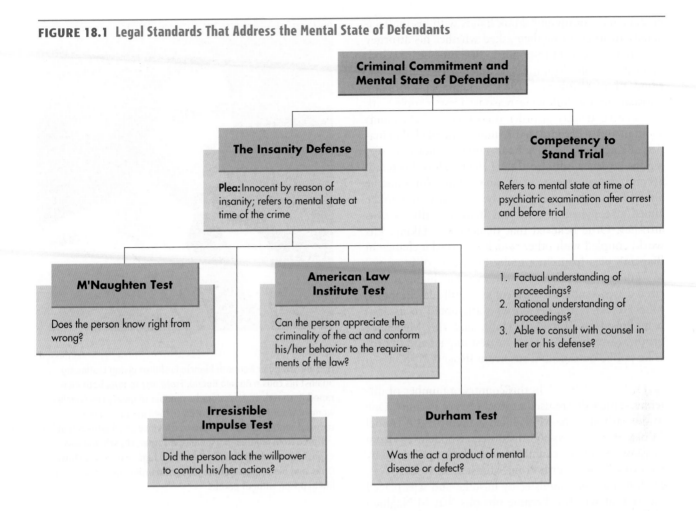

defendants who admit they have committed a crime but plead not guilty because they were mentally disturbed at the time the crime was committed. The insanity plea recognizes that under specific circumstances people may not be held accountable for their behavior. The fear that such a plea might be used by a guilty individual to escape criminal responsibility was portrayed in a popular film, *Primal Fear,* in which actor Richard Gere, playing a high-powered attorney, was duped into believing that his client suffered from a dissociative identity disorder (formerly known as multiple personality disorder). The client was found not guilty by reason of insanity at the trial, only to have Gere's character discover the ghastly truth. We need not go to the movies, however, to see the danger of misuse of the insanity plea. The Kenneth Bianchi case is a prime real-life example.

The question confronting the state prosecutors, defense attorney, and mental health experts in the Bianchi case was whether the defendant was a shrewd, calculating, cold-blooded murderer or a person with true dissociative identity disorder. It is important to note, however, that any number of psychiatric conditions may be used in an insanity plea.

Psychologist Martin Orne, an internationally recognized expert on hypnosis, was asked by the prosecution to examine Bianchi. Orne knew that Bianchi was either suffering from a dissociative personality disorder or was just a clever liar. He reasoned that if Bianchi was pretending, he would be highly motivated to convince others of his disorder. Orne thought that if he told Bianchi that multiple personalities rarely show just two distinct personalities, Bianchi might show still another personality to convince Orne that his was a true case. After hinting to Bianchi in the waking state that two personalities are rare, Orne placed Bianchi under hypnosis. Bianchi took the bait. Another personality—Billy—emerged. (Other experts were unable to draw out more than two personalities.)

Orne also noticed that Bianchi's behaviors were unusual for someone under hypnosis. For example, during one session Orne wanted Bianchi to hallucinate the presence of his attorney, so he suggested to Bianchi that his attorney was sitting in the room. Bianchi immediately got up and shook hands with his (halluci-nated) attorney. Orne then asked whether his attorney was shaven. Bianchi responded, "Oh, no. Beard. God, you can see him. You must be able to see him" ("The Mind of a Murderer," 1984). These behaviors are unusual for the following reasons. First, people with dissociative identity disorder almost never shake hands spontaneously because that requires a tactile hallucina-tion. Bianchi would have had to imagine not only see-ing his attorney but also feeling the touch of his hand. Second, the statement, "You can see him. You must be able to see him," seemed to be excessive and to be aimed at convincing Orne that Bianchi really saw his attorney. Orne believed that Bianchi was faking. His work, coupled with other evidence, forced a change in Bianchi's plea from "not guilty by reason of insanity" to "guilty." Unfortunately, the rare but highly publi-cized cases—such as those of the Hillside Strangler, John Hinckley (the person who attempted to assassi-nate President Ronald Reagan), and the Menendez brothers—seem to have the greatest impact and to pro-voke public outrage and suspicion (Rogers, 1987).

Legal Precedents   In this country, a number of dif-ferent standards are used as legal tests of insanity. One of the earliest is the M'Naghten Rule. In 1843, Daniel M'Naghten, a grossly disturbed woodcutter from Glasgow, Scotland, claimed that he was commanded by God to kill the English Prime Minister, Sir Robert Peel. He killed a lesser minister by mistake and was placed on trial, at which it became obvious that M'Naghten was quite delusional. Out of this incident emerged the **M'Naghten Rule,** popularly known as the "right-wrong" test, which holds that people can be acquitted of a crime if it can be shown that, at the time of the act, they (1) had such defective reasoning that they did not know what they were doing or (2) were unable to com-prehend that the act was wrong. The first part of the standard refers to a person's being unaware of the *nature* of an act (for example, strangling a person but believing one is squeezing a lemon) or the *quality* of an act (a disturbed person's belief that it would be amus-ing to cut off someone's head to watch him or her search for it in the morning) due to mental impairment. The M'Naghten Rule has come under tremendous crit-icism from some who regard it as being exclusively a cognitive test (knowledge of right or wrong), which does not consider volition, emotion, and other mental activity. Further, it is often difficult to evaluate a defen-dant's awareness or comprehension.

The second major precedent that strengthened the insanity defense was the **irresistible impulse test.** In essence, the doctrine says that a defendant is not crim-inally responsible if he or she lacked the will power to

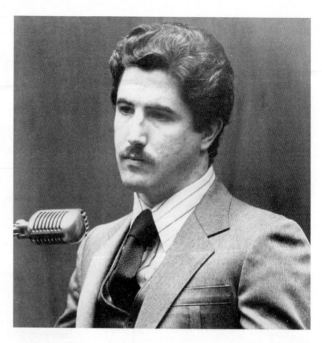

Faking Mental Illness to Use the Insanity Plea   Confessed Hillside Strangler Kenneth Bianchi is shown giving testimony against his cousin Angelo Buono. From 1977 to 1978, both men raped, tortured, and murdered a number of young Los Angeles women. Wanting to use the insanity plea in order to get a reduced sentence, Bianchi tried to convince psychiatrists that he suffered from multiple personality disorder. His scheme was exposed as a fake by psychologist and hypnosis expert Martin Orne, and Bianchi was found guilty of murder and sentenced to life in prison without parole.

control his or her behavior. Combined with the M'Naghten Rule, this rule broadened the criteria for using the insanity defense. In other words, a verdict of not guilty by reason of insanity could be obtained if it was shown that the defendant was unaware of or did not comprehend the act (M'Naghten Rule) or was irre-sistibly impelled to commit the act. Criticisms of the irresistible impulse defense revolve around what con-stitutes an irresistible impulse. D. L. Shapiro (1984, p. 30) asked the question, "What is the difference between an *irresistible* impulse (*unable* to exert con-trol) and an *unresisted* impulse (*choosing* not to exert control)?" For example, is a person with a history of antisocial behavior unable to resist his or her impulses, or is he or she choosing not to exert control? Neither the mental health profession nor the legal profession has answered this question satisfactorily.

In the case of *Durham v. United States* (1954), the U.S. Court of Appeals broadened the M'Naghten Rule with the so-called products test. An accused person was not considered criminally responsible if his or her unlawful act was the *product* of mental disease or defect. It was Judge David Bazelon's intent to (1) give the greatest possible weight to expert evaluation and testimony and (2) allow mental health professionals to define mental illness. The *Durham* standard also has its drawbacks. The term *product* is vague and difficult to define because almost anything can cause anything (as you have learned by studying the many theoretical viewpoints in this text). Leaving the task of defining mental illness to mental health professionals often results in having to define mental illness in every case. In many situations, relying on psychiatric testimony only serves to confuse the issues because both the prosecution and defense bring in psychiatric experts, who often present conflicting testimony (Otto, 1989; Shuman & Greenberg, 2003). Interestingly, Judge Bazelon eventually recognized these problems and withdrew support for the test.

In 1962, the **American Law Institute (ALI)**, in its **Model Penal Code**, produced guidelines to help jurors determine the validity of the insanity defense on a case-by-case basis. The guidelines combined features from the previous standards.

1. A person is not responsible for criminal conduct if at the time of such conduct as a result of mental disease or defect he lacks substantial capacity either to appreciate the criminality of his conduct or to conform his conduct to the requirements of the law.

2. As used in the Article, the terms "mental disease or defect" do not include an abnormality manifested by repeated criminal or otherwise antisocial conduct. (Sec. 401, p. 66)

It is interesting to note that the second point was intended to eliminate the insanity defense for people diagnosed as antisocial personalities.

With the attempt to be more specific and precise, the ALI guidelines moved the burden of determining criminal responsibility back to the jurors. As we have seen, previous standards, particularly the *Durham* standard, gave great weight to expert testimony, and many feared that it would usurp the jury's responsibilities. By using phrases such as "substantial capacity," "appreciate the criminality of his conduct," and "conform his conduct to the requirements of the law," the ALI standard was intended to allow the jurors the greatest possible flexibility in ascribing criminal responsibility.

In some jurisdictions, the concept of *diminished capacity* has also been incorporated into the ALI standard. As a result of a mental disease or defect, a person may lack the *specific intent* to commit the offense. For example, a person under the influence of drugs or alcohol may commit a crime without premeditation or intent; a person who is grief-stricken over the death of a loved one may harm the one responsible for the death. Although diminished capacity has been used primarily to guide the sentencing and disposition of the defendant, it is now introduced in the trial phase as well.

Such was the trial of Dan White, a San Francisco supervisor who killed Mayor George Moscone and Supervisor Harvey Milk on November 27, 1978. White blamed both individuals for his political demise. During the trial, his attorney used the now-famous "Twinkie defense" (White gorged himself on junk food such as Twinkies, chips, and soda) as partial explanation for his client's actions. White's attorney attempted to convince the jury that the high sugar content of the junk food affected his cognitive and emotional state and was partially to blame for his actions. Because of the unusual defense (the junk food diminished his judgment), White was convicted only of voluntary manslaughter and sentenced to less than eight years in jail. Of course, the citizens of San Francisco were outraged by the verdict and never forgave Dan White. Facing constant public condemnation, he eventually committed suicide after his release.

Guilty, but Mentally Ill   Perhaps no other trial has more greatly challenged the use of the insanity plea than the case of John W. Hinckley, Jr. Hinckley's attempt to assassinate President Ronald Reagan and Hinckley's subsequent acquittal by reason of insanity outraged the public, as well as legal and mental health professionals. Even before the shooting, the increasingly successful use of the insanity defense had been a growing concern in both legal circles and the public arena. Many had begun to believe that the criteria for the defense were too broadly interpreted. These concerns were strong, even though findings indicate that the insanity defense is used in less than 1 percent of cases, that its use is rarely successful, and that few defendants fake or exaggerate their psychological disorders (Callahan, Steadman, McGreevy, & Robbins, 1991; Silver, Cirincione, & Steadman, 1994; Steadman et al., 1993).

For quite some time, the *Hinckley* case aroused such strong emotional reactions that calls for reform were rampant. The American Psychiatric Association (1983), the American Medical Association (Kerlitz & Fulton, 1984), and the American Bar Association (1984) all advocated a more stringent interpretation of insanity. As a result, Congress passed the Insanity Reform Act of 1984, which based the definition of insanity totally on the individual's ability to understand what he or she did. The American Psychological Association's position on the insanity defense ran counter to these changes (Rogers, 1987). Its position is that even though a given verdict might be wrong, the standard is not necessarily wrong.

FIGURE 18.2 Factors in the Civil Commitment of a Nonconsenting Person

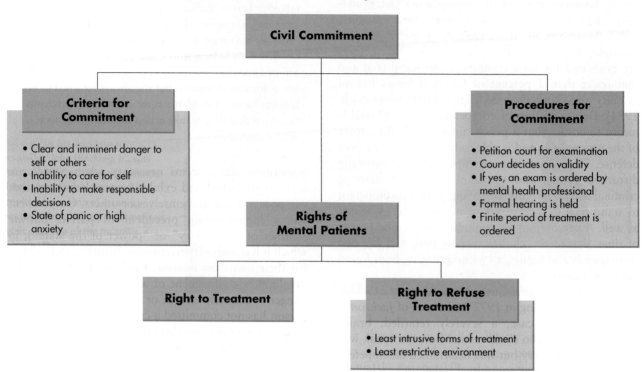

(Corey, Corey, & Callanan, 2003; Turkheimer & Parry, 1992).

1. *The person presents a clear and imminent danger to self or others.* An example is someone who is displaying suicidal or bizarre behavior (such as walking out on a busy freeway) that places the individual in immediate danger. Threats to harm someone or behavior viewed to be assaultive or destructive are also grounds for commitment.

2. *The person is unable to care for himself or herself or does not have the social network to provide for such care.* Most civil commitments are based primarily on this criterion. The details vary, but states generally specify an inability to provide sufficient forms of the following:

   • Food (person is malnourished, food is unavailable, and person has no feasible plan to obtain it)

   • Clothing (attire is not appropriate for climate or is dirty or torn, and person has no plans for obtaining others)

   • Shelter (person has no permanent residence, insufficient protection from climatic conditions, and no logical plans for obtaining adequate housing)

3. *The person is unable to make responsible decisions about appropriate treatment and hospitalization.* As a result, there is a strong chance of deterioration.

4. *The person is in an unmanageable state of fright or panic.* Such people may believe and feel that they are on the brink of losing control.

Certainly the example of the homeless lady would seem to fulfill the second criterion and possibly the third. In the past, commitments could be obtained solely on the basis of mental illness and a person's need for treatment, which was often determined arbitrarily. Increasingly, the courts have tightened up civil commitment procedures and have begun to rely more on a determination of whether the person presents a danger to self or others. How do we determine this possibility? Many people would not consider the homeless woman a danger to herself or others. Some, however, might believe that she could be assaultive to others and injurious to herself. Disagreements among the public may be understandable, but are trained mental health professionals more accurate in their predictions? Let's turn to that question.

Assessing Dangerousness   Most studies have indicated that mental health professionals have difficulty predicting whether their clients will commit dangerous acts and that they often overpredict violence (Buchanan, 1997; McNiel & Binder, 1991; Monahan & Walker, 1990). The fact that civil commitments are often based on a determination of **dangerousness**—the person's potential for doing harm to himself or herself or to others—makes this conclusion even more disturbing. The difficulty in predicting this potential seems linked to four factors.

1. *The rarer something is, the more difficult it is to predict.* As a group, psychiatric patients are not dangerous! Although there is some evidence that individuals suffering from severe psychotic disorders may have slightly higher rates of violent behavior (Hodgins, Mednick, Brennan, Schulsinger, & Engberg, 1996; Junginger, 1996; Monahan, 1993) than those found in the general population, this risk should not be a major concern. A frequent misconception shared by both the public and the courts is that mental illnesses are in and of themselves dangerous. Studies have indicated that approximately 90 percent of people suffering from mental disorders are neither violent nor dangerous (Swanson, Holzer, Ganju, & Jono, 1990), and few psychotic patients are assaultive: estimates range from 10 percent of hospitalized patients to about 3 percent in outpatient clinics (Tardiff, 1984; Tardiff & Koenigsburg, 1985; Tardiff & Sweillam, 1982). Homicide is even rarer: a psychiatric patient is no more likely to commit a homicide than is someone in the population at large (Monahan, 1981).

2. *Violence seems as much a function of the context in which it occurs as a function of the person's characteristics.* Although it is theoretically possible for a psychologist to accurately assess an individual's personality, we can have little idea about the situations in which people will find themselves. Shapiro (1984) advocated that the mental health professional needs to help the court define the term *dangerous* so that testimony can be restricted to a description of the patient's personality and the kinds of situations in which personality may deteriorate, lead to assaultive behavior, or both (see the Mental Health and Society feature "Predicting Dangerousness: The Case of Serial Killers and Mass Murderers").

3. *The best predictor of dangerousness is probably past criminal conduct or a history of violence or aggression.* Such a record, however, is frequently ruled irrelevant or inadmissible by mental health commissions and the courts.

4. *The definition of dangerousness is itself unclear.* Most of us would agree that murder, rape, torture,

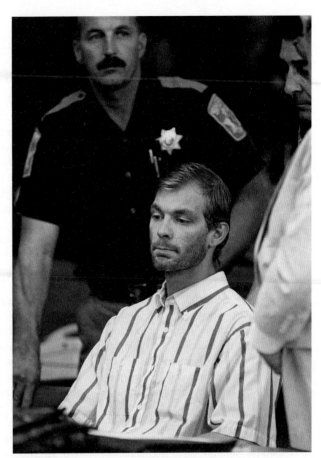

A Tragic Case of Failing to Predict Dangerousness
Convicted serial killer Jeffrey Dahmer killed at least seventeen men and young boys over a period of many years. Besides torturing many of his victims, Dahmer admitted to dismembering them and devouring their bodies in a celebration of cannibalism. Although Dahmer had been imprisoned in 1988 for sexual molestation, it would have been difficult to predict his degree of dangerousness. Despite an attempt to use the insanity plea, Dahmer was found guilty in 1994 and imprisoned. He was subsequently killed by another inmate.

and physical assaults are dangerous. But are we confining our definition to physical harm only? What about psychological abuse or even destruction of property?

Procedures in Civil Commitment

Despite the difficulties in defining dangerousness, once someone believes that a person is a threat to himself or herself or to others, civil commitment procedures may be instituted. The rationale for this action is that it (1) prevents harm to the person or to others, (2) provides appropriate treatment and care, and (3) ensures due process of law (that is, legal hearing). In most cases, people deemed in need of protective confinement can

MENTAL HEALTH AND SOCIETY

Predicting Dangerousness: The Case of Serial Killers and Mass Murderers

Jeffrey L. Dahmer admitted to killing his first victim in 1978 near his boyhood home. After killing his second victim, Dahmer stated he began to lose control of his necrophilia, a desire to have sex with the dead. Over a period of years until 1991 when he was arrested, he killed fifteen other men or young boys. Not only did he murder them, but he often killed them in hideous and torturous fashion. Once they were dead he would have sex with them, dismember their bodies, and feed on them in cannibalistic fashion. Dahmer pleaded "not guilty by reason of mental disease or defect," but he was subsequently found guilty and was killed by another inmate in prison.

In the worst mass shooting in the United States, thirty-five-year-old George Hennard smashed his pickup truck through a restaurant window, leaped out of the truck, and fired a high-powered automatic weapon into a lunchtime crowd. On that sunny afternoon in October 1991, Hennard killed twenty-two innocent patrons and workers in Killeen, Texas. Shortly after the slaughter, he put a bullet through his head and killed himself.

These examples of serial killers and mass murderers often make us wonder why such people were never identified as being potentially dangerous. Jeffrey Dahmer, for example, tortured animals as a small boy and was arrested in 1988 for molesting a child. Even though his father suspected his son was dangerous, Jeffrey Dahmer was released. And there appears to be sufficient evidence to suggest that mass murderer Hennard was a feared man who often acted in a paranoid way. In both situations, aberrant thoughts and behaviors appeared to go unrecognized or ignored.

Lest we be too harsh on psychologists and law enforcement officials, it is important to realize that few serial killers or mass murderers willingly share their deviant sexual or asocial fantasies. Furthermore, many of the problems in predicting whether a person will commit dangerous acts lie in (1) limited knowledge concerning the characteristics associated with violence, (2) lack of a one-to-one correspondence between danger signs and possible violence, (3) increasing knowledge that violent behavior is most often the result of many variables, and (4) recognition that incarceration—both criminal and civil— cannot occur on the basis of "potential danger" alone. Nevertheless, our limited experiences with mass murderers and serial killers have produced patterns and profiles of interest to mental health practitioners and law enforcement officials. Although similar, the profiles of mass murderers and serial killers also differ in some major ways.

---

be persuaded to *voluntarily* commit themselves to a period of hospitalization. This process is fairly straightforward, and many believe that it is the preferred one. *Involuntary* commitment occurs when the client does not consent to hospitalization.

Involuntary commitment can be a temporary emergency action or a longer period of detention that is determined at a formal hearing. All states recognize that cases arise in which a person is so grossly disturbed that immediate detention is required. Because formal hearings may take a long time, delaying commitment might prove adverse to the person or to other individuals.

Formal civil commitment usually follows a similar process, regardless of the state in which it occurs. First, a concerned person, such as a family member, therapist, or family physician, petitions the court for an examination of the person. If the judge believes there is responsible cause for this action, he or she will order an examination. Second, the judge appoints two professionals with no connection to each other to examine the person. In most cases, the examiners are physicians or mental health professionals. Third, a formal hearing is held in which the examiners testify to the person's mental state and potential danger. Others, such as family members, friends, or therapists, may also testify. The person is allowed to speak on his or her own behalf and is represented by counsel. Fourth, if it is determined that the person must enter treatment, a finite period may be specified; periods of six months to one year are common. Some states, however, have indefinite periods subject to periodic review and assessment.

Protection Against Involuntary Commitment

We have said that involuntary commitment can lead to a violation of civil rights. Some have even argued that criminals have more rights than the mentally ill. For example, a person accused of a crime is considered innocent until proven guilty in a court of law. Usually,

Profile of Serial Killers

Serial killers are usually white males, and they often suffer from some recognized psychiatric disorder, such as sexual sadism, antisocial personality, extreme narcissism, and borderline personality disorder. Few are psychotic, and psychoses do not appear to be the cause of their compulsion to kill. Almost all, however, entertain violent sexual fantasies and have experienced traumatic sex at a young age. Their earlier years are troubled with family histories of abuse, alcoholism, and criminal activity. Dahmer, for example, was sexually molested as a youngster. Most serial killers seem to exhibit little remorse for their victims, have little incentive to change, and seem to lack a value system. The compulsion to kill is often associated with what has been described as "morbid prognostic signs" (Schlesinger, 1989): breaking and entering for nonmonetary purposes; unprovoked assaults and mistreatment of women; a fetish for female undergarments and destruction of them; showing hatred, contempt, or fear of women; violence against animals, especially cats; sexual identity confusion, including underlying homosexual feelings; a "violent and primitive fantasy life"; and sexual inhibitions and preoccupation with rigid standards of morality (Youngstrom, 1991, p. 32).

Although we have come a long way in being able to compile a composite description of serial killers, some have challenged the accuracy of such profiles. In the 2002 Washington, D.C., sniping case, in which ten innocent people were shot (eight fatally), John Allen Muhammad and teenager Lee Boyd Malvo did not fit the descriptions profiled by experts. They were originally thought to be angry white men, with no military background and probably local residents. As it turned out, the snipers were African Americans, one had combat experience, and they were drifters.

Profile of Mass Murderers

Mass murderers are usually men who are social isolates and seem to exhibit inadequate social and interpersonal skills. They have been found to be quite angry and to be filled with rage. The anger appears to be cumulative and is triggered by some type of event, usually a loss. For example, they may view the end of a job or a relationship as a catastrophic loss. Most have strong mistrust of people and entertain paranoid fantasies, such as a wide-ranging conspiracy against them. They tend to be rootless and have few support systems such as family, friends, or religious or fraternal groups. Many researchers believe that the number of mass murders will increase as firearms proliferate in our society. Other social correlates affecting mass murders are an increasing sense of rootlessness in the country, general disenchantment, and loneliness. The more random the killings, the more disturbed, delusional, and paranoid the person is likely to be.

he or she is incarcerated only after a jury trial, and only if a crime is committed (not if there is only the possibility or even high probability of crime). Yet a mentally ill person may be confined without a jury trial and without having committed a crime if it is thought possible that he or she might do harm to self or others. In other words, the criminal justice system will not incarcerate people because they *might* harm someone (they must already have done it), but civil commitment is based on possible future harm. It can be argued that in the former case, confinement is punishment, whereas in the latter case it is treatment (for the individual's benefit). For example, it is often argued that mentally ill people may be incapable of determining their own treatment, and that, once treated, they will be grateful for the treatment they received. If people resist hospitalization, they are thus being irrational, which is a symptom of their mental disorder.

Critics do not accept this reasoning. They point out that civil commitment is for the benefit of those initiating commitment procedures (society) and not for the individual. Even after treatment, people rarely appreciate it. These concerns have raised and heightened sensitivity toward patient welfare and rights, resulting in a trend toward restricting the powers of the state over the individual.

Rights of Mental Patients   Many people in the United States are concerned about the balance of power among the state, our mental institutions, and our citizens. The U.S. Constitution guarantees certain "inalienable rights" such as trial by jury, legal representation, and protection against self-incrimination. As indicated in the chapter on abnormal behavior, the mental health profession has great power, which may be used wittingly or unwittingly to abridge individual freedom. In recent decades, some courts have ruled that commitment for any purpose constitutes a major deprivation of liberty that requires due process protection.

Until 1979, the level of proof required for civil commitments varied from state to state. In a case that set legal precedent, a Texas man claimed that he was denied due process because the jury that committed him was instructed to use a lower standard than "beyond a reasonable doubt" (more than 90 percent certainty). The appellate court agreed with the man, but when the case finally reached the Supreme Court in April 1979 (*Addington v. Texas*), the Court ruled that the state must provide only "clear and convincing evidence" (approximately 75 percent certainty) that a person is mentally ill and potentially dangerous before that person can be committed. Although these standards for confinement are higher than those advocated by most mental health organizations, this ruling nevertheless represented the first time that the Supreme Court considered any aspect of the civil commitment process. Under the advocacy of President Jimmy Carter, the U.S. Congress in 1980 passed the Mental Health Systems Act, protecting mental patients' rights and liberties. Some of these rights include the minimization of restrictions, reasonable explanation of treatment, refusal of treatment, confidentiality, and access to one's own records.

Due to decisions in several other cases (*Lessard v. Schmidt*, 1972, Wisconsin Federal Court; and *Dixon v. Weinberger*, 1975), states must provide the **least restrictive environment** for people. This means that people have a right to the least restrictive alternative to freedom that is appropriate to their condition. Only patients who cannot adequately care for themselves are confined to hospitals. Those who can function acceptably should be given alternative choices, such as boarding homes and other shelter.

Right to Treatment   One of the primary justifications for commitment is that treatment will improve a person's mental condition and increase the likelihood that he or she will be able to return to the community. If we confine a person involuntarily and do not provide the means for release (therapy), isn't this deprivation of due process? Several cases have raised this problem as a constitutional issue. Together, they have determined that mental patients who have been involuntarily committed have a **right to treatment**—a right to receive therapy that would improve their emotional state.

In 1966, in a lawsuit brought against St. Elizabeth's Hospital in Washington, D.C. (*Rouse v. Cameron*), the court held that (1) right to treatment is a constitutional right and (2) failure to provide treatment cannot be justified by lack of resources. In other words, a mental institution or the state could not use lack of funding facilities or labor power as reasons for not providing treatment. Although this decision represented a major advance in patient rights, the ruling provided no guidelines for what constitutes treatment.

This issue was finally addressed in 1972 by U.S. District Court Judge Frank Johnson in the Alabama federal court. The case (*Wyatt v. Stickney*) involved a boy with mental retardation who not only was not given treatment but also was made to live in an institution that was unable to meet even minimum standards of care. Indeed, the living conditions in two of the hospital buildings resembled those found in early asylums of the eighteenth century. Less than 50 cents a day was spent on food for each patient; the toilet facilities were totally inadequate and filthy; patients were crowded in group rooms with minimal or no privacy; and personnel (one physician per 2,000 patients) and patient care were practically nonexistent.

Judge Johnson not only ruled in favor of the right to treatment but also specified standards of adequate treatment, such as staff-patient ratios, therapeutic environmental conditions, and professional consensus about appropriate treatment. The court also made it clear that mental patients could not be forced to work (scrub floors, cook, serve food, wash laundry, and so on) or to engage in work-related activities aimed at maintaining the institution in which they lived. This practice, widely used in institutions, was declared unconstitutional. Moreover, patients who volunteered to perform tasks had to be paid at least the minimum wage to do them instead of merely being given token allowances or special privileges. This landmark decision ensures treatment beyond custodial care and protection against neglect and abuse.

Another important case (tried in the U.S. District Court in Florida), *O'Connor v. Donaldson* (1975), has also had a major impact on the right-to-treatment issue. It involved Kenneth Donaldson, who at age forty-nine was committed for twenty years to the Chattahoochee State Hospital on petition by his father. He was found to be mentally ill, unable to care for himself, easily manipulated, and dangerous. Throughout his confinement, Donaldson petitioned for release, but Dr. O'Connor, the hospital superintendent, determined that the patient was too dangerous. Finally, Donaldson threatened a lawsuit and was reluctantly discharged by the hospital after fourteen years of confinement. He then sued both O'Connor and the hospital, winning an award of $20,000. The monetary award is insignificant compared with the significance of the ruling. Again, the court reaffirmed the client's right to treatment. It ruled that Donaldson did not receive appropriate treatment and said that the state cannot constitutionally confine a nondangerous person who is capable of caring for himself or herself outside of an institution or who has willing friends or family to help. Further, it said that physicians, as well as institutions, are liable for improper confinements.

One major dilemma facing the courts in all cases of court-ordered treatment is what constitutes treatment. As discussed in earlier chapters, treatment can range from rest and relaxation to psychosurgery, medication, and aversion therapy. Mental health professionals believe that they are in the best position to evaluate the type and efficacy of treatment, a position supported by the case of *Youngberg v. Romeo* (1982). The court ruled that Nicholas Romeo, a boy with mental retardation, had a constitutional right to "reasonable care and safety," and it deferred judgment to the mental health professional as to what constitutes therapy.

Right to Refuse Treatment   Russell Weston, the man suffering from paranoid schizophrenia who killed two U.S. Capitol police officers in 1998, refused antipsychotic drugs (see the chapter-opening case study). As you recall, he was declared mentally incompetent to stand trial, and he refused to take medication to make him competent. Court-appointed psychiatrists have testified that his mental condition has worsened and that without treatment he could be dangerous. His attorneys, however, have supported his right to refuse treatment and have fought government officials on this point. Many believe that the refusal is based on a Supreme Court ruling (*Ford vs. Wainwright*) that the government cannot execute an incompetent convict. Thus it would seem ironic for any prisoner to agree to medication only to be executed. In January 2002, Russell Weston was forced by the courts to take antipsychotic medication based on the likelihood of improvement. Several other cases have come before the courts since then. In June 2003, the Supreme Court placed strict limits today on the ability to medicate mentally ill defendants forcibly to make them competent to stand trial. Such actions must be, according to the court, in the "best interest of the defendant." What this means will have to be played out in the future.

Although it may be easy for us to surmise the reason for Weston's attorneys to refuse treatment to make him better, does it make sense for others? Patients frequently refuse medical treatment on religious grounds or because the treatment would only prolong a terminal illness. In many cases, physicians are inclined to honor such refusals, especially if they seem to be based on reasonable grounds. But should mental patients have a right to refuse treatment? At first glance, it may appear illogical. After all, why commit patients for treatment and then allow them to refuse it? Furthermore, isn't it possible that mental patients may be incapable of deciding what is best for themselves? For example, a man with a paranoid delusion may

refuse treatment because he believes the hospital staff is plotting against him. If he is allowed to refuse medication or other forms of therapy, his condition may deteriorate more. The result is that the client may become even more dangerous or incapable of caring for himself outside of hospital confinement.

Proponents of the right to refuse treatment argue, however, that many forms of treatment, such as medication or electroconvulsive therapy (ECT), may have long-term side effects, as discussed in earlier chapters. They also point out that involuntary treatment is generally much less effective than treatment accepted voluntarily (Shapiro, 1984). People forced into treatment seem to resist it, thereby nullifying the potentially beneficial effects.

The case of *Rennie v. Klein* (1978) involved several state hospitals in New Jersey that were forcibly medicating patients in nonemergency situations. The court ruled that people have a constitutional right to refuse treatment (psychotropic medication) and to be given due process. In another related case, *Rogers v. Okin* (1979), a Massachusetts court supported these guidelines. Both cases made the point that psychotropic medication was often used only to control behavior or as a substitute for treatment. Further, the decisions noted that drugs might actually inhibit recovery.

In these cases, the courts supported the right to refuse treatment under certain conditions and extended the least restrictive alternative principle to include *least intrusive forms of treatment*. Generally, psychotherapy is considered less intrusive than somatic or physical therapies (ECT and medication). Although this compromise may appear reasonable, other problems present themselves. First, how do we define *intrusive treatment*? Are insight therapies as intrusive as behavioral techniques (punishment and aversion procedures)? Second, if patients are allowed to refuse certain forms of treatment and if the hospital does not have alternatives for them, can clients sue the institution? These questions remain unanswered.

Court-Ordered Assisted Treatment: Coercion or Caring?

In January 1999, Kendra Webdale waited for a subway train at a midtown Manhattan station. It was reported that Andrew Goldstein, twenty-nine years old, moved toward the woman and pushed her onto the tracks as a subway train pulled into the station. Riders watched in horror as the train struck Kendra Webdale, killing her on that fateful morning. Passengers surrounded the suspect and held him until the police arrived. It was found that Goldstein was carrying medical papers indicating

The Downside of Deinstitutionalization Homelessness has become one of the great social problems of urban communities. Many believe that deinstitutionalization has contributed to the problem, although it is not clear what proportion of homeless people are mentally ill. Scenes like this one, however, are becoming all too common.

1987). The quality of care in many of these places is marginal, forcing continuing and periodic rehospitalization of their residents (Turkheimer & Parry, 1992). People with mental illnesses constitute a substantial portion of the homeless population (Fischer & Breakey, 1991; Levine & Rog, 1990).

Much of the problem with deinstitutionalization appears to be the community's lack of preparation and resources to care for people with chronic mental illness. Many patients lack family or friends who can help them make the transition back into the community; many state hospitals do not provide patients with adequate skills training; many discharged patients have difficulty finding jobs; many find substandard housing that is worse than the institutions from which they came; many are not adequately monitored and receive no psychiatric treatment; and many become homeless (Westermeyer, 1987). It is difficult to estimate how many discharged mental patients have been added to the burgeoning ranks of the homeless. We do know that homelessness in the United States, especially in large, urban areas, is increasing at an alarming pace (Kondratas, 1991; Toro & Wall, 1991). Certainly, it is not difficult to see the number of people who live in transport terminals, parks, flophouses, homeless shelters, cars, and storefronts. It is hard to determine how many of these homeless people were deinstitutionalized before adequate support services were present in a community. We do know, however, that the homeless have significantly poorer psychological adjustment and higher arrests and conviction records (Lamb, 1984). The solution, although complex, probably does not call for a return to the old institutions of the 1950s but rather for the provision of more and better community-based treatment facilities and alternatives (Kiesler, 1991).

For patients involved in alternative community programs, the picture appears somewhat more positive. After reviewing reports of experimental studies on alternative treatment, a group of researchers concluded that such patients fared at least as well as those in institutions. Where differences were found, they favored the alternative programs (Braun et al., 1981). Such studies are few, however, and much remains to be done if deinstitutionalized patients are to be provided with the best supportive treatment.

The Therapist-Client Relationship

The therapist-client relationship involves a number of legal, moral, and ethical issues. Three primary concerns are issues of confidentiality and privileged communication; the therapist's duty to warn others of a risk posed by a dangerous client; and the therapist's obligation to avoid sexual intimacies with clients.

Confidentiality and Privileged Communication

Basic to the therapist-patient relationship is the premise that therapy involves a deeply personal association in which clients have a right to expect that whatever they say will be kept private. Therapists believe that genuine therapy cannot occur unless clients trust their therapists and believe that they will not divulge confidential communications. Without this guarantee, clients may not be completely open with their thoughts and may thereby lose the benefits of therapy. This assumption raises several questions. First, what professional ethics and legal statutes govern the therapist-client relationship? Under what conditions can a therapist breach the confidentiality of the relationship? Second, what if, in a conflict between clinical issues (need for trust) and legal ones (need to disclose), the therapist chooses trust? What are the consequences? Third, if a therapist decides to disclose information to a third party, what effects can the disclosure have on the therapist-client relationship? Last, how can a therapist discuss the limits of confidentiality in a way that would be least likely to disrupt the therapeutic relationship?

Confidentiality is an ethical standard that protects clients from disclosure of information without their consent. The importance of confidentiality is also shared by the public; in one study it was found that 74 percent of respondents thought everything told to a therapist should be confidential; indeed, 69 percent believed that whatever they discussed was never disclosed (Miller & Thelen, 1986). Confidentiality, however, is an ethical, not a legal, obligation. **Privileged communication,** a narrower legal concept, protects privacy and prevents the disclosure of confidential communications without a client's permission (Corey et al., 2003; Herlicky & Sheeley, 1988). An important part of this concept is that the "holder of the privilege" is the client, not the therapist. In other words, if a client waives this privilege, the therapist has no grounds for withholding information. Shapiro (1984) pointed out that our society recognizes how important certain confidential relationships are and protects them by law. These relationships are the husband-wife, attorney-client, pastor-congregant, and therapist-client relationships. Psychiatric practices are regulated in all fifty states and the District of Columbia, and forty-two states have privileged communication statutes (Herlicky & Sheeley, 1988).

Exemptions from Privileged Communication
Although states vary considerably, all states recognize certain situations in which communications can be divulged (Brown & Srebalus, 2003). Corey and associates (1998) summarized these conditions:

1. In situations that deal with civil or criminal commitment or competency to stand trial, the client's right to privilege can be waived. For example, a court-appointed therapist who determines that the client needs hospitalization for a psychological disorder may disclose the results of the examination to an appropriate third party (judge, mental health professionals, or those intimately involved in the decision-making process).

2. Disclosure can also be made when a client sees a therapist and introduces his or her mental condition as a claim or defense in a civil action. For example, a woman who sues an employer for harassment and uses "mental distress" to justify her claim may force the therapist to disclose information relevant to her claim.

3. When the client is younger than sixteen years of age or is a dependent elderly person and information leads the therapist to believe that the individual has been a victim of crime (incest, rape, or child and elder abuse), the therapist must provide that information to the appropriate protective services agency.

4. When the therapist has reason to believe that a client presents a danger to himself or herself (possible injury or suicide) or may potentially harm someone else, the therapist must act to ward off the danger.

Privilege in communication is not absolute. Rather, it strikes a delicate balance between the individual's right to privacy and the public's need to know certain information (Leslie, 1991). Problems arise when we try to determine what the balance should be and how important various events and facts are in individual cases.

The Duty-to-Warn Principle

At the beginning of the chapter, we briefly described the case of Prosenjit Poddar (*Tarasoff v. Board of Regents of the University of California,* 1976), a graduate student who killed Tatiana Tarasoff after notifying his therapist that he intended to take her life. Before the homicide, the therapist had decided that Poddar was dangerous and likely to carry out his threat, and he had notified the director of the Cowell Psychiatric Clinic that the client was dangerous. He also informed the campus police, hoping that they would detain the student. Surely the therapist had done all that could be reasonably expected. Not so, ruled the California Supreme Court. In the *Tarasoff* **ruling,** the court stated that when a therapist determines, according to the standards of the mental health profession, that a patient presents a serious danger to another, the therapist is obligated to warn the *intended victim.* The court went on to say that protective privilege ends where public peril begins. In general, courts have ruled that therapists have a responsibility to protect the public from dangerous acts of violent clients and have held therapists accountable for (1) failing to diagnose or predict dangerousness, (2) failing to warn potential victims, (3) failing to commit dangerous individuals, and (4) prematurely discharging dangerous clients from a hospital.

On June 13, 1996, however, the U.S. Supreme Court reasserted the importance of privileged communication between psychotherapist and clients. In *Jaffee v. Redmond,* the Court ruled that communications between licensed therapists and clients are protected from forced disclosure under federal law. Prior to this

A Duty to Warn Tatiana Tarasoff, a college student, was stabbed to death in 1969 by Prosenjit Poddar, a graduate student at the University of California at Berkeley. Although Poddar's therapist notified the university that he thought Poddar was dangerous, the California Supreme Court ruled that the therapist should have warned the victim as well.

 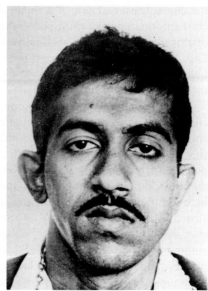

ruling, federal judges were relatively free to use their discretion in forcing therapists to disclose such information. The test case involved an on-duty police officer, Mary Lu Redmond, who shot and killed a suspect while attempting an arrest. Claiming that the constitutional rights of the victim had been violated, the family sued in federal court. The judge ordered Karen Beyer, a licensed clinical social worker, to turn over her notes on Redmond, whom she saw after the shooting. The therapist refused, citing privileged communication, a claim that was subsequently rejected by the judge. The jury awarded the family $545,000. The decision was reversed by the Court of Appeals for the Seventh Circuit, and that decision was upheld by the Supreme Court. For the first time, the Court officially recognized the therapist-client privilege for licensed social workers (it already exists for psychologists and psychiatrists) and leaves open the possibility that privilege also exists at the federal level for other licensed psychotherapists (mental health counselors, marriage and family therapists, and other counselors).

Criticism of the Duty-to-Warn Principle The *Tarasoff* ruling seems to place the therapist in the unenviable role of being a double agent (Bednar et al., 1991). Therapists have an ethical and legal obligation to their clients, but they also have legal obligations to society. Not only can these dual obligations conflict with one another, but they can also be quite ambiguous. Many situations exist in which state courts must rule to clarify the implications and uncertainties of the "duty-to-warn" rule (Fulero, 1988; see the Critical Thinking feature "Does the Duty-to-Warn Principle Apply to AIDS?").

Siegel (1979) loudly criticized the *Tarasoff* ruling, stating that it was a "day in court for the law and not for the mental health professions." He reasoned that if confidentiality had been an absolute policy, Poddar might have been kept in treatment, thus ultimately saving Tarasoff's life. Other mental health professionals have echoed this theme in one form or another. Hostile clients with pent-up feelings and emotions may be less likely to act out or become violent when allowed to vent their thoughts. The irony, according to critics, is that the duty-to-warn principle may actually be counterproductive to its intent to protect the potential victim.

Another controversial issue surrounding the duty-to-warn principle relates not just to determining danger but to when that determination should be made. Stimulated mainly by the *Tarasoff* ruling, mental health professionals and government and private institutions are developing guidelines for dealing with dangerous clients. These guidelines have several common elements. One is the recognition that the therapist's principal duty is to the client and that confidentiality is a crucial aspect of the therapeutic relationship.

Another is that therapy necessarily encourages people to engage in open dialogue with the therapist and to share their innermost thoughts and feelings. It is not unusual for clients to voice thoughts about ending their own lives or harming others. Relatively few of these threats are actually carried out, and therapists are not expected to routinely report all of them.

A third common element in the guidelines for dealing with dangerous clients is that the duty-to-warn principle can be invoked only in the most extraordinary circumstances. During the therapy session, however, the therapist should continue to treat the client and, if therapeutically appropriate, should attempt to dissuade the client from the threatened violence.

A final point is that somewhere in the therapy process, the therapist must discuss the limits of confidentiality and inform the client about the possible actions he or she must take to protect a third party. In other words, professionals are obligated to inform their clients that they have a duty to warn others about the threatened actions of their clients. Although some therapists fear that such actions might prevent the client from being open and honest, studies suggest that informing clients about the limits of confidentiality has little impact in inhibiting clients' disclosures and does not necessarily have negative consequences (Applebaum, 1994; Muehleman, Pickens, & Robinson, 1985).

The Family Educational Rights and Privacy Act and Confidentiality of College Student Life   In the chapter on suicide, we introduced the case of Elizabeth Shin, a nineteen-year-old MIT sophomore who set fire to herself and died on April 14, 2000. Two years after the suicide, her parents filed a $27 million wrongful death suit against MIT, accusing them of breach of contract, medical malpractice, and negligence on the part of university psychiatrists, student life staff, and campus police. The Shins contend that MIT knew their daughter had made suicide attempts, cut herself frequently, and suffered from depression but failed to inform them of her deteriorating mental state. Had they done so, they assert, Elizabeth Shin might still be alive today. They further claim that MIT broke the "business contract" with the family, which they say is implied in their daughter's college enrollment at MIT.

Not unlike the *Tarasoff* case, the outcome of the Shin's lawsuit has the power to set legal precedent and potentially radically change the Family Educational Rights and Privacy Act that prevents colleges and universities from disclosing any personal information about students, even to their parents. Colleges and universities generally assume that students are adults, and if required to report every problem to parents, they would infantilize students by sending the wrong message. Students may also be less inclined to share personal information with school officials if they knew such information may be reported back to their parents. Yet institutions of higher education are very aware that they are grappling to minister to an undergraduate population that seems to require more coddling and mental health care than ever before. One national study of counseling center client problems over thirteen years reveals that students are entering with more severe problems than in the past (Benton, Robertson, Tseng, Newton, & Benton, 2003). The outcome of the lawsuit is destined to have major implications not only for mental health law related to students but also for matters of student privacy and confidentiality.

Sexual Relationships with Clients

Therapeutic practice can also be legally regulated by civil lawsuits brought by clients against their therapists for professional malpractice. To be successful, however, these lawsuits must satisfy four conditions: (1) the plaintiff must have been involved in a professional therapeutic relationship with the therapist, (2) there must have been negligence in the care of the client, (3) demonstrable harm must have occurred, and (4) there must be a cause-effect relationship between the negligence and harm. If these four conditions are demonstrated, a jury may find the therapist guilty and award the plaintiff monetary damages. Although malpractice claims can be brought in any number of situations, by far the most common type involves sexual intimacies with a current or former client (Corey et al., 2003; Olarte, 1997).

Traditionally, mental health practitioners have emphasized the importance of separating their personal and professional lives. They reasoned that therapists need to be objective and removed from their clients because becoming emotionally involved with them was nontherapeutic. A therapist in a personal relationship with a client may be less confrontative, may fulfill his or her own needs at the expense of the client, and may unintentionally exploit the client because of his or her position (Corey et al., 1998; 2003). Although some people question the belief that a social or personal relationship is necessarily antitherapeutic, matters of personal relations with clients, especially those dealing with erotic and sexual intimacies, are receiving increasing attention.

Sexual misconduct of therapists is considered to be one of the most serious of all ethical violations. Indeed, virtually all professional organizations condemn sexual intimacies in the therapist-client relationship. The American Psychological Association (1995) states explicitly, "Psychologists do not engage in sexual intimacies with current patients or clients" (p. 474).

But how do practitioners view sexual intimacies with clients? How often do such intimacies really occur? Who does what to whom? Some studies indicate that being sexually attracted to a client or engaging in sexual fantasy about one is not uncommon among therapists (Pope, Tabachnick, & Keith-Spiegel, 1987; Pope & Tabachnick, 1993). Furthermore, complaints to state licensing boards about sexual misconduct by therapists have increased significantly (Zamichow, 1993). Although these are indisputable facts, the vast

CRITICAL THINKING

Does the Duty-to-Warn Principle Apply to AIDS?

George, a twenty-four-year-old graduate student, had known for some time that he was HIV infected. He entered counseling at the university psychiatric services center because of extreme feelings of guilt associated with his dishonesty in not disclosing his infection to a woman student with whom he had recently become intimate. He had hidden his medical condition from family, friends, and past lovers because of the social stigma involved and the fear that others would find out that he had often engaged in bisexual relationships. On numerous occasions, George had unprotected sex with his partners, but he had started to use condoms with his current woman friend. However, she did not like condoms and had encouraged George to avoid their use in lovemaking. Several times, George had complied with her request.

Before reading further, take a few minutes to contemplate your answers to these questions: If you were George's therapist, what would you do? What ethical or legal obligations do you have toward George and toward the larger society? Should you maintain the confidentiality of the therapeutic relationship or inform others about George's HIV condition? If you choose to disclose this information, whom would you notify? From your reading in the section on the *Tarasoff* decision, are there any guidelines that could help you decide?

Proponents of maintaining confidentiality believe that any violation of the therapeutic trust would decrease the likelihood that clients will discuss their health status with a counselor. Under the Family Educational Rights and Privacy Act (McGowan, 1991), student records are confidential, and strong prohibitions warn against releasing information. HIV- and AIDS-positive students are guaranteed confidentiality because of their right to privacy. In addition, a public diagnosis of HIV or AIDS may stigmatize the student and subject him or her to social ostracism and discrimination. Those who hold this position believe it would be more beneficial in the long run if the counselor explored with students their motives for concealing their condition and encouraged them to discuss it with their sexual partners.

Others, however, have less faith in the counselor's ability to persuade infected students to be honest with their partners (Hoffman, 1991). Studies indicate that dishonesty about one's sexual history and infectious state is quite common (Kegeles, Catania, & Coates, 1988): among gay or bisexual men who were diagnosed as HIV-positive, 12 percent said they did not plan to tell their primary sexual partners; 27 percent said they would not tell their nonprimary partners. In another study of heterosexual men, 20 percent said they would lie about being HIV-positive, and 35 percent said they had lied to female partners

---

majority of psychologists are able to control their sexual feelings and to behave in a professional manner.

In an early nationwide study of 500 male and 500 female psychologists, Holroyd and Brodsky (1977) reported that 5.5 percent of male therapists and 0.6 percent of female therapists have had sexual intercourse with clients. Sexual intimacy is almost always between male therapists and female clients. Of those who had sexual intercourse with clients, 80 percent were likely to repeat the practice. Of those responding, 88 percent of female and 70 percent of male therapists believed that erotic contact is never beneficial to clients. However, 4 percent of the respondents thought that erotic contact with clients was beneficial. Although in the minority, these therapists took the position that sexual intimacy may be beneficial to clients because it validates the clients as sexual beings, frees them from inhibitions and guilt, and allows them to enjoy their sexuality.

Critics of these arguments find them weak and self-serving (American Psychological Association, 1995;

Olarte, 1997). First, sexual intimacy represents an abuse of the therapist's power. Clients who discuss the most intimate aspects of their lives (sexual desires and struggles) are very vulnerable, and it is extremely easy for therapists to take advantage of their clients' trust and to exploit it. Second, sexual intimacy fosters dependency in clients, who look toward the therapist as an "ideal" and as someone who has "the answers." An individual's personal therapeutic goals become subordinate to a desire to please the therapist or to live up to his or her standards. Third, objectivity may also be lost. When therapists become sex partners, they cease to be therapists. Fourth, clients often feel exploited, used, embittered, and angry. Their self-esteem is also harmed.

Statistics on the harmful effects of sexual intimacy on clients have supported these conclusions. In a survey of 559 clients who became sexually involved with their therapists, 90 percent were deemed adversely affected (Bouhoutsos, Holroyd, Lerman, Forer, & Greenberg, 1983). The harm included mistrust of opposite-gender relationships, hospitalizations, deterioration of their

about their past sexual behavior (Elias, 1988). Some counselors would argue that breaking confidentiality is a small price to pay when a client's unknowing partner may be receiving the equivalent of a death sentence.

So far there have been no legal tests of the *Tarasoff* decision and its relationship to HIV infection (Corey et al., 1998). Furthermore, state laws are often confusing and conflict with one another. Pennsylvania law does not allow therapists to break confidentiality, but they are expected to persuade clients to change their behaviors voluntarily (Corey et al., 1998). Some states forbid disclosure to any third party. Others allow some disclosure to at-risk third parties by medical personnel but not by mental health professionals. Indeed, some state laws consider any such action malpractice. Most state statutes, however, are silent on this question.

The *Tarasoff* decision, however, does have important ramifications for

a therapist's decision to breach confidentiality. Three criteria have been identified as important in that decision (Hoffman, 1991):

1. *A (fiduciary) special relationship of trust must exist between the counselor and client.* A therapeutic relationship fulfills this criterion.
2. *There must be an identifiable potential victim.* Remember, the duty to warn extends only to identifiable victims rather than to all persons whom the client could conceivably infect. Anonymous partners or casual partners who are unknown to the counselor would not fall within the duty-to-warn principle. Partners who live with the person under a monogamous or exclusive relationship would probably meet this criterion.
3. *The assessment of dangerousness must be made.* Three factors need to be clarified under this criterion:

(1) the certainty of the client's HIV,
(2) the extent to which the client engages in behaviors that carry a high risk of HIV transmission, and
(3) the use or nonuse of safer-sex techniques.

Given these criteria, how would you apply them to the case of George? Perhaps it would be helpful to form small groups to discuss these issues and come to a decision. Remember, even with these criteria, many gray areas exist. For example, not all sexual practices are high risk with regard to transmission. Thus not all sexual practices would create a legal obligation to report. As mentioned, there have been no legal tests of the *Tarasoff* criteria with HIV-infected persons.

relationships with primary partners, and suicide. Many victims of therapist-client sexual contact showed responses that seemed similar to those of the rape syndrome and the battered-spouse syndrome, as well as symptoms displayed by victims of child abuse (Olarte, 1997; Pope, 1988; Pope & Vetter, 1991; Sherman, 1993). The Committee on Women in Psychology of the American Psychological Association (1989) took the position that sexual relationships between therapists and clients are never the fault of the client and that the therapist can never be excused for sexual misconduct.

Most professional organizations and states have procedures for filing and processing ethical complaints related to sexual intimacies between therapist and client. In the state of California, the Board of Medical Quality Assurance—the parent organization of the Psychology Examining Committee—has power to suspend or revoke the license of a therapist who engages in sexual misconduct with clients. And, as noted earlier, clients always have legal recourse to sue their therapists for malpractice. Therapists who engage in sex with

clients have few arguments they can use in court because the courts have generally rejected claims of consent (Austin, Moline, & Williams, 1990). Many cases of misconduct, however, probably go unreported because of the clients' shame and guilt over their "complicity." In any case, the consensus is that sexual intimacy with clients is unethical, antitherapeutic, and detrimental.

Cultural Competence and the Mental Health Profession

Many mental health professionals assert that the prevailing concepts of mental health and mental disorders are culture bound and that contemporary theories of therapy are based on values specific to a middle-class, white, highly individualistic, and ethnocentric population (American Psychological Association, 1992; Samuda, 1998; Sue & Sue, 2003). As a result, misdiagnosis and inappropriate treatments often victimize ethnic-minority clients. There are strong concerns that the services offered to culturally different clients are frequently antagonistic or inappropriate to their life experiences and that these services not only lack sensitivity and understanding but may also be oppressive and discriminating toward minority populations. These assertions about counseling and psychotherapy are echoed by many in our profession:

- "That it is a waste of time; that counselors do not accept, respect, and understand cultural differences" (Pine, 1972, p. 35).

- "A frequent and vigorous complaint of minority people who need care is that they often feel abused, intimidated, and harassed by non-minority personnel" (President's Commission on Mental Health, 1978, pp. 4–6).

- "In the psychotherapy relationship, characterized by close interpersonal interaction, aspects of racism may intrude readily. Differential experiences and effects of racism have not changed appreciably historically even though attention has been called to inequities in practice delivery and therapy process" (Jackson, 1983, p. 143).

- "Discriminatory practices result from ways in which the services are organized—selection procedures, points of comparison for promotion, etc. (in the case of staff) and diagnostic processes, selection criteria for types of treatment, indicators of 'dangerousness' etc. (in the case of patients)" (Fernando, 1988, p. 147).

- "As we stand at the threshold of the 21st century, mental health professionals, and psychologists more specifically, continue to be predominantly Caucasian; to be trained by predominantly Caucasian faculty members; and to be trained in programs in which ethnic issues are ignored, regarded as deficiencies, or included as an afterthought" (Meyers, Echemendia, & Trimble, 1991, p. 5).

These statements can be readily extended to other marginalized groups (women, gays/lesbians, disabled, etc.) in our society as well. Harsh as these allegations may appear, the American Psychological Association, in its most recent Ethical Principles of Psychologists and Code of Conduct (APA, 2002) has made it clear that working with culturally different clients is unethical unless the mental health professional has adequate training and expertise in multicultural psychology. Such a position has resulted in the development of "Guidelines for Providers of Psychological Services to Ethnic, Linguistic, and Culturally Diverse Populations" (American Psychological Association, 1993) and "Guidelines for Psychotherapy with Lesbian, Gay, and Bisexual Clients" (American Psychological Association, 2000).

In a historic move by the American Psychological Association (2003), the Council of Representatives passed "Guidelines on Multicultural Education, Training, Research, Practice, and Organizational Change for Psychologists." This document has now become official policy of the American Psychological

Changing Demographics and Therapy The Teaching Tolerance program, founded in 1991 by the Southern Poverty Law Center, supports the efforts of K–12 teachers and other educators to promote respect for differences and appreciation of diversity. This photo was taken at the Mix It Up at Lunch Day program, which encourages students to step outside their social boundaries through various activities.

Association and extends to nearly every realm of psychological practice. One of the most comprehensive guidelines on racial/ethnic minorities to be proposed, the document makes it clear that service providers need to become aware of how their own culture, life experiences, attitudes, values, and biases have influenced them. It also emphasizes the importance of cultural and environmental factors in diagnosis and treatment, and it insists that therapists respect and consider using traditional healing approaches intrinsic to a client's culture. Finally, it suggests that therapists learn more about cultural issues and seek consultation when confronted with cultural-specific problems.

Inherent in all these documents is their call for "cultural competence" and the conclusion that psychotherapy may represent biased, discriminatory, and unethical treatment if the racial/cultural backgrounds of clients are ignored and if the therapist does not possess adequate training in working with a culturally diverse population. From this perspective, mental health professionals have a moral and professional responsibility to become culturally competent if they work with people who differ from them in terms of race, culture, ethnicity, gender, sexual orientation, and so forth. To become culturally competent requires mental health professionals to strive toward attaining three goals (Sue & Sue, 2003): (1) to become aware of and deal with the biases, stereotypes, and assumptions that affect their practice; (2) to become aware of the culturally different client's values and worldview; and (3) to develop appropriate intervention strategies that take into account the social, cultural, historical, and environmental influences on culturally different clients. As we have seen, the increased awareness of multicultural influences in our understanding of abnormal psychology is reflected in the most recent version of the *Diagnostic and Statistical Manual of the American Psychiatric Association* (DSM-IV-TR; APA, 2000). For the first time since its publication in 1952, DSM is acknowledging the importance of culture in the diagnosis and treatment of mental disorders.

SUMMARY

Does insanity mean the same thing as being mentally disturbed?

- Insanity is a legal concept. Historically, several standards have been used.
- The M'Naghten Rule holds that people can be acquitted of a crime if it can be shown that their reasoning was so defective that they were unaware of their actions or, if aware of their actions, were unable to comprehend the wrongness of them.
- The irresistible impulse test holds that people are innocent if they are unable to control their behavior.
- The *Durham* decision acquits people if their criminal actions were products of mental disease or defects.
- The American Law Institute guidelines state that people are not responsible for a crime if they lack substantial capacity to appreciate the criminality of their conduct or to conform their conduct to the requirements of the law.
- Weaknesses in the standards and public outrage with the acquittal of some highly publicized people (such as John Hinckley, Jr.) have resulted in movements to restrict use of the insanity defense. The "guilty, but mentally ill" plea is an attempt to separate mental illness from insanity and to hold people responsible for their actions.

- The phrase "competency to stand trial" refers to defendants' mental state at the time they are being examined. It is a separate issue from criminal responsibility, which refers to past behavior at the time of the offense. Accused people are considered incompetent if they have difficulty understanding the trial proceedings or cannot rationally consult with attorneys in their defense. Although competency to stand trial is important in ensuring fair trials, being judged incompetent can have negative consequences, such as unfair and prolonged denial of civil liberties.

What legal means are available for hospitalizing or committing someone to a mental institution?

- Concern with denial of civil liberties is also present in civil commitment cases. People who have committed no crime can be confined against their will if it can be shown that (1) they present a clear and imminent danger to themselves or others, (2) they are unable to care for themselves, (3) they are unable to make responsible decisions about appropriate treatment and hospitalization, and (4) they are in an unmanageable state of fright or panic.
- Courts have tightened criteria and rely more than ever on the concept of dangerousness. Mental health professionals have great difficulty in predicting dangerousness because dangerous acts depend

as much on social situations as on personal attributes and because the definition is unclear.

■ Concern with patients' rights has become an issue because many practices and procedures seem to violate constitutional guarantees. As a result, court rulings have established several important precedents.

What is deinstitutionalization?

■ During the 1960s and 1970s, the policy of deinstitutionalization became popular: the shifting of responsibility for the care of mental patients from large central institutions to agencies within the local community.

■ Deinstitutionalization was considered a promising answer to the "least restrictive environment" ruling and to monetary problems experienced by state governments.

■ Critics, however, have accused the states of "dumping" former patients and avoiding their responsibilities under the guise of mental health innovations.

Is everything confidential in a therapy session? What are the exceptions?

■ Most mental health professionals believe that confidentiality is crucial to the therapist-client relationship.

■ Exceptions to this privilege include situations that involve (1) civil or criminal commitment and competency to stand trial, (2) a client's initiation of a lawsuit for malpractice or a civil action in which the client's mental condition is introduced, (3) the belief that child or elder abuse has occurred, (4) a criminal action, or (5) the danger a client poses to himself or herself or to others.

■ Although psychologists have always known that privileged communication is not an absolute right, the *Tarasoff* decision makes therapists responsible for warning a potential victim to avoid liability.

■ Mental health professionals are beginning to recognize that ethical and moral values permeate the therapeutic process. The most controversial issues involve erotic and sexual intimacy. Sexual intimacy with clients is almost universally condemned by therapists as immoral, unethical, and antitherapeutic.

What impact have the changing racial-cultural demographics had on the mental health profession?

■ Major demographic changes are forcing mental health professionals to consider culture, ethnicity, gender, and socioeconomic status as powerful variables in (1) the manifestation of mental disorders and (2) the need to provide culturally appropriate intervention strategies for minority groups.

■ Increasingly, mental health organizations are taking the position that it is unethical to treat members of minority groups without adequate training and expertise in cross-cultural psychology.

KEY TERMS

American Law Institute (ALI) Model Penal Code (p. 603)

civil commitment (p. 605)

competency to stand trial (p. 604)

confidentiality (p. 615)

criminal commitment (p. 600)

dangerousness (p. 607)

deinstitutionalization (p. 612)

due process (p. 605)

Durham standard (p. 603)

insanity defense (p. 600)

irresistible impulse test (p. 602)

least restrictive environment (p. 610)

mainstreaming (p. 613)

M'Naghten Rule (p. 602)

privileged communication (p. 615)

right to treatment (p. 610)

Tarasoff ruling (p. 615)

MULTIMEDIA PREVIEW

For additional study aids, we invite you to explore our media resources accompanying *Understanding Abnormal Behavior*, Eighth Edition. The Student CD-ROM includes videos, quizzing, and critical thinking activities that help to reinforce key concepts in a fun and engaging manner. The Student Web Site provides additional interactive activities, chapter outlines, and research links that further support and complement the text. All Web resources may be accessed by logging onto the Web site at **http://psychology.college.hmco.com/students**.

Glossary

Abnormal behavior Behavior that departs from some norm and that harms the affected individual or others

Abnormal psychology The scientific study whose objectives are to describe, explain, predict, and control behaviors that are considered strange or unusual

Acute stress disorder Exposure to a traumatic stressor that results in dissociation, reliving the experience, and attempts to avoid reminders of the events and that lasts for more than two days and less than thirty days

Agoraphobia An intense fear of being in public places where escape or help may not be readily available; in extreme cases, a fear of leaving one's home

Alcoholic Person who abuses alcohol and is dependent on it

Alcoholism Substance-related disorder characterized by abuse of, or dependency on, alcohol, which is a depressant

Altruistic suicide Suicide that is motivated by a desire to further group goals or to achieve some greater good

Alzheimer's disease A dementia in which brain tissue atrophies, leading to marked deterioration of intellectual and emotional functioning

American Law Institute (ALI) Model Penal Code A test of legal insanity that combines both cognitive criteria (diminished capacity) and motivational criteria (specific intent); its purpose is to give jurors increased latitude in determining the sanity of the accused

Amnestic disorder A disorder characterized by memory impairment as manifested by the inability to learn new information and the inability to recall previously learned knowledge or past events

Amniocentesis A screening procedure in which a hollow needle is inserted through the pregnant woman's abdominal wall and amniotic fluid is withdrawn from the fetal sac; used during the fourteenth or fifteenth week of pregnancy to determine the presence of Down syndrome and other fetal abnormalities

Amphetamine A drug that speeds up central nervous system activity and produces increased alertness, energy, and, sometimes, feelings of euphoria and confidence; also called "uppers"

Analogue study An investigation that attempts to replicate or simulate, under controlled conditions, a situation that occurs in real life

Anomic suicide Suicide that results when a person's relationship to society is unbalanced in some dramatic fashion

Anorexia nervosa An eating disorder characterized by a refusal to maintain a body weight above the minimum normal weight for the person's age and height; an intense fear of becoming obese, which does not diminish with weight loss; body image distortion; and, in females, the absence of at least three consecutive menstrual cycles otherwise expected to occur

Antisocial personality disorder A personality disorder characterized by a failure to conform to social and legal codes, by a lack of anxiety and guilt, and by irresponsible behaviors

Anxiety Feelings of fear and apprehension

Anxiety disorder A disorder that meets one of three criteria: the anxiety itself is the major disturbance; the anxiety is manifested only in particular situations; or the anxiety results from an attempt to master other symptoms

Assessment With regard to psychopathology, the process of gathering information and drawing conclusions about the traits, skills, abilities, emotional functioning, and psychological problems of an individual

Asthma A chronic inflammatory disease of the airways in the lungs, in which the airways become constricted, making it difficult to empty the lungs and therefore reducing the amount of air that can be inhaled

Attention deficit/hyperactivity disorder (ADHD) Disorders of childhood and adolescence characterized by socially disruptive behaviors—either attentional problems or hyperactivity—that are present before age seven and persist for at least six months

Autistic disorder A severe childhood disorder characterized by qualitative impairment in social interaction and/or communication; restricted, stereotyped interest and activities; and delays or abnormal functioning in a major area before the age of three

Aversion therapy Conditioning procedure in which the response to a stimulus is decreased by pairing the stimulus with an adverse stimulus

Aversive conditioning A classical conditioning technique in which an undesirable behavior is paired with an unpleasant stimulus to suppress the undesirable behavior

Avoidant personality disorder A personality disorder characterized by a fear of rejection and humiliation and a reluctance to enter into social relationships

Axon At the end of a neuron, a long, thin extension that sends signals to other neurons

Barbiturate Substance that is a powerful depressant of the central nervous system; commonly used to induce relaxation and sleep; and capable of inducing psychological and physical dependency

Base rate A phenomenon's natural occurrence in the population studied

Behavioral medicine A number of disciplines that study social, psychological, and lifestyle influences on health

Behavioral model A theory of psychopathology that is concerned with the role of learning in abnormal behavior

Binge-eating disorder A diagnostic category that is provided for further study in DSM-IV and that involves a large consumption of food over a short period of time at least twice weekly for six months; unlike bulimia, it does not involve extreme behavioral attempts to vomit or excessive exercise as compensation

Biofeedback therapy A therapeutic approach, combining physiological and behavioral approaches, in which a patient receives information regarding particular autonomic functions and is rewarded for influencing those functions in a desired direction

Biofeedback training A therapeutic technique in which the person is taught to voluntarily control a particular physiological function, such as heart rate or blood pressure

Biological marker Biological indicator of a disorder that may or may not be causal

Biological view The belief that mental disorders have a physical or physiological basis

Biopsychosocial approach The belief that biological, psychological, and social factors must all be considered in explaining and treating mental disorders

Bipolar disorder A category of mood disorders characterized by one or more manic or hypomanic episodes and, usually, by one or more depressive episodes

Body dysmorphic disorder A somatoform disorder that involves preoccupation with an imagined physical defect in a normal-appearing person, or an excessive concern with a slight physical defect

Borderline personality disorder A personality disorder characterized by intense fluctuations in mood, self-image, and interpersonal relationships

Brain pathology Dysfunction or disease of the brain

Brain trauma A physical wound or injury to the brain

Breathing-related sleep disorder Excessive daytime sleepiness that is caused by repeated awakenings due to a breathing obstruction (sleep apnea) or other breathing conditions that results in the disruption of sleep

Brief psychotic disorder Psychotic disorder that lasts no longer than one month

Bulimia nervosa An eating disorder characterized by recurrent episodes of binge eating (the rapid consumption of large quantities of food) at least twice a week for three months, during which the person loses control over eating and uses vomiting, laxatives, and excess exercise to control weight

Case study Intensive study of one individual that relies on observation, psychological tests, and historical and biographical data

Catatonic schizophrenia Rare schizophrenic disorder characterized by marked disturbance in motor activity—either extreme excitement or motoric immobility; symptoms may include motoric immobility or stupor; excessive purposeless motor activity; extreme negativism or physical resistance; peculiar voluntary movements; or echolalia or echopraxia

Cathartic method The therapeutic use of verbal expression to release pent-up unconscious conflicts

Cerebral blood flow measurement A technique for assessing brain damage, in which the patient inhales radioactive gas, and a gamma ray camera tracks the gas—and thus the flow of blood—as it moves throughout the brain

Cerebral infarction The death of brain tissue resulting from a decrease in the supply of blood serving that tissue

Cerebral tumor A mass of abnormal tissue growing within the brain

Cerebrovascular accident A sudden stoppage of blood flow to a portion of the brain, leading to a loss of brain function; also called *stroke*

Chronic tic disorder Childhood-onset disorder that last longer than one year and is characterized by involuntary, repetitive, and nonrhythmic movements or vocalizations

Circadian rhythm sleep disorder Excessive sleepiness or insomnia produced by a mismatch between the body's sleep-wake cycle and environmental cues such as due to "jet lag" or shift-work

Civil commitment The involuntary confinement of a person judged to be a danger to himself or herself or to others, even though the person has not committed a crime

Classical conditioning A principle of learning, in which involuntary responses to stimuli are learned through association

Classification system With regard to psychopathology, a system of distinct categories, indicators, and nomenclature for different patterns of behavior, thought processes, and emotional disturbances

Cluster headache Excruciating headache that produces stabbing or burning sensations in an eye or cheek

Cocaine Substance extracted from the coca plant; induces feelings of euphoria and self-confidence in users

Cognitive disorder A disorder characterized by behavioral disturbances that result from transient or permanent damage to the brain

Cognitive model A principle of learning holding that conscious thought mediates, or modifies, an individual's emotional state and/or behavior in response to a stimulus

Community psychology An approach to mental health that takes into account the influence of environmental factors and that encourages the use of community resources and agencies to eliminate conditions that produce psychological problems

Comorbidity The co-occurrence of different disorders

Competency to stand trial A judgment that a defendant has a factual and rational understanding of the proceedings and can rationally consult with counsel in presenting his or her own defense; refers to the defendant's mental state at the time of the psychiatric examination

Compulsion The need to perform acts or to dwell on thoughts to reduce anxiety

Compulsive sexual behavior Frequent, recurrent, and intrusive sexual thoughts or behavior (frequently called *sexual addiction*)

Computerized axial tomography (CAT) Neurological test that assesses brain damage by means of x-rays and computer technology

Concordance rate The likelihood that both members of a twin pair will show the same characteristic

Conditioned response (CR) In classical conditioning, the learned response made to a previously neutral stimulus that has acquired some of the properties of another stimulus with which it has been paired

Conditioned stimulus (CS) In classical conditioning, a previously neutral stimulus that has acquired some of the properties of another stimulus with which it has been paired

Conduct disorder Disorder of childhood and adolescence characterized by a persistent pattern of antisocial behaviors that violate the rights of others; repetitive and persistent behaviors include bullying, lying, cheating, fighting, temper tantrums, destruction of property, stealing, setting fires, cruelty to people and animals, assaults, rape, and truant behavior

Confidentiality An ethical standard that protects clients from disclosure of information without their consent; an ethical obligation of the therapist

Continuous amnesia An inability to recall any events that have occurred between a specific time in the past and the present time; the least common form of psychogenic amnesia

Conversion disorder A somatoform disorder in which there are complaints of physical problems or impairments of sensory or motor functions controlled by the voluntary nervous system, all suggesting a neurological disorder but with no underlying cause

Coronary heart disease (CHD) A narrowing of the arteries in or near the heart, resulting in the restriction or partial blockage of the flow of blood and oxygen to the heart

Correlation The extent to which variations in one variable are accompanied by increases or decreases in a second variable

Couples therapy Therapy of intimate partners in a relationship

Covert sensitization Aversive conditioning technique in which the individual imagines a noxious stimulus occurring in the presence of a behavior

Criminal commitment Incarceration of an individual for having committed a crime

Cultural relativism The belief that what is judged to be normal or abnormal may vary from one culture to another

Cultural universality The belief that the origin, process, and manifestation of disorders are equally applicable across cultures

Cyclothymic disorder A chronic and relatively continual mood disorder characterized by hypomanic episodes and depressed moods that do not meet the criteria for major depressive episode

Dangerousness A person's potential for doing harm to himself or herself or to others

Date rape drug Substance such as alcohol—but more frequently drugs such as gammahydroxybutyrate (GHB) and Rhohypnol—that is used to spike a woman's drinks for the purpose of sexual assault

Defense mechanism In psychoanalytic theory, an ego-protection strategy that shelters the individual from anxiety, operates unconsciously, and distorts reality

Deinstitutionalization The shifting of responsibility for the care of mental patients from large central institutions to agencies within local communities

Delirium A syndrome in which there is disturbance of consciousness and changes in cognition, such as memory deficit, disorientation, and language and perceptual disturbances

Delusion A false belief that is firmly and consistently held despite disconfirming evidence or logic

Delusional disorder A disorder characterized by persistent, nonbizarre delusions that are not accompanied by other unusual or odd behavior

Dementia A syndrome characterized by memory impairment and cognitive disturbances, such as aphasia, apraxia, agnosia, or disturbances in planning or abstraction in thought processes

Dendrite Rootlike structure that is attached to the body of the neuron and that receives signals from another neuron

Dependent personality disorder A personality disorder characterized by reliance on others and an unwillingness to assume responsibility

Dependent variable A variable that is expected to change when an independent variable is manipulated in a psychological experiment

Depersonalization disorder A dissociative disorder in which feelings of unreality concerning the self or the environment cause major impairment in social or occupational functioning

Depressant Substance that causes generalized depression of the central nervous system and a slowing down of responses; a sedative

Depression An emotional state characterized by intense sadness, feelings of futility and worthlessness, and withdrawal from others

Depressive disorders DSM-IV category including major depressive disorders, dysthymic disorder, and depressive disorders not otherwise specified; also known as *unipolar disorders* because no mania is exhibited

Detoxification Alcohol or drug treatment phase characterized by removal of the abusive substance; after that removal, the user is immediately or eventually prevented from consuming the substance

Diaschisis A process in which a lesion in a specific area of the brain disrupts other intact areas

Diathesis-stress model A theoretical model postulating that vulnerability to a disorder, either inherited or acquired, combines with the impact of stressors to produce the disorder

Diathesis-stress theory The theory that a predisposition to develop a mental illness—not the mental illness itself—is inherited and that this predisposition may or may not be activated by environmental forces

Disorganized schizophrenia A schizophrenic disorder characterized by grossly disorganized behaviors manifested by disorganized speech and behavior and flat or grossly inappropriate affect

Dissociative amnesia A dissociative disorder characterized by the partial or total loss of important personal information, sometimes occurring suddenly after a stressful or traumatic event

Dissociative disorder Mental disorder in which a person's identity, memory, or consciousness is altered or disrupted; includes dissociative amnesia, dissociative fugue, dissociative identity disorder (multiple-personality disorder), and depersonalization disorder

Dissociative fugue Confusion over personal identity accompanied by unexpected travel away from home; also called *fugue state*

Dissociative identity disorder A dissociative disorder in which two or more relatively independent personalities appear to exist in one person; formerly known as *multiple-personality disorder*

Dopamine hypothesis The suggestion that schizophrenia may result from excess dopamine activity at certain synaptic sites

Double-bind theory The suggestion that schizophrenia develops as a result of repeated experiences that the preschizophrenic child has with one or more family members (usually the mother and father) in which the child receives contradictory messages

Down syndrome A condition produced by the presence of an extra chromosome (trisomy 21) and resulting in mental retardation and distinctive physical characteristics

Due process Legal checks and balances that are guaranteed to everyone (the right to a fair trial, the right to face accusers, the right to present evidence, the right to counsel, and so on)

***Durham* standard** A test of legal insanity known as the products test—an accused person is not responsible if the unlawful act was the product of mental disease or defect

Dyspareunia Recurrent or persistent pain in the genitals before, during, or after sexual intercourse

Dyssomnia Sleep disorder involving problems in initiating or maintaining sleep that are due to abnormalities in terms of the amount, quality or the timing of sleep

Dysthymic disorder A disorder characterized by chronic and relatively continual depressed mood that does not meet the criteria for major depression

Egoistic suicide Suicide that results from an inability to integrate oneself with society

Electroconvulsive therapy (ECT) The application of electric voltage to the brain to induce convulsions; used to reduce depression; also called *electroshock therapy*

Electroencephalograph (EEG) A neurological test that assesses brain damage by measuring the electrical activity of brain cells

Encephalitis Brain inflammation that is caused by a viral infection and that produces symptoms of lethargy, fever, delirium, and long periods of stupor and sleep, also known as *sleeping sickness*

Encopresis An elimination disorder in which a child who is at least four years old defecates in his or her clothes, on the floor, or other inappropriate places, at least once a month for three months

Enuresis An elimination disorder in which a child who is at least five years old voids urine during the day or night into his or her clothes or bed or on the floor, at least twice weekly for at least three months

Epidemiological research The study of the rate and distribution of mental disorders in a population

Epilepsy Any disorder characterized by intermittent and brief periods of altered consciousness, often accompanied by seizures, and excessive electrical discharge from brain cells

Essential hypertension Chronic high blood pressure, usually with no known biological cause; the most common disease in the United States

Etiology The causes or origins of a disorder

Exhibitionism Disorder characterized by urges, acts, or fantasies about the exposure of one's genitals to strangers

Existential analysis A therapeutic approach that is concerned with the person's experience and involvement in the world as a being with consciousness and self-consciousness

Existential approach A set of attitudes that has many commonalities with humanism but is less optimistic, focusing (1) on human alienation in an increasingly technological and impersonal world, (2) on the individual in the context of the human condition, and (3) on responsibility to others as well as to oneself

Exorcism Ritual in which prayer, noise, emetics, and extreme measures such as flogging and starvation were used to cast evil spirits out of an afflicted person's body

Experiment A technique of scientific inquiry in which a prediction—an experimental hypothesis—is made about two variables; the independent variable is then manipulated in a controlled situation, and changes in the dependent variable are measured

Experimental hypothesis A prediction concerning how an independent variable affects a dependent variable in an experiment

Exposure therapy A therapy technique in which the patient is introduced to encounters (can be gradual or rapid) with the feared situation

Expressed emotion A type of negative communication pattern that is found in some families in which some members have schizophrenia and that is associated with higher relapse rates

External validity The degree to which findings of a particular study can be generalized to other populations or situations

Factitious disorder Disorder in which symptoms of physical or mental illness are deliberately induced or simulated with no apparent incentive

Family systems model A model of psychopathology that emphasizes the family's influence on individual behavior

Family therapy Group therapy that seeks to modify relationships within a family to achieve harmony

Female orgasmic disorder A sexual dysfunction in which the woman experiences persistent delay or inability to achieve an orgasm with stimulation that is adequate in focus, intensity, and duration after entering the excitement phase; also known as *inhibited orgasm*

Female sexual arousal disorder The inability to attain or maintain physiological response and/or psychological arousal during sexual activity

Fetal alcohol syndrome (FAS) A group of congenital physical and mental defects found in some children born to alcoholic mothers; symptoms include small body size and microcephaly, in which the brain is unusually small and mild retardation may occur

Fetishism Sexual attraction and fantasies involving inanimate objects, such as female undergarments

Field study An investigative technique in which behaviors are observed and recorded in the natural environment

Flat affect Little or no emotion in situations where strong reactions are expected

Flooding A behavioral treatment that attempts to extinguish fear by placing the client in continued *in vivo* (actual) or imagined anxiety-provoking situations; a form of exposure therapy

Free association A psychoanalytic method during which the patient says whatever comes to mind, regardless of how illogical or embarrassing it may seem, for the purpose of revealing the contents of the patient's unconscious

Frotteurism Disorder characterized by recurrent and intense sexual urges, acts, or fantasies or touching or rubbing against a nonconsenting person

Gender identity disorder Disorder characterized by conflict between a person's anatomical sex and his or her gender identity, or self-identification as male or female

General adaptation syndrome (GAS) A three-stage model for understanding the body's physical and psychological reactions to biological stressors

Generalized amnesia An inability to remember anything about one's past life

Generalized anxiety disorder (GAD) Disorder characterized by persistent high levels of anxiety and excessive worry over many life circumstances

Genetic linkage study Study that attempts to determine whether a disorder follows a genetic pattern

Genome The entire genetic material contained in the chromosomes of all living organisms

Genotype A person's genetic makeup

Gestalt therapy A humanistic-existential approach to therapy that emphasizes the importance of a person's total experience, which should not be fragmented or separated

Group therapy A form of therapy that involves the simultaneous treatment of two or more clients and may involve more than one therapist

Hallucination Sensory perception that is not directly attributable to environmental stimuli

Hallucinogen Substance that produces hallucinations, vivid sensory awareness, heightened alertness, or increased insight

Hardiness A concept developed by Kobasa and Maddi that refers to a person's ability to deal well with stress

Histrionic personality disorder A personality disorder characterized by self-dramatization, the exaggerated expression of emotions, and attention-seeking behaviors

Humanism Philosophical movement that emphasizes human welfare and the worth and uniqueness of the individual

Humanistic perspective The optimistic viewpoint that people are born with the ability to fulfill their potential and that abnormal behavior results from disharmony between the person's potential and his or her self-concept

Huntington's disease A rare, genetically transmitted degenerative disease characterized by involuntary twitching movements and eventual dementia

Hypochondriasis A somatoform disorder characterized by persistent preoccupation with one's health and physical condition, even in the face of physical evaluations that reveal no organic problems

Hypothesis A conjectural statement, usually describing a relationship between two variables

Iatrogenic Unintended effects of therapy; a change in behavior resulting from a medication prescribed or a psychological technique employed by the therapist

Implosion A behavioral treatment that attempts to extinguish a fear by having the client imagine the anxiety-provoking situation at full intensity

Impulse control disorder A disorder in which the person fails to resist an impulse or temptation to perform some act that is harmful to the person or to others; the person feels tension before the act and release after it

Incest Sexual relations between people too closely related to marry legally

Incidence Onset or occurrence of new cases of a given disorder over a specific time period

Independent variable A variable or condition that an experimenter manipulates to determine its effect on a dependent variable

Insanity defense The legal argument used by defendants who admit they have committed a crime but plead not guilty because they were mentally disturbed at the time the crime was committed

Intermittent explosive disorder Impulse control disorder characterized by separate and discrete episodes of loss of control over aggressive impulses, resulting in serious assaults on others or destruction of property

Internal validity The degree to which changes in the dependent variable are due solely to the effect of changes in the independent variable

Intoxication Condition in which a substance affecting the central nervous system has been ingested and certain maladaptive behaviors or psychological changes, such as belligerence and impaired function, are evident

Irresistible impulse test One test of sanity, which states that a defendant is not criminally responsible if he or she lacked the will power to control his or her behavior

Kleptomania An impulse control disorder characterized by a recurrent failure to resist impulses to steal objects

Law of effect The principle that behaviors associated with positive consequences will be repeated and behaviors associated with unpleasant consequences will be reduced

Learned helplessness Acquiring the belief that one is helpless and unable to affect the outcomes in one's life

Least restrictive environment A person's right to the least restrictive alternative to freedom that is appropriate to his or her condition

Lethality The probability that a person will choose to end his or her life

Life-change model An explanation of stress that assumes that all changes in a person's life—large or small, desirable or undesirable—can act as stressors and that the accumulation of small changes can be as powerful as one major stressor

Lifetime prevalence The total proportion of people in a population who have ever had a disorder in their lives

Localized amnesia The most common type of amnesia; an inability to recall all the events that happened during a specific period, often centered on some highly painful or disturbing event

Loosening of associations Continual shifting from topic to topic without any apparent logical or meaningful connection between thoughts

Magnetic resonance imaging (MRI) A technique to assess brain functioning, using a magnetic field and radio waves to produce pictures of the brain

Mainstreaming Integrating mental patients as soon as possible back into the community

Major depression A disorder in which a group of symptoms, such as depressed mood, loss of interest, sleep disturbances, feelings of worthlessness, and an inability to concentrate, are present for at least two weeks

Male erectile disorder An inability to attain or maintain an erection sufficient for sexual intercourse

Male orgasmic disorder Persistent delay or inability to achieve an orgasm after the excitement phase has been reached and sexual activity has been adequate in focus, intensity, and duration; usually restricted to an inability to ejaculate within the vagina (also known as *inhibited male orgasm*)

Malingering Faking a disorder to achieve some goal, such as an insurance settlement

Managed health care A term that refers to the industrialization of health care, whereby large organizations in the private sector control the delivery of services

Mania An emotional state characterized by elevated mood, expansiveness, or irritability, often resulting in hyperactivity

Marijuana The mildest and most commonly used hallucinogen; also known as "pot" or "grass"

Masochism A paraphilia in which sexual urges, fantasies, or acts are associated with being humiliated, bound, or made to suffer

Mass madness Group hysteria, in which large numbers of people exhibit similar symptoms that have no apparent cause

Meningitis Inflammation of the meninges, the membrane that surrounds the brain and spinal cord; can result in the localized destruction of brain tissue and seizures

Mental retardation Significant subaverage general intellectual functioning accompanied by deficiencies in adaptive behavior, with onset before age eighteen

Migraine headache Severe headache characterized by constriction of cranial arteries, followed by dilation of the cerebral blood vessels, resulting in moderate to severe pain

Milieu therapy A therapy program in which the hospital environment operates as a community and patients exercise a wide range of responsibility, helping to make decisions and to manage wards

M'Naghten rule A cognitive test of legal insanity that inquires whether the accused knew right from wrong when he or she committed the crime

Model An analogy used by scientists, usually to describe or explain a phenomenon or process that they cannot directly observe

Modeling The process of learning by observing models and later imitating them; also known as *vicarious conditioning*

Modeling therapy A therapeutic approach to phobias in which the person with the phobia observes a model in the act of coping with, or responding appropriately in, the fear-producing situation

Monoamine oxidase (MAO) inhibitor Antidepressant compound believed to correct the balance of neurotransmitters in the brain

Mood disorder Disorder characterized by disturbances in emotions that cause subjective discomfort, hinder a person's ability to function, or both; depression and mania are central to this type of disorder

Moral treatment movement A shift to more humane treatment of the mentally disturbed; its initiation is generally attributed to Philippe Pinel

Multicultural psychology A field of psychology that stresses the importance of culture, race, ethnicity, gender, age, socioeconomic class, and other similar factors in its efforts to understand and treat abnormal behavior

Narcissistic personality disorder A personality disorder characterized by an exaggerated sense of self-importance, an exploitative attitude, and a lack of empathy

Narcolepsy A dyssomnia characterized by irresistible sleep attacks of refreshing sleep that may be accompanied by cataplexy (loss of muscle tone) and elements of REM sleep

Narcotic Drug such as opium and its derivatives—morphine, heroine, and codeine—that depresses the central nervous system; acts as a sedative to provide relief from pain, anxiety, and tension; is addictive

Negative symptom In schizophrenia, a symptom that is associated with inferior premorbid social functioning and carries a poorer prognosis than a positive symptom; includes flat affect, poverty of speech, anhedonia, apathy, and avolition

Neuroleptic Antipsychotic drug that can help treat symptoms of schizophrenia but can produce undesirable side effects, such as symptoms that mimic neurological disorders

Neuron Nerve cell that transmits messages throughout the body

Neurotransmitter Chemical substance released by axon of sending neuron and involved in the transmission of neural impulse to the dendrite of receiving neuron

Nightmare disorder Disorder characterized by vivid and frightening dreams that cause repeated awakening during sleep or naps; when awakened, the individual rapidly becomes alert

Observational learning theory A theory of learning that holds that an individual can acquire behaviors simply by watching other people perform them

Obsession An intrusive and repetitive thought or image that produces anxiety

Obsessive-compulsive disorder Disorder characterized by intrusive and repetitive thoughts or images, or by the need to perform acts or dwell on thoughts to reduce anxiety

Obsessive-compulsive personality disorder A personality disorder characterized by perfectionism, a tendency to be interpersonally controlling, devotion to details, and rigidity

Operant behavior A voluntary and controllable behavior that "operates" on an individual's environment

Operant conditioning A theory of learning, applying primarily to voluntary behaviors, that holds that these behaviors are controlled by the consequences that follow them

Operational definitions Definitions of the variables under study

Oppositional defiant disorder (ODD) A childhood disorder characterized by a pattern of negativistic, argumentative, and hostile behavior in which the child often loses his or her temper, argues with adults, and defies or refuses adult requests; refusal to take responsibility for actions, anger, resentment, blaming others, and spiteful and vindictive behavior are common, but serious violations of other's rights are not

Organicity Damage or deterioration in the central nervous system

Pain disorder A somatoform disorder characterized by reports of severe pain that has no physiological or neurological basis, is greatly in excess of that expected with an existing condition, or lingers long after a physical injury has healed

Panic disorder Anxiety disorder characterized by severe and frightening episodes of apprehension and feelings of impending doom

Paranoid personality disorder A personality disorder characterized by unwarranted suspiciousness, hypersensitivity, and a reluctance to confide in others

Paranoid schizophrenia A schizophrenic disorder characterized by one or more systematized delusions or auditory hallucinations and the absence of such symptoms as disorganized speech and behavior or flat affect

Paraphilia Sexual disorder of at least six months' duration in which the person has either acted on, or is severely distressed by, recurrent urges or fantasies involving nonhuman objects, nonconsenting persons, or suffering or humiliation

Parkinson's disease A progressively worsening disorder characterized by muscle tremors; a stiff, shuffling gait; lack of facial expression; and social withdrawal

Pathognomonic Symptoms specific to a disorder

Pathological gambling An impulse control disorder in which the essential feature is a chronic and progressive failure to resist impulses to gamble

Pedophilia A disorder in which an adult obtains erotic gratification through urges, acts, or fantasies involving sexual contact with a prepubescent child

Personality disorder A disorder characterized by inflexible and maladaptive personality traits that cause significant functional impairment or subjective distress for the individual

Person-centered therapy A humanistic therapy that emphasizes the kind of person the therapist should be in the therapeutic relationship rather than the precise techniques to use in therapy

Pervasive developmental disorder Severe childhood disorder in which qualitative impairment in verbal and nonverbal communication and social interaction are the primary symptoms; includes autistic disorder, Rett's disorder, childhood disintegrative disorder, Asperger's disorder, and pervasive developmental disorders not otherwise specified

Phenotype The observable results of the interaction of a person's genotype and the environment

Phobia A strong, persistent, and unwarranted fear of some specific object or situation

Pleasure principle Usually associated with the id in Freudian theory; the impulsive, pleasure-seeking aspect of our being that seeks immediate gratification of instinctual needs regardless of moral or realistic concerns

Polysubstance dependence Substance dependence in which dependency is not based on the use of any single substance but on the repeated use of at least three groups of substances (not including caffeine and nicotine) for a period of twelve months

Positive symptom Symptom that is present during the active phase of schizophrenia and that tend to disappear with treatment; may include hallucinations and delusions, as well as disorganized speech and behavior, inappropriate affect, and formal thought disorders

Positron emission tomography (PET) A technique for assessing brain damage, in which the patient is injected with radioactive glucose and the metabolism of the glucose in the brain is monitored

Posthypnotic amnesia An inability to recall events that occurred during hypnosis

Posttraumatic stress disorder (PTSD) An anxiety disorder that lasts for more than thirty days; develops in response to a specific extreme stressor; characterized by intrusive memories of the traumatic event, emotional withdrawal, and heightened autonomic arousal

Premature ejaculation Ejaculation with minimal sexual stimulation before, during, or shortly after penetration

Prevalence The percentage of people in a population who have a disorder at a given point in time

Primary hypersomnia Excessive sleepiness during the day or prolonged sleep episodes that occur even when the individual's nocturnal sleep duration has been adequate

Primary insomnia A sleep disorder characterized by difficulty in initiating or maintaining sleep; complaints of difficulty of falling asleep and waking up during sleep are common

Primary prevention An effort to lower the incidence of new cases of behavioral disorders by strengthening or adding to resources that promote mental health and by eliminating community characteristics that threaten mental health

Privileged communication A therapist's legal obligation to protect a client's privacy and to prevent the disclosure of confidential communications without a client's permission

Prognosis A prediction of the future course of a particular disorder

Projective personality test A personality assessment technique in which the test taker is presented with ambiguous stimuli and is asked to respond to them in some way

Prospective study A long-term study of a group of people, beginning before the onset of a disorder, to allow investigators to see how the disorder develops

Psychoanalysis Therapy based on the Freudian view that unconscious conflicts must be aired and understood by the patient if abnormal behavior is to be eliminated

Psychodiagnosis An attempt to describe, assess, and systematically draw inferences about an individual's psychological disorder

Psychodynamic model A model based on the view that adult disorders arise from trauma or anxieties originally experienced in childhood but later repressed because they are too threatening for the adult to face

Psychological autopsy The systematic examination of existing information for the purpose of understanding and explaining a person's behavior before his or her death

Psychological test and inventory Instrument used to assess personality, maladaptive behavior, development of social skills, intellectual abilities, vocational interests, and cognitive impairment

Psychological view The belief or theory that mental disorders are caused by psychological and emotional factors, rather than organic or biological factors

Psychometrics Mental measurement, including its study and techniques

Psychopathology Clinical term meaning abnormal behavior

Psychopharmacology The study of the effects of drugs on the mind and on behavior; also known as *medication* and *drug therapy*

Psychophysiological disorder Any physical disorder that has a strong psychological basis or component

Psychosexual stages In psychoanalytical theory, the sequence of stages—oral, anal, phallic, latency, and genital—through which human personality develops

Psychosurgery Brain surgery performed for the purpose of correcting a severe mental disorder

Psychotherapy The systematic application, by a trained and experienced professional therapist, of techniques derived from psychological principles, for the purpose of helping psychologically troubled people; includes both insight-oriented and action-oriented therapies

Pyromania An impulse control disorder having as its main feature deliberate and purposeful fire setting on more than one occasion

Rape An act of intercourse accomplished through force or threat of force

Rape trauma syndrome A two-phase syndrome that rape victims may experience, including such emotional reactions as psychological distress, phobic reactions, and sexual dysfunction

Reactive attachment disorder A disorder that develops in infancy or early childhood when there is a failure to meet a child's physical or emotional needs and that affects the child's ability to form basic attachments and relate to others

Reactivity A change in the way a person usually responds, triggered by the person's knowledge that he or she is being observed or assessed

Reality principle Usually associated with the ego in Freudian theory; an awareness of the demands of the environment and of the need to adjust behavior to meet these demands

Reinforcing abstinence Giving behavioral reinforcements for abstinence from substance use

Relaxation training A therapeutic technique in which the person acquires the ability to relax the muscles of the body in almost any circumstances

Reliability The degree to which a procedure or test will yield the same results repeatedly, under the same circumstances

Residual schizophrenia A category of schizophrenic disorder reserved for people who have had at least one previous schizophrenic episode but are now showing an absence of prominent psychotic features; there is continuing evidence of two or more symptoms, such as marked social isolation, peculiar behaviors, blunted affect, odd beliefs, or unusual perceptual experiences

Resistance During psychoanalysis, the process in which the patient unconsciously attempts to impede the analysis by preventing the exposure of repressed material; tactics include silence, late arrival, failure to keep an appointment, and others

Right to treatment The concept that mental patients who have been involuntarily committed have a right to receive therapy that would improve their emotional state

Sadism Form of paraphilia in which sexually arousing urges, fantasies, or acts are associated with inflicting physical or psychological stress on others

Schema The set of underlying assumptions that is heavily influenced by a person's experiences, values, and perceived capabilities and that influence how he or she interprets events

Schizoid personality disorder A personality disorder characterized by social isolation, emotional coldness, and indifference to others

Schizophrenia A group of disorders characterized by severely impaired cognitive processes, personality disintegration, affective disturbances, and social withdrawal

Schizophrenia spectrum Disorders—such as "latent or borderline" schizophrenia, acute schizophrenic reactions, and schizoid and inadequate personality—that are believed to be genetically related to schizophrenia

Schizophreniform disorder Psychotic disorder that lasts more than one month but less than six months

Schizophrenogenic Causing or producing schizophrenia; a term generally used to describe a parent who is simultaneously or alternately cold and overprotecting, rejecting and dominating

Schizotypal personality disorder A personality disorder characterized by peculiar thoughts and behaviors and by poor interpersonal relationships

Scientific method A method of inquiry that provides for the systematic collection of data through controlled observation and for the testing of hypotheses

Secondary prevention An attempt to shorten the duration of mental disorders and to reduce their impact

Selective amnesia An inability to remember certain details of an incident

Selective serotonin reuptake inhibitors (SSRI) Medications that inhibit the central nervous system's neuronal uptake of serotonin; often prescribed for depression

Self-actualization An inherent tendency to strive toward the realization of one's full potential

Self-concept An individual's assessment of his or her own value and worth

Self-report inventory An assessment tool that requires test takers to answer specific written questions or to select specific responses from a list of alternatives; standardization helps reduce subjective responses by the test giver

Separation anxiety disorder (SAD) A childhood disorder characterized by excessive anxiety over separation from parents and home

Sexual addiction A popular term referring to a person's desire and need to engage in constant and frequent sexual behavior (frequently labeled *compulsive sexual behavior*)

Sexual arousal disorder Disorder characterized by problems occurring during the excitement phase and relating to difficulties with feelings of sexual pleasure or with the physiological changes associated with sexual excitement

Sexual desire disorder Sexual dysfunction that is related to the appetite phase and is characterized by a lack of sexual desire

Sexual dysfunction A disruption of any part of the normal sexual response cycle

Single-participant experiment An experiment performed on a single individual in which some aspect of the person's own behavior is used as a control or baseline for comparison with future behaviors

Skills training Teaching skills for resisting peer pressures or temptations, resolving emotional conflicts or problems, or for more effective communication

Sleep terror disorder Abrupt awakenings accompanied by screams of terror that occur during NREM sleep; during these episodes the individual is difficult to awaken or comfort and there is little recall of the event in the morning

Sleepwalking disorder Episodes of complex motor behavior (sitting up in bed, walking around, etc.) occurring during NREM sleep accompanied by reduced alertness and responsiveness; usually disappears spontaneously during adolescence

Social phobia An intense, excessive fear of being scrutinized in one or more social situations

Somatization disorder A somatoform disorder in which the person chronically complains of a number of bodily symptoms that have no physiological basis; complaints include at least four symptoms in different sites, two gastrointestinal symptoms, one sexual symptom, and one pseudoneurologic symptom

Somatoform disorder Mental disorder that involves physical symptoms or complaints that have no physiological basis; include somatization disorder, conversion disorder, pain disorder, hypochondriasis, and body dysmorphic disorder

Specific phobia An extreme fear of a specific object or situation; a phobia that is not classified as either agoraphobia or a social phobia

Stimulant Substance that is a central nervous system energizer, including elation, grandiosity, hyperactivity, agitation, and appetite suppression

Stress An internal response to a stressor

Stressor An external event or situation that places a physical or psychological demand on a person

Substance abuse Maladaptive pattern of recurrent use that extends over a period of twelve months; leads to notable impairment or distress; and continues despite social, occupational, psychological, physical, or safety problems

Substance dependence Maladaptive pattern of use extending over a twelve-month period and characterized by unsuccessful efforts to control use, despite knowledge of harmful effects; taking more of substance than intended; tolerance; or withdrawal

Substance-related disorder Disorder resulting from the use of psychoactive substances that affect the central nervous system, causing significant social, occupational, psychological, or physical problems, and that sometimes result in abuse or dependence

Sudden death syndrome Unexpected abrupt death that seems to have no specific physical basis

Suicidal ideation Thoughts about suicide

Suicide The intentional, direct, and conscious taking of one's own life

Synapse A minute gap between the axon of the sending neuron and the dendrites of the receiving neuron

Syndrome A cluster of symptoms that tend to occur together and that are believed to represent a particular disorder with its own unique cause, course, and outcome

Systematic desensitization A behavioral therapy technique in which relaxation is used to eliminate the anxiety associated with phobias and other fear-evoking situations

Systematized amnesia The loss of memory for only selected types of information, such as all members of one's family

Tarasoff **ruling** Often referred to as the "duty-to-warn" principle; obligates mental health professionals to break confidentiality when their clients pose clear and imminent danger to another person

Tension headache A headache thought to be produced by prolonged contraction of the scalp and neck muscles, resulting in vascular constriction

Tertiary prevention Efforts to facilitate the readjustment of the person to community life after hospital treatment for a mental disorder

Theory A group of principles and hypotheses that together explain some aspect of a particular area of inquiry

Therapy A program of systematic intervention whose purpose is to modify a client's behavioral, affective (emotional), or cognitive state

Tic Involuntary, repetitive, and nonrhythmic movement or vocalization

Token economy A treatment program, based on principles of operant conditioning, that rewards patients for appropriate behaviors with tokens, which can then be exchanged for hospital privileges, food, or weekend passes

Tolerance Condition in which increasing doses of a substance are necessary to achieve the desired effect

Tourette's syndrome A childhood disorder characterized by multiple motor and one or more verbal tics that may develop into coprolalia (compulsion to shout obscenities)

Transaction model of stress Explanation of stress that states that stress resides neither in the person alone nor in the situation alone, but rather between the two

Transference During psychotherapy, a process in which the patient reenacts early conflicts by carrying over and applying to the therapist feelings and attitudes that the patient has toward significant others (primarily parents) in the past

Transient tic disorder Childhood onset disorder that lasts longer than four weeks but less than one year and that is characterized by involuntary, repetitive, and nonrhythmic movements or vocalizations

Transsexualism A strong and persistent cross-gender identification and persistent discomfort with one's anatomical sex, which cause significant impairment in social, occupational, or other areas of functioning

Transvestic fetishism Intense sexual arousal obtained through cross-dressing (wearing clothes appropriate to the opposite gender); not to be confused with transsexualism

Trephining An ancient surgical technique in which part of the skull was chipped away to provide an opening through which evil spirits could escape

Trichotillomania An impulse control disorder characterized by an inability to resist impulses to pull out one's own hair

Tricyclic Antidepressant compound that relieves symptoms of depression and seems to work like an MAO inhibitor but produces fewer side effects with prolonged use

Unconditioned response (UCR) In classical conditioning, the unlearned response made to an unconditional stimulus

Unconditioned stimulus (UCS) In classical conditioning, the stimulus that elicits an unconditioned response

Undifferentiated schizophrenia A schizophrenic disorder in which the person's behavior shows prominent psychotic symptoms that do not meet the criteria for paranoid, disorganized, or catatonic schizophrenia

Undifferentiated somatoform disorder At least one physical complaint with no physical basis that has lasted for six months or more

Vaginismus Involuntary spasm of the outer third of the vaginal wall, preventing or interfering with sexual intercourse

Validity The extent to which a test or procedure actually performs the function it was designed to perform

Vascular dementia Dementia characterized by uneven deterioration of intellectual abilities and resulting from a number of cerebral infarctions

Voyeurism Urges, acts, or fantasies involving observation of an unsuspecting person disrobing or engaging in sexual activity

Withdrawal Condition characterized by distress or impairment in social, occupational, or other areas of functioning, or physical or emotional symptoms such as shaking, irritability, and inability to concentrate after reducing or ceasing intake of a substance

References

Abebimpe, V. R., Chu, C. C., Klein, H. E., & Lange, M. H. (1982). Racial and geographic differences in the psychopathology of schizophrenia. *American Journal of Psychiatry, 139,* 888–891.

Abel, G. G., Barlow, D. H., Blanchard, E. B., & Guild, D. (1977). The components of rapists' sexual arousal. *Archives of General Psychiatry, 34,* 895–903.

Abel, G. G., & Osborn, C. (1992). The paraphilias: The extent and nature of sexually deviant and criminal behavior. *Psychiatric Clinics of North America, 15,* 675–687.

Abeles, N., & Victor, T. (2003). Unique opportunities for psychology in mental health care for older adults. *Clinical Psychology: Science and Practice, 10,* 120–124.

Abeni, P. A. (2001). Stressful life events and skin diseases: Disentangling evidence from myth. *Psychotherapy and Psychosomatics, 70,* 118–136.

Abramowitz, A. J., & O'Leary, S. G. (1991). Behavioral interventions for the classroom: Implications for students with ADHD. *School Psychology Review, 20,* 220–234.

Abramowitz, J. S., Foa, E. B., & Franklin, M. E. (2003). Exposure and ritual prevention for obsessive-compulsive disorder: Effects of intensive versus twice-weekly sessions. *Journal of Consulting and Clinical Psychology, 71,* 394–398.

Abrams, K., Kushner, M. G., Medina, K. L., & Voight, A. (2002). Self-administration of alcohol before and after a public speaking challenge by individual with social phobia. *Psychology of Addictive Behaviors, 16,* 121–128.

Abrams, R., & Essman, W. B. (1982). *Electroconvulsive therapy.* Jamaica, NY: Medical & Scientific Books.

Abramson, J., Berger, A., Krubholz, H. M., & Vaccarino, V. (2001). Depression and risk of heart failure among older persons with isolated systolic hypertension. *Archives of Internal Medicine, 161,* 1725–1730.

Abramson, L. Y., Metalsky, G. I., & Alloy, L. B. (1989). Hopelessness in depression: A theory-based subtype of depression. *Psychological Review, 96(2),* 358–372.

Abramson, L. Y., Seligman, M. E. P., & Teasdale, J. D. (1978). Learned helplessness in humans: Critique and reformulation. *Journal of Abnormal Psychology, 87,* 49–74.

Addis, M. E. (1997). Evaluating the treatment manual as a means of disseminating empirically validated psychotherapies. *Clinical Psychology: Science and Practice, 4,* 1–11.

Adler, J., Hager, M., Zabarsky, M., Jackson, T., et al. (1984, April 23). The fight to conquer fear. *Newsweek,* pp. 66–72.

Adler, J., & Rogers, A. (1999, January 11). The new war against migraines. *Newsweek,* pp. 46–52.

Adler, R. H., Zamboni, P., Hofer, T., Hemmler, W., et al. (1997). How not to miss a somatic needle in the haystack of chronic pain. *Journal of Psychosomatic Research, 42,* 499–506.

Agras, W. S., Crow, S. J., Halmi, K. A., Mitchell, J. E., et al. (2000). Outcome predictors for the cognitive behavior treatment of bulimia nervosa: Data from a multisite study. *American Journal of Psychiatry, 157,* 1302–1308.

Agras, W. S., Rossiter, E. M., Arnow, B., Schneider, J. A., et al. (1992). Pharmacologic and cognitive-behavioral treatment for bulimia nervosa: A controlled comparison. *American Journal of Psychiatry, 149,* 82–87.

Ahles, T. A., Cassens, H. L., & Stalling, R. B. (1987). Private body consciousness, anxiety and the perception of pain. *Journal of Behavior Therapy and Experimental Psychiatry, 18,* 215–222.

Ahn, H. N., & Wampold, B. E. (2001). Where oh where are the specific ingredients? A meta-analysis of component studies in counseling and psychotherapy. *Journal of Counseling Psychology, 48,* 251–257.

Alanen, Y. O. (1994). An attempt to integrate the individual-psychological and interactional concepts of the origins of schizophrenia. *British Journal of Psychiatry, 164,* 56–61.

Alanen, Y. O. (1997). Vulnerability to schizophrenia and psychotherapeutic treatment of schizophrenic patients: Towards an integrated view. *Psychiatry, 60,* 142–157.

Albee, G. W. (2002). Just say no to psychotropic drugs! *Journal of Clinical Psychology, 58,* 635–648.

Aldridge-Morris, R. (1989). *Multiple personality. An exercise in deception.* Hove, United Kingdom: Erlbaum.

Alessandri, S. (1991). Play and social behavior in maltreated preschoolers. *Development and Psychopathology, 3,* 191–205.

Alexander, F. (1950). *Psychosomatic medicine.* New York: Norton.

Alexander, F. G., & Selesnick, S. T. (1966). *The history of psychiatry.* New York: Harper & Row.

Alexander, J. F., Holtzworth-Munroe, A., & Jameson, P. (1994). The process and outcome of marital and family therapy: Research review and evaluation. In A. E. Bergin & S. L. Garfield (Eds.), *Handbook of psychotherapy and behavior change* (pp. 595–630). New York: Wiley.

Alexander, J. R., Lerer, B., & Baron, M. (1992). Ethical issues in genetic linkage studies of psychiatric disorders. *British Journal of Psychiatry, 160,* 98–102.

Alford, G. S. (1980). Alcoholics Anonymous: An empirical outcome study. *Addictive Behaviors, 5,* 359–370.

Alford, G. S., Morin, C., Atkins M., & Schuen, L. (1987). Masturbatory extinction of deviant sexual arousal: A case study. *Behavior Therapy, 18,* 265–271.

Allanson, J., Bass, C., & Wade, D. T. (2002). Characteristics of patients with persistent severe disability and medically unexplained neurological symptoms: A pilot study. *Journal of Neurology, Neurosurgery and Psychiatry, 73,* 307–309.

Allen, L. A., Gara, M. A., Escobar, J. I., Waitzkin, H., & Silver, R. C. (2001). Somatization: A debilitating syndrome in primary care. *Psychosomatics, 42,* 63–67.

Allgeier, E. R., & Allgeier, A. R. (1998). *Sexual interactions.* Boston: Houghton Mifflin.

Althof, S. E., Turner, L. A., Levine, S. B., Risen, C., et al. (1987). Intracavernosal injection in the treatment of impotence: A prospective study of sexual, psychological, and marital functioning. *Journal of Sex and Marital Therapy, 13,* 155–167.

Amador, X. F., Falum, M., Andreasen, N. C., Strauss, D. H., et al. (1994). Awareness of illness in schizophrenia and schizoaffective and mood disorders. *Archives of General Psychiatry, 51,* 826–836.

American Association of Retired Persons. (1999, September-October). Sex and sexuality [Special issue]. *Modern Maturity.*

American Bar Association. Standing Committee on Association Standards for Criminal Justice. (1984). *Criminal justice and mental health standards.* Chicago: Author.

American Cancer Society. (2004). *Cancer statistics 2004.* Atlanta, GA: American Cancer Society.

American Dietetic Association. (2001). Position of the American Dietetic Association: Nutrition intervention in the treatment of anorexia nervosa, bulimia nervosa, and eating disorders not otherwise specified (EDNOS). *Journal of the American Dietetic Association, 101,* 810–819.

American Heart Association. (1998). *Biostatistical fact sheets.* Author.

American Psychiatric Association. (1980). *Diagnostic and statistical manual of mental disorders* (3rd ed.). [DSM-III]. Washington, DC: Author.

American Psychiatric Association. (1983). American Psychiatric Association statement on the insanity defense. *American Journal of Psychiatry, 140,* 681–688.

American Psychiatric Association. (1987). *Diagnostic and statistical manual of mental disorders* (3rd ed.). [DSM-III-R]. Washington, DC: Author.

American Psychiatric Association (1994). *Diagnostic and statistical manual of mental disorders* (4th ed.). [DSM-IV]. Washington, DC: Author.

American Psychiatric Association (1997). Practice guidelines for the treatment of patients with schizophrenia. *American Journal of Psychiatry, 154,* 1–40.

American Psychiatric Association (1998). Practice guidelines for the treatment of patients with panic disorder. *American Journal of Psychiatry, 155,* 1–34.

American Psychiatric Association. (2000). *Diagnostic and statistical manual of mental disorders* (4th ed., Text revision). Washington, DC: Author.

American Psychiatric Association. (2000). Practice guideline for the treatment of patients with eating disorders (revision). *American Journal of Psychiatry, 157,* 1–39.

American Psychological Association. (1989). *Ethical principles of psychologists.* Washington DC: Author.

American Psychological Association. (1992). Ethical principles of psychologists and code of conduct. *American Psychologist, 47,* 1597–1611.

American Psychological Association. (1993). Guidelines for providers of psychological services to ethnic, linguistic, and culturally diverse populations. *American Psychologist, 48,* 45–48.

American Psychological Association. (1995). *Ethical principles of psychologists and code of conduct.* Washington, DC: Author.

American Psychological Association. (2000). Guidelines for psychotherapy with lesbian, gay, and bisexual clients. *American Psychologist, 55*(12), 1440–1451.

American Psychological Association. (2002). Ethical principles of psychologists and code of conduct. *American Psychologist, 57,* 1060–1073.

American Psychological Association. (2003). Guidelines on multicultural education, training, research, practice, and organizational change for psychologists. *American Psychologist, 58,* 377–402.

APA Working Group on the Older Adult (1998). What practitioners should know about working with older adults. *Professional Psychology: Research and Practice, 29,* 413–427.

American Sleep Apnea Association. (2004a). *Tired of the sleepiness?* Washington, DC: Author.

American Sleep Apnea Association. (2004b). *Personal experiences: Bill's story: It was a big deal, after all.* Retrieved November 19, 2004, from http://www.sleepapnea.org/billstory.html

American Society of Aesthetic Plastic Surgery. (2004). *2003 ASAPS statistics.* Retrieved February 21, 2005, from http://www.surgery.org/press/statistics-2003.php

Anastasi, A. (1982). *Psychological testing.* New York: Macmillan.

Andersen, A. E. (2001). Progress in eating disorders research. *American Journal of Psychiatry, 158,* 515–517.

Andersen, B. L., & Cyranowski, J. M. (1995). Women's sexuality: Behaviors, responses, and individual differences. *Journal of Consulting and Clinical Psychology, 63,* 891–906.

Anderson, K. W., Taylor, S., & McLean, P. H. (1996). Panic disorder associated with blood-injury reactivity: The necessity of establishing functional relationships among maladaptive behaviors. *Behavior Therapy, 27,* 463–472.

Anderson, T., & Strupp, H. H. (1996). The ecology of psychotherapy research. *Journal of Consulting and Clinical Psychology, 64,* 776–782.

Andreasen, N. C. (1984). *The broken brain.* New York: Harper & Row.

Andreasen, N. C. (1989). Nuclear magnetic resonance imaging. In N. C. Andreasen (Ed.), *Brain imaging: Applications in psychiatry* (pp. 67–121). Washington, DC: American Psychiatric Press.

Andreasen, N. C., Arndt, S., Alliger, R., Miller, D., & Flaum, M. (1995). Symptoms of schizophrenia: Methods, meanings, and mechanisms. *Archives of General Psychiatry, 52,* 341–351.

Andreasen, N. C., Arndt, S., Swayze, V. W., II, Cizadlo, T., et al. (1994). Thalamic abnormalities in schizophrenia visualized through magnetic resonance image averaging. *Science, 266,* 294–298.

Andreasen, N. C., O'Leary, D. S., Flaum, M., & Nopoulous, P. (1997). Hypofrontality in schizophrenia: Distributed dysfunctional circuits in neuroleptic-naïve patients. *Lancet, 349,* 1730–1734.

Andreasen, N. C., Rezai, K., Alliger, R., Swayze, V. W., II, et al. (1992). Hypofrontality in neuroleptic-naïve patients and in patients with chronic schizophrenia. *Archives of General Psychiatry, 49,* 943–958.

Angermeyer, M. C., Holzinger, A., Kilian, R., & Matschinger, H. (2001). Quality of life—as defined by schizophrenic patients and psychiatrists. *International Journal of Social Psychiatry, 47,* 34–42.

Anorexia's web. (2001, September 7). *Current Events, 101,* 1–3.

Antony, M. M., Brown, T. A., & Barlow, D. H. (1997). Heterogeneity among specific phobia types in DSM-IV. *Behaviour Research and Therapy, 35,* 1089–1100.

Aoki, H., Kato, R., Hirano, K., Suzuki, T., et al. (2003). A case of sudden unexplained nocturnal death from overlooked Brugada syndrome at a pre-employment check-up. *Journal of Occupational Health, 45,* 70–73.

Aplin, D. Y., & Kane, J. M. (1985). Variables affecting pure tone and speech audiometry in experimentally simulated hearing loss. *British Journal of Audiology, 19,* 219–228.

Applebaum, P. S. (1987). The right to refuse treatment with antipsychotic medications: Retrospect and prospect. *American Journal of Psychiatry, 145,* 413–419.

Applebaum, P. S. (1994). *Almost a revolution: Mental health law and the limits of change.* New York: Oxford University Press.

Arango, C., Kirkpatrick, B., & Buchanan, R. W. (2000). Neurological signs and the heterogeneity of schizophrenia. *American Journal of Psychiatry, 157,* 560–565.

Arciniegas, D. B., & Dubovsky, S. L. (2001). Dementia due to other general medical conditions and dementia due to multiple etiologies. In G. O. Gabbard (Ed.), *Treatment of psychiatric disorders* (pp. 535–573). Washington, DC: American Psychiatric Press.

Ardizzone, J., & Scholl, G. T. (1985). Mental retardation. In G. T. Scholl (Ed.), *The school psychologist and the exceptional child.* Reston, VA: Council for Exceptional Children.

Arndt, S., Andreasen, N. C., Flaum, M., Miller, D., & Nopoulous, P. (1995). A longitudinal study of symptom dimensions in schizophrenia. *Archives of General Psychiatry, 52,* 352–360.

Arndt, W. B., Jr. (1991). *Gender disorders and the paraphilias.* Madison, CT: International Universities Press.

Aronson, T. A. (1987). A naturalistic study of imipramine in panic disorder and agoraphobia. *American Journal of Psychiatry, 144,* 1014–1019.

Asberg, M., Traskman, L., & Thoren, P. (1976). 5 HIAA in the cerebrospinal fluid: A biochemical suicide predictor? *Archives of General Psychiatry, 33,* 1193–1197.

Ash, P. (1949). The reliability of psychiatric diagnosis. *Journal of Abnormal and Social Psychology, 44,* 272–276.

Asian American Federation of New York. (2003). *Asian American mental health: A post–September 11th needs assessment.* New York: Asian American Federation of New York.

Asian Americans seen negatively. (2001). *San Francisco Chronicle,* p. A20.

Asmundson, G. J. G., & Norton, G. R. (1993). Anxiety sensitivity and its relationship to spontaneous and cued panic attacks in college students. *Behaviour Research and Therapy, 31,* 199–201.

Assalian, P. (1988). Clomipramine in the treatment of premature ejaculation. *Journal of Sex Research, 24,* 213–215.

Associated Press. (1994, January 30). Long-term HIV survivors intrigue scientists. *Bellingham Herald,* p. A10.

Associated Press (1998, August 14). Psychiatrist is sued over multiple bad personalities. *Seattle Post Intelligencer,* p. A12.

Associated Press. (2001, April 22). Two therapists found guilty in rebirthing therapy death. *Bellingham Herald,* p. A3.

Astin, M. C., Ogland-Hand, S. M., Foy, D. W., & Coleman, E. M. (1995). Posttraumatic stress disorder and childhood abuse in battered women: Comparisons with maritally distressed women. *Journal of Consulting and Clinical Psychology, 63,* 308–312.

Atkinson, D. R., Brown, M. T., Parham, T. A., Matthews, L. G., et al. (1996). African American client skin tone and clinical judgments of African American and European American psychologists. *Professional Psychology: Research and Practice, 27,* 500–505.

Atkinson, D. R., Morten, G., & Sue, D. W. (1998). *Counseling American Minorities: A cross-cultural perspective.* New York: McGraw-Hill.

Austin, K. M., Moline, M. M., & Williams, G. T. (1990). *Confronting malpractice: Legal and ethical dilemmas in psychotherapy.* Newbury Park, CA: Sage.

Ausubel, D. P. (1961). Causes and types of narcotic addiction: A psychosocial view. *Psychiatric Quarterly, 35,* 523–531.

Autism Society of Wisconsin. (2001). *Secretin and links.* Retrieved from http://www.gsw4autism.org/secretin.htm

Ax, R. K., & Resnick, R. J. (2001, March). Prescription privileges: An immodest proposal. *Monitor on Psychology, 27,* 53–54.

Ayalon, M., & Mercom, H. (1985). The teacher interview. *Schizophrenia Bulletin, 11,* 117–120.

Azar, B. (1995). Several genetic traits linked to alcoholism. *APA Monitor, 26,* 21–22.

Azorin, J.-M., Spiegel, R., Reminton, G., Vanelle, J.-M., et al. (2001). A double-blind comparative study of clozapine and risperidone in the management of severe chronic schizophrenia. *American Journal of Psychiatry, 158,* 1305–1313.

Babel, T. B., Warnke, P. C., & Ostertag, C. B. (2001). Immediate and long term outcome after infrathalamic and thalamic lesioning for intractable Tourette's syndrome. *Journal of Neurology, Neurosurgery, and Psychiatry, 70,* 666–671.

Bacon, N. M. K., Bacon, S. F., Atkinson, J. H., & Slater, M. A. (1994). Somatization symptoms in chronic low back pain patients. *Psychosomatic Medicine, 56,* 118–127.

Bagby, R. M., Rogers, R., Nicholson, R. A., Buis, T., et al. (1997). The effectiveness of the MMPI-2 validity indicators in the detection of defensive responding in clinical and nonclinical samples. *Psychology Assessment, 9,* 406–413.

Bahnson, C. B. (1981). Stress and cancer: The state of the art. *Psychosomatics, 22,* 207–209.

Bailey, D. S. (2003). Help the media prevent copycat suicides. *Monitor, 34,* 14.

Bak, M., Myin-Germeys, I., Hanssen, M., Bijl, R., et al. (2003). When does experience of psychosis result in a need for care? A prospective general population study. *Schizophrenia Bulletin, 29,* 349–356.

Baker, L. A., & Clark, R. (1990). Introduction to special feature on genetic origins of behavior: Implications for counselors. *Journal of Counseling and Development, 68,* 597–605.

Baker, R. R., Lichtenberg, P. A., & Moye, J. (1998). A practice guideline for assessment of competency and capacity of the older adult. *Professional Psychology: Research and Practice, 29,* 149–154.

Bakker, A., Spinhoven, P., Van Balkom, A. J. L. M., & Van Dyck, R. (2002). Relevance of assessment of cognitions during panic attacks in the treatment of panic disorder. *Psychotherapy and Psychosomatics, 71,* 158–162.

Baladerian, N. J. (1991). Abuse causes disabilities. In *Disability and the family.* Culver City, CA: Spectrum Institute.

Ball, J. D., Archer, R. P., Gordon, R. A., & French, J. (1991). Rorschach depression indices with children and adolescents: Concurrent validity findings. *Journal of Personality Assessment, 57,* 465–476.

Ballenger, J. C., Davidson, J. R. T., Lecrubier, Y., Nutt, D. J., et al. (2000). Consensus statement on generalized anxiety disorder from the International Consensus Group on depression and anxiety. *Journal of Clinical Psychiatry, 62,* 53–58.

Ballew, L., Morgan, Y., & Lippmann, S. (2003). Intravenous diazepam for dissociative disorder: Memory lost and found. *Psychosomatics, 44,* 346–349.

Balon, R., Pohl, R., Yeragani, V. K., Rainey, J. M., & Berchou, R. (1988). Follow-up study of control subjects with lactate- and isoproterenol-induced panic attacks. *American Journal of Psychiatry, 145,* 238–241.

Bancroft, J. (1989). *Human sexuality and its problems.* New York: Churchill-Livingstone.

Bandura, A. (1985). *Social foundations of thought and action.* Englewood Cliffs, NJ: Prentice-Hall.

Bandura, A. (1997). *Self-efficacy: The exercise of self-control.* New York: Freeman.

Bandura, A., Blanchard, E., & Ritter, B. (1969). Relative efficacy of desensitization and modeling approaches for inducing behavioral, affective, and attitudinal changes. *Journal of Personality and Social Psychology, 13,* 173–199.

Bandura, A., & Rosenthal, T. L. (1966). Vicarious classical conditioning as a function of arousal level. *Journal of Personality and Social Psychology, 3,* 54–62.

Banerjee, G., & Roy, S. (1998). Determinants of help-seeking behaviour of families of schizophrenic patients attending a teaching hospital in India: An indigenous explanatory model. *International Journal of Social Psychiatry, 44,* 199–214.

Barbaree, H. E., & Marshall, W. L. (1991). The role of male sexual arousal in rape: Six models. *Journal of Consulting and Clinical Psychology, 59,* 621–630.

Barber, J. (1997). Hypnosis and memory: A hazardous connection. *Journal of Mental Health Counseling, 19,* 305–317.

Barber, J. P., & Luborsky, L. (1991). A psychodynamic view of simple phobias and prescriptive matching: A commentary. *Psychotherapy, 28,* 469–472.

Barber, J. P., Morse, J. Q., Krakauer, I. D., Chittams, J., & Crits-Cristoph, K. (1997). Change in obsessive-compulsive and avoidant personality disorders following time-limited supportive-expressive therapy. *Journal of Psychotherapy, 34,* 133–143.

Barclay, L. (2004, September 14). Call for mandatory clinical trial registration, open access to results. *Medscape Medical News.* Retrieved October 19, 2004, from http//www.medscape.com/viewarticle/489219

Barkley, R. A., Anastopoulous, A. D., Guevremont, D. C., & Fletcher, K. E. (1992). Adolescents with attention deficit hyperactivity disorder: Mother-child-adolescent interactions, family beliefs and conflicts, and psychopathology. *Journal of Abnormal Child Psychology, 20,* 263–288.

Barkley, R. A., Fischer, M., Edelbrock, C., & Smallish, L. (1991). The adolescent outcome of hyperactive children diagnosed by research criteria–III. Mother-child interactions, family conflicts and maternal psychopathology. *Journal of Child Psychology and Psychiatry, 32,* 233–255.

Barlow, D. H. (1991). Introduction to the special issue on diagnoses, dimensions, and DSM-IV: The science of classification. *Journal of Abnormal Psychology, 100,* 243–244.

Barlow, D. H., Abel, G., & Blanchard, E. (1979). Gender identity change in transsexuals. *Archives of General Psychiatry, 36,* 1001–1007.

Barlow, D. H., Gorman, J. M., Shear, M. K., & Woods, S. W. (2000). Cognitive-behavioral therapy, imipramine, or their combination for panic disorder: A randomized controlled trial. *Journal of the American Medical Association, 283,* 2529–2536.

Baron, L., Straus, M. A., & Jaffee, D. (1988). Legitimate violence, violent attitudes, and rape: A test of the cultural spillover theory. In R. A. Prentky and V. L. Quisey (Eds.), Human sexual aggression: Current perspectives. *Annals of the New York Academy of Sciences, 528* (pp. 79–110). Salem, MA: New York Academy of Sciences.

Baron, M. (1991). Genetics of manic depressive illness: Current status and evolving concepts. In P. R. McHugh & V. A. McKusick (Eds.), *Genes, brain, and behavior* (pp. 153–164). New York: Raven Press.

Baron-Cohen, L., Leslie, A. M., & Frith, U. (1985). Does the autistic child have a "theory of mind"? *Cognition, 21,* 37–46.

Barraclough, B. M., Jennings, C., & Moss, J. R. (1977). Suicide prevention by the Samaritans: A controlled study of effectiveness. *Lancet, 2,* 237–238.

Barrett, G. V., & Depinet, R. L. (1991). A reconsideration of testing for competence rather than for intelligence. *American Psychologist, 46,* 1012–1024.

Barry, C. T., Frick, P. J., DeShazo, T. M., McCoy, M. G., et al. (2000). The importance of callous-unemotional traits for extending the concept of psychopathology to children. *Journal of Abnormal Psychology, 109,* 335–340.

Barsky, A. J., & Ahern, D. K. (2004). Cognitive behavior therapy for hypochondriasis: A randomized controlled trial. *Journal of the American Medical Association, 291,* 1464–1470.

Barsky, A. J., Cleary, P. D., Sarnie, M. K., & Klerman, G. L. (1993). The course of transient hypochondriasis. *American Journal of Psychiatry, 150,* 484–488.

Barsky, A. J., Wool, C., Barnett, M. C., & Cleary, P. D. (1995). Histories of childhood trauma in adult hypochondriacal patients. *American Journal of Psychiatry, 151,* 397–401.

Barsky, A. J., & Wyshak, G. (1990). Hypochondriasis and somatosensory amplification. *British Journal of Psychiatry, 157,* 404–409.

Barton, J. (2004, September 29). Mental health centers feel storm surge: Calls for help climb after hurricanes. *Columbian,* p. A3.

Bashore, T. R., Ridderinkhof, K. R., & Van der Molen, M. W. (1997). The decline of cognitive processing speed in old age. *Current Directions in Psychological Science, 6,* 163–169.

Basoglu, M., Livanou, M. L., & Salcioglu, E. (2003). A single session with an earthquake simulator for traumatic stress in earthquake survivors. *American Journal of Psychiatry, 160,* 788–790.

Bass, E., & Davis, L. (1988). *The courage to heal.* New York: Harper & Row.

Bassetti, C., & Aldrich, M. S. (1997). Idiopathic hypersomnia: A series of 42 patients. *Brain, 120,* 1423–1435.

Bassman, R. (2000). Agents, not objects: Our fights to be. *JCLP/In session: Psychotherapy in Practice, 56,* 1395–1411.

Bateson, G., Jackson, D., Haley, J., & Weakland, J. (1956). Toward a theory of schizophrenia. *Behavioral Science, 1,* 251–264.

Battaglia, M., Bertella, S., Politi, E., Bernardeschi, L., et al. (1995). Age at onset of panic disorder: Influence of familial liability to the disease and of childhood separation anxiety. *American Journal of Psychiatry, 152,* 1362–1364.

Baum, A., & Nesselhof, S. E. A. (1988). Psychological research and the prevention, etiology, and treatment of AIDS. *American Psychologist, 43*(11), 900–906.

Baum, A., & Posluszny, D. M. (1999). Health psychology: Mapping biobehavioral contributions to health and illness. *Annual Review of Psychology, 50,* 137–163.

Baumeister, R. F. (1988). Masochism as escape from self. *Journal of Sex Research, 25,* 28–59.

Beardslee, W. R., Wright, E., Rothberg, P. C., Salt, P., & Versage, E. (1996). Response of families to two preventative intervention strategies: Long-term differences in behavior and attitude change. *Journal of American Child and Adolescent Psychiatry, 35,* 774–782.

Beck, A. T. (1962). Reliability of psychiatric diagnosis: A critique of systematic studies. *American Journal of Psychiatry, 119,* 210–216.

Beck, A. T. (1974). The development of depression: A cognitive model. In R. J. Friedman & M. M. Katz (Eds.), *The psychology of depression: Contemporary theory and research.* New York: Wiley.

Beck, A. T. (1976). *Cognitive therapy and emotional disorders.* New York: International Universities Press.

Beck, A. T. (1985). Cognitive therapy, behavior therapy, psychoanalysis, and pharmacotherapy: A cognitive continuum. In M. Mahoney & A. Freeman (Eds.), *Cognition and psychotherapy.* New York: Plenum Press.

Beck, A. T. (1991). Cognitive therapy. *American Psychologist, 46,* 368–375.

Beck, A. T. (1997). Cognitive therapy: Reflections. In J. K. Zeig (Ed.), *The evolution of psychotherapy: The third conference.* New York: Brunner/Mazel.

Beck, A. T., Emery, G., & Greenberg, R. L. (1985). *Anxiety disorders and phobias: A cognitive perspective.* New York: Basic Books.

Beck, A. T., Freeman, A., & Associates. (1990). *Cognitive therapy of personality disorders.* New York: Guilford Press.

Beck, A. T., & Rector, N. A. (2000). Cognitive therapy of schizophrenia: A new therapy for the new millennium. *American Journal of Psychotherapy, 54,* 291–300.

Beck, A. T., Rush, A., Shaw, B., & Emery, G. (1979). *Cognitive therapy of depression.* New York: Guilford Press.

Beck, A. T., Ward, C. H., Mendelson, M., Mock, J. E., & Erbaugh, J. (1961). An inventory for measuring depression. *Archives of General Psychiatry, 4,* 561–571.

Beck, A. T., & Weishaar, M. E. (1989). Cognitive therapy. In R. J. Corsini & D. Wedding (Eds.), *Current psychotherapies* (pp. 285–320). Itasca, IL: Peacock.

Becker, A. E. (1995). *Body, self, and society: The view from Fiji.* Philadelphia: University of Pennsylvania Press.

Bednar, R. L., Bednar, S. C., Lambert, M. J., & Waite, D. R. (1991). *Psychotherapy with high-risk clients: Legal and professional standards.* Pacific Grove, CA: Brooks/Cole.

Bednar, R. L., & Kaul, T. J. (1978). Experiential group research: Current perspectives. In S. L. Garfield & A. E. Bergin (Eds.), *Handbook of psychotherapy and behavior change: An empirical analysis* (2nd ed.). New York: Wiley.

Beers, M. H., & Berkow, R. (Eds.) (1999). *The Merck manual of diagnosis and therapy* (17th ed.). Whitehouse Station, NJ: Merck Publications.

Beiser, M., Fleming, J. A. E., Iacono, W. G., & Lin, T.-Y. (1988). Redefining the diagnosis of schizophreniform disorder. *American Journal of Psychiatry, 145,* 695–700.

Belar, C. (1995). What distinguishes clinical health psychology, rehabilitation psychology, and neuropsychology? *Professional Psychology: Research and Practice, 26,* 349–351.

Belar, C. D., & Deardorff, W. W. (1995). *Clinical health psychology in medical settings: A practitioner's guidebook.* Washington, DC: American Psychological Association.

Bell-Dolan, D., & Wessler, A. E. (1994). Attribution style of anxious children: Extensions from cognitive theory and research on adult anxiety. *Journal of Anxiety Disorders, 8,* 79–94.

Bellack, A. S., & Hersen, M. (1980). *Introduction to clinical psychology.* New York: Oxford University Press.

Bellack, A. S., Hersen, M., & Himmelhoch, J. M. (1983). A comparison of social skills training. *Behavior Research & Therapy, 21,* 101–108.

Bellodi, L., Cavallini, M. C., Bertelli, S., Chiapparino, D., et al. (2001). Morbidity risk for obsessive-compulsive spectrum disorders in first-degree relatives of patients with eating disorders. *American Journal of Psychiatry, 158,* 563–569.

Benassi, V. A., Sweeney, P. D., & Dufour, C. L. (1988). Is there a relation between locus of control orientation and depression? *Journal of Abnormal Psychology, 97*(3), 357–367.

Bender, L. (1938). A visual-motor Gestalt test and its clincal use. *American Orthopsychiatric Association Research Monographs,* No. 3.

Benedict, J. G., & Donaldson, D. W. (1996). Recovered memories threaten all. *Professional Psychology: Research and Practice, 27,* 427–428.

Benight, C. C., Antoni, M. H., Kilbourn, K., Ironson, G., et al. (1997). Coping self-efficacy buffers psychological and physiological disturbances in HIV-infected men following a natural disaster. *Health Psychology, 16,* 248–255.

Benjamin, L. R., Benjamin, R., & Rind, B. (1998). The parenting experiences of mothers with dissociative disorders. *Journal of Marital and Family Therapy, 24,* 337–344.

Benjamin, L. S., & Karpiak, C. P. (2002). Personality disorders. In J. C. Norcross (Ed.), *Psychotherapy relationships that work* (pp. 423–440). New York: Oxford University Press.

Benjamin, L. S., & Wonderlich, S. A. (1994). Social perceptions and borderline personality disorder: The relation to mood disorders. *Journal of Abnormal Psychology, 103,* 610–624.

Bennett, L. F. C., & Sherman, R. (1983). Management of childhood "hyperactivity" by primary care physicians. *Journal of Developmental and Behavioral Pediatrics, 4,* 88–93.

Bennett, P., Wallace, L., Carroll, D., & Smith, N. (1991). Treating type A behaviours and mild hypertension in middle-aged men. *Journal of Psychosomatic Research, 35,* 209–223.

Benson, H., Shapiro, D., Tursky, B., & Schwartz, G. (1971). Decreased systolic blood pressure through operant conditioning techniques in patients with essential hypertension. *Science, 173,* 740–742.

Benton, S. A., Robertson, J. M., Tseng, W.-C., Newton, F. B., & Benton, S. L. (2003). Changes in counseling center client problems across 13 years. *Professional Psychology: Research and Practice, 34,* 66–72.

Ben-Tovim, D. I., Walker, K., Gilchrist, P., Freeman, R., et al. (2001). Outcome in patients with eating disorders: A five-year study. *Lancet, 357,* 1254–1257.

Beratis, S., Gabriel, J., & Hoidas, S., (1994). Age at onset in subtypes of schizophrenic disorders. *Schizophrenic Bulletin, 20,* 287–296.

Berenbaum, H., Raghavan, C., Le, H., Vernon, L. L., & Gomez, J. J. (2003). A taxonomy of emotional disturbances. *Clinical Psychology: Science and Practice, 10,* 206–226.

Berkowitz, A., & Perkins, H. W. (1988). Personality characteristics of children of alcoholics. *Journal of Consulting and Clinical Psychology, 56,* 206–209.

Berlow, S. J., Caldarelli, D. D., Matz, G. J., Meyer, D. H., & Harsch, G. G. (1981). Bacterial meningitis and SHL. *Laryngoscope, 4,* 1445–1452.

Berman, A. L., & Jobes, D. A. (1991). *Adolescent suicide: Assessment and intervention.* Washington, DC: American Psychological Association.

Berman, A. L., & Jobes, D. A. (1995). *Adolescent suicide: Assessment and intervention.* Washington, DC: American Psychological Association.

Berman, K. F., Torrey, E. F., Daniel, D. G., & Weinberger, D. R. (1992). Regional cerebral blood flow in monozygotic twins discordant and concordant for schizophrenia. *Archives of General Psychiatry, 49,* 927–934.

Bernard, J. (1976). Homosociality and female depression. *Journal of Social Issues, 32,* 213–238.

Bernstein, S. M., Steiner, B. W., Glaisler, J. T. D., & Muir, C. F. (1981). Changes in patients with gender identity problems after parental death. *American Journal of Psychiatry, 138,* 41–45.

Bersoff, D. N. (1981). Testing and the law. *American Psychologist, 36,* 1047–1057.

Bhadrinath, B. R. (1990). Anorexia nervosa in adolescents of Asian extraction. *British Journal of Psychiatry, 156,* 565–568.

Bickel, W. K., Amass, L., Higgins, S. T., Badger, G. J., & Esch, R. A. (1997). Effects of adding behavioral treatment to opiod detoxification with buprenorphine. *Journal of Consulting and Clinical Psychology, 65,* 803–810.

Binder, L. M. (1986). Persisting symptoms after mild head injury: A review of the postconcussive syndrome. *Journal of Clinical and Experimental Neuropsychology, 8,* 323–346.

Binder, R. L. (1988). Organic mental disorders. In H. H. Goldman (Ed.), *Review of general psychiatry* (pp. 252–265). Norwalk, CT: Appleton & Lange.

Binzer, M., Andersen, P. M., & Kullgren, G. (1997). Clinical characteristics of patients with motor disability due to conversion disorder: A prospective control group study. *Journal of Neurology, Neurosurgery, and Psychiatry, 63,* 83–87.

Binzer, M., Eisenmann, M., & Kullgren, G. (1998). Illness behavior in the acute phase of motor disability in neurological disease and in conversion disorder: A comparative study. *Journal of Psychosomatic Research, 44,* 657–666.

Biondi, M., Picardi, A., Bakker, A., Spinhoven, P., et al. (2003). Attribution of improvement to medication and increased risk of relapse of panic disorder with agoraphobia: Reply. *Psychotherapy and Psychosomatics, 72,* 110–111.

Bishop, G. E., Enkelmann, H. C., Tong, E. M. W., Why, Y. P., et al. (2003). Job demands, decisional control, and cardiovascular responses. *Journal of Occupational Health Psychology, 8,* 146–156.

Black, D. W., Noyes, R., Goldstein, R. B., & Blum, N. (1992). A family study of obsessive-compulsive disorder. *Archives of General Psychiatry, 49,* 362–368.

Black, S. T. (1993). Comparing genuine and simulated suicide notes: A new perspective. *Journal of Consulting and Clinical Psychology, 67,* 699–702.

Blakeslee, S. (1993, June 2). New therapies are helping men to overcome impotence. *New York Times,* p. C12.

Blampied, N. M. (2000). Single-case research designs: A neglected alternative. *American Psychologist, 55,* 960–961.

Blanchard, E. B. (1992). Psychological treatment of benign headache disorders. *Journal of Consulting and Clinical Psychology, 60,* 537–551.

Blanchard, J. J., Gangestad, S. W., Brown, S. A., & Horan, W. P. (2000). Hedonic capacity and schizotypy revisited: A taxometric analysis of social anhedonia. *Journal of Abnormal Psychology, 109,* 87–95.

Blanchard, J. J., Horan, W. P., & Brown, S. A. (2001). Diagnostic differences in social anhedonia: A longitudinal study of schizophrenia and major depressive disorder. *Journal of Abnormal Psychology, 110,* 363–371.

Blanchard, R. (1988). Nonhomosexual gender dysphoria. *Journal of Sex Research, 24,* 188–193.

Blanchard, R., Racansky, I. G., & Steiner, B. W. (1986). Phallometric detection of fetishistic arousal. *Journal of Sex Research, 22,* 452–462.

Blank, R. J. (1981). The partial transsexual. *American Journal of Psychiatry, 35,* 107–112.

Bleuler, E. (1911/1950). *Dementia praecox or the group of schizophrenias* (J. Zinkin, Trans.). New York: International Universities Press.

Blier, P., Szabo, S. T., Haddjeri, N., & Dong, J. (2000). Orbitofrontal cortex-basal ganglia system in OCD. *International Journal of Neuropsychopharmacology, 3,* 1–14.

Bliss, E. L. (1984). Hysteria and hypnosis. *Journal of Nervous and Mental Disease, 172,* 203–208.

Blomhoff, S., Haug, T. T., Helstron, K., Holme, I., et al. (2001). Randomized controlled general practice trial of sertraline, exposure therapy, and combined treatment in generalized social phobia. *British Journal of Psychiatry, 179,* 23–30.

Bloomberg, D. (2000, January/February). Bennett Braun case settled: Two-year loss of license, five years probation. *Skeptical Inquirer,* 7–8.

Blouin, A., Blouin, J., Aubin, P., Carter, J., et al. (1992). Seasonal patterns of bulimia nervosa. *American Journal of Psychiatry, 149,* 73–81.

Bogels, S. M., van Oosten, A., Muris, P., & Smulders, D. (2001). Family correlates of social anxiety in children and adolescents. *Behaviour Research and Therapy, 39,* 273–287.

Bogerts, B. (1993). Recent advances in the neuropathology of schizophrenia. *Schizophrenia Bulletin, 19,* 431–440.

Bohman, M., Cloninger, R., von Knorring, A. L., & Sigvardsson, S. (1984). An adoption study of somatoform disorders. *Archives of General Psychiatry, 41,* 872–878.

Bohne, A., Keuthen, N. J., Wilhelm, S., Deckersbach, T., & Jenike, M. A. (2002). Prevalence of symptoms of body dysmorphic disorder and its correlates: A cross-cultural comparison. *Psychosomatics, 43,* 486–490.

Boll, T. J. (1983). Neuropsychological assessment. In I. B. Weiner (Ed.), *Clinical methods in psychology.* New York: Wiley.

Boller, F., Kim, Y., & Detre, T. (1984). Assessment of temporal lobe disorder. In P. E. Logue & J. M. Schear (Eds.), *Clinical neuropsychology.* Springfield, IL: Thomas.

Bolton, P., Macdonald, H., Pickles, A., Rios, P., et al. (1994). A case-control family history of autism. *Journal of Child Psychology and Psychiatry, 35,* 877–900.

Bolton, P., Rutter, M., Butler, L., & Summers, D. (1989). Females with autism and the fragile X. *Journal of Autism and Developmental Disorders, 19,* 473–476.

Bongar, B. (1991). *The suicidal patient: Clinical and legal standards of care.* Washington, DC: American Psychological Association.

Bongar, B. (1992). Effective risk management and the suicidal patient. *Register Report, 18,* 1–3, 21–27.

Boon, S., & Draijer, N. (1993). Multiple personality disorder in the Netherlands: A clinical investigation of 71 patients. *American Journal of Psychiatry, 150,* 489–494.

Booth, G. K. (1988). Disorders of impulse control. In H. H. Goldman (Ed.), *Review of general psychiatry* (pp. 381–390). Norwalk, CT: Appleton & Lange.

Booth, R., & Rachman, S. (1992). The reduction of claustrophobia I. *Behaviour Research and Therapy, 30,* 207–221.

Borch-Jacobsen, M. (1997). Sybil—The making of a disease: An interview with Dr. Herbert Spiegel. *New York Review of Books, 44,* 60–64.

Borkovec, T. D., & Ruscio, A. M. (2001). Psychotherapy for generalized anxiety disorder. *Journal of Clinical Psychiatry, 62,* 37–42.

Bornas, X., Fullana, M. A., Tortella-Feliu, M., Llabres, J., & de la Banda, G. G. (2001). Computer-assisted therapy in the treatment of flight phobia. *Cognitive and Behavioral Practice, 8,* 234–240.

Bornstein, R. F. (1997). Dependent personality disorder in the DSM-IV and beyond. *Clinical Psychology, 4,* 175–187.

Bornstein, R. F. (1998). Reconceptualizing personality disorder diagnosis in the *DSM-V:* The discriminant validity challenge. *Clinical Psychology, 5,* 333–343.

Boucher, J., & Lewis, Y. (1992). Unfamiliar face recognition in relatively able autistic children. *Journal of Child Psychology and Psychiatry, 33,* 843–859.

Bouhoutsos, J., Holroyd, J., Lerman, H., Forer, B. R., & Greenberg, M. (1983). Sexual intimacy between psychotherapists and patients. *Professional Psychology: Research and Practice, 14,* 185–196.

Bouton, M. E., Mineka, S., & Barlow, D. H. (2001). A modern learning theory perspective on the etiology of panic disorder. *Psychological Review, 108,* 4–32.

Bouvard, M. A., Milliery, M., & Cottraux, J. (2004). Management of obsessive compulsive disorder. *Psychotherapy and Psychosomatics, 73,* 149–157.

Bownes, I. T., O'Gorman, E. C., & Sayers, A. (1991). Assault characteristics and post-traumatic stress disorder in rape victims. *Acta Psychiatrica Scandinavica, 83,* 27–30.

Boyajian, A. E., DuPaul, G. J., Handler, M. W., Eckert, T. L., & McGoey, K. E. (2001). The use of classroom based brief functional analysis with preschoolers at risk for ADHD. *School Psychology Review, 30,* 278–293.

Boyd-Franklin, N. (2003). *Black families in therapy.* New York: Guilford Press.

Bozzuto, J. C. (1975). Cinematic neurosis following *The Exorcist. Journal of Nervous and Mental Disease, 161,* 43–48.

Braaten, E. B., & Rosen, L. A. (2000). Self-regulation of affect in attention deficit-hyperactivity disorder (ADHD) and non-ADHD boys: Differences in empathic responding. *Journal of Consulting and Clinical Psychology, 68,* 313–321.

Bradley, S. J. (1995). Psychosexual disorders in adolescence. In J. M. Oldham & M. B. Riba (Eds.), *American Psychiatric Press Review of Psychiatry, 14,* Washington, DC: American Psychiatric Press.

Brammer, L. M., & Shostrom, E. (1982). *Therapeutic psychology.* Englewood Cliffs, NJ: Prentice-Hall.

Brandsma, J. (1979). *Outpatient treatment of alcoholism.* Baltimore: University Park Press.

Brannigan, G. G., Decker, S. L., & Madsen, D. H. (2004). *Innovative features of the Bender-Gestalt II and expanded guidelines for the use of the Global Scoring System* (Bender Visual-Motor Gestalt Test, 2nd ed., Assessment Service Bulletin No. 1). Itasca, IL: Riverside.

Braswell, L., & Kendall, P. C. (1988). Cognitive-behavioral methods with children. In K. S. Dobson (Ed.), *Handbook of cognitive-behavioral therapies* (pp. 167–213). New York: Guilford Press.

Braucht, G. (1982). Problem drinking among adolescents: A review and analysis of psychosocial research. In National Institute on Alcohol Abuse and Alcoholism, *Alcohol Monograph 4: Special Population Issues.* Washington, DC: U.S. Government Printing Office.

Braun, P., Kochonsky, G., Shapiro, R., Greenberg, S., et al. (1981). Overview: Deinstitutionalization of psychiatric patients: A critical review of outcome studies. *American Journal of Psychiatry, 138,* 736–749.

Brawman-Mintzer, O., Lydiard, R. B., Rickels, K., & Small, G. W. (1997). Biological basis of generalized anxiety disorder: Discussion. *Journal of Clinical Psychology, 58,* 16–23.

Bray, J. H., Adams, G. J., Getz, J. G., & McQueen, A. (2003). Individuation, peers, and adolescent alcohol use: A latent growth analysis. *Journal of Consulting and Clinical Psychology, 71,* 553–564.

Breier, A., Albus, M., Pickar, D., Zahn, T. P., et al. (1987). Controllable and uncontrollable stress in humans: Alterations in mood and neuroendocrine and psychophysiological function. *American Journal of Psychiatry, 144,* 1419–1425.

Bremner, J. D., Southwick, S. M., Johnson, D. R., Yehuda, R., & Charney, D. S. (1993). Childhood physical abuse and combat-related posttraumatic stress disorder in Vietnam veterans. *American Journal of Psychiatry, 150,* 235–239.

Brent, D. A., Bridge, J., Johnson, B. A., & Connolly, J. (1996). Suicidal behavior runs in families: A controlled family study of adolescent suicide victims. *Archives of General Psychiatry, 53,* 1145–1152.

Brent, D. A., Perper, J. A., & Allman, C. J. (1987). Alcohol, firearms, and suicide among youth. *Journal of the American Medical Association, 257,* 3369–3372.

Breslau, N., Davis, G. C., & Andreski, P. (1995). Risk factors for PTSD-related traumatic events: A prospective analysis. *American Journal of Psychiatry, 152,* 529–535.

Breuer, J., & Freud, S. (1957). *Studies in hysteria.* New York: Basic Books. (Original work published 1895)

Brewin, C. R., Andrews, B., & Valentine, J. D. (2000). Meta-analysis of risk factors for posttraumatic stress disorder in trauma-exposed adults. *Journal of Consulting and Clinical Psychology, 68,* 748–766.

Brewslow, N., Evans, L., & Langley, J. (1986). Comparisons among heterosexual, bisexual, and homosexual male sadomasochists. *Journal of Homosexuality, 13,* 83–107.

Briere, J. (1992). Methodological issues in the study of sexual abuse effects. *Journal of Consulting and Clinical Psychology, 60,* 196–203.

Brinkley, C. A., Newman, J. P., Widiger, T. A., & Lynam, D. R. (2004). Two approaches to parsing the heterogeneity of psychopathy. *Clinical Psychology: Science and Practice, 11,* 69–94.

Brislin, R. (1993). *Understanding culture's influence on behavior.* New York: Harcourt Brace Jovanovich.

Bristol, M. M., Cohen, D. J., Costello, E. J., Deckla, M. B., et al. (1996). State of the science in autism: Report to the National Institute of Health. *Journal of Autism and Developmental Disorders, 26,* 121–154.

Broman, S. H., Nichols, P. L., & Kennedy, W. A. (1975). *Preschool IQ: Prenatal and early developmental correlates.* Hillsdale, NJ: Erlbaum.

Brook, S. L., & Bowler, D. M. (1992). Autism by another name? Semantic and pragmatic impairments in children. *Journal of Autism and Developmental Disorders, 22,* 61–81.

Brooks, D. S., Murphy, D., Janota, I., & Lishman, W. A. (1987). Early-onset Huntington's chorea. *British Journal of Psychiatry, 151,* 850–852.

Brown, D., & Srebalus, D. J. (2003). *Introduction to the counseling profession.* Boston: Allyn & Bacon.

Brown, G. L., Ebert, M., Goyer, P., Jimerson, D. C., et al. (1982). Aggression, suicide, and serotonin: Relationships to CSF amine metabolites. *American Journal of Psychiatry, 139,* 741–746.

Brown, G. R., & Anderson, B. (1991). Psychiatric morbidity in adult inpatients with childhood histories of sexual and physical abuse. *American Journal of Psychiatry, 148,* 55–61.

Brown, G. W., & Harris, T. O. (1989). Depression. In G. W. Brown & T. O. Harris (Eds.), *Life events and illness* (pp. 49–93). New York: Guilford Press.

Brown, J. (2004, December 14). "Magic" opening for Burger King. *Miami Times,* p. 1a.

Brown, T. A., & Cash, T. F. (1990). The phenomenon of nonclinical panic: Parameters of panic fear, and avoidance. *Journal of Anxiety Disorders, 4*, 15–29.

Brown, T. A., Chorpita, B. R., & Barlow, D. H. (1998). Structural relationships among dimensions of the DSM-IV anxiety and mood disorder and dimensions of negative affect, positive affect, and autonomic arousal. *Journal of Abnormal Psychology, 107*, 179–192.

Brown, T. A., Di Nardo, P. A., Lehman, C. L., & Campbell, L. A. (2001). Reliability of DSM-IV anxiety and mood disorders: Implications for the classification of emotional disorders. *Journal of Abnormal Psychology, 110*, 49–58.

Bruch, H. (1978). Obesity and anorexia nervosa. *Psychosomatics, 19*, 208–221.

Bruch, M. A., Fallon, M., & Heimberg, R. G. (2003). Social phobia and difficulties in occupational adjustment. *Journal of Counseling Psychology, 50*, 109–117.

Bruch, M. A., & Heimberg, R. G. (1994). Differences in perceptions of parental and personal characteristics between generalized and nongeneralized social phobics. *Journal of Anxiety Disorders, 8*, 155–168.

Bryant, K. (2001, February 20). Eating disorders: In their own words. *Atlanta Constitution*, p. B4.

Bryant, R. A. (1997). Folie a familie: A cognitive study of delusional beliefs. *Psychiatry, 60*, 44–50.

Bryant, R. A., Guthrie, R. M., Moulds, M. L., & Harvey, A. G. (2000). A prospective study of psychophysiological arousal, acute stress disorder, and posttraumatic stress disorder. *Journal of Abnormal Psychology, 109*, 341–344.

Bryant, R. A., & McConkey, K. M. (1989). Visual conversion disorder: A case analysis of the influence of visual information. *Journal of Abnormal Psychology, 98*, 326–329.

Buchanan, A. (1997). The investigation of acting on delusions as a tool for risk assessment in the mentally disordered. *British Journal of Psychiatry, 170*, 12–14.

Buchanan, R. W., Breier, A., Kirkpatrick, B., Ball, P., & Carpenter, W. T. (1998). Positive and negative symptom response to clozapine in schizophrenic patients with and without the deficit syndrome. *American Journal of Psychiatry, 155*, 751–760.

Buchsbaum, M. S. (1990). The frontal lobes, basal ganglia, and the temporal lobes as sites for schizophrenia. *Schizophrenia Bulletin, 16*, 379–389.

Buckley, T. C., Blanchard, E. B., & Hickling, E. J. (1996). A prospective examination of delayed onset PTSD secondary to motor vehicle accidents. *Journal of Abnormal Psychology, 105*, 617–625.

Bulik, C. M., & Kendler, K. S. (2000). "I am what I (don't) eat": Establishing an identity independent of an eating disorder. *American Journal of Psychiatry, 157*, 1755–1760.

Bull, C. B. (2004). Binge eating disorder. *Current Opinion in Psychiatry, 17*, 43–48.

Bullard-Bates, P. C., & Satz, P. (1983). A case of pathological left-handedness. *Clinical Neuropsychology, 5*, 128–135.

Bunce, D., Kivipelto, M., & Wahlin, A. (2004). Utilization of cognitive support in episodic free recall as a function of apolipoprotein E and vitamin B12 or folate among adults aged 75 years and older. *Neuropsychology, 18*, 362–370.

Bunney, W. E., Pert, A., Rosenblatt, J., Pert, C. B., & Gallaper, D. (1979). Mode of action of lithium: Some biological considerations. *Archives of General Psychiatry, 36*, 898–901.

Burgess, A. W., Groth, A. N., & McCausland, M. P. (1981). *American Journal of Orthopsychiatry, 51*, 110–119.

Burgess, A. W., Hartman, C. R., McCausland, M. P., Powers, P. (1984). Response pattern in children and adolescents exploited through sex rings and pornography. *American Journal of Psychiatry, 141*, 656–662.

Burgess, A. W., & Holmstrom, L. L. (1979). Rape: Sex disruption and recovery. *American Journal of Orthopsychiatry, 49*, 648–657.

Burgy, M. (2001). The narcissistic function in obsessive-compulsive neurosis. *American Journal of Psychotherapy, 55*, 65–73.

Burke, W. J., & Bohac, D. L. (2001). Amnestic disorder due to a general medical condition and amnestic disorder not otherwise

specified. In G. O. Gabbard (Ed.), *Treatment of psychiatric disorders* (pp. 609–624). Washington, DC: American Psychiatric Press.

Burman, B., Mednick, S. A., Machon, R. A., Parnas, J., & Schulsinger, F. (1987). Children at high risk for schizophrenia: Parents and offspring perceptions of family relationships. *Journal of Abnormal Psychology, 96*, 364–366.

Burruss, J. W., Travella, J. I., & Robinson, R. G. (2001). Vascular dementia. In G. O. Gabbard (Ed.), *Treatment of psychiatric disorders* (pp. 515–534). Washington, DC: American Psychiatric Press.

Burt, D. B., Fuller, S. P., & Lewis, K. R. (1991). Brief report: Competitive employment of adults with autism. *Journal of Autism and Developmental Disorders, 21*, 237–242.

Burt, V. L., Whelton, P., Roccella, E. J., Higgins, M., et al. (1995). Prevalence of hypertension in the U.S. adult population: Results from the Third National Health and Nutrition Examination Survey, 1988–1991. *Hypertension, 25*, 305–313.

Bush, A., & Beail, N. (2004). Risk factors for dementia in people with Down Syndrome: Issues in assessment and diagnosis. *American Journal on Mental Retardation, 109*, 83–97.

Bushman, B. J., & Anderson, C. A. (2001). Media violence and the American public: Scientific facts versus media misinformation. *American Psychologist, 56*, 477–489.

Butcher, J. N. (1990). *The MMPI-2 in psychological treatment.* New York: Oxford University Press.

Butcher, J. N. (1995). Item content in the interpretation of the MMPI-2. In J. N. Butcher (Ed.), *Clinical personality assessment: Practical approaches* (pp. 302–316). New York: Oxford University Press.

Butcher, J. N. (Ed.). (1996). *International adaptations of the MMPI-2.* Minneapolis: University of Minnesota Press.

Butler, L. D., Duran, R. E. F., Jasiukaitis, P., Koopman, C., & Spiegel, D. (1996). Hypnotizability and traumatic experience. *American Journal of Psychiatry, 153*, 42–59.

Butler, R. N. (1984). Senile dementia: Reversible and irreversible. *Counseling Psychologist, 12*, 75–79.

Butzlaff, R. L., & Hooley, J. M. (1998). Expressed emotion and psychiatric relapse: A meta-analysis. *Archives of General Psychiatry, 55*, 547–553.

Byers, E. S., & Enos, R. J. (1991). Predicting men's sexual coercion and aggression from attitudes, dating history, and sexual response. *Journal of Psychology and Human Sexuality, 4*, 55–70.

Caccavale, J. (2002). Opposition to prescriptive authority: Is this a case of the tail wagging the dog? *Journal of Clinical Psychology, 58*, 623–633.

Cadoret, R. J., & Cain, C. (1981). Environmental and genetic factors in predicting adolescent antisocial behavior in adoptees. *Psychiatric Journal of the University of Ottawa, 6*, 220–225.

Cadoret, R. J., & Wesner, R. B. (1990). Use of the adoption paradigm to elucidate the role of genes and environment and their interaction in the genesis of alcoholism. In C. R. Cloninger & H. Begleiter (Eds.), *Genetics and biology of alcoholism* (pp. 31–42). Cold Spring Harbor, NY: Cold Spring Harbor Laboratory Press.

Calamari, J. E., Faber, S. D., Hitsman, B. L., & Poppe, C. J. (1994). Treatment of obsessive compulsive disorder in the elderly. *Journal of Behavior Therapy and Experimental Psychiatry, 25*, 95–104.

Calhoun, K. S., & Atkeson, B. M. (1991). *Treatment of rape victims.* Elmsford, NY: Pergamon.

Callahan, L. A., Steadman, H. J., McGreevy, M. A., & Robbins, P. C. (1991). The volume and characteristics of insanity defense pleas: An eight-state study. *Bulletin of the American Academy of Psychiatry and the Law, 19*, 331–338.

Camara, W. J., Nathan, J. S., & Puente, A. E. (2000). Psychological test usage: Implications in professional psychology. *Professional Psychology: Research and Practice, 31*, 141–154.

Cameron, R. P., Grabill, C. M., Hobfoll, S. E., Crowther, J. H., et al. (1996). Weight, self-esteem, ethnicity, and depressive symptomatology during pregnancy. *Health Psychology, 15*, 293–297.

Campbell, R. J. (1981). *Psychiatric dictionary* (5th ed.). New York: Oxford University Press.

Campbell, S. B., & Ewing, L. J. (1990). Follow-up of hard-to-manage preschoolers: Adjustment at age 9 and predictors of continuing symptoms. *Journal of Child Psychology and Psychiatry, 31,* 871–889.

Campo, J. A., Frederikx, M., Nijman, H. & Merckelback, H. (1998). Schizophrenia and changes in physical appearance. *Journal of Clinical Psychiatry, 59,* 197–198.

Canapary, D., Bongar, B., & Cleary, K. M. (2002). Assessing risk for completed suicide in patients with alcohol dependence: Clinicans' views of critical factors. *Professional Psychology: Research and Practice, 33,* 464–469.

Canetto, S. S., & Lester, D. (1995). The epidemiology of women's suicidal behavior. In S. S. Canetto & D. Lester (Eds.), *Women and suicidal behavior.* New York: Springer.

Cannon, T. D., Kaprio, J., Lonnqvist, J., Huttunen, M., & Koskenvuo, M. (1998). The genetic epidemiology of schizophrenia in a Finnish twin cohort. *Archives of General Psychiatry, 55,* 67–74.

Cantwell, D. P. (1996). Attention deficit disorder: A review of the past 10 years. *Journal of the American Academy of Child and Adolescent Psychiatry, 35,* 978–987.

Caplan, P. J. (1995). *They say you're crazy.* Reading, MA: Addison-Wesley.

Cardemil, E., & Barber, J. P. (2001). Building a model for prevention practice: Depression as an example. *Professional Psychology: Research and Practice, 32,* 392–401.

Carels, R. A., Cacciapaglia, H., Perez-Benitez, C. I., Douglass, O., et al. (2003). The association between emotional upset and cardiac arrhythmias during daily life. *Journal of Consulting and Clinical Psychology, 71,* 613–618.

Carey, B. (2004, August 10). For psychotherapy's claims, skeptics demand proof. *The New York Times,* pp. F1–2.

Carey, G. (1992). Twin imitation for antisocial behavior: Implications for genetic and family environment research. *Journal of Abnormal Psychology, 101,* 18–25.

Carey G., & DiLalla, D. L. (1994). Personality and psychopathology: Genetic perspectives. *Journal of Abnormal Psychology, 103,* 32–43.

Carey, K. B., & Carey, M. P. (1995). Reasons for drinking among psychiatric outpatients: Relationship to drinking patterns. *Psychology of Addictive Behavior, 9,* 251–257.

Carlat, D. J., Camargo, C. A., & Herzog, D. B. (1997). Eating disorders in males: A report on 135 patients. *American Journal of Psychiatry, 154,* 1127–1132.

Carlin, A. S., Hoffman, H. G., & Weghorst, S. (1997). Virtual reality and tactile argumentation in the treatment of spider phobia: A case report. *Behaviour Research and Therapy, 35,* 153–158.

Carlson, C. L., Pelham, W. E. Jr., Milich, R., & Dixon, J. (1992). Single and combined effects of methylphenidate and behavior therapy on the classroom performance of children with attention-deficit hyperactivity disorder. *Journal of Abnormal Child Psychology, 20,* 213–232.

Carlson, E. A. (1998). A prospective longitudinal study of disorganized attachment. *Child Development, 69,* 1107–1128.

Carlson, E. B., & Rosser-Hogan, R. (1991). Trauma experiences, posttraumatic stress, dissociation, and depression in Cambodian refugees. *American Journal of Psychiatry, 148,* 1548–1551.

Carnes, P. (1983). *Out of the shadows: Understanding sexual addiction.* Minneapolis, MN: CompCare.

Carney, M. A., Armeli, S., Tennen, H., Affleck, G., & O'Neil, T. P. (2000). Positive and negative daily events, perceived stress, and alcohol use: A diary study. *Journal of Consulting and Clinical Psychology, 68,* 788–798.

Carpenter, W. T., Conley, R. R., Buchanan, R. W., Breier, A., & Tamminga, C. A. (1995). Patient response and resource management: Another view of clozapine treatment of schizophrenia. *American Journal of Psychiatry, 152,* 827–832.

Carr, J. (1994). Annotation: Long-term outcome for people with Down syndrome. *Journal of Child Psychology and Psychiatry, 35,* 425–439.

Carskadon, M. A. (2004). Sleep difficulties in young people. *Archives of Pediatrics and Adolescent Medicine, 158,* 597–598.

Carson, R. C. (1991). Dilemmas in the pathway of the DSM-IV. *Journal of Abnormal Psychology, 100,* 302–307.

Carter, B., & McGoldrick, M. (2005). *The expanded family life cycle: Individual, family and social perspectives.* New York: Allyn & Bacon.

Carter, J. C., & Fairburn, C. G. (1998). Cognitive-behavioral self-help for binge eating disorder: A controlled effectiveness study. *Journal of Consulting and Clinical Psychology, 66,* 616–623.

Carter, M. M., Hollon, S. D., Carson, R., & Shelton, R. C. (1995). Effects of a safe person on induced distress following a biological challenge in panic disorder with agoraphobia. *Journal of Abnormal Psychology, 104,* 156–163.

Cartwright, R. (2004). Sleepwalking violence: A sleep disorder, a legal dilemma, and a psychological challenge. *American Journal of Psychiatry, 161,* 1149–1158.

Cartwright, S. (1967). "A report on the diseases and peculiarities of the Negro race" (1851). *DeBow's Review, Southern and Western States, 11* (New Orleans). Reprint New York: AMS Press.

Cash, R. (1998). Losing it? *Essence, 28,* pp. 34–37.

Castellanos, F. X., Giedd, J. N., Berquin, P. C., & Walter, J. M. (2001). Quantitative brain magnetic resonance imaging in girls with attention-deficit/hyperactive disorder. *Archives of General Psychiatry, 58,* 289–295.

Castle, D. J., & Murray, R. M. (1993). The epidemiology of late-onset schizophrenia. *Schizophrenia Bulletin, 22,* 691–699.

Catapano, F., Sperandeo, R., Perris, F., Lanzaro, M., & Maj, M. (2001). Insight and resistance in patients with obsessive-compulsive disorder. *Psychopathology, 34,* 62–69.

Catz, S. L., Kelly, J. A., Bogart, L. M., Benotsch, E. G., & McAuliffe, T. L. (2000). Patterns, correlates, and barriers to medication adherence among persons prescribed new treatments for HIV disease. *Healthy Psychology, 19,* 124–133.

Cauffman, E., & Steinberg, L. (1996). Interactive effects of menarcheal status and dating on dieting and disordered eating among adolescent girls. *Developmental Psychology, 32,* 631–635.

Cautela, J. R. (1966). Treatment of compulsive behavior by covert sensitization. *Psychological Record, 16,* 33–41.

Centers for Disease Control and Prevention. (1999). *Suicide deaths and rates per 100,000.* Retrieved from http://www.cdc.gov/ncipc/data/us9794/suic.htm

Centers for Disease Control and Prevention. (2003). *Chronic fatigue syndrome.* Retrieved November 14, 2004, from http://www.cdc.gov/ncidod/diseases/cfs/info.htm

Cesaroni, L., & Garber, M. (1991). Exploring the experience of autism through firsthand accounts. *Journal of Autism and Developmental Disorders, 21,* 303–313.

Chadwick, P., & Birchwood, M. (1994). The omnipotence of voices: A cognitive approach to auditory hallucinations. *British Journal of Psychiatry, 164,* 190–201.

Chadwick, P., Sambrooke, S., Rasch, S., & Davies, E. (2000). Challenging the omnipotence of voices: Group cognitive behavior therapy for voices. *Behaviour Research and Therapy, 38,* 993–1003.

Chamberlain, P., & Reid, J. B. (1998). Comparison of two community alternatives to incarceration for chronic juvenile offenders. *Journal of Consulting and Clinical Psychology, 6,* 624–633.

Chamberlain, P., & Rosicky, J. G. (1995). The effectiveness of family therapy in the treatment of adolescents with conduct disorders and delinquency. *Journal of Marital and Family Therapy, 21,* 441–459.

Chambless, D. L., Baker, M. J., Baucom, D. H., Beurtler, L.E., et al. (1998). Update on empirically validated therapies: II. *Clinical Psychologist, 51,* 3–16.

Chambless, D. L., & Hollon, S. D. (1998). Defining empirically supported therapies. *Journal of Consulting and Clinical Psychology, 66,* 7–18.

Chambless, D. M. (1993). Division 12 Board of Clinical Psychology, Task force on Promotion and Dissemination of Psychological Procedures. *Report adopted by the Division 12 Board—October 1993.* Unpublished document.

Chapey, R. (1994). Assessment of language disorders in adults. In

R. Chapey (Ed.), *Language intervention strategies in adult aphasia* (pp. 80–120). Baltimore: Williams & Wilkins.

Chapman, L. J., & Chapman, J. P. (1967). Genesis of popular but erroneous psychodiagnostic observations. *Journal of Abnormal Psychology, 72,* 193–204.

Charman, I., Swettenham, J., Baron-Cohen, S., Cox, A., et al. (1997). Infants with autism: An investigation of empathy, pretend play, joint attention and imitation. *Developmental Psychology, 33,* 781–789.

Chassin, L. C., Pillow, D. R., Curran, P. J., Molina, B. S., & Berrera, M. (1993). Relation of parental alcoholism to early adolescent substance use: A test of three mediating mechanisms. *Journal of Abnormal Psychology, 102,* 3–19.

Chen, E., Bloomberg, G. R., Fisher, E. B., & Strunk, R. C. (2003). Predictors of repeat hospitalizations in children with asthma: The role of psychosocial and socioenvironmental factors. *Health Psychology, 22,* 12–18.

Chen, H., Zhang, S., Hernan, M., Schwarzschild, M., et al. (2003). Nonsteroidal anti-inflammatory drugs and the risk of Parkinson disease. *Archives of Neurology, 60,* 1059–1064.

Chiles, J. A., Lambert, M. J., & Hatch, A. L. (1999). The impact of psychological interventions on medical cost offset: A meta-analytic review. *Clinical Psychology: Science and Practice, 6,* 204–220.

Chobanian, A. V., Bakris, G. L., Black, H. R., Cushman, W. C., et al. (2003). Seventh report of the Joint National Committee on Prevention, Detection, Evaluation, and Treatment of High Blood Pressure. *Hypertension, 42,* 1206–1274.

Chodoff, P. (1987). Letter to the editor. *American Journal of Psychiatry, 144,* 124.

Choi, P. Y. L., Pope, H. G., Jr., Olivardia, R., & Cash, T. F. (2002). Muscle dysphoria: A new syndrome in weightlifters. *British Journal of Sports Medicine, 36,* 375–377.

Chollar, S. (1988). Food for thought. *Psychology Today, 22,* 30–34.

Christenfeld, N., Gerin, W., Linden, W., Sanders, M., et al. (1997). Support effort effects on cardiovascular reactivity: Is a stranger as effective as a friend? *Psychosomatic Medicine, 59,* 388–398.

Christensen, L., & Duncan, K. (1995). Distinguishing depressed from nondepressed individuals using energy and psychosocial variables. *Journal of Consulting and Clinical Psychology, 63,* 495–498.

Christiansen, S. C., Martin, S. B., Schleicher, N. C., Koziol, J. A., & Zuraw, B. L. (1996). Current prevalence of asthma-related symptoms in San Diego's predominantly Hispanic inner-city children. *Journal of Asthma, 33,* 17–26.

Christopherson, E. R., & Mortweet, S. L. (2001). *Treatments that work with children.* Washington, DC: American Psychological Association.

Chua, S. E., & McKenna, P. J. (1995). Schizophrenia: A brain disease? A critical review of structural and functional cerebral abnormality in the disorder. *British Journal of Psychiatry, 166,* 563–582.

Chun, K. M., Eastman, K. L., Wang, G. C. S. & Sue, S. (1998). In N. W. S. Zane & L. C. Lee (Eds.), *Handbook of Asian American Psychology* (pp. 457–483), Thousand Oaks, CA: Sage.

Chung, R., & Okazaki, S. (1991). Counseling Americans of Southeast Asian descent: The impact of the refugee experience. In C. C. Lee & B. L. Richardson (Eds.), *Multicultural issues in counseling: New approaches to diversity* (pp. 107–126). Alexandria, VA: American Association for Counseling and Development.

Cinciripini, P. M., Lapitsky, L., Seay, S., Wallfisch, A., et al. (1995). The effects of smoking schedules on cessation outcome: Can we improve on common methods of gradual and abrupt nicotine withdrawal? *Journal of Consulting and Clinical Psychology, 63,* 388–400.

Clark, D. A. (1997). Twenty years of cognitive assessment: Current status and future directions. *Journal of Consulting and Clinical Psychology, 65,* 966–1000.

Clark, D. C., & Fawcett, J. (1992). Review of empirical risk factors for evaluation of the suicidal patient. In B. Bongar (Ed.), *Suicide: Guidelines for assessment, management, and treatment.* New York: Oxford University Press.

Clark, D. M. (1996). Panic disorder: From theory to therapy. In P. M. Salkovskis (Ed.), *Frontiers of cognitive therapy* (pp. 318–344). New York: Guilford Press.

Clark, M., Gosnell, M., Witherspoon, J., Huck, J., et al. (1984, December 3). A slow death of the mind. *Newsweek,* pp. 56–62.

Clarke, M. A., Bray, M. A., Kehle, T. J., & Truscott, S. D. (2001). A school-based intervention designed to reduce the frequency of tics in children with Tourette syndrome. *School Psychology Review, 30,* 11–22.

Clarke, A. D. B., & Clarke, A. M. (1987). Research on mental handicap, 1957–1958: A selective review. *Journal of Mental Deficiency Research, 31,* 317–328.

Clarkin, J. F., Hurt, S. W., & Mattis, S. (1999). Psychological and neurological assessment. In R. E. Hales, S. C. Yudofsky & J. A. Talbott (Eds.), *Textbook of psychiatry* (pp. 253–280). Washington, DC: American Psychiatric Press.

Clarkin, J. F., & Levy, K. N. (2004). The influence of client variables on psychotherapy. In M. J. Lambert (Ed.), *Bergin and Garfield's handbook of psychotherapy and behavior change* (pp. 194–226). New York: Wiley.

Clarkin, J. F., Marziali, E., & Munroe-Blum, H. (1991). Group and family treatments for borderline personality disorder. *Hospital and Community Psychiatry, 42,* 1038–1043.

Classen, C., Koopman, C., Hales, R., & Spiegel, D. (1998). Acute stress disorder as a predictor of posttraumatic stress symptoms. *American Journal of Psychiatry, 155,* 620–624.

Clay, R. A. (1997, April). Is assisted suicide ever a rational choice? *APA Monitor, 28,* 1, 43.

Clay, R. A. (2001). Marijuana youth treatment study produces promising results. *SAMHSA News, 9*(1), 17–19.

Cleckley, J. (1976). *The mask of sanity* (5th ed.). St. Louis, MO: Mosby.

Clemmensen, L. H. (1990). The "real-life test" for surgical candidates. In R. Blanchard & B. W. Steiner (Eds.), *Clinical management of gender identity disorders in children and adults* (pp. 119–136). Washington, DC: American Psychiatric Press.

Cloitre, M., Shear, M. K., Cancienne, J., & Zeitlin, S. B. (1994). Implicit and explicit memory for catastrophic associations to bodily sensation words in panic disorder. *Cognitive Therapy and Research, 18,* 225–240.

Clomipramine Collaborative Study Group. (1991). Clomipramine in the treatment of patients with obsessive-compulsive disorder. *Archives of General Psychiatry, 48,* 730–738.

Cloninger, C. R., Reich, T., Sigvardsson, S., von Knorring, A. L., & Bohman, M. (1986). The effects of changes in alcohol use between generations or the inheritance of alcohol abuse. In American Psychological Association (Ed.), *Alcoholism: A medical disorder: Proceedings of the 76th Annual Meeting of the American Psychological Association.*

Clothier, M. (1998, July 29). Exorcising the ghosts of war battle simulations: Virtually Better helps Vietnam vets face the past. *Atlanta Constitution,* p. D4.

Coffman, J. A. (1989). Computed tomography in psychiatry. In N. C. Andreasen (Ed.), *Brain imaging: Applications in psychiatry* (pp. 1–65). Washington, DC: American Psychiatric Press.

Cohen, A. M., & Weiner, W. J. (Eds.) (1994). *The comprehensive management of Parkinson's disease.* New York: Demos Publications.

Cohen, F. L., Nehring, W. M., & Cloninger, I. (1996). Symptom description and management in narcolepsy. *Holistic Nursing Practice, 10,* 44–53.

Cohen, M. J., Rickles, W. H., & McArthur, D. L. (1978). Evidence for physiological response stereotypy in migraine headaches. *Psychosomatic Medicine, 40,* 344–354.

Cohen, S., Frank, E., Doyle, W. J., Skoner, D. P., et al. (1998). Types of stressors that increase susceptibility in the common cold in healthy adults. *Health Psychology, 17,* 214–223.

Cohen, S., & Herbert, T. B. (1996). Health psychology: Psychological factors and physical disease from the perspective of human psychoneuroimmunology. *Annual Review of Psychology, 47,* 113–123.

Cohen, S., & Rodriguez, M. S. (1995). Pathways linking affective disturbances and physical disorders. *Health Psychology, 14,* 374–380.

Cohn, L. D., Adler, N. E., Irwin, C. E., Jr., Millstein, S. G., et al. (1987). Body-figure preferences in male and female adolescents. *Journal of Abnormal Psychology, 96,* 276–279.

Cole, D. A. (2004). Taxometrics in psychopathology research: An introduction to some of the procedures and related methodological issues. *Journal of Abnormal Psychology, 113,* 3–9.

Cole, S. W., Kemeny, M. E., & Taylor, S. E. (1997). Social identity and physical health: Accelerated HIV progression in rejection-sensitive gay men. *Journal of Personality and Social Psychology, 72,* 320–335.

Cole, S. W., Kemeny, M. E., Taylor, S. E., & Visscher, B. R. (1996). Elevated physical health risk among gay men who conceal their homosexual identity. *Health Psychology, 15,* 243–251.

Coleman, E. (1992). Is your patient suffering from compulsive sexual behavior? *Psychiatric Annals, 22*(6), 320–425.

Collins, K. O., & Comer, J. B. (2003). Maternal haloperidol treatment associated with dyskinesia in a newborn. *American Journal of Health System Pharmacology, 60,* 2253–2255.

Colon, E. A., Callies, A. L., Popkin, M. K., & McGlave, P. B. (1991). Depressed mood and other variables related to bone marrow transplantation survival in acute leukemia. *Psychosomatics, 32,* 420–425.

Colt, G. H., & Hollister, A. (1998, April). Were you born that way? *Life,* pp. 39–48.

Comings, D. E., Comings, B. G., Muhleman, G., Dietz, B., et al. (1991). The dopamine D2 receptor locus as a modifying gene in neuropsychiatric disorders. *Journal of the American Medical Association, 266,* 1793–1800.

Compas, B. E., Haaga, D. A. F., Keefe, F. J., Leitenberg, H., & Williams, D. A. (1998). Sampling of empirically supported psychological treatments from health psychology: Smoking, chronic pain, cancers, and bulimia nervosa. *Journal of Consulting and Clinical Psychology, 66,* 89–112.

Conger, J. J. (1951). The effects of alcohol on conflict behavior in the albino rat. *Quarterly Journal of Studies on Alcohol, 12,* 129.

Conn, D. K. (1991). Delirium and other organic mental disorders. In J. Sadavoy, L. W. Lazarus, & L. F. Jarvik (Eds.), *Comprehensive review of geriatric psychiatry* (pp. 11–336). Washington, DC: American Psychiatric Press.

Conners, M. E., & Morse, W. (1993). Sexual abuse and eating disorders: A review. *International Journal of Eating Disorders, 13,* 1–11.

Consensus Development Panel. (1982). Defined diets and childhood hyperactivity. *Clinical Pediatrics, 21,* 627–630.

Cook, C. A. L., Guerrerio, J. F., & Slater, V. E. (2004). Healing touch and the quality of life in women receiving radiation treatment for cancer: A randomized controlled trial. *Alternative Therapies in Health and Medicine, 10,* 34–41.

Cook, E. H., Jr. (1998). Genetics of autism. *Mental Retardation and Developmental Disabilities Research Reviews, 4,* 113–120.

Cook, E. W., III, Hodes, R. L., & Lang, P. J. (1986). Preparedness and phobia: Effects of stimulus content on human visceral conditioning. *Journal of Abnormal Psychology, 95,* 195–207.

Cooke, D. J., & Michie, C. (2001). Refining the construct of psychopathy: Towards a hierarchical model. *Psychological Assessment, 13,* 171–188.

Cooney, N. L., Litt, M. D., Morse, P. A., Bauer, L. O., & Gaupp, L. (1997). Alcohol cue reactivity, negative-mood reactivity, and relapse in treated alcoholic men. *Journal of Abnormal Psychology, 106,* 243–250.

Coons, P. M. (1986). Treatment progress in twenty patients with multiple personality disorder. *Journal of Nervous and Mental Disease, 174,* 715–721.

Coons, P. M. (1988). Misuse of forensic hypnosis: A hypnotically elicited false confession with the apparent creation of a multiple personality. *International Journal of Clinical and Experimental Hypnosis, 36,* 1–11.

Coons, P. M. (1994). Confirmation of childhood abuse in child and adolescent cases of multiple personality disorder and dissociative disorder not otherwise specified. *Journal of Nervous and Mental Disease, 182,* 461–464.

Coons, P. M., & Bowman, E. S. (1993). Dissociation and eating. *American Journal of Psychiatry, 150,* 171–172.

Coons, P. M., Milstein, V., & Marley, C. (1982). EEG studies of two multiple personalities and a control. *Archives of General Psychiatry, 39,* 823–825.

Cooper, A., & McCormack, W. A. (1992). Short-term group treatment for adult children of alcoholics. *Journal of Counseling Psychology, 39,* 350–355.

Cooper, A. J. (1969). A clinical study of coital anxiety in male potency disorders. *Journal of Psychosomatic Research, 13,* 143–147.

Cooper, J. E., Kendell, R. E., Gurland, B. J., Sharp, L., et al. (1972). *Psychiatric diagnosis in New York and London.* Maudsley Monograph Series No. 20. London: Oxford University Press.

Cooper, J. R., Bloom, F. E., & Roth, R. H. (1986). *The biochemical basis of neuropharmacology* (5th ed.). New York: Oxford University Press.

Cooper, M. L., Russell, M., & George, W. H. (1988). Coping, expectancies, and alcohol abuse: A test of social learning formulations. *Journal of Abnormal Psychology, 97,* 218–230.

Copolov, D. L., Mackinnon, A., & Trauer, T. (2004). Correlates of the affective impact of auditory hallucinations in psychotic disorders. *Schizophrenic Bulletin, 30,* 163–169.

Corbitt, E. M., & Widiger, T. A. (1995). Sex differences among the personality disorders: An exploration of the data. *Clinical Psychology: Science and Practice, 2,* 225–238.

Cordova, M. J., Cunningham, L. L. C., Carlson, C. R., & Andrykowski, M. A. (2001). Social constraints, cognitive processing, and adjustment to breast cancer. *Journal of Consulting and Clinical Psychology, 69,* 706–711.

Corey, G. (2001). *Theory and practice of counseling and psychotherapy* (6th ed.). Belmont, CA: Brooks/Cole.

Corey, G. (2004). *Theory and practice of group counseling* (6th ed.). Belmont, CA: Brooks Cole.

Corey, G. (2005). *Theory and practice of counseling and psychotherapy* (7th ed.). Belmont, CA: Brooks Cole.

Corey, G., Corey, M. S., & Callanan, P. (1998). *Issues and ethics in the helping professions.* Pacific Grove, CA: Brooks/Cole.

Corey, G., Corey, M. S., & Callanan, P. (2003). *Issues and ethics in the helping professions* (6th ed.). Pacific Grove, CA: Brooks Cole.

Corin, E. (1998). The thickness of being: Intentional worlds, strategies of identity, and experience among schizophrenics. *Psychiatry, 61,* 133–146.

Cormier, J. F., & Thelen, M. H. (1998). Professional skepticism of multiple personality disorder. *Professional Psychology: Research and Practice, 29,* 163–167.

Cormier, W. H., & Cormier, L. S. (1998). *Interviewing strategies for helpers: Fundamental skills and cognitive behavioral interventions* (4th ed.). Pacific Grove, CA: Brooks Cole.

Cornelius, J. R., Salloum, I. M., Mezzich, J., Cornelius, M. D., et al. (1995). Disproportionate suicidality in patients with comorbid major depression and alcoholism. *American Journal of Psychiatry, 152,* 358–364.

Corsini, R. J., & Wedding, D. (1995). *Current psychotherapies.* Itasca, IL: Peacock.

Cosand, B. J., Bourque, L. B., & Kraus, J. F. (1982). Suicide among adolescents in Sacramento County, California 1950–1979. *Adolescence, 17,* 917–930.

Cottone, R. R. (1992). *Theories and paradigms of counseling and psychotherapy.* Boston: Allyn & Bacon.

Council on Scientific Affairs. (1985). Scientific status of refreshing recollection by the use of hypnosis. *Journal of the American Medical Association, 253,* 1918–1923.

Courchesne, E. (1995). New evidence of cerebellar and brainstem hypoplasia in autistic infants, children, and adolescents: The MR imaging study by Hashimoto and colleagues. *Journal of Autism and Developmental Disorders, 25,* 19–22.

Courchesne, I., Yeung-Courchesne, R., Press, G. A., Hesselink, J. R.,

& Jernigan, T. L. (1988). Hypoplasia of cerebellar vermal lobules VI and VII in autism. *New England Journal of Medicine, 318,* 1349–1354.

Coursey, R. D., Alford, J., & Safarjan, B. (1997). Significant advances in understanding and treating serious mental illness. *Professional Psychology: Research and Practice, 28,* 205–216.

Coursey, R. D., Keller, A. B., & Farrell, E. W. (1995). Individual psychotherapy and persons with serious mental illness: The clients' perspective. *Schizophrenia Bulletin, 21,* 283–299.

Cousins, N. (1979). *Anatomy of an illness.* New York: Norton.

Cowley, G. (1990, February 12). Hanging up the knife. *Newsweek,* pp. 58–59.

Cowley, G. (1995). Blind to other minds. *Newsweek,* August 14, p. 67

Cowley, G., & Underwood, A. (1997, May 26). Why Ebonie can't breathe. *Newsweek,* 58–63.

Cox, B. J., Fergus, K. D., & Swinson, R. P. (1994). Patient satisfaction with behavioral treatments for panic disorder with agoraphobia. *Journal of Anxiety Disorders, 8,* 193–206.

Cox, D. J., & McMahon, B. (1978). Incidence of male exhibitionism in the United States as reported by victimized college students. *International Journal of Law and Psychiatry, 1,* 453–457.

Cox, W. M., & Klinger, E. (1988). A motivational model of alcohol use. *Journal of Abnormal Psychology, 97,* 168–180.

Coyne, J. C. (1976). Depression and the response of others. *Journal of Abnormal Psychology, 85,* 186–193.

Craig, M. E. (1990). Coercive sexuality in dating relationships: A situational model. *Clinical Psychology Review, 10,* 395–424.

Craik, F. I. (1994). Memory changes in normal aging. *Current Directions in Psychological Science, 3,* 155–158.

Crandall, C. S., Preisler, J. J., & Aussprung, J. (1992). Measuring life event stress in the lives of college students: The Undergraduate Stress Questionnaire (USQ). *Journal of Behavioral Medicine, 15,* 627–662.

Craufurd, D. (1994). Molecular biology of Huntington's Disease. In F. Owen & R. Itzhaki (Eds.), *Molecular and cell biology of neuropsychiatric diseases* (pp. 1–24). New York: Chapman and Hall.

Crespo-Facorro, B., Paradiso, S., Andreasen, N. C., O'Leary, D. S., et al. (2001). Neural mechanisms of anhedonia in schizophrenia: A PET study of response to unpleasant and pleasant odors. *Journal of the American Medical Association, 286,* 427–435.

Crimlisk, H. L., Bhatia, K., Cope, H., & David, A. (1998). Slater revisited: Six-year follow-up study of patients with medically unexplained motor symptoms. *British Medical Journal, 316,* 582–586.

Crits-Christoph, P. (1992). The efficacy of brief dynamic psychotherapy: A meta-analysis. *American Journal of Psychiatry, 149,* 151–158.

Cronkite, R. C., Moos, R. H., Twohey, J., Cohen, C., & Swindle, R., Jr. (1998). Life circumstances and personal resources as predictors of the ten-year course of depression. *American Journal of Community Psychology, 26,* 255–280.

Croteau, J. M., Lark, J. S., Lidderdale, M. A., & Chung, Y. B. (2005). *Deconstructing heterosexism in the counseling professions.* Thousand Oaks, CA: Sage.

Crowson, J. J., & Cromwell, R. L. (1995). Depressed and normal individuals differ both in selection and in perceived tonal quality of positive-negative messages. *Journal of Abnormal Psychology, 104,* 305–311.

Cruess, D. G., Antoni, M. H., Schneiderman, N., Ironson, G., et al. (2000). Cognitive-behavioral stress management increases free testosterone and decreases psychological distress in HIV-seropositive men. *Health Psychology, 19,* 12–20.

Cruz, I. Y., & Dunn, M. E. (2003). Lowering risk for early alcohol use by challenging alcohol expectancies in elementary school children. *Journal of Consulting and Clinical Psychology, 71,* 493–503.

Cummings, J. L., Trimble, M. R., & Hales, R. E. (1999). Clinical neuropsychiatry. In R. E. Hales, S. C. Yudofsky & J. A. Talbott (Eds.), *Textbook of psychiatry* (pp. 1667–1691). Washington, DC: American Psychiatric Press.

Cummings, N. A. (1995). Behavioral health after managed care: The next golden opportunity for professional psychology. *Register Report, 20,* 1, 30–33.

Cumsille, P. E., Sayer, A. G., & Graham, J. W. (2000). Perceived exposure to peer and adult drinking as predictors of growth in positive alcohol expectancies during adolescence. *Journal of Consulting and Clinical Psychology, 68,* 531–536.

Curran, P. J., Stice, E., & Chassin, L. (1997). The relation between adolescent alcohol use and peer alcohol use: A longitudinal random coefficients model. *Journal of Consulting and Clinical Psychology, 65,* 130–140.

Curry, V. (2001, May 20). School shooting affects students after three years. *Columbian,* p. C3.

Cutting, L. P., & Docherty, N. M. (2000). Schizophrenia outpatients' perceptions of their parents: Is expressed emotion a factor? *Journal of Abnormal Psychology, 109,* 266–272.

Cypress, B. K. (1980). *Characteristics of visits to female and male physicians: The national ambulatory medical care survey, 1977.* Hyattsville, MD: National Center for Health Statistics.

Cytryn, L., & McKnew, D. H., Jr. (1996). *Growing up sad: Childhood depression and its treatment.* New York: Norton.

Dahl, R. E. (1992). The pharmacologic treatment of sleep disorders. *Psychiatric Clinical America, 15,* 161–178.

Dahlstrom, W. G., & Welsh, G. S. (1965). *An MMPI handbook.* Minneapolis: University of Minnesota Press.

Daigneault, S. D. (2000). Body talk: A school-based group intervention for working with disordered eating behaviors. *Journal for Specialists in Group Work, 25,* 191–213.

Daley, S. E., Burge, D., & Hammen, C. (2000). Borderline personality disorder symptoms as predictors of four-year romantic relationship dysfunction in young women: Addressing issues of specificity. *Journal of Abnormal Psychology, 109,* 451–460.

Dammeyer, M. D., Nightingale, N. N., & McCoy, M. L. (1997). Repressed memory and other controversial origins of sexual abuse allegations: Beliefs among psychologists and clinical social workers. *Child Maltreatment, 2,* 252–263.

Dana, R. H. (1998). *Understanding cultural identity in intervention and assessment.* Thousand Oaks, CA: Sage.

Dana, R. H. (2000). Psychological assessment in the diagnosis and treatment of ethnic group members. In J. F. Aponte & J. Wohl (Eds.), *Psychological interventions and cultural diversity* (2nd ed., pp. 59–74). Boston: Allyn & Bacon.

Danto, B. L. (1971, Fall). Assessment of the suicidal person in the telephone interview. *Bulletin of Suicidology,* 48–56.

Dar, R., Rish, S., Hermesh, H., Taub, M., & Fux, M. (2000). Realism of confidence in obsessive-compulsive checkers. *Journal of Abnormal Psychology, 109,* 673–678.

Dardick, H. (2004, February 13). Psychiatric patient tells of ordeal in treatment. *Chicago Tribune,* p. 1.

Darrach, D. (1976, March 8). Poetry and poison. *Time.*

Dassori, A. M., Miller, A. L., & Saldana, D. (1995). Schizophrenia among Hispanics: Epidemiology, phenomenology, course, and outcome. *Schizophrenia Bulletin, 21,* 303–310.

Davey, G. C. L., McDonald, A. S., Hirisave, U., Prabhu, G. G., et al. (1998). A cross-cultural study of animal fears. *Behaviour Research and Therapy, 36,* 735–750.

Davidson, J., Allen, J. G., & Smith W. H. (1987). Complexities in the hospital treatment of a patient with multiple personality disorder. *Bulletin of the Menninger Clinic, 51,* 561–568.

Davidson, J. R. T. (2000). Pharmacotherapy of posttraumatic stress disorder: Treatment options, long-term follow-up and predictors of outcome. *Journal of Clinical Psychiatry, 61,* 52–56.

Davidson, J. R. T. (2001). Pharmacotherapy of generalized anxiety disorder. *Journal of Clinical Psychiatry, 62,* 46–50.

Davidson, J. R. T., Foa, E. B., Huppert, J. D., Keefe, F. J., et al. (2004). Fluoxetine, comprehensive cognitive behavioral therapy, and placebo in generalized social phobia. *Archives of General Psychiatry, 61,* 1005–1013.

Davidson, K., Hall, P., & MacGregor, M. (1997). Gender differences in the relation between interview-derived hostility scores and resting blood pressure. *Journal of Behavioral Medicine, 19,* 185–201.

Davis, J. D. (1983). Slaying the psychoanalytic dragon: An integrationist's commentary on Yates. *British Journal of Clinical Psychology, 22,* 133–134.

Davis, K. L., Kahn, R. S., & Ko, G. (1991). Dopamine in schizophrenia: A review and reconceptualization, *American Journal of Psychiatry, 148,* 1474–1486.

Davis, M. C., Mathews, K. A., Meilahn, E. N., & Kiss, J. E. (1995). Are job characteristics related to fibrinogen levels in middle-aged women? *Health Psychology, 14,* 310–318.

Davis, P. J., & Gibson, M. G. (2000). Recognition of posed and genuine facial expressions of emotion in paranoid and nonparanoid schizophrenia. *Journal of Abnormal Psychology, 109,* 445–450.

Davison, G. C., Williams, M. E., Nezami, E., Bice, T. L., & DeQuattro, V. (1991). Relaxation, reduction in angry articulated thoughts, and improvements in borderline essential hypertension and heart rate. *Journal of Behavioral Medicine, 14,* 453–468.

Dawson, G., & Castelloe, P. (1992). Autism. In C. E. Walker (Ed.), *Clinical psychology: Historical and research foundations.* New York: Plenum.

Day, S. X. (2004). *Theory and design in counseling and psychotherapy.* Boston: Houghton Mifflin.

de Jong, G. M., Timmerman, I. G. H., & Emmelkamp, P. M. G. (1996). The survey of recent life experience: A psychometric evaluation. *Journal of Behavioral Medicine, 19,* 529–542.

de Jong, P. J., Vorage, I., & van den Hout, M. A. (2000). Counterconditioning in the treatment of spider phobia: Effects on disgust, fear and valence. *Behaviour Research and Therapy, 38,* 1055–1069.

Dekker, J. (1993). Inhibited male orgasm. In W. O'Donohue & J. H. Geer (Eds.), *Handbook of sexual dysfunctions: Assessment and treatment* (pp. 279–301). Boston: Allyn & Bacon.

Delgado, P. L., & Gelenberg, A. J. (2001). Antidepressant and antimanic medications. In G. O. Gabbard (Ed.), *Treatment of psychiatric disorders* (pp. 1137–1179). Washington, DC: American Psychiatric Press.

DeLisi, L. E., Maurizio, A., Yost, M., Papparozzi, C. F., et al. (2003). A survey of New Yorkers after the Sept. 11, 2001, terrorist attacks. *American Journal of Psychiatry, 160,* 780–783.

Demaray, M. K., & Malecki, C. K. (2003). Perceptions of the frequency and importance of social support by students classified as victims, bullies, and bully/victims in an urban middle school. *School Psychology Review, 32,* 471–489.

Denisoff, E., & Endler, N. S. (2000). Life experiences, coping, and weight preoccupation in young adult women. *Canadian Journal of Behavioural Science, 32,* 97–103.

Dent, C. W., Sussman, S., Stacy, A. W., Craig, S., et al. (1995). Two-year behavior outcomes of Project Towards No Tobacco Use. *Journal of Consulting and Clinical Psychology, 63,* 676–677.

Dent, J., & Teasdale, J. D. (1988). Negative cognition and the persistence of depression. *Journal of Abnormal Psychology, 97,* 29–34.

Department of Health and Human Services. (1999). *Mental health: A report of the Surgeon General.* Rockville, MD: Author.

Depressing research. (2004). *Lancet, 363,* 1335.

Desmond, S., Price, J., Hallinan, C., & Smith, D. (1989). Black and White adolescents' perceptions of their weight. *Journal of School Health, 59,* 353–358.

des Portes, V., Hagerman, R. J., & Hendren, R.L. (2003). Pharmacotherapy. In S. Ozonoff, S. J. Rogers, & R. L. Hendren (Eds.), *Autism spectrum disorders: A research review for practitioners* (pp. 161–186). Arlington, VA: American Psychiatric.

Deutsch, A. (1949). *The mentally ill in America* (2nd ed.). New York: Columbia University Press.

DeVellis, B. M., & Blalock, S. J. (1992). Illness attributions and hopelessness depression: The role of hopelessness expectancy. *Journal of Abnormal Psychology, 101,* 257–264.

Devinsky, O. (1994). *A guide to understanding and living with epilepsy.* Philadelphia: F. A. Davis.

DeWaal, M. W. M., Arnold, I. A., Eekhof, J. A. H., & Van Hemert, A. M. (2004). Somatoform disorders in general practice. *British Journal of Psychiatry, 184,* 470–476.

Dewsbury, D. A. (1991). Psychobiology. *American Psychologist, 46,* 198–205.

Diaz-Asper, C. M., Schretlen, D. J., & Pearlson, G. D. (2004). Should clinicians use intelligence as a means of estimating expected neuropsychological test performance? *Journal of the International Neuropsychological Society, 10,* 82–90.

Dick, D. M., & Rose, R. J. (2002). Behavior genetics: What's new? What's next? *Current Directions in Psychological Science, 11,* 70–74.

Dick-Barnes, M., Nelson, R. O., & Aine, C. J. (1987). Behavioral measure of multiple personality: The case of Margaret. *Journal of Behavior Therapy and Experimental Psychiatry, 18,* 229–239.

Dickerson, S. S., & Kemeny, M. E. (2004). Acute stressors and cortisol responses: A theoretical integration and synthesis of laboratory research. *Psychological Bulletin, 130,* 355–391.

Dickey, R., & Steiner, B. (1990). Hormone treatment and surgery. In R. Blanchard & B. W. Steiner (Eds.), *Clinical management of gender identity disorders in children and adults* (pp. 137–158). Washington, DC: American Psychiatric Press.

Diekstra, R. F. (1990). Suicidal behavior in adolescents and young adults: The international picture. *Crisis, 10,* 16–35.

Diekstra, R. F., Kienhorst, C. W. M., & de Wilde, E. J. (1995). Suicide and suicidal behaviour among adolescents. In M. Rutter & D. J. Smith (Eds.), *Psychological disorders in young people.* Chichester, England: Wiley.

Di Gallo, A., Barton, J., & Parry-Jones, W. L., (1997). Road traffic accidents: Early psychological consequences in children and adolescents, *British Journal of Psychiatry, 170,* 358–363.

DiMatteo, M. R., Lepper, H. S., & Croghan, T. W. (2000). Depression is a risk factor for noncompliance with medical treatment. *Archives of Internal Medicine, 160,* 2101–2107.

Dingfelder, S. (2004). Treatment for the "untreatable." *Monitor on Psychology, 35,* 46–49.

Diokno, A. C., Brown, M. B., & Herzog, A. R. (1990). Sexual function in the elderly. *Archives of Internal Medicine, 150,* 197–200.

Dirmann, T. (2003, September 8). Ex-Spice Girl Geri Halliwell: How I beat my eating disorder. *US Weekly,* 60.

Dishion, T. J., McCord, J., & Poulin, F. (1999). When interventions harm: Peer groups and problem behavior. *American Psychologist, 54,* 755–764.

Dittmann, M. (2003). Fighting ageism. *Monitor on Psychology, 34,* 50–52.

Dodrill, C. B., & Matthews, C. G. (1992). The role of neuropsychology in the assessment and treatment of persons with epilepsy. *American Psychologist, 47,* 1139–1142.

Dogden, D. (2000). Science policy and the protection of children. *American Psychologist, 55,* 1034–1035.

Dollinger, S. J. (1983). A case of dissociative neurosis (depersonalization disorder) in an adolescent treated with family therapy and behavior modification. *Journal of Consulting and Clinical Psychology, 15,* 479–484.

Donenberg, G., & Baker, B. L. (1993). The impact of young children with externalizing behaviors on their families. *Journal of Abnormal Child Psychology, 21,* 179–198.

Dong, Q., Yang, B., & Ollendick, T. H. (1994). Fears in Chinese children and adolescents and their relations to anxiety and depression. *Journal of Child Psychology and Psychiatry, 35,* 351–363.

Donnerstein, E., & Linz, D. (1986). Mass media sexual violence and male viewers. *American Behavioral Scientist, 29,* 601–618.

Dorken, H., Stapp, J., & VandenBos, G. (1986). Licensed psychologists: A decade of major growth. In H. Dorken & Associates (Eds.), *Professional psychology in transition: Meeting today's challenge* (pp. 3–19). San Francisco: Jossey-Bass.

Draguns, J. G. (1996). Multicultural and cross-cultural assessment: Dilemmas and decisions. In G. R. Sodowsky & J. C. Impara (Eds.), *Multicultural assessment in counseling and clinical psychology* (pp. 37–84). Lincoln, NE: Buros Institute of Mental Measurements.

Drake, R. E., & Ehrlich, J. (1985). Suicide attempts associated with akathisia. *American Journal of Psychiatry, 142,* 499–501.

Drane, J. (1995). Physican-assisted suicide and voluntary active euthanasia: Social ethics and the role of hospice. *American Journal of Hospice and Palliative Care, 12,* 3–10.

Dressler, W. W., Dos Santos, J. E., & Viteri, F. E. (1986). Blood pressure, ethnicity, and psychosocial resources. *Psychosomatic Medicine, 48,* 509–519.

Drobes, D. J., & Tiffany, S. T. (1997). Induction of smoking urge through manual and in vivo procedures: Physiological and self-report manifestations. *Journal of Abnormal Psychology, 106,* 15–25.

Drossman, D. A. (1998). Presidential address: Gastrointestinal illness and the biopsychosocial model. *Psychosomatic Medicine, 60,* 258–267.

Drugs and talk therapy. (2004, October). *Consumer Reports,* 22–29.

Duberstein, P. R., & Conwell, Y. (1997). Personality disorders and completed suicide: A methodological and conceptual review. *Clinical Psychology 4,* 502–504.

Dubovsky, S., Franks, R., Lifschitz, M., & Coen, R. (1982). Effectiveness of verapamil in the treatment of a manic patient. *American Journal of Psychiatry, 139,* 502–504.

Dubovsky, S. L., & Buzan, R. (1999). Mood disorders. In R. E. Hales, S. C. Yudofsky & J. A. Talbott (Eds.), *Textbook of psychiatry* (pp. 479–565). Washington, DC: American Psychiatric Press.

Dugas, M. J., & Ladouceur, R. (2000). Treatment of GAD: Targeting intolerance of uncertainty in two types of worry. *Behavior Modification, 24,* 635–657.

Dunivin, D. L., & Orabona, E. (1999). Department of Defense Psychopharmacology Demonstration Project: Fellows' perspective on didactic curriculum. *Professional Psychology: Research and Practice, 30,* 510–518.

DuPaul, G. J., & Barkley, R. A. (1993). Behavioral contributions to psychopharmacology: The utility of behavioral methodology in medication treatment of children with attention deficit hyperactivity disorder. *Behavior Therapy, 24,* 47–65.

Durkheim, E. (1951/1897). *Suicide.* New York: Free Press.

Dutton, J. (1986, September 30). Doctors seek reason for bizarre syndrome. *Bellingham Herald,* p. C1.

Du Verglas, G., Banks, S. R., & Guyer, K. E. (1988). Clinical effects of fenfluramine on children with autism: A review of the research. *Journal of Autism and Developmental Disorders, 18,* 297–308.

Dworkin, S., VonKorff, M., & LeResche, L. (1990). Multiple pains and psychiatric disturbance. *Archives of General Psychiatry, 47,* 239–244.

Dykens, E. M., & Hodapp, R. M. (1997). Treatment issues in genetic mental retardation syndromes. *Professional Psychology: Research and Practice, 28,* 263–270.

Earle, C. C., & Neville, B. A. (2004). Underuse of necessary care among cancer survivors. *Cancer, 101,* 1712–1719.

Eaton, W. W., Holzer, C. E., III, Von Korff, M., Anthony, J. C., et al. (1984). The design of the Epidemiologic Catchment Area surveys. *Archives of General Psychiatry, 41,* 942–948.

Edelbrock, C., Rende, R., Plomin, R., & Thompson, L. A. (1995). A twin study of competence and problem behavior in childhood and adolescence. *Journal of Child Psychology and Psychiatry and Allied Disciplines, 36,* 775–785.

Edman, G., Asberg, M., Levander, S., & Schalling, D. (1986). Skin conductance habituation and cerebrospinal fluid 5-hydroxyindoleactic acid in suicidal patients. *Archives of General Psychiatry, 43,* 586–592.

Edwards, M. S., & Baker, C. J. (1981). Meningitis infections in children. *Journal of Pediatrics, 99,* 540–545.

Edwards, S., & Dickerson, M. (1987). On the similarity of positive and negative intrusions. *Behaviour Research and Therapy, 25,* 207–211.

Efron, R. (1956). The effect of olfactory stimuli in arresting uncinate fits. *Brain, 79,* 267–281.

Efron, R. (1957). The conditioned inhibitions of uncinate fits. *Brain, 80,* 251–262.

Egeland, J. A., Berhard, D. S., Pauls, D. L., Sussex, J. N., et al. (1987). Bipolar affective disorders linked to DNA markers on chromosome 11. *Nature, 325,* 783–787.

Egeland, J. A., & Hostetter, A. M. (1983). Amish study, I: Affective disorders among the Amish. *American Journal of Psychiatry, 140,* 56–61.

Ehlers, A., (1993) Introception and panic disorder. *Advances in Behavioural Research and Therapy, 15,* 3–21.

Ehlers, A., Margraf, J., Roth, W. T., Taylor, C. G., & Birbaumer, N. (1988). Anxiety induced by false heart rate feedback in patients with panic disorder. *Behaviour Research and Therapy, 26,* 1–11.

Eigenmann, P. A., & Haenggeli, C. A. (2004). Food colourings and preservatives: Allergy and hyperactivity. *Lancet, 364,* 9437–9438.

Eisen, A. R., & Silverman, W. K. (1998). Prescriptive treatment for generalized anxiety disorder in children. *Behaviour Therapy, 29,* 105–121.

Eisendrath, A. J. (1996). When Munchausen becomes malingering: Factitious disorder that penetrates the legal system. *Bulletin of the American Academy of Psychiatry and Law, 24,* 471–481.

Ekblad, S. (1990). The children's behaviour questionnaire for completion by parents and teachers in a Chinese sample. *Journal of Child Psychology and Psychiatry, 31,* 775–791.

Elias, M. (1988, August 15). Many lie about AIDS risk. *USA Today,* p. D–1.

Elkin, I. (1994). The NIMH Treatment of Depression Collaborative Research Program: Where we began and where we are. In A. E. Bergin & S. L. Garfield (Eds.), *Handbook of psychotherapy and behavior change* (4th ed., pp. 114–142). New York: Wiley.

Elkin, I., Gibbons, R. D., Shea, M. T., Sotsky, S. M., et al. (1995). Initial severity and differential treatment outcome in the National Institute of Mental Health Treatment of Depression Collaborative Research Program. *Journal of Consulting and Clinical Psychology, 63,* 841–847.

Ellason, J. W., & Ross, C. A. (1997). Two-year follow-up of inpatients with dissociative identity disorder. *American Journal of Psychiatry, 154,* 832–839.

Ellenberger, H. F. (1972). The story of "Anna O.": A critical review with new data. *Journal of the History of the Behavior Sciences, 8,* 267–279.

Ellickson, P. L., Hays, R. D., & Bell, R. M. (1992). Stepping through the drug use sequence: Longitudinal scalogram analysis of initiation and regular use. *Journal of Abnormal Psychology, 101,* 441–451.

Ellingson, R. (1954). Incidence of EEG abnormality among patients with mental disorders of apparently nonorganic origin: A critical review. *American Journal of Psychiatry, 111,* 363–375.

Ellis, A. (1962). *Reason and emotion in psychotherapy.* New York: Stuart.

Ellis, A. (1987). A sadly neglected cognitive element in depression. *Cognitive Therapy and Research, 11,* 121–146.

Ellis, A. (1989). Rational-emotive therapy. In R. J. Corsini & D. Wedding (Eds.), *Current psychotherapies* (pp. 197–238). Itasca, IL: Peacock.

Ellis, A. (1991). Rational-emotive treatment of simple phobias. *Psychotherapy, 28,* 452–456.

Ellis, A. (1997). The evolution of Albert Ellis and rational emotive behavior therapy. In J. K. Zeig (Ed.), *The evolution of psychotherapy: The third conference.* New York: Brunner/Mazel.

Ellis, L., & Ames, M. A. (1987). Neurohormonal functioning and sexual orientation: A theory of homosexuality-heterosexuality. *Psychological Bulletin, 101,* 233–258.

Ely, D. L., & Mostardi, R. A. (1986). The effects of recent life events stress, life assets, and temperament pattern on cardiovascular risk factors for Akron city police officers. *Journal of Human Stress, 12,* 77–91.

Emmelkamp, P. M. G. (1994). Behavior therapy with adults. In A. E. Bergin & S. L. Garfield (Eds.), *Handbook of psychotherapy and behavior change* (pp. 379–427). New York: Wiley.

Emmelkamp, P. M. G. (2004). Behavior therapy with adults. In M. J.

Lambert (Ed.), *Bergin and Garfield's handbook of psychotherapy and behavior change* (5th ed., pp. 393–446). New York: Wiley.

Emmelkamp, P. M. G., & Beens, H. (1991). Cognitive therapy with obsessive-compulsive disorder: A comparative evaluation. *Behaviour Research and Therapy, 29,* 293–300.

Emslie, G. J., & Rosenfeld, A. (1983). Incest reported by children and adolescents hospitalized for severe psychiatric problems. *American Journal of Psychiatry, 140,* 108–111.

Endler, N. (1982). *Holiday of darkness.* New York: Wiley.

Endler, N. (1990). *Holiday of darkness: A psychologist's journey out of his depression* (rev. ed.). Toronto: Wall & Thompson.

Enright, M. F., Welch, B. L., Newman, R., & Perry, B. M. (1990). The hospital: Psychology's challenge in the 1990s. American *Psychologist, 45,* 1057–1058.

Epilepsy Foundation of America. (1983). *Questions and answers about epilepsy.* Landover, MD: Author.

Erdely, S. R. (2004, March). What women sacrifice to be thin. *Redbook,* 114–120.

Erickson, D. J., Wolfe, J., King, D. W., King, L. A., & Sharkansky, E. J. (2001). Traumatic stress disorder and depression symptomatology in a sample of Gulf War veterans: A prospective study. *Journal of Consulting and Clinical Psychology, 69,* 41–49.

Erickson, W. D., Luxenberg, M. G., Walbek, N. H., & Seely, R. K. (1987). Frequency of MMPI two-point code types among sex offenders. *Journal of Consulting and Clinical Psychology, 55,* 566–570.

Erickson, W. D., Walbek, N. H., & Seely, R. K. (1988). Behavior patterns of child molesters. *Archives of Sexual Behavior, 17,* 77–86.

Eriksson, A. S., & de Chateau, P. (1992). Brief report: A girl aged two years and seven months with autistic disorder videotaped from birth. *Journal of Autism and Developmental Disorders, 22,* 127–129.

Erk, R. R. (2000). The framework for increasing understanding and effective treatment of attention-deficit/hyperactive disorder: Predominantly inattentive type. *Journal of Counseling and Development, 78,* 389–399.

Erlenmeyer-Kimling, L., Adamo, U. H., Rock, D., Roberts, S. A., et al. (1997). The New York High-Risk Project. *Archives of General Psychiatry, 54,* 1096–1102.

Ernst, E. (2004). The need for scientific rigor in studies of complementary and alternative medicine. *American Journal of Public Health, 94,* 1074.

Eronen, M., Angermeyer, M. C., & Schulze, B. (1998). The psychiatric epidemiology of violent behavior. *Social Psychiatry and Psychiatric Epidemiology, 33* (Suppl. 1), S13–S23.

Erwin, E. (1986). Establishing causal connections: Meta-analysis and psychotherapy. *Midwest Studies in Philosophy, 9,* 421–436.

Esman, A. H. (1994). Child abuse and multiple personality disorder. *American Journal of Psychiatry, 151,* 948.

Esser, G., Schmidt, M. H., & Woerner, W. (1990). Epidemiology and course of psychiatric disorders in school-age children: Results of a longitudinal study. *Journal of Child Psychology and Psychiatry, 31,* 243–263.

Estrada, A. U., & Pinsof, W. M. (1995). The effectiveness of family therapies for selected behavioral disorders of childhood. *Journal of Marital and Family Therapy, 21,* 403–440.

Evans, G., & Rey, J. (2001). In the echoes of gunfire: Practicing psychologists' response to school violence. *Professional Psychology: Research and Practice, 32,* 157–164.

Evans, S. J. (1997, April 11). How regular is your heartbeat? *Newsweek,* pp. 28–34.

Everson, S. A., Lynch, J. W., Kaplan, G. A., Lakka, T. A., et al. (1999). Stress-induced blood pressure reactivity and incident stroke in middle-aged men. *Psychosomatic Medicine, 61,* 125–126.

Ewing, C. P. (1998, February). Indictment fuels repressed-memory debate. *APA Monitor,* p. 52.

Exner, J. E. (1983). Rorschach assessment. In I. B. Weiner (Ed.), *Clinical methods in psychology.* New York: Wiley.

Exner, J. E. (1990). *A Rorschach workbook for the Comprehensive System* (2nd ed.). Asheville, NC: Rorschach Workshops.

Exner, J. E. (1995). In J. N. Butcher (Ed.), *Clinical personality assessment: Practical approaches* (pp. 10–18). New York: Oxford University Press.

Eysenck, H. J. (1952). The effects of psychotherapy: An evaluation. *Journal of Consulting Psychology, 16,* 319–324.

Fadden, G. (1998). Family intervention on psychosis. *Journal of Mental Health, 7,* 115–122.

Fagan, J., & McMahon, P. P. (1984). Incipient multiple personality in children: Four cases. *Journal of Nervous and Mental Disease, 172,* 26–36.

Fainaru, S. (1996, January 29). Ali shares his greatness with Cubans. *Boston Globe,* p. 2.

Fairburn, C. G., Cooper, Z., Doll, H. A., Norman, P., & O'Connor, M. (2000). The natural course of bulimia nervosa and binge eating disorder in young women. *Archives of General Psychiatry, 57,* 659–665.

Fairburn, C. G., Doll, H. A., Welch, S. L., Hay, P. J., et al. (1998). Risk factors for binge eating disorder: A community-based, case-control study. *Archives of General Psychiatry, 55,* 425–429.

Falloon, I. R. H. (1992). Early intervention for first episodes of schizophrenia: A preliminary exploration. *Psychiatry, 55,* 4–15.

Falloon, I. R. J., Boyd, J. L., & McGill, C. W. (1984). *Family care of schizophrenia.* New York: Guilford Press.

Fals-Stewart, W., & O'Farrell, T. J. (2003). Behavioral family counseling and naltrexone for male opioid-dependent patients. *Journal of Consulting and Clinical Psychology, 71,* 432–442.

Famularo, R., Kinscherff, R., Fenton, T., & Bolduc, S. M. (1990). Child maltreatment histories among runaways and delinquent children. *Clinical Pediatrics, 29,* 713–718.

Fang, C. Y., & Myers, H. F. (2001). The effects of racial stressors and hostility on cardiovascular reactivity in African American and Caucasian men. *Health Psychology, 20,* 64–70.

Faraone, S. V., Kremen, W. S., Lyons, M. J., Pepple, J. R., et al. (1995). Diagnostic accuracy and linkage analysis: How useful are schizophrenia spectrum phenotypes? *American Journal of Psychiatry, 152,* 1286–1290.

Faraone, S. V., Kremen, W. S., & Tsuang, M. T. (1990). Genetic transmission of affective disorders: Quantitative models and linkage analysis. *Psychological Bulletin, 108,* 109–127.

Faravelli, C., Giugni, A., Salvatori, S., & Ricca, V. (2004). Psychopathology after rape. *American Journal of Psychiatry, 161,* 1483–1485.

Farberow, N. L. (1970). Ten years of suicide prevention—Past and future. *Bulletin of Suicidology, 6,* 5–11.

Farley, F. (1986). World of the type T personality. *Psychology Today, 20,* 45–52.

Farmer, E. M. Z. (1995). Extremity of externalizing behavior and young adult outcomes. *Journal of Child Psychology and Psychiatry, 36,* 617–632.

Farrell, A. D., Stiles-Camplair, P., & McCullough, L. (1987). Identification of target complaints by computer interview: Evaluation of the computerized assessment system for psychotherapy evaluation research. *Journal of Consulting and Clinical Psychology, 55,* 691–700.

Farrell, A. D., & White, K. S. (1998). Peer influences and drug use among urban adolescents: Family structure and parent-adolescent relationship as protective factors. *Journal of Consulting and Clinical Psychology, 66,* 248–252.

Fauman, M. A. (1994). *Study guide to DSM-IV.* Washington, DC: American Psychiatric Press.

Fava, G. A., Zielezny, M., Savron, G., & Grandi, S. (1995). The long-term behavioral treatment for panic disorder with agoraphobia. *British Journal of Psychiatry, 166,* 87–92.

Federal Bureau of Investigation. (1991). *Uniform crime reports.* Washington, DC: U.S. Department of Justice.

Federal Bureau of Investigation. (1996). *Uniform crime reports for the United States, 1995.* Washington, DC: Government Printing Office.

Fedora, O., Reddon, J. R., & Yeudall, L. T. (1986). Stimuli eliciting sexual arousal in genital exhibitionists as possible clinical application. *Archives of Sexual Behavior, 15,* 417–427.

Feingold, B. F. (1977). Behavioral disturbances linked to the ingestion of food additives. *Delaware Medical Journal, 49,* 89–94.

Feitel, B., Margetson, N., Chamas, J., & Lipman, C. (1992). Psychosocial background and behavioral and emotional disorders of homeless and runaway youth. *Hospital Community Psychiatry, 43,* 155–159.

Feldman, H. A., Goldstein, I., Hatzichristou, D. G., Krane, R. J., & McKinlay, J. B. (1994). Impotence and its medical and psychosocial correlates: Results of the Massachusetts Male Aging Study. *Journal of Urology, 151,* 54–61.

Feldman, R. G., Mosbach, P., Thomas, C., & Perry, L. M. (1994). Psychosocial factors in the treatment of Parkinson's disease: A contextual approach. In A. M. Cohen & W. J. Weiner (Eds.), *The comprehensive management of Parkinson's disease* (pp. 193–208). New York: Demos Publications.

Feldman-Summers, S., & Pope, K. S. (1994). The experience of "forgetting" childhood abuse: A national survey of psychologists. *Journal of Consulting and Clinical Psychology, 62,* 636–639.

Fenichel, O. (1945). *The psychoanalytic theory of neuroses.* New York: Norton.

Fergusson, D. M., Horwood, L. J., & Lynskey, M. T. (1995). The stability of disruptive childhood behaviors. *Journal of Abnormal Child Psychology, 23,* 379–396.

Fernando, S. (1988). *Race and culture in psychiatry.* London: Croom Helm.

Ferster, C. B. (1965). Classification of behavior pathology. In L. Krasner & L. P. Ullman (Eds.), *Research in behavior modification.* New York: Holt, Rinehart & Winston.

Figley, C. R. (Ed.). (1985). *Trauma and its wake* (pp. 53–69). New York: Brunner/Mazel.

Fine, C. G. (1999). The tactical-integration model for the treatment of dissociative identity disorder and allied dissociative disorders. *American Journal of Psychotherapy, 53,* 361–376.

Finkelhor, D. (1980). Sex among siblings: A survey on prevalence, variety, and effects. *Archives of Sexual Behavior, 9,* 171–194.

Finkelhor, D., & Araji, S. (1986). Explanations of pedophilia: A four-factor model. *Journal of Sex Research, 22,* 145–161.

Fischer, D. G., & Elnitsky, S. (1990). A factor analytic study of two scales measuring dissociation. *American Journal of Clinical Hypnosis, 32,* 201–207.

Fischer, P. J., & Breakey, W. R. (1991). The epidemiology of alcohol, drug, and mental disorders among homeless persons. *American Psychologist, 46,* 1115–1128.

Flack, J. M., Amaro, H., Jenkins, W., Kunitz, S., et al. (1995). Panel I: Epidemiology of mental health. *Health Psychology, 14,* 592–600.

Flaherty, M. L., Infante, M., Tinsley, J. A., & Black, J. L., III (2001). Factitious hypertension by pseudoephedrine. *Psychosomatics, 42,* 150–153.

Flavin, D. K., Franklin, J. E., & Frances, R. J. (1990). Substance abuse and suicidal behavior. In S. J. Blumenthal & D. J. Kupfer (Eds.), *Suicide over the life cycle: Risk factors, assessment, and treatment of suicidal patients.* Washington, DC: American Psychiatric Press.

Fleer, J., & Pasewark, R. A. (1982). Prior public health agency contacts of individuals committing suicide. *Psychological Reports, 50,* 1319–1324.

Fleet, R. P., Lavoie, K. L., Martel, J.-P., Dupuis, G., et al. (2003). Two-year follow-up status of emergency department patients with chest pain: Was it a panic disorder? *Journal of the Canadian Association of Emergency Physicians, 5,* 247–252.

Fleming, I., Baum, A., Davidson, L. M., Rectanus, E., & McArdle, S. (1987). Chronic stress as a factor in physiologic reactivity to challenge. *Health Psychology, 6,* 221–237.

Flores, M. T., & Carey, G. (2000). *Family therapy with Hispanics: Toward appreciating diversity.* New York: Allyn & Bacon.

Foa, E. B. (2000). Psychosocial treatment of posttraumatic stress disorder. *Journal of Clinical Psychiatry, 61,* 43–53.

Foa, E. B., Dancu, C. V., Hembree, E. A., Jaycox, L. H., et al. (1999). A comparison of exposure therapy, stress inoculation training, and their combination in reducing posttraumatic stress disorder in female assault victims. *Journal of Consulting and Clinical Psychology, 67,* 194–200.

Foa, E. B., & Kozak, M. J. (1995). DSM-IV field trial: Obsessive-compulsive disorder. *American Journal of Psychiatry, 152,* 90–96.

Foa, E. B., Riggs, D. S., & Gershuny, B. S. (1995). Arousal, numbing, and intrusion: Symptom structure of PTSD following assault. *American Journal of Psychiatry, 152,* 116–119.

Foa, E. B., Rothbaum, B. O., & Furr, J. M. (2003). Augmenting exposure therapy with other CBT procedures. *Psychiatric Annals, 33,* 47–53.

Foley, V. (1989). Family therapy. In R. J. Corsini & D. Wedding (Eds.), *Current psychotherapies* (pp. 455–500). Itasca, IL: Peacock.

Follette, W. C., & Houts, A. C. (1996). Models of scientific progress and the role of theory in taxonomy development: A case study of the DSM. *Journal of Consulting and Clinical Psychology, 64,* 1120–1132.

Folstein, S., & Rutter, M. (1977). Infantile autism: A genetic study of 21 twin pairs. *Journal of Child Psychology, 18,* 297–321.

Folstein, S., & Rutter, M. (1988). Autism: Familial aggregation and genetic implications. *Journal of Autism and Developmental Disorders, 18,* 3–30.

Fombonne, E. (2003). Epidemiological surveys of autism and other pervasive developmental disorders: An update. *Journal of Autism and Developmental Disorders, 33,* 365–382.

Fontana, A., & Rosenheck, R. (1997). Effectiveness and cost of the inpatient treatment of posttraumatic stress disorder: Comparison of three models of treatment. *American Journal of Psychiatry, 154,* 758–765.

Forbes, G. B., Adams-Curtis, L. E., Rade, B., & Jaberg, P. (2001). Body dissatisfaction in women and men: The role of gender-typing and self-esteem. *Sex Roles, 44,* 461–484.

Fordyce, W. E. (1982). A behavioral perspective on chronic pain. *British Journal of Clinical Psychiatry, 21,* 313–320.

Fordyce, W. E. (1988). Pain and suffering: A reappraisal. *American Psychologist, 43,* 276–283.

Forgac, G. E., Cassel, C. A., & Michaels, E. J. (1984). Chronicity of criminal behavior and psychopathology in male exhibitionists. *Journal of Clinical Psychology, 40,* 827–832.

Forgac, G. E., & Michaels, E. J. (1982). Personality characteristics of two types of male exhibitionism. *Journal of Abnormal Psychology, 91,* 287–293.

Forsyth, J. P., Eifert, G. H., & Thompson, R. N. (1996). Systemic alarms in fear conditioning: II. An experimental methodology using 20 percent carbon dioxide inhalation as an unconditioned stimulus. *Behavior Therapy, 27,* 391–415.

Fortmann, S. P., & Killen, J. D. (1995). Nicotine gum and self-help behavioral treatment for smoking relapse prevention: Results from a trial using population-based recruitment. *Journal of Consulting and Clinical Psychology, 63,* 460–468.

Foxhall, K. (2001, March). How psychopharmacology training is enhancing some psychology practices. *Monitor on Psychology, 27,* 50–52.

Fox, R. E., & Sammons, M.,T. (1998). A history of prescription privileges. *Monitor on Psychology, 29,* 1–5.

Foxx, R., & Brown, R. (1979). Nicotine fading and self-monitoring for cigarette abstinence or controlled smoking. *Journal of Applied Behavior Analysis, 12,* 111–125.

Foxx, R. M., & Faw, G. D. (1992). An eight-year follow-up of three social skills training studies. *Mental Retardation, 30,* 63–66.

Frame, L., & Morrison, A. P. (2001). Causes of posttraumatic stress disorder in psychotic patients. *Archives of General Psychiatry, 58,* 305–306.

Frances, A. J., First, M. B., Widiger, T. A., Miele, G. M., et al. (1991). An A to Z guide to DSM-IV conundrums. *Journal of Abnormal Psychology, 100,* 407–412.

Francis, P. T., & Bowen, D. M. (1994). Neuronal pathology in relation to molecular biology and treatment of Alzheimer's disease. In F. Owen & R. Itzhaki (Eds.), *Molecular and cell biology of neuropsychiatric diseases* (pp. 24–54). New York: Chapman and Hall.

Franklin, D. (1987). The politics of masochism. *Psychology Today, 21,* 51–57.

Franklin, J. A. (1987). The changing nature of agoraphobic fears. *British Journal of Clinical Psychology, 26,* 127–133.

Franklin, J. E., & Frances, R. J. (1999). Alcohol and other psychoactive substance use disorders. In R. E. Hales, S. C. Yudofsky, & J. A. Talbott (Eds.), *Textbook of psychiatry* (pp. 363–423). Washington, DC: American Psychiatric Press.

Franklin, M. E., Abramowitz, J. S., Kozak, M. J., Levitt, J. T., & Foa, E. B. (2000). Effectiveness of exposure and ritual prevention for obsessive-compulsive disorder: Randomized compared with nonrandomized samples. *Journal of Consulting and Clinical Psychology, 68,* 594–602.

Free, M. L., & Oei, T. P. S. (1989). Biological and psychological processes in the treatment and maintenance of depression. *Clinical Psychology Review, 9,* 653–688.

Freedman, D. X. (1984). Psychiatric epidemiology counts. *Archives of General Psychiatry, 41,* 931–933.

Freeman, B. J. (1993). The syndrome of autism: Update and guidelines for diagnosis. *Infants and Young Children, 6,* 1–11.

Freeston, M. H., & Ladouceur, R. (1993). Appraisal of cognitive intrusions and response style: Replication and extension. *Behaviour Research and Therapy, 31,* 185–191.

Freeston, M. H., & Ladouceur, R. (1997). What do patients do with their obsessive thoughts? *Behaviour Research and Therapy, 35,* 335–347.

Freeston, M. H., Ladouceur, R., Gagnon, F., Thibodeau, et al. (1997). Cognitive-behavioral treatment of obsessive thoughts: A controlled study. *Journal of Consulting and Clinical Psychology, 65,* 405–413.

Freiberg, P. (1991). Suicide in family, friends is familiar to too many teens. *APA Monitor, 22,* 36–37.

Freinkel, A., Koopman, C., & Spiegel, D. (1994). Dissociative symptoms in media eyewitnesses of an execution. *American Journal of Psychiatry, 151,* 1335–1339.

Fremouw, W. J., Perczel, W. J., & Ellis, T. E. (1990). *Suicide risk: Assessment and response guidelines.* Elmsford, New York: Pergamon.

Freud, S. (1905). Psychical (or mental) treatment. In J. Strachey (Ed. & Trans.), *The complete psychological works* (vol. 7). New York: Norton.

Freud, S. (1938). The psychopathology of everyday life. In A. B. Brill (Ed.), *The basic writings of Sigmund Freud.* New York: Modern Library.

Freud, S. (1949). *An outline of psychoanalysis.* New York: Norton.

Freud, S. (1955). *Mourning and melancholia.* Standard ed., Vol. 14 (pp. 737–858). London: Hogarth Press. (Original work published 1917)

Freud, S. (1959). *Beyond the pleasure principle.* New York: Bantam. (Original work published 1909)

Freud, S., & Breuer, J. (1895). *Studies in hysteria.* Vienna: G. S.

Frick, P. J., & Lahey, B. B. (1991). Nature and characteristics of attention-deficit hyperactivity disorder. *School Psychology Review, 20,* 163–173.

Friedman, H. S., & Booth-Kewley, S. (1988). The "disease prone" personality: A meta-analytic view of the construct. *American Psychologist, 42,* 539–555.

Friedman, M. (1984). *Treating Type A behavior and your heart.* New York: Knopf.

Friedman, M., & Rosenman, R. H. (1974). *Type A behavior.* New York: Knopf.

Friedman, M. A., Detweiler-Bedell, J. B., Leventhal, H. E., Horne, R., et al. (2004). Combined psychotherapy and pharmacotherapy for the treatment of major depressive disorder. *Clinical Psychology: Science and Practice, 11,* 47–68.

Friedman, R. A. (2004, October 18). A patient's suicide, a psychiatrist's pain. *The New York Times,* p. F6.

Friedrich, J. (1985, January 7). Seven who have succeeded. *Time,* pp. 41–45.

Friedrich, W. N., Fisher, J., Broughton, D., Houston, M., & Shafran, C. (1998). Normative sexual behavior in children: A contemporary sample. *Pediatrics, 101,* 1–8.

Frisby, C. L. (1995). When facts and orthodoxy collide: The bell curve and the robustness criterion. *School Psychology Review, 24,* 12–19.

Frith, U. (1991). *Autism and Asperger syndrome.* Cambridge: Cambridge University Press.

Fritz, G. K., Rubenstein, S., & Lewiston, N. J. (1987). Psychological factors in fatal childhood asthma. *American Journal of Orthopsychiatry, 57,* 253–257.

Frost, R. O., Kim, H-J., Morris, C., Bloss, C., et al. (1998). Hoarding, compulsive buying, and reasons for saving. *Behaviour Research and Therapy, 36,* 657–664.

Frumkin, N. L., Palumbo, C. L., & Naeser, M. A. (1994). Brain imaging and its application to aphasia rehabilitation: CT and MRI. In R. Chapey (Ed.), *Language intervention strategies in adult aphasia* (47–79). Baltimore: Williams & Wilkins.

Fulero, S. M. (1988). Tarasoff: 10 years later. *Professional Psychology: Research and Practice, 19,* 184–190.

Furlong, F. W. (1991). Credibility of patients in psychiatric research. *American Journal of Psychiatry, 148,* 1423.

Furr, S. R., Westefeld, J. S., McConnell, G. N., & Jenkins, J. M. (2001). Suicide and depression among college students: A decade later. *Professional Psychology: Research and Practice, 32,* 97–100.

Gabbard, G. O. (2001). Psychodynamic psychotherapies. In G. O. Gabbard (Ed.), *Treatment of psychiatric disorders* (pp. 1227–1245). Washington, DC: American Psychiatric Press.

Gadow, K. D. (1986). *Children on medication* (Vol. 1). San Diego: College-Hill Press.

Gadow, K. D. (1991). Clinical issues in child and adolescent psychopharmacology. *Journal of Consulting and Clinical Psychology, 59,* 842–852.

Gallagher, D., & Frankel, A. S. (1980). Depression in (an) older adult(s): A moderate structuralist viewpoint. *Psychotherapy: Theory, Research, and Practice, 17,* 101–104.

Gallant, D. (2001). Alcoholism. In G. O. Gabbard (Ed.), *Treatment of psychiatric disorders* (pp. 665–678). Washington, DC: American Psychiatric Press.

Gamble, E., & Elder, S. (1983). Multimodal biofeedback in the treatment of migraine. *Biofeedback and Self-Regulation, 8,* 383–392.

Gangadhar, B., Kapur, R., & Kalyanasundaram, S. (1982). Comparison of electroconvulsive therapy with imipramine in endogenous depression: A double blind study. *British Journal of Psychiatry, 141,* 367–371.

Garbarino, S., Nobili, L., Beelke, M., Balestra, V., et al. (2002). Sleep disorders and daytime sleepiness in state police shiftworkers. *Archives of Environmental Health, 57,* 167–173.

Garber, H. J., & Ritvo, E. R. (1992). Magnetic resonance imaging of the posterior fossa in autistic adults. *American Journal of Psychiatry, 149,* 245–247.

Garcia, J. (1981). The logic and limits of mental aptitude testing. *American Psychologist, 36,* 1172–1180.

Garcia, J., McGowan, B. K., & Green, K. F. (1972) Biological constraints on conditioning. In A. H. Black & W. F. Prokasy (Eds.), *Classical conditioning II: Current research and theory.* New York: Appleton-Century-Crofts.

Garcia-Palacios, A., Hoffman, H., Carlin, A., Furness, T. A., III, & Botella, C. (2002). Virtual reality in the treatment of spider phobia: A controlled study. *Behaviour Research and Therapy, 40,* 983–993.

Gardner, M. (1998, December 16). Children and body images: Getting beyond Barbie. *Christian Science Monitor,* pp. 17–18.

Garfield, S. L. (1994). Research on client variables in psychotherapy. In A. E. Bergin & S. L. Garfield (Eds.), *Handbook of psychotherapy and behavior change* (pp. 190–228). New York: Wiley.

Garfield, S. L., & Bergin, A. E. (1994). Introduction and historical overview. In A. E. Bergin & S. L. Garfield (Eds.), *Handbook of psychotherapy and behavior change* (pp. 3–18). New York: Wiley.

Garfinkel, B. D., Froese, A., & Hood, J. (1982). Suicide attempts in children and adolescents. *American Journal of Psychiatry, 139,* 1257–1261.

Garfinkel, B. D., & Golumbek, H. (1983). Suicidal behavior in adolescence. In H. Golumbek & B. D. Garfinkel (Eds.), *The adolescent and mood disturbance.* New York: International Universities Press.

Garland, A. F., & Zigler, E. (1993). Adolescent suicide prevention: Current research and social policy implications. *American Psychologist, 48,* 169–182.

Garrett, M., & Silva, R. (2003). Auditory hallucinations, source monitoring, and the belief that "voices" are real. *Schizophrenia Bulletin, 29,* 445–451.

Gartner, A. F., & Gartner, J. (1988). Borderline pathology in postincest female adolescents. *Bulletin of the Menninger Clinic, 52,* 101–113.

Gass, C. S. (2002). Personality assessment of neurologically impaired patients. In J. N. Butcher (Ed.), *Clinical personality assessment: Practical approaches* (pp. 208–224). New York: Oxford University Press.

Gatz, M. (1990). Interpreting behavioral genetic results: Suggestions for counselors and clients. *Journal of Counseling and Development, 68,* 601–605.

Gatz, M., Smyer, M. A., & Lawton, M. P. (1980). The mental health system and the older adult. In L. W. Poon (Ed.), *Aging in the 1980s.* Washington, DC: American Psychological Association.

Gaub, M., & Carlson, C. L. (1997). Behavioral characteristics of *DSM-IV* ADHD subtypes in a school-based population. *Journal of Abnormal Child Psychology, 25,* 103–111.

Gawin, F. H. (1991). Cocaine addiction: Psychology and neurophysiology. *Science, 251,* 1580–1586.

Gaynor, J., & Hatcher, C. (1987). *The psychology of child firesetting.* New York: Brunner/Mazel.

Geddes, J. (2003). Efficacy and safety of electroconvulsive therapy in depressive disorders: A systematic review and meta-analysis. *Lancet, 361,* 799–808.

Gelard, M. S., & Sanford, E. E. (1987). Child abuse and neglect: A review of the literature. *School Psychology Review, 16,* 137–155.

Gelernter, J., O'Malley, S., Risch, N., Kranzler, H. R., et al. (1991). No association between an allele at the D2 dopamine receptor gene (DRD2) and alcoholism. *Journal of the American Medical Association, 266,* 1801–1807.

George, L. K., Landerman, R., Blazer, D. G., Anthony, J. C. (1991). Cognitive impairment. In L. N. Robins & D. A. Regier (Eds.), *Psychiatric disorders in America: The Epidemiologic Catchment Area study* (pp. 291–327). New York: Free Press.

George, M. S., & Ballenger, J. C. (1992). The neuroanatomy of panic disorder: The emerging role of the right parahippocampal region. *Journal of Anxiety Disorder, 6,* 181–188.

George, M. S., Trimble, M. R., Ring, H. A., Sallee, F. R., & Robertson, M. M. (1993). Obsessions in obsessive-compulsive disorder with and without Gilles de la Tourette's syndrome. *American Journal of Psychiatry, 150,* 93–97.

Gerhardt, P. (1998, August 2). Hearing my sister's voice. *Washington Post,* C01.

Gerin, W., Milner, D., Chawla, S., & Pickering, T. G. (1995). Social support as a moderator of cardiovascular reactivity in women: A test of the direct effects and buffering hypotheses. *Psychosomatic Medicine, 57,* 16–22.

Gerin, W., Pieper, C., Levy, R., & Pickering, T. G. (1992). Social support in social interaction: A moderator of cardiovascular reactivity. *Psychosomatic Medicine, 54,* 324–336.

Gershon, E. S., Berrettini, W. H., Nurnberger, J. I., Jr., & Goldin, L. R. (1989). Genetic studies of affective illness. In J. J. Mann (Ed.), *Models of depressive disorders: Psychological, biological, and genetic perspectives* (pp. 109–142). New York: Plenum.

Ghaziuddin, M., Tsai, L., Eilers, L., & Ghaziuddin, N. (1992). Brief report: Autism and herpes simplex encephalitis. *Journal of Autism and Developmental Disorders, 22,* 107–113.

Giancola, P. R., & Zeichner, A. (1997). The biphasic effects of alcohol on human physical aggression. *Journal of Abnormal Psychology, 106,* 598–607.

Gibbs, N. (1991, June 3). When is it rape? *Time,* pp. 48–54.

Giedd, J. N. (2001). Neuroimaging of pediatric neuropsychiatric disorders: Is a picture really worth a thousand words? *Archives of General Psychiatry, 58,* 443–445.

Gilbert, S. C. (2003). Eating disorders in women of color. *Clinical Psychology: Science and Practice, 10,* 1–16.

Gillberg, C. (1988). The neurobiology of infantile autism. *Journal of Child Psychology and Psychiatry, 29,* 257–266.

Gillberg, C. (1992). Autism and autistic-like conditions: Subclasses among disorders of empathy. *Journal of Child Psychology and Psychiatry, 33,* 813–842.

Gillberg, C. (1994). Debate and argument: Having Rett syndrome in ICD-10 PDD category does not make sense. *Journal of Child Psychology and Psychiatry, 35,* 377–378.

Gillis, J. J., Gilger, J. W., Pennington, B. F., & DeFries, J. C. (1992). Attention deficit in reading-disabled twins: Evidence for a genetic etiology. *Journal of Abnormal Child Psychology, 20,* 303–315.

Gillum, R. F. (1997). Sudden cardiac death in Hispanic American and African Americans. *American Journal of Public Health, 87,* 1461–1464.

Girard, F. (1984, August 5). State crime data called flawed, late. *Detroit News,* pp. 1, 12.

Girard, S. S., Toth, S. A., Davis, R. H., Donnelly, R. E., et al. (1998). Guidelines for the diagnosis and management of asthma. *Journal of American Academy of Physician Assistants, 11,* 45–48.

Glantz, K., Durlach, N. I., Barnett, R. C., & Aviles, W. A. (1996). Virtual reality (VR) for psychotherapy: From the physical to social environment. *Psychotherapy, 33,* 464–473.

Glassman, J. N. S., Magulac, M., & Darko, D. F. (1987). Folie a famille: Shared paranoid disorder in a Vietnam veteran and his family. *American Journal of Psychiatry, 144,* 658–660.

Glazer, W. M., Morgenstern, H., & Doucette, J. T. (1991). The prediction of chronic persistent versus intermittent tardive dyskinesia. *British Journal of Psychiatry, 158,* 822–828.

Gleaves, D. H. (1996). The sociocognitive model of dissociative identity disorder: A reexamination of the evidence. *Psychological Bulletin, 120,* 42–59.

Goff, D. C. (1993). Reply to Dr. Armstrong. *Journal of Nervous and Mental Disease, 181,* 604–605.

Goff, D. C., & Simms, C. A. (1993). Has multiple personality disorder remained consistent over time? *Journal of Nervous and Mental Disease, 181,* 595–600.

Goisman, R. M., Warshaw, M. G., Steketee, G. S., & Fierman, E. J. (1995). DSM-IV and the disappearance of agoraphobia without a history of panic disorder: New data on a controversial diagnosis. *American Journal of Psychiatry, 152,* 1438–1442.

Goldberg, D. (1996). Psychological disorders in general medical settings. *Social Psychiatry, 31,* 1–2.

Goldberg, T. E., Hyde, T. M., Kleinman, J. E., & Weinberger, D. R. (1993). Course of schizophrenia: Neuropsychological evidence for a static encephalopathy. *Schizophrenia Bulletin, 19,* 797–802.

Golden, C. J. (1989). The Nebraska Neuropsychological Children's Battery. In C. R. Reynolds & E. Fletcher-Janzen (Eds.), *Handbook of clinical child neuropsychology* (pp. 193–204). New York: Plenum Press.

Golden, C. J., Graber, B., Blose, I., Berg, R., et al. (1981). Differences in brain densities between chronic alcoholic and normal control patients. *Science, 211,* 508–510.

Golden, C. J., Moses, J. A., Coffman, J. A., Miller, W. R., & Strider, F. D. (1983). *Clinical neuropsychology.* New York: Grune & Stratton.

Golden, C. J., Moses, J. A., Fishburne, F. J., Engum, E., et al. (1981). Cross-validation of the Luria-Nebraska Neuropsychological Battery for the presence, lateralization, and location of brain damage. *Journal of Consulting and Clinical Psychology, 49,* 491–507.

Golden, G. S. (1987). Tic disorders in childhood. *Pediatrics in Review, 8,* 229–234.

Golden, J. (1988). A second look at a case of inhibited sexual desire. *Journal of Sex Research, 25,* 304–306.

Goldenberg, H., & Goldenberg, I. (1995). Family therapy. In R. J.

Corsini & D. Wedding (Eds.), *Current psychotherapies* (5th ed.). Itasca, IL: Peacock.

Goldenhar, L. M., Swanson, N. G., Hurrell, J. J., Jr., Ruder, A., & Deddens, J. (1998). Stressors and adverse outcomes for female construction workers. *Journal of Occupational Health Psychology, 3,* 19–32.

Goldfein, J. A., Devlin, M. J., & Spitzer, R. L. (2000). Cognitive behavioral therapy for the treatment of binge eating disorder: What constitutes success? *American Journal of Psychiatry, 157,* 1051–1056.

Goldfried, M. R., & Castonguay, L. G. (1992). The future of psychotherapy integration. *Psychotherapy, 29,* 4–10.

Goldfried, M. R., & Davison, G. C. (1976). *Clinical behavior therapy.* San Francisco: Holt, Rinehart & Winston.

Goldfried, M. R., Greenberg, L. S., & Marmar, C. (1990). Individual psychotherapy: Process and outcome. *Annual Review of Psychology* (Vol. 41, pp. 659–688). Palo Alto, CA: Annual Reviews.

Goldfried, M. R., & Safran, J. D. (1986). Future directions in psychotherapy integration. In J. C. Norcross (Ed.), *Handbook of eclectic psychotherapy* (pp. 463–483). New York: Brunner/Mazel.

Golding, J. M., Sanchez, R. P., & Sego, S. A. (1996). Do you believe in repressed memories? *Professional Psychology: Research and Practice, 27,* 429–437.

Golding, J. M., Smith, G. R., & Kashner, T. M. (1991). Does somatization disorder occur in men? *Archives of General Psychiatry, 48,* 231–235.

Goldman, H. H. (1988). Psychiatric epidemiology and mental health services research. In H. H. Goldman (Ed.), *Review of general psychiatry* (pp. 143–156). Norwalk, CT: Appleton & Lange.

Goldman, H. H., & Foreman, S. A. (1988). Psychiatric diagnosis and psychosocial formulation. In H. H. Goldman (Ed.), *Review of general psychiatry* (pp. 136–142). Norwalk, CT: Appleton & Lange.

Goldman, L. S., Genel, M., Bezman, R. J., & Slanetz, P. J. (1998). Diagnosis and treatment of attention-deficit/hyperactivity disorder in children and adolescents. *Journal of the American Medical Association, 279,* 1100–1107.

Goldman, M. J., & Gutheil, T. G. (1991). Bruxism and sexual abuse. *American Journal of Psychiatry, 148,* 1089.

Goldstein, A. (1999). *Low level aggression: First steps on the ladder to violence.* Champaign, IL: Research Press.

Goldstein, A. P., & Kodluboy, D. W. (1998). *Gangs in school: Signs, symbols and solutions.* Champaign, IL: Research Press.

Goldstein, J. M. (1997). Sex differences in schizophrenia: Epidemiology, genetics, and the brain. *International Review of Psychiatry, 9,* 399–408.

Goleman, D. (1992). Therapies offer hope for sex offenders. *New York Times,* pp. C1, C11.

Golier, J. A., Yehuda, R., Bierer, L. M., Mitropoulou, V., et al. (2003). The relationship of borderline personality disorder to posttraumatic stress disorder and traumatic events. *American Journal of Psychiatry, 160,* 2018–2024.

Goma, M., Perez, J., & Torrubia, R. (1988). Personality variables in antisocial and prosocial disinhibitory behavior. In T. E. Moffitt & S. A. Mednick (Eds.), *Biological contributions to crime causation* (pp. 211–222). Boston: Martinus Nijhoff Publishers.

Gonzalez, J. S., Penedo, F. J., Antoni, M. H., Duran, R. E., et al. (2004). Social support, positive state of mind, and HIV treatment adherence in men and women living with HIV/AIDS. *Health Psychology, 23,* 413–418.

Goodlin-Jones, B. L., & Solomon, M. (2003). Contributions of psychology. In S. Ozonoff, S. J. Rogers, & R. L. Hendren (Eds.), *Autism spectrum disorders: A research review for practitioners* (pp. 55–86). Arlington, VA: American Psychiatric.

Goodwin, D. W. (1979). Alcoholism and heredity. *Archives of General Psychiatry, 36,* 57–61.

Goodwin, D. W. (1985). Alcoholism and alcoholic psychoses. In H. I. Kaplan & B. J. Sadock (Eds.), *Comprehensive textbook of psychiatry* (Vol. 4, pp. 1016–1025). Baltimore: Williams & Wilkins.

Goodwin, D. W., & Guze, S. B. (1984). *Psychiatric diagnosis* (3rd ed.). New York: Oxford University Press.

Gordon, A. (2001). Eating disorders: 2. Bulimia nervosa. *Hospital Practice, 36,* 71–73.

Gorman, J. M. (2001). Generalized anxiety disorder. *Clinical Cornerstone, 3,* 37–46.

Gorman, J. M., Kent, J. M., Sullivan, G. M., & Coplan, J. D. (2000). Neuroanatomical hypothesis of panic disorder, revised. *American Journal of Psychiatry, 157,* 493–505.

Gotham, H. J., Sher, K. J., & Wood, P. K. (1997). Predicting stability and change in frequency of intoxication for the college years to beyond: Individual-difference and role transition variables. *Journal of Abnormal Psychology, 106,* 619–629.

Gotlib, I. H. (1992). Interpersonal and cognitive aspects of depression. *Current Directions in Psychological Science, 1*(5), 149–154.

Gottesman, I. I. (1978). Schizophrenia and genetics: Where are we? Are you sure? In L. C. Wynne, R. L. Cromwell, & S. Matthysse (Eds.), *The nature of schizophrenia: New approaches to research and treatment* (pp. 59–69). New York: Wiley.

Gottesman, I. I. (1991). *Schizophrenia genesis.* New York: W. H. Freeman & Co.

Gottesman, I. I., & Shields, J. (1982). *Schizophrenia: The epigenetic puzzle.* New York: Cambridge University Press.

Gottlieb, A. M., Killen, J. D., Marlatt, G. A., & Taylor, C. B. (1987). Psychological and pharmacological influences in cigarette smoking withdrawal: Effects of nicotine gum and expectancy on smoking withdrawal symptoms and relapse. *Journal of Consulting and Clinical Psychology, 55,* 606–608.

Gould, R. A., Buckminster, S., Pollack, M. H., Otto, M. W., & Yap, L. (1997). Cognitive-behavioral and pharmacological treatment for social phobia: A meta-analysis. *Clinical Psychology: Science and Practice, 4,* 291–306.

Gould, R. A., Otto, M. W., Pollack, M. H., & Yap, L. (1997). Cognitive behavioral and pharmacological treatment of generalized anxiety disorder. A preliminary meta-analysis. *Behavior Therapy, 28,* 285–305.

Gould, S. J. (1994, November 28). Curveball. *New Yorker,* 139–149.

Graham, J. R. (1990). MMPI-2: *Assessing personality and psychopathology.* New York: Oxford University Press.

Graham-Bermann, S. A., & Levendovsky, A. A. (1998). Traumatic stress symptoms in children of battered women. *Journal of Interpersonal Violence, 13,* 111–128.

Gramling, S. E., Clawson, E. P., & McDonald, M. K. (1996). Perceptual and cognitive abnormality of hypochondriasis: Amplification and physiological reactivity in women. *Psychosomatic Medicine, 58,* 423–431.

Grant, J. E., Kim, S. W., & Crow, S. J. (2001). Prevalence and clinical features of body dysmorphic disorder in adolescent and adult psychiatric inpatients. *Journal of Clinical Psychiatry, 62,* 517–522.

Green, R. (1987). *The "sissy boy syndrome" and the development of homosexuality.* New Haven: Yale University Press.

Green, R., & Blanchard, R. (1995). Gender-identity disorders. In H. I. Kaplan & B. J. Sadock (Eds.), *Comprehensive textbook of psychiatry* (Vol. 6, pp. 1345–1360). Baltimore: Williams & Wilkins.

Green, R., Mandel, J. B., Hotvedt, M. E., Gray, J., & Smith, L. (1986). Lesbian mothers and their children: A comparison with solo parent heterosexual mothers and their children. *Archives of Sexual Behavior, 15,* 167–184.

Greenan, D. E., & Tunnell, G. (2003). *Couple therapy with gay men.* New York: Guilford Press.

Greenberg, B. D., Altemus, M., & Murphy, D. L. (1997). The role of neurotransmitters and neurohormones in obsessive-compulsive disorder. *International Review of Psychiatry, 9,* 31–44.

Greenberger, E., Chen, C., Tally, S. R., & Dong, Q. (2000). Family, peer, and individual correlates of depressive symptomatology among U.S. and Chinese adolescents. (2000). *Journal of Consulting and Clinical Psychology, 68,* 209–219.

Greene, R. L. (1991). *The MMPI-2/MMPI: An interpretive manual.* Boston: Allyn & Bacon.

Greene, R. W., Biederman, J., Faraone, S. V., & Oullette, C. (1996). Toward a new psychometric definition of social disability in children with attention-deficit hyperactivity disorder. *Journal of the American Academy of Child and Adolescent Psychiatry, 35,* 571–578.

Greenhill, L., Abikoff, H., Arnold, L., Cantwell, D., et al. (1998). *Psychopharmacological treatment manual: NIMH multimodal treatment study of children with attention deficit hyperactivity disorder (MTA study).* New York: Psychopharmacology Subcommittee of the MTA Steering Committee.

Greeno, C. G., Wing, R. R., & Shiffman, S. (2000). Binge eating antecedents in obese women with and without binge eating disorder. *Journal of Consulting and Clinical Psychology, 68,* 95–102.

Greer, S. (1991). Psychological response to cancer and survival. *Psychological Medicine, 21,* 43–49.

Grencavage, L. M., & Norcross, J. C. (1990). Where are the commonalities among the therapeutic common factors? *Professional Psychology: Research and Practice, 21,* 372–378.

Gresham, F. M., Beebe-Frankenberger, M. E., & MacMillan, D. L. (1999). A selective review of treatment of children with autism: Description and methodological considerations. *School Psychology Review, 28,* 559–575.

Griffith, E. E., Gonzalez, C. A., & Blue, H. C. (1999). The basics of cultural psychiatry. In R. E. Hales, S. C. Yudofsky & J. A. Talbott (Eds.), *Textbook of psychiatry* (pp. 1463–1492). Washington, DC: American Psychiatric Press.

Grilly, D. M. (2002). *Drugs and human behavior.* New York: Allyn & Bacon.

Grinker, R. R., & Robbins, F. P. (1954). *Psychosomatic case book.* New York: Blakiston.

Groopman, L. C., & Cooper, A. M. (2001). Narcissistic personality disorder. In G. O. Gabbard (Ed.), *Treatment of psychiatric disorders* (pp. 2309–2326). Washington, DC: American Psychiatric Press.

Gross, P. R., & Eifert, G. H. (1990). Components of generalized anxiety: The role of intrusive thoughts vs. worry. *Behaviour Research and Therapy, 28,* 421–428.

Groth, A. N., Burgess, A. W., & Holstrom, L. (1977). Rape: Power, anger, and sexuality. *American Journal of Psychiatry, 134,* 1239–1243.

Grove, M. W., Lebow, B. S., Clementz, B. A., Cerri, A., et al. (1991). Familial prevalence and coaggregation of schizotypy indicators: A multitrait family study. *Journal of Abnormal Psychology, 100,* 115–121.

Guerin, P. J., Jr., & Chabot, D. R. (1992). Development of family systems theory. In D. K. Freedheim (Ed.), *History of psychotherapy* (pp. 225–260). Washington, DC: American Psychological Association.

Gunderson, J. G., & Links, P. S. (2001). Borderline personality disorder. In G. O. Gabbard (Ed.), *Treatment of psychiatric disorders* (pp. 2273–2291). Washington, DC: American Psychiatric Press.

Gur, R. E., Cowell, P., Turetsky, B. I., Gallacher, F., et al. (1998). A follow-up magnetic resonance imaging study of schizophrenia. *Archives of General Psychiatry, 55,* 145–152.

Gureje, O., Simon, G. E., Ustun, T. B., & Goldberg, D. P. (1997). Somatization in cross-cultural perspective: A World Health Organization study in primary care. *American Journal of Psychiatry, 154,* 989–995.

Gurman, A. S., & Kniskern, D. P. (1978). Research on marital and family therapy: Progress, perspective, and prospect. In S. L. Carfield & A. E. Bergin (Eds.), *Handbook of psychotherapy and behavior change: An empirical analysis* (2nd ed.). New York: Wiley.

Gustafson, R., Popovich, M., & Thomsen, S. (2001). Subtle ad images threaten girls more. *Marketing News, 35,* 12–13.

Gutierrez, P. M., & Silk, K. R. (1998). Prescription privileges for psychologists: A review of the psychological literature. *Professional Psychology: Research and Practice, 29,* 213–222.

Guttmacher, L. B., & Nelles, C. (1984). In vivo desensitization alteration of lactate-induced panic: A case study. *Behavior Therapy, 15,* 369–372.

Guttman, M. (1995, October 27–29). The Ritalin generation. *USA Weekend,* pp. 4–6.

Haas, K., & Haas, A. (1993). *Understanding human sexuality.* St. Louis, MO: Mosby.

Haenen, M. A., de Jong, P. J., Schmidt, A. J. M., Stevens, S., & Visser, L. (2000). Hypochondriacs' estimation of negative outcomes: Domain-specificity and responsiveness to reassuring and alarming information. *Behaviour Research and Therapy, 38,* 819–833.

Hafner, H., an der Heiden, W., Behrens, S., Gattaz, W. F., et al. (1998). Causes and consequences of gender difference in age at onset of schizophrenia. *Schizophrenia Bulletin, 24,* 99–113.

Hagen, M. A. (2003). Faith in the model and resistance to research. *Clinical Psychology: Science and Practice, 10,* 172–178.

Hagerman, R. J. (1996). Biomedical advances in development psychology: The case of fragile X syndrome. *Developmental Psychology, 32,* 416–424.

Halderman, D. C. (2002). Gay rights, patient rights: The implications of sexual orientation conversion therapy. *Professional Psychology: Research and Practice, 33,* 260–264.

Haley, J. (1963). *Strategies of psychotherapy.* New York: Grune & Stratton.

Haley, J. (1977). *Problem-solving therapy.* San Francisco: Jossey-Bass.

Haley, J. (1980). *Leaving home.* New York: McGraw-Hill.

Haley, J. (1987). *Problem-solving therapy* (2nd ed.). New York: Jossey-Bass.

Haley, J. (2003, October 31). Defendant's wife testifies about his multiple personas. *Bellingham Herald,* p. B4.

Hall, G. C. (1996). *Theory-based assessment, treatment, and prevention of sexual aggression.* New York: Oxford University Press.

Hall, G. C., Windover, A. K., & Maramba, G. C. (1998). Sexual aggression among Asian Americans: Risk and protective factors. *Cultural Diversity and Mental Health, 4,* 305–318.

Hall, G. C. N., & Hirschman, R. (1991). Toward a theory of sexual aggression: A quadripartite model. *Journal of Consulting and Clinical Psychology, 59,* 662–669.

Hall, J. E. (1995). A perspective on the evolving health care environment: Quality, integrity, reliability and value. *Register Report, 20,* 2–3.

Hall, N. R. S. (1988). The virology of AIDS. *American Psychologist, 43,* 907–913.

Hall, R. G., Sachs, D. P. L., Hall, S. M., & Benowitz, N. L. (1984). Two-year efficacy and safety of rapid smoking therapy in patients with cardiac and pulmonary disease. *Journal of Consulting and Clinical Psychology, 52,* 574–581.

Hall, S. M., Tunstall, C. D., Ginsberg, D., Benowitz, N. L., & Jones, R. T. (1987). Nicotine gum and behavioral treatment: A placebo controlled trial. *Journal of Consulting and Clinical Psychology, 55,* 603–605.

Hallak, J. E. C., Crippa, J. A. S., & Zuardi, A. W. (2000). Treatment of koro with citalopram. *Journal of Clinical Psychology, 61,* 951–952.

Halmi, K. A., Sunday, S. R., Strober, M., Kaplan, A., et al. (2000). Perfectionism in anorexia nervosa: Variation by clinical subtype, obsessionality, and pathological eating disorder. *American Journal of Psychiatry, 157,* 1799–1805.

Hamilton, M. (1982). Symptoms and assessment of depression. In E. S. Paykel (Ed.), *Handbook of affective disorders* (pp. 3–11). New York: Guilford.

Hammen, C. (1991). Generation of stress in the course of unipolar depression. *Journal of Abnormal Psychology, 100,* 555–561.

Hammen, C., Davilla, J., Brown, G., Ellicott, A., & Gitlin, M. (1992). Psychiatric history and stress: Predictors of severity of unipolar depression. *Journal of Abnormal Psychology, 101,* 45–52.

Hammen, C., & Peters, S. (1978). Interpersonal consequences of depression: Responses to men and women enacting a depressed role. *Journal of Abnormal Psychology, 87,* 322–332.

Hammen, C. L. (1985). Predicting depression: A cognitive-behavioral perspective. In P. Kendall (Ed.), *Advances in cognitive-behavioral research and therapy* (Vol. 4). New York: Academic Press.

Hammond, W. R., & Yung, B. (1993). Psychology's role in the

public health–response to assaultive violence among young African-American men. *American Psychologist, 48,* 142–154.

Hanback, J. W., & Revelle, W. (1978). Arousal and perceptual sensitivity in hypochondriacs. *Journal of Abnormal Psychology, 87,* 523–530.

Hans, S. L., Auerbach, J. G., Styr, B., & Marcus, J. (2004). Offspring of parents with schizophrenia: Mental disorders during childhood and adolescence. *Schizophrenia Bulletin, 30,* 303–315.

Hans, S. L., Marcus, J., Henson, L., Auerbach, J. G., & Mirsky, A. F. (1992). Interpersonal behavior of children at risk for schizophrenia. *Psychiatry, 55,* 314–335.

Hanson, R. F., & Spratt, E. (2000) Reactive attachment disorder: What we know about the disorder and implications for treatment. *Child Maltreatment, 5*(2), 137–145.

Harding, C. M., Zubin, J., & Strauss, J. S. (1992). Chronicity in schizophrenia: Revisited. *British Journal of Psychiatry, 161,* 27–37.

Hare, R. D. (1968). Psychopathy, autonomic functioning and the orienting responses. *Journal of Abnormal Psychology, 73,* 1–24.

Hare, R. D. (1970). *Psychopathy: Theory and research.* New York: Wiley.

Hare, R. D. (1975). Anxiety, stress, and psychopathy. In I. Sarason & C. Spielberger (Eds.), *Stress and anxiety* (Vol. 2). Washington, DC: Hemisphere Publishing.

Hare, R. D., Hart, S. D., & Harpur, T. J. (1991). Psychopathology and the DSM-IV criteria for antisocial personality disorder. *Journal of Abnormal Psychology, 100,* 391–398.

Harenstam, A., Theorell, T., & Kaijser, L. (2000). Coping with anger-provoking situations, psychosocial working conditions, and the ECG-detected signs of coronary heart disease. *Journal of Occupational Health Psychology, 5,* 191–203.

Harlow, H. F., & Harlow, M. (1962). Social deprivation in monkeys. *Scientific American, 207* (5), 136–146.

Harlow, J. M. (1868). *Recovery from the passage of an iron bar through the head. Publication of the Massachusetts Medical Society, 2,* 327.

Harpur, T. J., Hare, R. D., & Hakstian, A. R. (1989). Two-factor conceptualization of psychopathology: Construct validity and assessment implications. *Psychological Assessment: A Journal of Consulting and Clinical Psychology, 1,* 6–17.

Harrington, R. C. (2001). Childhood depression and conduct disorder: Different routes to the same outcome? *Archives of General Psychiatry, 58,* 237–240.

Harris, E. C., & Barraclough, B. (1997). Suicide as an outcome for mental disorders. *British Journal of Psychiatry, 170,* 205–228.

Harris, J. C. (2001). Psychiatric disorders in mentally retarded persons. In G. O. Gabbard (Ed.), *Treatment of psychiatric disorders* (pp. 75–107). Washington, DC: American Psychiatric Press.

Harris, J. C. (2004). Anxiety (Angst). *Archives of General Psychiatry, 61,* 15.

Harris, S. L. (1995). Autism. In M. Hersen & R. T. Ammerman (Eds.), *Advanced abnormal psychology.* Hillsdale, NJ: Lawrence Erlbaum.

Harrison, K. (2001). Ourselves, our bodies: Thin-ideal media, self-discrepancies, and eating disorder symptomatology in adolescents. *Journal of Social and Clinical Psychology, 20,* 289–299.

Harrison, K., & Cantor, J. (1997). The relationship between media exposure and eating disorders. *Journal of Communication, 47,* 40–67.

Harrow, M., Herbener, E. S., Shanklin, A., Jobe, T. H., et al. (2004). Followup of psychotic outpatients: Dimensions of delusions and work functioning in schizophrenia. *Schizophrenia Bulletin, 30,* 147–161.

Hart, S. D., & Hare, R. D. (1989). Discriminant validity of the psychopathology checklist in a forensic psychiatric population. *Psychological Assessment: A Journal of Consulting and Clinical Psychology, 1,* 211–218.

Hartman-Stein, P. (2004). Psychologists develop new roles with Parkinson's patients. *National Psychologist, 13,* 4–5.

Harvey, A. G., & Bryant, R. A. (1998). The relationship between acute stress disorder and posttraumatic stress disorder: A prospective evaluation of motor vehicle accident survivors. *Journal of Consulting and Clinical Psychology, 66,* 507–512.

Harvey, A. G., Bryant, R. A., & Dang, S. T. (1998). Autobiographical memory in acute stress disorder. *Journal of Consulting Clinical Psychology, 66,* 500–506.

Harvey, A. G., Clark, D. M., Ehlers, A., & Rapee, R. M. (2000). Social anxiety and self-impression. *Behaviour Research and Therapy, 38,* 1183–1192.

Hashimoto, T., Tayama, M., Murakawa, K., Yoshimoto, T., et al. (1995). Development of brainstem and cerebellum in autistic patients. *Journal of Autism and Developmental Disorders, 25,* 1–18.

Haslam, N. (2003). The dimensional view of personality disorders: A review of the taxometric evidence. *Clinical Psychology Review, 23,* 75–93.

Hastings, J. D., & Robbennolt, J. K. (2004). Physician-assisted suicide. *Monitor, 35*(9), 86.

Hatcher, S. (1989). A case of doll phobia. *British Journal of Psychiatry, 155,* 255–257.

Hathaway, S. R., & McKinley, J. C. (1943). *Manual for the Minnesota Multiphasic Personality Inventory.* New York: Psychological Corporation.

Haug Schnabel, G. (1992). Daytime and nighttime enuresis: A functional disorder and its ethological decoding. *Behavior, 120,* 232–262.

Haugaard, J. J. (2000). The challenge of defining child sexual abuse. *American Psychologist, 55,* 1036–1039.

Hauser, W. A. (1994). The distribution of mild and severe forms of epilepsy. In M. R. Trimble & W. E. Dodson (Eds.), *Epilepsy and quality of life* (pp. 249–257). New York: Raven Press.

Hawton, K. (1987). Assessment of suicide risk. *British Journal of Psychiatry, 150,* 145–153.

Hawton, K., Catalan, J., Martin, P., & Fagg, J. (1986). Long-term outcome of sex therapy. *Behaviour Research and Therapy, 24,* 665–675.

Hayes, S. (1995). *Now the battles are substantive.* Reno: Content Press.

Hayes, S. C., Brownell, K. D., & Barlow, D. H. (1983). Heterosexual skills training and covert sensitization: Effects on social skills and sexual arousal in sexual deviants. *Behaviour Research and Therapy, 21,* 383–392.

Hayes, S. C., & Chang, G. (2002). Invasion of the body snatchers: Prescription privileges, professional schools, and the drive to create a new behavioral health profession. *Clinical Psychology: Science and Practice, 9,* 264–275.

Hayes, S. C., Wilson, K. G., Gifford, E. V., Follette, V. M., & Strosahl, K. (1996). Experimental avoidance and behavioral disorders: A functional dimensional approach to diagnosis and treatment. *Journal of Consulting and Clinical Psychology, 64,* 1152–1168.

Hayley, M. (2004, July 21). Type "pro-ana" into any internet search engine and you'll get disturbing glimpse of a deadly obsession with thin. *Canadian Press Newswire,* p. 1.

Haynes, S. N. (2001). Clinical applications of analogue behavioral observation: Dimensions of psychometric evaluation. *Psychological Assessment, 13,* 73–85.

Hays, R. B., Turner, H., & Coates, T. J. (1992). Social support, AIDS-related symptoms, and depression among gay men. *Journal of Consulting and Clinical Psychology, 60*(3), 463–469.

Hayward, P., Wardie, J., & Higgitt, A. (1989). Benzodiazepine research: Current findings and practical consequences. *British Journal of Psychiatry, 28,* 307–327.

Hedlund, S., & Rude, S. S. (1995). Evidence of latent depressive schemas in formerly depressed individuals. *Journal of Abnormal Psychology, 104,* 517–525.

Heffernan, K. (1994). Sexual orientation as a factor in risk for binge eating and bulimia nervosa: A review. *International Journal of Eating Disorders, 16,* 335–347.

Heiby, E. M. (1983). Depression as a function of the interaction of self- and environmentally controlled reinforcement. *Behavior Therapy, 14,* 430–433.

Heilbrun, A. B., Jr., & Loftus, M. P. (1986). The role of sadism and peer pressure in the sexual aggression of male college students. *Journal of Sex Research, 22,* 320–332.

Heinrichs, R. W. (1993). Schizophrenia and the brain. *American Psychologist, 48,* 221–233.

Heinssen, R. K., & Cuthbert, B. N. (2001). Barrier to relationship formation in schizophrenia: Implications for treatment, social recovery, and translational research. *Psychiatry, 64,* 126–132.

Heinssen, R. K., Liberman, R. P., & Kopelowicz, A. (2000). Psychosocial skills training for schizophrenia: Lessons from the laboratory. *Schizophrenia Bulletin, 26,* 21–33.

Hellmich, N. (2001, July 25). Super-thin, super-troubling. *USA Today,* p. D7.

Hellstrom, K., Fellenius, J., & Öst, L-G. (1996). One versus five sessions of applied tension in the treatment of blood phobia. *Behaviour Research and Therapy, 34,* 101–112.

Helms, J. E. (1992). Why is there no study of cultural equivalence in standardized cognitive ability testing? *American Psychologist, 47,* 1083–1101.

Hendin, H. (1995). Assisted suicide, euthanasia, and suicide prevention: The implications for the Dutch experience. *Suicidal Life Threatening Behavior, 25,* 193–205.

Hendin, H., Pollenger, A., Singer, P., & Ulman, R. (1981). Meanings of combat and the development of posttraumatic stress disorder. *American Journal of Psychiatry, 131,* 1490–1493.

Hendren, R., & Mullen, D. (1997). Conduct disorder in childhood. In J. M. Weiner (Ed.), *Textbook of child and adolescent psychiatry* (2nd ed., pp. 427–440). Washington, DC: American Psychiatric Press.

Hendrie, H. C. (2001). Exploration of environmental and genetic risk factors for Alzheimer's disease: The value of cross-cultural studies. *Current Directions in Psychological Science, 10,* 98–101.

Herlicky, B., & Sheeley, V. L. (1988). Privileged communication in selected helping professions: A comparison among statutes. *Journal of Counseling & Development, 65,* 479–483.

Herman, J., & Hirschman, L. (1981). Families at risk for father-daughter incest. *American Journal of Psychiatry, 38,* 967–970.

Herman, S., Russell, D., & Trocki, K. (1986). Long-term effects of incestuous abuse in childhood. *American Journal of Psychiatry, 154,* 1293–1296.

Herring, R. D. (1999). *Counseling with Native American Indians and Alaska Natives.* Thousand Oaks, CA: Sage.

Herrnstein, R. J., & Murray, C. (1994). *The bell curve: Intelligence and class structure in American life.* New York: Free Press.

Herschell, A. D., McNeil, C. B., & McNeil, D. W. (2004). Clinical child psychology's progress in disseminating empirically supported treatments. *Clinical Psychology: Science and Practice, 11,* 267–288.

Herschkowitz, S., & Dickes, R. (1978). Suicide attempts in a female-to-male transsexual. *American Journal of Psychiatry, 135,* 368–369.

Hersen, M., Bellack, A., & Himmelhoch, J. (1980). Treatment for unipolar depression with social skills training. *Behavior Modification, 4,* 547–556.

Herzog, W., Kronmuller, K.-T., Hartmann, M., Bergmann, G., & Kroger, F. (2000). Family perception of interpersonal behavior as a predictor in eating disorders: A prospective, six-year follow-up study. *Family Process, 39,* 359–374.

Hessl, D., Dyer-Friedman, J., Glaser, B., Wisbeck, J., et al. (2001). The influence of environmental and genetic factors on behavior problems and autistic symptoms in boys and girls with Fragile X Syndrome. *Pediatrics, 108,* 88.

Heston, L. L. (1966). Psychiatric disorders in foster-home-reared children of schizophrenic mothers. *British Journal of Psychiatry, 122,* 819–825.

Heston, L. L., & Denny, D. (1968). Interactions between early life experience and biological factors in schizophrenia. In D. Rosenthal & S. Kety (Eds.), *The transmission of schizophrenia.* New York: Pergamon Press.

Hewitt, P. L., Newton, J., Flett, G. L., & Callander, L. (1997). Perfectionism and suicide ideation in adolescent psychiatric patients. *Journal of Abnormal Psychology, 25,* 95–101.

Hidalgo, R. B., & Davidson, J. R. T. (2000). Posttraumatic stress disorder: Epidemiology and health-related considerations. *Journal of Clinical Psychiatry, 61,* 5–13.

Hill, A. J., & Bhatti, R. (1995). Body shape perception and dieting in preadolescent British Asian girls: Links with eating disorders. *International Journal of Eating Disorders, 17,* 175–183.

Hill, C. E., & Lambert, M. J. (2004). Methodological issues in studying psychotherapy processes and outcomes. In M. J. Lambert (Ed.), *Bergin and Garfield's handbook of psychotherapy and behavior change* (pp. 84–135). New York: Wiley.

Hill, D., & Watterson, D. (1942). Electroencephalographic studies of the psychopathic personality. *Journal of Neurology and Psychiatry, 5,* 47–64.

Hiller, W., Leibbrand, R., Rief, W., & Fichter, M. M. (2002). Predictors of course and outcome in hypochondriasis after cognitive-behavioral treatment. *Psychotherapy and Psychosomatics, 71,* 318–327.

Hills, C. E. (1990). Is individual therapy process really different from group therapy process: The jury is still out. *Counseling Psychologist, 18,* 126–130.

Hillson, J. M., & Kuiper, N. A. (1994). Stress and coping model of child treatment. *Clinical Psychological Review, 14,* 261–285.

Hillyer, J. (1964). Reluctantly told. In B. Kaplan (Ed.), *The inner world of mental illness.* New York: Harper & Row.

Hilsenroth, M. J., Fowler, J. C., Padawer, J. R., & Handler, L. (1997). Narcissism in the Rorschach revisited: Some reflections on empirical data. *Psychological Assessment, 9,* 113–121.

Hinshaw, S. (1987). On the distinction between attentional deficits/hyperactivity and conduct problems/aggression in child psychopathology. *Psychological Bulletin, 101,* 443–463.

Hirose, S. (2003). The causes of underdiagnosing akathisia. *Schizophrenia Bulletin, 29,* 547–552.

Hirschfeld, R. M., & Shea, T. (1985). Affective disorders: Psychosocial treatment. In H. I. Kaplan & B. J. Sadock (Eds.), *Comprehensive textbook of psychiatry* (4th ed., pp. 786–810). Baltimore: Williams & Wilkins.

Ho, D. D., Neumann, A. U., Perelson, A. S., Chen, W., et al. (1995). Rapid turnover of plasma virions and CD4 lymphocytes in HIV-1 infection. *Nature, 373,* 123–126.

Ho, E. D. F., Tsang, A. K. T., & Ho, D. Y. F. (1991). An investigation of the calendar calculation ability of a Chinese calendar savant. *Journal of Autism and Developmental Disorders, 21,* 315–327.

Hobson, R. P. (1987). The autistic child's recognition of age- and sex-related characteristics of people. *Journal of Autism and Developmental Disorders, 17,* 63–79.

Hodgins, D. C., Currie, S. R., & El-Guebaly, N. (2001). Motivational enhancement and self-help treatments for problem gambling. *Journal of Consulting and Clinical Psychology, 69,* 50–57.

Hodgins, D. C., El-Guebaly, N., & Armstrong, S. (1995). Prospective and retrospective reports of mood states before relapse to substance use. *Journal of Consulting and Clinical Psychology, 63,* 400–407.

Hodgins, S., Mednick, S. A., Brennan, P. A., Schulsinger, F., & Engberg, M. (1996). Mental disorder and crime. *Archives of General Psychiatry, 53,* 489–496.

Hoehn-Saric, R., McLeod, D. R., Funderburk, F., & Kowalski, P. (2004). Somatic symptoms and physiologic responses in generalized anxiety disorder and panic disorder: An ambulatory monitor study. *Archives of General Psychiatry, 61,* 913–921.

Hoehn-Saric, R., Pearlson, G. D., Harris, G. J., Machlin, S. R., & Camargo, E. E. (1991). Effects of fluoxetine on regional cerebral blood flow in obsessive-compulsive patients. *American Journal of Psychiatry, 148,* 1243–1245.

Hoff, A. L., Kremen, W. S., Weineke, M. H., Lauriello, J., et al. (2001). Association of estrogen levels with neuropsychological performance in women with schizophrenia. *American Journal of Psychiatry, 158,* 1134–1139.

Hoffman, K. B., Cole, D. A., Martin, J. M., Tram, J., & Seroczynski, A. D. (2000). Are the discrepancies between self- and others' appraisals of competence predictive or reflective of depressive symptoms in children and adolescents? A longitudinal study: Part 2. *Journal of Abnormal Psychology, 109,* 651–662.

Hoffman, L. (1998). *Eating disorders.* Rockville, MD: National Institutes of Health.

Hoffman, M. A. (1991). Counseling the HIV-infected client: A psychosocial model for assessment and intervention. *Counseling Psychologist, 19,* 467–542.

Hoffmann, S. G. (2000). Self-focused attention before and after treatment of social phobia. *Behaviour Research and Therapy, 38,* 717–725.

Hofmann, S. G., Ehlers, A., & Roth, W. T. (1995). Conditioning theory: A model for the etiology of public speaking anxiety? *Behaviour Research and Therapy, 33,* 567–571.

Hofmann, S. G., Lehman, C. L., & Barlow, D. H. (1997). How specific are specific phobias? *Journal of Behavior Therapy and Experimental Psychiatry, 28,* 233–240.

Hoffmann, S. G., Moscovitch, D. A., Kim, H.-J., & Taylor, A. N. (2004). Changes in self-perception during treatment of social phobia. *Journal of Consulting and Clinical Psychology, 72,* 588–596.

Hoge, C. W., Castro, C. A., Messer, S. C., McGurk, D., et al. (2004). Combat duty in Iraq and Afghanistan, mental health problems and barriers to care. *New England Journal of Medicine, 351,* 13–22.

Hohmann, A. A., Larson, D. B., Thompson, J. W., & Beardsley, R. S. (1988, November). *Psychotropic medication prescription in U.S. ambulatory medical care.* Paper presented at the American Public Health Association Annual Meeting, Boston, Massachusetts.

Holahan, C. (2001a, August 28). Hidden eating disorders concealment is growing, specialists say. *Boston Globe,* p. C4.

Holahan, C. (2001b, August 4). Yahoo removes pro-eating-disorder Internet sites. *Boston Globe,* p. A2.

Holahan, C. J., & Moos, R. H. (1991). Life stressors, personal and social resources, and depression: A four-year structure model. *Journal of Abnormal Psychology, 100,* 31–38.

Holbrook, T., & Weltzin, T. E. (1998). Eating disorders in males. *Treatment Today, 10,* 52–53.

Holcomb, H. H., Links, J., Smith, C., & Wong, D. (1989). Positron emission tomography: Measuring the metabolic and neurochemical characteristics of the living human nervous system. In N. C. Andreasen (Ed.), *Brain imaging: Applications in psychiatry* (pp. 235–370). Washington, DC: American Psychiatric Press.

Holden, C. (1986). Proposed new psychiatric diagnoses raise charges of gender bias. *Science, 231,* 327–328.

Holden, N. L. (1987). Late paraphrenia or the paraphrenias? A descriptive study with a 10-year follow-up. *British Journal of Psychiatry, 150,* 635–639.

Hollender, M. H. (1980). The case of Anna O.: A reformulation. *American Journal of Psychiatry, 137,* 797–800.

Hollon, S. D., & Beck, A. T. (1994). Cognitive and cognitive-behavioral therapies. In A. E. Bergin & S. L. Garfield (Eds.), *Handbook of psychotherapy and behavior change* (pp. 428–466). New York: Wiley.

Hollon, S. D., & Fawcett, J. (2001). Combined medication and psychotherapy. In G. O. Gabbard (Ed.), *Treatment of psychiatric disorders* (pp. 1247–1266). Washington, DC: American Psychiatric Press.

Hollon, S. D., DeRubeis, R. J., & Seligman, M. E. P. (1992). Cognitive therapy and the prevention of depression. *Applied and Preventive Psychology, 1,* 89–95.

Hollon, S. D., Thase, M. E., & Markowitz, J. C. (2002). Treatment and prevention of depression. *Psychological Science in the Public Interest, 3,* 39–77.

Holloway, J. D. (2003). Understanding compulsive sexual behavior. *APA Monitor, 34,* 20.

Holloway, J. D. (2004). Lawsuits could change managed-care landscape. *Monitor on Psychology, 35*(3), 30–31.

Holmes, T. H., & Rahe, R. H. (1967). The Social Readjustment Rating Scale. *Journal of Psychosomatic Research, 11,* 213–218.

Holmes, T. S., & Holmes, T. H. (1970). Short-term intrusion into the life style routine. *Journal of Psychosomatic Research, 14,* 121–132.

Holroyd, J., & Brodsky, A. (1977). Psychologists' attitudes and practices regarding erotic and nonerotic physical contact with patients. *American Psychologist, 32,* 839–843.

Holroyd, K. A., France, J. L., Cordingley, G. E., & Rockicki, L. A. (1995). Enhancing the effectiveness of relaxation-thermal biofeedback training with propranolol hydrochloride. *Journal of Consulting and Clinical Psychology, 63,* 327–330.

Holroyd, S., & Baron-Cohen, S. (1993). Brief report: How far can people with autism go in developing a theory of mind? *Journal of Autism and Developmental Disorders, 23,* 379–385.

Honda, K., & Goodwin, R. D. (2004). Cancer and mental disorders in a national community sample. *Psychotherapy and Psychosomatics, 73,* 235–242.

Hong, G. K., & Domokos-Cheng Ham, M. (2001). *Psychotherapy and counseling with Asian American clients.* Thousand Oaks, CA: Sage.

Hood, B., Bruck, D., & Kennedy, G. (2004). Determinants of sleep quality in the healthy aged: The role of physical, psychological, circadian and naturalistic light variables. *Age and Ageing, 33,* 159–165.

Hooper, J. (1998, August). Science in the sack: Beyond Viagra. *Health and Fitness,* pp. 108–113.

Hoover, D. W., & Milich, R. (1994). Effects of sugar ingestion expectancies on mother-child interactions. *Journal of Abnormal Child Psychology, 22,* 501–515.

Horne, R. L., Pettinati, H. M., Sugerman, A. A., & Varga, E. (1985). Comparing bilateral to unilateral electroconvulsive therapy in randomized study with EEG monitoring. *Archives of General Psychiatry, 42,* 1087–1092.

Horowitz, M. J. (2001). Histrionic personality disorder. In G. O. Gabbard (Ed.), *Treatment of psychiatric disorders* (pp. 2293–2307). Washington, DC: American Psychiatric Press.

Houston, B. K., Babyak, M. A., Chesney, M. A., Black, G., & Ragland, D. R. (1997). Social dominance and 22-year all-cause mortality in men. *Psychosomatic Medicine, 59,* 5–12.

Houston case may sink Texas sodomy law. (1998, November 7). *San Francisco Chronicle,* p. A7.

Hovanitz, C. A., & Wander, M. R. (1990). Tension headache: Disregulation at some levels of stress. *Journal of Behavioral Medicine, 13,* 539–560.

Hovarth, K., Stefanatos, G., Sokolski, K. N., Wachtel, R., et al. (1998). Improved social and language skills after secretin administration in patients with autistic spectrum disorders. *Journal for the Association for Academic Minority Physician, 9,* 9–15.

Howard, K. (1994). Quality assurance in psychotherapy: An application of research to clinical cases. In Scientific Program Committee (Ed.), *Proceedings of the 16th International Congress of Psychotherapy,* Seoul: Korean Academy of Psychotherapists.

Howard, R. (1992). Folie a deux involving a dog. *American Journal of Psychiatry, 149,* 414.

Howard, R., Rabins, P. V., Seeman, M. V., & Jeste, D. V. (2000). International late onset schizophrenia group: Late-onset schizophrenia and very-late-onset schizophrenia-like psychosis—An international consensus. *American Journal of Psychiatry, 157,* 172–178.

Hu, S., Pattatucci, A. M. L., & Patterson, C. L. L. (1995, November). Linkage between sexual orientation and chromosome Xq28 in males but not in females. *Nature Genetics, 11,* 248–256.

Hubble, M. A., Duncan, B. L., & Miller, S. D. (Eds.). (1999). *The heart and soul of change.* Washington, DC: American Psychological Association.

Hudson, J. I., Manoach, D. S., Sabo, A. N., & Sternbach, S. E. (1991). Recurrent nightmares in posttraumatic stress disorder: Association with sleep paralysis, hypnopompic hallucinations, and REM sleep. *Journal of Nervous and Mental Disease, 179,* 572–573.

Hudziak, J. J., Beijsterveldt, C. E. M., Althof, R. R., Stanger, C., et al. (2004). Genetic and environmental contributions to the Child Behavior Checklist Obsessive-Compulsive Scale: A cross-cultural twin study. *Archives of General Psychiatry, 61,* 608–617.

Hull, J. C., & Bond, C. F. (1986). Social and behavioral consequences of alcohol consumption and expectancy: A meta-analysis. *Psychological Bulletin, 99,* 347–360.

Humphrey, D. (1991). *Final exit.* Eugene, OR: Hemlock Society.

Hunsley, J., Crabb, R., & Mash, E. J. (2004). Evidence-based clinical assessment. *Clinical Psychologist, 57,* 25–32.

Hunter, R., Blackwood, W., & Bull, J. (1968). Three cases of frontal meningiomas presenting psychiatrically. *British Medical Journal, 3,* 9–16.

Hunter, R., & Macalpine, I. (1963). *Three hundred years of psychiatry, 1535–1860.* London: Oxford University Press.

Huppert, J. D., Schultz, L. T., Foa, E. B., Barlow, D. H., et al. (2004). Differential response to placebo among patients with social phobia, panic disorder, and obsessive-compulsive disorder. *American Journal of Psychiatry, 161,* 1485–1487.

Hurley, R. A., Saxena, S., Rauch, S. L., Hoehn-Saric, R., & Taber, K. H. (2002). Predicting treatment response in obsessive-compulsive disorder. *Journal of Neuropsychiatry and Clinical Neurosciences, 14,* 249–255.

Hurtig, A. L., & Rosenthal, I. M. (1987). Psychological findings in early treated cases of female pseudohermaphroditism caused by virilizing congenital adrenal hyperplasia. *Archives of Sexual Behavior, 16,* 209–223.

Hussong, A. M., Hicks, R. E., Levy, S. A., & Curran, P. J. (2001). Specifying the relations between affect and heavy alcohol use among young adults. *Journal of Abnormal Psychology, 110,* 449–461.

Hutchings, B., & Mednick, S. A. (1977). Criminality in adoptees and their adoptive and biological parents: A pilot study. In S. A. Mednick & K. L. Christianson (Eds.), *Biosocial bases of criminal behavior.* New York: Garden Press.

Hynd, G. W., Hern, K. L., Voeller, K. K., & Marshall, R. M. (1991). Neurobiological basis of attention-deficit hyperactivity disorder. *School Psychology Review, 20,* 174–186.

Ina, S. (1997). Counseling Japanese Americans. In C. C. Lee (Ed.), *Multicultural issues in counseling.* Alexandria, VA: American Counseling Association.

Ingraham, L. J., Kugelmass, S., Frenkel, E., Nathan, M., & Mirsky, A. F. (1995). Twenty-five–year follow-up of the Israeli high-risk study: Current and lifetime psychopathology. *Schizophrenia Bulletin, 21,* 183–192.

Inman, T. H., Vickery, C. D., Berry, D. T. R., Lamb, D. G., et al. (1998). Development and initial validation of a new procedure for evaluating adequacy of effort given during neuropsychological testing: The Letter Memory Test. *Psychological Assessment, 10,* 128–139.

Irizarry, L. (2004, August 8). Widespread starvation: A proliferation of web sites are promoting anorexia, which shows that sometimes, there is no safety in numbers. *Times-Picayune,* p. 1.

Irving, L. M. (2001). Media exposure and disordered eating: Introduction to the special section. *Journal of Social and Clinical Psychology, 20,* 259–263.

Irwin, A., & Gross, A. M. (1990). Mental retardation in childhood. In M. Hersen & C. G. Last (Eds.), *Handbook of child and adult psychopathology* (pp. 325–336). New York: Pergamon Press.

Irwin, H. J. (1998). Attitudinal predictors of dissociation: Hostility and powerlessness. *Journal of Psychology, 132,* 389–404.

Irwin, M., Daniels, M., Smith, T. L., Bloom, E., & Weiner, H. (1987). Impaired natural killer cell activity during bereavement. *Brain, Behavior, and Immunity, 1,* 98–104.

Isenberg, S. A., Lehrer, P. M., & Hochron, S. (1992). The effects of suggestion and emotional arousal on pulmonary function in asthma: A review and a hypothesis regarding vagal medication. *Psychosomatic Medicine, 54,* 192–216.

Issenman, R. M., Filmer, R. B., & Gorski, P. A. (1999). A review of bowel and bladder control development in children: How gastrointestinal and urologic conditions relate to problems in toilet training. *Pediatrics, 103,* 1346–1352.

Ito, Y., Teicher, M. H., Glod, C. A., & Ackerman, E. (1998).

Preliminary evidence for aberrant cortical development in abused children: A qualitative EEG study. *Journal of Neuropsychiatry and Clinical Neuroscience, 10,* 293–307.

Ivey, A. E., D'Andrea, M., Ivey, M., & Simek-Morgan, L. (2002). *Theories of counseling and psychotherapy: A multicultural perspective.* Boston: Allyn & Bacon.

Ivnik, R. J., Smith, G. E., Malec, J. F., Petersen, R. C., & Tangalos, E. G. (1995). Long-term stability and intercorrelations of cognitive abilities in older persons. *Psychological Assessment, 7,* 155–161.

Iwamasa, G. Y., Larrabee, A. L., & Merrit, R. D. (2000). Are personality disorder criteria ethnically biased? A card-sort analysis. *Cultural Diversity and Ethnic Minority Psychology, 6,* 284–296.

Jablensky, A. V., Morgan, V., Zubrick, S. R., Bower, C., & Yellachich, L. A. (2005). Pregnancy, delivery, and neonatal complications in a population cohort of women with schizophrenia and major affective disorder. *American Journal of Psychiatry, 162,* 79–91.

Jackson, A. M. (1983). A theoretical model for the practice of psychotherapy with black populations. *Journal of Black Psychology, 10,* 19–27.

Jackson, B., & Farrugia, D. (1997). Diagnosis and treatment of adults with attention deficit hyperactive disorder. *Journal of Counseling and Development, 75,* 312–319.

Jackson, C. T., Covell, N. H., & Essock, S. M. (2004). Differential effectiveness of clozapine for patients nonresponsive to or intolerant of first generation antipsychotic medications. *Schizophrenia Bulletin, 30,* 219–223.

Jackson, J. L., Calhoun, K., Amick, A. E., Maddever, H. M., & Habif, V. (1990). Young adult women who experienced childhood intrafamilial sexual abuse: Subsequent adjustment. *Archives of Sexual Behavior, 19,* 211–221.

Jackson, K. M., Sher, K. J., Gotham, H. J., & Wood, P. K. (2001). Transitioning into and out of large-effect drinking in young adulthood. *Journal of Abnormal Psychology, 110,* 378–391.

Jackson, M., & Claridge, G. (1991). Reliability and validity of a psychotic traits questionnaire (STQ). *British Journal of Psychiatry, 30,* 311–323.

Jackson, T. (2003, December 17). Malvo's case in hands of Va. jury: Insanity argued in sniper case. *The Washington Post,* p. A01.

Jacobs, D., & Klein, M. E. (1993). The expanding role of psychological autopsies. In A. A. Leenaars (Ed.), *Suicidology.* Northvale: Jason Aronson.

Jacobsen, L. K., Giedd, J. N., Castellanos, F. X., Vaituzis, A. C., et al. (1998). Progressive reduction of temporal lobe structures in childhood-onset schizophrenia. *American Journal of Psychiatry, 155,* 678–685.

Jacobsen, P. B., Bovbjerg, D. H., Schwartz, M. D., Hudis, C. A., et al. (1995). Conditioned emotional distress in women receiving chemotherapy for breast cancer. *Journal of Consulting and Clinical Psychology, 63,* 108–114.

Jacobson, E. (1938). *Progressive relaxation.* Chicago: University of Chicago Press.

Jacobson, E. (1967). *Tension in medicine.* Springfield, IL: Thomas.

Jacobson, N. S., & Anderson, E. A. (1982). Interpersonal skill and depression in college students: An analysis of the timing of self-disclosures. *Behavior Therapy, 13,* 271–282.

Jacobson, S., & Alex, P. (2001, February 19). Waist management: Men aren't immune to eating disorders, but they do their best to disguise them. *Record,* p. 1.

James, R. K., & Gilliland, B. E. (2003). *Counseling and psychotherapy.* Boston: Allyn & Bacon.

Jamison, K. R. (1996). Manic-depressive illness, genes, and creativity. In L. L. Hall (Ed.), *Genetics and mental illness: Evolving issues for research and society* (pp. 111–132). New York: Plenum Press.

Janssen, K. (1983). Treatment of sinus tachycardia with heart-rate feedback. *Psychiatry and Human Development, 17,* 166–176.

Janus, S. S., & Janus, C. L. (1993). *The Janus report on sexual behavior.* New York: Wiley.

Jason, L. A. (1998). Tobacco, drug and HIV prevention media

interventions. *American Journal of Community Psychology, 26,* 151–187.

Jawed, S. Y. (1991). A survey of psychiatrically ill Asian children. *British Journal of Psychiatry, 158,* 268–270.

Jellinek, E. M. (1971). Phases of alcohol addiction. In G. Shean (Ed.), *Studies in abnormal behavior.* Chicago: Rand McNally.

Jenike, M. A. (2001). A forty-five-year-old woman with obsessive-compulsive disorder. *Journal of the American Medical Association, 285,* 2121–2128.

Jenike, M. A. (2004). Obsessive-compulsive disorder. *New England Journal of Medicine, 350,* 259–265.

Jenner, F. A., Gjessing, L. R., Cox, J. R., Davies-Jones, A., et al. (1967). A manic-depressive psychotic with a persistent forty-eight-hour cycle. *British Journal of Psychiatry, 113,* 895–910.

Jenner, J. A., Nienhuis, F. J., Wiersma, D., & van de Willige, G. (2004). Hallucination focused integrative treatment: A randomized controlled trial. *Schizophrenia Bulletin, 30,* 133–145.

Jensen, P. S. (2003). Foreword. In S. Ozonoff, S. J. Rogers, & R. L. Hendren (Eds.), *Autism spectrum disorders: A research review for practitioners* (pp. xv–xix). Arlington, VA: American Psychiatric.

Jensen, P. S., Bhatara, V. S., Vitiello, B., Hoagwood, K., et al. (1999). Proactive medication prescribing practices for U.S. children: Gaps between research and clinical practice. *Journal of the American Academy of Child and Adolescent Psychiatry, 38,* 557–565.

Jilek, W. G. (2001). Cultural factors in psychiatric disorders. Paper presented at the Twenty-sixth Congress of the World Federation for Mental Health, July.

Johnson, D. A. W., Ludlow, J. M., Street, K., & Taylor, R. D. W. (1987). Double-blind comparison of half-dose and standard-dose flupenthixol decanoate in the maintenance treatment of stabilized out-patients with schizophrenia. *British Journal of Psychiatry, 151,* 634–638.

Johnson, K. W., Anderson, N. B., Bastida, E., Kramer, B. J., et al. (1995). Macrosocial and environmental influences on minority health. *Health Psychology, 14,* 601–612.

Johnson, S. L., Sandrow, D., Meyer, B., Winters, R., et al. (2000). Increases in manic symptoms after life events involving goal attainment. *Journal of Abnormal Psychology, 109,* 721–727.

Johnson, W. G. (1990). Multifactorial diseases and other disorders with non-Mendelian inheritance. In H. E. Hendrie, L. G. Mendelsohn, & C. Readhead (Eds.), *Brain aging: Molecular biology, the aging process and neurodegenerative disease* (pp. 5–19). Bern, Germany: Hans Huber.

Johnston, C., Fine, S., Weiss, M., & Weiss, J. (2000). Effects of stimulant medication treatment on mothers and children's attribution for the behavior of children with ADHD. *Journal of Abnormal Child Psychology, 28,* 371–382.

Joiner, T. E., Heatherton, T. F., Rudd, M. D., & Schmidt, N. B. (1997). Perfectionism, perceived weight status, and bulimic symptoms: Two studies testing a diathesis-stress model. *Journal of Abnormal Psychology, 106,* 145–153.

Jones, D. R., Harrell, J. P., Morris-Prather, C. E., Thomas, J., & Omowale, N. (1996). Affective and physiological responses to racism. The role of Afrocentrism and mode of presentation. *Ethnicity and Disease, 6,* 109–122.

Jones, J. M. (1995). Headache: Benign or catastrophic? *Physician Assistant, 19,* 25–44.

Jones, J. M. (1996). Treating acute pain in a desperate headache. *Journal of the American Academy of Physician Assistants, 9,* 26–50.

Jones, J. M., Bennett, S., Olmsted, M. P., Lawson, M. L., & Rodin, G. (2001). Disordered eating attitudes and behaviours in teenaged girls: A school-based study. *Canadian Medical Association Journal, 165,* 547–551.

Jones, K. L., Shainberg, L. W., & Byer, C. O. (1977). *Sex and people.* New York: Harper & Row.

Joseph, E. (1991). Psychodynamic personality theory. In K. Davis, H. Klar, & J. J. Coyle (Eds.), *Foundations of psychiatry.* Philadelphia: Saunders.

Joseph, J. (2001). Separated twins and the genetics of personality differences: A critique. *American Journal of Psychology, 114,* 1–30.

Joseph, S. A., Brewin, C. R., Yule, W., & Williams, R. (1993). Causal attributions in posttraumatic stress in adolescents. *Journal of Child Psychology and Psychiatry, 34,* 247–253.

Joyce, C. (1988). Assault on the brain. *Psychology Today, 22,* 38–44.

Julkunen, J., Idanpaan-Heikkila, U., & Saarinen, T. (1993). Components of type A behavior and the first-year prognosis of a myocardial infarction. *Journal of Psychosomatic Research, 37,* 11–18.

Junginger, J. (1996). Psychosis and violence: The case for a content analysis of psychotic experience. *Schizophrenia Bulletin, 22,* 91–103.

Just, N., & Alloy, L. B. (1997). The response styles of depression: Tests and an extension of the theory. *Journal of Abnormal Psychology, 106,* 221–229.

Kabot, S., Masi, W., & Segal, M. (2003). Advances in the diagnosis and treatment of autism spectrum disorders. *Professional Psychology: Research and Practice, 34,* 26–33.

Kahn, A. U., Staerk, M., & Bonk, C. (1974). Role of counterconditioning in the treatment of asthma. *Journal of Psychosomatic Research, 18,* 88–92.

Kaivanto, K. K., Estlander, A. M., Moneta, G. B., & Banharanta, H. (1995). Isokinetic performance in low back pain patients: The predictive power of the self-efficacy scale. *Journal of Occupational Rehabilitation, 5,* 87–99.

Kamphaus, R. W., Petoskey, M. D., & Rowe, E. W. (2000). Current trends in psychological testing of children. *Professional Psychology: Research and Practice, 31,* 155–164.

Kamphuis, J. H., & Telch, M. J. (2000). Effects of distraction and guided threat reappraisal on fear reduction during exposure-based treatments for specific fears. *Behaviour Research and Therapy, 38,* 1163–1181.

Kanas, N. (1988). Psychoactive substance use disorders: Alcohol. In H. H. Goldman (Ed.), *Review of general psychiatry* (pp. 286–298). Norwalk, CT: Appleton & Lange.

Kanaya, T., Scullin, M. H., & Ceci, S. J. (2003). The Flynn Effect and U.S. policies: The impact of rising IQ scores on American society via mental retardation diagnoses. *American Psychologist, 58,* 778–790.

Kanayama, G., Pope, H. G., Jr., & Hudson, J. I. (2001). "Body image" drugs: A growing psychosomatic problem. *Psychotherapy and Psychosomatics, 70,* 61–64.

Kane, J. M., & Freeman, H. L. (1994). Towards more effective antipsychotic treatment. *British Journal of Psychiatry, 165,* 22–31.

Kane, J. M., Woerner, M., Borenstein, M., Wegner, J., & Lieberman, J. (1986). Investigating the incidence and prevalence of tardive dyskinesia. *Psychopharmacology Bulletin, 22,* 254–258.

Kanfer, F. H., & Phillips, J. S. (1969). A survey of current behavior therapies and a proposal for classification. In C. M. Franks (Ed.), *Behavior therapy: Appraisal and status.* New York: Wiley.

Kang, S. H., Chen, A. M., Lew, R., Min, K., et al. (1997). Behavioral risk factor survey of Korean Americans: Alameda County, California, 1994. *MMWR, 46,* 774–777.

Kanner, L. (1943). Autistic disturbances of affective content. *Nervous Child, 2,* 217–240.

Kanner, L., & Lesser, L. I. (1958). Early infantile autism. *Pediatrics Clinic of North America, 5,* 711–730.

Kaplan, H. S. (1974). No nonsense therapy for six sexual malfunctions. *Psychology Today, 8,* 76–80, 83, 86.

Kaplan, M. (1983). A woman's view of DSM-III. *American Psychologist, 38,* 786–792.

Karlsson, H., Bachmann, S., Schroder, J., McArthur, J., et al. (2001). Retroviral RNA identified in the cerebrospinal fluids and brains of individuals with schizophrenia. *Proceedings of the National Academy of Science, 98,* 4634–4639.

Karmarck, T. W., Muldoon, M. F., Shiffman, S., Sutton-Tyrrell, K., et al. (2004). Experiences of demand and control in daily life as correlates of subclinical carotid atherosclerosis in a healthy older sample. *Health Psychology, 23,* 24–32.

Karno, M., & Golding, J. M. (1991). Obsessive-compulsive disorder. In L. N. Robins & D. A. Regier (Eds.), *Psychiatric disorders in America: The Epidemiologic Catchment Area study* (pp. 204–219). New York: Free Press.

Karno, M., Hough, R. L., Burnam, A., Escobar, J. I., et al. (1987). Lifetime prevalence of specific psychiatric disorders among Mexican Americans and non-Hispanic whites in Los Angeles. *Archives of General Psychiatry, 44,* 695–701.

Karon, B. P. (1995). Provision of psychotherapy under managed health care: A growing crisis and national nightmare. *Professional Psychology: Research and Practice, 26,* 5–9.

Kasari, C., Sigman, M. D., Baumgartner, P., & Stipek, D. J. (1993). Pride and mastery in children with autism. *Journal of Child Psychology and Psychiatry, 34,* 353–362.

Kaslow, N. J., & Aronson, S. G. (2004). Recommendations for family interventions following a suicide. *Professional Psychology: Research and Practice, 35,* 240–246.

Kaszniak, A. W., Nussbaum, P. D., Berren, M. R., & Santiago, J. (1988). Amnesia as a consequence of male rape: A case report. *Journal of Abnormal Psychology, 97,* 100–104.

Katschnig, H., & Amering, M. (1994) Long-term treatment risk/benefit ratio and therapeutic outcome. *Clinical Neuropharmacology, 15,* 178–179.

Kaufman, A. S., Kamphaus, R. W., & Kaufman, N. L. (1985). The Kaufman Assessment Battery for Children (K-ABC). In C. S. Newmark (Ed.), *Major psychological assessment instruments* (pp. 249–276). Boston: Allyn & Bacon.

Kaufman, A. S., & Kaufman, N. L. (1983). *Kaufman Assessment Battery for Children. Circle Pines,* MN: American Guidance Services.

Kaul, T. J., & Bednar, R. L. (1986). Experiential group research: Results, questions, and suggestions. In S. L. Garfield and A. E. Bergin (Eds.), *Handbook of psychotherapy and behavior change: An evaluative analysis.* New York: Wiley.

Kavanagh, D. J. (1992). Recent developments in expressed emotions and schizophrenia. *British Journal of Psychiatry, 160,* 601–620.

Kawachi, I., Sparrow, D., Vonkonas, P. S., & Weiss, S. T. (1994). Symptoms of anxiety and risk of coronary heart disease: The Normative Aging Study. *Circulation, 90,* 2225–2229.

Kazdin, A. E. (1987). Treatment of antisocial behavior in children: Current status and future directions. *Psychological Bulletin, 102,* 187–203.

Kazdin, A. E. (1994). Psychotherapy for children and adolescents. In A. E. Bergin & S. L. Garfield (Eds.), *Handbook of psychotherapy and behavior change* (pp. 543–594). New York: Wiley.

Kazdin, A. E. (1998). Treatment manuals in clinical practice: Introduction to the series. *Clinical Psychology, 5,* 361–362.

Kazdin, A. E., Siegel, T. C., & Bass, D. (1992). Cognitive problem-solving skills training and parent management training in the treatment of antisocial behavior in children. *Journal of Consulting and Clinical Psychology, 60,* 733–747.

Keel, P. K., Mitchell, J. E., Miller, K. B., Davis, T. L., & Crow, S. J. (1999). Long-term outcome of bulimia nervosa. *Archives of General Psychiatry, 56,* 63–69.

Kegeles, T., Catania, J., & Coates, T. (1988). Intentions to communicate positive HIV status to sex partners (letters to the editor). *Journal of the American Medical Association, 259,* 216–217.

Keith, S. J., Regier, D. A., & Rae, D. S. (1991). Schizophrenic disorders. In L. N. Robins & D. A. Regier (Eds.), *Psychiatric disorders in America* (pp. 33–52). New York: Free Press.

Kellner, R. (1985). Functional somatic symptoms and hypochondriasis. *Archives of General Psychiatry, 42,* 821–833.

Kellner, R., Hernandez, J., & Pathak, D. (1992). Hypochondriacal fears and beliefs, anxiety, and somatization. *British Journal of Psychiatry, 160,* 525–532.

Kelly, J. A., & Murphy, D. A. (1992). Psychological interventions with AIDS and HIV: Prevention and treatment. *Journal of Consulting and Clinical Psychology, 60*(4), 576–585.

Kendall, P. C., Brady, E. U., & Verduin, T. L. (2001). Comorbidity in childhood anxiety disorders and treatment outcomes. *Journal of the American Academy of Child and Adolescent Psychology, 40,* 787–794.

Kendall, P. C., Holmbeck, G., & Verduin, T. (2004). Methodology, design, and evaluation in psychotherapy research. In M. J. Lambert (Ed.), *Bergin and Garfield's handbook of psychotherapy and behavior change* (pp. 16–43). New York: Wiley.

Kendall-Tackett, K. A., Williams, L. M., & Finkelhor, D. (1993). Impact of sexual abuse on children: A review and synthesis of recent empirical studies. *Psychological Bulletin, 113,* 164–180.

Kendler, K. S. (1988). Familial aggregation of schizophrenia and schizophrenic spectrum disorders. *Archives of General Psychiatry, 45,* 377–383.

Kendler, K. S., & Hays, P. (1982). Familial and sporadic schizophrenia: A symptomatic, prognostic, and EEG comparison. *American Journal of Psychiatry, 139,* 1557–1562.

Kendler, K. S., Hettema, J. M., Butera, F., Gardner, C. O., & Prescott, C. A. (2003). Life event dimensions of loss, humiliation, entrapment and danger in the prediction of onsets of major depression and generalized anxiety. *Archives of General Psychiatry, 60,* 789–796.

Kendler, K. S., Karkowski-Shuman, L., O'Neill, F. A., & Straub, R. E. (1997). Resemblance of psychotic symptoms and syndromes in affected sibling pairs from the Irish study of high-density schizophrenia families: Evidence for possible etiologic heterogeneity. *American Journal of Psychiatry, 154,* 191–198.

Kendler, K. S., MacLean, C., Neale, M., Kessler, R., et al. (1991). The genetic epidemiology of bulimia nervosa. *American Journal of Psychiatry, 148,* 1627–1637.

Kendler, K. S., Myers, J., Prescott, C. A., & Neale, M. C. (2001). The genetic epidemiology of irrational fears and phobias in men. *Archives of General Psychiatry, 58,* 257–265.

Kendler, K. S., Neale, M. C., Kessler, R. C., Heath, A. C., & Eaves, L. J. (1992). Generalized anxiety disorder in women. *Archives of General Psychiatry, 49,* 267–271.

Kendler, K. S., Silberg, J. L., Neale, M. C., Kessler, R. C., et al. (1991). The family history method: Whose psychiatric history is being measured? *American Journal of Psychiatry, 148,* 1501–1504.

Kennedy, R. (2002). PTSD: The trauma after the trauma. *Medscape Psychiatry and Mental Health, 2.* Retrieved January 12, 2003, from http://medscape.com/viewarticle/441133

Kent, J. M., Papp, L. A., Martinez, J. M., Browne, S. T., et al. (2001). Specificity of panic response to CO_2 inhalation in panic disorder: A comparison with major depression and premenstrual dysphoric disorder. *American Journal of Psychiatry, 158,* 58–67.

Kerlitz, I., & Fulton, J. P. (1984). *The insanity defense and its alternatives: A guide to policy makers.* Williamsburg, VA: National Center for State Courts.

Kernberg, O. (1976). Technical considerations in the treatment of borderline personality organization. *Journal of the American Psychoanalytic Association, 24,* 795–829.

Kernberg, O. F. (1975). *Borderline conditions and pathological narcissism.* New York: Jason Aronson.

Kessler, R. C. (2003). Epidemiology of women and depression. *Journal of Affective Disorders, 74,* 5–13.

Kessler, R. C., McGonagle, K. A., Zhao, S., Nelson, C. B., et al. (1994). Lifetime and twelve-month prevalence of DSM-III-R psychiatric disorders in the United States. *Archives of General Psychiatry, 51,* 8–19.

Kessler, R. C., Sonnega, A., Bromet, E., Hughes, M., & Nelson, B. (1995). Posttraumatic stress disorder in the National Comorbidity Survey. *Archives of General Psychiatry, 52,* 1048–1068.

Kessler, R. C., Stein, M. B., & Berglund, P. (1998). Social phobia subtypes in the National Comorbidity Survey. *American Journal of Psychiatry, 155,* 613–619.

Kety, S. S., Wender, P. H., Jacobsen, B., Ingraham, L. J., et al. (1994). Mental illness in the biological and adoptive relatives of schizophrenic adoptees. *Archives of General Psychiatry, 51,* 442–455.

Khanna, S., Desai, N. G., & Channabasavanna, S. M. (1987). A treatment package for transsexualism. *Behavior Therapy, 2,* 193–199.

Kiecolt-Glaser, J. K., Dura, J. R., Speicher, C. E., Trask, O. J., et al. (1991). Spousal caregivers of dementia victims: Longitudinal changes in immunity and health. *Psychosomatic Medicine, 53,* 345–362.

Kiecolt-Glaser, J. K., & Glaser, R. (1992). Psychoneuroimmunology: Can psychological interventions modulate immunity? *Journal of Consulting and Clinical Psychology, 60,* 569–575.

Kiecolt-Glaser, J. K., & Glaser, R. (1993). Mind and immunity. In D. Goleman & J. Gurin (Eds.), *Mind/body medicine* (pp. 39–64). New York: Consumer Reports Books.

Kiecolt-Glaser, J. K., & Glaser, R. (1995). Psychoneuroimmunology and health consequences: Data and shared mechanisms. *Psychosomatic Medicine, 57,* 269–274.

Kiecolt-Glaser, J. K., Glaser, R., Cacioppo, J. T., MacCallum, R. C., et al. (1997). Marital conflict in older adults: Endocrinological and immunological correlates. *Psychosomatic Medicine, 59,* 339–349.

Kiecolt-Glaser, J. K., Glaser, R., Dyer, C., Shuttleworth, E. C., et al. (1987). Chronic stress and immune function in family care-givers of Alzheimer's disease victims. *Psychosomatic Medicine, 49,* 523–535.

Kienhorst, I. C., de Wilde, E. J., Diekstra, R. F. W., & Wolters, W. H. G. (1995). Adolescents' image of their suicide attempt. *Journal of the American Academy of Childhood and Adolescent Psychiatry, 34,* 623–628.

Kiesler, C. A. (1991). Homelessness and public policy priorities. *American Psychologist, 46,* 1245–1252.

Killen, J. D., Fortmann, S. P., Schatzberg, A. F., Hayward, C., et al. (2000). Nicotine patch and paroxetine for smoking cessation. *Journal of Consulting and Clinical Psychology, 68,* 883–889.

Killen, J. D., Robinson, T. N., Haydel, K. F., Hayward, C., et al. (1997). Prospective study of risk factors for the initiation of cigarette smoking. *Journal of Consulting and Clinical Psychology, 65,* 1011–1016.

Kilmann, P., Sabalis, R., Gearing, M., Bukstel, L., & Scovern, A. (1982). The treatment of sexual paraphilias: A review of the outcome research. *Journal of Sex Research, 18,* 193–252.

Kilmann, P. R., & Auerbach, R. (1979). Treatments of premature ejaculation and psychogenic impotence: A critical review of the literature. *Archives of Sexual Behavior, 8,* 81–100.

Kim, M.-S., Ha, T. H., & Kwon, J. S. (2004). Neurological abnormalities in schizophrenia and obsessive-compulsive disorder. *Current Opinion in Psychiatry, 17,* 215–220.

Kim, U., & Berry, J. W. (1993). *Indigenous psychologies.* Newbury Park, CA: Sage.

Kimerling, R., & Calhoun, K. S. (1994). Somatic symptoms, social support, and treatment seeking among sexual assault victims. *Journal of Consulting and Clinical Psychology, 62,* 333–340.

Kinderman, P., & Bentall, R. P. (1996). Self-discrepancies and persecutory delusions: Evidence for a model of paranoid ideation. *Journal of Abnormal Psychology, 105,* 106–113.

Kinderman, P., & Bentall, R. P. (1997). Casual attributions in paranoia and depression: Internal, personal, and situational attributions for negative events. *Journal of Abnormal Psychology, 106,* 341–345.

King, N. J., Clowes-Hollins, V., & Ollendick, T. H. (1997). The etiology of dog phobia. *Behaviour Research and Therapy, 35,* 77.

King, N. J., Eleonora, G., & Ollendick, T. H. (1998). Etiology of childhood phobias: Current status of Rachman's three pathways theory. *Behaviour Research and Therapy, 36,* 297–309.

King, N. J., Gullione, E., Tonge, B. J., & Ollendick, T. H. (1993). Self-reports of panic attacks and manifest anxiety in adolescents. *Behaviour Research and Therapy, 31,* 11–116.

King, R. M., & Wilson, G. V. (1991). Use of a diary technique to investigate psychosomatic relations in atopic dermatitis. *Journal of Psychosomatic Research, 35,* 697–706.

Kinsey, A. C., Pomeroy, W. B., & Martin, C. E. (1948). *Sexual behavior in the human male.* Philadelphia: W. B. Saunders.

Kinsey, A. C., Pomeroy, W. B., Martin, C. E., & Gebhard, P. H. (1953). *Sexual behavior in the human female.* Philadelphia: Saunders.

Kinzie, J. D., Frederickson, R. H., Ben, R., Fleck, J., & Karls, W. (1984). Posttraumatic stress disorder. *American Journal of Psychiatry, 141,* 645–650.

Kircher, T. T., Liddle, P. F., Brammer, M. J., Williams, S. C. R., et al. (2001). Neural correlates of formal thought disorder in schizophrenia: Preliminary findings from a functional magnetic resonance imaging study. *Archives of General Psychiatry, 58,* 769–774.

Klagsbrun, F. (1976). *Too young to die: Youth and suicide.* Boston: Houghton Mifflin.

Klein, D. N., Norden, K. A., Ferro, T., Leader, J. B., et al. (1998). Thirty-month naturalistic follow-up study of early-onset dysthymic disorder: Course, diagnostic stability, and prediction of outcome. *Journal of Abnormal Psychology, 107,* 338–348.

Kleinberg, J., & Galligan, B. (1983). Effects of deinstitutionalization on adaptive behavior of mentally retarded adults. *American Journal of Mental Deficiency, 88,* 21–27.

Kleinman, A. (1991, April). *Culture and DSM-IV: Recommendations for the introduction and for the overall structure.* Paper presented at the Conference on Culture and DSM-IV, Pittsburgh.

Kleinmutz, B. (1967). *Personality measurement: An introduction.* Homewood, IL: Dorsey.

Klerman, G. L. (1982). Practical issues in the treatment of depression and mania. In E. S. Paykel (Ed.), *Handbook of affective disorders.* New York: Guilford Press.

Klerman, G. L., Weissman, M. M., Markowitz, J., Glick, I., et al. (1994). Medication and psychotherapy. In A. E. Bergin & S. L. Garfield (Eds.), *Handbook of psychotherapy and behavior change* (pp. 734–782). New York: Wiley.

Klerman, G. L., Weissman, M. M., Rounsavelle, B. J., & Chevron, E. S. (1984). *Interpersonal psychotherapy of depression.* New York: Basic Books.

Klesges, R. C., Winders, S. E., Meyers, A. W., Eck, L. H., et al. (1997). How much weight gain occurs following smoking cessation? A comparison of weight gain using both continuous and point prevalence abstinence. *Journal of Consulting and Clinical Psychology, 65,* 286–291.

Klin, A. (1991). Young autistic children's listening preferences in regard to speech: A possible characterization of the symptom of social withdrawal. *Journal of Autism and Developmental Disorders, 21,* 29–42.

Klin, A., Volkmar, F. R., & Sparrow, S. S. (1992). Autistic social dysfunction: Some limitations of the theory of mind hypothesis. *Journal of Child Psychology and Psychiatry, 33,* 861–876.

Klopfer, B., & Davidson, H. (1962). *The Rorschach technique.* New York: Harcourt, Brace & World.

Klott, J., & Jongsma, A. E. (2004). *The suicide and homocide risk assessment and prevention treatment planner.* Hoboken, NJ: Wiley.

Kluft, R. P. (1987). Dr. Kluft replies. *American Journal of Psychiatry, 144,* 125.

Kluft, R. P. (1996). Treating the traumatic memories of patients with dissociative identity disorder. *American Journal of Psychiatry, 153,* 103–108.

Kluft, R. P., & Foote, B. (1999). Dissociative identity disorder: Recent developments. *American Journal of Psychotherapy, 53,* 283–286.

Kluger, J. (2003). Medicating young minds. *Time, 162,* 48–58.

Klusman, L. E. (1998). Military health care providers' views on prescribing privileges for psychologists. *American Psychologist, 53,* 223–229.

Knapp, S., & VandeCreek, L. (1996). Risk management for psychologists: Treating patients who recover lost memories of childhood abuse. *Professional Psychology, Research and Practice, 27,* 452–459.

Kneisel, P. J., & Richards, G. P. (1988). Crisis intervention after the suicide of a teacher. *Professional Psychology: Research and Practice, 19,* 165–169.

Knopf, I. J. (1984). *Childhood psychopathology* (2nd ed.). Englewood Cliffs, NJ: Prentice-Hall.

Knott, J., Platt, E., Ashley, M., & Gottlieb, J. (1953). A familial evaluation of the electroencephalogram of patients with primary behavior disorder and psychopathic personality. *EEG and Clinical Neurophysiology, 5,* 363–370.

Kobasa, S. C., Hilker, R. J., & Maddi, S. R. (1979). Psychological hardiness. *Journal of Occupational Medicine, 21,* 595–598.

Kockott, G., & Fahrner, E.-M. (1987). Transsexuals who have not undergone surgery: A follow-up study. *Archives of Sexual Behavior, 16,* 511–522.

Koegel, R. L., Screibman, L., Loos, L. M., Dirlich-Wilheim, H., et al. (1992). Consistent stress profiles in mothers of children with autism. *Journal of Autism and Developmental Disorders, 22,* 205–216.

Koh, K. B. (1998). Emotion and immunity. *Journal of Psychosomatic Research, 45,* 107–115.

Kohlenberg, R. J., & Tsai, M. (1991). *Functional analytic psychotherapy.* New York: Plenum.

Kohler, J. (2001, March 30). Therapists on trial in death of girl, 10. *Washington Post,* p. A19.

Kohon, G. (1987). Fetishism revisited. *International Journal of Psychoanalysis, 68,* 213–228.

Kolarsky, A., & Madlatfousek, J. (1983). The inverse rule of preparatory erotic stimulation in exhibitionists: Phallometric studies. *Archives of Sexual Behavior, 12,* 123–148.

Kolb, B., Gibb, R., & Robinson, T. E. (2003). Brain plasticity and behavior. *Current Directions in Psychological Science, 12,* 1–4.

Kolko, D. J., & Kazdin, A. E. (1991). Children who set fires. *Journal of Clinical Child Psychology, 20,* 191–201.

Kolko, D. J., Loar, L. L., & Sturnick, D. (1990). Inpatient social-cognitive skills training groups with conduct disordered and attention deficit disordered children. *Journal of Child Psychology and Psychiatry, 31,* 734–748.

Kondratas, A. (1991). Ending homelessness. *American Psychologist, 46,* 1226–1231.

Kopelman, M. D. (1987). Amnesia: Organic and psychogenic. *British Journal of Psychiatry, 144,* 293–298.

Kopelman, M. D. (2002). Disorders of memory. *Brain, 125,* 2152–2190.

Kopelowicz, A. (1998). Adapting social skills training for Latinos with schizophrenia. *International Review of Psychiatry, 10,* 47–50.

Koppitz, E. M. (1975). *The Bender-Gestalt test for young children: Vol. II. Research and application, 1963–1973.* Needham Heights, MA: Allyn & Bacon.

Koran, L., Thienemann, M., & Davenport, R. (1996). Quality of life for patients with obsessive-compulsive disorder. *British Journal of Psychiatry, 156,* 51–54.

Korchin, S. J. (1976). *Modern clinical psychology.* New York: Basic Books.

Kosky, R. (1983). Childhood suicidal behavior. *Journal of Child Psychology and Psychiatry, 24,* 457–468.

Koss, M. P. (1993). Detecting the scope of rape: A review of prevalence research methods. *Journal of Interpersonal Violence, 8,* 198–222.

Koss, M. P., Gidycz, C. A., & Wisniewski, N. (1987). The scope of rape: Incidence and prevalence of sexual aggression and victimization in a national sample of higher education students. *Journal of Consulting and Clinical Psychology, 55,* 162–170.

Kottler, J. A. (2002). *Theories in counseling and therapy.* Boston: Allyn & Bacon.

Kottler, J. A., & Brown, R. W. (1992). *Introduction to therapeutic counseling.* Belmont, CA: Brooks/Cole.

Kovacs, M., Devlin, B., Pollock, M., Richards, C., & Mukerji, P. (1997). A controlled family history study of childhood-onset depressive disorder. *Archives of General Psychiatry, 54,* 613–623.

Kovacs, M., Goldston, D., & Gatsonis, C. (1993). Suicidal behaviors and childhood-onset depressive disorders: A longitudinal investigation. *Journal of American Academy of Childhood and Adolescent Psychiatry, 32,* 8–20.

Kraepelin, E. (1923/1883). Textbook of psychiatry (8th ed.). New York: Macmillan.

Krakow, B., Hollifield, M., Johnston, L., Koss, M., et al. (2001). Imagery rehearsal therapy for chronic nightmares in sexual assault survivors with posttraumatic stress disorder. *Journal of the American Medical Association, 286,* 1–18.

Kramer, B. (1973, November 16). Mass hysteria: An age-old illness still crops up in modern times. *Wall Street Journal,* p. 36b.

Krantz, S. E., & Moos, R. H. (1988). Risk factors at intake predict nonremission among depressed patients. *Journal of Consulting and Clinical Psychology, 56,* 863–869.

Kranzler, H. R., & Anton, R. F. (1994). Implications of recent neuropsychopharmacologic research for understanding the etiology and development of alcoholism. *Journal of Consulting and Clinical Psychology, 62,* 1116–1126.

Kraus, R. P., & Nicholson, I. R. (1996). AIDS-related obsessive compulsive disorder: Deconditioning based in fluoxetine-induced inhibition of anxiety. *Journal of Behavior Therapy and Experimental Psychiatry, 27,* 51–56.

Kremer, L. (1999, January 2). Whatever happened to … Jody Roberts drops plan for book and television movie about her life. *News Tribune,* p. B1.

Kresin, D. (1993). Medical aspects of inhibited sexual desire disorder. In W. O'Donahue, & J. Geer (Eds.), *Handbook of sexual dysfunctions.* Boston: Allyn & Bacon.

Krieger, N., & Sidney, S. (1996). Racial discrimination and blood pressure: The CARDIA study of young black and white adults. *American Journal of Public Health, 86,* 1370–1380.

Krueger, R. F., Caspi, A., Moffitt, T. E., & Silva, P. A. (1998). The structure and stability of common mental disorders (DSM-III-R): A longitudinal-epidemiological study. *Journal of Abnormal Psychology, 107,* 216–227.

Kubany, E. S., Hill, E. E., Owens, J. A., Iannce-Spencer, C., et al. (2004). Cognitive trauma therapy for battered women with PTSD (CTT-BW). *Journal of Consulting and Clinical Psychology, 72,* 3–18.

Kubiszyn, T. W., Meyer, G. J., Finn, S. E., Eyde, L. D., et al. (2000). Empirical support for psychological assessment in clinical health care settings. *Professional Psychology: Research and Practice, 31,* 119–130.

Kuhn, B., Marcus, B., & Pitner, S. (1999). Treatment guidelines for primary nonretentive encopresis and stool toileting refusal. *American Family Physician, 59,* 2171–2178.

Kuipers, E. L., Garety, P., Fowler, D., & Dunn, G. (1997). London-East Anglia randomized controlled trial of cognitive-behavioural therapy for psychosis: I. Effects of treatment phase. *British Journal of Psychiatry, 171,* 319–325.

Kumanyika, S., Wilson, J., & Guilford-Davenport, M. (1993). Weight-related attitudes and behaviors of Black women. *Journal of the American Dietetic Association, 93,* 416–422.

Kumperscak, H. G., Paschke, E., Gradisnik, P., Vidmar, J., & Bradac, S. U. (2005). Adult metachromatic leukodystrophy: Disorganized schizophrenia-like symptoms and postpartum depression in 2 sisters. *Neuroscience, 30,* 33–36.

Kurdyak, P. A. (2004). Do food additives cause hyperactivity in preschool children? *Canadian Medical Association Journal, 171,* 450–451.

Kurth, J. H., & Kurth, M. C. (1994). Role of monoamine oxidase genetics in the etiology of Parkinson's disease. In A. Lieberman, C. W. Olanow, M. B. Youdin, & K. Tipton (Eds.), *Monoamine oxidase inhibitors in neurological diseases* (pp. 113–126). New York: Marcel Dekker.

Kusek, K. (2001). Could a fear wreak havoc on your life? *Cosmopolitan, 230,* 182–184.

Kushner, H. I. (1995). Women and suicidal behavior: Epidemiology, gender, and lethality in historical perspective. In S. S. Canetto & D. Lester (Eds.), *Women and suicidal behavior.* New York: Springer.

Kushner, M. (1965). The reduction of a long-standing fetish by means of aversive conditioning. In L. P. Ullmann & L. Krasner (Eds.), *Case studies in behavior modification.* New York: Holt, Rinehart & Winston.

Kutner, N. G., Bliwise, D. L., & Zhang, R. (2004). Linking race and well-being within a biopsychosocial framework: Variation in subjective sleep quality in two racially diverse older adult samples. *Journal of Health and Social Behavior, 45,* 99–113.

Lacey, J. I., Bateman, D. E., & Van Lehn, R. (1953). Autonomic response specificity. *Psychosomatic Medicine, 15,* 8–21.

Lackner, J. M., Carosella, A. M., & Feuerstein, M. (1996). Pain expectancies, pain, and functional self-efficacy expectancies as determinants of disability in patients with chronic low back disorders. *Journal of Consulting and Clinical Psychology, 64,* 212–220.

Lader, M., & Bond, A. J. (1998). Interaction of pharmacological and psychological treatments of anxiety. *British Journal of Psychiatry, 173,* 41–48.

Ladouceur, R., Dugas, M. J., Freeston, M. H., Leger, E., et al. (2000). Efficacy of a cognitive-behavioral treatment for generalized anxiety disorder. *Journal of Consulting and Clinical Psychology, 68,* 957–964.

Ladouceur, R., Freeston, M. H., Fournier, S., Rheaume, J., et al. (2000). Strategies used with intrusive thoughts: A comparison of OCD patients with anxious and community controls. *Journal of Abnormal Psychology, 109,* 179–187.

LaGreca, A. M., Silverman, W. K., Vernberg, E. M., & Prinstein, M. J. (1996). Symptoms of posttraumatic stress in children after Hurricane Andrew: A prospective study. *Journal of Consulting and Clinical Psychology, 64,* 712–723.

LaGreca, A. M., & Stringer, S. A. (1985). The Wechsler Intelligence Scale for Children–Revised. In C. S. Newmark (Ed.), *Major psychological assessment instruments* (pp. 277–322). Boston: Allyn & Bacon.

Lahey, B., Hartdagen, S. E., Frick, P. J., McBurnett, K., et al. (1988). Conduct disorder: Parsing the confounded relation to parental divorce and antisocial personality. *Journal of Abnormal Psychology, 97,* 334–337.

Lahey, B. B., Loeber, R., Hart, E. L., Frick, P. J., et al. (1995). Four-year longitudinal study of conduct disorders in boys: Patterns and predictors of persistence. *Journal of Abnormal Psychology, 104,* 89–93.

Lai, J. Y., & Linden, W. (1992). Gender anger expression style, and opportunity for anger release determine cardiovascular reaction to and recovery from anger provocation. *Psychosomatic Medicine, 54,* 297–310.

Laird, J., & Green, R. J. (1996). *Lesbians and gays in couples and families.* San Francisco: Jossey-Bass.

Laker, B. (1992, April 14). A nightmare of memories. *Seattle Post-Intelligencer,* pp. C1–C2.

Lakkis, J., Ricciardelli, L. A., & Williams, R. J. (1999). Role of sexual orientation and gender-related traits in disordered eating. *Sex Roles, 41,* 1–16.

Lam, R. W., Lee, S. K., Tam, E. M., Grewal, A., & Yatham, L. N. (2001). An open trial of light therapy for women with seasonal affective disorder and comorbid bulimia nervosa. *Journal of Clinical Psychiatry, 62,* 164–168.

Lamb, H. R. (1984). Deinstitutionalization and the homeless mentally ill. *Hospital Community Psychiatry, 35,* 899–907.

Lamberg, L. (2002). Long hours, little sleep: Bad medicine for physicians-in-training? *Journal of the American Medical Association, 287,* 303–306.

Lambert, E. W., Wahler, R. G., Andrade, A. R., & Bickman, L. (2001). Looking for the disorder in conduct disorder. *Journal of Abnormal Psychology, 110,* 110–123.

Lambert, M. J. (1992). Implications of outcome research for psychotherapy integration. In J. C. Norcross & M. R. Goldstein (Eds.), *Handbook of psychotherapy integration* (pp. 94–129). New York: Basic Books.

Lambert, M. J., & Bergin, A. E. (1994). The effectiveness of psychotherapy. In A. E. Bergin & S. L. Garfield (Eds.), *Handbook of psychotherapy and behavior change* (pp. 143–189). New York: Wiley.

Lambert, M. J., & Ogles, B. M. (2004). The efficacy and effectiveness of psychotherapy. In M. J. Lambert (Ed.), *Bergin and Garfield's handbook of psychotherapy and behavior change* (5th ed., pp. 139–193). New York: Wiley.

Lambert, M. J., Shapiro, D. A., & Bergin, A. E. (1986). The effectiveness of psychotherapy. In S. L. Garfield & A. E. Bergin (Eds.), *Handbook of psychotherapy and behavior change* (3rd ed., pp. 157–212). New York: Wiley.

Lambert, M. V., Senior, C., Phillips, M. L., Sierra, M., et al. (2001). Visual imagery and depersonalization. *Psychopathology, 34,* 259–264.

Lambert, N. M. (1988). Adolescent outcomes for hyperactive children. *American Psychologist, 43,* 786–799.

Lambley, P. (1974). Treatment of transvestism and subsequent coital problems. *Journal of Behavior Therapy and Experimental Psychiatry, 5,* 101–102.

Landesman S., & Butterfield, E. C. (1987). Normalization and deinstitutionalization of mentally retarded individuals. *American Psychologist, 42,* 809–816.

Landrigan, C. P., Rothschild, J. M., Cronin, J. W., Kaushal, R., et al. (2004). Effect of reducing interns' work hours on serious medical errors in intensive care units. *New England Journal of Medicine, 351,* 1838–1848.

Langer, E. J., & Rodin, J. (1976). The effects of choice and enhanced personal responsibility for the aged: A field experiment in an institutional setting. *Journal of Personality and Social Psychology, 34,* 191–198.

Langevin, R. (1990). Sexual anomalies and the brain. In W. L. Marshall, D. R. Laws, & H. E. Barbaree (Eds.), *Handbook of sexual assault: Issues, theories, and treatment of the offender* (pp. 103–114). New York: Plenum Press.

Langevin, R., Bain, J., Wortzman, G., Hucker, S., et al. (1988). Sexual sadism: Brain, blood, and behavior. In R. A. Prentky and V. L. Quisey (Eds.), *Human sexual aggression: Current perspectives. Annals of the New York Academy of Sciences, 528* (pp. 79–110). Salem, MA: New York Academy of Sciences.

Langevin, R., Paitich, D., Ramsay, G., Anderson, C., et al. (1979). Experimental studies of exhibitionism. *Archives of Sexual Behavior, 8,* 307–331.

Lara, M. E., Klein, D. N., & Kasch, K. L. (2000). Psychosocial predictors of the short-term course and outcome of major depression: A longitudinal study of a nonclinical sample with recent-onset episodes. *Journal of Abnormal Psychology, 109,* 644–650.

Laraia, M. T., Stuart, G. W., Frye, L. H., Lydiard, R. B., & Ballenger, J. C. (1994). Childhood environment of women having panic disorder with agoraphobia. *Journal of Anxiety Disorders, 8,* 1–17.

Larkin, K. T., & Zayfert, C. (1996). Anger management training with mild essential hypertensive patients. *Journal of Behavioral Medicine, 19,* 415–433.

Larson, C. A., & Carey, K. B. (1998). Caffeine: Brewing trouble in mental health settings? *Professional Psychology, Research and Practice, 29,* 373–376.

Last, C. G., & Perrin, S. (1993). Anxiety disorders in African-American and white children. *Journal of Abnormal Child Psychology, 21,* 153–162.

Laudenslager, M. L., Ryan, S. M., Drugan, R. C., Hyson, R. L., & Maier, S. F. (1983). Coping and immunosuppression: Inescapable but not escapable shock suppresses lymphocyte proliferation. *Science, 220,* 568–570.

Laughlin, H. P. (1967). *The neuroses.* Washington, DC: Butterworth.

Lauman, E. O., Gagnon, J. H., Michael, R. T., & Michaels, S. (1994). *The social organization of sexuality.* Chicago: University of Chicago Press.

Laws, D. R., & Marshall, W. L. (1990). A conditioning theory of the etiology and maintenance of deviant sexual preference and behavior. In W. L. Marshall, D. R. Laws, & H. E. Barbaree (Eds.), *Handbook of sexual assault: Issues, theories, and treatment of the offender* (pp. 209–230). New York: Plenum Press.

Lazarus, A. A. (1967). In support of technical eclecticism. *Psychological Reports, 21,* 415–416.

Lazarus, A. A. (1983). *Psychological stress.* New York: McGraw-Hill.

Lazarus, A. A. (1984). Multimodal therapy. In R. J. Corsini (Ed.), *Current psychotherapies.* Itasca, IL: Peacock.

Lazarus, P. (2001, May). Breaking the code of silence: What schools can do about it. *NASP Communique*, 28–29.

Lazarus, R. S. (1966). *Psychological stress and the coping process.* New York: McGraw-Hill.

Leary, P. M. (2003). Conversion disorder in childhood: Diagnosed too late, investigated too much? *Journal of the Royal Society of Medicine, 96*, 436–444.

Leary, W. E. (1992, December 10). Medical panel says most sexual impotence in men can be treated without surgery. *New York Times*, p. D20.

Lecci, L., & Cohen, D. J. (2002). Perceptual consequences of an illness concern induction and its relation to hypochondriacal tendencies. *Health Psychology, 21*, 147–156.

Leckman, J. F., Walker, D. E., & Cohen, D. J. (1993). Premonitory urges in Tourette's syndrome. *American Journal of Psychiatry, 150*, 98–102.

LeDoux, J. C., & Hazelwood, R. R. (1985). Police attitude and beliefs toward rape. *Journal of Police Science Administration, 13*, 211–220.

Lee, S. (1997). A Chinese perspective of somatoform disorders. *Journal of Psychosomatic Research, 43*, 115–119.

Lee, S., Hsu, L. K., & Wing, Y. K. (1992). Bulimia nervosa in Hong Kong Chinese patients. *British Journal of Psychiatry, 161*, 545–551.

Lee, T. M. C., Chen, E. Y. H., Chan, C. C. H., Paterson, J. G., et al. (1998). Seasonal affective disorder. *Clinical Psychology: Science and Practice, 5*, 275–290.

Leekham, S. R., & Prior, M. (1994). Can autistic children distinguish lies from jokes? A second look at second-order belief attribution. *Journal of Child Psychology and Psychiatry, 35*, 901–915.

Leenaars, A. A. (1992). Suicide notes, communication, and ideation. In R. W. Maris, A. L. Berman, J. T. Maltsberger, & R. I. Yufit (Eds.), *Assessment and prediction of suicide*. New York: Guilford.

Leferink, K. (1998). Private and public in the lives of chronic schizophrenic patients. *Psychiatry, 61*, 147–162.

Leff, J. (1994). Working with the families of schizophrenic patients. *British Journal of Psychiatry, 164*, 71–76.

Leff, J., Wig, N. N., Bedi, H., Menon, D. K., et al. (1990). Relatives' expressed emotion and the course of schizophrenia in Chandigarh. *British Journal of Psychiatry, 156*, 351–356.

Legato, M. J. (1996). What we know about coronary artery disease in women. *Physician Assistant, 20*, 93–100.

Lehman, A. F., Kreyenbuhl, J., Buchanan, R. W., & Dickerson, F. B. (2004). The schizophrenia patient outcome research team (PORT): Updated treatment recommendations 2003. *Schizophrenia Bulletin, 30*, 193–207.

Lehman, A. F., & Steinwachs, D. M. (1998). At issue: Translating research into practice: The schizophrenia patient outcome research team (PORT) treatment recommendations. *Schizophrenia Bulletin, 24*, 1–10.

Lehmann, H. E. (1985). Affective disorders: Clinical features. In H. I. Kaplan & B. J. Sadock (Eds.), *Comprehensive textbook of psychiatry* (Vol. 4, pp. 786–810). Baltimore: Williams & Wilkins.

Lehrer, P. M., Sargunaraj, D., & Hochron, S. (1992). Psychological approaches to the treatment of asthma. *Journal of Consulting and Clinical Psychology, 60*, 639–643.

Lehrer, P. M., Vaschillo, E., Vachillo, B., Lu, S-E., et al. (2004). Biofeedback treatment for asthma. *Chest, 126*, 352–361.

Leibbrand, R., Hiller, W., & Fichter, M. M. (2000). Hypochondriasis and somatization: Two distinct aspects of somatoform disorders. *Journal of Clinical Psychology, 56*, 63–72.

Leiblum, S. R., & Rosen, R. C. (1991). Couples therapy for erectile disorders: Conceptual and clinical considerations. Special issue: The treatment of male erectile disorders. *Journal of Sex and Marital Therapy, 17*, 147–159.

Leichtman, M. (1995). Behavioral observations. In J. N. Butcher (Ed.), *Clinical personality assessment: Practical approaches* (pp. 251–266). New York: Oxford University Press.

Leland, J. (1997). A risky Rx for fun. *Newsweek*, p. 74.

Lemonick, M. D. (2004a, February 6). Prescription for suicide? *Time, 163*, 59–60.

Lemonick, M. D. (2004b, October 11). In search of sleep. *Time*, 100.

Lenzenweger, M. F. (2001). Reaction time slowing during high-load, sustained-attention task performance in relation to psychometrically identified schizotypy. *Journal of Abnormal Psychology, 110*, 290–296.

Lenzenweger, M. F., Cornblatt, B. A., & Putnick, M. (1991). Schizotypy and sustained attention. *Journal of Abnormal Psychology, 100*, 84–89.

Lerner, J. V., Hertzog, C., Hooker, K. A., Hassibi, M., & Thomas, A. (1988). A longitudinal study of negative emotional states.

Lerner, P. M. (1995). Assessing adaptive capacities by means of the Rorschach. In J. N. Butcher (Ed.), *Clinical personality assessment: Practical approaches* (pp. 317–328). New York: Oxford University Press.

Lesieur, H. R. (1989). Current research into pathological gambling and gaps in the literature. In H. J. Shaffer, S. A. Stein, B. Gambino, & T. N. Cummings (Eds.), *Compulsive gambling: Theory, research, and practice* (pp. 223–248). Lexington, MA: Lexington Books.

Leslie, R. (1991, July/August). Psychotherapist-patient privilege clarified. *California Therapist*, 11–19.

Lester, D. (1989). *Can we prevent suicide?* New York: AMS Press.

Lester, D. (1991). Do suicide prevention centers prevent suicide? *Homeostasis in Health and Disease, 33*(4), 190–194.

Lester, D. (1994). Are there unique features of suicide in adults of different ages and developmental stages? *Omega Journal of Death and Dying, 29*, 337–348.

Lester, R., & Petrie, T. A. (1998). Physical, psychological, and societal correlates of bulimic symptomatology among African American college women. *Journal of Counseling Psychology, 45*, 315–321.

Leung, N., Thomas, G., & Waller, G. (2000). The relationship between parental bonding and core beliefs in anorexic and bulimic women. *British Journal of Clinical Psychology, 39*, 205–210.

Levenstein, C., Prantera, C., Varvo, V., Scribano, M. L., et al. (1993). Development of the Perceived Stress Questionnaire: A new tool for psychosomatic research. *Journal of Psychosomatic Research, 37*, 19–32.

Levenston, G. K., Patrick, C. J., Bradley, M. M., & Lang, P. J. (2000). The psychopath as observer: Emotion and attention in picture processing. *Journal of Abnormal Psychology, 109*, 373–385.

Levine, D. S., & Willner, S. G. (1976, February). The cost of mental illness, 1974. *Mental Health Statistical Note No. 125* (pp. 1–7). Washington, DC: National Institute of Mental Health.

Levine, I. S., & Rog, D. J. (1990). Mental health services for homeless mentally ill persons: Federal initiatives and current service trends. *American Psychologist, 45*, 963–968.

Levinthal, C. F. (2005). *Drugs, behavior, and modern society*. New York: Allyn & Bacon.

Lewinsohn, P. M. (1974). A behavioral approach to depression. In R. J. Friedman & M. M. Katz (Eds.), *The psychology of depression: Contemporary theory and research*. New York: Wiley.

Lewinsohn, P. M. (1977). The behavioral study and treatment of depression. In M. Hersen, R. M. Eisler, & P. M. Miller (Eds.), *Progress in behavior modification*. New York: Academic Press.

Lewinsohn, P. M., Hoberman, H. M., & Rosenbaum, M. (1988). A prospective study of risk factors for unipolar depression. *Journal of Abnormal Psychology, 97*, 251–264.

Lewinsohn, P. M., Hoberman, H. M., Teri, L., & Hautzinger, M. (1985). An integrative theory of depression. In S. Reiss & R. R. Bootzin (Eds.), *Theoretical issues in behavioral therapy* (pp. 331–359). Orlando, FL: Academic Press.

Lewinsohn, P. M., Hopps, H., Roberts, R. E., Seeley, J. R., & Andrews, J. A. (1993). Adolescent psychopathology: I. Prevalence and incidence of depression and other DSM-III-R disorders in high school students. *Journal of Abnormal Psychology, 102*, 133–144.

Lewinsohn, P. M., Joiner, T. E., & Rohde, P. (2001). Evaluation of cognitive diathesis-stress models in predicting major depressive disorder in adolescents. *Journal of Abnormal Psychology, 110*, 203–215.

Lewinsohn, P. M., Pettit, J. W., Joiner, T. E., & Seeley, J. R. (2003).

The symptomatic expression of major depressive disorder in adolescents and young adults. *Journal of Abnormal Psychology, 112,* 244–252.

Lewinsohn, P. M., Zeiss, A. M., & Duncan, E. M. (1989). Probability of relapse after recovery from an episode of depression. *Journal of Abnormal Psychology, 97,* 387–398.

Lewis, B. L. (2001). Health psychology specialty practice opportunities in a rural community hospital: Practicing local clinical science. *Professional Psychology: Research and Practice, 32*(1), 59–64.

Lezon, D. (2002, May 25). Everybody a stranger. *Houston Chronicle,* A33.

Li, G. (1995). The interaction effect of bereavement and sex on the risk of suicide in the elderly: An historical cohort study. *Social Science and Medicine, 40,* 82.

Liberini, P., Faglia, L., Salvi, F., & Grant, R. P. J. (1993). Cognitive impairment related to conversion disorder: A two-year follow-up study. *Journal of Nervous and Mental Disease, 181,* 325–327.

Liberman, R. P., & Green, M. F. (1992). Whither cognitive-behavioral therapy for schizophrenia. *Schizophrenia Bulletin, 18,* 27–35.

Libman, E., Creti, L., Amsel, R., Brender, W., & Fichten, C. S. (1997). What do older good and poor sleepers do during periods of nocturnal wakefulness? *Psychology and Aging, 12,* 170–182.

Lichstein, K. L., Riedel, B. W., Lester, K. W., & Aguillard, R. N. (1999). Occult sleep apnea in a recruited sample of older adults with insomnia. *Journal of Consulting and Clinical Psychology, 67,* 405–410.

Lichstein, K. L., Wilson, N. M., & Johnson, C. T. (2000). Psychological treatment of secondary insomnia. *Psychology and Aging, 15,* 232–240.

Lichtenstein, E. (1982). The smoking problem: A behavioral perspective. *Journal of Consulting and Clinical Psychology, 50,* 804–819.

Lichtenstein, E., & Danaher, B. (1976). Modification of smoking behavior: A critical analysis of theory, research, and practice. In M. Hersen, R. Eisler, & P. Miller (Eds.), *Progress in behavior modification: 3.* New York: Academic Press.

Lichtenstein, E., & Glasgow, R. E. (1977). Rapid smoking: Side effects and safeguards. *Journal of Consulting and Clinical Psychology, 45,* 815–821.

Lichtenstein, E., & Glasgow, R. E. (1992). Smoking cessation: What we have learned over the past decade? *Journal of Consulting and Clinical Psychology, 60,* 518–527.

Lichtenstein, E., & Rodrigues, M. (1977). Long-term effects of rapid smoking treatment for dependent cigarette smokers. *Addictive Behaviors, 2,* 109–112.

Lickey, M. E., & Gordon, B. (1991). *Medicine and mental illness.* New York: W. H. Freeman.

Lieberman, J. A. (1995). Signs and symptoms. *Archives of General Psychiatry, 52,* 361–363.

Light, K. C., Brownley, K. A., Turner, J. R., Hinderliter, A. L., et al. (1995). Job status and high-effort coping influence work blood pressure in women and Blacks. *Hypertension, 25,* 554–559.

Lilienfeld, S. O., Lynn, S. J., Kirsch, I., Chaves, J. F., et al. (1999). Dissociative identity disorder and the sociocognitive model: Recalling the lessons of the past. *Psychological Bulletin, 125,* 507–523.

Lilienfeld, S. O., Wood, J. M., & Garb, H. N. (2000). The scientific status of projective techniques. *Psychological Science in the Public Interest, 1,* 17–66.

Lin, K. M., Cheung, F., Smith, M., & Poland, R. E. (1997). The use of psychotropic medications in working with Asian patients. In E. Lee (Ed.), *Working with Asian Americans: A guide for clinicians* (pp. 388–399). New York: Guilford Press.

Lindamer, L. A., Lohr, J. B., Caligiuri, M. P., & Jeste, D. V. (2001). Relationship of gender and age of onset of schizophrenia to severity of dyskinesia. *Journal of Neuropsychiatry and Clinical Neurosciences, 13,* 399–401.

Linehan, M. M. (1987). Dialectical behavior therapy for borderline personality disorder. Theory and method. *Bulletin of the Menninger Clinic, 51,* 261–276.

Linehan, M. M. (1993). *Cognitive-behavioral treatment of borderline personality disorder.* New York: Guilford Press.

Linn, V. (2004, June 26). Headache "beast" holds tight grip on sufferers. *Seattle Post-Intelligencer,* p. A1.

Lipman, A. J., & Kendall, P. C. (1992). Drugs and psychotherapy: Comparison, contrasts, and conclusions. *Applied and Preventive Psychology, 1,* 141–148.

Liposuction vs. American fat. (1998). *USA Today, 127,* pp. 8–9.

Li-Repac, D. (1980). Cultural influences on clinical perceptions: A comparison between Caucasian and Chinese-American therapists. *Journal of Cross-Cultural Psychology, 11,* 327–342.

Lisak, D. (1991). Sexual aggression, masculinity, and fathers. *Signs, 16,* 238–262.

Lishman, W. A. (1978). *The psychological consequences of cerebral disorder.* Oxford, England: Blackwell.

Litman, R. E. (1987). Hospital suicides: Lawsuits and standards. *Suicide and Life-Threatening Behavior, 12,* 212–220.

Livesley, W. J., Schroeder, M. L., Jackson, D. N., & Jang, K. L. (1994). Categorical distinctions in the study of personality disorder: Implications for classification. *Journal of Abnormal Psychology, 103,* 6–17.

Lockley, S. W., Cronin, J. W., Evans, E. E., Cade, B. E., et al. (2004). Effect of reducing interns' weekly work hours on sleep and attentional failures. *New England Journal of Medicine, 351,* 1829–1837.

Loeber, R. (1990). Development and risk factors of juvenile antisocial behavior and delinquency. *Clinical Psychology Review, 10,* 1–42.

Loening-Baucke, V. (2000). Clinical approach to fecal soiling in children. *Clinical Pediatrics, 39,* 603–607.

Loesch, D. Z., Bui, Q. M., Grigsby, J., Butler, E., et al. (2003). Effect of the Fragile X status categories and the Fragile X mental retardation protein levels on executive functioning in males and females with Fragile X. *Neuropsychology, 17,* 646–657.

Loewenstein, R. (1994). Diagnosis, epidemiology, clinical course, treatment, and cost effectiveness of treatment for dissociative disorders and MPD: Report submitted to the Clinton administration task force on health care reform. *Dissociation, 7,* 3–11.

Loftus, E. F. (1993). The reality of repressed memories. *American Psychologist, 48,* 518–537.

Loftus, E. F., Garry, M., & Feldman, J. (1994). Forgetting sexual trauma: What does it mean when 38 percent forget? *Journal of Consulting and Clinical Psychology, 62,* 1177–1181.

Longstaffe, S., Moffatt, M. E., & Whalen, J. C. (2000). Behavioral and self-concept changes after six months of enuresis treatment: A randomized, controlled trial. *Pediatrics, 105,* 935–940.

Lopez, S. R., & Hernandez, P. (1987). When culture is considered in the evaluation and treatment of Hispanic patients. *Psychotherapy, 24,* 120–126.

Lopez, S. R., Hipke, K. N., Polo, A. J., Jenkins, J. H., et al. (2004). Ethnicity, expressed emotion, attributions, and course of schizophrenia: Family warmth matters. *Journal of Abnormal Psychology, 113,* 428–439.

LoPiccolo, J. (1985). Advances in diagnosis and treatment of male sexual dysfunction. *Journal of Sex and Marital Therapy, 11,* 215–232.

LoPiccolo, J. (1991). Postmodern sex therapy for erectile failure. In R. C. Rosen & S. R. Leiblum (Eds.), *Erectile failure: diagnosis and treatment.* New York: Guilford.

LoPiccolo, J. (1995). Sexual disorders and gender identity disorders. In R. J. Comer, *Abnormal Psychology.* New York: W. H. Freeman.

LoPiccolo, J. (1997). Sex therapy: A postmodern model. In S. J. Lynn & J. P. Garske (Eds.), *Contemporary psychotherapies: Models and methods.* New York: Guilford.

LoPiccolo, J., & Freidman, J. R. (1988). Broad spectrum treatment of low sexual desire: Integration of cognitive, behavioral, and systemic treatment. In S. Leiblum & R. Rosen (Eds.), *Sexual desire disorders.* New York: Guilford.

LoPiccolo, J., & Stock, W. E. (1986). Treatment of sexual dysfunction. *Journal of Consulting and Clinical Psychology, 54,* 158–167.

Lorion, R. P. (1990). Developmental analyses of community phenomena. In P. Tolan, C. Keys, F. Chertok, & L. Jason (Eds.), *Researching community psychology* (pp. 32–41). Washington, DC: American Psychological Association.

Lovaas, O. I. (1977). *The autistic child: Language development through behavior modification.* New York: Halsted Press.

Lovaas, O. I. (1987). Behavioral treatment and normal educational and intellectual functioning in young autistic children. *Journal of Consulting and Clinical Psychology, 55,* 3–9.

Lovaas, O. I., Schaeffer, B., & Simmons, J. Q. (1965). Building social behavior in autistic children by use of electric shock. *Journal of Experimental Research in Personality, 1,* 99–109.

Lovejoy, M. (2001). Disturbances in the social body: Differences in body image and eating problems among African American and white women. *Gender and Society, 15,* 239–261.

Lowe, C. F., & Chadwick, P. D. J. (1990). Verbal control of delusions. *Behavior Therapy, 21,* 461–479.

Lubell, S. (2004, February 19). On the therapist's couch, a jolt of virtual reality. *The New York Times,* p. G5.

Luborsky, L., Diguer, L., Seligman, D. A., Rosenthal, R., et al. (1999). The researcher's own therapy allegiances: A "wild card" in comparisons of treatment efficacy. *Clinical Psychology: Science and Practice, 6,* 95–106.

Luecken, L. J., Suarez, E. C., Kuhn, C. M., Barefoot, J. C., et al. (1997). Stress in employed women: Impact of marital status and children at home on neurohormone output and home strain. *Psychosomatic Medicine, 59,* 352–359.

Lundberg, G. D. (2004). Should the unpublished results of clinical trials be available to other researchers and physicians? *Medscape General Medicine, 3,* 1.

Lundervold, D. A., & Belwood, M. F. (2000). The best kept secret in counseling: Single-case ($N = 1$) experimental designs. *Journal of Counseling and Development, 78,* 92–102.

Luparello, T., Lyons, H. A., Bleecker, E. R., & McFadden, E. R. (1968). Influences of suggestion on airway reactivity in asthmatic subjects. *Psychosomatic Medicine, 30,* 819–825.

Luria, A. R. (1982). *Language and cognition.* New York: Oxford University Press.

Lydiard, R. B. (1996). Recent developments in the psychopharmacology of anxiety disorders. *Journal of Consulting and Clinical Psychology, 64,* 660–668.

Lydiard, R. B., Brady, K. T., & Austin, L. S. (1994). To the editor. *American Journal of Psychiatry, 151,* 462.

Lyke, M. L. (2004a, August 27). I'm afraid something is going to set me off. *Seattle Post-Intelligencer,* p. A8.

Lyke, M. L. (2004b, August 27). Once a "people person," vet couldn't leave home. *Seattle Post-Intelligencer,* p. A8.

Lykken, D. F. (1957). A study of anxiety in the sociopathic personality. *Journal of Abnormal and Social Psychology, 55,* 6–10.

Lykken, D. T. (1982). Fearlessness: Its carefree charm and deadly risks. *Psychology Today, 16,* 20–28.

Lynn, S. J., & Nash, M. R. (1994). Truth in memory: Ramifications for psychotherapy and hypnotherapy. *American Journal of Clinical Hypnosis, 36,* 194–206.

Lynskey, M. T., & Fergusson, D. M. (1995). Childhood conduct problems, and adolescent alcohol, tobacco, and illicit drug use. *Journal of Abnormal Child Psychology, 23,* 281–302.

Mace, C. J., & Trimble, M. R. (1996). Ten-year prognosis of conversion disorder. *British Journal of Psychiatry, 169,* 282–288.

MacEachron, A. E. (1983). Institutional reform and adaptive functioning of mentally retarded persons: A field experiment. *American Journal of Mental Deficiency, 88,* 2–12.

Machon, R. A., Mednick, S. A., & Huttunen, M. O. (1997). Adult major affective disorder after prenatal exposure to an influenza epidemic. *Archives of General Psychiatry, 54,* 322–328.

Machover, K. (1949). *Personality projection in the drawing of the human figure: A method of personality investigation.* Springfield, IL: Thomas.

MacKenzie, K. R. (1994). Using personality measurements in clinical practice. In P. T. Costa & T. A. Widiger (Eds.), *Personality disorders and the five-factor model of personality* (pp. 237–250). Washington, DC: American Psychological Association.

Mackenzie, T. B., & Popkin, M. K. (1987). Suicide in the medical patient. *International Journal of Psychiatry in Medicine, 17,* 3–22.

Maddi, S. R. (1972). *Personality theories.* Homewood, IL: Dorsey.

Madle, R. A. (1990). Mental retardation in adulthood. In M. Hersen & C. G. Last (Eds.), *Handbook of child and adult psychopathology* (pp. 337–352). New York: Pergamon Press.

Magni, G., & Schifano, F. (1984). Psychological distress after stroke. *Journal of Neurology, Neurosurgery and Psychiatry, 47,* 567–568.

Maher, W. B., & Maher, B. A. (1985). Psychopathology: I. From ancient times to the eighteenth century. In G. A. Kimble & K. Schlesinger (Eds.), *Topics in the history of psychology* (Vol. 2). Hillsdale, NJ: Erlbaum.

Mahler, S. (2004). Shocked back to life. *Health, 18,* 99.

Mahoney, D. M. (2000). Panic disorder and self states: Clinical and research illustrations. *Clinical Social Work Journal, 28,* 197–212.

Malamuth, N. M. (1981). Rape proclivity among males. *Journal of Social Issues, 37,* 138–157.

Malamuth, N. M., & Briere, J. (1986). Sexual violence in the media: Indirect effects on aggression against women. *Journal of Social Issues, 42,* 75–92.

Malamuth, N. M., & Check, J. V. P. (1983). Sexual arousal to rape depictions: Individual differences. *Journal of Abnormal Psychology, 92,* 55–67.

Malamuth, N. M., Sockloskie, R. J., Koss, M. P., & Tanaka, J. S. (1991). Characteristics of aggressors against women: Testing a model using a national sample of college students. *Journal of Consulting and Clinical Psychology, 59,* 670–681.

Malatesta, V. J., & Adams, H. E. (1984). The sexual dysfunctions. In H. E. Adams & P. B. Sutker (Eds.), *Comprehensive handbook of psychopathology* (pp. 725–776). New York: Plenum Press.

Malison, R. T., McDougle, C. J., Van Dyck, C. H., Scahill, L., et al. (1995). $[^{123}I]\beta$-CIT SPECT imaging of striatal dopamine transporter binding in Tourette's disorder. *American Journal of Psychiatry, 152,* 1359–1361.

Mallik, I. (2001). Hypertension. *Heart, 86,* 251.

Mallinckrodt, B., McCreary, B. A., & Robertson, A. K. (1995). Co-occurrence of eating disorders and incest: The role of attachment, family environment, and social competencies. *Journal of Counseling Psychology, 42,* 178–186.

Maltais, M. (2001, May 31). E-briefing: Body of knowledge: The Web offers a wealth of information about self-image and resources for the size and shape conscious. *Los Angeles Times,* p. T3.

Man accused of stalking Kournikova. (2005, February 9). *Bellingham Herald,* p. B2.

Mancuso, C. E., Tanzi, M. G., & Gabay, M. (2004). Paradoxical reactions to benzodiazepines: Literature review and treatment options. *Pharmacotherapy, 24,* 1177–1185.

Manderscheid, R. W., & Sonnenschein, M. A. (1992). *Mental health, United States, 1992.* Rockville, MD: U.S. Department of Health and Human Services.

Mangweth, B., Pope, H. G., Jr., Kemmler, G., Ebenbichler, C., et al. (2001). Body image and psychopathology in male body builders. *Psychotherapy and Psychosomatics, 70,* 38–42.

Manjiviona, J., & Prior, M. (1995). Comparison of Asperger syndrome and high-functioning autistic children on a test of motor impairment. *Journal of Autism and Developmental Disorders, 25,* 23–39.

Mann, J. J. (1989). Neurobiological models. In J. J. Mann (Ed.), *Models of depressive disorders: Psychological, biological, and genetic perspectives* (pp. 143–177). New York: Plenum Press.

Mann, S. J., & James, G. D. (1998). Defensiveness and essential hypertension. *Journal of Psychosomatic Research, 45,* 139–148.

Marantz, S., & Coates, S. (1991). Mothers of boys with gender identity disorder: A comparison of matched controls. *Journal of the American Academy of Child and Adolescent Psychiatry, 30,* 310–315.

Marcus, J., Hans, S. L., Nagler, S., Auerbach, J. G., et al. (1987).

Review of the NIMH Israeli kibbutz-city study and the Jerusalem Infant Developmental study. *Schizophrenia Bulletin, 13,* 425–437.

Margolin, G., & Gordis, E. B. (2004). Children's exposure to violence in the family and community. *Current Directions in Psychological Science, 13,* 152–155.

Margolin, R. (1991). Neuroimaging. In J. Sadavoy, L. W. Lazarus, & L. F. Jarvik (Eds.), *Comprehensive review of geriatric psychiatry* (pp. 245–271). Washington, DC: American Psychiatric Press.

Margraf, J., Barlow, D. H., Clark, D. M., & Telch, M. J. (1993). Psychological treatment of panic: Work in progress on outcome, active ingredients, and follow-up. *Behaviour Research and Therapy, 31,* 1–8.

Margraf, J., Ehlers, A., & Roth, W. T. (1987). Panic attacks associated with perceived heart rate acceleration: A case report. *Behavior Therapy, 18,* 84–89.

Margraf, J., Ehlers, A., Roth, W. T., Clark, D. B., et al. (1991). How "blind" are double-blind studies? *Journal of Consulting and Clinical Psychology, 59,* 184–187.

Mariani, M. A., & Barkley, R. A. (1997). Neuropsychological and academic functioning in preschool boys with attention deficit hyperactivity disorder. *Developmental Neuropsychology, 13,* 111–129.

Marine, C. (1998, September 29). No intercourse means no sex. *San Francisco Examiner,* A4.

Maris, R. W., Berman, A. L., & Silverman, M. M. (2000). *Comprehensive textbook of suicidology.* New York: Guilford Press.

Marks, I., Shaw, S., & Parkin, R. (1998). Computer-aided treatments of mental health problems. *Clinical Psychology: Science and Practice, 5,* 151–170.

Marlatt, G. A. (1978). Craving for alcohol, loss of control and relapse: A cognitive-behavioral analysis. In P. E. Nathan & G. A. Marlatt (Eds.), *Experimental and behavioral approaches to alcoholism.* New York: Plenum.

Marlatt, G. A. (1983). The controlled-drinking controversy: A commentary. *American Psychologist, 38,* 1097–1110.

Marlatt, G. A., Baer, J. S., Kivlahan, D. R., Dimeff, L. A., et al. (1998). Screening and brief intervention for high-risk college student drinkers: Results from a two-year follow-up assessment. *Journal of Consulting and Clinical Psychology, 66,* 604–615.

Marlatt, G. A., Demming, B., & Reid, J. (1973). Loss-of-control drinking in alcoholics: An experimental analogue. *Journal of Abnormal Psychology, 81,* 233–241.

Marlatt, G. A., & Gordon, J. R. (1985). *Relapse prevention: Maintenance strategies in the treatment of addictive behaviors.* New York: Guilford Press.

Marlowe, N. I. (1992). Pain sensitivity and headache: An examination of the central theory. *Journal of Psychosomatic Research, 36,* 17–24.

Marmar, C. R. (1988). Personality disorders. In H. H. Goldman (Ed.), *Review of general psychiatry* (pp. 401–424). Norwalk, CT: Appleton & Lange.

Marmor, J., & Woods, S. M. (1980). *The interface between the psychodynamic and behavioral therapies.* New York: Plenum Medical.

Marmot, M. G., & Syme, S. L. (1976). Acculturation and coronary heart disease in Japanese-Americans. *American Journal of Epidemiology, 104,* 225–247.

Marquardt, W. H. (2000). Update on migraine management. *Journal of the American Academy of Physician Assistants, 13,* 60–72.

Marrugat, J., Sala, J., Masia, R., Pavesi, M., et al. (1998). Mortality differences between men and women following first myocardial infarction. *Journal of the American Medical Association, 280,* 1405–1409.

Marsa, L. (2000, April 3). Children's health issue—The drug dilemma: The increased use of powerful psychiatric medicines in children under six has raised concerns about overmedication and long-term effects. *Los Angeles Times,* p. S1.

Marsella, A. J. (1988). Ethnocultural issues in the assessment of psychopathology. In S. Wetzler (Ed.), *Measuring mental illness.* (pp. 7–21). Washington, DC: American Psychiatric Press.

Marsh, D. T., & Johnson, D. L. (1997). The family experience of mental illness: Implications for intervention. *Professional Psychology: Research and Practice, 28,* 229–237.

Marsh, D. T., Lefley, H. P., Evans-Rhodes, D., Ansell, V. I., et al. (1996). The family experience of mental illness: Evidence for resilience. *Psychiatric Rehabilitation Journal, 20,* 3–12.

Marsh, J. C. (1988). What have we learned about legislative remedies for rape? In R. A. Prentky & V. L. Quisey (Eds.), *Human sexual aggression: Current perspectives. Annals of the New York Academy of Sciences, 528* (pp. 79–110). Salem, MA: New York Academy of Sciences.

Marshall, G. N., & Schell, T. L. (2002). Reappraising the link between peritraumatic dissociation and PTSD symptom severity: Evidence from a longitudinal study of community violence survivors. *Journal of Abnormal Psychology, 111,* 626–636.

Marshall, J. (1998, February 23). Memoir of anorexia and bulimia is a harrowing story. *Seattle Post-Intelligencer,* pp. D1–D2.

Marshall, W. L. (1988). Behavioral indices of habituation and sensitization during exposure to phobic stimuli. *Behaviour Research and Therapy, 26,* 67–77.

Marshall, W. L., & Barbaree, H. E. (1990). Outcome of comprehensive cognitive-behavior treatment programs. In W. L. Marshall & D. R. Laws (Eds.), *Handbook of sexual assault: Issues, theories, and treatment of the offender* (pp. 363–385). New York: Plenum Press.

Marshall, W. L., Jones, R., Ward, T., Johnston, P., & Barbaree, H. E. (1991). Treatment outcome with sex offenders. *Clinical Psychology Review, 11,* 465–486.

Martin, P. R. (1993). *Psychological management of chronic headaches.* New York: Guilford Press.

Martin, P. R., & Seneviratne, H. M. (1997). Effects of food deprivation and a stressor on head pain. *Health Psychology, 16,* 310–318.

Martin, R. A. (2001). Humor, laughter, and physical health: Methodological issues and research findings. *Psychological Bulletin, 127,* 504–519.

Martin, S. (1995). APA to pursue prescription privileges. *APA Monitor, 26,* 6.

Maser, J. D., Kaelber, C., & Weise, R. E. (1991). International use and attitudes toward DSM-III and DSM-III-R: Growing consensus in psychiatric classification. *Journal of Abnormal Psychology, 100,* 271–279.

Masi, G., Favilla, L., Mucci, M., Poli, P., & Romano, R. (2001). Depressive symptoms in children and adolescents with dysthymic disorder. *Psychopathology, 34,* 29–35.

Maslow, A. H. (1954). *Motivation and personality.* New York: Harper & Row.

Masserman, J., Yum, K., Nicholson, J., & Lee, S. (1944). Neurosis and alcohol: An experimental study. *American Journal of Psychiatry, 101,* 389–395.

Masson, J. M. (1988). *Against therapy: Emotional tyranny and the myth of psychological healing.* New York: Atheneum.

Masterman, D. L., & Cummings, J. L. (2001). Alzheimer's disease. In G. O. Gabbard (Ed.), *Treatment of psychiatric disorders* (pp. 481–514). Washington, DC: American Psychiatric Press.

Masters, W. H., & Johnson, V. E. (1966). *Human sexual response.* Boston: Little, Brown.

Masters, W. H., & Johnson, V. E. (1970). *Human sexual inadequacy.* London: Churchill.

Masters, W. H., & Johnson, V. E. (1979). *Homosexuality in perspective.* Boston: Little, Brown.

Masters, W. H., Johnson, V. E., & Kolodny, R. C. (1992). *Human sexuality.* New York: HarperCollins.

Masterson, J. F. (1981). *The narcissistic and borderline disorders: An integrated developmental approach.* New York: Brunner/Mazel.

Mataix-Cols, D., Marks, I. M., Greist, J. H., Kobak, K. A., & Baer, L. (2002). Obsessive compulsive symptom dimensions as predictors of compliance with and response to behavior therapy: Results from a controlled trial. *Psychotherapy and Psychosomatics, 71,* 255–261.

Mataix-Cols, D., Wooderson, S., Lawrence, N., Brammer, M. J., et al.

(2004). Distinct neural correlates of washing, checking, and hoarding symptom dimensions in obsessive-compulsive disorder. *Archives of General Psychiatry, 61,* 564–576.

Matarazzo, J. D. (1986). Computerized clinical psychological test interpretations. Unvalidated plus all mean and no sigma. *American Psychologist, 41,* 14–41.

Matarazzo, J. D. (1992). Psychological testing and assessment in the twenty-first century. *American Psychologist, 47,* 1007–1018.

Materka, P. R. (1984). Families caring, coping with Alzheimer's disease. *Michigan Today, 16,* 13–14.

Mather, M., Canli, T., English, T., Whitfield, S., et al. (2004). Amygdala responses to emotionally valenced stimuli in older and younger adults. *Psychological Science, 15,* 259–263.

May, D. C., & Turnbull, N. (1992). Plastic surgeons' opinions of facial surgery for individuals with Down syndrome. *Mental Retardation, 30,* 29–33.

May, R. (1967). *Psychology and the human dilemma.* New York: Van Nostrand.

Mayberg, H. S., Silva, J. A., Brannan, S. K., Tekell, J. L., et al. (2002). The functional neuroanatomy of the placebo effect. *American Journal of Psychiatry, 159,* 728–738.

Mazure, C. M. (1998). Life stressors as risk factors in depression. *Clinical Psychology: Science and Practice, 5,* 291–313.

Mazza, J., & Overstreet, S. (2000). Children and adolescents exposed to community violence: A mental health perspective for school psychologists. *School Psychology Review, 29,* 86–101.

McAnulty, R. D., & Burnette, M. M. (2003). *Fundamentals of human sexuality: Making healty decisions.* New York: Allyn & Bacon.

McAnulty, R. D., & Burnette, M. M. (2004). *Exploring human sexuality: Making healthy decisions.* New York: Allyn & Bacon.

McBride, M. C. (1990). Autonomy and the struggle for female identity: Implications for counseling women. *Journal of Counseling and Development, 69,* 22–26.

McCarthy, K. (2002). Family dynamics affect asthma in at-risk kids. *Psychology Today, 35,* 30–31.

McCauley, E., & Ehrhardt, A. A. (1984). Follow-up of females with gender identity disorders. *Journal of Nervous and Mental Disease, 172,* 353–358.

McClain, P. (1995). *Centers for Disease Control and Prevention,* Atlanta, GA.

McCord, W., & McCord, J. (1964). *The psychopath: An essay on the criminal mind.* Princeton, NJ: Van Nostrand.

McCormick, R. A., & Taber, J. I. (1988). Attributional style in pathological gamblers in treatment. *Journal of Abnormal Psychology, 97,* 368–370.

McCracken, L. M., & Larkin, K. T. (1991). Treatment of paruresis with in vivo desensitization: A case report. *Journal of Behavior Therapy and Experimental Psychiatry, 22,* 57–62.

McCrady, B. S. (1994). Alcoholics Anonymous and behavior therapy: Can habits be treated as diseases? Can diseases be treated as habits? *Journal of Consulting and Clinical Psychology, 62,* 1159–1166.

McCrae, R. R. (1994). A reformulation of Axis II: Personality and personality-related problems. In P. T. Costa & T. A. Widiger (Eds.), *Personality disorders and the five-factor model of personality* (pp. 303–310). Washington, DC: American Psychological Association.

McCreary, D. R., & Sadava, S. W. (2001). Gender differences in relationships among perceived attractiveness, life satisfaction, and health in adults as a function of body mass index and perceived weight. *Psychology of Men and Masculinity, 2,* 108–116.

McCullough, P. K., & Maltsberger, J. T. (2001). Obsessive-compulsive personality disorder. In G. O. Gabbard (Ed.), *Treatment of psychiatric disorders* (pp. 2341–2351). Washington, DC: American Psychiatric Press.

McDaniel, S. H., & Speice, J. (2001). What family psychology has to offer women's health: The examples of conversion, somatization, infertility treatment, and genetic testing. *Professional Psychology: Research and Practice, 32,* 44–51.

McDermut, W., Miller, I. W., & Brown, R. A. (2001). The efficacy of group psychotherapy for depression: A meta-analysis and review of the empirical research. *Clinical Psychology: Science and Practice, 8,* 98–116.

McDowell, D. M. (2001). Club drugs. In G. O. Gabbard (Ed.), *Treatment of psychiatric disorders* (pp. 749–758). Washington, DC: American Psychiatric Press.

McElroy, S. L., & Arnold, L. M. (2001). Impulse-control disorders. In G. O. Gabbard (Ed.), *Treatment of psychiatric disorders* (pp. 2435–2471). Washington, DC: American Psychiatric Press.

McGee, R., & Stanton, W. R. (1992). Sources of distress among New England adolescents. *Journal of Child Psychology and Psychiatry, 33,* 999–1010.

McGee, R., Williams, S., Bradshaw, J., Chapel, J. L., et al. (1985). The Rutter scale for completion by teachers: Factor structure and relationships with cognitive abilities and family adversity for a sample of New Zealand children. *Journal of Psychology and Psychiatry, 26,* 727–739.

McGilley, B. M., & Pryor, T. L. (1998). Assessment and treatment of bulimia nervosa. *American Family Physician, 57,* 2743–2750.

McGonagle, K. A., & Kessler, R. C. (1990). Chronic stress, acute stress, and depressive symptoms. *American Journal of Community Psychology, 18,* 681–706.

McGowan, S. (1991, November). Confidentiality and the ethical dilemma. *Guidepost, 34,* 1, 6, 10.

McGue, M., & Christensen, K. (1997). Genetic and environmental contributions to depression symptomology: Evidence from Danish twins 75 years of age and older. *Journal of Abnormal Psychology, 106,* 439–448.

McGuire, L., Junginger, J., Adams, S. G., Burright, R., & Donovick, P. (2001). Delusions and delusional reasoning. *Journal of Abnormal Psychology, 110,* 259–266.

McGuire, P. A. (1999). More psychologists are finding that discrete uses of humor promote healing in their patients. *APA Monitor Online, 30,* 1–5.

McGuire, R. J., Carlisle, J. M., & Young, B. G. (1965). Sexual deviations as conditioned behavior: A hypothesis. *Behavior Research and Therapy, 2,* 185–190.

McIntosh, J. L. (1991). Epidemiology of suicide in the U.S. In A. A. Leenaars (Ed.), *Lifespan perspectives of suicide.* New York: Plenum.

McIntosh, J. L. (1992). Epidemiology of suicide in the elderly. *Suicidal and Life-Threatening Behavior, 22,* 15–35.

McKenzie, N., Marks, I., & Liness, S. (2001). Family and past history of mental illness as predisposing factors in posttraumatic stress disorder. *Psychotherapy and Psychosomatics, 70,* 163–167.

McKeon, P., & Murray, R. (1987). Familial aspects of obsessive-compulsive neurosis. *British Journal of Psychiatry, 151,* 528–534.

McLarnon, L. D., & Kaloupek, D. G. (1988). Psychological investigation of genital herpes recurrence: Prospective assessment and cognitive-behavioral intervention for a chronic physical disorder. *Health Psychology, 1,* 231–249.

McLean, P. D., Whittal, M. L., Thordarson, D. S., Taylor, S., et al. (2001). Cognitive versus behavior therapy in the group treatment of obsessive-compulsive disorder. *Journal of Consulting and Clinical Psychology, 69,* 205–214.

McLellan, A. T., Alterman, A. I., Metzger, D. S., Grissom, G. R., et al. (1994). Similarity of outcome predictors across opiate, cocaine, and alcohol treatments: Role of treatment services. *Journal of Consulting and Clinical Psychology, 62,* 1141–1158.

McLeod, B. (1985). Real work for real pay. *Psychology Today, 19,* 42–50.

McLin, W. M. (1992). Introduction to issues in psychology and epilepsy. *American Psychologist, 47,* 1124–1125.

McNally, R. J. (1999). Theoretical approaches to the fear of anxiety. In S. Taylor (Ed.), *Anxiety sensitivity: Theory, research, and treatment of the fear of anxiety* (pp. 3–16). Hillsdale, NJ: Erlbaum.

McNally, R. J., Clancy, S. A., Schacter, D. L., & Pitman, R. K. (2000). Personality profiles, dissociation, and absorption in women reporting repressed, recovered, or continuous memories of childhood sexual abuse. *Journal of Consulting and Clinical Psychology, 68,* 1033–1037.

McNamee, H. B., Mello, N. K., & Mendelson, J. H. (1968). Experimental analysis of drinking patterns of alcoholics: Concurrent psychiatric observations. *American Journal of Psychiatry, 124,* 1063–1069.

McNiel, D. E., & Binder, R. L. (1991). Clinical assessment of the risk of violence among psychiatric inpatients. *American Journal of Psychiatry, 148,* 1317–1321.

McQueen, P. C., Spence, M. W., Garner, J. B., Pereira, L. H., & Winson, E. J. T. (1987). Prevalence of major mental retardation and associated disabilities in the Canadian Maritime Provinces. *American Journal of Mental Deficiency, 91,* 460–466.

Meares, A. (1979). Mind and cancer. *Lancet, 22,* 978.

Mears, F. G. (2004). Antidepressant adverse events. *National Psychologist, 13,* 6–7.

Mednick, S. A. (1970). Breakdown in individuals at high risk for schizophrenia: Possible predispositional perinatal factors. *Mental Hygiene, 54,* 50–63.

Mednick, S. A., Cannon, T., Parnas, J., & Schulsinger, F. (1989). Twenty-seven-year follow-up of the Copenhagen high-risk for schizophrenia project: Why did some of the high-risk offspring become schizophrenic? *Schizophrenia Research, 2,* 14.

Mednick, S. A., & Christiansen, K. O. (Eds.). (1977). *Biosocial bases of criminal behavior.* New York: Gardner Press.

Mednick, S. A., & Kandel, E. (1988). Genetic and perinatal factors in violence. In T. E. Moffitt & S. A. Mednick (Eds.), *Biological contributions to crime causation* (pp. 40–54). Boston: Martinus Nijhoff.

Meehl, P. E. (1962). Schizotaxia, schizotypia, schizophrenia. *American Psychologist, 17,* 827–838.

Mehler, P. S. (2003). Bulimia nervosa. *New England Journal of Medicine, 349,* 875–881.

Meichenbaum, D. H. (1977). *Cognitive-behavior modification: An integrative approach.* New York: Plenum.

Meichenbaum, D. H. (1985). *Stress-inoculation training.* New York: Pergamon Press.

Meichenbaum, D. H. (1993). The personal journey of a psychotherapist and his mother: In G. Brannigan & M. R. Merrens (Eds.), *The undaunted psychologist: Adventures in research.* New York: McGraw-Hill.

Meichenbaum, D. H., & Cameron, R. (1982). Cognitive behavior therapy. In G. T. Wilson & C. M. Franks (Eds.), *Contemporary behavior therapy: Conceptual and empirical foundations.* New York: Guilford Press.

Meier, M. J. (1992). Modern clinical neuropsychology in historical perspective. *American Psychologist, 47,* 550–558.

Meissner, W. W. (2001). Paranoid personality disorder. In G. O. Gabbard (Ed.), *Treatment of psychiatric disorders* (pp. 2227–2236). Washington, DC: American Psychiatric Press.

Melges, F., & Bowlby, J. (1969). Types of hopelessness in psychopathological process. *Archives of General Psychiatry, 20,* 690–699.

Meller, P. J., & Ohr, P. S. (1996). The assessment of culturally diverse infants and preschool children. In L. A. Suzuki, P. J. Meller, & J. G. Ponterotto (Eds.), *Handbook of multicultural assessment.* San Francisco: Jossey-Bass.

Meloy, J. R. (2001). Antisocial personality disorder. In G. O. Gabbard (Ed.), *Treatment of psychiatric disorders* (pp. 2251–2271). Washington, DC: American Psychiatric Press.

Meltzer, H. Y. (2000). Side effects of antipsychotic medications: Physician's choice of medication and patient compliance. *Journal of Clinical Psychiatry, 61,* 3–4.

Mendlein, J. M., Freedman, D. S., Peter, D. G., Allen, B., et al. (1997). Risk factors for coronary heart disease among Navajo Indians: Findings from the Navajo Health and Nutrition Survey. *Journal of Nutrition, 127,* 2099–2105.

Mendlowicz, M. V., Rapaport, M. H., Fontenelle, L., Jean-Louis, G., et al. (2002). Amnesia and neonaticide. *American Journal of Psychiatry, 159,* 498.

Menzies, R. G., & Clarke, J. C. (1995). Danger expectancies and insight in acrophobia. *Behaviour Research and Therapy, 33,* 215–221.

Menzies, R. P. D., Fedoroff, J. P., Green, C. M., & Isaacson, K. (1995). Prediction of dangerous behavior in male erotomania. *British Journal of Psychiatry, 166,* 529–536.

Mercer, J. R. (1979). *System of Multicultural Pluralistic Assessment (SOMPA): Technical manual.* New York: Psychological Corporation.

Mercer, J. R. (1988). Death of the IQ paradigm: Where do we go from here? In W. J. Lonner & V. O. Tyler (Eds.), *Cultural and ethnic factors in learning and motivation: Implications for education.* Bellingham, WA: Western Washington University.

Merryman, K. (1997, July 17). Medical experts say Roberts may well have amnesia: Parts of her life match profile of person who might lose memory. *News Tribune,* pp. A8–A9.

Merskey, H. (1992). The manufacture of personalities: The production of multiple personality disorder. *British Journal of Psychiatry, 160,* 327–340.

Merskey, H. (1995). Multiple personality disorder and false memory syndrome. *British Journal of Psychiatry, 166,* 281–283.

Merz, C. N. B. (1997, April 11). Heart Disease: The stress connection. *Newsweek,* pp. 9–16.

Messer, S. B. (2001). Empirically supported treatments: What's a nonbehaviorist to do? In B. D. Slife, R. N. Williams, & S. H. Barlow (Eds.), *Critical issues in psychotherapy* (pp. 45–59). Thousand Oaks, CA: Sage.

Meyer, G. J., Finn, S. E., Eyde, L. D., Kay, G. G., et al (2001). Psychological testing and psychological assessment: A review of evidence and issues. *American Psychologist, 56,* 128–165.

Meyer, G. J., Finn, S. E., Eyde, L. D., Kay, G. G., et al (2003). Psychological testing and psychological assessment: A review of evidence and issues. In A. E. Kazdin (Ed.) *Methodological issues and strategies in clinical research* (pp. 265–345). Washington, DC: America Psychological Association.

Meyer, J., & Peter, D. (1979). Sex reassignment: Follow-up. *Archives of General Psychiatry, 36,* 1010–1015.

Meyer, R. G. (1989). *The clinician's handbook.* Needham Heights, MA: Allyn & Bacon.

Meyer, R. G., & Osborne, Y. V. H. (1982). *Case studies in abnormal behavior.* Boston: Allyn & Bacon.

Meyer, W. S., & Keith, C. R. (1991). Homosexual and preoedipal issues in the psychoanalytic psychotherapy of a female-to-male transsexual. In C. W. Socarides & V. D. Volkan (Eds.), *The homosexualities and the therapeutic process* (pp. 75–96). Madison, CT: International Universities Press.

Meyers, H., Echemedia, F., & Trimble, J. E. (1991). American Indians and the counseling process. In P. B. Pedersen (Ed.), *Handbook of cross-cultural counseling.* Westport, CT: Greenwood.

Meyers, W. A. (1991). A case history of a man who made obscene telephone calls and practiced frotteurism. In G. I. Fogel & W. A. Myers (Eds.), *Perversions and near-perversions in clinical practice* (pp. 109–126). New Haven, CT: Yale University Press.

Michael, R. T., Gagnon, J. H., Lauman, E. O., & Kolata, G. (1994). *Sex in America: A definitive survey.* New York: Little, Brown.

Miklowitz, D. J. (1994). Family risk indicators in schizophrenia. *Schizophrenia Bulletin, 20,* 137–148.

Mileno, M. D., Barnowski, C., Fiore, T., Gormley, J., et al. (2001). Factitious HIV syndrome in young women. *AIDS Reader, 11,* 263–268.

Milich, R., & Pelham, W. E. (1986). Effects of sugar ingestion on the classroom and playground behavior of attention deficit disordered boys. *Journal of Consulting and Clinical Psychology, 54,* 714–718.

Miller, D. J., & Thelen, M. H. (1986). Knowledge and beliefs about confidentiality in psychotherapy. *Professional Psychology, 17,* 15–19.

Miller, G. A., & Keller, J. (2000). Psychology and neuroscience: Making peace. *Current Directions in Psychological Science, 9,* 212–215.

Miller, G. E., & Cohen, S. (2001). Psychological interventions and the immune system: A meta-analytic review and critique. *Health Psychology, 20,* 47–63.

Miller, H. L., Coombs, D. W., & Leeper, J. D. (1984). An analysis of the effects of suicide prevention facilities on suicide rates in the United States. *American Journal of Public Health, 74,* 340–343.

Miller, J. B. (1976). *Toward a new psychology of women.* Boston: Beacon Press.

Miller, J. N., & Ozonoff, S. (2000). The external validity of Asperger disorder: Lack of evidence from the domain of neuropsychology. *Journal of Abnormal Psychology, 109,* 227–238.

Miller, L. K. (1999). The savant syndrome: Intellectual impairment and exceptional skill. *Psychological Bulletin, 125,* 31–46.

Miller, M., & Kantrowitz, B. (1999, January 25). Unmasking Sybil. *Newsweek,* pp. 66–68.

Miller, M. N., & Pumariega, A. J. (2001). Culture and eating disorders: A historical and cross-cultural review. *Psychiatry, 64,* 93–110.

Miller, S. B., Friese, M., Dolgoy, L., Sita, A., et al. (1998). Hostility, sodium consumption, and cardiovascular response to interpersonal stress. *Psychosomatic Medicine, 60,* 71–77.

Miller, S. D., & Triggiano, P. J. (1992). The psychophysiological investigation of multiple personality disorder: Review and update. *American Journal of Clinical Hypnosis, 35,* 47–61.

Millon, T. (1975). Reflections on Rosenhan's "On being sane in insane places." *Journal of Abnormal Psychology, 84,* 456–461.

Millon, T. (1981). *Disorders of personality: DSM-III-R, Axis II.* New York: Wiley-Interscience.

Millon, T. (1983). The DSM-III: An insider's perspective. *American Psychologist, 38,* 804–814.

Millon, T. (1994). Personality disorders: Conceptual distinctions and classification issues. In P. T. Costa & T. A. Widiger (Eds.), *Personality disorders and the five-factor model of personality* (pp. 279–301). Washington, DC: American Psychological Association.

Millon, T., & Everly, G. S. (1985). *Personality and its disorders.* New York: Wiley.

Milstein, V. (1988). EEG topography in patients with aggressive violent behavior. In T. E. Moffitt & S. A. Mednick (Eds.), *Biological contributions to crime causation* (pp. 121–134). Boston: Martinus Nijhoff.

Milstone, C. (1997). Sybil minds. *Saturday Night, 112,* 35–42.

The mind of a murderer (pts. 1–2). (1984, March 19 & 26). Prod. Michael Barnes. *Frontline,* Public Broadcasting Service, New York.

Minde, K. K. (1977). Children in Uganda: Rates of behavioural deviations and psychiatric disorders in various school and clinic populations. *Journal of Child Psychology and Psychiatry, 18,* 23–27.

Mineka, S., & Sutton, S. K. (1992). Cognitive biases and the emotional disorders. *Psychological Science, 3*(1), 65–69.

Mintz, J., Mintz, L., & Goldstein, M. (1987). Expressed emotion and relapse in first episodes of schizophrenia. *British Journal of Psychiatry, 151,* 314–320.

Minuchin, S. (1974). *Families and family therapy.* Cambridge, MA: Harvard University Press.

Minuchin, S., Rosman, B., & Baker, L. (1978). *Psychosomatic families: Anorexia nervosa in context.* Cambridge, MA: Harvard University Press.

Mirsky, A. F., Kugelmass, S., Ingraham, L. J., Frenkel, E., & Nathan, M. (1995). Overview and summary: Twenty-five–year follow-up of high-risk children. *Schizophrenia Bulletin, 21,* 227–237.

Mischel, W. (1968). *Personality and assessment.* New York: Wiley.

Mitchell, A. (1998, June 17). Controversy over Lott's view of homosexuality. *New York Times,* p. 24.

Modestin, J. (1992). Multiple personality disorder in Switzerland. *American Journal of Psychiatry, 149,* 88–92.

Mogg, K., Philippot, P., & Bradley, B. P. (2004). Selective attention to angry faces in clinical social phobia. *Journal of Abnormal Behavior, 113,* 160–165.

Mohr, D. C., & Beutler, L. E. (1990). Erectile dysfunction: A review of diagnostic and treatment procedures. *Clinical Psychology Review, 10,* 123–150.

Monahan, J. (1981). *The clinical prediction of violent behavior.* Rockville, MD: National Institute of Mental Health.

Monahan, J. (1993). Limiting therapist exposure to Tarasoff liability: Guidelines for risk containment. *American Psychologist, 48,* 242–250.

Monahan, J., & Walker, L. (Eds.). (1990). *Social science in law: Cases and materials* (2nd ed.). Westbury, NJ: Foundation Press.

Money, J. (1987). Masochism: On the childhood origin of paraphilia, opponent-process theory, and antiandrogen therapy. *Journal of Sex Research, 23,* 273–275.

Money, J. (1996). *Lovemaps: Clinical concepts of sexual/erotic health and pathology, paraphilia, and gender transpositions in childhood, adolescence, and maturity.* New York: Irvington.

Monroe, M., & Simons, A. D. (1991). Diathesis-stress theories in the context of life stress research: Implications for the depressive disorders. *Psychological Bulletin, 110,* 406–425.

Monroe, S. M., Thase, M. E., & Simons, A. D. (1992). Social factors and the psychobiology of depression: Relations between life stress and rapid eye movement sleep latency. *Journal of Abnormal Psychology, 101,* 528–537.

Mooney, J. (1988, November 18). A flight from pain for Vietnam veterans. *Seattle Post-Intelligencer,* p. B2.

Moos, R. H., Cronkite, R. C., & Moos, B. S. (1998). Family and extrafamily resources and the ten-year course of treated depression. *Journal of Abnormal Psychology, 107,* 450–460.

Morenz, B. & Becker, J. V. (1995). The treatment of youthful sex offenders. *Applied and Preventive Psychology, 4,* 247–256.

Morey, L. C. (1988). Personality disorders in DSM-III and DSM-III-R: Convergence, coverage, and internal consistency. *American Journal of Psychiatry, 145,* 573–577.

Morey, L. C., & Ochoa, E. S. (1989). An investigation of adherence to diagnostic criteria: Clinical diagnosis of the DSM-III personality disorders. *Journal of Personality Disorders, 3,* 180–192.

Morey, L. C., & Zanarini, M. C. (2000). Borderline personality: Traits and disorder. *Journal of Abnormal Psychology, 109,* 733–737.

Morgan, D. L., & Morgan, R. K. (2001). Single-participant research design: Bringing science to managed care. *American Psychologist, 56,* 119–127.

Morgan, S. B., & Brown, T. L. (1988). Luria-Nebraska Neuro-psychological Battery–Children's Revision: Concurrent validity with three learning disability subtypes. *Journal of Consulting and Clinical Psychology, 56,* 463–466.

Morgan, W. J., Crain, E. F., Gruchalla, R. S., O'Connor, G. T., et al. (2004). Results of a home-based environmental intervention among urban children with asthma. *New England Journal of Medicine, 351,* 1068–1080.

Morgenstern, J., Labouvie, E., McCrady, B. S., Kahler, C. W., & Frey, R. M. (1997). Affiliation with Alcoholics Anonymous after treatment: A study of its therapeutic effects and mechanisms of action. *Journal of Consulting and Clinical Psychology, 65,* 768–777.

Moriarity, J., Collie, A., Olson, D., Buchanan, J., et al. (2004). A prospective controlled study of cognitive function during an amateur boxing tournament. *Neurology, 62,* 1497–1502.

Morihisa, J. M., Rosse, R. B., Cross, C. D., Balkoski, V., & Ingraham, C. A. (1999). Laboratory and other diagnostic tests in psychiatry. In R. E. Hales, S. C. Yudofsky, & J. A. Talbott (Eds.), *Textbook of psychiatry* (pp. 281–316). Washington, DC: American Psychiatric Press.

Morriss, R. K., & Gask, L. (2002). Treatment of patients with somatized mental disorder: Effect of reattribution training on outcomes under the direct control of the family doctor. *Psychosomatics, 43,* 394–399.

Moscicki, E. K. (1995). Epidemiology of suicidal behavior. Special issue: Suicide prevention: Toward the year 2000. *Suicidal Life Threatening Behavior, 25,* 22–35.

Moser, C., & Levitt, E. E. (1987). An exploratory-descriptive study of a sadomasochistically oriented sample. *Journal of Sex Research, 23,* 322–337.

Moser, G., Wenzel-Abatzi, T-A., Stelzeneder, M., & Wenzel, T. (1998). Globus sensation: Pharnygoesophageal function, psychometric and psychiatric findings, and follow-up in eighty-eight patients. *Archives of Internal Medicine, 158,* 1365–1372.

Mrazek, D. A. (1993). Asthma: Stress, allergies, and the genes. In D. Goleman & J. Gurin (Eds.), *Mind/body medicine* (pp. 193–205). New York: Consumer Reports Books.

Muehleman, T., Pickens, B. K., & Robinson, F. (1985). Informing clients about the limits to confidentiality, risks, and their rights: Is self-disclosure inhibited? *Professional Psychology: Research and Practice, 16,* 385–397.

Muenzenmaier, K., Castille, D. M., Shelley, A.-M., Jamison, A., et al. (2005). Comorbid posttraumatic stress disorder and schizophrenia. *Psychiatric Annals, 35,* 50–56.

Mueser, K. T., Goodman, L. B., Trumbetta, S. L., Rosenberg, S. D., et al. (1998). Trauma and posttraumatic stress disorder in severe mental illness. *Journal of Consulting and Clinical Psychology, 66,* 493–499.

Mueser, K. T., Sengupta, A., Schooler, N. R., Bellack, A. S., et al. (2001). Family treatment and medication dosage reduction in schizophrenia: Effects on patient social functioning, family attitudes, and burden. *Journal of Consulting and Clinical Psychology, 69,* 3–12.

Mukai, T. (1996). Mothers, peers, and perceived pressure to diet among Japanese adolescent girls. *Journal of Research on Adolescence, 6,* 309–324.

Mulder, R. T., Beautrais, A. L., Joyce, P. R., & Fergusson, D. M. (1998). Relationship between dissociation, childhood sexual abuse, childhood physical abuse, and mental illness in a general population sample. *American Journal of Psychiatry, 155,* 806–811.

Mulholland, A. M., & Mintz, L. B. (2001). Prevalence of eating disorders among African American women. *Journal of Counseling Psychology, 48,* 111–116.

Mulkens, S. A. N., de Jong, P. J., & Merckelbach, H. (1996). Disgust and spider phobia. *Journal of Abnormal Psychology, 105,* 464–468.

Mullan, M., & Brown, F. (1994). The clinical features of Alzheimer's disease and the search for clinico-aetiologic correlates. In D. Nicholson (Ed.), *Anti-dementia agents: Research and prospects for therapy* (pp. 1–12). San Diego: Academic Press.

Mumford, D. B., Whitehouse, A. M., & Choudry, I. Y. (1992). Survey of eating disorders in English-medium schools in Lehore, Pakistan. *International Journal of Eating Disorders, 11,* 173–184.

Mundo, E. Bareggi, S. R., Pirola, R., & Bellodi, L. (1997). Long-term pharmacotherapy of obsessive-compulsive disorder: A double-blind controlled study. *Journal of Clinical Psychopharmacology, 17,* 4–10.

Munoz, R. F., Glish, M., Soo-Hoo, T., & Robertson, J. (1982). The San Francisco mood survey project: Preliminary work toward the prevention of depression. *American Journal of Community Psychology, 10,* 317–330.

Munoz, R. F., Ying, Y. W., Bernal, G., Perez-Stable, E. J., et al. (1995). Prevention of depression with primary care patients: A randomized controlled trial. *American Journal of Community Psychology, 23,* 199–222.

Munoz, R. H., & Sanchez, A. M. (1996). *Developing culturally competent systems of care for state mental health services.* Boulder, CO: WICHE.

Muris, P., & Merckelbach, H. (2000). How serious are common childhood fears? II. The parent's point of view. *Behaviour Research and Therapy, 38,* 813–818.

Muris, P., Merckelbach, H., & Clavan, M. (1997). Abnormal and normal compulsions. *Behaviour Research and Therapy, 35,* 249–252.

Muris, P., Merckelbach, H., & Collaris, R. (1997). Common childhood fears and their origins. *Behaviour Research and Therapy, 35,* 929–936.

Muris, P., Merckelbach, H., & de Jong, P. J. (1995). Exposure therapy outcome in spider phobics: Effects of monitoring and blunting coping styles. *Behaviour Research and Therapy, 33,* 461–464.

Muris, P., Merckelbach, H., Ollendick, T. H., King, N. J., & Bogie, N. (2001). Children's nighttime fears: Parent-child ratings of frequency, content, origins, coping behaviors and severity. *Behaviour Research and Therapy, 39,* 13–28.

Murphree, O. D., & Dykman, R. A. (1965). Litter patterns in the offspring of nervous and stable dogs: I. Behavioral tests. *Journal of Nervous and Mental Disorders, 141,* 321–332.

Murphy, J. K., Stoney, C. M., Alpert, B. S., & Walker, S. S. (1995). Gender and ethnicity in children's cardiovascular reactivity: Seven years of study. *Health Psychology, 14,* 48–55.

Murray, E. J. (1983). Beyond behavioral and dynamic therapy. *British Journal of Clinical Psychology, 22,* 127–128.

Murray, H. A., & Morgan, H. (1938). *Explorations in personality.* New York: Oxford University Press.

Mustanski, B. S., Viken, R. J., Kaprio, J., & Rose, R. J. (2003). Genetic influences on the association between personality risk factors and alcohol use and abuse. *Journal of Abnormal Psychology, 112,* 282–289.

Myers, J. K., Weissman, M. M., Tischler, G. L., Holzer, C. E., et al. (1984). Six-month prevalence of psychiatric disorders in three communities. *Archives of General Psychiatry, 41,* 959–967.

Myers, L. L. (1997). Exposure therapy in the brief treatment of an elevator phobia. *Scandinavian Journal of Behavior Therapy, 26,* 22–26.

Nademanee, K., Veerakul, G., Nimmannit, S., Chaowakul, V., et al. (1997). Arrhythmogenic marker for sudden unexplained death syndrome in Thai men. *Circulation, 96,* 2595–2600.

Nagin, D. S., & Tremblay, R. E. (2000). Parental and early childhood predictors of persistent physical aggression in boys from kindergarten to high school. *Archives of General Psychiatry, 58,* 389–394.

Nagler, S., Marcus, J., Sohlberg, S. C., Lifshitz, M., & Silberman, E. K. (1985). Clinical observation of high-risk children. *Schizophrenia Bulletin, 11,* 107–111.

Naglieri, J. A., Drasgow, F., Schmit, M., Handler, L., et al. (2004). Psychological testing on the Internet: New problems, old issues. *American Psychologist, 59,* 150–162.

Nakao, M., Nomura, S., Shimosawa, T., Yoshiuchi, K., et al. (1997). Clinical effects of blood pressure biofeedback treatment on hypertension by autoshaping. *Psychosomatic Medicine, 59,* 331–338.

Nardi, A. E., Valenca, A. M., Nascimento, I., Mezzasalma, M. A., & Zin, W. A. (2001). Hyperventilation in panic disorder and social phobia. *Psychopathology, 34,* 123–126.

Nash, J. M. (1997, March 24). Gift of love. *Time,* pp. 81–82.

Nash, M. R., Drake, S. D., Wiley, S., & Khalsa, S. (1986). Accuracy of recall by hypnotically age-regressed subjects. *Journal of Abnormal Psychology, 95,* 298–300.

Nathan, P. E. (1976). Alcoholism. In H. Leitenberg (Ed.), *Handbook of behavior modification and behavior therapy.* Englewood Cliffs, NJ: Prentice-Hall.

Nathan, P. E. (1988). The addictive personality is the behavior of the addict. *Journal of Consulting and Clinical Psychology, 56,* 183–188.

Nathan, P. E. (1991). Substance use disorders in the DSM-IV. *Journal of Abnormal Psychology, 100,* 356–361.

Nathan, P. E. (1998). Practice guidelines: Not yet ideal. *American Psychologist, 53,* 290–299.

National Anxiety Foundation. (2003). *Obsessive-compulsive disorder.* Retrieved October 17, 2004, from http://www.lexington-on-line.com/naf.ocd.2.html

National Association of Anorexia Nervosa and Associated Disorders. (2004). *Eating disorder information.* Retrieved March 9, 2005, from http://www.anad.org/site/anadweb/content.php?type1&id=6982

National Center for Health Statistics. (1988). Advance report of final mortality statistics, 1986. *NCHS Monthly Vital Statistics Report, 37*(6). Hyattsville, MD: U.S. Public Health Service.

National Center for Health Statistics. (1989). *Vital statistics of the United States, 1987 (Vol. 2): Mortality.* Washington, DC: U.S. Government Printing Office.

National Center for Health Statistics. (1994). Advance report of final mortality statistics, 1991. *Monthly Vital Statistics Report, 42.*

National Center for Health Statistics. (2001a). *Asthma.* Hyattsville, MD: U.S. Department of Health and Human Services.

National Center for Health Statistics. (2001b). *Hypertension*. Hyattsville, MD: U.S. Department of Health and Human Services.

National Center for Health Statistics. (2003). *US Mortality, 2001*. Washington, DC: Centers for Disease Control and Prevention.

National Council on the Aging. (1998, September, 29). *San Francisco Chronicle*, A4.

National Institute of Child Health and Human Development. (1999, September 30). NICHD funded researchers discover gene for Rett's syndrome. *News Alert*, pp. 1–3. Retrieved from http://156.40.88.3/new/releases/retgene.htm

National Institutes of Health. (2004a). *Brain basics: Understanding sleep*. Retrieved November 16, 2004, from http://www.ninds.nih.gov/disorders/brain_basics/understanding_sleep_pr.htm

National Institutes of Health. (2004b). *Facts about narcolepsy*. Retrieved November 16, 2004, from http://www.nh1bi.nih.gov/health/public/sleep/narcolep.txt

National Institute of Mental Health. (1985). *Mental Health: United States, 1985*. Washington, DC: U.S. Government Printing Office.

National Institute of Mental Health. (1995). *Mental illness in America: The National Institute of Mental Health agenda*. Rockville, MD: Author.

National Institute of Mental Health. (1999). *Facts about panic disorder*. Washington, DC: National Institute of Mental Health.

National Institute of Mental Health. (2000). *Anxiety disorders*. Bethesda, MD: U.S. Department of Health and Human Services.

National Institute of Mental Health. (2001). *When someone has schizophrenia*. Washington, DC: U.S. Government Printing Office.

National Institute of Neurological Disorders and Stroke. (2001a). *Autism fact sheet*. Bethesda, MD: National Institutes of Health.

National Institute of Neurological Disorders and Stroke. (2001b). *NINDS headache information fact sheet*. Bethesda, MD: National Institutes of Health.

National Institute of Neurological Disorders and Stroke. (2004). *NINDS hypersomnia information*. Retrieved November 19, 2004, from http://www.ninds.nih.gov/disorders/hypersomnia/hypersomnia_pr.htm

National Institute on Drug Abuse. (1991). *National household survey on drug abuse: Main findings 1990*. Washington, DC: U.S. Government Printing Office.

National Institute on Drug Abuse. (2004). *MDMA (Ecstacy) abuse* (Research Report Series). Rockville, MD: National Institute on Drug Abuse.

National Sleep Foundation. (2000). *2000 Omnibus Sleep in America Poll*. Retrieved November 16, 2004, from http://www.sleepfoundation.org/publications/2000poll.cfm.

National Sleep Foundation. (2002). *2002 Sleep in America poll*. Washington, DC: Author

National Sleep Foundation. (2004a). *REM behavior disorder*. Retrieved November 16, 2004, from http://www.sleepfoundation.org/remdis.cfm

National Sleep Foundation. (2004b). *Sleep apnea*. Retrieved November 16, 2004, from http://www.sleepfoundation.org/publications/sleepap.cfm

National Sleep Foundation. (2004c). *2004 Sleep in America poll*. Washington, DC: Author.

National Sleep Foundation. (2004d). *When things go bump in the night: Nightmares, sleep terrors, and REM behavior disorder*. Retrieved November 16, 2004, from http://www.sleepfoundation.org/nightmares.cfm

National Victim Center. (1992). *Rape in America: A Report to the Nation*. Charleston, SC: Crime Victims Research and Treatment Center.

Neagoe, A. D. (2000). Abducted by aliens: A case study. *Psychiatry, 63*, 202–207.

Nelson, C. B., Heath, A. C., & Kessler, R. C. (1998). Temporal progression of alcohol dependence symptoms in the U. S. household population: Results from the National Comorbidity Survey. *Journal of Consulting and Clinical Psychology, 66*, 474–483.

Nelson, K. B., Grether, J. K., Croen, L. A., Dambrosia, J. M., et al. (2001). Neuropeptides and neurotrophins in neonatal blood of children with autism or mental retardation. *Annals of Neurology, 49*, 597–606.

Nelson, L. D., & Adams, K. M. (1997). Challenges for neuropsychology in the treatment and rehabilitation of brain-injured patients. *Psychological Assessment, 9*, 368–373.

Nelson-Gray, R. O. (1991). DSM-IV: Empirical guidelines from psychometrics. *Journal of Abnormal Psychology, 100*, 308–315.

Nemeroff, C. B. (1998). Psychopharmacology of affective disorders in the twenty-first century. *Biological Psychiatry, 44*, 517–525.

Nestler, E. J., & Malenka, R. C. (2004). The addicted brain. *Scientific American, 290*, 50–57.

Netting, J. (2001, February 17). The newly sequenced genome bares all. *Science News*. Retrieved May 4, 2005, from http://www.sciencenews.org/articles/20010217/fob1.asp

Neugebauer, R. (1979). Medieval and early modern theories of mental illness. *Archives of General Psychiatry, 36*, 477–483.

Neumark-Sztainer, D., Hannan, P. J., & Stat, M. (2000). Weight-related behaviors among adolescent girls and boys. *Archives of Pediatric Adolescent Medicine, 154*, 569–577.

Nevid, J. S., Fichner-Rathus, L., & Rathus, S. A. (1995). *Human sexuality*. Boston: Allyn & Bacon.

Newman, J. P., & Schmitt, W. A. (1998). Passive avoidance in psychopathic offenders: A replication and extension. *Journal of Abnormal Psychology, 107*, 527–532.

Newman, L. E., & Stoller, R. J. (1974). Nontranssexual men who seek sex reassignment. *American Journal of Psychiatry, 131*, 437–441.

Newmark, C. S. (1985). The MMPI. In C. S. Newmark (Ed.), *Major psychological assessment instruments* (pp. 11–64). Boston: Allyn & Bacon.

Neziroglu, F., & Yaryura-Tobias, J. A. (1997). A review of cognitive behavioral and pharmacological treatment of body dysmorphic disorder. *Behavior Modification, 21*, 324–340.

Niaura, R. S., Rohsenow, D. J., Binkoff, J. A., Monti, P. M., et al. (1988). Relevance of cue reactivity to understanding alcohol and smoking relapse. *Journal of Abnormal Psychology, 97*, 133–152.

Nichols, M. P., & Schwartz, R. C. (2005). *The essentials of family therapy*. New York: Allyn & Bacon.

Nicholson, R. A., & Berman, J. S. (1983). Is follow-up necessary in evaluating psychotherapy? *Psychological Bulletin, 93*, 261–278.

Nicholson, R. A., & Kugler, K. E. (1991). Competent and incompetent criminal defendants: A quantitative review of comparative research. *Psychological Bulletin, 109*, 355–370.

Nicotine: Powerful grip on the brain. (1995, September 22). *Los Angeles Times*, pp. A1, A37.

Nietzel, M. T., Bernstein, D. A. & Milich, R. (1994). *Introduction to clinical psychology* (4th ed.). Englewood Cliffs, NJ: Prentice-Hall.

Nigg, J. T., Lohr, N. E., Westen, D., Gold, L. J., & Silk, K. R. (1992). Malevolent object representations in borderline personality disorder and major depression. *Journal of Abnormal Psychology, 101*, 61–67.

Nilsson, L-L., Grawe, R. W., Levander, S., & Lovaas, A-L. (1998). Efficacy of conversational skills training of schizophrenic patients in Sweden and Norway. *International Review of Psychiatry, 10*, 54–57.

Nisenson, L. G., Berenbaum, H., & Good, T. L. (2001). The development of interpersonal relationships in individuals with schizophrenia. *Psychiatry, 64*, 111–125.

Nitzkin, J., & Smith, S. A. (2004). *Clinical preventive services in substance abuse and mental health update: From science to services* (DHHS Publication No. SMA 04-3906). Rockville, MD: Substance Abuse and Mental Health Services Administration, Center for Mental Health Services.

Noble, E. P. (1990). Alcoholic fathers and their sons: Neuropsychological, electrophysiological, personality, and family correlates. In C. R. Cloninger & H. Begleiter (Eds.), *Genetics and biology of alcoholism* (pp. 159–170). Cold Spring Harbor, NY: Cold Spring Harbor Laboratory Press.

Noble, J., & McConkey, K. M. (1995). Hypnotic sex change: Creating and challenging a delusion in the laboratory. *Journal of Abnormal Psychology, 104*, 69–74.

Nolen-Hoeksema, S. (1987). Sex differences in unipolar depression: Evidence and theory. *Psychological Bulletin, 101,* 259–282.

Nolen-Hoeksema, S. (1991). Responses to depression and their effects on the duration of depressive episodes. *Journal of Abnormal Psychology, 100,* 569–582.

Nolen-Hoeksema, S., Girgus, J. S., & Seligman, M. E. (1992). Predictors and consequences of childhood depressive symptoms: A 5-year longitudinal study. *Journal of Abnormal Psychology, 101,* 405–422.

Norcross, J. C. (2004). Empirically supported treatments (ESTS): Context, consensus, and controversy. *The Register Report, 30,* 12–14.

Norcross, J. C., & Freedheim, D. K. (1992). Into the future: Retrospect and prospect in psychotherapy. In D. K. Freedheim (Ed.), *History of psychotherapy: A century of change* (pp. 881–900). Washington, DC: American Psychological Association.

Norcross, J. C., & Newman, C. F. (1992). Psychotherapy integration: Setting the context. In J. C. Norcross & M. R. Goldfried (Eds.), *Handbook of psychotherapy integration* (pp. 3–45). New York: Basic Books.

Norcross, J. C., & Prochaska, J. O. (1988). A study of eclectic (and integrative) views revisited. *Professional Psychology: Research and Practice, 19,* 170–174.

Norfleet, M. A. (2002). Responding to society's needs: Prescription privileges for psychologists. *Journal of Clinical Psychology, 58,* 599–610.

North, C. S., Smith, E. M., & Spitznagel, E. L. (1997). One-year follow-up of survivors of a mass shooting. *American Journal of Psychiatry, 154,* 1696–1702.

North, M. M., North, S. M., & Coble, J. R. (1997). Virtual reality therapy for fear of flying. *American Journal of Psychiatry, 154,* 130.

Northup, J., & Gulley, V. (2001). Some contributions of functional analysis to the assessment of behaviors associated with ADHD and the effects of stimulant medication. *School Psychology Review, 30,* 227–238.

Norton, P. J., & Hope, D. A. (2001). Analogue observational methods in the assessment of social functioning in adults. *Psychological Assessment, 13,* 59–72.

Noyes, R., Jr., Langbehn, D. R., Happel, R. L., Stout, L. R., et al. (2001). Personality dysfunction among somatizing patients. *Psychosomatics, 42,* 320–329.

Nussbaum, N. L., & Bigler, E. D. (1989). Halstead-Reitan neuropsychological test batteries for children. In C. R. Reynolds & E. Fletcher-Janzen (Eds.), *Handbook of clinical child neuropsychology* (pp. 181–191). New York: Plenum Press.

Nutt, D. J. (2001). Neurobiological mechanisms in generalized anxiety disorder. *Journal of Clinical Psychiatry, 62,* 22–27.

Nwachuku, U., & Ivey, A. (1991). Culture specific counseling: An alternative approach. *Journal of Counseling and Development, 70,* 106–111.

Nystul, M. S. (2003). *Introduction to counseling.* Boston: Allyn & Bacon.

O'Connor, B. P. & Dyce, J. A. (1998). A test of models of personality disorder configuration. *Journal of Abnormal Psychology, 107,* 3–16.

O'Connor, K. (1987). The interaction of hostile and depressive behaviors: A case study of a depressed boy. *Journal of Child and Adolescent Psychotherapy, 3,* 105–108.

O'Connor, T. G., McGuire, S., Reiss, D., Hetherington, E. M., & Plomin, R. (1998). Co-occurrence of depressive symptoms and antisocial behavior in adolescence: A common genetic liability. *Journal of Abnormal Psychology, 107,* 27–37.

Office of National Drug Control Policy. (1998). *1997 national household survey on drug abuse: Selected findings.* Washington, DC: Author.

Ofshe, R. J. (1992). Inadvertent hypnosis during interrogation: False confession due to dissociative state; misidentified multiple personality and the satanic cult hypothesis. *International Journal of Clinical and Experimental Hypnosis, 40,* 125–156.

Ogden, C. L., Fryar, C. D., Carroll, M. D., & Flegal, K. M. (2004). *Mean body weight, height, and body mass index, United States 1960–2002. Advance data from vital and health statistics* (no. 347). Hyattsville, MD: National Center for Health Statistics.

Ohaeri, J. U., & Odejide, O. A. (1994). Somatization symptoms among patients using primary health care facilities in a rural community in Nigeria. *American Journal of Psychiatry, 151,* 728–731.

O'Hara, M. W. (2003). Postpartum depression. *Clinician's Research Digest, 29,* 12.

Ohman, A., & Hultman, C. M. (1998). Electrodermal activity and obstetric complications in schizophrenia. *Journal of Abnormal Psychology, 107,* 228–237.

Ohman, A., & Mineka, S. (2001). Fears, phobias, and preparedness: Toward an evolved module of fear and fear learning. *Psychological Review, 108,* 483–522.

Okazaki, S. (1997). Sources of ethnic differences between Asian American and white American college students on measures of depression and social anxiety. *Journal of Abnormal Psychology, 106,* 52–60.

Okazaki, S., & Sue, S. (1995). Cultural considerations in psychological assessment of Asian Americans. In J. N. Butcher (Ed.), *Clinical personality assessment: Practical approaches* (pp. 107–119). New York: Oxford University Press.

Oke, N. J., & Schreibman, L. (1990). Training social imitations to a high-functioning autistic child: Assessment of collateral behavior change and generalization in a case study. *Journal of Autism and Developmental Disorders, 20,* 479–497.

O'Kearney, R. O. (1993). Additional considerations in the cognitive-behavioral treatment of obsessional ruminations—A case study. *Journal of Behavior Therapy and Experimental Psychiatry, 24,* 357–365.

Olarte, S. W. (1997). Sexual boundary violations. In *The Hatherleigh guide to ethics in therapy* (pp. 195–209). New York: Hatherleigh Press.

Olfson, M., Shaffer, D., Marcus, S. C., & Greenberg, T. (2003). Relationship between antidepressant medication treatment and suicide in adolescents. *Archives of General Psychiatry, 60,* 978–982.

Olivardia, R., Pope, H. G., Jr., & Hudson, J. I. (2000). Muscle dysphoria in male weightlifters: A case-control study. *American Journal of Psychiatry, 157,* 1291–1296.

Oliver, J., Shaller, C. A., Majovski, L. V., & Jacques, S. (1982). Stroke mechanisms: Neuropsychological implications. *Clinical Neuropsychology, 4,* 81–84.

Olkin, R. (1999). *What psychotherapists should know about disability.* New York: Guilford Press.

Ollendick, T. H., & King, N. J. (1998). Empirically supported treatments for children with phobic and anxiety disorders: Current status. *Journal of Clinical Child Psychology, 27,* 156–167.

Olmos de Paz, T. (1990). Working-through and insight in child psychoanalysis. *Melanie Kelin and Object Relations, 8,* 99–112.

O'Neill, A., & Fernandez, J. M. (2000). Dissociative disorder associated with a colloid cyst of the third ventricle: Organic or psychogenic amnesia? *Psychotherapy and Psychosomatics, 69,* 108–110.

Onstad, S., Skre, I., Edvardsen, J., Torgersen, S., & Kringlen, E. (1991). Twin concordance for DSM-III-R schizophrenia. *Acta Psychiatrica Scandinavica, 83,* 395–401.

Opler, M. K. (1967). *Culture and social psychiatry.* New York: Atherton Press.

Oren, D. A., & Rosenthal, N. E. (2001). Light therapy. In G. O. Gabbard (Ed.), *Treatment of psychiatric disorders* (pp. 1295–1306). Washington, DC: American Psychiatric Press.

Orr, S. P., Lasko, N. B., Shalev, A. Y., & Pitman, R. K. (1995). Physiologic responses to loud tones in Vietnam veterans with post-traumatic stress disorder. *Journal of Abnormal Psychology, 104,* 75–82.

Orr, S. P., Metzger, L. J., Lasko, N. B., Macklin, M. L., et al. (2000). De Novo conditioning in trauma-exposed individuals with and without posttraumatic stress disorder. *Journal of Abnormal Psychology, 109*, 290–298.

Ortega, A. N., McQuaid, E. L., Canino, G., Goodwin, R. D., & Fritz, G. K. (2004). Comorbidity of asthma and anxiety and depression in Puerto Rican children. *Psychosomatics, 45*, 93–99.

Osbourne, L. (2001, May 6). Regional disturbances. *New York Times Magazine*, pp. 6–14.

Öst, L.-G. (1987). Age of onset in different phobias. *Journal of Abnormal Psychology, 96*, 223–229.

Öst, L.-G. (1992). Blood and injection phobia: Background and cognitive, physiological, and behavioral variables. *Journal of Abnormal Psychology, 101*, 68–74.

Öst, L.-G., Alm, T., Brandberg, M., & Breitholtz, E. (2001). One vs. five sessions of exposure and five sessions of cognitive therapy in the treatment of claustrophobia. *Behaviour Research and Therapy, 39*, 167–183.

Öst, L.-G., & Hugdahl, K. (1981). Acquisition of phobias and anxiety response patterns in clinical patients. *Behaviour Research and Therapy, 19*, 439–447.

Öst, L.-G., & Westling, B. E. (1995). Applied relaxation vs. cognitive behavior therapy in the treatment of panic disorder. *Behaviour Research and Therapy, 33*, 145–158.

Othmer, E., & Othmer, S. C. (1994). *The clinical interview using DSM-IV. Volume 1: Fundamentals.* Washington, DC: American Psychiatric Press.

Otto, M. W., Pollack, M. H., & Sabatino, S. A. (1996). Maintenance of remission following cognitive behavior therapy for panic disorder: Possible deleterious effects of concurrent medication treatment. *Behavior Therapy, 27*, 473–482.

Otto, R. K. (1989). Bias and expert testimony of mental health professionals in adversarial proceedings: A preliminary investigation. *Behavioral Science and Law, 7*, 267–273.

Overholser, J. C., & Beck, S. (1986). Multimethod assessment of rapists, child molesters, and three control groups in behavioral and psychological measures. *Journal of Consulting and Clinical Psychology, 54*, 682–687.

Ozer, E. J., Best, S. R., Lipsey, T. L., & Weiss, D. S. (2003). Predictors of posttraumatic stress disorder and symptoms in adults: A meta-analysis. *Psychological Bulletin, 129*, 52–73.

Ozonoff, S., & Rogers, S. J. (2003). From Kanner to the millennium. In S. Ozonoff, S. J. Rogers, & R. L. Hendren (Eds.), *Autism spectrum disorders: A research review for practitioners* (pp. 3–36). Arlington, VA: American Psychiatric.

Palfrey, J. S., Levine, M. D., Walker, D. K., & Sullivan, M. (1985). The emergence of attention deficits in early childhood: A prospective study. *Developmental and Behavioral Pediatrics, 6*, 339–348.

Pallack, M. (1995). Managed care's evolution during the health care revolution. *National Psychologist, 4*, 12.

Pallanti, S., Quercioli, L., & Hollander, E. (2004). Social anxiety in outpatients with schizophrenia: A relevant cause of disability. *American Journal of Psychiatry, 161*, 53–57.

Palmer, K. S. (2001, May 10). Colleges start to realize men need body-image help too. *USA Today*, p. A15.

Panagiotopoulos, C., McCrindle, B. W., Hick, K., & Katzman, D. K. (2000). Electrocardiographic findings in adolescents with eating disorders. *Pediatrics, 105*, 1100–1105.

Paniagua, F. A. (1998). *Assessing and treating culturally diverse clients.* Thousand Oaks, CA: Sage.

Papolos, D., & Papolos, J. (1999). *The bipolar child: The definitive and reassuring guide to childhood's most misunderstood disorder.* New York: Broadway Books.

Papp, L. A., Klein, D. F., Martinez, J., Schneier, F., et al. (1993). Diagnostic and substance specificity of carbon-dioxide-induced panic. *American Journal of Psychiatry, 150*, 250–257.

Parham, T. A. (2002). *Counseling persons of African descent.* Thousand Oaks, CA: Sage.

Parham, T. A., White, J. L. & Ajamu, A. (1999). *The psychology of blacks: An African-centered perspective* (3rd ed.). Englewood Cliffs, NJ: Prentice-Hall.

Parker, S., Nichter, M., Vuckovic, N., Sims, C., & Ritenbaugh, C. (1995). Body image and weight concerns among African-American and White adolescent females: Differences that make a difference. *Human Organization, 54*, 103–114.

Parnas, J. (1987). Assortative mating in schizophrenia: Results from the Copenhagen high-risk study. *Psychiatry, 50*, 58–64.

Parrott, C. (1998). Treating binge eating disorder. *Counseling Psychology Quarterly, 11*, 265–281.

Paternite, C. E., Loney, J., & Roberts, M. A. (1995). External validation of oppositional disorder and attention deficit disorder with hyperactivity. *Journal of Abnormal Child Psychology, 23*, 453–469.

Patrick, C. J., Cuthbert, B. N., & Lang, P. J. (1994). Emotion in the criminal psychopath: Fear image processing. *Journal of Abnormal Psychology, 103*, 523–534.

Patterson, C. H. (1980). *Theories of counseling and psychotherapy.* New York: Harper & Row.

Patterson, G. R. (1986). Performance models for antisocial boys. *American Psychologist, 41*, 432–444.

Patterson, S. M., Matthews, K. A., Allen, M. T., & Owens, J. F. (1995). Stress-induced hemoconcentration of blood cells and lipids in healthy women during acute psychological stress. *Health Psychology, 14*, 319–324.

Paul, G. L. (1985). Can pregnancy be a placebo effect: Terminology, designs, and conclusions in the study of psychosocial and pharmacological treatments of behavioral disorders. In L. White, B. Tursky, & G. Schwartz (Eds.), *Placebo: Clinical phenomenon and new insights.* New York: Guilford Press.

Pauli, P., Marquardt, C., Hartl, L., Nutzinger, D. O., et al. (1991). Anxiety induced by cardiac perceptions in patients with panic attacks: A field study. *Behaviour Research and Therapy, 29*, 137–145.

Paulson, T. (1999, May 11). UW team joins study of autism treatment: Story of hormone secretin is like "Lorenzo's Oil." *Seattle Post Intelligencer*, p. C1, 3, 5.

Paykel, E. S. (Ed.). (1982). *Handbook of affective disorders.* New York: Guilford Press.

Payne, R. L. (1992). First person account: My schizophrenia. *Schizophrenia Bulletin, 18*, 725–728.

Penava, S. J., Otto, M. W., Maki, K. M., & Pollack, M. H. (1998). Rate of improvement during cognitive-behavioral group treatment for panic disorder. *Behaviour Research and Therapy, 36*, 665–673.

Pendery, M. L., Maltzman, I. M., & West, L. J. (1982). Controlled drinking by alcoholics? New findings and a reevaluation of a major affirmative study. *Science, 217*, 169–175.

Penn, D. L., Mueser, K. T., Tarrier, N., Gloege, A., et al. (2004). Supportive therapy for schizophrenia: Possible mechanisms and implications for adjunctive psychosocial treatments. *Schizophrenia Bulletin, 30*, 101–112.

Penn, N. E., Kar, S., Kramer, J., Skinner, J., & Zambrana, R. E. (1995). Panel VI: Ethnic minorities, health care systems, and behavior. *Health Psychology, 14*, 641–646.

Penninx, B. W. J. H., Beekman, A. T. F., Honig, A., Deeg, D. J. H., et al. (2001). Depression and cardiac mortality: Results from a community-based longitudinal study. *Archives of General Psychiatry, 58*, 221–227.

Perez, J. E. (1999). Clients deserve empirically supported treatments, not romanticism. *American Psychologist, 54*, 205–206.

Perls, F. (1969). *Gestalt therapy verbatim.* Moab, UT: Real People Press.

Perner, L. E. (2001, August). Literal detours: Propositions on abstraction in high functioning autistic individuals. Paper presented at the meeting of the American Psychological Association, San Francisco.

Perodeau, G. M. (1984). Married alcoholic women: A review. *Journal of Drug Issues, 14*, 703–720.

Perris, C. (1966). A study of bipolar (manic-depressive) and unipolar recurrent depressive psychosis. *Acta Psychiatrica Scandinavica* (Suppl. 194).

Perry, J. C. (2001). Dependent personality disorder. In G. O. Gabbard (Ed.), *Treatment of psychiatric disorders* (pp. 2353–2368). Washington, DC: American Psychiatric Press.

Perse, T. L., Greist, J. H., Jefferson, J. W., Rosenfeld, R., & Dar, R. (1987). Fluvoxamine treatment of obsessive-compulsive disorder. *American Journal of Psychiatry, 144,* 1543–1548.

Persky, V. W., Kempthorne-Rawson, J., & Shekelle, R. B. (1987). Personality and the risk of cancer: 20 years follow-up of the Western Electric Company. *Psychosomatic Medicine, 49,* 435–449.

Persons, J. B. (1986). The advantages of studying psychological phenomena rather than psychiatric diagnosis. *American Psychologist, 41,* 1252–1260.

Persons, J. B. (1991). Psychotherapy outcome studies do not accurately represent current models of psychotherapy: A proposed remedy. *American Psychologist, 46,* 99–106.

Petersen, A. C., Compas, B. E., Brooks-Gunn, J., Stemmler, M., Ey, S., & Grant, K. E. (1993). Depression in adolescence. *American Psychologist, 48,* 155–168.

Peterson, B. S., Pine, D. S., Cohen, P., & Brook, J. S. (2001). Prospective, longitudinal study of tic, obsessive-compulsive and attention-deficit/hyperactivity disorders in an epidemiological sample. *Journal of the American Academy of Child and Adolescent Psychiatry, 40,* 685–695.

Peterson, L., & Brown, D. (1994). Integrating child injury and abuse-neglect research: Common histories, etiologies, and solutions. *Psychological Bulletin, 116,* 293–315.

Petry, N. M., Martin, B., Cooney, J. L., & Kranzler, H. R. (2000). Give them prizes, and they will come: Contingency management for treatment of alcohol dependence. *Journal of Consulting and Clinical Psychology, 68,* 250–257.

Peveler, R. (1998). Understanding medically unexplained physical symptoms: Faster progress in the next century than in this? *Journal of Psychosomatic Research, 45,* 93–97.

Pfeiffer, R. F., & Ebadi, M. (1994). Pharmacologic management. In A. M. Cohen & W. J. Weiner (Eds.), *The comprehensive management of Parkinson's disease* (pp. 9–38). New York: Demos Publications.

Pfuhlmann, B., & Stober, G. (1997). The importance of differentiated psychopathology of catatonia. *Acta Psychiatrica Scandinavia, 95,* 357–359.

Phares, E. J. (1984). *Clinical psychology: Concepts, methods, and professions.* Homewood, IL: Dorsey.

Phelan, J. C., Bromet, E. J., & Link, B. G. (1998). Psychiatric illness and family stigma. *Schizophrenia Bulletin, 24,* 115–126.

Phelps, B. J. (2000). Dissociative identity disorder: The relevance of behavior analysis. *Psychological Record, 50,* 235–249.

Phelps, L., Brown, R. T., & Power, T. J. (2002). *Pediatric psychopharmacology: Combining medical and psychosocial interventions.* Washington, DC: American Psychological Association.

Phillips, A., & Daniluk, J. C. (2004). Beyond "survivor": How childhood sexual abuse informs the identity of adult women at the end of the therapeutic process. *Journal of Counseling and Development, 82,* 177–184.

Phillips, D. P., Todd, E. R., & Wagner, L. M. (1993). Psychology and survival. *Lancet, 342,* 1142–1145.

Phillips, D. P., Van Voorhees, C. A., & Ruth, T. E. (1992). The birthday: Lifeline or deadline? *Psychosomatic Medicine, 54,* 532–542.

Phillips, K. A., & Gunderson, J. G. (1999). Personality disorders. In R. E. Hales, S. C. Yudofsky & J. A. Talbott (Eds.), *Textbook of psychiatry* (pp. 795–823). Washington, DC: American Psychiatric Press.

Phillips, K. A., McElroy, S. L., Dwight, M. M., Eisen, J. L., & Rasmussen, S. A. (2001). Delusionality and response to open-label fluvoxamine in body dysmorphic disorder. *Journal of Clinical Psychiatry, 62,* 87–91.

Phillips, K. A., McElroy, S. L., Keck, P. E., Pope, H. G., Jr., & Hudson, J. I. (1993). Body dysmorphic disorder: Thirty cases of imagined ugliness. *American Journal of Psychiatry, 150,* 302–308.

Phillips, K. A., & Rasmussen, S. A. (2004). Change in psychosocial functioning and quality of life of patients with body dysmorphic disorder treated with fluoxetine: A placebo-controlled study. *Psychosomatics, 45,* 438–444.

Physician's desk reference (57th ed.). (2003). Montvale, NJ: Thompson Healthcare.

Pianta, R. C., & Egeland, B. (1994). Relation between depressive symptoms and stressful life events in a sample of disadvantaged mothers. *Journal of Consulting and Clinical Psychology, 62,* 1229–1234.

Piasecki, T. M., Jorenby, D. E., Smith, S. S., Fiore, M. C., & Baker, T. B. (2003). Smoking withdrawal dynamics: I. Abstinence distress in lapsers and abstainers. *Journal of Abnormal Psychology, 112,* 3–13.

Pigott, T. A. (1996). OCD: Where the serotonin selectivity story begins. *Journal of Clinical Psychiatry, 57,* 11–20.

Pigott, T. A., & Murphy, D. L. (1991). In reply. *Archives of General Psychiatry, 48,* 858–859.

Pigott, T. A., & Seay, S. (1997). Pharmacotherapy of obsessive-compulsive disorder. *International Review of Psychiatry, 9,* 133–147.

Pike, J. L., Smith, T. L., Hauger, R. L., Nicassio, P. M., et al. (1997). Chronic life stress alters sympathetic, neuroendocrine, and immune responsivity to an acute psychological stressor in humans. *Psychosomatic Medicine, 59,* 447–457.

Pike, K. M., Dohm, F.-A., Streigel-Moore, R., Wilfley, D. E., & Fairburn, C. G. (2001). A comparison of black and white women with binge eating disorder. *American Journal of Psychiatry, 158,* 1455–1461.

Pilisuk, M. (1975). The legacy of the Vietnam veteran. *Journal of Social Issues, 31*(4), 3–12.

Pine, G. J. (1972). Counseling minority groups: A review of the literature. *Counseling and Values, 17,* 35–44.

Pines, M. (1983, October). *Science,* pp. 55–58.

Pittman, F. (1994, January/February). A buyer's guide to psychotherapy. *Psychology Today,* pp. 50–53, 74, 76–78, 80–81.

Platt, J. J. (1986). *Heroin addiction: Theory, research, and treatment.* New York: Wiley.

Plienis, A. J., Hansen, D. J., Ford, F., Smith, S., Jr., Stark, L. J., & Kelly, J. A. (1987). Behavioral small group training to improve the social skills of emotionally-disordered adolescents. *Behavior Therapy, 18,* 17–32.

Plomin, R. (1989). Environment and genes: Determinant of behavior. *American Psychologist, 44,* 105–111.

Plomin, R., & Crabbe, J. (2000). DNA. *Psychological Bulletin, 126,* 806–828.

Plomin, R., & Daniels, D. (1987). Why are children in the same family so different from one another? *Behavioral and Brain Sciences, 10,* 1–15.

Plomin, R., Owen, M. J., & McGuffin, P. (1994). The genetic basis of complex human behaviors. *Science, 264,* 1733–1739.

Polivy, J., Schueneman, A. L., & Carlson, K. (1976). Alcohol and tension reduction: Cognitive and physiological effects. *Journal of Abnormal Psychology, 85,* 595–600.

Polaschek, D. L. L. (2003). Relapse prevention, offense process models, and the treatment of sexual offenders. *Professional Psychology: Research and Practice, 34,* 361–367.

Pollard, C. A., Pollard, H. J., & Corn, K. J. (1989). Panic onset and major events in the lives of agoraphobics: A test of continuity. *Journal of Abnormal Psychology, 98,* 318–321.

Ponterotto, J. G., & Casas, J. M. (1991). *Handbook of racial/ethnic minority counseling research.* Springfield, IL: Thomas.

Poon, L. W., & Siegler, I. C. (1991). Psychological aspects of normal aging. In J. Sadavoy, L. W. Lazarus, & L. F. Jarvik (Eds.), *Comprehensive review of geriatric psychiatry* (pp. 117–145). Washington, DC: American Psychiatric Press.

Pope, H. G., Jr., Gruber, A. J., Mangweth, B., Bureau, B., et al. (2000). Body image perception among men in three countries. *American Journal of Psychiatry, 157,* 1297–1301.

Pope, H. G., Jr., & Hudson, J. I. (1992). Is childhood sexual abuse a risk factor for bulimia nervosa? *American Journal of Psychiatry, 149,* 455–463.

Pope, H. G., Jr., Mangweth, B., Negrao, A. B., Hudson, J. I., & Cordas, T. A. (1994). Childhood sexual abuse and bulimia nervosa: A comparison of American, Austrian, and Brazilian women. *American Journal of Psychiatry, 151,* 732–737.

Pope, H. G., Jr., Oliva, P. S., Hudson, J. I., Bodkin, J. A., & Gruber, A. J. (1999). Attitudes toward DSM-IV dissociative disorders diagnoses among board-certified American psychiatrists. *American Journal of Psychiatry, 156,* 321–323.

Pope, H. G., Jr., Olivardia, R., Borowiecki, J. J., III, & Cohane, G. H. (2001). The growing commercial value of the male body: A longitudinal survey of advertising in women's magazines. *Psychotherapy and Psychosomatics, 70,* 189–193.

Pope, K. S. (1988). How clients are harmed by sexual contact with mental health professionals: The syndrome and its prevalence. *Journal of Counseling and Development, 67,* 222–226.

Pope, K. S., & Tabachnick, B. G. (1993). Therapists' anger, hate, fear, and sexual feelings: National survey of therapist responses, client characteristics, critical events, formal complaints, and training. *Professional Psychology: Research and Practice, 24,* 142–152.

Pope, K. S. Tabachnick, B. G., & Keith-Spiegel, P. (1987). Ethics of practice: The beliefs and behaviors of psychologists as therapists. *American Psychologist, 42,* 993–1166.

Pope, K. S., & Vetter, V. A. (1991). Prior therapist-patient sexual involvement among patients seen by psychologists. *Psychotherapy, 28,* 429–438.

Popper, C., & West, S. A. (1999). Disorders usually first diagnosed in infancy, childhood, or adolescence. In R. E. Hales, S. C. Yudofsky & J. A. Talbott (Eds.), *Textbook of psychiatry* (pp. 825–954). Washington, DC: American Psychiatric Press.

Portnoff, L. A., Golden, C. J., Wood, R. E., & Gustavson, J. L. (1983). Discrimination between schizophrenic and parietal lesion patients with neurological tests of parietal involvement. *Clinical Neuropsychology, 5,* 175–178.

Poulton, R., Trainor, P., Stanton, W., McGee, R., et al. (1997). The (in)stability of adolescent fears. *Behaviour Research and Therapy, 35,* 159–163.

Poulton, R., Waldie, K. E., Craske, M. G., Menzies, R. G., & McGee, R. (2000). Dishabituation processes in height fear and dental fear: An indirect test of the non-associative model of fear acquisition. *Behaviour Research and Therapy, 38,* 909–919.

Pound, E. J. (1987). Children and prematurity. In A. Thomas & J. Grimes (Eds.), *Children's needs: Psychological perspectives* (pp. 441–450). Washington, DC: National Association of School Psychologists.

Powell, A. D., & Kahn, A. S. (1995). Racial differences in women's desires to be thin. *International Journal of Eating Disorders, 17,* 191–195.

Powell, C. J. (1982, August). *Adolescence and the right to die: Issues of autonomy, competence, and paternalism.* Paper presented at the meeting of the American Psychological Association, Washington, DC.

Powell, D. H., & Whitla, D. K. (1994). Normal cognitive aging: Toward empirical perspectives. *Current Directions in Psychological Science, 3,* 27–31.

President's Commission on Mental Health. (1978). *Report from the President's Commission on Mental Health.* Washington, DC: U.S. Government Printing Office.

President's New Freedom Commission on Mental Health. (2003). *Achieving the promise: Transforming mental health care in America* (DHHS Publication No. SMA-03-3832). Rockville, MD: Author.

Press Association. (2001). Schizophrenia test is "Accurate." *APA Online.* Retrieved May 4, 2005, from http://www.psycport.com/news/2001/02/21/eng-preassociation_health_long/eng-preassociation_health_long_140546_217_396443067119_html

Pribor, E. F., & Dinwiddie, S. H. (1992). Psychiatric correlates of incest in childhood. *American Journal of Psychiatry, 149,* 52–56.

Price, L. J., Fein, G., & Feinberg, I. (1980). Neurological assessment of cognitive function in the elderly. In L. W. Poon (Ed.), *Aging in the 1980s.* Washington, DC: American Psychological Association.

Prichard, J. C. (1837). *Treatise on insanity and other disorders affecting the mind.* Philadelphia: Haswell, Barrington & Haswell.

Priester, M. J., & Clum, G. A. (1992). Attributional style as a diathesis in predicting depression, hopelessness, and suicide ideation in college students. *Journal of Psychopathology and Behavioral Assessment, 14,* 111–122.

Prigatano, G. P., Fordyce, D. J., Zeiner, H. K., Roueche, et al. (1984). Neuropsychological rehabilitation after closed head injury in young adults. *Journal of Neurology and Neuropsychology, 47,* 505–513.

Prochaska, J. O., & Norcross, J. C. (1994). Stages of change and decisional balance for twelve problem behaviors. *Health Psychology, 13,* 39–46.

Prochaska, J. O., & Norcross, J. C. (1999). *Systems of psychotherapy: A transtheoretical analysis* (4th ed.). Pacific Grove, CA: Brooks Cole.

Prochaska, J. O., & Norcross, J. C. (2003). *Systems of psychotherapy: A transtheoretical analysis* (5th ed.). Pacific Grove, CA: Brooks Cole.

Psychosomatic medicine: Doctors see positive effects of humor on health. (2004, June 16). *Immunotherapy Weekly, 135.*

Pueschel, S. M. (1991). Ethical considerations relating to prenatal diagnosis of fetuses with Down syndrome. *Mental Retardation, 29,* 185–190.

Quan, S. F., & Zee, P. (2004). A sleep review of systems: Evaluating the effects of medical disorders on sleep in the older patient. *Geriatrics, 59,* 37–43.

Quay, H. C. (1965). Psychopathic personality as pathological stimulation seeking. *American Journal of Psychiatry, 122,* 180–183.

Rabkin, J. G., McGrath, P. J., Quitkin, F. M., Tricamo, E., et al. (1990). Effects of pill-giving on maintenance of placebo response in patients with chronic depression. *American Journal of Psychiatry, 147,* 1622–1626.

Rabkin, J. G., Williams, J. B. W., Remien, R. H., Goetz, R., et al. (1991). Depression, distress, lymphocyte subsets, and human immunodeficiency virus symptoms on two occasions in HIV-positive homosexual men. *Archives of General Psychiatry, 48,* 11–119.

Rachman, S. (1966). Sexual fetishism: An experimental analogue. *Psychological Record, 16,* 293–296.

Rachman, S., & DeSilva, P. (1987). Abnormal and normal obsessions. *Behaviour Research and Therapy, 16,* 233–248.

Rachman, S., & Hodgson, R. (1980). *Obsessions and compulsions.* Englewood Cliffs, NJ: Prentice-Hall.

Radloff, L. S., & Rae, D. S. (1981). The components of the sex difference in depression. In R. G. Simmons (Ed.), *Research in community and mental health* (Vol. 2). Greenwood, CT: JAI Press.

Rahe, R. H. (1994). The more things change ... *Psychosomatic Medicine, 56,* 306–307.

Raine, A., Mellingen, K., Liu, J., Venables, P., & Mednick, S. A. (2003). Effect of environmental enrichment at ages 3–5 years on schizotypal personality and antisocial behavior at ages 17 and 23 years. *American Journal of Psychiatry, 160,* 1627–1635.

Ramer, J. C., & Miller, G. (1992). Overview of mental retardation. In G. Miller & J. C. Ramer (Eds.), *Static encephalopathies of infancy and childhood* (pp. 1–10). New York: Raven Press.

Ranchor, A. V., Sanderman, R., Bouma, J., Buunk, B. P., & van den Heuvel, W. J. (1997). An exploration of the relation between hostility and disease. *Journal of Behavioral Medicine, 20,* 223–240.

Rand, C., & Kuldau, J. (1990). The epidemiology of obesity and self-defined weight problem in the general population: Gender, race, age, and social class. *International Journal of Eating Disorders, 9,* 329–343.

Rao, S. M., Huber, S. J., & Bornstein, R. A. (1992). Emotional changes with multiple sclerosis and Parkinson's disease. *Journal of Consulting and Clinical Psychology, 60,* 369–378.

Rapaport, K., & Burkhart, B. R. (1984). Personality attitudinal characteristics of sexually coercive college males. *Journal of Abnormal Psychology, 93,* 216–221.

Rapee, R. M. (1995). Psychological factors influencing the affective response to biological challenge procedures in panic disorder. *Journal of Anxiety Disorders, 9,* 59–74.

Rappaport, J., & Cleary, C. P. (1980). Labeling theory and the social psychology of experts and helpers. In M. S. Gibbs, J. R. Lachenmeyer, & J. Sigal (Eds.), *Community psychology: Theoretical and empirical approaches.* New York: Gardner Press.

Raps, C. S., Peterson, C., Reinhard, K. E., Abramson, L. Y., & Seligman, M. E. P. (1982). Attributional styles among depressed patients. *Journal of Abnormal Psychology, 91,* 102–108.

Rassin, E., Muris, P., Schmidt, H., & Merckelbach, H. (2000). Relationships between thought-action fusion, thought suppression and obsessive-compulsive symptoms: A structural equation modeling approach. *Behaviour Research and Therapy, 38,* 889–897.

Ratey, J. J., Grandin, T., & Miller, A. (1992). Defense behavior and coping in an autistic savant: The story of Temple Grandin, PhD. *Psychiatry, 55,* 382–391.

Rathus, S. A., Nevid, J. S., & Fichner-Rathus, L. (2005). *Abnormal psychology.* New York: Allyn & Bacon.

Ratican, K. L. (1992). Sexual abuse survivors: Identifying symptoms and special treatment considerations. *Journal of Counseling and Development, 71,* 33–38.

Rea, M. M., Tompson, M. C., Miklowitz, D. J., Goldstein, M. J., et al. (2003). Family-focused treatment versus individual treatment for bipolar disorder: Results of a randomized clinical trial. *Journal of Consulting and Clinical Psychology, 71,* 482–492.

Read, J. P., Kahler, C. W., & Stevenson, J. F. (2001). Bridging the gap between alcoholism treatment research and practice: Identifying what works and why. *Professional Psychology: Research and Practice, 32,* 227–238.

Read, S. (1991). The dementias. In J. Sadavoy, L. W. Lazarus, & L. F. Jarvik (Eds.), *Comprehensive review of geriatric psychiatry* (pp. 287–309). Washington, DC: American Psychiatric Press.

Reading, C., & Mohr, P. (1976). Biofeedback control of migraine: A pilot study. *British Journal of Social and Clinical Psychology, 15,* 429–433.

Rechlin, T., Loew, T. H., & Joraschky, P. (1997). Pseudoseizure "status." *Journal of Psychosomatic Research, 42,* 495–498.

Reed, G. M., Levant, R. F., Stout, C. E., Murphy, M. J., & Phelps, R. (2001). Psychology in the current mental health marketplace. *Professional Psychology: Research and Practice, 32*(1), 65–70.

Rees, L. (1964). The importance of psychological, allergic, and infective factors in childhood asthma. *Journal of Psychosomatic Research, 1,* 253–262.

Regier, D. A., Boyd, J. H., Burke, J. D., Rae, D. S., et al. (1988). One-month prevalence of mental disorders in the U.S.: Based on five Epidemiologic Catchment Area (ECA) sites. *Archives of General Psychiatry, 45,* 977–986.

Regier, D. A., Narrow, W. E., Rae, D. S., Manderscheid, R. W., et al. (1993). The de facto U.S. Mental and Addictive Disorders Service System: Epidemiologic Catchment Area prospective one-year prevalence rates of disorders in services. *Archives of General Psychiatry, 50,* 85–94.

Reich, J. (1987). Sex distribution of DSM-III personality disorders in psychiatric outpatients. *American Journal of Psychiatry, 144,* 485–488.

Reid, W. H. (1981). The antisocial personality and related symptoms. In J. R. Lion (Ed.), *Personality disorders: Diagnosis and management.* Baltimore: Williams & Wilkins.

Reid, W. H., & Mason, M. (1998). Psychiatric hospital utilization in patients treated with clozapine for up to 4.5 years in a state mental health care system. *Journal of Clinical Psychiatry, 59,* 189–194.

Reilly, D. (1984). Family therapy with adolescent drug abusers and their families: Defying gravity and achieving escape velocity. *Journal of Drug Issues, 14,* 381–389.

Reisberg, B., Ferris, S. H., & Crook, T. (1982). Signs, symptoms, and course of age-associated cognitive decline. In S. Corkin, K. L. Davis, J. H. Growdon, E. Usdin, & R. J. Wurtman (Eds.), *Alzheimer's disease: A report of progress.* New York: Raven Press.

Reiser, D. E. (1988). The psychiatric interview. In H. H. Goldman (Ed.), *Review of general psychiatry* (pp. 184–192). Norwalk, CT: Appleton & Lange.

Reiss, S., Peterson, R. A., Gursky, D. M., & McNally, R. J. (1986). Anxiety sensitivity, anxiety frequency, and the prediction of fearfulness. *Behaviour Research and Therapy, 24,* 1–8.

Repressed memory claims expected to soar. (1995, May). *National Psychologist, 4,* 3.

Reschly, D. J. (1992). Mental retardation: Conceptual foundations, definitional criteria, and diagnostic operations. In S. R. Hooper, G. W. Hynd, & R. E. Mattison (Eds.), *Developmental disorders: Diagnostic criteria and clinical assessment* (pp. 23–67). Hillsdale, NJ: Lawrence Erlbaum Associates.

Research Task Force of the National Institute of Mental Health. (1975). *Research in the service of mental health* (DHEW Publication No. ADM 75–236). Washington, DC: U.S. Government Printing Office.

Resnick, M., Yehuda, R., & Pitts, R. K. (1992, March 24). JAMA cited in young Indians prone to suicide, study finds. *New York Times,* p. D24.

Reus, V. I. (1988). Affective disorders. In H. H. Goldman (Ed.), *Review of general psychiatry* (pp. 332–348). Norwalk, CT: Appleton & Lange.

Reynolds, C. R., Kamphaus, R. W., & Rosenthal, B. L. (1989). Applications of the Kaufman Assessment Battery for Children (KABC) in neuropsychological assessment. In C. R. Reynolds & E. Fletcher-Janzen (Eds.), *Handbook of clinical child neuropsychology* (pp. 181–191). New York: Plenum Press.

Rhee, S. H., Waldman, I. D., Hay, D. A., & Levy, F. (1999). Sex differences in genetic and environmental influences in DSM-III-R ADHD. *Journal of Abnormal Psychology, 108,* 24–41.

Rhodes, L., Bailey, C. M., & Moorman, J. E. (2004). Asthma prevalence and control characteristics by race/ethnicity: United States, 2002. *Morbidity and Mortality Weekly Reports, 53,* 145–148.

Ricca, V., Mannucci, E., Zucchi, T., Rotella, C. M., & Faravelli, C. (2000). Cognitive-behavioral therapy for bulimia nervosa and binge eating disorder: A review. *Psychotherapy and Psychosomatics, 69,* 287–295.

Ricciardelli, L. A., & McCabe, M. P. (2004). A biopsychosocial model of disordered eating and the pursuit of muscularity in adolescent boys. *Psychological Bulletin, 130,* 179–205.

Rice, D. P., & Miller, L. S. (1998). Health economics and cost implications of anxiety and other mental disorders in the United States. *British Journal of Psychiatry, 173,* 4–9.

Richards, J. C., Alvarenga, M., & Hof, A. (2000). Serum lipids and their relationships with hostility and angry affect and behaviors in men. *Health Psychology, 19,* 393–398.

Richardson, L. F. (1998). Psychogenic dissociation in childhood: The role of the counseling psychologist. *Counseling Psychologist, 26,* 69–100.

Rickels, K., & Schweizer, E. (1997). The clinical presentation of generalized anxiety in primary-care settings: Practical concepts of classification and management. *Journal of Clinical Psychology, 58,* 4–9.

Richwine, L. (2004a, September 21). *Antidepressants need stronger pediatric use warnings, advisory panel concludes.* Retrieved November 19, 2004, from http://www.medscape.com/viewarticle/489269

Richwine, L. (2004b). *U.S. reviewer claims pressure in antidepressant probe.* Retrieved November 19, 2004, from http://www.medscape.com/viewarticle/489987

Ridgway, A. R., Northup, J., Pellegrin, A., LaRue, R., & Hightshoe, A. (2003). The benefits of recess for children with and without attention-deficit/hyperactivity disorder. *School Psychology Quarterly, 18,* 253–268.

Ridley, C. R. (1995). *Overcoming unintentional racism in counseling and therapy: A practitioner's guide to intentional intervention.* Thousand Oaks, CA: Sage.

Rief, W., & Hiller, W. (2003). A new approach to the assessment of the treatment effects of somatoform. *Psychosomatics, 44,* 492–496.

Rietveld, S., Everaerd, W., & van Beest, I. (2000). Excessive breathlessness through emotional imagery in asthma. *Behaviour Research and Therapy, 38,* 1005–1014.

Rietveld, S., van Beest, I., & Everaerd, W. (2000). Psychological confounds in medical research: The example of excessive cough in asthma. *Behaviour Research and Therapy, 38,* 791–800.

Rifkin, A., Ghisalbert, D., Dimatou, S., Jin, C., & Sethi, M. (1998).

Dissociative identity disorder in psychiatric inpatients. *American Journal of Psychiatry, 155,* 844–845.

Rind, B., Tromovitch, P., & Bauserman, R. (1998). A meta-analysis examination of assumed properties of child sexual abuse using college samples. *Psychological Bulletin, 124,* 22–53.

Rios, M. (2001, January). Genomics and the future of the pharmaceutical industry. *Pharmaceutical Technology.* Retrieved May 4, 2005, from http://www.findarticles.com.

Riskind, J. H., Moore, R., & Bowley, L. (1995). The looming of spiders: The fearful perceptual distortion of movement and menace. *Behaviour Research and Therapy, 33,* 171–178.

Ritvo, E. R., Freeman, B. J., Yuwiler, A., Geller, E., Yokota, A., Schroth, P., & Novak, P. (1984). Study of fenfluramine in outpatients with the syndrome of autism. *Journal of Pediatrics, 105,* 823–828.

Ritvo, E. R., Jorde, L. B., Mason-Brothers, A., Freeman, B. J., et al. (1989). The UCLA–University of Utah epidemiologic survey of autism: Recurrent risk estimates and genetic counseling. *American Journal of Psychiatry, 146,* 1032–1036.

Rivas-Vazquez, R. A. (2001). Cholinesterase inhibitors: Current pharmacological treatments for Alzheimer's disease. *Professional Psychology: Research and Practice, 32,* 433–436.

Rivas-Vazquez, R. A., & Blais, M. A. (1997). Selective serotonin reuptake inhibitors and atypical antidepressants: A review and update for psychologists. *Professional Psychology: Research and Practice, 28,* 526–536.

Rivas-Vazquez, R. A., Blais, M. A., Rey, G. J., & Rivas-Vazquez, A. A. (2000). Atypical antipsychotic medications: Pharmacological profiles and psychological implications. *Professional Psychology: Research and Practice, 31,* 628–640.

Roberto, L. (1983). Issues in diagnosis and treatment of transsexualism. *Archives of Sexual Behavior, 12,* 445–473.

Roberts, G. W. (1991). Schizophrenia: A neuropathological perspective. *British Journal of Psychiatry, 158,* 8–17.

Roberts, W. (1995). Postvention and psychological autopsy in the suicide of a 14-year-old public school student. *School Counselor, 42,* 322–330.

Robins, L. N. (1966). *Deviant children growing up: A sociological and psychiatric study of sociopathic personality.* Baltimore: Williams & Wilkins.

Robins, L. N. (1991). Conduct disorder. *Journal of Child Psychology and Psychiatry, 32,* 193–212.

Robins, L. N., Helzer, J. E., Weisinann, M. M., Orvaschel, H., et al. (1984). Lifetime prevalence of specific psychiatric disorders in three sites. *Archives of General Psychiatry, 41,* 949–958.

Robins, L. N., & Kulbok, P. (1988). Epidemiological studies in suicide. *Psychiatric Annual, 18,* 619–627.

Robins, L. N., Locke, B. Z., & Regier, D. A. (1991). An overview of psychiatric disorders in America. In L. N. Robins & D. A. Regier (Eds.), *Psychiatric disorders in America: The Epidemiologic Catchment Area study* (pp. 328–366). New York: Free Press.

Robins, L. N., & Regier, D. A. (Eds.) (1991). *Psychiatric disorders in America: The Epidemiologic Catchment Area study.* New York: Free Press.

Robins, L. N., Tipp, J., & Przybeck, T. (1991). Antisocial personality. In L. N. Robins & D. A. Regier (Eds.), *Psychiatric disorders in America: The Epidemiologic Catchment Area study* (pp. 258–290). New York: Free Press.

Robinson, J. P., Shaver, P. R., & Wrightsman, L. S. (Eds.). (1991). *Measures of personality and social psychological attitudes.* San Diego, CA: Academic Press.

Roelofs, K., Keijsers, G. P. J., Hoogduin, K. A. L., Naring, G. W. B., & Moene, F. C. (2002). Childhood abuse in patients with conversion disorder. *American Journal of Psychiatry, 159,* 1908–1913.

Rogers, C. R. (1951). *Client-centered therapy.* Boston: Houghton Mifflin.

Rogers, C. R. (1959). A theory of therapy, personality, and interpersonal relationships, as developed in client-centered framework. In S. Koch (Ed.), *Psychology: A study of science* (Vol. 3). New York: McGraw-Hill.

Rogers, C. R. (1961). *On becoming a person.* Boston: Houghton Mifflin.

Rogers, C. R. (1980). *A way of being.* Boston: Houghton Mifflin.

Rogers, C. R. (1987). The underlying theory: Drawn from experiences with individuals and groups. *Counseling and Values, 32,* 38–45.

Rogers, J. R. (1990). Female suicide: The trend toward increased lethality in method of choice and its implications. *Journal of Counseling and Development, 69,* 37–41.

Rogers, J. R. (1992). Suicide and alcohol: Conceptualizing the relationship from a cognitive-social paradigm. *Journal of Counseling and Development, 70,* 540–543.

Rogers, R. L., & Petrie, T. A. (2001). Psychological correlates of anorexic and bulimic symptomatology. *Journal of Counseling and Development, 79,* 178–187.

Rohsenow, D. J., Monti, P. M., Hutchinson, K. E., Swift, R. M., et al. (2000). Naltrexone's effects on reactivity to alcohol cues among alcoholic men. *Journal of Abnormal Psychology, 109,* 738–742.

Rohsenow, D. J., Monti, P. M., Martin, R. A., Michalec, E., & Abrams, D. B. (2000). Brief coping skills treatment for cocaine abuse: 12-month substance use outcomes. *Journal of Consulting and Clinical Psychology, 68,* 515–520.

Roland, C. B. (1993). Exploring childhood memories with adult survivors of sexual abuse: Concrete reconstruction and visualization techniques. *Journal of Mental Health Counseling, 15,* 363–372.

Romme, M. A., Honig, A., Noorthoorn, E. O., & Escher, A. D. M. A. C. (1992). Coping with hearing voices: An emancipatory approach. *British Journal of Psychiatry, 161,* 99–103.

Root, M. P. (1990). Disordered eating in women of color. *Sex Roles, 22,* 525–536.

Root, M. P. (1996). *The multiracial experience.* Thousand Oaks, CA: Sage.

Root, R. W., & Resnick, R. J. (2003). An update on the diagnosis and treatment of attention-deficit/hyperactivity disorder. *Professional Psychology: Research and Practice, 34,* 34–41.

Rosen, G. (1995). *The Aleutian Enterprise* sinking and posttraumatic stress disorder: Misdiagnosis in clinical and forensic settings. *Professional Psychology, 26,* 82–87.

Rosen, J. C., Reiter, J., & Orosan, P. (1995). Assessment of body image in eating disorders with the body dysmorphic disorder examination. *Behaviour Research and Therapy, 33,* 77–84.

Rosen, R. C., & Leiblum, S. R. (1987). Current approaches to the evaluation of sexual desire disorders. *Journal of Sex Research, 23,* 141–162.

Rosen, R. C., & Leiblum, S. R. (1995). Hypoactive sexual desire. *Psychiatric Clinics of North America, 13,* 107–121.

Rosenfarb, I. S., Goldstein, M. J., Mintz, J., & Nuechterlein, K. H. (1995). Expressed emotion and subclinical psychopathology observable within the transactions between schizophrenic patients and their family members. *Journal of Abnormal Psychology, 104,* 259–267.

Rosenfeld, B. (2004). *Assisted suicide and the right to die.* New York: Guilford Press.

Rosenfield, A. H. (1985). Discovering and dealing with deviant sex. *Psychology Today, 19,* 8–10.

Rosenhan, D. L. (1973). On being sane in insane places. *Science, 179,* 250–258.

Rosenstreich, D. L., Eggleston, P., & Kattan, M. (1997). The role of cockroach allergy and exposure to cockroach allergen in causing morbidity among inner-city children with asthma. *New England Journal of Medicine, 336,* 1356–1363.

Rosenthal, D. (1970). *Genetic theory and abnormal behavior.* New York: McGraw-Hill.

Rosenthal, D. (1971). *Genetics of psychopathology.* New York: McGraw-Hill.

Rosenthal, J., & Jacobson, L. (1968). *Pygmalion in the classroom.* New York: Holt, Rinehart & Winston.

Rosenthal, P., & Rosenthal, S. (1984). Suicidal behavior by preschool children. *American Journal of Psychiatry, 141,* 520–525.

Rossiter, L. F. (1983). Prescribed medicines: Findings from the National Medical Care Expenditure Survey. *American Journal of Public Health, 73,* 1312–1315.

Sloane, R. B., Staples, F. R., Cristol, A. H., Yorkston, N. J., & Whipple, K. (1975). *Psychotherapy versus behavior therapy.* Cambridge, MA: Harvard University Press.

Slovenko, R. (1995). *Psychiatry and criminal culpability.* New York: Wiley.

Slutske, W. S., Eisen, S., Xian, H., True, W. R., et al. (2001). A twin study of the association between pathological gambling and antisocial personality disorder. *Journal of Abnormal Psychology, 110,* 297–308.

Slutske, W. S., Heath, A. C., Dinwiddie, S. H., Madden, P. A. F., et al. (1997). Modeling genetic and environmental influences in the etiology of conduct disorder: A study of 2,682 adult twin pairs. *Journal of Abnormal Psychology, 106,* 266–279.

Slutske, W. S., Heath, A. C., Dinwiddie, S. H., Madden, P. A. F., et al. (1998). Common genetic risk factors for conduct disorders and alcohol dependence. *Journal of Abnormal Psychology, 107,* 363–374.

Slutske, W. S., Jackson, K. M., & Sher, K. J. (2003). The natural history of problem gambling from age 18 to 29. *Journal of Abnormal Psychology, 112,* 263–274.

Smalley, S. L., & Asarnow, R. F. (1990). Brief report: Cognitive subclinical markers in autism. *Journal of Autism and Developmental Disorders, 20,* 271–278.

Smith, A., & Sugar, O. (1975). Development of above normal language and intelligence twenty-one years after left hemispherectomy. *Neurology, 25,* 813–818.

Smith, C. (2002, August 7). Persecuted parents or protected children. *Seattle Post Intelligencer,* pp. A1, A10.

Smith, C. S. (2003, September 27). Son's wish to die, and mother's help, stir French debate. *The New York Times,* pp. A1, A4.

Smith, D., & Kraft, W. A. (1983). DSM-III: Do psychologists really want an alternative? *American Psychologist, 38,* 777–785.

Smith, D. E., & Landry, M. J. (1988). Psychoactive substance use disorders: Drugs and alcohol. In H. H. Goldman (Ed.), *Review of general psychiatry* (pp. 266–285). Norwalk, CT: Appleton & Lange.

Smith, G. C., Clarke, D. M., Handrinos, D., Dunsis, A., & McKenzie, D. P. (2000). Consultation-liaison psychiatrists' management of somatoform disorders. *Psychosomatics, 41,* 481–489.

Smith, G. T., Goldman, M. S., Greenbaum, P. E., & Christiansen, B. A. (1995). Expectancy for social facilitation from drinking: The divergent paths of high-expectancy and low-expectancy adolescents. *Journal of Abnormal Psychology, 104,* 32–40.

Smith, J. E., Meyers, R. J., & Delaney, H. D. (1998). The community reinforcement approach with homeless alcohol-dependent individuals. *Journal of Consulting and Clinical Psychology, 66,* 541–548.

Smith, K. (1988, May). Loving him was easy. *Reader's Digest,* pp. 115–119.

Smith, K., & Bryant, R. A. (2000). The generality of cognitive bias in acute stress disorder. *Behaviour Research and Therapy, 38,* 709–715.

Smith, M. L., & Glass, G. V. (1977). Meta-analysis of psychotherapy outcome studies. *American Psychologist, 32,* 752–760.

Smith, M. L., Glass, G. V., & Miller, T. I. (1980). *The benefits of psychotherapy.* Baltimore: The Johns Hopkins University Press.

Smith, N. M., Floyd, M. R., Scogin, F., & Jamison, C. S. (1997). Three-year follow-up of bibliotherapy for depression. *Journal of Consulting and Clinical Psychology, 65,* 324–327.

Smith, T. W., Ruiz, J. M., & Uchino, B. N. (2000). Vigilance, active coping, and cardiovascular reactivity during social interaction in young men. *Health Psychology, 19,* 382–393.

Smith, T. W., Turner, C. W., Ford, M. H., Hunt, S. C., et al. (1987). Blood pressure reactivity in adult male twins. *Health Psychology, 6,* 209–220.

Smyer, M. A. (1984). Life transitions and aging: Implications for counseling older adults. *Counseling Psychologist, 12,* 17–28.

Snowden, L. R., & Cheung, F. K. (1990). Use of inpatient mental health services by members of ethnic minority groups. *American Psychologist, 45,* 347–355.

Snowden, D. A., Greiner, L. H., Mortimer, J. A., Riley, K. P., et al.

(1997). Brain infarction and the clinical expression of Alzheimer's Disease. *Journal of the American Medical Association, 277,* 813–817.

Snyder, R. D., Stovring, J., Cushing, A. H., Davis, L. E., & Hardy, T. L. (1981). Cerebral infarction in childhood bacterial meningitis. *Journal of Neurology, Neurosurgery, and Psychiatry, 44,* 581–585.

Snyder, S. (1986). *Drugs and the brain.* New York: Scientific American Library.

Sohlberg, S. C. (1985). Personality and neuropsychological performance of high-risk children. *Schizophrenia Bulletin, 11,* 48–65.

Solano, L., Costa, M., Salvati, S., Coda, R., et al. (1993). Psychosocial factors and clinical evolution in HIV-1 infection: A longitudinal study. *Journal of Psychosomatic Research, 37,* 39–51.

Solomon, R. L. (1977). An opponent-process theory of motivation: The affective dynamics of drug addiction. In J. D. Maser & M. E. Seligman (Eds.), *Psychopathology: Experimental models.* San Francisco: Freeman.

Solomon, R. L. (1980). The opponent-process theory of acquired motivation: The costs of pleasure and the benefits of pain. *American Psychologist, 35,* 691–712.

Sommers-Flanagan, J., & Sommers-Flanagan, R. (2004). *Counseling and psychotherapy theories in context and practice.* Hoboken, NJ: Wiley.

Sontag, D. (2002, April 28). Who was responsible for Elizabeth Shin? *The New York Times Magazine,* 1–17.

Sorenson, S. B., & Siegel, J. M. (1992). Gender, ethnicity, and sexual assault: Findings from a Los Angeles study. *Journal of Social Issues, 48,* 93–104.

Sorenson, S. B., & White, J. W. (1992). Adult sexual assault: Overview of research. *Journal of Social Issues, 48,* 1–8.

Sotillo, C., Rodriguez, C., & Salazar, V. (1998). Dissemination of a social skills training program for chronic schizophrenic patients. *International Review of Psychiatry, 10,* 51–53.

Southwick, S. M., Morgan, C. A. III, Nicolaou, A. L., & Charney, D. S. (1997). Consistency of memory for combat-related traumatic events in veterans of Operation Desert Storm. *American Journal of Psychiatry, 154,* 173–177.

Sovani, A., & Thatte, S. (1998). Effects of psychosocial interventions on motor speed and accuracy of chronic positive, negative and mixed symptom schizophrenics. *International Journal of Social Psychiatry, 44,* 117–126.

Spangler, D. L., Simons, A. D., Monroe, S. M., & Thase, M. E. (1997). Comparison of cognitive models of depression: Relationships between cognitive constructs and cognitive diathesis-stress match. *Journal of Abnormal Psychology, 106,* 395–403.

Spanos, N. P. (1978). Witchcraft in histories of psychiatry: A critical analysis and an alternative conceptualization. *Psychological Bulletin, 85,* 417–439.

Spanos, N. P. (1994). Multiple identity enactments and multiple personality disorder: A sociocognitive perspective. *Psychological Bulletin, 116,* 143–165.

Spanos, N. P., Menary, E., Gabora, N. J., DuBreuil, S. C., & Dewihirst, B. (1991). Secondary identity enactments during hypnotic past-life regression: A sociocognitive perspective. *Journal of Personality and Social Psychology, 61,* 308–320.

Spanos, N. P., Weekes, J. R., & Bertrand, L. D. (1985). Multiple personality: A social psychological perspective. *Journal of Abnormal Psychology, 94,* 362–376.

Spark, R. F. (1991). *Male sexual health: A couple's guide.* Mount Vernon, NY: Consumer Reports Books.

Spearing, M., & Hendrix, M. L. (1988, October). Recent NIMH research sheds light on depression. *The Bell: National Mental Health Association,* pp. 4, 12.

Spector, I. P., & Carey, M. P. (1990). Incidence and prevalence of sexual dysfunctions: A critical review of the empirical literature. *Archives of Sexual Behavior, 19,* 389–408.

Speer, D. C. (1971). Rate of caller re-use of a telephone crisis service. *Crisis Intervention, 3,* 83–86.

Speer, D. C. (1972). *An evaluation of a telephone crisis service.* Paper presented at the meeting of the Midwestern Psychological Association, Cleveland, Ohio.

Spencer, S. L., & Zeiss, A. M. (1987). Sex roles and sexual dysfunction in college students. *Journal of Sex Research, 23,* 338–347.

Spencer, T. J., Biederman, J., Faraone, S., & Mick, E. (2001). Impact of tic disorder on ADHD outcome across the life cycle: Findings from a large group of adults with and without ADHD. *American Journal of Psychiatry, 158,* 611–617.

Spiess, W. F., Geer, J. H., & O'Donohue, W. T. (1984). Premature ejaculation: Investigation of factors in ejaculatory latency. *Journal of Abnormal Psychology, 93,* 242–245.

Spiro, A. III, Aldwin, C. M., Ward, K. D., & Mroczek, D. K. (1995). *Health Psychology, 14,* 563–569.

Spitzer, B. L., Henderson, K. A., & Zivian, M. T. (1999). Gender differences in population versus media body sizes: A comparison over four decades. *Sex Roles, 40,* 545–565.

Spitzer, R. L. (1975). On pseudoscience in science, logic in remission, and psychiatric diagnosis: A critique of Rosenhan's "On being sane in insane places." *Journal of Abnormal Psychology, 84,* 442–452.

Spitzer, R. L., Gibbon, M., Skodol, A. E., Williams, J. B., & First, M. B. (Eds.). (1994). *DSM-IV: Casebook.* Washington, DC: American Psychiatric Press.

Spitzer, R. L., Gibbon, M., & Williams, J. B. (1996). *Structured clinical interview of DSM-IV Axis I disorders.* New York: New York State Psychiatric Institute, Biometrics Research Department.

Spitzer, R. L., Skodol, A. E., Gibbon, M., & Williams, J. B. W. (1981). *DSM-III casebook.* Washington, DC: American Psychiatric Association.

Spivak, B., Trottern, S. F., Mark, M., Bleich, A., & Weizman, A. (1992). Acute transient stress-induced hallucinations in soldiers. *British Journal of Psychiatry, 160,* 412–414.

Srinivasan, T. N., Suresh, T. R., & Jayaram, V. (1998). Emergence of eating disorders in India: Study of eating distress syndrome and development of a screening questionnaire. *International Journal of Social Psychiatry, 44,* 189–198.

Srole, L., & Fischer, A. K. (1980). The midtown Manhattan longitudinal study vs. "the mental paradise lost" doctrine: A controversy joined. *Archives of General Psychiatry 37,* 209–221.

Srole, L., Langer, T. S., Michael, S. T., Opler, M. K., & Rennie, T. A. (1962). *Mental health in the metropolis: The midtown Manhattan study.* New York: McGraw-Hill.

Staal, M. A., & Hughes, T. G. (2002). Suicide prediction in the U.S. Air Force: Implications for practice. *Professional Psychology: Research and Practice, 33,* 190–196.

Staal, W. G., Pol, H. E. H., Schnack, H. G., van Haren, N. E. M., et al. (2001). Structural abnormalities in chronic schizophrenia at the extremes of the outcome spectrum. *American Journal of Psychiatry, 158,* 1140–1142.

Staats, A. W., & Heiby, E. M. (1985). Paradigmatic behaviorism's theory of depression: Unified, explanatory, and heuristic. In S. Reiss & R. R. Bootzin (Eds.), *Theoretical issues in behavioral therapy* (pp. 279–330). Orlando, FL: Academic Press.

Stack, S. (1987). Celebrities and suicide: A taxonomy and analysis, 1948–1983. *American Sociological Review, 52,* 401–412.

Stacy, A. W., Newcomb, M. D., & Bentler, P. M. (1991). Cognitive motivation and drug use: A 9-year longitudinal study. *Journal of Abnormal Psychology, 100,* 502–515.

Stacy, M., & Roeltgen, D. (1991). Infection of the central nervous system in the elderly. In S. Duckett (Ed.), *The pathology of the aging human nervous system* (pp. 374–392). Philadelphia: Lea & Febiger.

Stader, S. R., & Hokanson, J. E. (1998). Psychosocial antecedents of depressive symptoms: An evaluation using daily experiences methodology. *Journal of Abnormal Psychology, 107,* 17–26.

Stalberg, G., Ekerwald, H., & Hultman, C. M. (2004). At issue: Siblings of patients with schizophrenia: Sibling bond, coping patterns, and fear of possible schizophrenia heredity. *Schizophrenia Bulletin, 30,* 445–451.

Stanley, M., & Mann, J. J. (1983). Increased serotonin-z binding sites in frontal cortex of suicide victims. *Lancet, 2,* 214–216.

Stanley, M. A., Beck, J. G., Novy, D. M., Averill, P. M., et al. (2003). Cognitive-behavioral treatment of late-life generalized anxiety disorder. *Journal of Consulting and Clinical Psychology, 71,* 309–319.

Stanley, M. A., & Turner, S. M. (1995). Current status of pharmacological and behavioral treatment of obsessive-compulsive disorder. *Behavior Therapy, 26,* 163–186.

Stanton, A. L., Danoff-Burg, S., Cameron, C. L., Bishop, M., et al. (2000). Emotionally expressive coping predicts psychological and physical adjustment to breast cancer. *Journal of Consulting and Clinical Psychology, 68,* 875–882.

Stark, E. (1984). The unspeakable family secret. *Psychology Today, 18,* 38–46.

Stark, J. (2004, July 25). Twin sisters, a singular affliction. *Bellingham Herald,* p. A1.

Stark, M. J. (1992). Dropping out of substance abuse treatment: A clinically oriented review. *Clinical Psychology Review, 12,* 93–116.

Steadman, H. J., Monahan, J., Robbins, P. C., Appelbaum, P., et al. (1993). From dangerousness to risk assessment: Implications for appropriate research strategies. In S. Hodgins (Ed.), *Mental disorder and crime.* New York: Sage Publications.

Steege, J. F., Stout, A. L., & Carson, C. C. (1986). Patient satisfaction in Scott and small-Carrion penile implant recipients: A study of 52 patients. *Archives of Sexual Behavior, 15,* 171–177.

Steele, C. M., & Josephs, R. A. (1988). Drinking your troubles away II: An attention-allocation model of alcohol's effect on psychological stress. *Journal of Abnormal Psychology, 97,* 196–205.

Steele, C. M., & Josephs, R. A. (1990). Alcohol myopia: Its prized and dangerous effects. *American Psychologist, 45,* 921–933.

Steele, M. S., & McGarvey, S. T. (1997). Anger expression, age, and blood pressure in modernizing Samoan adults. *Psychosomatic Medicine, 59,* 632–637.

Steffen, J. J., Nathan, P. E., & Taylor, H. A. (1974). Tension-reducing effects of alcohol: Further evidence and methodological considerations. *Journal of Abnormal Psychology, 83,* 542–547.

Steffenburg, S., & Gillberg, C. (1989). The etiology of autism. In C. Gillberg (Ed.), *Diagnosis and treatment of autism* (pp. 63–82). New York: Plenum Press.

Stein, D. J. (2001). Comorbidity in generalized anxiety disorder: Impact and implications. *Journal of Clinical Psychiatry, 62,* 29–34.

Stein, M., Miller, A. H., & Trestman, R. L. (1991). Depression, the immune system, and health and illness. *Archives of General Psychiatry, 48,* 171–177.

Stein, M. B., Chartier, M. J., Hazen, A. L., & Kozak, M. V. (1998). A direct-interview family study of generalized social phobia. *American Journal of Psychiatry, 155,* 90–97.

Steinberg, J. S., Arshad, A., Kowalski, M., Kukar, A., et al. (2004). Increased incidence of life-threatening ventricular arrhythmias in implantable defibrillator patients after the World Trade Center attack. *Journal of the American College of Cardiology, 44,* 1261–1264.

Steinbrook, R. (2004). The AIDS epidemic in 2004. *New England Journal of Medicine, 351,* 115–117.

Stenberg, J-H., Jaaskelainen, I. P., & Royks, R. (1998). The effect of symptom self-management training on rehospitalization for chronic schizophrenia in Finland. *International Review of Psychiatry, 10,* 58–61.

Stepanski, E., Rybarczyk, B., Lopez, M., & Stevens, S. (2003). Assessment and treatment of sleep disorders in older adults: A review for rehabilitation psychologists. *Rehabilitation Psychology, 48,* 23–36.

Steptoe, A. (1991). Invited review: The links between stress and illness. *Journal of Psychosomatic Research, 35,* 633–644.

Stern, J., Murphy, M., & Bass, C. (1993). Personality disorders in patients with somatisation disorder: A controlled study. *British Journal of Psychiatry, 163,* 785–789.

Sternberg, K. J., Lamb, M. B., Greenbaum, C., & Cicchetti, D. (1992). Effects of domestic violence on children's behavior problems and depression. *Developmental Psychology, 29,* 44–52.

Stevens, J. (1987). Brief psychoses: Do they contribute to the good prognosis and equal prevalence of schizophrenia in developing countries? *British Journal of Psychiatry, 151,* 393–396.

Stewart, W. F., Lipton, R. B., Celentano, D. D., & Reed, M. L. (1992). Prevalence of migraine headache in the United States. *Journal of the American Medical Association, 267,* 64–69.

Stice, E., & Bearman, S. K. (2001). Body-image and eating disturbances prospectively predict increases in depressive symptoms in adolescent girls: A growth curve analysis. *Developmental Psychology, 37,* 597–607.

Stice, E., & Shaw, H. (2004). Eating disorder prevention programs: A meta-analytic review. *Psychological Bulletin, 130,* 206–227.

Stice, E., Shaw, H., & Nemeroff, C. (1998). Dual pathway model of bulimia nervosa: Longitudinal support for dietary restraint and affect-regulation mechanisms. *Journal of Social and Clinical Psychology, 17,* 129–149.

Stice, E., Telch, C. F., & Rizvi, S. L. (2000). Development of validation of the Eating Disorder Diagnostic Scale: A brief self-report measure of anorexia, bulimia, and binge-eating disorder. *Psychological Assessment, 12,* 123–131.

Stiles, J. (1998). The effects of early focal brain injury on lateralization of cognitive form. *Current Directions in Psychological Science, 7,* 21–26.

Stillion, M. J., & McDowell, E. E. (1996). *Suicide across the life span: Premature exits* (2nd ed.). Washington, DC: Taylor & Francis.

Stillion, M. J., McDowell, E. E., & May, J. H. (1989). *Suicide across the life span: Premature exits.* Washington, DC: Hemisphere.

Stock, W. E. (1991). Feminist explanations: Male power, hostility, and sexual coercion. In E. Grauerholz & M. A. Koralewski (Eds.), *Sexual coercion: A sourcebook on its nature, causes, and prevention* (pp. 61–73). Lexington, MA: Lexington Books.

Stocks, J. T. (1998). Recovered-memory therapy: A dubious practice technique. *Social Work, 43,* 423–436.

Stone, A. A., Smyth, J. M., Kaell, A., & Hurewitz, A. (2000). Structured writing about stressful events: Exploring potential psychological mediators of positive health effects. *Health Psychology, 19,* 619–624.

Stone, M. H. (2001). Schizoid and schizotypal personality disorders. In G. O. Gabbard (Ed.), *Treatment of psychiatric disorders* (pp. 2237–2250). Washington, DC: American Psychiatric Press.

Stone, W. L., & Lemanek, K. L. (1990). Parental report of social behaviors in autistic preschoolers. *Journal of Autism and Developmental Disorders, 20,* 513–522.

Stones, A., & Perry, D. (1997). Survey questionnaire data on panic attacks gathered using the World Wide Web. *Depression and Anxiety, 6,* 86–87.

Stoolmiller, M., Eddy, J. M., & Reid, J. B. (2000). Detecting and describing preventative intervention effects in a universal school-based randomizing trial: Targeting delinquent and violent behavior. *Journal of Consulting and Clinical Psychology, 68,* 296–306.

Story, M., Neumark-Sztainer, D., Sherwood, N., Stang, J., & Murray, D. (1998). Dieting status and its relationship to eating and physical activity behaviors in a representative sample of U. S. adolescents. *Journal of the American Dietetic Association, 98,* 1127–1135.

Stout, C., Kotses, H., & Creer, T. L. (1997). Improving perception of air flow obstruction in asthma patients. *Psychosomatic Medicine, 59,* 201–206.

Streissguth, A. P. (1994). A long-term perspective of FAS. *Alcohol Health and Research World, 18,* 74–81.

Streissguth, A. P., Landesman-Dwyer, S., Martin, J. C., & Smith, D. W. (1980). Teratogenic effects of alcohol in humans and laboratory animals. *Science, 209,* 353–361.

Strickland, B. R. (1992). Women and depression. *Current Directions in Psychological Science, 1*(4), 132–135.

Striegel-Moore, R. H., Dohm, F. A., Kraemer, H. C., Taylor, C. B., et al. (2003). Eating disorders in white and black women. *American Journal of Psychiatry, 160,* 1326–1331.

Stripling, S. (1986, August 3). Crossing over. *Seattle Post Intelligencer,* pp. K1–K2.

Strobeck, C. (2002, August). What it feels like to have an obsessive compulsive disorder. *Esquire, 138,* 76–77.

Strober, M., Freeman, R., Diamond, C. L. J., & Kaye, W. (2000). Controlled family study of anorexia nervosa and bulimia nervosa: Evidence of shared liability and transmission of partial syndromes. *American Journal of Psychiatry, 157,* 393–401.

Stroebe, M., & Stroebe, W. (1991). Does "grief work" work? *Journal of Consulting and Clinical Psychology, 59,* 479–482.

Strohman, R. (2001, April). Beyond genetic determinism. *California Monthly, 111*(5), 24–27.

Strom, L., Pettersson, R., & Andersson, G. (2000). A controlled trial of self-help treatment of recurrent headache conducted via the Internet. *Journal of Consulting and Clinical Psychology, 68,* 722–727.

Stromberg, C., Lindberg, D., & Schneider, J. (1995, January). A legal update on forensic psychology. *The Psychologists' Legal Update, No. 6.* Washington, DC: National Register of Health Service Providers in Psychology.

Strong, B., & DeVault, C. (1994). *Human sexuality.* Mountain View, CA: Mayfield.

Strong, J. E., & Farrell, A. D. (2003). Evaluation of the computerized assessment system for psychotherapy evaluation and research (CASPER) interview with a psychiatric inpatient population. *Journal of Clinical Psychology, 59,* 967–984.

Strong, S. M., Williamson, D. A., Netemeyer, R. G., & Geer, J. H. (2000). Eating disorder symptoms and concerns about body differ as a function of gender and sexual orientation. *Journal of Social and Clinical Psychology, 19,* 240–255.

Strous, R. D., Alvir, J. M., Robinson, D., Gal, G., et al. (2004). Premorbid functioning in schizophrenia, treatment response, and medication side effects. *Schizophrenia Bulletin, 30,* 265–272.

Strupp, H. H., & Hadley, S. W. (1977). *Psychotherapy for better or worse: An analysis of the problem of negative effects.* New York: Jason Aronson.

Stuart, F. M., Hammond, D. C., & Pett, M. A. (1987). Inhibited sexual desire in women. *Archives of Sexual Behavior, 16,* 91–106.

Stuss, D. T., Gow, C. A., & Hetherington, C. R. (1992). "No longer Gage": Frontal lobe dysfunction and emotional changes. *Journal of Consulting and Clinical Psychology, 60,* 349–359.

Substance Abuse and Mental Health Services Administration. (2004). Overview of findings from the 2003 National Survey on Drug Use and Health (NSDUH Series H–24, DHHS Publication No. SMA 04–3963). Rockville, MD: Author.

Suddath, R. L., Christison, G. W., Torrey, E. F., & Weinberger, D. R. (1990). Cerebral anatomical abnormalities in monozygotic twins discordant for schizophrenia. *New England Journal of Medicine, 322,* 789–794.

Sue, D. (1979). Erotic fantasies of college students during coitus. *Journal of Sex Research, 15,* 299–305.

Sue, D. W. (1995). Toward a theory of multicultural counseling and psychotherapy. In J. A. Banks & C. A. Banks, *Handbook of research on multicultural education.* New York: Macmillan.

Sue, D. W. (2001). Multidimensional facets of cultural competence. *The Counseling Psychologist, 29,* 790–821.

Sue, D. W., Carter, R. T., Casas, J. M., Fouad, N. A., et al. (1998). *Multicultural counseling competencies: Individual and organizational development.* Thousand Oaks, CA: Sage.

Sue, D. W., Ivey, A. E., & Pedersen, P. B. (1996). *A theory of multicultural counseling and psychotherapy.* Pacific Grove, CA: Brooks Cole.

Sue, D. W., & Sue, D. (1999). *Counseling the culturally different Theory and practice* (3rd ed.). New York: Wiley.

Sue, D. W., & Sue, D. (2003). *Counseling the culturally diverse: Theory and practice.* Hoboken, NJ: Wiley.

Sue, S., & Abe, J. (1988). *Predictors of academic achievement among Asian American and white students.* New York: College Board.

Sue, S., & Morishima, J. K. (1982). *The mental health of Asian Americans.* San Francisco: Jossey-Bass.

Sue, S., & Nakamura, C. Y. (1984). An integrative model of physiological and social/psychological factors in alcohol consumption among Chinese and Japanese Americans. *Journal of Drug Issues, 14,* 349–364.

Sugar, M. (1995). A clinical approach to childhood gender identity disorder. *American Journal of Psychotherapy, 49,* 260–281.

Sugiura, T., Sakamoto, S., Tanaka, E., Tomada, A., & Kitamura, T. (2001). Labeling effects of Seishin-Bunretsu-Byou, the Japanese translation for schizophrenia: An argument for relabeling. *International Journal of Social Psychiatry, 47,* 43–51.

Suicide belt. (1986, February 24). *Time, 116,* 56.

Suicide rate climbing for Black teens. (1998, March 20). *San Francisco Chronicle,* p. A17.

Sullivan, P. F., Bulik, C. M., Fear, J. L., & Pickering, A. (1998). Outcome of anorexia nervosa. *American Journal of Psychiatry, 155,* 939–946.

Sulser, F. (1979). Pharmacology: New cellular mechanisms of antidepressant drugs. In S. Fielding & R. C. Effland (Eds.), *New frontiers in psychotropic drug research.* Mount Kisco, NY: Futura.

Sundberg, N. D., Taplin, J. R., & Tyler, L. E. (1983). *Introduction to clinical psychology.* Englewood Cliffs, NJ: Prentice-Hall.

Sundel, M., & Sundel, S. S. (1998). Psychopharmacological treatment of panic disorder. *Research of Social Work Practice, 8,* 426–451.

Sundstrom, E. (2004). First person account: The clogs. *Schizophrenia Bulletin, 30,* 191–192.

Suokas, J., & Lonnqvist, J. (1995). Suicide attempts in which alcohol is involved: A special group in general hospital emergency rooms. *Acta Psychiatrica Scandinavia, 91,* 36–40.

Susman, E. (2002). Many HIV patients carry mutated drug-resistant strains. *Lancet, 359,* 49–50.

Sussman, S., Dent, C. W., McAdams, L. A., Stacy, A. W., et al. (1994). Group self-identification and adolescent cigarette smoking: A one-year prospective study. *Journal of Abnormal Psychology, 103,* 576–580.

Sutherland, S. M. (2001). Avoidant personality disorder. In G. O. Gabbard (Ed.), *Treatment of psychiatric disorders* (pp. 2327–2340). Washington, DC: American Psychiatric Press.

Suzuki, K., Takei, N., Kawai, M., Minabe, Y., & Mori, N. (2003). Is Taijin Kyofusho a culture-bound syndrome? *American Journal of Psychiatry, 160,* 1358.

Swann, W. B., Jr., Wenzlaff, R. M., Krull, D. S., & Pelham, B. W. (1992). Allure of negative feedback: Self-verification strivings among depressed persons. *Journal of Abnormal Psychology, 101*(2), 193–306.

Swanson, J., Holzer, C., Ganju, V., & Jono, R. (1990). Violence and psychiatric disorder in the community: Evidence from the Epidemiological Catchment Area Surveys. *Hospital Community Psychiatry, 41,* 761–770.

Swanson, J. W. (1994). Mental disorder, substance abuse, and community violence: An epidemiological approach. In J. Monahan & H. J. Steadman (Eds.), *Violence and mental disorder: Developments in risk assessment* (pp. 101–136). Chicago: University of Chicago Press.

Swartz, M., Landerman, R., George, L. K., Blazer, D. G., & Escobar, J. (1991). Somatization disorder. In L. N. Robins and D. A. Regier (Eds.). *Psychiatric disorders in America* (pp. 220–255). New York: Free Press.

Swedo, S. E., Rapoport, J. L., Leonard, H., Lenane, M., & Cheslow, D. (1989). Obsessive-compulsive disorder in children and adolescents. *Archives of General Psychiatry, 46,* 335–341.

Sweet, J. J. (1983). Confounding effects of depression on neuropsychological testing: Five illustrative cases. *Clinical Neuropsychology, 5,* 103–108.

Swindler, J. (2004, September 10). Latest death at NYU tests new mental health program. *Columbia Spectator,* p. A1.

Sylvain, C., Ladouceur, R., & Boisvert, J.-M. (1997). Cognitive and behavioral treatment of pathological gambling: A controlled study. *Journal of Consulting and Clinical Psychology, 65,* 727–732.

Syvalahti, E. K. G. (1994). I. The theory of schizophrenia: Biological factors in schizophrenia. *British Journal of Psychiatry, 164,* 9–14.

Szapocznik, J., Feaster, D. J., Mitrani, V. B., Prado, G., et al. (2004). Structural ecosystems therapy for HIV-seropositive African American women: Effects on psychological distress, family hassles, and family support. *Journal of Consulting and Clinical Psychology, 72,* 288–303.

Szasz, T. (1986). The case against suicide prevention. *American Psychologist, 41,* 806–812.

Szasz, T. S. (1963). *Law, liberty, and psychiatry.* New York: Macmillan.

Szasz, T. S. (1987). Justifying coercion through theology and therapy. In J. K. Zeig (Ed.), *The evolution of psychotherapy.* New York: Brunner/Mazel.

Szymanski, S., Kane, J. M., & Lieberman, J. A. (1991). A selective review of biological markers in schizophrenia. *Schizophrenia Bulletin, 17,* 99–111.

Tabakoff, B., Whelan, J. P., & Hoffman, P. L. (1990). Two biological markers of alcoholism. In C. R. Cloninger & H. Begleiter (Eds.), *Genetics and biology of alcoholism* (pp. 195–204). Cold Spring Harbor, NY: Cold Spring Harbor Laboratory Press.

Tager-Flusberg, H., & Sullivan, K. (1994). Predicting and explaining behavior: A comparison of autistic, mentally retarded, and normal children. *Journal of Child Psychology and Psychiatry, 35,* 1059–1075.

Takamura, J. C. (1998). An aging agenda for the twenty-first century: The opportunities and challenges of population longevity. *Professional Psychology: Research and Practice, 29,* 411–412.

Takeuchi, D. T., & Uehara, E. S. (1996). Ethnic minority mental health services: Current research and future conceptual directions. In B. L. Levin & J. Petrila (Eds.), *Mental health services: A public health perspective.* New York: Oxford University Press.

Takeuchi, J. (2000). Treatment of a biracial child with schizophreniform disorder: Cultural formulation. *Cultural Diversity and Ethnic Minority Psychology, 6,* 93–101.

Tamminga, C. A., & Frost, D. O. (2001). Changing concepts in the neurochemistry of schizophrenia. *American Journal of Psychiatry, 158,* 1365–1366.

Tarasoff vs. The Board of Regents of the University of California, 17 Cal. 3d 435, 551 P.2d, 334, 131 Cal. Rptr. 14, 83 Ad. L. 3d 1166 (1976).

Tardiff, K. (1984). Characteristics of assaultive patients in private psychiatric hospitals. *American Journal of Psychiatry, 141,* 1232–1235.

Tardiff, K., & Koenigsberg, H. W. (1985). Assaultive behavior among psychiatric outpatients. *American Journal of Psychiatry, 142,* 960–963.

Tardiff, K., & Sweillam, A. (1982). Assaultive behavior among chronic inpatients. *American Journal of Psychiatry, 139,* 212–215.

Tarkan, C. L. (1998). Diary of an eating disorder. *Joe Weider's Shape, 18,* 116–119.

Tarter, R. E., & Vanyukov, M. (1994). Alcoholism: A developmental disorder. *Journal of Consulting and Clinical Psychology, 62,* 1096–1107.

Task Force on Promotion and Dissemination of Psychological Procedures. (1995). Training in and dissemination of empirically-validated psychological treatments: Report and recommendations. *Clinical Psychologist, 48,* 3–23.

Tassin, J. P., Trovero, F., Blanc, G., Herve, D., & Glowinski, J. (1994). Interactions between noradrenaline and dopamine neurotransmission in the rat prefrontal cortex and their consequences on dopaminergic subcortical function. In M. Briley & M. Marien (Eds.), *Noradrenergic mechanisms in Parkinson's disease* (pp. 107–125). Ann Arbor, MI: CRC Press.

Tatman, S. M., Peters, D. B., Greene, A. L., & Bongar, B. (1997). Graduate student attitudes toward prescription privilege training. *Professional Psychology: Research and Practice, 28,* 515–517.

Tavris, C. (1991). The mismeasure of woman: Paradoxes and perspectives in the study of gender. In J. D. Goodchilds (Ed.), *Psychological perspectives on human diversity in America* (pp. 91–136). Washington, DC: American Psychological Association.

Taylor, E. H. (1990). The assessment of social intelligence. *Psychotherapy, 27,* 445–457.

Taylor, S. (1995). Anxiety sensitivity: Theoretical perspectives and recent findings. *Behaviour Research and Therapy, 33,* 243–258.

Taylor, S., Woody, S., Koch, W. J., McLean, P. D., & Anderson, K. W. (1996). Suffocation fear alarms and efficacy of cognitive behavioral therapy for panic disorder. *Behavior Therapy, 27,* 115–126.

Taylor, S. E., Kemeny, M. E., Bower, J. E., Gruenewald, T. L., & Reed, G. M. (2000). Psychological resources, positive illusions, and health. *American Psychologist, 55,* 99–109.

Telch, C. F., & Stice, E. (1998). Psychiatric comorbidity in women with binge eating disorder: Prevalence rates from a non-treatment-seeking example. *Journal of Consulting and Clinical Psychology, 66,* 768–776.

Telch, M. J., Lucas, J. A., & Nelson, P. (1989). Nonclinical panic in college students: An investigation of prevalence and symptomatology. *Journal of Abnormal Psychology, 98,* 300–306.

Tellegen, A., Lykken, D. T., Bouchard, T. J., Jr., Wilcox, K. J., et al. (1988). Personality similarity in twins reared apart and together. *Journal of Personality and Social Psychology, 54,* 1031–1039.

Temoshok, L., & Dreher, H. (1992). *The type C connection: The mind-body link to cancer and your health.* New York: Penguin.

Teri, L., & Wagner, A. (1992). Alzheimer's disease and depression. *Journal of Consulting and Clinical Psychology, 60*(3), 379–391.

Terman, L. M., & Merrill, M. A. (1960). *Stanford-Binet intelligence scale.* Boston: Houghton Mifflin.

Terr, L. C. (1991). Childhood traumas: An outline and overview. *American Journal of Psychiatry, 148,* 10–20.

Thacker, A. J. (1994). Formal communication disorder: Sign language in deaf people with schizophrenia. *British Journal of Psychiatry, 165,* 818–823.

Thapar, A., Gottesman, I. I., Owen, M. J., O'Donovan, M. C., & McGuffin, P. (1994). The genetics of mental retardation. *British Journal of Psychiatry, 164,* 747–758.

Tharp, B. R. (2003). Contributions of neurology. In S. Ozonoff, S. J. Rogers, & R. L. Hendren (Eds.), *Autism spectrum disorders: A research review for practitioners* (pp. 111–132). Arlington, VA: American Psychiatric.

Tharp, R. G. (1991). Cultural diversity and treatment of children. *Journal of Consulting and Clinical Psychology, 59,* 799–812.

Thase, M. E. (2001). Depression-focused psychotherapies. In G. O. Gabbard (Ed.), *Treatment of psychiatric disorders* (pp. 1181–1226). Washington, DC: American Psychiatric Press.

Theorell, T., Blomkvist, V., Jonsson, H., Schulman, S., et al. (1995). Social support and the development of immune function in human immunodeficiency virus infection. *Psychosomatic Medicine, 57,* 32–36.

Thigpen, C. H., & Cleckley, H. M. (1984). On the incidence of multiple personality disorder: A brief communication. *International Journal of Clinical and Experimental Hypnosis, 32,* 63–66.

Thom, A., Sartory, G., & Johren, P. (2000). Comparison between one-session psychological treatment and benzodiazepine in dental phobia. *Journal of Consulting and Clinical Psychology, 68,* 378–387.

Thomas, A., Chess, S., & Birch, H. G. (1968). *Temperament and behavior disorders in children.* New York: New York University Press.

Thomas, P. (1995). Thought disorder or communication disorder: Linguistic science provides a new approach. *British Journal of Psychiatry, 166,* 287–290.

Thompson, P. M., Vidal, C., Giedd, J. N., Gochman, P., et al. (2001). Mapping adolescent brain change reveals dynamic wave of accelerated gray matter loss in very early-onset schizophrenia. *Proceedings of the National Academy of Science, 98,* 11650–11655.

Thorndike, R. L., Hagen, E. P., & Sattler, J. M. (1986). *The Stanford-Binet intelligence scale: Guide for administration and scoring* (3rd ed.). Chicago: Riverside.

Thorpe, S.J., & Salkovskis, P. M. (1998). Studies on the role of disgust in the acquisition and maintenance of specific phobias. *Behaviour Research and Therapy, 36,* 877–893.

Tienari, P., Wynne, L. C., Moring, J., Lahti, I., et al. (1994). The Finnish adoptive family study of schizophrenia: Implications for family research. *British Journal of Psychiatry, 164,* 20–26.

Tierney, J. (1988, July 3). Research finds lower-level workers bear brunt of workplace stress. *Seattle Post Intelligencer,* pp. K1–K3.

Tiffany, S. T. (1990). A cognitive model of drug urges and drug-use behavior: Role of automatic and nonautomatic processes. *Psychological Review, 97,* 147–168.

Tiggemann, M., & Kuring, J. K. (2004). The role of body objectification in disordered eating and depressed mood. *British Journal of Clinical Psychology, 43,* 299–311.

Tikhonova, I. V., Gnezditskii, V. V., Stakhovskaya, L. V., & Skvortsova, V. I. (2003). Neurophysiological characterization of transitory global amnesia syndrome. *Neuroscience and Behavioral Physiology, 33,* 171–175.

Titone, D., Levy, D. L., & Holzman, P. S. (2000). Contextual insensitivity in schizophrenic language processing: Evidence from lexical ambiguity. *Journal of Abnormal Psychology, 109,* 761–767.

Tjosvold, D., & Tjosvold, M. M. (1983). Social psychological analysis of residences for mentally retarded persons. *American Journal of Mental Deficiency, 88,* 28–40.

Tobin, J. J., & Friedman, J. (1983). Spirits, shamans, and nightmare death: Survivor stress in a Hmong refugee. *American Journal of Orthopsychiatry, 53,* 439–448.

Tolan, P. H., Gorman-Smith, D., Huesmann, L. R., & Zelli, A. (1997). Assessment of family relationship characteristics: A measure to explain risk for antisocial behavior and depression among urban youth. *Psychological Assessment, 9,* 212–223.

Tolan, P. H., & Thomas, P. (1995). The implications of age of onset for delinquency risk II: Longitudinal data. *Journal of Abnormal Child Psychology, 23,* 157–180.

Tolin, D. F., Lohr, J. M., Sawchuk, C. N., & Lee, T. C. (1997). Disgust and disgust sensitivity in blood-injection-injury and spider phobia. *Behaviour Research and Therapy, 35,* 949–953.

Tollefson, G. D., Beasley, C. M., Jr., Tran, P. V., & Street, J. S. (1997). Olonzapine versus haloperidol in the treatment of schizophrenia and schizoaffective disorders: Results of an international collaborative trial. *American Journal of Psychiatry, 154,* 457–465.

Tollefson, G. D., Rampey, A. H., Potvin, J. H., Jenike, M. A., et al. (1994). A multicenter investigation of fixed-dose fluoxetine in the treatment of obsessive-compulsive disorder. *Archives of General Psychiatry, 51,* 559–567.

Tolman, A. O., & Mullendore, K. B. (2003). Risk evaluations for the courts: Is service quality a function of specialization? *Professional Psychology: Research and Practice, 34,* 225–232.

Tolton, J. C. (2004). First person account: How insight poetry helped me to overcome my illness. *Schizophrenia Bulletin, 30,* 469–470.

Torgalsboen, A-K., & Rund, B. R. (1998). "Full recovery" from schizophrenia in the long term: A ten-year follow-up of eight former schizophrenic patients. *Psychiatry, 61,* 20–34.

Toro, P. A. & Wall, D. D. (1991). Research on homeless persons: Diagnostic comparisons and practice implications. *Professional psychology: Research and practice, 22,* 479–488.

Torpy, J. M. (2002). Heart disease and women. *Journal of the American Medical Association, 288,* 3230–3232.

Toth, S. L., Manly, J. T., & Cicchetti, D. (1992). Child maltreatment and vulnerability to depression. *Developmental Psychopathology, 4,* 97–112.

Tourette Syndrome Association. (2001). *Tourette syndrome fact sheet.* Bayside, NY: Tourette Syndrome Association.

Townsley, A. (2004). Night terrors: What you need to know. *Pediatrics for Parents, 21,* 7.

Tremeau, F., Malaspina, D., Duval, F., Correa, H., et al. (2005). Facial expressiveness in patients with schizophrenia compared to depressed patients and non-patient comparison subjects. *American Journal of Psychiatry, 162,* 92–101.

Trierweiler, S. J., Neighbors, H. W., Munday, C., Thompson, E. E., et al. (2000). Clinician attributions associated with the diagnosis of schizophrenia in African American and non–African American patients. *Journal of Consulting and Clinical Psychology, 68,* 171–175.

Tripp, M. M., & Petrie, T. A. (2001). Sexual abuse and eating disorders: A test of a conceptual model. *Sex Roles, 44,* 17–32.

Tross, S., & Hirsch, D. A. (1988). Psychological distress and neuropsychological complications of HIV infection and AIDS. *American Psychologist, 43*, 929–934.

Troxel, W. M., Matthews, K. A., Bromberger, J. T., & Tyrrell, K. S. (2003). Chronic stress burden, discrimination, and subclinical carotid artery disease in African American and Caucasian women. *Health Psychology, 22*, 300–309.

Trull, T. J. (1995). Borderline personality disorder features in nonclinical young adults: 1. Identification and validation. *Psychological Assessment, 7*, 33–41.

Trull, T. J., Useda, J. D., Conforti, K., & Doan, B.-T. (1997). Borderline personality disorder features in nonclinical young adults, Part 2: Two-year outcome. *Journal of Abnormal Psychology, 106*, 307–314.

Tsai, G., & Gray, J. (2000). The Eating Disorders Inventory among Asian American college women. *Journal of Social Psychology, 140*, 527–529.

Tsoi, W. F. (1993). Male and female transsexuals: A comparison. *Singapore Medical Journal, 33*, 182–185.

Tucker, E. (2002, August 28). 2 men missing since 9/11 found alive in hospitals. *Houston Chronicle*, p. 15.

Tuller, D. (2004, June 21). Gentlemen, start your engines? *The New York Times*, pp. F1, F11.

Tuomisto, M. T. (1997). Intra-arterial blood pressure and heart rate reactivity to behavioral stress in normotensive, borderline, and mild hypertensive men. *Health Psychology, 16*, 554–565.

Turkheimer, E., & Parry, C. D. H. (1992). Why the gap? *American Psychologist, 47*, 646–655.

Turner, W. J. (1995). Homosexuality, Type 1: An Xq28 phenomenon. *Archives of Sexual Behavior, 24*, 109–134.

Tutkun, H., Sar, V., Yargic, L. I., & Ozpulat, T. (1998). Frequency of dissociative disorders among psychiatric inpatients in a Turkish university clinic. *American Journal of Psychiatry, 155*, 800–805.

Tylka, T. L., & Subich, L. M. (2004). Examining a multidimensional model of eating disorder symptomatology among college women. *Journal of Counseling Psychology, 51*, 314–328.

Tyrer, P., Lee, I., & Alexander, J. (1980). Awareness of cardiac function in anxious, phobic, and hypochondriacal patients. *Psychological Medicine, 10*, 171–174.

U.S. Advisory Board on Child Abuse and Neglect. (1995). *A national shame: Fatal child abuse and neglect in the United States* (5th report). Washington, DC: Government Printing Office.

U.S. Bureau of the Census. (1988). *Statistical abstract of the United States* (108th ed.). Washington, DC: U.S. Government Printing Office.

U.S. Bureau of the Census. (1992). *We, the American ...* Washington, DC: U.S. Government Printing Office.

U.S. Bureau of the Census. (1995). *Population profile of the United States*. Washington, DC: U.S. Government Printing Office.

U.S. Bureau of the Census. (2001). *Population profile of the United States*. Washington, DC: U.S. Government Printing Office.

U.S. Department of Health and Human Services. (1991). *Depression: What you need to know*. Rockville, MD: NIMH 60-FL-1485-0.

U.S. Department of Health and Human Services. (1995a). Down syndrome prevalence at birth–United States, 1983–1990. *Morbidity and Mortality Weekly Report, 43*, 617–623.

U.S. Department of Health and Human Services. (1995b). Update: Trends in fetal alcohol syndrome. *Morbidity and Mortality Weekly Report, 44*, 249–251.

U.S. Senate Committee on the Judiciary. (1991). Violence against women: The increase of rape in America 1990. *Response to the Victimization of Women and Children, 14* (79, No. 2), 20–23.

U.S. Surgeon General. (1999). *Mental health: A report of the Surgeon General*. Washington, DC: U.S. Government Printing Office.

Uchino, B. N., & Garvey, T. S. (1997). The availability of social support reduces cardiovascular reactivity to acute psychological stress. *Journal of Behavioral Medicine, 20*, 15–27.

Ullmann, L. P., & Krasner, L. (1965). Introduction. In L. P. Ullmann & L. Krasner (Eds.), *Case studies in behavior modification*. New York: Holt, Rinehart & Winston.

Ullmann, L. P., & Krasner, L. (1975). *A psychological approach to abnormal behavior* (2nd ed.). Englewood Cliffs, NJ: Prentice-Hall.

United States Public Health Service. (1999). *The Surgeon General's call to action to prevent suicide*. Washington, DC: U.S. Public Health Services.

Vaillant, G. E. (1975). Sociopathy as a human process: A viewpoint. *Archives of General Psychiatry, 32*, 178–183.

Vaillant, G. E. (1994). Ego mechanisms of defense and personality psychopathology. *Journal of Abnormal Psychology, 103*, 44–50.

Vaillant, G. E., & Perry, J. C. (1985). Personality disorders. In H. I. Kaplan & B. J. Sadock (Eds.), *Comprehensive textbook of psychiatry* (4th ed., pp. 958–986). Baltimore: Williams & Wilkins.

Valenstein, M., Blow, F. C., Copeland, L. A., McCarthy, J. F., et al. (2004). Poor antipsychotic adherence among patients with schizophrenia: Medication and patient factors. *Schizophrenia Bulletin, 30*, 255–264.

Valentiner, D. P., Foa, E. B., Riggs, D. S., & Gershuny, B. S. (1996). Coping strategies and posttraumatic stress disorder in female victims of sexual and nonsexual assault. *Journal of Abnormal Psychology, 105*, 455–458.

Valera, E. M., & Berenbaum, H. (2003). Brain injury in battered women. *Journal of Consulting and Clinical Psychology, 71*, 797–804.

Van den Bergh, O., Stegen, K., & Van de Woestijne, K. P. (1997). Learning to have psychosomatic complaints: Conditioning of respiratory behavior and somatic complaints in psychosomatic patients. *Psychosomatic Medicine, 59*, 13–23.

Van Der Molen, G. M., van den Hout, M. A., Vroemen, J., Lousberg, H., & Griez, E. (1986). Cognitive determinants of lactate-induced anxiety. *Behaviour Research and Therapy, 24*, 677–680.

Van Evra, J. P. (1983). *Psychological disorders of children and adolescents*. Boston: Little, Brown.

van Heerden, B., Stein, D. J., Carey, P., Seedat, S., & Warwick, J. (2004). SPECT imaging of body dysmorphic disorder. *Neurosciences, 16*, 357–359.

Van Horn, J. D., & McManus, I. C. (1992). Ventricular enlargement in schizophrenia. *British Journal of Psychiatry, 160*, 687–697.

Van Ommeren, M., de Jong, J. T. V. M., & Komproe, B. S. (2001). Psychiatric disorders among tortured Bhutanese refugees in Nepal. *Archives of General Psychiatry, 58*, 475–483.

Van Oppen, P., De Haan, E., Van Balkom, A. J. L. M., Spinhoven, P., et al. (1995). Cognitive therapy and exposure in vivo in the treatment of obsessive disorder. *Behaviour Research and Therapy, 33*, 378–390.

Van Pragg, H. M. (1983). CSF 5-H1AA and suicide in non-depressed schizophrenics, *Lancet, 2*, 977–978.

Vanderlinden, J., Norre, J., & Vandereycken, W. (1992). *A practical guide to the treatment of bulimia nervosa*. New York: Brunner/Mazel.

Vaughan, S., & Fowler, D. (2004). The distress experienced by voice hearers is associated with the perceived relationship between the voice hearer and the voice. *British Journal of Clinical Psychology, 43*, 143–147.

Vaughn, C., & Leff, J. (1981). Patterns of emotional response in relatives of schizophrenic patients. *Schizophrenia Bulletin, 7*, 43–45.

Vazquez, J. M. (1997). Puerto Ricans in the counseling process: The dynamics of ethnicity and its societal context. In C. C. Lee (Ed.), *Multicultural issues in counseling*. Alexandria, VA: American Counseling Association.

Veale, D., Boocock, A., Gournay, K., & Dryden, W. (1996). Body dysmorphic disorder: A survey of fifty cases. *British Journal of Psychiatry, 169*, 196–201.

Vedantam, S. (2001). Drug found to curb kid's debilitating social anxiety. *Washington Post*, p. A1.

Vega, W., & Rumbaut, R.G. (1991). Ethnic minorities and mental health. *Annual Review of Sociology, 17*, 351–383.

Vernberg, E. M., LaGreca, A. M., Silverman, W. K., & Prinstein, M. J. (1996). Prediction of posttraumatic stress symptoms in children after Hurricane Andrew. *Journal of Abnormal Psychology, 105*, 237–248.

Vincent, M. A., & McCabe, M. P. (2000). Gender differences among adolescents in family, and peer influences on body dissatisfaction, weight loss, and binge eating disorders. *Journal of Youth and Adolescence, 29*, 205–221.

Visintainer, M. A., Volpicelli, J. R., & Seligman, M. E. P. (1982). Tumor rejection in rats after inescapable or escapable shock. *Science, 216*, 437–439.

Vita, A., Bressi, S., Perani, D., Invernizzi, G., et al. (1995). High-resolution SPECT study of regional cerebral blood flow in drug-free and drug-naive schizophrenic patients. *American Journal of Psychiatry, 152*, 876–882.

Vita, A., Dieci, M., Giobbio, G. M., Azzone, P., et al. (1991). CT scan abnormalities and outcome in chronic schizophrenia. *American Journal of Psychiatry, 148*, 1577–1579.

Vogel, G., Vogel, F., McAbee, R., & Thurmond, A. (1980). Improvement of depression by REM sleep deprivation. *Archives of General Psychiatry, 37*, 247–253.

Vogler, R. E., & Bartz, W. R. (1983). *The better way to drink*. New York: Simon & Schuster.

Vojdani, A., & Thrasher, J. D. (2004). Cellular and humoral immune abnormalities in Gulf War veterans. *Environmental Health Perspectives, 112*, 840–846.

Volavka, J. (1995). *Neurobiology of violence*. Washington, DC: American Psychiatric Press.

Volden, J., & Lord, C. (1991). Neologisms and idiosyncratic language in autistic speakers. *Journal of Autism and Developmental Disorders, 21*, 109–130.

Volkmar, F. R., Cicchetti, D. V., Dykens, E., Sparrow, S. S., et al. (1988). An evaluation of the Autism Behavior checklist. *Journal of Autism and Developmental Disorders, 18*, 81–97.

Volkmar, F. R., Klin, A., Schultz, R. T., Rubin, E., & Bronen, R. (2000). Asperger's disorder. *American Journal of Psychiatry, 157*, 262–267.

Vontress, C. E., & Epps, L. R. (1997). Historical hostility in the African American client: Implications for counseling. *Journal of Multicultural Counseling and Development, 25*, 170–185.

Vossekuil, G., Reddy, M., Fein, R., Borum, R., & Modzeleski, W. (2000). *U.S. Secret Service Schools Initiative: An interim report on the prevention of targeted violence in schools*. Washington, DC: U.S. Secret Service, National Threat Assessment Center.

Wachtel, P. L. (1982). Vicious circles: The self and the rhetoric of emerging and unfolding. *Contemporary Psychoanalysis, 18*, 280–282.

Wade, T. D., Bulik, C. M., Sullivan, P. F., Neale, M. C., & Kendler, K. S. (2000). The relationship between risk factors for binge eating and bulimia nervosa: A population-based female twin study. *Health Psychology, 19*, 115–123.

Waehler, C. A., Kalodner, C. R., Wampold, B. E., & Lichtenberg, J. W. (2000). Empirically supported treatments (ESTs) in perspective: Implications for counseling psychology. *Counseling Psychologist, 28*, 657–671.

Wagner, A. K., Zhang, F., Soumerai, S. B., Walker, A. M., et al. (2004). Benzodiazepine use and hip fracture in the elderly: Who is at greatest risk? *Archives of Internal Medicine, 164*, 1567.

Wahass, S., & Kent, G. (1997). A cross-cultural study of the attitudes of mental health professionals toward auditory hallucinations. *International Journal of Social Psychiatry, 43*, 184–192.

Wahlberg, K.-E., Wynne, L. C., Oja, H., & Keskitalo, P. (1997). Gene-environment interaction in vulnerability to schizophrenia: Findings from the Finnish adoptive family study of schizophrenia. *American Journal of Psychiatry, 154*, 355–362.

Wakefield, J. (1988). Female primary orgasmic dysfunctions: Masters and Johnson versus DSM-III-R on diagnosis and incidence. *Journal of Sex Research, 24*, 363–377.

Wakefield, J. C. (1992). The concept of mental disorder. *American Psychologist, 47*, 373–388.

Waldrop, D., Lightsey, O. R., Ethington, C. A., Woemmel, C. A., & Coke, A. L. (2001). Self-efficacy, optimism, health competence, and recovery from orthopedic surgery. *Journal of Counseling Psychology, 48*, 233–238.

Walker, L. E. (1991). Posttraumatic stress disorder in women: Diagnosis and treatment of battered woman syndrome. *Psychotherapy, 28*, 21–29.

Walkup, J. (1995). A clinically based rule of thumb for classifying delusions. *Schizophrenia Bulletin, 21*, 323–331.

Wallace, C. J. (1998). Social skills training in psychiatric rehabilitation: Recent findings. *International Review of Psychiatry, 10*, 9–19.

Walsh, B. T., & Devlin, M. J. (1998). Eating disorders: Progress and problems. *Science, 280*, 1387–1390.

Walter, H. J. (2001). Substance abuse and substance use disorders. In G. O. Gabbard (Ed.), *Treatment of psychiatric disorders* (pp. 325–338). Washington, DC: American Psychiatric Press.

Wampold, B. E., Lichtenberg, J. W., & Waehler, C. A. (2002). Principles of empirically supported interventions in counseling psychology. *Counseling Psychologist, 30*, 197–217.

Ward, C. H., Beck, A. T., Mendelson, M., Mock, J. E., & Erbaught, J. K. (1962). The psychiatric nomenclature: Reasons for diagnostic disagreement. *Archives of General Psychiatry, 7*, 198–205.

Ward, T., & Stewart, C. A. (2003). The treatment of sex offenders: Risk management and good lives. *Professional Psychology: Research and Practice, 34*, 353–360.

Wardle, J., Robb, K. A., Johnson, F., Griffith, J., et al. (2004). Socioeconomic variation in attitudes to eating and weight in female adolescents. *Health Psychology, 23*, 275–282.

Warner, R. (1986). Hard times and schizophrenia. *Psychology Today, 20*, 50–51.

Warner, T. D., & Roberts, L. W. (2004). Scientific integrity, fidelity, and conflicts of interest. *Current Opinion in Psychiatry, 17*, 381–385.

Wartik, N. (1994, February). Fatal attention. *Redbook*, pp. 62–69.

Warwick, H. M. C., & Marks, I. M. (1988). Behavioural treatment for illness phobia and hypochondriasis. *British Journal of Psychiatry, 152*, 239–241.

Wasserman, E., & Gromisch, D. (1981). *Survey of clinical pediatrics*. New York: McGraw-Hill.

Wassertheil-Smoller, S., Shumaker, S., Ockene, J., Talavera, G. A., et al. (2004). Depression and the cardiovascular sequelae in post-menopausal women: The women's health initiative. *Archives of Internal Medicine, 164*, 289–299.

Waterman, J., & Lusk, R. (1986). Scope of the problem. In K. MacFarlane (Ed.), *Sexual abuse of young children: Evaluation and treatment* (pp. 3–14). New York: Guilford Press.

Watkins, B., & Bentovim, A. (1992). The sexual abuse of male children and adolescents: A review of current research. *Journal of Child Psychology and Psychiatry, 33*, 197–248.

Watson, D., Weber, K., Assenheimer, J. S., Clark, L. A., et al. (1995). Testing a tripartite model: I. Evaluating the convergent and discriminant validity of anxiety and depression symptom scales. *Journal of Abnormal Psychology, 104*, 3–14.

Watson, D. L., & Tharp, R. G. (1997). *Self-directed behavior: Self-modification for personal adjustment*. Pacific Grove, CA: Brooks Cole.

Watson, J. B., & Rayner, R. (1920). Conditioned emotional responses. *Journal of Experimental Psychology, 3*, 1–14.

Watson, J. B., & Rayner, R. (2000). Conditioned emotional reactions. *American Psychologist, 55*, 313–317.

Watson, R. (2004). MEPs lead demand to get sudden unexplained deaths recognized as a syndrome. *British Medical Journal, 327*, 886.

Wax, E. (2000, March 6). Immigrant girls are starving to be American, studies find. *Washington Post*, p. B1.

Webster, J. S., & Scott, R. P. (1983). The effects of self-instruction training in attention deficit following head injury. *Clinical Neuropsychology, 5*, 69–74.

Webster-Stratton, C. (1991). Annotation: Strategies for helping families with conduct disordered children. *Journal of Child Psychology and Psychiatry, 32*, 1047–1062.

Wechsler, D. (1981). *Wechsler Adult Intelligence Scale*. New York: Harcourt, Brace, Jovanovich.

Wedding, D. (1995). Current issues in psychotherapy. In R. J. Corsini & D. Wedding (Eds.). *Current psychotherapies* (pp. 419–437). Itasca, IL: Peacock.

Weems, C., Silverman, W. K., & LaGreca, A. M. (2000). What do youth referred for anxiety problems worry about? *Journal of Abnormal Child Psychology, 28,* 63–72.

Weems, C. F., Hayward, C., Killen, J., & Taylor, C. B. (2002). A longitudinal investigation of anxiety sensitivity in adolescence. *Journal of Abnormal Psychology, 111,* 471–477.

Wehmeier, P. M., Barth, N., & Remschmidt, H. (2003). Induced delusional disorder. *Psychopathology, 36,* 37–45.

Weiden, P. J., Mann, J. J., Haas, G., Mattson, M., & Frances, A. (1987). Clinical nonrecognition of neuroleptic-induced movement disorders: A cautionary study. *American Journal of Psychiatry, 144,* 1148–1553.

Weiller, J., Bisserbe, C., Maier, W., & Lecrubier, Y. (1998). Prevalence and recognition of anxiety syndromes in five European primary care settings. *British Journal of Psychiatry, 173,* 18–23.

Weinberg, T. S. (1987). Sadomasochism in the United States: A review of recent sociological literature. *Journal of Sex Research, 23,* 50–69.

Weiner, B. (1975). On being sane in insane places: A process (attributional) analysis and critique. *Journal of Abnormal Psychology, 84,* 433–441.

Weiner, I. B. (1995). How to anticipate ethical and legal challenges in personality assessments. In J. N. Butcher (Ed.), *Clinical personality assessment: Practical approaches* (pp. 95–106). New York: Oxford University Press.

Weiner, I. B. (2003). Prediction and postdiction in clinical decision making. *Clinical Psychology: Science and Practice, 10,* 335–338.

Weiner, I. W. (1969). The effectiveness of suicide prevention programs. *Mental Hygiene, 53,* 357–373.

Weiner, R. D., & Krystal, A. D. (2001). Electroconvulsive therapy. In G. O. Gabbard (Ed.), *Treatment of psychiatric disorders* (pp. 1267–1293). Washington, DC: American Psychiatric Press.

Weinman, J., & Petrie, K. J. (1997). Illness perceptions: A new paradigm for psychosomatics. *Journal of Psychosomatic Research, 42,* 113–116.

Weintraub, W. (1981). Compulsive and paranoid personalities. In J. R. Lion (Ed.), *Personality disorders: Diagnosis and management.* Baltimore: Williams & Wilkins.

Weiser, B. (2000, December 16). Judge rules defendant's amnesia is feigned in terror case. *New York Times,* p. B2.

Weishaar, M. E., & Beck, A. T. (1992). Clinical and cognitive predictors of suicide. In R. W. Maris, A. L. Berman, J. T. Maltsberger, & R. I. Yufit (Eds.), *Assessment and prediction of suicide.* New York: Guilford.

Weisman, A. G., Nuechterlein, K. H., Goldstein, M. J., & Snyder, K. S. (1998). Expressed emotion, attributions, and schizophrenia symptoms dimensions. *Journal of Abnormal Psychology, 107,* 355–359.

Weisman, A. G., Nuechterlein, K. H., Goldstein, M. J., & Snyder, K. S. (2000). Controllability perceptions and reactions to symptoms of schizophrenia: A within-family comparison of relatives with high and low expressed emotions. *Journal of Abnormal Psychology, 109,* 167–171.

Weiss, B., Weisz, J. R., Politano, M., Carey, M., et al. (1992). Relations among self-reported depressive symptoms in clinic referred children versus adolescents. *Journal of Abnormal Psychology, 101,* 391–397.

Weiss, D. S. (1988). Personality assessment. In H. H. Goldman (Ed.), *Review of general psychiatry* (pp. 221–232). Norwalk, CT: Appleton & Lange.

Weiss, J. M., Glazer, H. I., & Pohorecky, L. A. (1975). Coping behavior and neurochemical changes: Alternative explanation for the original "learned helplessness" experiments. In G. Serban & A. Ling (Eds.), *Relevance of the animal model to the human.* New York: Plenum.

Weissberg, M. (1993). Multiple personality disorder and iatrogenesis: The cautionary tale of Anna O. *International Journal of Clinical and Experimental Hypnosis, 41,* 15–34.

Weissman, M. M. (1993). The epidemiology of personality disorders: A 1990 update. *Journal of Personality Disorders, Supplement 1,* 44–62.

Weissman, M. M., Bland, R. C., Canino, G. J., Faravelli, C., et al. (1997). The cross-national epidemiology of panic disorder. *Archives of General Psychiatry, 54,* 305–309.

Weissman, M. M., Bruce, M. L., Leaf, P. J., Florio, L. P., & Holzer, C. (1991). Affective disorders. In L. N. Robins & D. A. Regier (Eds.), *Psychiatric disorders in America: The Epidemiologic Catchment Area study* (pp. 53–80). New York: Free Press.

Welch Shaw, S., & Linehan, M. M. (2002). High-risk situations associated with parasuicide and drug use in borderline personality disorder. *Journal of Personality Disorders, 16,* 561–569.

Wells, A., & Papageorgiou, C. (1999). The observer perspective: Biased imagery in social phobia, agoraphobia, and blood/injury phobia. *Behaviour Research & Therapy, 37,* 653–658.

Wells, C. E. (1978). Role of stroke in dementia. *Stroke, 9,* 1–3.

Wells, K. B., Sturm, R., Sherbourne, C. D., & Meredith, L. S. (1996). *Caring for depression.* Cambridge, MA: Harvard University Press.

Wen, P. (2001, April 10). Thinking the unspeakable, the "silent epidemic" of obsessive dark thoughts. *Boston Globe,* p. B6.

Wender, P. H., & Klein, D. F. (1981, February). The promise of biological psychiatry. *Psychology Today, 15,* 25–41.

Wender, P. H., Rosenthal, D., Rainer, J. D., Greenhill, L., & Sarlan, M. B. (1977). Schizophrenics' adopting parents. *Archives of General Psychiatry, 34,* 777–784.

Wenger, N. K. (1997). Coronary heart disease: An older woman's health risk. *British Medical Journal, 315,* 1085–1089.

Werth, J. L. (1996). *Rational suicide? Implications for mental health professionals.* New York: Taylor & Francis.

Wertheim, E. H., Paxton, S. J., Schutz, H. K., & Muir, S. L. (1997). Why do adolescent girls watch their weight? An interview study examining sociocultural pressures to be thin. *Journal of Psychosomatic Research, 42,* 345–355.

Westen, D. (1991). Cognitive-behavioral interventions in the psychoanalytic psychotherapy of borderline personality disorders. *Clinical Psychology Review, 11,* 211–230.

Westen, D., Novotny, C. M., & Thompson-Brenner, H. (2004). The empirical status of empirically supported psychotherapies: Assumptions, findings, and reporting in controlled clinical trials. *Psychological Bulletin, 130,* 631–663.

Westermeyer, J. (1987). Public health and chronic mental illness. *American Journal of Public Health, 77,* 667–668.

Wetherell, J. L., Gatz, M., & Craske, M. G. (2003). Treatment of generalized anxiety disorder in older adults. *Journal of Consulting and Clinical Psychology, 71,* 31–40.

Wetter, D. W., Fiore, M. C., Gritz, E. R., Lando, H. A., et al. (1998). The Agency for Health Care Policy and Research smoking cessation clinical practice guideline: Findings and implications for psychologists. *American Psychologist, 53,* 657–669.

Weze, C., Leathard, H. L., Grange, J. M., & Stevens, G. (2004). Evaluation of healing by gentle touch in thirty-five clients with cancer. *European Journal of Oncological Nursing, 8,* 40–49.

Weze, C., Leathard, H. L., & Stevens, G. (2004). Evaluation of healing by gentle touch for the treatment of musculoskeletal disorders. *American Journal of Public Health, 94,* 50–52.

Whalen, C. K., & Henker, B. (1991). Therapies for hyperactive children: Comparisons, combinations, and compromises. *Journal of Consulting and Clinical Psychology, 59,* 126–137.

Whipple, E., & Webster-Stratton, C. (1991). The role of parental stress in physically abusive families. *Child Abuse and Neglect, 15,* 279–291.

White, G. M. (1982). The role of cultural explanations in "somatization" and "psychologization." *Social Science Medicine, 16,* 1519–1530.

White, J. H. (2000). The prevention of eating disorders: A review of the research on risk factors with implications for practice. *Journal of Child and Adolescent Psychiatric Nursing, 13,* 76–88.

White, J. L., & Parham, T. A. (1990). *The psychology of Blacks.* Englewood Cliffs, NJ: Prentice-Hall.

White, P. D., & Moorey, S. (1997). Psychosomatic illnesses are not "all in the mind." *Journal of Psychosomatic Research, 42,* 329–333.

Whitehill, M., DeMeyer-Gapin, S., & Scott, T. J. (1976). Stimulus seeking in antisocial preadolescent children. *Journal of Abnormal Psychology, 85,* 101–104.

Whiteside, S. P., & Abramowitz, J. S. (2004). Obsessive-compulsive symptoms and the expression of anger. *Cognitive Therapy and Research, 28,* 259–268.

Whittal, M. L., & Goetsch, V. L. (1995). Physiological, subjective, and behavioral responses to hyperventilation in clinical and infrequent panic. *Behaviour Research and Therapy, 33,* 415–422.

Whittal, M. L., Suchday, S., & Goetsch, V. L. (1994). The panic attack questionnaire: Factor analysis of symptom profiles and characteristics of undergraduates who panic. *Journal of Anxiety Disorders, 8,* 237–245.

Whittington, C. J., Kendall, T., Fonagy, P., Cottrell, D., & Cotgrove, A. (2004). Selective serotonin reuptake inhibitors in childhood depression: Systematic review of published versus unpublished data. *Lancet, 363,* 1341–1346.

Whybrow, P. C., Akiskal, H. S., & McKinney, W. T., Jr. (1984). *Mood disorders: Toward a new psychobiology.* New York: Plenum.

Wickramasekera, I. (1976). Aversive behavior rehearsal for sexual exhibitionism. *Behavioral Therapy, 1,* 167–176.

Widiger, T. A., & Coker, L. A. (2002). Assessing personality disorders. In J. N. Butcher (Ed.), *Clinical personality assessment: Practical approaches* (pp. 407–434). New York: Oxford University Press.

Widiger, T. A., & Shea, T. (1991). Differentiation of Axis I and Axis II disorders. *Journal of Abnormal Psychology, 100,* 399–406.

Widiger, T. A., & Spitzer, R. L. (1991). Sex bias in the diagnosis of personality disorders: Conceptual and methodological issues. *Clinical Psychology Review, 11,* 1–22.

Widiger, T. A., Trull, T. J., Clarkin, J. F., Sanderson, C., & Costa, P. T. (1994). A description of the DSM-III-R and DSM-IV personality disorders with the five-factor model of personality. In P. T. Costa & T. A. Widiger (Eds.), *Personality disorders and the five-factor model of personality* (pp. 41–58). Washington, DC: American Psychological Association.

Widom, C. S. (1976). Interpersonal and personal construct systems in psychopaths. *Journal of Consulting and Clinical Psychology, 44,* 614–623.

Widom, C. S. (1977). A methodology for studying noninstitutionalized psychopaths. *Journal of Consulting and Clinical Psychology, 45,* 674–683.

Wiens, A. N. (1983). The assessment interview. In I. B. Weiner (Ed.), *Clinical methods in psychology.* New York: Wiley.

Wiersma, D., Nienhuis, F. J., Sloof, C. J., & Giel, R. (1998). Natural course of schizophrenic disorders: A fifteen-year follow-up of a Dutch incidence cohort. *Schizophrenia Bulletin, 24,* 75–85.

Wiesel, F.-A. (1994). II. The treatment of schizophrenia. *British Journal of Psychiatry, 164,* 65–70.

Wijsman, M. (1990). Linkage analysis of alcoholism: Problems and solutions. In C. R. Cloninger & H. Begleiter (Eds.), *Genetics and biology of alcoholism* (pp. 317–326). Cold Spring Harbor, NY: Cold Spring Harbor Laboratory Press.

Wilding, T. (1984). Is stress making you sick? *American Health, 6,* 2–5.

Wilfley, D. E., Dounchis, J. Z., Stein, R. I., Welch, R. R., et al. (2000). Comorbid psychopathology in binge eating disorder: Relationship to eating disorder severity at baseline and following treatment. *Journal of Consulting and Clinical Psychology, 68,* 641–649.

Wilfley, D. E., Pike, K. M., Dohm, F.-A., Striegel-Moore, R. H., & Fairburn, C. G. (2001). Bias in binge eating disorder: How representative are recruited clinic samples? *Journal of Consulting and Clinical Psychology, 69,* 383–388.

Williams, J. B. (1999). Psychiatric classification. In R. E. Hales, S. C. Yudofsky & J. A. Talbott (Eds.), *Textbook of psychiatry* (pp. 227–252). Washington, DC: American Psychiatric Press.

Williams, K. E., Chambless, D. L., & Steketee, G. (1998). Behavioral treatment of obsessive-compulsive disorder in African Americans:

Clinical issues. *Journal of Behavior Therapy and Experimental Psychiatry, 29,* 163–170.

Williams, L. M., & Finkelhor, D. (1990). The characteristics of incestuous fathers: A review of recent studies. In W. L. Marshall, D. R. Laws, & H. E. Barbaree (Eds.), *Handbook of sexual assault: Issues, theories, and treatment of the offender* (pp. 231–256). New York: Plenum Press.

Williams, R. (1974). The problem of match and mismatch. In L. Miller (Ed.), *The testing of black children.* Englewood Cliffs, NJ: Prentice-Hall.

Williams, R. B., Jr., Barefoot, J. C., Haney, T. L., Harrell, F. E., Jr., et al. (1988). Type A behavior and angiographically documented coronary atherosclerosis in a sample of 2,289 patients. *Psychosomatic Medicine, 50,* 139–152.

Williams, R. J., & Chang, S. Y. (2000). A comprehensive and comparative review of adolescent substance abuse treatment outcome. *Clinical Psychology: Science and Practice, 7,* 138–166.

Williams, R. J., Taylor, J., & Ricciardelli, L. A. (2000). Brief report: Sex-role traits and self-monitoring as dimensions in control: Women with bulimia nervosa versus controls. *British Journal of Clinical Psychology, 39,* 317–320.

Williamson, D., Robinson, M. E., & Melamed, B. (1997). Patient behavior, spouse responsiveness, and marital satisfaction in patients with rheumatoid arthritis. *Behavior Modification, 21,* 97–106.

Wilson, G. T. (1984). Clinical issues and strategies in the clinical practice of behavior therapy. In C. M. Franks, G. T. Wilson, K. D. Brownell, & P. Kendall (Eds.), *Annual review of behavior therapy: Theory and practice* (p. 8). New York: Guilford Press.

Wilson, G. T., & O'Leary, K. D. (1980). *Principles of behavior therapy.* Englewood Cliffs, NJ: Prentice-Hall.

Wilson, G. T., & Shafran, R. (2005). Eating disorders guidelines from NICE. *Lancet, 365,* 79–81.

Wilson, M. S., & Meyer, E. (1962). Diagnostic consistency in a psychiatric liaison service. *American Journal of Psychiatry, 19,* 207–209.

Wilson, R. S., & Bennett, D. A. (2003). Cognitive activity and risk of Alzheimer's disease. *Current Directions in Psychological Science, 12,* 87–91.

Wincze, J. P., Bansal, S., & Malamud, M. (1986). Effects of medrox progesterone acetate on subjective arousal, arousal to erotic stimulation, and nocturnal penile tumescence in male sex offenders. *Archives of Sexual Behavior, 15,* 293–305.

Wincze, J. P., Hoon, E. F., & Hoon, P. W. (1978). Multiple measure analysis of women experiencing low sexual arousal. *Behaviour Research and Therapy, 16,* 43–49.

Windle, M., & Windle, R. C. (2001). Depressive symptoms and cigarette smoking among middle adolescents: Prospective associations and intrapersonal and interpersonal influences. *Journal of Consulting and Clinical Psychology, 69,* 215–226.

Wing, J. K. (1980). Social psychiatry in the United Kingdom: The approach to schizophrenia. *Schizophrenia Bulletin, 6,* 557–565.

Wing, L. (1981). Asperger's syndrome: A clinical account. *Psychological Medicine, 11,* 115–129.

Winnett, R. L., Bornstein, P. H., Cogsuell, K. A., & Paris, A. E. (1987). Cognitive-behavioral therapy for childhood depression: A levels-of-treatment approach. *Journal of Child and Adolescent Psychotherapy, 4,* 283–286.

Winokur, G., Clayton, P. J., & Reich, T. (1969). *Manic depressive illness.* St. Louis: Mosby.

Winton, E. C., Clark, D. M., & Edelmann, R. J. (1995). Social anxiety, fear of negative evaluation, and the detection of negative emotion in others. *Behaviour Research and Therapy, 33,* 193–196.

Wise, M. G., & Tierney, J. G. (1999). Impulse control disorders not elsewhere classified. In R. E. Hales, S. C. Yudofsky & J. A. Talbott (Eds.), *Textbook of psychiatry* (pp. 773–793). Washington, DC: American Psychiatric Press.

Wise, M. G., Gray, K. F., & Seltzer, B. (1999). Delirium, dementia, and amnestic disorders. In R. E. Hales, S. C. Yudofsky & J. A. Talbott (Eds.), *Textbook of psychiatry* (pp. 317–362). Washington, DC: American Psychiatric Press.

Wise, M. G., Hilty, D. M., & Cerda, G. M. (2001). Delirium due to a general medical condition, delirium due to multiple etiologies, and delirium not otherwise specified. In G. O. Gabbard (Ed.), *Treatment of psychiatric disorders* (pp. 387–412). Washington, DC: American Psychiatric Press.

Wise, R. A. (1988). The neurobiology of craving: Implications for understanding and treatment of addiction. *Journal of Abnormal Psychology, 97,* 118–132.

Wise, T. N., Fagan, P. J., Schmidt, C. W., & Ponticas, Y. (1991). Personality and sexual functioning of transvestitic fetishists and other paraphilics. *Journal of Nervous and Mental Disorders, 179,* 694–698.

Witkiewitz, K., & Marlatt, G. A. (2004). Relapse prevention for alcohol and drug problems: That was zen, this is tao. *American Psychologist, 59,* 224–235.

Wittchen, H.-U., Zhao, S., Kessler, R. C., & Eaton, W. W. (1994). DSM-III-R generalized anxiety disorder in the National Comorbidity Survey. *Archives of General Psychiatry, 51,* 355–364.

Woike, B. A., & McAdams, D. P. (2001). TAT-based personality measures have considerable validity. *APS Observer, 14,* 10.

Wolfe, J., Sharkansky, E. J., Read, J. P., & Dawson, R. (1998). Sexual harassment assault as predictors of PTSD symptomatology among U.S. female Persian Gulf War military personnel. *Journal of Interpersonal Violence, 13,* 40–57.

Wolfensberger, W. (1988). Common assets of mentally retarded people that are commonly not acknowledged. *Mental Retardation, 26,* 63–70.

Woliver, R. (2000, March 26). 44 personalities, but artist shines. *New York Times,* pp. 6–9.

Wolkin, A., Rusinek, H., Vaid, G., & Arena, L. (1998). Structural magnetic resonance image averaging in schizophrenia. *American Journal of Psychiatry, 155,* 1064–1073.

Wolkin, A., Sanfilipo, M., Wolf, A. P., Angrist, B., et al. (1992). Negative symptoms and hypofrontality in chronic schizophrenia. *Archives of General Psychiatry, 49,* 959–965.

Wolpe, J. (1958). *Psychotherapy by reciprocal inhibition.* Stanford, CA: Stanford University Press.

Wolpe, J. (1973). *The practice of behavior therapy.* New York: Pergamon.

Wolpe, J. (1982). *The practice of behavior therapy* (3rd ed.). Elmsford, NY: Pergamon Press.

Wolraich, M. L., Wilson, D. B., & White, J. W., (1995). The effect of sugar on behavior or cognition in children. *Journal of the American Medical Association, 274,* 1617–1621.

Wood, C. (1986). The hostile heart. *Psychology Today, 20,* 10–12.

Woodard, C. R. (2004). Hardiness and the concept of courage. *Consulting Psychology Journal: Practice and Research, 56,* 173–185.

Woodruff, P. G., & Fahy, J. V. (2001). Asthma: Prevalence, pathogenesis, and prospects for novel therapies. *Journal of the American Medical Association, 286,* 1–10.

Woodside, D. B., Garfinkel, P. E., Lin, E., Goering, P., et al. (2001). Comparisons of men with full or partial eating disorders, men without eating disorders, and women with eating disorders in the community. *American Journal of Psychiatry, 158,* 570–574.

Woody, G. E., & Cacciola, J. (1994). Review of remission criteria. In T. A. Widiger, A. J. Frances, H. A. Pincus, M. B. First, R. Ross, & W. Davis (Eds.), *DSM-IV Sourcebook* (Vol. 1, pp. 67–80). Washington, DC: American Psychiatric Association.

Woody, S. R., Chambless, D. L., & Glass, C. R. (1997). Self-focused attention in the treatment of social phobia. *Behaviour Research and Therapy, 35,* 117–129.

Woody, S. R., & Sanderson, W. C. (1998). Manuals for empirically supported treatments: 1998 update. *Clinical Psychologist, 51,* 17.

Wootton, J. M., Frick, P. J., Shelton, K. K., & Silverthorn, P. (1997). Ineffective parenting and childhood conduct problems: The moderating role of callous-unemotional traits. *Journal of Consulting and Clinical Psychology, 65,* 301–308.

World Health Organization. (1973). Report on the international pilot study of schizophrenia (Vol. 1). Geneva: World Health Organization.

World Health Organization. (1987). The Dexamethasone Suppression Test in depression. *British Journal of Psychiatry, 150,* 459–462.

Wren, C. (2002). Sudden death in children and adolescents. *Heart, 88,* 426–434.

Wyler, A. R., Masuda, M., & Holmes, T. H. (1971). Magnitude of the life events and seriousness of illness. *Journal of Psychosomatic Medicine, 33,* 115–122.

Yalom, I. D. (1970). *The theory and practice of group psychotherapy.* New York: Basic Books.

Yarhouse, M. A., & Burkett, L. A. (2002). An inclusive response to LGB and conservative religious persons: The case of same-sex attraction and behavior. *Professional Psychology: Research and Practice, 33,* 235–241.

Yassa, R., & Jeste, D. V. (1992). Gender differences in tardive dyskinesia: A critical review of the literature. *Schizophrenia Bulletin, 18,* 701–715.

Yasumatsu, K. (1993). One's own body odor and eye-to-eye phobias in high school students: A cross-sectional questionnaire study. Japanese *Journal of Child and Adolescent Psychiatry, 34,* 261–267.

Yee, D. (2005, February 11). Panel urges shots to halt meningitis. *Contra Costa Times,* p. A17.

Yehuda, R. (2000). Biology of posttraumatic stress disorder. *Journal of Clinical Psychiatry, 61,* 14–21.

Yehuda, R., & McFarlane, A. C. (1995). Conflict between current knowledge about posttraumatic stress disorder and its original conceptual basis. *American Journal of Psychiatry, 152,* 1705–1713.

Yen, S., Shea, M. T., Sanislow, C. A., Grilo, C. M., et al. (2003). Axis I and Axis II disorders as predictors of prospective suicide attempts: Findings from the Collaborative Longitudinal Personality Disorders Study. *Journal of Abnormal Psychology, 112,* 375–381.

Yeung, A., & Deguang, H. (2002). Somatoform disorders. *Western Journal of Medicine, 176,* 253–256.

Yonkers, K. A., Zlotnick, C., Allsworth, J., & Warshaw, M. (1998). Is the course of panic disorder the same in women and men? *American Journal of Psychiatry, 155,* 596–602.

Young, A. S., Sullivan, G., Burnam, M. A., & Brook, R. H. (1998). Measuring the quality of outpatient treatment for schizophrenia. *Archive of General Psychiatry, 55,* 611–615.

Young, E. C., & Kramer, B. M. (1991). Characteristics of age-related language decline in adults with Down syndrome. *Mental Retardation, 29,* 75–79.

Young, M. (1980). Attitudes and behavior of college students relative to oral-genital sexuality. *Archives of Sexual Behavior, 9,* 61–67.

Young, M. A., Meaden, P. M., Fogg, L. F., Cherin, E. A., & Eastman, C. I. (1997). Which environmental variables are related to the onset of seasonal affective disorder? *Journal of Abnormal Psychology, 106,* 554–562.

Young, T., Skatrud, J., & Peppard, P. E. (2004). Risk factors for obstructive sleep apnea in adults. *Journal of the American Medical Association, 291,* 2013–2016.

Youngren, M. A., & Lewinsohn, P. M. (1980). The functional relation between depression and problematic interpersonal behavior. *Journal of Abnormal Psychology, 89,* 333–341.

Youngstrom, N. (1991). Spotting serial killer difficult, experts note. *APA Monitor, 22,* 32.

Yu-Fen, H., & Neng, T. (1981). Transcultural investigation of recent symptomatology of schizophrenia in China. *American Journal of Psychiatry, 138,* 1484–1486.

Yumoto, S., Kakimi, S., Ogawa, Y., Nagai, H., et al. (1995). Aluminum neurotoxicity and Alzheimer's disease. In I. Hanin, M. Yoshida, & A. Fisher (Eds.), *Alzheimer's and Parkinson's diseases: Recent developments* (pp. 223–229). New York: Plenum Press.

Zamichow, N. (1993, February 15). The dark corner of psychology. *Los Angeles Times,* p. A1.

Zanarini, M. C., Parachini, E. A., Frankenburg, F. R., & Holman, J. B. (2003). Sexual relationship difficulties among borderline patients and Axis II comparison subjects. *Journal of Nervous and Mental Disease, 191,* 479–482.

Zayas, E. M., & Grossberg, G. T. (1998). The treatment of psychosis in later life. *Journal of Clinical Psychiatry, 59,* 5–9.

Zhang, A. Y., & Snowden, L. R. (1999). Ethnic characteristics of mental disorders in five U.S. communities. *Cultural Diversity and Ethnic Minority Psychology, 5,* 134–146.

Zhang, M., Wang, M., Li, J., & Phillips, M. R. (1994). Randomized-control trial of family intervention for 78 first-episode male schizophrenic patients. An eighteen-month study in Suzhou, Jiangsu. *British Journal of Psychiatry, 165,* 96–102.

Zheng, Y.-P., & Lin, K.-M. (1994). A nationwide study of stressful life events in mainland China. *Psychosomatic Medicine, 56,* 296–305.

Zigler, E. (1967). Familial mental retardation: A continuing dilemma. *Science, 155,* 292–298.

Zigler, E., & Bergman, W. (1983). Discerning the future of early childhood intervention. *American Psychologist, 38,* 893–905.

Zigler, E., Taussig, C., & Black, K. (1992). Early childhood intervention: A promising preventative for juvenile delinquency. *American Psychologist, 47,* 997–1006.

Zilbergeld, B. (1983). *The shrinking of America.* Boston: Little, Brown.

Zilboorg, G., & Henry, G. W. (1941). *A history of medical psychology.* New York: Norton.

Zipursky, R. B., Lambe, E. K., Kapur, S., & Mikulis, D. J. (1998). Cerebral gray-matter volume deficits in first-episode psychosis. *Archives of General Psychiatry, 55,* 540–546.

Zito, J. M., Craig, T. J., Wanderling, J., & Siegel, C. (1987). Pharmaco-epidemiology in 136 hospitalized schizophrenic patients. *American Journal of Psychiatry, 144,* 778–782.

Zito, J. M., Safer, D. J., dos Reis, S., Gardner, J. F., et al. (2000). Trends in the prescribing of psychotropic medications to preschoolers. *Journal of the American Medical Association, 283,* 1025–1030.

Zucker, K. J. (1990). Gender identity disorders in children: Clinical descriptions and natural history. In R. Blanchard & B. W. Steiner (Eds.), *Clinical management of gender identity disorders in children and adults* (pp. 1–24). Washington, DC: American Psychiatric Press.

Zuckerman, M. (1996). Sensation seeking. In C. G. Costello (Ed.), *Personality characteristics of the personality disordered* (pp. 317–330). New York: Wiley.

Zuger, B. (1984). Early effeminate behavior in boys: Outcome and significance for homosexuality. *Journal of Nervous and Mental Disease, 172,* 90–97.

Zullow, H. M., Oettingen, G., Peterson, C., & Seligman, M. E. (1988). Pessimistic explanatory style in the historical record: Caving LBJ, presidential candidates, and East versus West Berlin. *American Psychologist, 43,* 673–682.

Zwillich, T. (2004, October 20). *States failing to fight rising obesity rates.* Retrieved November 19, 2004, from http://my.webmed.com/content/article/95/103430.htm

Zverina, J., Lachman, M., Pondelickova, J., & Vanek, J. (1987). The occurrence of atypical sexual experience among various female patient groups. *Archives of Sexual Behavior, 16,* 321–326.

Credits

Text Credits

Chapter 1: p. 28 Excerpt in "Managed Care: Will Someone Please Help Me!" from "Rosenhan Revisited," by Christopher M. Scribner in *Professional Psychology: Research and Practice*, 2001, Vol. 32, No. 2, pp. 215–216. Copyright © 2001 by the American Psychological Association. Adapted with permission. **Chapter 3:** p. 91 *Table 3.3:* Reprinted with permission from the *Diagnostic and Statistical Manual of Mental Disorders*, Copyright 2000. American Psychiatric Association. **Chapter 4:** p. 111 *Table 4.1:* Reproduced with permission from *Pediatrics*, Vol. 101, Page e9, Copyright © 1998 by the AAP. p. 122 *Figure 4.3:* Reprinted from *Journal of Counseling & Development*, Winter 2000, Vol. 78, p. 99. ACA. Reprinted with permission. No further reproduction authorized without written permission from the American Counseling Association. **Chapter 5:** p. 139 *Figure 5.3:* Reprinted with permission from American Journal of Psychiatry, Copyright 2002. American Psychiatric Association. p. 144 *Table 5.2:* Reprinted by permission of the author(s). p. 160 *Figure 5.7:* Reprinted by permission Elsevier Science. **Chapter 7:** p. 204 *Figure 7.1:* From "Circulation" from Nademanee, K. et al., "Arrhythmogenic Marker for Sudden Unexplained Death Syndrome in Thai Men," in *Circulation*, 96 (October 21, 1997), p. 2598. Reprinted by permission of Lippincott, Williams & Wilkins. p. 218 *Figure 7.2:* Pennix et al., "Depression and Cardiac Mortality: Results From a Community Assessed Longitudinal Study," *Archives of General Psychiatry*, Vol. 58, pp. 221–226. Reprinted by permission of American Medical Association. p. 226 *Figure 7.5:* © 1997 *Newsweek*, Inc. All rights reserved. Reprinted by permission. **Chapter 8:** p. 258 *Figure 8.2:* Reprinted from The 1964 Nebraska Symposium on Motivation, by permission of the University of Nebraska Press. Copyright © 1964 by the University of Nebraska Press. **Chapter 10:** p. 313 *Figure 10.2:* From *Our Sexuality* 5th edition by Crooks/Baur. © 1993. Reprinted with permission of Wadsworth, a division of Thomson Learning: www.thomsonrights.com. Fax 800-730-2215. **Chapter 13:** p. 427 *Figure 13.1:* Amador, X. F. et al. (1994), "Awareness of illness in schizophrenia and schizoaffective and mood disorders," *Archives of General Psychiatry*, Vol. 51, pg. 830. Reprinted by permission of American Medical Association. **Chapter 14:** p. 486 *Table 14.3:* Copyright © 1995 by the National Association of School Psychologists, Bethesda MD. Reprinted with permission of the publisher. **Chapter 16:** p. 537 *Figure 16.2:* Reprinted with permission from *American Journal of Psychiatry*, Copyright 2001. American Psychiatric Association. p. 540 *Figure 16.3:* From S. Kety, L. P. Rowland, R. L. Sidman, & S. W. Matthysse, eds., *The Genetics of Neurological and Psychiatric Disorders* (New York: Raven Press, 1983). Reprinted by permission of Raven Press. p. 546 *Table 16.6:* Reprinted with permission from *American Journal of Psychiatry*, Copyright 2000. American Psychiatric Association.

Photo Credits

Chapter 1: p. 6 Stone/Getty Images. p. 9 Jeffrey Dunn Studios. p. 10 (top) Jerry Irwin/Getty Images. p. 10 (bottom) Jeff Greenberg/PhotoEdit. p. 11 (top) ©1996 Dick Hemingway. p. 11 (bottom) Ariel Skelley/Corbis. p. 14 Reuters/Corbis. p. 17 Joseph Sohm/ChromoSohm Inc./Corbis. p. 19 Neg. #312263 photo by Julius Krishner, 1928/Courtesy Dept. of Library Services, American Museum of Natural History. p. 21 Corbis/Bettmann. p. 23 Archives of American Psychology. p. 24 Stock Montage. p. 25 Science Photo Library/Photo Researchers, Inc. p. 31 NASA/Corbis/Sygma. **Chapter 2:** p. 42 Washington University in St. Louis, School of Medicine. p. 44 Library of Congress/Woodfin Camp & Associates. p. 45 (right) Laura Dwight/Peter Arnold, Inc. p. 45 (left) Roseanne Olson/Tony Stone Images. p. 49 The Granger Collection.

p. 51 Mary Kate Denny/PhotoEdit. p. 52 AP/Wide World Photos. p. 53 Bob Daemmrich/Stock Boston. p. 58 Corbis. p. 60 Ariel Skelley/Corbis. p. 61 (left) Stone/Getty Images. p. 61 (right) Stone/Getty Images. **Chapter 3:** p. 76 (right) Rainbow. p. 76 (left) David Young Wolff/PhotoEdit. p. 78 Rorschach H: Diagnostics. p. 79 ©1971 By the President and Fellows of Harvard College. p. 84 Copyright ©2004 by The Riverside Publishing Company. All rights reserved. Photo depiction of the Standford-Binet Intelligence Scales, Fifth Edition reproduced with permission of the publisher. p. 87 (left) Dan McCoy/Rainbow. p. 87 (right) Dan McCoy/Rainbow. p. 87 (bottom) Dan McCoy/Rainbow. p. 88 Dan McCoy/Rainbow. p. 98 Jose Luis Pelaez, Inc./Corbis. p. 100 Leo Abbett Cartoons. **Chapter 4:** p. 107 Dan McCoy/Rainbow. p. 114 Leo Abbett Cartoons. p. 115 Christopher Morrow/Stock Boston. p. 118 (left) D. Gorton/Time Magazine. p. 118 (right) D. Gorton/Time Magazine. p. 119 Stone/Getty Images. p. 120 James Robert Fuller/Corbis. p. 123 Peter Menzel/Human Genome Project Cal. Tech./Stock Boston. p. 127 Jeff Greenberg/Rainbow. **Chapter 5:** p. 135 Scala/Art Resource. p. 137 The New Yorker Collection 1987 Roz Chast from cartoonbank.com All rights reserved. p. 145 (left) Reuters/Corbis. p. 145 (right) Corbis. p. 145 (bottom) David Ulmer/Stock Boston. p. 150 Cartoonists and Writers Syndicate. p. 153 Michael Newman/PhotoEdit. p. 155 Thomas R. Fletcher/Stock Boston. p. 162 Catherine Leuthold/Corbis. p. 164 Bob Daemmrich/Stock Boston. p. 167 Marianne Armshaw/Wide World Photos. **Chapter 6:** p. 174 Getty Images. p. 176 George Tooker, The Subway, 1950. Egg tempera 18 1/8 x 26 1/8 in. The Whitney Museum of American Art, New York. Purchase, with funds from The Juliana Force Purchase Award 50.23. p. 179 Gordon M. Grant. p. 181 Jacques Jangoux/Photo Researchers, Inc. p. 185 ©1989 Debra Lex/People Weekly. p. 191 Steve Smith/Outline. p. 194 The New Yorker Collection 1987 Roz Chast from cartoonbank.com All rights reserved. p. 195 The Image Bank. p. 198 The Granger Collection. p. 199 Michael Newman/PhotoEdit. **Chapter 7:** p. 207 (left) Jonathan Nourok/PhotoEdit. p. 207 (right) Mark Richards/PhotoEdit. p. 208 Gary A. Conner/PhotoEdit. p. 210 (left) Bob Daemmrich/The Image Works. p. 210 (right) Ariel Skelley/Corbis. p. 211 John S. Abbott. p. 212 NIBSC/Science Photo Library/Photo Researchers, Inc. p. 214 Mark Richards/PhotoEdit. p. 218 Newport Daily News Press. p. 220 Dan McCoy/Rainbow. p. 222 Spencer Platt/Getty Images. p. 223 Michael Newman/PhotoEdit. p. 229 Michael Newman/PhotoEdit. p. 231 Michael A. Keller/Corbis. **Chapter 8:** p. 240 Michael Newman/PhotoEdit. p. 242 Cartoons by Brad Veley. p. 244 (top) Photofest. p. 245 Bureau L.A. Collection/Corbis. p. 246 Shooting Star. p. 251 Corbis. p. 251 Leo Abbett Cartoons. p. 253 PhotoEdit. p. 258 Craig Prentis/Allsport/Getty Images. p. 260 Mary Kate Denny/PhotoEdit. p. 264 Photofest. p. 265 Michael Freeman/Corbis. **Chapter 9:** p. 275 David Simson/Stock Boston. p. 278 Daniel Hulshizer/AP/Wide World Photos. p. 279 Christobal Corral Vega/HBO Films/ZUMA/Corbis. p. 281 Michael Newman/PhotoEdit. p. 282 J. Griffin/The Image Works. p. 284 Gerry Gropp/Sipa. p. 285 Tom Prettyman/PhotoEdit. p. 286 Rufus S. Folkks/Corbis. p. 289 Tony Freeman/PhotoEdit. p. 292 Photofest. p. 296 Spencer Grant/PhotoEdit. p. 298 Rob Crandall/Rainbow. p. 299 Billy E. Barnes/Stock Boston. p. 303 Cartoonists and Writers Syndicate. **Chapter 10:** p. 309 (left) Jeff Greenberg/PhotoEdit. p. 309 (right) Amy C. Etra/PhotoEdit. p. 312 Ira Wyman /Corbis-Sygma. p. 315 (right) Dennis Brack/Black Star. p. 315 (left) Theo Westenberger Photographer. p. 316 Sondra Dawes/The Image Works. p. 321 ©The New Yorker Collection 2000 Eric Lewis from cartoonbank.com. All Rights Reserved. p. 326 Rob Rogers reprinted by permission of United Features Syndicate, Inc.

Name Index

Subject Index

I-18